MW01672295

... of Accounting in Information Systems
Illinois State University

COMPUTING CONCEPTS

Wadsworth Publishing Company
Belmont, California
A Division of Wadsworth, Inc.

To Wendy and Michael

Computer Science Editor: Frank Ruggirello
Developmental Editor: Alan Venable
Editorial Assistant: Rhonda Gray
Production: Hal Lockwood, Bookman Productions
Print Buyer: Martha Branch
Art Editor: Jane Brundage, Bookman Productions
Interior and Cover Design: Vargas/Williams/Design
Copy Editor: Betty Duncan
Photo Researchers: Sarah Bendersky, Darcy Lanham, Judy Mason, Monica Suder
Technical Illustrator: Illustrious, Inc.
Compositor: Graphic Typesetting Service
Printer: Arcata Graphics, Kingsport
Cover Photo: TIB/West/ Eric Meola © 1991

3 4 5 6 7 8 9 10—96 95 94 93 92
ISBN Computing Concepts: 0-534-17538-4

2 3 4 5 6 7 8 9 10—96 95 94 93 92
ISBN Computing Concepts Plus Four Software Tools: 0-534-16200-2

Library of Congress Cataloging-in-Publication Data

Duffy, Tim,
Computing concepts plus four software tools / Tim Duffy. — [2nd ed.]
p. cm.
Previous ed. published under title: Four software tools plus applications and concepts.
Includes index.
ISBN 0–534–16200–2
1. Microcomputers—Programming. 2. Application software.
I. Duffy, Tim. Four software tools plus applications and concepts.
II. Title.
QA76.6.D82 1992 91–43267
004.16—dc20 CIP

CONTENTS

The following software sections are included in the large volume, *Computing Concepts Plus Four Software Tools,* second edition, or are available, along with other software applications, as individual books. For detailed tables of contents, see the beginning of each individual software section.

ESSENTIAL DOS 3.3

ESSENTIAL WORDPERFECT 5.0/5.1

ESSENTIAL LOTUS 1-2-3 (VERSION 2.2)

ESSENTIAL dBASE III PLUS

PREFACE

PURPOSE

This computer concepts book and its associated software-training materials teach computer literacy and software competency. These materials are designed for both majors and nonmajors in a quarter or semester course that uses the microcomputer as the primary vehicle for introducing students to computer concepts and problem solving. As typically expected in this type of course, there are no prerequisites.

APPROACH

In the nine core chapters of *Computing Concepts*, students learn what they need to know to function effectively in an increasingly computerized world. The choice of topics was determined by market studies, discussions with and letters from past adopters, roundtable discussions, and discussions with and evaluation from my students.

Students acquire software competency by completing a set of software-training chapters that focus on current releases of various major software packages. Included in one volume with the *Concepts* chapters or available as separate booklets, these materials emphasize hands-on problem solving. Carefully prepared, hands-on tutorials are provided within each chapter. Closely related end-of-chapter exercises reinforce the tutorial learning and expand the student's mastery over a broader range of applications.

A FLEXIBLE PACKAGE

This text has been designed to provide maximum flexibility to adopters. The materials are available in three basic formats, from which combinations can be chosen:

- *Computing Concepts Plus Four Software Tools:* A spiral-bound, one-volume package that includes the nine chapters on computer concepts and the following hands-on sections: DOS 3.3 and Windows (2 chapters); word processing and desktop publishing using WordPerfect 5.0/5.1 (three chapters); spreadsheets and graphing using Lotus 1-2-3 2.2 (four chapters); and database management using dBASE III Plus (three chapters).
- *Computing Concepts:* Nine concepts chapters covering the basic knowledge students need to enter a computerized workplace.
- *Software Essentials:* Separately bound booklets offering a hands-on introduction to selected major software packages:

  DOS 3.3 and 5.0

  WordPerfect 5.0/5.1

  Lotus 1-2-3 2.2 and 2.3

  Quattro Pro 3.0.

  dBASE III Plus

  dBASE IV 1.1

  Paradox 3.5

  Windows 3.1

These hands-on separates have been designed specifically to complement *Computing Concepts*. To order *Computing Concepts* in combination with various separates, please contact your Wadsworth sales representative.

SPECIAL FEATURES IN *COMPUTING CONCEPTS*

This text builds on the well-received first edition of *Four Software Tools Plus Applications and Concepts*. Based on input from adopters, roundtable participants, market studies, and teacher and student reviews, the following changes have been made:

- **Illustrated Timelines** Many users feel that the history of computers is important, but they cannot devote large blocks of time to teaching it. This problem is addressed by the inclusion of timelines at the beginning of each chapter. The timelines provide a brief history of events related to the chapter content, upon which teachers can expand as they feel necessary.
- **Personal Cases** Each chapter begins with a personal case problem that allows the student to identify more closely with the main issues raised in the chapter. As the chapter progresses, so does the personal case. Each case is revisited at the end of the chapter to show how the overall case problem is resolved.
- **Future Trends and Other Features** Each chapter includes a Future Trends box and other boxed features that call attention to a wide variety of personal, technical, and social issues raised by the continuing rapid pace of technological change in the computer industry.
- **Knowledge Applied in Chapter Exercises** Besides various types of informational review exercises, each chapter ends with two special sections. "In Your Own Case" invites students to apply what they have learned in the chapter to some aspect of their own circumstances. "Questions for Thought" asks students to think further about the broader ramifications of concerns and problems discussed in the chapter.

IMPROVEMENTS IN SOFTWARE INSTRUCTION

- **Hints/Hazards Boxes** Many Hints/Hazards boxes throughout the software tools instruction inform students about the tricks they can use and potential traps they may encounter when using a particular software tool.
- **Keyboard Icons** Keyboard icons appear frequently in headings and tables. These icons help the student identify and remember specific keystrokes.

WORKING IN A HANDS-ON ENVIRONMENT

Computing Concepts and its allied materials work best in a hands-on environment. The step-by-step exercises make most sense when an individual is sitting at a computer and can immediately see the results of his or her actions. A symbol such as the one shown in the margin indicates hands-on material.

Each software package covered in this series of tools is treated in enough detail to satisfy the requirements of a computer novice. However, the text assumes that the software has already been configured for the student's use. If a package has not been configured for a specific machine, refer to the documentation for that package.

The software packages can be covered in any order. However, I encourage you to cover at least the first three chapters of *Computing Concepts* before going on to one of the software tools.

HARDWARE REQUIREMENTS FOR HANDS-ON SOFTWARE

An IBM PC or compatible computer with two disk drives and 320K of memory is required for most tools in this series. Note that you need 512K and a hard disk to run dBASE IV. You will also need a color monitor/graphics adapter board to properly display Lotus 1-2-3 graphics on the screen. A printer (with graphics capabilities if you wish to print Lotus graphs) is also required for printing documents, reports, graphs, and worksheets.

The hard disk (fixed disk) has resulted in many changes in the way computer concepts and use are taught in the classroom. During the past few years, the prices of hard disk technology have plummeted. Because this technology is now affordable for most colleges and universities, this text includes instructions for running software from a fixed disk and covers hard disk topics such as directories.

LEARNING AIDS AND SAMPLE FILES

Exercises are provided at the end of each chapter to give students quick feedback on their progress. Besides the written exercises, hands-on computer exercises are included at the end of the software chapters to provide feedback through challenging applications of material covered in the chapter. A number of sample diskette files—including sample worksheets, text files, and database files—have been provided for use with text lessons and exercises.

TEACHING AIDS

An Instructor's Manual is provided without charge to each adopter of *Computing Concepts* or *Computing Concepts Plus Four Software Tools.* The manual contains a lecture outline and transparency masters for each chapter. Adopters of *Computing Concepts Plus Four Software Tools* also receive a disk containing all the finished worksheets at the end of each spreadsheet chapter and, as a bonus, a Lotus 1-2-3 GRADBOOK template instructors can use for tracking students' grades. The GRADBOOK template, which is completely macro-driven, makes the tedious process of tracking grades much easier.

A computerized test generator is also available to adopters of *Computing Concepts Plus Four Software Tools.* The test generator, which includes true/false, multiple-choice, fill-in-the-blank, and short-answer test questions, makes the process of creating tests easy. Contact your Wadsworth representative.

ACKNOWLEDGMENTS

When I first started writing the original textbook, *Four Software Tools,* I did not realize what a tremendous effort such an endeavor entailed. I soon learned that a multitude of people are needed to make a textbook a success. These individuals include family, friends, colleagues, and many people in the publishing business. I am deeply indebted to my wife Wendy, who initially encouraged me to start on the first version of this text. Without her encouragement, the original text might never have been finished.

In this particular book I am tremendously indebted to the work of Alan Venable, the developmental editor for Wadsworth. Alan and I worked closely on this book, sending manuscript endlessly back and forth through the mail: exchanging ideas on the content, trying to cut length, adjusting the style to the audience, and making it read well. This was really my first experience developing a text in this fashion, and I am really pleased with the end product. Alan, thanks for all your help! This book is really a tribute to your patience and effort.

I would also like to thank the reviewers of this book: Harvey Blessing, Essex Community College; Mark Ciampa, Volunteer State Community College; Richard B. Daehler-Wilking, College of Charleston; Kevin Duggan, Midlands Technical College; Gerald Fischer, Niagara County Community College; Charles Hofmann, La Salle University; Robert Horton, University of Wisconsin–Whitewater; Peter Irwin, Richland College; Roy Johnson, Nanyang Technological University, Singapore; Cynthia Kachik, Santa Fe Community College; Richard G. Lee, Northern Virginia Community College; Elizabeth Magalski, Marquette University; Trudy Montoya, Aims Community College; J. D. Oliver, Prairie View A & M; Leonard Presby, William Paterson State College; Herb Rebhun, University of Houston–Downtown Campus; Holly Roe, University of Texas–San Antonio; LoriLee Sadler, Indiana University; Judith Scheeren, Westmoreland County Community College; Sandra Stalker, Northshore Community College; Richard Stearns, Parkland College; Sue Ellen Taylor, West Texas State University; Marilyn Wilkins, Eastern Illinois University; and Linda Woolard, Southern Illinois University.

The efforts of the individuals at Wadsworth Publishing Company must also be acknowledged because they are responsible for turning a last-minute manuscript into a professional final copy. Frank Ruggirello, publisher, is without equal in the publishing business. Frank is always a joy to talk with or to visit. Frank continues to be a rabid Giants fan. I always look forward to attending a game at the "Stick" when I visit Wadsworth on business.

Hal Humphrey of Wadsworth did a great job of shepherding this project from start to finish. Hal was responsible for making certain that all parties involved got their work done on schedule.

Hal Lockwood and Jane Brundage of Bookman Productions did a phenomenal job of completing this four-color project on such a tight schedule. There were times when it appeared to be an impossible task to get the book finished, but Hal and Jane's expert management of the project, along with their patience, brought it to a successful conclusion.

A frequently overlooked ingredient in the success of a textbook is the sales staff of a publishing company. Without their marketing efforts, any text, no matter how good, fails. There is no doubt in my mind that Wadsworth has one of the finest, most professional staffs in the country. I want to especially thank Ragu Raghavan, Peggy Hopp, Lisa Bettendorf, Reita Kinsman, Bob Ross, Gerry Levine, Jack Fox, Rusty Johnson, and Doni Marquart. I also want to thank our campus representative, Danny Murphy. Many of these individuals, including those not mentioned because of space considerations, will always be considered personal friends.

Finally, my wife Wendy and my son Michael are the two most important people in my life. Michael, especially, made this project a challenge. His sudden appearances beside the computer for a hug and a cuddle in Dad's lap are much appreciated. It is increasingly difficult to reserve large blocks of writing time when requests are made to accompany Michael to the basement to run Lionel trains, build a castle with blocks, or go for a bicycle ride around the block.

1

THE COMPUTER

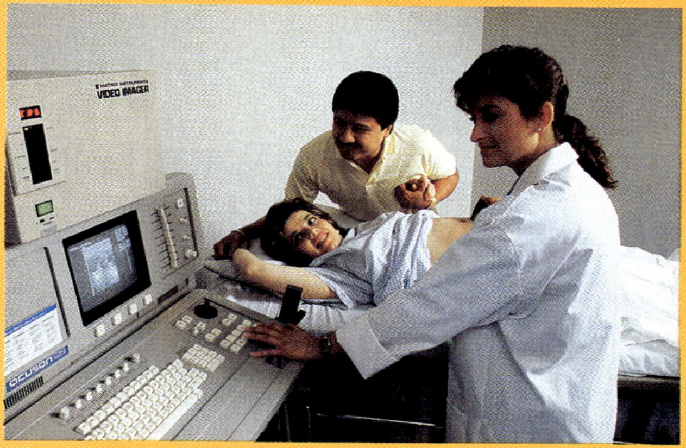

CHAPTER OBJECTIVES

After completing this chapter, you should be able to

- **Define a computer**
- **Differentiate the five parts of a microcomputer system**
- **Explain the stored-program concept**
- **Trace the four generations of computers**
- **Describe the types of computers**
- **Describe the hierarchy of data**
- **Describe in general how a computer accesses and processes data**
- **Intelligently explore the computer landscape of a work or school environment**

MODERN COMPUTING TECHNOLOGY

1942	The Atanasoff–Berry computer (ABC) is produced.
1944	The first electromechanical computer, the Mark I, is introduced. It is based on the work of Howard Aiken of Harvard in conjunction with IBM.
1945	John von Neumann develops the stored-program concept.
1946	J. Presper Eckert, Jr., and John Mauchley complete ENIAC.
1947	Bell Laboratories develop the transistor.
1951	UNIVAC I tabulates the 1950 census.
1953	IBM introduces the 650 computer.
1954	The first commercial, nongovernment computer is delivered to a General Electric plant in Louisville, Kentucky. First compiler language—FORTRAN (FORmula TRANslator)—is developed.
1956	IBM becomes the world's largest manufacturer of computers.
1959	Grace Hopper develops the first compiler for COBOL.
1960	Transistors replace vacuum tubes for computer storage. The first minicomputer, the DEC PDP-1, is introduced.
1964	IBM introduces the 360 computer.
1965	Integrated circuits are applied to computer technology.
1966	The first solid-state, hand-held calculator is offered by Texas Instruments.
1971	The Cray-1 supercomputer is introduced. The first commercially available microprocessor is introduced.
1975	MIT's Altair, the first commercially produced microcomputer, is marketed.
1977	The Apple II is introduced.
1981	The IBM PC is introduced.
1982	The computer is named "Man of the Year" by *Time* magazine.
1984	The Apple Macintosh is introduced.

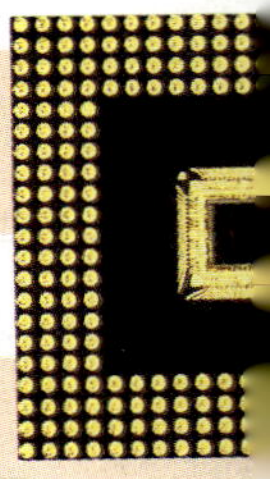

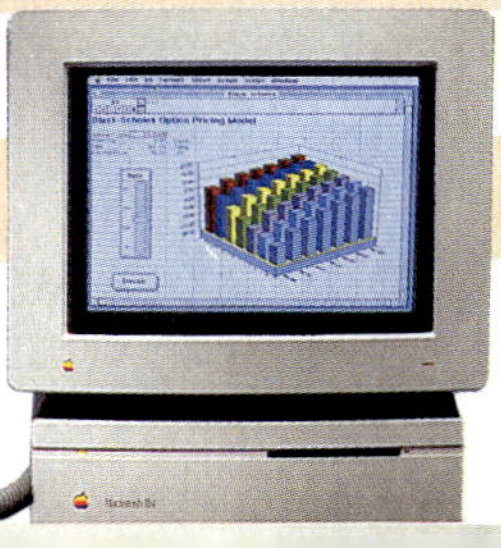

PERSONAL CASE

Computers in the Corporate Workplace

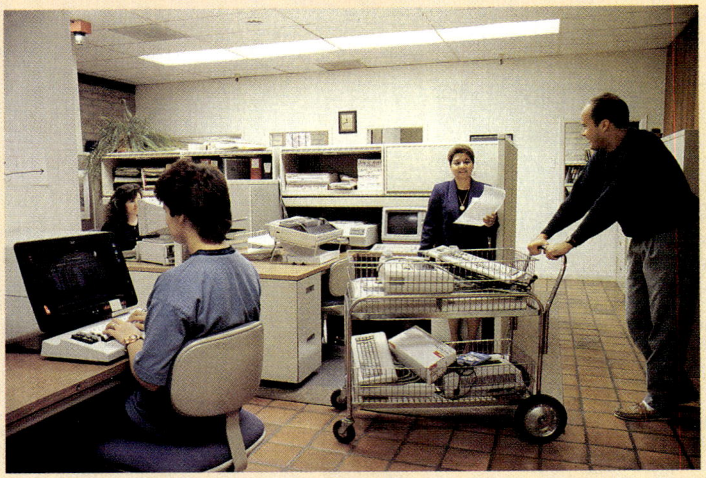

KATHERINE SEYMOUR has just returned to work with USQ Corporation. For the past eight years, she's been raising a family and advancing her education. Now that her youngest child has entered first grade, Katherine has rejoined USQ as an executive assistant. Immediately, she sees one tremendous change in the workplace: Computers are everywhere. Some sit on desks; others seem to comprise whole workstations. One group of large machines takes up a whole room. Cables run everywhere throughout the offices, connecting boxes and machines. Also surprising to Katherine are the vivid, finely detailed images on some of the computer screens, as colorful as her son's Nintendo. Before, the business computers she had seen were displaying only drab columns of text or numbers.

Late on Katherine's first day, a co-worker at a nearby desktop computer prints out a report. Their boss looks it over.

"This is great," she says. "At last we have sales stratification info in a form we all can understand! Good job!"

"It wasn't hard," the co-worker says. "I got all the data from the DP mainframe computer, and the form I used is just a worksheet template that is used to manipulate data from our MIS computer network. I used my PC to request the data and reformat some of the numbers."

Katherine leaves work that day knowing she's got some catching up to do. Her first problem will be getting comfortable with the microcomputer that sits on her desk. Her second problem will be figuring out what all these other computers are, how they're connected, and how they might also help her do her job.

Katherine has just become part of the ongoing technological revolution: the computer society. Information is power, and the computer is the information machine.

THE COMPUTER REVOLUTION

Although as late as the mid-1970s computers were used by relatively few people, the computer has already had a greater impact on our society than any other device invented in the second half of the twentieth century. In business, computers now help design and manufacture products, shape marketing campaigns, and track and process everything from inventory to accounts receivable and payable to payroll. In education, they help in teaching, scheduling classes, and recording grades. In the medical professions, computers assist in diagnosing and monitoring patients and regulating treatment. Scientists use computers to analyze our solar system, forecast weather patterns, and conduct experiments.

Of all computer types, the microcomputer has been the most helpful in improving our ability to control information and solve problems. The microcomputer is used by Fortune 500 companies and small businesses alike to file information, produce documents and correspondence, and perform time-consuming financial calculations and projections. It has boosted the productivity of workers at all organizational levels, from the mail room to the board room, as well as those who work independently. The microcomputer is your point of entry to a whole new range of information, connections, and abilities. Knowing about computers can revolutionize your life and career.

In this chapter, we look at computers and the computing process in general, as well as the microcomputer you'll be using with this book.

COMPUTERS AND MICROCOMPUTER SYSTEMS

A **computer** is a general-purpose electronic device that performs high-speed arithmetic and logical operations according to internal instructions, which are executed without human intervention. The most common type of computer these days is the microcomputer. Loosely speaking, a **microcomputer** is a computer of the size that can generally be used by one person at a time and can be placed on your lap or on a desktop.

As you sit down at a microcomputer, you become part of a *microcomputer information system* (MIS) (Figure 1.1), which consists of people, hardware, software, data/information, and documentation.

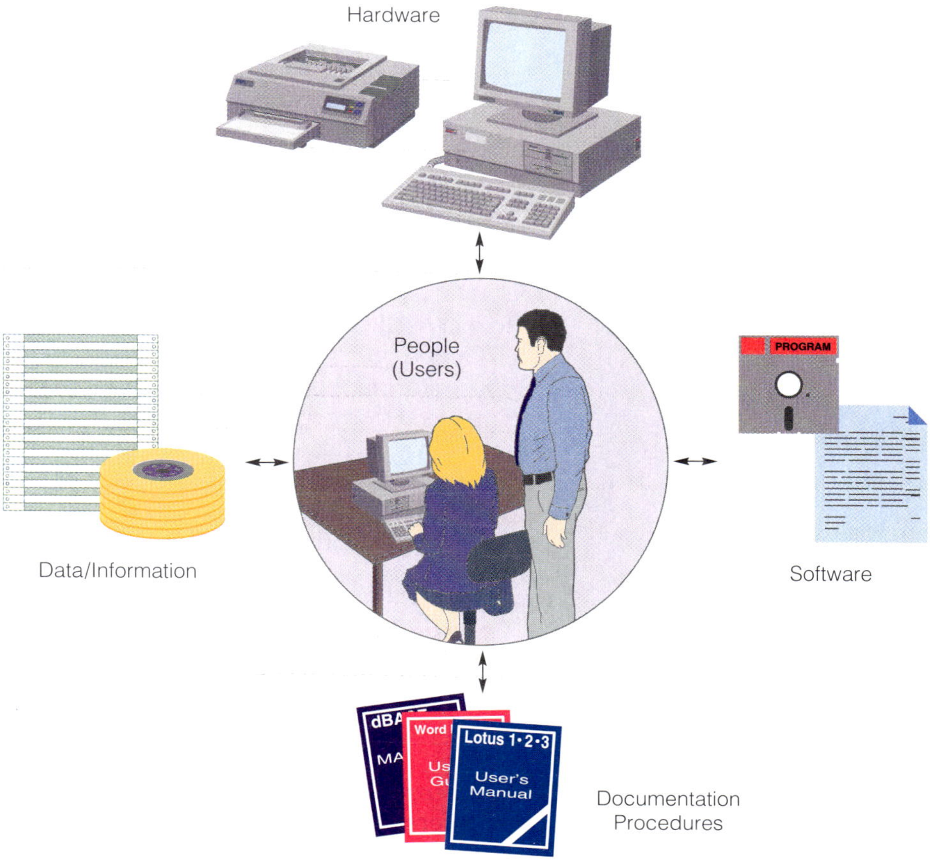

Figure 1.1

A microcomputer-based information system includes five not-so-equal parts. The most important part is the person who uses it. He or she determines the success or failure of the other four parts: hardware, software, data/information, and documentation.

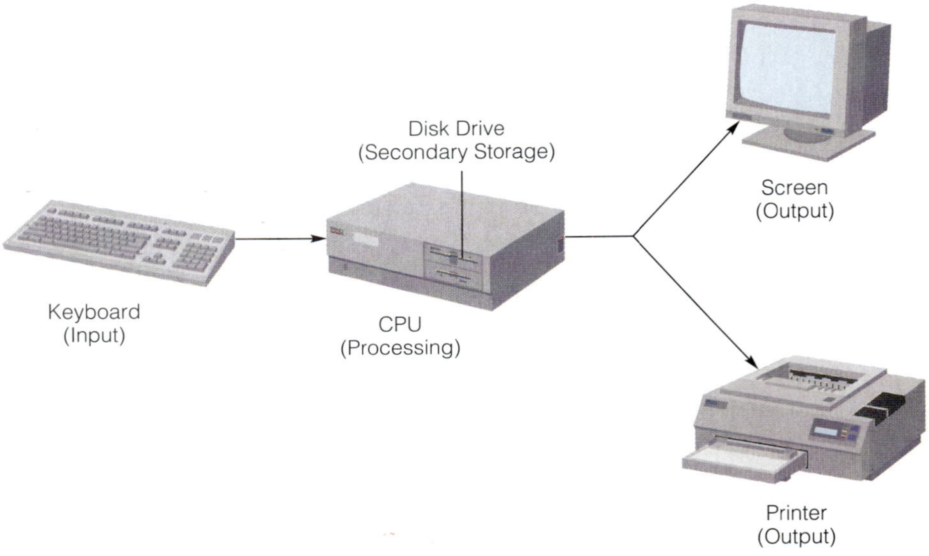

Figure 1.2
Four basic functions of microcomputer hardware: input, processing, output, and secondary storage.

Microcomputer **hardware** includes all machines that comprise the computer. These may be housed in one unit or may be a number of separate devices. Computer hardware must perform four vital functions (Figure 1.2):

1. Input: The user enters data and instructions into the computer, for instance, by keyboard.
2. Processing: The computer manipulates or processes those instructions and data.
3. Output: The computer communicates its results back to the user, for instance, by display on a video monitor or in print.
4. Secondary storage: The computer places information in electronic storage from which it can be retrieved at a later time.

Input, output, and secondary storage devices are commonly called **peripherals** because they lie outside the central processor. A complete computer hardware system may all be housed in one casing, or it may consist of a number of separately housed components.

Throughout the various pieces of hardware, all modern computers use chips to store and process information. A **chip** is a silicon wafer containing miniature electronic components called semiconductors. One computer may have many chips performing a variety of functions. The chip or chips that perform the computer's processing, or "thinking," is called the **central processing unit (CPU).** The CPU processes data and performs arithmetic and logical calculations. Informally, the box that houses these chips and other devices of the microcomputer may also be referred to as the CPU. Computer hardware is discussed more fully in Chapter 2.

Software is the electronically coded instructions **(programs)** that direct the functioning of the computer toward some particular application. Software is discussed in detail in Chapter 3. **Documentation** refers to the instructions, or procedures manuals, provided to the user on how to operate hardware and software.

When you use a library to do research for a class paper, you employ a complex information system that includes both tangible and intangible elements. Among the tangible elements are yourself, the card catalog, other files that indicate where to find information, and the source books and papers containing the information you seek. The intangible elements include your research goals, the file information you use to locate your source books, and the information you find in those source books.

A microcomputer system is also an information system with tangible and intangible parts. The tangible elements include you (the computer user), the computer's hardware, and the instructional texts that guide you in operating the system. Intangible elements include all the information you need to run the system, including data, processed data, software, and procedures. Data and processed data are the primary materials of problem solving. Software is the set of instructions the computer uses to manipulate the data. **Procedures** are written instructions that guide you in the use of software and hardware. For example, you may refer to a procedures manual when it's time to change the paper in a printer.

HISTORY OF THE ELECTRONIC COMPUTER

This brief history will help you understand that the computer revolution is still in progress. It should also help you see the microcomputer as a machine that is capable of communicating with a broader network of information and computing resources.

In essence, computers began big and were centralized, then got smaller and were many times decentralized. Now, small computers are being linked back to the big ones and to each other, so that in effect a small computer has the resources of the bigger computer. The following history is an approach to classify computers within a rapidly changing stream of events.

Prior to the midtwentieth century, people used mechanical computers to perform calculations, tabulate large numbers, and control a variety of large machines such as industrial weaving looms. Electronic computers were first developed during the 1930s and 1940s. From 1939 to 1942, John Atanasoff, an Iowa State College physics professor, and his graduate-student assistant Clifford Berry developed a computing device that performed mathematical calculations (Figure 1.3). Called the Atanasoff–Berry Computer (ABC), it used vac-

Figure 1.3
The ABC computer (1942)—the first electronic computer designed.

Figure 1.4
The ENIAC computer (1946).

uum tubes to process data, making it the first entirely electronic computer. Although Atanasoff and Berry never completed their computer, it served as a model for many future computer designs.

The first electronic computer completed was the ENIAC (Electronic Numerical Integrator and Computer) (Figure 1.4), financed by the U.S. Army for use in World War II. It was designed by University of Pennsylvania professors John Mauchly and J. Presper Eckert, Jr., to compute artillery ballistic tables. The 30-ton ENIAC filled a 20-foot by 40-foot room, contained 18,000 vacuum tubes, and could perform mathematical computations 1000 times faster than adding machines of the time. This mammoth computer had to be programmed by manually wiring it to three walls of plug-boards containing more than 6000 switches. Entering a new program was a tedious process requiring days or even weeks.

In 1945 John von Neumann, who had worked with Eckert and Mauchly at the University of Pennsylvania, published a paper on the stored-program concept. The **stored-program concept** permitted the reading of a program into a computer's memory and then executing the program instructions without rewiring the computer. The first computer to use the stored-program concept was the EDVAC (Electronic Discrete-Variable Automatic Computer), developed by von Neumann, Eckert, and Mauchly.

Stored programs gave computers tremendous flexibility and reliability and were far faster and less error-prone than were manually wired programs. A computer with a stored-program capacity could be used for numerous applications by loading and executing the appropriate programs.

Up to this point, programs and data could be entered into a computer only in the form of numbers written in **binary notation**, which is the only code that computers ultimately "understand." (Chapter 2 explains binary numbers.) The next major computer-design breakthrough was the development of translators that allowed people to communicate with computers by means other than binary numbers. In 1952 Grace Murray Hopper, a U.S. Navy officer, developed the first compiler, a program that can translate English-like statements into machine-readable binary code. She later developed the COBOL (COmmon Business-Oriented Language) compiler, a project jointly sponsored by private business, education, and the federal government during the late 1950s. COBOL allowed a computer program that had been written for one manufacturer's computer to be run on another manufacturer's computer without being rewritten. Suddenly, programs were easily transported, and the business world started accepting computers with enthusiasm.

HOLLERITH'S PUNCHED-CARD COMPUTING SYSTEM

Herman Hollerith (1860–1929) is credited with making the first commercially viable punched-card computing system. Hollerith worked feverishly from 1882 until 1889 on punched-card equipment that could be used for counting the 1890 census. He worked on his "census machine" while he was an instructor at MIT, as well as while he was a clerk in the U.S. Patent Office.

Before going to MIT, he had become friends with Colonel John Shaw Billings, director of statistics for the census. Billings was convinced that information about each U.S. citizen could be recorded on a punched card and that this would make the information easy to count.

Hollerith designed a punched card the size of the dollar bill at the time, a size convenient for storage in cabinets. After much testing, he developed a machine that could count 10,000 occurrences of any characteristic that had been coded on the cards (only one characteristic could be counted per pass). Hollerith's equipment (Figure 1.5) defeated two other contenders and was chosen by the Census Bureau for performing the 1890 tabulation.

The equipment Hollerith leased to the U.S. government read 50 to 80 cards a minute and took over two years to count the 62.6 million residents. (In contrast, the 1990 census required less than 9 months to generate the

Figure 1.5
The Hollerith tabulating machine used for the 1890 census.

Box continues

initial tally of over 260 million people.) After Hollerith's success with the U.S. census, a number of foreign countries—including Austria, Canada, and Russia—investigated using his equipment to perform the census, and Hollerith began to lease it to them. In 1896 he formed the Tabulating Machine Company. In 1912 Hollerith sold the rights of his company to a holding company that eventually became IBM. Thomas J. Watson, Sr., who became the driving force of IBM, was brought in to lead the company.

This punched-card system became the primary method of input used by many generations of computers. Since its invention in the 1880s, billions of punched cards have been used to provide program and data input for computers.

COMPUTER GENERATIONS

Four generations of computers are differentiated by their electronic components. Vacuum tubes were used for the first generation of computers, transistors for the second, integrated circuit chips for the third, and large-scale integrated (LSI) and very large-scale integrated (VLSI) chips for the fourth (Figure 1.6).

The First Generation, 1951 to 1958 First-generation computers used vacuum tubes for processing information. Operators entered data and programs in a special code on punched cards (Figure 1.7). Internal storage was provided by a rapidly rotating drum on which a reader/recorder device placed magnetic spots. Like their radio counterparts, vacuum-tube computers were far bulkier and generated far more heat than contemporary models.

Eckert and Mauchly helped usher in the first-generation era by forming a private computer company and building UNIVAC I, which the Census Bureau used to tabulate the 1950 census (Figure 1.8).

International Business Machines (IBM), which was selling punched-card equipment and had unsuccessfully competed for the 1950 census contract,

Figure 1.6
A set of vacuum tubes, a transistor unit, an integrated chip, and a VLSI. A transistorized device can typically hold hundreds of electronic components, an integrated chip can contain thousands of electronic components, and a VLSI chip can contain hundreds of thousands of electronic components.

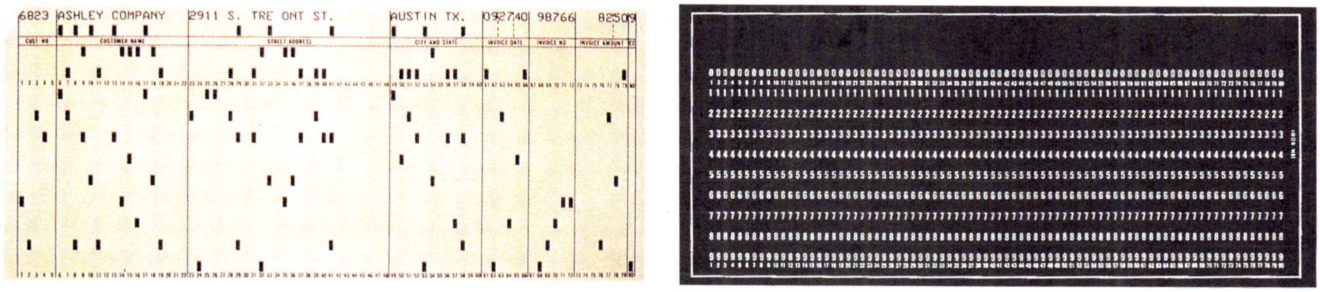

Figure 1.7

A punched card was used to enter data into first-generation computers. The perforations on each of the columns on the card indicate a specific digit, alphabetic character, or other symbol. The code, developed by Hollerith, uses the top 3 rows as zone rows and the bottom 10 rows as numeric rows to represent numbers, letters, and special characters. Each card of this type provides a maximum of 80 characters of input. Some programs required thousands of cards to be fed in batches into the computer to be read by a processing device that had mechanical "fingers" to sense the holes in the card. Punched cards continued to be used for entering data into computers until around 1986.

Figure 1.8

UNIVAC tabulated the 1950 census.

started manufacturing electronic computers and quickly became a strong contender in the market (Figure 1.9).

Although expensive and of limited use, computers soon gained acceptance by business and government. By the mid-1950s, IBM and Remington Rand,

Figure 1.9
Introduced in 1953, IBM's 650 computer made it a strong contender in the market.

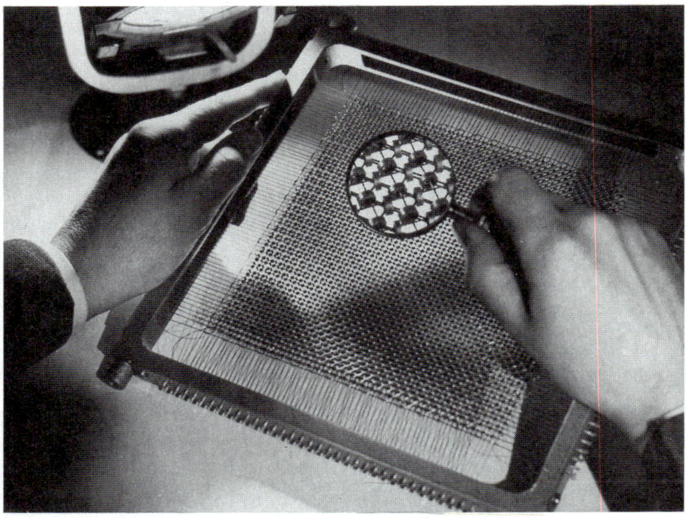

Figure 1.10
Magnetic core used as internal memory storage for second- and third-generation computers. A total of nine screens stacked on top of one another were needed to represent a character. A character was represented as a series of magnetized or nonmagnetized cores.

which had purchased Eckert and Mauchly's company, had emerged as the dominant computer manufacturers. Their clients included Sylvania, General Electric, and the federal government. Since 1956 IBM has been the world's largest manufacturer of computers.

The Second Generation, 1958 to 1964 In 1947 three Bell Laboratories scientists won the Nobel Prize by developing a transistor that was faster, more reliable, and 200 times smaller than the vacuum tube and that required less electricity. The transistor made possible a new generation of faster, more compact, cooler computers. Compare a vacuum-tube radio to a transistorized radio to get an idea of how this new technology reduced computer size.

Second-generation computers also used magnetic cores instead of magnetic drums for internal storage. These cores comprised tiny, wired rings of magnetic material on which instructions and data could be stored (Figure 1.10).

Computer programs, or software, also improved. COBOL (COmmon Business-Oriented Language), developed during the first-generation era, became commercially available. Programs written for one computer now could be transferred to another computer with minimal effort. Writing a program no longer required a thorough understanding of computer hardware.

Figure 1.11
The Whirlwind I computer, which was used as the first flight simulator

Figure 1.12
The IBM 360 mainframe computer.

Second-generation computers were substantially smaller and faster than vacuum-tube computers and were used for a variety of new applications such as airline-reservation systems, air-traffic control, and general-purpose simulations. Business began to diligently apply the computer to basic record-keeping tasks like inventory management, payroll, and accounting. The U.S. Navy used second-generation computers to construct the world's first flight simulator, Whirlwind I (Figure 1.11).

The Third Generation, 1964 to 1970 Third-generation computers emerged with the development of integrated circuits—silicon chips on which thousands of electronic components have been placed together, or integrated. Computers again became smaller, faster, cooler, and more energy-efficient.

Before the advent of integrated circuits, computers were designed for either mathematical or business applications but not both. Integrated circuits enabled computer manufacturers to increase program flexibility and to standardize their model lines. The IBM 360 (Figure 1.12), one of the first commercial computers

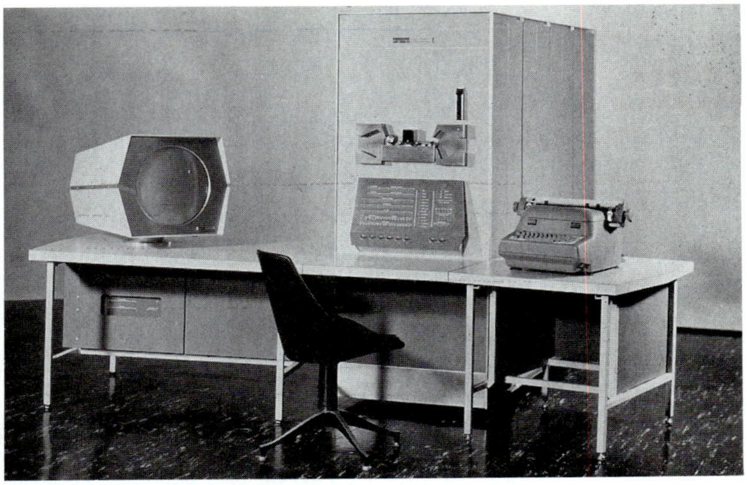

Figure 1.13

DEC PDP-1, one of the most popular early minicomputers. It can also be viewed as one of the very first personal computers. This machine was especially popular among scientists, engineers, and university researchers because it provided computer power that was directly controlled by its users.

to use integrated circuitry, could perform both file processing and mathematical analysis. Customers could upgrade their 360 to a larger IBM model and still run their existing programs.

With the introduction of the 360, IBM captured 70 percent of the market, driving RCA, General Electric, and Xerox out of the large-computer field. However, the 360's standardization permitted the growth of storage-device manufacturers, whose competitively priced peripheral equipment was compatible with the IBM series.

To avoid competing directly with IBM, Digital Equipment Corporation (DEC) redirected its efforts toward small computers. Far less costly to buy and operate than large computers, minicomputers were first developed during the second-generation computer era and came into widespread use in the 1960s and 1970s. In 1960 DEC introduced its first minicomputer, the PDP-1 (Figure 1.13), and by 1969 had a line of best-selling minicomputers.

Integrated-circuit technology also prompted the emergence of the software industry. Standard programs were rewritten to work in contemporary integrated-circuit computers and in hardware still on the drawing boards. This upward compatibility enabled businesses to continue using their existing software after they upgraded their computer hardware.

The Fourth Generation, 1971 to Today Two improvements in computer technology mark the beginning of fourth-generation computers: the replacement of magnetic-core memory by silicon-chip memory and the placing of much more circuitry on each chip. Intel Corporation took this idea to its logical conclusion by creating the **microprocessor**, a single chip containing all the circuitry required to make it programmable.

The microprocessor chip's compact size made personal computers possible. A single chip can now contain two of the CPU's components, the control and arithmetic/logic units. A third component, primary memory, is performed by other chips.

Today, LSI (large-scale integration) and VLSI (very large-scale integration) technology enables hundreds of thousands of electronic components to be

FUTURE TRENDS

Fifth-Generation Computers

There is some difference of opinion of exactly what will constitute a **fifth-generation computer.** In 1980 the Japanese began an effort to build what they called an "intelligent" computer making extensive use of artificial intelligence.

Artificial intelligence is the field of study that tries to apply human thought processes used in problem solving to the computer. If we can ever incorporate these processes in a computer, we will be able to communicate with computers in much the same fashion that we communicate with other human beings, in what is often called a **natural language.** For a computer to use natural language, it would need a knowledge base that is similar to the knowledge held by each human being. Such a computer could communicate in something close to human speech. However, there has yet to appear such a computer.

Some individuals think that the fifth generation of computers will be multiple processors hooked together to solve a particular problem. Such computers, called **parallel processors,** would hook together hundreds or even thousands of processors to solve problems simultaneously.

stored on one chip (Figure 1.14). Using VLSI, a manufacturer can make a small computer that rivals the power of a room-sized first-generation computer.

Applications for fourth-generation computers have been more involved with handling data tasks remotely via terminals for large computers. Many entrepreneurs made a tremendous impact on the computer industry by applying existing technology in new ways. Adam Osborne, for example, was responsible for developing and marketing the first portable computer.

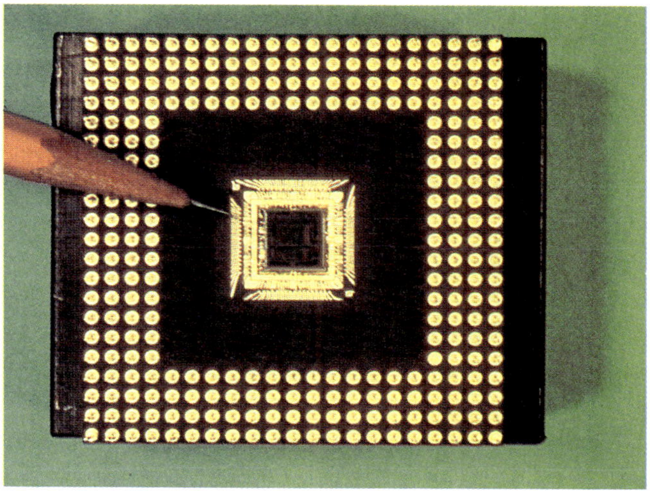

Figure 1.14

A VLSI circuit. Hundreds of thousands of electronic components are embedded in an extremely small component. This compact size makes this type of computer faster.

CLASSIFICATIONS OF TODAY'S COMPUTERS

Any classification of computers is arbitrary. Classifications based on price or size are quickly outdated by new technology. However, today's computers can be roughly divided into microcomputers, minicomputers (quickly disappearing), mainframes, and supercomputers, each type characterized by size, price, speed of operation, and memory/processing capabilities.

Microcomputers are the smallest, least costly, and most popular computers on the market (Figure 1.15a). Microcomputers range from around $1000 to around $15,000. Some models rival the power of minicomputers and older mainframes. Businesses use microcomputers for everything from spreadsheets to desktop publishing.

Thanks to microprocessors, microcomputers are small enough to fit on top of a desk or, in some cases, in a briefcase. Microcomputers can function as stand-alone units or be hooked up with other microcomputers or a mainframe to expand their capabilities. Microcomputers are sold like appliances in depart-

(a) (b) (c) (d)

Figure 1.15

Today's computers. (a) A typical microcomputer system—a Compaq. (b) A Prime minicomputer and peripherals. (c) A typical mainframe computer room. (d) A Cray-2 supercomputer.

ment, discount, and computer-specialty stores. The availability of low-cost, easy-to-use programs plays a major role in consumer acceptance of microcomputer brands.

Minicomputers were first developed during the 1960s to perform specialized tasks such as handling data communications (Figure 1.15b). Today's minicomputers rival some mainframes in power and are used in word processing, industrial automation, and multioperator applications.

Minicomputers are smaller, cheaper, and easier to maintain and install than mainframes. Prices range from around $50,000 to several hundred thousand dollars.

The minicomputer industry is today in a tremendous state of flux. Operations that were once performed by minis are now performed by increasingly powerful micros, and minicomputer vendors suffered a period of severe retrenchment during the 1980s. Several operators linked to the same minicomputer can still access resources such as printers and disk storage faster than operators on a network of microcomputers. However, some pundits predict there will be no demand for minicomputers by the middle of the 1990s.

Mainframe computers are large, fast systems capable of supporting several hundred input and output devices (Figure 1.15c). Large businesses, universities, banks, and hospitals rely on mainframe computers for their tremendous operational speed and processing capacity. For example, mainframe computers handle the hundreds of thousands of reservation orders that travel agents make each day with an airline. Mainframe computers range in price from several hundred thousand to several million dollars.

Mainframe computers are frequently used as repositories of huge amounts of data. These data can be accessed by mainframe users or by micro users whose terminals are connected to the mainframe.

Mainframe computers produce considerable heat, so environmental temperature and humidity must be controlled by special systems. They also require large support staffs. Typically, the computer vendor (seller) trains the user's staff and provides maintenance support. In turn, the staff operates and programs the mainframe computer.

Supercomputers are the fastest, most expensive computers (Figure 1.15d). They can run numerous different calculations simultaneously, thereby processing in a minute what would take a personal computer several weeks or months. Scientists at Sandia National Laboratory in New Mexico built a supercomputer consisting of 1024 processors. Each processor has the computing capability of a smaller computer and is assigned a separate part of one massive problem, which is worked on by all the processors simultaneously. Called the Hypercube, this supercomputer solves problems 1000 times faster than a typical mainframe computer.

Most supercomputers are used for scientific work, particularly for creating mathematical models of the real world. Called **simulation,** this process is especially useful in seismology, oil exploration, weather forecasting, and predicting the spread of pollution. Supercomputers cost millions of dollars, and only a few are produced each year.

COMPUTERS AS PROBLEM-SOLVING TOOLS

Because it can manipulate data using an internally held program, the computer is generally defined to be a problem-solving tool. Initially, computers were used to automate basic record-keeping processes such as student enrollment, class scheduling, general-ledger bookkeeping, and payrolls. Since then, computers have handled increasingly higher-level applications involving the selection of an appropriate solution to a problem from many possible alternatives. One of the most complicated applications involves evaluating input from thousands of different weather stations in order to predict the weather. No matter how small or large the computer, they all store and manipulate data in essentially the same way.

The following discussion focuses on computers as they are used in most business applications. This is dramatically different from instruction-intensive processing applications such as chess or mathematical simulations. To play chess, for instance, a computer must evaluate a small bit of input data and then execute tremendous amounts of internally contained program logic (perhaps thousands of different operations) to determine its next move. By contrast, file-oriented business applications usually have just a few actions to be performed for each record processed. At the same time, they may involve processing large volumes of data against numerous file records.

DATA AND INFORMATION

Data are raw facts that have not been processed or manipulated. Hours worked, employee name, and Social Security number are all examples of data that could be processed. **Information** is data that have been processed or manipulated. For instance, data on hours worked and pay rate can be used to calculate a person's gross-pay information.

What constitutes data or information depends on a person's point of view: One person's information may be another person's data. For example, suppose a traveler needs to fly to San Francisco. The traveler gives a travel agent data on where he's going, when he wants to fly, and how much he's prepared to pay. The agent uses these data and flight-availability data to decide what flight to book. The flight number and reservation are the information produced by the agent using the traveler's data. At the airline's corporate headquarters, the traveler's reservation becomes part of booking data by which the airline plans its flights.

DATA STORAGE AND THE HIERARCHY OF DATA

Data storage follows a linear hierarchy, beginning with the smallest piece of datum and ending with the largest:

1. Character
2. Field, or item
3. Record
4. File
5. Database

A **character** (such as a letter of the alphabet or a numerical digit) is the smallest humanly useful piece of datum. (Chapter 2 explains how characters are represented by pieces of computer data called bits and bytes.) A **field**, or **item**, contains one or more related characters that describe an attribute of an entity (or subject) for which data are being stored. For example, an entity of an accounts-receivable system may be a particular customer, whereas the entity's attributes might be described by such data fields as customer name, address, current balance, and so on.

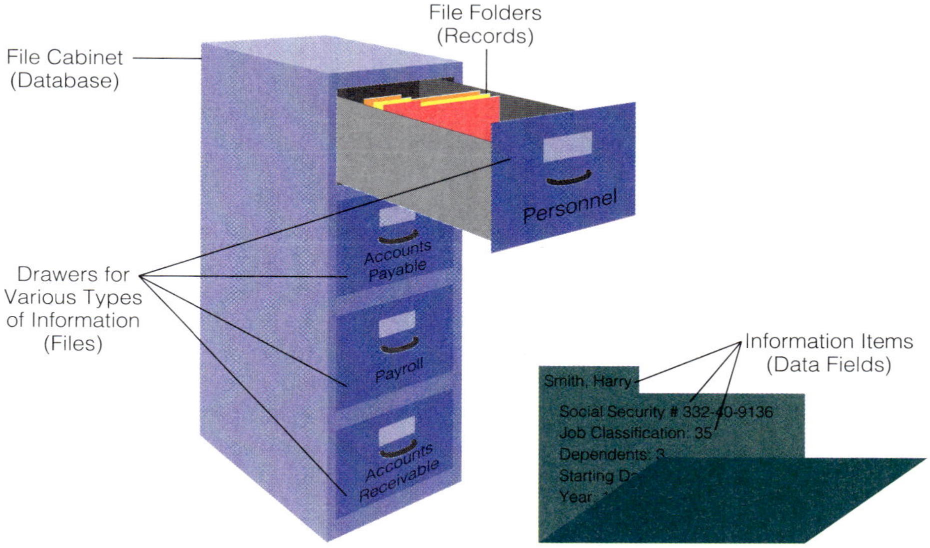

Figure 1.16
A manual filing system embodies the same hierarchy of data items as is found in a computer database.

A **record** is a grouping of related fields devoted to the various attributes of one entity. In our accounts-receivable example, a record might contain the following fields:

- Customer number
- Customer name
- Customer address
- Credit limit
- High historical balance
- Current accounts-receivable balance
- Date customer record was established
- Date of last activity

A computer record is analogous to a file folder in a manual filing system.

Logically related records are collected in a **file.** The collection of all accounts-receivable records in a computer is the accounts-receivable file (Figure 1.16), just as the collection of all manual-system file folders in a filing cabinet is the manual file.

A **database** includes all the organization's files that have been cross-indexed and structured for updating and data retrieval. A corporation's database may include payroll, accounts-receivable, and accounts-payable files (Figure 1.17). A computer database is comparable to one or more manual filing cabinets.

HOW A COMPUTER LOCATES AND PROCESSES DATA

There are two basic ways to organize data within a file: the sequential-access method and the direct-access method.

The **sequential-access method** stores records in ascending or descending order by **record key,** data that identify one record from others. Student Social Security numbers serve as record keys in many colleges' sequential files. The file must be searched in sequence, a relatively slow process.

Figure 1.17
Some of the many types of files typically found in a corporate database.

- Accounts-payable master file
- Accounts-payable receipts summary
- Accounts-receivable adjustments transaction file
- Accounts-receivable master file
- Back-order file
- Bill of materials file
- Budget master file
- Cash-disbursements transaction file
- Cash-receipts transaction file
- Completed picking ticket file
- Customer change file
- Customer master file
- Customer order transaction file
- Customer sales recap file
- Daily sales file
- Employee/payroll master file
- Finished-goods file
- Fixed-assets master file
- General-ledger master file
- General-ledger transaction summary
- Inventory master file
- Invoice accounts-receivable summary file
- Invoice transaction file
- Marketing file
- Parts master file
- Pending purchase-order file
- Product change file
- Product master file
- Product sales recap file
- Purchase order file
- Purchase order master file
- Raw-materials file
- Receiving report file
- Regional inventory master file
- Routing file
- Sales force sales recap file
- Sales-order file
- Sales transaction file
- Shipping notice file
- Standard costs master file
- Tax rates file
- Time-card file
- Vendor master file
- Work-center status file
- Work in process inventory file

Sequential access is suitable for processing many records at once on magnetic tapes or disks, which are among the most affordable computer-storage media. Sequential filing is used for preparing payroll checks on payday, for example.

The **direct-access method** uses algorithms or indexes to locate a record. An **algorithm** is a series of steps that are followed to solve a problem. An **index** lists key fields, which in turn contain all the file's records and their locations.

PERSONAL CASE PROGRESS

Working at a Terminal

Looking around during a break, Katherine watches various co-workers at their computer stations. One operator's equipment seems to consist simply of a screen and keyboard.

"This isn't a full computer," the operator says. "It's just a *terminal* that connects me with the mainframe computer. Right now I'm not really interacting with the mainframe. I'm entering some expense figures into a file for batch processing later tonight. The mainframe will take all figures in my file and add them to its database in one batch. This way I can enter the data quickly and let the computer take time to process it later."

A worker at another terminal enters a few characters on the screen and waits for the computer's response.

"We call this real-time processing," she says. "First I ask the computer a question, and then the computer answers it. Then I ask another question. It's like holding a conversation. Everything's happening here and now."

Direct access is particularly useful for applications where information is required as questions occur. For example, if someone wants to book a seat on Flight 225, she could telephone a travel agent and find out the flight's booking status while speaking with the agent.

In processing data, computers use both master files and transaction files. A **master file** holds semipermanent summary data about an entity. Within the records in the master file, some fields (for instance, a Social Security number field) must differ from one record to another. Also, some data fields will change and some will remain the same when the master record is updated by information from a transaction file.

A **transaction file** is a transitory or temporary file containing data about some business action. Information in the transaction file is entered and used to update master file records. The transaction file is then discarded or saved as part of a history file.

In the early days of computing, most processing was done in a batch-processing mode, whereby records are grouped together and processed all at once with information from a transaction file containing changes to many different records. With **batch processing**, a specific file update or information request (query) is processed only when needed or as a regular schedule dictates.

PERSONAL CASE REVISITED

The Central Computer Facility

At USQ Corporation, new or returning employees are given a tour of the company's central computer facility. On her tour, Katherine sees a series of four large interconnected IBM mainframe computers that are used for centralized data processing. These computers are controlled from a command center that includes 10 large display screens hung from the ceiling that give status reports about the computers, programs that are running, and any problems that are occurring. Operators use keyboard devices to communicate with the control software of the computer system.

The guide points out the tape cassette readers that are used to read the digital cassette tapes containing the files to be processed by the computers. He also points out row upon row of disk drives (over 40 in all), which are used to store data that are accessed for real-time applications.

Katherine sees a large DEC minicomputer, which processes electronic mail for the corporation. This machine handles thousands of messages traveling by computers from one part of the corporation to another each hour. Within the actual building complex of the corporation, these messages travel by cable. Any employee with a microcomputer or terminal hooked to one of these links is capable of sending messages to others on the network. An employee working outside the office can get mail from his or her "mailbox" by contacting the computer via telephone.

In another room, a rack of cabled devices called modems track the real-time purchase transactions by customers who enter their purchases using microcomputers at their own offices.

Katherine sees several large printers supplied with rolls of paper, 5 or 6 feet in diameter, for generating reports. More rolls of this paper are waiting along the wall on metal carts with pneumatic lifts. In many areas of the tour, Katherine sees that the floor has been raised to evidently allow all the wiring required for the tape drives, disk drives, computers, and other peripherals.

Katherine notes the emphasis on security around the central computers. The few entrances have magnetic-card readers and numeric keypads that must be used to gain access, and the central security office has television surveillance of internal and external views of the facility.

Most businesses require such controlled access to protect the important data that are typically held and processed in such a facility. Data about customers, employees, competitors, as well as data about sales transactions, collections, and payables, are considered to be important corporate assets.

When Katherine returns to her office, she takes a closer look at her own equipment. She finds out that the hardware on her desk is an IBM microcomputer called a PS/2 Model 70. Besides the operating system software, which her colleague says is already stored on a hard disk in her computer, Katherine finds she's been given packages containing software programs for a database, word processing, and an electronic spreadsheet. The colleague shows the documentation that tells her how to run these software packages and says that USQ gives classes on how to use the programs. She's also excited to hear that her computer is connected to a Novell network that has 65 other users and a large company database.

Katherine learns that her co-worker prepared his successful report by using a special utility program that allows him to selectively extract information from the sales database contained on the corporate mainframe. He was able to use this data on his spreadsheet program, sort it, summarize it, and generate a report. Katherine says she's impressed.

"Don't worry," he says. "We'll get you up to speed. Just remember that people are the most important part of the system."

Ø95 SIDE 2
NAME:
NUMBER: SCH#
DA IN OUT DAILY REG. OT1 OT2
SIGNATURE:
REMARKS:

Figure 1.18
One type of source document—a time card.

In business applications, batch processing starts with a preprinted form called the **source document** on which information about a business occurrence or transaction is recorded. A source document used for computing payroll is the time card, which lists an employee's Social Security number, name, regular hours worked, and overtime hours worked (Figure 1.18). Source documents are gathered periodically and then transcribed (keyed) into a transaction file by data-entry operators.

The transcribed information is fed into the computer and examined by an **edit program** to ensure that it is properly recorded. For instance, if the transaction is a time card, the edit program will check to see if the record is for a valid employee and if the numbers entered in the hours-worked and overtime fields are reasonable amounts. Transactions deemed to be in error by the edit program are returned to the payroll department for correction, then re-entered into the transaction file. Finally, the entire batch of payroll records is processed.

Batch processing is most useful when it is convenient to intermittently process a large number of transactions against records in a file. However, the transcription step is time-consuming and error-prone, and the files are only as current as the last processing run.

Real-time processing means updating or processing each transaction as it is entered into a computer and transmitting the resultant information back to the operator. Thus, at any given time, a real-time file will be as current as the last entered information. Most travel agents use real-time processing to make airline reservations (the transactions) because flight prices and space availability are constantly changing and must be continually updated. Real-time processing is better than batch processing in many ways, and many batch-processing systems have been converted to real-time systems.

CHAPTER REVIEW

Computers have had a greater impact on our daily lives than any other device invented in the second half of the twentieth century. A computer is an electronic device that performs arithmetic and logical operations, contains a stored program, and has internal storage. The stored-program concept enables any given computer to execute various programs that can be loaded into its memory.

Computer history is marked by four technological generations. First-generation computers used vacuum tubes as the primary electronic components.

Second-generation computers were made of transistors, and some commercial models featured compilers. Third-generation computers were composed of integrated circuits and featured standardized architecture, which permitted upward compatibility of software. Fourth-generation computers rely on large-scale and very large-scale integrated circuits and process by real-time systems.

The four types of computers by size are microcomputer, minicomputer, mainframe computer, and supercomputer. Microcomputers are desktop size or smaller and provide general-purpose functions. Minicomputers can support multiple users but for many purposes are being replaced by microcomputers. Mainframe computers are very large, support hundreds of users, and require a controlled-temperature environment. Supercomputers are the largest, fastest computers and are used for extremely complex modeling and problem solving. A computer system comprises input, processing, output, and storage portions.

Data are raw facts that computers process; information is processed data. A computer operator enters data or instructions through an input device. Secondary storage devices provide long-term storage. Output devices display information in either humanly readable or machine-readable form.

Data are stored by the computer in a hierarchy of forms that includes characters, fields, records, files, and databases. Stored data can be accessed by the sequential-access or direct-access method. Sequential access requires that all intervening records be read until the desired record key is located. Direct-access methods use either an algorithm or an index to locate and access a record.

Two modes for processing data are batch and real-time. In batch processing, records are grouped and then processed all at once, whereas real-time systems process transactions as they occur. Batch processing can use either a sequential-access or direct-access filing system, but real-time processing requires direct-access files.

KEY TERMS AND CONCEPTS

algorithm
artificial intelligence
batch processing
binary notation
central processing unit (CPU)
character
chip
computer
computer system
data
database
direct-access method
documentation
edit program
field (item)
fifth-generation computer
file
hardware
hierarchy of data
index
information
mainframe computer
master file
microcomputer
microprocessor
minicomputer
natural language
parallel processor
peripheral
procedures
program
real-time processing
record
record key
sequential-access method
simulation
software
source document
stored-program concept
supercomputer
transaction file

CHAPTER QUIZ

Multiple Choice

1. The term *permanent* is most frequently associated with which of the following?
   a. Keyboard input device
   (b.) Secondary storage
   c. Main memory
   d. Control unit
   e. None of the above

2. Which of the following is *not* considered to be hardware?
   a. Input device
   (b.) Diskette
   c. Output device
   d. CPU
   e. All of the above

3. Which of the following *cannot* be stored in main memory?
   a. Program instructions
   b. Data
   c. Intermediate results
   (d.) All of the above can be stored in main memory.

4. Which of the following computers could be small enough to fit in a briefcase?
   (a.) Microcomputer
   b. Minicomputer
   c. Mainframe computer
   d. Supercomputer
   e. None of the above

5. Which of the following computers is used for large, complex simulations?
   a. Microcomputer
   b. Minicomputer
   c. Mainframe computer
   (d.) Supercomputer
   e. None of the above

True/False

6. The process of manually transferring information from a source document to a machine-readable form is known as transportation. false

7. Most computers today make use of silicon chips. true

8. Batch processing operates on a group of transactions and processes them at the same time. true

9. Mainframe computers are being used to replace supercomputers. false

10. Real-time processing requires direct-access files. true

Answers

1. b 2. b 3. d 4. a 5. d 6. f 7. t 8. t 9. f 10. t

Exercises

1. Define the following terms:
   a. Computer
   b. Stored-program concept
   c. Transcription
   d. Direct-access method
   e. Batch processing
   f. Master file

2. __________ operations involve comparing two data items.

3. The __________ concept requires program instructions to be stored within the computer.

4. The term __________ refers to processed data.

5. The major benefit of a stored program is that it provides a tremendous flexibility and __________ to the user.

6. The __________ portion of a computer system allows you to enter instructions or data.

7. Data inside a computer are usually stored in __________ format.

8. The class of computer that many times is replaced by a microcomputer is the __________.

9. The class of computer that can cost less than $1000 is the __________.

10. The class of computer that can have hundreds of display terminals is the __________.

11. The smallest element in the hierarchy of data is the __________.

12. A method of arranging 0's and 1's to represent a character is referred to as binary __________.

13. The element in the hierarchy of data that is used to store something related to an attribute is called a(n) __________.

14. The element in the hierarchy of data that is used to store data about an entity is a(n) __________.

15. A collection of logically related records is a(n) __________.

16. The item that identifies a record is called a(n) __________.

17. The __________ -access method typically stores records in order by record key.

18. The __________ -access method uses an algorithm or index to store or locate a record.

19. The processing mode that requires grouping of transactions is called __________ processing.

20. Real-time processing mode requires __________ -access files.

21. The major components of the four computer generations are __________, __________, __________, and __________.

22. The device that is generally viewed to be the precursor of all computers is called the __________ computer and was designed but not completely developed by __________ and __________.

23. The ____________ is generally viewed as the first commercially available computer.

24. ____________ is usually credited with developing the stored-program concept.

25. Although the company known as ____________ was late in manufacturing computers, it now dominates the marketplace.

IN YOUR OWN CASE

1. Explore the presence of computers on your campus. Visit the computer labs or computer centers at your school. What types of computers are contained there? How were they acquired? Who uses them? What do they use them for? Are these machines connected to other machines? Where else on campus are computers? Who uses them? Are they interconnected? Why? (If your campus is large, you may want to confine your study to one particular school or department.)

2. Talk with someone who is knowledgable about the history of computers on your campus. When were computers first introduced? Why? What changes have taken place in recent years? To what extent do these changes represent attempts to solve particular problems? To what extent do they reflect changes in available technology?

3. Explore the use of computers in your campus library system. What terminals and computerized services are available for your use? What training is available on how to use them? Become at least a novice user of computer facilities in your library.

4. If you are employed off campus, explore whatever computer system may be connected with your employment. Prepare a profile of the system. How can you become a more effective user of it?

QUESTIONS FOR THOUGHT

1. Explore the enrollment system used for your college or university. Is this a batch or real-time system? Try to imagine what types of processes would have to be used if this process were done manually instead of by computer. Mentally, go through the procedures of how such a manual system would work in allowing students to select their classes while keeping track of the number of students currently enrolled such that the maximum enrollment figure is not exceeded. Imagine doing this for all classes at your institution.

2. How do today's more powerful microcomputers compare with the first computers that were marketed during the 1950s? What are the differences in size, speed, and cost? What are the differences in programming languages between the two types of computers? What are the differences in the requirements of support staff in running the two types of computers?

3. List the computer-driven applications that you come into contact with each day. What would happen if the computers driving these applications stopped functioning? What would be the impact of such an occurrence on your life and on your ability to function on a day-to-day basis?

2

MICROCOMPUTER HARDWARE

CHAPTER OBJECTIVES

After completing this chapter, you should be able to

- **Define the microcomputer's four main hardware parts**
- **Define basic technical terms related to microcomputers**
- **Discuss various input devices**
- **Describe the parts of the processing unit**
- **Discuss output devices**
- **Discuss secondary-storage media for microcomputers**
- **Handle diskettes properly**
- **Evaluate microcomputer hardware-purchasing options**

EVOLUTION OF THE MICROCOMPUTER

1966	Texas Instruments introduces the first solid-state hand-held calculator.
1975	The first commercial microcomputer, the MIT's Altair, is introduced. It is programmed by flipping switches on the front of the computer. Several thousand are sold.
1977	Steve Jobs and Steve Wozniak develop Apple II, using the Z80 microprocessor chip. It was originally produced and sold out of a garage.
1978	The 8088 Intel chip, a 16-bit processor chip using an 8-bit bus, is introduced.
1980	The price of dot-matrix printers drops below $1000. Formerly, less reliable printers cost up to $2000.
1981	The IBM PC is developed with 8088 Intel chip. Disk drives, electronic components, and software are also provided by third-party vendors. The IBM PC immediately becomes the de facto standard for business. Adam Osborne introduces the first "luggable" portable computer—25 pounds.
1984	Apple markets the Macintosh with 3.5-inch disks. It is advertised as an easy-to-use "computer for the rest of us." The 80286 Intel chip, a 16-bit processor chip using a 16-bit bus, is introduced. The IBM AT using Intel 80286 chip is introduced and is much faster than the original PC.
1986	The 80386 Intel chip, a 32-bit chip using a 32-bit bus, is introduced and is still faster.
1987	IBM PS/2 family of computers and VGA graphics is introduced.
1988	The 80386SX Intel chip, a 32-bit processor chip using a 16-bit bus, is introduced.
1989	The price of laser printers drops under $1000. The 80486 chip with built-in math coprocessor chip is introduced and executes more instructions twice as fast as the 80386 chip.

ALTAIR 8800 COMPUTER

IBM

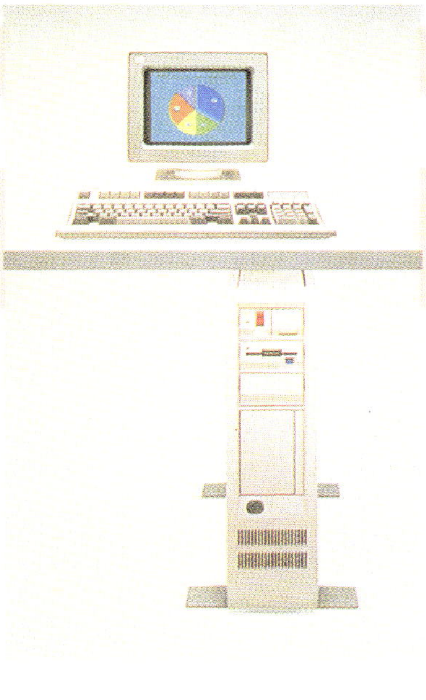

PERSONAL CASE

Buying a Computer

JOHN DILLINGHAM is a partner in Valid Investments, a financial advisory company. Having used his company's Compaq microcomputer at the office to handle several clients' investments, John is thinking of buying a microcomputer for home. John is a typical microcomputer user. Even though he uses the Compaq almost daily, he wasn't involved in its purchase or the choice of software, and he knows fairly little about it beyond how to use it to perform a few specific tasks.

John likes the Compaq but wonders whether other computers might be better and/or cheaper for his own uses. He also wants information on devices like scanners and light pens, which he doesn't have at work.

John could buy a few books about computers, but he doesn't have much time to spend reading them. He decides instead to enroll in an evening seminar, "Introduction to Micros," at City College, taught by Don Carpenter.

"Where should I start?" he asks him.

Don suggests that John begin by deciding what software programs he will want to use and then buy the hardware that will run them. Regarding the computer hardware system itself, that will have to serve four functions: *input, processing, secondary storage (disk),* and *output.* Depending on his budget and needs, he may consider a wide variety of hardware. The system he buys will fall into the category of the *microcomputer,* also called a **personal computer (PC).**

Don urges John, along with the programs he may want to run, to consider *compatibility.* Because John will probably want to bring Compaq file diskettes home from the office to work on them in the evening, he will want a computer that is compatible with the Compaq—in other words, a system that can run the same programs and use the same file diskettes. Currently, two basic families of computers are in the business world—Apple and IBM. Most other microcomputers are designed to be IBM-compatible or Apple-compatible. Some compatibles made by other companies use many of the same chips as the Apple or IBM computers and resemble them in other ways. These computers are called "clones" and can run at least some of the Apple- or IBM-oriented software. In addition, the distinction between IBM and Apple computers is not absolute. For instance, some Apple computers can read and create IBM-compatible files, and some (but fewer) IBM computers can create files compatible with some Apples. Compaq is an IBM-compatible, as are about 80 percent of all computers used by business.

"Why isn't everything compatible with everything else?" John asks.

"Theoretically, it could be," says Don, "but, of course, there's always the question of profits. Sometimes it's more profitable to put out a product that's compatible with everything else. Sometimes it's more profitable to make your customers buy everything from your system and nothing from the competitors. In 1977 Apple began publishing its computers' specifications so other companies could manufacture hardware and software that Apple owners could use to upgrade their equipment. This 'open-architecture' policy was very popular with consumers, so IBM did the same thing for a while. But some of the clones have sold so well that both companies have moved away from completely open architecture.

"For some people, it's a hard choice between the Apple and IBM sides," he says. "A lot of people think the Apple Macintosh has the easiest method for entering instructions for average users, and the 'Mac' took over a lot of the market in the late '80s and early '90s. But things have been changing. For instance, Microsoft makes some software called Windows that make IBM machines about as easy to use as the Mac."

John's problem is to find the right configuration of input, processing, secondary storage, and output hardware to meet his needs. He wants the system to be compatible with the microcomputer at work and reasonably priced.

HARDWARE COMPONENTS

The input, processing, memory, and output hardware covered in this text typically belongs to the IBM and IBM-compatible family of computers, but most of the concepts apply also to the Apple line. Like the central processing "heart" of the computer, most of the peripheral devices that the computer requires also contain computer chips, tiny integrated circuits embedded in wafers of silicon (Figure 2.1).

Figure 2.1
Manufacturing a computer chip.

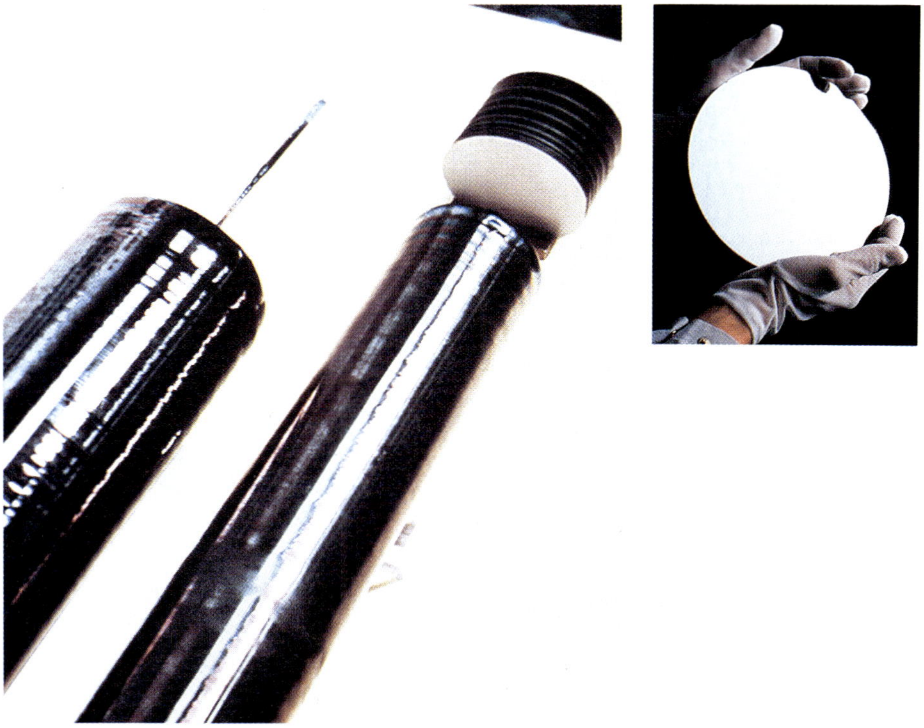

Making a computer chip requires ▶ obtaining a common material called silicon in uncommonly pure form. Molten silicon can be used to produce purified crystals up to 8 inches in diameter and 4 feet in length.

The crystals are sliced with a diamond saw and polished into wafers less than 4/1000 inch thick.

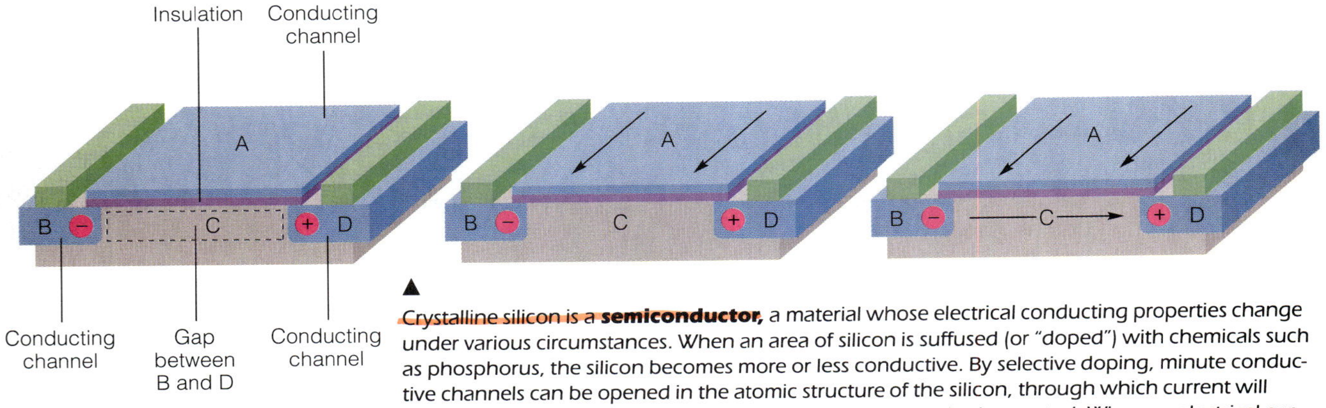

▲ Crystalline silicon is a **semiconductor,** a material whose electrical conducting properties change under various circumstances. When an area of silicon is suffused (or "doped") with chemicals such as phosphorus, the silicon becomes more or less conductive. By selective doping, minute conductive channels can be opened in the atomic structure of the silicon, through which current will readily flow. Barrier regions of low-conductive silicon can also be created. When an electrical current passes nearby a low-conductive region, the electrical field created by the current can cause the low-conductive region to become more conductive. When this happens, an electrical charge may pass through the region as though a "gate" had been opened.

These tiny, nonmechanical gate arrangements for switching current on or off are called **transistors.** A single microprocessor chip may contain more than a million transistors in one **integrated circuit.** Patterns of electrical flow through this circuit produce the electrical signals of computer output.

A microprocessing chip may take ▶ dozens of engineers several years to design. The goal is a complex set of blueprints that show how the silicon will have to be treated at successive levels on the chip to create the channels and transistors. Computers are used extensively to design and test the blueprint. For humans to read them, the blueprints must be thousands of times larger than the ultimate pattern on the chip.

A computer-directed electron beam shrinks and cuts the shape of each level of the design onto a photographic plate or "mask" about the size of a postcard. Each mask is used to stencil a tiny image of one level of the design onto each chip. The design may require as many as 15 levels or masks.

▼

Each level requires numerous stages ▶ of heating, masking, etching, doping, and coating.

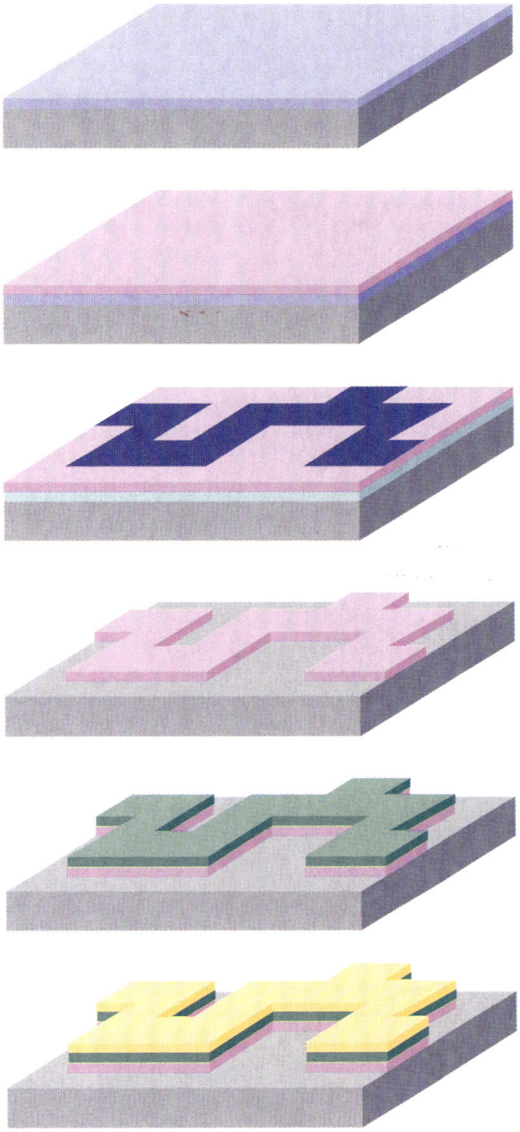

Silicon wafer is heated in the presence of oxygen or steam to create silicon dioxide layer.

A photoresist layer is applied.

The wafer is masked to expose only the pattern of desired channels of conduction.

After exposure to ultraviolet light and developing, exposed areas harden. Unexposed areas dissolve in solvents.

Doping adds coating that allows conduction or insulation.

Top aluminum coating permits connection to wires and so on outside the chip.

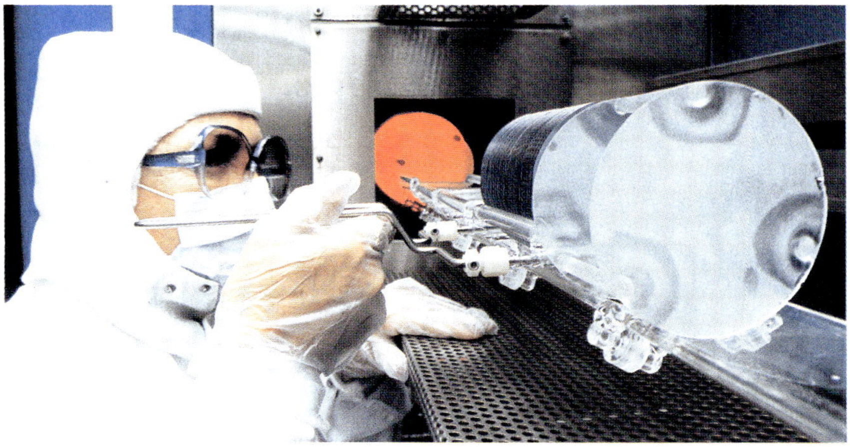

Designing and manufacturing a chip is extremely complex and expensive. However, once the manufacturing process begins, each silicon wafer produces hundreds of chips in a highly automated process.

Vulnerable to flaws and contaminations, the chips are tested individually by computer and by human inspection, and the faulty chips are marked for discard.

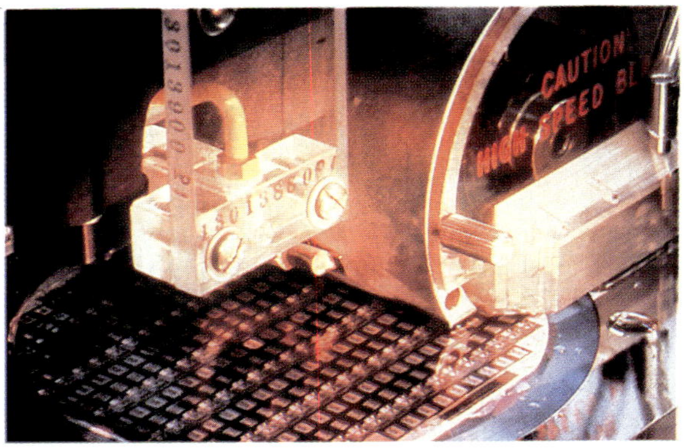

Individual chips are cut from the wafer with a diamond scribe.

A chip may need to have more than 150 wire leads or prongs attached for input and output.

The chip is sealed in a protective plastic case.

Still more testing is conducted on the bonded chip.

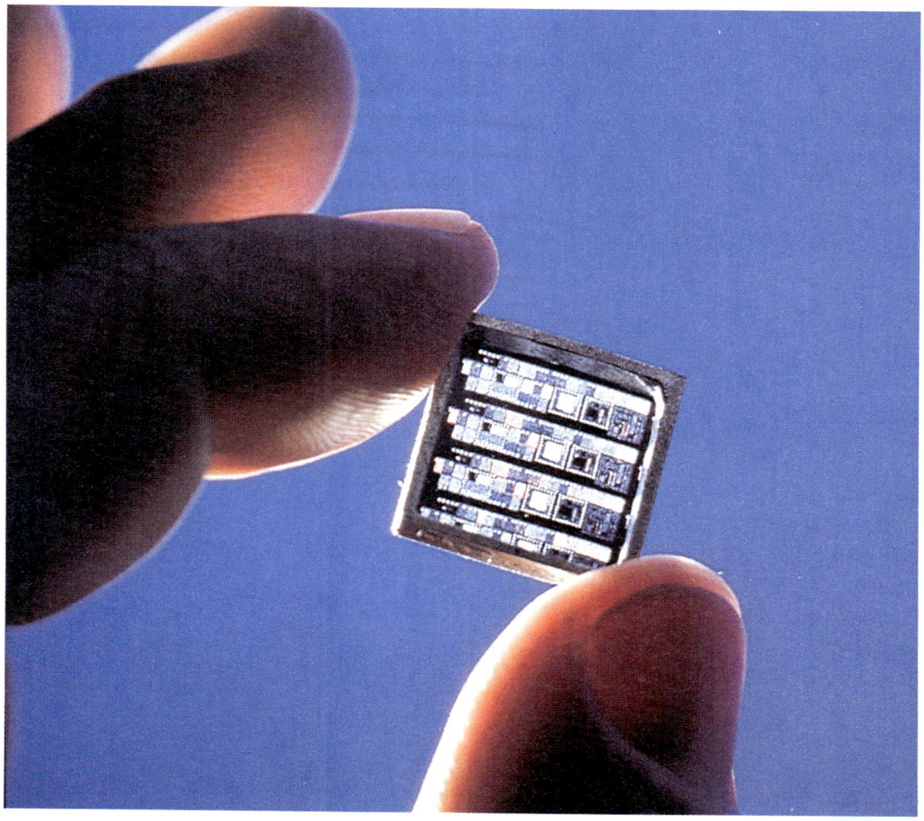

The microchip: The culminating invention of the twentieth century?

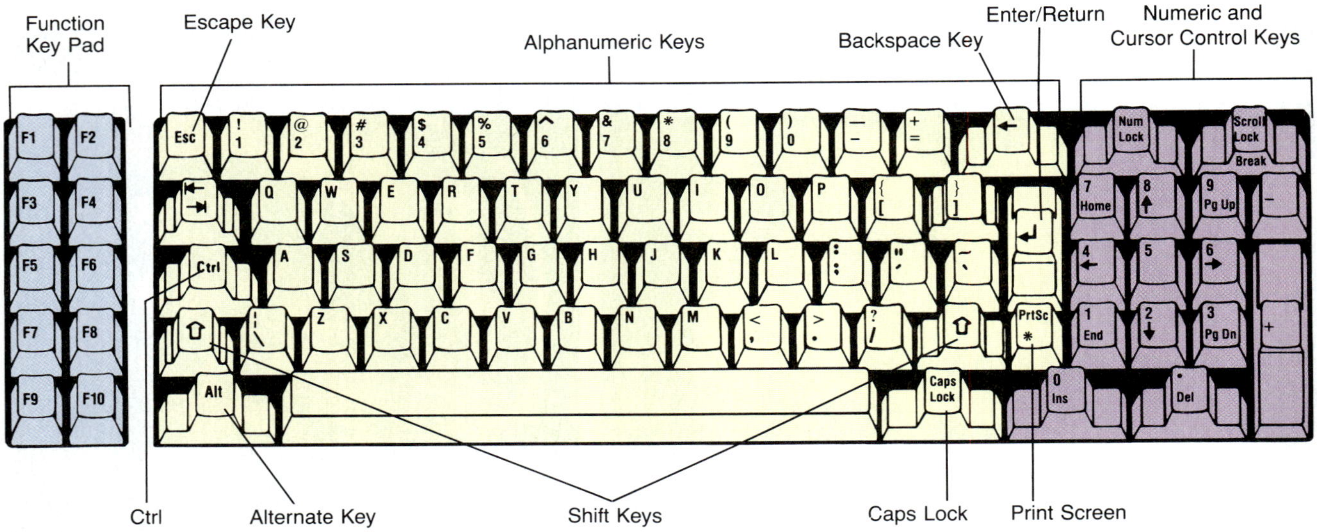

Figure 2.2
An IBM PC keyboard has three parts: function keys, alphanumeric keys, and a numeric keypad.

INPUT DEVICES

People use manual input devices to enter data into a computer and to give commands to manipulate the data.

Keyboard The standard input device for the microcomputer is the **keyboard.** The typical keyboard has three parts: function keys (in the left-hand part of the keyboard or across the top), alphanumeric keys (in the middle), and the numeric keypad (in the right-hand area) (Figure 2.2).

Function keys (usually labeled F1, F2, and so forth) are a set of keys that can be reserved by a software program to perform special functions such as saving or retrieving files. Different programs use these keys in different ways.

The **alphanumeric keys** are used to enter alphabetic, numeric, and punctuation characters.

The **numeric keypad** lets you quickly enter numbers and numeric symbols, do mathematical calculations, and move the cursor.

Table 2.1 lists other keys. A 101-key keyboard has a top row of function

Table 2.1 PC Keyboard Input and Cursor Control Keys

Name of Function	*Keys*	*Name of Function*	*Keys*
Alternate	Alt	Home	Home
Arrows: up, down, right, left	↑ ↓ → ←	Insert	Ins
Backspace	BackSpace ←	Number Lock	NumLock
Break	Break	Page Down	PgDn
Caps Lock	CapsLock	Page Up	PgUp
Control	Ctrl	Print Screen	PrtSc
Delete	Del	Scroll Lock	ScrollLock
End	End	Shift	Shift ⇑
Enter/Return	Enter ↵	Tab	Tab ⇄
Escape	Esc	+ (plus)	+
Function	F1 to F10	− (minus)	−

THE CASE AGAINST QWERTY

The alphanumeric keys on computer keyboards are usually arranged in the same sequence as they are on a standard typewriter. Invented over a century ago, the **QWERTY** arrangement was intended to make typing difficult, to slow the typist's fingers to a speed that would not jam the mechanism of early typewriters. However, on the modern computer keyboard, the QWERTY layout is a liability because the computer can accept keystrokes many times faster than the human can type them.

In the 1930s, August Dvorak and William Dealey studied the QWERTY layout to determine exactly what was wrong with it. They found that it overused the commonly weaker left hand and underused the stronger right hand. It also overworked some fingers and underworked others. Dvorak and Dealey also determined that in an 8-hour day of typing on a QWERTY keyboard, the typist's fingers traveled as much as 15–20 miles! They went on to invent the **Dvorak** keyboard (Figure 2.3), which, unlike the QWERTY, has the most frequently used characters in the home position. Among other advantages, the Dvorak keyboard reduces the distance the fingers must travel in a day to about 1 mile.

Some computer users have switched to the Dvorak keyboard layout. This can be done by buying a Dvorak keyboard or buying software that rearranges the functions of the keys on a standard keyboard so that, for instance, the QWERTY *D* becomes the Dvorak *E* key. The main problem lies in retraining people to use the new keyboard. Once people have learned to type on the QWERTY keyboard, most don't want to bother learning a new way.

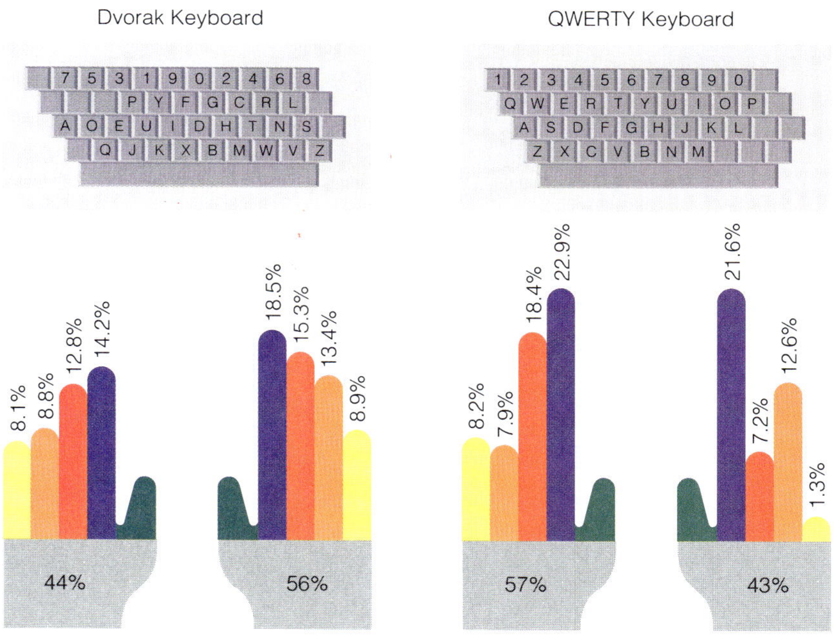

Figure 2.3

The Dvorak and QWERTY keyboards. The percentages on each hand and length of fingers indicate the comparative amount of work each performs on the different keyboards. Adapted from Dvorak, August. "There is a better typewriter." *National Business Education Quarterly* XII, 2 December 1943.

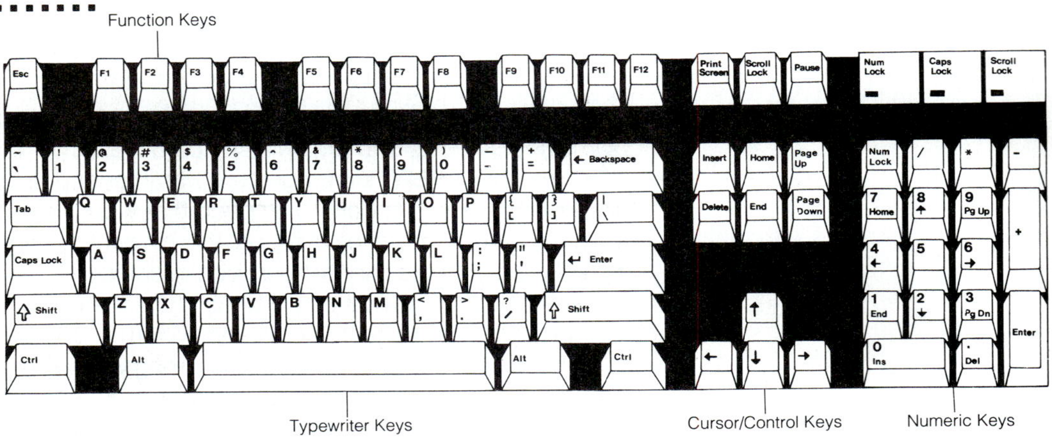

Figure 2.4
A 101-key keyboard.

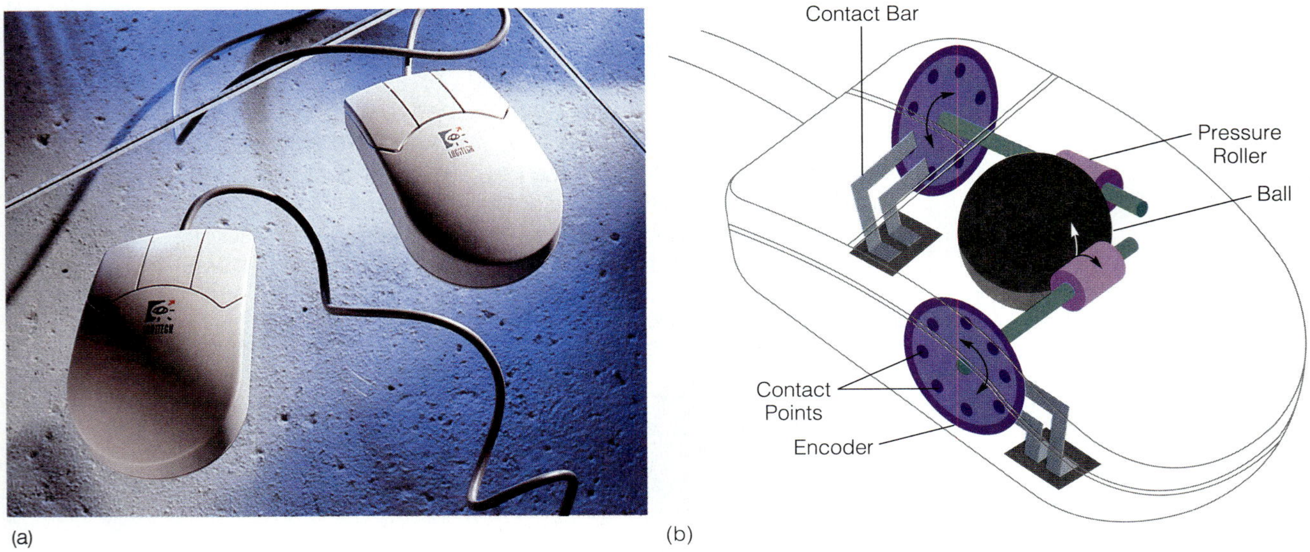

Figure 2.5
(a) A Logitech mouse. (b) The internal parts of a mechanical mouse.

keys, a redesigned numeric keypad, and additional cursor movement keys (Figure 2.4).

Many microcomputers can use a variety of other input devices including the mouse, touch pad/tablet, pens, voice-recognition unit, touch screen, and bar code-recognition unit.

Mouse The second most popular input device is a pointer tool called the mouse. The user drags the mouse across a flat surface to maneuver a pointer on the monitor screen. The most popular forms of mice ride on a $\frac{3}{4}$-inch steel or rubber ball whose rolling motions become electrical impulses to the computer. Buttons on the mouse let you get the computer's attention and issue commands (Figure 2.5).

Figure 2.6
A typical graphics tablet.

Figure 2.7
A light pen.

For many functions, such as selecting text and graphics, the mouse is far faster than the keyboard. However, mice do not fully replace the keyboard, and mice cannot be used with all software. Apple Macintosh software usually supports mice, whereas IBM and IBM-compatible software sometimes does not.

Touch Pads/Tablets A graphics **tablet** (also called a **digitizing tablet**) consists of a flat drawing surface and a pointing tool that functions like a pencil. The tablet turns the pointer's movements into digitized data that can be read by special computer programs (Figure 2.6). Tablets range from palm to desktop size.

Light Pen A **light pen** looks like an oversized writing pen attached to an electric cord and requires special software support (Figure 2.7). It works somewhat like an ordinary pen but uses light instead of ink. By pressing the light pen to the monitor screen, a user can select program operations (menu items) or draw images.

Light pens are used for order-entry work in large warehouses, point-of-sale recording in department stores, and applications like computer-aided design in design and graphics studios.

Other Pen-Based Input "Clipboard computers" let you use a special pen or stylus for printing neatly on a touch-sensitive screen. Software then interprets the handwriting and displays it in computer script. You can also enter information by checking boxes that appear on the screen or by circling words or numbers. Several systems are already on the market, some more accurate than others (Figure 2.8).

Many consider these pen-based systems a tremendous breakthrough that will very shortly allow us to perform many tasks that previously required a keyboard. New clipboard computers will receive, alter, and send faxes. With such technology, lawyers will be able to do legal research directly from the courtroom during a trial. Insurance agents and adjustors will also benefit greatly from this technology.

Figure 2.8

A pen-based computer from Grid Systems, a subsidiary of Tandy. This computer lets salespeople, police, inventory clerks, and others enter information much as they would on a paper form.

EDITING USING A CLIPBOARD

Using a clipboard computer, you can write directly on the etched-glass screen with the stylus just as you would with pen and paper. The writing is transformed into crisp, computer-readable typescript as you write. To add a phrase, draw a little caret under the insertion point and write.

The Go Corporation has standardized 11 gestures or symbols that can be made with a penlike device to give instructions to Pen Point, an operating system for this new generation of computers (Figure 2.9).

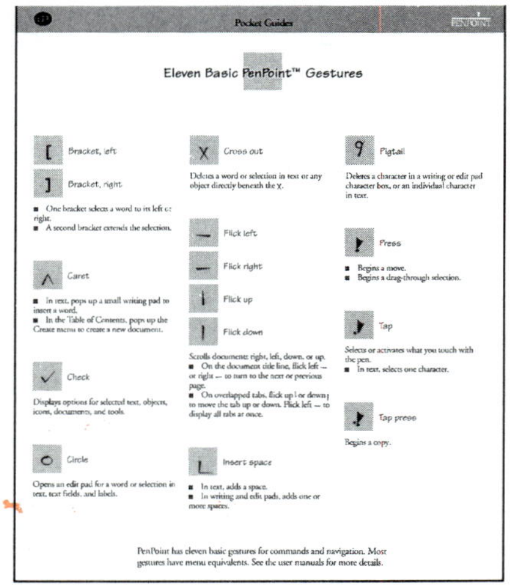

Figure 2.9

Pen-drawn signals of the Pen Point operating system.

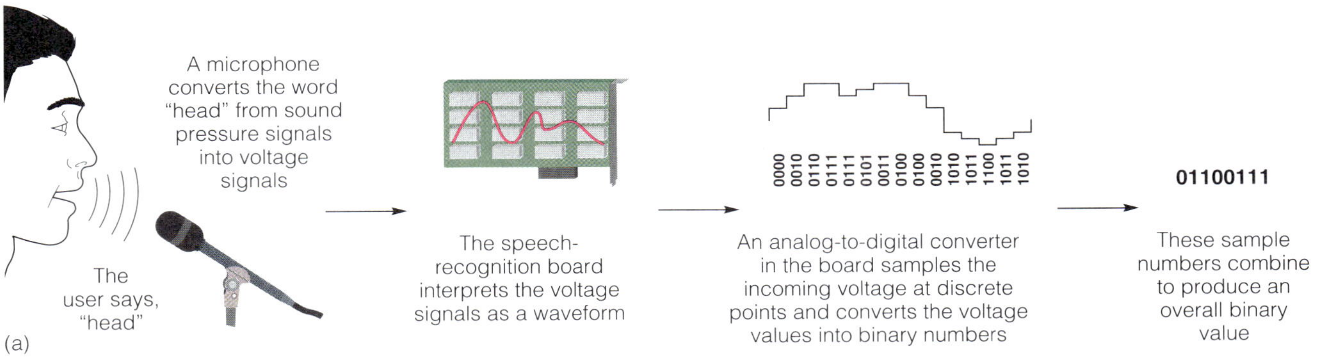

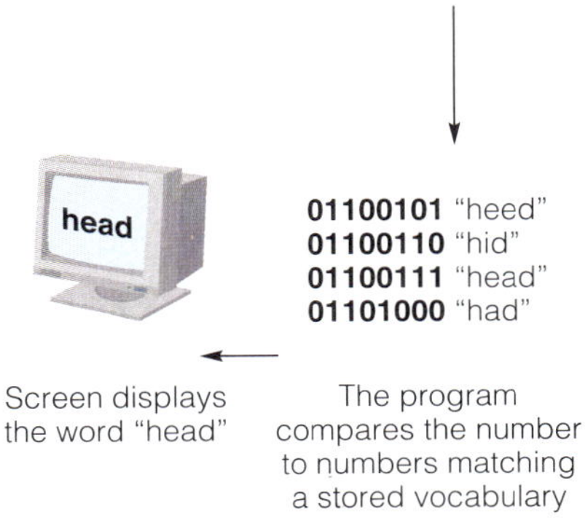

(b)

Figure 2.10
(a) The IBM voice-input control board. (b) A relatively simple voice-input application: when the child says the right word, the animal smiles.

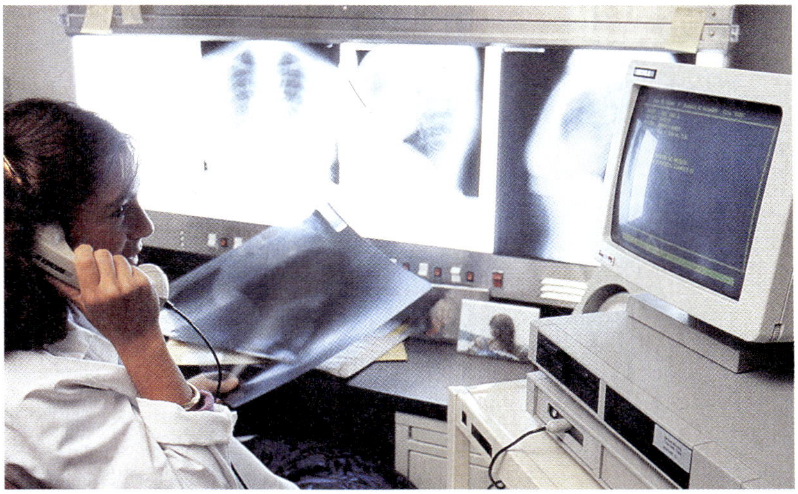

Figure 2.11
A radiologist can dictate reports into the Kurzweil Voice RAD system, edit on the system's computer screen, and order an instant printout. This time-saving system solves problems with delays in transcribing reports dictated to tape. Benefits include improved patient care and more efficient billing.

Voice Input **Voice-input devices** convert a person's voice into digital signals. Most of these systems have to be "trained" to recognize commands that are given verbally by a user. The computer matches the spoken word patterns with patterns that are stored in the computer. Several companies produce a board that can be inserted within a computer that recognizes hundreds of different words or commands (Figure 2.10).

Voice recognition is used by the medical profession to enable physicians to quickly compile reports but also to save money and help guard against malpractice suits. Over 300 Kurzweil Voicemed (Figure 2.11) systems are currently installed in more than 200 different medical sites across the nation.

Figure 2.12
A bar-code scanner/reader.

This newer type of voice-recognition technology makes use of speaker-independent technology. This means that a computer does not have to be trained to recognize the speech of a single person. It can recognize the same words from many different individuals. Thanks to the immensely greater processing power of today's computers, systems now can recognize up to 30,000 different words. These newer systems have an accuracy rate of 90 percent or better.

By the end of the 1990s, we may routinely be able to interact with computers by using vocal commands. Imagine writing a term paper by simply dictating the text. Computers will probably be able to take dictation much faster than people can type.

Touch Screens **Touch screens** let you give commands to a computer simply by touching certain spots on the screen. However, few software programs can work with them, and consumers have complained that the touch screen is too far away from the keyboard. Consequently, touch screens have fallen out of favor.

Large department stores use this type of technology to help customers locate various goods or services within the store. Generally, the user presses a box corresponding to an item on a menu, and the program responds by displaying one or more screens of information.

Automated Input Automated input devices enter data with minimal human intervention. These devices drastically reduce human data-entry errors.

You have no doubt had experience with bar-code readers at a grocery or other retail store (Figure 2.12). **Bar-code readers** are photoelectric scanners that read the vertical stripes that comprise the bar code. The bar-code reader is usually an integral part of what is frequently called a point-of-sale (POS) terminal. Grocery stores make use of the universal product code (UPC). Bar-code information helps a computer identify the product, store its description and price, track inventory for the store, and print an itemized receipt for the customer.

Figure 2.13
An example of a hand-held bar-code scanner.

Figure 2.14
An HP ScanJet desktop scanner and a scanned image.

Some readers are mounted on a fixed surface; others are held in the hand (Figure 2.13).

Scanners convert text, photographs, and black-and-white or color graphics into computer-readable form and transfer the information to a computer (Figure 2.14). Capable of scanning a page of print and graphics in mere seconds, scanners provide fast, easy, and accurate (99.5 percent) entry of printed information into a computer using optical character-recognition (OCR) software.

Most scanners are sold with software that controls the scanning device and allows adjustments for output resolution, image size, and image-brightness and contrast levels. After an image has been scanned, it can be modified or saved in secondary storage (see also Chapters 4 and 5).

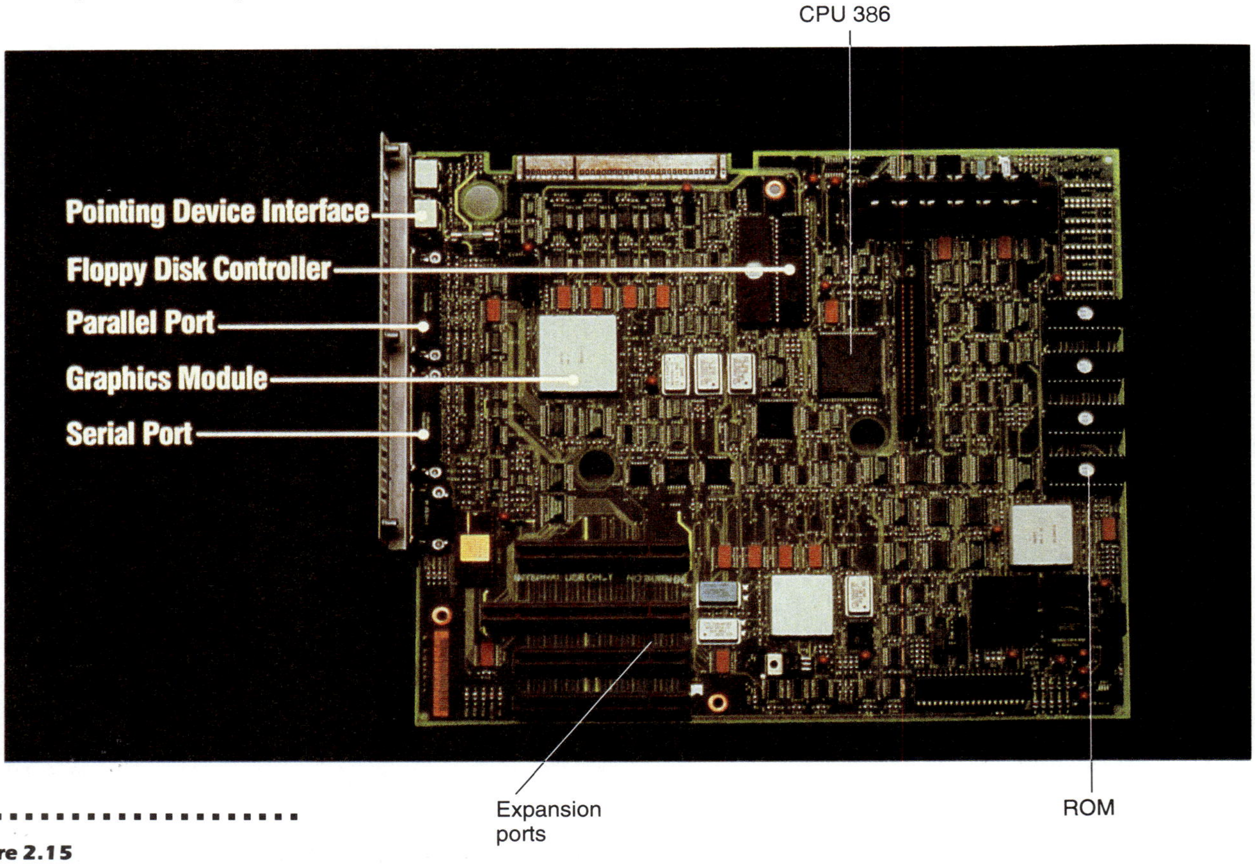

Figure 2.15
Parts of the processing unit of a typical IBM PC microcomputer system board.

Figure 2.16
The three parts of the CPU are the control unit, the arithmetic/logic unit, and primary storage. DOS (system software), program instructions, and data are stored in primary memory. The control unit evaluates and executes instructions (for example, multiply rate by hours to determine gross pay). The arithmetic/logic unit copies the contents of rate (2) and hours (5), performs the calculation, and generates a result of 10. This result is then placed in the area of memory reserved for gross pay.

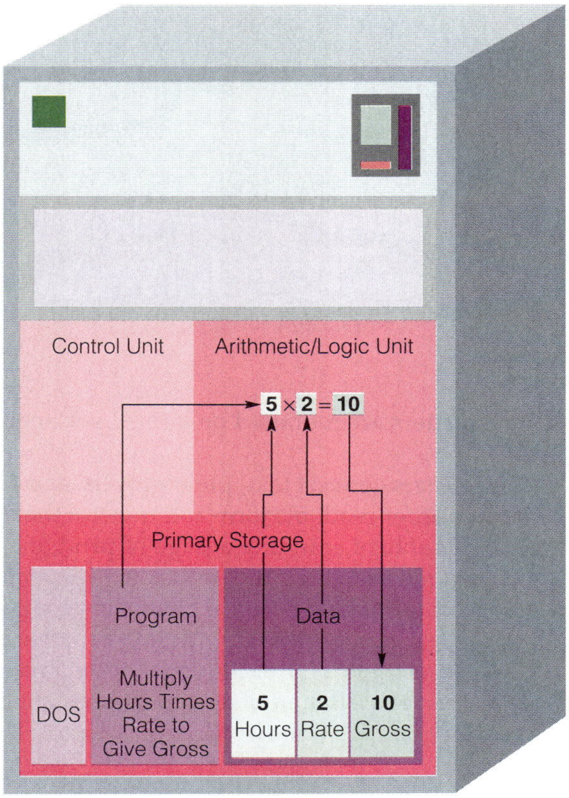

PROCESSING

Computers manipulate information in the **processing unit** (or **processor**), which includes the microcomputer's "brain" and all devices that connect it with input and output hardware. The processor has four parts: microprocessor, primary memory, buses and boards, and interfaces (Figure 2.15).

Microprocessors The brain of a microcomputer system is the **microprocessor,** typically called the *central processing unit* (CPU). The CPU is responsible for controlling data flow and executing program instructions on the data. It can add, subtract, multiply, and divide and compare numbers and characters. The CPU is divided into three parts: primary storage (or memory), the control unit, and the arithmetic/logic unit (Figure 2.16).

WHO NEEDS MICROPROCESSORS?

Since the first hand-held calculator was introduced in 1966 using solid-state circuitry, microprocessor chips have become an integral part of our lives. They are used to control microwave ovens; watches; automobile antilock braking systems; automotive sensors that display the status of doors, water reservoirs, and oil; fax machines; refrigerators; cellular phones; beepers; computers; automatic teller machines; bread makers; copy machines; and many other conveniences.

These microprocessors are typically an integral part of any of these appliances. The instructions needed to control a specific appliance or gadget are hard-wired into the microprocessor circuitry. This means that such a device can only do the one task for which it was programmed.

Consider the microwave oven. The integrated microprocessor lets you enter the amount of time and the task to be performed. If you have a frozen roast, you might want to set the microwave to defrost for 20 minutes and then switch to a cooking mode for 30 minutes. You can enter all these instructions, and then the microprocessor executes them, allowing you time to do other things.

These integrated microprocessors can also alert you to problems that might occur, thereby fulfilling a control function. A copier, for example, has sensors that alert the microprocessor to such errors as jammed paper, depleted toner, or empty paper tray. Once the microprocessor receives such a message, it may issue a beep on the copier and light an indicator to show the user the source of the difficulty.

One automobile manufacturer, BMW, is using this integration of computer technology in cars that can make corrections for possible driver mistakes. BMW's Heading Control system contains a camera above the rear-view mirror to track the center stripe and the line along the right side of the road. If the driver gets too close to either of these markers, a small electric motor integrated into the steering system is activated to put things right. Possible later versions will be able to evaluate road conditions and differentiate between broken and solid (no passing allowed) lines. A system could then evaluate whether it's okay to pass.

Drivers might feel a slight tug on the steering wheel as a correction is being made. They can, however, override the computer by continuing with whatever they were doing. BMW estimates that this system will be available in its cars about 1996.

As noted in Chapter 1, a computer performs all operations in binary notation—1 meaning on, 0 meaning off. This system parallels the on-off nature of electronic components. Figure 2.17 displays some examples of decimal numbers and their binary equivalents. The binary system allows computers to represent numbers and perform arithmetic operations much as people do using a decimal system. Binary codes can also be used to represent letters of the alphabet and other symbols. The basic unit of this system is called a byte, which is a sequence of 8 bits. Every character entered on the keyboard is instantly translated into such a combination of binary digits called a binary equivalent.

A computer system's binary code determines how any specific character is

Figure 2.17
Decimal numbers and their binary equivalents.

Decimal	*Binary*
0	0
1	1
2	10
3	11
4	100
5	101
6	110
7	111
8	1000
9	1001
10	1010

Figure 2.18
ASCII code for single numeric digits and for uppercase and lowercase letters of the alphabet. ASCII code can also represent punctuation marks and other symbols.

Binary	*Hex*	*Decimal*	*Symbol*	*Binary*	*Hex*	*Decimal*	*Symbol*
0100000	20	32	space	1001011	4B	75	K
0100001	21	33	!	1001100	4C	76	L
0100010	22	34	"	1001101	4D	77	M
0100011	23	35	#	1001110	4E	78	N
0100100	24	36	$	1001111	4F	79	O
0100101	25	37	%	1010000	50	80	P
0100110	26	38	&	1010001	51	81	Q
0100111	27	39	'	1010010	52	82	R
0101000	28	40	(	1010011	53	83	S
0101001	29	41	)	1010100	54	84	T
0101010	2A	42	*	1010101	55	85	U
0101011	2B	43	+	1010110	56	86	V
0101100	2C	44	,	1010111	57	87	W
0101101	2D	45	—	1011000	58	88	X
0101110	2E	46	.	1011001	59	89	Y
0101111	2F	47	/	1011010	5A	90	Z
0110000	30	48	0	1100001	61	97	a
0110001	31	49	1	1100010	62	98	b
0110010	32	50	2	1100011	63	99	c
0110011	33	51	3	1100100	64	100	d
0110100	34	52	4	1100101	65	101	e
0110101	35	53	5	1100110	66	102	f
0110110	36	54	6	1100111	67	103	g
0110111	37	55	7	1101000	68	104	h
0111000	38	56	8	1101001	69	105	i
0111001	39	57	9	1101010	6A	106	j
0111010	3A	58	:	1101011	6B	107	k
0111011	3B	59	;	1101100	6C	108	l
0111100	3C	60	<	1101101	6D	109	m
0111101	3D	61	=	1101110	6E	110	n
0111110	3E	62	>	1101111	6F	111	o
0111111	3F	63	?	1110000	70	112	p
1000000	40	64	@	1110001	71	113	q
1000001	41	65	A	1110010	72	114	r
1000010	42	66	B	1110011	73	115	s
1000011	43	67	C	1110100	74	116	t
1000010	44	68	D	1110101	75	117	u
1000101	45	69	E	1110110	76	118	v
1000110	46	70	F	1110111	77	119	w
1000111	47	71	G	1111000	78	120	x
1001000	48	72	H	1111001	79	121	y
1001001	49	73	I	1111010	7A	122	z
1001010	4A	74	J				

Table 2.2 The Intel Family of Produced Chips Used by IBM/Compatible Computers

Chips	Year Introduced	Bits Processed	Bus Width	Speed	Addressable Memory
8088	1978	16 bits	8 bits	4.77–10MHz	1 megabyte
80286*	1984	16 bits	16 bits	6–12MHz	Real—1 megabyte
80386	1986	32 bits	32 bits	16–33MHz	4 gigabytes
80386SX	1988	32 bits	32 bits	16–20MHz	4 gigabytes
80486†	1989	32 bits	32 bits	25–50MHz	64 gigabytes

*This chip can access only 1 megabyte (M) of real memory (more with extended memory). It can also access up to 16M of protected memory (a mode that has to have software written especially for it and is defined later).
†This chip has a built-in math coprocessor.

represented in binary digits. Most microcomputers use the **American Standard Code for Information Interchange (ASCII)** (pronounced "ask-ee") to represent data (Figure 2.18). Notice that uppercase and lowercase letters have different binary codes. To a computer, *a* does not mean the same thing as *A*.

Microcomputer processors vary widely in their primary-storage capacity and other characteristics, depending on whether the CPU uses 8-bit, 16-bit, or 32-bit chips. An 8-bit microprocessor uses 8 bits (1 byte) at a time and so forth (Table 2.2). Eight-bit microprocessors have a maximum addressable (usable) storage of 64K, or 65,536 bytes; 16-bit microprocessors, 1000K, or over 1 million bytes; and 32-bit microprocessors, 16,000K, or over 16 million bytes. (The term *addressable* typically refers to the primary memory storage that is available to the processor to store the operating system, program, and data.) Some 8-bit computers get around their storage limitation by using **banked memory.** For example, the Apple IIe has two banks of 64K each, giving it a total memory capacity of 128K. However, the IIe can access only one bank at a time.

MEASURING COMPUTER STORAGE

A **bit** (short for binary digit) is the smallest **binary** unit; it can be a 1 or a 0. Computers use groups of bits as information chunks, much as people use words to send and receive messages.

A **byte** is the smallest information chunk. It includes 8 bits and can hold any of 256 different values, depending on how the bits are ordered. Individual bytes represent specific numerals or characters. To store the letters *CPU* in memory, a computer would need 3 bytes—one for each character.

A **kilobyte (K)** equals 1024 bytes. To make it easier to calculate a CPU's storage capacity, most computer users think of a K as being 1000 bytes. A 256K system, for instance, is popularly thought of as being able to store 256,000 bytes, but it actually can hold 262,144 (256 × 1024) bytes.

A **megabyte (M)** equals 1000K, or 1,024,000 bytes, but is commonly thought of as 1 million bytes. Hard-disk storage is measured in megabytes.

A **gigabyte (G)** equals 1000M, or 1,073,741,824 bytes, commonly thought of as 1 billion bytes. Very large disk-storage devices are measured in gigabytes.

Microprocessors also vary considerably in their operating speed. Operating speed is a function of the bit size of the CPU chips, the system's clock speed, and the presence of coprocessing units. A CPU's speed increases with bit size, so 16-bit computers are usually much faster than 8-bit ones.

Clock speed, measured in millions of cycles per second (megahertz, or MHz), indicates how fast a computer can process information and is a function of the ease with which electricity passes through the CPU. Most computers perform a single processing step in one clock cycle. The faster its clock, the quicker a computer can run through its cycles. Most microcomputer clocks operate at 4 to 50 MHz. A computer with a 16-MHz clock performs calculations four times faster than a computer with a 4-MHz clock. Some computers let you control the speed of the clock using an option sometime referred to as **turbo**.

The **coprocessor** is an optional chip used primarily for mathematical manipulation, freeing the CPU to concentrate on other tasks. However, the coprocessor will perform its function only if the computer software is programmed to call on it for mathematical applications. Otherwise, the software will use the slower CPU. Coprocessors are typically used for applications that require a tremendous amount of mathematical calculations that tend to slow a machine. Such applications include computer-aided design (CAD), statistics, and large computation-intensive spreadsheets.

Primary Memory A computer's **primary memory,** or internal storage, must be able to hold the operating system, instructions for manipulating data, and the data itself. Primary-memory capacity determines the length and therefore often the complexity of programs and the size of data files a computer can handle. In computers with little memory, complex programs have to be broken down into subprograms to fit. Storage capacity also determines how much data can be stored in the computer, thus limiting, for example, the size of a document it can hold. Within certain limits, additional memory can be obtained by installing additional memory chips.

Computers use two types of primary memory: **read-only memory (ROM)** and **random-access memory (RAM)**. ROM stores certain programs and information needed by the computer. These instructions are permanently "burned" into the ROM chip and cannot be changed by an operator, hence "read-only." This is called **nonvolatile memory** because it is not wiped out when the power is turned off.

Basic instructions needed to start the computer (the "bootstrap loader") are usually put in ROM memory. Sometimes utility programs and software packages are too. ROM-resident programs include the BASIC program found in some IBM PCs and the spreadsheet programs in some portable computers.

RAM also can hold data and programs vital to the computer's functioning. In RAM, however, information can be changed, stored, and erased by the user. The amount of RAM affects what software programs can be run and how much data can be processed. A spreadsheet package like Lotus 1–2-3 may require every byte of a computer's RAM. The more user-friendly a program is, the more RAM it generally needs.

RAM is **volatile memory**—unless stored to disk, it is lost when the computer is turned off (except in computers having special batteries to power RAM).

Buses and Boards **Buses** are processing components that facilitate information transfer between the CPU and its peripherals. Suppose you command a computer to print a particular document. The CPU sends that command and the document to the bus system. The bus system holds on to this information while it alerts the printer that the document is coming, then sends the document on to be printed.

PERSONAL CASE PROGRESS

Looking at Chips

JOHN asks a salesperson at a local computer store her advice about what type of processor chip he needs.

"Have you ever looked inside a computer?" she asks.

When John says he hasn't, she opens a processing unit and shows him what's inside.

John learns that much of the software currently being written for the 80386 and 80486 families of computers (and especially future software) cannot be run on older computers. He also finds that the 80386SX family of computers costs about the same amount of money as an older 80286 computer. He concludes that, if he can afford it, he's better off buying a minimum of an 80386SX-equipped machine.

UPGRADING RAM

When the operating system for IBM and compatible computers was designed, it arbitrarily limited the maximum amount of base RAM to 640K for ordinary use. At first, this was not a problem (even though RAM must hold DOS, the software, and the data) because not much RAM was needed for most business applications. As software developers created more and more features, they quickly ran out of RAM. To quench this thirst for RAM, developers "tricked" the operating system into recognizing more RAM by using the following types of memory extenders:

- **Expanded memory** is banked memory used for the 8088 chip to increase memory. Many blocks of memory can be switched or swapped into the available 640K of memory and then accessed by the computer. Special controlling software (the Lotus-Intel-Microsoft Expanded Memory Specification, or LIM-EMS) is required.
- **Extended memory** is directly accessible to the CPU at addresses higher than 1M. This requires an 80286-or-higher processor chip as well as additional controlling software for IBM-compatible systems.

Figure 2.19
Adding a peripheral to the system may require inserting an interface board in an empty expansion slot.

There are two basic types of bus systems—open and closed. On the computer's **main system board** (sometimes called a **motherboard**), an **open-bus system** provides expansion slots that let you expand the system as needed. The IBM XT, for example, has eight expansion slots. A peripheral is added to the computer system by plugging an appropriate interface board into an expansion slot (Figure 2.19). The IBM PC, IBM compatibles, and the Apple II computer are all open-bus computers.

Closed-bus systems are equipped with sockets called established ports that accept peripheral connecting cables (Figure 2.20). To expand a closed-bus system, the computer operator merely plugs a peripheral into a port. No additional board is needed. However, the computer can accept only as many peripherals as it has ports to accept them.

Interfaces **Interfaces,** or adapter **boards,** are circuit-filled components that let a computer communicate with its peripherals. An interface may translate computer output for a printer or turn a scanner's input into binary computer code.

Interfaces are either parallel or serial. A **parallel interface** transmits all the bits contained in a byte of storage simultaneously. At least eight wires, one for each bit, are needed to carry the information. However, most parallel devices have additional wires to handle a variety of data-checking and message-carrying functions. The standard method of parallel data transmission is called **Centronics.**

A **serial interface** transmits a byte 1 bit at a time. Only two wires are needed, one to send bits and the other to receive them. Other lines accommodate data-checking and message-carrying functions. No real standards for serial transmission have been established in the computer industry, and, conse-

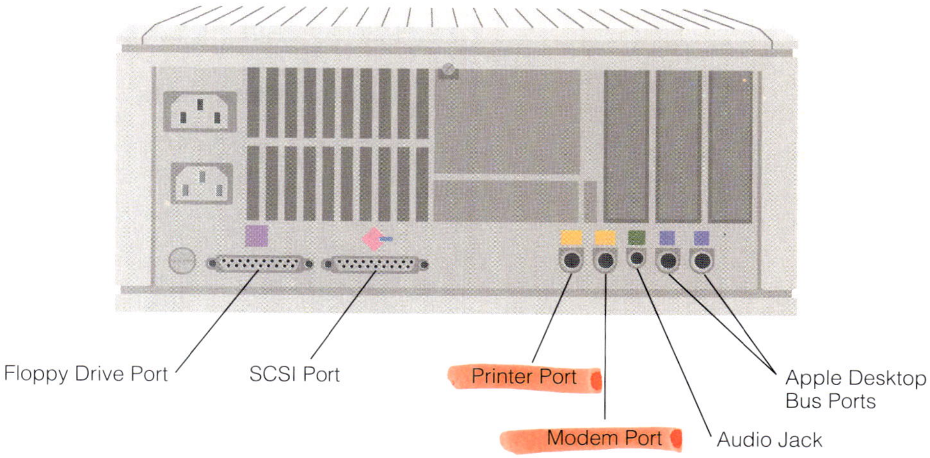

Figure 2.20
Port sockets of an Apple Macintosh II closed-bus system.

BUS ARCHITECTURES

A bus can be viewed as a transportation network, or highway, that transfers data from one point to another. As the processor chips have gained more bits, this highway network inside the computer has gained more "travel lanes" for moving data. Currently, three methods (architectures) accomplish this task:

Industry Standard Architecture (ISA)
This is the bus system that was generated for the original IBM PC. It started as an 8-bit-wide data path; with the introduction of the 80286 machine, it moved to 16-bit-wide and then to a 32-bit-wide passage with the subsequent 80386 and 80486. Many older expansion or interface boards (circuit boards that can be inserted into the computer) can be moved from one computer to another without worry.

Microchannel Architecture (MCA)
This architecture was introduced by IBM with some of its PS/2 computers in 1987. It requires special expansion boards. One of its advantages is its ability to do multitasking, which allows faster processing of data.

Extended Industry Standard Architecture (EISA)
This is a competing 32-bit standard architecture that was proposed in 1988 by nine manufacturers of IBM-compatible computers, led by Compaq. The intention of this standard was not only to combat IBM's incompatible architecture, but to propose a system that could use some of the boards of the ISA architecture.

quently, serial interfaces are more difficult to work with than parallel ones. Parallel transmission is faster, but serial transmission lets information be transmitted farther (parallel devices usually restrict cable length to 15 feet or less). Disk drives and printers usually use parallel transmission, though a few printers use serial transmission; terminals and modems usually use serial transmission.

PERSONAL CASE PROGRESS

Portable Computers

One of John's partners at Valid Investments has just bought a portable computer to use on-site at client businesses, and John looks it over.

She says she had been considering portables ever since Adam Osborne brought out the hefty Osborne-1 computer in 1981, but she began to take them seriously when they got small enough to fit in a briefcase or stow under an airplane seat. Many early portables were disappointingly weak compared with desktop computers, but newer models are becoming more durable and practical as the power of microprocessing chips increases and the size of the computer decreases.

Most portable computers consist of a battery-powered laptop computer that has a highly readable **liquid crystal display (LCD)** or **plasma display monitor,** one or more disk

(a)

(b)

Figure 2.21

Two full-featured portable microcomputers. (a) Zenith Data Systems Z-181 portable with an 8088c microprocessor chip. (b) Compaq LTE 3865/20 personal computer.

(a) (b)

Figure 2.22
Notebook computers. (a) Hewlett Packard 95LX and (b) Poquet PC.

drives (usually 3.5-inch drives), and a hard disk (Figure 2.21). Some of these weigh less than 6 pounds. Battery-powered portables can be used almost anytime and anywhere. During a recent flight back home, she used hers to write a summary of an out-of-town meeting. Notebook-sized computers, as the name implies, are even smaller (about the size of a three-ring notebook). Pocket computers (Figure 2.22) are the smallest (at the time of publication), weighing in at around 2 pounds.

However, John finds out that buying a portable does involve some trade-offs. One problem is the size of the keyboard. Many portables have nonstandard keyboards with important keys in places other than where John would like to see them. Also, some portables use lightweight plastic in places where sturdier desktop models use steel, and someone suggests that this makes the portables more susceptible to damage. Some reports also indicate that the screen technology used in these portables is more prone to malfunctions than that used in regular monitors.

John's partner says, "If portability isn't your main concern, you probably don't want a portable for your first computer."

OUTPUT DEVICES

Output devices convert the information that comes out of a computer into screen images, print, or other forms. Consumers often evaluate a microcomputer system according to the quality of output it produces, demanding that it be accurate, easy-to-read, and rapidly available.

Monitors The **monitor,** or video screen, is the primary output device. (Figure 2.23). Some displays are built into the main computer box, while others are attachable.

Monochrome monitors display images in one color, such as black, green, or amber, usually against a black or white background. With some monitors it is possible to reverse the colors, showing, for instance, either light type on a dark background or dark type on a light background. Other monitors are capable of showing a wide range of colors.

Many monitors developed for personal computers in the early 1980s were alphanumeric, capable of showing print characters but not graphic images. Today's monitors are more often capable of showing both characters and graphics. The typical display shows 25 lines of type, each up to 80 characters long.

Monitors vary greatly in the sharpness and quality of the image they produce, and different types of monitors are more or less appropriate for specific uses. Until recently, monochrome monitors were typically used for sustained day-to-day office applications such as word processing because they provided crisp character resolution that was easier on the eyes than most color monitors. Inexpensive monochrome monitors are still satisfactory for many office uses, but more versatile (and more costly) color monitors also now provide good alphanumeric resolution.

Most monitors allow you to adjust the brightness of the image and the level of contrast between text and any background shading. Also available are antiglare devices that fit over the screen to minimize eyestrain and reduce the reflection of ambient lighting.

Televisions and standard computer video monitors create images with a **cathode-ray-tube (CRT),** a vacuum tube that fires electrons at a phosphor-coated screen (Figure 2.24). Thousands of tiny glowing dots of energized phosphor called **pixels** (short for picture elements) form the screen's images. The more pixels a screen contains, the sharper the image. To keep the pixels glowing, the CRT must rebombard the screen 15 to 30 times a second in a process called *refreshing*. Figure 2.25 shows seven types of monitors including flat-screen, nonvideo technology.

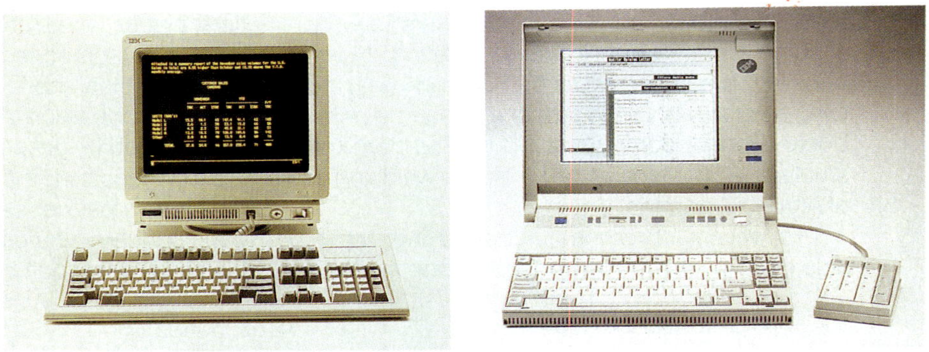

(a) (b)

Figure 2.23

Monitors. (a) The IBM 3476 model ER computer has a detached monochrome monitor, shown here with amber letters on a black background. (b) The IBM PS/2 model L40 SX, a portable computer, has a monochrome, flat-screen monitor built right into the top half of the folding case.

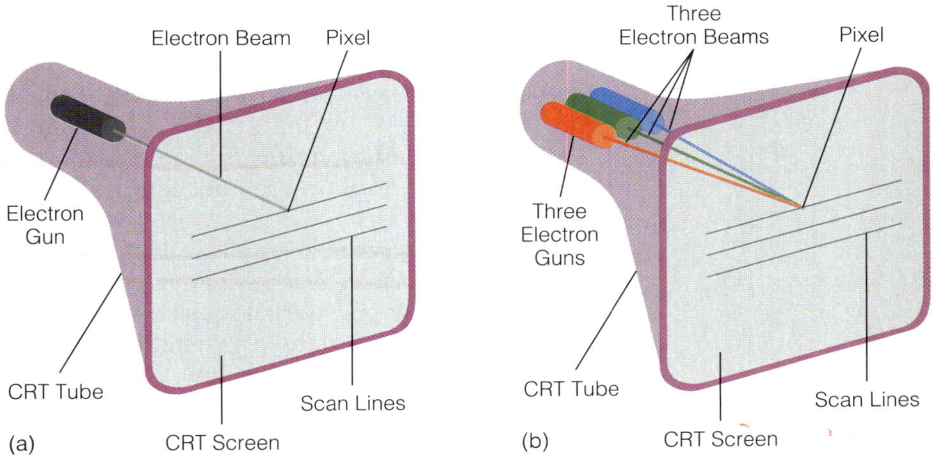

(a) (b)

Figure 2.24

(a) Monochrome and (b) color CRTs.

Figure 2.25

Seven types of video display. (a) **Television:** Adequate display for games. Poor, eye-fatiguing resolution inadequate for uses such as word processing. For best performance, it must be attached to a radio-frequency (rf) modulator. (b) **One-color display monitor:** One active color, such as black-on-white background or amber-on-black. Better resolution than televisions but still fatiguing to the eye. One variety, the monochrome monitor, uses many more pixels per character and produces a crisper display. (c) **Color monitor:** Excellent for graphics, graphs, and games. Not good for spreadsheets or word processing because the images frequently tear in the screen and the pixels often appear multicolored. (d) **Flat-screen monitor:** Developed for laptop computers. Uses types of display that do not need a large tube, such as LCD (liquid crystal display—like that in many watches and calculators) or plasma display. LCD screens have black characters on a white or gray background, are lightweight, and sometimes suffer from poor readability. Plasma display terminals use an energized gas much like neon lights. (e) **Enhanced graphics adapter (EGA) monitor:** Good resolution, with 64 or more different colors displayed on 640 × 350-pixel screens. (f) **Video graphics array (VGA) monitor:** Clearer, more vivid graphics than almost any other display device. Especially useful in computer-aided design (CAD) applications, business graphics, and video games. 640 × 480-pixel screens use 262,144 colors, 16 to 256 of which (depending on the amount of display memory) can be displayed at the same time. Monochrome VGAs offer up to 64 shades of gray. (g) **Super video graphics array (SVGA) monitor:** Clearest video currently available. Uses a 1,024 × 768-pixel screen. Number of displayable colors varies according to the memory allocated to the display.

(a) Television

(b) One-color display monitor

(c) Color monitor

(d) Flat-screen monitor

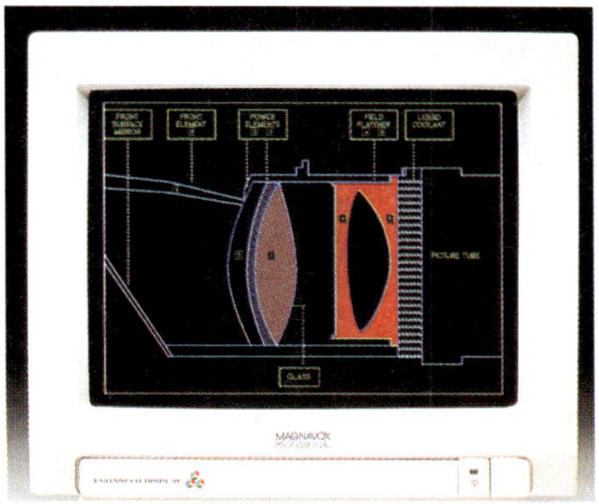

(e) EGA monitor

(f) VGA monitor

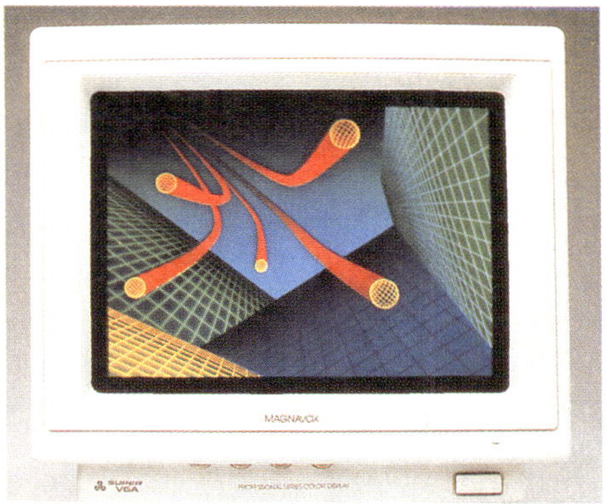

(g) SVGA monitor

Printers Printers transfer output to paper using dot-matrix, thermal, daisy-wheel, ink-jet, and laser technologies (Figure 2.26). Nonimpact printers can only generate one copy of a page at a time, whereas impact printers can use carbon or multicopy forms to print multiple copies.

Figure 2.26
Print output devices.

IMPACT DEVICES

Dot-matrix printer: The most popular microcomputer printer. A moving print head with 7 to 24 tiny print pins strikes an inked ribbon to form dotted characters on paper. The more print pins in the print head, the better the quality of type. May have a near letter quality (NLQ) print mode for higher quality (slower print speed) output. Speed: 80 to 450 characters per second (cps).

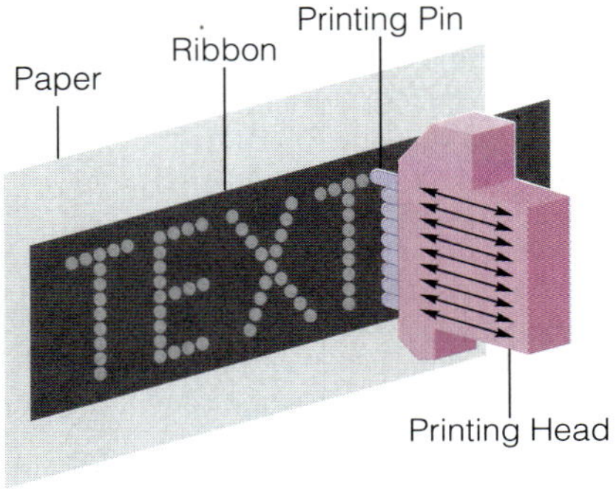

Letter-quality printer: Typewriter-quality characters created by a daisy wheel or print thimble. Now typically being replaced by low-cost laser printers. Speed: 10 to 60 cps.

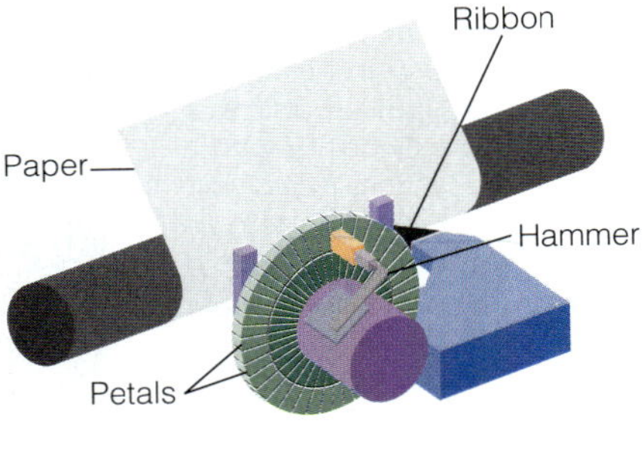

Plotter: Moving pen (sometimes the paper also moves) creates high-quality graphics such as architectural drawings. Flat-bed or drum design. Newer plotters can produce multi-color drawings. Popularity has declined since the advent of the laser printer.

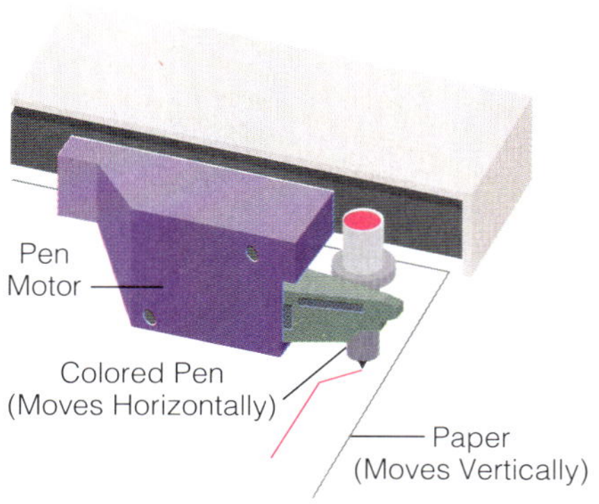

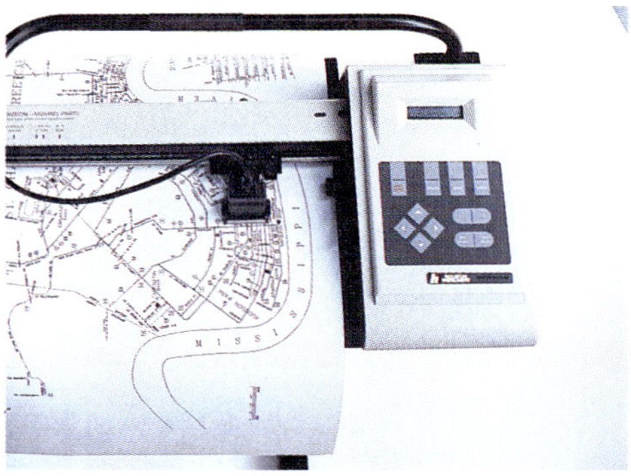

NONIMPACT DEVICES

Thermal printer: Prints similar to dot matrix, but characters are formed by burning dots onto special paper. Speed: about 80 cps.

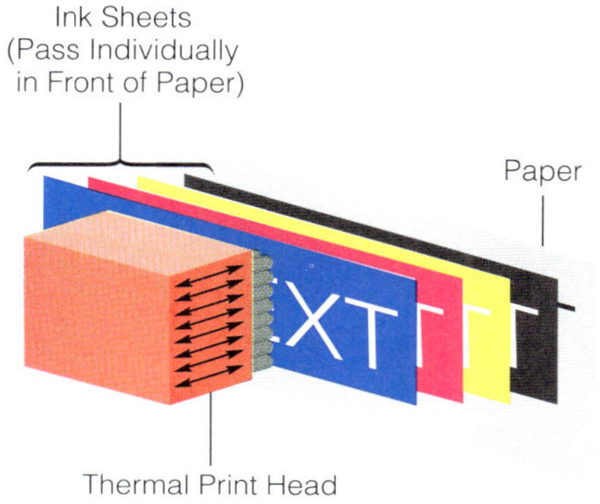

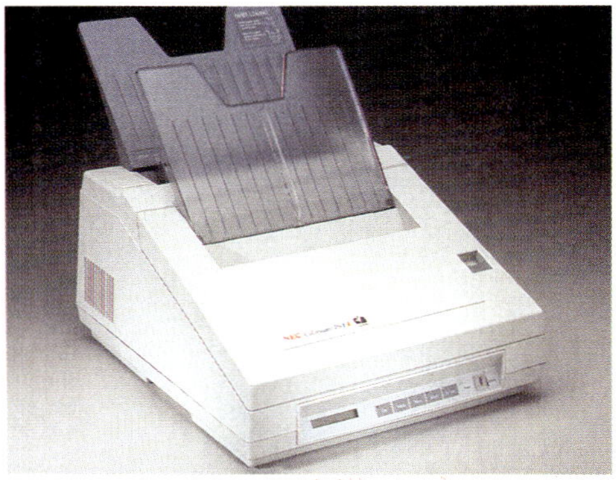

Ink-jet printer: Shoots little jets of ink from disposable cartridges onto paper. Great variation in legibility, but the best of them print letter-quality. Speed: over 200 cps.

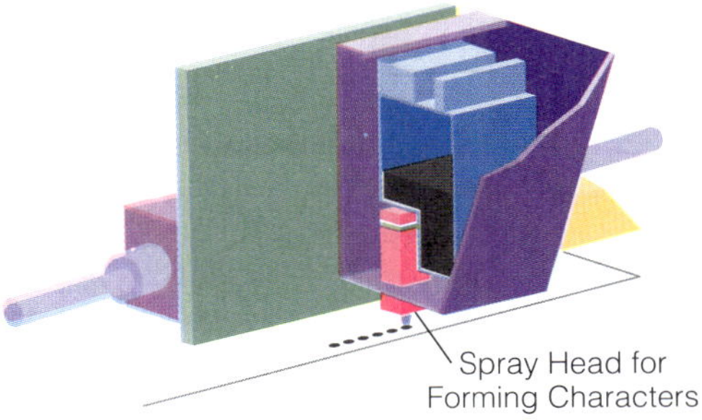

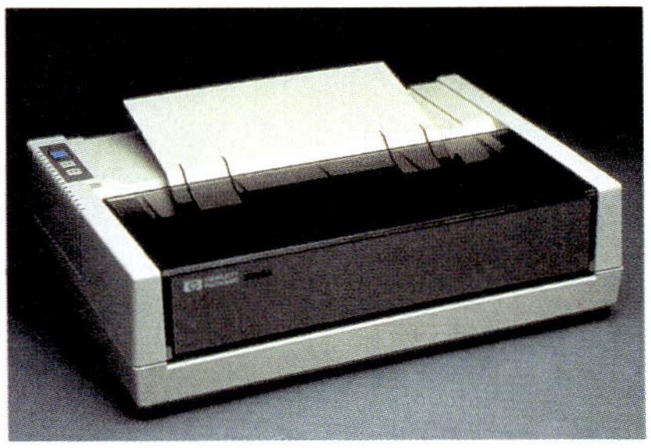

Laser printer: Creates type and graphics through a photocopying process. Laser beam traces characters onto a photosensitive drum, then bonds toner (an inklike solution) to paper with heat. The high resolution (about 300 dots per inch) is essential to desktop publishing. Initial high prices now much lower. Speed: 4 to 16 pages per minute.

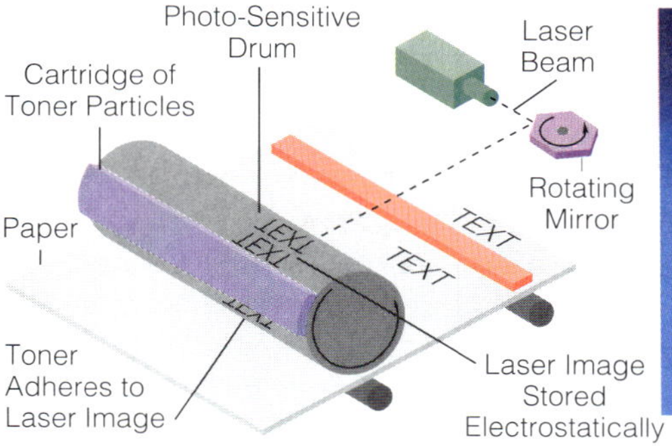

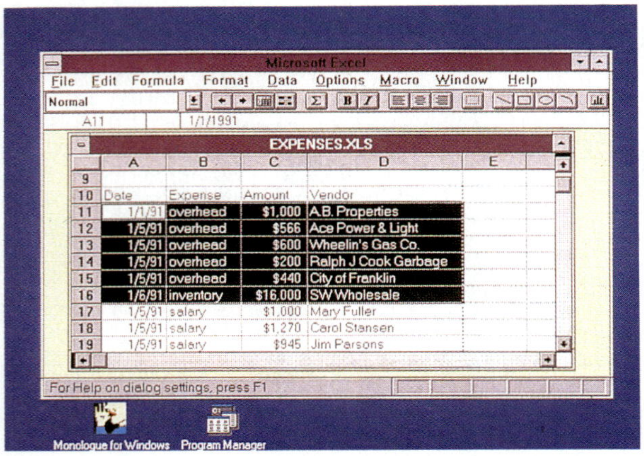

Figure 2.27
Monologue 2.0 and other software packages convert lines of characters to speech.

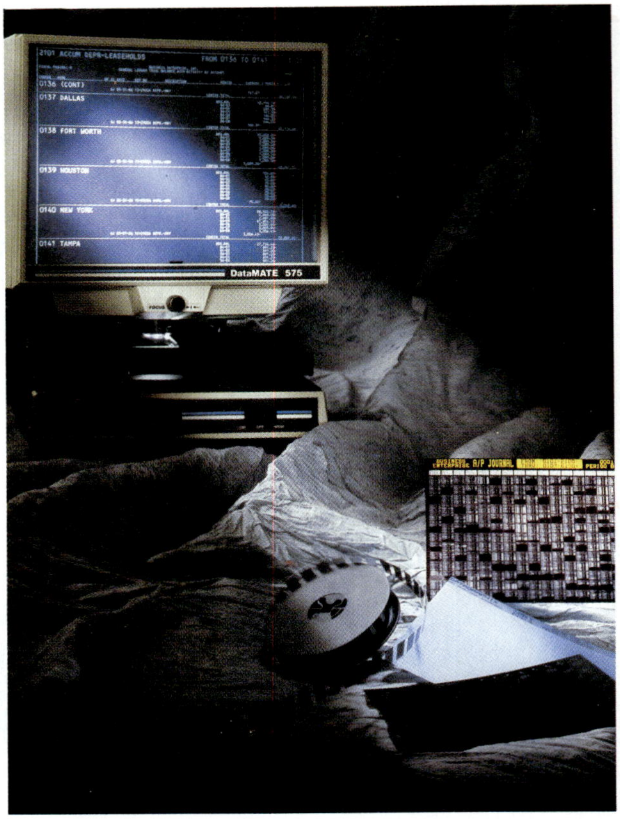

Figure 2.28
This small sheet of microfiche can hold up to 200 pages of print.

Voice Output Voice output may simply involve replaying previously recorded words or phrases. In the phone company's "time-and-temperature" service, for instance, various phrases for each possible time or temperature are recorded and, based on the current time and temperature, played back to the caller. In grocery stores, POS recordings may announce product names and prices. Voice output can also be used as a reinforcement and pronunciation coach to students who are studying a foreign language.

Voice applications packages such as Monologue 2.0 provide speech capability by converting any text string to speech signals, which can be played on an audio speaker. Thus, a user can mark typed information on the screen for the computer to pronounce. This type of application can be used with word processing, spreadsheet, or other types of applications (Figure 2.27). Some packages have to be trained to properly pronounce nonphonetic words such as "ocean."

Computer Output Microfilm Computer output microfilm (COM) stores relatively unchanging data. How much room, for example, would it take to store all the parts catalogs used by a Sears repair department? How much room would it take to store the newspapers from the major cities of the United States for the past 20 years? How much room would it take to store the name and address information of policyholders for a national insurance company? To save space, COM was developed to produce very small images on 4-inch by 6-inch sheets of microfiche (Figure 2.28) or rolls of microfilm.

(a)
(b)

Figure 2.29
(a) Typical 3.5-inch disk and (b) 5.25-inch disk.

The main disadvantage of COM is the need for an enlarging device for reading. Some people complain about going to special locations to use the readers and about eyestrain from their use.

SECONDARY STORAGE

In contrast to primary storage, **secondary storage** is separate from the CPU and can store data indefinitely (the memory is not lost when the power is turned off). Data from secondary storage can be fed into the computer from a diskette or other storage medium when the user determines that the computer needs that information.

The process of transferring data into a computer is known as the **read process.** The process of transferring data out of a computer back to secondary storage is known as the **write process.**

Diskettes For years, tapes were the only nonvolatile storage medium available. Tape storage requires a computer to run sequentially through the tape until a desired file of data is found, just as a stereo owner has to run through an audiotape to locate a particular song. Today, the standard secondary storage medium for microcomputers is the **diskette,** also called the **disk** or **floppy disk.** In contrast to tapes, diskettes let the computer locate files quickly by going directly to any track on the disk, just as one can immediately locate and play any song on a compact disk album.

A disk is simply a Mylar plastic circle that has a ferrous oxide coating capable of holding magnetic spots. Disks come in different sizes (identified by diameter). The most common sizes are 3.5 inches and 5.25 inches. The Mylar circles are encased in plastic covers. The term *floppy* alludes to the 5.25-inch disk's physical flimsiness and its flexibility in providing storage (Figure 2.29). Before a new disk can be used, it must be prepared so that the computer can recognize it and record data on it. This process is called **formatting.**

5.25-Inch Disk As shown in Figure 2.30, two round holes are visible at the center of the disk. The larger one, called the **centering hole,** is clamped by the disk drive, which then rotates the disk inside its protective cover. A piece of lubricated fabric inside the cover traps foreign particles, decreases drag, and protects the Mylar from scratching. On good-quality disks, the centering hole is reinforced by a plastic ring. The smaller hole to the right of the centering hole is the **timing hole.** It indicates the beginning of a track or sector and tells the disk drive where to start reading or writing.

Figure 2.30

(a) Features of a typical 5.25-inch disk. (b) A 5.25-inch disk, showing clusters, tracks, and sectors.

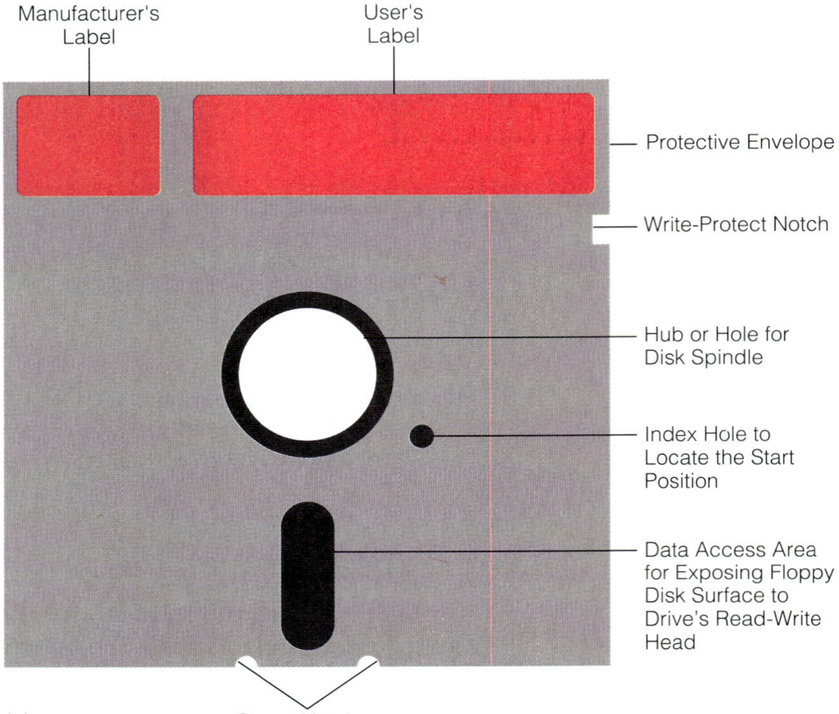

(a)

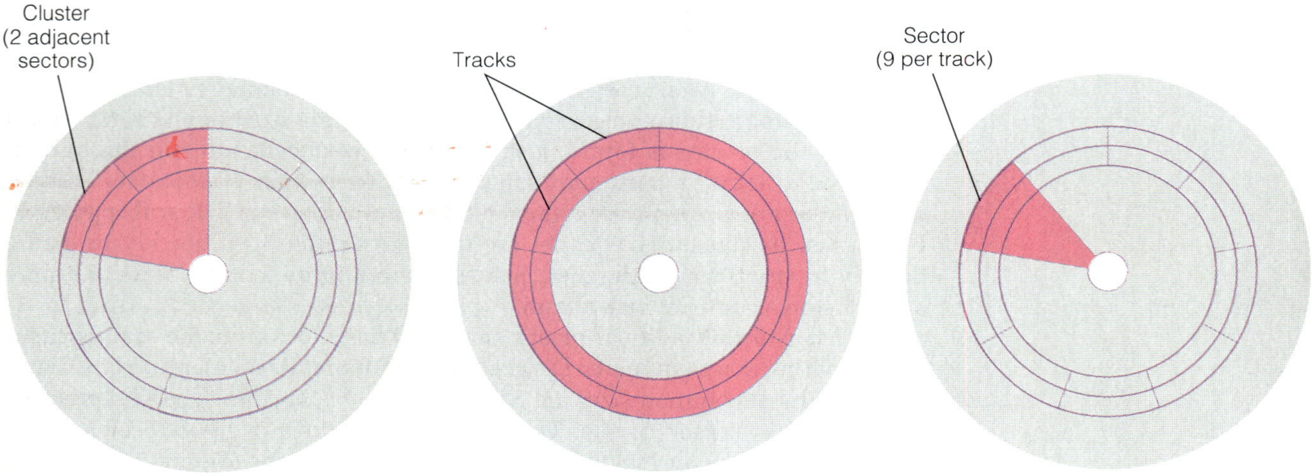

(b)

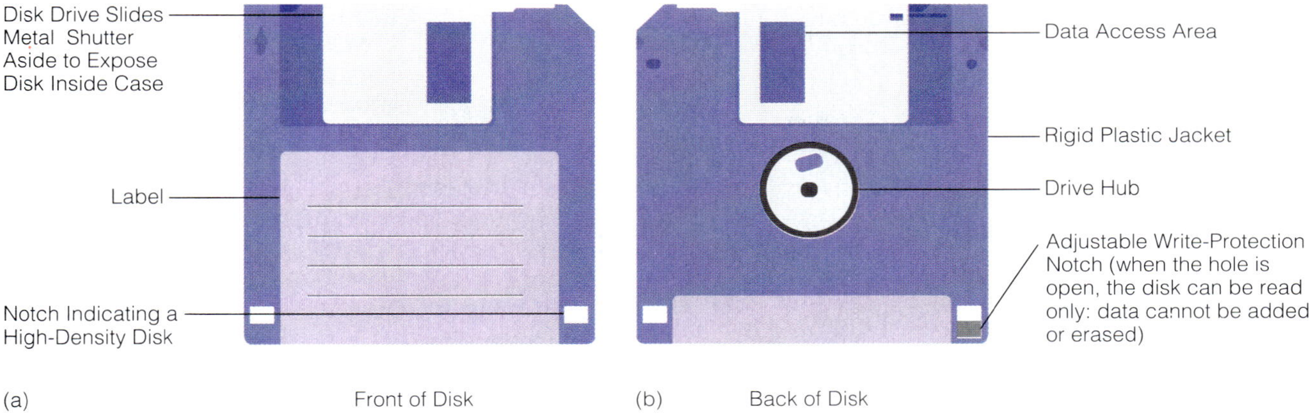

Figure 2.31
Features of the 3.5-inch disk.

Below the centering hole is an oval opening called the **read/write access hole.** Through this hole, read/write heads read from or record to the disk. Information is stored on the disk in concentric circles called **tracks** (Figure 2.31c). Each track is subdivided into **sectors,** each of which can store 512 bytes. There are nine sectors per track, 40 tracks per disk side, and two sides per disk; thus, each 5.25-inch disk has a storage capacity of 368,640 bytes (512 × 9 × 40 × 2). Disk storage is also measured in kilobytes, and a 5.25-inch disk holds 360K.

If there is only one timing hole on the disk, the disk is soft-sectored; if there is more than one hole, the disk is hard-sectored. **Soft-sectored disks** are divided into sectors by the computer during the formatting process. **Hard-sectored disks** have already been sectored at the factory. Apple and IBM computers and IBM compatibles use soft-sectored disks. Hard-sectored disks cannot be used in computers with disk drives designed for soft-sectored disks, nor will soft-sectored disks work in hard-sectored disk drives.

The two small cutouts below the read/write access hole are stress notches, which allow the disk to bend without creasing. Along the upper right-hand edge of the disk is a rectangular notch known as the **write-protect notch.** Covering this notch with a piece of tape prevents alteration of the disk's information, but the disk remains readable. Many software program disks do not have a write-protect notch, so their information is permanently safeguarded from alteration or erasure.

3.5-Inch Disks The 3.5-inch disk epitomizes the "smaller-is-larger" progress of computer technology. A typical **double-density 3.5-inch disk** (Figure 2.31) disk holds twice the information of a double-density 5.25-inch disk, or 720K (newer disks hold 1.44M). First popularized on the Apple Macintosh computer, this style of disk is now the industry standard.

The 3.5-inch disk has other advantages besides its greater storage, including its hard-plastic protective shell. A metal shutter also protects the read/write opening of the disk, so there is no need for protective envelopes. This shutter automatically opens when the disk is placed in the drive.

The notched corner of the disk also prevents it from being inserted improperly in the drive. A hole in the lower left-hand corner of the 3.5-inch disk is for write protection. When the slider covers the write-protect hole, the disk can be both read from and written to. When the hole is uncovered, the disk is **write-**

FUTURE TRENDS

An Information Appliance?

Not only is disk size shrinking, but the computer and all its other components are predicted, as well, to shrink dramatically by the year 2000. A number of technology visionaries are predicting that the PC will become an "information appliance." These machines will contain up to 100 million transistors, up from 1 million today. They will run up to eight times faster than today's 80486 computers. These machines will have a stylus and screen replacing the current keyboard. The device will also double as a telephone and allow information to be passed extremely rapidly using fiber-optic cables and satellites, thereby supporting multimedia and teleconferencing. This multifaceted machine is expected to weigh in at only 15 pounds (Figure 2.32). When this machine is fully operational, 264-megabit memory chips will be available. Today, a 64-megabit memory chip can store Shakespeare's complete works (1.6 million words). With the portability this machine no doubt will have, a user will be able to access data anywhere, whether a microcomputer bulletin board or a remote corporate database, limited only by the type of communication line the carrier provides. And this machine most likely will have a stylus for handwritten input and the ability to recognize and respond to spoken commands and dictation.

Figure 2.32
A multifaceted information appliance.

protected. The presence of a second hole at the bottom of the disk indicates a 1.44M (high-density) disk.

Regardless of the varying sizes and densities, all disks used by the standard Apple and IBM-compatible microcomputer operating systems are divided into tracks and sectors, and all store 512 bytes in a sector. Table 2.3 notes the differences among the disks.

Table 2.3 Disk Types

	5.25-Inch Double-Density	*5.25-Inch High-Density*	*3.5-Inch Double-Density*	*3.5-Inch High-Density*
Number of tracks	40	80	80	80
Sectors per track	9	15	9	18
Total sectors	720	2400	1440	2880
Total storage	360K	1.2M	720K	1.44M

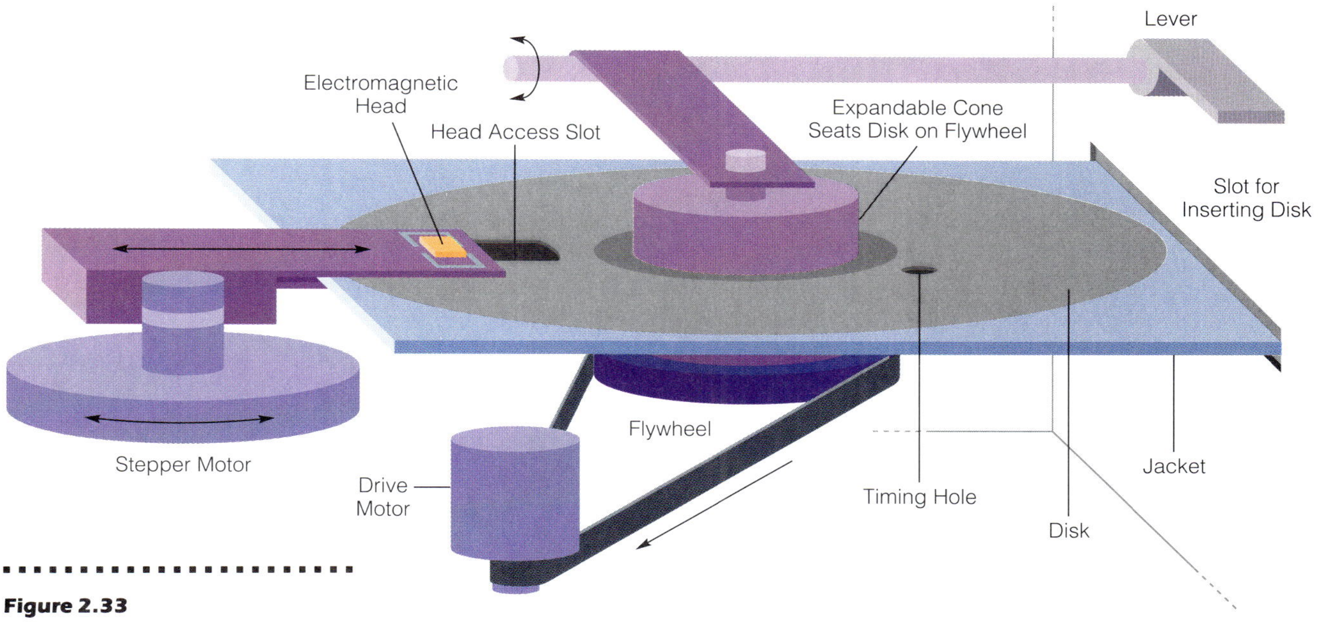

Figure 2.33
A floppy disk drive.

How Floppy Disk Drives Work Information is read from and recorded to the disk by a **disk drive** (Figure 2.33). An expandable cone inside the drive clamps the disk onto a flywheel, which rotates the Mylar disk inside its jacket. A system of lights and light sensors locates the beginning of a track containing the data that the user is seeking. After motors position the read/write heads at the appropriate track, data are read from or written onto the disk.

NEW READ/WRITE TECHNOLOGY FOR DISKS?

Data has historically been written to disk using a serial technique. That is, the 0's and 1's used to represent characters are stored one after another and lined up in a row. Such serial storage limits how closely 0's and 1's can be packed. After a certain data density is achieved, it is extremely expensive to pack data closer together.

Some disk manufacturers are now using a parallel-storage technique to store bits 1 byte at a time instead of 1 bit at a time. Now, instead of sensing a string of 0's and 1's, the disk read/write head senses a stack of 0's and 1's that have been recorded in the magnetic substrate.

Parallel recording dramatically increases the storage capacity of disks. Currently, a serially recorded 3.5-inch disk can store 1.44M of data, whereas a parallel disk holds up to 2.88M. Eventually, such disks may hold as much as 20M.

The diskette material used for parallel recording is different from the current 3.5-inch diskette material, and parallel storage is therefore not currently compatible with serial storage. This means that new drives as well as diskettes are needed. However, some manufacturers of these new drives are trying to make them compatible with the older disk as well.

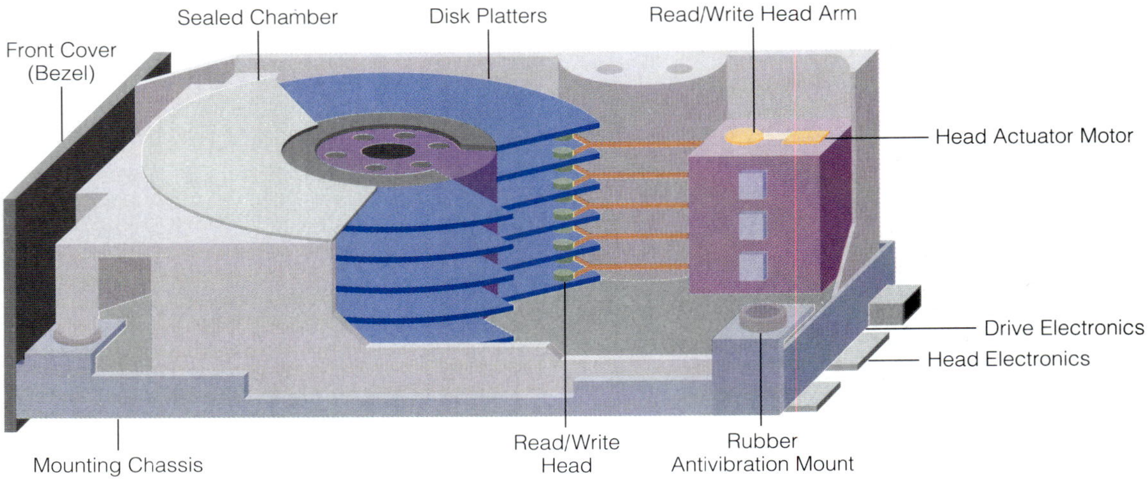

Figure 2.34
Parts of a hard disk.

Hard Disks Hard disk systems are becoming increasingly popular for storing microcomputer information because they store more data and retrieve it faster than do floppy disks. **Hard disks** contain one or more rigid platters for recording data (Figure 2.34), each coated with a metal oxide that holds magnetic charges. Read/write heads hover fourteen-millionths of an inch above the disk surface. The platters rotate on a spindle at about 3600 rpm, 12 times faster than floppy disks (the faster a disk rotates, the quicker the read/write heads can locate a track of information).

Hard disk units may have a removable disk **cartridge** or a fixed disk in a sealed housing, commonly known as the Winchester disk (Figure 2.35). The Winchester was first developed by IBM for use on mainframe computers and is the more popular disk system. Some units have both.

Hard disk platters vary in diameter and in capacity. Units storing 40M or more are now affordable for the average consumer. The diameter of the platters varies from 2 to 5.25 inches, and the amount of data that can be stored on a hard disk also varies greatly.

Whatever form of secondary storage you are using, it is very important to keep backup copies of important data. This applies to hard disks as well as floppies. In removable-cartridge disks, contaminants such as hair or dust can collect on a platter, tripping the read/write head and causing it to strike the Mylar disk. Take care to keep these cartridges clean and dust-free. Due to their sealed housing, Winchester disks rarely have this problem.

A different type of removable disk is the Bernoulli (Figure 2.36), which uses diskette-type material to store large amounts of data (up to 90M). This type of media is much less susceptible to head crashes.

On a system with removable-cartridge disks, you can back up your data by copying onto a backup cartridge that is shelved for safekeeping. Winchester disks are more difficult to back up. Most can have their data copied onto floppy disks, but this is a lengthy process, and it takes 28 5.25-inch floppies to store all the information on a full 10M hard disk. An alternative is a tape-cartridge system that can copy 10 to 120M of data in a few minutes.

Optical Disk (CD ROM) Floppy disks and hard disks record information using magnetic spots. Another, newer form of secondary storage is called the **compact disk (CD),** which stores data optically with the same technology used

(a)

(b)

(c)

Figure 2.35

(a) A Gigafile model FH-31200 provides 1.2 gigabytes of storage capacity. The drive has an average access time of better than 14 milliseconds. (b) The Conner 3.5-inch "Hopi Series" is available in capacities of 60M, 80M, and 120M. (c) A Tallgrass tape backup system using minicartridge (PAT) storage technology.

Figure 2.36

A transportable Bernoulli drive and removable disk.

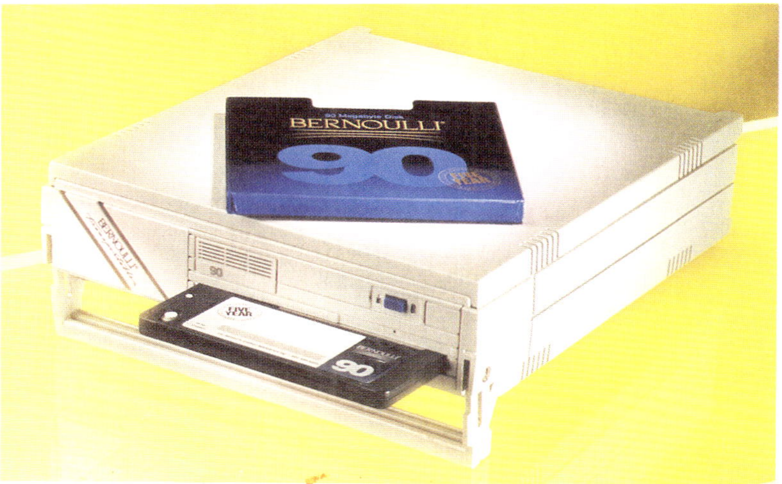

DISKETTE DO'S AND DON'TS

Do's

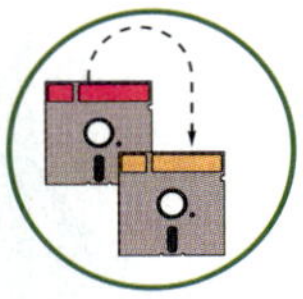

1. Copy (back up) all records! Never trust a single disk with important data or files.

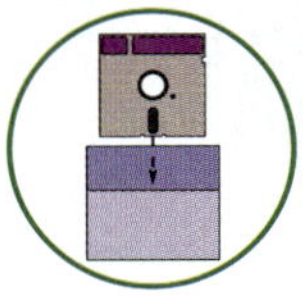

2. When finished using a disk, place it inside its protective paper envelope to keep out dust, coffee, and other contaminants.

3. Store disks vertically, like record albums. Laying disks flat or at an angle will bend and warp them.

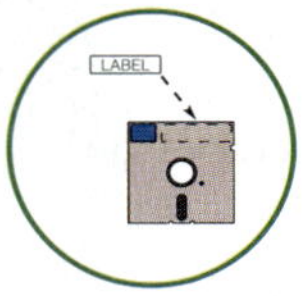

4. Place a label on every disk; this will simplify locating it when needed.

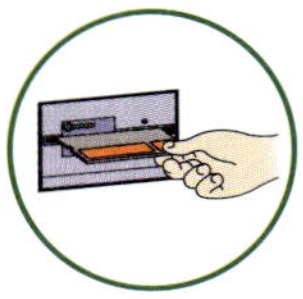

5. Be especially careful when inserting a disk into the disk drive. It's very easy to crease a disk by catching it on a piece of internal machinery. If you do crease a disk, back it up immediately.

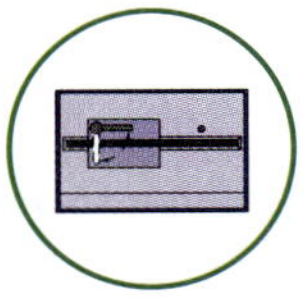

6. Close the disk-drive door gently to allow the disk to center properly. Snapping the door shut can catch the disk off center and damage it.

7. Handle disks with care; carelessness can destroy hours of computer work in an instant.

Don'ts

1. Never write on a disk's plastic cover (only with 5.25-inch disks) with pencil or ballpoint pen—doing so could damage the Mylar. Fill in the label prior to affixing it to the disk. If you must write on a label already on the disk, use a felt-tip pen and a light hand.

2. Don't touch the disk's Mylar surface with fingers, tissue, or solvents or place an unprotected disk on a dusty surface.

3. Don't bend or crease disks. Special protective packages are available for mailing disks.

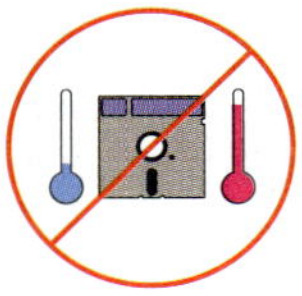

4. Don't place disks in direct sunlight, on top of radiators, in the trunks of cars, next to cold windowsills, or otherwise expose them to temperature extremes.

5. Don't expose disks to airport X-ray machines or library security devices.

6. Keep disks away from magnetic fields, which are generated by magnets, some color monitors, and older telephones.

Figure 2.37
Typical optical storage disks: A laser videodisk, a compact disk, and a rewritable compact disk.

Figure 2.38
The NeXT computer. This computer is touted by many computer pundits as representing a new breakthrough in the use of microcomputer technology.

for music CD recordings (Figure 2.37). Lasers burn information into the CD as bubbles, which later can be read by another laser. However, on many systems, the burned-in information cannot be erased or altered. These are called WORM drives ("Write-Once-Read-Many").

Recent improvements in CD ROM technology allow the laser to melt existing data bubbles and then store new data in the form of new bubbles over melted areas. This type of technology, which started out being called CD ROM because it was unerasable, now bears the name magneto-optical (MO). In effect, some CD ROM (MO) devices now work in much the same fashion as read/write magnetic disks, which erase and record over the same areas on a disk. The NeXT computer (Figure 2.38) designed by Steve Jobs makes use of this erasable CD ROM technology.

PERSONAL CASE REVISITED

Surrounded by Hardware

JOHN has talked to many people before buying his computer hardware and has thought about the question of compatibility between the computer at the office and the one he wants at home. He has also identified the main software programs that he and his family expect to run on the home computer.

Based on his needs and research, he decides on the following types of hardware:

Input	Keyboard and mouse
Processor	IBM-compatible unit with at least 2M of RAM
Secondary storage	5.25-inch drive, 3.5-inch drive, and hard disk with at least 80M of storage
Output	VGA monitor or SVGA monitor and dot-matrix printer

This isn't everything John wants, but it's what he needs initially. He intends to get an open-bus system with plenty of slots for expansion.

The computers at work are supported by a 24-hour service-and-repair agreement with a service vendor (meaning that service will be provided within 24 hours, providing that the next day is a workday); but given his more casual needs at home and the high dependability ratings of the hardware he is considering, he decides to save some money by foregoing this level of service for his own computer. He decides instead to purchase a machine from a competitively priced mail-order business that guarantees service within 3 working days. John consults a popular microcomputer journal and finds such a mail-order business that offers an 80386 computer with the following characteristics at a reasonable price:

- 4M RAM
- 1.2M 5.25-inch drive
- 1.44M 3.5-inch drive
- 200M hard disk drive
- SVGA monitor
- One parallel and two serial ports
- 101-key keyboard
- Mouse

This mail-order business also offers a 24-hour-a-day telephone support service. With a little apprehension, John makes a telephone call and orders the computer.

One CD ROM can hold 5G or more (roughly 5 billion characters), compared with the 200 to 300M capacity of a large hard disk. This high-storage feature and the safety or reliability of its storage method make CD ROM disks ideal for archival, backup, and recovery applications.

In the past few years, the CD ROM technology has continued to grow at about 100 percent a year, but it still occupies only a small niche within the com-

Figure 2.39
Britannica Software's *Compton's MultiMedia Encyclopedia.*

puter industry. Experts predict that use of CD ROM will increase in **multimedia projects,** which present information using combined media such as sound, graphics, animation, video, and text.

Other proven uses for CD ROM include large financial databases, actuarial tables, and other extremely large bodies of data. Microsoft publishes the CD ROM Bookshelf reference library that includes a spelling checker; *Roget's II: Electronic Thesaurus;* electronic versions of *Bartlett's Familiar Quotations,* the *World Almanac, The American Heritage Dictionary,* and *The Chicago Manual of Style;* a U.S. zip code directory; a grammar checker; a collection of customizable templates for standard business forms; and the Business Information Sources directory.

Encyclopedias have also recently become available on CD ROM. Britannica Software, for example, has published a version of *Compton's MultiMedia Encyclopedia* (Figure 2.39), with over 10 million words, 15,000 photos, and an hour of spoken words and music. All this information is indexed and linked via a graphical interface to make access easier. A user navigates the encyclopedia by using keywords or a graphical gateway. Graphical gateways include photos, maps, electronic bookmarks, an interactive time line, and a 150,000 word dictionary.

Other reference materials include the *Guinness Book of World Records* and *Grolier's Electronic Encyclopedia.* Games are also being marketed on CD ROM. Although this type of product has yet to take off in the United States, it is extremely popular in Japan.

CD ROM technology shows great promise but is not without its problems. For example, compatibility is not guaranteed, and a CD will not necessarily work on a drive other than the one for which it was manufactured. CD ROMs are also inherently slower than hard disk drives.

INPUT/OUTPUT DEVICES

Fax (facsimile transmission) machines are endemic in the business world and can be connected to computers for both input and output, as described in Chapter 6.

Figure 2.40
Computerized check-sorting machine being used in a bank.

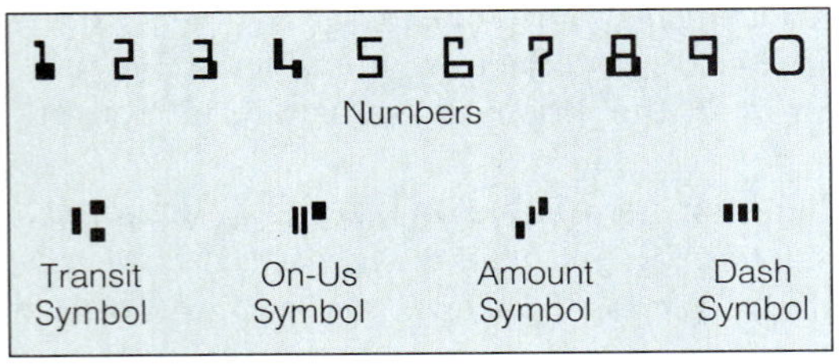

(a)

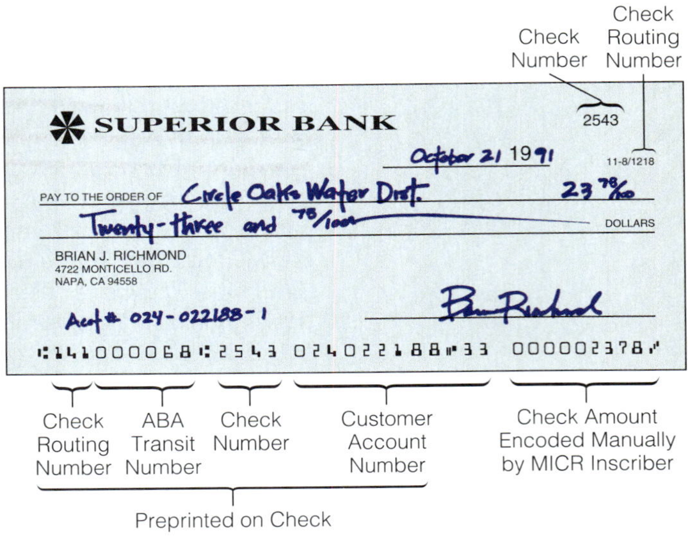

(b)

Figure 2.41
(a) The MICR character set. (b) MICR characters and symbols are printed at the bottom of each check. Some information is preprinted on the check. The amount of the check is added by the receiving bank.

Magnetic-ink character recognition (MICR) is a method used by the banking industry for recording the account number with magnetic ink at the bottom of each check and then adding additional information after the check is written and processed. Processing the huge volume of checks written requires the use of a special reader/sorter (Figure 2.40). Once a check has been written, information such as the amount of the check is coded onto the check in special MICR characters (Figure 2.41a), and the check is returned to you along with a bank statement (because of processing expense, some banks send you the actual check only if you specially request it). A sample of a check can be seen in Figure 2.41b.

Optical mark recognition (OMR) is sometimes referred to as mark sense because a machine senses pencil marks on paper. This system is frequently used in scoring multiple-choice tests. Marks are recorded in pencil on an answer sheet, which the OMR system evaluates. A light-beam device converts the marks to signals that the computer uses to compare responses with an answer key.

CHAPTER REVIEW

The hardware component comprises input, processing, output, and storage. The microprocessor chip serves as the hardware component's brain.

Common input devices include the keyboard, mouse, touch pad and tablet, pen, voice input, touch screen, bar-code reader, and scanner.

Centering around the microprocessor (CPU), processing hardware includes primary memory (ROM and RAM), buses and boards, and interfaces. The byte (one character) is the smallest useful bit of data. RAM stores data and program instructions inside the computer in a special binary code called ASCII. ROM is used primarily by the computer rather than for user-selected data or programs.

A number of different types of output devices such as monitors and printers can be attached to a microcomputer system. Information can be stored on a nonvolatile storage medium, the most popular being the disk.

Microcomputer secondary storage is usually provided by a disk drive. Tape and CD ROM can also be used for secondary storage.

KEY TERMS AND CONCEPTS

alphanumeric keys
American Standard Code for Information Interchange (ASCII)
banked memory
bar-code reader
binary
bit
board
bus
byte
cartridge
cathode-ray tube (CRT)
centering hole
Centronics
characters per second (cps)
clock speed
closed-bus system
color monitor
compact disk (CD)
computer output microfilm (COM)
coprocessor
daisy wheel printer
digitizing tablet
disk drive
diskette (disk)
dot-matrix printer
double-density disk
Dvorak
enhanced graphics adapter (EGA) monitor
expanded memory
extended industry standard architecture (EISA)
extended memory
fax (facsimile transmission) machine
floppy disk
formatting
function key
gigabyte (G)
hard disk
hard-sectored disk
industry standard architecture (ISA)
ink-jet printer
interface
keyboard
kilobyte (K)
laser printer
letter-quality printer
light pen
liquid crystal display (LCD) monitor
magnetic-ink character recognition (MICR)
main system board
megabyte (M)
microchannel architecture (MCA)
microprocessor
monitor
monochrome monitor
motherboard
mouse
multimedia project
multipurpose monitor
nonvolatile memory
numeric keypad
open-bus system
optical disk (CD ROM)
optical mark recognition (OMR)
parallel interface
personal computer (PC)
pixel
plasma display monitor
plotter
primary memory
printer
print thimble
processing unit (processor)

QWERTY
random-access memory (RAM)
read-only memory (ROM)
read process
read/write access hole
scanner
secondary storage
sectors
serial interface
soft-sectored disk
supervideo graphics array (SVGA) monitor
tablet
thermal printer
timing hole
touch screen
tracks
turbo
video graphics array (VGA) monitor
voice-input device
volatile memory
write process
write-protected
write-protect notch

CHAPTER QUIZ

Multiple Choice

1. Which of the following items is part of the microcomputer?
   a. RAM (random-access memory)
   b. Interface
   c. ROM (read-only memory)
   d. Bus
   e. All of the above

2. Which of the following is *not* an output device?
   a. Printer
   b. Plotter
   c. Monitor
   d. Keyboard
   e. All of the above are output devices.

3. Which of the following statements is correct?
   a. RAM is the nonvolatile memory.
   b. ROM is the memory used to hold data and instructions.
   c. The bus moves data and instructions from one part of the computer to another.
   d. The laser printer uses new technology to make it an input device.

4. Which of the following terms do(es) *not* apply to a disk?
   a. Sector
   b. Track
   c. Soft sectored
   d. Byte
   e. All of the above terms apply to a disk.

5. Which of the following statements is false?
   a. About eight "families," or types, of microprocessors are currently on the market.
   b. A 32-bit processor will probably be slower than an 8-bit processor.
   c. RAM restrictions will not usually restrict the type of software you are allowed to run on your computer.
   d. b and c.
   e. All of the above

True/False

6. An impact letter-quality printer is typically faster than a dot-matrix printer.

7. A disk is an example of nonvolatile storage.

8. As a general rule of thumb, the more bits a microprocessor chip can handle at one time, the more memory it can address and the faster it operates.

9. Hard disks are typically faster and more reliable than are floppy disks.

10. Monochrome display monitors are easier to read than are one-color monitors because they use more pixels.

Answers

1. e 2. d 3. c 4. e 5. e 6. f 7. t 8. t 9. t 10. t

Exercises

1. Define or describe each of the following:
   a. Bit
   b. Byte
   c. ASCII
   d. RAM
   e. ROM
   f. Bus
   g. Centronics
   h. Pixel
   i. Track
   j. Sector
   k. K
   l. M

2. Four typical input devices for a microcomputer are ____________, ____________, ____________, and ____________.

3. The standard code used for storing information in microcomputers is the ____________ code.

4. Differences among 8-, 16-, and 32-bit microprocessing computer chips limit the amount of addressable ____________ memory.

5. Memory that is only capable of 64K functioning at one time but that has a total storage capacity of 128K is called ____________ memory.

6. The type of monitor that displays characters with the pixels (dots) close together is the ____________ display.

7. ____________ memory is available to the user, but ____________ memory is used only by the machine.

8. The unit of storage required to hold a numeric digit or character is called a(n) ____________.

9. A(n) ____________ interface transmits 1 bit at a time, whereas a(n) ____________ interface transmits at least 8 bits at once.

10. The terms *diskette* and ____________ *disk* are synonymous.

11. A kilobyte (K) of memory is equal to about ____________ bytes, and a megabyte (M) of memory equals about ____________ bytes of storage.

12. List some advantages and disadvantages using hard disk–storage devices (at least two each).

13. Why is the human element so important in a microcomputer system? Do you know of any examples of individuals not satisfied with their microcomputers because they were inappropriate to their particular problem?

14. A printer that prints characters using dot patterns is called a(n) __________ printer.

15. A(n) __________ chip greatly speeds processing that involves mathematical manipulation.

16. An input device that is moved across the surface of a flat area and that issues instructions by pressing one or more buttons is a(n) __________.

17. An input device that can digitize images contained on a sheet of paper is called a(n) __________.

18. The individual spots on a monitor screen used to generate a character are referred to as __________.

19. A printer that is rated at a speed of pages per minute is the __________ printer.

20. A type of secondary storage that cannot be erased is called __________.

IN YOUR OWN CASE

1. Review John's decision to buy the microcomputer system described in the Personal Case Revisited. Based on what you know about John and about computer hardware, how well do his choices match his needs? Is his hardware complete? What different or additional equipment might you recommend?

2. What hardware components would you need for a computer system that would meet your needs? What type of computer, printer, and other peripherals would you want for your system? Consult a microcomputing journal or visit a microcomputer store to research products and prices. List the various components along with their cost. Base your choice on the amount of money you actually have available for such a purchase. (If you're presently out of funds, use a budget of up to $3000.) Explain why you chose those specific components.

3. If you already own a computer system, what different or additional hardware might you want? Consult a microcomputing journal or visit a microcomputer store to research products and prices. List the various components along with their cost. Give yourself a budget of up to $1500. Explain why you chose specific components.

4. Write a three-word sentence in binary code. Exchange with a classmate and decipher.

QUESTIONS FOR THOUGHT

1. Assume that you are looking for a used computer to use for word processing only. If you had the opportunity to buy a used 8088 computer system for $400 or an 80286 computer system for $500, and all of the peripherals were the same, which would you buy?

2. What type of monitor and printer would best serve your present needs? What criteria did you use to make this decision?

3. What does the time line on page 32 suggest has been the general nature of development in computer hardware?

3

SOFTWARE

CHAPTER OBJECTIVES

After completing this chapter, you should be able to

- ***Discuss the three types of software***
- ***Discuss programming software***
- ***Discuss operating systems***
- ***Describe the five major types of application software***
- ***Understand menu systems***
- ***Evaluate application software in relation to our own needs***

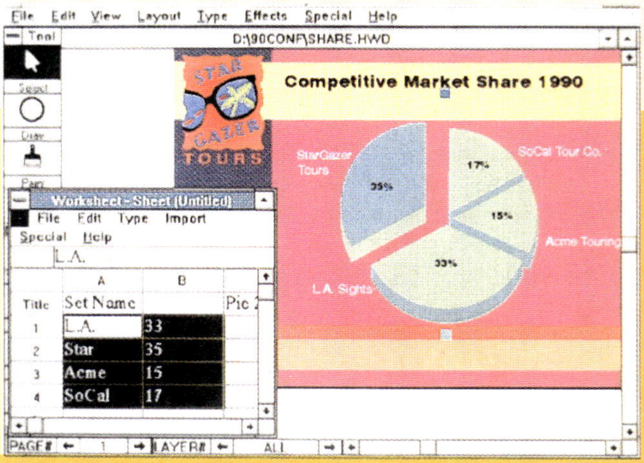

THE DEVELOPMENT OF COMPUTER SOFTWARE

1954	IBM develops the FORTRAN (FORmula TRANslation) programming language.
1959	CODASYL, the Committee on Data Systems Languages, creates COBOL (COmmon Business-Oriented Language). Grace Hopper develops the first COBOL compiler, which allows COBOL programs to be run on many different computers.
1965	John Kemeny and Thomas Kurtz develop BASIC (Beginner's All-Purpose Instruction Code) at Dartmouth College.
1971	Niklaus Wirth develops Pascal for teaching structured-programming techniques. Dennis Ritchie develops the UNIX operating system at Bell Laboratories.
1972	Bell Laboratories introduces the C programming language.
1975	Bill Gates and Paul Allen found Microsoft Corporation after they adapt BASIC to the Altair MITS microcomputer.
1978	Don Flystra and Dan Bricklin develop VisiCalc, the first electronic spreadsheet software.
1979	MicroPro International introduces WordStar, one of the first full-featured word processing packages for the microcomputer.
1981	MS DOS (Microsoft) becomes the standard disk operating system for the IBM PC. Ashton-Tate introduces dBASE II, the first relational database for microcomputers.
1983	Lotus 1-2-3 replaces VisiCalc as the standard spreadsheet for the IBM PC.
1984	Apple introduces the graphic user interface for the Macintosh.
1988	Microsoft and IBM introduce OS/2.
1990	Microsoft introduces the windows operating environment for the IBM.

True

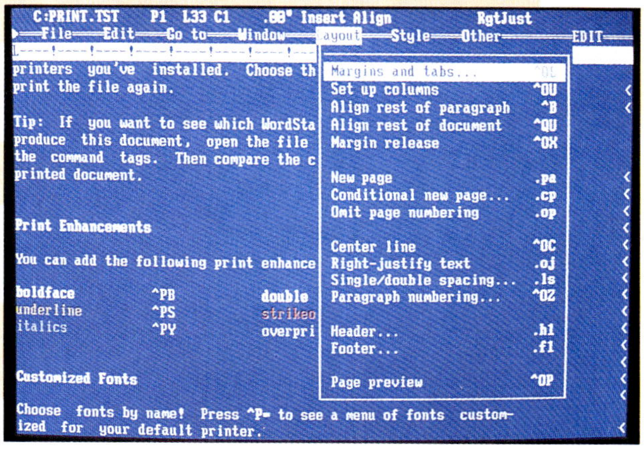
C:PRINT.TST P1 L33 C1 .80" Insert Align RgtJust
File Edit Go to Window Layout Style Other EDIT
printers you've installed. Choose th
print the file again.
Tip: If you want to see which WordSta
produce this document, open the file
the command tags. Then compare the c
printed document.
Print Enhancements
You can add the following print enhance
boldface ^PB double
underline ^PS strikeo
italics ^PY overpri
Customized Fonts
Choose fonts by name! Press ^P= to see a menu of fonts custom-
ized for your default printer.
Margins and tabs... ^OL
Set up columns ^OU
Align rest of paragraph ^B
Align rest of document ^QU
Margin release ^OX
New page .pa
Conditional new page... .cp
Omit page numbering .op
Center line ^OC
Right-justify text .oj
Single/double spacing... .ls
Paragraph numbering... ^OZ
Header... .h1
Footer... .f1
Page preview ^OP

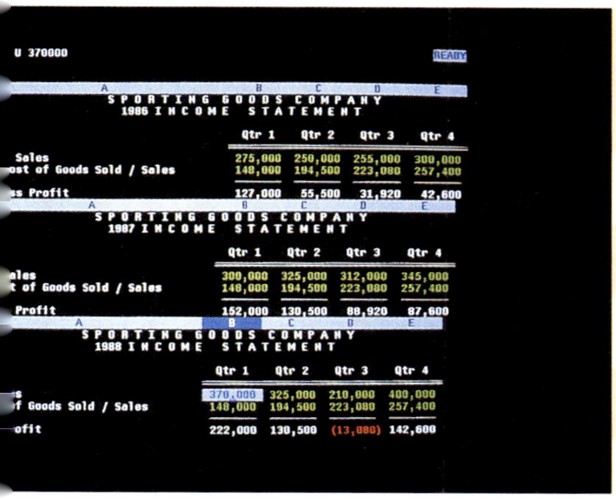
U 370000
READY
SPORTING GOODS COMPANY
1986 INCOME STATEMENT
Qtr 1 Qtr 2 Qtr 3 Qtr 4
Sales 275,000 250,000 255,000 300,000
ost of Goods Sold / Sales 148,000 194,500 223,080 257,400
ss Profit 127,000 55,500 31,920 42,600
SPORTING GOODS COMPANY
1987 INCOME STATEMENT
Qtr 1 Qtr 2 Qtr 3 Qtr 4
ales 300,000 325,000 312,000 345,000
t of Goods Sold / Sales 148,000 194,500 223,080 257,400
Profit 152,000 130,500 88,920 87,600
SPORTING GOODS COMPANY
1988 INCOME STATEMENT
Qtr 1 Qtr 2 Qtr 3 Qtr 4
370,000 325,000 210,000 400,000
f Goods Sold / Sales 148,000 194,500 223,080 257,400
ofit 222,000 130,500 (13,080) 142,600

Version
3.0
For DOS Systems
5¼" high-density
(1.2 MB) disk version
Microsoft. Windows.
Graphical Environment

PERSONAL CASE

Computers in the Law Office

For the past ten years, Rhonda Gray has been the legal secretary for a small law office. For about eight years, she has been preparing legal briefs using a stand-alone, dedicated word processing machine bought from Dedication Systems. Twice during that time, the firm has upgraded her equipment.

The firm received notice last month that Dedications Systems is going out of business and will continue servicing their equipment only through the end of the year. Because the lawyers were considering replacing or again upgrading the system soon anyway, no one feels too badly. The managing partner has Rhonda to select a microcomputer system that will handle the kinds of software that will be introduced in the next three to five years. He also wants her to look at various software packages and determine what she thinks is best for word processing and certain other tasks that she has not been doing on a computer. In particular, he wants her to select the following:

- A communications package for doing on-line searches of case law in the LEXUS legal database
- An electronic spreadsheet package for tracking office budgets
- A time-and-billing system for tracking time on cases and billing clients

Rhonda has fairly little trouble deciding to go with one of the latest IBM-compatible microcomputer hardware systems. With regard to choosing software, however, she feels more uncertain. She's an expert on one word processing software system but is no expert at evaluating other software. At this point, she's not even sure what to call the kinds of programs she needs. She does know that buying software is an important and, in some ways, complex question. Her first decision is to invest some time in learning what kinds of programs are available and how they match her needs.

Software is the sets of instructions computers use to manipulate and process data. Without software, the computer is a useless collection of hardware. Load software into a computer, and the machine acts as if it has received an instant education; suddenly it "knows" how to operate and how to think.

There are three general categories of software: programming languages, operating systems, and application programs (Figure 3.1). All three types are needed to make computers usable by the average person.

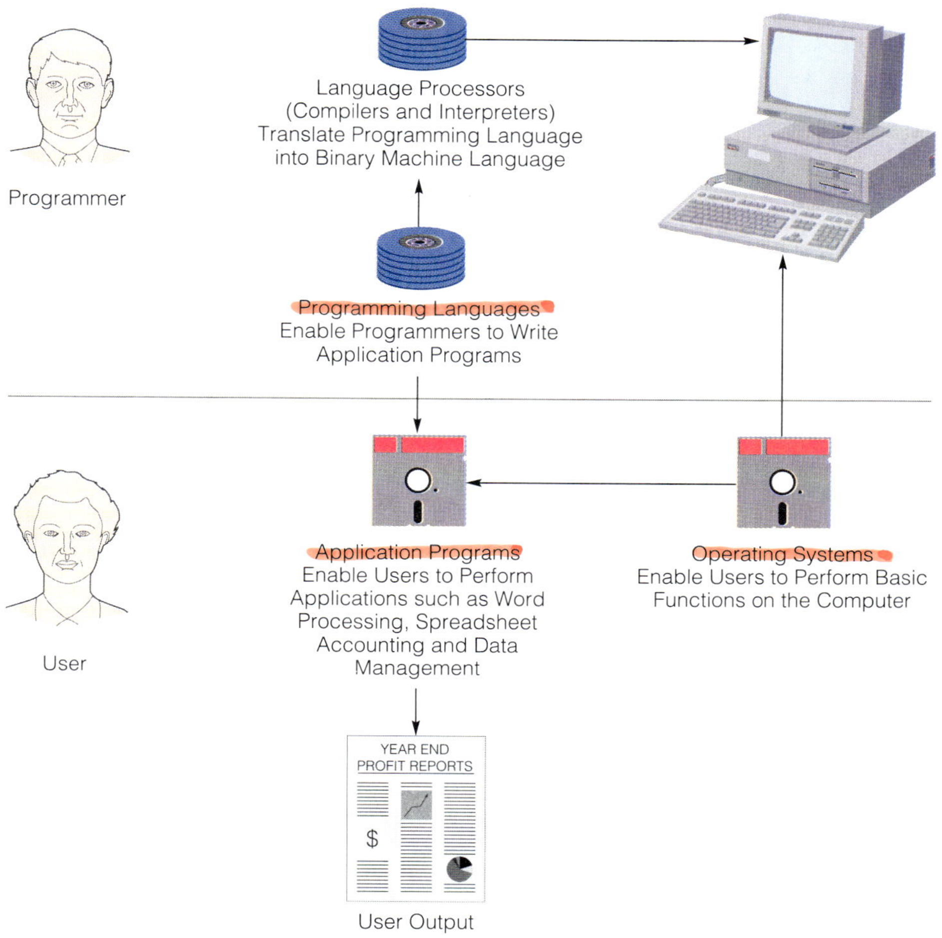

Figure 3.1
Types of software.

LANGUAGE PROCESSORS AND PROGRAMMING LANGUAGES

HOW PROGRAMS COMMUNICATE WITH COMPUTERS

Programming languages bridge a gap between computers, which work only with binary numbers, and people, who more often prefer to use words or other number systems. Expressing instructions entirely in binary code is excruciatingly slow, difficult, and error-ridden even for the most skilled and experienced programmers. Programming languages let programmers write English-like statements, numbers, and mathematical symbols (Figure 3.2), which computers then convert into binary code by programs called language processors. Programmers use programming languages to construct specific software programs such as word processing or electronic spreadsheets, which in turn can be used by a person with no knowledge of programming.

Programmers categorize programming languages according to their readability. **Low-level languages** are difficult for people to understand and require programmers to code instructions in considerable detail. **High-level languages** use more English-like statements that even novice programmers can master with minimal training.

Language processors translate programming language instructions into binary code much as a bilingual person might translate Swahili into English. The set of program instructions written in a programming language is the **source code**. The set of translated binary instructions that the computer can execute is the **object code**.

Figure 3.2
An example of source code: a portion of a COBOL program.

```
ID DIVISION
PROGRAM-ID. PROG1.
ENVIRONMENT DIVISION.
INPUT-OUTPUT SECTION.
FILE-CONTROL.
        SELECT INVENTORY-FILE ASSIGN TO PFMS.
        SELECT PRINT-FILE ASSIGN TO PFMS
DATA DIVISION
FILE SECTION.
FD      INVENTORY-FILE
        LABEL RECORDS ARE STANDARD
        RECORD CONTAINS 20 CHARACTERS
        DATA RECORD IS INVENTORY-REC.
01      INVENTORY-REC.
        02  PART-NO             PIC X(5).
        02  DESCRIPTION         PIC X(15).
FD      PRINT-FILE
        LABEL RECORDS ARE STANDARD
        RECORD CONTAINS 133 CHARACTERS
        VALUE OF FILE-ID IS 'PRINTER1'
        DATA RECORD IS PRINT-REC.
01      PRINT-REC.
        02   FILLER             PIC X(5).
        02   PART-NO-OUT        PIC X(5).
        02   FILLER             PIC X(10).
        02   DESCRIPTION-OUT    PIC X(15).
        02   FILLER             PIC X(98).
PROCEDURE DIVISION.
START-HERE.
        OPEN INPUT INVENTORY-FILE OUTPUT PRINT-FILE.
READ-TIME.
        READ INVENTORY-FILE AT END GO TO EOJ.
        MOVE SPACES TO PRINT-REC.
        MOVE PART-NO TO PART-NO-OUT.
        MOVE DESCRIPTION TO DESCRIPTION-OUT.
        WRITE PRINT-REC AFTER ADVANCING 2 LINES.
        GO TO READ-TIME.
EOJ.
        CLOSE INVENTORY-FILE PRINT-FILE.
        STOP RUN.
```

Language processors are either compilers or interpreters. **Compiler** software translates a source-code program into machine-language object code all at once, while checking for any errors that the programmer might have made. The object program, which is the program that performs all actual processing, becomes operative if the source program contains no errors. In contrast, an **interpreter** translates source code one instruction at a time, just as an interpreter might translate a speech one sentence at at time.

Because they need to translate a program only once, compiled programs are generally three to five times faster than interpreted programs. Thus, COBOL, a high-level program that uses a compiler, is faster than interpreted BASIC or the internal programming of dBASE database software, which typically uses an interpreter.

In writing programs, programmers usually follow a set of procedures called the system development life cycle, which provides guidance on how to tackle complicated problems through system analysis (see Chapter 8). This applies whether the program is for general consumption or for a special need.

Some programming languages such as BASIC are simple enough that laypersons can learn to use them within a few hours; others such as the C language are used only by well-trained professionals. In either case, it can take hundreds or thousands of hours to write a good tailor-made program. Eventually, you may want to try writing some programs as an exercise to learn about programming or because you have some need that isn't met by existing programs, but otherwise you should probably avoid trying to write your own programs while you are still a novice. Most people's programming needs are met by affordable commercial software.

SOME COMMON PROGRAMMING LANGUAGES

The most common programming languages are **BASIC** (Beginner's All-purpose Symbolic Instruction Code) (Figure 3.3), **COBOL** (COmmon Business-Oriented Language), and **Pascal**. Some programming languages, especially BASIC, the most popular of all, have numerous versions. Consequently, a program written on one computer often must be changed before it can be run on another computer. Some database packages, such as dBASE, have a built-in programming language (Figure 3.4).

FORTRAN was developed by IBM in the 1950s and was designed for use in applications that involved mathematical manipulation. Pascal, created in 1971 by Niklaus Wirth of Switzerland, was originally designed to teach structured-programming techniques. It has since evolved to a regular production language for developing systems.

The **C language** has become especially important for microcomputers. Since its development in 1972 by Dennis Ritchie at Bell Laboratories, this lan-

```
10 REM Sample Program #1 - Example of an interactive program
20 INPUT "Please enter your first name ",FIRST$
30 PRINT "Hi, ";FIRST$;", thanks for visiting me."
40 END




1LIST  2RUN←  3LOAD"  4SAVE"  5CONT←  6,"LPT1  7TRON←  8TROFF←  9KEY  0SCREEN
```

(a)

(b)

Figure 3.3

(a) A BASIC program that prompts the user for his or her first name and then thanks the user for visiting. (b) John Kemeny and Thomas Kurtz demonstrate their True BASIC.

Figure 3.4
A portion of a dBASE program.

```
IF # > 0
   @ 5,0 SAY "Sorry, there are no records in the database"
   STORE 1 TO count
   DO WHILE count < 50
      STORE count + 1 TO count
   ENDDO
   RELEASE count
   ERASE
   RETURN
ENDIF
SET INDEX TO
GO TOP
DO WHILE T
   STORE " " TO pause

   STORE T to badans
   STORE " " TO mchoice
   IF *
     @ 1,50 SAY "DELETED"
   ELSE
     @ 1,50 SAY "        "
   ENDIF
   @ 1,72 SAY DATE()
   @ 5,0 SAY "Product Number:"
   @ 5,16 SAY Prd:num
   @ 7,0 SAY "Product Description:"
   @ 7,21 SAY Prd:desc
   @ 9,0 SAY "Product Cost:"
```

Figure 3.5
Portions of (a) Pascal and (b) C program code.

```
program demo ( input, output )
begin
     writeln ( 'This is programming in Pascal!') ;
     writeln ( 'It looks a lot like C, doesn't it?' ) ;
     writeln ( 'Yes' ) ;
end .
```

(a)

```
#include <demo.h>
main (  )



      printf ( "This is programming in C!\n" ) ;
      printf ( "It is very similar to Pascal, isn't it?\n" ) ;
      printf ( "Yes\n" ) ;
}
```

(b)

guage has become one of the most prevalent languages used for microcomputer software (Figure 3.5). This particular langauge allows the programmer to have the same access to hardware as the assembler language. The real advantage to programs written in C is that they can be run on just about any computer.

OPERATING SYSTEMS

Operating system software coordinates the computer's hardware and supervises the input, output, storage, and processing functions. Operating systems let you issue commands to the computer such as "open a file," "make a printed copy of what appears on the screen," or "copy file x from disk b to disk a."

A **disk operating system (DOS)** is the set of software instructions that keeps track of the minute-to-minute housekeeping tasks required for the operation of the computer. These tasks include keeping track of files and where they are stored, saving and retrieving files, allocating storage space, and providing for accepting input and output from the defined devices.

Every computer has some type of operating system, which must be activated when the computer is turned on. If the operating system is recorded in ROM or present on the computer's hard disk, the operating system generally activates automatically when the computer is turned on. If it is not, you have to insert a diskette containing the operating system in order to activate it.

Operating systems set many practical limits on a computer's usefulness. In addition, a computer's operating system dictates how diskettes used on the computer must be formatted in order to hold storage files. An operating system also provides a program or routine to properly prepare or format diskettes.

TYPES OF OPERATING SYSTEMS

There are currently two generic types of operating systems: character-based and graphic user interface. The character-based operating system is best exemplified by the operating system historically used by IBM and IBM-compatible computers. DOS tells you it is ready to receive a command by displaying a **DOS prompt** (A> or C>, for example) on the screen; you respond by entering an instruction to be executed, character-by-character from the keyboard (Figure 3.6).

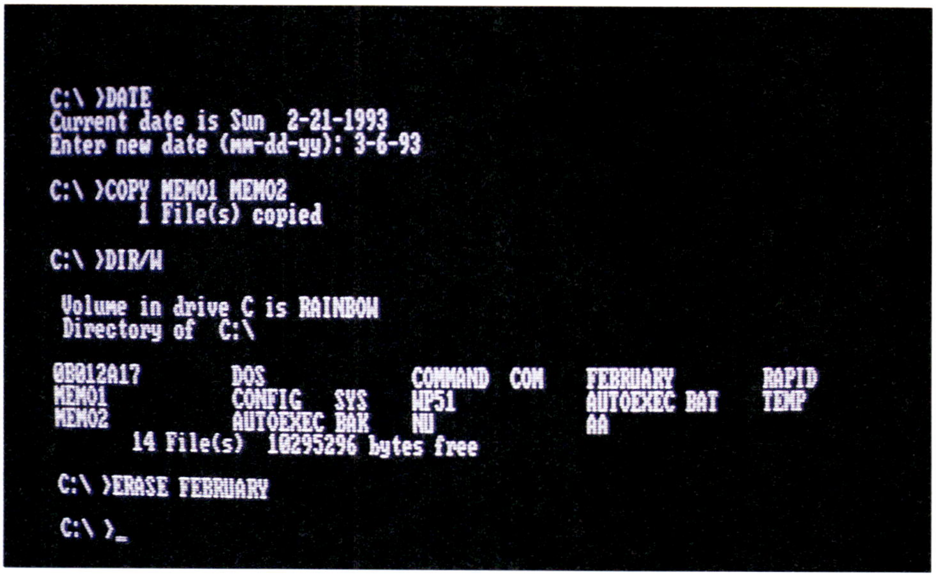

Figure 3.6
Screen dialogue between a user and the IBM PC DOS operating system version. The user has instructed DOS to (1) change the current date stored in the system's memory; (2) create a copy of a file called MEMO1 and call the copy MEMO2; (3) list the files and directories available on directory C; and (4) erase a file called FEBRUARY.

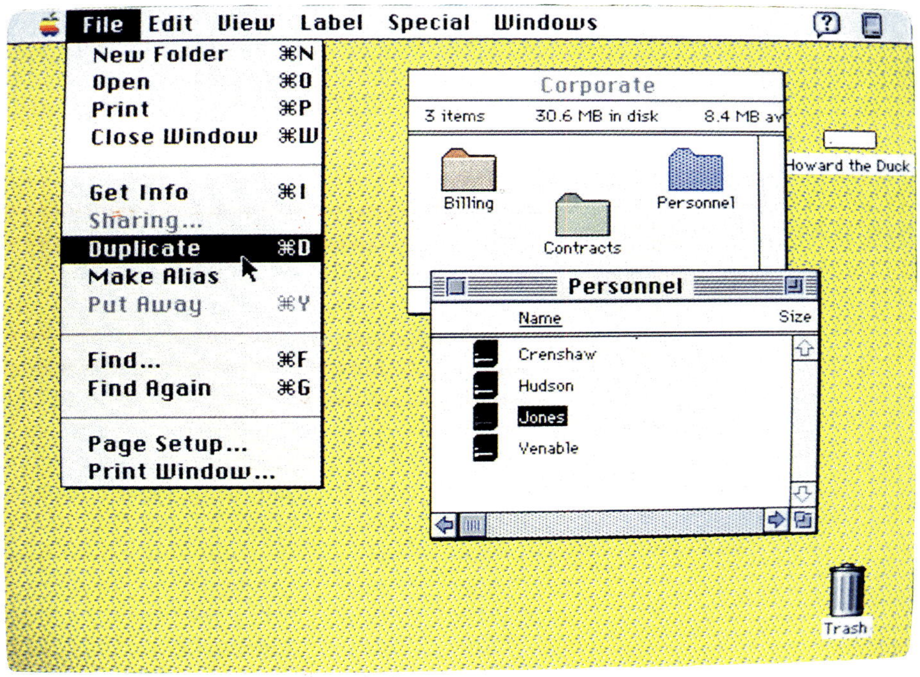

Figure 3.7

The Apple Macintosh GUI operating system. Using a mouse to move the arrow pointer and to signal choices, the user has opened a file directory called "Corporate" and a subdirectory called "Personnel." After highlighting the icon for a data file called "Jones," the user is now instructing the system to create a duplicate copy of the file.

The graphic user interface (GUI) makes use of a mouse for a pointing device and lets you point to *icons* (tiny symbols or pictures that represent some task to be performed) and click a button on the mouse to execute that particular operation or task. This easy-to-use interface software is an overlay over the operating system of a computer and passes instructions made by the user to the operating system. The Macintosh had the first commercially successful GUI for microcomputers (Figure 3.7). Microsoft has since introduced the Windows interface for IBM-compatible computers.

As noted in Chapter 2, some pen-based computers also have a different operating system. Although it is still too soon to predict how operating systems are going to evolve, it appears likely that different types of computers will continue to use different operating systems. Differing systems are not a great problem as long as data files can be transferred from one system to another.

An application software package always includes the programming that is necessary to run the application on a particular type of operating system. If the computer does not have that system, the application will not run. However, major application software such as WordPerfect or Lotus 1-2-3 are generally marketed in a variety of versions to match each of the major operating systems.

The following discussion of the primary IBM PC operating system, DOS, gives some idea of what operating systems do and how they operate.

DOS

The IBM personal computer disk operating system (DOS) is a collection of programs designed so that you can easily create and manage files, run programs, and use the system devices attached to the computer. The software company **Microsoft** developed PC DOS for IBM when IBM decided to market a microcomputer. Microsoft markets virtually the same operating system, under the name **MS DOS,** to many of the manufacturers of IBM-compatible computers. The two operating systems are identical for all intents and purposes.

DOS dictates how programs are executed on IBM and IBM-compatible microcomputers. For example, it is the DOS, not the hardware, that limits IBM-style machines to 640K of addressable base RAM.

OTHER OPERATING SYSTEMS

Besides Microsoft's disk operating system, a number of other types of operating systems can be used on an IBM-style microcomputer. They include the following:

- **OS/2** is an operating system that was jointly announced in 1988 by Microsoft and IBM for 80286 and 80386 computers. It lets a user have more than one application active at a time.
- **UNIX** was developed at Bell Laboratories, and the first commercial version was released in 1971. One advantage of UNIX is its extensive library of support tools, developed for the computer programmer, to aid in program development. This operating system tends to be used in networking applications. UNIX is not compatible with application programs that have been designed to run on DOS.
- **DR DOS 5.0** was developed by Digital Research and released in 1990 and updated to DR DOS 6.0 in 1991. It is the first operating system for the regular PC that breaks the 640K limit on base memory. It is compatible with existing application programs that run on earlier versions of DOS. It also contains a GUI to make it easier for users to enter commands (Figure 3.8).

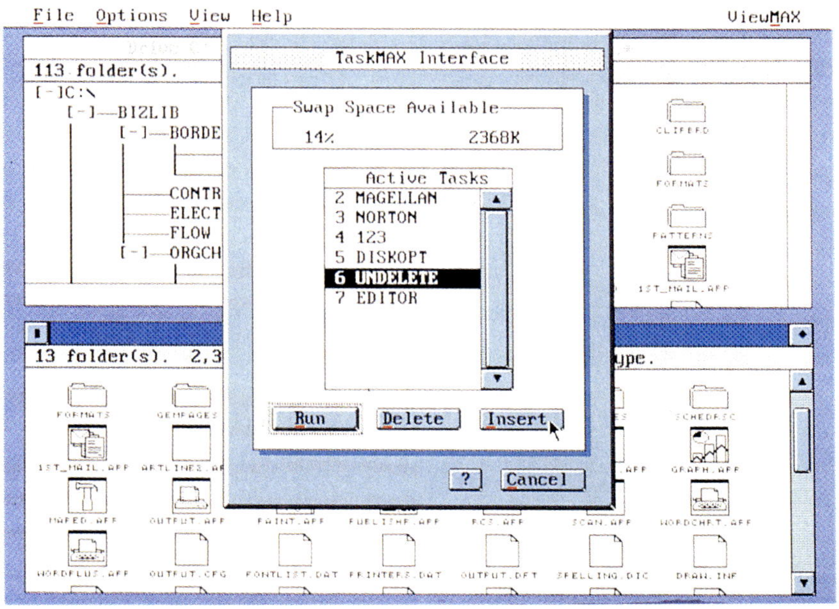

Figure 3.8
TaskMAX as seen through the graphical user interface of DR DOS 6.0.

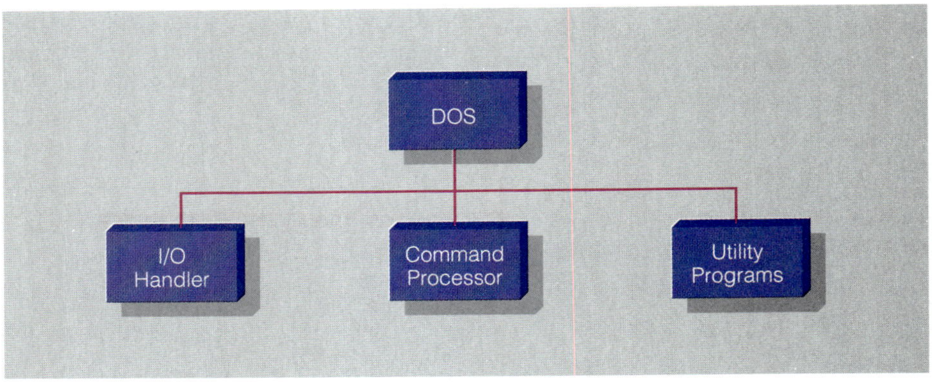

Figure 3.9
Component parts of DOS.

Parts of DOS MS DOS contains three program parts: the I/O (input/output) handler, the command processor, and utility programs (Figure 3.9).

I/O Handler The I/O handler manages input and output, encoding and decoding all data transferred between application programs and peripherals such as monitors, keyboards, disk drives, and printers. It also contains routines for preparing data to be stored on a disk, whether the data consist of a program, a document, or something else. The I/O handler comprises "hidden" files called IO.SYS and DOS.SYS.

Command Processor The command processor has built-in functions (also called subprograms) that handle most DOS tasks, including copying files, running programs, and examining a disk's table of contents to determine what files are stored on it. The file COMMAND.COM contains the command processor.

Utility Programs Utility programs perform housekeeping tasks that don't readily fit in the command processor. They are referred to as external files because they are stored as separate files (usually on the same disk as the rest of DOS). Utilities handle tasks like formatting disks, comparing files and/or disks, and reporting the available free space on a disk.

The above DOS programs are stored on a disk in four pieces:

1. The **boot record** is a special program, placed on every disk formatted by DOS, responsible for loading the rest of DOS into the PC. The boot record is contained on every formatted disk, regardless of whether it contains DOS.
2. The **IO.SYS** program acts as the I/O handler, managing all input and output to and from the computer.
3. The **DOS.SYS** program acts as the DOS file manager and contains file-related functions that can be used by DOS to store and retrieve files.
4. The **COMMAND.COM** program accepts DOS commands and runs the appropriate subprograms.

Versions of DOS Since first creating its PC DOS and MS DOS, Microsoft has written several versions of each. These versions are numbered in the style that is generally used for numbering updated versions of software programs. Issues of DOS include 1.1, 2.0, 2.1, 3.0, 3.1, 3.2, 3.3, 4.0, 4.01, and 5.0. The digit to the left of the decimal indicates the **version** of the operating system, each version being a major change in the system; the digit to the right of the decimal indicates

Table 3.1 Versions of DOS and the Amount of Space Each Occupies on Disk and When Loaded into RAM

DOS Version	Disk Space (Bytes)	RAM Memory Required (Bytes)
1.1	13,663	12,400
2.0	39,660	24,576
2.1	40,320	26,576
3.0	58,926	37,024
3.1	62,122	37,040
3.2	68,668	43,712
3.3	78,555	54,992
4.0	106,431	55,088

the **release** of the operating system, each release representing more minor changes. The 1.0, 2.0, and 3.0 versions represent the first releases of their respective versions.

Version 1.x (1.0, 1.1, and so on) was the original operating system for the IBM PC computer and compatibles. It supported only floppy disk drives. This operating system truly represents the infancy of the PC. Many of the commands that now appear in the operating system did not even exist in this earliest version. Also, many of the commands in this first version have been significantly altered to perform other tasks besides those originally expected of them.

Version 2.x was developed specifically for the IBM XT microcomputer. This version was the first to support a hard disk drive and to allow the creation of directories and subdirectories for storing programs and files in separate areas on a disk.

Version 3.x appeared about the same time as the IBM AT microcomputer. Although Version 3.x does not take advantage of the full power of the 80286 microprocessor chip and was not designed specifically for the AT, it still enhanced the power of the new computer. Version 3.x releases provided a number of advanced features. Version 3.2 introduced support for networking (connection of several computers to a shared printer or other peripheral devices) and 3.5-inch disk drives.

Version 4.x has added a DOS shell to allow the user to more easily operate DOS. This DOS shell provides a graphics/menu interface that lets you "point" to files that are to be operated on.

Version 5.0 greatly expanded the user interface and also allowed better, more efficient use of memory above the base of 640K.

Each succeeding DOS version has been able to perform increasingly complex tasks and, consequently, has required a corresponding increase in the memory space required to store the DOS program files. Table 3.1 shows the growth of DOS.

APPLICATION PROGRAMS

Application programs are precoded sets of computer instructions designed to meet relatively standardized data processing needs. The computer operator need only select the right application program for the job, just as you would choose the proper tool to tighten a bolt. Application software can be viewed on a continuum. Some software can only be used for a specific purpose, problem, or application, whereas other software can be used to address many different problems or applications.

SPECIAL-USE APPLICATION SOFTWARE

Software writers have created many special-purpose application programs, each designed to solve only one type of problem. Examples include the following:

- Personal accounting
- Educational programs
- General ledger
- Accounts receivable and payable
- Payroll
- Mailing lists
- Grading programs for teachers
- Computer games

This kind of software can only be used to fill a relatively narrow need. An accounts-receivable package, for example, can be used to track only accounts-receivable information. It cannot be used for maintaining a database of all customers for a firm.

Practical software programs have also been written for personal use (Figure 3.10). Financial programs are available for tracking checkbook activity, credit charges, and tax-deductible expenses and for generating monthly income and balance statements. Sophisticated stock-portfolio programs enable users to access the Dow Jones database and to buy or sell stocks from their homes.

Figure 3.10
Personal-use software programs can help you do everything from balancing your checkbook to buying and selling stocks.

Educational software is in plentiful supply, addressing everything from learning the alphabet to preparing for the SAT exam. These programs use techniques such as simulation, drill and practice, and computerized tutorials. Children can learn programming and improve their problem-solving skills with the computer programming language called LOGO. Educational software offers many advantages. Students can benefit from computer-assisted instruction nearly any time—at night, on weekends, or during regular school hours. With computerized drill-and-practice programs, students receive instant verification or correction of their answers. Moreover, computerized instruction can be specially programmed to meet the needs of the individual student. In a drill-and-practice exercise, for example, a student can be given specific review information when he or she misses a question.

Business software is also abundant. Packages are available for nearly every business problem, from general ledger to payroll. Many such programs have proved their soundness by withstanding the scrutiny of public accounting firms. Some software packages address specific industries such as real estate or the health professions.

PRODUCTIVITY SOFTWARE

In the past few years, a new type of software has emerged that saves time by performing repetitive tasks quickly. Two examples of such **productivity software** are desktop organizers and DOS shells.

Desktop Organizers Picture the typical executive's desk: A leaning stack of papers clutters one corner. At another corner is a jumble of gadgets, which include the telephone, clock, and Rolodex. Legal pads and memos form a paper mountain in the center, under which a calendar and calculator lie hidden. The executive is speaking on the telephone, frantically trying to find a scrap of paper with some vital information on it.

Software designers have devised the desktop organizer as the solution to the cluttered desktop. **Desktop organizers** can include calculators, notepads, automatic dialers, and appointment calendars, all neatly tucked away in the computer's memory and ready for instant access. Because most desktop organizers are RAM-resident programs, there is no need to insert a disk to call to the screen a calendar, notepad, or other desktop tool. You simply issue a command.

The first commercial desktop organizer was SideKick, a highly successful RAM-resident program developed by Borland International (Figure 3.11). It displays several desktop tools in a separate window on the screen. You can use your favorite spreadsheet package to enter formulas, then invoke SideKick's calculator to check the work without exiting from the spreadsheet.

Figure 3.11
(a) Calculator window of SideKick, which can be invoked from within another software package, such as Lotus 1-2-3. (b) Other Sidekick windows.

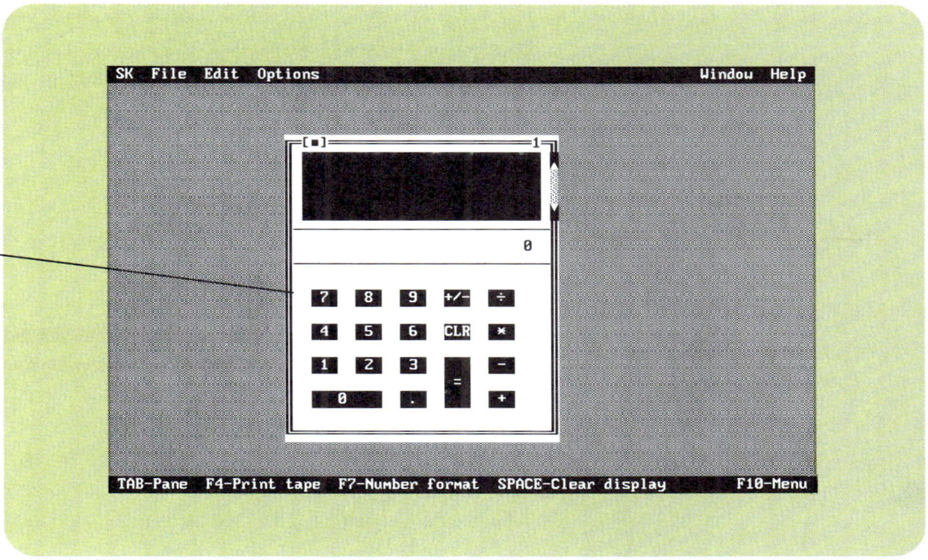

(a)

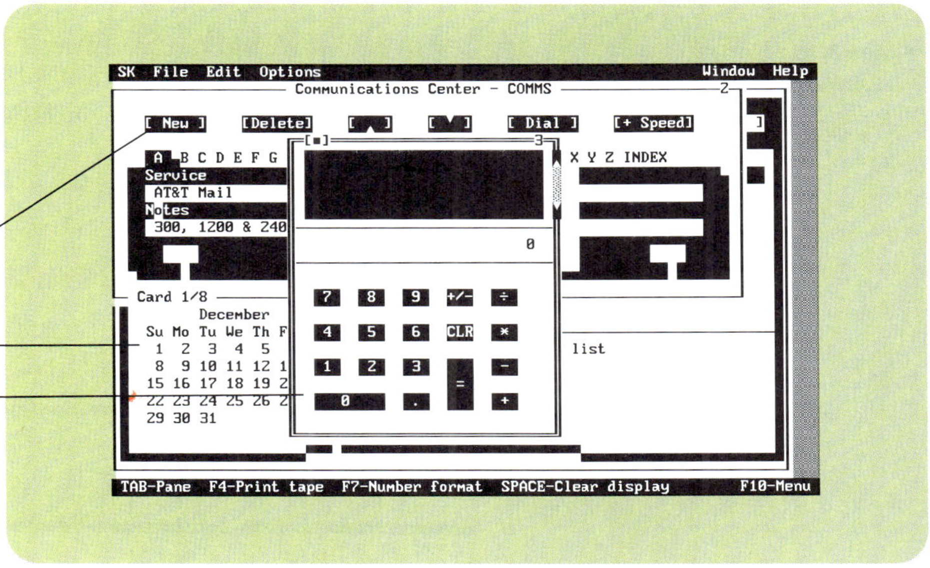

(b)

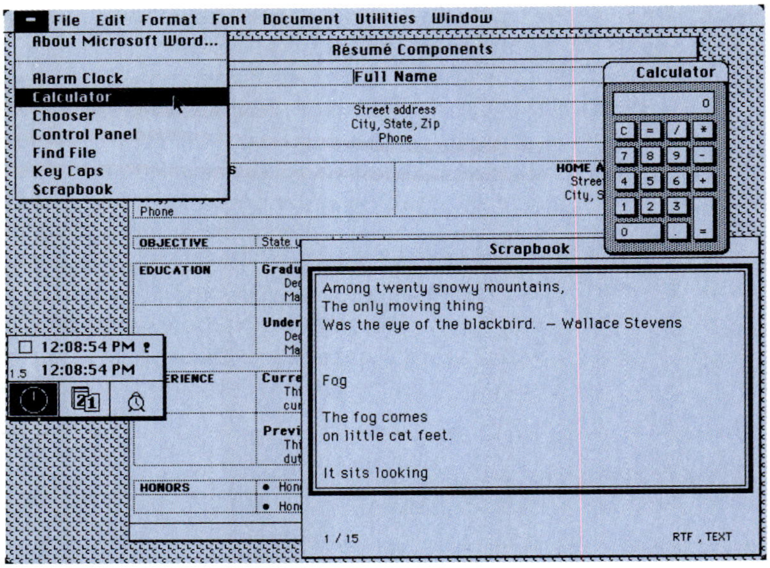

Figure 3.12
Desktop organizer on the Macintosh, showing the calculator, the scrapbook, and the alarm clock features.

Apple MacIntosh computers have a built-in set of desk accessories that can be used at any time, including an alarm clock, calculator, scrapbook, and other features (Figure 3.12).

DOS Shells **DOS shell** software packages help users with minimal knowledge of the disk operating system to quickly do things such as copying files. The user simply tags the files to be copied and indicates where the copies should go. DOS shell programs often use a mouse. One well-received DOS Shell is PC Tools, which performs a wide variety of chores such as providing file backup and allowing you to access control of one computer from another computer keyboard (Figure 3.13). Many shells also have viewers that show the contents

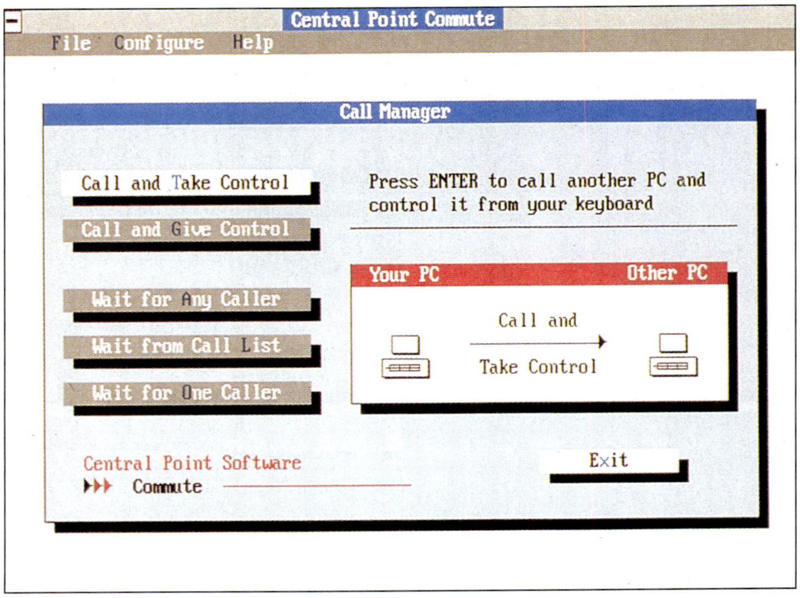

Figure 3.13
PC Tools from Central Point Software provides the Call Manager shell, which allows you to control other PCs.

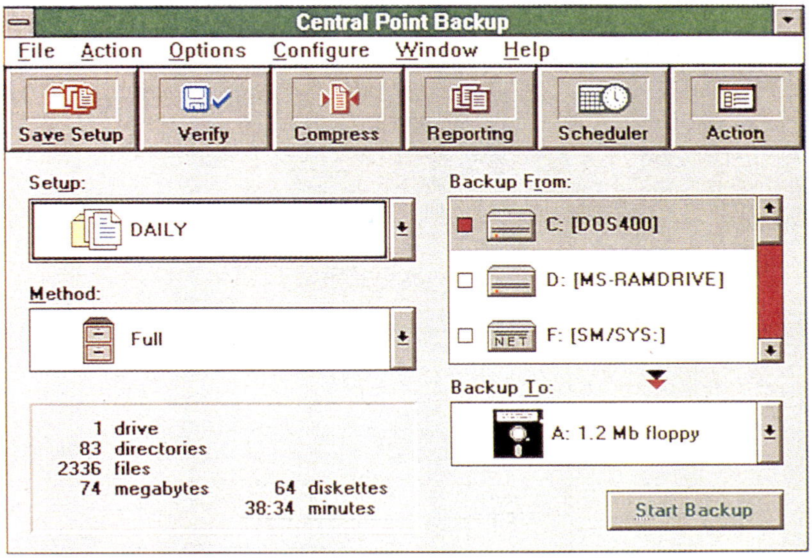

Figure 3.14

The PC Tools Backup routine allows you to easily back up the contents of a fixed disk.

of a file without your running the software that created that file (Figure 3.14). PC Tools has viewers for 30 different software packages.

GENERAL-PURPOSE APPLICATION SOFTWARE

General-purpose application software serves five core applications: electronic spreadsheets, word processing, data communications, database management, and graphics (Figure 3.15).

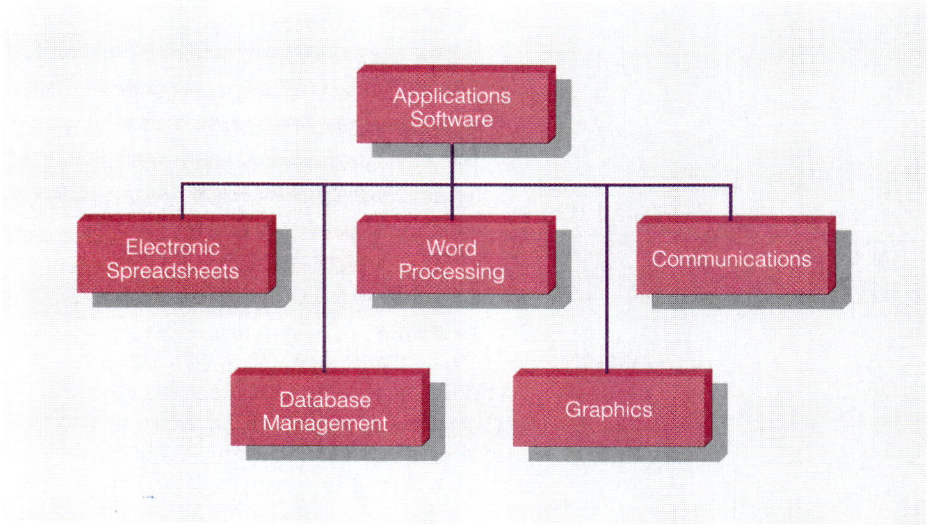

Figure 3.15

The five core software applications: electronic spreadsheets, word processing, data communications, database management, and graphics.

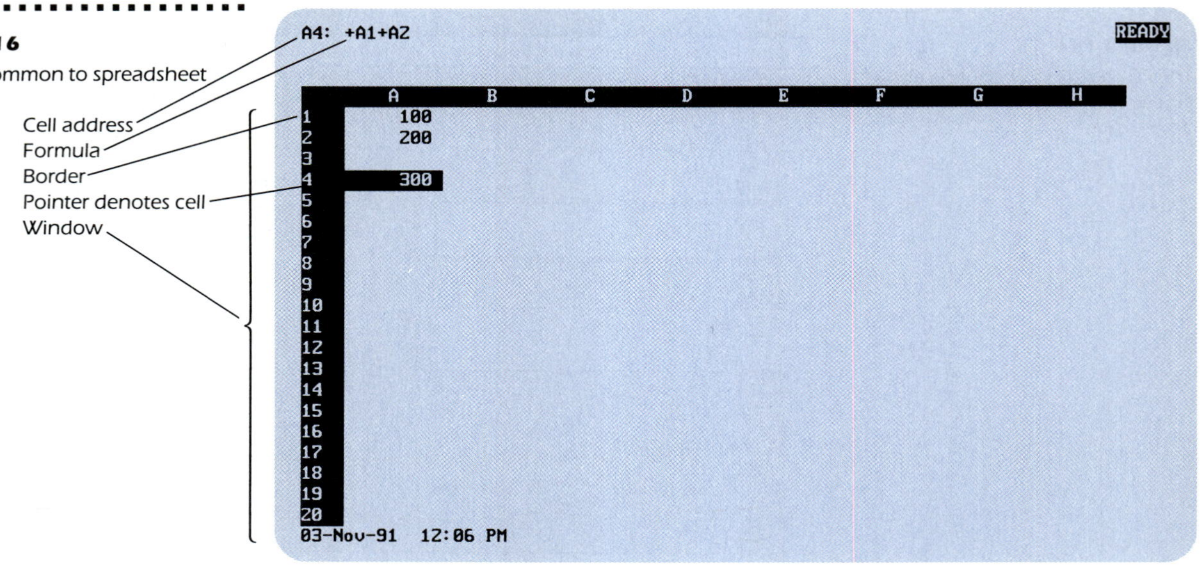

Figure 3.16
Features common to spreadsheet software:

Electronic Spreadsheets **Electronic spreadsheet** programs let you manipulate various data that can be arranged in rows and columns. A cell (the point where a row and a column intersect) can contain text, a number, or a formula that establishes its relationship with other cells. Whenever you change the contents of one cell, the spreadsheet automatically recalculates other cell values. Spreadsheets free you from the tedium of recalculating by hand, thereby saving an enormous amount of time.

Figure 3.16 uses Lotus 1-2-3 to illustrate some common features of spreadsheet software:

1. The **border** contains the letters and numbers that identify the rows and columns.
2. The **cell** is the entity at the intersection of a column and a row.
3. The **cell address** is identified by column-and-row method. This is cell A4.
4. The **formula** tells Lotus 1-2-3 to add the contents of cell A1 to the contents of cell A2 and store the sum in cell A4 where the formula is located.
5. The **pointer** is a high-intensity rectangle that moves from cell to cell when you press an Arrow key. The pointer indicates on which cell you are currently working.
6. The **window** is the portion of the worksheet that is visible on your monitor.

Sophisticated spreadsheet packages do much more than manipulate rows and columns of numbers. Some have advanced features such as "if-then-else" logic and "less-than/greater-than" tests. These operations are used in tasks such as calculating payroll. A less-than/greater-than test can pick out those employees who worked more than 40 hours in a week. The if-then-else operation can calculate these employees' wages according to a different rate. In effect, this operation says to the computer, "If an employee's weekly hours total more than 40, then calculate his or her wages according to an overtime formula." Built-in functions provide other advanced features such as determining the minimum, maximum, or average value in a range of numbers.

VISICALC

VisiCalc, the first spreadsheet software, was originally designed for the Apple II computer by Harvard Business School graduate students Robert Frankston and Dan Bricklin (Figure 3.17). VisiCalc led many businesspeople to view the microcomputer as a useful business tool rather than as a toy. Many current microcomputer spreadsheet packages far surpass the original VisiCalc.

VisiCalc helped popularize Apple microcomputers. Spreadsheet packages such as **Lotus 1-2-3** spurred businesses to purchase the IBM PC.

Figure 3.17
VisiCalc and its inventors.

Some spreadsheets also allow the importing or exchanging of information from other application programs. This lets you perform additional calculations with data already processed and print out reports. The following are only a few of many business and personal spreadsheet applications:

- Materials and labor requirements
- Product planning
- Production forecasting
- Marketing
- Merger and acquisition of real estate
- Cash-flow analysis
- Checkbook registers
- Personal balance sheet

PERSONAL CASE PROGRESS

Sources of Software Information

How does someone get reliable information about what software to buy when he or she may not know anything about software, let alone the quality of the competing products? Rhonda belongs to a club of legal secretaries and decides to call Peter Cortines, another member, whose firm has recently made similar decisions. They meet for lunch to discuss Rhonda's software selection problems.

Peter suggests a number of sources of software information: computer magazines, user groups, computer stores, and computer manufacturers.

Computer magazines such as *Byte, PC Magazine, PC World, MacUser,* and *MacWorld* frequently issue "report cards" on new software packages (Figure 3.18). They also rate and compare products by various scales based on the strengths and weaknesses found during the testing process.

User groups are local computer clubs whose members meet and exchange information about computers in general or specifically (for example, Apple, IBM, or Amiga). Some user groups have attracted regional or national attention. They are good sources of information about software, hardware, and how to operate them. Many also distribute public domain software utility programs, personal software, and games at a nominal cost to members.

Computer stores also are good sources of information. Many are staffed by people who can help you select an appropriate software package. In a reliable store, staff will take the time to evaluate your needs and recommend the program that meets them best.

The usefulness of an electronic spreadsheet alone has justified many microcomputer purchases by both individuals and businesses.

Word Processing How often, in drafting a letter or report, have you filled a wastebasket with "reject" paper? How often have you crossed out lines or tried to squeeze additional comments on the sides of the page? How often have you wished you could easily move a paragraph from one place to another?

Word processing simplifies the task of writing, editing, and printing a document. It also improves personal productivity by letting you duplicate a docu-

Some computer manufacturers include ("bundle") software free with each computer they sell. Although some of this software may not be the current best-seller in its market, it may still be what you need.

Rhonda thanks Peter for this information, to which he adds his own personal comments on the software being used where he works.

"It's good you asked me about this," he says. "The best way to learn about software is to talk with people who know and use it."

REPORT CARD **INFO WORLD**

SPREADSHEET SOFTWARE

Lotus 1-2-3 for Windows

VERSION 1.0

Criterion	*(Weighting)*	Score
Performance		
Formulas/Analysis	*(100)*	Good
Compatibility	*(50)*	Very Good
Speed	*(75)*	Satisfactory
Database	*(75)*	Very Good
Graphics	*(100)*	Good
Output	*(75)*	Satisfactory
Macros	*(50)*	Poor
Consolidation/ linking	*(50)*	Very Good
Capacity	*(50)*	Very Good
Networkability	*(50)*	Satisfactory
Documentation	*(50)*	Satisfactory
Ease of learning	*(50)*	Very Good
Ease of use	*(75)*	Poor
Support		
Support policies	*(25)*	Very Good
Technical support	*(25)*	Satisfactory
Value	*(100)*	Satisfactory
Final score		5.6

PRODUCT SUMMARY

Company: Lotus Development Corp., 55 Cambridge Parkway, Cambridge, MA 02142; (617) 577-8500.
List Price: $595
Requires: IBM PC/AT, PS/2, or compatible; DOS 3.11 or later; Windows 3.0; 2 megabytes of RAM.
Pros: Traditional 1-2-3 slash commands still work; compatible with prior 1-2-3 macros; customizable icon bar; Solver capability built in.
Cons: Macro transcript feature doesn't work; screen update problems; cannot read Excel 3.0 file format; no dialog box macro commands; no auditing features; documentation is weak in parts.
Summary: The Windows version of 1-2-3 essentially matches the features found in 1-2-3 Release 3.1, but with a vastly improved user interface. Unfortunately, this product was released with some significant problems.

Figure 3.18
Infoworld's "Report Card."

ment without retyping it or recall the document 6 months later without having to leaf through a ton of paper to find it. Word processing does not necessarily reduce the time it takes to produce a first-draft report from scratch, but it does provide the means to revise and generate an almost perfect document without having to spend hours retyping drafts.

Word processing software enhancements can also check and correct spelling, check grammar, and suggest synonyms. Figure 3.19 shows some common word processing features.

Figure 3.19
Common word processing features.

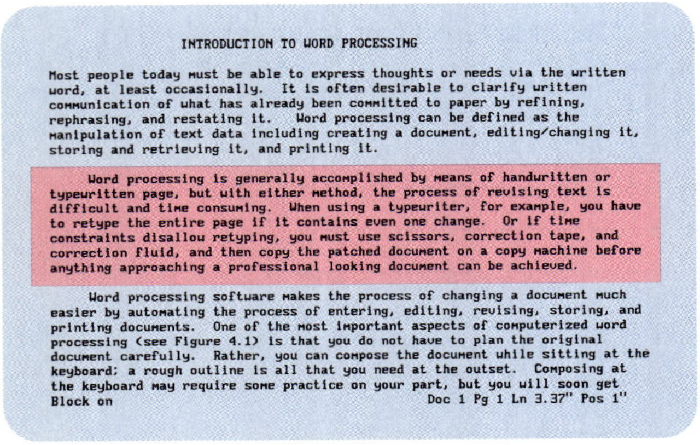

Block marks a portion of text and for deletion, movement, or some other operation.

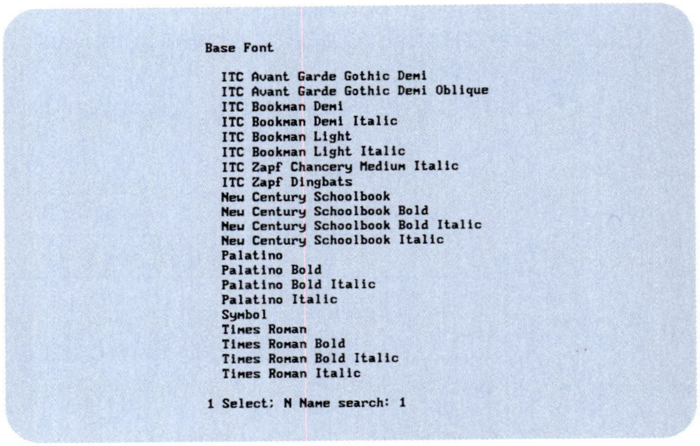

Font changes the size and appearance of text to be printed.

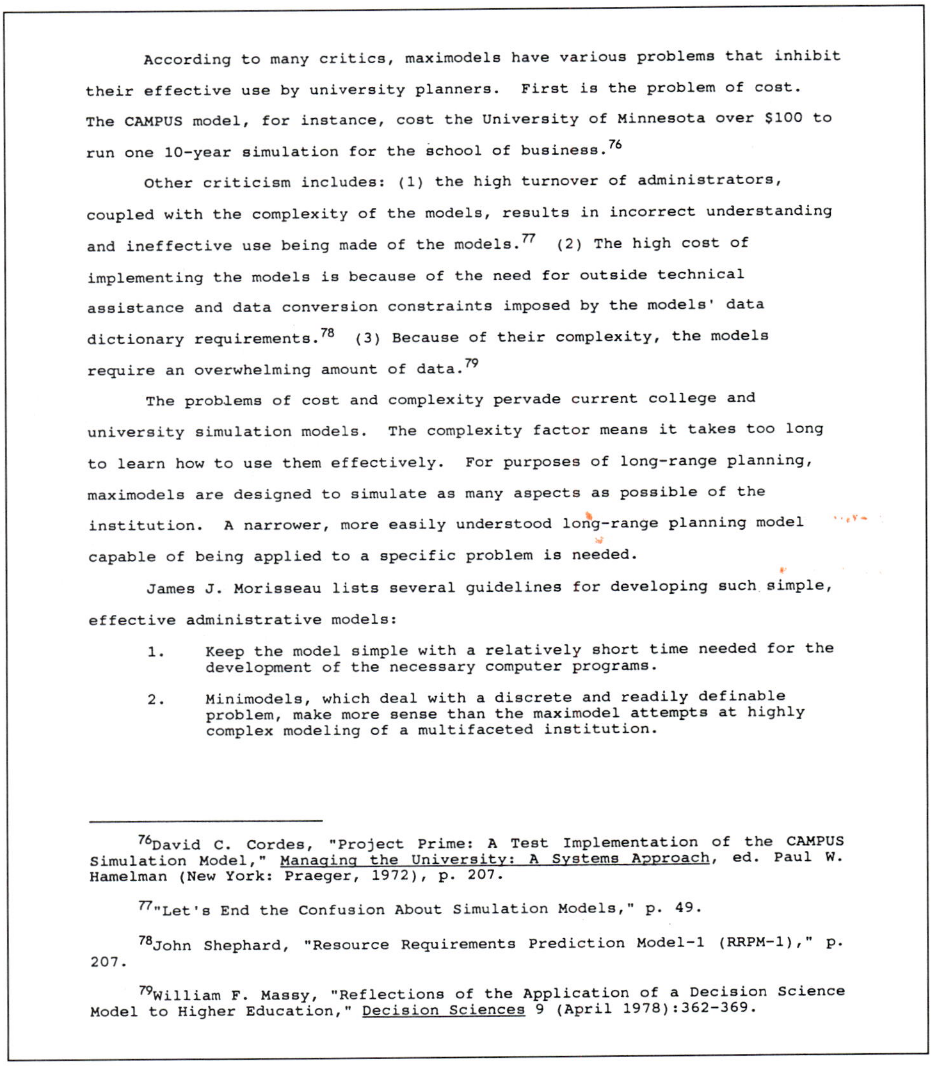

According to many critics, maximodels have various problems that inhibit their effective use by university planners. First is the problem of cost. The CAMPUS model, for instance, cost the University of Minnesota over $100 to run one 10-year simulation for the school of business.[76]

Other criticism includes: (1) the high turnover of administrators, coupled with the complexity of the models, results in incorrect understanding and ineffective use being made of the models.[77] (2) The high cost of implementing the models is because of the need for outside technical assistance and data conversion constraints imposed by the models' data dictionary requirements.[78] (3) Because of their complexity, the models require an overwhelming amount of data.[79]

The problems of cost and complexity pervade current college and university simulation models. The complexity factor means it takes too long to learn how to use them effectively. For purposes of long-range planning, maximodels are designed to simulate as many aspects as possible of the institution. A narrower, more easily understood long-range planning model capable of being applied to a specific problem is needed.

James J. Morisseau lists several guidelines for developing such simple, effective administrative models:

1. Keep the model simple with a relatively short time needed for the development of the necessary computer programs.

2. Minimodels, which deal with a discrete and readily definable problem, make more sense than the maximodel attempts at highly complex modeling of a multifaceted institution.

---

[76]David C. Cordes, "Project Prime: A Test Implementation of the CAMPUS Simulation Model," Managing the University: A Systems Approach, ed. Paul W. Hamelman (New York: Praeger, 1972), p. 207.

[77]"Let's End the Confusion About Simulation Models," p. 49.

[78]John Shephard, "Resource Requirements Prediction Model-1 (RRPM-1)," p. 207.

[79]William F. Massy, "Reflections of the Application of a Decision Science Model to Higher Education," Decision Sciences 9 (April 1978):362-369.

Footnote/Endnote automatically places footnotes at the bottom of a page and keeps balanced the number of lines of text on the page and the number of lines of footnotes.

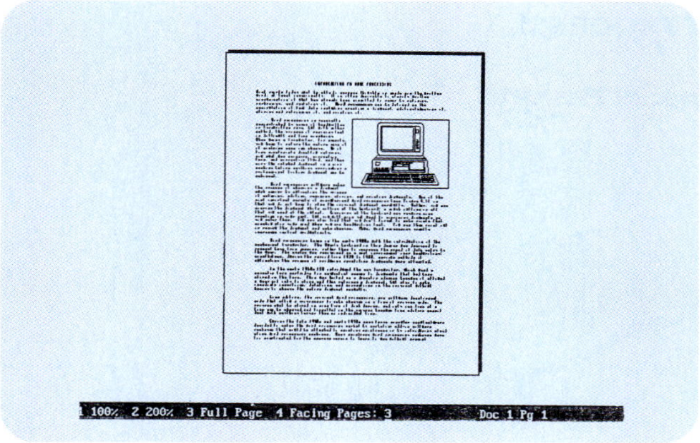

Graphics places text and graphics on the same page.

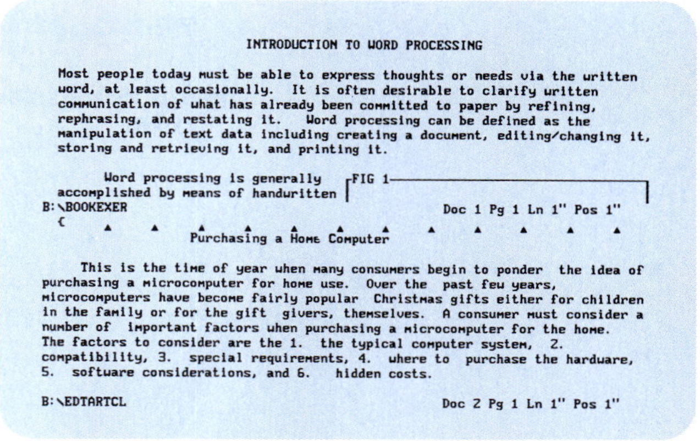

Split screen lets you divide the screen to have two different views of the same document or two entirely different documents available for editing.

Spell check identifies questionable words, suggests possible replacements, and then replaces the suspect word with an identified replacement in a document.

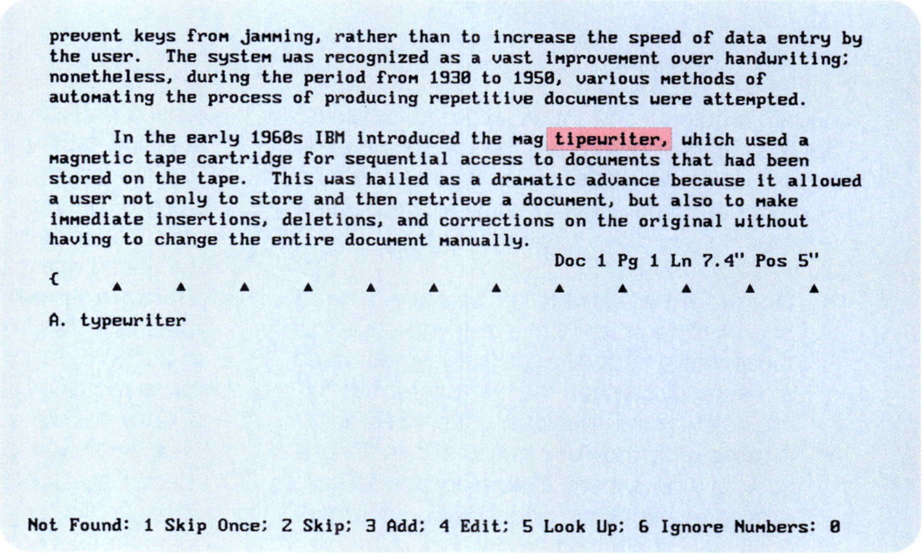

Thesaurus Provides synonyms or antonyms for selected word in a document.

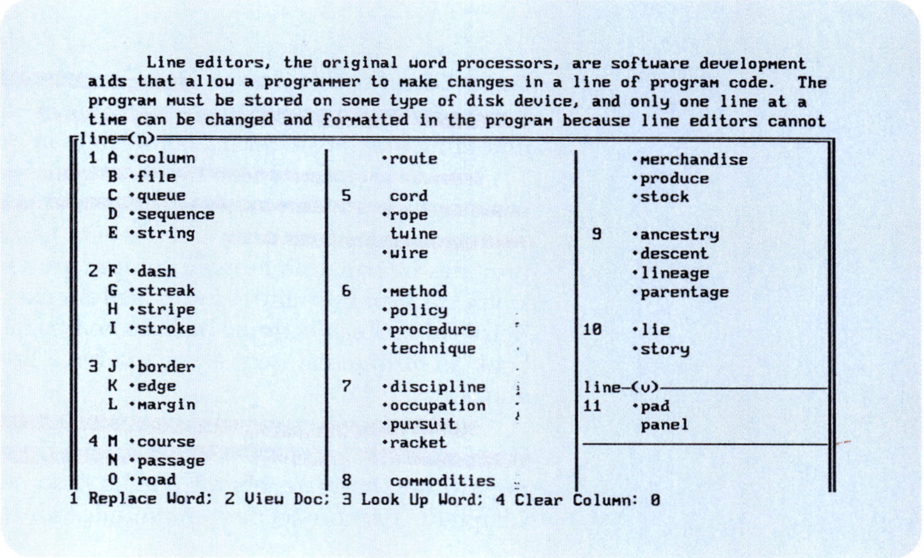

PERSONAL CASE PROGRESS

Word Processing Special Features

Legal, medical, and other word processing applications sometimes require special features. From her experience as a legal secretary, Rhonda can identify several unusual features she wants in her word processing software:

- **Document assembly** lets you take a number of different files from a disk and assemble those into one document (sometimes called a master document) that will print the different files together, paginating them in order.
- A **table of authorities** lists all of the citations used in a document. Before advanced word processing software, legal secretaries generally put off creating the table of authorities until a brief had been typed. The word processing table-of-authorities feature lets the typist mark the authorities as they are being typed. The program then generates a table of all citations automatically after the document has been typed.
- **Paragraph numbering** automatically numbers and renumbers different segments of contracts, regulations, and definitions, as often required in legal documents.
- **Fonts** allows a variety of type sizes and styles (for example, italic) for wills and trusts, deeds and contracts, summonses, pleadings, and other documents in letter-quality or near-typeset quality.

Data Communications **Data communications** software lets individuals and businesses transmit vital information—for example, information about an unfolding merger—over telephone lines in minutes.

Microcomputers communicate over long distances by means of a **modem,** which translates the computer's binary signals into audible sounds, which can be sent via telephone lines. The modem has helped spawn a new industry that provides information to microcomputer owners. For instance, you can receive stock information and buy or sell stocks through the Dow Jones News/Retrieval. Other electronic bulletin boards allow microcomputer subscribers to book an airline seat, rent a car, reserve a hotel room, and purchase consumer goods.

Microcomputers can also be linked into a **local area network (LAN),** which lets them share resources such as hard disks and printers. LANs involve installing various interface boards, cables, and software rather than modems. See Chapter 6 for more on data communications.

USES OF COMMUNICATIONS SOFTWARE

- A **bulletin board system (BBS)** is a private telecommunications facility usually set up by a microcomputer hobbyist. A bulletin board is usually created as a means for individuals interested in a particular topic to communicate about it.
- An **information service** is a for-profit service that makes available news, stock quotes, travel services, and other types of information to subscribers via modem hookups. These include CompuServe, Prodigy, Dow Jones, and others.
- **Electronic mail** is the use of electronic communications equipment to send text-based messages such as letters, memos, or reports. This is a "forward-and-store" type of communication, which means that the individual receiving the message does not have to be present when it is sent. When that person is ready to read his or her mail, he or she calls it up on the screen.

Database Management **Database management** software organizes, updates, and stores records and files in virtually unlimited ways. For example, suppose a large business has placed information about each employee in a computerized database file. The business gets a request from the government for information on how many of its employees are over age 55. Without computer assistance, personnel department workers can spend hours searching employee file folders for this information. However, if employee birth dates are recorded in the database, a personnel worker can simply tell the computer to search for files containing birth dates of a given year and earlier, and the computer produces a list of employees.

A database management software package saves vast amounts of time in accessing information from a file. The first relational database created for microcomputers was dBASE II. See Chapter 7 for more on database management.

COMMON DATABASE TERMS

Database	A collection of related information about a subject that can be organized in a useful manner.
Field	A space for a specific piece of information in a record.
Query	The ability to address a question to the database and receive the answer in the form of the appropriate data.
Record	A unit of data about an entity or transaction. A record is composed of fields.
Report	Selected information from a database formatted and displayed or printed out in an easy-to-read format.
Sort	The ability to physically rearrange records into a specified order.

PERSONAL CASE PROGRESS

Shopping for Software

The expense of a software package does not stop with the initial purchase. Based on her experience with the dedicated word processing system, Rhonda knows that changes will occur in all her major software. She decides to stop at a local software store, look at some packages, and inquire about what future changes are likely to cost.

A salesperson talks with her about the problem, pointing out that software companies are constantly trying to improve their programs by correcting any errors that are found by users. They are also adding features that have been requested by current users or that will differentiate their product from the competition. From time to time (usually shortly after she has purchased a software package and registered as a user), Rhonda is likely to receive information about a newer version. Updating to this newer version usually costs a fraction of the original purchase price.

After receiving the update notice, Rhonda will probably be allowed to examine the new features and decide whether or not to buy the update. Some packages, like WordPerfect and Lotus 1-2-3, have had a variety of updates over the years to stay competitive in the marketplace. Lotus has had, at this time, nine updates of its 1-2-3 package.

Rhonda concludes that a software package that costs about $500 might cost $1000 to $1500 over its useful life, including several updates. This cost will escalate if the software company charges for any support.

Graphics People can comprehend a well-made graph much faster than the printed statistics it represents. As a means of imparting information, graphics can offer similar advantages over reading or listening. Whereas word processing has increased the ease of producing reams of printed information, computer graphics have increased the comprehension and speed with which printed information can be absorbed.

Some popular software programs that can convert raw data into **graphic displays** are Harvard Graphics, Applause II, PowerPoint, Corel Draw, and Lotus 1-2-3 (Figure 3.20). Plotters and color printers can produce hard copies of graphs created on a computer screen, and some devices make photographic slides of computer-generated graphics.

Computer graphics can also be used in a wide variety of applications in business, advertising, design and manufacture, and the arts and entertainment industries. See Chapter 4 for more about graphics and graphics software.

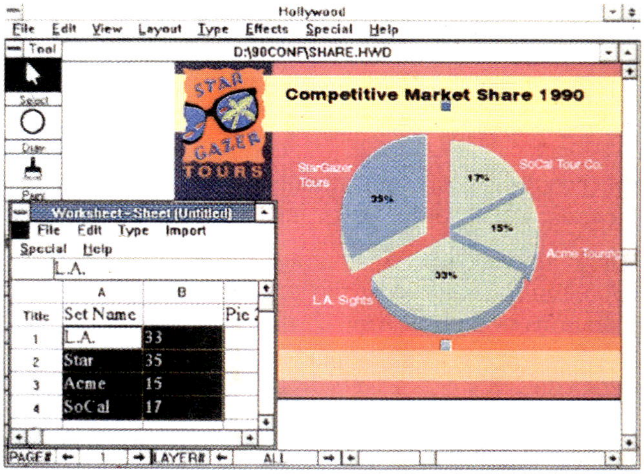

(a)

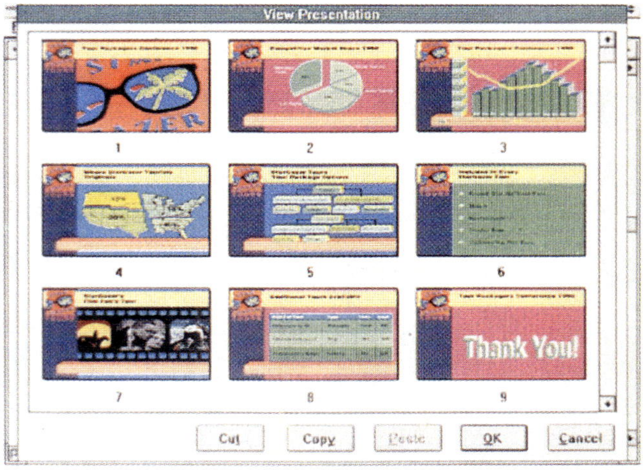

(b)

Figure 3.20
Effective use of graphics to present information.

(c)

INTEGRATED SOFTWARE

Microcomputer users can derive great benefits from the five core applications. However, these applications offer even more advantages when their problem-solving capabilities are combined.

Lotus 1-2-3 is one such **integrated package.** It contains a powerful spreadsheet with low-level database management and medium-level graphics. An operator writing a business report with Lotus 1-2-3 could exit out of the spreadsheet package and open the graphics package to create an illustrative graph, then return to the spreadsheet at the exact place he or she left off. The report generated using a package like WordPerfect 5.1 could mix graphs, text, and statistics for maximum impact. Since the advent of Lotus 1-2-3, several packages (including Framework, Symphony, and Intuit) have combined all five core applications.

FUTURE TRENDS

Figure 3.21
Experiments in virtual reality.

Approaching Human Experience

Two trends that promise to have an impact on software are virtual reality and intuitive software.

Virtual Reality This system uses hardware and software to make it appear to the individual using the program that he or she is involved in an artificial environment. This technology is being developed and applied at various levels of sophistication. For instance, several computer home game systems have gloves or footpads that can be used to control the game with movements somewhat more like what a real situation might require, rather than simply pressing a button. At a more sophisticated level, computer artists are attempting to create virtual reality systems that surround an individual in a comprehensive realm of visual, aural, and tactile sensations (Figure 3.21).

Intuitive Programs This software aims at making programs easier to use. Many people who have difficulties in using automatic teller machines, microwave ovens, or VCRs also have problems using computer software. Why? Because all these machines or programs force them to act in accordance with arbitrary rulesthat come with the device or package. Even with the supposedly user-friendly GUI packages, arbitrary rules must be followed in ways that people don't necessarily think.

The fundamental issue may be that current computers simply don't "think" like people in some respects. All people, to some extent, make intuitive leaps of judgment or solve problems by thinking by analogy rather than always following rigid sets of rules. People can also think inductively, recognizing trends with just a few samples of input.

In the future, computers—as well as the software that control them—will be able to think more like people. Currently, computer scientists are developing neural networks that can reason more like human beings. Other techniques such as building commonsense knowledge bases are also being applied.

Combined with voice input and output, these techniques will make computers and their programs easier to use.

SOFTWARE MENUS: MAKING SOFTWARE EASIER TO USE

Early microcomputer software was so complex that consumers often spent many hours reading documentation before they could use it. People complained loudly about the lack of user-friendly programs. Software developers responded by adding screen menus and prompts. Like an index that helps readers locate information in a book, a **menu** tells you where to find information in a program.

Menus greatly improve the "friendliness" of programs by reducing the number of commands you need to learn. Like a menu in a restaurant, a program menu offers an array of choices. Selecting an option either executes a command or brings to the screen a submenu of options. Prompts are often included in the menu to guide you step-by-step.

Menus of just about every conceivable type have been incorporated into software. Some software requires a special command to bring a menu onto the screen, whereas other software automatically displays a menu. Menu structures are either horizontal or vertical, with pull-down and pop-up variations.

Horizontal Menus Horizontal menus appear across the screen in one or two rows of text. You can issue a command on the menu in a variety of ways: Press a function key, type the first letter in the name of the command, press the numeric key that corresponds to the command's selection number, or highlight the command with a pointer and press Enter.

Lotus 1-2-3 displays a two-line menu along the top of the worksheet screen (Figure 3.22). The first line contains various menu selections, and the second contains submenu options or descriptions of what the highlighted commands will do. Note that no two menu selections start with the same first letter. This lets you select the proper command by entering just its first character. Lotus 1-2-3 also lets you select a command by highlighting the proper menu selection and pressing Enter. Once invoked, the Lotus 1-2-3 Main Menu stays on the screen until the command task has been carried out.

Many software packages have more than 100 commands that can be executed via menus and submenus. The menu system lists groups of commands under specific menu options. For example, in Lotus 1-2-3, any command dealing with a print operation is found under the Print command option of Lotus's Main Menu. Submenus facilitate the logical progression from one menu to the next.

Vertical Menus Vertical menus occupy more screen area than do horizontal menus. Some vertical menus (like those used in WordStar) occupy only half a

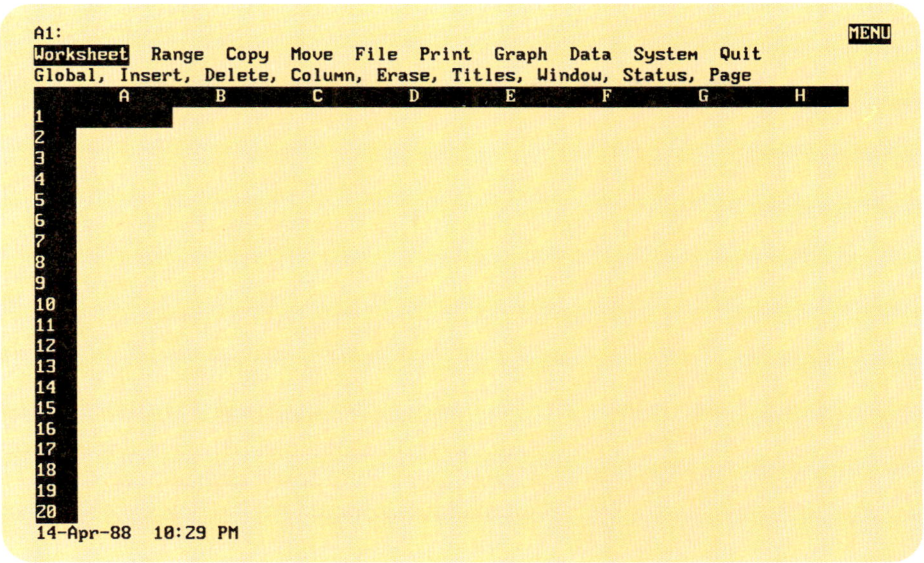

Figure 3.22
Lotus 1-2-3 Main Menu structure.

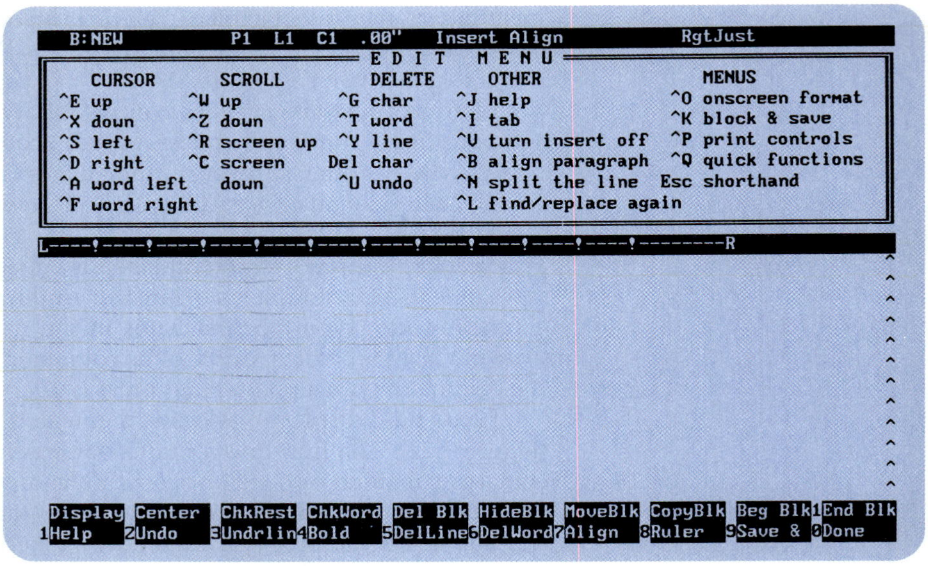

Figure 3.23
WordStar half-screen vertical menu.

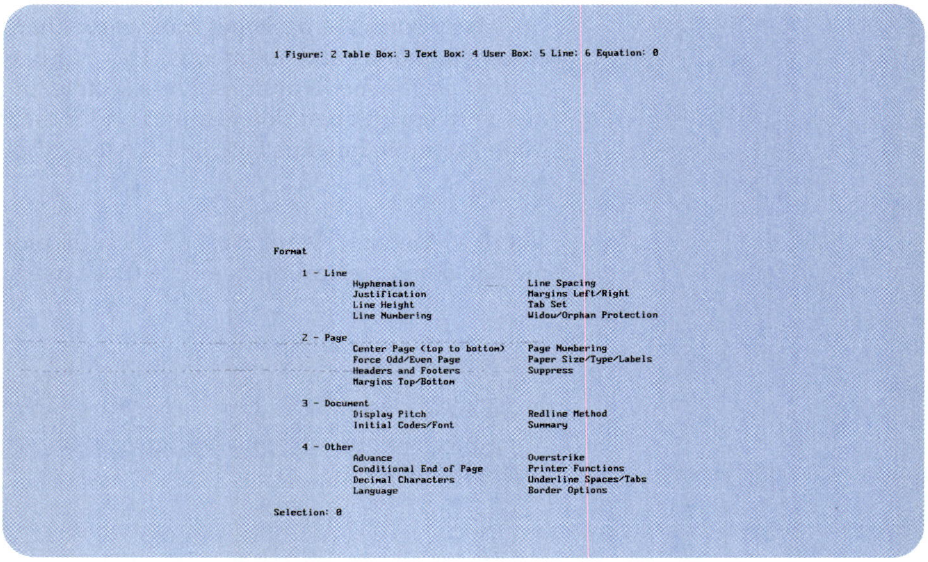

Figure 3.24
WordPerfect (a) horizontal and (b) vertical menus.

screen (Figure 3.23), whereas others (like some used in WordPerfect) take up the entire screen. Some packages use both horizontal and vertical menus (Figure 3.24).

Typically, vertical menus display more selection items and are more informative than horizontal menus. Vertical menus can be in full-screen, pull-down, or pop-up form. Pull-down and pop-up menus disappear after the user enters a command.

Pull-Down Menus Like window shades, these menus pull down from a horizontal menu bar located along the top of the screen (Figure 3.25). Use the Right or Left Arrow key to select a menu heading. Underneath the heading, the computer displays a vertical menu. Using Up and Down Arrow keys, you then select from this menu and press Enter to execute the command.

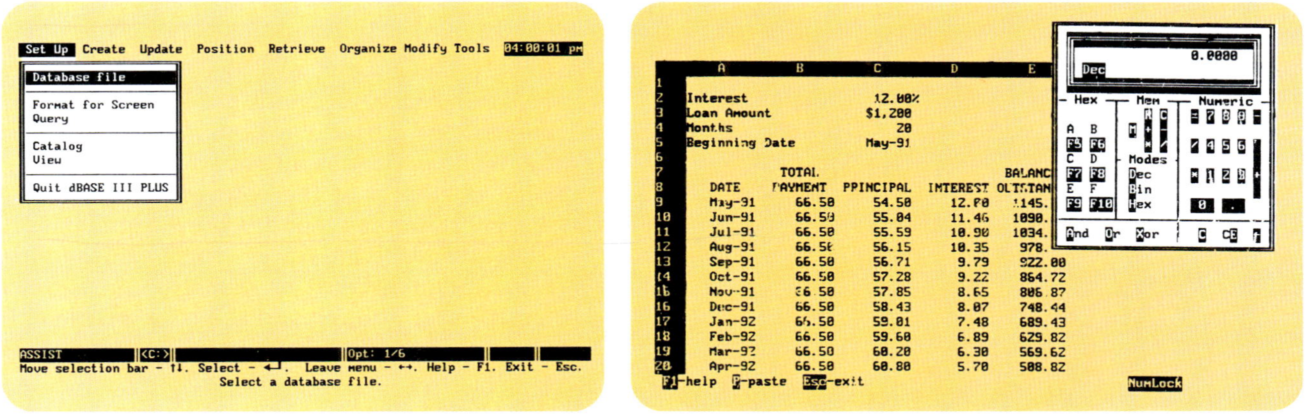

(a) (b)

Figure 3.25
(a) dBASE III Plus menus on the PC screen, which pull down one at a time; (b) pull-down menus on the Macintosh.

Pop-Up Menus These menus pop up on the screen. Typically, pop-up menus are created by **RAM-resident programs.** They are loaded into RAM when the computer is turned on and retained there until the computer is turned off or a special command is issued to purge the program from memory. Thus, pop-up menus operate independently of the software application being run. When you activate a pop-up menu (using a special keystroke sequence), the computer suspends whatever software it is executing and presents the utility program. After selecting some function from the menu, you can then return to the original program. Sometimes these pop-up menus are also referred to as **windows** because they form a windowlike image on the screen (not to be confused with the GUI term *windows*).

SOFTWARE AND MEMORY

Programs require varying amounts of storage file space and running space in a computer's RAM. The more elaborate and user-friendly the software, the more space it is likely to take. Later versions of popular software tend to require more RAM and secondary storage (although not always) than an earlier, simpler version.

Software packages usually state on their packaging how much computer memory is required to run them. On computers with less than optimal memory or without a hard disk drive, it may be possible to configure that package so that some features, such as help screens, are not available. In this manner, a user might still be able to run a program from a floppy disk drive, but the necessity of inserting diskettes and other inconveniences may make this slow and impractical.

SOFTWARE SUPPORT AND INSTRUCTION

Part of a software package is the documentation that explains how to use it. Unfortunately, the quality of documentation frequently falls short of the quality of the actual program. In addition, problems can arise that are not directly addressed in the documentation. For instance, if there is a minor error in the program (or a typo in the documentation), a user may issue an instruction to perform a specific task only to find that the software apparently doesn't work.

Problems related to the actual operation of the software can often be resolved by calling the customer support number found in the documentation. You must be a registered user of the software before you can receive this service. If you are, you will probably be helped at no cost or at a nominal fee. A customer assistance operator can usually "step" you through and solve the problem. If there is an actual error in the program, they will probably send you a corrected version.

If you are having difficulty in learning how to use certain software, you may be able to take a class at the computer store where you purchased the computer (this may have been included in the cost of the computer). Community colleges and universities present credit and noncredit courses on how to operate certain software. Private companies also offer classes to the public on how to use various popular packages.

Besides taking a class, you can also find books on how to use specific software. Most bookstores have a complete section of these publications. These books often teach how to use the software much, much better than does the original documentation.

The popular computer magazines also have articles on how to use a specific command or feature of popular packages. Some packages such as Lotus 1-2-3 and WordPerfect have complete magazines devoted to their use. Subscription information often comes with the documentation for such packages.

CHAPTER REVIEW

The three basic types of software for microcomputers are programming languages, operating systems, and application programs. Users do not have to know how to program to make effective use of today's microcomputers. If a user does decide to program, he or she will probably use a high-level language such as BASIC or Pascal. The instructions of these programming languages must be converted into a machine-understandable format before they can be executed by the computer. The translation process is performed by either a compiler or an interpreter.

The disk operating system (DOS), a critical piece of software that is loaded into the machine at start-up time, allows the user to perform laborious tasks (formatting a disk, copying files, or listing the directory of a disk) with ease. A graphical user interface (GUI) such as Microsoft Windows is an arrangement by which the user can control the operating system by selecting and manipulating icons on the monitor.

Application programs are prewritten programs that solve specific user problems. The five basic problem areas addressed by application software are electronic spreadsheets, word processing, database management, data communications, and graphics. A number of these general applications can be combined in one set of integrated software. Integration lets the user pass data/information quickly from one application to another and to manipulate or process it without having to leave one application and start another.

Most software developers also include some type of menu systems to make their software easier to use. These menus can be horizontal, half- or full-screen,

PERSONAL CASE REVISITED

Installing New Software

RHONDA buys the latest version of Microsoft DOS. To make the software system easier to use, she has also purchased a copy of PC Tools. This package lets her move easily from one directory to another and comes with a built-in backup program that allows her to easily back up the entire contents of her fixed disk. This system can also be controlled by a mouse.

The word processing package that Rhonda chooses is the latest version of WordPerfect. Besides being the best-selling word processing package, it has many features she needs for legal work. For instance, it can automatically number paragraphs and assemble printable master documents from numerous separate files. WordPerfect also easily handles many different fonts and can generate high-quality output on a laser printer.

Based on reviews that appeared in various computer journals, Rhonda selects the PROCOMM communications package for communication with LEXUS, the subscription case-law database. PROCOMM is inexpensive, easily customized, and extremely reliable.

She has also narrowed her selection of electronic spreadsheet packages to Excel and Lotus 1-2-3. Both of these packages sell well and have received good reviews. She wants to check with some of her colleagues who are actively using these packages, to get their input.

Rhonda has written to three vendors of time-and-billing systems to obtain more information about those packages. She notes that this type of software is more specialized and, as a result, more expensive than typical off-the-shelf application software. She needs to ask the lawyers some questions about whether they may want to change some bills by writing off part of the work performed for selected clients. She also wants to know how each package assembles a client's bill. For instance, can overhead costs be factored into it?

or pull-down in nature. Menus typically give you selection alternatives and brief explanations of each alternative.

Information about software packages can be obtained from a number of sources. Magazine articles many times compare the features of comparable software. User groups also provide information about advantages or disadvantages of software. Other users are also a good source of information.

KEY TERMS AND CONCEPTS

application program
BASIC
block
boot record
border
bulletin board system (BBS)
cell
C language
COBOL
COMMAND.COM
command processor
compiler
database
database management
data communications
desktop organizer
disk operating system (DOS)
document assembly
DOS prompt
DOS shell
DOS.SYS
DR DOS 5.0
editing
electronic mail
electronic spreadsheet
field
font
footnote/endnote
formula
FORTRAN
graphic display
graphics
high-level language
IO.SYS
information service
integrated package
interpreter
intuitive program
I/O handler
language processor
local area network (LAN)
Lotus 1-2-3
low-level language
mailmerge
menu
Microsoft
modem
MS DOS
object code
operating system
OS/2
paragraph numbering
Pascal
pointer
productivity software
programming language
query
RAM-resident program
record
release
report
software
sort
source code
spell check
split screen
table of authorities
thesaurus
UNIX
utility program
version
virtual reality
VisiCalc
window
word processing
word wrap

CHAPTER QUIZ

Multiple Choice

1. Which of the following is *not* an example of application software?
   a. WordPerfect
   b. VisiCalc
   c. BASIC
   d. dBASE III Plus
   e. All of the above are examples of application software.

2. Which of the following is *not* a benefit of word processing?
   a. Easy to make changes
   b. Allows user to move parts of a document to new locations
   c. Increases efficiency
   d. May check your spelling
   e. All of the above are benefits of word processing.

3. Which of the following statements about operating systems is false?
   a. A program can be run using any operating system.
   b. The operating system keeps track of where files are stored.
   c. The operating system provides for communication with the disk device.
   d. None of the above

4. Which of the following statements about programming languages is false?
   a. Pascal was originally developed to teach structured programming.
   b. FORTRAN is a good business programming language.
   c. The machine-executable version of a program is called the object code.
   d. A piece of software that translates an entire program so that it is understandable by the computer is called a compiler.

5. Which of the following represents a special-use software package?
   a. Electronic spreadsheet
   b. Database management
   c. Graphics
   d. Accounts receivable

True/False

6. A command-based disk operating system makes use of icons for entering instructions.

7. A program interpreter translates only one source-program instruction to machine language at a time.

8. The MS DOS and PC DOS operating systems are not compatible.

9. A modem is required before communications software can be used.

10. A hidden cost of software that accrues over its lifetime is the cost of obtaining updates.

Answers

1. c 2. e 3. a 4. b 5. d 6. f 7. t 8. f 9. t 10. t

Exercises

1. Define or describe each of the following:
   a. Software
   b. Compiler
   c. Interpreter
   d. Application program
   e. Electronic spreadsheet
   f. Word processing
   g. Modem
   h. Database management
   i. Integration
   j. DOS

2. A software ____________ provides alternatives from which you can make selections.

3. A(n) ____________ menu takes up one or more lines on your monitor screen.

4. Some menu systems, like Lotus 1-2-3, may require you to pass through several ____________ in order to perform an operation.

5. Menus that take up the entire screen are called __________ .

6. Menus that are associated with a menu line at the top of a screen are called because they appear as a menu option is selected.

7. A(n) __________ translates a program all at once, whereas a(n) __________ translates a program a statement at a time.

8. The __________ code of a program is written by a programmer.

9. The five core software applications are __________ , __________ , __________ , __________ , and __________ .

10. The device that translates digital signals into audible noises that can be transmitted across telephone lines is called a(n) __________ .

11. __________ allows you to pass data quickly from one application to another.

12. The __________ interfaces between the user and the hardware.

13. The __________ language was developed by Niklaus Wirth as an educational tool.

14. The piece of software that takes care of performing various housekeeping tasks is called the __________ .

15. The Apple Macintosh and Microsoft Windows uses __________ for entering commands to the system.

16. The first electronic spreadsheet package was __________ .

17. An electronic medium that allows you to receive stock information, rent a car, or reserve a hotel room is a(n) __________ .

18. __________ combines several applications under one piece of software.

19. __________ software makes users of that software feel as if they are actually taking an active part in a game or simulation.

20. The use of electronic communications equipment to send text-based messages such as letters, memos, or reports is called __________ .

IN YOUR OWN CASE

1. Research an application software package that would solve a problem or perform a task in which you are interested. Which packages are its major competitors? What are the relative strengths and weaknesses of the software package that you have selected? Based on your research, would you still purchase this package?

2. If you have already run some application package on your own computer, find someone running a different package that performs the same general function or a more advanced version of the same program

that you are using. Talk with that person about the differences between your software. Do you see any reasons you might want to change or upgrade?

QUESTIONS FOR THOUGHT

1. Given the type of software Rhonda is purchasing, would the hardware system that Dave Dillingham bought in Chapter 2 be likely to meet Rhonda's needs as well? How or how not?

2. What types of general software packages do you have use for? Detail your applications.

3. Can you think of any special-purpose software packages that you or someone you know might be able to use? List the applications and describe the special processing required.

4

GRAPHICS

0 Points Layer: 1 Color: 9
ROOT MENU
ARC/CIRC
BLOCKS 1
BLOCKS 2
DISPLAY
EDIT
FILES
HIDE
INFO
LINES
NOTES
PARAMETER
POINTS
SOLIDS
SHADE
SURFACES
End

CHAPTER OBJECTIVES

After completing this chapter, you should be able to

- ***Describe what hardware is needed for graphics applications***
- ***Discuss the need for image processing in paper-intensive businesses***
- ***Understand what presentation graphics packages can do***
- ***Describe the four common types of graphs and the steps used in creating a graph***
- ***Discuss computer-aided design and other graphics applications***

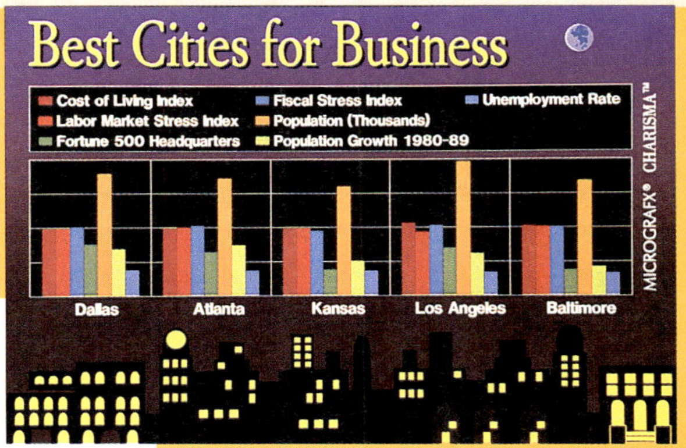

THE DEVELOPMENT OF COMPUTER GRAPHICS

1944	MIT introduces the first computer with a CRT capable of displaying graphics, the Whirlwind.
1949	SAGE introduces the first hand-held photocell "light gun," the precursor of the light pen.
1956	TX-0 and TX-2 computers (MIT) combine transistor circuitry, video display, and light pen, to allow human–machine interaction.
1960	Interactive computer graphics program Sketchpad for TX-2 makes MIT graduate student developer Ivan Sutherland "the father of computer graphics."
1962	The Society for Information Display (SID) is founded.
1963	General Motors develops computer-aided design (CAD) using Sketchpad and DAC-1.
1964	Rand Corporation introduces the graphic tablet.
1972	Atari markets the first computer-based video game "Pong."
1977	Apple markets Apple II, the first computer presenting text and graphics on the same screen.
1982	Pac-Man is introduced.
1983	Lotus Development Corporation introduces Lotus 1-2-3, the commercially successful business spreadsheet package with built-in graphics.

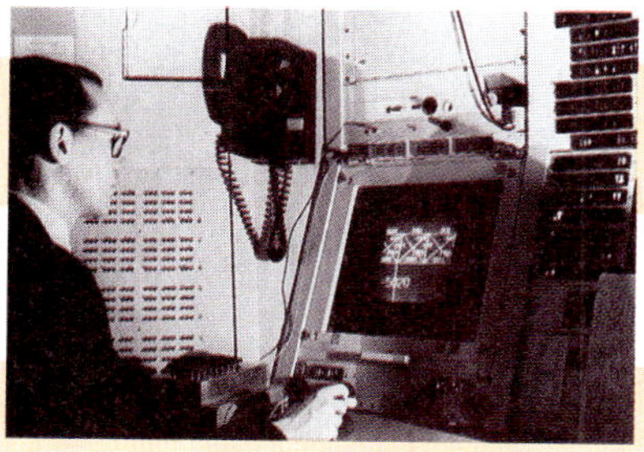

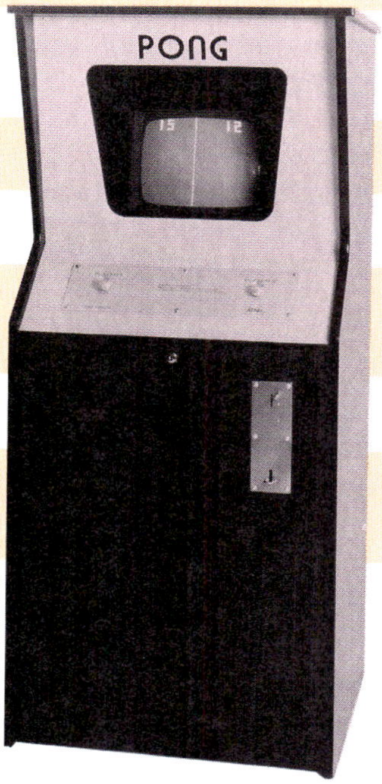
PONG

PERSONAL CASE

Computers and Graphic Design

DAVE MORI's first "client" as a marketing consultant was a pet store owner wanting some free advice about how to place an ad in the local paper. Since then, Dave has gradually built up a modest-paying clientele of stores and services around the county. Recently, he's employed Peter Schell as a market research assistant and, on several occasions, has hired Celeste Richards, a talented graphic designer, to perform or supervise free-lance artwork. A "word man" himself, Dave appreciates Celeste's frankness and her ability to work out visual problems. In fact, he values her enough to think he might one day ask her in as a business partner.

Right now, Dave has a shot at the account of the local semiprofessional soccer team, the Talons. Attendance at the games is down, and the owner feels it's time for some advertising and a new image. Dave wants this account because not only would it be fun but it would also enhance the appeal of his small business to other, more profitable clients. He's given the owner a few ideas, such as creating a new team logo. The owner seems to like his ideas but is also being courted by a larger company from a nearby city. He doubts that Dave's company is big enough to handle the business. Dave is puzzled. He knows his company is certainly big enough and creative enough to help the Talons. At lunch with Celeste one day, he asks her, "Why don't these guys see how much talent we really have to offer?"

"I see two problems," she says. "The first problem is your image as a low-budget operation. I think potential clients sometimes wonder whether you have enough resources. The second problem is that you need to show this client some visual concepts that will really impress him and make him see what you can do for them. That's another image problem."

Dave's not entirely pleased at the term *low budget* and asks Celeste to say more about it. In response, she mentions several things, including the somewhat dull-looking charts that Peter shows their clients to explain his market research and the unimaginative look of his company letterhead. Frankly, she says, she thinks Dave should invest in some computer graphics power. She sees a lot of uses for it.

"Isn't computer graphics expensive?" asks Dave.

"It is," she says, "but you're already using computers for other purposes, and the additional investment should pay off in the long run. You need to understand the potential of computer graphics."

Dave decides he should learn enough about computer graphics to know what it can do for his growing company. Can it make his existing staff more productive and successful? Should he consider investing in some serious graphics capabilities? Should he possibly invite Celeste on board, buy the equipment she wants, and thereby save on some free-lance costs?

Most people see computers as data processors, word processors, and number crunchers. But computers are as well suited to displaying information as they are to processing it. Given the vital roles that both graphics and computers play in communication, it's not surprising that software designers have turned the computer into a powerful image maker. Computer graphics applications are growing rapidly in such diverse areas as business, publishing, education, entertainment, aesthetic design, fine arts, mathematics, science, engineering, architecture, medicine, and cartography.

This chapter examines the hardware needed to support computer graphics. It discusses the graphics features of commercial packages such as Lotus 1-2-3 and various presentation graphics packages and describes the types of charts and graphs microcomputers can create. It introduces graphics editor and drawing tools programs and other graphics applications.

GRAPHICS HARDWARE

PROCESSING

To support graphics software, computers without built-in graphics circuitry require a special adapter graphics card. Although many manufacturers indicate that graphics can be handled with a computer containing an 80286 microprocessor chip, an 80386 chip is almost a prerequisite for handling sophisticated applications.

INPUT DEVICES

Common input devices for drawing and other functions include the mouse, the digitizer board (pen and tablet), and the scanner (Figure 4.1). **Scanners** digitize images recorded on paper so that they can be put into computerized storage.

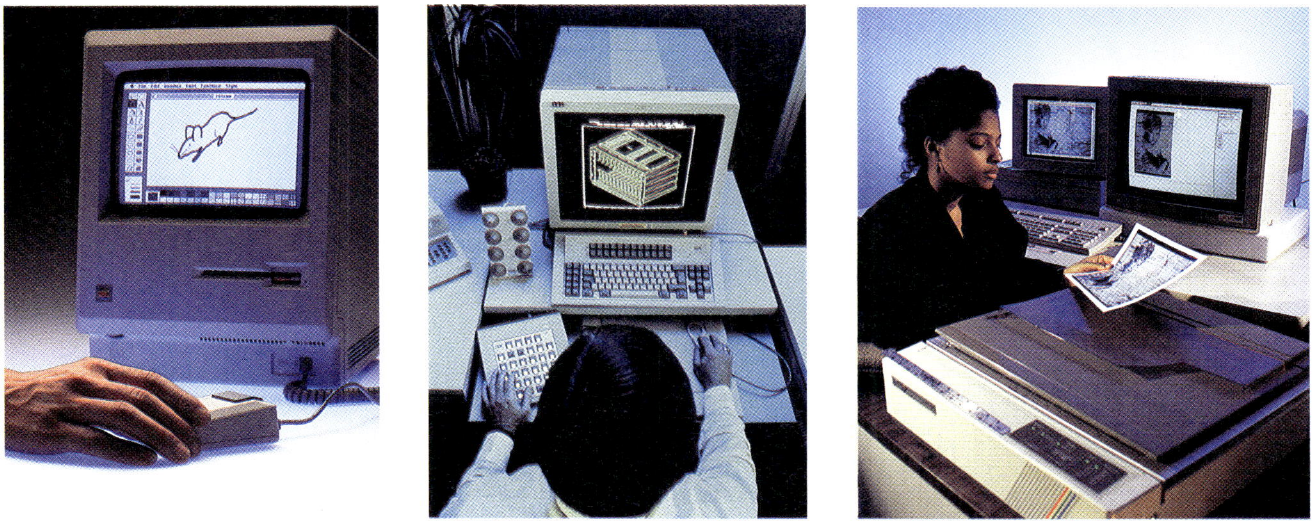

(a) Mouse (b) Digitizer Board (c) Scanner

Figure 4.1
Common graphics input devices.

The digitized image can then be retrieved and modified or included in another graphic. Black-and-white scanners can show up to 64 gradations of gray, producing an image almost like a black-and-white photo. Color scanners are also available.

OUTPUT DEVICES

Graphics systems require monitors and printers or plotters capable of displaying graphics. For even moderately sophisticated work, VGA or SVGA monitors and boards are desirable. Graphics output can also be made directly onto film.

A computer creates graphic screen images by converting data into numbers that correspond to its screen's X/Y (width/height) coordinates. The numbers dictate which of the screen's pixels are to be used to create the image. Graphic images can be displayed to a screen as bits (dots) or vectors (lines).

Early in the evolution of computer graphics, screen technology quickly surpassed the capabilities of available software. The software drivers (programs that allow the computer to communicate with an I/O device) of packages like Lotus 1-2-3 did not interface well enough with high-quality color monitors to produce multicolored charts. The situation changed with the introduction of faster computers, EGA/VGA graphics boards, and EGA/VGA monitors (see Chapter 2). Today's graphics software and sophisticated screens can produce graphics containing up to 256,000 colors (provided there is enough memory for the video display).

Color-print technology is now catching up with screen output. Plotters and dot-matrix printers, the historical standard printing devices, have limited capabilities for combining text and graphics. Plotters, good at drawing color graphics, generate choppy text. Some dot-matrix printers can't produce graphics, and, of those that can, only the most advanced produce high-quality color output.

Desktop publishing systems are blazing the trail to better color printing, and the corporate world yearns for more advanced systems. In response, manufacturers have produced laser printers that generate high-quality text and graphics and are quieter and faster than plotters and dot-matrix printers. Although they do not yet equal the most sophisticated screen display, laser printers will figure prominently in the future of color graphics.

STORAGE DEVICES

Graphic images can take up tremendous amounts of disk storage. A simple black-and-white scanned image, for example, can take up several hundred thousand bytes. The amount of storage required increases dramatically for high-quality, color images because it is necessary to store a color code for each dot required by a graphic image. Intel and IBM have attacked this problem by designing special circuitry that compresses the individual data for groups of dots. For example, in a photo of someone wearing a blue blazer, the dots making up the blazer compose large numbers of dots within the photo. These adjacent dots can be represented together by a color and a repetition factor. Stored using these data-compression techniques, a graphic image requires only about 10 percent of the storage space otherwise required. IBM now sells a board with its multimedia product to provide this capability. Intel foresees computers in the near future that have this feature built into the motherboard.

TYPES OF COMPUTER GRAPHICS APPLICATIONS

Let's look at five common computer graphics applications: image processing, presentation graphics, graphics editors and drawing tools, computer animation, and computer-aided design graphics.

IMAGE PROCESSING

For years businesspeople have been "drowning in paper," and companies continue to spend millions of dollars each year to store, track, and retrieve paper documents. A single business may need hundreds of filing cabinets to store its paper records. However, more and more companies are turning to image processing to solve these problems.

Image processing involves using a scanning device to store an electronic image of a document on disk (usually some type of laser-based technology like CD ROM) and then later retrieve that document (Figure 4.2). This type of technology has been around for about 20 years, but only recently has the quality of the output justified its widespread use.

The United Services Automobile Association (USAA) Insurance Company of San Antonio, Texas, has a large image-processing system. USAA receives approximately 10,000 letters a day for its property and casualty unit, and storage for those letters occupied 39,000 square feet of office space.

With IBM image-processing equipment, these files have been scanned and stored on optical computer disks on a system that takes up less than 100 square feet. The system index tracks each letter and relates it to other documents in the system. Now, instead of taking several days to respond to a client's call, company representatives at 1500 CRTs can quickly call up the letters and information from over 2 million customer files. The images are so detailed that they can show handwritten notations in the margins or photographs showing damage to an insured vehicle.

The great advantages of image processing are speed of retrieval, accessibility to networks of users, and savings in space and costs of retrieval. Drawbacks include the still comparatively high storage-processing cost per sheet. The costliest aspect is scanning the backlog of existing documents. Also, improvements

Figure 4.2
Image processing saves a company's office space as well as time and money.

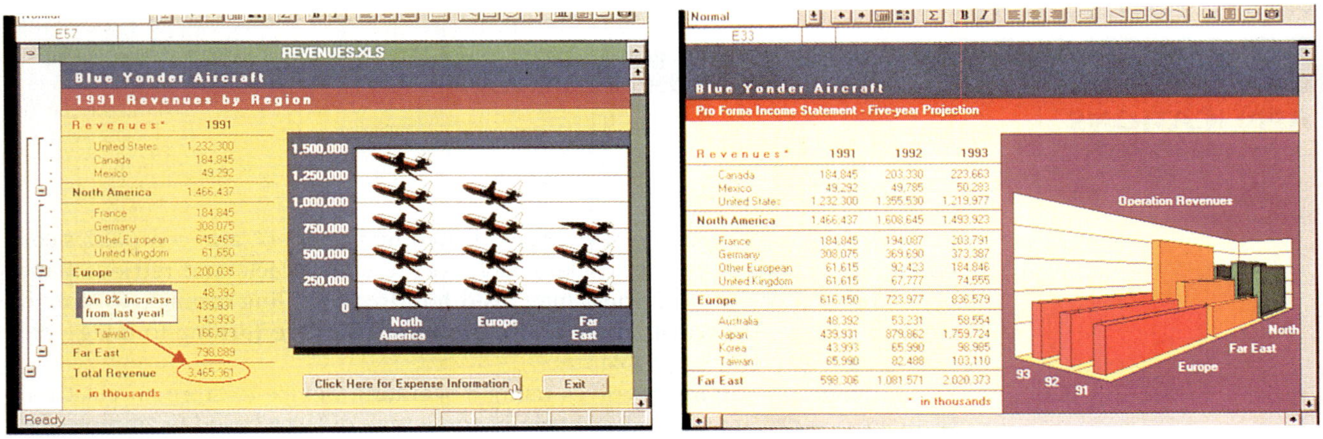

(a) (b)

Figure 4.3

Presentation graphics. Packages can add special text and enhanced graphics.

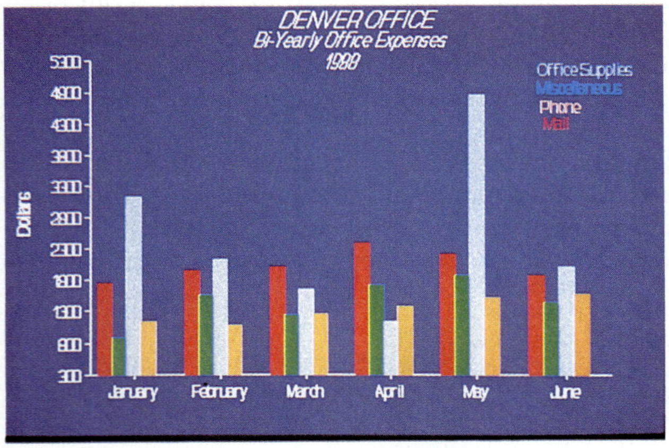

(a) Side-by-side bar chart, using PlanPerfect

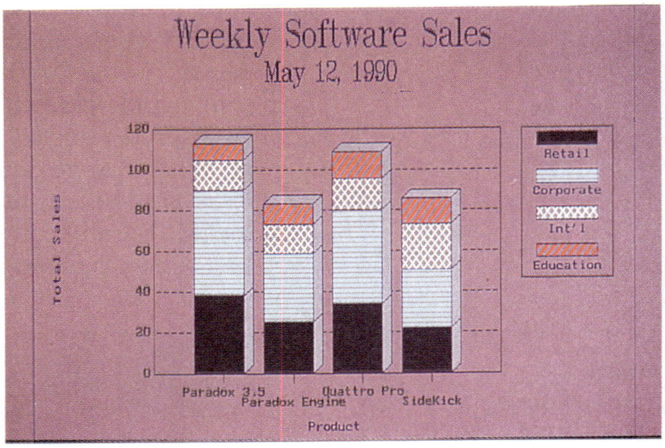

Stacked bar chart, using Paradox 3.5

Figure 4.4

Types of charts and graphs. (a) A **bar chart** shows horizontal or vertical bars. A stacked-bar chart (right) layers bars to form a larger bar representing a category's combined total. A side-by-side bar chart (left) compares data in distinct categories. (b) A **line graph** shows lows, highs, and trends with a line or series of lines. Line graphs are ideal for showing trends over time or the distribution of one variable over another. An area line graph can represent combined entries much like a stacked-bar chart. (c) A **pie chart** compares the proportional parts of a whole. Pie charts are useful for comparing component shares with one another and with the combined total. (d) A **scatter plot,** or **XY graph,** shows points whose coordinates represent values on the **X (horizontal)** and **Y (vertical) axes.** Scatter plots show how variables are related to each other. (e) A **hi-lo graph** is often used by newspapers to show the high and low selling points of stocks. Hi-lo graphs emphasize the range between the highest and lowest values within a category by connecting them with a line.

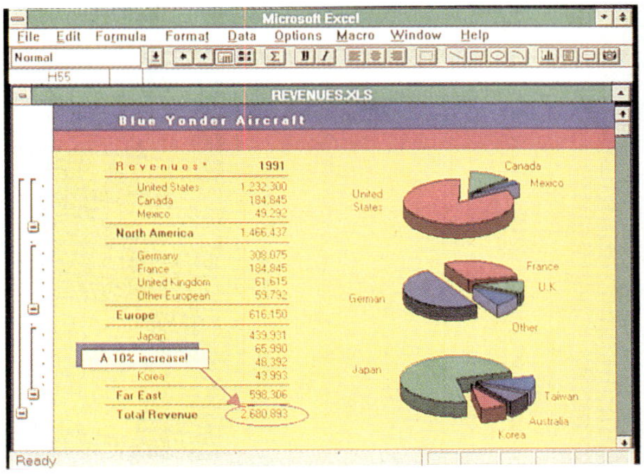

(c) Pie chart, using Microsoft Excel

are needed in the algorithms used for storing the document and the way indexes are used for updating, tracking, and retrieving documents. If a document is not properly indexed, for example, it can be lost forever.

Image-processing applications will continue to grow because 95 percent of business information is still on paper.

PRESENTATION GRAPHICS

One of the most daunting forms of printed information is the statistical spreadsheet. Yet a user can interpret hundreds of statistics at a glance if the numbers are rendered into a well-designed graph.

Presentation graphics software lets users with little artistic skill turn numeric information and data relationships into attractive and informative graphs and charts (Figure 4.3). Businesspeople use presentation graphics to highlight key information, direct thinking, show relationships, and make comparisons. Studies show that people perceive presentations that include graphics to be better organized, more interesting, more comprehensible, and more persuasive than presentations that do not. Figure 4.4 shows five common types of graphs.

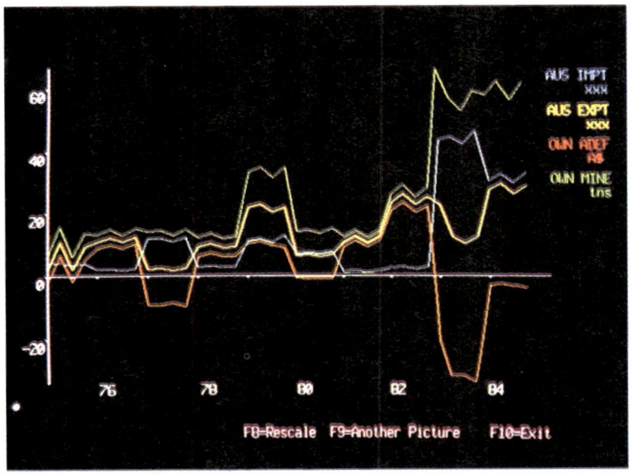

(b) Line graph, using IBM's Data Interpretation System

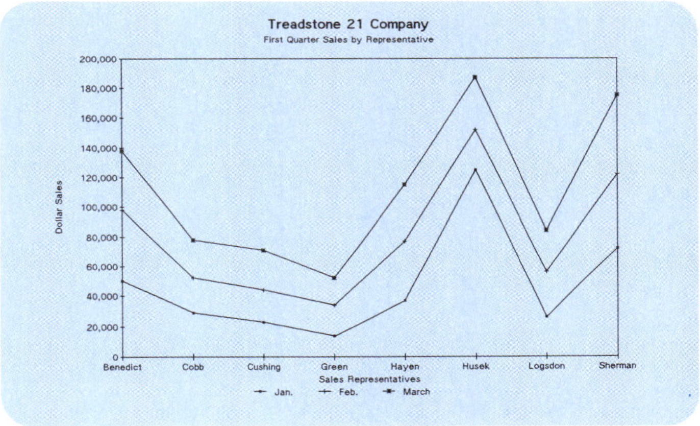

Area line graph

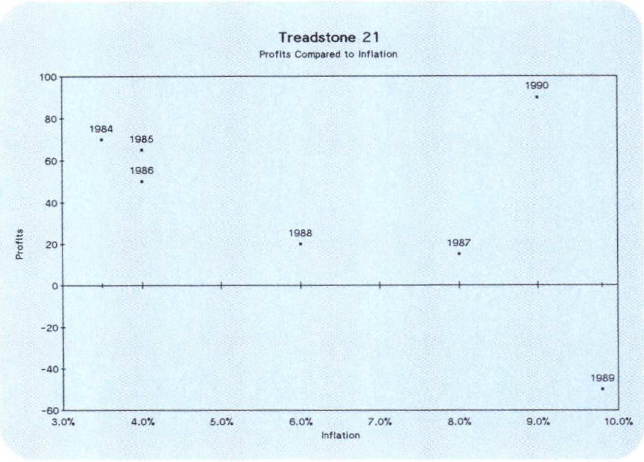

(d) Scatter plot or XY graph

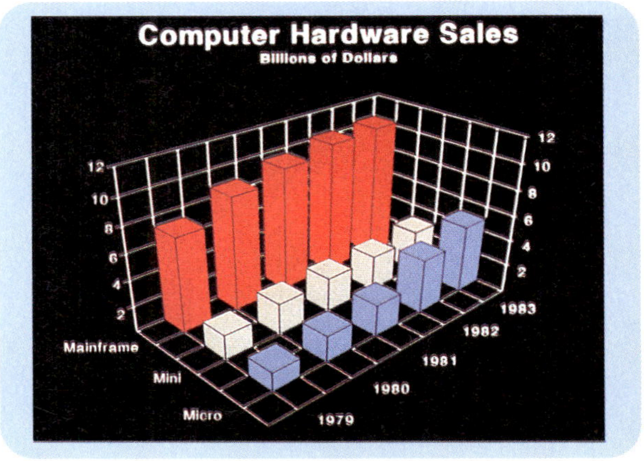

(e) Hi-lo graph

Creating Graphs Presentation graphics software lets you create and then modify a graph. To create a graph, select the data that are to be graphed and specify labels that will appear on the graph, as well as other explanatory text that may be required. Graphs and charts always need some sort of text or identifying labels to indicate what they are depicting.

Some software packages include integrated graphics capabilities for creating graphics from the package's spreadsheets or databases. There are also **stand-alone presentation packages** that can graph data from the keyboard or from spreadsheets and databases. These can be used with packages that lack their own graphics software, such as dBASE III Plus.

Creating Graphs with Integrated Software Lotus 1-2-3, Symphony, Microsoft Works, and Excel each have their own integrated graphics programs. Let's consider Lotus as an example. Suppose you want to graph sales for a grocery store on the worksheet in Figure 4.5a. First, enter the Lotus 1-2-3 Graphs Menu. Next, select from a submenu the graph type that would best represent the data. Lotus

Figure 4.5

Creating a bar graph with Lotus 1-2-3. (a) The worksheet from which the graph is created, (b) the preliminary graph, and (c) the final version.

A1: READY

COMPSALS

Department	Last Year	This Year	Change	% Change
Deli	700.00	575.00	(125.00)	-18%
Bakery	1,000.00	1,100.00	100.00	10%
Liquor	1,200.00	1,400.00	200.00	17%
Grocery	2,500.00	2,900.00	400.00	16%
Produce	950.00	1,000.00	50.00	5%
Meat	1,500.00	1,410.00	(90.00)	-6%
Store Total	7,850.00	8,385.00	535.00	7%

03-Nov-91 04:13 PM

(a)

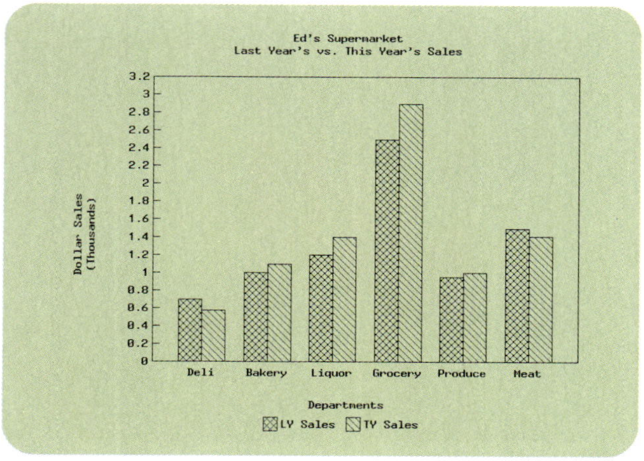

(b)

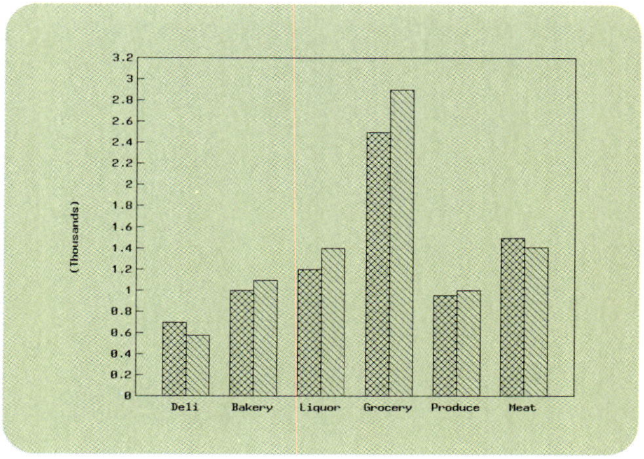

(c)

1-2-3 lets you choose a Line, Bar, XY, Stacked-Bar, or Pie graph, and you choose the Line graph.

After selecting the graph type, enter the set(s) of data points (the data ranges) to be graphed. Lotus 1-2-3 lets you select up to six data ranges from the worksheet, to which you assign the successive letters A–F from the Graph Menu's options. In Figure 4.5a, only three data ranges will be graphed (one for each month), which will be called A, B, and C. Next, use another submenu to select the range that will name the department along the X axis of the graph. The graph depicted in Figure 4.5b is now ready for preliminary viewing or printing.

The final step in completing the graph is supplying it with title lines and a legend that tells what each bar represents. These will name the graph and further identify the data being represented along the X and Y axes. To distinguish among the different bars, assign each month a different symbol, color, or style of hatching (shading lines). Figure 4.5c shows the completed graph. The legend along the bottom of the graph shows the hatching used for each month.

Creating Graphs with Stand-Alone Presentation Packages Stand-alone packages usually can generate a greater variety and more sophisticated graphics than can integrated packages (Figure 4.6). For example, some stand-alone packages can store screen images and later display them in a specific sequence (like a slide-show presentation) on the computer screen, in a printout, or in camera-generated pictures.

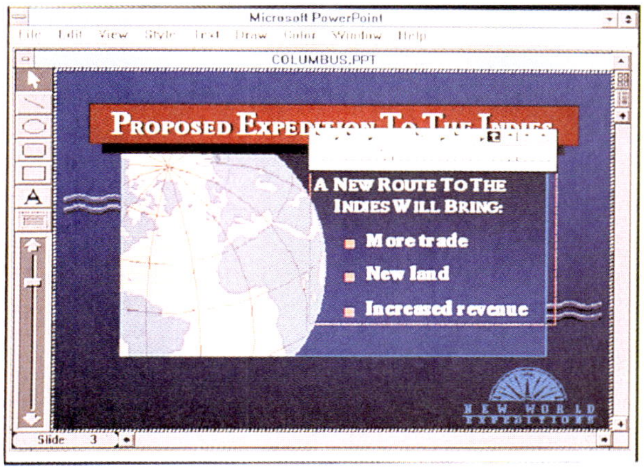

(a)

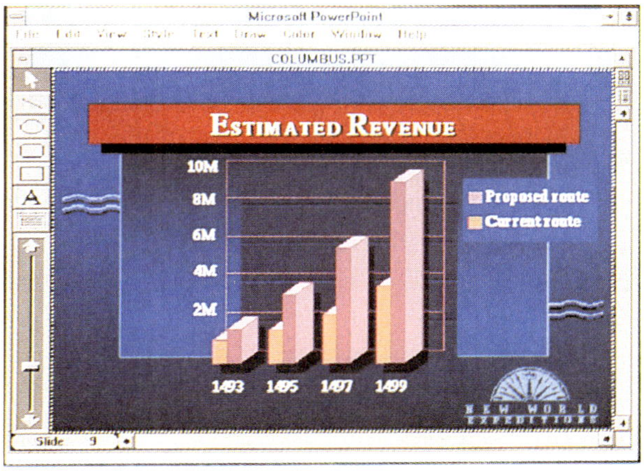

(b)

Figure 4.6

Graphs produced with stand-alone graphics packages—PowerPoint from Microsoft.

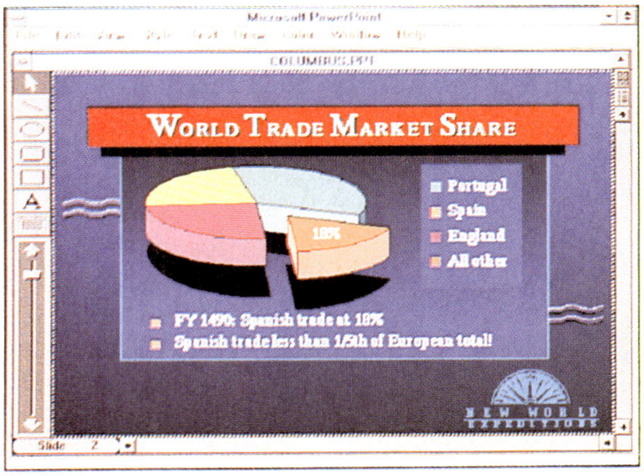

(c)

PERSONAL CASE PROGRESS

Looking at Pie Charts

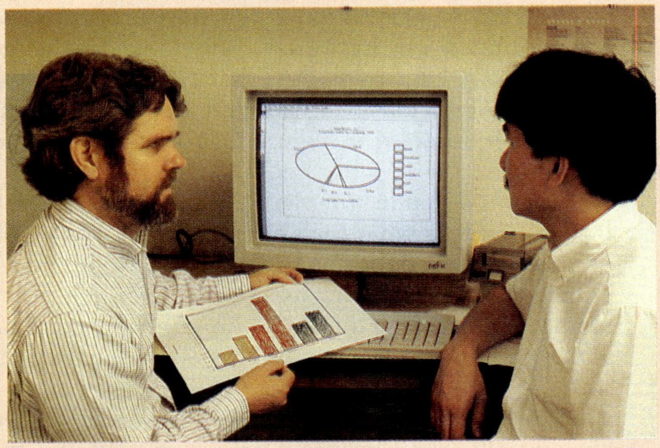

DAVE looks over some of the charts that his market research assistant Peter has been preparing for client presentations. Peter has been using the graphics function of Lotus 1-2-3 to summarize consumer data and convert it into several types of charts, which he prints in black and white and then colors by hand.

'I'm sure that bar graph is accurate," says Dave, "but it isn't very inspiring."

"Then take a look at this," says Peter. "It's a demo disk for a stand-alone graphics presentation package that might work better."

Dave and Peter boot up the demo program and find it promising. One of its more basic features lets them view the circular face of a pie chart from an oblique angle. It can also make circles or bars look three-dimensional and fill them in with various styles and degrees of shading.

"A package like this could be a good investment," says Dave. "Let's compare this with some competing products and see which one suits us best."

Packages such as Ashton-Tate's Applause II or Microsoft's PowerPoint let you incorporate data from another program into a chart, create screen images of slides (the screen image can then be sent to a service bureau and copied to 35-mm film) for presentations, create outlines, and perform other graphics-related tasks.

Some products come with clip art (pictures) that can be included in presentation graphics. **Clip art** refers to public domain images, either in books or on disks, that you can use free of charge and without credit in a publication. Some of these packages contain a built-in editor (more or less like a word processing package) that lets you quickly make changes to graphic text images. Some presentation graphics packages let you include *animated* clip art for screen display. Such an image is called a **sprite** and comes ready-made from companies such as Aldus, Lotus Development, and Microsoft. It lets you include animation without going through all of the tortuous programming required to create animation from scratch. You do not have to know anything about programming to include it in a presentation. However, this animated clip art has much less movement than most of the animation you are used to seeing.

GRAPHICS EDITORS AND DRAWING TOOLS

Graphics editors and **drawing tools** turn the computer screen into a luminous canvas or drawing pad on which you can create and then modify graphic images using computerized art tools (Figure 4.7). Some currently popular prod-

Figure 4.7
What's possible with computer graphics drawing tools and editors.

(a)

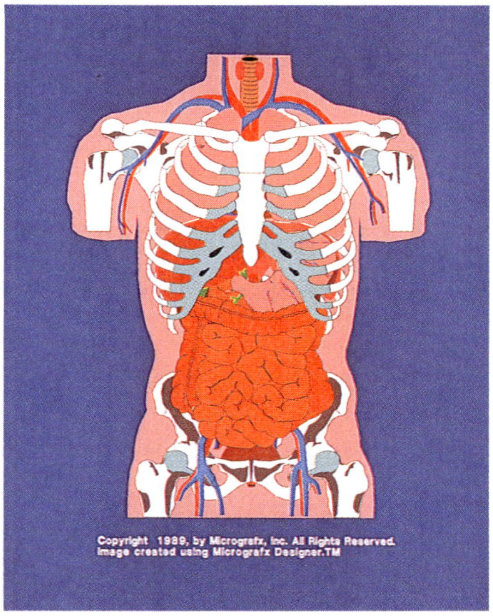

(b)

(c)

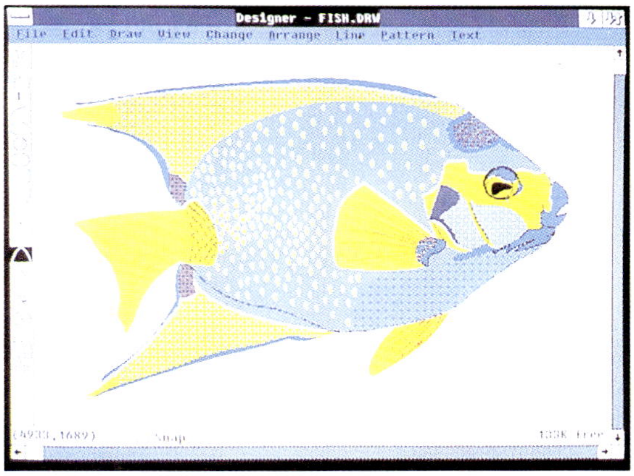

(d)

(e)

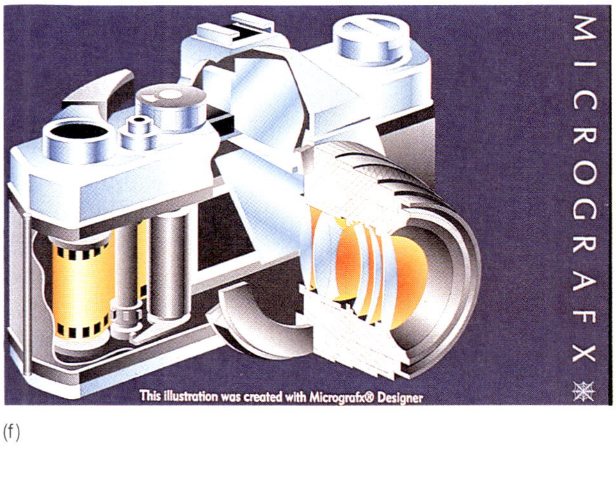

(f)

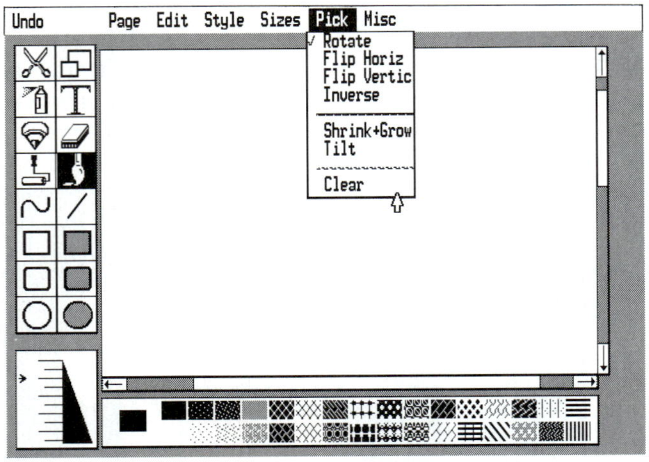

(a)

(b)

Figure 4.8

(a) The PC Paintbrush screen. (b) A finished image. Note how the mouse pointer indicates a pull-down menu selection.

ucts are PC Paintbrush, PC Paintbrush IV Plus, Publisher's Paintbrush, Hot Shot Graphics, Microsoft Paintbrush, Corel Draw, and Adobe Illustrator. With these programs, you can create business graphics such as company logos and visual devices for reports, newsletters, and financial statements. You can save the image to a disk file and recall it later to incorporate in a document or poster that you have created with other software programs.

Most of these packages present you with a "toolbox," a menu, a palette of colors or patterns, a variety of shapes such as boxes and circles, some method of controlling line width, and an enlargement feature that lets you "zoom in" on and modify details of the drawing. Figure 4.8 shows the screen of PC Paintbrush.

Let's look at MacPaint, by Claris, to see how paint programs work. MacPaint is a very inexpensive package for novices on the Apple Macintosh. It supports a two-button mouse for drawing, giving commands, and selecting tools and menu options. The mouse's movements are represented on the screen by either a dot (while on the drawing area) or an arrow (when off the drawing area). Using the mouse as a pointer, select a pull-down menu and highlight an option (see Figure 4.8). In the screen's lower left-hand corner is the drawing-width scale, from which you choose a drawing-line thickness by positioning the pointer on the proper setting and pressing a button on the mouse.

From the palette at the bottom of the screen, you can choose various colors (up to 16 in a given image) and patterns of shading, which you activate by positioning the pointer on the appropriate box and clicking the mouse. The box immediately to the right of the drawing-width scale indicates the active color or shading pattern.

The toolbox, located on the screen's left-hand side, contains various tools for drawing, erasing, airbrushing, setting type, and filling in areas with colors or patterns. Each tool is represented by an icon. Figure 4.9 shows the steps leading to a completed drawing.

Figure 4.9
Creating a graphic with MacPaint.

(a) Finished graphic

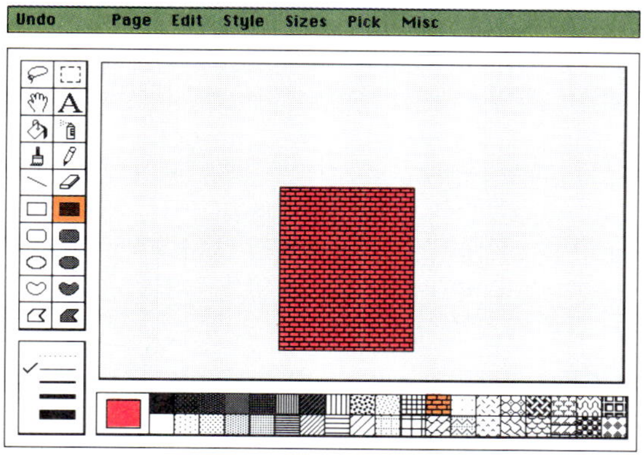

(b) Using the rectangle tool, construct the shaft of the clock tower.

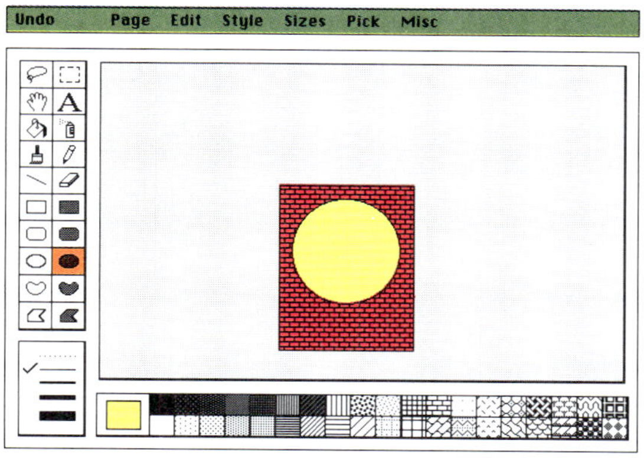

(c) Using the circle tool, create the outer clock face.

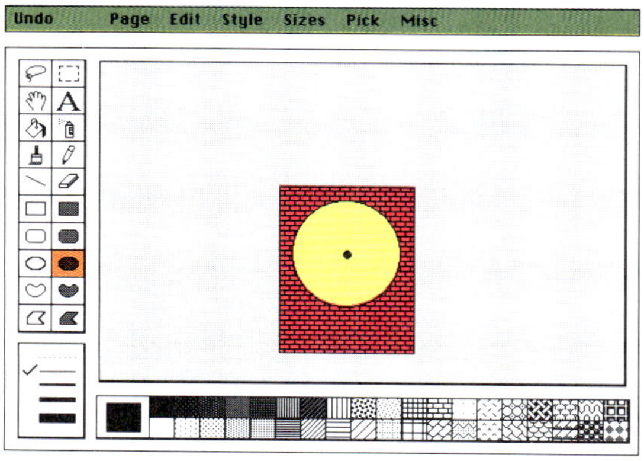

(d) Again using the circle tool, create the inner clock mechanism.

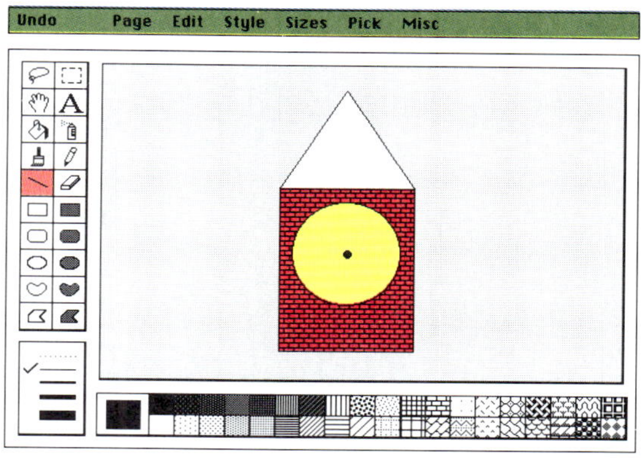

(e) Using the line tool, insert the roof of the clock tower.

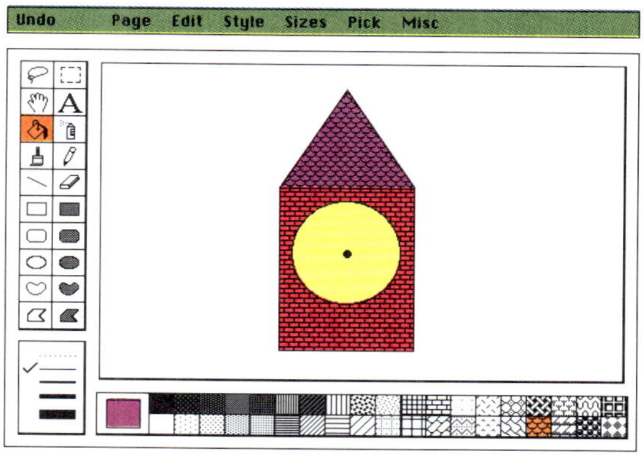

(f) Using the fill tool, color the roof of the clock tower.

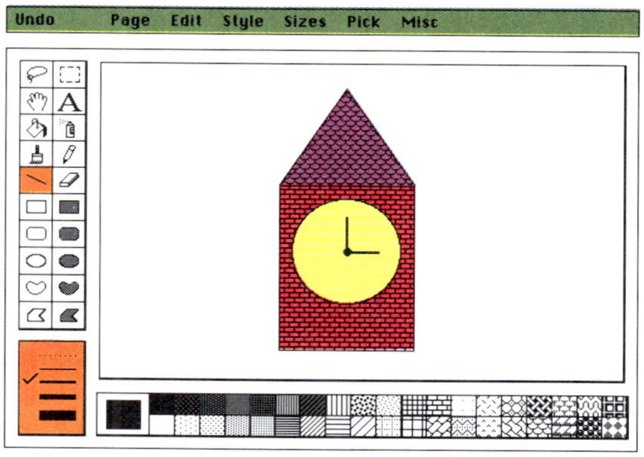

(g) Using the line tool and selecting a heavier line weight, draw the hands on the clock.

(h) Using the type tool, set the numbers on the clock face.

FEATURES TO TEST IN DRAWING SOFTWARE

- **WYSIWYG** (pronounced "wizzy-wig") is "What-You-See-Is-What-You-Get." Does the image appear on the screen the way it will also appear when printed? Screen and printer output should be as similar as possibile.
- Speed depends on software and hardware. Can you move images quickly around the screen? Can you duplicate and regenerate images quickly? You don't want to have to wait 20 or 30 seconds for the image to be regenerated.
- A drawing program should be able to import clip art from an existing library into a text document or another graphic image. The package should also have a library of such images. How extensive is the library? How useful are the images?
- Does the drawing package allow you to use the scanner as an input device? What type of scanners are supported? Can you scan a black-and-white photo using gray scale? Can you scan color?
- Are different printing **fonts** (styles of type) accepted by the software? Can you easily control the style as well as the size of type that is to be displayed on the screen and the printed output?

The more advanced drawing packages use scanners to digitize images and graphic digitizing boards for drawing. More advanced packages also give more choices for varying fonts and sizes of text characters that appear in the graphic image.

Many drawing packages can be used to import and touch up photographic images. The process begins with scanning the photo to create a high-quality digitized image, which can then be displayed on a computer screen and changed.

Figure 4.10
Changes can be made to a photographic image by digitized retouching. (a) An artist can use a graphics tablet to show, for example, how different cosmetics would look. (b) For advertising purposes, blemishes and imperfections can be eliminated.

(a)

(b)

Using a digital graphics pad and an electronic pen, the artist can reshape an eye, alter a nose, darken the complexion, change colors, or import features from other photos. This type of technology has been used to prepare fake skyline backdrops for television studios, delete unflattering or unneeded parts of portraits, and restore receding hairlines. This ability to essentially remake photos is of real concern to those involved with photo journalism because skilled artists using sophisticated equipment can retouch photos and fake even massive changes that are virtually undetectable (Figure 4.10).

CD ROM CLIP-ART LIBRARIES

Libraries of clip-art images were first made available on diskettes. As clip art has become more elaborate and required more and more storage space, CD ROM has become the preferred method of storage for both IBM and Macintosh computers (Figure 4.11). A single clip-art image may require many tens of thousands of bytes of storage. A single CD ROM will have up to 650M of storage and can usually store about 300 images. Holding images in CD ROM helps keep fixed disk space free for other uses. The one disadvantage to CD ROM is that it is slow—about the speed of a typical diskette drive. This means that very large clip-art files may take a lot of time to load into memory.

CD ROM libraries are now available from manufacturers of CD ROM drives and from third-party vendors. Subject matter may include business, cartoons, computers, technology, travel, animals, maps, sports, religion, people, and buildings.

Figure 4.11

Clip art ranges from simple icons to highly detailed full-screen images. The latter take up a great deal of storage.

PERSONAL CASE PROGRESS

Shopping for Graphics Software

Most of Celeste's colleagues use the Macintosh computer. To find out whether IBM systems are comparable, she and Dave visit a computer store specializing in computer graphics. Bob Garcia, the manager, became intrigued with computer graphics while he was working as a graphic artist for a large insurance company. His business serves both Macintosh and IBM graphics users. Bob says that, although Apple initially had a tremendous lead over IBM, over the last few years IBM and compatible equipment have gained a lot of ground.

Bob advises Dave on the hardware requirements of high-end graphics and demonstrates some of the software. Dave is startled at how much a quality color system will cost, especially given the price of printers. For black-and-white output, a regular laser printer starting at around $1200 can be used, but Dave can expect to spend over $10,000 for a color printer.

Aware that he can't afford to purchase immediately, Dave asks Bob if he can provide them with actual graphics services on a fee basis. Bob says he can, and they agree on an hourly rate.

For some applications, Bob says his work will be much easier and cost less if Celeste will do some initial data preparation using a presentation graphics package on Dave's current 80286 AT machine. Bob indicates that this involves creating some of the initial graphic images, taking the first pass at building any charts, or doing the initial presentation outlines. Dave and Celeste make a note to be sure that the stand-alone graphics software package they buy will allow this.

Celeste gives Bob some rough sketches for the Talons' logo and asks him to spend a little time working them up in color graphics.

COMPUTER ANIMATION

Computer graphic technology is also being applied to animated cartoons, historically an extremely labor-intensive process. Every second of animation requires 24 individual images, or *cels,* so a 30-minute cartoon takes roughly 43,000 cels. By the traditional method, each cel is outlined in ink on an acetate sheet by an artist and then hand painted.

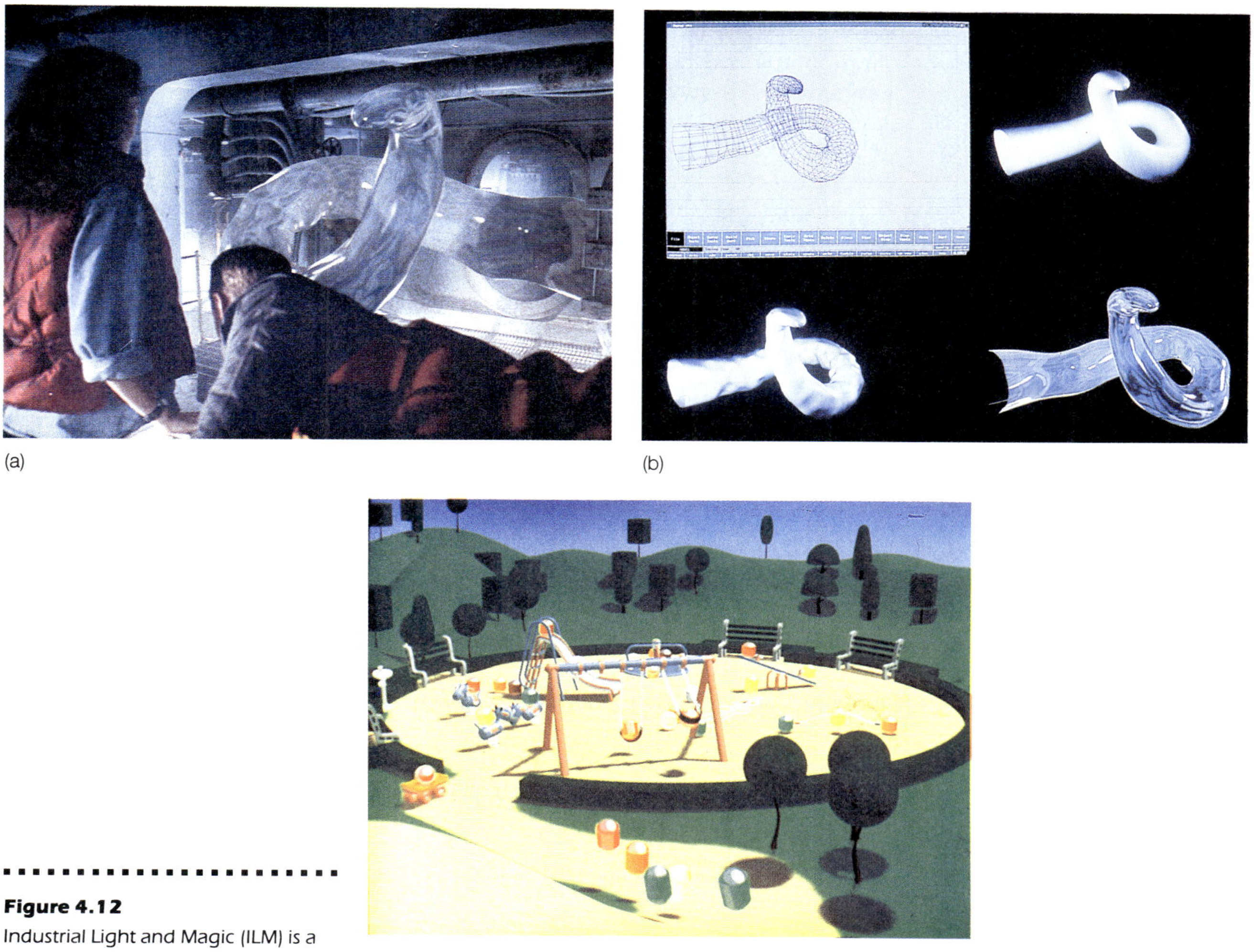

(a) (b) (c)

Figure 4.12
Industrial Light and Magic (ILM) is a leader in computerized animation.

More and more now, individual cels are being drawn on computers. This method takes less (but still a lot) of time because it lets the artist modify cels more easily. It also lets a filmmaker merge cartoons with photography. "Who Framed Roger Rabbit" by Touchstone Pictures earned recognition for this technique. George Lucas's company, Industrial Light and Magic, has won several Oscars for its instrumental computer animation work on this and other film series such as "Star Wars" and "Back to the Future" (Figure 4.12).

Computer animators also use scanners to enter film images, which can then be altered quickly with computer drawing tools. The changed image can then be transferred to video and then back to film.

Using computers for animation takes a fast computer and a tremendous amount of storage. A single cel may require 5 to 20M of storage.

Besides its use in cartoons, computer-generated animation has also become a means of creating television commercials. These types of commercials take much time and money to produce. It is common for a 30-second computer-animated commercial to cost $300,000.

COMPUTER-AIDED DESIGN GRAPHICS

Computer-aided design graphics help designers draw everything from automobiles to skyscrapers. Applications such as **computer-aided design (CAD), computer-aided manufacturing (CAM),** and **computer-aided engineering (CAE)** make use of design graphics and have greatly reduced design and manufacturing costs in some fields.

Using CAD/CAM programs, industrial designers can create in a day drawings that used to take weeks to complete. CAD/CAM programs can rotate a drawing, layer it to show detail, and display it in various scales or three dimensions.

Industry's enthusiastic use of CAD has also led architects, electrical engineers, theatrical designers, landscape designers, illustrators and artists, film animators, and others to use it (Figure 4.13).

Computers shorten design time because not only drawing and revising can be done more quickly but also designs can be tested on CAE systems before they are manufactured. Before CAE, new product ideas were tested by first being turned into prototypes, expensive early-version models, which engineers subjected to various tests of durability and suitability. Now, a designer can

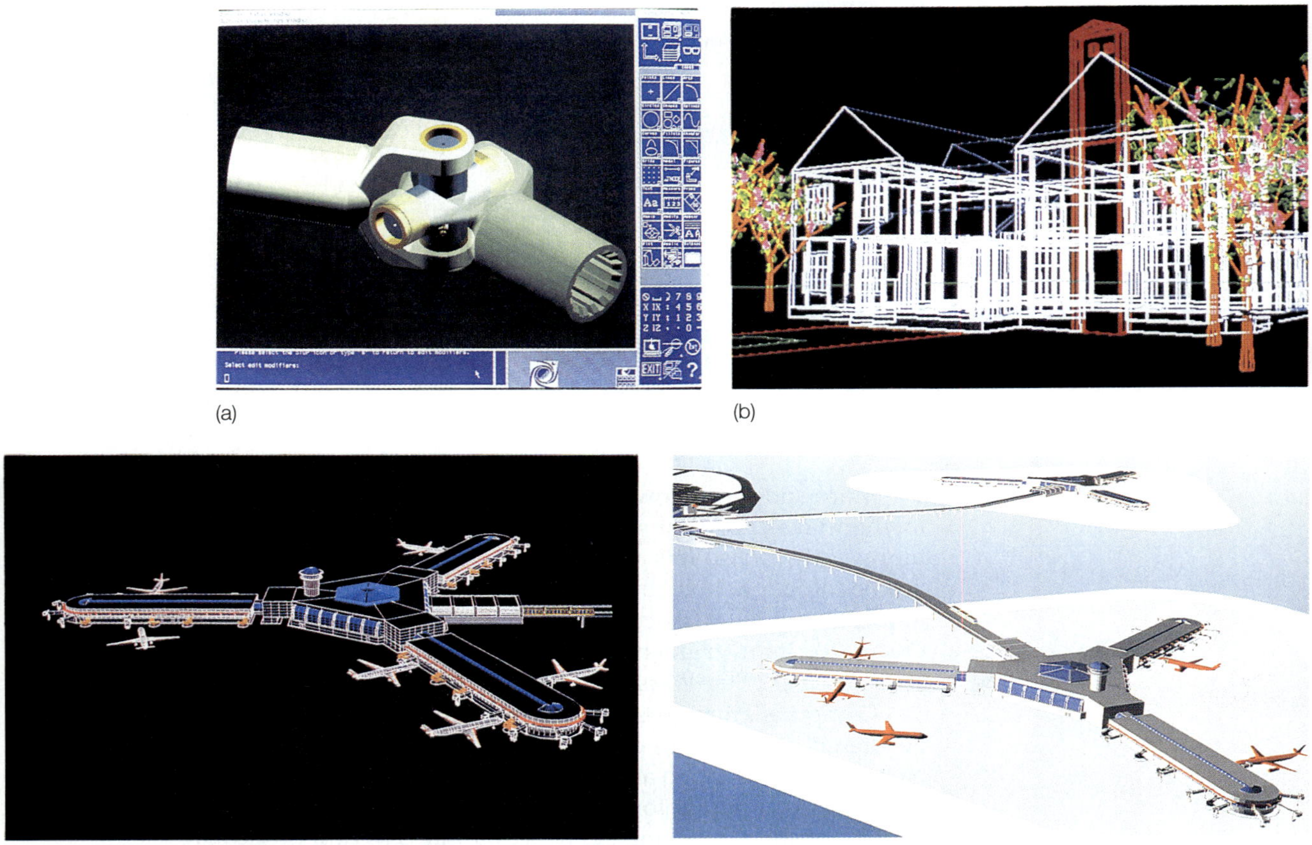

(a) (b) (c) (d)

Figure 4.13

Computer-aided design software can be used to design almost anything: (a) a hinge, (b) a house, (c) and (d) a new wing of the Orlando International Airport.

MEDICAL USES OF GRAPHICS

For a decade or so, computer graphics have been aiding medical diagnosis. Now three-dimensional graphics are also helping surgeons prepare for sophisticated surgery. A program called Analyze by Dr. Richard Robb, director of Biotechnology Computer Resources at the Mayo Clinic/Foundation in Minnesota, lets physicians practice surgery on a computer workstation before the actual surgery is performed.

To accomplish this, a patient's internal organ is first measured and modeled three dimensionally by computers associated with a technique called magnetic resonance imaging (MRI). The MRI computer creates a series of images that represent cross sections of the organ. These combine to display a three-dimensional picture of tissues and/or skeletal structures on a monitor. The surgeon can then manipulate this picture, progressing through each structural layer. This experience helps the physician in various ways—for instance, in determining and rehearsing the best route for surgical entry (Figure 4.14).

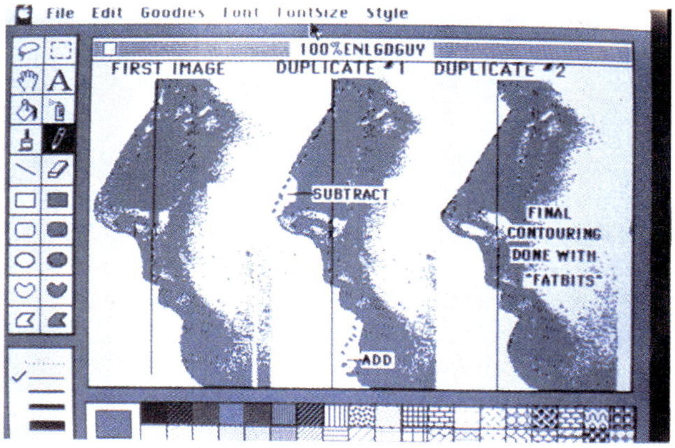

(a)

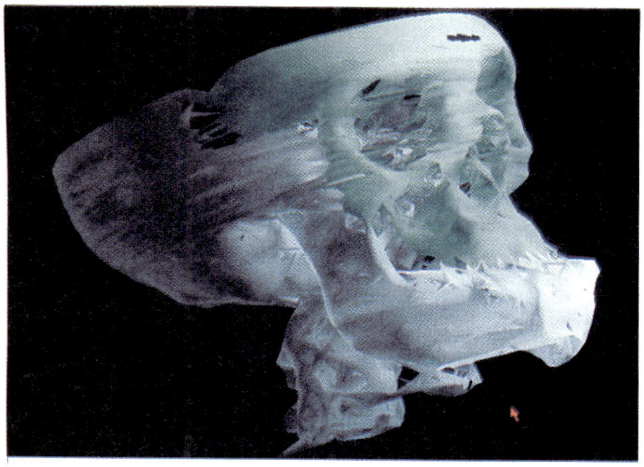

(b)

Figure 4.14

Three-dimensional graphic images. (a) End result of plastic surgery. (b) Skull prior to facial reconstruction.

PERSONAL CASE REVISITED

Closing the Deal

Things come together for Dave at his company's presentation to the Talons owner. His soon-to-be client is impressed by the logo Dave's team has created, as well as their marketing insights.

"I think new uniforms are in order," he says.

Dave decides that quality computer graphics are essential to his business success. Although he still doesn't have the money to purchase all the graphics hardware he wants, he begins to explore leasing a system. As part of the agreement, Bob suggests that Celeste receive 6 to 8 weeks of on-the-job training on the leased equipment. Dave suggests to Celeste that the training be her first assignment as a full-time member of the business.

create a product with CAD and test it on a CAE system more rigorously than is possible using real-world prototypes.

CAM systems help produce goods by creating artwork masters (such as blueprints), compiling lists of required components, and controlling machine operations. For example, a CAM program may be used to precisely control assembly-line robots that weld together car-body panels.

CAM can also help in estimating production costs. An architect can use a CAD package to design a floor plan, then use CAM to estimate the cost of its construction. If the floor plan is changed, the CAM system will automatically re-estimate the cost.

The toy-model company Lionel Trains has made extensive use of CAD. For instance, this Michigan business uses CAD to design its locomotives, get an idea of the machining that will be involved in producing it, and estimate its costs. CAD then helps Lionel to quickly generate plans for various train pieces and produce detailed plans for making them. These techniques were instrumental in the resurgence of Lionel in the late 1980s.

FUTURE TRENDS

Changing Graphics in the 1990s

The 1990s will see a number of changes in how graphic images are handled by computers:

- Three-dimensional imagery will replace two-dimensional imagery as the standard for advanced graphic packages.
- **Control software,** similar to PostScript (see Chapter 5), will change how graphic information is displayed to the screen or dispatched to the printer.
- Editing, to modify graphic images, will become much easier. Changes will be possible in more general fashion, rather than pixel-by-pixel.
- Transferring the exact color of an image from one ouput device to another will be easier. Standards will be created to facilitate this.
- Exhaustive libraries of images and shapes will become available to graphics users. These libraries will let the user easily change the size, orientation, and color of the image. Users will be able to merge these images seamlessly into an existing image on the screen.

CHAPTER REVIEW

Graphics enhance communication by connecting pictures with ideas and words. Businesses rely on graphics to summarize numeric information in readily understandable pictorial form.

Before you can create graphics on a computer system, the system must have a built-in or an added-on graphics circuitry, a monitor (a color screen is needed for some applications), and a hard-copy output device such as a pen plotter, laser printer, or dot-matrix printer. Some applications also take large amounts of storage.

Image processing and presentation graphics are two common business applications. Presentation graphics render numeric data into charts and graphs. Four common types of graphs are the bar chart, line graph, pie chart, and scatter plot. Presentation graphics also may be used to create signs, Gantt charts, and organization charts.

Graphics editors or paint software is used to generate drawings or to edit existing graphic images that are stored on disk. Once a picture has been correctly drawn or scanned, it can be printed separately, inserted in a desktop-published document, or included in another graphic. Most paint programs have a drawing area, palette, toolbox, and menus for issuing commands. Animation is another application based on scanning, drawing, and editing functions.

Computer-aided design (CAD) software exemplifies design graphics packages used in design and manufacturing. This software helps accomplish in minutes tasks that once required hours or days. Originally used by manufacturing concerns, CAD packages are now popular with a variety of businesses. Designers often link CAD packages to computer-aided engineering (CAE) software, in order to test new product designs, and to computer-aided manufacturing (CAM) software, in order to facilitate the manufacturing process by generating parts lists and managing industrial robotics.

KEY TERMS AND CONCEPTS

bar chart
clip art
computer-aided design (CAD)
computer-aided engineering (CAE)
computer-aided manufacturing (CAM)
computer animation
control software
drawing tool
font
graphics editor
hi-lo graph
image processing
line graph
pie chart
presentation graphics
scanner
scatter plot (XY graph)
sprite
stand-alone presentation graphics package
WYSIWYG
X (horizontal) axis
Y (vertical) axis

CHAPTER QUIZ

Multiple Choice

1. Which of the following is a use for computer graphics?
   a. Computer games
   b. Presentation charts
   c. Organization charts
   d. None of the above
   e. All of the above

2. Which of the following is or might be required for computer graphics applications?
   a. A graphics board
   b. A color monitor
   c. A pen plotter
   d. A laser printer
   e. All of the above

3. Which of the following is *not* found in the toolbox of PC Paintbrush?
   a. Spray can
   b. Drawing-width scale
   c. Scissors
   d. Paintbrush
   e. All of the above are tools found in the toolbox.

4. Which of the following is *not* a part of defining a graph?
   a. Specifying the data to plot
   b. Specifying the titles
   c. Specifying the width of the bars
   d. Specifying the axes labels
   e. All of the above are tasks in defining a graph.

5. CAD packages can be used for which of the following applications?
   a. Landscaping design
   b. House design
   c. Theatrical design
   d. All of the above
   e. None of the above

True/False

6. Numeric data can be easily summarized via a graph.

7. Pen plotters are usually preferred over laser printers as output devices for graphic displays.

8. One benefit of presentation graphics software packages is that they let you change a graph until it exactly suits your purpose.

9. Graphics editors/drawing tools software cannot usually be used by a novice.

10. Computer-aided design packages are used only in manufacturing.

Answers

1. e 2. e 3. b 4. c 5. d 6. t 7. f 8. t 9. f 10. f

Exercises

1. The ____________ microprocessor is powerful enough to quickly generate graphics.

2. Two types of presentation-graphics packages are ____________ and ____________.

3. When building a graph, you have to provide a number of different pieces of information to the software package. Three of these pieces of information include ____________, ____________, and ____________.

4. An example of a software package with an integrated graphics module is ____________.

5. An example of a stand-alone presentation graphics package is ____________.

6. Four basic types of graphs that can be generated are ____________, ____________, ____________, and ____________.

7. The output device for graphics that is preferred most is the ____________.

8. A(n) ____________ generates excellent graphics, but text quality is limited.

9. A graphics display device that represents lines as continuous lines between two points rather than as dots uses ____________.

10. The software package that is capable of producing organization charts is ____________.

11. Software packages that let you create a drawing are called ____________.

12. Paint programs usually use a device called a(n) ____________ for issuing instructions and drawing.

13. The area of the screen called the ____________ has a number of devices used in creating a drawing.

14. The ____________ contains the different colors or patterns used in a drawing.

15. The ____________ assumes different shapes, depending on whether you are inside or outside the drawing area.

16. The size of a line is determined by the ________ .

17. Selecting a menu option from the menu lines results in a ________ menu appearing on the screen.

18. The software application that was first used extensively in the engineering field is ________ .

19. Three features that can be included in the CAD package are ________ , ________ , and ________ .

20. The ________ can be used to develop parts lists, pricing, and instructions that will later be used by robots in assembling a product.

IN YOUR OWN CASE

1. Do you have a computer? If not, find out where you can try producing some computer graphics—on campus, at work, or at the home of a friend. Produce a simple image of some sort.

2. Do you own a computer that does not have graphics capabilities? Find out what hardware and software you would need to give you graphics power. Consider the pros and cons of making such a purchase.

3. If you own a computer with graphics capabilities, are you presently taking full advantage of this? What might you do to access or expand these capabilities? Consider the pros and cons.

QUESTIONS FOR THOUGHT

1. In your estimation, how much does effective use of computer graphics depend on artistic ability?

2. How can computer graphics applications help you in your academic work or your current or intended career?

3. How could computer graphics be useful to some other organization to which you belong? How might you help the organization gain this resource?

5

DESKTOP PUBLISHING

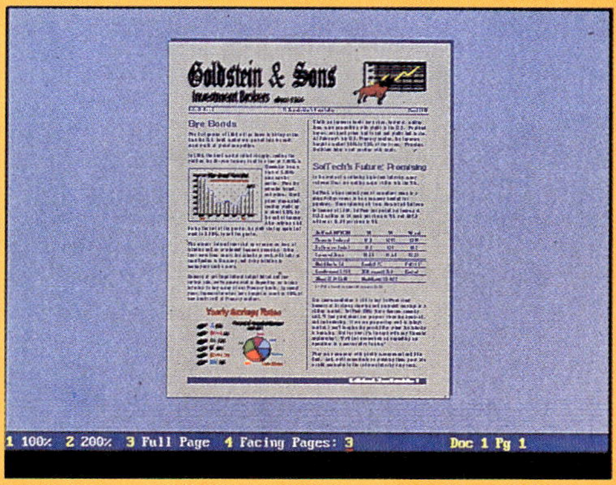

CHAPTER OBJECTIVES

After completing this chapter, you should be able to

- **Define and describe desktop publishing**
- **Describe the hardware needs of desktop publishing**
- **Differentiate between bit-mapped and formula-generated characters**
- **Discuss the use of scanners in desktop publishing**
- **Discuss desktop-publishing software**

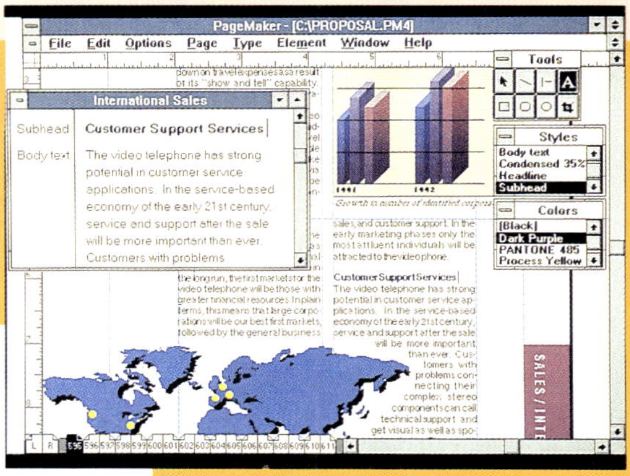

THE EVOLUTION OF DESKTOP PUBLISHING

1966	IBM introduces the Selectric Composer, a typewriter-like device with multiple typefaces and type sizes.
1970s	Dynabook, an experimental computer, shows text on screen in various printable typefaces (Xerox). Dynabook also lets the user draw or paint on screen and create new fonts and icons.
1981	Star system displays typographic fonts in the exact face and point size (Xerox). It also displays graphics.
1984	Apple introduces the Macintosh.
1985	Paul Brainard, president of Aldus Corporation, proposes the term *desktop publishing*. Hewlett-Packard introduces the first laser printer, the LaserJet. Apple introduces the LaserWriter printer along with PostScript, to produce varying sizes of type. First DTP package for microcomputers, PageMaker, gives Apple Macintosh the lead in desktop publishing.
1991	Color laser printers sell for less than $10,000.

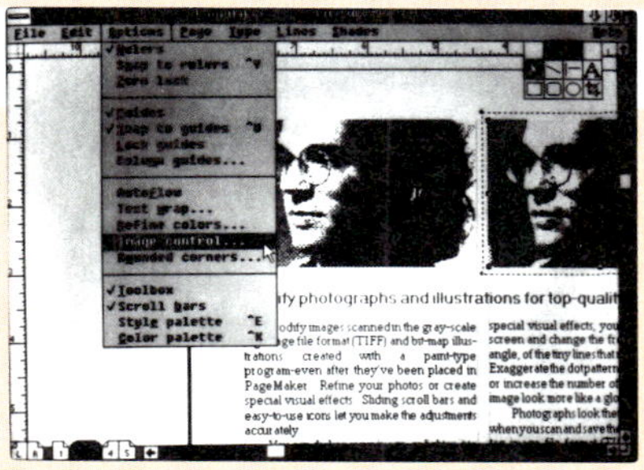
File
Edit
Options
Page
Type
Lines
Shades
Rulers
Snap to rulers
Zero lock
Guides
Snap to guides
Lock guides
Column guides...
Autoflow
Text wrap...
Define colors...
Image control...
Rounded corners...
Toolbox
Scroll bars
Style palette
Color palette

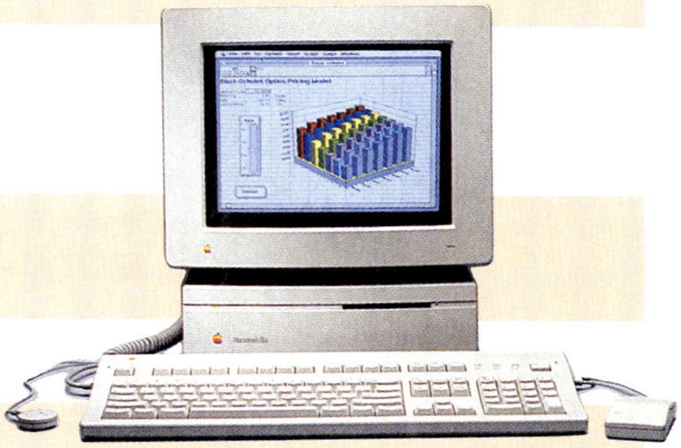

PERSONAL CASE

Computers and Desktop Publishing

GAIL FRANKLIN is a partner with a regional accounting firm. Because of her unusual skills in interpersonal relations and written communication, she has recently been placed in charge of the company's public relations. Among other things, Gail wants to publish a newsletter for the firm's clients, potential clients, and other businesspeople.

To start the newsletter, Gail has requested articles about topics of general interest from the accountants and other professional staff in the company.

Assisting Gail with the newsletter is William Caskin, an audit senior (an individual who has been with the company for 2 or more years) who has extensive background using microcomputers and knows several word processing programs. After soliciting several good articles, Gail and William decide to contract out the design and actual preparation of the newsletter to a service that specializes in this type of work. Their role, so they think, will be simply editing the articles and passing them along on diskette files for use by the production service.

When they take their first diskettes down to the service, they are overwhelmed with questions about what they want in terms of a layout and the design of the masthead (the title and other information displayed at the head of the newsletter). They also find themselves spending several hours discussing graphs and photos they'd planned to publish and discover they need a graphic artist to render the graphs in suitable form. What Gail and William envisioned as an afternoon task evolves into a 4-day chore as they shunt back and forth among designers, graphic artists, and typesetters. At the end of the fifth day, they examine a galley (prepress copy) and find numerous glaring errors.

Having gone this far, Gail publishes her first issue through the service. In the future, though, William suggests they create the newsletter themselves using some desktop-publishing software and one of the firm's IBM-compatible microcomputers. But what exactly do they need? Gail and William decided to visit a local computer store that specializes in desktop publishing.

Traditional publishing is an expensive, time-consuming, specialized operation. Writers write copy; editors review it for content; copyeditors revise the writing and correct spelling, punctuation, and grammar; graphic artists create a design; typesetters set the text; proofreaders review galley proofs for errors; and printers operate the press. **Desktop publishing (DTP)** on the microcomputer is a cheaper, quicker, less specialized alternative. Today, a user with a mere semblance of artistic ability, a little publishing know-how, and access to a $5000 to $10,000 DTP system can be a publisher.

The potential market for desktop publishing is staggering. Nearly every company needs brochures, catalogs, stationery, price lists, newsletters, financial reports, training manuals, and business cards. DTP systems have already saved the corporate world millions of dollars in professional printing costs. Industry pundits predict that demand for DTP systems will climb steeply for some years to come.

DESKTOP PUBLISHING DEFINED

The term *desktop publishing* was coined by Paul Brainard, the entrepreneur who founded Aldus Corporation (developer of PageMaker software). DTP systems produce high-quality publications with microcomputer technology that can merge text and graphics on the printed page and produce text in a variety of fonts (styles of type) and sizes.

Although DTP systems range in quality, good systems are affordable and can be operated reasonably well without extensive technical training or unusual talent. Less than expertly produced desktop publications often fall short of the standards of professional publishers, but aesthetic criticisms have hardly slowed the growing and effective use of DTP systems by churches, schools, public relations firms, advertising agencies, and quick-print shops.

In fact, desktop publishing is now revolutionizing professional publishing. Most technical illustrations throughout the publishing industry are now done with desktop publishing (historically, the machine of choice has been an Apple Macintosh). Complete, full-color national magazines such as Apple's *MacWeek* are now being created entirely on DTP systems.

In book publishing, desktop publishing has caused book designers to become more involved in what used to be considered strictly production jobs. For instance, they can set type for headings and sometimes separate colors—jobs previously done by specialists.

Desktop publishing has also raised the level of understanding of design and typography issues among nonspecialists. For instance, until desktop publishing became relatively common, people outside these areas typically knew nothing about fonts. Now people tend to know.

HARDWARE FOR DESKTOP PUBLISHING

DTP systems require a computer with high-speed processing power and enough storage capacity to handle large programs and voluminous data. The computer should have at least the power of an AT (a much faster version of the IBM PC) and a minimum of 2M of RAM. Running a DTP program on the relatively slow PC tends to try the user's patience.

DTP monitor screens should be large enough and sophisticated enough to display both an entire page and a blown-up portion of text (Figure 5.1). This is especially true for DTP programs with What-You-See-Is-What-You-Get, or WYSIWYG ("wizzy-wig"), capability.

Other useful additions to a DTP system include a fixed disk, a mouse, a scanner, and a laser printer. A fixed disk's larger storage capacity lets you piece together publications quickly and easily. Laser printers and scanners are especially helpful in producing publications with high-quality graphics.

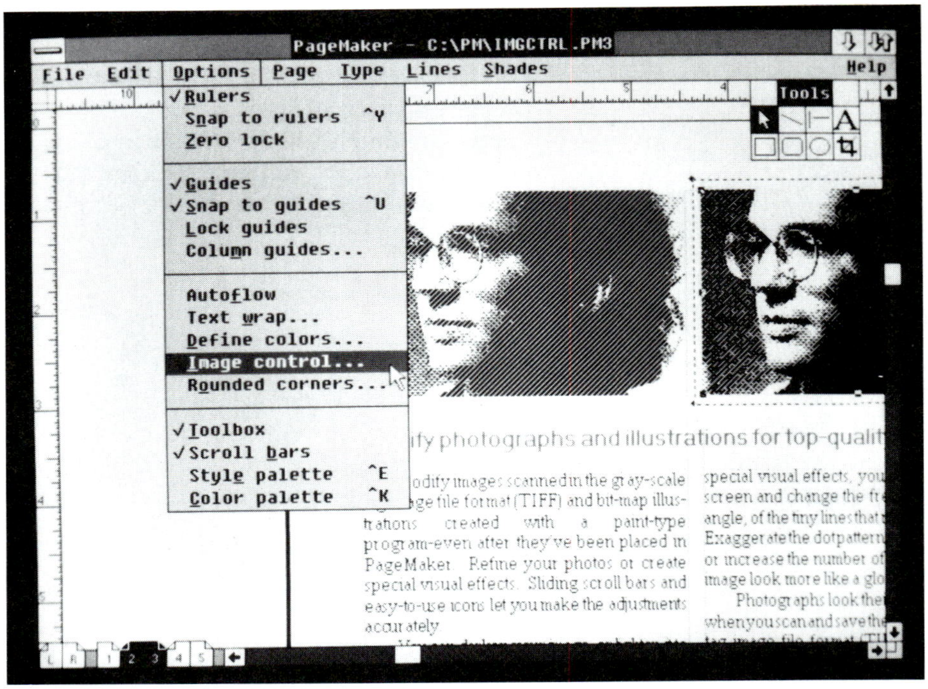

Figure 5.1
A blown-up, or zoomed, screen display of a document produced on a DTP system.

PRINTERS

Hewlett-Packard and Apple have set the market's standards for DTP system printers.

Hewlett-Packard Laser Printers In 1985 Hewlett-Packard introduced LaserJet, the market's first **laser printer.** Quiet in operation and able to print 300 dpi (dots-per-inch) resolution, the LaserJet was heralded as the high-tech replacement for slow, noisy daisy-wheel printers. It could print eight pages of letter-quality text per minute and had two resident fonts, Courier 10 pitch and 16 pitch. The LaserJet's success prompted other computer manufacturers to rush their own laser printers to market. Competitors enticed consumers to buy their machines by offering multiple fonts and type sizes.

In 1987 Hewlett-Packard discontinued its LaserJet and has since introduced a number of different printers. Hewlett-Packard and H-P compatible printers share a number of common characteristics. They usually come with a minimum of 512K of memory. Most of these printers are purchased for printing letter-quality, word processed documents quickly and quietly. However, users quickly discover that these are excellent printers for DTP systems.

These printers produce **bit-mapped,** or dot-pattern, **fonts.** Hewlett-Packard has wired different styles, sizes, and orientations of Courier characters into the ROM of each machine (Figure 5.2). To print in typefaces other than those residing in the laser's ROM, the user has to download additional fonts into the printer's RAM or plug a special font cartridge into the printer.

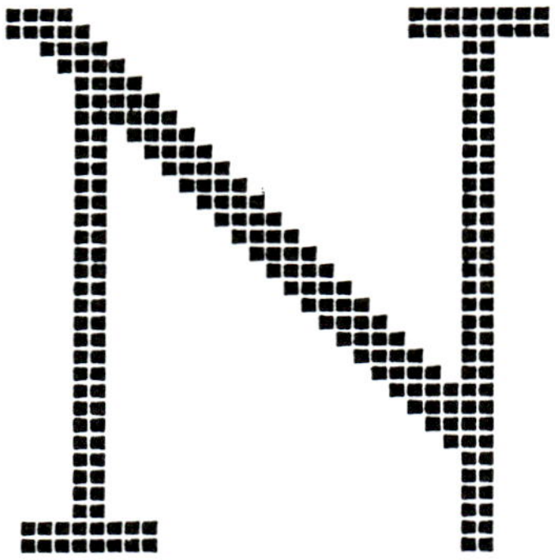

Figure 5.2
An example of a character generated via a bit map. Bit-mapped fonts consist of characters that have been drawn pixel-by-pixel—like this 12-point *N*—to be printed at a specific resolution, in this case, 300 dpi.

Downloading fonts into a printer reduces the amount of RAM the printer can use for printing text and graphics. This is of particular concern with laser printers, which produce an entire page at once and must have all of a page's text in memory before printing. If the laser printer's RAM is too full to accept an entire page's worth of data from the computer, the printer outputs the text or graphic it has in memory and prints any leftover material on a second page.

This is one reason why many people purchase additional RAM for their printer and expand it to at least 2M.

A printer with limited RAM also can be overloaded by data-rich, high-resolution graphics. For example, a laser printer, with only 512K of memory, is not capable of printing a full-page graphic at 300 dpi—such a piece contains too much information. Only by reducing the laser printer's printing resolution to 70 to 150 dpi (about the quality of a standard dot-matrix printer) will the user be able to print the page.

Hewlett-Packard's printers generate characters with **page-control language (PCL),** a simple language designed to load bit-mapped fonts and graphics into the printer. Characters created in this control language cannot be scaled or manipulated in the printer; the user must perform these operations with the application software. Accordingly, the user's application software must have a special driver for the LaserJet in order to output on the laser printer.

Apple Laser Printers Shortly after the LaserJet appeared on the market, Apple introduced its LaserWriter and has since introduced a number of other laser printers. This original printer had 13 resident fonts, 1.5M of RAM, and could generate high-quality graphics and a wide range of character sizes. LaserWriter uses a technology that ties in with **PostScript,** a special **page-description language (PDL),** developed by Adobe Systems.

LaserWriter uses a different technique than does LaserJet for forming characters. Instead of bit-mapped fonts, it uses hard-wired PostScript code to create mathematical descriptions of the various arcs, circles, and straight lines (Figure 5.3). Because it stores characters as mathematical descriptions, the LaserWriter must process a considerable amount of information before printing a page of text or graphics; this is why it needs so much RAM. However, using PostScript to produce characters and graphics permits the user to size and rotate material to be printed more easily than does bit-mapping production. In addition, PostScript's PDL sends a whole page's worth of information to the printer at a

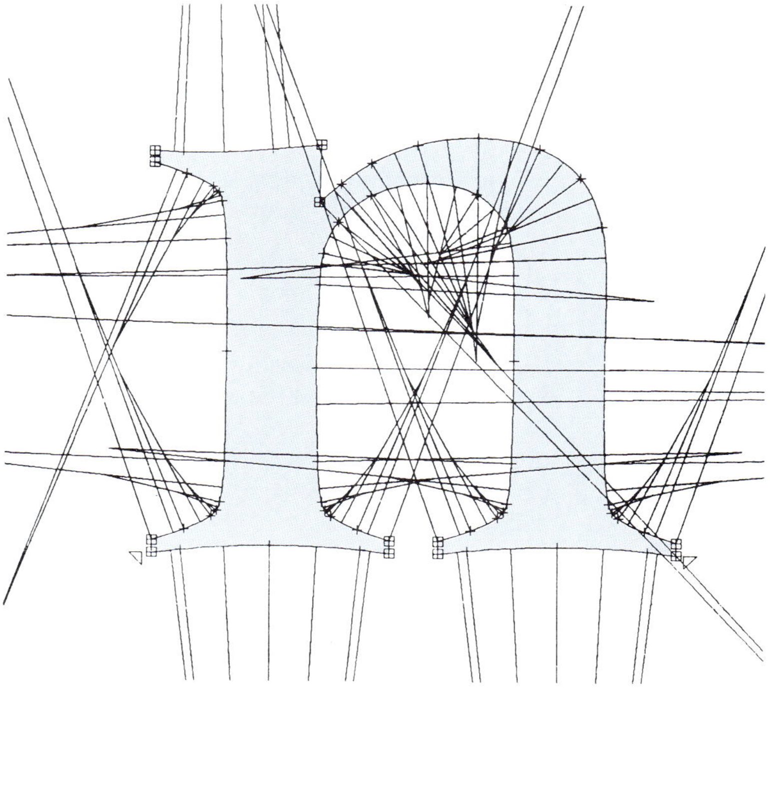

Figure 5.3
An outline font describes a character mathematically. (Courtesy of Bitstream)

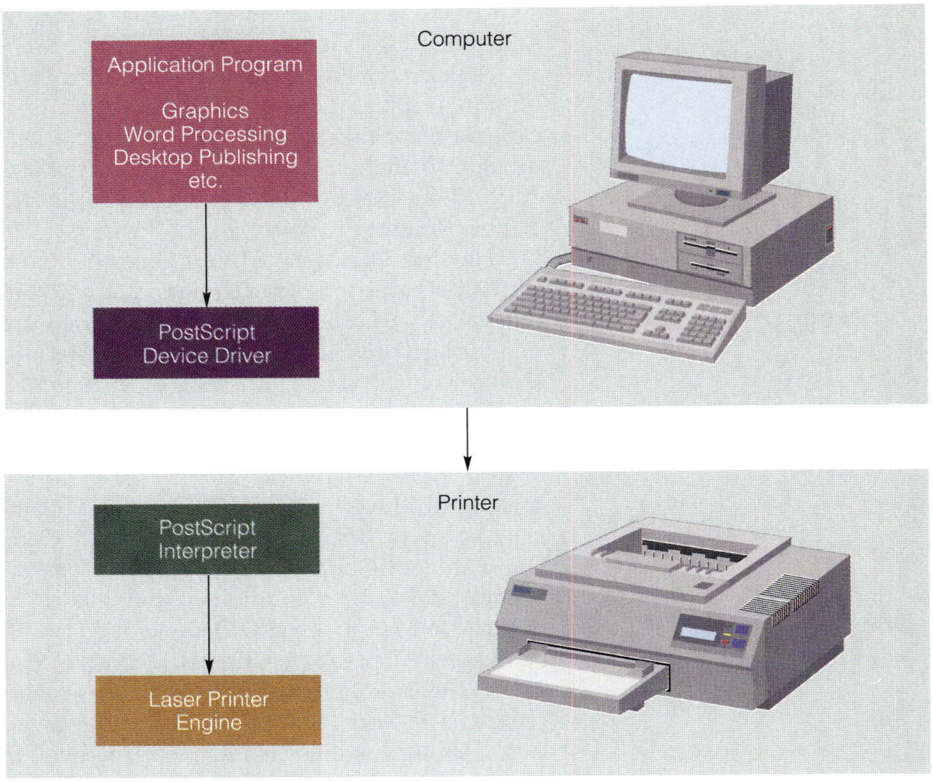

Figure 5.4
PostScript uses a device driver and interpreter for printing.

time, which complements perfectly the full-page output method of laser printers.

Apple was the first company to market an entire DTP system, which includes the LaserWriter, Macintosh microcomputer, and page-composition software, and LaserWriter has proved very successful. As a result, many manufacturers have introduced printers that rely on PostScript, which has become a standard PDL for word processors, graphics packages, spreadsheets, and other applications in both the Apple and IBM environments. Any PostScript printer accepts print instructions from any application software that has a PostScript device-driver program. The driver program encodes the data into the proper format and routes it to the printer's PostScript interpreter. The printer then builds the document's image in its RAM (Figure 5.4).

SCANNERS

Scanners are light-sensing devices that digitize print materials and convert them into bit-mapped images (see Chapter 2). In desktop publishing, scanners can be used to store photographs or other images, which the user can resize, rotate, or otherwise modify with a graphics editor package, as described in Chapter 4. Finished images can be inserted into a DTP document to add appeal and information.

Special software is needed to control a scanner. This software may come with the scanner at the time of purchase or be purchased separately. A package like Publisher's Paintbrush (Z-Soft) can be used both to control a scanner during the digitization process and modify the scanned image.

(a)

(b)

Figure 5.5
(a) A clear, high-resolution image. (b) A grainy image generated via changing the dither rating.

Most scanners are sold with software that performs the digitizing process. Users also can drive a scanner with an **optical character recognition (OCR)** program, which scans printed material and stores it to a word processing file. OCR software can save a user hours of manually typing in text. However, most OCR software can only read specific fonts; files created by scanning inappropriate type styles will contain a high number of errors. Some packages represent each error with the symbol @.

Scanners have two "reading" modes from which the user must choose. **Bi-level mode** scans only black and white. This mode works well for line graphics such as found in simple charts. When reading a graphic in bi-level mode, the scanner compares each bit with a value. Bits above the value are rendered in black; those that are below, in white.

Dither mode digitizes a range of grays, such as are found in photographs and other complex graphics. In dither mode, a scanner represents grays as patterns of white-and-black dots, just as newspaper photographs do. The dots give the image a slightly grainy appearance. The poorer a photograph's resolution, the grainier will be its scanned image (Figure 5.5).

SOFTWARE FOR DESKTOP PUBLISHING

Most DTP packages are basically page-composition tools that permit users to electronically assemble text and graphics. They offer text- and graphics-formatting commands, rudimentary text editing (for making corrections or typing in phrases), and limited graphic capabilities for embellishing assembled documents. Typically, users don't draft text and graphics on a DTP program but, rather, import them from other applications.

For example, although text can be typed directly into a DTP file, the user is better off composing copy on a high-end word processor that offers features that most DTP packages don't have, such as spelling checkers or search and replace. Similarly, users often create graphics with a paint program. After passing the

PERSONAL CASE PROGRESS

Contemplating a DTP System

GAIL and WILLIAM make an appointment and visit a store that specializes in DTP systems. Frank Kincaid, the store's DTP expert, first asks about the accounting business's hardware platform.

Apple has historically dominated the DTP field. In fact, the early leading DTP software package, PageMaker, was originally developed for the Apple Macintosh and was almost single-handedly responsible for getting Apple accepted by U.S. business. However, popular PageMaker versions now also run on the IBM. Windows has been a unifying force for standardization of software packages for the IBM platform, and since its introduction, DTP packages have become increasingly common on IBM computers and their compatibles.

Frank learns that Gail's company is an IBM-compatible shop with a number of 80386 and 80286 machines, each containing a minimum of 1M of RAM. The 80386 machines each have 4M of RAM, whereas the 80286 machines vary from 1 to 2M of RAM. The company's machines also have 150M fixed disks, VGA monitors with 1M of RAM, and high-density 3.5-inch disk drives. The company also has a laser printer that contains PostScript.

Although an 80286 machine with 1M of RAM will perform desktop publishing, Frank recommends that they use one of the 80386 machines. He suggests they purchase a copy of PageMaker for publishing their newsletter. He says this package is ideal for such small projects and offers a tremendous amount of control over various design considerations.

Frank suggests that they purchase a large monitor that will be capable of displaying a full page of document text on the screen. Although people who do a great deal of desktop publishing typically use a monitor that can show two pages (a "spread") at a time, the one-page screen seems adequate for the newsletter. Gail and William agree.

Frank shows them several scanners and asks what features they may be seeking. For instance, would they use it for color or just for black and white? Gail decides to go with a less expensive scanner that comes bundled with name-brand software for scanning images. They put off buying more elaborate scanner software until they have tried out what they have.

The meeting with Frank leaves William feeling that he doesn't really have the graphics and typography skills required for the actual preparation of the newsletter. He and Gail decide to look around the company for someone else who can help them in this regard.

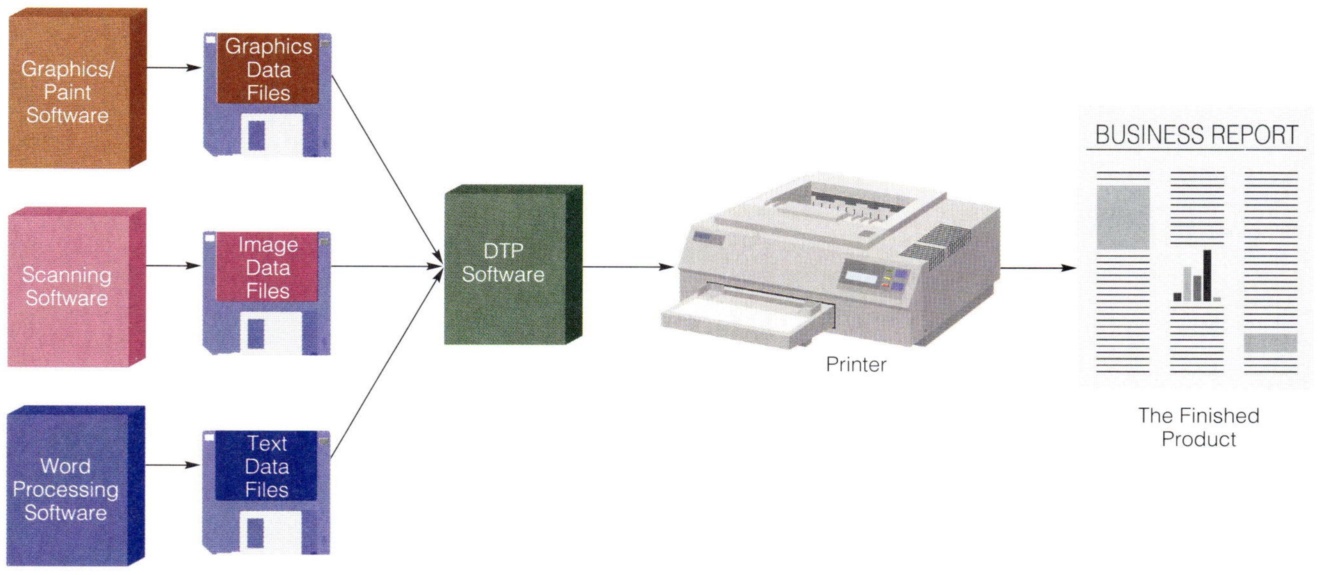

Figure 5.6
Files involved in desktop publishing with PageMaker and other application software.

text or graphics file to a DTP program, the user can call up the material and assemble it to create a document (Figure 5.6).

Among the most popular DTP software packages on the market are PageMaker by Aldus, Xerox Ventura Publisher by Xerox, GEM Desktop Publisher by Digital Research, and Office Publisher by Laser Friendly.

SOME QUESTIONS TO ASK ABOUT DTP SOFTWARE

- Is it easy to learn? Does it provide on-screen help menus?
- Is it easy to use?
- Does it provide a "workbench" environment in which you can post an element off to the side of the page before you place it on the page?
- Is it best for short or long documents?
- Does it have features that may help in the formatting and design specifications of longer documents? Does it have a master style sheet for the document? Can you change the style for specific pages?
- How much precision does it offer in placing and formatting elements?
- Is it WYSIWYG? Both novice users wanting something easy to learn and high-end users who need detailed screen display are best off with WYSIWYG.
- Is it *truly* WYSIWYG? Poor screen resolution or poor interaction between screen and software may lead to important differences between what appears on the screen and what prints out.
- Can it automatically create indexes, footnotes, and tables of contents? Some non-WYSIWYG programs are best in these respects and may be preferable for long publications such as books that require a consistent appearance throughout.

FUTURE TRENDS

Desktop Publishing Versus Word Processing

The distinctions between word processing and DTP packages are beginning to blur. DTP packages are including more and more word processing capabilities such as global search and replace, spelling checkers, and thesauri. High-end word processing packages now provide such DTP features as the ability to select different fonts, change the font size, and merge text with graphic images, as well as incorporating graphic lines of varying thickness.

The merging of these two software lines has presented problems and opportunities for users. Historically, high-quality output required creating a text file on a word processing package like WordPerfect and then transferring the file to a DTP package for additional formatting and graphics.

Future DTP programs will likely do away with much of the need to import text and graphics. Soon, DTP packages by themselves may serve to create all the text and graphics for many kinds of documents.

Some users who do not have sophisticated DTP needs find that a package like WordPerfect more than fulfills their needs.

In the following pages, we'll explore PageMaker for the IBM PC to see how DTP software generally works. Introduced in 1985 for the Apple Macintosh, **PageMaker** was the first WYSIWYG DTP package developed for microcomputers. PageMaker instantly displays all document changes to the screen, is very user-friendly, and is now used by many desktop publishers.

DESIGNING AND CREATING DOCUMENTS

Before laying out text and graphics with PageMaker or any DTP system, form a rough idea of how the document should look. In this document-design step, answer the following questions:

- What size paper will be used?
- Will the pages be single- or double-sided (printed on one side or both sides)?
- What elements will appear on each page? Are footers, headers, lines between columns, and so forth required?
- How many columns will each page have?
- Will the pages be printed in **portrait** (tall-and-narrow) or **landscape** (short-and-wide) **format?**
- What fonts and type sizes will be used for headings, captions, and body text?

A number of design reference books can guide you in designing your document. One basic rule is that no more than two fonts should be used in the text of a document. Too many different type styles look confusing. A good way to avoid design problems is to have a professional create a document model that provides you with typeface specifications, general layout, and other design characteristics (such as borders and embellishments).

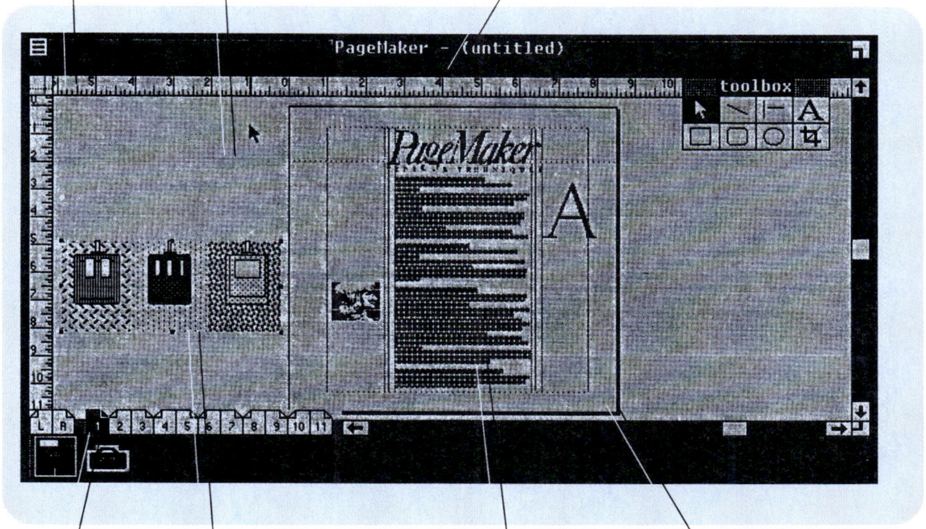

Figure 5.7
Laying out text and graphics on the PageMaker drawing board.

Having a rough idea of what the finished document should look like, you can assemble and manipulate the text and graphics with DTP software. With PageMaker, the screen serves as a drawing board on which to organize the document's components (Figure 5.7).

IMPORTANT DESKTOP-PUBLISHING TERMS

- **Camera-ready** Photographs, art, or complete pages in a finished form that the printer can photograph for making print plates.
- **Clip art** Public domain art that you can use free of charge and without credit in a publication.
- **Encapsulated PostScript** A file format that lets you print line art with smooth edges and resize the graphic image on-screen. Such images can be created in graphics programs that produce PostScript code.
- **Folio** The page number.
- **Galley** Proofs of type before it is arranged on the page; used for proofreading and layout.
- **Grid** A series of nonprinting vertical and horizontal rules used to determine placement of text and graphics on the page.
- **Kerning** The process of adjusting the space between characters, generally done only in headlines and other display type.
- **Point** The basic measurement of typography. One point equals about $\frac{1}{72}$ inch.
- **Serif** A line or curve projecting from the end of a letter. Styles of type that have such projections, such as SERIF. **Sans serif** type lacks these projections —SANS SERIF.
- **Spread** Two facing pages of a publication.
- **White space** The areas of the page without text or graphics; used as a deliberate element in good graphic design.

PERSONAL CASE REVISITED

The New Newsletter

WILLIAM consults the personnel director to see if there are any employees with any graphic arts experience. In the employee database, the personnel director finds Tom Fowler, an entry-level accountant who has been with the company for about a year-and-a-half and has an art minor from college. She pulls his folder and finds from his college transcripts that Tom took several graphic arts classes. William calls Tom's manager to see if Tom has some hours available for the newsletter project.

Finding that he does, and tentatively allocating this time to the newsletter, Tom and his manager meet with William. Tom is really pleased at the prospect. Gail and William show Tom the first edition of the newsletter and some other DTP samples they like, then give him pretty much of a free hand in redesigning the newsletter.

Tom's design impresses several outside recipients of the newsletter, who approach the company about the possibility of producing a newsletter for them. Gail explores the idea of setting up a new revenue-generating unit within the company—desktop publishing of newsletters for interested clients.

How much of a PageMaker document can be read at any one time depends on the monitor. A large-screen, or full-page, monitor lets you read an entire $8\frac{1}{2}$-inch by $11\frac{1}{2}$-inch page without scrolling. On a standard-size screen, you must zoom in on the page to read text (Figure 5.8). A document displayed in actual size will have its text shown in **"greeked,"** or simulated, form.

As shown in Figure 5.7 the PageMaker screen has a series of pull-down menus containing commands for manipulating the document's elements. At the top and along the left side of the screen is a ruler for measuring and aligning text and graphics. In the upper right-hand corner of the screen is a **toolbox** containing several graphic design tools. The area around the document page is the **pasteboard,** where text and graphics may be moved off the page until they are needed. Numbers at the bottom of the screen tell what pages are being displayed. Figure 5.9 shows finished documents that were created using PageMaker and several other DTP packages.

Figure 5.8

A PageMaker document viewed using PageMaker's Actual Size command.

(a)

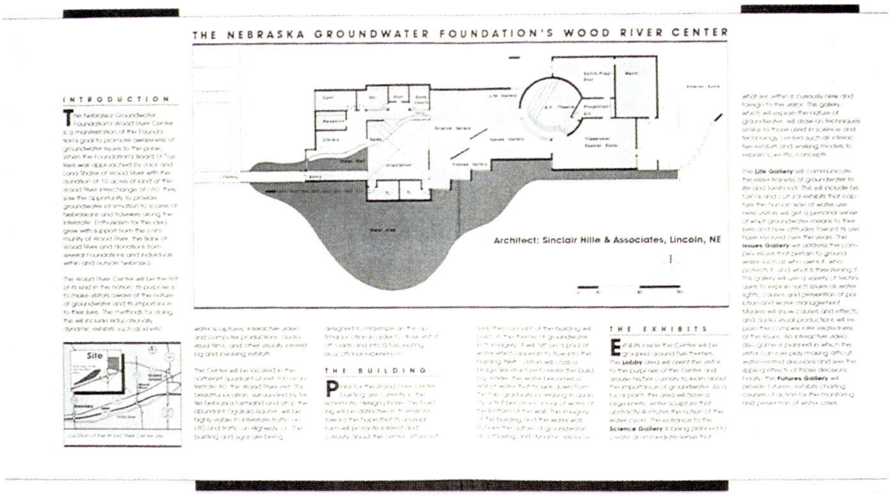

(b)

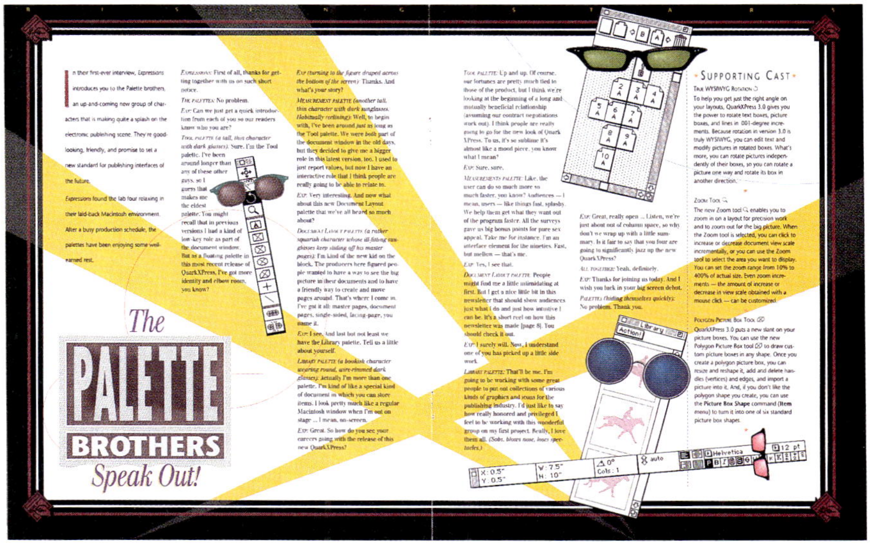

(c)

Figure 5.9

Documents created with desktop publishing: (a) Aldus PageMaker. (b) Ventura Publishing. (c) Quark Express.

CHAPTER REVIEW

Desktop publishing (DTP) has dramatically helped many types or organizations. Desktop publishing can generate professional-looking documents at a fraction of the cost of traditional publishing methods. DTP systems use microcomputer technology to produce a variety of fonts and type sizes and to merge text and graphics into one document. Typical systems cost $5000 to $10,000 and can be used by people with minimal publishing skills.

Minimum hardware requirements for a DTP system include a high-quality monitor, fixed disk, mouse, laser printer, scanner, and a computer with at least the power of an AT-class machine and 2M of RAM.

Laser printers come in two classes: those that support PostScript printing and those that do not. Printers that support PostScript define text characters as mathematical formulas. Other printers use a bit-mapping scheme to generate characters. Users can augment the selection of type styles that can be printed on a bit-mapped printer by loading extra fonts into the printer's RAM.

Users can incorporate line drawings and photographs into a DTP document by digitizing them with a scanner. When driven by optical character recognition (OCR) software, scanners can read paper-based text and images and store them to word processing text files.

DTP software let users combine and manipulate word processing text files, scanned images, and graphics created with a paint program into a single, high-quality document. WYSIWYG DTP packages display a document to the screen exactly the way it will look when printed.

Before assembling a document with a DTP package, the user needs a rough idea of what the document should look like—what size paper it will use, how many columns will be on each page, the width of the margins, and so on. To make their work easier and their finished publications more attractive, desktop publishers can base their document's design on a professionally made model.

KEY TERMS AND CONCEPTS

bi-level mode
bit-mapped font
camera ready
clip art
desktop publishing (DTP)
dither mode
encapsulated PostScript
folio
galley
greeked text
grid
kerning
landscape format
laser printer
optical character recognition (OCR)
page-control language (PCL)
page-description language (PDL)
PageMaker
pasteboard
point
portrait format
PostScript
sans serif
scanner
serif
spread
toolbox
white space

CHAPTER QUIZ

Multiple Choice

1. Which of the following characteristics do *not* apply to desktop publishing?
   a. Ability to use microcomputer hardware
   b. Ability to merge text with graphics
   c. Requires an expert in graphic design
   d. Ability to support multiple fonts and type sizes
   e. All of the above are characteristics of desktop publishing.

2. Which of the following hardware is usually *not* associated with desktop publishing?
   a. Fixed disk
   b. Mouse
   c. Scanner
   d. Laser printer without graphics capability
   e. All of the above are associated with desktop publishing.

3. Which of the following statements about laser printers is false?
   a. Only bit-mapped printers can generate graphics.
   b. A PostScript printer takes less time to generate a page than do other laser printers.
   c. A bit-mapped character is generated using mathematical formulas.
   d. None of the above are false.
   e. All of the above are false.

4. Which of the following statements about PostScript printers is true?
   a. Text cannot be rotated on a page.
   b. A software package generating PostScript output must have a PostScript printer driver.
   c. An interpreter to evaluate instructions to the printer is not required.
   d. All of the above are false.
   e. Only b and c are true.

5. What software packages can be used to prepare files for a DTP document?
   a. Paint/draw programs
   b. Word processing programs
   c. Scanning software
   d. All of the above
   e. None of the above

True/False

6. DTP packages can be used by people with limited graphic design background.

7. A scanner lets you scan only a line image or a photograph.

8. PostScript printers let you have any size character without loading a new bit map for the characters to be printed.

9. Scanning software many times lets you control the quality of the scanned image.

10. The pasteboard lets you temporarily store an image or text.

Answers

1. c 2. d 3. e 4. b 5. d 6. t 7. f 8. t 9. t 10. t

Exercises

1. Define the following terms:
   a. Desktop publishing
   b. Bit-mapped font
   c. PostScript
   d. PageMaker

2. The market for desktop publishing is expected to ____________ over the next few years.

3. A person with a(n) ___________ of skills can use a DTP system.

4. A(n) ___________ is a device that digitizes images.

5. A(n) ___________ monitor lets you see an entire page of a document on the screen at a time.

6. The first laser printers were introduced by the companies ___________ and ___________ .

7. A character that is described to the printer according to the dots needed to make that character is called a(n) ___________ printer.

8. The language that is used to describe a character to a printer via mathematical formulas is called a(n) ___________ .

9. The LaserWriter uses a language called ___________ , developed by Adobe Systems, to describe characters.

10. Laser printers print a(n) ___________ of text/graphics at a time.

11. A graphics laser printer requires more ___________ than does a laser printer that prints only text.

12. The scanner software that is used to read text from a page is called ___________ software.

13. ___________ mode is used by a scanner to represent various shades of gray.

14. Various application packages that can be used to prepare files for processing, using PageMaker, are ___________ , ___________ , and ___________ .

15. Simulated text on a PageMaker screen is called ___________ text.

IN YOUR OWN CASE

1. Find some newsletters, reports or other materials in your home, at school, or at your workplace that were produced with desktop publishing. Compare these materials with publications you know to have come from traditional publishing companies. In what ways does desktop publishing seem less powerful than more elaborate methods? In what ways might it be superior?

2. Find a DTP system on your campus, at your workplace, or in some other organization with which you are affiliated. How is this system being used?

3. Identify some organization you know fairly well that could make good use of desktop publishing. Talk with several people in the organization about the uses and feasibility of acquiring a DTP system.

4. Visit a computer outlet and inspect a DTP system. What would a system cost that would suit your level of needs and experience?

QUESTIONS FOR THOUGHT

1. Make a list of 10 to 20 applications for which desktop publishing can be used.

2. In what ways does the idea of running a small DTP operation appeal to you? In what ways does it not?

3. Suppose someone offered to put up the money for you to start such a business. Would you seriously consider the offer? What problems would you expect to encounter? What rewards?

6

DATA COMMUNICATIONS

CHAPTER OBJECTIVES

After completing this chapter, you should be able to

- **Discuss the basic concepts of data communications**
- **Discuss modems**
- **Differentiate between serial and parallel transmission**
- **Discuss protocols of communications software**
- **Discuss distributed data processing and local area networks**
- **Discuss some of the media that are used for transmitting messages**
- **Discuss various types of networks for linking computers**

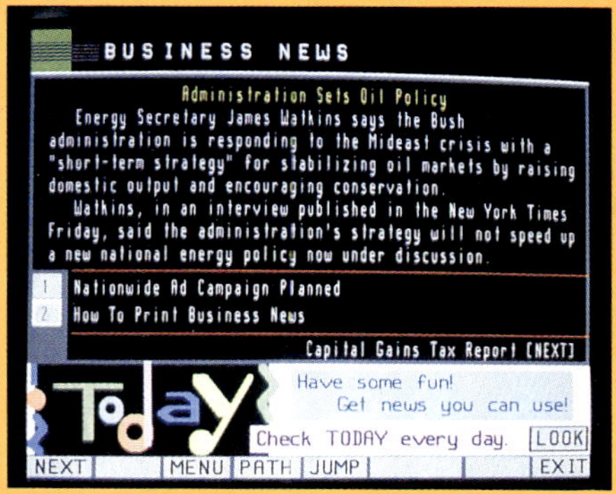

THE DEVELOPMENT OF DATA COMMUNICATION

1835	Samuel Morse invents the telegraph, the first electronic communications device permitting instant, one-way communication over long distances.
1875	Alexander Graham Bell invents the telephone, the first two-way verbal communications device.
1877–1984	AT&T is founded and becomes the largest telecommunications provider in the United States until its divestiture in 1985.
1915	The first transcontinental and first transatlantic phone service is introduced.
1940	Remote processing experiments produce the first terminal (Bell Laboratories).
1954	Remote Job Entry (RJE) communications (IBM) allows data input from and output to locations remote from the computer.
1958	NASA launches the first U.S. communications satellite.
1959	The FCC approves private microwave communications networks.
1963	Satellite SYNCOM II is launched in geosynchronous orbit. Satellites in this orbit (about 22,300 miles above Earth) are permanently stationed over one point on the planet and therefore constantly available for communication.
1964	IBM provides the first full-scale communications system for business: on-line airline reservations sytem for American Airlines.
1968	U.S. Supreme Court "Carterphone" decision legalizes attaching non-AT&T phones and other devices to telephone lines.
1969	Picturefone, the first video telephone, is introduced.
1979	The Source and CompuServe Information Services go on-line to the public.
1983	Cellular telephone networks are introduced. AT&T installs the first fiber-optic line between Washington, D.C., and New York.
1987	PC fax boards are introduced.
1989	Two million people use cellular phones.

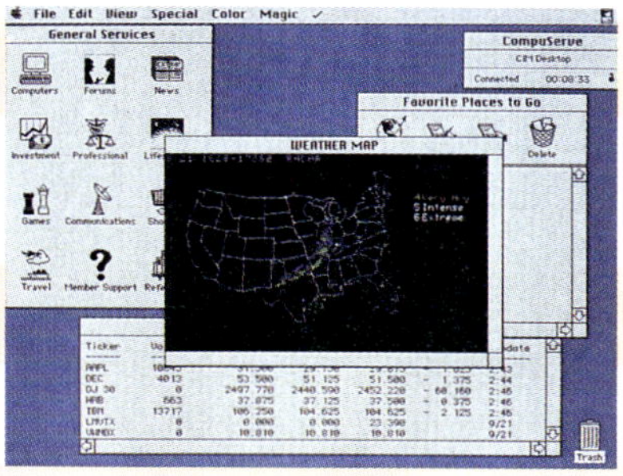

File Edit View Special Color Magic
General Services
CompuServe
Favorite Places to Go
WEATHER MAP
Computers
Forums
News
Investment
Professional
Delete
Games
Communications
Travel
Member Support
Trash

PERSONAL CASE

Data Communications and the Small Business

CLIFFORD and JOAN LUCERNE have been in the auction business for 14 years. They have held many profitable auctions for such items as Disney animation cels, antique coins, paintings and sculpture, antique furniture, and toy trains.

Cliff and Joan attribute their success in part to their finding specialty collections to auction and inviting potential bidders who have a special interest in these collections. They also personally supervise the advertising of their specialty auctions and ensure that information about their auctions appears in the appropriate regional special-interest journals and national special-interest journals such as *Antique Trader* and *Antique Monthly.*

The Lucernes hold their auctions in a comfortable warehouse near the center of town, which they have remodeled to provide office space, food service, and exhibition space and seating. In the last 10 years, the Lucernes have computerized much of their business. They currently have two microcomputers at their office, which are in constant use by their eight employees, and one at home. The computers are used for the accounting associated with each auction, information tracking about important customers (interests, what is purchased, amount, and so on), general accounting, payroll, and database information about the magazines in different special-interest areas.

In the past two years, employee demand for computer time has been enormous, and Joan has been using the computer at home more and more just to let others use the office computers. As a result, she is constantly carrying data diskettes back-and-forth from between office and home and sometimes finds she has data diskettes at home that other people need. Even between the two computers at work, employees are frequently passing diskettes back-and-forth in order to keep information current for use in both computers. In view of these problems, the Lucernes are interested in connecting their computers into some kind of network. At the same time, the various magazines in which they advertise are asking for more and more lead time in the placement of an ad, and the Lucernes are having problems meeting these deadlines. They would therefore like to use telecommunications to speed communication with these publishers.

Because of computers, people produce far more information than they did a few decades ago. This has created the need to quickly transfer vast amounts of computer-generated data from one place to another. Accordingly, the past decade has witnessed a boom in computer data communications. This technology lets computers and their operators "talk" in highly efficient networks and has profoundly affected our control of information. Organizations can distribute information-processing resources throughout their structures and cut labor, paperwork, and turnaround time.

This chapter examines how computers communicate. **Data communications** (also sometimes called **telecommunications**) is the transfer of information from one computer or terminal to another computer by phone lines, satellite transmission, microwave links, coaxial cable, or radio transmission. Through telecommunications you can work at home and transmit the results electronically to a distant office (the "electronic cottage concept"); retrieve financial information from and sell or purchase stock on the Dow Jones Network; send and receive electronic mail; or electronically search a computerized bibliography and receive a listing of selected articles, books, and papers.

DATA TRANSMISSION

For two computers to communicate, they must each recognize the transmission format in which the data are being transmitted, transmit and receive at an established rate, "know" the direction the data are being sent, and operate according to common rules (protocols) governing data transfer. The device used by microcomputers to communicate over telephone lines is called a modem. Let's take a detailed look at modems and the requirements of transmission.

DATA CONVERSION AND MODEMS

Data can be transmitted in either analog (continuous wave) or digital (binary) form (Figure 6.1). As noted in Chapter 2, computers process data in binary code, and binary code is transmitted in **digital signals,** alternations between two distinct states—the presence (1) or the absence (0) of voltage. In contrast, telephones handle and transmit sound waves, which are **analog signals.** To be transmitted over standard telephone copper lines, computer-stored data must first be converted from digital to **analog** form.

Recently, telephone companies have begun to construct communication lines out of optical fibers instead of copper cables. Fiber-optic cables readily carry digital transmission signals. Nevertheless, analog data transmission will likely continue for some years. Signals received in analog form must be recon-

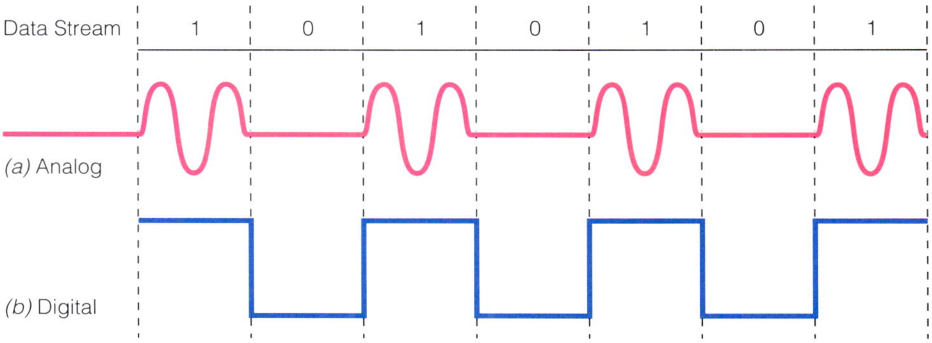

Figure 6.1

(a) Analog signals (such as sound) are waves. (b) Digital signals are represented by the presence or absence of voltage.

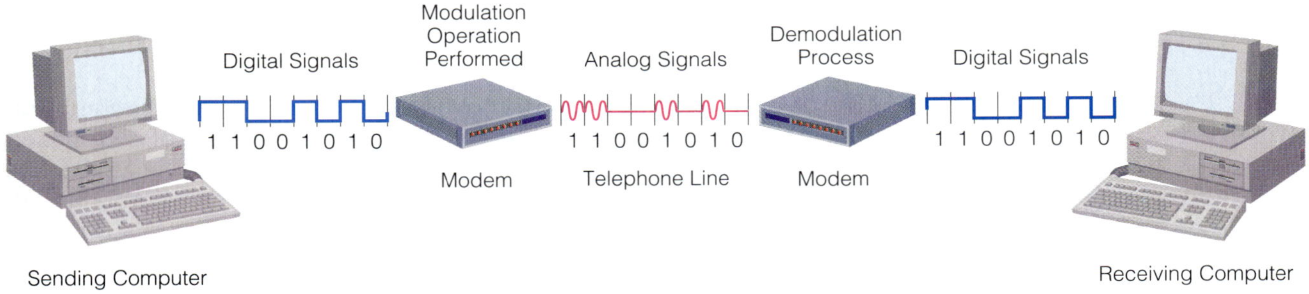

Figure 6.2
Sending and receiving computer data across telephone lines require converting digital signals to analog (sound) signals and back again.

verted into digital signals for the receiving computer. The process of converting a digital signal to an analog signal is called **modulation;** converting analog signals into digital signals is called **demodulation** (Figure 6.2). The device that performs this task is called a **modem** (short for modulation-demodulation).

Modems can be either external or internal (Figure 6.3). An **internal modem** is a circuit board that fits into an expansion slot of an open-bus computer. An **external modem** is a separate box that connects to a microcomputer's serial interface. The most common serial interface is the RS-232. Internal modems are designed to be used with specific computers, whereas external modems typically work with a variety of computers. External modems require an external power source and usually cost more than internal modems. Many portable computers have built-in modems. Modems generally come complete with any software that is necessary to their basic operation.

Most modems use a standardized plug that connects directly to a telephone-jack receptacle. Many modems also allow users to plug a telephone into the modem so that the telephone functions normally when the modem is not in use.

Figure 6.3
Modems.

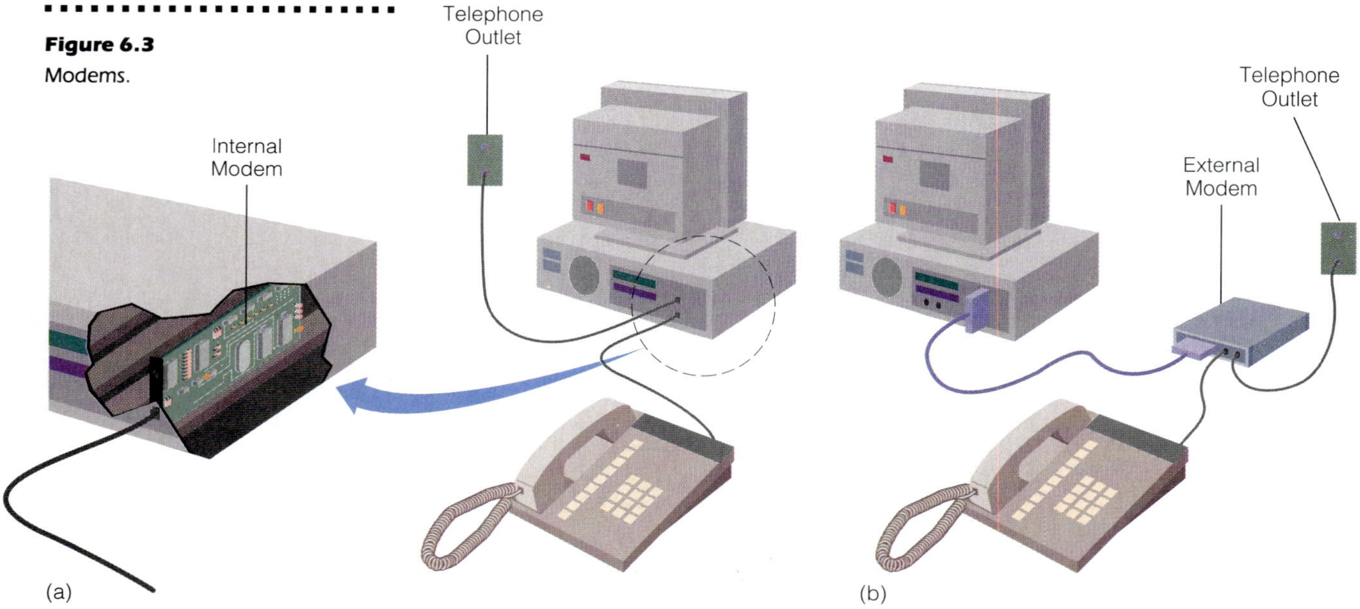

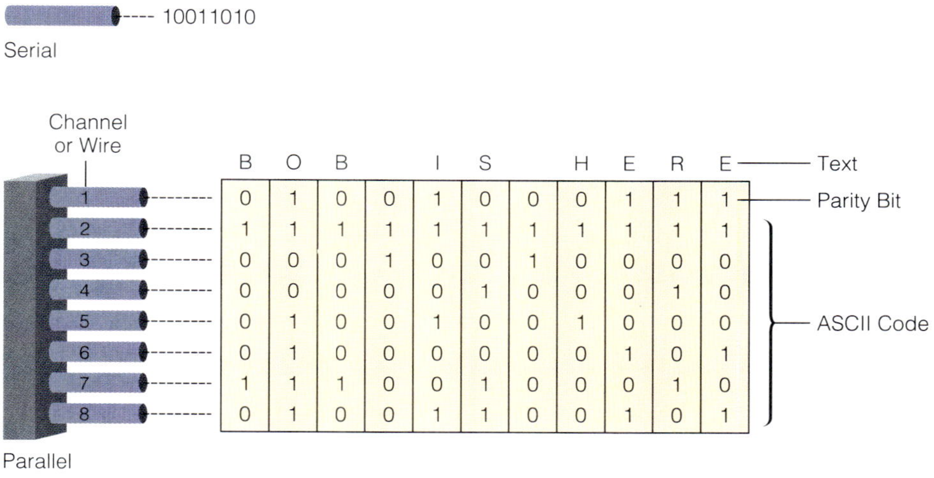

Figure 6.4

Serial transmission sends 1 bit at a time. Parallel transmission sends 1 byte at a time.

TRANSMISSION SPEED

Data can be communicated in either serial or parallel transmission (Figure 6.4). Computers always transmit over telephone lines in serial form. **Serial transmission** sends information 1 bit at a time over a single communication link. Serial-transmission speed is measured in bits per second (bps). The term *baud* is often erroneously used as a synonym for bits per second, but *baud* actually refers to the number of signaling events per second. Bps and **baud rates** can be equivalent in transmissions of 300 baud, but not at transmissions of 1200 baud or faster, in which several bits are sent in every signal event.

Parallel transmission sends all 8 bits needed to represent one character (1 byte) at once and requires at least eight connecting wires, one for each bit.

Parallel-transmission speed is measured in characters per second (cps) and is usually faster than serial transmission. However, parallel transmission is limited to around 15 feet, so it is most suitable for transmissions between a computer and nearby connecting peripherals such as disk drives and printers.

Modems vary in **transmission speed** from about 300 to 9600 bps (or 33 to 1066 cps). The upper rate for microcomputer modems is 9600 bps, and the price of the hardware tends to rise with speed. Businesses want faster modems to save time and money on long-distance telephone calls. However, there is a practical limit on a modem's baud rate because the grade, or **bandwidth,** of a communications line dictates maximum transmission speed. For example, high-speed modems (over 9600 bps and not generally available for microcomputers) may not be able to transmit at full rate over regular telephone cables because such lines are of insufficient bandwidth.

DIRECTION OF DATA TRANSMISSION

Data transmission over a communications line can be directed in three ways—simplex, half-duplex, and full-duplex (Figure 6.5). **Simplex transmission** occurs in one direction; data can be sent but not received or received but not sent. Radio and television broadcasting towers are simplex transmitters, and radios and televisions are simplex receivers. Simplex transmission is rarely used in computer communication because information processing usually requires that data be both sent and received.

Half-duplex transmission sends or receives data, but not both simultaneously. CB radios and home intercoms are half-duplex transmitters. To send a

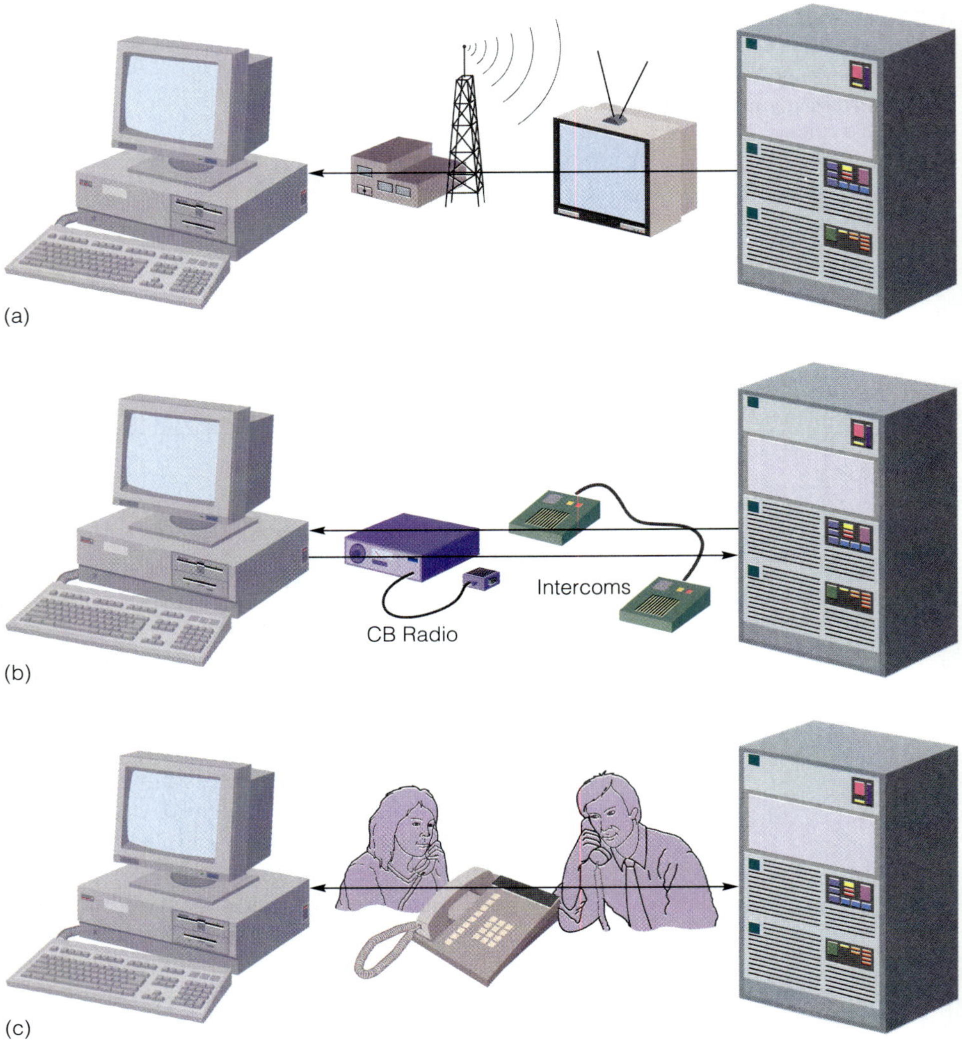

Figure 6.5
(a) Simplex-transmission devices only send or only receive data. (b) Half-duplex devices send and receive data, but not simultaneously. (c) Full-duplex devices simultaneously send and receive data.

message on these devices, a person must press a button while speaking and release the button while receiving a response.

Full-duplex transmission sends and receives information simultaneously. A telephone is a full-duplex device because both parties can talk simultaneously.

PROTOCOL

In sending or receiving data, computers follow a set of rules called a **protocol.** There are two protocol modes, asynchronous and synchronous (Figure 6.6). **Asynchronous protocol** transmits data one character at a time and uses several control features, including inserting a start bit before each character and one or more stop bits after each character. This control process is called **handshaking.**

Synchronous protocol sends and receives groups of characters, called packets, at fixed quantities and intervals. The transmitting terminal or computer must be able to store these blocks of characters. Synchronous protocol is much faster and more complex than is asynchronous protocol. It is rarely used in microcomputer-based communication links but is standard for IBM mainframe computers.

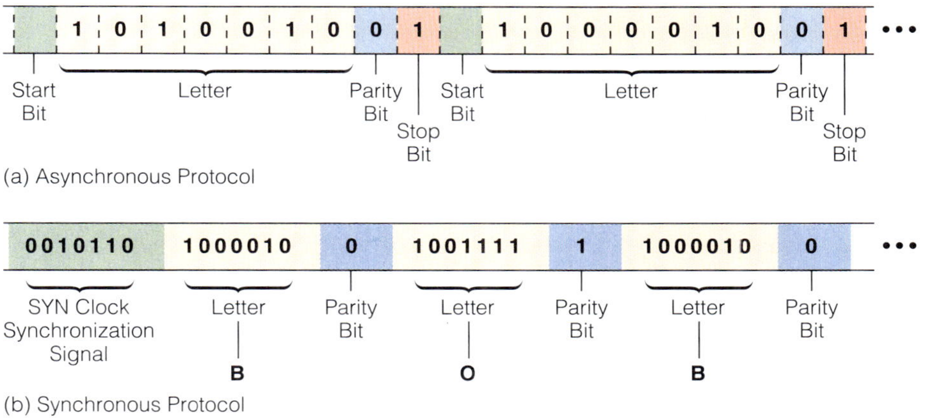

Figure 6.6
The difference between (a) asynchronous- and (b) synchronous-transmission protocols.

FAX MACHINES

Fax (facsimile transmission) machines can operate as stand-alone devices or as part of a microcomputer system in conjunction with a modem. Fax machines scan a paper document containing text or graphics and encode it as a series of electronic instructions that represent light and dark areas. The fax machine then sends these instructions over telephone lines to a receiving fax, which converts the signals back to an image and writes that image to paper through a process like photocopying.

GARBAGE FAX

The fax has become such an integral part of our everyday life that people now use it for ordering pizzas from the local pizzeria or for placing orders to the local deli. Many radio stations allow you to enter their contests not only by mailing in contest entries but also by sending them by fax. Newspapers commonly allow you to place your classified ads using facsimile transmission.

Some companies even make money by collecting telephone numbers of fax users and selling these numbers to other companies who want to advertise to those same fax users (fax users are considered to be more well-to-do than other people within society).

It is not uncommon for fax users to come home at night or arrive at work in the morning only to find page after page of this "garbage," or unsolicited fax material, at their machine. This can be especially vexing to users that were expecting an important fax only to find that the garbage faxes had used up all of the paper and, as a result, the expected message was aborted. The problem is compounded by all but the most expensive fax machines being required to use a special paper that is expensive compared to regular paper (it costs about 6 cents a page to receive a fax).

The problem reached such proportions that members of the U.S. Congress submitted legislation that would ban this practice of sending unsolicited fax messages during the 1990 session. The legislation died in committee when President Bush promised to veto it.

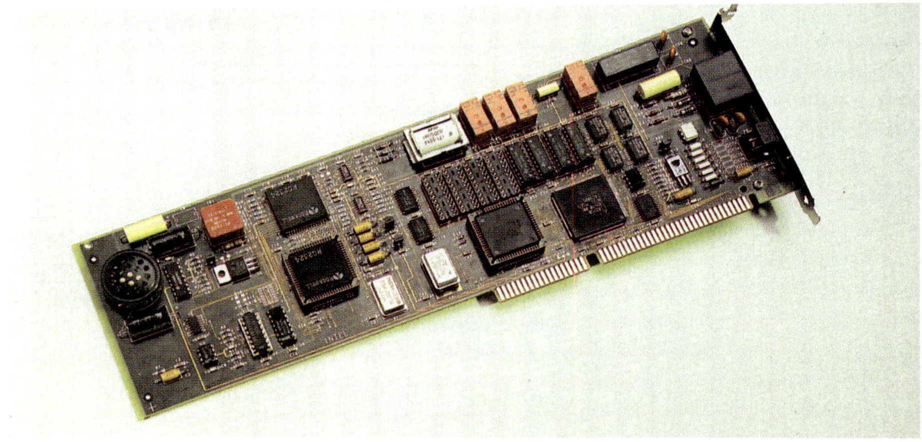

Figure 6.7
The internal Intel Satisfaxion board.

Fax machines can be installed within a computer via an interface board (Figure 6.7). This lets you create a document using, for example, your word processing package and send it by modem to another fax receiver station. To transmit an image that is currently on paper, your computer must be equipped with a scanner to first digitize the image.

An internal fax has two advantages: (1) It can print on regular paper rather than the usual chemically treated stock; (2) when you receive a fax message, you can review it first on your monitor and decide whether it's worth printing.

Disadvantages, according to some fax-board users, are that the computer may have to be left on for long periods simply to receive incoming faxes and that the fax board consumes many computer resources. Some users avoid this latter problem by installing 4M or more of RAM memory on their computers.

COMMUNICATIONS SOFTWARE FOR SPECIAL FUNCTIONS

Whereas modems generally come with the software necessary to run them, computers may require additional special software to perform such functions as terminal emulation, file transfers, accessing a specific computer, and log-on procedures.

Terminals that computer systems commonly link up with include ASCII terminals, dumb terminals, and teletypes. A **dumb terminal** is a terminal that contains no built-in processing powers; it simply sends and receives data. **Terminal emulation** software lets a microcomputer serve as a terminal for another system.

File transfer entails the uploading and downloading of files. **Uploading** means sending a file to another computer; **downloading** means accessing another computer's file and storing it in the downloaded computer. These functions let you send and receive electronic mail, obtain free public domain programs from bulletin board services, or issue stock puts and calls using the Dow Jones Network.

Modems and the appropriate software can also perform automatic telephone-dialing **(auto-dial)** and -answering **(auto-answer)** tasks. A modem may automatically dial computer telephone numbers that you have entered on a keyboard. Auto-answer lets you call the computer from another location and access information stored in the computer. To do this, the receiving modem and computer must be connected and running. Dialing directories is a software feature that lets you store and auto-dial frequently used computer numbers. At your command, the computer dials a number and logs on with the dialed system by providing such information as your access code and password.

PERSONAL CASE PROGRESS

Faxes and Modems

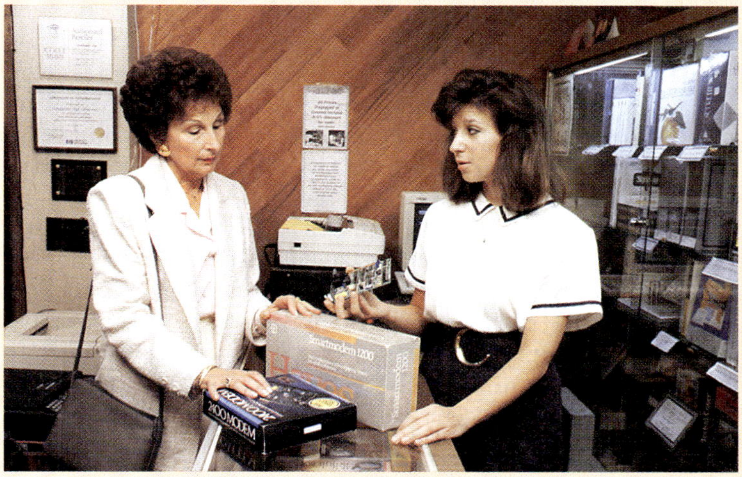

JOAN calls several magazines in which she has advertised auctions. All of them, she finds, now have fax machines for receiving advertising copy and communicating back-and-forth about production. Most will fax an image of the final advertising copy back to Joan for verification that the ad is correct.

Several prominent magazines also say they can download geographically selected lists of subscriber names and addresses. They can send this information to the Lucernes in various word processing formats, including WordPerfect, which the Lucernes use in their office. The Lucernes can then use these lists for mailings directly to the subscribers. Joan determines that the cost is reasonable and decides that this might be worthwhile for those "rush" auctions that do not allow enough lead time for proper advertising.

Joan decides to investigate modems and fax machines. At a local computer store, the salesperson tries to interest Joan in an "all-in-one" facsimile and modem card. However, Joan would also have to buy a scanner (price about $1400) to convert hard-copy images to digital images. She would also need to leave the computer on 24 hours a day to receive fax messages. Joan decides to buy a low-end standalone fax machine for about $750.

She also plans to purchase two internal 2400 bps modems for about $120 each. One will be installed in the computer at home and the other in one of the office computers, so that she can transfer data back-and-forth between home and office. Although 9600 bps modems are available, they are more expensive ($500 to $700), and the Lucernes do not need that much speed.

NETWORKS

Computer communication is not restricted to two machines at a time. Data exchange and resource sharing can be extended to several geographically dispersed computers of varying types and capacities. A computer network can be either a distributed data processing network or a local area network.

DISTRIBUTED DATA PROCESSING

A **distributed data processing (DDP)** network distributes and manages resources among several microcomputers, minicomputers, mainframe computers, or any combination of computer types. DDP systems can save money and improve reliability. For example, some businesses employ a DDP system of one mainframe computer and several microcomputers because they find it easier and cheaper to do certain tasks on microcomputers than on the mainframe.

Employees can use each DDP computer, or **node,** as a stand-alone processing system for individual application needs. This is one of the major advantages of a DDP system. For example, suppose a large brewery switched from using a single mainframe computer to a DDP system that included microcomputers and the mainframe. Using their own microcomputer node, employees at the brewery's distribution centers now can record their monthly beer sales to the DDP's data records. Such on-site use helps reduce error because it puts data processing resources into the hands of those who are most familiar with their application needs instead of a few central-computer operators. However, DDPs make all users responsible for maintaining accurate, updated files.

DDP systems can be tailored to an organization's needs. An organization may supply its autonomous branches with application nodes so that the branches can process their own data. Conversely, a branch that relies on the organization's central computer for all its processing needs may require only a simple terminal. For example, the brewery installs a microcomputer at each of its distribution warehouses so each can track inventory. Suppose, however, that the brewery is small and has only a single nearby-distribution warehouse. With minimal processing needs, the warehouse might require just a simple terminal with which to send data to the brewery's computer for processing.

Constructing a DDP can present several difficulties: Telephone-line charges may be too high; the system may have to use the business's existing hardware, which may be ill suited for distributed data linkage; and widely varying user needs may necessitate a complex system design. Also, storage of multiple copies of key files must be kept to a minimum on a DDP because every change in a file's data must be recorded on all copies. Security, too, can be problematic on a DDP. The more nodes a system has, the easier it is for unauthorized users to gain access to sensitive data. Special safeguards may be needed.

LOCAL AREA NETWORKS

A **local area network (LAN)** is a system of interlinked microcomputers. Most LAN systems are confined to a single building and have a maximum operating radius of 1000 to 7000 feet, depending on the network selected. Nodes are usually connected to the network by coaxial cable.

LANs link computers and peripherals, permit data transmission between computers, and provide for such features as electronic mail. **Electronic mail** is a computer-based message system that routes word processed text—memos, letters, reports—among users of a LAN system. The prime advantage of electronic mail is speed. A user can electronically mail a message to another user and receive a response in a matter of seconds.

LANs work at very high speeds; data often are transmitted over the coaxial cables at 50 megabits per second or faster. Accordingly, LANS are ideal for applications requiring large data files or processing large amounts of data.

LANs allow sharing of such resources as laser printers and fixed disks. However, peripheral prices have declined so dramatically in recent years that such resource sharing is no longer a primary rationale for installing a LAN. In fact, a company with modest processing needs may find it less expensive to purchase several printers or fixed disks than to connect a few such components in a LAN system.

ELECTRONIC MEETINGS USING NETWORKS

Many businesses are adopting a decision-making tool, called Group Decision Support Systems (GDSS), for groups of individuals. This new technology is taking the stress out of face-to-face meetings: No longer can one person shout down or make other members in a group defensive about their views (Figure 6.8).

In the electronic meeting, up to 50 people sit around a table or in tiered rows around the room. Each person is equipped with a computer screen and keyboard and participates through this media in the meeting. A LAN and controlling software track and sort by topic anything typed in by participants. These typed messages can then be displayed on a projection screen, and discussion can be ordered and controlled by a facilitator. The **facilitator** is a neutral party who directs the discussion and keeps it on track. The group does not know who is the author of any given message, so each participant is essentially anonymous. In this environment, participants do not feel constrained about presenting their opinions honestly. Even the shyest quickly lose their inhibitions.

IBM is one of the biggest backers of the electronic meeting concept. They orginally provided the University of Arizona with $2 million to perfect the technique and develop the software. IBM has also built 18 electronic meeting rooms, plans many others, and is actively marketing the idea.

This type of meeting dramatically enhances productivity. In a study reported by the University of Arizona, electronic meetings were as much as 55 percent faster than traditional ones. Unnecessary chitchat is eliminated, and discussions do not digress.

One perceived problem with electronic meetings is that the end product is the result of a group effort and no one can take credit for a great idea. A benefit is the absence of verbal brawls.

Figure 6.8
An electronic meeting.

The greatest advantage users derive from a LAN is the ability to share key data files and databases, thereby reducing data redundancy and increasing data integrity. LANs make vital stored information—such as customer, payroll, or patient master files—available to several users at once. To avoid confusion, file sharing requires software that lets one user "lock" onto records that he or she is using, thus preventing others from using it until he or she has updated and released the record. Locking ensures accurate updating of records and guarantees that the next user gets the most recent version of the records.

File security is another important LAN advantage. An organization installing a LAN can add a variety of security controls to system files. Log-on/password controls allow only those individuals who know a designated password and log-on procedures to access the network. Trustee security limits user access to specific network directories for each specific user. Directory security dictates the type of actions users can take within a network directory. File-attributes security establishes whether a particular user can write to or merely read from a file.

The Novell Corporation produces a popular LAN with at least three parts (Figure 6.9). In this system, one microcomputer serves as a file server, which stores common-use software including that which monitors the network operation. Printers and fixed disk storage hook directly to the file server. Other microcomputers then serve as nodes or workstations. Cabling and connection hardware link each node to the file server via the interface cards (circuit cards that go in the file server and workstations). A **bridge** is an optional component that allows a network to communicate with other, both like and unlike, network topologies. An asynchronous communications server (ACS) **gateway** lets the network communicate by modem with other computers.

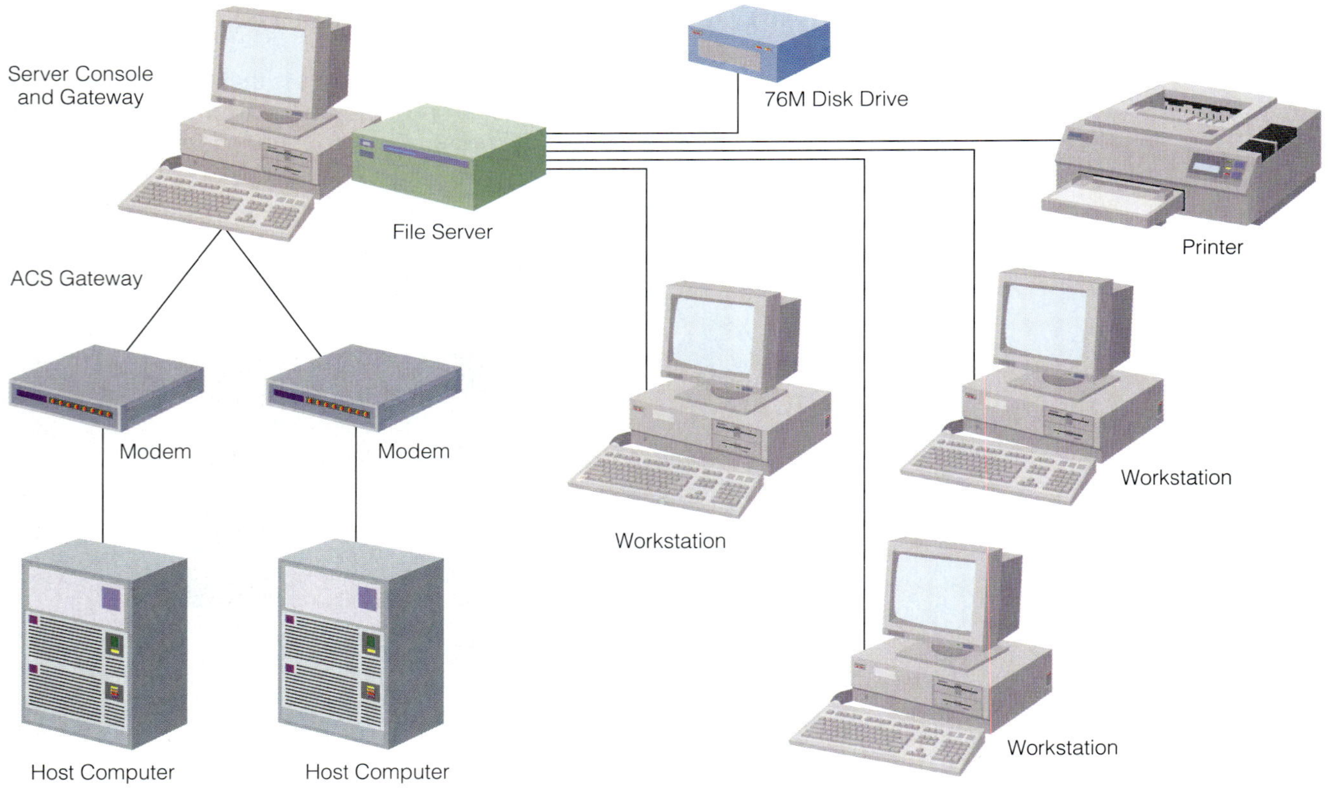

Figure 6.9

The Novell LAN system. The host computers, which may contain the file servers, reside outside the LAN.

DATA-TRANSMISSION CONSIDERATIONS

Most businesses want their communication systems to send as much data as possible and as fast as possible to lower transmission costs. A business can promote these ends by carefully selecting an appropriate transmission medium and using special hardware that boosts transmission speed.

COMMUNICATION MEDIA

Computer networks require some form of transmission medium, a channel or route that will carry the data much like a highway carries automobiles. Communication media vary widely in efficiency and cost. Typically, a business selects a medium based on speed, cost, and message-range considerations. Figure 6.10 shows three types of media.

Twisted-pair wiring is the most common and inexpensive communication medium for small LANs with an operating speed of 1 megabit per second or slower. This medium, which is frequently used in telephone systems, consists of two twisted, insulated copper wires. Twisted-pair wires have a low bandwidth and transmit relatively few characters per second.

Coaxial cable, which is used to hook television sets to cable service, consists of copper wire surrounded by insulation, which itself is surrounded by a signal shield of metal mesh. More costly than twisted-pair wiring, coaxial cable will carry up to 10 megabits per second and is used to connect higher-speed LANs.

Fiber optics is a relatively new technology that is replacing copper wires as the dominant message-transmission medium for both telephone and computer-network systems. Fiber-optic cables consist of hair-thin glass strands that carry light pulses (Figure 6.11). Fiber-optic cables are less expensive and far more efficient than comparable coaxial cables. These cables are often paired so that mes-

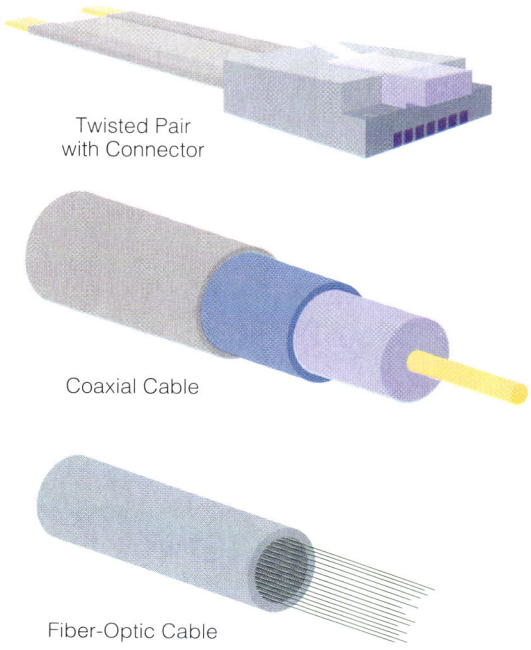

Figure 6.10
Types of communications media: twisted-pair wiring, several types of coaxial cable, and fiber-optic cable.

Figure 6.11
Fiber optics is revolutionizing the communications industry.

sages can be sent most efficiently in both directions. A standard coaxial cable can carry around 5000 voice channels, whereas a much thinner fiber-optic cable can carry 10 times that amount. As telephone companies convert to fiber optics, data-communication capabilities will increase dramatically.

REPAIRING FIBER-OPTIC CABLES

One problem with using fiber-optic cables to carry telephone messages (both voice and computer) is their tremendous bandwidth. This means that if one pair of fiber-optic cables is disrupted a tremendous number of calls can be disrupted. The problem becomes even more severe when you realize that in contrast to a pair of copper cables, which can support 24 simultaneous telephone calls, a pair of fiber-optic cables can support 37,500 calls; an average fiber-optic cable bundle many times contains about 72 fibers; and a large cable contains about 144 fibers.

For instance, on January 4, 1991, an AT&T maintenance crew mistakenly cut through a fiber-optic cable in Newark, New Jersey, disrupting approximately 40 percent of AT&T's long-distance service into and out of New York.

Once severed, a fiber optic cable is not easily repaired. Splicing requires perfectly aligning the two optic cores along six different dimensions: not only the *x* (width), *y* (height), and *z* (depth) dimensions but also the three angular dimensions. If they are not aligned correctly, light leaks out, and the signal is weakened. In addition, the splice has to be strong enough to withstand vibration and constant changes in temperature for thousands of hours.

The splicing process used to take many hours and the use of a microscope. However, splices can now be performed in about three hours. An easier way to compensate for a cut or disrupted fiber-optic cable is to reroute the calls to other fiber-optic cables, and such alternate routes are now becoming more available.

Modems and telephone lines suffice for connecting widely separated computers that communicate in low-volume data. However, regular phone lines are often inadequate for high-volume transmission. Businesses that must daily transmit high volumes of data often rent or lease a dedicated line, which is specially prepared to reduce background noise and transmit at higher speeds.

Data transmission doesn't always require wires or cables every step of the way. Microwave signals, short radio waves that are transmitted between relay towers, are frequently used in telephone-communication systems. Businesses can employ microwave transmission to quickly and inexpensively relay data throughout a computer-communication system. Using such a transmission can be more affordable than leasing a dedicated telephone line.

Satellite communication enables users to send microwave computer data vast distances. Today, mainframe computers easily send data from one country to another via satellite transmission (Figure 6.12).

MULTIPLEXORS AND CONCENTRATORS

When multiple users are connected to a computer by separate lines, the computer continually polls, or checks, each station to see if there are data to be sent.

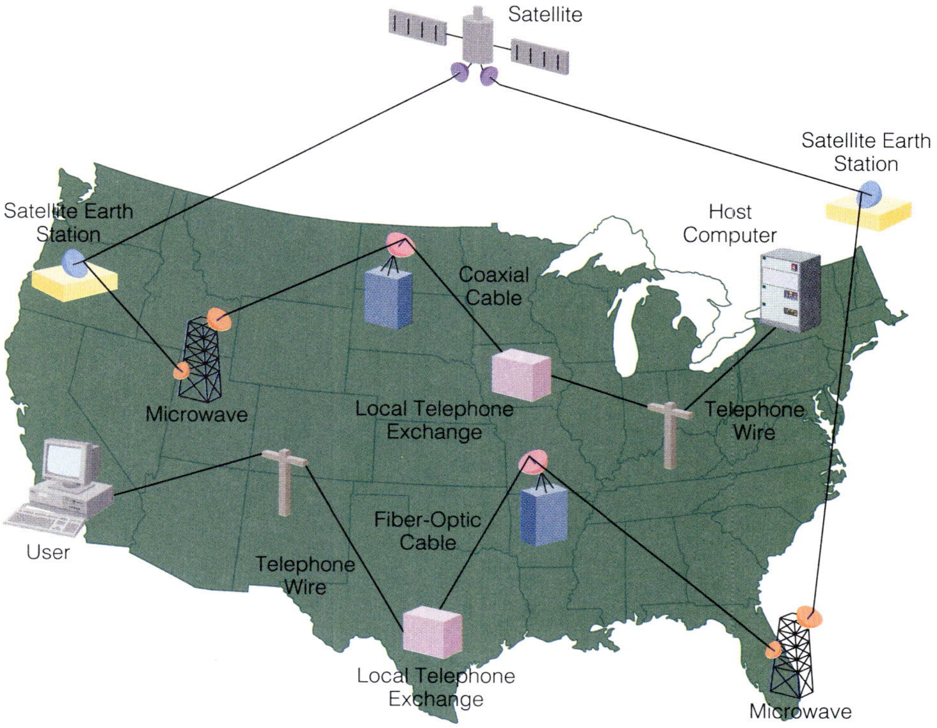

Figure 6.12
Satellite communication allows data to be sent over great distances. It can be connected to other communication networks utilizing telephone systems, microwave transmissions, or direct cable connections.

This **polling** process occurs many times each second (Figure 6.13). To increase the speed and efficiency of this system, especially when long-distance telephone lines are used, many businesses install special hardware called multiplexors and concentrators. These devices increase a communication system's efficiency by

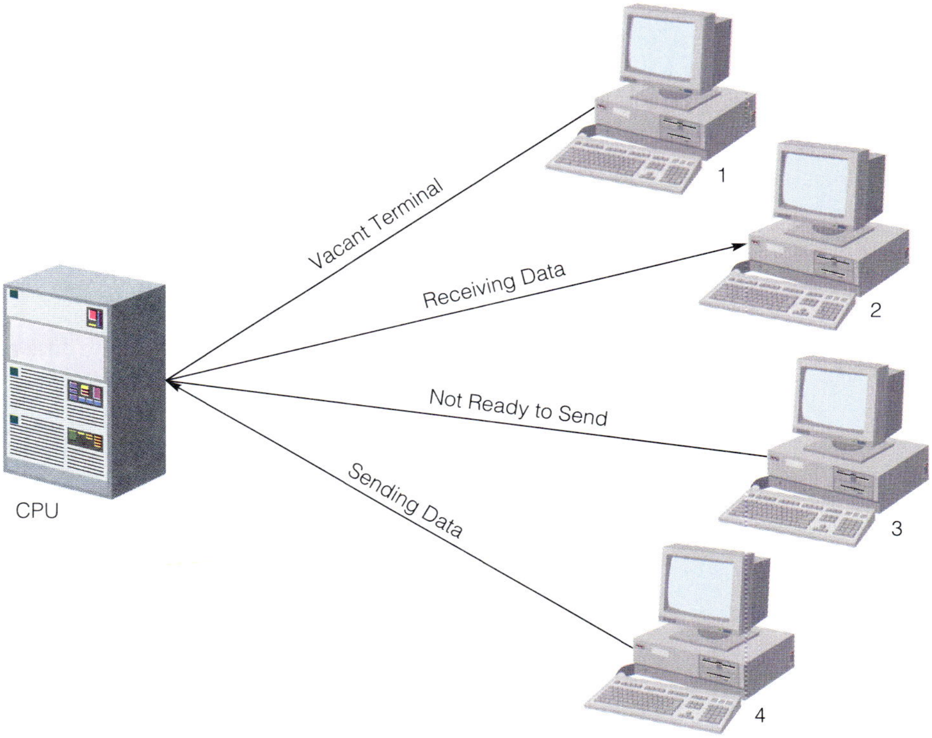

Figure 6.13
Multiple-line terminal communication with a computer. The computer is constantly checking each terminal to see if data are ready to be sent.

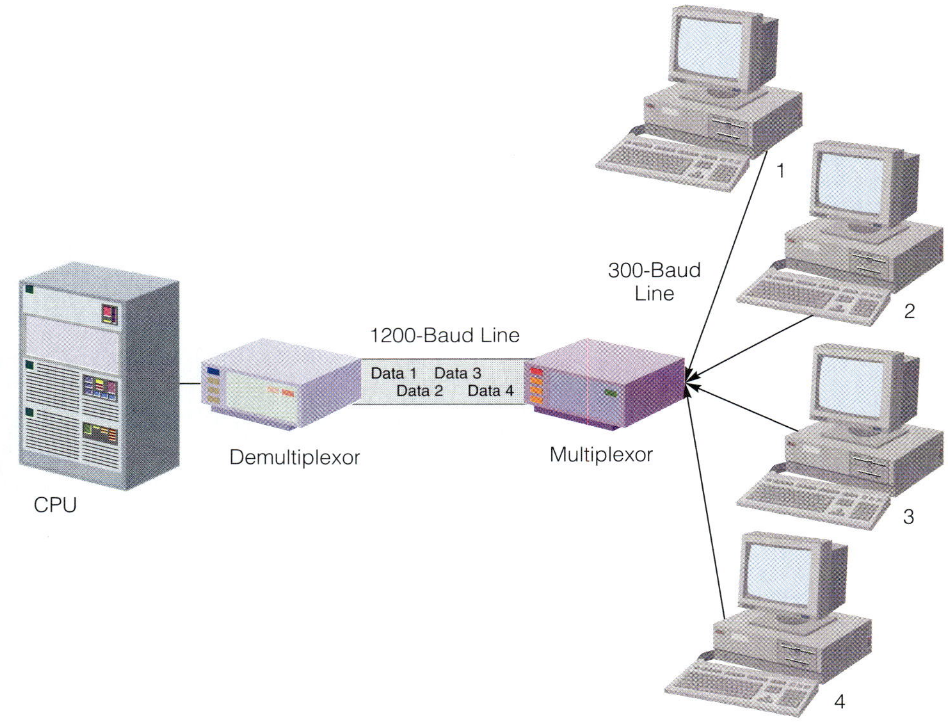

Figure 6.14
A multiplexor accepts input from several terminals, combines it, and sends it to the receiving computer where it is decombined.

letting more peripherals be connected to a computer at a lower cost per connection and by relieving the receiving computer's CPU of many housekeeping and control functions.

A **multiplexor** routes the output from several terminals or computers into a single channel (Figure 6.14). This allows one telephone link to carry a transmission that normally would require several links. It also permits faster baud transmission. For example, a multiplexor can route four 300-baud terminal lines into a 1200-baud link to a distant computer. The multiplexor allocates to each terminal line one-fourth of the fast line's capacity (see Figure 6.14).

The receiving computer demultiplexes, or breaks down, the transmission into its component messages and routes them to the proper application programs.

A **concentrator** is a multiplexor with built-in computer circuitry (Figure 6.15). It, too, combines several slow lines into one fast line but in a more efficient way. Concentrators give busy terminals more time than slow or unoccupied terminals.

Concentrators can be programmed to compress data, send the data over the telephone line, and then uncompress the data at the other end. And, unlike multiplexors, concentrators can detect errors and correct them. Concentrators can also convert messages from one binary code to another (from ASCII or EBCDIC, for example), allowing otherwise incompatible terminals to link to the same network.

FRONT-END PROCESSOR

A **front-end processor** is a minicomputer that, besides performing general-purpose processing, frees a DDP's mainframe computer from such time-consuming housekeeping tasks as polling terminals for data, synchronizing the message packet, and error checking (Figure 6.16).

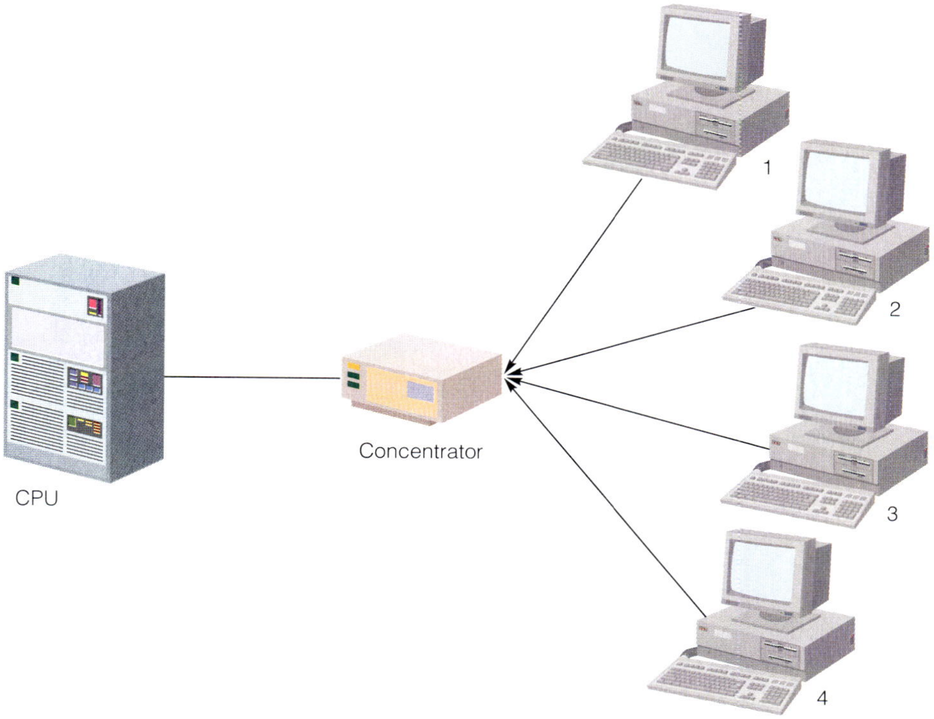

Figure 6.15
A concentrator is an intelligent multiplexor.

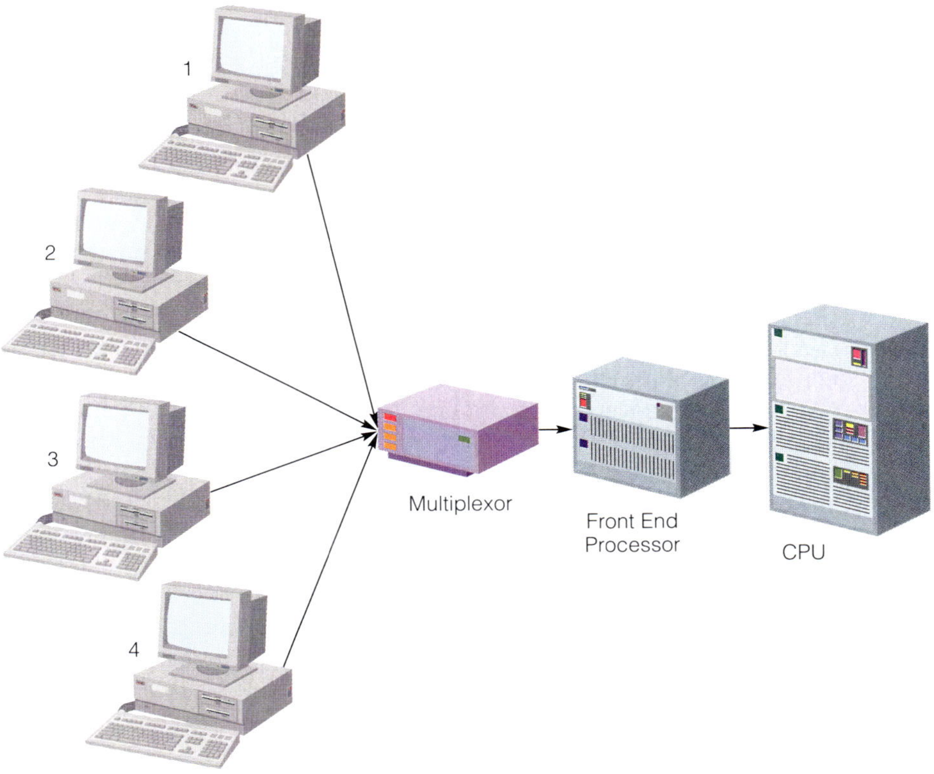

Figure 6.16
A front-end processor relieves the mainframe of many housekeeping tasks involved with data communications.

PERSONAL CASE PROGRESS

The GEnie

As Cliff and Joan install the modem board and software on one of their computers, they notice an advertising brochure about subscribing to an electronic on-line information service called GEnie—an information resource utility offered by General Electric.

GEnie includes a variety of features, including bulletin boards for special-interest groups in real estate, investment, law, medicine, and small business. In essence, each bulletin board is an arrangement by which individuals can use their modem to electronically post messages to other users on the GEnie system. Each of these bulletin boards offers a library of related software and text files that can be downloaded to the subscriber's computer. The software may be public domain or that provided by GEnie or various vendors. The text files may include documentation on how to perform some task or process. GEnie also offers NewsGrid, a feature providing recent news.

Most interesting to the Lucernes, however, is GEnie's Quotes Securities Database, which offers daily closing stock quotes. They find they can get historical quotes back to May 1985. GEnie also lets them create 10 theoretical portfolios with 100 stocks in each and tracks the daily gains and losses of these stocks. Clifford sees this feature as a way to test some of his stock market assumptions without actually making certain investments and incurring any actual losses.

GEnie comes with an interface program called the Aladdin shell, which the Lucernes can download and install on their computer. This interface makes the service easy to use and eliminates any need for training.

The Lucernes do a little research, comparing GEnie with other similar information and bulletin board services such as The Source and CompuServe. They find that numerous software companies such as Ashton-Tate, Borland, Microsoft, WordPerfect, and others also provide bulletin boards and various types of data communications with their products.

Clifford and Joan believe that a service will be worth the investment principally because it will give them help in using software that they run and information about the stock market. In the end, they choose GEnie, whose price is especially good. The monthly subscription is $4.95, and they will pay connect charges as low as $6 an hour during off-hours of the morning and evening. They will also get daily closing stock quotes free of any hourly charges. To keep their usage charges down, they decide to use the service no more than two hours a week.

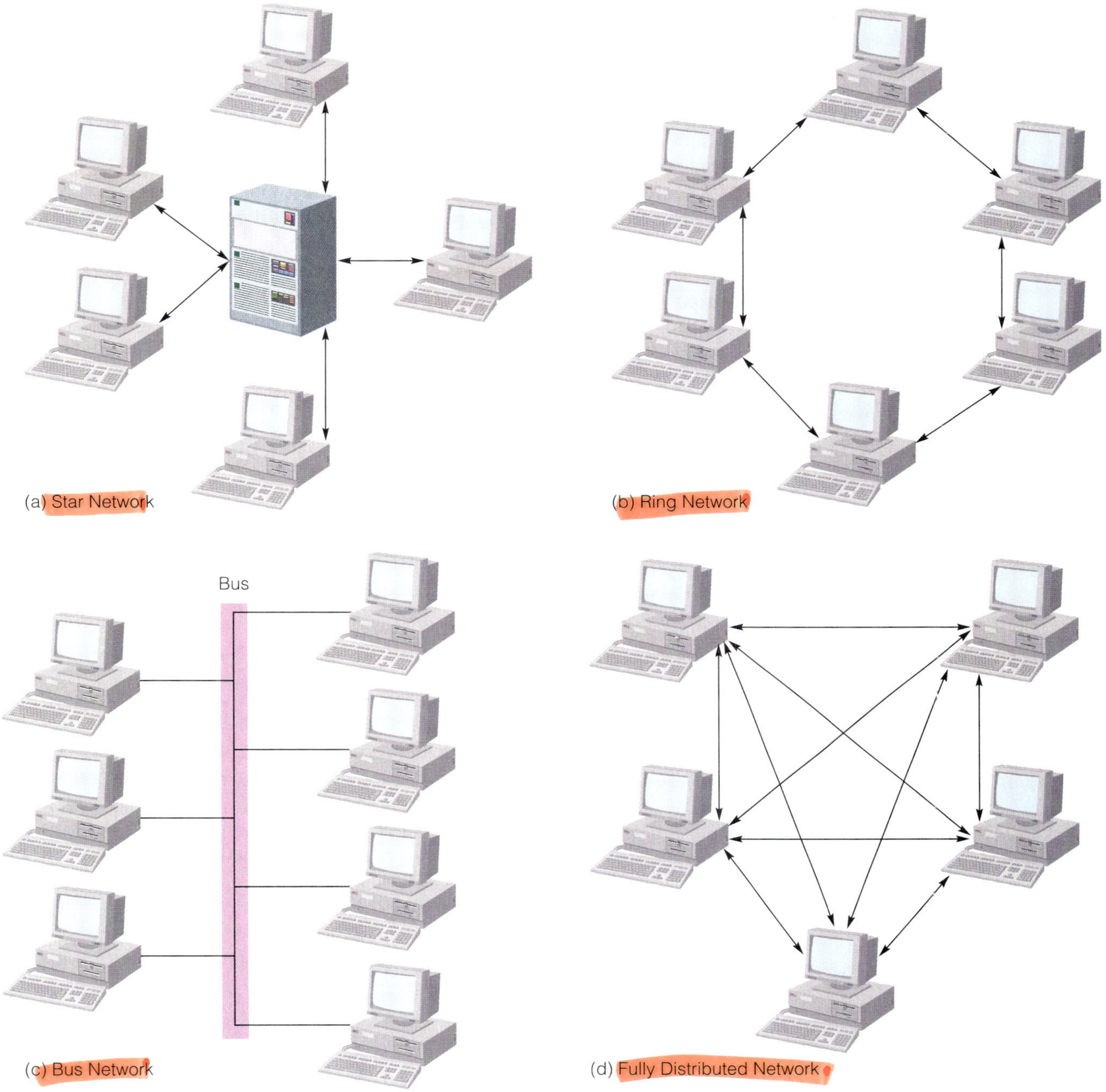

Figure 6.17
Network topologies: (a) star network, (b) ring network, (c) bus network, and (d) fully distributed network.

NETWORK TOPOLOGIES

The arrangement pattern of computers in a DDP is called the system's **network topology.** A network topology can assume many configurations (Figure 6.17)

In a **star network,** computer nodes radiate like spokes from a central, or hub, computer. A node on the network can be a computer of any size. Communication between spoke computers must pass through the hub computer. A bank with computers at several branches might use a star topology. Each branch processes its transactions with an on-site node, then stores the day's data on the master data files at the main-office hub computer.

A **ring network** joins computers in a circle. A message destined for a specific node travels to it through each node around the ring. Many ring networks control data exchange with a token-passing protocol. A **token** is a control signal that is passed from one node to the next, indicating which node is allowed to transmit. Only one token is passed around, so just one computer can transmit at a time. The major liability of a ring network is that if one node becomes inoperative the entire network fails.

A **bus network** connects several nodes or computers with a single cable along which computers can send messages in either direction. To send a message, a computer temporarily seizes control of the cable or bus and transmits. Bus networks are prone to message congestion (called contention) and delay and tend to be less efficient than other topologies.

In a **fully distributed network,** all nodes can communicate directly with each other. This topology speeds communication between computers, but the additional hardware and software costs often make it too expensive.

FUTURE TRENDS

Teleconferencing: The Wave of the Future?

Figure 6.18
Interest in teleconferencing by business has increased because international travel has become more expensive and more risky.

Since its introduction in 1969, the video telephone has enjoyed little success, even though long-distance rates have declined and the technology has gotten more sophisticated. However, the 1991 United Nations police action in Kuwait renewed some interest in it. Alarmed at the possibility of terrorism on international flights, some companies, like Unisys, decided to forbid to employees international travel for company-related work and turned to computer-based **teleconferencing** instead.

PictureTel is a leader in teleconference technology (Figure 6.18), selling its System 4000 for about $40,000 in 1991. Companies could either buy the system or rent what they needed for a given conference, including special telephone lines capable of carrying 768,000 bps (equivalent to about 12 simultaneous voice connections), equipment, facilities, and the services of operators skilled with the cameras and other machinery. The approximate cost of $3600 for a 2-hour teleconference was still cheaper than flying a team of executives to Europe.

PictureTel equipment also interfaces to VCRs and document scanners. It can link output from microcomputers and let users encrypt the transmission signal of a conference for security purposes.

PictureTel is currently working with Intel, the computer chip manufacturer, to develop a series of plug-in adapter cards for cheaper desktop conferencing. This new technology may eventually sell for as low as $60 a card.

Other companies that have developed equipment and support for video conferencing include US Sprint (Meeting Channel), Compression Labs, Matsushita, AT&T, and Sony. The major problem for these companies is achieving compatibility. Video phones and teleconferencing will not become as popular as the fax machine unless standards (especially data-compression standards) are developed and followed.

PERSONAL CASE REVISITED

Installing the Network

CLIFF and JOAN buy two more office computers to meet current demands and provide for growing future needs.

One of the primary goals that Cliff and Joan have in hooking the computers together is the ability to access and share the key data files that keep track of and coordinate the accounting for the many different items sold at each auction. As part of his research into networks, Cliff talks with his good friend Gerry Drake, a professor of data communications at State University who does extensive consulting for business networks.

After hearing what Cliff wants to do, Gerry tells him there are a number of systems from which to choose, ranging in price from $300 to $5000. He recommends an Ethernet-based LAN called LANtastic. LANtastic uses a peer-to-peer type of communication, in which any machine on the network can be used as a file server. It supports such features as file-and-record locking as well as the dial-up port that the Lucernes will want for a modem link-up to their home. It works at a speed of 10 megabits per second. With the number of computers that Cliff and Joan will be supporting, the response speed will be no different than that of a system that requires one computer to be dedicated to the file-serving function.

Gerry says the initial price will be about $600 for the operating system, wiring, and boards for two computers and about $200 for each additional node. He points out that this relatively inexpensive system will not support features found on more expensive, robust systems. Beyond file-and-record locking, security is not very elaborate, and the system will not perform the "roll back" function that resets the system to the state that it had before a particular problem occurred and allows for restoring the system.

CHAPTER REVIEW

In the past decade, intercomputer data communication has become vitally important in the corporate world. Telecommunication between computers usually occurs over some type of telephone network. To be transmitted, computer signals must be converted into and out of analog form by modems attached to the sending and receiving computers.

Data must be communicated over telephone lines in serial mode, or 1 bit at a time. Information can be transmitted between a computer and peripherals in parallel mode, or one character at a time. The transmission of data over a telephone line can be in simplex, half-duplex, or full-duplex form. Because users need to both send and receive data, computers usually transmit in either half-duplex or full-duplex mode.

A protocol is a set of transmitting rules. Asynchronous protocol transmits one character at a time and is the most common method of transmitting data. The synchronous method sends packets, or groups of characters, at a time. This protocol is most often used with IBM mainframe computers.

Communications software is a set of programs that handles the sending and receiving of data. It usually carries out such functions as terminal emulation, uploading and downloading files, and auto-dial and auto-answer.

The process of distributing and managing computer resources is called distributed data processing (DDP). A number of advantages and disadvantages are associated with DDP systems. Computer networks are connected by twisted-pair wires, coaxial cable, fiber-optic cables, dedicated telephone lines, microwave-communication links, or satellite-communication links.

Local area networks (LANs) let users share data files and high-cost peripherals and support features such as electronic mail. LANs are usually contained in one building. A LAN should provide for several levels of security.

Efficiency of communication is a major concern to network users. Multiplexors, concentrators, and front-end processors all help speed the process.

The topology of a computer network is the pattern of arrangement of the computers. Network topologies include the star, ring, bus, and fully distributed systems. Ring networks use a token to indicate which computer can transmit data.

KEY TERMS AND CONCEPTS

analog signal
asynchronous protocol
auto-answer
auto-dial
bandwidth
baud rate
bridge
bus network
coaxial cable
concentrator
data communications
demodulation
digital signal
distributed data processing (DDP)
downloading
dumb terminal
electronic mail
external modem
facilitator
fax (facsimile transmission) machine
fiber optics
front-end processor
full-duplex transmission
fully distributed network
gateway
half-duplex transmission
handshaking
internal modem
local area network (LAN)
modem
modulation
multiplexor
network topology
node
parallel transmission
polling
protocol
ring network
serial transmission
simplex transmission
star network
synchronous protocol
telecommunication
teleconferencing
terminal emulation
token
transmission speed
twisted-pair wiring
uploading

CHAPTER QUIZ

Multiple Choice

1. Which network topology is sometimes referred to as a hub network?
   a. Ring
   b. Star
   c. Bus network
   d. Fully distributed
   e. None of the above

2. Which network topology makes use of a token to control the computer that has access to the network?
   a. Ring
   b. Star
   c. Bus network
   d. Fully distributed
   e. None of the above

3. Which of the following statements is false?
   a. Digital communication commonly takes place using telephone lines.
   b. A modem is only used with fiber-optic cables.
   c. A digital signal still requires the use of at least one modem.
   d. All of the above
   e. None of the above

4. Which of the following is *not* a concern for security on a LAN?
   a. Which word processor is used?
   b. Does the person have read/write privileges to this file?
   c. Does this password have access rights to this directory?
   d. None of the above is a security concern for a LAN.

5. Which of the following is usually false with respect to telephone-transmitted computer links?
   a. Data are usually transmitted digitally.
   b. Simplex transmission is frequently used.
   c. Synchronous transmission is infrequently used.
   d. All of the above

True/False

6. Fiber-optic cables can be used for transmitting digital data.

7. Only an external modem can be used on an open-bus computer.

8. The grade, or bandwidth, of a telephone line dictates the speed of a data transmission.

9. The "handshake" is simply the set of rules that are followed when transmitting data.

10. Downloading refers to copying a file from a computer and transferring it to your computer via a communication link.

Answers

1. b 2. a 3. d 4. a 5. d 6. t 7. f 8. t 9. t 10. t

Exercises

1. Define the following terms:
   a. Distributed data processing
   b. Telecommunications
   c. Protocol
   d. Handshaking
   e. Network topology
   f. LAN

2. The transmission of any data over a communications link is called ___________.

3. The process of translating a digital signal to an analog signal is called ___________.

4. The device that performs the modulation–demodulation process is called a(n) ___________.

5. The measurement in units of ___________ is used to measure the number of bits per second (bps) for data transmission.

6. Data transmitted 1 byte at a time refers to ___________ transmission of data, whereas data transmitted 1 bit at a time refers to ___________ transmission.

7. The grade, or ___________, of a communications line determines the speed at which data can be sent.

8. The ___________ data transmission only sends or receives data.

9. The ___________ data transmission both sends and receives data simultaneously.

10. The ___________ data transmission sends and receives data, but not simultaneously.

11. The ___________ transmission protocol sends information one character at a time.

12. The process of preceding and following a character with stop and start bits is a process called ___________.

13. The process of sending a file from your computer to another computer via a communications link is called ___________.

14. The process of distributing computer power and then managing a network is called ___________.

15. A computer in a network is sometimes referred to as a(n) ___________.

16. The medium usually used to connect telephones is referred to as ___________.

17. A cousin of this communications medium is also used to connect televisions.

18. The process called ___________ is used to check to see if a terminal has data to send.

19. A(n) ___________ is a device that uses a high-speed communications line to combine low-speed messages.

20. A(n) ___________ is a device that can allocate line time based on terminal activity.

21. A(n) ____________ network topology has each computer connected to one in front and one in back.

22. A(n) ____________ is a control signal passed from one computer to the next to determine which computer on the network can send data.

23. A(n) ____________ network topology connects several computers with one cable.

24. The biggest advantage of a LAN is the ability to share ____________ between users.

25. The areas of security that should be addressed for a LAN are ____________, ____________, ____________, and ____________.

IN YOUR OWN CASE

1. What uses could you make of a computer with a modem? What data services or communications abilities would this open up for you as a student, in your employment, or in some personal capacity?

2. If you already own or have access to a computer with a modem, what are you currently doing with it? How might you expand your use of data communications?

3. Explore the modem market. What features are offered? What features do you believe are desirable? What are the relative costs of modems that transmit at various speeds?

4. Explore the current use of LANs at your school or workplace. Is there any way in which introducing LAN technology might improve the quality of your work or education? Where would you want to introduce it? How would it make a difference?

QUESTIONS FOR THOUGHT

1. In a typical week, where do you already encounter data-communication technology? Where might you expect to find it in the next few years? In 10 years?

2. Ten years from now, what other uses do you expect to emerge for data-communication technology?

7

INTRODUCTION TO DATABASE MANAGEMENT

CHAPTER OBJECTIVES

After completing this chapter, you should be able to

- **Contrast the traditional approach to information processing with the database approach**
- **Discuss the relationship between a database management system (DBMS) and a database**
- **Discuss the advantages and disadvantages of a DBMS**
- **Describe the functional parts of a DBMS**
- **Tell what a database administrator does**
- **Discuss some database organization methods**
- **Describe the key elements in an effective database**

THE EVOLUTION OF DATABASE MANAGEMENT

1957	IBM introduces RAMAC, the first computing device to include a direct-access storage device (DASD) for magnetically storing disk files in its hardware configuration. It can store up to 5 million characters of data.
1964	The term *database,* first used by U.S. military, appears in the literature.
1964–1968	There is dramatic development and increased use of more advanced programming languages and complex operating systems.
1969	IBM introduces IMS, a hierarchical database.
1970s	With sharply dropping costs, increased capacity of DASDs leads to quick, cost-effective systems for accessing data.
1971	E. F. Codd publishes "A Relational Model of Data for Large Shared Data Banks" in *Communications of the ACM.* He presents the underlying principles of relational database theory. CODASYL Systems Committee sets standards for the network database structure.
1979	The number of hard disk devices in the United States tops 179,000. Combined total storage: approximately 18,887 gigabytes (G) of information.
1981	Ashton-Tate introduces dBASE II, the first relational database for microcomputers.
1984	Ashton-Tate introduces dBASE III. The number of hard disk devices tops 1 million. Combined total storage: approximately 56,400G.
1985	IBM introduces DB2, a relational database for mainframe computers.
1988	Ashton-Tate introduces dBASE IV.
1990	Ashton-Tate introduces dBASE IV Release 1.1.

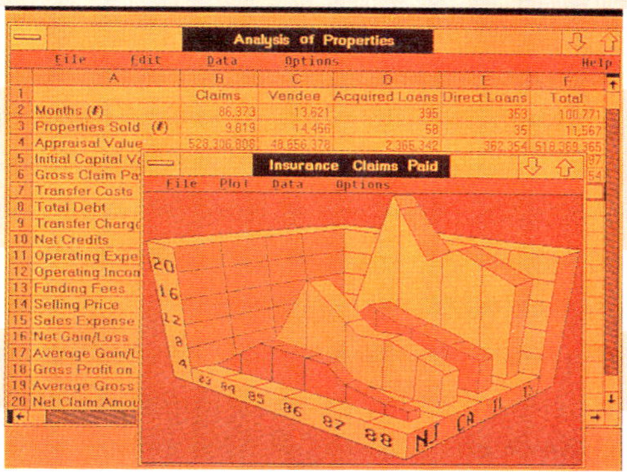

Analysis of Properties
File Edit Data Options Help
Claims Vendee Acquired Loans Direct Loans Total
Months (#)
Properties Sold (#)
Appraisal Value
Initial Capital Va
Gross Claim Pa
Transfer Costs
Total Debt
Transfer Charg
Net Credits
Operating Expe
Operating Incon
Funding Fees
Selling Price
Sales Expense
Net Gain/Loss
Average Gain/L
Gross Profit on
Average Gross
Net Claim Amou
Insurance Claims Paid
File Plot Data Options

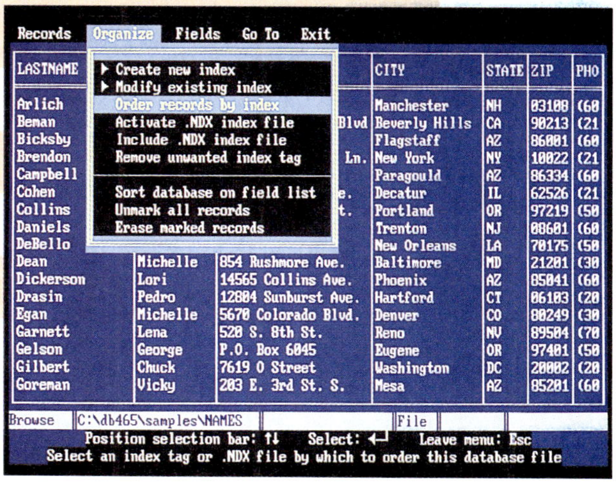

Records Organize Fields Go To Exit
Create new index
Modify existing index
Order records by index
Activate .NDX index file
Include .NDX index file
Remove unwanted index tag
Sort database on field list
Unmark all records
Erase marked records
LASTNAME CITY STATE ZIP PHO
Arlich Manchester NH 03108
Beman Beverly Hills CA 90213
Bicksby Flagstaff AZ 86001
Brendon New York NY 10022
Campbell Paragould AZ 86334
Cohen Decatur IL 62526
Collins Portland OR 97219
Daniels Trenton NJ 08601
DeBello New Orleans LA 70175
Dean Michelle 854 Rushmore Ave. Baltimore MD 21201
Dickerson Lori 14565 Collins Ave. Phoenix AZ 85041
Drasin Pedro 12804 Sunburst Ave. Hartford CT 06103
Egan Michelle 5670 Colorado Blvd. Denver CO 80249
Garnett Lena 520 S. 8th St. Reno NV 89504
Gelson George P.O. Box 6045 Eugene OR 97401
Gilbert Chuck 7619 O Street Washington DC 20002
Goreman Vicky 203 E. 3rd St. S. Mesa AZ 85201
Browse C:\db465\samples\NAMES File
Position selection bar: ↑↓ Select: ↵ Leave menu: Esc
Select an index tag or .NDX file by which to order this database file

PERSONAL CASE

Database Management and the College Administrator

WESLEY FRAMPTON is in charge of registration and class scheduling for Meredith College, a small liberal arts school. Meredith offers its 2200 students baccalaureate degrees in 20 different disciplines. Over the years, it has become famous for the quality of its undergraduate instruction, and more than 55 percent of its graduates go on to graduate programs around the country.

The registration and scheduling process has been a time-consuming manual procedure ever since the school was founded in the 1870s. At this time, each student signs up for an average of five classes, requiring Wes to keep track of roughly 11,000 (2200 × 5) class assignments, as well as other information. Wes is interested in using his microcomputer to expedite this process. He has talked with a number of vendors providing software designed specifically for his type of needs and has found a database management package written in dBASE IV that the college can afford.

Wes has decided to try to solve the registration and scheduling problem using this package and thinks it may also solve the information problems of other administrators at the college. The package does not have all features found on mainframe packages, but Wes thinks it may be adequate.

A **database** is a collection of logically related records or files. A database consolidates many records previously stored in separate files so that a common pool of records serves as a single central file for many processing applications needing that type of data. A **database management system (DBMS)** is the collection of hardware and software that organizes the data and provides access to the database. The software portion of a DBMS provides the mechanisms used to create a computerized database file; to add, delete, or change data within the file; to change how data are stored within database files; to search the database for data that meet certain criteria; and to perform other data-handling chores.

Some DBMSs also have a hardware portion. The hardware portion usually consists of a small computer whose role is to keep track of the addresses of records in indexes. Only DBMS applications that have a need for very fast record access make use of this hardware feature because it raises the cost of the DBMS substantially.

The DBMS for large business organizations requires a number of staff members and large expenditures for hardware, software, and the training of employees. Two examples of mainframe database management software for business are IBM's Information Management System (IMS) and DB2.

DBMSs can also run on microcomputers with software packages such as dBASE III Plus and dBASE IV. These programs require far less expertise and training to use than do their mainframe cousins.

In this chapter, we first examine the traditional manner of supplying information to a user from files not integrated into one database and then the database approach. We discuss the parts of a DBMS, the database itself, and the role played by the database administrator.

PROGRAMMING: THE TRADITIONAL APPROACH TO INFORMATION PROCESSING

The **traditional approach** to providing information to an individual user or organization is file-oriented. Each application or department has its own set of master and transaction files, which are used for storing, processing, and retrieving data (Figure 7.1). Although each application data file is divided into records and fields (as described in Chapter 1), no particular correspondence exists between the organization of one data file and another. The files and programs for each application are designed specifically for that application, and no provision has been made for sharing data between applications or departments of the organization. Each functional area of an organization has its own set of files

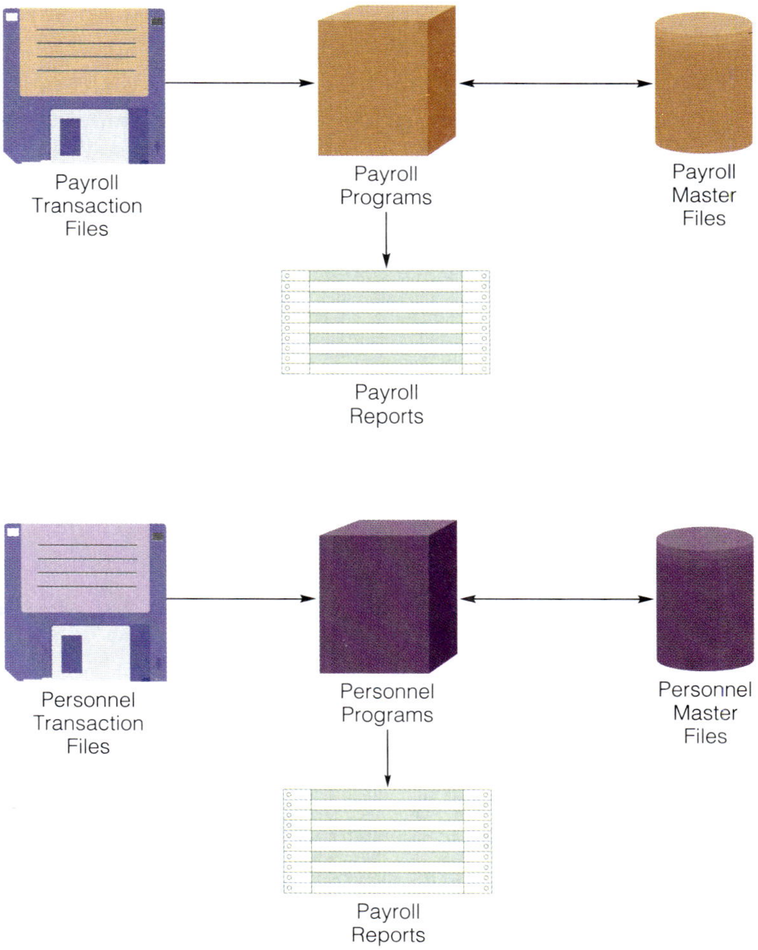

Figure 7.1
With the traditional approach to information processing, each application has its own set of master and transaction files.

and programs for manipulating that data. For example, if a person's zip code is changed in the company's personnel department files, the zip code is not then automatically changed in the company's payroll department files. Similarly, if the personnel department's data fields are altered so that staff can enter a nine-character zip code instead of the older five-character version, no similar change may necessarily be made in payroll's data fields.

The traditional approach centers around separate transaction and master files for each separate application. The manner in which data are stored **(record structure)** cannot readily be altered. For instance, once a file has been created with a certain number of fields, each of a certain length, neither the number nor size of the fields may easily be changed.

PROBLEMS OF THE TRADITIONAL APPROACH

Although still frequently used, the traditional approach has some built-in problems. These involve data redundancy, data integrity, interdependency of programs and data files, and lack of flexibility.

Data Redundancy Storing identical information in multiple files is called **data redundancy.** This practice means that the same data have to be recorded by more than one application. The record structures in Figure 7.2 show that a number of fields are identical between payroll and personnel files. Storing and maintaining the same data in two files rather than one is obviously more costly than doing so for one file because it requires double storage space and double the amount of work.

Data Integrity Keeping data of these common fields identical between applications is also a problem. Data such as a person's zip code should be identical from one file to another, but when separate files are kept, discrepancies often develop. When data in a specific entity's records are inconsistent from one file to another, **data integrity** is impaired. Lack of data integrity produces errors in the reports generated from one file or the other and causes various problems.

Figure 7.2
The fields typically found in the payroll and personnel master files.

Payroll File Fields	Personnel File Fields
Social Security Number	Social Security Number
Department Number	Department Number
Name	Name
Address	Address
City	City
State	State
Zip	Zip
Regular Pay Rate	Job Title
Overtime Pay Rate	Date Hired
Number of Exemptions	
Marital Code	
Quarter-to-Date Gross Pay	
Year-to-Date Gross Pay	
Year-to-Date Net Pay	

For instance, Joe, an employee of your company, moves. It's around the end of the year, and Joe wants to make certain that he receives his W-2 form (summary of earnings for the year that is sent to the IRS for tax purposes) at his new address. Joe is a very busy person but takes the time to let the payroll department know of his changed address. Naturally, he assumes that any notices the company sends him will now reach him at the new address. Not realizing that the other departments keep entirely separate records, Joe stops receiving notices from personnel about possible advancement within the company.

Interdependency of Program and Data Files Another problem with the traditional approach to information processing is that changing the characteristics of the fields within an established file is often difficult or impossible. If a field is to be added, deleted, or changed, a new file must first be created that reflects the desired change. A program must then be written that reads a record from the old file and copies this record in the new format to the new file. If a new field has been added to the record, the information that will go in that field must be entered manually for each record.

Lack of Flexibility In a traditional information system, changing some characteristic of one file is often extremely difficult because any programs or other files that access the first file must also be changed. This reduces the **flexibility** (the ability to quickly make a change) of such systems. Because every report generated by a system requires a special program to be written, operators find it extremely difficult to respond quickly to requests for special reports. Often the complexity of the program and its logic design make the cost of obtaining the report greater than its benefits.

Still another problem is that each field contained in a file must be defined perfectly so that the program can properly access the file. This means that any time a field is added, deleted, or changed in a file, any program that accesses the changed file must be changed so that the program's description of the file matches the changed file.

THE POWER OF DATABASE MANAGEMENT SYSTEMS

Databases and DBMSs respond to these traditional problems, both in the mainframe environment and on microcomputer systems. In essence, the DBMS integrates many formerly separate sets of data and provides a complete set of programs that serves as the interface between one or many users and their various applications. In a DBMS, data can be created, deleted, or changed in one integrated database that can issue a wide variety of routine and special reports. The term *integrated* refers to the ability of the DBMS to logically relate one record with another such that any data related to a specific topic can easily be retrieved via simple requests to the DBMS (Figure 7.3). In a large organization using mainframe computers, DBMS users gain access to data by requesting reports via some application program. On a microcomputer DBMS system, the user typically has more direct access, entering instructions at the keyboard.

The database approach to information processing also allows greater data independence, eliminates data redundancy, increases data integrity, integrates data from various files, enhances security, and standardizes reports.

Data Independence With the traditional approach to information processing, the data needed for a separate application were handled in a separate set of transaction–master files. With database information processing, all data needed

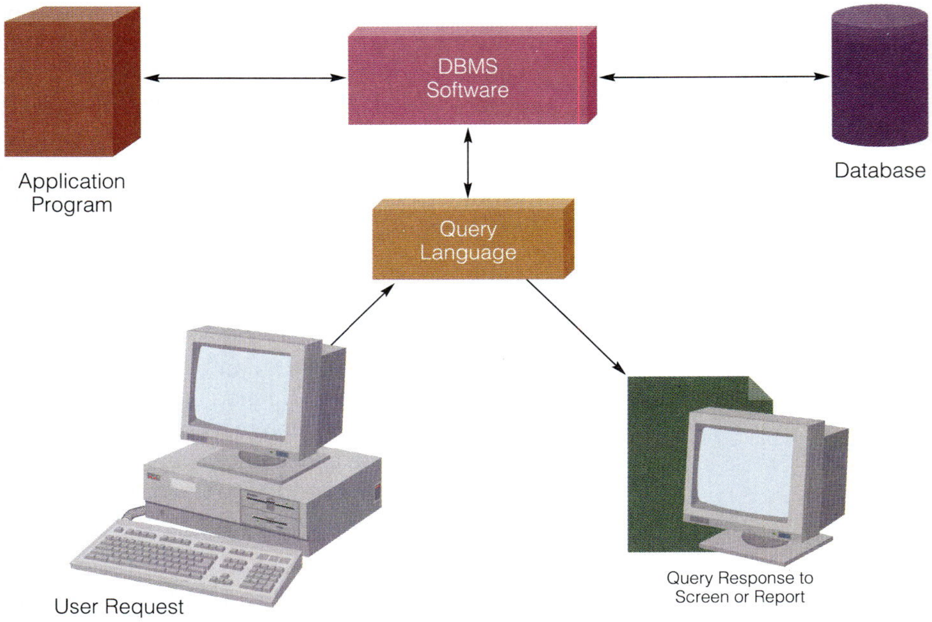

Figure 7.3
The DBMS for many mainframe applications acts as the interface between a user (or application program) and the database.

for a number of related applications can be stored in one general database. If any changes must be made to the data, they can be made without changing each program that accesses the database. This is possible because a DBMS provides for two views of the data stored in it.

The **physical view** of the database is related to the actual location of the data on a storage device. Experts who lay out the inner workings of the DBMS are aware of this view, but ordinary users aren't aware of it and do not need to be. The **logical view** represents records and fields of data as they are needed by the user or programmer. All that the user must know is the name of the file and data fields within the file that he or she wishes to access. DBMS software accesses the data and makes it available to the user.

Eliminated Data Redundancy and Increased Data Integrity Because all data related to a number of related applications are stored in one place, if a piece of datum must be changed, it only has to be changed in one location.

Integrated Data from Other Files A user can gather data from a number of files within the database and apply this combined data to a particular report or other application. This is done by creating relationships between records in one file and records in other files. This greatly enhances flexibility.

Enhanced Security Through Management of Data Access Advanced DBMS packages can be instructed to examine a user's request for data and verify that the particular user is allowed to "see" the data found in a requested field. This ability to deny unauthorized users access to restricted data greatly enhances **data security** and further ensures data integrity.

Standardized Reports and Queries A DBMS allows a user to request that a program produce a standardized report. It also lets the user pose shorter queries (requests for data in a specified format). The database can be used by a personnel program that was written to generate a report of employees' birthdays so that a small gift can be sent to them. Or it can be queried to list or count selected records of individuals who meet certain criteria related to age or gender.

PERSONAL CASE PROGRESS

Getting Information from Student Records

One reason Wes wants a DBMS is reflected in a recent incident. Wes had received a call from the college president, who had received a request from a data-reporting agency that provides information for the *Chronicle of Higher Education,* a weekly journal for colleges and universities. The agency wants some demographic information about students in independent colleges and wants Meredith in its sample. The information, which the agency is seeking, is the number of men and women in each class (freshman, sophomore, junior, and senior).

Unfortunately, the request sat on the president's desk for a few days, and by the time it reached Wes, he had only about a week to respond.

The information itself was contained in three five-drawer filing cabinets. The student records were stored in manila folders and in alphabetic order. All Wes had to do was go through each folder, determine the gender and class of each student, and record that data on a sheet of paper, but he didn't have time to do that. In the end, he had to hire a work–study student to do it. It took many hours and was not the most exciting job the student had ever had.

How would Wes have handled the request if his student records had been on a DBMS? Instead of leafing through thousands of folders, Wes would have sat briefly at his computer keyboard, accessing the student database pictured in Figure 7.4. Each row in the figure depicts a record, and each column depicts a field of data within the record. The class information is recorded as FRE for freshman, SOP for sophomore, JUN for junior, and SEN for senior. For the gender of an individual, F is female, and M is male.

For the freshman class, the actual commands that Wes would have entered, to receive the information he was seeking, would have been:

```
.USE STUDENTS
.COUNT FOR CLASS = 'FRE' AND SEX = 'M'
.COUNT FOR CLASS = 'FRE' AND SEX = 'F'
```

As a result, a count of all male and female freshman records would have come up on the screen. The entire process would have taken at most about 10 minutes.

Figure 7.4
Portions of a student database file, which Wes could have used.

SS#	Major	Last Name	First Name	Sex	Address
323-45-6732	SOC	Anderson	Jane	F	1536 N. Delmore Lane
345-23-4959	ACC	Billingham	George	M	113 Delane Dr.
567-36-7948	HIS	Boling	Susan	F	6789 W. University
283-85-3905	MTH	Clayburn	Cliff	M	2345 N. Adelaide
203-59-2848	PHI	Crane	Fraser	M	1676 W. Freud
345-56-2342	SOC	Croxton	Roberta	F	234 N. Main St.
202-76-4848	ENG	Doring	Fran	F	1674 W. Gregory

PARTS OF A DATABASE MANAGEMENT SYSTEM

The programs of a DBMS comprise four parts: a query language, a report generator, a data-definition language, and a data-manipulation language.

QUERY LANGUAGE

For most DBMS users, the query language is the easiest way to get information from the database, especially when routine periodic reports do not have exactly what is needed. The **query language** lets you interrogate the DBMS about specific data.

For example, suppose you are using the DBMS of dBASE III Plus to track an inventory of merchandise. You have a method for deciding when to reorder certain items when the number of those items in stock falls below a certain number, which you call the "reorder value." Here is a query you might want to pose to find out if any items need to be reordered:

> List all inventory items that have an on-hand value less than the reorder value.

Here is a query you might pose in order to keep your eye on your "big ticket" items, to ensure that no major pilferage is occurring:

> List all inventory items that have a total inventory value greater than $7500.

(The inventory value is calculated by multiplying the unit cost by the number on hand.) Learning to prepare such queries requires just a few hours of introduction to the dBASE III Plus package and its query language. Figure 7.5 shows the structure of a dBASE III Plus inventory file for this example. The actual commands you would enter to produce the queries are as follows:

```
USE INVENTRY
LIST FOR ONHAND<REORDER
LIST FOR PRICE*ONHAND>7500
```

Figure 7.6 shows the results of the requests.

Figure 7.5
The structure of the dBASE INVENTRY inventory file. This structure indicates the type of data and the size of each field within each record contained in a database file.

```
Structure for database: B:Inventry.dbf
Number of data records: 25
Date of last update: 01-01-92
Field  Field Name  Type       Width  Dec
    1  INVID       Character   10
    2  NAME        Character   36
    3  ONHAND      Numeric      4
    4  REORDER     Numeric      4
    5  OPTIMUM     Numeric      7      2
    6  PRICE       Numeric      7      2
**Total**                      69
```

Record#	INVID	NAME	ONHAND	REORDER	OPTIMUM	PRICE
1	3625a1	crt lamp	13	50	100	149.00
6	3970-8a1	multipurpose back shelf	25	30	50	110.00
7	4400a1	workstations	9	12	20	699.00
8	4430a1	workstations	5	8	15	650.00
9	4440	triangle extension	15	18	20	185.00
10	4442	rectangle extension	100	120	150	175.00
12	4446	wristrest	35	45	50	39.00
13	4838	footrest	120	130	150	35.00
14	4858a1	manager's chair	8	10	12	549.00
15	4857	associate's chair	12	15	18	359.00
16	4856	clerical chair	33	40	54	299.00
17	4765	associate's chair	55	60	75	340.00
18	4447a1	copyholder	88	92	99	120.00
19	4270	42" customizer	30	40	45	190.00

(a)

Record#	INVID	NAME	ONHAND	REORDER	OPTIMUM	PRICE
3	8093a1	serial microbuffer	45	30	100	379.00
5	6582a1	computer vacuum	85	75	120	139.00
10	4442	rectangle extension	100	120	150	175.00
16	4856	clerical chair	33	40	54	299.00
17	4765	associate's chair	55	60	75	340.00
18	4447a1	copyholder	88	92	99	120.00
30	4288a1	suspension bar	4853	21	34	33.00
42	7177a1	tape i.d. system	1000	900	1000	115.00
44	2955	applesaver	89	92	95	99.00
66	7180	data strike data eraser	110	120	160	69.00
69	6580	portable computer vacuum	99	120	135	112.00
100	4003	84" high data storage	18	36	84	575.00

(b)

Figure 7.6

Output from several queries to a dBASE III Plus inventory file: (a) LIST FOR ONHAND<REORDER. (b) LIST FOR PRICE*ONHAND>7500.

REPORT GENERATOR

Report generators are most frequently found in microcomputer-based DBMS packages. A **report generator** greatly simplifies generating a formatted report with appropriate report headings, page numbers, report date, column headings, grand totals, and so on. Figure 7.7 shows an example of a report generated using the dBASE III Plus report generator with the inventory file.

Page no. 1
01/01/92

Inventory Sales Report

Item	Description	Price	Units Sold	Extension
3625a1	crt lamp	149.00	9	1341.00
3970-8a1	multipurpose back shelf	110.00	5	550.00
4270	42" customizer	190.00	88	16720.00
4271	72" customizer	250.00	2	500.00
4272a1	42" side extension	115.00	50	5750.00
4273	72" side extension	135.00	1	135.00
4276	flat shelf	68.00	85	5780.00
4278a1	suspension bar	39.00	45	1755.00
4279	back extension foot	40.00	9	360.00
4400a1	workstations	699.00	9	6291.00
4430a1	workstations	650.00	5	3250.00
4440	triangle extension	185.00	2	370.00
4442	rectangle extension	175.00	7	1225.00
4444	copyholder	99.00	55	5445.00
4446	wristrest	39.00	0	0.00
4447a1	copyholder	120.00	18	2160.00
4545a1	ready files set	39.50	20	790.00
4765	associate's chair	340.00	55	18700.00
4838	footrest	35.00	12	420.00
4856	clerical chair	299.00	28	8372.00
4857	associate's chair	359.00	35	12565.00
4858a1	manager's chair	549.00	5	2745.00
6137a1	IBM nylon cartridge ribbon	5.95	10	59.50
6582a1	computer vacuum	139.00	85	11815.00
8093a1	serial microbuffer	379.00	45	17055.00
Total		5208.45	685	124153.50

Figure 7.7
A finished report using the dBASE III Plus report generator.

DATA-DEFINITION LANGUAGE

The **data-definition language (DDL)** defines the logical structure (or **schema**) of the database. The schema defines the characteristics of records within a file: the fields to be contained in each record, their names, the type of data that can be stored in the field, and the field length.

A **subschema** is the way in which a specific application program or user is allowed to access the data found in a file. It can limit access to fields and define the access rights (read-only or read-with-write privileges) of specific programs or users. For instance, in a payroll application, a payroll clerk should be able to field bona fide questions from employees about their paychecks. To answer these questions, a subschema may therefore let the clerk view fields such as pay rate, hours worked, gross pay, net pay, and year-to-date totals. However, the same subschema might prevent the clerk from changing any of these values.

DO DATABASES INVADE THE RIGHT TO PRIVACY?

In 1990 Lotus Corporation announced plans to commercially develop a database that was to include demographic data on 120 million American consumers. This information would be sold to small businesses who could use it to target their business contacts. Called Market Place, the package was to be distributed on CD ROM. After its announcement, the company received more than 30,000 requests from people wanting to strike their names from the database.

The furor ignited by the announcement of the product illustrates the concern that many individuals feel about data collected about them by a third party. Most people were not concerned that the data had been collected but how that data might potentially have been used.

The data to be contained in the database included name, address, age range, gender, marital status, dwelling type, estimated household income (range), product or life-style category, and shopping habits. It did not include telephone numbers, credit data, purchase history, actual income, or actual age.

Lotus Corporation had planned to tailor the database to the needs of various small businesses, selling it in 5000-name units. To prevent the product's getting into the wrong hands, potential buyers would have been required to sign a contract guaranteeing ethical usage of the data. Potential buyers also would have been checked against a "known violators" list and other business databases to ensure that they were legitimate businesses. Privacy advocates, however, pointed out that this information could be mixed with other databases.

Much of the concern over this particular product could be described by the phrases "too little too late" or "locking the barn after the horse was stolen." Most of this type of data has been available to medium- and large-size businesses for years. This type of data has been collected, updated, and combined with data from other vendors for years. A whole discipline called *geodemographics* has evolved to track the purchase characteristics of anyone who makes a credit purchase that can be later tracked by computer. This type of data has then been analyzed to generate purchase characteristics of just about all neighborhoods in the United States. About 20 different purchase profiles have been developed by the firms manipulating these data to predict purchase patterns of differing neighborhoods. This information is routinely sold to any business that wants it as "consumer profile" data.

Some grocery stores that let consumers buy their staples with a credit card routinely make this information available to market research firms, thereby avoiding the 2 to 3 percent handling costs usually charged for accepting credit cards. This type of data is not anonymous. That is, it can be tracked directly to the individual who purchased those goods using the credit card.

A number of attempts have been made to enact legislation, like that currently in effect in Europe, to place controls over how this type of data is managed and distributed by business. So far, however, these attempts have been thwarted.

DATA-MANIPULATION LANGUAGE

The **data-manipulation language (DML)** includes all commands that let a user store, retrieve, change, delete, or sort data or records within the database. The following shows some common dBASE III Plus commands and what they let the user do:

BROWSE	Views a file and specifies the fields to be included.
CREATE	Defines a dBASE file
DISPLAY	Displays a record or a group of records to the screen.
LIST	Displays all records or a group of records that meet certain criteria.
SORT	Reorders how records are stored in the file.

Each command can be customized further with additional information about the fields to be included or certain values to be used in executing the command. The DML evaluates all requests for data that have been issued through the query language of the DBMS.

In many microcomputer-based DBMS systems, the DDL and DML are combined into one language, which is usually referred to as the DML. A separate DDL is most commonly found in mainframe-based DBMS systems where the need for many different users to access a single database and the subsequent need for security is far greater than it is in microcomputer systems.

THE DATABASE ADMINISTRATOR

The data contained in a database are extremely important to both small and large organizations. In large organizations, however, more people have access to the database, make changes to the database, and take actions that can directly or indirectly harm the data contained in the database. In such cases, a **database administrator (DBA)** is usually appointed by management and provided with a staff that works with users to create, maintain, and safeguard the data in the database. For a microcomputer-based DBMS, it falls on the individual user to do what a DBA does for the larger company.

A DBA in any environment has several important roles. These include maintaining a data dictionary, a transaction log, configuration control, security, and proper backup of the database (Figure 7.8).

DEVELOPING AND MAINTAINING A DATA DICTIONARY

Because a database can be used by multiple users, keeping data names unique within an application is important. The **data dictionary** defines the meaning of each piece of datum (each field) in the database; it includes data names (names of fields), type of data, and field size and describes any interrelationships between one piece of datum and another.

Many DBMS systems now combine the DDL with an active data dictionary, which the DBMS uses as a reference tool. When a data item is requested, the DBMS automatically refers to the data dictionary to determine the location of the requested data.

MAINTAINING A TRANSACTION LOG

A **transaction log** contains a complete audit trail of all activity of a database for a given period of time. This log aids in the backup process if any data are

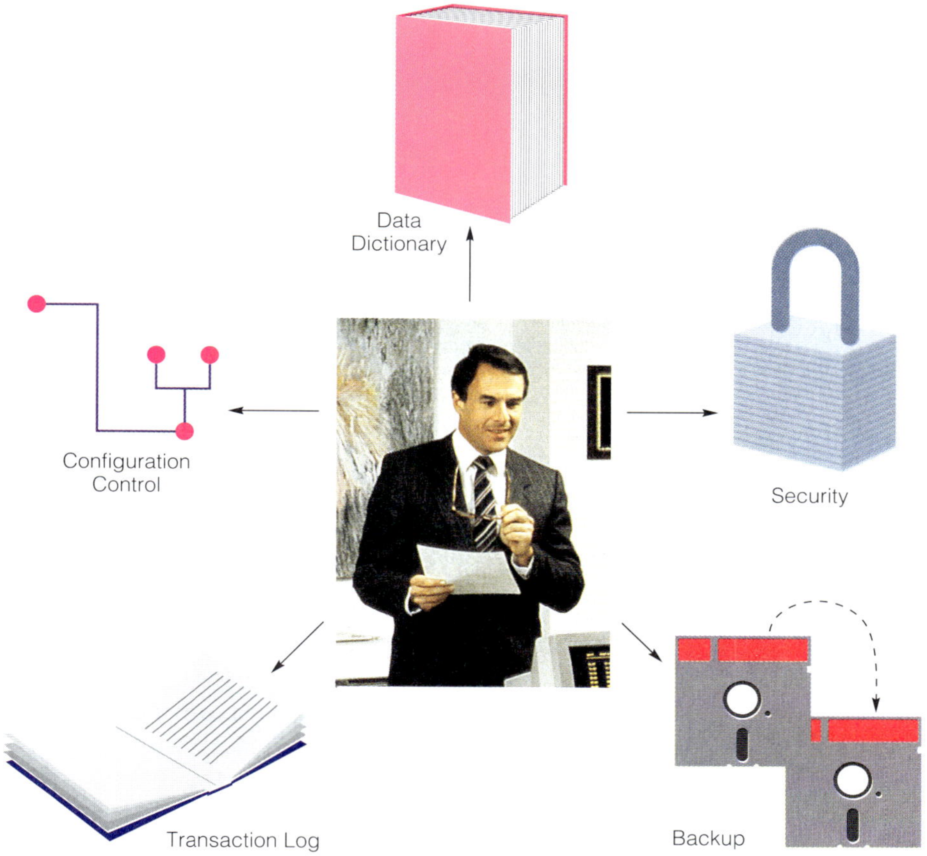

Figure 7.8
The DBA maintains the system.

destroyed; the log has a record of all changes, which can be used to re-create or restore the database to its original condition before it was damaged or erased. The transaction log also provides the means to track any unauthorized access to the database. The transaction log keeps track of not only what was done to the database but also who did it. Not all DBMS packages for microcomputers have transaction-logging abilities. dBASE III Plus does have a HISTORY command, however, which lets you record instructions that are entered from the keyboard. Mainframe- or minicomputer-based DBMSs automatically dump information from the transaction log to a tape or disk file.

PROVIDING CONFIGURATION CONTROL

In an organizational database, fields should not be added or deleted by one user without the agreement of other users. **Configuration control** allows only the DBA to make such changes to the schema of a database.

The DBA also works with users to determine what types of edit controls should be placed on any new field. The DBA can instruct the DBMS about what type of data is expected in a particular field and cause it to perform validity checks to ensure that only appropriate data types or values have been entered.

ENSURING SECURITY

Security includes deciding what access a given use is permitted to a given data field or file. For instance, users can be classified as having no access to a field or file, read-only access, or read-and-write access.

FUTURE TRENDS

The Library as a Database

Your college or university library may be using CD ROM to hold the library's collection of books, monographs, or other works that are useful to you and your professors. Collections of articles found in the *Business Index to Periodicals* are also found on CD ROM. Along with the citation of a book or article, some of these CD ROM bibliographic services also provide a summary or abstract of the article. Up to this time, however, the actual text of the article has not been available on CD ROM. After the bibliographic citation has been obtained, you still have to physically search the library for the actual book or article. This is about to change. A number of universities are now working with vendors to provide not only the actual text but also any graphics that are included in the book or article. The chemistry department of Cornell University has been working with a vendor to provide this service for chemistry articles. Developers hope that this system, called Chemistry On-Line Retrieval Experiment (CORE), will have 70,000 articles from 20 scientific journals available to students and researchers.

Such databases typically consist of four parts: ASCII text files, an index, graphics from the cited articles, and reproductions of entire pages from selected articles. The text, indexes, and graphic portions are stored on magnetic medium; the page reproductions are stored on CD ROM.

Security also includes providing for efficient recovery if a disaster strikes and the information in the database is lost (see Chapter 9).

ENSURING BACKUP AND RECOVERY

The DBA ensures that proper backup of the database is performed. **Backup** refers to the copies and a record of all changes that have been made to the database. If something happens to damage or destroy the database, the data can be reconstructed **(recovered)** using the backup. The transaction log assists in this by recording any changes and transactions that have been processed on the database. The backup copy of a database can be saved to a removable disk device, tape, or, when the file is small, a diskette.

DATABASE ORGANIZATION METHODS

The way a database is organized determines how fast data can be retrieved and how complex your interaction with the database can be. Some methods are much slower than others because they require large portions of a file to be read before a record is located. Two methods frequently used for mainframe-based systems are network and hierarchical structures. The following discussion focuses on two other types more commonly used on microcomputers— sequential list structures and relational structures.

SEQUENTIAL LIST STRUCTURES

The **sequential list structure** is a traditional method of database organization that links records through the use of pointers. A **pointer** is a data item in a

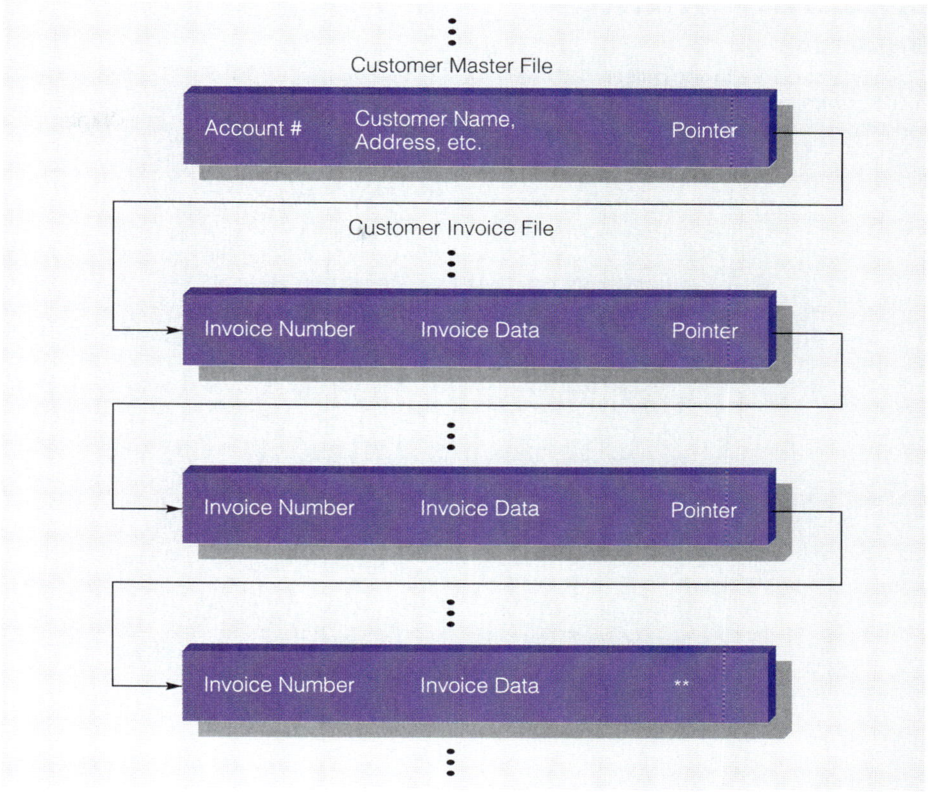

Figure 7.9
List structure keeping track of invoice items for a single customer.

record that identifies the storage location of another record that is logically related.

For example, suppose a retail company that issues credit cards to its customers wants to track each customer's charges for the current month in order to issue a monthly invoice. Each cardholder's name, address, and account number are recorded as a record in the company's customer master file. Throughout the month, the credit card transactions of various customers are recorded chronologically in a separate file of transactions. From these files, a **list structure** can be used to generate an individual customer's invoice. Every record in the customer master file contains a field that points to the record location of the first invoice for that customer in the invoice file (Figure 7.9). The first invoice record is linked to all later invoices for the customer. The last invoice in the chain is identified by a special character. Through these links, the customer's various transactions are assembled for the invoice.

RELATIONAL STRUCTURES

Another database organization method, the **relational structure,** consists of one or more tables on which data are stored in the form of relations. Finding data in a relational structure involves creating links from one table to another.

For example, relational tables can link a college course number or title with the name of its instructor and the location of the class (Figure 7.10). Suppose you want to find out who teaches English 110 and where the class meets. To find the name of the instructor, you order a search of the course–instructor relation, which produces the name Meyer. To find the course location, you search the course–location relation, which provides the location, Stevenson 101.

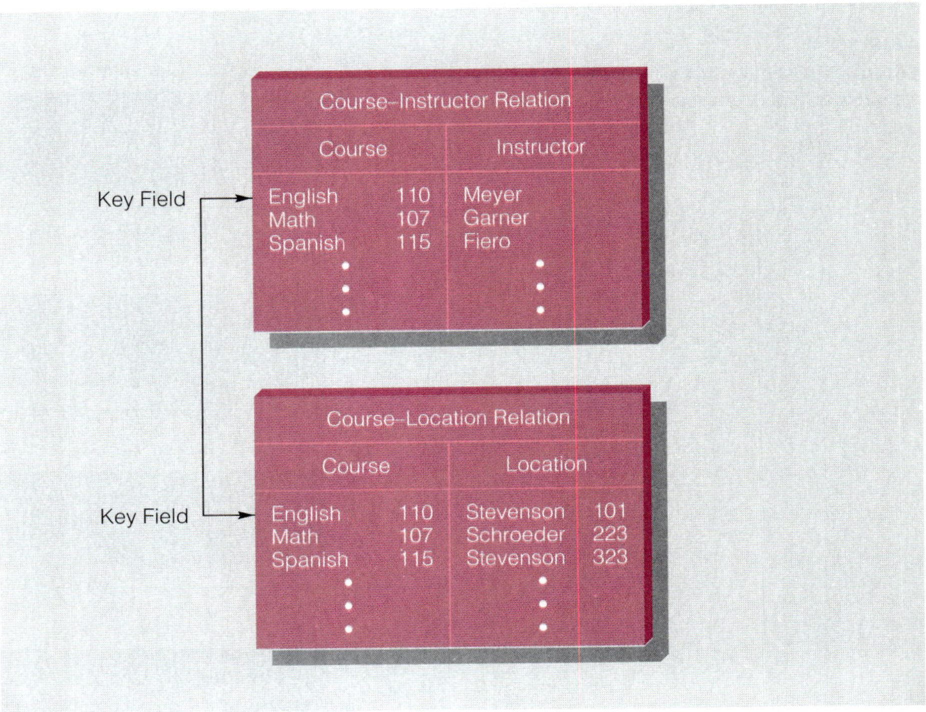

Figure 7.10
Relational structure linking college courses with professors, locations, and other data categories.

Many other relations are, of course, possible. Suppose, for instance, you want to know the name of any instructor who was teaching a class in Stevenson 101. This would involve first using the course–location relation to determine which courses meet in that classroom and then using the course–instructor relation to find Professor Meyer.

Relational structures are a relatively new and very popular database structure for microcomputer packages.

Indexing in Relational Structures Indexes are an essential component of any relational database. **Indexes** enable the user to keep track of the various relations in the database environment and to access any record in a file quickly and easily. Each index in a relational database contains one or more key fields for ordering a file. When you use an index, the physical record remains in the same physical position in the file, but the key of each record (along with its record number) is placed in the index, producing a file that has been logically reordered by one or more key fields.

In an index, information is held sequentially and in multiple data levels. This produces a structure like an inverted tree. Once a branch in the tree is chosen, you never have to go backward; only the subbranches of the chosen branch need to be considered. Figure 7.11, for example, illustrates two levels of an index, each of which divides its portion of the data into smaller parts at junctions, or branching points, called **nodes.** The top level is the **root node,** at which every search for a particular record key starts. The root node in Figure 7.11 has three keys: Alabama, Hawaii, and Kansas. All alphabetic entries from Alabama to Hawaii are pointed to by the Alabama key and found in the lower-left node; all those from Hawaii to Kansas are in the middle node; and all those from Kansas on are in the lower-right node.

Suppose the indexing program is required to find the record for Indiana. The program first looks at the root node; and because Indiana is between

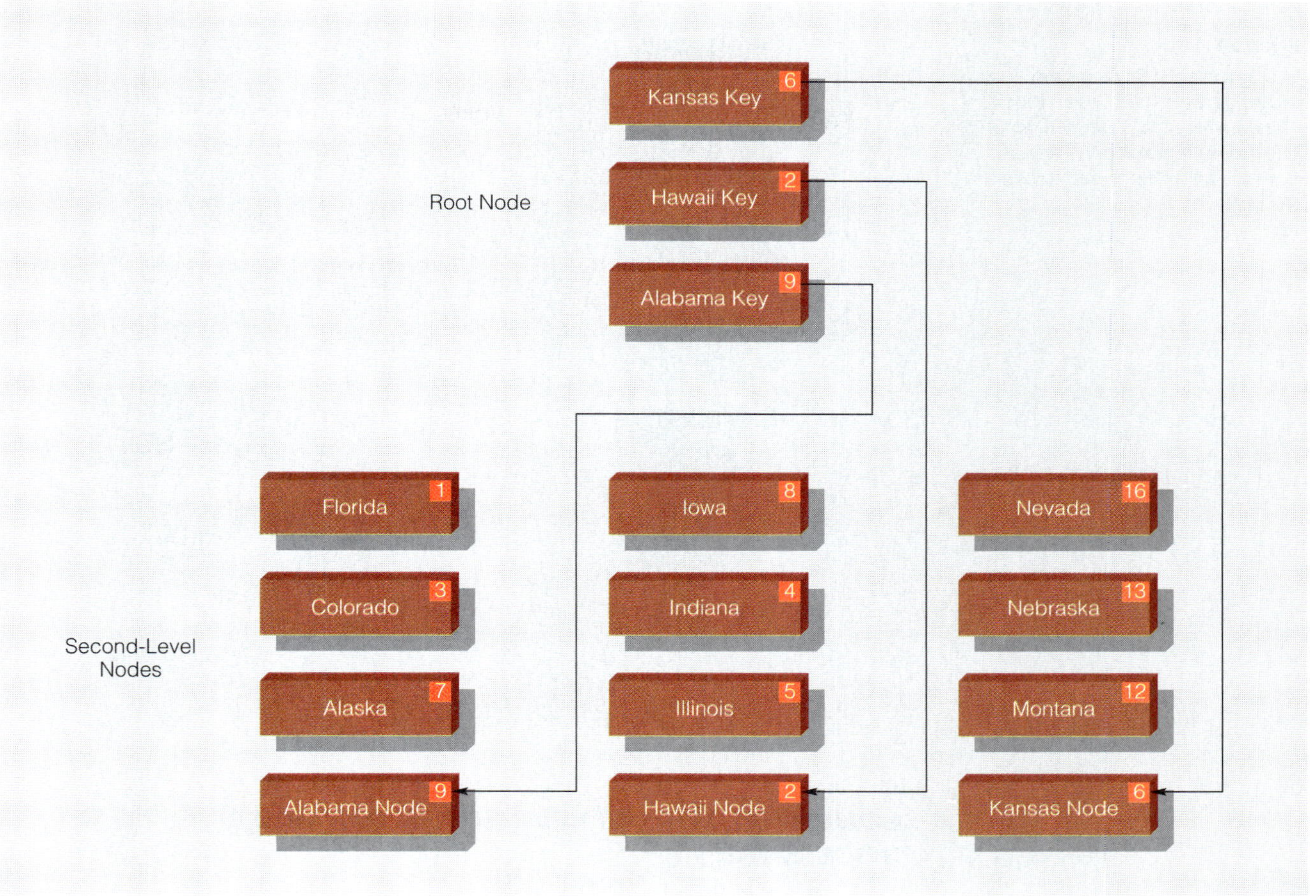

Figure 7.11
Customer address file, indexed in state order.

Hawaii and Kansas alphabetically, the program examines only the middle node, where it finds Indiana. In this case, the index has only two levels, but it could have many.

The index merely contains the location of the desired record(s) in the database file. Accessing an actual relational database record via the index requires two steps. First, the index must be searched to find the location of the desired record in the file. Second, the desired record must be accessed in the file. Database management software can usually access a record from a hard disk in about 2 to 3 seconds. Figure 7.12 illustrates this point.

The subdivision of indexes produces the ability to run through a file rapidly. Fast access to every key depends on the index tree being in balance. As keys are added, the index grows, and the nodes fill. When a node gets full, the database management software splits it, creating two half-full nodes that can now accommodate additional records.

Indexing has the distinct advantage of being able to maintain data in several orders at the same time. Information about clients or customers can be ordered simultaneously by last name, Social Security number, city, and state. Indexes can therefore be used to cross-reference a data file, giving a relational database tremendous accessing power.

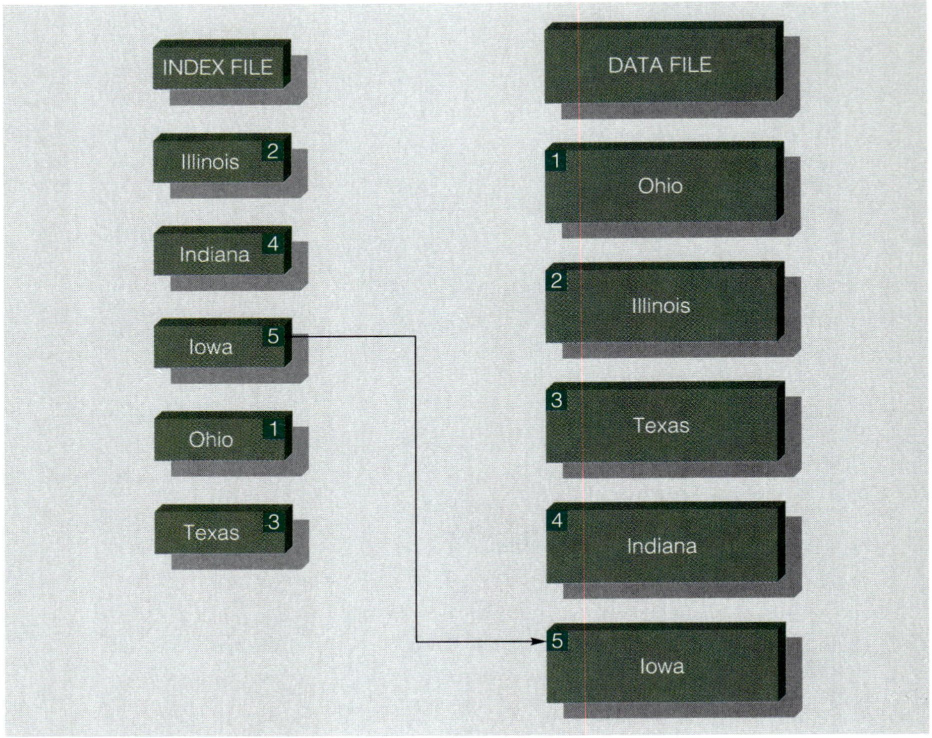

Figure 7.12
The process dBASE follows in accessing an address found in an index. The data file holds complete records. The index file holds only the data from the field being used to create the index.

SEQUENTIAL VERSUS RELATIONAL DATABASE PROCESSING

Coupled with its indexing functions, relational file organization is much more efficient than the traditional sequential method and greatly improves computer performance. For instance, users do not have to wait repeatedly for time-consuming file sorts to be performed, access to data is much quicker, and adding records to existing files is quicker. Because of its ability to index, a relational microcomputer DBMS is adequate for many database needs.

Table 7.1 summarizes these and other differences between the sequential file and relational database techniques.

Table 7.1 Differences Between Traditional Sequential File Processing and Indexed Relational Database Processing

Action	*Sequential File Processing*	*Relational Database Processing (One Index)*
Building a file or adding a record	Appends newer records after older records and sorts when finished.	Appends newer records after older records and updates index.
Preparing for processing	Places records in ascending or descending order according to the contents of one or more fields.	Leaves records in original order but generates an index of required key fields that point to the corresponding record on disk.
Accessing a record	Performs a sequential search.	Uses an index to find the location of a record and goes to that location on disk.
Obtaining a different file order	Resorts the file.	Uses another index or generates a new index.

PERSONAL CASE PROGRESS

REGISTER

WES FRAMPTON buys dBASE IV Release 1.1 for the college, along with the registration and scheduling package REGISTER. dBASE is a relational database, which has a fair number of advanced features that Wes thinks he can use. He also arranges the purchase of a 350M hard disk to hold the various data files, which are needed by the system, and a tape backup unit, which can easily make backup copies of the various programs and files on disk.

Wes has full support from his superiors for this project. They realize that once he gets the registration information on the computer, it will also provide other staff with valuable data. For instance, Wes will be able to provide student names and addresses quickly to the college telephone operator. Parental data will also be available early in the semester. Some of Wes's data will also be useful, after a student graduates, to the people responsible for fund-raising.

REGISTER needs a number of files, or databases, to track information. It needs at least a file for student information, a class file, and a teacher file. Information for these files is to be entered by student workers and college staff. Because the college does not want sensitive information about its students available to just anyone, Wes will be making extensive use of the REGISTER's password feature. For instance, it will be used to prevent student workers from looking at or changing the grades of students in the database.

Once the bulk of the data has been entered by his staff, Wes will probably need to create some other files and develop formats for some of the special reports that administrators will need to have printed, especially at the start of each new semester.

Wes also begins to investigate the possibility of getting some additional equipment that will allow him to generate automatically class schedules by directly reading/scanning the student schedule forms. He also begins to look at the cost of making some of this information available to other college offices via a network.

DESIGNING A DATABASE

The key to designing an effective database is in how its fields are designed. As noted earlier, each record within a database holds information that is essentially parallel in purpose and structure to the information in other records in the database. Each record has the same pattern of fields, though any given field within a given record may or may not have had data entered in it. For instance, in a customer file, the first field of any record might hold the customer's surname;

FUTURE TRENDS

Standardizing Database Languages

One problem that has become readily apparent to anyone who has used several relational database packages is that the languages used by the various packages differ tremendously. This complicates and lengthens the process of learning to use a different package. Standardizing language interface would help with this problem. Standardization is even more important with respect to the problem of communications between mainframe databases and microcomputers.

Why would a microcomputer user want to access data on a mainframe? Although microcomputers can hold what appears to be a lot of data, approximately 97 percent of corporate-specific data is found on mainframe computers, and microcomputer users often want to download (copy) data that meet their specific needs.

One means that has been developed to achieve this communication is the **database server,** usually located at the mainframe site. A database server is different from a file server. A file server is a large disk of files that can be shared by multiple users. A database server is a computer that processes high-level database requests.

With a file server, each machine is responsible for its own processing. This means that every bit of information required for a given task (including intermediate results) needs to be transmitted to the workstation over the local area network and then possibly be transmitted back if a shared answer is to be generated. With a database server, the request is transmitted from the node, all processing is done locally on the server, and only the answer is sent back from the server.

Database servers are being used increasingly in conjunction with a standardized **system query language (SQL).** The SQL helps move data from one environment (such as the mainframe) and makes it available to another environment (such as the microcomputer).

As more and more data are required from mainframe databases for use by differing database packages, the use of the SQL server or some other type of technology will be required.

the second field might hold the given name; the third might hold the customer's middle initial, if any; and so on.

Whether relationally or sequentially based, a DBMS relies on information from one or more fields to define the keys in which the records of the database are ordered, identified, and retrieved. Several keys are commonly used. The **primary key** is the unique identifier for a particular record, most often a unique record number, say, record number 5. When a database is in physical primary key order, record number 5 occupies the fifth position in the database. A **secondary key** can also be defined by information from one or more other fields within the database and used to arrange the database in some other order. For instance, you might create a secondary key containing a Social Security number field to put a file of employee records in order by that number.

Because the information in the fields provides the basis for any system of keys, it is crucial for the fields to isolate those bits of information that you may need to use as keys. In this regard, it's important to remember that whereas humans can often identify separate bits of information within a field, computers

DATABASE FOR PRICING ART?

Pricing art is a chancy proposition. The best way to determine the price for a given piece is to sell it. Another way to price a given piece is to know what it or comparable works by the same artist have sold for in the past.

To facilitate this process, a business called Centrox has developed a package to track and price art. This package is updated quarterly to include prices for comparable works of painting and sculpture sold by 172 auction houses and high-resolution graphics of all the artwork. In addition, it includes a registry of stolen art and a listing of works that subscribers wish to sell (at no commission to Centrox).

For example, suppose you want to sell one of your paintings by van Gogh; you enter a search, and all of the van Goghs that have been sold in the last two years, along with the appropriate price and image, appear on the screen (Figure 7.13).

Such special-purpose database systems are expensive. In a base cost of $9000, Centrox includes a computer and special monitor powerful enough to produce high-resolution color images. For a slightly higher cost, Centrox also provides a scanner.

This type of system is of special interest to insurance firms that provide coverage for artwork as well as to banks that lend money against the purchase of artwork. It also interests the Internal Revenue Service, which can use it for deciding whether someone has correctly shown the value of a piece of art that's listed in a tax return.

Figure 7.13

A selection of paintings displayed on the Centrox screen.

generally cannot. For instance, consider the following four lines from a customer address file:

Alfred A. Conant
2645 W. Hartford
Moosejaw, IL 61703
(309)367–8934

PERSONAL CASE REVISITED

The System in Action

WES finds that the REGISTER database system allows him to perform quickly tasks that had previously taken him much time and routing through filing cabinets. A case in point is finding which classes are taken by Sam Thomas.

Student information is in one file, and class information is in another; each file has an index file. The program first looks at the student file, checking through the student index by name (Figure 7.14). This leads (through several index levels not shown) to the index entry containing Sam Thomas's name and student ID (4417). The database program now switches to the class file indexed by student ID (Figure 7.15), searching for the first occurrence of 4417. This process points to record 1. The program is satisfied that

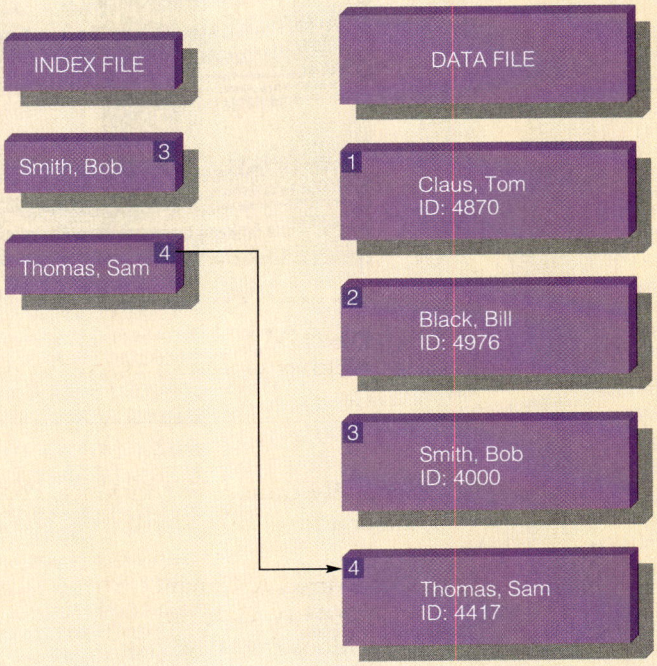

Figure 7.14
Index entries of the student file, containing name and student ID.

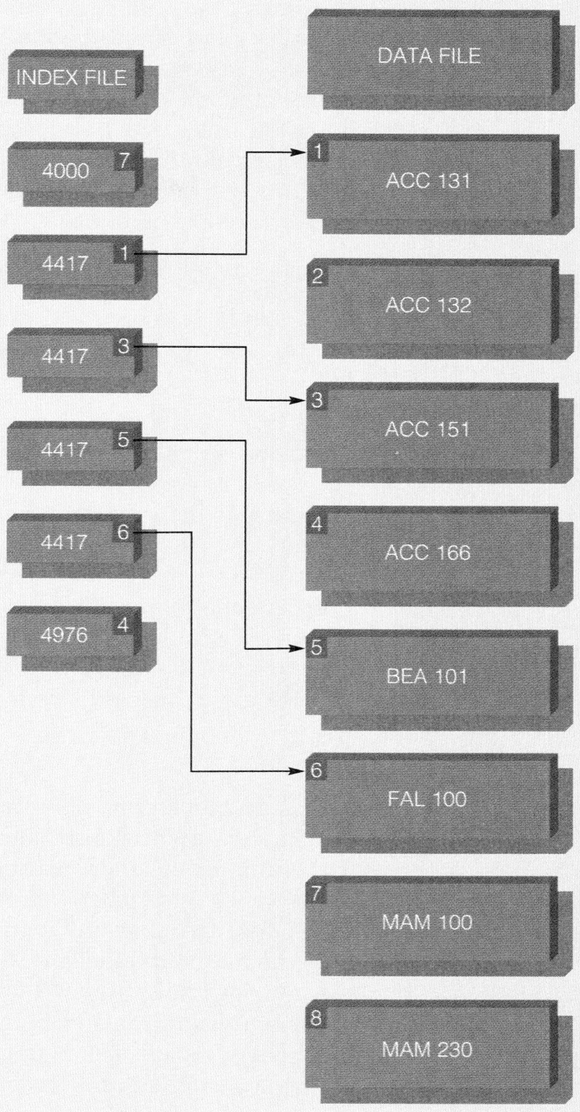

Figure 7.15
Index entries for student 4417, pointing to classes-attended records.

no other classes for this individual exist because the class index file is ordered so that all 4417 class entries occur together in the class index file.

The REGISTER system has been up and running for just over one year. The technical part of the system works well, but Wes has found that some of his co-workers are a bit sensitive over their inability to get at pieces of data to which Wes thinks they should not have access. He has had several complaints directed at him in meetings, as well as complaints to his superior.

He has also found it necessary to impress on his co-workers that they maintain the secrecy of their passwords. Wes remembers the unpleasant episode where one of the clerks in the registrar's office gave his password to a student worker to do some of the work that should have been done by only that clerk. With the password, the student accessed the grade database and changed some of her grades and the grades of some friends. Wes was able to detect the changes via his daily perusal of the change log generated by REGISTER, but some unpleasant disciplinary proceedings were necessary with respect to both the clerk and the student.

While more work can be done by the same number of people, Wes sometimes wonders how he became responsible for such sensitive data. He also realizes that the technical problems can be solved more easily than the people problems.

How many fields should it take to store these lines in a record? Storing the customer's name in one field is possible. However, the computer cannot sort records by last names because it doesn't know that Alfred is a first name and Conant a last name. Nor can the computer readily tell an address from a telephone number. Thus, designers and users of databases must take care to lay out fields and enter data in rigid, predictable patterns that let the computer process information in the database solely on the basis of its field, without any understanding of the meaning of the data. In practice, the preceding customer information requires eight fields:

First Name	Address	Phone
Middle Initial	City	
Last Name	State	
	Zip	

The name is divided into three fields so that records can be sorted by last name, and the first name can be used independently of the middle initial. Divisions in the address line let you rearrange records within the database by city, state, or zip code.

Well-designed fields give you great flexibility in choosing secondary keys. With the above fields, for instance, to produce a report in order by customer names, you could create a key based on first and last names. By changing the keys to last name and city or state, you could produce another report in order by customer name and location.

CHAPTER REVIEW

The traditional approach to information processing requires that each application have its own set of master and transaction files. This arrangement leads to such problems as data redundancy, lack of data integrity, program and data dependency, and lack of flexibility.

A database management system (DBMS) is a set of software that resides between a user and the data stored in a database. The view of the data stored in the database (logical view) is translated by the DBMS software so that it can easily retrieve the data from the database (the physical view). A DBMS has four basic parts: the query language, a report generator, a data-definition language, and a data-manipulation language.

An organization's database administrator (DBA) is responsible for the day-to-day planning and control of the database. It is the DBA who is responsible for maintaining a data dictionary and transaction log. It is also the DBA, along with members of the staff, who ensure that the integrity of data stored in the database is maintained. Data integrity is maintained by keeping out unauthorized users. This person is also responsible for ensuring proper backup and control of the database.

A number of organization methods are used to arrange data in a database. Sequential list structures are one traditional method. The relational structure is fast, easy to use, and therefore increasingly popular.

The heart of the relational method is the index, which uses a treelike structure for holding record keys. The index lets you access a record directly; it contains the field from each record indexed, along with the record's location on disk. The index is split into branches, and data are kept in sequence within a node of each branch. As a result, only a small portion of the index has to be searched to find the location of any record.

One of the greatest benefits of a relational database is that a general understanding of how indexes work is all you need to know before using the index feature.

The index also lets you use pieces of data to link one or more files together for processing. For instance, finding a piece of information in one record in turn lets you access another record directly from a second file.

Database files, records, and fields should be designed with future processing needs in mind. For instance, this means separating name fields into last name, first name, and middle initial fields so that the computer can arrange the information in alphabetic order by last name.

KEY TERMS AND CONCEPTS

backup and recovery
configuration control
database
database administrator (DBA)
database management system (DBMS)
database server
data-definition language (DDL)
data dictionary
data independence
data integrity
data-manipulation language (DML)
data redendancy
data security
flexibility
index
list structure
logical view
node
physical view
pointer
primary key
program and data dependency
query language
record structure
relational structure
report generator
root node
schema
secondary key
sequential list structure
subschema
system query language (SQL)
traditional approach
transaction log

CHAPTER QUIZ

Multiple Choice

1. Which of the following individuals is responsible for maintaining security of a DBMS?
   a. Systems analyst
   b. Programmer
   c. User
   d. Management
   e. None of the above

2. Which data-storage entity is used to store information about a transaction?
   a. File
   b. Record
   c. Element
   d. Field
   e. None of the above

3. Which entity or device allows a database to be defined?
   a. Node
   b. Data-definition language
   c. Query language
   d. Data-manipulation language
   e. None of the above

4. Which of the following statements about index structures is (are) true?
   a. An index contains a number of branches.
   b. The field being indexed and the address on disk are stored for each record.
   c. Once a search is started for a record in an index, it will probably require going through at least one branch to find the desired record.

d. Branches must be in balance (contain about the same number of entries) for searches to be efficient.
e. All of the above

5. In which database organizations can ordered data be viewed as a table?
 a. Relational
 b. Hierarchical
 c. Network
 d. List structure
 e. None of the above

True/False

6. In discussions about managing databases on microcomputers, *database* and *file* usually mean the same thing.

7. A properly designed record layout lets you easily order the file in a number of different ways.

8. Managing a database includes such tasks as creating reports and adding, deleting, and changing records.

9. In most large businesses, the librarian controls access to the database.

10. Even though data are not in the proper order in a relational database, the index holds information that lets you order the file logically.

Answers

1. e 2. b 3. b 4. e 5. a 6. t 7. t 8. t 9. f 10. t

Exercises

1. Define or describe each of the following:
 a. Database management system
 b. Database
 c. Database administrator
 d. Data-definition language
 e. Relational structure
 f. Root node
 g. Index

2. The __________ approach has a set of files for each information-processing activity.

3. Two problems with the traditional approach are __________ and __________.

4. The problem with the traditional approach that does not allow changes to be easily made to a file is called __________ dependence.

5. The four parts of a DBMS are __________, __________, __________, and __________.

6. How a user accesses data from the database is called the __________ view, and how the data are stored in the database is called the __________ view.

7. A __________ of a database holds data about any accesses or changes that have been made to a database.

8. __________ means that only a DBA can make changes to the schema of a database.

9. The part of a database called the __________ lets you add fields or create new files within the database.

10. The __________ for a database holds information about each piece of datum, such as data name, type of data, and field size, found in the database and any interrelationships for this piece of datum.

11. The __________ structure uses tables to organize the records in the file logically.

12. Creating a new relation involves simply creating a new __________ .

13. The top node of an index is called the __________ .

14. The index contains __________ and __________ about each record in an indexed file.

15. Data in an index are stored __________ .

16. The field that identifies a record is called a(n) __________ .

17. A(n) __________ holds one piece of information contained in a record.

18. In designing a record, it is important that the __________ organize the fields properly for later processing.

19. The process of creating reports and adding, deleting, and changing records is called __________ the database.

20. A commonly used microcomputer-based DBMS is __________ or __________ .

IN YOUR OWN CASE

1. Suppose, with your microcomputer, that you can construct one or more database files for your own personal use. What specific collections of information would you want to have in the database? Why? Design a set of fields for the records in one such file.

2. Does your school library have information about various public or commercial databases? Where else might you find out about such things? Identify several databases available to microcomputer users of which you could make good use. Find out how to gain access to these sources.

QUESTIONS FOR THOUGHT

1. How do you feel about the Market Place database project described in this chapter? What criticisms do you have? Do you think the project should have gone ahead?

2. Suppose you and three other people were sharing a microcomputer at school or at work for a variety of database applications. How would yo work things out so that the typical DBA functions were reliably being performed?

8

MANAGEMENT INFORMATION SYSTEMS AND SYSTEM ANALYSIS

CHAPTER OBJECTIVES

After completing this chapter, you should be able to

- **Describe the characteristics of a system**
- **Describe a management information system**
- **List the three levels of decision making and discuss their needs**
- **Define system analysis**
- **List and discuss the phases in the system development life cycle**
- **Describe the function of data-flow diagrams and decision tables**
- **Discuss some of the problems of implementing or changing a system**

THE DEVELOPMENT OF MANAGEMENT

1956 John McCarthy of MIT coins the phrase *artificial intelligence,* and work begins toward developing expert systems and decision-support systems.

1957 The first issue of *Datamation,* a business-oriented journal explaining computers and how they are used by organizations, is published.

1959 The first major description of COBOL is completed. COBOL later becomes the most widely used programming language for commercial purposes.
Xerox introduces the first office photocopier.

1962 National Machine Accountants Association becomes the Data Processing Management Association (DPMA), a social and professional development support organization for MIS personnel.
H. Ross Perot forms Electronic Data Systems (EDS), an early nationwide consulting firm for MIS.

1967 The first issue of *ComputerWorld,* a weekly journal supporting business and information systems, is published.

1968 Edsgar Dijkstra's article "Go to Statement Considered Harmful" in *Communications of the ACM* advocates avoiding the use of Go To statements.

1971 Gerald Weinberg's *The Psychology of Computer Programming* espouses "egoless programming" and creates a basis for structured walkthroughs of programming logic and code.

1975 Douglas Ross and Kenneth Schoman, Jr., introduce structured analysis and design methodology.
Principles of Program Design presents Michael Jackson's methodology of structured programming.
Techniques of Program Structure and Design presents Edward Yourdon's methodology of structured programming.

1986 *ComputerWorld* publishes issue number 1000.

INFORMATION SYSTEMS

PERSONAL CASE

A Management Information System for a Chain Store

MARY BRANDON owns a chain of five drugstores, Brandon's Pharmacy, in a midwestern metropolitan area of 200,000 people. Mary believes her company's competitiveness is hampered by the lack of certain information in the reports currently generated by her manual record-keeping system. For example, she does not receive information that lets her easily determine the types and quantities of pharmaceuticals her staff should be ordering.

She has also discovered that her pharmaceutical departments are less competitive because they do not currently offer some services provided by the big chain drugstores. Mary has set a strategic goal of improving her stores' services in these competitive areas. She also wants to track her inventory better in order to reduce costs and ensure that merchandise is available when needed.

Mary thinks that she should computerize her record-keeping system. She decides to talk to some members of her local Business Women's Association about reputable consulting organizations that might help her.

In this chapter, we examine the roles that information and computers play in decision making. We look at various types of decisions, who makes them, and what information they require. We examine management information systems, which provide decision-making information, and system analysis, the process of designing such systems.

As you read this chapter, bear in mind the following:

- Business organizations rely on information to meet their primary goals: decreasing costs and increasing productivity.
- Organizations incur half their operational costs handling information.
- Most managerial problems are solvable with better information.
- Managers often don't know what information they require to improve their decision making.

WHAT IS A SYSTEM?

Let's note briefly some important aspects of any system. A **system** is a set of interrelated parts that work together. An automobile is a system of transport. Streets, stop signs, streetlights, and the like are a system of paths and signals through which the automobile can move.

Systems often possess capabilities not inherent in any component part. This quality of a system being greater than the sum of its parts is called **synergism.**

A **subsystem** is a system that is part of a larger system. Your body is a system of vital biological subsystems (circulation, respiration, metabolism, and so on). As a system, a business, too, is made up of numerous functions or subsystems. For example, a cash-receipts subsystem serves an organization's more encompassing financial-reporting system. Data from a firm's cash-receipts subsystem is fed to its accounts-receivable subsystem, which in turn provides information to the general ledger. The general ledger then provides information to the financial-reporting system, which managers use to determine the financial health of the company.

SYSTEM CHARACTERISTICS

The following characteristics are important in understanding any system.

Purpose Systems must have a specific purpose. The purpose of the circulatory system is to maintain life. The goal of most companies is to make a profit for its shareholders. The objective of a payroll system is to fulfill contractual obligations related to remuneration of employees.

Boundaries A **boundary** defines the limits of a system or subsystem. Anything outside the boundary is considered part of the system's **environment.** For example, a department might be described as a subsystem contained within a certain boundary; several departments that work together might be seen as existing within another boundary. An environment consists of all those things that lie outside a system and are therefore beyond its control. Because an automobile manufacturer cannot dictate events outside the factory, such as inflation rate, changes in tax laws, or the price of gasoline, these factors are all part of its environment.

Boundaries between subsystems are not as well defined as the boundary between a system and its environment. This is because subsystems are interdependent; they cannot be completely separate from one another if the system is to function. The point where subsystems overlap is called the **interface.** The interface is where the subsystems connect, where one subsystem's output becomes another's input. No change occurs at the interface. For example, the U.S. Postal Service acts as the interface when a cardholder sends a check to pay a VISA bill, but the passage of the check from the cardholder to the VISA company does not change the Postal Service.

Interaction with the Environment Although distinct from their environment, systems must interact with it. Systems accept and process environmental inputs and generate outputs, which they send back into the environment (Figure 8.1). For example, a payroll system accepts time-card information from the environment (in this case, other departments residing outside the payroll system's boundary), processes those inputs, and sends outputs back into the environment in the form of paychecks.

Environmental inputs to an automobile plant would include raw materials such as sheet metal and assembly parts. The plant would process these parts

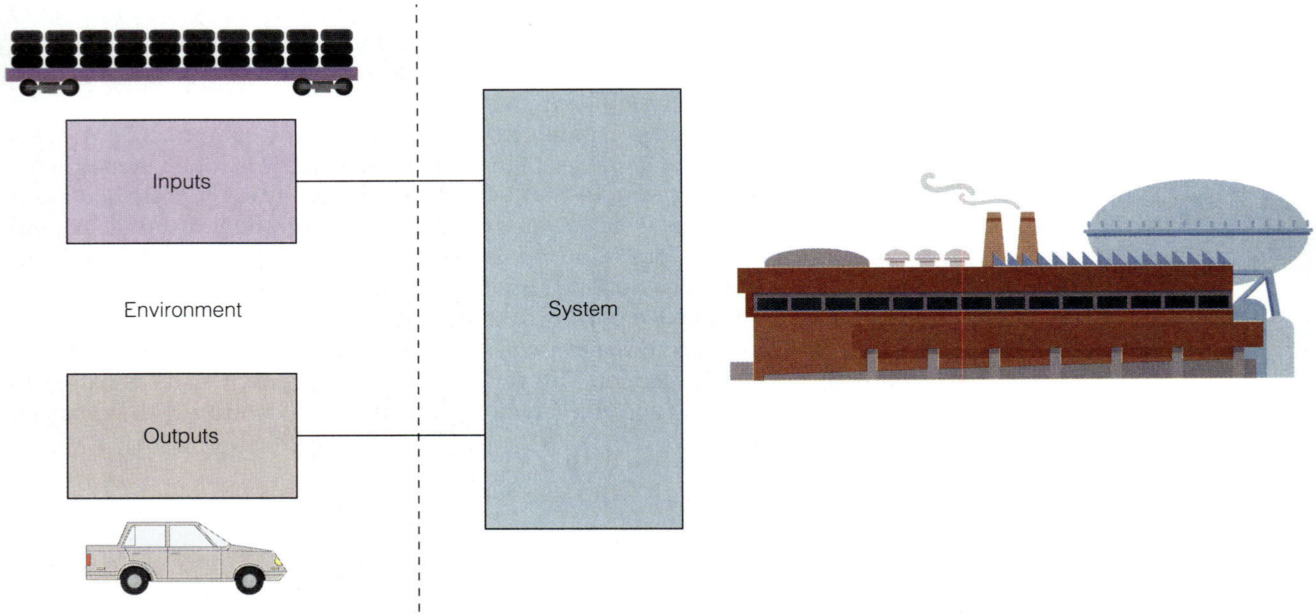

Figure 8.1
A system interacts with its environment.

through stamping, assembling, and painting. The output would be the finished automobile.

A system cannot function properly without interacting with its environment. No system that involves humans is closed—that is, not interacting with and not depending on its environment. If a factory produces cars that consumers in the environment don't want, it will go out of business. The factory will also as surely be forced to close its doors if it cannot procure raw materials from the environment.

Feedback Finally, all systems need some means to regulate and correct themselves, to maintain a steady state. A system regulates itself through the feedback process. **Feedback** is accomplished by sampling output from one part of the system and sending it back into the system as input (Figure 8.2). Through feedback the system can check the functioning of its component parts. If a sample output is not within established tolerances, the system takes corrective action.

A common example of a feedback loop is the thermostat, which heating and cooling systems use to maintain a set temperature. A house thermostat set to 70 degrees turns on the furnace when the temperature drops below 70 degrees. The furnace heats the home until the temperature climbs back to 70 degrees, at which point the switch in the thermostat shuts off the furnace. Environmental temperature provides the input to the thermostat.

Feedback also can take the form of quality control. For example, a feedback device may check parts to ensure that they are milled to within set tolerances. Parts that exceed the tolerances can be remilled or removed from the assembly line.

Black-Box Concept Because the transformation of inputs into outputs can be extremely complex, the process is often represented in simplified, graphic form by the **black-box concept.** Rather than describing the process in detail, the black box defines it as simply input, process, and output (Figure 8.3). To con-

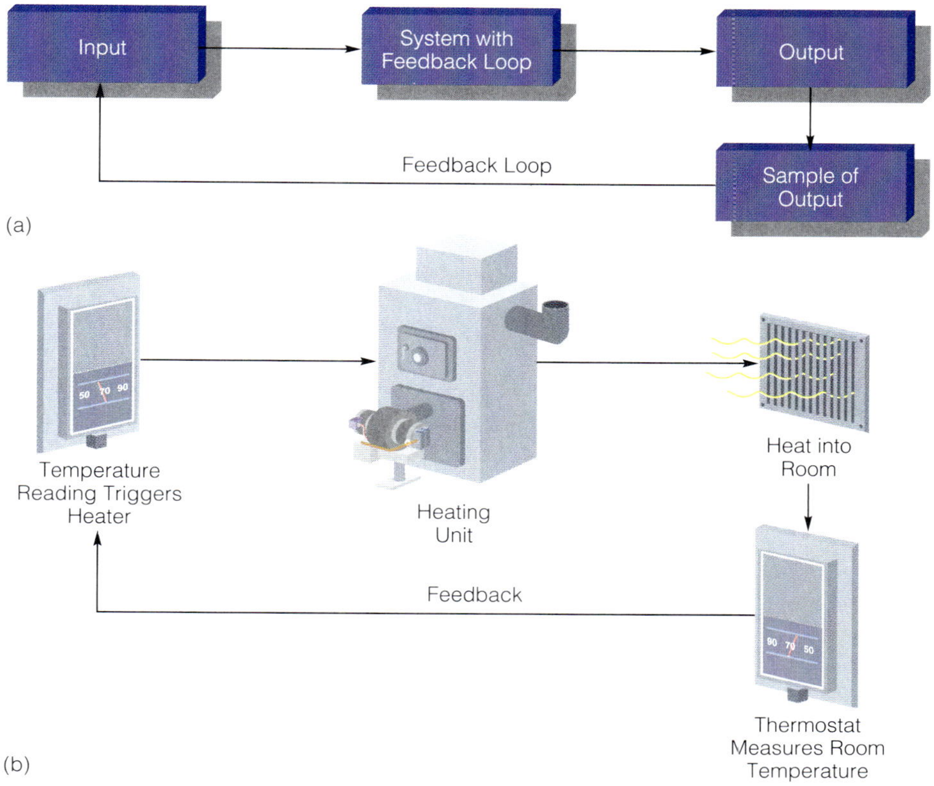

Figure 8.2
A system with a feedback loop.

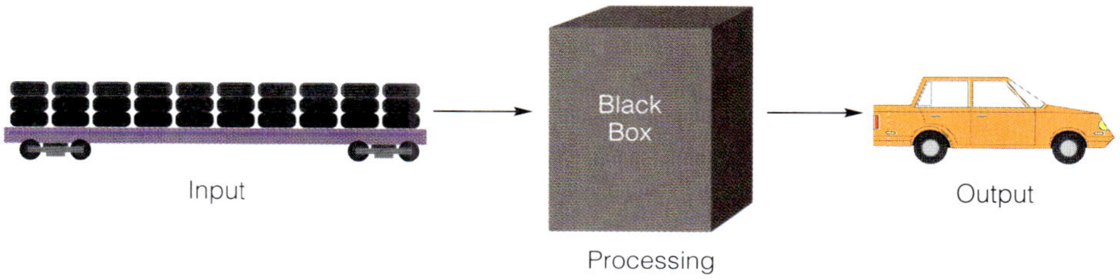

Figure 8.3
The black-box concept.

struct a black box, the user only needs to know the input and output components. The transformation step, in which input is processed to generate output, is represented as a black box. The black box enables managers to easily conceptualize a complex task or series of tasks.

MANAGEMENT INFORMATION SYSTEMS

A **management information system (MIS)** is a formal process using both manual and computerized tools to control information. The goal of an MIS is to provide managers with vital decision-making information when they need it.

DECISION-MAKING LEVELS

Management can be divided into top, middle, and low levels. Top-level managers generally make strategic decisions, middle-level managers make tactical

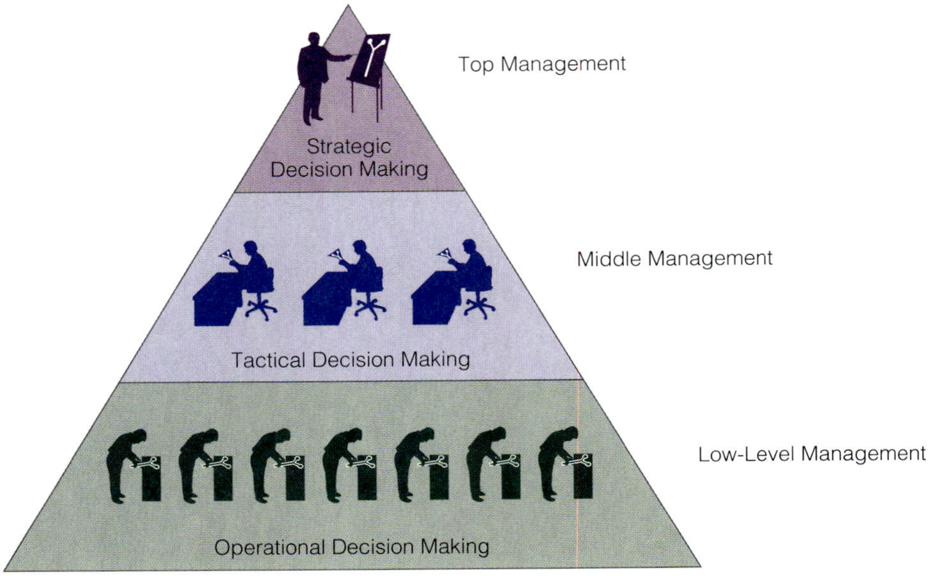

Figure 8.4

To be effective, an MIS needs to provide information for three types of decision making: strategic, tactical, and operational. Strategic decision making involves setting the goals for the company such as deciding which regions of the country should be targeted for market penetration and where to build facilities. Tactical decision making involves middle-level management meeting with other managers to decide how the budget is to be allocated to meet the strategic goals. Operational decision making involves making those decisions necessary to meet constraints set by the budget, to meet the company's strategic goals.

decisions, and low-level managers make operational decisions. Each level requires a different mix of decision-making information (Figure 8.4).

Strategic decision making means setting objectives for an organization and devising long-range plans. This includes deciding what new products to manufacture, which new markets to target, where to build new plants, and how to raise capital. Because their decision making is directed toward the future on a wide—even global—scale, top-level managers have a great need for external information such as economic forecasts, employment trends, and resource availability.

Tactical decision making implements strategic decisions by allocating an organization's resources. Tactical decision makers typically make decisions about personnel, budgeting, production scheduling, and allocation of working capital.

Operational decision making ensures that employees perform tasks efficiently by measuring their output against preset standards. Operational decision makers answer such questions as who is assigned what job, whether to accept credit, how much inventory to reorder, and what raw materials are needed.

The decision-making process varies from level to level, as Table 8.1 shows. Low-level managers usually have highly structured roles, which are standardized in written operational procedures. Because they deal with day-to-day operations, these managers often need instant (real-time) access to information from within the organization but have less need for environmental information. Low-level managers work at problems that require fairly rapid decisions. They tend to make fewer independent judgments than do tactical and strategic decision makers.

Table 8.1 Characteristics of the Three Levels of Decision Making

Characteristic	Level Low (Operational)	 Middle (Tactical)	 High (Strategic)
Degree of structure	High	Moderate	Low
Need for external information	Low	Moderate	High
Need for internal information	High	Moderate	Low
Need for real-time information	High	Moderate	Low
Degree of judgment	Low	Moderate	High

High-level managers perform roles almost opposite those of low-level managers. They have no written procedures to guide them in solving the problems they face, so they frequently exercise independent judgment. They often need external information because they decide what direction their organization should take in the future to compete against other companies.

Between these two extremes are middle-level managers, whose roles are moderately structured. They need moderate amounts of both internal and external information to perform their duties: external information in order to understand the strategies formulated by high-level managers and internal information in order to direct low-level managers on how to implement those strategies in the workplace.

TYPES OF DECISIONS

Within these three decision-making levels, the MIS must address two types of decisions, structured and unstructured.

Structured decisions occur most frequently at the operational level and can be addressed by established procedures. For example, a loan officer engages in structured decision making when granting or denying a car loan to a person, based on the applicant's age, income, years employed, credit standing, and so on. In a manual environment, written procedures dictate whether the applicant should receive the loan. For example, the procedures may state that the loan should be denied if the applicant is unemployed or younger than 18 years of age. Although structured decisions can be executed on a computer, they are routinely performed without computers.

Unstructured decisions resolve ill-defined or unstructured problems. Typically, these decisions are made at the strategic level and entail future-oriented problems such as what products to produce or which markets to penetrate. These problems involve many variables that are difficult to quantify. To solve them, decision makers often turn to computer tools that enable them to project the outcome of several alternatives.

REPORTING METHODS TO AID DECISION MAKING

To satisfy their decision-making needs, the various management levels require information presented to them in specific forms. Lower-level managers need prompt, detailed information for everyday decisions involving such things as payroll, inventory, accounts receivable, and manufacturing. Middle- and top-level managers need their data organized so that they can summarize it across functional lines (for example, the total payroll for a particular period). Accordingly, whereas managers at the lowest levels may use certain reports, MISs are designed mainly to provide decision makers with the following special reports.

Scheduled Reports **Scheduled reports** usually contain large amounts of detailed information. Often irrelevant to the highest levels of management, these reports may be most meaningful at somewhat lower levels. Scheduled reports may be generated on a daily, weekly, or other regular basis. Although currently most are circulated on paper, scheduled reports increasingly are being displayed on monitor screens as real-time processing replaces batch processing.

Exception Reports **Exception reports** alert management that an activity or process needs corrective action. An exception report could, for example, list customers with bills outstanding 90 or more days.

Demand Reports A manager will request a **demand report** to obtain specific information. For example, a vice president of sales may request a demand report detailing which sales representatives earned more than $100,000 in commissions for the year. Operators can produce a demand report in minutes by using a software package such as dBASE.

Predictive Reports Managers use **predictive reports** in their planning process. Users create these reports by commanding the appropriate software to construct what-if scenarios, which may involve statistical and modeling techniques such as simulation or regression. (Regression has to do with determining the predictive powers of specific variables.) For example, a manager who wants to project how the penetration of a new market would affect the company's revenues could command Lotus 1-2-3 to compute several what-if alternatives. The alternatives could include how different unit-sales levels and fixed- and variable-product costs would affect net income. The manager could alter any item in the model, and the software will project a result.

MANAGEMENT INFORMATION SYSTEMS VERSUS TRANSACTION-PROCESSING SYSTEMS

A **transaction-processing system** (often referred to as **data processing**) processes transactions and outputs the results. It represents the bulk of computerized processing.

Transaction-processing systems enable users to process on computers such business tasks as inventory control, payroll, and accounts receivable. After a transaction has been processed, a manager can examine its impact and take further actions. For example, when someone records an item-purchase transaction, the transaction-processing system then reduces the item's amount-on-hand value in an inventory file by the appropriate amount. Later, the inventory manager can examine the amount-on-hand value to determine whether it must be reordered. If it must, he or she can automatically generate a purchase order.

Transaction-processing systems are well suited to providing prompt (real-time) internal information. Therefore, their primary users have been operational managers. Tactical and strategic managers rarely employ transaction processing because it does not provide the type of information they need to make decisions.

An MIS always has a transaction-processing component, but a transaction-processing system by itself does not constitute an MIS. However, a transaction-processing system can be upgraded to become an MIS, by the addition of query functions that allow it to generate decision models. It can thus become a decision-support tool for upper-level managers.

PERSONAL CASE PROGRESS

Consulting with a System Analyst

At a meeting of the Business Women's Association, Mary talks to several colleagues who have had success working with Goldstein and Associates, a consulting business. She calls the company and talks with one of its associates, Harold Stern, who meets with her a few days later to discuss her problems and see whether his company can assist her. Mary tells him that her primary concern is to meet her strategic goal of improving personal service to customers but that she has some other problems in mind also:

- Mary's pharmacies are sometimes short of needed drugs and at other times overloaded with slow-moving medications. While avoiding shortages, she wants to reduce inventory-carrying costs and thereby reduce her prices to customers. To do this, she needs predictive information about the quantities and types of drugs to order from the wholesale house.
- Mary wants her staff to respond quickly to customers' request for refills. To do this, they need detailed information concerning previously filled prescriptions. Customers also need this type of information for insurance and tax purposes. Each store currently gives a detailed receipt with each purchase, but many customers lose the slip and ask for the information again later. Thus, for several reasons, Mary needs to have prescription information stored and readily retrievable.
- She wants her pharmacists to be able to quickly identify generic equivalents to brand-name drugs and provide these to customers who want them.
- About 37 percent of Mary's prescription business is in deliveries. She wants to use a computer to help plan efficient routes for delivering prescription efficiently in terms of delivery time and gasoline.
- Medications frequently cause side effects, when taken either alone or in combination with another medication. Mary's pharmacists need a database of potential problems that they can follow in providing warning labels and verbally instructing customers.
- Pharmacies sometimes receive recall alerts for certain drugs. Mary wants hers to be able to quickly locate all customers taking a specific medication in case it is recalled.

Discussing Mary's business organization, Harold describes it as being extremely flat. Mary is the president of the corporation, her husband is vice president, and some relatives occupy other offices as required by law. Mary, however, is the effective general manager and the only family member actively involved with the business. Each store is managed by a chief pharmacist who takes care of day-to-day tasks like staffing.

Harold agrees that his company can probably assist Brandon Pharmacy with its problems. He agrees to do a preliminary investigation and promises Mary that they will try to control costs by using prepackaged programs as much as possible.

A TREND TOWARD OUTSOURCING

One of the trends of the 1990s is outsourcing. In **outsourcing,** a business splits off its own information systems functions from the rest of the company. To do this, it sells those functions (including hardware, staffing, and other resources) to a third-party outsourcing company and then leases these services back from the third party on a long-term basis.

Outsourcing may be chosen for a variety of reasons: The information systems department may be perceived as a cost center rather than as an income-generating center; the company has not been operating its own information services efficiently; or the company does not have the in-house expertise to provide a service like data communications. Whatever the reason, some businesses that have contracted with outsourcing vendors estimate that within 10 years they can save 35 percent of their information-processing costs.

Among major organizations that buy outsourced information systems and then lease them back to the seller are Andersen Systems, McDonnell Douglas, and Electronic Data Systems. Such organizations look for potential clients that can provide them with additional programming and design expertise and people who have skills in data communications, CASE (discussed later), and project management. They are also interested in obtaining clients that have plenty of unused computer time available that can, in turn, be sold to other clients.

DECISION-SUPPORT SYSTEMS AND MANAGEMENT INFORMATION SYSTEMS

MISs excel at providing information for routine, predictable decisions, and they permit easy access of large data stores. However, they have been less successful in providing support for unstructured decisions, such as where the company should locate its next factory.

A **decision-support system (DSS),** an optional extension of an MIS, provides user-friendly languages or programs that retrieve or store data and perform modeling to solve unstructured problems. A **model** is a mathematical representation of the problem or system being examined. Many decision makers use microcomputers with spreadsheet software for decision-support purposes. Many of these packages, such as Lotus 1-2-3, let the user combine spreadsheet, graphics, and database management to model a problem. The user can alter the model easily when the environment suddenly changes.

In large organizations, the MIS staff provides decision makers with appropriate information. Systems analysts ascertain managers' information needs and develop programs or a system of programs to meet them.

SYSTEM ANALYSIS

Few people in a complex system know how their actions affect the system as a whole. For example, a vice president of manufacturing may decide to increase production 20 percent without realizing how much more personnel, raw materials, and inventory space will be required.

DOWNSIZING

Downsizing has two meanings in relation to an MIS. Downsizing can refer to an organization that has to reduce the size of its information systems apparatus and staff. Over the last few years, this has often occurred in various U.S. financial and service businesses such as banking and insurance.

Downsizing can also refer to the use of microcomputers for tasks previously assigned to minicomputers or mainframe computers. Within the past few years, high-end microcomputers have rivaled the powers of these larger machines and taken over functions from them, such as networking. Besides costing less than larger computers, microcomputers also typically experience less "downtime" (less time when they aren't functioning for one reason or another).

Downsizing to microcomputers has been aided by improved microcomputer disk storage technology, which has become both much larger and less costly over the last few years. A technique called mirrored imaging has also made microcomputer data storage more reliable. **Mirrored imaging** involves storing the same data to two disk storage devices. If the first storage device becomes inoperative, the second storage device is still available as a backup.

Trends toward outsourcing and downsizing might be perceived as reasons for people not to enter the information systems field because of a perceived decline in jobs. In fact, despite these trends, a University of Georgia study ranks the job of systems analyst as the fifth fastest growing profession (3.6 percent annual growth), a figure also supported by Department of Labor statistics. In addition, most individuals displaced by such outsourcing and downsizing are easily able to move to other companies.

System analysis is the procedure of analyzing and developing systems. It is also a process for helping management improve an organization by studying and modeling the organization's systems. System analysis is performed by a **systems analyst,** who serves as an adviser to the organization. A systems analyst usually provides management with several alternative ways to solve a particular problem. Although the analyst may recommend a particular solution, management makes the final decision.

A systems analyst may recommend changes in a company's manual procedures or recommend a new, computerized information system. An analyst helps an organization decide what actions will yield the most return on the money invested in the system. The system analysis will succeed or fail based on economic or strategic criteria.

An organization might investigate the feasibility of developing a new information system for various reasons:

Rapid Growth Rapid growth strains existing systems. Transactions may increase so much that the company's staff cannot process them without putting in extensive overtime.

Data Considerations Managers may require more accurate data to improve their decision making. The primary benefit of computerized systems is accuracy; a correctly designed computerized system always correctly processes properly entered data.

Changes in Technology Companies can adopt technologically advanced hardware to process data more efficiently, saving both time and money.

Reducing Human Effort Computerizing applications usually helps people process transactions much faster and handle more work. This is especially important in locations where it is difficult to find clerical staff.

SYSTEM DEVELOPMENT LIFE CYCLE

System analysis is performed in a series of formal steps called the **system development life cycle (SDLC)** (Figure 8.5). The SDLC is typically used to build a system from scratch or to make major changes to an existing system. The topic of system analysis is an involved process and takes two and sometimes three courses to properly cover. Keep in mind that the following discussion involves just a concise summary. During the active life of a system, analysts often will repeat many of the following SDLC steps:

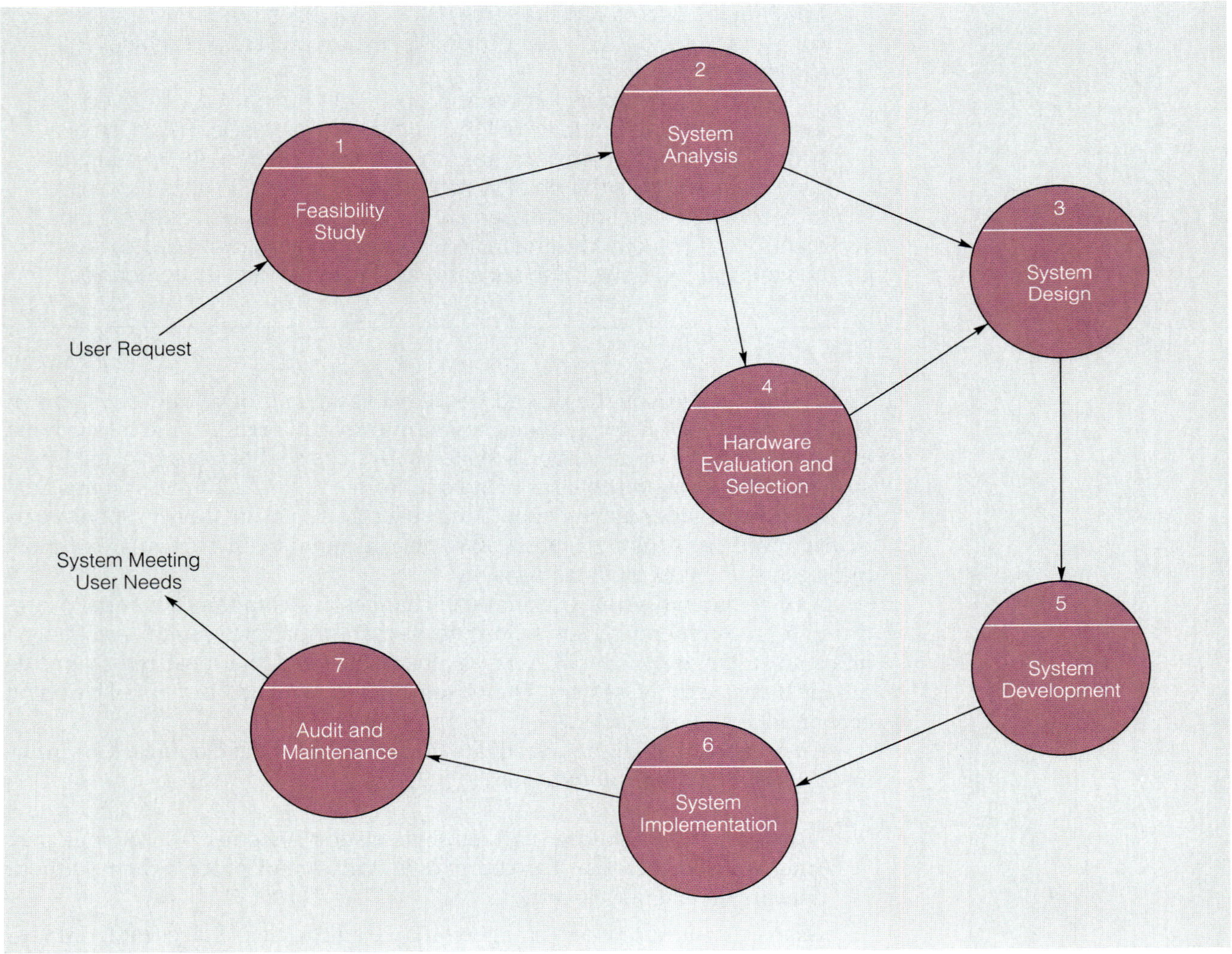

Figure 8.5
The system development life cycle.

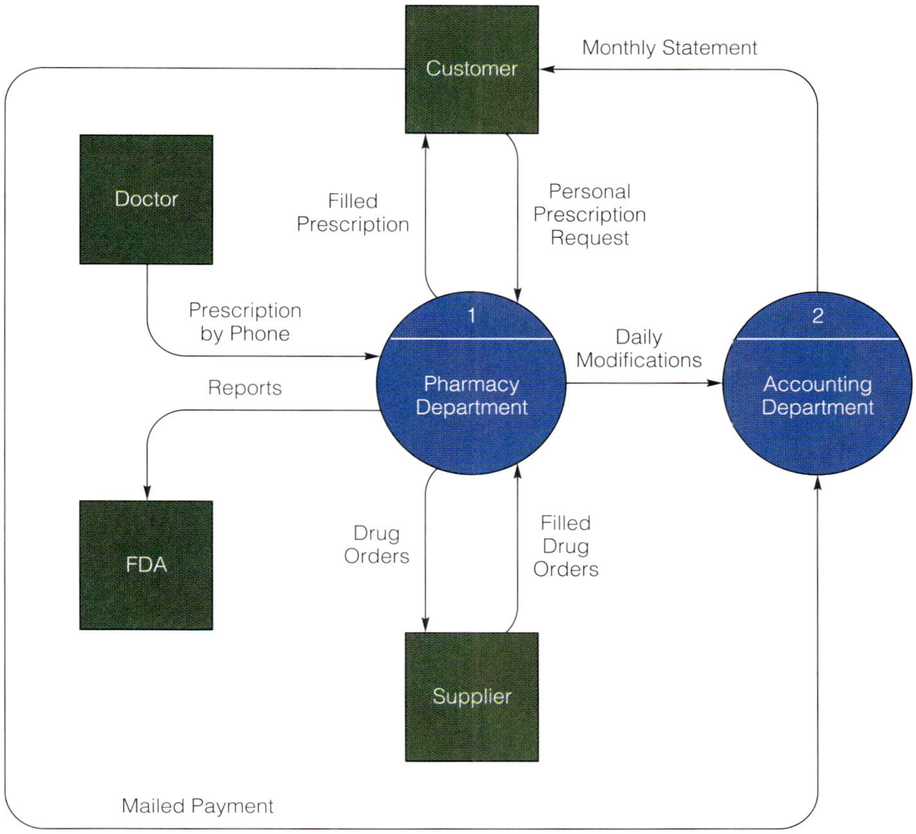

Figure 8.6
A physical data-flow diagram showing the overall view of the Brandon's Pharmacy system.

1. *Feasibility Study.* A **feasibility study** defines the problem and determines whether it can be solved within budget constraints. The system analysis team usually limits its data gathering to interviews.
2. *System Analysis.* The team gathers data (using observation or questionnaires) on all aspects of the organization's existing information system and documents it in the form of **data-flow diagrams.** Figure 8.6 shows an overview data-flow diagram for Brandon's Pharmacy. Figure 8.7 explains some of the symbols typically used in data-flow diagrams and how they would be used to describe the Brandon's Pharmacy accounting process.

   The systems analysis team identifies how the system works as a whole, describes the subsystems' roles, and documents any problems. It may also document and describe the contents of the company's record files in a **data dictionary** (Figure 8.8) (see Chapter 7). In additon, it may describe procedures using **pseudocode,** a highly **structured English** (Figure 8.9). **Decision tables** are another descriptive tool (Figure 8.10). The team formulates possible solutions and describes what needs to be done to achieve them. It then sends a system analysis report to management.
3. *System Design.* The analysis team designs the solution selected by management. The team decides what the system's parts should be and how those parts should function. It develops a test plan for evaluating the system's accuracy and soundness.

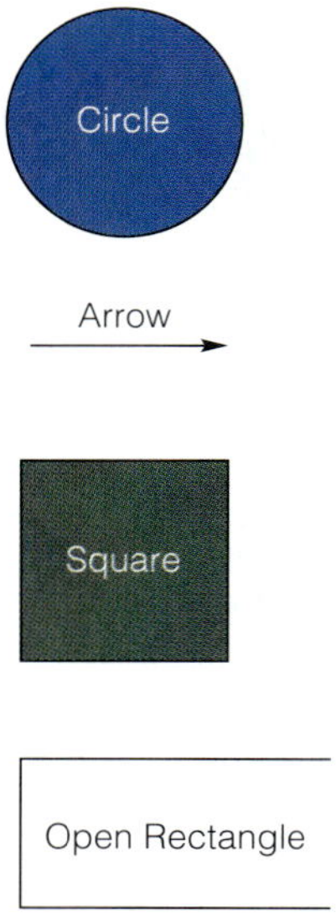

A Process or Data Transformation: Some type of manipulation that is performed on the data. This could take the form of modifying, adding, or deleting data.

A Data Flow: Data that are being passed from one process to another. This could be in the form of either input to a process or output from a process. These data flows are sometimes referred to as interfaces.

An External Entity: An individual or organization that exists outside the system. An external entity can be either an originator or recipient of data generated/processed by the system.

A Data Store: A temporary or permanent file for data. This can take the form of a 3-inch by 5-inch card file, filing cabinet, or computerized storage. The medium is irrelevant—all that really matters is that a storage process be identified.

(a)

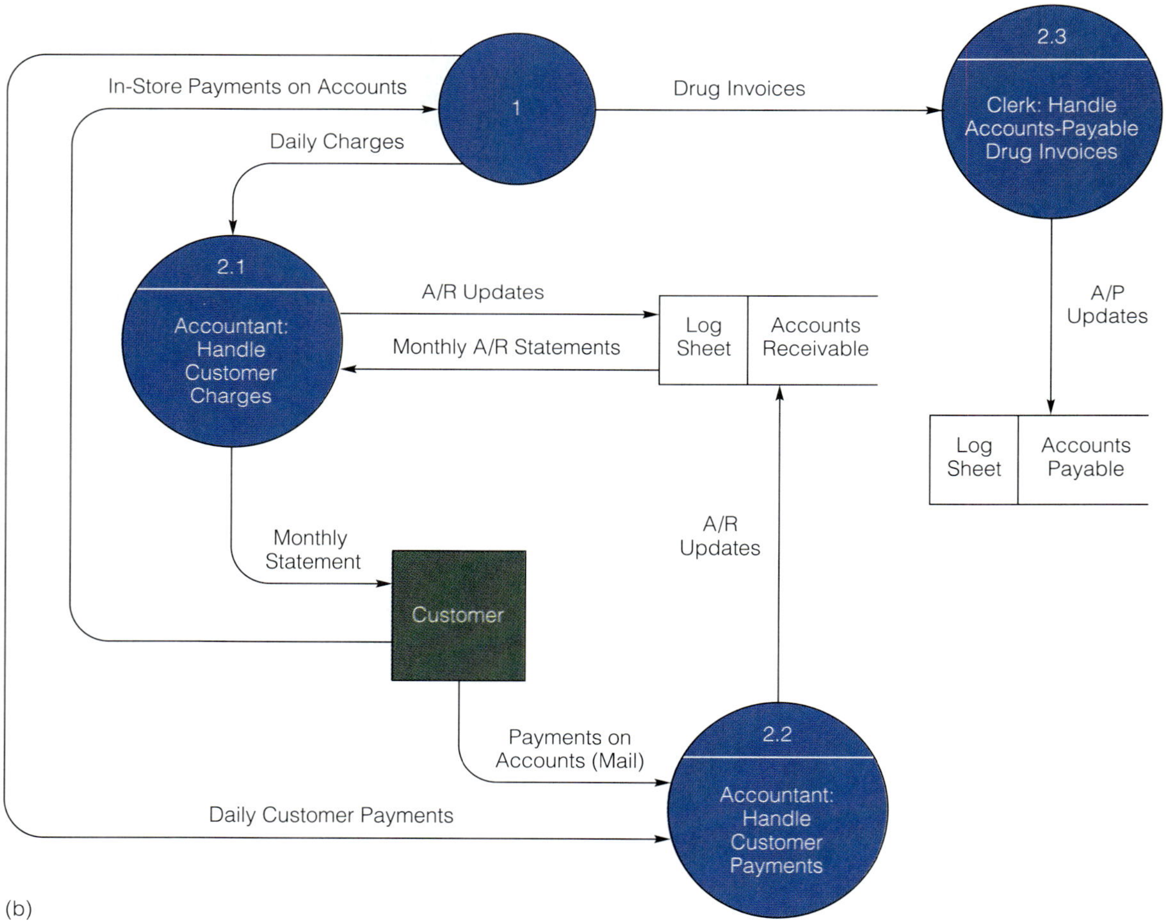

(b)

Figure 8.7

(a) Symbols used in a data-flow diagram. (b) A data-flow diagram of the Brandon's Pharmacy accounting process.

```
CUSTOMER NAME
         CUSTOMER ADDRESS, which consists of the
         following:
             One or both of the following:
                 STREET ADDRESS
                 POST OFFICE BOX NUMBER
             CITY
             STATE
             ZIP
```

Figure 8.8
An entry in the data dictionary defining a customer address field.

Sequence Structure
```
(DO)
  Do operation X
  Do operation Y
```

Selection Structure
```
(IF-THEN-ELSE)
If condition X is true
THEN
  Do operation Y
ELSE
  Do operation Z
ENDIF
```

Loop Structure
```
(DO-WHILE)
  Do X while Y is true
```

Case Structure
```
(SELECT-CASE)
Select the rule that
applies:
Case 1   A<1
  Do operation X
Case 2   A≥1 and A≤10
  Do operation Y
Case 3   A>10
  Do operation Z
```

(a)

```
If the amount of the prescription exceeds $75
       IF the customer has a bill more than 90 days old
       THEN
                Do not extend credit
       ELSE (customer's credit is good)
                Extend credit
       ENDIF
ELSE (prescription amount is $75 or less)
       If the customer has a bill more than 90 days old
       THEN
                Get pharmacist's approval
       ELSE (the customer's credit is good)
                Extend credit
       ENDIF
ENDIF
```

(b)

Figure 8.9
(a) The four basic structured-English constructs (or "primitives") and (b) a nested implementation of the selection structure.

Figure 8.10
A decision table for Brandon's Pharmacy.

Credit Approval Policy	Rules 1	2	3	4
Condition Stub	**Condition Entry**			
1. Prescriptions > $75	Y	N	Y	N
2. Bill overdue by 90+ days	Y	Y	N	N
Action Stub	**Action Entry**			
1. Extend credit			Y	Y
2. Deny credit	Y			
3. Get pharmacist's approval		Y		

Figure 8.11
A portion of structured English (pseudocode) used for designing an accounting module for Brandon's Pharmacy.

```
DOWHILE not end of file (there are still more records)

    Read a record
    IF today's date is greater than 90 days from the
    date of last payment
        Compute the total owed
        Compute penalties
        Compute grand total
        Place overdue notice on bill
    ELSE
        Compute the total owed
    ENDIF
    Print the bill
    ENDDO
```

4. *Hardware Evaluation and Selection.* The team members select and procure the hardware that best fulfills their system design needs.
5. *System Development.* The team determines what software the new system requires, procures or designs the software, and tests it. Writing the programs involves first designing the logic of a program using structured English (Figure 8.11) and then having the logic of the program reviewed by team members in a process referred to as a **structured walkthrough.** After the structured walkthrough has been completed, the program code can be written and tested. **Testing** involves **stub testing,** ensuring that the program works; **string testing,** ensuring that files are passed from one program to another; and **system testing,** ensuring that all parts of the system work.
6. *System Implementation.* Installing a new system is referred to as system conversion. The organization implements the new system and trains its personnel in its use.
7. *System Audit and Maintenance.* During the **system audit** and maintenance stage, the analysis team evaluates the new system on how well it solves the problems identified in the system analysis (or feasibility study) phase. Required changes or improvements are made, and the system is reevaluated.

PERSONAL CASE PROGRESS

From Feasibility Study to Implementation

The first thing Goldstein Associates determines is the feasibility of computerizing Mary Brandon's business, answering the question whether she should pursue the project from a cost-benefit perspective—that is, whether the benefits of the system outweigh the costs of implementing it.

By interviewing Mary and her pharmacist managers and by gathering and analyzing various documents, the Goldstein team determines that a computerized system would indeed help the pharmacies with the problems Mary has defined. For instance, they determine that a system would be able to do such things as generate a year-to-date summary for any patient within 1 minute and generic equivalents for prescriptions within 3 to 5 seconds.

After a contract for services has been arranged, the team proceeds through its analysis of the existing system and the following steps of the SDLC, in which hardware including retail sales terminals and microcomputers is selected. As it turns out, they can satisfy Mary's database needs fairly inexpensively through the programmable features of dBASE III Plus. Her accounting needs are also met by tailoring software that has already been developed for pharmacies.

In planning the implementation of the new system, Harold Stern and Mary decide to start out by putting the system in place at one store, training the entire staff of all the stores, and then rotating the staff through the store with the new system for training. This way, they will be able to work out any bugs in one store before starting the system in other locations, and they will have a staff in the other four stores who is already familiar with the new system.

AUTOMATING SYSTEM ANALYSIS

Analyzing and designing systems has, until recent years, been highly labor-intensive. In the last few years, two techniques have been introduced to make developing systems easier: prototyping and CASE.

Prototyping **Prototyping** involves analyzing the current system, identifying the information needs, and developing a model for a new system. Prototyping techniques follow one of two basic approaches. One approach is to develop a scaled-down version of the system that is capable of performing some rudimentary processing of transactions. This type of prototype lets the analyst test and verify that he or she is on the right track before going very far.

FUTURE TRENDS

The New Millenium

Those who like to predict doom and gloom for the new millenium may be partly right, at least for software developers. Unless they are changed, in the year 2000 the date-handling capabilities of most current programs will suffer a major logic error.

Programs that manipulate dates must follow some system for representing the days, months, and years efficiently. In the year 2000, however, the way these units have been identified up until now will, in many cases, become invalid. For example, the date February 20, 1990, is currently represented in the year/month/day (YY/MM/DD) format as the number 900220. Similiarly, January 15, 1992, is recorded as 920115. This arrangement is convenient because it allows the computer to simply compare the size of the numbers and from that to determine, for example, which date is earlier. However, following this system, January 1, 2000, would be numbered as 000101 and would therefore be perceived by computers as an earlier date than 920115.

This particular problem was created in 1968 when the Federal Information Processing Standard (FIPS) came out with the YY/MM/DD format. FIPS has since approved a four-digit year format, called the ANSI standard X3.30, to remedy the problem, but the new standard must still somehow be implemented on thousands of computers and programs.

Another problem that will crop up concerns the leap year. Some computer programs try to dodge the leap year complication. For instance, whereas some automated teller machines recognize February 29 as a valid leap year date, others simply regard it as the same date as March 1. The usual algorithm for calculating a leap year is that a leap year is divisible by 4, but not by 100. But, in fact, the year 2000 will be a leap year, and it is divisible by both 4 and 100—a fact that many people who developed computer-based algorithms to handle dates overlooked.

A number of businesses apparently face tremendous difficulties in responding to this change. Some have stated that it will take at least 300 person years just to implement this one change in all company programs and data that would be affected.

The other approach is to get an actual system up and running as quickly as possible (usually in less than a week). Rather than being a scaled-down version, this prototype is a limited but, in some respects, fully functioning system, which can then be used to process the information. This type of prototyping involves several repetitions of the analysis and development phases with the user. As the model is enhanced, it can perform more and more of the user's processing needs. The subsequent iterations involve minimal time on the part of the analyst and the user.

With either approach to prototyping, there are two keys to success: First, the user(s) must be committed to providing timely feedback. Second, the prototype must be easy to modify in response to user requests for change. Such modifications are usually accomplished using fourth-generation languages. A **fourth-generation language (4GL)** uses high-level, English-like instructions to retrieve and format data for inquiries and reports. Some languages that qualify as 4GLs are RAMIS II, EASYTRIEVE Plus, FOCUS, NOMAD2, and DATATRIEVE. Some prototypes are also created using the dBASE language.

PERSONAL CASE REVISITED

The Training

DIANNE BONNER is in charge of training the employees of Brandon's Pharmacy. Noting that the pharmacists are, on average, 10 to 15 years older than the clerical staff, she decides the former might be more comfortable if they were together and did not feel that they were in competition with the younger employees. Dianne decides to conduct two different series of sessions, one for the pharmacists of the various stores and one for the clerical staffs.

During the sessions, Dianne sees that some of the staff are having difficulty. She resolves to pay special attention to them, eliciting and answering whatever questions they have. From several years' experience, Dianne knows that older employees may take a bit longer to learn a task, but once they learn it, they often understand the underlying concepts better and can explain them well to others.

Many of the clerical staff are high school or college students who have grown up with computers. They typically learn how to use computer systems in less time than their older counterparts. However, she knows that *cyberphobia* (fear of machines, especially computers) can affect persons of all ages. She's not surprised to find one cyberphobic young man, Barney, who resists all efforts to learn how to use the computer terminals and system. She decides to consult with Mary Brandon on how to proceed with Barney.

CASE CASE (for computer-aided software engineering) is a group of software tools that emerged in the 1980s to help analysts automate several portions of a system analysis project. The tools help generate much of the documentation required to describe a system and are an improved replacement for the pencil and paper most analysts previously used.

One CASE software product that was developed specifically for use on microcomputers is the Excelerator package. Excelerator helps an analyst design, validate, and prepare specifications for applications and information systems. Once a design has been decided on, some CASE tools can create the program specifications used in coding or even generate programs themselves. They can also be used in coding, debugging, and maintaining programs.

CASE tools range in price from about $1000 to $100,000, which puts this type of technology out of the reach of many small- or medium-size businesses. However, in the past few years, some CASE tools have emerged as shareware. With these, the user can test the software before purchasing a license.

CHAPTER REVIEW

All information systems are open systems—that is, they accept input from an environment, process that input, and send output back to the environment. Systems employ feedback to ensure that intermediate processes generate output that is consistent with established standards. Any complex system can be depicted graphically with the black-box concept.

A management information system (MIS) is a formal process that uses manual and computerized tools to provide management with timely decision-making information. MISs serve three levels of decision making: strategic, tactical, and operational. Information is provided in the form of reports—scheduled, exception, demand, and predictive.

An MIS provides decision makers with the information they need to make structured decisions. Unstructured decisions require decision-support systems (DSS). A DSS represents problems in mathematical terms. Spreadsheets are common DSS tools for microcomputers.

An information systems department provides the information that management needs. It builds information systems through the process of system analysis and the system development life cycle (SDLC). The SDLC can be followed to computerize manual information systems or improve computerized systems.

The SDLC includes feasibility studies, system analysis, system design, hardware evaluation and selection, system development, implementation, and audit and maintenance. System analysis and the SDLC require a great deal of labor, but the processes have been automated somewhat recently through the use of protoyping techniques and CASE tools.

KEY TERMS AND CONCEPTS

black-box concept
boundary
CASE
data dictionary
data-flow diagram
data processing
decision-support system (DSS)
decision table
demand report
downsizing
environment
environmental interaction
exception report
feasibility study
feedback
fourth-generation language (4GL)
interface
management information system (MIS)
mirrored imaging
model
operational decision making
outsourcing
predictive report
prototyping
pseudocode
scheduled report
strategic decision making
string testing
structured decision
structured English
structured walkthrough
stub testing
subsystem
synergism
system
system analysis
system analyst
system audit
system development life cycle (SDLC)
system testing
tactical decision making
testing
transaction-processing system
unstructured decisions

CHAPTER QUIZ

Multiple Choice

1. Which of the following is a type of decision that is supported by an MIS?
   a. Tactical decision
   b. Operational decision
   c. Strategic decision
   d. Both a and b
   e. All of the above

2. Which of the following statements is false?
   a. MISs work best for unstructured types of decisions found in the strategic decision-making process.
   b. The heart of DSSs is the model of the problem being investigated.
   c. A DSS allows you to ask what-if questions about a problem.
   d. A common microcomputer-based tool in a DDS is an integrated spreadsheet package.

3. Which of the following is *not* true of systems?
   a. A feedback loop is established to check the output to ensure that it follows preset standards.
   b. Systems have little, if any, interaction with their environment.
   c. The area outside the boundaries of the system is called the environment.
   d. The area of overlap between two systems is called an interface.

4. Which of the following is *not* a phase found in the SDLC?
   a. System development
   b. System analysis
   c. Programming
   d. System implementation
   e. None of the above

5. Which of the following data-gathering or documentation tools is (are) used by an analyst during the system analysis phase of a project?
   a. Data-flow diagrams
   b. Structured English
   c. Interviews
   d. Questionnaires
   e. All of the above

True/False

6. A DSS is not part of an MIS.

7. Strategic planning makes use of masses of internal information.

8. Structured decisions can be most easily supported by an MIS.

9. Systems analysts require little involvement by management concerning selection of what systems to computerize.

10. A walkthrough allows other analysts to examine the logic of a module, to ensure that it will perform a task properly.

Answers

1. e 2. a 3. b 4. c 5. e 6. f 7. f 8. t 9. f 10. t

Exercises

1. Define or describe each of the following:
   a. Management information system
   b. Decision-support system
   c. System
   d. System analysis
   e. System development life cycle

2. The ____________ level of decision making deals with the allocation of resources that are required to meet the objectives of an organization.

3. The ____________ level of decision making deals with the day-to-day operations of the organization to ensure that processes stay within the parameters of preset standards.

4. The ____________ level of decision making deals with the future.

5. ____________ decisions are those decisions for which preset standards have already been established.

6. A(n) ____________ is an entity used to present information to a user and can be on either paper or a CRT.

7. A(n) ____________ report is one that is generated at regular intervals.

8. A(n) ____________ report is generated at the request of the user using some type of query language.

9. A DSS is most frequently used to help with ____________ decisions.

10. The key part of a DDS involves building a(n) ____________ or mathematical representation of the problem.

11. A(n) ____________ is a set of interrelated parts that work toward a common goal.

12. ____________ is the concept that the whole is greater than the sum of its parts.

13. The overlap of two systems or subsystems where no processing occurs is called the ____________ .

14. A(n) ____________ system interacts with its environment.

15. The process of sampling output and sending it back into the system as input to verify that it is within established parameters is referred to as ____________ .

16. The ____________ concept allows any system to be depicted as input, process, and output.

17. ____________ is the process of studying and modeling systems.

18. The phases that are used in the system analysis process represent methodology that is called the ____________ .

19. The ____________ phase of the SDLC defines the problem and determines whether a system can be cost-justified.

20. A data-flow diagram uses four symbols to document any system. List and state the purpose of each symbol: ____________ , ____________ , ____________ , and ____________ .

21. A(n) ____________ is used during the system analysis phase to document each data item.

22. The output of the system analysis phase that is received by management is called the __________ .

23. __________ resembles structured English with input, output, and control statements and is used to design the logic for a module.

24. A __________ is conducted by other analysts to verify that the logic of a module functions as it is supposed to function.

25. __________ testing verifies that information is passed correctly from one file to the next.

26. __________ conversion ensures that the files have been properly created for the new system.

27. Before employees can use the new system, they have to be __________ or educated as to how the new system operates.

28. The process of examining the new system to ensure that it operates as it is supposed to is called the __________ .

IN YOUR OWN CASE

1. Identify a group or organization with which you are associated that includes several levels of management or responsibility. What types of formal or informal reports or information do persons at various levels of this organization depend on? What improvements would you like to see in the kinds of information individuals in that organization receive?

2. Are you part of an organization that has a management information system? Make some inquiries about how the system operates. Clarify your own role with regard to the information you receive or the information you are responsible for conveying to others. How might a system analysis benefit your organization?

QUESTIONS FOR THOUGHT

1. How good do you think you would be as a member of a system analysis team? At which steps in the SDLC process would you be most effective? Which would be most difficult for you? Why?

2. What kinds of internally gathered information help organizations compete with other organizations? What kinds of externally gathered information do they need to compete? How can computers help in gathering, storing, or retrieving such information?

9

ETHICS, SOCIAL ISSUES, AND COMPUTER SECURITY

CHAPTER OBJECTIVES

After completing this chapter, you should be able to

- ***Discuss some questions about computer education***
- ***Discuss some questions related to job security and to computer monitoring of employees***
- ***Discuss the ergonomics of computers***
- ***Define and discuss computer crime***
- ***Discuss software piracy***
- ***Discuss viruses and how to avoid them***
- ***Discuss individual privacy questions related to computers***
- ***Discuss methods of computer security and control***

SOCIETY AND COMPUTERS: SOME SOCIAL

1970	Fair Credit Reporting Act of 1970 lets individuals inspect their files and challenge the accuracy of information.
1973	Equity Funding scandal draws national attention to the need for computer controls.
1974	Privacy Act of 1974 regulates how federal government manages information collected on citizens.
1978	Right to Financial Privacy Act limits government access to customer records of financial institutions. Total number of computers in the United States tops 500,000.
1981	Journal articles first warn about hazards of sitting in front of a computer or terminal for long hours.
1983	Total number of computers in the United States tops 10 million.
1984	Comprehensive Crime Control Act makes accessing federal files a felony.
1986	Computer Fraud and Abuse Act strengthens and enhances the 1984 legislation.
1987	Lotus Corporation drops copy protection on Lotus 1-2-3. This was the last major software package to be copy-protected.
1988	A software "worm" released into Internet sabotages over 6000 computers.

MILESTONES

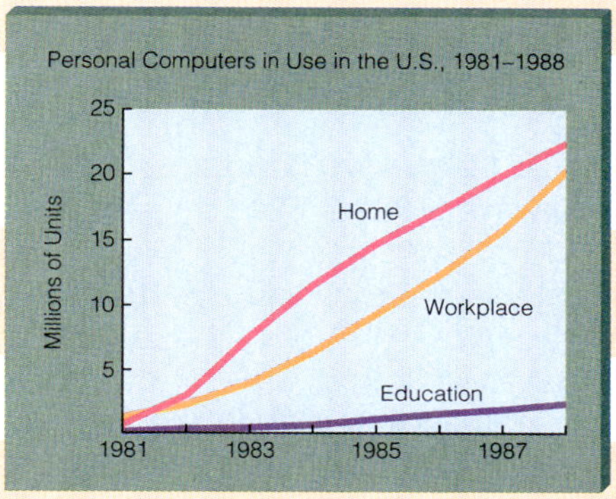
Personal Computers in Use in the U.S., 1981–1988
Millions of Units
25
20
15
10
5
Home
Workplace
Education
1981
1983
1985
1987

Lotus 1-2-3/G
Lotus 1-2-3/G

PERSONAL CASE

Computers and Ethical Issues

Yesterday, Ben and his wife Jill Milligan went to buy the sports car they've always wanted. The deal was struck with the understanding that the auto dealership would arrange 2-year financing for the couple through a local bank.

Today Ben receives a call at work from the manager of the dealership, who apologetically lets him know that his request for a loan has been turned down by the bank due to a bad credit rating.

"What's wrong with my credit?" he asks the manager.

"Well," she replies, "they say you defaulted on an earlier car loan. They also say you're about $5000 behind on some credit payments."

Ben can't believe it. None of these things are true. In fact, Ben is an upper-middle-level manager for SX Corporation where he's worked for 16 years, currently earns about $75,000 a year, and has no outstanding debts except for the mortgage on his house. Furthermore, Jill is a high school science teacher for the town of Belmont, earning about $34,000 a year. Until recently, the couple has struggled some to finance their two daughters' college educations, but now they really have no economic problems.

Ben calls the bank that refused his loan and gets no satisfaction. As a matter of fact, the situation worsens. The banker says that a report from the local credit bureau also shows that Ben is divorced and behind on his child-support payments. Ben strenuously denies these allegations.

"Mr. Milligan," says the banker, "Maybe you should go to the credit bureau and get this straightened out."

"I'll do just that," says Ben.

A distressed Ben visits the credit bureau office obtains a free copy of his credit report, which the office is legally required to give to anyone who has been refused credit within the past 30 days. As he reads it, Ben realizes that there are apparently two Ben Milligans in Belmont and that the information in his credit report is actually about the other man. After some further inquiries, the credit bureau clerk realizes this is true and promises to get the mistake corrected.

On his way back to work, a stunned Ben Milligan wonders how many other people go through such frustrating experiences. When he gets to the office, Ben calls his banker and requests that he call the credit bureau to confirm that the error has been corrected.

Imagine the social chaos that would ensue if computers were to suddenly cease to operate. Patients in hospitals would die, trains and airplanes would become unsafe, roads would become snarled with cars as traffic lights failed, communications would break down, and production and manufacturing would come to a standstill. The more dependent we become on computers, the more concerned we must be about protecting their operation and determining that they serve not only our material purposes but also our ethical concerns.

Ethics is the study of conduct and moral judgment. In this chapter, we address the ethical use of the computer by government, businesses, and individuals. We examine what obligation schools have to teach computer use. We also raise issues about computers in the workplace. We discuss the individual's right to privacy and whether the gathering of computer data on people violates that right. Finally, we look at ways users can safeguard their computer systems.

EDUCATION AND COMPUTER LITERACY

In the near future, say some business and education professionals, an individual who wants a good job will find it is as important to possess computer skills as to know the three *R*s. If this is so, we are ethically bound to incorporate computer instruction in school curricula and ensure that students are computer literate by the time they are ready to enter the work force.

Definitions of computer literacy vary. Some define it as being able to write a program that enables a computer to perform some task. By such a standard, our educational system should be introducing elementary grade students to simple languages such as BASIC or LOGO. Others equate computer literacy with lower-level skills such as using various application software. Still others insist that computer literacy projects should mainly teach about the impact computers have on society.

COMPUTERS IN THE WORKPLACE

We know that computers have made blue- and white-collar workers more productive, but we know little about how employees view computers. One thing we do know is that many workers are worried that their skills will be rendered obsolete by computer technology. In fact, computers have eliminated several employment positions, changed how workers perform their duties, and created a variety of new jobs.

JOB SECURITY

Few studies have been done on how computers are affecting job security. Computer advocates claim that computer technology has created millions of new jobs, but detractors say it has put millions out of work. Conscientious companies retrain those employees who lose jobs to computerization. Generally, those jobs that require the least technical skills have been the first to be computerized. For example, many manufacturing jobs that require routine welding, sorting, or assembly tasks are now performed by robots. In the office, manual filing and typing chores are being replaced by computerized counterparts (Figure 9.1).

Computerization has also increasingly affected middle management. Historically, much of the work performed by middle managers involved summarizing data and generating reports for higher management. In the 1980s, as more and more businesses began to implement true computer management information systems (and as foreign competition grew), jobs for these middle-level managers declined dramatically.

Figure 9.1
Computer-automated assembly.

PERFORMANCE MONITORING

Computerized monitoring of employee work performance is a potentially explosive issue. Managers can program computers to track how many mistakes a typist or a data-entry clerk makes, how much time a worker spends away from a terminal, or how many transactions an accountant handles in a day.

Computer monitoring has become so common that a Computer Spying Hotline has been started by the union-affiliated National Association of Working Women in Cleveland. Such organizations argue that this type of monitoring, especially when it is poorly applied, puts employees under serious stress. A study of 762 monitored and nonmonitored terminal users, conducted jointly by the University of Wisconsin and the Communications Workers of America, found that monitored employees suffer more tension, exhaustion, neck pain, and sore wrists than nonmonitored employees.

HEALTH CONSIDERATIONS

Millions of employees suffer eye, back, and muscle strain from spending their workdays at a computer.

Hazards of Monitors Unions and other employee groups continue to ask what health risks may arise from the long-term use of monitors. The question has not yet been answered conclusively. Some studies suggest that monitor use is hazardous; others suggest it is not.

The Environmental Protection Agency (EPA) and the Federal Drug Administration (FDA) continue to study closely the use of monitors in the workplace. The EPA was spurred to action after a study it conducted identified 60-hertz magnetic fields from power lines as a possible but as yet unproved cause of cancer in humans. Although screens have come under study for their radiation emissions, the EPA's study appears to focus more on the fields created by the use of any electrical appliance. The FDA is conducting a comprehensive study of the effects of electromagnetic radiation from video display terminals and television sets.

Many manufacturers of monitors are not waiting for these studies to be completed before addressing this issue. Some already make monitors that emit lower levels of radiation. In 1991 the necessary modifications added about $100 to the price of the monitor, but this figure should decline as the technology is employed more widely.

Looking at a monitor all day may or may not be dangerous, but there is little doubt it can cause red eyes and sore muscles. Users can minimize eyestrain by taking a break after every hour of viewing. They can also ergonomically design their workplaces to reduce muscle strain and increase efficiency.

Ergonomics **Ergonomics** is the art and science of adapting work and working conditions to suit the individual worker. For example, hardware manufacturers now build sloping keyboards for a more comfortable typing position and put monitors on swivel bases so that screens can be adjusted to suit the user's viewing angle. They also produce a variety of screen colors—including white, green, and amber—which reduce eyestrain. Ergonomically designed furniture helps office workers reduce backache and muscle strain (Figure 9.2). Ergonomically designed work environments cost more than traditional offices, but increased productivity more than compensates for the added expense.

COMPUTER CRIME

Computer crime is the commission of unlawful acts by using computer technology. Some experts claim that only one-tenth of the computer crimes commit-

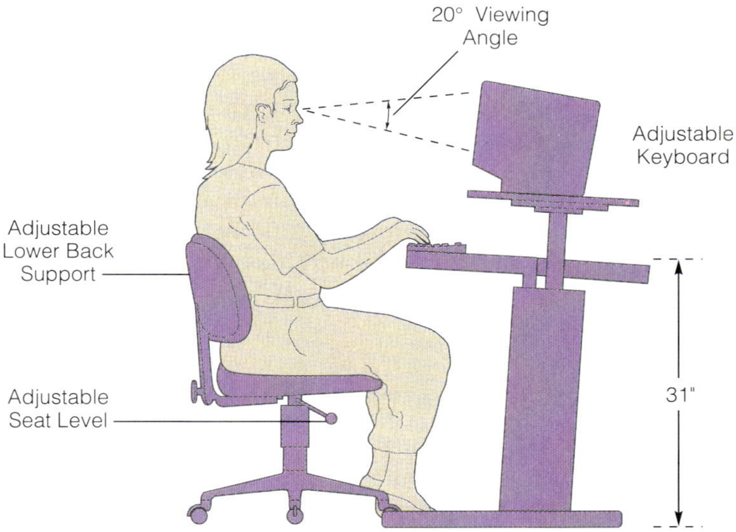

Figure 9.2
Examples of ergonomic furniture.

ted in the United States are actually reported. One reason for this lopsided ratio is that many businesses are reluctant to report computer crime for fear it will cause stockholders to lose confidence in them. The following are several varieties of computer crime.

FRAUDULENT TRANSACTIONS

Equity Funding (1973) A former favorite of Wall Street investors, Equity Funding Corporation comprised a group of investment and insurance companies. Several top-level managers from some of these companies colluded to attract additional investors by lying about company profits. They also created 50,000 bogus insurance policies on the computer and sold them, packaged with bona fide policies, to other insurance companies. The group coded the fake policies in such a way that the company's auditors could not distinguish them from bona fide policies. Out of $3 billion in policies, $2.1 billion were fraudulent. The fraud was uncovered, and more than 20 individuals were convicted on federal charges.

Union Dime When police raided a bookie's office, they found that one of the biggest bettors was a bank teller who was betting over $30,000 a week. The bank was informed and found that the teller had been entering fraudulent records to the computer to cover the skimming of money from bank accounts. The bank lost more than $1 million.

Pacific Telephone Jerry Schneider is a computer wizard who built his own computer system at the age of 10 years. Years later Schneider began raiding the garbage dumpsters of Pacific Telephone to retrieve the company's discarded computer printouts and other documents providing account numbers, passwords, and computer procedures. Using this information, Schneider would dial into the Pacific Telephone inventory-control system, order equipment to be delivered to himself, and then erase all traces of the transaction.

Schneider became so successful that he had to hire assistants. One of those assistants, who had asked his boss for a raise and been turned down, reported Schneider to the police.

Enough Is Enough! A young Englishman stole 50,000 pounds (£) from the company that employed him and then manipulated computer data to cover the theft. The fraud was discovered, but management declined to prosecute for fear the publicity would worry the company's stockholders. The young man then demanded management provide him with a letter of recommendation, which it did. He used this recommendation to obtain a job at another company. Four years later, the company traced a £150,000 fraud to him. Again, management refused to prosecute, and again the thief demanded a letter of recommendation. But the thief pushed too hard when he demanded £3500 in severance pay. The company filed charges.

DESTRUCTIVE HACKING

The 414 gang was a group of teenage Wisconsin computer hackers who used microcomputers to gain access to computer systems across the country. Gang members would obtain or guess passwords to a system, examine files, run programs, and discover as much about the system as possible. During their electronic forays, they damaged key files of several companies. They also penetrated a hospital system used to monitor critically ill patients. A physician stated several people could have died if the gang had damaged the system. The members of the 414 gang wound up having their computers confiscated, and some had to pay fines.

VIRUSES

A newer form of computer crime is the spreading of software **viruses.** Like their biological counterparts, these viruses can infect many parts of the host system—application programs, data files, and disk operating systems—and are self-replicating. Systems can be infected by on-line services, electronic bulletin boards, and users swapping disks. Once in a computer's RAM, the virus can infect other programs loaded for execution.

Software viruses wreak havoc by destroying data, modifying data, or sabotaging printing. The bug may command the computer to display the message "GOTCHA" and reboot the system, causing everything in RAM to be lost; it may destroy the file allocation table so that files cannot be found by the operating system; or it might reformat a disk containing crucial information, thus destroying its contents—a particularly harmful event for a fixed disk user.

Software viruses are created and released by programmers, sometimes as a prank but often for malicious purposes. "Scores," the most widespread virus to infect Apple Macintosh microcomputers, was originally designed to attack custom applications used by a Texas company. The virus creates difficulty in running certain Apple programs and printing from applications and causes systems to crash when certain applications are started.

SOFTWARE PIRACY

Software piracy is the illegal duplication of software, a continual problem for the software industry. Software manufacturers estimate that for every popular microcomputer application package sold, pirates make four unauthorized duplications. Piracy costs software developers billions of dollars a year and increases the cost of original copies to the typical consumer.

VIRUS "VACCINES"

A number of software companies have introduced products designed to search out and destroy software viruses (Figure 9.3). These programs can be used to scan files contained on disk or in RAM for storage patterns (bit configurations) that match known viruses. Scanning each foreign diskette, before you use it on your system, can dramatically reduce the probability of contracting a known virus. Unfortunately, however, these programs are of little use when a new virus is introduced. Be prepared to purchase updates as the virus-prevention software is updated to fight new viral strains.

Norton Anti-Virus, Certus LAN, Data Physician, Virex-PC, Virucide, and Vi-Spy are some common antiviral software.

A hardware approach to detecting a viral infection is to install a circuit board, such as Thunderbyte, which is preprogrammed with algorithms to search for virus characteristics. The circuit board is placed in the computer like any other board, whereupon any software loaded into the computer is automatically checked. These systems can also be used to prevent unauthorized disk formatting and detects any write operations that bypass the operating system.

Figure 9.3

Icons of several common virus applications. Such antiviral software can be used to locate, and then eliminate, viruses found in RAM or on disk.

Illegal copying may be done by persons or companies wanting to use free copies of particular software packages, or it may be committed with the intention of selling pirated software. In trying to avoid purchasing software, businesses have been caught making up to 100 unauthorized copies or more of a single software program. Selling pirated software copies is particularly prevalent in foreign countries, especially Brazil, Taiwan, and Saudi Arabia.

BATTLING PIRACY ON THE CORPORATE FRONT

To battle piracy, the Software Publishers Association (SPA) started a Copyright Protection Fund in 1988 to battle piracy. According to SPA officials, software companies are losing $2.4 billion in sales a year to pirates.

The SPA is aggressive. They (1) issue cease-and-desist orders, (2) do audits in lieu of litigation, and (3) they do litigate. Once it has been informed of potential corporate piracy, it writes to the firm and indicates that the firm has two choices: submit itself to an audit of its software by SPA staff or face litigation and all the corresponding publicity. Most CEOs decide to submit to the audit to avoid the negative publicity.

The SPA also takes a more pro-active approach through education. It provides brochures such as "Software Use and the Law" and "Is It Okay to Copy My Colleague's Software?" for distribution to employees (Figure 9.4). It also provides a copy of a program called SPAudit that can be copied by anyone within the business to track who has which software package within the company. SPAudit is used to check the directories of a hard disk and develop a list of any 645-plus copyrighted programs that might be contained on that disk. This list can then be compared with a company list of software purchase orders. If there is no purchase order, most likely the software is pirated.

Figure 9.4
Brochures available from the SPA.

The primary legal protection software manufacturers have is **copyright** protection. This is the easiest and least expensive form of protection a software manufacturer can obtain, but it does not provide as much protection as a patent would. Federal laws are unclear about what rights a copyright provides a software developer, but courts have awarded as much as $100,000 in damages for copyright infringement for each pirated copy of certain licensed software.

Many manufacturers have tried placing copy-protection features on their software disks to prevent piracy. However, many people strongly object to copy-protection schemes, which they feel wrongfully penalize honest software

Figure 9.5
Example of the Ashton-Tate license agreement.

Software License Agreement

Ashton-Tate®

Important: Please read this page before opening the disk package. By opening the package, you show your agreement to the terms of this license.

THIS IS A LICENSE. IT GIVES YOU CERTAIN LIMITED RIGHTS TO USE THE SOFTWARE, SOFTWARE COPIES, AND RELATED MATERIALS. YOU DO NOT BECOME THE OWNER OF, AND ASHTON-TATE RETAINS TITLE TO, ALL THE SOFTWARE, SOFTWARE COPIES AND RELATED MATERIALS. ALL RIGHTS NOT SPECIFICALLY GRANTED IN THIS LICENSE ARE EXPRESSLY RESERVED BY ASHTON-TATE.

Refund

If you don't wish to follow the terms of this license agreement, you may obtain a full refund by returning this package with your receipt to the place of purchase within three (3) days, provided you have not opened the sealed disk packet. Your right to return this product for a refund for this reason expires on the fourth day after purchase. For upgrade/update only, call Customer Service at **(213) 329-9989** for the upgrade/update return policy.*

Definitions

In this license agreement, the following terms shall have the following meanings: "Software" means the computer programs contained in the disks in this package, together with any updates subsequently supplied by Ashton-Tate. "Software Copies" means the actual copies of all or any portion of the Software, including back-ups, updates, and merged or partial copies permitted hereunder or subsequently supplied by Ashton-Tate. "Related Materials" means all of the printed materials provided In this package or subsequently supplied by Ashton-Tate for use with the Software.

Permitted Uses/You may:

- Load into RAM and use the Software on a single terminal or a single workstation of a computer (or its replacement). You may use the LAN version of this Software, if applicable, on a local area network with up to five (5) workstations or up to five (5) workstations of a multi-user computer. Additional workstations must be separately licensed by Ashton-Tate.
- Install the Software onto a permanent storage device (a hard disk drive).
- Make and maintain up to three (3) back-up copies of the Software, provided they are used only for back-up purposes **(or by you personally on another workstation, such as one at another location, so long as the Software is not used on more than one machine at one time)** and you keep possession of the back-ups. In addition, all the information appearing on the original disk labels (including the copyright notice) must be copied onto the backup labels.

Uses Not Permitted/You may not:

- Make copies of the Software, except as permitted above.
- Make copies of the Related Materials.
- Use the Software in a network or multiple user arrangement unless you have sufficient copies of the LAN version for the terminals or workstations from which the Software will actually be accessed.
- Rent, lease, sublicense, time-share, lend or transfer the Software, Software Copies, Related Materials or your rights under this license except that transfers may be made with Ashton-Tate's prior written authorization.
- Alter, decompile, disassemble or reverse-engineer the Software, or make any attempt to unlock or bypass the initialization system used on initialized disks.
- Remove or obscure any copyright or trademark notices.

Additional Restrictions

In the event this Software is of any of the following types, the applicable additional restrictions apply:

- Educational Product. The educational Software, Software Copies, and Related Materials may only be used for internal educational purposes.
- Upgrade Products. Any upgrade Software, Software Copies, and Related Materials may only be used upon destruction of the prior version of the Software upgraded.
- U.S. Domestic Products. Software, Software Copies, and Related Materials may not be used outside of the United States without the prior written authorization of Ashton-Tate.
- International Products. The United States Department of Commerce imposes certain restrictions on exports of technical data Including Software, Software Copies, and Related Materials, to certain destinations.
- United Kingdom Products. You may not use or resell the Software, Software Copies, and Related Materials outside of EEC member countries.

Duration

This agreement is effective from the day you open the sealed disk packet. Your license continues for fifty years for United States domestic products and twenty-five years for international and United Kingdom products or until you return to Ashton-Tate the original disks and any back-up copies, whichever comes first.

If you breach this agreement, Ashton-Tate may terminate this license upon notifying you in writing. You will be required to return all Software, Software Copies, and Related Materials. Ashton-Tate may also enforce all other rights at law or in equity.

General

This agreement represents our entire understanding and agreement regarding the Software, Software Copies, and Related Materials, and supersedes any prior purchase order, communications, advertising, or representations. This license may be modified by a written amendment signed by an authorized Ashton-Tate officer; if any provision of this agreement shall be found to be unlawful, void, or for any reason unenforceable, it shall be deemed severable from, and shall in no way affect the validity or enforceability of the remaining provisions of this agreement. This agreement shall be governed by California law.

U.S. Government Restricted Rights

The Software, Software Copies and Related Materials are provided with RESTRICTED RIGHTS. Use, duplication, or disclosure by the Government Is subject to restrictions as set forth in subdivision (c)(1)(ii) of the Rights in Technical Data and Computer Software Clause at 48 C.F.R. 252.227-7013. Contractor/Manufacturer is Ashton-Tate Corporation, 20101 Hamilton Avenue, Torrance, California 90509-9972.

BY OPENING THE PACKAGE CONTAINING THE SOFTWARE DISKS, YOU ACKNOWLEDGE THAT YOU HAVE READ EVERY PROVISION OF THIS AGREEMENT.

This Software is subject to the LIMITED WARRANTY specified on the reverse side.

users by making it difficult for them to create legitimate backup copies of legally purchased software. Copy-protection schemes also may harm a computer's disk operating system. As a result, most software producers no longer install copy protection on their popular application packages.

Many software developers do not sell actual software to consumers but rather offer a form of **license agreement,** specifically the right to use a particular package on one computer (Figure 9.5). These "shrink-wrap licenses" often provide neither warranty on the software nor compensation provisions if the software malfunctions. The intent of such policies is to prevent users from buying a software program, copying it, and then returning the purchased copy, claiming it is defective.

Eventually, the courts will determine whether shrink-wrap licenses are valid. In the meantime, there is much confusion over how software can be used. For instance, no one is sure whether a user who purchases a word processing

CHARACTERISTICS OF A COMPUTER CRIMINAL

Donn Parker, an expert on computer crime, gives the following profile of the typical computer criminal:

- Male
- White-collar employee
- 18 to 30 years of age
- In a trusted position within the company
- Never been in trouble before
- Behavior not markedly different in other respects from that of his or her peers
- Trying to overcome some type of personal problem, typically financial
- Considers his or her acts justifiable because they are against a corporation rather than a person

It should be noted that the gender pattern is changing as more women enter the white-collar work force. Computer criminals tend to be young probably because financial burdens are often heaviest early in one's career. Often the criminal is supporting a family on limited resources. The unlikelihood of having committed previous crimes probably derives from the fact that the typical computer criminal simply would not rob someone at gunpoint. Stealing from a faceless entity like a corporation seems like another matter. Computer criminals will be less frequently white-collar workers as the computer becomes a more common tool for people in other lines of work.

software disk licensed for one computer can use the disk both at the office and at home if it is for the same work.

Shrink-wrap licenses are particularly problematic for schools. With software groups offering bounties for information about illegal copies, many schools have initiated policies stating that anyone caught copying school-owned software can be flunked and expelled from school. The easiest way to avoid trouble is to not copy software unless you have purchased it yourself.

FEDERAL LAWS ABOUT COMPUTER CRIME

The **Comprehensive Crime Control Act of 1984** prohibits unauthorized individuals from accessing computer records to obtain information protected by the Right to Financial Privacy Act of 1978 or data contained in the files of a consumer-reporting agency. It also prohibits them from using, modifying, destroying, or disclosing information stored on government-owned computers or sabotaging government computers or software.

The **Computer Fraud and Abuse Act of 1986** goes much further. It defines a variety of computer-related activities as criminal and specifies punishments. Fines can be up to $250,000 or twice the value of stolen data, and prison sentences can range from 1 to 20 years, depending on the offense and whether it is a first offense.

This act applies only to computers used by the federal government and federally insured financial institutions and to computer crimes affecting interstate or foreign commerce. It makes it a felony to access such a computer in order to

Figure 9.6
Thoroughly tested software is essential for controlling such sensitive systems as those that run nuclear power plants.

alter or destroy data such as medical records or to use the computer to steal amounts over $1000. It also makes it a misdemeanor to trespass in a "federal interest computer" or to traffic in stolen passwords.

The act of 1986 was first used to prosecute Robert Morris, a computer science graduate at Cornell University. Morris was found guilty of introducing a "worm" into a nationwide computer network (Internet) that sabotaged over 6000 computers in November 1988. He was sentenced to 3 years of probation and ordered to perform 400 hours of community service.

SOFTWARE DEVELOPMENT

Ethical software developers thoroughly test their software before selling it. This can be a life or death matter when the software runs systems that monitor hospital patients, control air traffic, regulate traffic lights, provide switching for railways, or automate nuclear power plants (Figure 9.6).

Consider the following case. A programmer made a minor change in the program used to update the New York City Welfare Department's master file. The programmer considered the revision "trivial" and did not test the program after making the change. In the following months, welfare recipients whose names were listed in the master file died, moved away, or lost their eligibility to receive payments.

Normally, these recipients would have been deleted from the welfare rolls when the master file was updated, but the change caused the updated program to ignore batch-entered deletions to the master file and kept open files that should have been closed. For 3 months, the system's printers spewed out thousands of checks to people who were dead, had left the city, or were no longer entitled to payments. Field workers began to report that welfare pay-

PERSONAL CASE PROGRESS

The Evils of Piracy

BEN MILLIGAN is walking through the office one afternoon and passes one of his employees, John Parrish, working away on his computer. When Ben stops to chat, he notices that John has the latest release of a best-selling graphics-based spreadsheet package running on his computer. This surprises Ben because the SX Corporation is standardized on other spreadsheet software—and because Ben's signature would have been necessary to approve its purchase. He asks John where he got it.

John replies, "I got it from my next-door neighbor, a tax consultant."

Ben feels a panic attack hitting. For one thing, John has placed the SX Corporation at risk by using the pirated software at work. For another, John has committed software piracy by copying the software from his friend. Ben tells John about the SPA and how it monitors such actions. John is surprised to hear that what he has done is both illegal and actionable. In some embarrassment, he deletes the pirated program files from his fixed disk and assures Ben there will be no recurrence.

ments were still being paid to closed cases. By the time the error was discovered, $7.5 million had been paid to people whose names should have been deleted from the files.

Welfare workers were able to find out who received the checks but getting the money back was another matter. Most of the checks were for less than $300, and the cost of retrieving the money through suits and prosecutions could easily have cost more than the entire amount. In the end, New York City taxpayers wound up paying millions of dollars for the programmer's mistake.

INDIVIDUAL PRIVACY AND COMPUTERS

Privacy has been defined as the claim of individuals, groups, or institutions to determine for themselves when, how, and to what extent personal information about them is communicated to others. Some people believe that the enormous capacity of computers to store and retrieve information makes it easy for government or businesses to infringe on our right to privacy.

Institutions that store data on individuals include schools, banks, credit offices, drivers license bureaus, state and federal internal revenue offices, law

Figure 9.7
Libraries compare their data records on books and borrowers against other computer information systems to keep track of things.

enforcement offices, libraries, insurance companies, and many more. The federal government alone has thousands of data-collection and -storage systems.

An applicant for a bank loan will be asked for information on his or her place of employment, outstanding loans, names and current balances of any credit cards, and other similar information. The applicant will be asked to sign a statement allowing the bank to check the applicant's credit status. Usually, such data are used to our benefit. However, it is also possible for this information to be used against us.

Data stored in one computerized information system can be matched against data in other systems (Figure 9.7). For example, by matching a computer record of federal government employees and a computer listing of student loan defaulters, the government identified more than 47,000 of its own workers who failed to pay back their student loans.

In another example of record matching, the employees of a federal agency charged with the recovery of arrears child-support payments were themselves computer-checked for compliance with child-support laws. The government discovered 540 employees who were behind in child-support payments.

Such matching can be performed with any number of computerized information systems. Opponents of computer matching decry the process as a danger to privacy and want it controlled. Proponents claim record matching is an effective method to discover fraud and enforce the law.

Electronic funds transfer (EFT) systems also pose a threat to privacy. An EFT system electronically transfers an individual's paycheck to a bank account. The person then may use a debit card to make purchases of groceries, gasoline, books, and so on. The amount of each purchase is automatically debited from the individual's account, recorded, and transferred to the appropriate vendor's account. This system is very popular among vendors because it makes bad check writing a thing of the past. Banks benefit in that the system cuts the paperwork required to process checks.

At the end of the month, the bank sends its EFT-account holders a detailed listing of all the places they made purchases. However, such systems paint a detailed financial portrait of account holders. The question is, Who is allowed access to this information? Some people believe that these systems pose an unprecedented threat to privacy and freedom, arguing that government access to EFT information smacks of "Big Brother" control.

The U.S. Supreme Court has yet to review a case that has demanded a direct ruling on exactly what rights to privacy a citizen has under the Constitution. However, in a number of landmark cases, the Court has ruled that a right to privacy is implied by the First, Third, Fourth, Fifth, and Ninth Amendments.

FEDERAL PRIVACY LEGISLATION

The U.S. Congress and several state legislatures have passed legislation to safeguard an individual's privacy. Some important federal legislation on privacy includes the following:

- Congress passed the **Fair Credit Reporting Act of 1970** to mitigate problems associated with the collection and use of information from credit, insurance, and employment records. Under the law, credit bureaus and investigatory reporting agencies must permit people on whom they maintain records the opportunity to inspect their files. If an individual challenges the accuracy of a file, the organization holding the records must review the data and correct any errors.
- The **Freedom of Information Act of 1970** allows individuals access to data about themselves stored in a federal government database or file.
- The **Educational Privacy Act** permits parents and students access to students' educational records. No federal funds will be made available to an educational agency that has a policy of denying parents and students the right to inspect and review relevant educational records. Also, educational records can only be disclosed to state and local authorities who have need for this information according to laws of those jurisdictions and to state and federal educational agencies. The rights provided for under this act may be waived by the student.
- The **Privacy Act of 1974** stipulates that the government must annually report all of its data banks in the Federal Register. It further regulates how the federal government manages information collected on citizens. Federal agencies must report how they intend to use the data; if an agency plans to use it for any but the stated purpose, it must first acquire the permission of the affected individual. Individuals have the right to review information stored about them, except when the files contain classified information or are part of a law enforcement database. If the individual feels that his or her file information is inaccurate, the act provides a set of procedures for correcting the data.
- The **Right to Financial Privacy Act of 1978** limits government access to customers' records of financial institutions, thus protecting, to some degree, the confidentiality of personal financial data. Prior to this legislation, government investigators could access microfilm records of this data and examine them without the owner's knowledge.

It seems inevitable that computers will store information on individuals. But in a democracy, the citizenry must decide how to reconcile this gathering of information with the right to privacy.

COMPUTER SECURITY AND CONTROLS

Organizations can help safeguard the privacy of data and reduce their chances of becoming computer crime victims by instituting a **security system.** A security system must include an **internal control** program: organizational procedures designed to protect computer facilities, hardware, software, and databases.

Information is one of the most precious resources an organization possesses. The goal of computer security and internal control is to protect that resource. However, a company must strike an appropriate balance between security costs and the replacement costs of the assets being protected. Before

> **PRIVACY AND E-MAIL**
>
> Local area networks have greatly increased the use of electronic mail software to send messages within a network. Of course, many of these messages are not strictly work-related. Some companies make it a point to monitor E-mail. This has led to numerous complaints by employees and some lawsuits over violation of privacy.
>
> Some of these lawsuits have been thrown out by lower courts, which have rejected any right to privacy on employer-owned systems. Some of these rulings will no doubt be challenged with appeals.
>
> When you are using an E-mail system, keep in mind that messages may be monitored.

implementing extensive security measures, many businesses undertake a risk-analysis study to determine their security needs and how much meeting those needs will cost.

The cost of security may involve more than the price of installing a system. Unnecessarily strict internal controls can interfere with an organization's work flow. Employees may try to speed their work by circumventing such controls, creating havoc with the security system in the process.

Controls can be broken into three basic categories: general controls, program controls, and documentation.

GENERAL CONTROLS

General controls regulate access to a computer system. They include access controls, hardware controls, organization controls, system controls, data and procedural controls, and hazard controls.

Access Controls **Access controls** protect computer equipment and facilities. This may require nothing more than locating computer equipment behind a locked door. Or it may involve elaborate hardware or procedures: closed-circuit camera surveillance of computer rooms, combination door locks, or ID card checks at entry points (Figure 9.8). Typical access controls for a mainframe environment include locating the computer equipment in a windowless room separate from the organization's offices.

Figure 9.8
An ID card system of access to a secured mainframe environment.

Passwords often control access to networked systems, especially those with remote terminals. Users must enter the password when they log on. Some password systems notify security personnel if the user doesn't provide the right password within three tries. This prevents unauthorized users from guessing their way onto the system. Some on-line systems are designed to automatically log off a user who has not entered data for a specific period of time—say, 20 minutes. This prevents unauthorized individuals from using an unattended computer or terminal.

Organizations can restrict access to specific data in various ways. Companies using mainframe computers often employ a data librarian to control who gains access to data files. A locked drawer may provide sufficient access control for microcomputer diskettes or other removable storage media.

Hardware Controls **Hardware controls** are incorporated into computers themselves to regulate who can use them. Besides requiring passwords, mainframe computers and minicomputers may also be equipped with **console logs,** devices that record what actions users perform on the machines. These devices even log what tapes were mounted on which drives by the operators, which files the operator altered, and what responses the operator gave to the computer's prompts or instructions.

Organization Controls **Organization controls** divide data processing operations among several users. For example, one person may collect accounts-receivable data, whereas another person records it. Such division of labor makes fraud or other crimes more difficult because they will have to involve collaboration. A company's organization controls may direct that programming and operating computers be done by different individuals, that a librarian control the data files, or that operators rotate when running sensitive programs.

Organizational controls can also be used to ensure the smooth functioning of the company. For example, companies often separate their computer department from other departments so that it can function with the best interests of the organization in mind. By contrast, if computer department personnel report, for instance, to a manager in the comptroller's office, they can wind up devoting more attention to the comptroller's needs than to others in the company.

System Controls **System controls** ensure the proper development of information systems. Most important is the participation of users and management in a system's development (see Chapter 8). Implementing a new system also requires conversion controls such as record counts and file comparisons to ensure that all the old system's records are safely converted. The company must then test the new system. Finally, to keep system errors to a minimum, a company must control what changes can be made to a system and who can make them.

Data and Procedural Controls **Data controls** safeguard data or ensure their proper entry. In batch processing, workers often send a batch-control slip along with the documents that operators are feeding into the computer. These control slips state how many documents are in the batch and provide control totals that can be used to check the accuracy of the transcription. For example, a control total for an accounts-receivable application might be the grand total of all charges made by the customers listed in a file.

Hash, or "nonsense," totals can also be used to check the accuracy of transcription. These totals are nonsense in that they don't truly represent a sum in the way control totals do. An example of a hash total would be the summed value of Social Security numbers in all records processed.

Control and hash totals serve to detect when records have been excluded

CONTROL FOR MICROCOMPUTERS

What methods of protection or control apply specifically to microcomputers?

1. Lock the room where the microcomputer is kept. If this isn't possible, limit access to the computer by purchasing a lock for the power switch and/or diskette drives. Make use of the key (if present) to lock and unlock the keyboard (Figure 9.9).
2. To protect the equipment from theft, purchase special lockdowns for bolting or chaining the computer and its peripherals to walls or tables.
3. Buy software that lets you store files in encrypted format. Encryption software also requires passwords to be given before encrypted files can be read by other programs.
4. If encryption software is not available or desirable, store sensitive files to diskette rather than hard disk. Lock up the diskettes when not in use.
5. Use software utilities such as the Norton Utilities, Mace Utilities, and PC Tools to restore erased files on a formatted disk.
6. Because erased files can be restored using one of the above utilities, special steps must be taken to completely destroy the contents of a file so that it can't be reconstructed. For instance, a program like Sweep'r can record zeros to all bytes in the file and then erase the file.

Figure 9.9
PC-LOK from Inmac.

from processing. These totals can be compared from one processing step to the next. If the totals match, then all records have been processed. If the totals do not match, the operator purposely or mistakenly did not include a record or records for processing.

Perhaps the most important data control involves the creation and safeguarding of backup files. Backup files are copies of original files; they can serve as replacements if the original files are destroyed. Backup files are sometimes stored away from a company's computer center so they are safe even if the computer center is struck by fire or other major mishap. Data controls also help ensure that records that have been suspended from processing due to errors are corrected and appropriately processed.

Procedural controls are sets of written instructions for those who operate and maintain a computer system. Operators can consult these when there is a problem. If the problem is not adequately covered in the procedures, the instructions should provide the name and telephone number of someone who can give assistance.

Hazard Controls Emergency **hazard controls** anticipate fire, flood, earthquake, or other disasters. For example, fire-protection measures might include installing smoke detectors and fire-extinguishing systems.

More comprehensive emergency plans provide contingency actions if a company loses its entire computer operation. For example, two businesses could agree to share computer equipment and processing with one another if one should lose its system. However, unless the businesses are very small, this is rarely a viable alternative. Larger companies sometimes establish contingency contracts with vendors who will provide computer hardware in the event of a disaster. In such cases, the business can continue to process data if it has safeguarded its backup software and databases.

PROGRAM CONTROLS

Program controls verify that data are entered and processed properly and that the resultant information is correctly expressed as output. These controls are commonly referred to as input, processing, and output controls.

Input Controls **Input controls** are vital because they help ensure that the data entered into a system are correct. Input controls can include batch-control slips (in batch systems) and limit tests, which determine if the value entered in a field exceeds an established maximum. For example, a limit test for a payroll application could check weekly time-card totals to ensure that no employee has more than, say, 60 work hours. Tests can also be performed to check whether field data are numeric, a field contains blanks, a field contains a positive or negative value, or the name of an employee or entity on whom data are being recorded exists in the master file.

The program or module that contains the various program-control checks is usually called the *edit program* in a batch system and the *edit module* in a real-time system. Batch records found to contain errors are suspended from processing and recorded to a list of such records. In real-time processing, the computer usually displays the erroneous field with an error message so that the user can immediately make corrections.

Processing Controls **Processing controls** provide evidence that data are being processed properly. A common processing control is the **control total,** which the program generates. The user then can compare the control total with the output of the previous step and note and correct any discrepancies in the totals.

Other processing controls include external labeling on disks or tape. Proper labeling ensures that the user loads the right storage medium for a job.

Logic controls within a program ensure that key values in an application are reasonable. For example, it would be unreasonable for the inventory-on-

PERSONAL CASE REVISITED

Out to Lunch

BEN has been reading articles about companies whose data and programs stored on company microcomputers have disappeared. He's also noticed that many machines at SX Corporation are left running and untended while employees leave their work area to run some type of errand. Ben is worried about corporate assets being at risk and the potential for damage to the company.

But what to do? He's not by nature a police officer, and he can see the problem goes beyond a few people whom he knows well enough to talk with easily about it. He thinks the company needs to assess the problem and how to deal with it and to get some savvy advice.

Ben decides to request that the company send him to a seminar conducted by the Security Institute dealing with securing microcomputers and terminals in the corporate workplace, a 3-day session in San Diego led by experts in security and internal control.

hand value to be negative. If this occurs, the program should display an error message.

Output Controls **Output controls** involve reconciling the control totals from one job step to another and scanning the output to ensure that the data were processed correctly. They can also involve delivering output to the authorized individual.

DOCUMENTATION

People tend to think of documentation as a necessary evil, not as a control device. However, a system's documentation is one of its most important assets. It provides information on the analysis, design, and implementation of the system and serves as a reference for the system's users. New employees can use system documentation as a training tool. Large organizations often maintain system documentation libraries.

CHAPTER REVIEW

Ethical use of computers entails a wide variety of considerations. Educators are concerned with how to construct curricula that will help students become computer literate. In the workplace, employers should provide safe and efficient computer environments for their employees, including ergonomically designed furniture and computer equipment.

Computer crime is the commission of unlawful acts with computer hardware, software, or data. The most pervasive computer crime is software piracy, the illicit duplication of software.

Ethical software development calls for proper testing of new software; software that fails to perform as the developers promise can inflict harm on companies and society.

Privacy is the claim of individuals, groups, and institutions to determine for themselves when, how, and to what extent personal information about them is communicated to others. Computerization is making it increasingly difficult to ensure privacy. Innovations such as electronic funds transfer (EFT) systems and computer record matching threaten to provide institutions with intimate details of our daily lives. The Fair Credit Reporting Act of 1970 and the Privacy Act of 1974 have played important roles in protecting the privacy of individuals.

Security and internal-control systems protect a company's computer assets from theft or unauthorized use. These controls are divided into general controls, program controls, and documentation controls. The general controls are divided into access controls, hardware controls, organization controls, system controls, data and procedural controls, and hazard, or emergency, controls.

KEY TERMS AND CONCEPTS

access controls
Comprehensive Crime Control Act of 1984
computer crime
Computer Fraud and Abuse Act of 1986
console log
control total
copyright
data controls
Educational Privacy Act
electronic funds transfer (EFT)
ergonomics
ethics
Fair Credit Reporting Act of 1970
Freedom of Information Act of 1970
general controls
hardware controls
hazard controls
input controls
internal control
license agreement
organization controls
output controls
privacy
Privacy Act of 1974
procedural controls
processing controls
program controls
Right to Financial Privacy Act of 1978
security system
software piracy
system controls
virus

CHAPTER QUIZ

Multiple Choice

1. Which of the following would *not* be considered an ethical concern related to computers?
   a. Copying software from business for personal use
   b. Looking at other users' E-mail when they are not at their computer
   c. Proper testing of software systems that deal with life-threatening applications
   d. Proper testing of a trial-balance worksheet
   e. All of the above are of ethical concern.

2. Which of the following statements is (are) false?
   a. Illegal copying of software is fine as long as it is only used at home.
   b. Software developers are clearly protected by copyright and patent laws.
   c. Some software developers have banded together to find and prosecute people who illegally copy their software.
   d. All of the above
   e. Only a and b

3. Which of the following is *not* a characteristic of a typical computer criminal?
   a. The person is young.
   b. The person is suffering financial difficulty.
   c. The person's actions differ dramatically from their peers due to financial stress.
   d. The person has never been in trouble before.
   e. All of the above are characteristics of a computer criminal.

4. Which of the following presents a possible source of violation of privacy?
   a. Improper review of school records
   b. Improper use of credit information
   c. Access to EFT information
   d. All of the above
   e. None of the above

5. Maintaining and reviewing a console log is an example of which control?
   a. Access control
   b. Hardware control
   c. Organization control
   d. Systems control
   e. None of the above

True/False

6. Ethics applied to computers also involves concern with employees' welfare in the workplace.

7. The Privacy Act of 1974 applies to businesses as well as to the federal government.

8. A password is an example of the application of an access control.

9. Hazard controls involve contingency plans for ensuring that an organization can still provide for information needs in the event of a natural disaster.

10. Documentation is not a form of internal control.

Answers

1. e 2. e 3. c 4. d 5. b 6. t 7. f 8. t 9. t 10. f

Exercises

1. Define the following terms:
   a. Ethics
   b. Ergonomics
   c. Privacy
   d. Security
   e. Internal control

2. The term ____________ refers to the computer keeping track of an employee's performance.

3. Furniture that is ____________ helps ease backache and muscle strain.

4. The term ____________ refers to the illegal duplication of application software.

5. The theft, attack, misappropriation, or misuse of computer hardware, software, or data is called ____________ .

6. Four characteristics typical of computer criminals are ____________ , ____________ , ____________ , and ____________ .

7. The claim of individuals to determine for themselves when, how, and to what extent information about them is communicated to others is known as ____________ .

8. The ____________ is federal legislation that only applies to data banks maintained by the federal government.

9. The ____________ Act protects U.S. citizens from unlimited government access to records in financial institutions.

10. ____________ is the set of policies, procedures, and safeguards that are taken by an organization to protect its assets.

11. The three families of controls are ____________ , ____________ , and ____________ .

12. A locked door to the computer room is an example of a(n) ____________ control.

13. A batch-control slip is an example of a(n) ____________ control.

14. ____________ controls provide for contingencies in the case of a natural disaster.

15. Ensuring that testing is properly carried out is an example of a(n) ____________ control.

16. A console log is an example of a(n) ____________ control.

17. ____________ controls verify that information is being entered, processed, and output properly in an application.

18. A(n) ____________ control examines a document to ensure that calculations were properly performed.

19. A(n) ____________ control ensures that the printouts are delivered to the appropriate person within an organization.

20. Besides describing a system, ____________ is used as a training aid and a control.

IN YOUR OWN CASE

1. What ethical issues related to computers have you personally encountered? What problems have arisen? How have you dealt with them? Does the information in this chapter give you any new perspectives on these problems? How so?

2. If you own a computer or work in a computerized environment, is enough being done to ensure the security of the equipment, software, and data? What further security of control measures should you, your school, or your company take?

3. What are the rules regarding software piracy at your school or workplace? How well are they adhered to? What changes do you think should be made in the rules or their enforcement?

QUESTIONS FOR THOUGHT

1. Do you think it is ethical for companies to use a computer equipped with voice output to make "cold" sales calls to prospective customers? Why or why not?

2. Should law enforcement agencies have ready access to data files from financial institutions, schools, or social agencies for use in attempting to locate lawbreakers or potential lawbreakers?

3. Children in elementary school are increasingly using the computer to study and complete their homework. Do you think this dependence on the computer will result in a loss of important skills in math or other areas? Why or why not?

GLOSSARY

access controls: Protect the computer equipment and facilities.

algorithm: A series of steps that manipulate the record key to find a record.

alphanumeric keys: Keys with numbers, letters, and special characters that appear on a keyboard device.

American Standard Code for Information Interchange (ASCII): Often called USASCII, this code is a standard method of representing a character with a number inside the computer. Knowledge of the code is important only if you write programs.

analog signals: Transmission of data via sounds.

application program: Precoded set of generalized instructions for the computer, written to accomplish a certain goal. Examples of such programs include a general ledger package, a mailing list program, and PacMan.

arithmetic/logic unit: Performs the arithmetic operations of addition, subtraction, multiplication, and division and any comparisons required by the program.

arrow keys: Keys (down, up, right, and left) found on the numeric keyboard and typically used to move a pointer or cursor.

artificial intelligence: The attempt to construct computer-based hardware/software systems that think like a human being.

ASCII: *See* **American Standard Code for Information Interchange.**

asynchronous protocol: Transmits data one character at a time.

auto-answer: A feature found in some modems that allows the computer to answer the phone.

auto-dial: Feature frequently found in modems that lets you place a call to a specified number without having to dial it yourself.

backup and recovery: Backup refers to copies made of the database used to restore (recover) from any disasters. This ensures that no data (or only a minimal amount) are lost.

bandwidth: Refers to the grade of transmission media. The wider the bandwidth, the greater the number of bits per second can be transmitted.

banked memory: Usually two sets of 64K memory used to give a computer a total memory of 128K. Only one set of 64K can be active at a time.

bar chart: Horizontal or vertical bars that are stacked, floating, or clustered side-by-side.

bar-code reader: An electronic device that reads data represented in the parallel lines of the universal product code (UPC).

BASIC: Acronym for Beginners All-Purpose Symbolic Instruction Code, a common, easy-to-learn computer programming language. The advanced version of BASIC is called BASICA. BASIC was developed by Kemeney and Kurtz at Dartmouth College in 1963 and has proved to be the most popular language for personal computers.

batch processing: Records grouped together and processed all at once.

baud rate: Speed at which modems can transmit characters across telephone lines. A 300-baud modem can transmit about 30 characters per second.

BBS: *See* **bulletin board system.**

bi-level mode: A scanning mode that only scans black and white.

binary: Number system consisting of two digits, 0 and 1, with each digit in a binary number representing a power of 2. Most digital computers are binary. A binary signal is easily expressed by the presence or absence of an electrical current or magnetic field.

binary notation: The use of 0's and 1's to create characters or numbers on which the computer then performs operations.

bit: Binary digit, the smallest amount of information a computer can hold. A single bit specifies a single value of 0 or 1. Bits can be grouped to form larger values. *See* **byte.**

bit-mapped font: Text characters that are built using a pattern of dots.

black-box concept: Used to break a complex task into simple inputs, process, and outputs.

block: Designated portion of text, consisting of one or more lines, that is to be copied, moved, or deleted.

board: A plastic card that holds chips and contains circuitry for a computer or peripheral devices.

boot record: Record that resides on sector 1 of track 0 of a file and contains the program responsible for loading the rest of DOS into the microcomputer.

border: Set of labels for the rows and columns of a worksheet. The columns are labeled with letters, and the rows are labeled with numbers.

boundary: Defines the limits of a component, the collection of components, or the entire system.

bridge: The component of a local area network that lets it communicate with other networks.

bug: Error. A hardware bug is a physical or electrical malfunction or design error; a software bug is an error in programming, either in the logic of the program or in typing.

bulletin board system (BBS): A system consisting of a computer and one or more modems that is used to store messages, programs, or data for anyone having access to the system.

bus: Entity that enables the computer to pass information to a peripheral and to receive information from a peripheral.

bus network: Connects several nodes or computers with a single cable along which computers can send messages in either direction.

byte: Basic unit of measure of a computer's memory. A byte usually has 8 bits, so its value can be from 0 to 255. Each character can be represented by 1 byte in ASCII.

camera ready: A high-quality printed output that is ready for reproduction.

cartridge: Removable hard disk storage unit that typically holds ten or more megabytes of storage.

CASE (computer-assisted systems engineering): Software that facilitates the process of systems analysis and development.

cathode-ray tube (CRT): The tube that produces the image on a monitor screen.

CD: *See* **compact disk.**

CD ROM: *See* **optical disk.**

cell: Intersection point of a row and a column in a spreadsheet. It is referenced by the cell address COLUMN/ROW.

centering hole: Large hole on a diskette that allows the Mylar plastic disk inside the diskette envelope to center on the capstan for proper rotation.

central processing unit (CPU): Device in a computer system that contains the arithmetic unit, the control unit, and the main memory. Also referred to as the computer.

Centronics: Standard method of passing information through a parallel data port.

character: Any graphic symbol that has a specific meaning to people. Letters (both uppercase and lowercase), numbers, and various symbols (such as punctuation marks) are all characters.

characters per second (cps): A measurement of printing speed most often applied to dot-matrix and impact printers.

chip: Electronic entity containing one or more semiconductors on a wafer of silicon, within which an integrated circuit is formed.

C language: A popular language for microcomputers that provides a tremendous amount of control over the computer.

clip art: Art that is ready to be placed within a desktop publishing application.

clock speed: Measured in millions of cycles per second (megahertz, or MHz), indicates how fast a computer can process information and is a function of the ease with which electricity passes through the CPU.

closed-bus system: Type of computer system that comes with plugs, called established ports, that accept device cables from the peripheral.

coaxial cable: The same type of cable often used to connect a television set. Capable of carrying up to 10 megabits of data at a time.

COBOL: Acronym for COmmon Business-Oriented Language, a high-level language oriented toward organizational data processing procedures.

code: Method of representing something in terms of something else. The ASCII code represents characters in terms of binary numbers; the BASIC language represents algorithms in terms of program statements. *Code* also may refer to programs, usually in low-level languages. Invisible command to WordPerfect that tells it how to display or print text.

color monitor: Monitor sometimes referred to as RGB (red, green, and blue).

COM: *See* **computer output microfilm.**

COMMAND.COM: Command processor of DOS, containing built-in functions or subroutines that enable user to copy a file or get a directory listing of a disk.

command processor: The portion of the operating system that stores DOS commands that will be contained in RAM once DOS is loaded into RAM.

compact disk (CD): A laser technology disk that stores computer data. Basically the same as the compact disk now commonly used for recorded music.

compiler: Software that translates a program into machine language. As it performs this translation, it also checks for errors made by the programmer.

Comprehensive Crime Control Act of 1984: Prohibits an unauthorized person from accessing computer records to obtain information protected by the Right to Financial Privacy Act of 1978 or data in the files of a consumer-reporting agency.

computer: Any device that can receive and store a set of instructions and then act on those instructions in a predetermined and predictable fashion. The definition implies that both the instructions and the data on which the instructions act can be changed; a device whose instructions cannot be changed is not a computer.

computer animation: The process of using computer-generated images to produce animation, or cartoons.

computer crime: The commission of unlawful acts by using computer technology.

Computer Fraud and Abuse Act of 1986: An attempt by Congress to define computer crime and establish penalties.

computer output microfilm (COM): A process of using photographic techniques and reduction to hold large amounts of data in computer storage.

computer system: Composed of input, storage, processing, and output components.

concentrator: A multiplexor with built-in circuitry that makes the transmission process more efficient. Also performs rudimentary editing on the data to be transmitted.

configuration control: Allows only the DBA to make changes to the schema of a database.

console log: Devices that record what actions users perform on the machines. These devices even log what tapes were mounted on which drives by the operators, which files the operator altered, and what responses the operator gave to the computer's prompts or instructions.

control total: A total generated by a program to assist an operator in determining whether data have been entered or processed correctly. Typical control totals include the total number of records processed or the grand total of an amount field.

coprocessor: Microprocessor chip that is placed in a microcomputer to take the burden of manipulating numbers off the CPU, allowing it to perform other tasks.

cps: *See* **characters per second.**

CPU: *See* **central processing unit.**

CRT: *See* **cathode-ray tube.**

daisy wheel printer: Letter-quality printer that uses a solid-font printing mechanism (the mechanism is shaped like a flower or a thimble).

data (datum): Information of any kind.

database: Collection of data related to one specific type of application. *Database* is often used synonymously with *file*.

database administrator (DBA): An individual appointed by management, who works with users to create, maintain, and safeguard the data found in the database.

database management system (DBMS): Complete set of programs that help users to organize, update, and store records and files in virtually unlimited ways.

database server: In some LANs, a special computer dedicated exclusively to the database needs of the network users.

data communications: The electronic transfer of data from one computer device to another.

data controls: Safeguard data or ensure their proper entry. Batch-control slips with control totals and hash totals are examples.

data-definition language (DDL): Used to design the logical structure of the database. Used to give information such as field name, data type, and size, as well as limit access to these data.

data dictionary: Contains the meaning of each piece of datum found in the database; it includes data names, type of data, field size; and describes any interrelationships between this piece of datum with other data items.

data-flow diagram: Graphical method for documenting systems. A physical data-flow diagram documents the current system, whereas a logical data-flow diagram documents the design of the new system.

data integrity: Relates to the problem of errors occurring in data that are stored in files.

data-manipulation language (DML): Has all the stored routines that allow a user to store, retrieve, change, delete, or sort data or records within the database.

data processing: The process of manipulating data to produce information for use in making decisions.

data redundancy: The same data are stored in more than one location.

DBA: *See* **database administrator.**

DBMS: *See* **database management system.**

DDL: *See* **data-definition language.**

DDP: *See* **distributed data processing.**

debug: To find hardware or software faults and eliminate them.

decision-support system (DSS): Provides user-friendly languages or programs that a decision maker can employ to retrieve or store data and perform modeling to solve unstructured problems.

decision table: The graphic representation of a decision-making process that contains the following parts: decision stub, decision entry, action stub, and action entry.

demand report: Used to obtain information that may be needed for a specific problem.

demodulation: The conversion of analog signals to digital signals.

desktop organizer: Primarily RAM-resident software package that can include such capabilities as calculators, notepads, automatic dialers, and appointment calendars.

desktop publishing (DTP): Gives the user typeset quality such as you see in newspapers and textbooks. Also allows you to combine text with pictures.

digital signals: Represent the values 0 and 1 by the presence or absence of voltage.

digitizing tablet: A flat drawing surface used with some graphics applications. The tablet lets a user enter commands with a drawing device rather than a mouse or keyboard.

direct-access method: Uses algorithms or indexes to locate a record.

disk: A rotating flexible or rigid medium on whose surface data can be stored and later retrieved through an electromagnetic or other process.

disk drive: Rectangular box, connected to or situated inside the computer, that reads and writes into diskettes.

disk operating system (DOS): *See* **DOS.**

distributed data processing (DDP): Distributes and manages resources among several computers or terminals.

dither mode: Scanning mode that scans shades of grays.

DML: *See* **data-manipulation language.**

documentation: The written text or manual that details how to use a computer device or piece of software.

DOS: Acronym for disk operating system, the program responsible for enabling you to interact with the many parts of a computer system. DOS (pronounced "doss") is the interface between you and the hardware. To perform system functions, DOS commands are typed on the keyboard, but DOS is actually a collection of programs designed to make it easy to create and manage files, run programs, and use system devices attached to the computer.

DOS prompt: Indicates that DOS is ready to receive an instruction. It also tells which drive DOS will try to execute the instruction against, unless told otherwise. Typical DOS prompts are A>, B>, C>, or D>.

DOS shell: A piece of software that makes the disk operating system easier to use by introducing menus or some type of graphic user interface.

DOS.SYS: Hidden DOS file that handles any information to be passed to disk.

dot-matrix printer: Printer that generates characters by firing seven or nine tiny print heads against a ribbon.

double-density disks: Have approximately twice the storage of a single-density disk because they use a higher quality read/write surface on the disks, so that data can be stored in a denser format.

double-sided disks: Disks on which data can be stored on both surfaces. A double-sided disk has been certified (tested) on both sides.

downloading: Entails receiving a file from another computer.

downsizing: The process of moving applications from a mainframe environment to a microcomputer environment. It may also refer to performing a given amount of work with fewer people.

drawing tool: A set of tools contained in a graphics package for drawing lines, filling areas of the screen with specific colors or patterns, or performing other tasks such as erasing.

DR DOS 5.0: A disk operating system from Digital Research that contains a graphic user interface and allows users to utilize RAM above 640K.

DSS: *See* **decision-support system.**

DTP: *See* **desktop publishing.**

dumb terminal: An ASCII terminal that contains no built-in processing powers; it simply sends and receives data.

Dvorak: A keyboard design offered as an alternative to the QWERTY keyboard.

editing: Verifying that the text of a document has been entered correctly.

EFT: *See* **electronic funds transfer.**

EGA monitor: *See* **enhanced graphics adapter monitor.**

EISA monitor: *See* **extended industry standard architecture.**

electronic funds transfer (EFT): A banking system that electronically records deposits and withdrawals as they occur.

electronic mail: A type of software that provides for the easy sending and receiving of messages from one computer to another.

electronic spreadsheet: Program used to manipulate data that can be expressed in rows and columns.

enhanced graphics adapter (EGA) monitor: Video device capable of presenting clear, vivid graphics. Uses a 640 × 350 (or more) dot resolution to present crisper, more colorful images.

environmental interaction: Any system that accepts inputs from the environment, processes those inputs, and generates outputs back into the environment.

ergonomics: The science of adapting work and working conditions to suit the individual worker.

ethics: The study of conduct and moral judgment.

exception report: Alerts management that an activity or process needs correction.

expanded memory: RAM above the 640K base memory limit.

expansion board: Printed circuit board that can be inserted into an open-bus expansion slot, expanding the computer configuration to include such items as modems and plotters.

extended industry standard architecture (EISA): The alternative standard to the MCA architecture of IBM's PS/2 hardware.

extended memory: In a microcomputer, memory higher than 1M.

external modem: Connects to a microcomputer's serial interface.

facilitator: An independent, "third-party" person in a group decision-support environment who keeps discussion on track and in other ways helps conduct the meeting.

Fair Credit Reporting Act of 1970: Requires credit bureaus and investigatory reporting agencies to let people on whom they maintain records inspect their files.

fax (facsimile transmission) machine: A device for transmitting or receiving text or images over telephone lines.

feasibility study: Defines a problem and determines whether a solution can be implemented within budget constraints.

feedback: The process of sampling output to make certain that it is within pre-established limits. Data are then sent back to the system as input.

fiber optics: A relatively new technology that is replacing copper wires as the dominant message-transmission medium for both telephone and computer networked systems.

field: Subdivision of a record that holds one piece of data about a transaction.

fifth-generation computers: Computers that will incorporate many of the concepts of artificial intelligence. These machines will have a natural language, receive voice input, be extremely easy to use, and process data 10,000 times faster than existing computers.

file: Collection of data or programs that serves a single purpose. A file is stored on a diskette and given a name so that you can recall it.

flexibility: A system's ability to make changes quickly.

floppy disk: A term usually applied to 8-inch and 5.25-inch diskettes. The flexible nature of this medium makes the term self-explanatory.

font: Character set for printing. Pica, Elite, Helvetica, Courier, and Orator are among the many common fonts.

footnote/endnote:

formatting: Process performed to prepare a diskette for use.

formula: Series of characters containing cell references and arithmetic operators for numeric data manipulation.

fourth-generation language (4GL): A high-level language that is easy to learn and is capable of generating many low-level instructions for each instruction entered.

Freedom of Information Act of 1970: A Congressional act that makes much information available for public perusal.

front-end processor: A minicomputer that, besides performing general-purpose processing, frees a DDP's mainframe computer from such time-consuming housekeeping tasks as polling terminals for data, synchronizing the message packet, and error checking.

full-duplex transmission: Sends and receives information simultaneously.

fully distributed network: All nodes can communicate directly with each other.

function key: One of 10 keys (F1–F10) that allows special functions to be entered with a single user keystroke. Computer programs (DOS, BASIC, and so on) use these keys for different purposes.

G: *See* **gigabyte.**

general controls: Regulate access to the computer system.

gigabyte (G): A term that represents about 1 billion bytes of data.

graphics editor: Allows you to edit existing computer graphics or to create your own art.

greeked text: Lines displayed to represent text as it will appear in a printed document.

half-duplex transmission: Sends or receives data, but not both simultaneously.

handshaking: The number of stop and start bits used for sending and receiving data.

hard disk: Rigid medium for storing computer information, usually rated in megabytes (millions of bytes) of storage capacity.

hard-sectored disk: A disk with a fixed number of sectors per track.

hardware: Physical parts of a computer.

hardware controls: Incorporated into computers to regulate who can use the machines.

hazard controls: Provide provisions in case fire, flood, earthquake, or other disasters threaten a company's computer system.

high-level language: Language that is more intelligible to humans than it is to machines.

hi-lo graph: Often used by newspapers to show the high and low selling points of stocks. Emphasizes the range between the highest and lowest values within a category by connecting them with a line.

image processing: The process of transferring visual images from paper into electronic form for computerized storage and retrieval.

index: Keeps track of relations in a relational database environment and provides access to any record in a file.

information: Data that have been processed or manipulated. Gross pay (calculated by multiplying hours worked by pay rate) is an example of information.

ink-jet printer: Printer that sprays ink in droplets onto paper to form characters. It is much quieter than a dot-matrix or letter-quality printer.

input controls: Represent some of the most vital controls, for they help ensure that the data that users enter into a system are correct.

integrated software: Software that combines several general software applications into one software package.

interface: Adapter or circuit board containing the electrical components that connect a peripheral with the computer's bus system.

internal control: Policies and procedures used to safeguard an organization's assets.

internal modem: A circuit board that fits into an expansion slot of an open-bus computer.

interpreter: Program, usually written in machine language, that understands and executes a higher-level language one statement at a time.

intuitive program: A program written in such a way that the choice of the next command is always evident to the user.

I/O handler: The DOS function that provides for communications links with peripherals. The DOS I/O handler is contained in the IO.SYS file.

IO.SYS: Hidden file in DOS that manages each character that is typed, displayed, printed, received, or sent through any communications adapter.

K: *See* **kilobyte.**

kerning: The adjustment of spacing between alphanumeric characters displayed on the screen or, more often, in printed output. Kerning takes into account the differing widths and shapes of various characters.

keyboard: System hardware used to input characters, commands, and functions to the computer. The keyboard consists of 83 or 101 keys and is organized into three sections: function keys, typewriter keyboard, and numeric keypad.

kilobyte (K): Abbreviation for the Greek prefix *kilo-*, meaning *thousand*. In computer-related usage, K usually represents the quantity 2^{10}, or 1024. A kilobyte of storage represents 1024 bytes.

LAN: *See* **local area network.**

landscape format: Text printed on a sheet of paper in 11″ wide × 8½″ deep format.

language processor: Software that translates a high-level language such as COBOL or BASIC into machine-understandable code.

laser printer: Printer that uses laser-based technology to form characters on paper via electronic charges and then places toner on the charges to display the characters. The toner is fixed in place by a heat process.

LCD monitor: *See* **liquid crystal display monitor.**

letter-quality printer: Printer that generates output of a quality comparable to that produced on a typewriter.

light pen: Works somewhat like ordinary pen, but it uses light and a computer screen instead of ink and paper to record information.

line graph: Illustrates lows, highs, and trends with a line or series of lines. Line graphs are ideal for showing trends over time or the distribution of one variable over another.

liquid crystal display (LCD) monitor: Frequently used on notebook-size portable computers.

local area network (LAN): A collection of nearby computers that have been linked to share data, programs, and peripherals.

logical view: The manner in which a user or an application accesses a database through a subschema.

Lotus 1-2-3: Popular electronic spreadsheet package.

low-level language: Language that is more intelligible to machines than to humans.

M: *See* **megabyte.**

magnetic-ink character recognition (MICR): A set of magnetically sensitive printed symbols together with the devices and procedures used to interpret them. MICR is widely used by banks to enter dollar amounts and other banking information onto checks so that the checks can be read by computer.

mainframe computer: A large, fast system capable of supporting several hundred input and output devices such as keyboards and monitor screens.

main system board (motherboard): The central board in a computer, typically containing memory chips, processor chip, and other components.

management information system (MIS): A formal process using both manual and computerized tools to control information.

master file: Holds semipermanent summary data about an entity.

MCA: *See* **microchannel architecture.**

megabyte (M): One million characters of storage, a quantity usually used as a measure of available storage on a hard disk.

menu: A list of commands from which to select.

merge: The process of automatically combining fixed information from a word processing template file with variable information from another file in order to produce a series of similar but not identical documents. For instance, a merge can combine a form letter with a list of names and addresses to produce "personalized form letters" in which the body of the letter stays the same, but the addressee information varies.

MICR: *See* **magnetic-ink character recognition.**

microchannel architecture (MCA): The architecture introduced by IBM for some of its PS/2 computers. MCA provides for multitasking (performing several jobs seemingly at once).

microcomputer: Computer based on a microprocessor (8-bit or 16-bit) that can execute a single user's program.

microprocessor: Integrated circuit that understands and executes machine-language programs.

Microsoft: Company that originally developed PC DOS for IBM (an operating system known, with some minor differences, as MS DOS).

minicomputer: Smaller, cheaper, and easier to maintain and install than a mainframe but in declining demand because of increasing power of the microcomputer.

mirrored imaging: A process by which information is stored to at least two memory devices each time a write operation is performed. If data on one device are lost, the other serves as a backup.

MIS: *See* **management information system.**

model: Symbolic representation of an entity or process that is difficult to observe.

modem: Acronym for modulator-demodulator, a device that converts digital computer signals into analog telephone signals (audible sounds that can be sent via telephone) and reverses the procedure at the other end of the line.

modulation: The conversion of digital signals to analog signals.

monitor: TV-like device that gives users of microcomputer equipment video feedback about their actions and the computer's actions.

monochrome monitor: A device similar to a one-color monitor except that monochrome pixels are much closer together, producing clearer characters.

motherboard: Another name for the *main system board*.

mouse: Hand-held controller that electronically signals the computer to move the cursor on the display screen. The same movements can be accomplished via the cursor control pad.

MS DOS: Operating system developed by Microsoft. It is the same as PC DOS except that there is no ROM BASIC provision. Most IBM-compatible computers use this operating system.

multimedia: Transmitting text and graphics in real time.

multiplexor: A device that routes the output from several terminals or computers into a single channel. This allows one telephone link to carry a transmission that normally would require several such links.

natural language: A language designed so human beings and machines can interact easily.

node: A computer or terminal capable of sending and receiving data from other computers or terminals on a network.

nonvolatile memory: Form of storage that does not lose its content when the system's power is turned off. It may take the form of bubble memory, or it may be powered by batteries.

numeric keypad: Section of the keyboard containing numeric entry and editing keys.

object code: Machine-language code created by the compiler and executed by the computer.

OCR: *See* **optical character recognition.**

open-bus system: Contains expansion slots that let users expand the system as needed. A peripheral is added to the computer by plugging it into an expansion slot with an interface board.

operating system: Interface between the computer and the user, which provides the user with flexible and manageable control over the resources of the computer.

operational decision making: Ensures that employees perform tasks efficiently by measuring their output against preset standards.

optical character recognition (OCR): Using a scanner driven by the appropriate software that allows text to be read from a typed piece of paper.

optical disk (CD ROM): A slow, high-density storage medium typically measured in gigabytes.

optical mark recognition: A system of input based on a scanning device that locates and interprets pencil or pen markings on a piece of paper, such as a multiple-choice questionnaire.

organization controls: Divide data processing operations among several users so that if fraud is perpetrated there must be collusion among several people.

OS/2: An operating system used on 80286-chip computers and later machines. OS/2 allows more than one program to be in RAM at once.

output: Computer-generated data whose destination is the screen, disk, printer, or some other output device.

output controls: Involve reconciling control totals from one job step to another and scanning the output to make certain that the data were processed correctly. They can also involve delivering output to the authorized individual.

outsourcing: A business arrangement whereby one company sells its information systems functions to another company and then leases back computer and programming time.

page-control language (PCL): A language designed to load bit-mapped fonts and graphics into a printer.

page-description language (PDL): Creates characters using outline fonts developed from formulas.

PageMaker: A very popular package for desktop publishing.

parallel interface: Interface arrangement that transmits all 9 bits (8 data and 1 parity) of a character at one time.

parallel processing: The simultaneous use of several CPU chips within one computer to process information.

parallel transmission: Sends data 1 byte at a time.

Pascal: A language designed for teaching structured programming techniques.

pasteboard: The area around a document in desktop publishing.

PC: *See* **personal computer.**

PCL: *See* **page-control language.**

PDL: *See* **page-description language.**

peripheral: Something attached to the computer that is not part of the computer itself. Most peripherals are input and/or output devices.

personal computer (PC): Computer equipped with memory, languages, and peripherals, well suited for use in a home, office, or school.

physical view: The exact manner in which data are stored to devices used in a database.

pie chart: Compares the proportional parts of a whole. Useful for comparing component shares with one another and with the combined total.

pixel: Dot that is turned on or off depending on what character is being displayed on the screen.

plotter: Device that moves a pen on X and Y axes to draw graphs or pictures. For one of the axes, the paper may move instead of the pen.

point: A printer's measurement, about $\frac{1}{72}$ of an inch.

pointer: Reverse-video bar, sometimes referred to as the cursor. Its width depends on the width of the cell it is referencing. In a database, it is the data item in a record that identifies the storage location of another record that is logically related. It may also indicate the current record being processed. The exact role of the pointer depends on the type of database-structuring technique in use.

polling: The process of a computer checking to see if there are data at a node location ready for transmission.

portrait format: Text printed on a sheet of paper in 8½ wide × 11″ deep format.

PostScript: The PDL language developed by Adobe systems for PageMaker.

predictive report: Used in the planning process to construct what-if scenarios.

presentation graphics: Turns numeric information and data relationships into graphics—charts and graphs.

primary key: In dBASE, the record number; in sorting, the major sort field.

primary memory: Internal memory used by the computer for several different functions. It can contain data, program instructions, or intermediate results of calculations.

printer: Device used to make a permanent copy of any output.

print thimble: Device used by impact letter-quality printers to form characters on paper.

privacy: The claim of individuals, groups, or institutions to determine for themselves when, how, and to what extent personal information about them is communicated to others.

Privacy Act of 1974: Regulates how the federal government manages information collected on citizens.

procedural controls: Written instructions for those who operate and maintain a computer system.

procedures: Written instructions on how to use hardware or software.

processing controls: Provide evidence that data are being processed properly. A typical example is the control total.

processing unit: *See* **central processing unit.**

processor: *See* **central processing unit.**

productivity software: Allows a person to be more productive. These packages include such applications as desktop organizers and outline software.

program: Set of instructions that tells the computer how to perform a certain task. DOS, BASIC, and the Instructor are all programs.

program controls: Verify that data are entered and processed properly and that the resulting information is correctly outputted.

programming language: Special means of providing instructions to the computer to get it to perform a specific task. Examples of programming languages are BASIC, COBOL, Pascal, and FORTRAN.

protocol: Set of rules used for sending or receiving data.

prototyping: The process of creating a new information system by first rapidly developing a scaled-down or functionally limited model. The prototype model is subsequently modified with the aid of fourth-generation languages.

pseudocode: Programlike code that does not follow the exact syntax of a language. Used for designing and documenting the logic of a module.

query: A question that is asked of and processed by a database management system.

query language: A simple, easy-to-learn language used to interface with the database that lets users quickly generate needed reports.

QWERTY: The standard keyboard arrangement for keys located above the "home"keys.

RAM: *See* **random-access memory.**

RAM-resident program: Means that once the program is loaded into memory, it stays there until either the machine is turned off or you tell it to erase itself.

random-access memory (RAM): Main memory of a computer. The acronym RAM can be used to refer either to the integrated circuits that make up this type of memory or to the memory itself. The computer can store values in distinct locations in RAM and then recall them, or it can alter and restore them.

read-only memory (ROM): Memory usually used to hold important programs or data that must be available to the computer when power is first turned on. Information in ROM is placed there during the process of manufacture and is unalterable. Information stored in ROM does not disappear when power is turned off.

read process: Transfers data into a computer from a secondary storage device.

read/write access hole: Oval opening on a diskette that allows the read/write heads to record or access information.

real-time processing: Updates each master file by processing each transaction as it is entered into a computer and transmits the resulting information back to the user.

record: Entity that contains information about a specific business happening or transaction.

record key: Data that identify one record from others. Student Social Security numbers serve as record keys in many colleges' sequential files. The file must be searched in sequence; if the desired record is passed, the operator must return to the start of the file and search again.

record structure: The fields, data type, and field length.

relational structure: Structural arrangement consisting of one or more tables. Data are stored in the form of relations in these tables.

release: The latest version of a piece of software. The latest release of a software package typically has enhancements as well as corrections of errors found in prior releases.

report generator: Portion of the query language that lets a user quickly generate reports on paper or video medium.

Right to Privacy Act of 1978: A Congressional act limiting government access to customer records of financial institutions.

ring network: Joins each computer in the system to two other computers, in opposing directions, forming a circle.

ROM: *See* **read-only memory.**

sans serif: A style of type without serifs.

scanner: Converts text, photographs, and black-and-white graphics into computer-readable form and transfers the information to a computer.

scatter plot (or XY graph): Two-dimensional graph of points whose coordinates represent values on the X (horizontal) and Y (vertical) axes.

scheduled report: Generated at set intervals and usually contains much detailed information.

schema: How data are physically stored in the database.

SDLC: *See* **system development life cycle.**

secondary key: Defining key used to order information within the primary key.

secondary storage: Separate from the CPU, it can store data indefinitely—usually on a magnetic disk. Holds most of the data processed by a computer.

sectors: One part of a track. For the IBM microcomputer, each track is divided into eight or nine sectors of 512 bytes each. This sector holds the data.

sequential-access method: Stores records in a file in ascending or descending order by record key, data that identify one record from others.

serial interface: Transmits 1 byte 1 bit at a time.

serial transmission: Sends data 1 bit at a time.

serif: A short ornamental stroke or line stemming out at an angle from the end of a printed character.

simplex transmission: Data can be sent but not received or received but not sent.

soft-sectored disk: Has each track divided into sectors during the format process.

software: Program that gives the hardware something to do.

software piracy: Illicit duplication of software.

sort: The process of physically rearranging records within a file.

source code: Set of program instructions written in a high-level language.

source document: The original paper document that holds information about a record or transaction.

speller: Software that checks the spelling of words in a document.

split screen: The ability to divide a monitor screen in half and display a different document or graphic images on each half.

sprite: A graphic image in some animation packages that can be manipulated to produce animation, or movement.

SQL: *See* **system query language.**

stand-alone presentation graphics package: A software program through which text or graphic files can be passed to create images for presentations.

star network: Computer nodes radiate like spokes from a central or hub computer.

stored-program concept: Permits the reading of a program into a computer's memory and then executing the program instructions without rewiring the computer.

strategic decision making: Includes setting objectives for an organization and devising long-range plans.

string testing: Verifies that interprogram control results in files being transferred properly from one program to the next.

structured decisions: Any decisions made via existing procedures.

structured English: Plain English with certain restrictions, which derive from its structural similarity to program code.

structured walkthrough: Process of having a number of individuals review a program or worksheet and check it for accuracy, logic, and readability.

stub testing: Involves designing dummy modules, with a minimum of program code, that let a programmer verify that linkage between modules function properly.

subschema: How data are accessed by a user or an application.

supercomputer: The fastest, most expensive computers manufactured. They can run numerous different calculations simultaneously, thereby processing in 1 minute what would take a personal computer several weeks or months.

synchronous protocol: Transmits data in groups of characters, called packets, at fixed quantities and intervals.

synergism: The concept that the whole is greater than the sum of its parts.

system: A set of interrelated parts that work together to achieve a common goal.

system analysis: Procedure of developing MISs that provide managers with the information they need to make decisions.

system analyst: A person responsible for examining an existing information system and suggesting improvements to the system.

system audit: A step in the SDLC in which it is verified that a system is meeting expectations and processing data appropriately.

system controls: Ensure the proper development of information systems.

system development life cycle (SDLC): A series of formalized steps used in system analysis.

system query language (SQL): A standardized language through which queries are directed to databases.

system testing: Verifies that the manual and computerized parts of the system function properly.

tablet: A flat drawing surface and a pointing tool that functions like a pencil. The tablet turns the pointer's movements into digitized data that can be read by special computer programs. Tablets range from palm- to desktop-size.

tactical decision making: Implements strategic decision by allocating an organization's resources (personnel, budgeting, production scheduling, and allocation of working capital).

telecommunications: Data communication using communications facilities.

teleconferencing: Creating a meeting by transmitting voice and visual images back-and-forth between physically remote individuals.

terminal: A device for passing information to a computer, generally consisting of a keyboard for entering data or instructions and a screen for displaying output.

terminal emulation: Enables a microcomputer to serve as a computer terminal for another system.

testing: The process of verifying that all processes and procedures are working properly. This includes input, processing, output, and file generation procedures.

thermal printer: Uses specially treated paper to "burn" in dots to form characters.

thesaurus: Software that allows you to obtain synonyms.

timing hole: Small hole to the right of the centering hole on a diskette.

token: A control signal passed from one node to the next, indicating which node is allowed to transmit.

toolbox: An icon-based menu with tools that can be used in desktop publishing.

touch screen: Lets user enter instructions by touching a menu selection or indicating which text to include in an instruction by tracking through the text with a finger.

tracks: Concentric circles of storage on a disk's read/write surface on which data are stored.

traditional approach: File-based processing.

transaction file: Contains data about some business action and is by nature transitory. After its information is inputted, the transaction file is discarded.

transaction log: Contains complete audit trail of all activity of a database for a given time.

transaction-processing system: Another name for *data processing*.

transmission speed: The speed at which data are transmitted across communications links.

unstructured decisions: Resolve ill-defined or unstructured problems (these are typically made at strategic level).

uploading: Sends a file from one computer to another computer.

version: *See* **release.**

VGA monitor: *See* **video graphics array monitor.**

video graphics array (VGA) monitor: Video adapter introduced by IBM with its PS/2 line of computers. This analog system can display 262,144 different colors or shades of colors.

virus: A self-replicating piece of software that may or may not cause severe danger to a user's computer system.

virus vaccines: Special software packages designed to detect and remove viruses.

VisiCalc: First spreadsheet introduced for microcomputers.

volatile memory: Memory that is erased when the electrical current to the computer is turned off.

white space: The blank space left on a page to make it more readable.

Windows: A graphic user interface developed by Microsoft for use by IBM and compatible computers.

word processing: Automated manipulation of text data via a software package that usually provides the ability to create, edit, store, and print documents easily.

word wrap: Feature that automatically places a word on the next line when it will not fit on the current line.

write process: Transfers data out of a computer back to secondary storage.

write-protected: Diskettes that have been protected from having information stored on them, being altered, or being deleted; this is accomplished by placing a write-protect tab over the small rectangular hole on the side of a diskette.

write-protect notch: Rectangular notch at upper right-hand edge of some disks. Covering notch with a piece of tape prevents alteration of disk's information, but disk remains readable.

WYSIWYG: The acronym for What-You-See-Is-What-You-Get. Generally used with word processing and graphics applications to indicate that how an image appears on the screen is also how it will look in print.

X (horizontal) axis: The left-to-right axis.

Y (vertical) axis: The up-and-down axis.

PHOTO CREDITS

Personal cases by Jonathan Fischer (pp. 6, 23, 24, 34, 53, 56, 72, 84, 100, 104, 106, 113, 122, 130, 136, 140, 150, 156, 160, 170, 177, 186, 189, 198, 203, 215, 218, 228, 235, 243, 245, 254, 264, 271)

Chapter 1 Page 2: top, courtesy of International Business Machines; bottom, copyright Robert Holmgren; p. 3: top, copyright Tony Stone; bottom, copyright Peter Menzel; p. 4: top, photo courtesy of Hewlett-Packard Company; bottom, courtesy of Apple Computer, Inc.; p. 5: top, Iowa State University, News Service Photo Dept.; middle and middle left, courtesy of International Business Machines; bottom left, courtesy of Apple Computer, Inc.; bottom right, photo by Paul Shambroom, courtesy of Cray Research, Inc.; Figure 1.3: Iowa State University, News Service Photo Dept.; Figures 1.4–1.7: Courtesy of International Business Machines; Figure 1.8: Courtesy of UNISYS Corporation; Figures 1.2, 1.9, 1.10: Courtesy of International Business Machines; Figure 1.11: The M.I.T. Museum; Figure 1.13: Courtesy of Digital Equipment Corporation; Figure 1.14: Photo courtesy of Hewlett-Packard Company; Figure 1.15: (a) Reprinted with permission of Compaq Computer Corporation. All rights reserved; (b) Photo courtesy of Hewlett-Packard Company; (c) Photo courtesy of International Business Machines; (d) Photo by Paul Shambroom, courtesy of Cray Research, Inc.

Chapter 2 Page 30: Copyright Ralph Mercer/Tony Stone; p. 31: top, photo courtesy of Hewlett-Packard Company; bottom, copyright Chuck O'Rear/West Light; p. 33: top left, courtesy of Texas Instruments Incorporated; top right, courtesy of The Computer Museum; middle top, left; bottom, courtesy of Intel Corporation; middle right and bottom left, photo courtesy of International Business Machines; Figure 2.1: p. 35, left, courtesy of AT&T; right, courtesy of International Business Machines; p. 36: middle, courtesy of Ken Whitmore/Tony Stone; bottom, courtesy of Rockwell International; p. 37: bottom left, copyright Dan McCoy/Rainbow; bottom right, courtesy of Rockwell International; p. 38: top, copyright 1990 Sumatech; middle left, copyright Dan McCoy/Rainbow; middle right, courtesy of AT&T; bottom, photo courtesy of Hewlett-Packard Company; p. 39: top left, photo courtesy of Hewlett-Packard Company; top right and middle, courtesy of AT&T; bottom, TIB/WEST/John Stuart © 1991; Figure 2.4: Courtesy of International Business Machines; Figure 2.5: (a) Courtesy of Logitech Corporation; Figure 2.6: Reprinted with permission of Compaq Computer Corporation. All rights reserved; Figure 2.7: Photo courtesy of International Business Machines; Figure 2.8: Courtesy of GRID Systems Corporation; Figure 2.9: Courtesy of GO Corporation; Figure 2.10: (b) Copyright Hank Morgan/Rainbow; Figure 2.11: Courtesy of Kurzweil Applied Intelligence; Figure 2.12: Photo courtesy of International Business Machines; Figure 2.13: Courtesy of Symbol Technologies, Inc.; Figure 2.14: Photo courtesy of Hewlett-Packard Company; Figure 2.15: Photo courtesy of International Business Machines; Figure 2.19: Courtesy of Plus Development Corporation; Figure 2.21: (a) Courtesy of Apple Computer, Inc.; (b) Courtesy of Poquet Computer Corporation; Figure 2.22: (a) Photo courtesy of Hewlett-Packard Company; (b) Reprinted with permission of Compaq Computer Corporation. All rights reserved; Figure 2.23: (a), (b) Photos courtesy of International Business Machines; Figure 2.25: (a) Courtesy of Mitsubishi Electronics; (b), (e) Courtesy of Radius, Inc.; (d) Courtesy of Hundai Electronics America; (c), (g) Courtesy of Phillips Consumer Electronics; (f) Courtesy of Samsung Information Systems America, Inc.; Figure 2.26: Dot-matrix printer courtesy of Fujitsu America; print thimble courtesy of NEC Technologies, Inc.; daisywheel courtesy of Data Products; plotter courtesy of Houston Instruments, a Summagraphics company; thermal printer courtesy of NEC Technologies, Inc.; ink-jet printer photo courtesy of Hewlett-Packard Company; laser printer courtesy of C-Tech Electronics Inc.; Figure 2.27: Courtesy of First Byte; Figure 2.28: Courtesy of Anacomp, Inc.; Figure 2.29: (a), (b) TIB/WEST/ A. M. Rosario © 1991; Figure 2.32: Courtesy of Empruve Inc.; Figure 2.35: (a) Courtesy of Microscience International Corporation; (b) Photo courtesy of Seagate Technology, Inc.; (c) Courtesy of Tallgrass Technologies; Figure 2.36: Courtesy of IOMEGA Corporation; Figure 2.37: Courtesy of 3M Corporation; Figure 2.38: Courtesy of NEXT Computer, Inc.; Figure 2.39: Courtesy of Britannica Software, Inc.; Figure 2.40: Copyright Drew Jimsan/Tony Stone

Chapter 3 Page 80: top, copyright 1990 Peter Menzel; bottom, copyright Hank Morgan/Science Source; p. 83: top, Dartmouth News Service, copyright Stuart Bratesman; right, copyright Ira Wyman; bottom left, courtesy of WordStar International Inc.; bottom right, courtesy of Microsoft Corporation; Figure 3.3: (b) Dartmouth News Service, copyright Stuart Bratesman; Figure 3.6: Courtesy of International Business Machines; Figure 3.7: Courtesy of Apple Computer, Inc.; Figure 3.8: Courtesy of Digital Research; Figure 3.10: Copyright Lorraine Rorke, The Image Works; Figure 3.11: (a), (b) Courtesy of Borland International; Figure 3.12: Courtesy of Apple Computer, Inc.; Figure 3.13: Courtesy of Central Point Software; Figure 3.14: Courtesy of Central Point Software; Figure 3.17: Copyright Ira Wyman; Figure 3.20: (a), (b) Courtesy of International Business Machines; (c) Courtesy of Ashton-Tate Corporation; Figure 3.21: Courtesy of Rory Lysaght

Chapter 4 Page 119: top, copyright Alexander Tsiaras/Science Source; middle, copyright 1990 Peter Menzel and Evans and Southerland; bottom, courtesy of Micrografx; p. 121: top left, courtesy of The M.I.T. Museum; top right, courtesy of The Computer Museum; middle left, courtesy of Atari Games Corporation; middle right, courtesy of Apple Computer, Inc.; Figure 4.1: (a) Copyright Roger Tully/Tony Stone; (b) Courtesy of International Business Machines; (c) Copyright Hank Morgan/Science Source; Figure 4.2: Courtesy of Wang Laboratories, Inc.; Figure 4.3: Courtesy of Micro-soft Corporation; Figure 4.4: (a) Courtesy of WordPerfect Corporation; (b) Courtesy of Borland International; (c) Courtesy of Microsoft Corpor-ation; Figure 4.5: (b) Sheila Terry/Science Photo Library; (c) Precision Visuals International/Science Photo Library; Figure 4.6: (a)–(c) Courtesy of Microsoft Corporation; Figure 4.7: (a) Courtesy of Adobe Systems Inc. © 1991; (b), (f) Courtesy of Micrografx; (c) Courtesy of Glenn Harrison; (e) Courtesy of Vanloese; Figure 4.8: (b) Courtesy of Z Soft Company; Figure 4.10: (a) Copyright Hank Morgan/Rainbow; (b) Copyright Musi-lek Photography; Figure 4.11: Clip art courtesy of Dubl-Clik Software, Inc.; Figure 4.12: (a), (b) Courtesy of Industrial Light and Magic; (c) © 1991 Pixar; Figure 4.14: (a), (b) Copyright John Griffin/The Image Works

Chapter 5 Page 146: Courtesy of Quark Inc.; p. 147: top, courtesy of Photocraft; middle, photo courtesy of Hewlett-Packard Company; bottom, courtesy of Aldus Corporation; p. 149: top left, courtesy of International Business Machines; top right, courtesy of Apple Computer, Inc.; middle, courtesy of Aldus Corporation; bottom, photo courtesy of Hewlett-Packard Company; Figure 5.1: Courtesy of Aldus Corporation; Figure 5.3: Courtesy of Bitstream; Figure 5.5: (a), (b) Courtesy of Anthro Corporation; Figure 5.8: Courtesy of Aldus Corporation; Figure 5.9: (a) Courtesy of Ventura Software Inc.; (c) Courtesy of Quark Inc.

Chapter 6 Page 166: Copyright Dan McCoy/Rainbow; p. 167: top, courtesy of Hayes Microcomputer Products; bottom left, copyright T. J. Florian/Rainbow; bottom right, Prodigy; p. 169: top left, courtesy of The Bettman Archive; top right, courtesy of NASA; middle, courtesy of AT&T Bell Laboratories; bottom left, courtesy of CompuServe Incorporated; bottom right, courtesy of Russ Glover; Figure 6.8: Courtesy of Katherine Lambert; Figure 6.11: Lawrence Manning/West Light; Figure 6.18: Courtesy of AT&T

Chapter 7 Page 194: Courtesy of Centrox Corporation; p. 195: top, courtesy of International Business Machines; bottom, photo courtesy of Hewlett-Packard Company; p. 197: top left and bottom left, courtesy of International Business Machines; top right, courtesy of UNISYS Corporation; bottom right, courtesy of Ashton-Tate Corporation; Figure 7.8: Photo courtesy of Hewlett-Packard Company; Figure 7.13: Courtesy of Centrox Corporation

Chapter 8 Page 224: Copyright Steve Chenn/West Light; p. 225: top, copyright Robert Holmgren; bottom left, copyright Pierre Kopp/West Light; bottom right, copyright Jeff Zaruba/Tony Stone; p. 227: top, copyright Blair Seitz/Photo Researchers; middle, copyright Jeff Zaruba/Tony Stone; bottom, copyright Jim Pickerell/West Light

Chapter 9 Page 250: Copyright Charles Thatcher/Tony Stone; p. 251: top, courtesy of Apple Computer, Inc.; bottom, copyright Charles Thatcher/Tony Stone; p. 253: top, photo courtesy of Hewlett-Packard Company; bottom, courtesy of Lotus Development Corporation; Figure 9.1: Copyright Dan McCoy/Rainbow; Figure 9.5: Courtesy of Ashton-Tate Corporation; Figure 9.6: Copyright Tony Stone; Figure 9.7: TIB/WEST/Chuck Mason © 1991; Figure 9.8: Copyright Dick Luria/Science Source; Figure 9.9: Courtesy of Inmac

INDEX

ESSENTIAL
DOS 3.3

Tim Duffy
Professor of Accounting in Information Systems
Illinois State University

ESSENTIAL DOS 3.3

Wadsworth Publishing Company
Belmont, California
A Division of Wadsworth, Inc.

Computer Science Editor: Frank Ruggirello
Developmental Editor: Alan Venable
Editorial Assistant: Rhonda Gray
Production: Hal Lockwood, Bookman Productions
Print Buyer: Martha Branch
Art Editor: Jane Brundage, Bookman Productions
Interior and Cover Design: Vargas/Williams/Design
Copy Editor: Betty Duncan
Photo Researchers: Sarah Bendersky, Darcy Lanham, Judy Mason, Monica Suder
Technical Illustrator: Illustrious, Inc.
Compositor: Graphic Typesetting Service, Los Angeles
Printer: Arcata Graphics, Kingsport, Tennessee

2 3 4 5 6 7 8 9 10—96 95 94 93 92
ISBN: 0-534-18722-6

To Wendy and Michael

CONTENTS

PREFACE

PURPOSE

This *Software Essentials* book and its associated software-training materials teach software competency. These materials are designed for both majors and non-majors in a quarter or semester course that uses the microcomputer as the primary vehicle for introducing students to problem solving. As typically expected in this type of course, there are no prerequisites.

APPROACH

Students acquire software competency by completing a set of software-training chapters that focus on current releases of various major software packages. To achieve that competency, each software package is presented in a separate booklet emphasizing hands-on problem solving. Carefully prepared, hands-on tutorials are provided within each chapter. Closely related end-of-chapter exercises reinforce the tutorial learning and expand the student's mastery over a broader range of applications.

Software packages covered in this series include

- DOS 3.3 and 5.0.
- WordPerfect 5.0/5.1.
- Lotus 1-2-3 2.2 and 2.3.
- Quattro Pro 3.0.
- dBASE III Plus.
- dBASE IV 1.1.
- Paradox 3.5.
- Windows 3.1.

IMPROVEMENTS IN SOFTWARE INSTRUCTION

I have always made the greatest possible effort to make hands-on instruction direct and meaningful. For this series in *Software Essentials,* the hands-on passages have been extensively reviewed and revised to make the booklets in the series more effective for the teacher and learning easier for the beginning student. Important changes include the following:

- **Self-Contained Modules** Each software module is self-contained. Each has its own front matter, chapter numbering, glossary, and command summary.
- **Expanded Hands-On Learning** The number of hands-on exercises has been increased dramatically. Particularly, the number of shorter exercises has been increased.
- **Use of Second Color** All hands-on exercise commands in the text appear in second color. This allows the student to quickly identify what keystrokes to enter and to distinguish them from additional explanation about a software feature or command.

- **Hints/Hazards Boxes** Many Hints/Hazards boxes inform students about the tricks they can use and potential traps they may encounter when using a particular software tool.
- **Keyboard Icons.** Keyboard icons appear frequently in headings and tables. These icons help the student to identify and remember specific keystrokes.

WORKING IN A HANDS-ON ENVIRONMENT

Software Essentials and its allied materials work best in a hands-on environment. The step-by-step exercises make most sense when an individual is sitting at computer and can immediately see the results of his or her actions. A symbol such as the one shown in the margin indicates hands-on material.

Each software package covered in this series is treated in enough detail to satisfy the requirements of a computer novice. However, each software booklet assumes that the software has already been configured for the student's use. If a package has not been configured for a specific machine, refer to the documentation for that package.

HARDWARE REQUIREMENTS FOR HANDS-ON SOFTWARE

An IBM PC or compatible computer with two disk drives and 320K of memory is required for most tools in this series. Note that you need 512K and a hard disk to run dBASE IV. You will also need a color monitor/graphics adapter board to properly display Lotus 1-2-3 graphics on the screen. A printer (with graphics capabilities if you wish to print Lotus graphs) is also required for printing documents, reports, graphs, and worksheets.

The hard disk (fixed disk) has resulted in many changes in the way computer concepts and use are taught in the classroom. During the past few years, the prices of hard disk technology have plummeted. Because this technology is now affordable for most colleges and universities, this text includes instructions for running software from a fixed disk.

LEARNING AIDS AND SAMPLE FILES

Exercises are provided at the end of each chapter to give students quick feedback on their progress. Besides the written exercises, hands-on computer exercises are included at the end of the software chapters to provide feedback through challenging applications of material covered in the chapter. A number of sample diskette files—including sample worksheets, text files, and database files—have been provided for use with text lessons and exercises.

ESSENTIAL

DOS 3.3

1

INTRODUCTION TO DOS

CHAPTER OBJECTIVES

After completing this chapter, you should be able to

- **Distinguish between internal and external DOS commands**
- **Start (boot) the computer system**
- **Change the default drive**
- **Write appropriate filenames**
- **Describe how DOS uses various keys and how it uses wild cards**
- **Understand the format of DOS commands**
- **Use the Directory (DIR) command**
- **Prepare a diskette for use with the FORMAT command**
- **Use the DATE and TIME commands**

In Chapter 3 of "Computing Concepts," we explained the function of operating systems in general and gave some information on the IBM PC **disk operating system (DOS).** In this chapter, we discuss more about DOS and introduce several DOS commands required for daily use of the IBM PC. For more information about DOS or about differences in the commands contained in other versions, refer to the **Microsoft MS DOS** reference manual that comes with your version of DOS.

DOS commands are either internal or external. **Internal commands are built into the command processor file COMMAND.COM. External commands reside in separate, external files** (also called utilities). For example, the FORMAT command is contained in a file called FORMAT.COM. External commands must be read from the appropriate file before they can be executed. This means that a disk containing that file must be available in one of the drives for DOS to execute it.

Besides COMMAND.COM and various external files, DOS also includes two files called **IO.SYS,** which handles input and output, and **DOS.SYS, which acts as a file manager.** IO.SYS and DOS.SYS are hidden program files that reside on the same disk as COMMAND.COM but are not listed when you issue the Directory command to call up a list of files contained on the disk.

When DOS is placed on a disk, it consumes considerable storage space. In fact, recent versions of DOS require over 100K of storage space, leaving about 260K of storage available on a typical 5.25-inch double-density disk for programs and data. Once DOS has been loaded, the hidden files take up to 50K of your computer's RAM. DOS does not have to be placed on **data disks** but should be copied, if possible, onto any disk that will be used to hold application programs.

THE BOOT PROCESS

Starting a computer has long been known as the **boot process,** a term derived from the old expression "pulling oneself up by the bootstraps." Two basic ways initiate the boot process: the **cold start** (starting the computer when the power is off) and the **system reset, or warm start.**

When a computer is started cold or warm, the CPU executes the bootstrap loader, a small program contained in ROM. The bootstrap loader checks the disk directory to ensure that the disk has, in consecutive storage locations, the IO.SYS and DOS.SYS programs, which are then loaded in order into RAM.

The IO.SYS program executes next, checking to see what peripherals are attached to the computer and preparing them for use. For example, the IO.SYS initializes a printer, signaling it to stand by to receive information. After IO.SYS has finished, the DOS.SYS program performs **initialization** work that allows data to be passed to a disk and stored. Next, the COMMAND.COM file is automatically brought in from the disk and placed in RAM, completing the boot process.

After the boot process is completed, DOS checks for an AUTOEXEC.BAT file on the boot disk. **AUTOEXEC.BAT** files are command files that you can create, for instance, to tell the computer to automatically start up a certain application program. If there is such a file, DOS executes its commands.

If it does not find an AUTOEXEC.BAT file, it will next display date and time prompts. If your computer has its own internal clock/calendar hardware, it will most likely show the correct date and time. If it doesn't, it will probably display the date 01-01-80. If you want to accept the date and time the computer gives you, press Enter. If you want to change the date, respond to the prompt requesting you to enter a new date. DOS asks you to type the date in a month/day/year format (MM/DD/YY).

In between the numbers for month, day, and year, you must enter some form of delimiter. A **delimiter** is any sort of punctuation that shows where one part of a command ends and the next part begins. Enter the date using either dashes or slashes as delimiters (mm-dd-yy or mm/dd/yy). Complete the command by pressing Enter. The date entered will be recorded in the directory for any files that are created or changed during this session.

Next, the computer asks for the time in the hh:mm format, which you must enter using colons as delimiters (for example, 10:42 for 10:42 A.M. or 22.42 for 10:42 P.M.). The time entered will serve as the starting time for the time recorded in the directory for any files that are created or changed during this session. After the date and time have been entered, the computer displays something like the following three lines at the top of the screen:

```
The IBM Personal Computer DOS
Version 3.30 (C)Copyright International Business Machines Corp 1981, 1987
             (C)Copyright Microsoft Corp. 1981, 1986
C>
```

Depending on your system, you may see C>, A> or B>. Each of these is the **DOS prompt.** It means that DOS is waiting for you to enter a command.

Starting DOS if the Computer Power Is Off (Cold Start)

1. To load DOS into memory, insert the DOS disk or the program disk with DOS (label side up and thumb on label) in disk drive A (the left-hand disk drive).
2. Close the drive door. (If you have a fixed disk, leave the drive door open and turn on the machine.)
3. If peripherals are attached, turn their power switches to the ON position.
4. Turn the system unit power switch (located on the right-hand side, toward the rear of the machine) to the ON position.

Restarting DOS if the Computer Is Already On (System Reset, or Warm Start)

1. To load DOS into memory, insert the DOS disk or the program disk with DOS (label side up and thumb on label) in disk drive A.
2. Close the drive door. (If you have a fixed disk, leave the drive door open and turn on the machine.)
3. Press and hold down both Ctrl and Alt; then press Del. Release the three keys.

When first turned on in a cold start, a computer performs a memory check to ensure that all RAM locations are capable of storing and retrieving data correctly. This memory check is not performed during a system reset. The memory check consumes most of the computer's start-up time, and the more memory a machine has, the longer the check takes. Microcomputers may take anywhere from 3 to about 45 seconds to start and load DOS.

USING DOS: AN INTRODUCTION

HARDWARE CONFIGURATIONS

One of the problems in writing a text like this is that a computer can take many different types of configurations. One user's computer may have two 5.25-inch disk drives; another's might have a 3.5-inch disk drive and a hard disk drive; another's a 5.25-inch disk drive, a 3.5-inch disk drive, and a hard disk drive; yet another's two 3.5-inch disk drives and a hard disk drive; and so forth.

When you are referring to a specific drive or other storage device on your computer, you must call it by the name that DOS uses, which will be some letter of the alphabet, *A* through *N*. If you have fixed disk, it is typically referred to as device C (though part of that disk may also be called D and another part E). Your diskette drives are referred to as A and B. If the drives sit next to one another, the left-hand drive is usually A. If the drives are stacked on top of one another, the top drive is usually A (Figure 1.1).

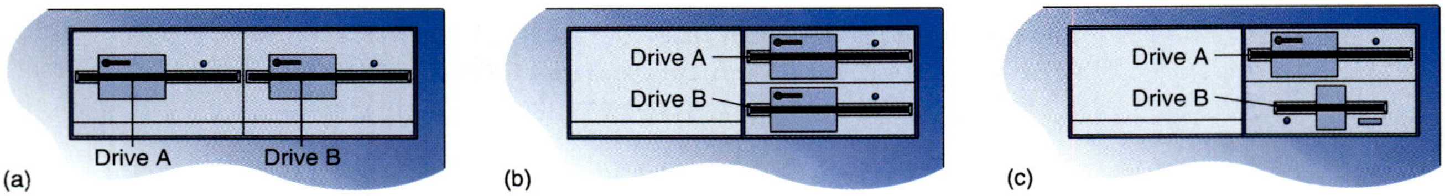

Figure 1.1
How DOS names the computer's disk drives in (a) a side-by-side configuration, (b) a stacked configuration, and (c) a stacked configuration with one 5.25" disk drive and one 3.5" disk drive.

CHANGING DEFAULT DRIVES

The C in C> (the DOS prompt) designates the **default disk drive** to DOS, telling it which disk the computer will automatically use to retrieve a file or execute a command. Unless you specify another drive, DOS searches only the default-drive disk for filenames. The default drive can be thought of as the drive currently in use.

The boot program tries to start a computer by trying to find DOS on whatever disk is in drive A. If it finds a disk in A that does not contain DOS, it responds with an error message and asks you to put in the correct disk. If it does not find a disk in A, it checks to see if there is a hard disk with DOS. If DOS is on the disk in drive A, the default drive remains A. If DOS is on the hard disk, the default drive becomes C. Additional drives attached to the computer are specified by consecutive letters: B for the second, C for the third, and so on.

You can change the default drive by typing the designation letter of the desired drive in either uppercase or lowercase letters, followed by a colon, and pressing Enter. (DOS always translates lowercase letters into uppercase.) For example, to change from disk drive A to drive B, change the prompt as follows:

Screen shows A>	Original drive
Type `B:`	Specifies new drive designation
Press Enter	Makes the change
Screen shows B>	New drive, new prompt

B is now the default (current) drive. DOS will now search only the disk located in disk drive B to execute commands or find filenames, unless you specify another drive. Try this on your computer.

HINTS/HAZARDS

If you have a computer with a fixed disk and only one diskette drive, you may be a bit confused by the fact that DOS will refer to the diskette drive—or let you refer to it—sometimes as drive A and sometimes as drive B. Don't worry about this. Referring to the same drive by different names is sometimes necessary—for instance, when you are using the same drive to copy material from one diskette to another by alternately inserting one diskette and then the other into the same drive.

Changing Default Drives

Type `B:`	Changes the default drive and the prompt to B>.
Enter	Executes the command.
Type `A:`	Changes the default drive and the prompt to A>.
Enter	Executes the command.

DIRECTORIES

Every disk that is used with DOS contains a **directory** of the files on that disk. This directory is also called the root directory, and its framework is created during the disk-preparation (format) process. The directory of a disk can be listed by using the Directory (DIR) command, as will be shown in more detail later in the chapter. Figure 1.2 shows a typical disk directory. The first column shows the filename of each file in the directory. The second column contains an additional part of the filename, the file extension. (Not all filenames have extensions.) The third column shows the file size in bytes. The fourth and fifth columns show the data and time when the file was created or last changed.

Next to the root directory on the disk (but not displayed on the screen) is a system area known as the **file allocation table (FAT).** Its job is to keep track of which sectors store particular files and to inventory available space on the disk so that new files can be created and stored in unused areas. Each disk has one directory and two copies of the FAT. If the system has a problem reading the first copy of the FAT, it reads the second.

Examining a Directory

1. Place the student data disk (or some other disk containing files) in drive A of your computer and issue the Directory command:

Type `DIR`	Issues the command.
Enter	Executes the command.

2. Identify the following items of information displayed to the screen:
   Filename
   File extension
   File size
   Date and time of creation
3. How much space is left on the disk?

Figure 1.2
A typical disk directory.

```
A>dir
 Volume in drive A has no label
 Directory of A:\

   CH8EX7   WK2       896   3-01-92    8:05p
   CH10EX1A AHV      4608   2-28-92    7:53p
   CH8EX8             512   3-01-92    8:21p
   CH8EX9             896   3-01-92    8:28p
   EDTARTCL         10880   3-03-92    8:34a
   CH10EX5A          1024   2-28-92    8:00p
   CUSTOMER DBF      1598   1-01-80    2:06a
   BLUEWS4         106240   3-02-92    4:50p
   FOOTNOTE          2048   2-27-92    7:30p
   BLUEWS7          52864   3-01-92    8:56p
   EXER1             1024   3-03-92    8:35a
   CH9EX8   DBF      1110   3-02-92   10:31a
   BOOKEXER          9216   3-27-92    8:42a
   CH9EX9   WK1      1810   3-02-92   10:40a
   BLUEWS9          53888   3-02-92    5:24p
   SMLBUSNS          3328   3-01-92    2:59p
   NEWLETTR         11136   2-27-92    5:08p
   PROTDATA          8448   3-02-92   11:54a
   BLUEWS5          57984   3-01-92    8:24p
   BLUEWS8          48768   3-02-92    5:04p
   BLUEWS6          69632   3-01-92    8:46p
   CH7EX6            3712   3-01-92    5:05p
       22 File(s)      176128 bytes free
```

FILENAMES

A file is a collection of related information that can be either data (data file) or instructions for manipulating data (program file). Users keep track of the files on a disk by name.

HINTS/HAZARDS

Within any given list of files displayed in a directory, each filename must be unique. If a disk has a file named MICRO.1 on it and you store a second file named MICRO.1 on that disk, the computer will destroy the original MICRO.1 and replace it with the second.

Within space and special-character limitations, you can name files almost anything you wish. Disk **filenames** can be one to eight characters in length and can be followed by a one- to three-character **filename extension**, separated by a period. A student data file for grades, for example, might be called STUDGRAD.TXT. The components of this name are labeled in Figure 1.3.

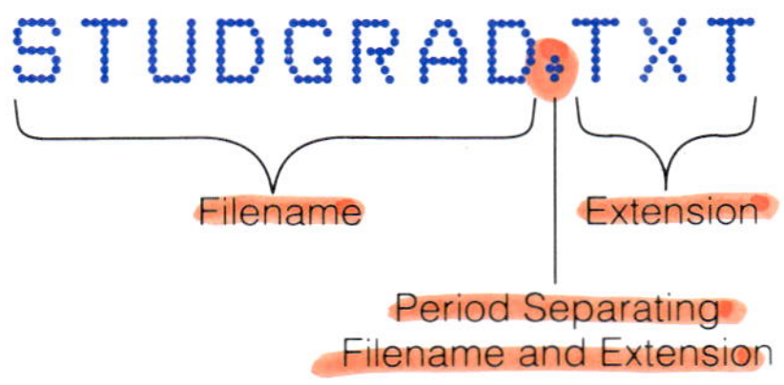

Figure 1.3
Components of a filename.

In creating a new file, you can give a filename extension or omit it. However, to access an existing file that has an extension, you must type the complete name, separating the filename from the extension using a period and leaving no blank spaces between them. (You may notice that the directory in Figure 1.2 shows one or more spaces between the filename and the extension and does not show the period—this was arbitrarily done by Microsoft.) DOS can generally locate a file with an extension only if you enter both the filename and the extension. The only exceptions to this concern the DOS file extensions .BAT, .EXE, and .COM.

The following characters can be used for filenames and extensions:

A–Z	!	}	&	)	~
0–9	'	-	#	-	'
$	(	^	@	{	

All other characters are invalid. An invalid character is assumed to be a delimiter, which truncates the filename. Embedded spaces (blanks within the filename or filename extension) are not allowed.

Generally, special characters should not be used in filenames because some software packages do not accept them. In addition, Microsoft may use special characters as DOS commands in future versions of the operating system program. For example, the %, <, >, and \ characters were allowable in DOS 1.0 and DOS 1.1 but are invalid in all versions of the software from DOS 2.0 on.

The following filenames and extensions would be acceptable filenames in DOS Version 3.30:

HOMERUNS
HOMERUNS.ABC
123HOMER
H
#.@

The following would not be acceptable:

REGGIEJACKSON	(more than eight characters)
75%.GRD	(disallowed character)
.WED	(no filename)
HOMER?.NOW	(disallowed character)

Filenames should reflect the data held in the files. For example, a student drafting an English term paper on a computer could title the file ENGTP—an abbreviation for English term paper.

HINTS/HAZARDS

When selecting filenames, try to make them self-documenting. This may be difficult because DOS limits you to just eight characters. You can alleviate this problem somewhat with the use of a file extension that descriptively names your file. For example, you can give any file containing a letter an .LTR file extension, a file containing a memo an .MEM file extension, a file containing a term paper a .TP file extension, and a file containing an annotated bibliography a .BIB file extension.

The root directory of a 360K disk can store as many as 112 files or a single document of 360K if it is the only file on the disk. A hard disk, however, does not have this limitation, and DOS allows a file to be up to 32 billion bytes in size.

SPECIAL DOS KEYS

Control Keys **Control keys** perform a variety of functions in connection with entering commands or lines of input. Table 1.1 lists the control keys.*

DOS Editing Keys **DOS editing keys** let you make changes to the last DOS command entered, which can save many keystrokes (Table 1.2). The instruction

Table 1.1 Control Keys

Control Keys	*Function*
Enter ↵	Makes a line or command available to the computer.
Ctrl + Break	Stops a program that is executing.
Ctrl + S	Temporarily stops output to the screen so that it can be examined (restart the output by again pressing Ctrl + S).
Shift + PrtSc (or Ctrl + P)	Toggles (turns) the printer echo either ON or OFF. Prints the exact contents of the screen.
Esc	Cancels the current line (many programs also use this key to stop processing or to get out of some difficulty).
BackSpace ←	Moves the cursor back one position.
Function keys F1, F2, . . .	Cuts down on the number of keystrokes required to enter a command.
NumLock	Activates either the numeric keypad or the Arrow keys and other special function keys.

**Throughout this text, the following system is used to show how keystrokes are combined. When two or three keystrokes are separated by plus signs (for example, Ctrl + Del), hold down the first key while pressing the remaining key(s). When two keystrokes are separated by a comma (for example, F2, Del), simply press each key in the order given.*

Table 1.2 DOS Editing Keys

Editing Keys	*Function*
Del	Skips one character in the current line.
Esc	Cancels the current line without changing the data in the instruction buffer.
F1	Copies and displays one character from the instruction buffer to the cursor position in the current line.
F2	Copies all characters from the instruction buffer up to a specified character and places them in the current line.
F3	Copies all remaining characters from the instruction buffer up to the current line.
F4	Skips all characters in the instruction buffer up to a specified character.
F5	Places the current line in the instruction buffer for more editing.
Ins	Inserts characters at the current cursor location using this toggle.

buffer, referenced with some of the keys in Table 1.2, is a temporary holding area that retains your last command so that it can be quickly executed again.

The F3 key is probably the most important of the **function keys.** Pressing it reissues the prior command, which has been held in the instruction buffer.

DOS COMMAND SYNTAX

Syntax refers to the rules that apply when you enter commands into a computer. According to the syntax of DOS, issuing a DOS command begins by typing the name of the command. This is usually followed by one or more **parameters**—information of any kind that is entered in addition to the command name. For example, the name of the file to be copied and the destination drive for the copy are parameters for the COPY command.

As noted previously, a delimiter is a character that shows where one part of a command ends and another part begins. The most commonly used delimiter is a space (usually represented in instruction manuals as the character b̸). Other common delimiters are the comma, semicolon, equal sign, and Tab key. A period is *not* a delimiter. Commands and parameters must always be separated by delimiters, but there must never be a space or other delimiter between a colon that appears between a drive name and a following filename. The following examples are correct:

ERASE FILE01.DOC
RENAME OLDFILE NEWFILE
DIR B:REPORT.DOC
COPY A:FILE03 B:
DIR B:FILE04.DOC

The following are incorrect:

B:REPORT DOC	(period missing between filename and extension)
A: REPORT.DOC	(unallowed space between drive and filename)
DIR A:FILE04. DOC	(unallowed space between filename and extension)

HINTS/HAZARDS

You can never go wrong placing a space after a DOS command, if you wish to follow that command with any parameters.

You can end commands while they are running by pressing Ctrl + Break (or Ctrl + C). It may take a while for the command to affect the computer.

Drives can act in either of two ways: A **source drive** is one from which data are transferred, and a **target drive** is one to which data are transferred. Depending on the particular operation involved, any drive may function as either the source drive or the target drive.

HINTS/HAZARDS

If you are using a networked device, you cannot use the following commands:

CHKDSK
DISKCOPY
FORMAT
LABEL
RECOVER
SYS

If you do try to use such a command, DOS generally responds with the following message:

```
Cannot <command> to a network device
```

The <command> entry is the name of the command that you entered at the keyboard.

HOW THIS BOOK PRESENTS DOS COMMAND INFORMATION

In the following pages, information about each DOS command is presented in the following order: (1) the name of the command; (2) the purpose (function) of the command; (3) the syntactic format (word order, spacing, and punctuation) of the command, with any optional parameters; (4) the nature of the command, identifying whether it is part of the COMMAND.COM file (internal) or is a utility (external); and (5) any remarks or explanations about the command.

The following tells how to read the syntactic format for each command, for example, the DOS command CHKDSK [d:][filename][/F][/V]:

1. Any words shown in capital letters must be entered exactly as shown. They can, however, be entered as any combination of uppercase and lowercase letters because DOS automatically changes all letters to uppercase.
2. Items shown in lowercase letters ask you to supply some variable information, such as the name of a specific file or disk drive.
3. Items in brackets ([ ]) are optional.
4. Ellipses (. . .) indicate that the item they accompany can be repeated as many times as desired.
5. All punctuation (except brackets)—commas, equal signs, question marks, colons, slashes, and so on—must be included where shown.

GLOBAL FILENAME CHARACTERS

Global filename characters, also known as **wild cards,** let you execute a command against several files whose names have one or more characters in common. The two wild cards used in DOS are the question mark **(?)** and the asterisk **(*).** A ? in a filename or extension indicates that any character can occupy that position or the position can be vacant. The use of wild cards is illustrated in the following discussion of the **Directory (DIR) command.**

THE DIRECTORY (DIR), FORMAT, DATE, AND TIME COMMANDS

DIRECTORY (DIR) COMMAND

Function This command lists all file-related information for specified files or families of files. The entity being listed can be a disk or a subdirectory (see Chapter 2). The list includes the filename, extension (if any), file size, and date and time of creation (or updating).

Format `DIR [d:][filename][.ext]][/P][/W]`

Type Internal.

Remarks and Examples Here are some examples of the DIR command:

A>DIR This lists all file entries from the root directory on the default drive. A typical directory listing might look like this:

```
Volume in drive A has no label
Directory of A:\
CH8EX7   WK2       896  3-01-92   8:05p
CH10EX1A AHV      4608  2-28-92   7:53p
CH8EX8             512  3-01-92   8:21p
CH8EX9             896  3-01-92   8:28p
EDTARTCL         10880  3-03-92   8:34a
CH10EX5A          1024  2-28-92   8:00p
CUSTOMER DBF      1598  1-01-80   2:06a
BLUEWS4         106240  3-02-92   4:50p
FOOTNOTE          2048  2-27-92   7:30p
BLUEWS7          52864  3-01-92   8:56p
EXER1             1024  3-03-92   8:35a
CH9EX8   DBF      1110  3-02-92  10:31a
BOOKEXER          9216  2-27-92   8:42a
CH9EX9   WK1      1810  3-02-92  10:40a
BLUEWS9          53888  3-02-92   5:24p
SMLBUSNS          3328  3-01-92   2:59p
NEWLETTR         11136  2-27-92   5:08p
PROTDATA          8448  3-02-92  11:54a
BLUEWS5          57984  3-01-92   8:24p
BLUEWS8          48768  3-02-92   5:04p
BLUEWS6          69632  3-01-92   8:46p
CH7EX6            3712  3-01-92   5:05p
      22 File(s)    176128 bytes free
```

The filename, extension, size of the file, creation date, and time of creation are given for each file on the disk. At the end of the listing, the amount of available storage on the disk is given.

A>DIR B: This lists all entries on the disk in drive B.

You can also use the wild-card characters ? and * with the filename and extension parameters. For example:

A>DIR REPORT?.? This lists all directory entries on the default drive with filenames of seven characters beginning with REPORT. The listed entries may have any character in the seventh position. Files that would be listed by the above DIR command include

REPORT
REPORTS.PDQ
REPORT3
REPORTB.2

An * in a filename or extension indicates that any character can occupy that position and any remaining positions in the filename or extension:

DIR W*.* This lists all directory entries on the default drive that have filenames beginning with W and having any or no extension. The filenames in this example may be from one to eight characters in length, and the extensions may be from one to three characters in length. (The second * in the above command tells DOS to list any files that start with a

W with or without a file extension.) Files that would be listed by the above DIR command include

WS	COM
WSOVLY1	OVR
WINSTALL	COM
WORK01	

B>DIR C*.* This lists all files in drive B that start with a C. The listing might look like this:

```
Volume in drive B has no label
Directory of B:\
CH8EX7              896   3-01-92   8:05p
CH10EX1A           4608   2-28-92   7:53p
CH8EX8              512   3-01-92   8:21p
CH8EX9              896   3-01-92   8:28p
CH9EX8    DBF      1110   3-02-92  10:31a
CH9EX9    WK1      1810   3-02-92  10:40a
CH10EX5A           1024   2-28-92   8:00p
CUSTOMER DBF       1598   1-01-92   2:06a
CH7EX6             3712   3-01-92   5:05p
        9 File(s)    176128 bytes free
```

Only files that begin with a C are included in this listing.

C>DIR *.COM This lists all entries on the disk (or directory) in the default drive that have an extension of .COM. The listing might look like this:

```
Volume in drive C has no label
Directory of C:\WS5\
README    COM    29212  8-17-92   5:00p
SWITCH    COM      571  8-17-92   5:00p
WSLIST    COM    64000  8-04-92   5:00p
GOODCLK   COM       50  8-04-92   5:00p
KEYSET    COM     1256  8-04-92   5:00p
        5 File(s)    526336 bytes free
```

A>DIR/P Adding the /P parameter causes the display to pause after 23 lines have been shown. The screen then displays the message `Strike a key when ready....` This command is useful when the disk or subdirectory contains more files than the screen can show at one time. Under such conditions, the DIR command alone causes filenames to scroll off the top of the screen as it displays names that are farther down the list.

B>DIR/W This command displays only the filenames and extensions of the disk files. The /W parameter produces a five-column-wide display of the files, and the amount of available storage is also given:

```
Volume in drive B has no label
Directory of B:\
CH8EX7         CH10EX1A       CH8EX8         CH8EX9         EDTARTCL
CH10EX5A       CUSTOMER DBF   BLUEWS4        FOOTNOTE       BLUEWS7
EXER1          CH9EX8    DBF  BOOKEXER       CH9EX9    WK1  BLUEWS9
SMLBUSNS       NEWLETTR       CH3            PROTDATA       BLUEWS5
BLUEWS8        BLUEWS6        CH7EX6
      23 File(s)    175104 bytes free
```

Chapter 2 discusses other commands related to directories and subdirectories.

Issue the following DIR commands against your student data disk (press Enter after each command). This exercise assumes that the disk is in drive A:

`DIR *.C*`	Gets a listing of all files that have a C as the first character of the file extension.
`DIR B*.*`	Gets a listing of any file that begins with a B.
`DIR *.C13`	Gets a listing of any file that has a C13 as the file extension.

FORMAT COMMAND

The following presents the **FORMAT command** in its simplest version, which is all you need at the moment. Chapter 2 gives more variations.

Function Data are stored on a disk's narrow, concentric recording rings called tracks, which are further divided into sectors. Before a disk can store data, it must be organized by the formatting (initializing) process, which magnetically marks the boundaries of the tracks and sectors. These magnetic tracks lay out information boundaries on the disk, somewhat like traffic lanes dictating the routes and directions of cars.

For DOS to recognize a disk and to track files on it, the disk must be formatted with the FORMAT command:

Format `FORMAT [d:][/S]`

Type External.

Remarks and Examples A disk needs to be formatted only the first time it is used. FORMAT verifies the storage integrity of every sector of a disk. It finds and write-protects tracks that have bad (nonrecordable) sectors, sets up the directory, establishes the FAT, and puts the boot record program at the beginning of the disk. It can also create a copy of DOS on a new disk.

The command FORMAT A:/S both formats the disk in drive A and places DOS on the disk. Use this command if you want to store application software to the disk and boot the system with the disk.

The command FORMAT A: formats the disk in drive A but does not place DOS on it. This should be used for disks that will store only data.

HINTS/HAZARDS

Do not perform the following exercise in relation to a hard drive (C:). Formatting a hard disk will erase all program and data files from the disk.

The following exercise involves formatting a **diskette.** For this exercise, you will need a new 3.5-inch or 5.25-inch diskette or a diskette that does not contain any files that need to be saved because formatting will erase all existing files. First, confirm that the diskette doesn't contain files to be saved: Insert the diskette in a drive and issue the DIR command to see the directory of files. Then enter the following commands.

`FORMAT B:`	Formats the disk as a data disk.
`DIR`	Issues the Directory command.

You should receive a `No files` message.

How DOS Uses the 5.25-Inch Double-Density Disk Most disk drives record 48 tracks per inch (tpi) on diskette, but only a $\frac{5}{6}$-inch-wide strip of disk actually holds tracks. With 48-tpi drives, then, only 40 usable tracks are actually created. These tracks are labeled 0 through 39.

Each track is usually divided into 8 or 9 sectors. A PC, unless told to do otherwise, will automatically divide a track into 9 sectors, creating 720 total sectors on a disk (40 tracks $\times$ 9 sectors $\times$ 2 sides). Of these 720 sectors, 12 are reserved by the system to be used as follows:

To hold the FAT (two copies, with two sectors per copy): 4 sectors

To hold the directory: 7 sectors

To hold the boot program in the boot record: 1 sector

Therefore, 708 sectors (with a total user storage of 362,496 bytes) remain available on a disk formatted without the operating system.

Other types of disks, such as the 3.5-inch disk, use more sectors to hold directory and FAT information.

Space within a track is allocated in increments called **clusters.** A cluster on a single-sided disk is one sector; a cluster on a double-sided disk consists of two adjacent sectors. The operating system will allocate just one cluster to a file, then wait until that cluster is filled before assigning another.

Another important disk concept is the **cylinder.** A floppy disk contains 40 tracks on each side of the disk, with each track on the top side lying directly above the corresponding track on the bottom side. All like-numbered tracks on all recording surfaces constitute a cylinder. On floppy disks, 2 tracks make up each cylinder; on a hard disk, up to 10 tracks to a cylinder (Figure 1.4).

Figure 1.4
The like-numbered tracks from all disks in a hard drive create a cylinder.

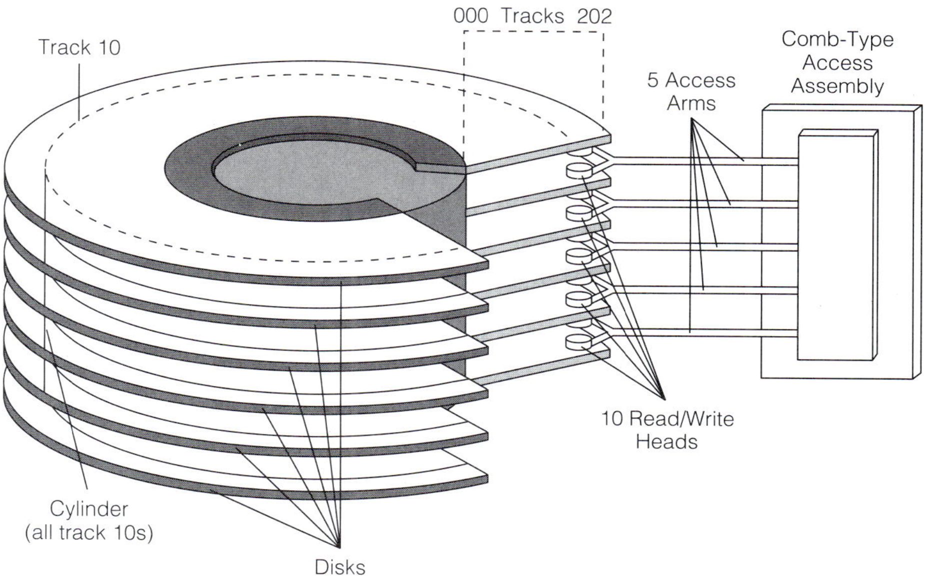

DOS refers to the bottom of the disk as side 0 and to the top as side 1. On a double-sided disk, DOS starts storing data on the outermost track (referred to as track 0) of side 0, filling sectors 0 through 8. It then goes to side 1 to use track 0, sectors 0 through 8; then back to side 0 to use track 1, sectors 0 through 8; and so on. This process continues until the entire disk is full. (If the disk is single-sided, of course, DOS does not switch sides.)

The cylinder concept lets the disk drive access information much faster than would otherwise be possible. The read/write heads need only be activated electronically from one side to another until the cylinder of storage is filled, at which point the read/write head can position itself mechanically to the next cylinder. Mechanical delay is always more time-consuming than electronic delay.

DATE COMMAND

Function Some computers come with built-in clock/calendar circuitry. With such a computer, you do not have to reset the date and time every time you start the computer. If you have a computer without such circuitry or you want to change the internally held date, you must use the **DATE command.** This command changes the date that has been stored by DOS (today's date). Ultimately, the date is placed in the directory entry for any files that are created or altered and resaved during this session.

Format `DATE mm-dd-yy.`

Type Internal.

Remarks and Examples For example, to change the system date to January 15, 1993, enter the command DATE 1-15-93. If you have entered a valid date, it will be the new date accepted by DOS. If you press Enter after DATE, the DATE command produces the following prompt:

```
Current date is day mm-dd-yy
Enter new date: __
```

The system displays the day of the week in the day location. Don't worry that you have never told it the day of the week; DOS has a formula for calculating this information.

To leave the date unchanged, press Enter.

The valid delimiters within the date are hyphens (-) and slashes (/); therefore, the dates 4-23-93 and 4/23/93 are both correct. DOS also lets you mix these delimiters, so the date 4/23-93 also works.

DOS does not let you enter a date prior to 1-1-80. Apart from that, any date is acceptable as today's date as long as the digits are in the correct ranges for each field. This means, for example, that you can't enter 16 for a month (12 is the maximum) or 35 for a day (31 is the maximum). If you make a mistake, DOS displays the error message `Invalid date.`

HINTS/HAZARDS

You can save a keystroke by entering the new date to be used by DOS following the DATE command. For example, to change the system date to January 15, 1993, enter the following command at the keyboard:

```
DATE 1-15-93
```

TIME COMMAND

Function The **TIME command** lets you enter a new time for the system. This time then becomes a part of any directory entry of a new file.

Format `TIME [hh:mm:ss.xx].`

Type Internal.

Remarks and Examples Upon receiving a valid time entry, DOS stores that information and updates it until a new time is entered. In the latter case, the system displays the following prompt:

```
Current time is hh:mm:ss.xx
Enter new time: __
```

In this prompt, hh stands for hours, mm for minutes, ss for seconds, and xx for hundredths of a second.

To leave the time as currently set, press Enter.

A 24-hour clock pattern is used. This means that 1:00 P.M. is entered as 13:00. Most people are concerned only with hours and minutes; entering the seconds and hundredths of a second is not required.

If you enter partial time information (for example, just hours), the remaining fields are shown as zeros.

The valid delimiters for time fields are colons (:)—separating hours, minutes, and seconds—and the period (.)—separating seconds and hundredths of a second.

If you enter an invalid time or invalid delimiter, the message `Invalid time` appears.

In the following example, when Enter is pressed, the time recorded by the system will be changed to 18:25:00.00:

```
A>TIME
Current time is 00:25:16.65
Enter new time:18:25 __
```

CHAPTER REVIEW

The two basic types of DOS commands are internal and external. Internal commands are part of the DOS file COMMAND.COM. To execute one of these commands, you need only enter the command from the keyboard. External commands reside on disk(ette) as separate files outside COMMAND.COM. To execute one of these commands, the disk it is on must reside in the default drive or in a drive that you specify with a drive identifier.

Booting a computer means starting it up, either from a cold start (power off) or a warm start or reset (power already on).

Information stored on a disk is contained in files. Each file must have a unique filename. DOS filenames can be one to eight characters long, followed optionally by a period and an extension name of one to three characters.

DOS uses disk drives in executing commands. It also uses information contained on special areas of the disk or in files. Global characters (wild cards) can access some of this information if it is file-related.

Each DOS command has characteristics in common with other DOS commands; DOS also makes use of a common format notation. All disk-oriented commands have unique features that can be expressed adequately only when discussed in detail.

The Directory command (DIR) lets you see a list of the files on your hard disk or diskette. The DOS FORMAT command prepares a disk for use with DOS. The DATE and TIME commands let you set the date and time that your system uses.

KEY TERMS AND CONCEPTS

AUTOEXEC.BAT
boot process
cluster
cold start
COMMAND.COM
control key
cylinder
data disk
DATE command
default disk drive
delimiter
directory
Directory (DIR) command
diskette
disk operating system (DOS)
DOS editing keys
DOS prompt
DOS.SYS
external command
file allocation table (FAT)
filename
filename extension
FORMAT command
function key
global filename characters
initialization
internal command
IO.SYS
Microsoft
MS DOS
parameter
source drive
syntax
system reset
target drive
TIME command
warm start
wild card
?
*

CHAPTER QUIZ

Multiple Choice

1. What information is entered in addition to a DOS command?
   a. Delimiter
   b. Extension
   c. Modifier
   d. Parameter

2. Which of the following are acceptable filenames for DOS Versions 2.0 and higher?
   a. INVENTORY.303
   b. DOC\23.bk!
   c. ///.AHV
   d. 2978
   e. -#.9$

3. Which of the following are acceptable delimiters in DOS?
   a. Comma
   b. Space
   c. Equal sign
   d. Period
   e. Semicolon

4. Which of the statements below is false?
   a. A DOS filename can have up to eight characters.
   b. A DOS filename must have an extension.
   c. A period must appear between a filename and its extension.
   d. The filename extension can have from one to three characters.
   e. All of the above are true.

5. DOS is *not* made up of which of the following parts?
   a. Boot record
   b. IO.SYS
   c. DOS.SYS
   d. COMMAND.COM
   e. It is composed of all the above parts.

True/False

6. You do not have to format a disk before you use it for the first time.

7. The difference between a cold start (cold boot) and a warm start (system reset) is that the RAM memory is not checked during the system reset.

8. Only the disk on the default drive is checked during a search for files, unless the computer is otherwise instructed.

9. DOS keeps track of where files are stored by using the file allocation table (FAT).

10. Global characters (wild cards) are normally not much help in using DOS commands.

Answers

1. a 2. d, e 3. a, b, c, e 4. b 5. e 6. f 7. t 8. t 9. t 10. f

Exercises

1. Define or describe each of the following:
   a. DOS
   b. Cold start (cold boot)
   c. Warm start (system reset)
   d. Default drive

2. Describe the difference between an internal command and an external command.

3. List and describe the two parts of a filename. Place an asterisk to the left of the required part(s).

4. List the five pieces of information given by the DIR command for each file.

5. The ____________ command prepares a disk for use.

6. A(n) ____________ boot requires that the power to the machine be off beforehand.

7. The disk that is automatically searched is the ____________ disk.

8. Of the 720 sectors created on the 5.25-inch disk, only 708 are available to the user. The remaining sectors are taken up by ____________, ____________, and ____________.

9. The wild-card character ____________ identifies a variable in only one position.

10. If a file was originally created with a file extension, that extension must be used any time that the file is referenced in the future. List three exceptions to this rule.

11. Up to ____________ files can be stored on a single disk.

COMPUTER EXERCISES

1. Enter the characteristics of your computer system(s) at your (a) school and (b) home/elsewhere.
   a. What is the amount of RAM memory? ____________ K
      How many diskette drives? ____________
      What is the size of the diskette drive? ____________
      How many bytes can be stored on a diskette? ____________
      Do you have a fixed disk? ____________
      What is the size of the fixed disk? ____________
      What is the type of display? ____________
      What is the type of printer? ____________
      What is the speed of the printer? ____________
      Which software packages are installed for your computer? ____________
   b. What is the amount of RAM memory? ____________ K
      How many diskette drives? ____________
      What is the size of the diskette drive? ____________
      How many bytes can be stored on a diskette? ____________
      Do you have a fixed disk? ____________
      What is the size of the fixed disk? ____________
      What is the type of display? ____________
      What is the type of printer? ____________
      What is the speed of the printer? ____________
      Which software packages are installed for your computer? ____________

2. Place your student data disk in drive A. Enter the following DIR commands:
   a. Display the directory, one page at a time.
   b. Display the directory using the wide parameter option. Enter the following commands. Enter how many files are displayed for each of the commands:
   c. DIR E*.*
   d. DIR CH?EX*.*
   e. DIR CH*.*
   f. DIR *.WK1
   g. DIR *.*

3. What happens when you press F3?

4. List the three keys that are used for a system reset (warm start) and then perform one.

5. Format a disk using the /S parameter to place the system on a diskette. Once the format procedure is finished, issue a DIR command against that disk. You should see only the COMMAND.COM file on that disk.

6. Again format this disk, but format it as a data disk (this is necessary if you want to get rid of the hidden DOS files). Issue a DIR command against that disk. You should now receive a `File not found` message because reformatting has erased the COMMAND.COM file.

7. If your computer has only one diskette drive, issue the command A: to change the default drive to A. Issue a DIR command and note the files that are displayed. Issue a B: command to change the default drive to B. Issue another DIR command and note the files that are displayed. There should be no difference. The contents of the physical drive (the diskette drive) do not change as the drive name (logical drive) is changed.

8. Issue a system reset command (Ctrl + Alt + Del). What two pieces of information does DOS automatically prompt you for when the boot process is finished (provided there is no AUTOEXEC.BAT file present)?

9. When you performed the system reset, did the correct date and time appear? If a date other than 1-1-80 appeared, your computer contains built-in clock/calendar circuitry. Does your computer have this built-in circuitry?

10. Issue the two commands below against your student data disk. What is the difference between the files that are displayed?
    a. DIR CH?EX*.*
    b. DIR CH??EX*.*

11. What is the DOS prompt that automatically appears on the screen after the boot process is finished for a diskette-based system?

12. What is the DOS prompt that automatically appears on the screen after the boot process is finished for a hard disk–based system?

2

MORE DOS COMMANDS AND WINDOWS

CHAPTER OBJECTIVES

After completing this chapter, you should be able to

- **Create a subdirectory**
- **Use common directory-building commands**
- **Use the active directory**
- **Use various other DOS commands**
- **Use the Windows graphics user interface**

This chapter continues the previous chapter's coverage of DOS commands that are commonly used with microcomputers.

MORE NOTES ON DISK DIRECTORIES

In its **root directory,** any disk drives operating with DOS can hold a certain number of files, or subdirectories. A **subdirectory** is a smaller directory nested within a larger one. A 5.25-inch double-sided floppy disk can hold up to 112 files, or subdirectories. Table 2.1 shows the capacities of various types of disks.

Subdirectories can contain more files or even more subdirectories. Although DOS limits the number of entries in a root directory, it does not limit the number of entries within a subdirectory.

Learning to use subdirectories is very important for two reasons. First, they allow you to have many more files on a disk than it can otherwise contain. Second, they let you organize your disk more effectively. For instance, you can create a subdirectory that groups together all of the program or data files for a particular application. In Figure 2.1, all of the word processing program files are held in a word processing subdirectory. Within this subdirectory are nested three more subdirectories for filing data files (memos, letters, reports, and so on) pertaining to work, school, or home.

One problem with this type of directory structure is that program and data files are mixed in a single directory, making it difficult to find a specific data file. Each subdirectory depicted can be divided into other subdirectories. For example, besides holding the database program files, the database directory can hold two subdirectories that subdivide the data files according to whether they are for business or personal use.

DOS DIRECTORY COMMANDS

Although a subdirectory is like a root directory in some ways, it is actually a file. Because a subdirectory is a file, it must be named. However, the procedure for creating a subdirectory is different from that for creating an ordinary file. The following commands are used to create, display, and delete subdirectories:

- Make Directory (MKDIR) [MD] builds a file to contain the new directory entries.
- Change Directory (CHDIR) [CD] moves to another directory and makes that the active directory.
- Remove Directory (RMDIR) [RD] deletes the file containing the directory.
- TREE displays all directories on the disk.

The first three commands are internal. They can be executed either by their complete DOS name (in parentheses) or by their abbreviated name [in brackets].

Table 2.1 File Capacities of Various Types of Disks

Disk Type	*Maximum Number of Files or Subdirectories*
Single-sided	64
Double-sided	112
High-density (AT or 3.5-inch)	224
Hard disk	512

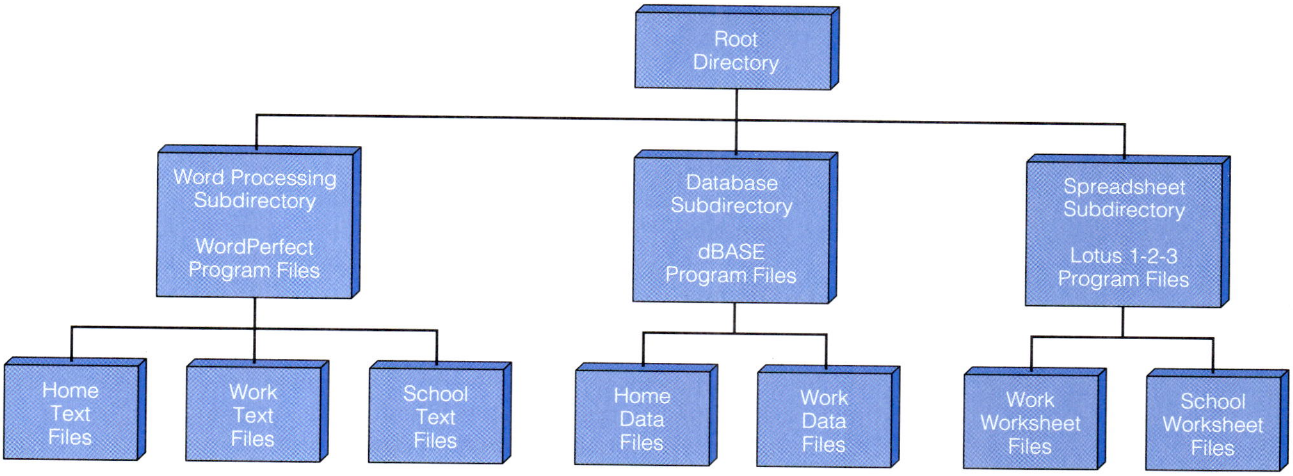

Figure 2.1
Project subdirectories within applications' subdirectories.

TREE is an external command and resides as a separate file on disk. These commands are explained more fully below.

Before you make a subdirectory, plan how you want to store data on your disk. You may decide to store programs and information by application type or you may plan to store programs and information by project. A third possibility is to combine these two techniques, storing information by project within an application (Figure 2.1).

You can use the Directory (DIR) command to list files in a subdirectory. If that subdirectory is currently the active directory, simply issue the DIR command by itself to list the files in that subdirectory. You can also use the DIR command to list the files in a lower-level subdirectory of the currently active subdirectory. For instance, suppose your DOS prompt shows WP51 as the name of the active subdirectory, C:\WP51>, and 123-22 is the name of a subdirectory within WP51. The following command lists the files in subdirectory 123-22: C:\WP51>DIR 123-22. The following command lists all files in 123-22 that bear the .WRK filename extension: C:\WP51>DIR 123-22*.WRK.

MAKE DIRECTORY (MKDIR OR MD) COMMAND

Function Once you have an idea of how you want to store your information, you can build the subdirectories that will hold the information. The **MKDIR (MD) command** creates a subdirectory on a specified drive named by the characters following the command. The complete name for a file, including the complete subdirectory name on which it is found, is referred to as the **path.** For example, the entry C:\1-2-3\WORK\SALES.WK1 refers to the SALES.WK1 file that resides in the WORK subdirectory of the 1-2-3 directory on drive C.

Format `MD [d][path]` or `[MKDIR [d:][path]`.

Type Internal.

Remarks and Examples You can use the abbreviated form MD for the MKDIR command. The path entry in the format refers to the exact location of a file or directory on disk.

The following commands create a directory called WORK on the default drive C:

```
C>MD WORK
C>MKDIR WORK
```

The following commands create a directory called HOME on drive A. The default drive remains C:

```
C>MD A:HOME
C>MKDIR A:HOME
```

Use the [d:] parameter to specify the drive on which you wish to create the subdirectory. If no drive is specified, the default drive is assumed.

DOS specifies no limit to the number of directories that you can create. The only limitation is the amount of storage available on your default device. Nor is there a limit to how many times a filename can appear on a disk as long as each occurrence is in a different subdirectory.

After each MD command is entered, the specified drive starts to record information about the new subdirectory. You can issue a DIR command, and your screen displays information about the created subdirectory. You might, for example, see something like the following if you created a subdirectory called WP:

```
Volume in drive A is TIM DUFFY
Directory of A:
WP              <DIR>        3-29-92      12:05a
                 x File(s)   290792 bytes free
```

Upon issuing a DIR command, you will notice that DOS is treating the subdirectory as a file. You can differentiate a subdirectory from a file by the <DIR> (abbreviation for directory) message, which is displayed in place of the file-size data. Notice that the date on which the subdirectory was created (the system date stored in the machine at start-up time) is also listed.

Also notice that the bytes-free entry that appears on your screen changes as any subdirectories are created. Each subdirectory takes a minimum of 1K, or 1024 characters, of storage.

CHANGE DIRECTORY (CHDIR OR CD) COMMAND

Function Once you have created subdirectories, you can reach a subdirectory via the **CHDIR command.** It changes the current DOS directory or displays the current directory of the default drive.

Format `CD [d:][path]` or `CHDIR [d:][path]`.

Type Internal.

Remarks and Examples You can use the abbreviated form CD for the CHDIR command. Use the [d:] parameter to specify the drive on which the subdirectory that you want to change resides or on which you want to display the current directory.

Assume that you have created the WP subdirectory and enter the following commands:

A>CD\WP This moves you from the root directory to the word processing (WP) subdirectory. To ensure that you have moved to the right subdirectory, issue the DIR command to see where you are. The following output appears on your monitor:

```
Volume in drive A is TIM DUFFY
Directory of A:\WP
.      <DIR>      3-29-92    12:08a
..     <DIR>      3-29-92    12:08a
     2 File(s) 292840 bytes free
```

The output generated by such a DIR command is just a bit different from the output of the root directory. Notice that the second line of this directory listing contains A:\WP. This denotes the active subdirectory. You can always tell when you are at the root directory because the output of the DIR command will give you the default drive followed only by a backslash, for example, A:\. DOS creates the . and .. entries to hold housekeeping information about the files that are stored in this directory.

The CD command provides you with a fair amount of flexibility in moving around a disk containing subdirectories:

CD This moves you from the current subdirectory to the root directory.

CD.. This moves you from the current subdirectory to the next higher directory.

CD This lets you find out where you are in a subdirectory tree. DOS will respond by naming the current active directory or subdirectory.

HINTS/HAZARDS

One problem that many people have using subdirectories is remembering exactly where they are in the directory structure. This problem is easily remedied by using the **PROMPT PG command.** Once that command is entered, the path of the active directory is given as the DOS prompt. Instead of seeing A appear, for example, you might see A:\DB> as the prompt. To turn this off, enter the command PROMPT at the DOS prompt.

The Active (Current) Directory The **active** (current) **directory** concept is especially important in a hard disk or high-density disk environment. After you have moved to a subdirectory in your hard disk, you can switch the default drive to one of your disk drives, and DOS will remember which is the active subdirectory. If you copy files from the disk to the hard disk drive that contains the active (current) subdirectory, they will be placed in that subdirectory.

HINTS/HAZARDS

When you want to issue a CD command that is to be used one level beneath the current (active) directory, the backslash is not a required character. For example, instead of entering the command CD \DB, you can enter the command CD DB.

REMOVE DIRECTORY (RMDIR OR RD) COMMAND

Function The **RMDIR (RD) command** removes the subdirectory of the name composed of the characters following the command.

Format `RD [d:][path]` or `RMDIR [d:][path]`.

Type Internal.

Remarks and Examples Assume that the DB subdirectory is no longer needed. Not wanting to waste the disk space taken up by this directory and its files, you decide to erase it with the RMDIR (RD) command. First, all files must be deleted from the directory with the DEL *.* command (this command will be discussed in detail later in the chapter). If you forget to remove any file from the subdirectory, DOS will display the following error message:

```
Invalid path, not a directory
or directory not empty
```

If you receive this error message, simply go to that directory and erase the rest of the files from it; then issue the RD command to remove the subdirectory.

You cannot remove root directories from a disk.

To work along with the following subdirectories exercise, place your student data disk in drive A.

`A>MD\WP`	Creates the word processing subdirectory (see Figure 2.1).
`A>MD\DB`	Creates the database subdirectory (see Figure 2.1).
`A>MD\SS`	Creates the spreadsheet subdirectory (see Figure 2.1).

After each command is entered, drive A starts to record information from that subdirectory's files.

`DIR` Displays the following information on your screen:

```
Volume in drive A is TIM DUFFY
Directory of A:\
WP        <DIR>            3-29-92     12:05a
DB        <DIR>            3-29-92     12:05a
SS        <DIR>            3-29-92     12:05a
      12 File(s) 292840 bytes free
```

The number of bytes free will probably be different on your disk.

Notice that this listing shows that DOS is treating the subdirectories as files. The original listing had *x* files, but after you created the subdirectories, it has three more files. You can differentiate a subdirectory from a file by the <DIR> message, which is displayed in place of the file-size data. The date on which the subdirectory was created (the system date stored in the machine at start-up time) is also listed.

Also notice that the bytes-free entry has changed since the three subdirectories were created. Each subdirectory takes a minimum of 1K, or 1024 characters, of storage. Continue entering these commands:

`PROMPT $P$G`	Activates the path as part of the DOS prompt.
`CD\WP`	Makes the WP subdirectory the active subdirectory.
`DIR`	Issues a Directory command.

Note that there are now two files with a . and a .. filename. Remember, DOS uses these to track information about the files stored in a subdirectory.

`MD SCHOOL`	Creates the subdirectory SCHOOL.
`MD PERSONAL`	Creates the subdirectory PERSONAL.
`CD\SCHOOL`	Moves to the SCHOOL subdirectory.

Notice that the DOS prompt has `A:\WP\SCHOOL>`.

`CD..`	Returns to the WP subdirectory.
`CD\PERSONAL`	Positions to the PERSONAL subdirectory.

Notice that the DOS prompt has `A:\WP\PERSONAL`.

`C:`	Changes the default drive to C.
`DIR A:`	Issues a Directory command against drive A.

Notice that the second line indicates that you are getting a directory listing of `A:\WP\PERSONAL`. You receive this listing because the PERSONAL subdirectory is the active or current directory for drive A. This means that this was the last directory that you were in on drive A.

`A:`	Returns to drive A.
`CD\`	Returns to the root directory.

Notice that you could have entered two CD.. commands to accomplish the same task. The CD\ command saves keystrokes when you are several subdirectory levels below the root directory. Continue as follows:

`CD\WP`	Moves to the WP subdirectory.
`RD SCHOOL`	Deletes the SCHOOL subdirectory.
`RD PERSONAL`	Deletes the PERSONAL subdirectory.
`CD..`	Returns to the root directory.
`RD WP`	Deletes the WP subdirectory.
`RD DB`	Deletes the DB subdirectory.
`RD SS`	Deletes the SS subdirectory.

TREE COMMAND

Function You may someday use a microcomputer system that is not familiar, in which case you may not know what subdirectories are on a disk or which files are in which subdirectory. The DOS **TREE command** will then be extremely helpful. It displays all subdirectories on a disk and, using an optional parameter, lists the files of the root directory and each subdirectory.

Format `[d:][path] TREE [d:][/F].`

Type External.

Remarks and Examples Use the [d:] and [path] optional parameters that appear before the TREE command to tell DOS in what drive and in what subdirectory this external file resides. Use the optional [d:] following the TREE command to tell DOS in which drive to execute the command. Use the optional [/F] parameter to tell DOS to list each file contained in each subdirectory.

Suppose a root directory contains the subdirectories SS, WP, and DB. For that directory, the TREE command without any of its parameters creates the following output:

```
TREE(Command)
DIRECTORY PATH LISTING FOR VOLUME TIM DUFFY
Path: \SS
Sub-directories: None
Path: \WP
Sub-directories: None
Path: \DB
Sub-directories: None
```

If this information is not enough, the /F parameter will list any files found in a subdirectory besides the subdirectory name. The command TREE /F creates the following display:

```
DIRECTORY PATH LISTING FOR VOLUME TIM DUFFY
      Path: \SS
      Sub-directories: None
      Files:           None
      Path: \WP
      Sub-directories: None
      Files:           FORMAT.COM
      Path:  \DB
      Sub-directories: None
      Files:           FORMAT.COM
```

DISK COMMANDS

The remainder of this chapter covers other commonly used DOS commands, which have been grouped into two families. **Disk commands** are discussed in this section. The **file commands** COPY, ERASE, RENAME, and TYPE are discussed in the following section. Each section begins with a brief description of the commands, followed by details and examples.

The **CHKDSK command** examines the directory and file allocation table (FAT) of a disk and produces disk and memory status reports. CHKDSK can also repair errors in the directories or FAT. This is the only command that lets you verify the amount of RAM that has been installed for the computer (up to 640K of base RAM).

The **DISKCOPY command** copies the entire contents of the disk that is in the specified source drive onto the disk that is in the specified target drive—exactly as the information appears on the source disk.

The basic FORMAT command was introduced in Chapter 1. This section provides further details. The FORMAT command initializes the disk in the designated or default drive so that it conforms to a recording format that DOS can use. As it executes, FORMAT analyzes the entire disk for defective sectors, initializes the directory, sets up space for the FAT, and records the boot program in the boot record.

CHECK DISK (CHKDSK) COMMAND

Function This command lets you analyze the directory and the FAT of a disk and produces disk and memory status reports. CHKDSK can also repair errors in the directories or FAT.

Format `CHKDSK [d:][filename][/F][/V].`

Type External.

Remarks and Examples CHKDSK temporarily makes the drive specified in [d:] the default drive. If CHKDSK ends prematurely (because, for example, you replied N to a disk error message), the default drive changes to the drive that CHKDSK was checking.

The command CHKDSK by itself does not automatically correct errors found in the directory or FAT. This is good in that it allows you to first analyze errors and consider the consequences of making corrections. It is generally inadvisable to make corrections unless there is a major problem; if the error is in the directory or FAT itself, a large part of the data on the disk can be lost.

The [/F] parameter causes CHKDSK to automatically correct errors in the directory and FAT.

The [/V] parameter brings a series of messages to the screen, identifying the status of each file.

CHKDSK [FILENAME] tells if the file specified (in this case, [FILENAME]) has been stored in contiguous sectors on disk. When a disk has recently been formatted, the 512 individual byte sectors used to store files will store input files contiguously. After some files have been erased and other files added, however, DOS will still attempt to store any new files or additions to existing files in the first vacant sector. Occasionally, a large file will end up being stored in a number of nonadjacent sectors as a result. Such a file, referred to as a **fragmented file,** will slow DOS's reading speed because the read/write heads will have to be moved physically to a number of different locations on disk.

For most applications, a fragmented file has no effect on the speed at which that file gets retrieved. Fragmentation is almost an automatic by-product of how files are stored on disk. If you are constantly adding information to a file, that file will be fragmented.

If a file is large and the number of noncontiguous locations reported by CHKDSK is large, the COPY command can eliminate this fragmentation because the COPY command copies a file onto contiguous sectors. This may improve performance.

CHKDSK does not prompt you to insert a disk in the specified drive; it automatically assumes that the disks are in the appropriate drives and begins to execute shortly after Enter has been pressed.

The status report displayed by CHKDSK contains the following pieces of information:

Disk Report

Total disk space

Number of bytes used for hidden or system files

Number of bytes used for user files

Bytes used by tracks containing bad sectors

Bytes available for use

RAM Report

Bytes of total memory (RAM)

Bytes of available (unused) memory

After the disk has been checked, error messages (if any) and a status report are displayed. The report shows disk information such as the following:

362496 bytes total disk space

48128 bytes in 2 hidden files

135168 bytes in 12 user files

(4608 bytes in bad sectors)

179200 bytes available on disk

It also shows information about RAM:

654336 bytes total memory (total RAM memory)

584192 bytes free (unused RAM memory)

Notice that two hidden files are reported in the above. These are the DOS system files IO.SYS and DOS.SYS, which are hidden from normal directory searches.

You should run CHKDSK occasionally for each disk to ensure the integrity of the file structures. Here are some examples of the uses of CHKDSK:

C>CHKDSK B: This runs the CHKDSK program that resides on drive C against the disk in drive B.

A>CHKDSK B:/F This tells CHKDSK to correct any errors in the above example. Respond yes (Y) to the prompt about fixing errors when CHKDSK is through.

A>CHKDSK REPORT This tells DOS to find out if the file REPORT is fragmented.

C>CHKDSK A:*.* This tells DOS to find out whether any file on the disk in drive A is fragmented.

B>C:CHKDSK With B as the default drive, this executes the CHKDSK utility located on the disk in drive C against the files on the disk in drive B.

C>CHKDSK With C as the default drive, this executes the CHKDSK utility and examines the hard disk.

DISK COPY (DISKCOPY) COMMAND

Function This command copies the contents of the disk in the specified source drive onto the disk in the specified target drive—exactly as the information appears on the source disk. When this command is executed, you end up with two identical disks.

Format `DISKCOPY [d:][d:][/1].`

Type External.

Remarks and Examples The first parameter specified is the source drive, and the second is the target drive. The [/1] parameter causes DISKCOPY to copy only side 0 (the first side) of the disk, regardless of whether the disk is single- or double-sided (for most applications, this parameter is not used).

The same drives (or different ones) can be specified as source and target. If the drives are the same, a single-drive copy operation is performed. This requires you to insert, alternately, the source and target disks. DISKCOPY prompts you throughout the process. Here are examples of the command:

A>DISKCOPY A: B: This causes DOS to load in the DISKCOPY file from the default disk drive. The contents of a disk to be placed in drive A are to be copied to a disk to be placed in drive B. The following message is displayed:

```
Insert source disk in drive A:
Insert target disk in drive B:
Strike any key when ready:
```

The DISKCOPY program then checks to see if the disk in drive B is formatted. If it isn't, DISKCOPY formats it. It then performs the copy process and after copying displays the following prompt:

```
Copy another (Y/N)? __
```

If you press Y, the next copy is done on the originally specified drives, and DISKCOPY again prompts you to insert the source and target disks. If you press N, the command ends.

A>DISKCOPY B: A: In this case, the source disk is in drive B, and the target disk is in drive A.

HINTS/HAZARDS

DISKCOPY destroys all pre-existing files on the target disk as soon as the copying process begins. Be sure you understand how the command works before you use it.

A>DISKCOPY A: A: In this case, because both parameters specify the same drive, a single-drive copy operation is performed. The DISKCOPY program prompts you to insert first the source disk, which is then read. After the source disk is read, DISKCOPY prompts you to insert the target disk.

Disks subjected to much file creation and deletion activity become fragmented because disk space is allocated to files on the basis of the first available opening. Because a disk with fragmented files can degrade performance by requiring excessive head movement and rotational delays in finding, reading, or writing a file, use the CHKDSK *.* command on busy disks from time to time to identify the extent of fragmentation. If a lot of fragmentation exists, use the COPY command instead of DISKCOPY to eliminate it.

Use the following command, for example, to copy all files (in unfragmented order) from the disk in drive A to the disk in drive B: COPY A:*.* B:.

HINTS/HAZARDS

It is safest to use preformatted disks when using DISKCOPY. Make certain that no bad sectors exist on the target disk. Because the copy generated is a mirror image, good data can end up being placed in a bad sector during a DISKCOPY operation.

HINTS/HAZARDS

When you use the DISKCOPY command, be consistent in specifying the source and target drives. Otherwise, you may insert your original disk in the target drive and a blank, formatted disk in the source drive. In this situation, you end up with two blank, formatted disks along with a severe case of heartburn.

FORMAT COMMAND

Function Chapter 1 presented this command in its simplest versions. Besides initializing in the DOS recording format, FORMAT analyzes the entire disk for defective sectors, initializes the directory, sets up space for the FAT, and records the boot program in the boot record.

Format `FORMAT [d:][/S][/1][/8][/V][/B][/4][/t:yy][/n:xx].`

Type External.

Remarks and Examples All new disks must be formatted. An unformatted disk is unrecognizable to DOS. The following examples demonstrate the basic command as well as the numerous parameters:

> **A>FORMAT B:** This is the basic command to format a disk in drive B with nine-sector tracks. This disk (identified as a data disk) can be used only to store data. The system cannot be booted from such a disk; if booting is attempted, DOS will display the following message:
>
> ```
> Non-System disk or disk error
> Replace and strike any key when ready
> ```

When you issue the FORMAT command, the system begins by issuing the following message:

```
Insert new disk for drive B:
and strike any key when ready
```

After you insert the appropriate disk and strike any key, the system issues the following message while disk formatting is taking place:

```
Formatting...
```

Once the formatting is complete, the system issues a message like this:

```
...Format complete

362496 bytes total disk space
362496 bytes available on disk

Format another (Y/N)? __
```

Enter Y to format another disk; enter N to end the FORMAT program.

During the formatting process, discovery of any defective sectors in a track results in the entire track's being marked RESERVED. This prevents any sectors in the **reserved track** from being allocated to a data file. DOS reports the total amount of defective space with an additional message such as `4608 bytes in bad sectors` and subtracts this from the total bytes available on the disk.

HINTS/HAZARDS

DOS is so careful when it is formatting a disk that it is sometimes too conservative when marking bad sectors. Therefore, if you again perform a FORMAT on a disk containing bad sectors, those sectors may disappear after this preparation process has been performed.

HINTS/HAZARDS

Formatting destroys any previously existing data on the disk. Do *not* format a disk that contains data you will need later, or it will be lost forever.

C>FORMAT B:/S This does all that the basic FORMAT command does. In addition, it copies the IO.SYS, DOS.SYS, and COMMAND.COM files from the default drive onto the newly formatted, nine-sectored disk in drive B. The new disk is now a **system disk,** with all the operating system files necessary to boot the system. You can then copy an application program onto this same disk, thus creating a disk that will both boot the system and load a program. If you wish to have any external DOS utility programs also on this disk, they must be copied from a DOS master disk.

Once the formatting is complete, the system issues a message like this:

```
Formatting...Format complete
System transferred

362496 bytes total disk space
40960 bytes used by system
(4608 bytes in bad sectors)
316928 bytes available on disk
```

C>FORMAT A:/1 This formats a disk for single-sided use.

C>FORMAT A:/8 This tells FORMAT to prepare the disk with eight sectors per track, instead of the default number of nine per track. You should let DOS use the default number so that you gain the additional 40K of disk space.

C>FORMAT A:/V This causes DOS to prompt you for a volume label name. It cannot be used with the /8 parameter. The name you give can include up to 11 characters. Thereafter, the volume name will appear when the DIR or CHKDSK command is executed, identifying the disk for you.

C>FORMAT B:/B This creates a disk with eight sectors per track and leaves room for IBMBIO.COM and IBMDOS.COM to be placed on the disk at a later time with the SYS command. Because it does not record these files onto the disk, any version of the IBM operating system can be placed there.

C>FORMAT A:/4 Depending on the version of DOS and the type of disk drives that you have, you can specify the type of disk to be formatted. The /4 parameter formats a 5.25-inch 360K disk using a high-density disk drive; otherwise, DOS formats the disk as a 1.2M disk. Do not use this parameter if you have regular 360K disk drives.

C>FORMAT B:/t:yy This parameter is supported beginning with DOS 3.3. It lets you tell DOS the number of tracks on a 3.5-inch disk and formats a 3.5-inch disk to the number of tracks specified. For 720K disks and 1.44M disks, this value is 80 (/t:80).

C>FORMAT B:/n:xx This parameter is also supported beginning with DOS 3.3. It lets you specify the number of sectors per track, if it is different from the default setting. For example, you can format a 3.5-inch 720K disk in a 3.5-inch 1.44M drive. The command would be FORMAT B:/N:9 (to specify 9 sectors per track instead of the drive's default of 18 sectors).

HINTS/HAZARDS

Never format a 5.25-inch double-density disk as a high-density disk. The surface quality of a double-density disk is not good enough to retain the packed magnetic charges created by a high-density disk drive. If you try to format a double-density disk in this way, the result may be that you lose important files.

FILE COMMANDS

The **COPY command** copies one file or a number of files with similar names to another disk or subdirectory. It also copies the contents of one file into a new file with a different name on the same disk.

The **ERASE (DEL) command** deletes a specific file or group of files from the disk or subdirectory in the designated drive. (If no drive is specified, the default is used.)

The **RENAME (REN) command** changes the name of an existing file to a new name.

The **TYPE command** displays the contents of a file to the screen. It lets you view a file without first starting another program that might normally be used in processing that file.

COPY COMMAND

Function This command copies one file (the source) or, in some cases, a number of files with similar names to another disk or subdirectory (the target). It also copies one or more files and creates a new file with a different name on the same disk or subdirectory. In the latter case, a different name must be given to the new copy.

Format

```
COPY [/A][/B][filespec][/A][/B] [d:][filename[.ext]][/A][/B]
```

or

```
COPY [/A][/B][filespec][/A][/B] [d:][filename[.ext]][/A][/B][/V]
```

Type Internal.

Remarks and Examples The parameter [filespec] is the source file. The parameter [d:][filename[.ext]] is the target file.

When you are copying files, the source file can be on just about any device (A, B, C, D, and so on). The target (where the file is going) can also be on any device. Unless told otherwise via a drive identifier, DOS assumes that the file being copied resides on the default drive/directory. You can indicate the drive to receive the copy (target) by specifying a drive identifier. You can also include the subdirectory name if you want to copy the file to a directory other than the root directory.

Only the commonly used aspects of the COPY command are discussed here. For additional coverage, refer to the DOS manual. Here are some examples of the uses of COPY:

A>COPY REPORT B: This copies the file REPORT from drive A onto the disk contained in drive B. Because no new filename is specified, it has the same name as the original file. For this reason, the source drive and the target drive must be different; otherwise, an error message is displayed.

A>COPY B:FILE01 This copies the file FILE01 from the disk in disk drive B onto the disk in the default drive A, with no change in the filename.

A>COPY *.* B: This copies all files from the disk in the default drive A onto the disk in drive B. The filenames remain unchanged, and each is displayed as its file is copied. This method is very useful if the files on the default-drive disk are fragmented.

C>COPY FILE01 FILE01.BAK This copies the file FILE01 and names the copy FILE01.BAK. Because no other drive has been specified, both files are on the disk in the default drive (C).

C>COPY FILE01 B:FILE01.BAK This does the same thing as the previous command, except that the new copy, FILE01.BAK, is placed on the disk in drive B.

A>COPY FILE01.ABC b:*.XXX This copies the file FILE01.ABC from the disk in drive A onto the disk in drive B. It names the copy in drive B FILE01.XXX.

A>COPY FILE01 C:\123-22\HOME This copies the file FILE01 from the disk in drive A to the HOME directory underneath the 123-22 directory found on drive C. The name stays the same.

HINTS/HAZARDS

You can use the COPY command even though you only have one disk drive on your computer. If, for example, you enter the command A>COPY FILE1 B:, DOS first reads the file and then displays a prompt telling you to insert a new disk in drive B and press a key when you are ready. Once you do this, the file is written to the new disk.

Copying Between Subdirectories The COPY command also copies files between subdirectories of disks. For example, suppose that your current active subdirectory (WP) is on drive A. Also suppose that you have changed your default drive from A to C but want to copy the file MEMO.TXT back to your active subdirectory on drive A. All that is required is to enter the following command.

C>COPY MEMO.TXT A:

Because DOS remembers which is the active subdirectory, it automatically copies the file to that subdirectory (WP).

When you are copying information from one directory to another, remember that both the directory and the filename must be used. For example, if you want to copy the MEMO.TXT from the root directory to the DB directory, enter the following DOS command:

A>COPY MEMO.TXT \DB

This command translates as follows: Take the file MEMO.TXT and copy it to the DB subdirectory; use the existing name. Now, if you want to refer to the MEMO.TXT file as it exists in the DB subdirectory while you are in the root directory, enter \DB\MEMO.TXT. When you refer to files in directories other than the active directory, you must use their full names. The subdirectory is part of that name. While remaining at the root directory, copy the MEMO.TXT file from the DB subdirectory to the WP subdirectory by using the following command:

A>COPY \DB\MEMO.TXT \WP

Again, you must specify all sending information (the path), which in this case is the name of the subdirectory and the name of the file, and all receiving information, which (unless you are going to change the name of the file) is only the receiving directory.

ERASE (OR DEL) COMMAND

Function This command deletes a specific file or group of files from a disk or subdirectory. (If no drive is specified, the default drive is used.)

Format `ERASE filespec` or `DEL filespec`.

Type Internal.

Remarks and Examples You can use the shortened form **DEL** in place of ERASE. The global characters ? and * can be used in the filename and in the extension. Use global characters with caution, however, because several files can easily be erased with a single command. If proper care is not taken in using this command, you may inadvertently delete all files on a disk or directory.

Here are examples of the ERASE, or DEL, command:

A>ERASE FILE01.PRG This erases the file FILE01.PRG from the disk in drive A.

A>ERASE B:FILE02.PRG This erases the file FILE02.PRG from the disk in drive B.

C>ERASE d:*.* This tells DOS to erase all files on the disk (or directory) in the specified drive. DOS responds with the message `Are you sure (Y/N)?` Then press Y and Enter to erase or press N and Enter to cancel the command.

The system files IO.SYS and DOS.SYS, however, cannot be erased because they are hidden files and are not accessible to you.

C:\WP51>ERASE \123-22\HOM*.WK? The DOS prompt for this command shows that the active subdirectory is WP51 from drive C. Any file from the 123-22 subdirectory starting with the letters HOM is deleted as long as the first two characters of the extension are WK.

HINTS/HAZARDS

The regular version of PC DOS cannot restore a file once it has been erased from disk. DOS utilities such as the Norton Utilities, Mace Utilities, and PC Tools have a program that performs this task. Also, a number of such utilities are available as public domain software. If you accidentally erase a file, do not save any data to the disk; make a copy of the disk using DISKCOPY before you try to recover the deleted file. If you make a mistake recovering the file, the deleted file will still be on your backup disk. You may have a special version of DOS that has an "unerase" utility. For example, the 3.3 Plus version of MS DOS, provided with Zenith computers, contains the command GDU to recover accidentally deleted files. GDU is an external command with the format GDU d:filename.

RENAME (OR REN) COMMAND

Function This command changes the name of an existing file specified in the first parameter to the new name and extension specified in the second parameter.

Format `REN[AME] filespec filename[.ext.].`

Type Internal.

Remarks and Examples You can use the abbreviated form REN for the RENAME command. The global characters ? and * can also be used with this command. Here are examples:

> **C>RENAME B:FILE03 NEWFILE** This renames the file FILE03 on drive B as NEWFILE.
>
> **C>REN B:FILE03 *.XY** This renames the file FILE03 on drive B as FILE03.XY.

TYPE COMMAND

Function This command causes the contents of the requested file to be displayed on the screen.

Format `TYPE filespec.`

Type Internal.

Remarks and Examples Press Ctrl + PrtSc if you want the contents of a file to be printed as they are being displayed. Press Ctrl + S to cause the output to pause and then press any key to continue scrolling.

Text files appear in a legible format; other files, however, such as object program files, may contain unreadable nonalphabetic or nonnumeric characters.

In the following example, file FILE03.PRG on the disk in drive A will be displayed on the screen: `C>TYPE A:FILE03.PRG.`

WINDOWS

Windows is a **graphics user interface (GUI)** created by Microsoft for the MS DOS family of computers. It is the most popular GUI for these computers. Depending on the type of microprocessor chip used by a computer, Windows lets you have several application programs active or running at the same time.

ENTERING COMMANDS

Instead of requiring you to type commands at the keyboard, Windows provides graphic screens containing menus and **icons** (graphic figures on the screen that represent a particular object or command). Using a mouse or pointing device, or entering commands from the keyboard, you activate and make selections from menus and activate programs represented by icons.

The Windows **desktop** is the screen area on which all Windows operations take place. It includes the entire screen. Any windows that appear on the screen, as well as any icons, are part of the desktop.

When you move the pointer over the surface of a window or use it to answer prompts in a dialog box, the shape of the pointer may change. For example, the pointer is an arrow when you are selecting a menu option but changes to a hand when you are using the Help feature.

Three commands can be issued using the left-hand button of a mouse: clicking, double-clicking, and dragging. Clicking is a single press and release of the button. Double-clicking is pressing the button twice in quick succession. Dragging involves holding down the button while you move the mouse.

STARTING WINDOWS

If the WIN command appears in an AUTOEXEC.BAT file, your computer will automatically start Windows when the computer is booted. To start Windows from DOS, enter the command WIN. You can tell Windows to start and then immediately run another program by placing the program name following the WIN command. For example, the command WIN PM4 tells the computer to start Windows and activate PageMaker 4.0.

Windows uses extensive secondary windows and dialog boxes. For example, executing a command may cause a new window to appear, overlapping a previous window, or make a dialog box appear. A dialog box contains a number of options that are available to you in using Windows or some application program.

PROGRAM MANAGER

When Windows starts to run, the Program Manager screen appears (Figure 2.2). Most windows generated by Windows have the same parts or characteristics. You can always verify where you are in Windows by examining the **title bar,** which contains the name of the window/application being run. In the left-hand portion of the title bar is the **control menu** button. This menu lets you arrange keyboard access to manipulations that otherwise require a mouse.

Each window displayed by Windows contains two buttons in the right-hand portion of the title bar. Clicking on the **minimize button** (down arrow) causes the window to disappear and an icon representing the window to appear at the bottom of the desktop. Clicking on the **maximize button** (up arrow) enlarges the window to take up the entire screen. Once a window has been maximized, the minimize button is replaced by a **restore button** (up and down arrows), which restores the window to its previous size.

The **menu bar** contains the menu options for the window. Windows is fairly consistent in how menu items are arranged and what types of commands are used in the submenus. This consistency and standardization makes different Windows applications easier to learn.

Figure 2.2
The first Windows screen, the Program Manager.

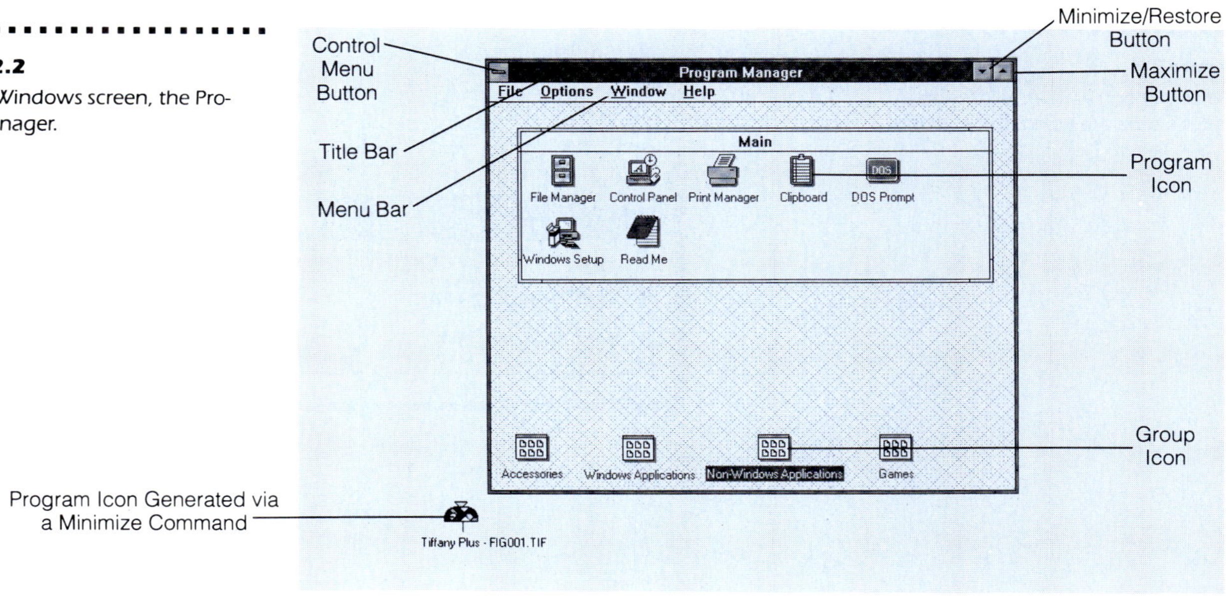

You can choose an option from the menu bar by clicking on it or by the Alt key together with the underlined character of the option. (For instance, Alt + F activates the File submenu of the menu bar.) A pull-down submenu then appears on the screen (Figure 2.3). Highlight an option from the submenu by clicking on it. If the option contains an ellipsis, a dialog box will appear (Figure 2.4). Menu commands are executed by double-clicking.

A window screen may also have a vertical **scroll bar** on the right-hand border (see Figure 2.3). Clicking the up and down arrow buttons moves the information up or down a line. The **scroll box** shows the relative location of the cursor in the displayed text or document. This button can be dragged up or down to move the cursor quickly to any part of the document.

The Main Menu of the Program Manager screen shows **program icons,** which can be double-clicked to activate various Windows programs. Each icon has a graphic portion and a label.

Figure 2.3
The pull-down menu for the File command of the menu bar.

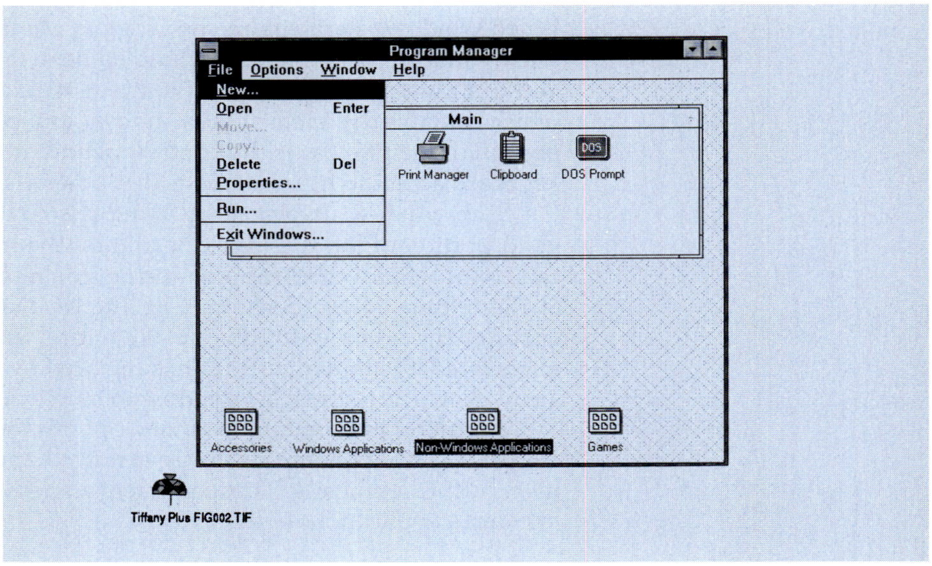

Figure 2.4
A menu option with an ellipses generates a separate menu box.

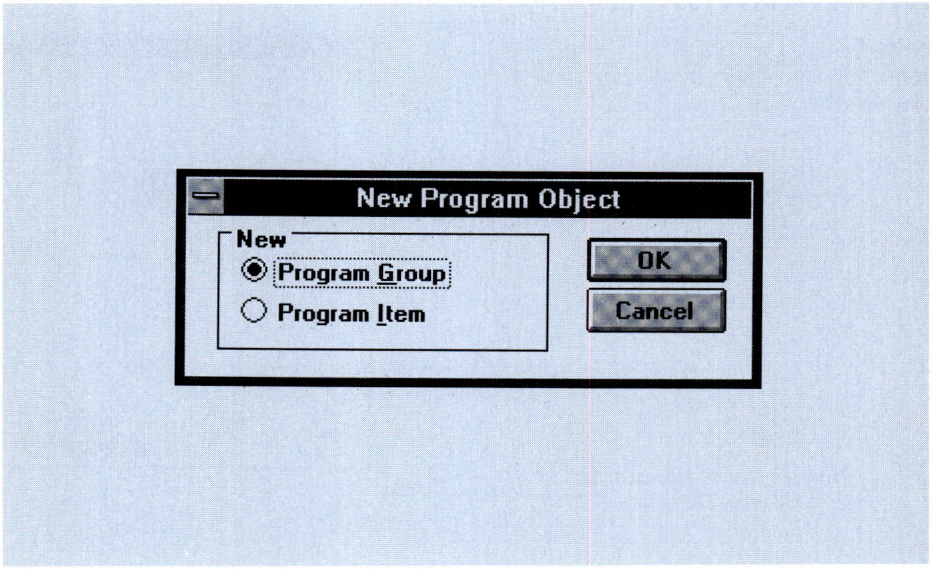

RUNNING WINDOWS APPLICATIONS

The icons at the bottom of the desktop are called **group icons.** Each activates an application window (Figure 2.5) from which specific programs can be selected. (If you do not have a Windows Applications group icon on your screen, click the Window command of the menu bar and then double-click the Windows Application command in the pull-down menu.)

To execute the Excel program from Figure 2.5, double-click on that icon. Windows now displays the full-screen window for Excel (Figure 2.6). Notice that Excel's menu bar is like the ones contained in Windows.

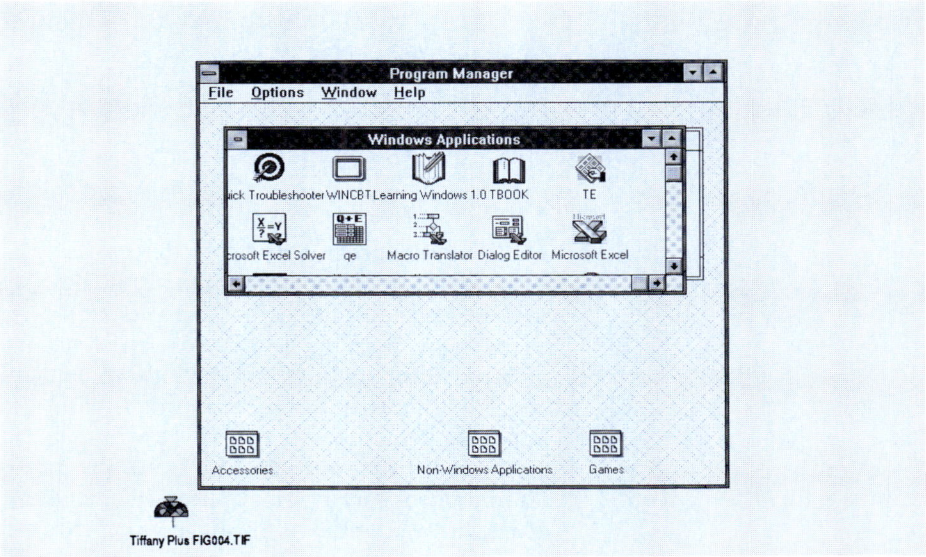

Figure 2.5
When the group icon Windows Applications is double-clicked, this window appears.

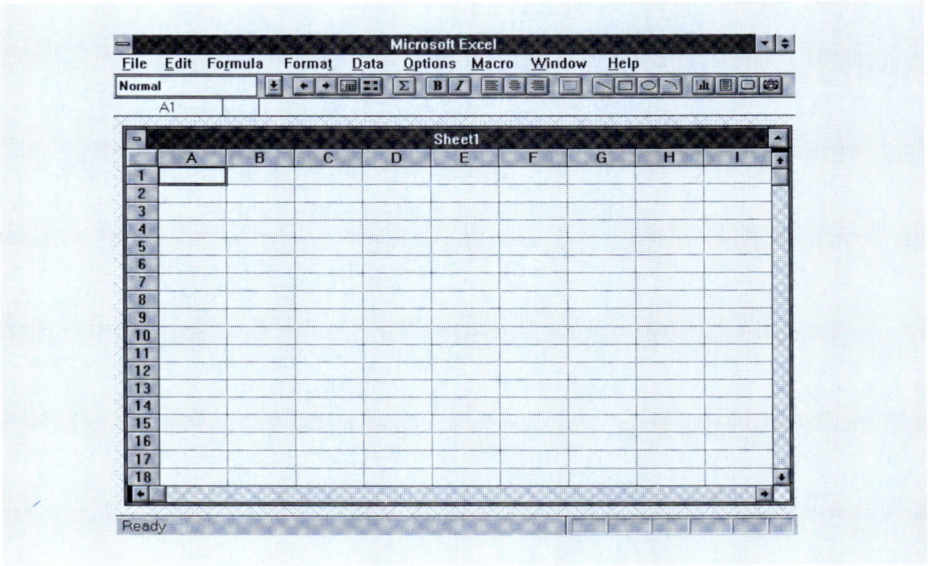

Figure 2.6
The window for some applications, like Excel, takes up the entire screen.

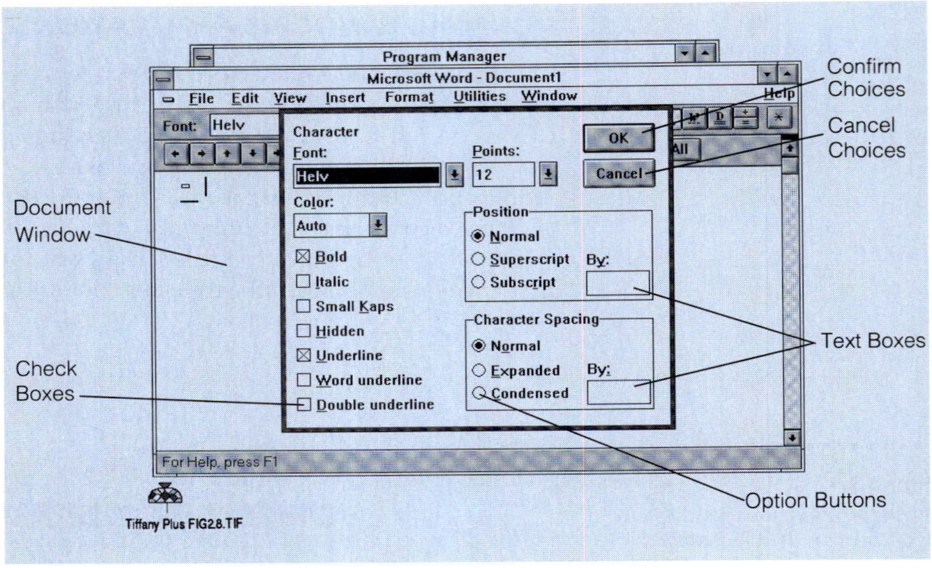

Figure 2.7
A Font dialog box generated by Microsoft Word.

Once you are in a Windows-supported application program, you can issue a command that displays a dialog box like Figure 2.7, which was generated by clicking on the Font entry of the Microsoft Word screen. Entries in boxes can be changed by pointing to the box, clicking, entering the appropriate text, and pressing Enter. Sets of option buttons let you select only one option. Check boxes let you check more than one option. The OK and Cancel buttons in the upper right-hand box let you accept or cancel changes to the box.

To exit from an application, use the File Menu of the menu bar. The Exit option closes any open application files along with the data files. The Close command will remove the application from the desktop, but it won't clear the application from your PC's memory or, in some cases, save the file.

If you just want to move a window out of the way to make more room on the desktop, minimize the window into an icon. This way, the application still resides in memory and can be restored by double-clicking the icon.

FILE MANAGER

The File Manager is a Windows program that performs functions similar to various DOS file commands such as DIR, COPY, and ERASE. To activate it, double-click its icon in the Program Manager window. The File Manager window now appears on the screen (Figure 2.8). Once Windows has been installed, it automatically knows the configuration of your system. The **drive icons** indicate which drives can be examined. The volume entry shows the active/default drive.

Each device can be activated by double-clicking on its icon. A directory tree for the activated drive appears on the screen. The tree shows directories as file folder icons. Executable files are depicted as rectangular icons. Data files are shown as paper with a folded upper right-hand corner. A plus sign (+) inside a file folder icon indicates that within the folder additional folders ("child directories") are currently hidden. To make the folders appear, click on the icon. This changes the plus sign to a minus sign (−) and causes the hidden folders to be

Figure 2.8
The directory tree of the File Manager displays the files and directories on the default drive.

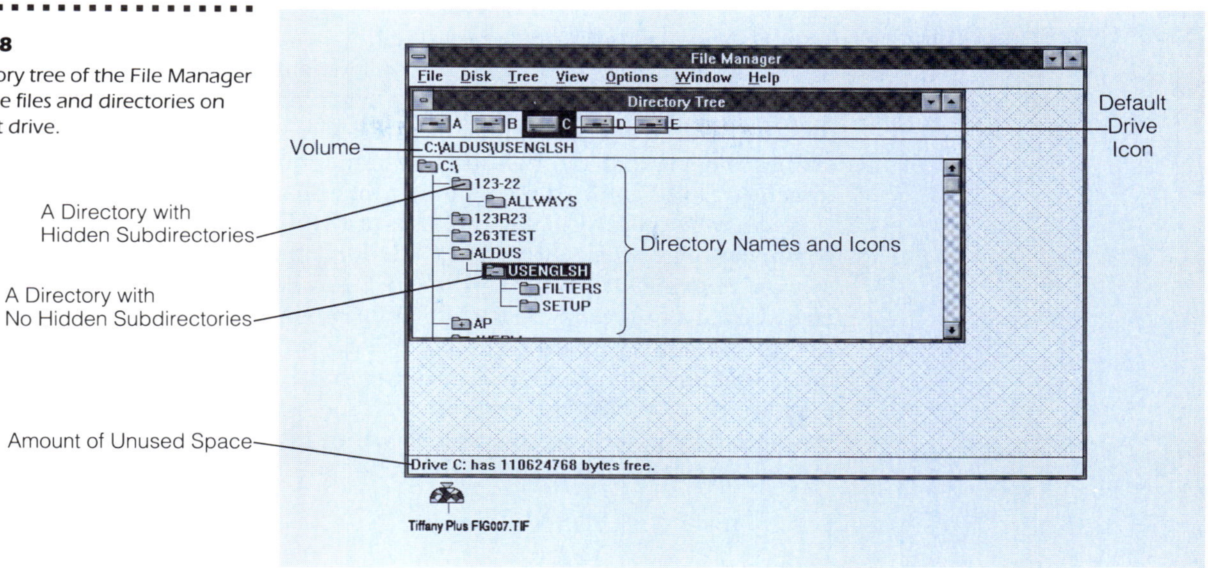

Figure 2.9
The detailed file listing of the WP51 directory.

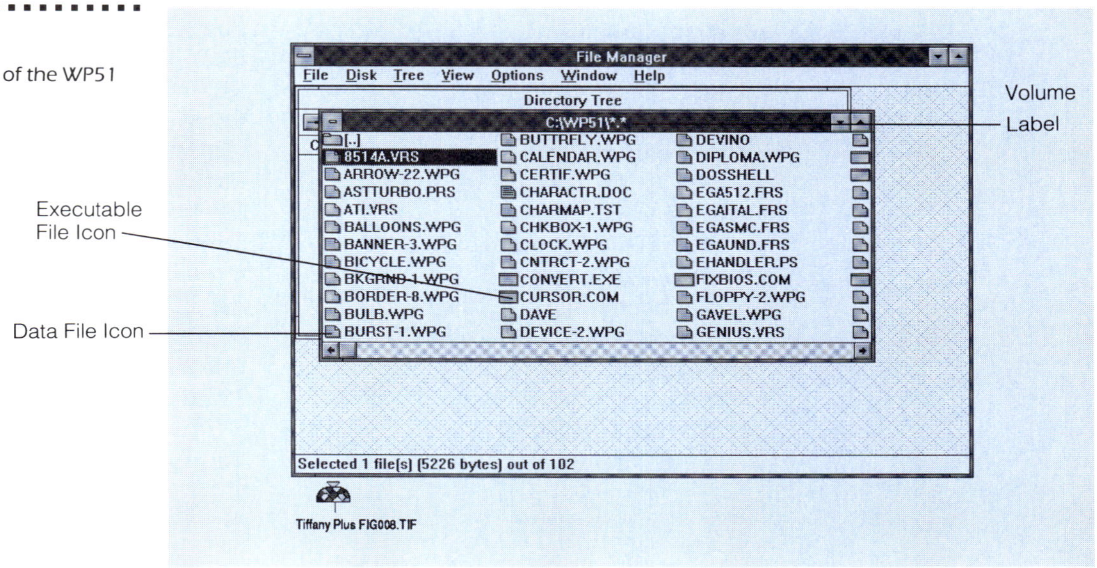

shown as subdirectories. Clicking the parent folder icon once again hides the child directories again and converts the minus sign back to a plus sign. You can scroll through the listing of files and directories by using the scroll bar on the right-hand side of the window.

To get a listing of the files in a directory, double-click the desired folder icon (Figure 2.9). The volume label now contains the drive and subdirectory being examined. To return control to the parent directory, double-click the .. entry in the upper left-hand corner or issue a Close command from the Control Menu box. To start an executable program file, double-click its icon. To perform a task such as deleting or copying a file, click the filename and choose the appropriate command from the menu bar.

CHAPTER REVIEW

Directories and subdirectories divide disk storage space into functional units. This lets you place all word processing files in one directory, all spreadsheet files in another directory, and all data management files in still another directory. Directories are most appropriate on a hard disk but can be used as easily on diskettes. The major advantage of directories, besides allowing you to group similar files, is that the file-number limitations that DOS places on the root directory can be avoided by building a subdirectory.

A number of directory commands are available in DOS. The MKDIR (MD) command builds a directory. The CHDIR (CD) command allows downward or upward movement from one directory to another. Once all files have been erased from a directory, the RMDIR (RD) command can delete a directory.

The Windows graphics user interface provides a convenient alternative method of interaction with the computer that does not rely on typing DOS commands. Windows displays various icons and menus from which commands can be selected by pointing or by clicking with a mouse. Windows also lets you run several application programs at the same time.

KEY TERMS AND CONCEPTS

active directory
CHDIR (CD) command
CHKDSK command
control menu
COPY command
DEL (Delete) command
desktop
disk command
DISKCOPY command
drive icon
ERASE (DEL) command
file command
fragmented file
graphics user interface (GUI)
group icon
icon
maximize button
menu bar
minimize button
MKDIR (MD) command
path
program icon
PROMPT PG command
RENAME (REN) command
reserved track
restore button
RMDIR (RD) command
root directory
scroll bar
scroll box
subdirectory
system disk
title bar
TREE command
TYPE command
Windows

CHAPTER QUIZ

Multiple Choice

1. Which of the statements below is false with respect to copying files using IBM PC DOS?
   a. DISKCOPY is the command that re-forms fragmented files.
   b. COPY can create a copy of a file on the same disk, but a different name must then be used.
   c. COPY can create a backup file on another disk.
   d. DISKCOPY creates an exact copy of a disk's contents. It does this sector-by-sector and track-by-track.

2. The FORMAT command does all but which of the following tasks?
   a. Divides each track into eight or nine sectors.
   b. Marks any track having a bad sector(s) as reserved.
   c. Builds the directory.

d. Builds the file allocation table (FAT).
e. Performs all the above tasks.

3. Which of the following commands takes you directly to the root directory?
   a. CD
   b. CD ..
   c. CD\
   d. CD root

4. Which of the commands below *cannot* use the * or ? wild cards?
   a. ERASE
   b. COPY
   c. CHKDSK
   d. DISKCOPY
   e. DIR
   f. All of the above can use wild cards.

5. Which of these commands will cause the contents of FILE1 on a disk in drive A to be copied to a disk in drive B?
   a. A>COPY FILE1 A:
   b. B>COPY A:FILE1
   c. A>COPY FILE1 A:FILE1.BAK
   d. Both a and b
   e. All of the above

True/False

6. If you do not give a drive specifier in a command, DOS assumes that the command you have just entered is to be executed against the default drive.

7. An external command must reside on the default disk unless a drive specifier is given.

8. The COMMAND.COM file contains the external DOS commands.

9. The ERASE and DEL commands can be used interchangeably.

10. The computer can be booted from a data disk.

Answers

1. a 2. e 3. c 4. d. 5. b 6. t 7. t 8. f 9. t 10. f

Exercises

1. Define or describe each of the following:
   a. COPY versus DISKCOPY
   b. System disk versus data disk
   c. Path

2. List three internal DOS commands.

3. List three external DOS commands.

4. Without changing the default drive, give the following COPY commands:
   a. Copy FILE1 from the default disk A and create FILE1.BAK on drive A.
   b. Copy FILE1 from the default disk A onto the disk in drive B.
   c. Copy FILE1 from disk B and copy it onto the disk in default drive A, using the same name.
   d. Copy FILE1 from disk B and copy it onto the disk in default drive A, using the name FILE1.BAK.

5. The default drive is A. Enter the command that would erase FILE1 from the disk in drive B, without changing the default drive.

6. The DOS command that re-forms fragmented files is the ____________ command.

7. The DOS command that examines the directory and prints a listing of files is the ____________ command.

8. List two commands that can delete unwanted files.

9. The command that creates a "carbon" copy of the disk in drive A onto the disk in drive B is ____________.

10. List two commands that can tell you the amount of available space on a disk.

11. The COPY command that will also copy all the files of one disk onto another disk is the COPY ____________.

12. What happens when you enter the command ERASE*.*? What prompt do you receive? What happens if you continue?

13. The directory created automatically on any disk device during the format process is called the ____________ directory.

14. A double-sided 5.25-inch disk can store a maximum of ____________ files without using directories.

15. Directories are created by using the DOS ____________ command.

16. Directories are erased by using DOS ____________ command.

17. Before a directory can be removed, all files must be removed using the DOS ____________ command.

18. The directory command that is part of PC DOS but not MS DOS is the ____________ command.

19. A directory is actually viewed by DOS as a(n) ____________ of data.

20. The ____________ command finds out where you are in a series of directories and subdirectories.

21. The __________ command tells DOS to display the path of the current directory as part of the DOS prompt.

22. The __________ command tells DOS to use the default drive at the DOS prompt.

23. Windows is known as a(n) __________ interface.

24. When using Windows, many commands can be entered using the hand-held __________ instead of the keyboard.

25. The __________ is the screen area on which all Windows operations take place.

26. __________ is a single press of a mouse key.

27. __________ involves holding down a mouse button and, at the same time, moving the mouse.

28. The Windows __________ button changes the window to an icon at the bottom of the screen.

29. When using the Windows File Manager, if an entry is a subdirectory with files contained in it, the file folder will have a(n) __________ sign.

30. The __________ bar of a Windows screen contains the name of the window/application being run.

COMPUTER EXERCISES

1. Run CHKDSK on your disk. Fill in the following blanks:
   __________ bytes total disk space
   __________ bytes in ______ hidden files
   __________ bytes in ______ user files
   __________ bytes in bad sectors
   __________ bytes available on disk
   __________ bytes total memory
   __________ bytes free

2. If you have one, run CHKDSK on your fixed disk. Fill in the following blanks:
   __________ bytes total disk space
   __________ bytes in ______ hidden files
   __________ bytes in ______ user files
   __________ bytes in bad sectors
   __________ bytes available on disk
   __________ bytes total memory
   __________ bytes free

3. The date of creation for the SEMPCINT.DOC file is __________. The command that you used to obtain this information was the __________ command.

4. Make a backup of the SEMPCINT.DOC file on your disk, using the COPY command. Enter the command that you used: ________.

5. Run CHKDSK again on your disk. Fill in any of the following blanks that changed from Exercise 2.
   ________ bytes total disk space
   ________ bytes in ______ hidden files
   ________ bytes in ______ user files
   ________ bytes in bad sectors
   ________ bytes available on disk
   ________ bytes total memory
   ________ bytes free

6. Use the COPY command to do the following:
   a. Copy the SEMPCINT.DOC file to the SEMPCINT.BKP file on the same disk. Enter the command you used: ________.
   b. Copy the SEMPCINT.DOC file to another disk using the same name. Enter the command you used: ________.
   c. Copy the SEMPCINT.DOC file to another disk using the name SEMPCINT.BKP. Enter the command you used: ________.

7. Erase all copies of the SEMPCINT.BKP file. Enter the commands you used: ________ and ________.

8. Change the name of the SEMPCINT.DOC file to PCOUTLIN. Enter the command you used: ________.

9. What other command covered in this chapter would also let you change the filename? ________.

10. Use the TYPE command to list the file PCOUTLIN to the screen. Enter the command you used: ________. This is an example of a DOS text file. Notice that you can read all characters. Issue the TYPE command again and be ready with a Ctrl + S to make the display pause. Enter other Ctrl + S commands to display other pages of the file.

11. Use the TYPE command to list one of the DOS command files (CHKDSK.COM, for instance). Enter the command you used: ________. This is an example of a machine-executable file. Notice that many characters from the IBM character set that are not normally seen are displayed on your screen. These are examples of the 256 different characters that your computer can readily use.

12. Use the FORMAT command to prepare any disks that you will be using this term. Be sure to format them as data disks. You do not want the system program on any of these disks.

13. This exercise is intended to reinforce the directory concepts introduced in this chapter. It requires that you have the data disk that is used with this text in drive A. A number of directories (Figure 2.10) will be constructed on this disk, and some files will be placed in those directories. Two files from this disk will be copied to another disk (either to drive B on a two-disk computer or to drive C on a computer with a fixed disk). Once this exercise is completed, all directories and the two disk files will be erased.

Figure 2.10
Directories to be created for Exercise 13.

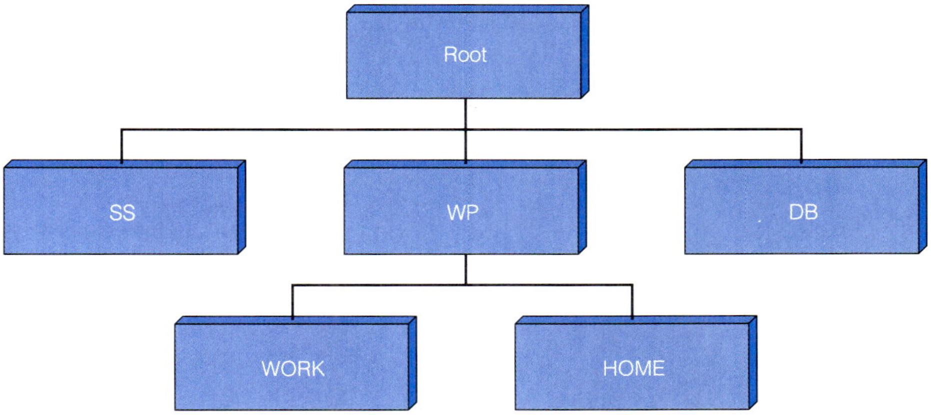

The directories and any subdirectories, which they might have and that you are to create, appear below:

a. Create the directories. Make certain that you have the A> DOS prompt.

MD SS	Makes the SS subdirectory.
MD WP	Makes the WP subdirectory.
ME DB	Makes the DB subdirectory.
CD WP	Changes to the WP subdirectory.
MD HOME	Makes the HOME subdirectory.
MD WORK	Makes the WORK subdirectory.

b. PROMPT PG Activates the path as part of the DOS prompt.

c. Use some Change Directory (CD) commands:

CD HOME	Changes to the HOME subdirectory.
CD..	Changes to the WP subdirectory.
CD..	Changes to the root directory.
CD WP	Changes to the WP subdirectory.
CD WORK	Changes to the WORK subdirectory.

d. Use the command that goes directly to the root instead of using CD.. commands:

CD\ Moves directly to the root directory.

e. COPY E*.WK1 SS Copies the two worksheet files that begin with the letter E to the SS directory. Notice that you do not have to place the drive identifier on the receiving path specification as long as the directory resides on the default drive.

f. COPY R*.* WP\WORK Copies the file that begins with an R to the WORK subdirectory.

g. From the root, issue two directory commands for subdirectories:

```
DIR WP\WORK
DIR SS
```

h. Copy two files to either drive B or C:

```
COPY PCOUTLIN B:
COPY EXER1B B:
```

i. `CD WP\WORK` Moves to the WORK subdirectory, using only one CD command. You do not have to go down one directory at a time, if you know the path of the subdirectory.

j. `B:` Changes the default drive to the disk to which you copied the files in Step h.
`COPY PCOUTLIN A:` Copies the PCOUTLIN file to the active directory. Notice that all you do to accomplish this is refer to drive A.
`DIR A:` Verifies that the copy worked correctly.

k. `COPY EXER1B A:WP` Copies the EXER1B file to the WP subdirectory.
`DIR A:WP` Verifies that the copy worked. Notice that, because the directory is on a disk other than the default, you must use the drive identifier.

l. `COPY PCOUTLIN A:WP\HOME` Copies the file PCOUTLIN to the HOME subdirectory.
`DIR A:WP\HOME` Verifies that the copy worked.

m. Return to the root directory of drive A.

`A:`	Returns to drive A.
`CD\`	Issues the return to the root directory.

n. `RD WP` Tries to remove the WP subdirectory. You should receive an error message indicating that the directory is not empty.

o. Erase the files from each of the subdirectories and then remove the subdirectories. Be certain that you issue each of the following directory commands exactly as entered and check the DOS prompt to ensure that you are at the correct location. Otherwise, you might erase all files contained in the root directory. Respond Y to each prompt warning you about erasing all files from the directory:

```
CD DB
DEL *.*
CD
CD WP\HOME
DEL *.*
CD ..
CD WORK
DEL *.*
CD ..
RD HOME
RD WORK
CD\
CD SS
DEL *.*
CD\
RD SS
RD DB
RD WP
```

p. `PROMPT` Turns off the path for the DOS prompt.
q. Delete the two files from either drive B or C:

```
B:
DEL PCOUTLIN
DEL EXER1B
```

DOS COMMAND SUMMARY

CD	Changes to a directory
CHKDSK	Checks the status of a disk and prepares the status report.
COPY	Copies one or more files.
DATE	Changes the system date.
DEL (or ERASE)	Deletes one or more files.
DIR	Lists the files in the directory.
DISKCOPY	Copies a complete disk.
ERASE (or DEL)	Deletes one or more files.
FORMAT	Prepares a disk for use.
MD	Creates a subdirectory.
PROMPT	Changes the system prompt.
RD	Removes a subdirectory.
RENAME	Renames disk files.
TIME	Changes the system time.
TREE	Lists subdirectories and files.
TYPE	Displays file contents on the monitor screen.

DOS COMMANDS BY FUNCTION AND TYPE

Time	**DATE, TIME**
File	**COPY, DEL, DIR, ERASE, RENAME, TYPE**
Disk	**CHKDSK, DISKCOPY, FORMAT, CD, RD, MD, TREE**
System	**PROMPT**

Internal Commands	*External Commands (Utilities)*
CD	**CHKDSK**
COPY	**DISKCOPY**
DATE	**FORMAT**
DEL	**TREE**
DIR	
ERASE	
MD	
PROMPT	
RD	
RENAME	
TIME	
TYPE	

GLOSSARY

?: The wildcard symbol that represents one character at this position.

***:** The wildcard symbol that represents any number of characters at this position and to the right.

active directory: The active directory on a disk device is the last directory that you were in via a CD command. Any files copied to the disk name (with no path specified) get copied to this directory.

Arrow keys: Keys (Down, Up, Right, and Left) found on the numeric keyboard and typically used to move a pointer or cursor.

AUTOEXEC.BAT: File that is executed by the computer as soon as the boot process is completed. This type of file is used in building a turnkey application that requires very little input from a user before starting.

Backspace key: Key used to erase the last character typed. It is labeled with an arrow that points toward the left.

boot process: Process of starting the computer. During the boot process, a memory check is performed, the various parts of DOS are loaded, and the date and time are requested.

break: Function for halting the program in progress. Usually the program returns to some higher-level program such as DOS, BASIC, or the main application program, but not all programs have this function. It is invoked by holding down the Ctrl key while pressing Scroll Lock.

CHDIR (CD): DOS command that lets you move to another directory and make that the active directory.

CHKDSK: DOS command that checks the status of a disk and prepares the status report.

cluster: Entity composed of two adjacent sectors. Storage is allocated to a file one cluster at a time.

cold start: Booting process used to begin operating a computer that has just been turned on.

COMMAND.COM: Command processor of DOS, containing built-in functions or subroutines that let you copy a file or get a directory listing of a disk.

Control key: General-purpose key whose uses include invoking breaks, pauses, system resets, clear screens, print echos, and various edit commands. In instructions, the Control key is often represented as a caret (^).

control menu: In the left-hand portion of the title bar is the Control Menu button, which provides access to a menu that provides keyboard access to many window manipulations that otherwise require a mouse.

COPY: DOS command that copies one or more files onto the current disk or onto another disk. In spreadsheets, it lets you copy the contents of a cell into one or more other cells.

cylinder: Entity composed of all like-numbered tracks from all recording surfaces of a disk.

data disk: A formatted disk that does not contain DOS. Data disks are used only to store user files.

DATE: DOS command that changes the system date.

default disk drive: Disk drive that is accessed automatically by the microcomputer when a file-oriented command is executed.

DEL: DOS command that deletes one or more files from disk.

delimiter: Character that indicates to the computer where one part of a command ends and another part begins. Typical delimiters are the space, the period, and the comma.

desktop: The screen area on which all Windows operations take place.

DIR: DOS Directory command that lists the files in the directory.

directory: Part of a diskette that holds the names of files stored on it. The directory also contains information about file size, file extensions, their location on diskette, and the dates and times files were created or changed.

disk commands: The subset of DOS commands that affect the disk, including CHKDSK, DISKCOPY, and FORMAT.

DISKCOPY: DOS command that copies a complete disk.

diskette: Square recordlike objects that store information from the computer.

disk operating system: *See* **DOS.**

DOS: Acronym for disk operating system, the program responsible for enabling you to interact with the many parts of a computer system. DOS (pronounced "doss") is the interface between you and the hardware. To perform system functions, DOS commands are typed on the keyboard, but DOS is actually a collection of programs designed to make it easy to create and manage files, run programs, and use system devices attached to the computer.

DOS editing keys: Keys that let the user make changes to the last DOS command entered, which can save many keystrokes.

DOS prompt: The characters that indicate which drive is the default drive and that DOS is waiting for a command to be entered (for example, A>, B>, C>).

drive icons: The drive icons indicate which drives can be examined on your system (Windows automatically knows the configuration of your system after it has been installed).

ERASE (DEL): DOS command that deletes one or more files from disk.

external DOS commands: Utility commands that are not part of the COMMAND.COM command processor. They reside on disk as separate files.

FAT: *See* **file allocation table.**

file allocation table (FAT): Entity that keeps track of which sectors belong to which files and of how much available space remains on the diskette (so that new files can be created and stored in unused areas of the diskette).

file commands: The subset of DOS commands that affect the files, including COPY, ERASE, RENAME, and TYPE.

filename: Unique identifier of a file, composed of one to eight characters. If an optional one- to three-character extension is used, there must be a period between the filename and the filename extension.

filename extension: One- to three-character portion of a filename. Extensions are typically used to indicate families of files, such as backups (.BK!), regular database files (.DBF), and indexes (.NDX).

FORMAT: DOS command that prepares a disk so that it can be used by the computer. It defines every sector of a diskette, finds and write-protects any tracks with bad sectors, sets up the directory, sets up the file allocation table, and puts the boot record program at the beginning of the diskette. *Format* also refers to how data are stored in a worksheet cell, for example, as character or numeric data.

fragmented file: A file whose sectors are not in adjacent locations. A fragmented file can be stored on a disk in a number of different physical locations.

function key: One of 10 keys (F1–F10) that allow special functions to be entered with a single user keystroke. Computer programs (DOS, BASIC, and so on) use these keys for different purposes.

global filename characters: DOS characters (? and *) that specify a number of files via a single command.

graphic user interface (GUI): A graphic means of allowing a user to enter commands using a mouse as a pointing device rather than typing the commands from the keyboard.

group icons: As the name implies, these represent groups of applications that can be activated via a separate window.

GUI: *See* **graphic user interface.**

IO.SYS: Hidden file in DOS that manages each character that is typed, displayed, printed, received, or sent through any communications adapter.

DOS.SYS: Hidden DOS file that handles any information to be passed to disk.

icon: A graphic image that represents a command or program. The command or program is invoked or executed by using a mouse to position the pointer on the icon and signaling with a click.

initialization: Process during the boot routine when the computer activates the various peripherals hooked to the computer.

internal DOS command: Command that is part of the COMMAND.COM command processor.

menu bar: The menu bar contains the menu options that can be selected for this window. One of the benefits of Windows is that it provides a fair amount of consistency in how menu items are arranged and what types of commands can be expected in the submenus. This consistency and standardization make different Windows applications easier to learn.

Microsoft: Company that originally developed PC DOS for IBM (an operating system known, with some minor differences, as MS DOS).

minimize/maximize buttons: Each window displayed by the Windows GUI contains two buttons in the right-hand portion of the title bar: the minimize and maximize buttons. When you click on the minimize (down arrow) button, Windows substitutes an icon for the window and moves the icon to the bottom of the desktop. When you click on the maximize (up arrow) button, Windows enlarges the window to take up the entire screen.

MKDIR (MD): The DOS command that creates a subdirectory.

MS DOS: Operating system developed by Microsoft. It is the same as PC DOS except that there is no ROM BASIC provision. This operating system is used by most IBM-compatible computers.

parameter: Modifying piece of information that constitutes part of a DOS or dBASE command. It might, for example, indicate which files or fields are to be included in an operation.

path: The complete name for a file, including the complete subdirectory name.

Print Screen key: Key that, when pressed with the Shift key, results in the screen contents being printed.

program icons: A graphic representation of a program.

PROMPT PG: DOS command that lets a user designate a path as part of the DOS prompt.

PrtSc: Key label for the Print Screen key.

RENAME (REN): DOS command that renames a disk file.

reserved tracks: Tracks of disk storage that contain a bad sector and have been set aside so that data cannot be recorded on them.

restore button: Once the maximize command is issued, Windows substitutes the minimize button with a restore (up and down arrows) button, which, when clicked, restores the window to its previous size.

RMDIR (RD): DOS command that deletes a subdirectory.

root directory: The main directory of a disk. Subdirectories are created below the root directory on a disk medium.

scroll bar: A window screen may also have a vertical scroll bar on the right-hand border. The up and down arrow buttons, when clicked, move the information up or down a line.

scroll box (slider): This shows the relative location of the cursor in the displayed text or document. This button can be dragged to move the cursor quickly from one part of the screen to another. You can also move the display up or down a screen at a time by clicking above or below the slider.

source drive: Drive that contains any files to be copied.

subdirectory: Like a root directory except that it is itself a file and contains DOS housekeeping entries in a regular directory; it does not have the size limitation of the root directory.

syntax: Structure of instructions in a language. If you make a mistake in entering an instruction and garble the syntax, the computer sometimes responds with the message Syntax error.

system: The command that lets you exit a software package to DOS, issue DOS commands, and then return to the software package previously exited.

system disk: Disk that has been formatted and contains DOS. This type of disk can be used to boot the system.

system reset: System function that restarts your computer just like a power on/off. This is accomplished by pressing the Del key while holding down the Ctrl and Alt keys. Three keys are required to ensure that you know what you are doing and to avoid an accidental system reset.

target drive: Disk to which files will be copied.

TIME: DOS command that changes the time for the system.

title bar: This contains the name of the window/application being run.

TREE: DOS command that lists all directories and subdirectories along with any files that might also be resident.

TYPE: DOS command that displays file contents on the screen.

warm start: Booting process used to restart a computer after you have lost control of its language or operating system.

wild cards: Characters that let you include a number of files or fields in an operation by using only one command.

Windows: The graphic user interface that makes using the computer and running programs easier. This interface allows use of the mouse as a pointing tool.

INDEX

DOS

Internal Commands

CLS	DIR	TYPE
COPY	ERASE	VER
DATE	RENAME	VOL
DEL	TIME	

External Commands

CHKDSK	PRINT
DISKCOPY	SORT
FORMAT	SYS
MORE	

Redirection

<	Specify input other than the keyboard
>	Specify output other than the printer
>>	Specify output other than the printer and add this to the end of an existing line

DOS

Copy:

A>COPY fn B:	Copy a file from the default drive to drive B:
A>COPY fna fnb	Copy a file to the same disk under another name
A>COPY B:fn	Copy a file from drive B: to the default
A>COPY B:fn fna	Copy a file from drive B: and place it on the default under a different name

A>Copy *.* B:	Copy all files from a: to b:
A>Copy file? B:	Copy any file beginning with FILE and any character in position 5.

DOS

CHKDSK

A>CHKDSK b:	Check the status of the disk in drive B:
A>CHKDSK fn	Check the file, fn, for fragmentation
A>CHKDSK B:*.*	Check all the files on drive B: for fragmentation
A>CHKDSK B:*.*/F	Check drive B: for fragmentation and fix any problems

Format

FORMAT B:	Format the disk in drive B: w/o DOS
FORMAT B:/S	Format the disk in drive B: with DOS
FORMAT B:/V	Format the disk w/o DOS and record a label
FORMAT B:S/V	Format the disk with DOS and record a label

DOS

Directory Piping Commands

DIR¦SORT	Sort the directory by file name
DIR¦SORT/ + 10	Sort the directory by file extension
DIR¦SORT/ + 14	Sort the directory by file size
DIR¦SORT/ + 25	Sort the directory by date
DIR¦SORT>DIR1	Sort the directory and place output in file DIR1

MORE<filename	Display the contents of filename to the monitor a screen at a time
DIR¦SORT¦MORE	Display the directory in sorted order to the monitor a screen at a time

ESSENTIAL WORDPERFECT 5.0/5.1

Tim Duffy
Professor of Accounting in Information Systems
Illinois State University

ESSENTIAL WORDPERFECT 5.0/5.1

Wadsworth Publishing Company
Belmont, California
A Division of Wadsworth, Inc.

Computer Science Editor: Frank Ruggirello
Developmental Editor: Alan Venable
Editorial Assistant: Rhonda Gray
Production: Hal Lockwood, Bookman Productions
Print Buyer: Martha Branch
Art Editor: Jane Brundage, Bookman Productions
Interior and Cover Design: Vargas/Williams/Design
Copy Editor: Betty Duncan
Photo Researchers: Sarah Bendersky, Darcy Lanham, Judy Mason, Monica Suder
Technical Illustrator: Illustrious, Inc.
Compositor: Graphic Typesetting Service, Los Angeles
Printer: Arcata Graphics, Kingsport, Tennessee

3 4 5 6 7 8 9 10—96 95 94 93 92
ISBN: 0-534-18727-7

CONTENTS

PREFACE

PURPOSE

This *Software Essentials* book and its associated software training materials teach software competency. These materials are designed for both majors and non-majors in a quarter or semester course that uses the microcomputer as the primary vehicle for introducing students to problem solving. As typically expected in this type of course, there are no prerequisites.

APPROACH

Students acquire software competency by completing a set of software-training chapters that focus on current releases of various major software packages. To achieve that competency, each software package is presented in a separate booklet emphasizing hands-on problem solving. Carefully prepared, hands-on tutorials are provided within each chapter. Closely related end-of-chapter exercises reinforce the tutorial learning and expand the student's mastery over a broader range of applications.

Software packages covered in this series include

- DOS 3.3 and 5.0.
- WordPerfect 5.0/5.1.
- Lotus 1-2-3 2.2 and 2.3.
- Quattro Pro 3.0.
- dBASE III Plus.
- dBASE IV 1.1.
- Paradox 3.5.
- Windows 3.1.

IMPROVEMENTS IN SOFTWARE INSTRUCTION

I have always made the greatest possible effort to make hands-on instruction direct and meaningful. For this series in *Software Essentials*, the hands-on passages have been extensively reviewed and revised to make the booklets in the series more effective for the teacher and learning easier for the beginning student. Important changes include the following:

- **Self-Contained Modules** Each software module is self-contained. Each has its own front matter, chapter numbering, glossary, and command summary.
- **Expanded Hands-On Learning** The number of hands-on exercises has been increased dramatically. Particularly, the number of shorter exercises has been increased.
- **Use of Second Color** All hands-on exercise commands in the text appear in second color. This allows the student to quickly identify what keystrokes to enter and to distinguish them from additional explanation about a software feature or command.

- **Hints/Hazards Boxes** Many Hints/Hazards boxes inform students about the tricks they can use and potential traps they may encounter when using a particular software tool.
- **Keyboard Icons** Keyboard icons appear frequently in headings and tables. These icons help the student identify and remember specific keystrokes.

WORKING IN A HANDS-ON ENVIRONMENT

Software Essentials and its allied materials work best in a hands-on environment. The step-by-step exercises make most sense when an individual is sitting at a computer and can immediately see the results of his or her actions. A symbol such as the one shown in the margin indicates hands-on material.

Each software package covered in this series is treated in enough detail to satisfy the requirement of a computer novice. However, each software booklet assumes that the software has already been configured for the student's use. If a package has not been configured for a specific machine, refer to the documentation for that package.

HARDWARE REQUIREMENTS FOR HANDS-ON SOFTWARE

An IBM PC or compatible computer with two disk drives and 320K of memory is required for most tools in this series. Note that you need 512K and a hard disk to run dBASE IV. You will also need a color monitor/graphics adapter board to properly display Lotus 1-2-3 graphics on the screen. A printer (with graphics capabilities if you wish to print Lotus graphs) is also required for printing documents, reports, graphs, and worksheets.

The hard disk (fixed disk) has resulted in many changes in the way computer concepts and use are taught in the classroom. During the past few years, the prices of hard disk technology have plummeted. Because this technology is now affordable for most colleges and universities, this text includes instructions for running software from a fixed disk.

LEARNING AIDS AND SAMPLE FILES

Exercises are provided at the end of each chapter to give students quick feedback on their progress. Besides the written exercises, hands-on computer exercises are included at the end of the software chapters to provide feedback through challenging applications of material covered in the chapter. A number of sample diskette files—including sample worksheets, text files, and database files—have been provided for use with text lessons and exercises.

1

INTRODUCTION TO WORDPERFECT

CHAPTER OBJECTIVES

After completing this chapter, you should be able to

- **Understand basic concepts of word processing**
- **Use common word processing terminology**
- **Discuss the steps involved in using word processing packages**
- **List the various parts of the WordPerfect package**
- **Interpret the parts of the status line of the entry screen**
- **Use a number of cursor movement commands**
- **Use a number of elementary WordPerfect commands**
- **Use the Speller feature**

INTRODUCTION TO WORDPERFECT

This text will teach you how to use WordPerfect Versions 5.0 and 5.1. **WordPerfect,** one of the best word processing software packages on the market, includes a number of important features.

Word Processing The WordPerfect **word processing** program lets you type a document into RAM and later store it to disk. Once you have created a document, you can revise and rearrange it, copy it, print it, or perform various other operations on it.

WordPerfect sets no limit on the size of document file you can create. In theory, for example, you could create a 1000-page file. However, the size is limited by the limits of whatever storage medium you are using and by other practical considerations.

Speller and Thesaurus The WordPerfect **Speller** lets you find and correct spelling errors in a document. Its dictionary contains over 100,000 words and lets you add or delete words. Speller offers its own "best guess" when a word appears misspelled. It can also count the words in a document.

Thesaurus contains about 10,000 words, including synonyms and antonyms. At your command, it displays words from this list on the screen to help you find a substitute for some word that you are trying to replace with a better word.

Desktop Publishing WordPerfect includes a number of features that make it an effective tool for lower-level desktop publishing applications.

Additional Features WordPerfect also includes a number of powerful additional features not covered in this brief text. For instance, the **Merge feature** lets you combine (merge) information such as a list of names and addresses with a standard letter, so that you can create a series of individualized letters with little more effort than it takes to type one letter. WordPerfect also lets you perform math within a document, build a table of contents or an index, make drawings, and do a number of other things.

This text will give you a solid introduction to the word processing features of WordPerfect. It will also show you how to use Speller and a number of features related to desktop publishing. When you have completed this text, you will probably be familiar enough with how WordPerfect works to learn to use many other features on your own with the assistance of WordPerfect's built-in Help feature and the documentation that comes with the WordPerfect software package.

The symbol **5.1** indicates a feature not found in WordPerfect Version 5.0 but available in Version 5.1.

STARTING WORDPERFECT

How you start WordPerfect depends on whether you are using a diskette or hard disk system.

Diskette-Based System

1. If your WordPerfect disk also contains DOS, boot the computer with that disk in drive A. If not, boot it with the DOS disk. Enter the date and time if you want this information in the directory entries of the files you create.
2. Unless instructed otherwise, place your WordPerfect diskette in drive A and the disk that is to hold your document files in drive B. To get

WordPerfect to store files on the diskette in drive B, change the default to drive B. To do this, type `B:` at the A> prompt and press Enter.

3. To start WordPerfect, type `WP` at the B> prompt and press Enter.

Hard Disk–Based System

1. Boot the computer and activate the directory in which your WordPerfect program and data files reside. To do this, use the Change Directory (CD) command. For example, if your WordPerfect directory is named WP, type `CD \WP` and press Enter.
2. At the DOS prompt for the active directory, type `WP` and press Enter to start WordPerfect. Any files that you create will be saved to the active directory.

Once you issue the WP command to start WordPerfect, WordPerfect briefly displays a copyright screen. The Note line on the copyright screen indicates on which drive the WordPerfect files are located. If you start WordPerfect from a diskette and the files also reside in a directory called WP on the hard disk, this directory will be displayed instead of drive A. The `* Please Wait *` message informs you that the required WordPerfect files are being loaded by the computer.

WORDPERFECT SCREEN

Once the WordPerfect program is loaded, the screen in Figure 1.1 appears. The dash in the upper left-hand corner of the screen is the cursor. The **status line** is the single line of information at the bottom of the screen; it is the twenty-fifth line on your screen. In this example, C: \WP51\FILENAME indicates an existing file that is being edited. This entry is absent when you are creating a new, as yet unnamed, document.

The WordPerfect screen is initially blank except for the following in the lower right-hand corner: WordPerfect lets you open two document files at one time and manipulate both, a feature that will be discussed in detail later. The Doc 1 entry of the status line indicates that the first document is on the screen:

```
Doc 1 Pg 1 Ln 1" Pos 1"
```

The Pg entry gives the current page number. The Ln entry gives the current location of the cursor on the page. If line spacing has been set for double spacing (2), this entry will advance $\frac{1}{3}$ inch each time Enter is pressed (1 inch, 1.33 inches, 1.66 inches, and so forth). If the line spacing is set for single spacing, these entries are in increments of $\frac{1}{6}$ inch (1 inch, 1.16 inches, 1.33 inches, and so forth).

The Pos indicator tells the position of the cursor in inch increments on a line of text and provides other information. Notice that the Pos indicator in Figure

Figure 1.1

A clear screen with the status line at the bottom.

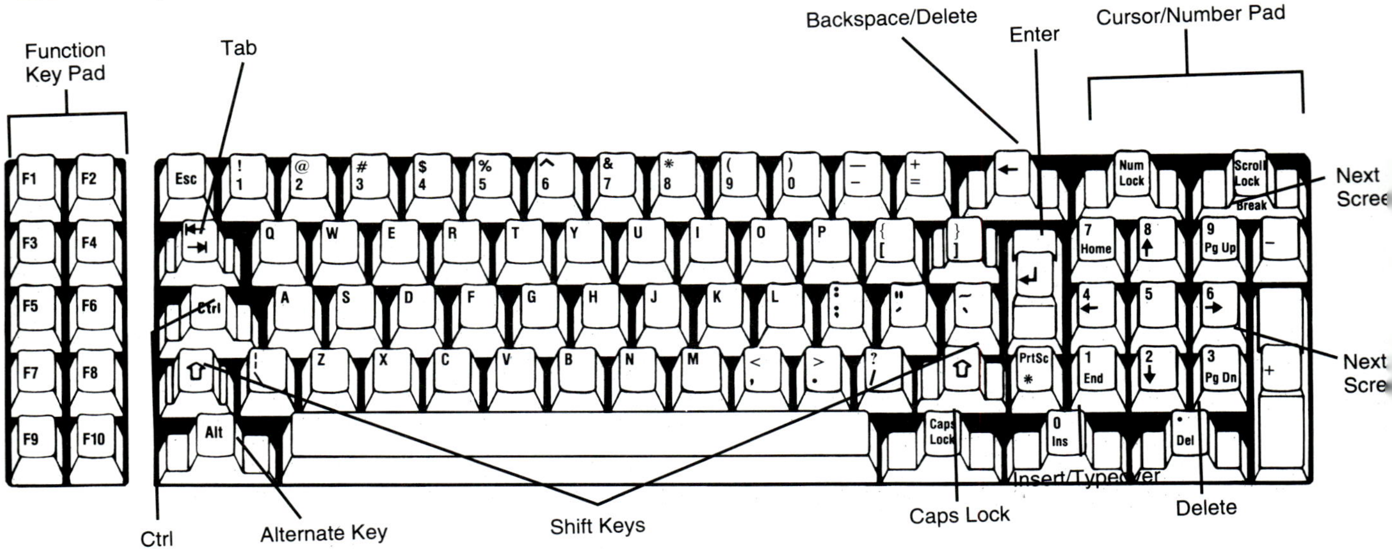

Figure 1.2

The WordPerfect keyboard. Function keys work alone or in combination with the Ctrl, Shift, and Alt keys.

1.1 contains the value of 1 inch even though the cursor appears to be in the left-most position on the screen. The position displayed on the screen is the lineal position of the cursor in inches on the line in which this character will appear on the printed document. As the cursor is moved, this value changes according to the characters per inch (font size) that have been specified for this document. For example, if 10 characters per inch have been specified, this value changes by increments of 1/10 inch (for example, 1.1 inches, 1.2 inches, and 1.3 inches). The various characteristics of the document will be covered later.

When the position indicator appears as Pos, the Caps Lock key is off; when it appears as POS, the Caps Lock key is on, and only uppercase characters will be typed. The number that follows Pos also informs you of the status of other features. If you invoke Boldface, then the number appears in boldface. If you invoke Underline, then the number appears underlined. If the POS indicator is blinking, it tells you that the Num Lock key of your keyboard is active.

The **text window** is composed of the 24 blank lines above the status line. As you enter text, the window fills with lines of text. The maximum amount of text that can be displayed on a standard monitor at one time is 24 lines.

ENTERING AND CANCELING COMMANDS: KEYBOARD

WordPerfect makes extensive use of function keys in conjunction with the Ctrl, Shift, and Alt keys to enter commands (Figure 1.2). To ease the learning process, a labeled template fits over the function keys (Figure 1.3a). This template shows which combination of keys executes a specific command or calls forth a menu from which you can make selections.*

**Throughout this text, the following system is used to show how keystrokes are combined. When two or three keystrokes are separated by addition signs (for example, Alt + F2), you must hold down the Alt key while you press the F2 key. When two keystrokes are separated by a comma (for example, F5, Enter) simply press and release each key in sequence.*

Figure 1.3
The 40 WordPerfect function key commands: (a) PC/XT keyboard; (b) enhanced keyboard.

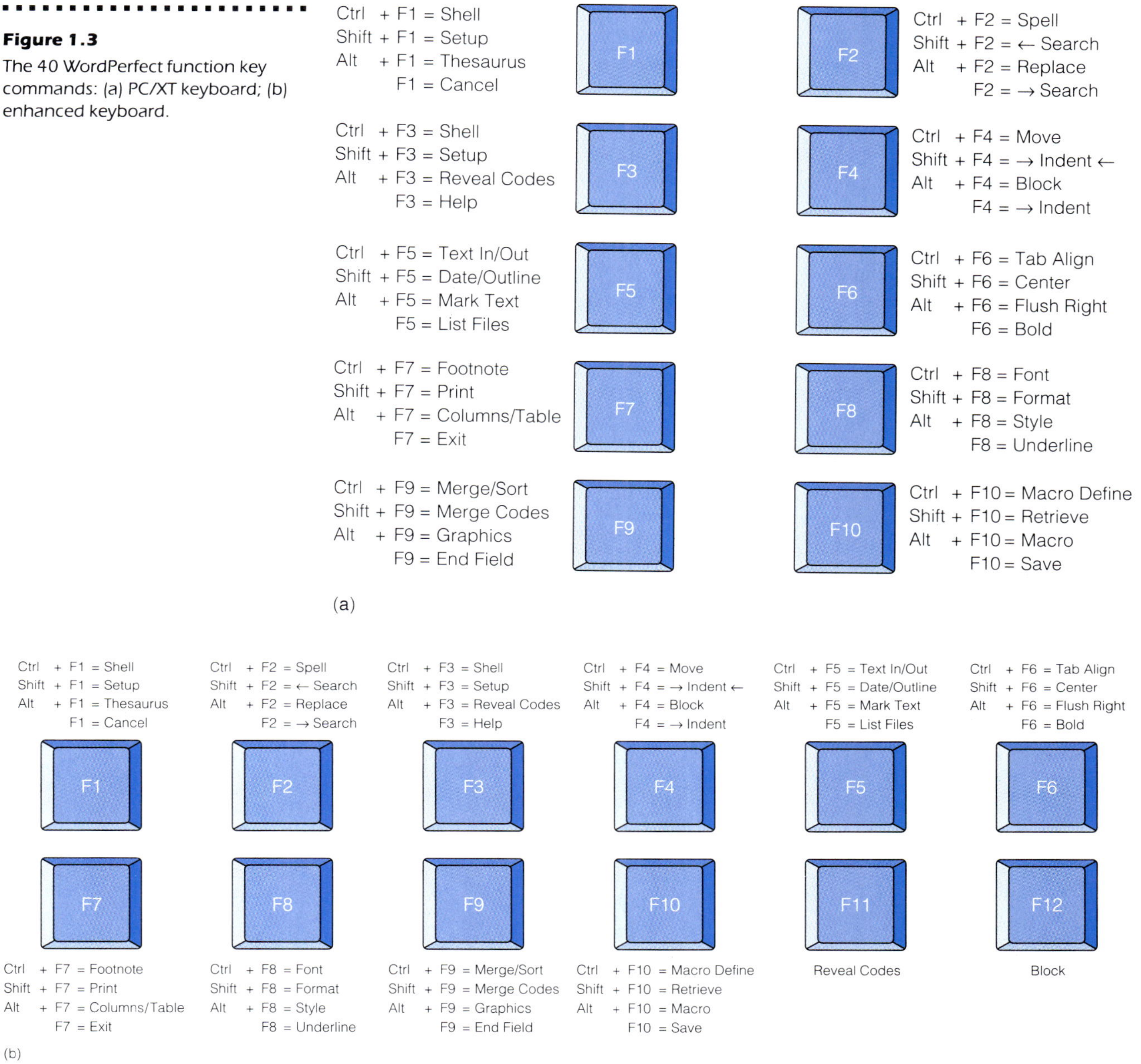

Figure 1.4

An example of the horizontal Font Menu.

```
1 Size; 2 Appearance; 3 Normal; 4 Base Font; 5 Print Color: 0
```

Figure 1.5

(a) An example of the full-screen Format Menu; (b) an example of the full-screen Page submenu for the Format command.

```
Format

     1 - Line
              Hyphenation                        Line Spacing
              Justification                      Margins Left/Right
              Line Height                        Tab Set
              Line Numbering                     Widow/Orphan Protection

     2 - Page
              Center Page (top to bottom)        Page Numbering
              Force Odd/Even Page                Paper Size/Type
              Headers and Footers                Suppress
              Margins Top/Bottom

     3 - Document
              Display Pitch                      Redline Method
              Initial Codes/Font                 Summary

     4 - Other
              Advance                            Overstrike
              Conditional End of Page            Printer Functions
              Decimal Characters                 Underline Spaces/Tabs
              Language

Selection: 0
```

(a)

```
Format: Page

     1 - Center Page (top to bottom)    No

     2 - Force Odd/Even Page

     3 - Headers

     4 - Footers

     5 - Margins - Top                  1"
                   Bottom               1"

     6 - Page Numbering

     7 - Paper Size                     8.5" x 11"
               Type                     Standard

     8 - Suppress (this page only)


Selection: 0
```

(b)

WordPerfect, a menu or submenu is either horizontal (Figure 1.4) or full-screen (Figure 1.5). With so many different commands available, however, it is easy to inadvertently press the wrong key sequence and have an unexpected menu appear.

F1 or F7
Cancel/Exit

Canceling Commands WordPerfect provides two commands for canceling a menu or for interrupting a command once it has started to execute: Cancel (F1) and Exit (F7). If, for example, you want to issue a Format (Shift + F8) command but instead issue a Font (Ctrl + F8) command, exit that menu by issuing either F1 (Cancel) or F7 (Exit). The difference between the commands is that F7 always returns you immediately to your document. F1 backs up one command in a menu structure. It may therefore take several Cancel (F1) commands to return you to your document if you are several levels within a WordPerfect menu hierarchy.

5.1

ENTERING COMMANDS: PULL-DOWN MENUS

WordPerfect 5.1 introduces an alternative to the above standard menu structure: pull-down menus. Pull-down menus provide an alternative method of entering commands that can be used with or without a mouse.

The menu bar (Figure 1.6) provides nine different choices from which to select. Activate this menu by pressing the right key of a mouse or by entering the command Alt + = from the keyboard. To select a menu option from the keyboard, enter the first letter of the command or use the Arrow key to highlight the appropriate command and press Enter. Using a mouse, move the cursor via the mouse to the desired command and press the left button. Once a command is selected, a pull-down menu such as those depicted in Figure 1.7a to 1.7i is displayed.

Once a pull-down menu is activated, make a selection from the keyboard by entering the highlighted character of the desired command. You can also use Arrow keys to reposition the highlighting bar; press Enter once the desired command is highlighted. Using a mouse, move the mouse until the cursor is at the desired menu option and press the left button to select that menu item. To exit from the menu (the same as F7), press the right mouse button.

A command, once selected, may display a WordPerfect full-screen menu. In such a case, the mouse can no longer be used for selecting menu options. You must enter all commands using the keyboard. Some commands, however, result in a pop-out menu box appearing on the screen, as shown in Figure 1.7h. Notice the pop-out menus contain an arrow in the right-most portion of the highlighted command option. When such a box appears, continue making command selections using the same tool.

USING A MOUSE

To make effective use of a mouse, you must be acquainted with a number of terms. These include clicking, double-clicking, dragging, and dual click/release. Each serves to give a different instruction to the software.

Clicking involves quickly pressing and then releasing one of the buttons of the mouse. **Double-clicking** involves quickly pressing and releasing the same

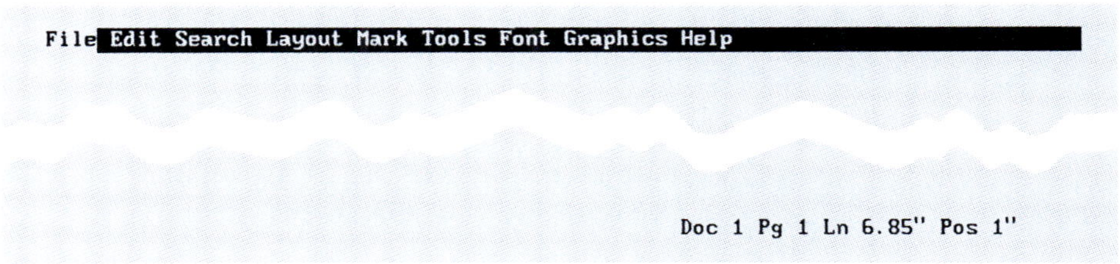

Figure 1.6

The menu bar for the pull-down menu.

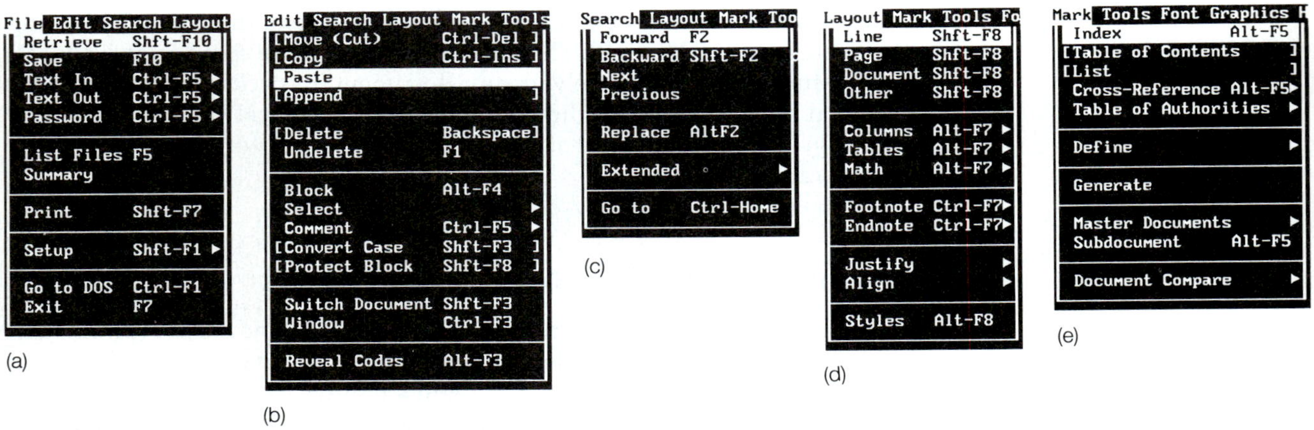

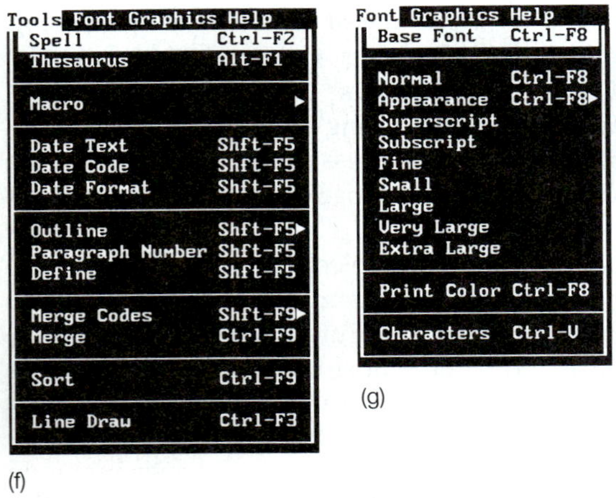

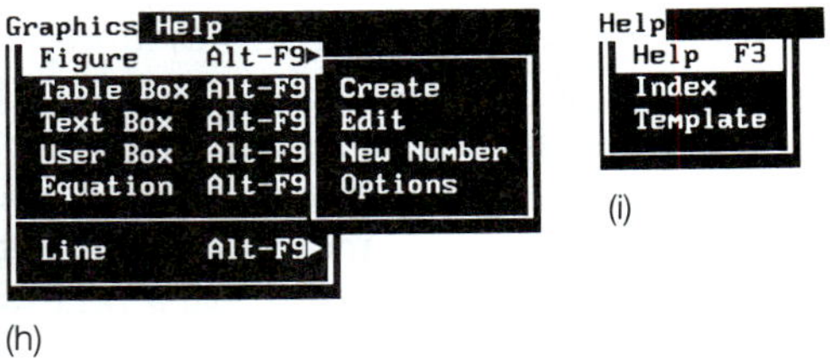

Figure 1.7

The pull-down menus that are displayed by selecting commands from the menu bar: (a) the File option menu; (b) the Edit option menu; (c) the Search option menu; (d) the Layout option menu; (e) the Mark option menu; (f) the Tools option menu; (g) the Font option menu; (h) the Graphics option menu; (i) the Help option menu.

5.1

button twice. **Dragging** involves pressing a button, holding it down, and then moving the mouse. A **dual click/release** involves holding down both buttons and releasing them simultaneously.

In the discussion of WordPerfect commands contained within this text, both methods of entering commands (regular menus and pull-down menus) are covered. The keys required for executing a WordPerfect command are provided along with the options from the File Menu in any text exercises.

F3 Help

HELP FEATURE

WordPerfect contains a built-in Help feature that can be invoked by pressing the Help (F3) key. To get information about a command or function, press F3, followed by the first letter of the command or the desired function key. Figure 1.8 depicts a Help screen that appears when you press F5 (List Files) after F3.

Experiment with the Help feature. Begin by pressing F3 and a letter of the alphabet (for example, *L*). Try another letter. When you are finished, press Enter to return to your document screen.

Figure 1.8

A Help screen for the List Files (F5) command.

```
List

     Displays a list of files or equation commands, depending on when you press
     this key.  Pressing List (F5) at the normal editing screen invokes the
     List Files feature which lists all files that match the filename template
     (pattern) given.  When WordPerfect displays the template (e.g.,
     c:\files\*.*), press Enter to display all the files in the current default
     directory, or edit the template to display the directory and files you
     wish to view.

     To perform an action on a file, move the cursor to the file before
     selecting the action.  To perform an action on several files at once, mark
     each of the files (i.e., move to each file and press *) and then select
     the action.  You can then delete, print, copy, or search the marked files.
     To print the directory listing, press Print (Shift-F7).

     Pressing List at a "Filename:" prompt (e.g., Graphics Box Definition,
     Style Definition) allows you to use List Files to find and retrieve a
     file.  Pressing List in the Equation Editor moves the cursor to the list
     of equation commands.

1 Retrieve; 2 Delete; 3 Move/Rename; 4 Print; 5 Short/Long Display;
6 Look; 7 Other Directory; 8 Copy; 9 Find; N Name Search

Selection: 0                                   (Press ENTER to exit Help)
```

OPERATING WORDPERFECT

ENTERING A DOCUMENT

You can type your document without worrying about the approach of the end of a line (as you would have to on a typewriter) because WordPerfect automatically moves a word that is too long for a line down to the next line via the **word-wrap** feature. The only time you have to enter a **hard return** (press the Enter key) is at the end of a paragraph.

5.1

WordPerfect also keeps track of dormant hard returns. A **dormant hard return** is a carriage return that appears as the first line of a page. Usually you don't want a blank line here, so WordPerfect converts the hard return to a dormant return and suppresses the blank line until the text before it has expanded and the blank line is needed.

To practice entering text, type the following paragraphs. Use the Tab key (located above the Ctrl key) to indent. Don't be concerned if the text on your screen looks slightly different from that below and don't correct errors. We discuss how to delete text and correct errors later.

```
   A file is a collection of related information in the form of data
or of instructions for manipulating that information. In other words,
files can be either data files or program files. You keep track of
files on a disk by name. Each filename must be unique; if you try to
record a file using a name that already exists on the disk, the
content of the previous file will be destroyed and replaced with the
content of the new file.
   With a few exceptions, you can name your file anything you wish.
Disk filenames can be one to eight characters in length and can be
followed by a filename extension that is preceded by a period and is
one to three characters in length. For example, a student data file
for grades might be called STUDGRAD.TXT.
```

SAVING A DOCUMENT (FILE) TO DISK

Two function keys save a file to disk. The first (F10) returns you to the document, and the second (F7) lets you start a new document or return to DOS.

F10

Select Save from the File Menu

SAVE

The Save (F10) command saves (stores) the current document in a file on disk. If the file is new, you are prompted to enter a filename. If the file is an old one that has been retrieved from disk, the filename is first displayed with a prompt. For example,

```
Document to be Saved: C:\WP\EXERCISE
```

Notice that the drive name is displayed along with the subdirectory, if any, and the filename. Press Enter. You will now be asked if you want to overwrite the existing file with the new one:

```
Replace C:\WP\EXERCISE? No (Yes)
```

Respond with a Y. After the file has been saved, you are returned to the document and can resume editing. This procedure saves any changes that have been made to your document. You should do this regularly while working on a file, even though WordPerfect does provide a backup facility (to be discussed later).

F7

Select Exit from the File Menu

EXIT

If you want to save a file and then leave WordPerfect or create or edit another document, press the Exit (F7) key. You will then be asked if you want to save the file, to which you respond Y. After the file has been saved on disk, WordPerfect displays the following prompt:

```
Exit WP? No (Yes)     (Cancel to return to document)
```

If you respond N, the existing document is erased from RAM, and you receive a blank screen ready for new text; if you answer Y, you are returned to DOS. If you issue the Cancel (F1) command, you are returned to your document.

SAVE THE EXERCISE FILE

The next commands will illustrate how you can issue the Save (F10) command or the Exit (F7) command to save the two-paragraph exercise file that has just been created:

F10	(Or select Save from the File Menu) Issues the Save command to save your two-paragraph practice file. WordPerfect responds with the prompt `Document to be saved:`.
Type `INPUT1`	Gives the name of the file to which this document is to be saved.
Enter	Executes the Save command. Once the file is saved, notice that the path of the file appears in the status line (for example, A:\INPUT1).

Once you have saved a file, you might want to enter more text or make changes to the existing text in your document. As a general rule, it is a good idea to save the document with any changes every 10 to 15 minutes. This means that you only have to redo the last 15 minutes if a power failure occurs. To save your changes, issue the following commands:

F10	(Or select Save from File Menu) Issues the Save command. WordPerfect now responds with a prompt, including the path of the file, `Document to be saved: A:\INPUT1`.
Enter	Indicates that this is the name to use. WordPerfect now responds with the prompt `Replace A:\INPUT1? No (Yes)`.
Y	Accepts the Replace option. WordPerfect then issues the prompt `Saving A:\INPUT1` and saves the file to disk.

Continue adding text and making changes to your file until it is time either to leave WordPerfect or to erase this document and start on another. To save the file and erase the screen for another document, issue the following instructions:

F7	(Or select Exit from the File Menu) Issues the Exit command. WordPerfect now asks, `Save document? Yes (No)`.
Y	Indicates yes. WordPerfect responds with the prompt `Document to be saved: A:\INPUT1`.
Enter	Accepts the name INPUT1. WordPerfect now asks, `Replace A:\INPUT1? No (Yes)`.
Y	Indicates yes. WordPerfect now asks, `Exit WP? No (Yes)`.
N	Tells WordPerfect that you do not wish to exit. WordPerfect now erases the screen, and you are ready to start on a new document.

To exit WordPerfect, all that is required is to answer yes to the prompt `Exit WP? Yes (No)`. At that time, you are returned to the DOS prompt.

IMPORTANT When you want to leave WordPerfect, always use the Exit command. Remove the WordPerfect program disk (when you are using a diskette-based system) only when the DOS prompt (A>, B>, C>, or D>) appears on the screen. If you remove the program disk while the drive is running, the file may not be properly saved.

If you turn off the computer without first properly exiting WordPerfect, a number of temporary files that are used by WordPerfect are left open. The next time that you start WordPerfect, the prompt `Are there any other versions of WordPerfect running on this machine?` appears on the screen. In such a situation, enter an N for no and press Enter.

Shift + F10

Select Retrieve from the File Menu

RETRIEVING A FILE

WordPerfect provides two different commands for loading a file into RAM from disk. The first command is the Retrieve (Shift + F10) command. Use this command when you remember the filename. Once this command is issued, the prompt `Document to be retrieved:` appears on the screen. Now enter the name of the desired file and press Enter. That document is now loaded into RAM. If

Figure 1.9

The List Files screen.

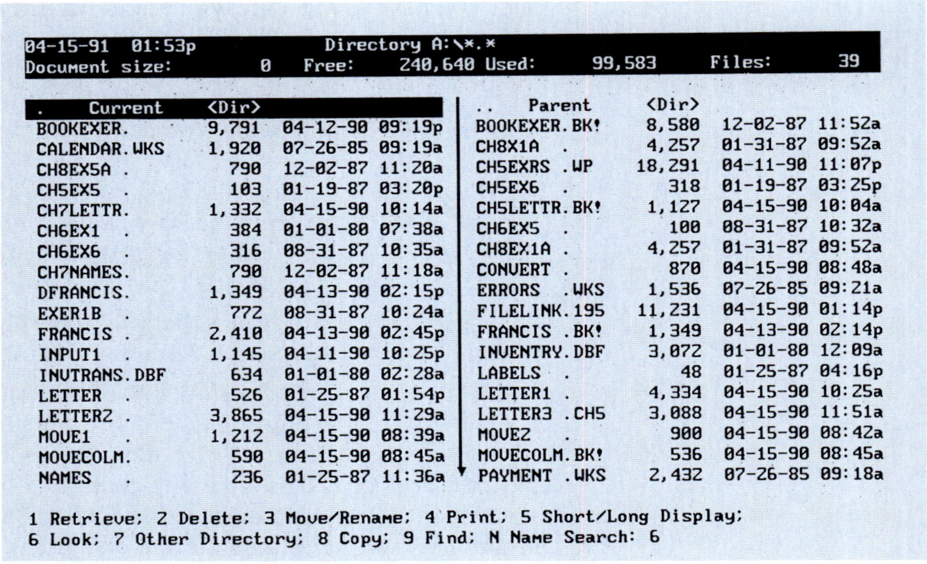

```
04-15-91  01:53p              Directory A:\*.*
Document size:        0   Free:    240,640 Used:       99,583      Files:       39

 .   Current    <Dir>                          ..    Parent     <Dir>
 BOOKEXER.      9,791  04-12-90 09:19p   BOOKEXER.BK!    8,580  12-02-87 11:52a
 CALENDAR.WKS   1,920  07-26-85 09:19a   CH8X1A   .      4,257  01-31-87 09:52a
 CH8EX5A .        790  12-02-87 11:20a   CH5EXRS  .WP   18,291  04-11-90 11:07p
 CH5EX5   .       103  01-19-87 03:20p   CH5EX6   .        318  01-19-87 03:25p
 CH7LETTR.      1,332  04-15-90 10:14a   CH5LETTR.BK!    1,127  04-15-90 10:04a
 CH6EX1   .       384  01-01-80 07:38a   CH6EX5   .        100  08-31-87 10:32a
 CH6EX6   .       316  08-31-87 10:35a   CH8EX1A .       4,257  01-31-87 09:52a
 CH7NAMES.        790  12-02-87 11:18a   CONVERT .         870  04-15-90 08:48a
 DFRANCIS.      1,349  04-13-90 02:15p   ERRORS   .WKS   1,536  07-26-85 09:21a
 EXER1B   .       772  08-31-87 10:24a   FILELINK.195   11,231  04-15-90 01:14p
 FRANCIS .      2,410  04-13-90 02:45p   FRANCIS  .BK!   1,349  04-13-90 02:14p
 INPUT1   .     1,145  04-11-90 10:25p   INVENTRY.DBF    3,072  01-01-80 12:09a
 INVTRANS.DBF     634  01-01-80 02:28a   LABELS   .         48  01-25-87 04:16p
 LETTER   .       526  01-25-87 01:54p   LETTER1 .       4,334  04-15-90 10:25a
 LETTER2 .      3,865  04-15-90 11:29a   LETTER3  .CH5   3,088  04-15-90 11:51a
 MOVE1    .     1,212  04-15-90 08:39a   MOVE2    .        900  04-15-90 08:42a
 MOVECOLM.        590  04-15-90 08:45a   MOVECOLM.BK!      536  04-15-90 08:45a
 NAMES    .       236  01-25-87 11:36a   PAYMENT  .WKS   2,432  07-26-85 09:18a

1 Retrieve; 2 Delete; 3 Move/Rename; 4 Print; 5 Short/Long Display;
6 Look; 7 Other Directory; 8 Copy; 9 Find; N Name Search: 6
```

you already have a document opened, that file is loaded into the current document beginning at the location occupied by the cursor.

If you have forgotten the filename, issue the List Files (F5) command. After that command is issued, a prompt appears verifying that the current active drive/directory is the one desired. To verify that this is correct, press Enter. A screen containing a list of files now appears (Figure 1.9). To select a file, use the cursor keys on the numeric keypad to highlight the desired file and press R to issue a Retrieve command. The file is now loaded into RAM. If you currently have a document in RAM, the prompt `Retrieve into current document? No (Yes)` appears at the bottom of the screen. If you respond yes, the file is retrieved into the current document beginning at the cursor location.

OTHER FILE MANEUVERS USING LIST FILES (F5)

(F5) LIST FILES

Select List Files from Retrieve Menu

The List Files (F5) command solves memory loss and other problems. The List Files (F5) command allows you to view a directory of all files on disk; find the files that contain a specific word or phrase; read or scan a document; retrieve a document to the screen; delete, rename, print, or copy a file; and retrieve an ASCII file.

When you first issue the List files (F5) command, WordPerfect prompts for the name of the disk and subdirectory to be displayed, with the current disk and subdirectory as the default. At this time, you can change the directory by pressing = and entering the name of a new directory, or you can press Enter to accept the current one. A screen like Figure 1.9 now appears on your monitor.

The top lines of the screen provide the date, time, disk/directory name, size of the document in memory, and amount of space available on disk. The middle portion contains, for each of the various files on disk, the name, size, date, and time of creation. Use the cursor keys to move the bar from one file to the next. The bottom two lines contain a menu of various tasks that can be performed.

To execute a command, move the bar to a filename and then press a number key or the highlighted character to select a menu option.

1 Retrieve This command retrieves a file. *Never retrieve any WordPerfect program files (any file that starts with WP or any file with a .COM or .EXE file extension) because you can damage them and ruin your copy of the program.*

2 Delete This command displays the message `Delete filename? No (Yes)`. If you press Y, the file will be deleted.

3 Move/Rename This command lets you rename a file. Simply enter the new name at the prompt `New Name:___`.

4 Print This command sends a file to the printer.

5 Short/Long Display This command lets you alternate between displaying two filenames or one filename per line.

6 Look This command lets you view a file without loading it into RAM, by displaying it a page at a time to the screen. You can use cursor commands to scroll through the file, but you cannot make changes to the file. Press F1 to return to List Files screen.

7 Other Directory This command lets you access files from another directory or disk. WordPerfect will then use the indicated directory or disk for saving or retrieving files.

8 Copy This command lets you copy the indicated file to another file, disk, or directory.

9 Find This command lets you find all files in the current directory that contain a word or phrase that matches a pattern that you provided.

N Name This command lets you position the cursor to the first file that begins with the character(s) that you enter from a keyboard.

Marking Files The List Files command copies, deletes, finds, moves, or prints a group of files by "marking" each file with an asterisk (*). When you wish to perform one of these commands, highlight the file and then enter the asterisk. Continue until all desired files have been marked. Once all files have been marked, select one of the commands from the List Files Menu and enter any information required by that command.

Once a file has been marked, it can be "unmarked" by again highlighting that file and entering another asterisk. All files can be marked or unmarked for a task by entering the command Home + *.

As the various files are marked and unmarked using the asterisk, the Files indicator at the top of the screen changes to indicate the amount of storage used by the marked files.

To get out of the List Files screen, press 0 or F1.

Practice exiting from and retrieving your INPUT1 document using the Exit (F7) command, the Retrieve (Shift + F10) command, and the Retrieve option of the List Files command (F5, Enter, 1).

WORKING WITHIN A DOCUMENT

MOVING AROUND THE DOCUMENT

Cursor movement commands move the cursor over the text in the text window (Table 1.1). The cursor movement commands of WordPerfect are executed by using the 10-key numeric keypad (Figure 1.10) or other keys with arrow symbols, depending on your keyboard.

Some tasks performed by some cursor horizontal-movement commands are not readily apparent until a document has lines that extend beyond the edge of the screen. For example, the function of the Home + Right Arrow command is not obvious until this type of application is encountered. Until you have a document in which the lines are longer than the width of the screen, the (1) Home, Right Arrow, (2) Home, Home, Right Arrow, and (3) End commands all appear to perform the same cursor movement command.

PAGE BREAKS

WordPerfect lets you see where a page break will appear when the file is printed. This signal, the **soft page break,** occurs when one page is full and another page is about to begin. To indicate a soft page break, WordPerfect automatically places a line of dashes (--------) across the screen. It appears after the

Table 1.1 Cursor Movement Commands

Keys	*Cursor Movement*
Horizontal Movement	
→	To the right one position
←	To the left one position
Ctrl + →	To first character of next word to the right
Ctrl + ←	To first character of next word to the left
End	To right end of the line
Home, →	To right end of line
Home, ←	To the left end of line
Home, Home, →	To the extreme right edge of the document
Home, Home, ←	To the extreme left edge of the document
Vertical Movement	
↑	Up one line
↓	Down one line
Home, Home, ↑	To the beginning of the file
Home, Home, ↓	To the end of the file
PgUp	To the first line of text on the previous page
PgDn	To the first line of text on the next page
−	Up one screen (24 lines) of text
+	Down one screen (24 lines) of text
Ctrl + Home, #	This positions the cursor at the top of the indicated page number (#). For example, if you want to move the cursor to the top of page 10, enter Ctrl + Home (whereupon you receive the prompt `Go to`); then type 10 and press Enter. After the repositioning message disappears from the top of the screen, you are the top of page 10.

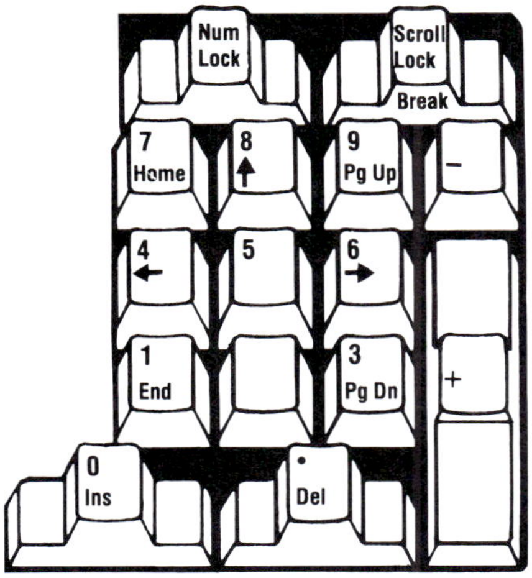

Figure 1.10
Various functions of the numeric keypad that are supported on IBM and IBM-compatible computers.

last line of text for a page on the screen but does not become part of your document. It is placed on the screen to aid you in keeping "widow" or "orphan" lines out of your document. A **widow** is the first line of a paragraph that appears alone at the bottom of a page. An **orphan** is the last line of a paragraph that appears alone at the top of a page.

Ctrl + Enter
Hard Page Break

A **hard page break,** caused by entering the command Ctrl + Enter, becomes part of the document. A hard page break occurs on a page at any place you have issued the Ctrl + Enter command. After this command, the cursor moves to the next page. WordPerfect uses a line of equal signs (= = = = = = = =) across the screen to indicate a hard page break. A hard page break can be deleted from a document by positioning the cursor at the end of the line immediately above the row of equal signs and pressing Del.

REVEALING HIDDEN CODES

Alt + F3
Reveal Codes

Many WordPerfect commands insert a hidden code in the document that causes something to happen at that point on the screen. For instance, the Hard Page Break command inserted a Hard Page code [HPg]. You can reveal these codes with the Reveal Codes (Alt + F3) command.

Press Alt + F3 to reveal the codes in your INPUT1 document. Notice that the screen is divided to show a few lines of your document without the codes and the same lines with the codes revealed. Try moving around the document with the cursor movement keys. Find the [HPg] code. Notice the Soft Return [SRt] codes that appear automatically at the end of each line and the Hard Return [HRt] codes that appear where you pressed Enter at the end of each paragraph. Press Alt + F3 again to return your screen to normal.

Making corrections on the screen while the codes are revealed is possible, but the computer responds more slowly than normal, and the presence of the codes is confusing to most users. However, the Reveal Codes command is often very useful when you are editing a document and want to locate hidden commands that you want to delete. It is also useful when the screen looks wrong in some way that you can't explain without seeing what hidden codes may be operating.

Retrieve your INPUT1 document and try out some of the cursor movements keys described in Table 1.1. Create a page break somewhere in the middle of the document. Delete the page break.

EDITING TEXT

After text has been entered, you will want to correct spelling and grammatical errors, delete unwanted words, and smooth punctuation. Many times, however, you will detect typing errors as soon as you make them. WordPerfect makes it easy for you to correct errors while entering text. You simply move the cursor back to the error and correct it.

Although you may catch some errors as you type, you will eventually want to print out the rough draft of your document and mark any errors for correction. You should print out the document rather than proofing it on the screen because you're still too intimately involved with the work on the screen to see even obvious errors. This also can occur with printed output but less often because you can take more time and review the document away from the computer.

After you have marked the corrections on paper, it is fairly easy to make changes using the following WordPerfect commands: cursor movement commands to move through the document, commands to insert new text into the body of the document, and commands to delete unwanted text.

Inserting Text You can add new text within a document in two ways: with the insert option (the WordPerfect default) or the typeover option.

Ins
Insert/Typeover

Insert Option The Ins key is a "toggle." That is, pressing the key turns on or off the insert function. The message `Typeover` appears in place of the filename when typeover is invoked. The **insert** option of WordPerfect is the default. To insert text into a document, place the cursor at the desired location and enter the new characters. These appear to the left of the cursor. Existing text is moved to the right on the same line. If text extends beyond the right-hand margin, it will be re-formed as soon as you issue a vertical cursor movement command.

Typeover Option Sometimes you want to insert text that will replace existing text. To do so, press the Ins key toggle to turn on the **typeover** option. WordPerfect now says `Typeover` on the status line where the filename usually appears. You return to the insert option by pressing Ins again.

Enter Key and Space Bar in Typeover Modes Both the Enter key and the Space Bar play a role in editing data. When pressed, the Enter key signals the end of a paragraph by inserting a hard return, and any text to the right of the cursor is moved to the next line. The Enter key can also be used to insert one blank line—each time it is pressed—between existing lines of text.

The Space Bar can be used to slide existing text to the right in a line. Each time it is pressed, any existing text moves to the right one position. The Enter key inserts blank lines in a document in either mode.

When you edit a document, you delete text from some lines and insert text in others. This deletion and insertion of text gives a line a ragged appearance. WordPerfect automatically issues a re-form command to realign the text within the left- and right-hand margins whenever you press an Up or Down cursor key.

Use your INPUT1 file to practice the insert and typeover methods of correction:

1. Move your cursor to rest underneath the letter *f* in *file*. With insert mode on, type `computer` followed by a space.
2. Move your cursor under the *n* in *new* at the end of the paragraph. Change to typeover mode and type `file you have just created`.
3. Move your cursor to the end of the first sentence and press Enter. For the moment, leave the cursor in this position.

Deleting Text WordPerfect lets you delete text one character at a time, one word at a time, part of a word at a time, part of a line at a time, and the rest of a page. Look before you delete. WordPerfect is somewhat forgiving with the Delete commands because deleted text from the last three Delete commands can be restored using the Undelete command. The Undelete feature will be discussed after the Delete commands.

Del and Backspace

Deleting Characters

Deleting One Character at a Time WordPerfect provides two commands for deleting material one character at a time. The Del key deletes the character at the cursor position. The Backspace key deletes the character to the left of the cursor. All text is moved to the left automatically as characters are deleted.

Deleting Codes with Del and Backspace As mentioned previously, WordPerfect embeds special codes in text to tell the monitor how to display text, to tell the printer how text is to be printed, and to accomplish any number of other special tasks. When you delete text one character at a time and one of these special codes is encountered, WordPerfect responds with a message such as `Delete [name of code]? No (Yes)`. To delete this code, enter a Y. To keep the code, press N or Enter.

Rejoining a Split Paragraph The Del command can be used to rejoin a split paragraph. A split paragraph occurs when you inadvertently press Enter and insert one or more hard returns.

For instance, in the previous exercise you inserted a hard return that split the first paragraph. To restore the paragraph, position your cursor one space to the right of *information*. (If you wish, press Alt + F3 to confirm that the cursor is highlighting the [HRt] code.) Press Del. The Hard Return code is now deleted, and the paragraph is restored.

Deleting One Word at a Time (Ctrl + Backspace) To delete one word at a time, position the cursor beneath any character of the word and press Ctrl + Backspace. This deletes the entire word and any trailing space to the next word, as shown in Table 1.2.

Deleting Part of a Word (Home, Del; Home, Backspace) WordPerfect also lets you delete the right- or left-hand portion of a word. Home, Del deletes any characters in a word to the right of the cursor. Home, Backspace deletes any characters in a word to the left of the cursor.

Deleting a Line or a Portion of a Line (Ctrl + End) Ctrl + End deletes the rest of a line (and any embedded codes) to the right of the cursor or deletes an entire line. The Ctrl + End command deletes an entire line of text when the cursor is at the beginning of the line. If the line is part of a paragraph and contains a **soft**

Table 1.2 Summary of Delete Commands

Keys	*Deletion*	*Deletion Shaded*
Del	Character at cursor	content of the new file.
BackSpace ←	Character to left of cursor	content of the new file.
Ctrl + BackSpace ←	Word at the cursor location	content of the new file.
Home, Del	Portion of word from cursor location to end of word	content of the new file.
Home, BackSpace ←	Portion of word from cursor location to the beginning of word	content of the new file.
Ctrl + End	To the end of the line	content of the new file.
Ctrl + PgDn	To the end of the page	

return (automatically placed within the document by the word-wrap feature), the text is moved up one line, replacing the deleted line. When a line that contains a hard carriage return (inserted by pressing Enter) is deleted, a blank line (holding the carriage return) remains. The carriage return itself must be deleted by pressing Del.

Deleting to the End of the Page (Ctrl + PgDn) Ctrl + PgDn deletes all text and codes from the cursor position to the end of the current page. When you press Ctrl + PgDn, the following message appears: `Delete Remainder of Page? No (Yes)`. Press Y to delete the text, or if you change your mind, press N or Enter.

Shift + F1

Select Undelete from the Edit Menu

Restoring Deleted Text WordPerfect saves the last three pieces of text that have been deleted. A deletion, in this sense, is any group of characters that is erased between two moves of the cursor. There is no limit to the number of characters in any of these three deletions, and any of the delete commands are included.

When you want to retrieve deleted text, move the cursor to the location where you want the text reinserted; then press F1 (Cancel/Undelete) to display the Retrieve Menu:

```
Undelete: 1 Restore; 2 Previous Deletion: 0
```

The last piece of text to be deleted is now highlighted in your document at the cursor location. If this is the correct piece of text, press 1; otherwise, press 2 to display the previous deleted text, and so on. Pressing 0 or Enter cancels the operation.

Remember, the location of your cursor plays an important role in the text-restoration process. If you suddenly realize that the cursor is not at the proper location, press 0 or Enter to end this restore session.

Position the cursor under *c* in *collection* in the INPUT1 document. Press Ctrl + Backspace to delete the word. Go to the word *related* and delete that word. Position your cursor at *of*, just after where *collection* used to be. Press F1 (Cancel/Undelete). The screen displays the Undelete Menu:

```
Undelete: 1 Restore; 2 Previous Deletion: 0
```

Press 2 to see the previously deleted word *collection*. Press 1 to restore *collection*.

Position the cursor at *information*. Press F1 and follow the prompts to restore *related*.

Shift + F8

Select Line from the Layout Menu

Line Spacing Up to this point, we have used only single spacing (or whatever your default line spacing was set to). You can change the spacing of a WordPerfect document to any number of lines. For instance, you can easily single-, double-, or even triple-space it. WordPerfect provides this ability through the Format (Shift + F8) command, which produces the Format Menu in Figure 1.11. This menu lets you change a number of characteristics about your document. Right now we are interested only in resetting the **line spacing,** so we select the Line option. Note that both the 1 and the L of this option appear in high-intensity video (or a different color with a color monitor). You can enter either of these characters to get to the Line submenu (Figure 1.12).

Now enter S for spacing and enter a new number to change the spacing: 2 for double spacing and 3 for triple spacing. Press Enter.

When you issue the spacing command, a code is embedded within the text at the cursor location to tell WordPerfect how to display and print the text. Only the text following the cursor is affected by the spacing command; if you want the entire document respaced, be sure to position the cursor at the beginning of the document before you enter the command. Any text following the code is now **re-formed.**

Any portion of a document (for example, a paragraph) can be spaced differently by moving the cursor to the desired paragraph and resetting the spacing. The rest of the document is now re-formed to the new spacing. Next position the cursor at the beginning of the next paragraph and issue a spacing command to return to the previous spacing. The document now has the first portion and the last portion with one spacing and the middle portion with another.

Use the spacing command to double-space your INPUT1 file. Position the cursor at the beginning of the file and enter the following:

Shift + F8	Gets the Format Menu (see Figure 1.11).
1	Selects the Line option (see Figure 1.12).
6	Selects Line Spacing.
2	Specifies double spacing.
Enter	Returns you to Selection prompt.
F7	Exits the menu.

Figure 1.11

The Format Menu screen appears when you enter the Format (Shift + F8) command.

```
Format

     1 - Line
              Hyphenation                     Line Spacing
              Justification                   Margins Left/Right
              Line Height                     Tab Set
              Line Numbering                  Widow/Orphan Protection

     2 - Page
              Center Page (top to bottom)     Page Numbering
              Force Odd/Even Page             Paper Size/Type
              Headers and Footers             Suppress
              Margins Top/Bottom

     3 - Document
              Display Pitch                   Redline Method
              Initial Codes/Font              Summary

     4 - Other
              Advance                         Overstrike
              Conditional End of Page         Printer Functions
              Decimal Characters              Underline Spaces/Tabs
              Language

Selection: 0
```

Figure 1.12
The Line submenu of the Format command (Shift + F8) contains the Line Spacing option for resetting the spacing of a document.

```
Format: Line

     1 - Hyphenation                          No

     2 - Hyphenation Zone - Left              10%
                            Right             4%

     3 - Justification                        Full

     4 - Line Height                          Auto

     5 - Line Numbering                       No

     6 - Line Spacing                         1

     7 - Margins - Left                       1"
                   Right                      1"

     8 - Tab Set                              Rel: -1", every 0.5"

     9 - Widow/Orphan Protection              No


Selection: 0
```

The INPUT1 file should now appear double-spaced. Save the re-formed INPUT1 file with F7 to clear the screen. If you wish to continue with this session, do not exit WordPerfect.

SPELLER

Ctrl + F2

Select Speller from the Tools Menu

The Speller option helps you proofread a document by comparing every word in the document with the words contained in the Speller dictionary of over 100,000 words. Among other things, Speller can

- Create and maintain a personal dictionary for words that are not in the main dictionary.
- Check spelling by page, block, or entire document.
- Find alternative spellings by a phonetic or pattern look-up.
- Detect double occurrences of words (for example, the the) and delete the second occurrence.
- Detect nonwords in the document.
- Count the words that were checked for spelling.

WordPerfect uses three special files to perform a spelling check:

Main dictionary (WP{WP}US.LEX) The WP{WP}US.LEX file is the main dictionary file of over 100,000 words. Because of its large size, it is on a separate disk.

Supplemental dictionary (WP{WP}US.SUP) The WP{WP}US.SUP file contains words that you add to WordPerfect's dictionary, such as words related to your specific discipline. It can be edited directly by WordPerfect. If WordPerfect cannot find a word in the main dictionary file, it also searches this file.

Speller utility (SPELL.EXE) The SPELL.EXE File lets you modify and create dictionaries by adding, correcting, or deleting words.

How you start Speller depends on your system.

Diskette-Based System On a diskette-based system, first retrieve the document to RAM. Then remove the data disk from the disk drive (usually drive B) and replace it with the Speller (dictionary) diskette. Press Ctrl + F2 (Spell) to start the spelling check. Using a mouse, select the Spell option from the Tools Menu. You must leave the Speller disk in drive B while the spelling check is in process.

Hard Disk–Based System On a hard disk–based system, first retrieve the document to RAM. Press Ctrl + F2 (Spell) to start the spelling check.

This method assumes that both dictionaries are in the same directory as your WordPerfect files. If WordPerfect is unable to find the dictionary files, it displays a message in the status line similar to the following:

```
Main dictionary not found. Enter name: C:\WP\WP{WP}US.LEX
```

If the dictionary files are in a subdirectory or another directory, you must change to that directory.

Once the Speller command has been given, the following menu appears:

```
Check: 1 Word; 2 Page; 3 Document; 4 New Sup Dictionary; 5 Look Up; 6 Count: 0
```

If you want to check only the word or page at the current cursor location, select option 1 or 2, respectively. Option 3 checks the entire document. Option 4 displays a message similar to that below:

```
Enter new main dictionary name: WP{WP}US.LEX
```

You can now enter the name of a separate main dictionary of your own creation to use in the spelling check. For instance, if you are a medical student, you might use a dictionary of medical terms.

After you have chosen the new main dictionary, WordPerfect asks if you want to use a new supplementary dictionary:

```
Enter new supplementary dictionary name: WP{WP}US.SUP
```

If you do, enter its name.

Option 5, the Look Up option, helps with words you don't know how to spell by looking for words in the main dictionary that include a particular pattern of letters. The words found are displayed at the bottom of the screen.

Option 6, the Count option, counts the words in your document without doing a spelling check and displays the number at the end of the document.

Once the proofing has started, the screen displays the message `* Please Wait *` until WordPerfect encounters a group of characters in your document that it cannot find in its dictionary. Then, your screen splits into two parts, with text from your document at the top with the suspect word highlighted in reverse video and speller information at the bottom (Figure 1.13). Let's examine the lines at the bottom of the screen:

```
Not found: 1 Skip Once; 2 Skip; 3 Add; 4 Edit; 5 Look Up; 6 Ignore Numbers: 0
```

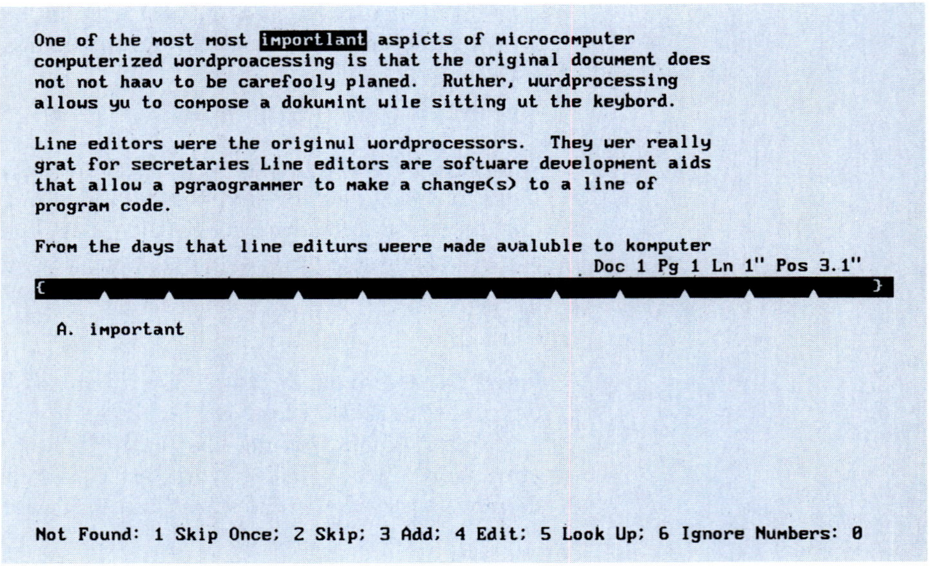

Figure 1.13
The spelling screen of WordPerfect, showing the suspect word and suggested words for the EXER1B test file.

The `Not found` message is not relevant if suggestions for replacing the suspect word are displayed. Type the letter of the correct suggestion, and any occurrence of that word in your document is corrected. If the correct spelling is not displayed on the screen but options A through X appear, press Enter to display the next screen of suggestions.

A suspect word is not always misspelled; WordPerfect may simply not have your particular word in its dictionary. In this case, you can take the Skip Once or Skip option. With the Skip option, WordPerfect asks no further questions about that word during the current proofing session. The Add option adds the word to the supplementary dictionary, and Speller then resumes proofing.

If the suspect word is indeed incorrect and WordPerfect does not have a correction in its dictionary, select the Edit option to correct the word. The cursor now appears beneath the suspect word so that you can correct the spelling manually. When you are finished, press Enter to continue proofing.

A word may be misspelled in such a way that WordPerfect cannot make any suggestions. In this case, select the Look Up option. When the message `Word Pattern: _` appears, type a pattern of characters that may resemble the correct spelling of the suspect word. If this still does not locate the correct word, consult a printed dictionary and select the Edit option to correct the word manually.

WordPerfect provides wild-card characters for the Look Up operation. You can represent a single letter, of which you are uncertain, by a question mark (?) and more than one letter by an asterisk (*). For example, if you enter the character string *p?ck*, the words *pack, peck, pick, pock,* and *puck* are displayed on the screen. The Look Up character string *pack** generates *pack, package, packaged,* and so on.

Select option 6, Ignore Numbers, if you do not want WordPerfect to stop on every character string containing a numeric digit.

One handy feature of the Speller is that it can locate double occurrences of a word (for example, the the). When a **double word** is found, the menu below is displayed:

```
Double Word: 1 2 Skip; 3 Delete 2nd; 4 Edit; 5 Disable Double Word Checking
```

Options 1 and 2 resume proofing. The Delete 2nd option deletes the second occurrence of the double word and resumes proofing.

This exercise introduces you to WordPerfect Speller. First, retrieve file EXER1B and then issue the following commands:

Ctrl + F2	Issues the Speller command.
D	(Or select the Spell command from the Tools option of the Alternate Menu) Selects the Document option. The spell-check process now begins, and WordPerfect stops at the *most most* double-word occurrence.
3	Selects option 3 to delete the second occurrence. WordPerfect now stops on the misspelled word *importlant*.
A	Accepts the correct spelling: *important*. WordPerfect corrects that error and then stops at the misspelled word *aspicts*.
A	Accepts the correct spelling: *aspects*. WordPerfect corrects that error and then stops at the word *wordproacessing*.
4	Selects the Edit option because WordPerfect can find no correct spellings for this word. Now place a space after *word*, delete the *a*, and then press F7 to return to the spell-check process.

You can now continue the spell-check. To terminate a spell-check session, issue the Cancel (F1) command. After you have finished a spell-check session or interrupted a session, WordPerfect provides a count of the words checked in the lower left-hand corner of the screen.

PRINTING THE DOCUMENT

WordPerfect lets you print a file that resides either in RAM or on disk; you are not required to save the file to disk before you can print. The Print command is evoked by Shift + F7 and displays the menu in Figure 1.14.

Shift + F7

Select Print from the File Menu

PRINTING A DOCUMENT EXERCISE

WordPerfect provides three different methods for printing a file. Two methods use the Print (Shift + F7) command, and the third method uses the List Files (F5) command. A file can be printed from RAM or from a file on disk.

This first example illustrates how a document can be loaded into RAM and then printed. Although this example illustrates a Retrieve command followed directly by a Print command, most times editing would occur between these two commands. If the EXER1B file is still on your screen, clear it with the Exit (F7) command but do not exit WordPerfect.

F10	(Or select Retrieve from the File Menu) Issues the Retrieve command.
Type `INPUT1`	Names the file to be retrieved.
Enter	Executes the command.
Shift + F7	(Or select Print from the File Menu) Issues the Print command.

Figure 1.14

The Print Menu appears when you enter the Print (Shift + F7) command.

```
Print

     1 - Full Document
     2 - Page
     3 - Document on Disk
     4 - Control Printer
     5 - Multiple Pages
     6 - View Document
     7 - Initialize Printer

Options

     S - Select Printer                      HP LaserJet IIP
     B - Binding Offset                      0"
     N - Number of Copies                    1
     U - Multiple Copies Generated by        WordPerfect
     G - Graphics Quality                    High
     T - Text Quality                        High


Selection: 0
```

F	Tells WordPerfect to print the entire document. Once the Print command has executed, you are returned to your document in RAM. Resume editing the document.

The second method also uses the Print (Shift + F7) command. The file to be printed, however, is not currently in RAM. This means that you must remember the filename that you wish to print.

Shift + F7	(Or select Print from the File Menu) Issues the Print command.
D	Selects the Document on Disk option.
Type INPUT1, Enter	Enters the name of the file to print. WordPerfect now responds with the prompt (All).
Enter	Executes the command to Print all.

The third method uses the List Files (F5) command. Highlight the file to be printed and issue the Print command. This command is useful when you can't remember the filename to print.

F5	(Or select List Files from the File Menu) Issues the List Files command.
Enter	Indicates that the default is the desired drive/directory.
INPUT1	(Highlight the INPUT1 file using the cursor keys.)
P	Issues the Print command. WordPerfect now responds with the prompt (All).
Enter	Executes the command.
F1	Exits from the List Files screen.

After selecting any one of the three print methods, you may see the message * Please Wait * at the bottom of your screen. This message is displayed while WordPerfect takes the time to copy the contents of the file to be printed to

Figure 1.15
WordPerfect preset print default.

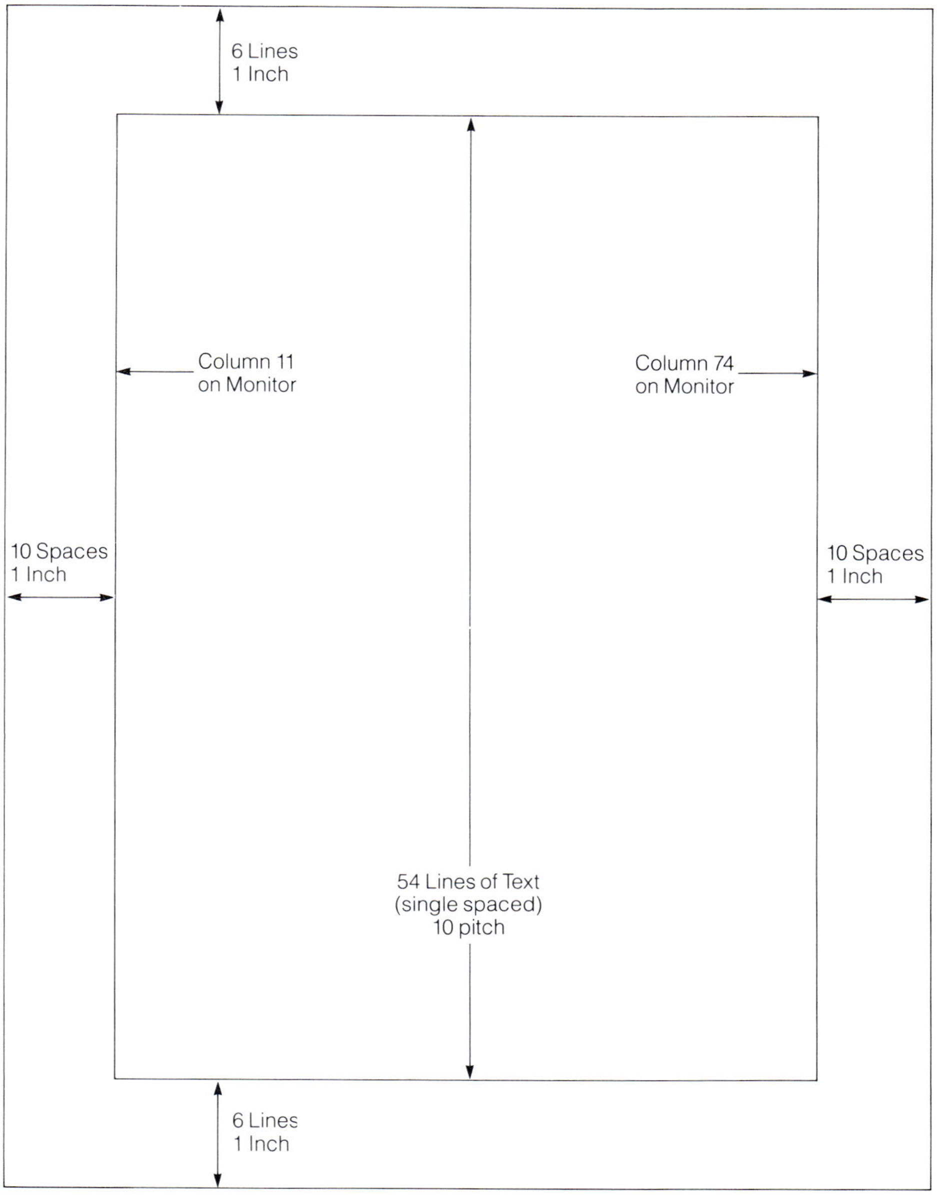

another file that it uses to actually print the document. Once this copy process is completed, you are returned to the List Files screen or to your document in RAM.

Notice that the text on your screen has a ragged right-hand margin and that the printed text has a smooth right-hand margin (**right justification**). This smooth right-hand margin is one of the print defaults of WordPerfect. We'll see later how to turn this off.

The appearance of a printed document (Figure 1.15) depends on a number of WordPerfect defaults. Some are the following: all margins are 1 inch, there are 54 printable lines of text per page, all documents are single spaced, and pica pitch (10 characters per inch) is in effect. How to change these print defaults will be discussed in a later chapter.

CHAPTER REVIEW

WordPerfect is a command-driven word processing package with many special features. These commands involve using the function keys alone or in conjunction with the Ctrl, Shift, and Alt keys. When you start WordPerfect, you first see a clear screen with a status line, which contains information about the location of the cursor and also provides an area for displaying prompts or menus to the user.

The area above this status line is called the entry window. Twenty-four line "chunks" of text that are being entered or edited are displayed in this window.

Cursor movement commands allow you to move the cursor in the document. The simple, horizontal, and vertical cursor movement commands provide you with flexibility in moving around a document.

Editing is the process of making changes to an existing document. Changes can be made in insert or typeover mode. Insert moves existing text to the right. Typeover simply replaces existing characters with new characters. Other editing commands include commands for deleting text, breaking paragraphs, and changing the line spacing.

The Speller option checks the spelling of any document file quickly against a main dictionary and a supplemental dictionary. The appropriate part of the document is displayed (with a suspect word in reverse video) so that you can see the word in context. Speller provides an easy-to-follow menu of alternative actions regarding the suspect word.

KEY TERMS AND CONCEPTS

clicking
cursor movement
deleting text
desktop publishing
dormant hard return
double-clicking
double word
dragging
dual click/release
hard page break
hard return
insert
line spacing
main dictionary
Merge feature
orphan
re-form
right justification
soft page break
soft return
Speller
status line
supplementary dictionary
text window
Thesaurus
typeover
widow
WordPerfect
word processing
word wrap

CHAPTER QUIZ

Multiple Choice

1. Which of the following is *not* used for word processing?
   a. Line editor
   b. Typewriter
   c. Dedicated word processor
   d. Microcomputer with WordPerfect
   e. All of the above
   f. None of the above

2. Which of the following statements about WordPerfect is(are) false?
   a. It was originally developed for the CP/M operating system.
   b. It allows a document to be as large or larger as the amount of available RAM.

c. It is a tremendously popular word processing package.
d. It requires that you store a document before you can print it.
e. All of the above statements are true.

3. Which of the following statements is(are) true?
   a. WordPerfect is used for entering, editing, and printing documents.
   b. WordPerfect can be used for generating synonyms.
   c. The Merge option allows you to personalize a "form" letter.
   d. All of the above

4. Select the following WordPerfect command(s) that affect one word at a time:
   a. Left Arrow
   b. − (minus key)
   c. Ctrl + Backspace
   d. Ctrl + End
   e. Ctrl + Right Arrow
   f. Ctrl + Left Arrow

5. Which of the following is *not* typically contained on the status line?
   a. Filename
   b. Page number
   c. Amount of available RAM
   d. Line location

True/False

6. Word processing can be accomplished with either a typewriter or a computer.

7. When using word processing software, you must first carefully plan how your document is going to appear.

8. WordPerfect limits document size to the amount of available RAM memory.

9. A command-driven word processing package forces you to have the menu on the screen at all times.

10. The Enter/Return key is pressed at the end of each line in a paragraph.

Answers

1. e 2. a, d 3. d 4. c, e, f 5. c 6. t 7. f 8. f 9. f
10. f

Exercises

1. Define or describe each of the following:
   a. Word wrap
   b. Hard return
   c. Status line
   d. Page break

2. Pressing the mouse button and then releasing it is called ____________.

3. The feature that automatically moves a word that will not fit on the current line down to the next line is called ____________.

4. The ____________ key is pressed only at the end of a paragraph.

5. The line at the bottom of the data-entry window is called the ____________ line.

6. ____________ movement commands move the cursor over the text.

7. The line of dashes (--------) in a document is called a(n) ____________.

8. A(n) ____________ line occurs when the first line of a new paragraph appears by itself at the bottom of the page.

9. A(n) ____________ line occurs when the last line of a paragraph appears by itself at the top of the page.

10. The WordPerfect command ____________ re-forms a paragraph so that it will fit in new margins.

11. The WordPerfect command ____________ deletes one line of text from a document.

12. The WordPerfect command ____________ changes the line spacing in a document.

13. The ____________ command is used to exit WordPerfect properly.

14. WordPerfect uses a line of ____________ to indicate a hard page break.

15. The go to a specific page command is ____________.

16. The type of menu that is activated via WordPerfect's optional menu bar is called a(n) ____________ menu.

17. This menu is activated by pressing the ____________-hand button on a mouse or by entering the command ____________ from the keyboard.

18. Holding down a button and then moving a mouse is a process known as ____________.

19. The cancel/exit keyboard command ____________ moves you back a level in a multiple-level menu structure within WordPerfect.

20. The cancel/exit keyboard command ____________ drops you out of a multiple-level menu structure and returns you to your document.

21. The Speller command ____________ finds a word by using wild-card characters.

22. The Speller command ____________ finds words that sound like the suspect word.

COMPUTER EXERCISES

1. Saving files. Use the Copy command from the List Files screen to copy the file SMLBUSNS to a file called CH1EX1. Retrieve the file called CH1EX1. Use the Save (F10) command to save the file. Print the file. Use the Exit (F7) command to clear the screen but remain in WordPerfect.

2. Canceling commands. Issue the following commands:

Shift + F8	Issues the Format command to display the Format Menu.
P	Selects the Page command to display the Page submenu.
H	Selects the Header command.
F1 (3)	Exits from this series of commands. You should now be returned to your document.

Again issue the following commands:

Shift + F8	Issues the Format command.
P	Selects the Page command.
H	Selects the Header command.
F7	Exits the menus. You should be immediately taken back to your document.

Notice that you may need more than one Cancel (F1) command to exit from a series of menu commands, but you only need one Exit (F7) command.

3. List Files. Use the List Files (F5) command screen to mark three files for printing. Remember, the asterisk is used to mark files before a command is issued. The files to be printed are INPUT1, EXER1B, and NAMES.

4. Load the file called BOOKEXER. Change the spacing to double spacing. Exit without saving the file.

5. Use the Copy command on the List Files screen to copy the contents of file EXER1 into a file called CH1EX5. Now edit the file CH1EX5. Delete the words and characters underlined below that are found in the file. Correct any spelling errors and wrong punctuation. When you have finished making changes to the text, print and save the document.

   One of the most most importlant aspicts of microcomputer computerized word proacessing is that the original document does not not haav to be carefooly planed, Ruther, wurdprocessing allows yu to compose a dokumint wile sitting ut the keybord.

   Line editors were the originul word processors. They wer really grat for secretaries Line editors are software development aids that allow a pgraogrammer to make a change(s) to a line of program code.

   From the days that line editurs weere made avaluble to komputer programers for making online chaunges to pograms, usirs huv been taking adnatage of the kompooter to perform basic editing functions such as making hay while entering data, to perform basic editing functions such moving, copying, inserting, and deleting tixt.

6. Retrieve the file CH1EX5. Position the cursor to the beginning of the file. Reset the line spacing to double spacing. Print the file. Exit (F7) without saving the file.

7. Clear the WordPerfect screen. Enter the following text and save it to a file called CH1EX7. After you have entered the text, print it. Once the file is saved, review the printout and make any necessary corrections. Save the file with these corrections and print the file again. Insert a hard page

break after the first paragraph and print the document. Use the Exit command to clear the screen, but do not save the file.

One major difference among microcomputer-based word processing packages is how they handle document size. Some packages limit the size of a document to the amount of available RAM, making 10 to 16 pages the effective maximum. In contrast, what could be referred to as virtual-file allocation word processing packages contain only about 6 to 12 pages of a document in RAM at one time, saving the remainder on disk.

A recent trend in microcomputer word processing software has been the introduction of supplementary writing aid programs such as spelling checkers, grammar checkers, and thesauri. Some word processing software comes with these options built in, whereas others make them installable at additional cost. Add-on programs compatible with many word processing packages are also available from third-party vendors.

Word processing, which allows the user to create, edit, and print documents easily, will continue to expand in importance in the workplace. Packages such as spelling and grammar checkers help the typical businessperson be more productive. Enhancements to packages make them easier to use and help increase business productivity.

8. Enter the following text and save it to a file called CH1EX8. After you have finished entering the text, print it. Review the printout and make any necessary corrections. Save the file and erase the screen. Using the List Files (F5) command, print the file.

Introduction to Database

The term "database" evokes different images for different people, but the concept is not technical. It is as easy to envision as a filing cabinet in an office. The filing cabinet and its contents are the database. Anytime that the pieces of paper pertaining to a specific function, such as a Customer Address file in the filing cabinet, are rearranged in a meaningful order (for example, alphabetically by last name), some sort of data management function has been performed.

Thus, the average office filing cabinet is a database. It doesn't do anything; it just holds information. Whenever a drawer of the filing cabinet is opened to find a record (for example, the record for the customer Smith), the database must be searched. This process of searching the database is actually a way to manage it. Databases are typically stored in some order, usually alphabetically by last name, city, or region. This provides for easier database management.

Before proceeding further, some key terms, which pertain to the topic of database, must be defined. A database is the same type of entity as the file cabinet in an office. The database holds information that is related to a specific type of application. In this context, it is viewed to be synonymous with a file.

A record relates to the "entity" that contains information about a specific business "happening" or transaction in the database. There are typically many records in a database. Each record holds information about a business transaction.

One or more fields are used to comprise a record. It is the concept of the field that allows information to be stored about a transaction or business event. Each field is capable of holding information about one part of the event. For example, the LASTNAME field holds information about the last name of the individual who created the transaction.

The information from one or more fields of a record are used to form a key. A key is composed of one or more fields and is used to identify records in a file. The record key is usually used to make the process of retrieving records from a file easier. The key is also important for placing a file in order. Many times the records in a file will be placed in key order.

A file uses a number of different keys. The primary key is the unique identifier for each record and in a database is the physical record number of this record. If this record occupies the fifth-record location, it has the record number 5. This 5 is also the primary key for this record.

The other type of key is the secondary key. Data are usually arranged within a file in some type of order based on the contents of one or more fields known as the secondary key. For example, a file might be arranged in order by the Social Security field, or it might be placed in order by name. You are typically not limited to the number of keys that you wish to develop for an application.

9. Enter the following text and save it to a file called CH1EX9. After you have finished entering the text, print it. Review the printout, make any necessary corrections, and print the changed file.

Introduction to the Computer

The computer has had a greater impact on our society than any other device intended in the second half of the twentieth century. As late as the mid-1970s, relatively few people used computers. For many people today, computers are as much a part of a daily life as automobiles, telephones, and electric lights.

In business, computers track and process inventory, accounts receivable, accounts payable, and payroll. They are used in education to schedule classes, train students, and record grades. In the medical professions, computers diagnose and monitor patients. Scientists use computers to analyze our solar system, forecast weather patterns, and conduct experiments.

Of all the computer types, the microcomputer has been most helpful in improving our ability to control information and solve problems. The microcomputer is used alike by Fortune 500 companies and small businesses to file information, produce documents and correspondence, and perform time-consuming financial calculations and projections. It has boosted the productivity of workers at all organizational levels, from the mail room to the board room. Because it has a tireless capacity to perform practice exercises and simulations, the microcomputer is also an excellent teaching tool for primary- and secondary-school students.

10. Enter the following letter. Save the file to disk to a file called CH1EX10.

The Basket Tree
Box 1049
Bloomington, IL 61701

August 23, 1992

Hal Jamieson
Heritage Enterprises
1059 S. Main Street
Normal, IL 61761

Dear Mr. Jamieson, ↓ 2

This letter is to confirm our agreement for the lease of the property at 12 Normandy Village in Normal, Illinois, beginning October 1. The price that we agreed on Thursday is satisfactory. Per our agreement, if a year's rent is paid by February 15, I can take a 10 percent deduction against the total rent. ↓ 2

On September 1, I will take possession of the property to prepare it for occupancy, without incurring any additional rental obligation.

↓ 2

I understand that any changes in the color scheme or carpeting are my financial responsibility. I will also be responsible for heating, cooling, and water costs, but Heritage Enterprises will have R40-rated insulation installed in the ceiling no later than November 1 of this year.

↓ 2

I look forward to being at Normandy Village for several years.

↓ 2

Sincerely yours,

↓ 4

Jim
The Basket Tree

11. Use the Copy command on the List Files screen to copy the contents of file SMLBUSNS into a file called CH1EX11. Now edit the file called CH1EX11. The contents of the new file CH1EX11 appear below. Locate any errors and misspellings and correct them here in the text. Then edit the file called CH1EX11 using WordPerfect and correct the errors in the file. When you have finished making changes to the text, save the file back to disk and print it.

Micro Computers for Small Business

An individul startin a smull business does knot typically have an immediate need for a micro computer. However, sooner or later an entrepeneur will, bekause of increasd busness, accounting needs, or to enable better planing seriously konsider purchasing a mikro computer system.

A number of record keeping/processing tasks that a computer can perform well that might prompt an individual to consider purchasing a computer include: accounting applications (accounts receivable, akounts payable, genral leger, inventry, and payroll), wurd processing, data base management, and spreadsheets.

Iff won or more of the above applications is a likely candidate for placing on a micro computer, you can typically automate that application without exxtremely high costs. There are a wide number of pakages pakages that have been developed for solving any of the above applikations. You shuld try to find a package that solves your specific prooblem before you consider iring a consultant to right a program. A good application program will most at most $500. To hire a consooltant to write a package specifically for your business might cost in excess of $10,000.

Historikally, the aqqounting applications were handled by a public accountant. Today, however, more and more public accounting firms are encouraging their klients to porchase a computer system system. Accounting firms are finding that it is costing too much of their time, and resulting in inflated billings to clients, if their clients rely on an accounting firm to keep the buks.

Muny accounting pakages are marketed in modules. That is, there is a separate accounts receivable module, a separate accounts pyable module and so forth. Each of these can be purchased separately. In the last few yers, a number of integrated accounting packages have been placed on the market that are able to handle a number of these applikations all at once and also can be be purchased for a very very low cost. One such package is DAC Easy Accounting which retails for $69. It operates on IBM and IBM compatible computers and handls all accounting applications exept payroll. It was designed specifically with small busiensses in mind.

A person owning a small business does not have to computerize all accounting aplications at one time. It might be wise to automate the acounts recievable process first and then proseed with another application. If you decide to automate your accounting prosedures using a system of independent modules, however, make sertain that the first package (module) that you purchase is capable of passing data to subsequent applications software. Don't make the mistake of buying one package from one vendor and another package from anuther vendor. You may end up having to reenter large amounts of data simply because the packages are not able to communicate with each other and share data.

2

MORE ON SAVING, PRINTING, AND EDITING

CHAPTER OBJECTIVES

After completing this chapter, you should be able to

- **Use effective file backup techniques**
- **Use the various print options that are available in the Print Options Menu**
- **Use the Margin, Tab, Indent, and Center commands**
- **Use the Block command together with the Boldface, Underline, Center, Redline and Strikeout, Cut, and Copy commands**
- **Use the Block command in other ways**
- **Use the Move command**
- **Use the Search and Replace commands**
- **Use the dual document feature**

This chapter continues the discussion of saving files and introduces the backup feature of WordPerfect. It also covers additional printing options and various special text-entry and editing problems such as tab and margin settings and the powerful Block, Search, and Replace commands.

SAVING AND BACKING UP YOUR FILES

As explained in Chapter 1, WordPerfect lets you save a file at any time while you are working on it with the Save (F10) command. You should get into the habit of saving the file on which you are working periodically—say, every 10 or 15 minutes or after entering about two pages of text. Doing so will prevent accidental loss of your work if a sudden power failure wipes out everything not already safely saved to disk.

When you exit WordPerfect with the Exit (F7) command, you can either save the work you have just done or discard it. If you save it under its existing filename, you will destroy the previous version of the file. If you discard your current work, the previous version of the file will not be altered because, when you retrieve a working file, WordPerfect copies that file into a **temporary file.** This is the file on which you work, rather than on the original. If there is not enough room in RAM for the temporary file, WordPerfect creates an overflow file called {WP}.TV1 on the WordPerfect disk to hold the extra text. When you next save the document, the temporary file becomes permanent, replacing the old file on disk, if there was one.

BACKUP FEATURE OF WORDPERFECT

For further file security, besides saving files frequently, you can use WordPerfect's automatic backup feature. This feature is not one of WordPerfect's default options, so if you want to use it you must specifically activate this feature. Instructions on how to do this are included at the beginning of the Command Summary at the end of these WordPerfect chapters. Once you have installed the backup feature as one of your program defaults, it will work automatically whenever you use WordPerfect.

The backup feature of WordPerfect automatically creates backup copies of your files and names these files with the backup filename extension .BK!. The content of the **backup file** is identical to the content of your document before the last time you executed either Save command. For instance, if you open an existing file called REPORT, edit it, save REPORT, and exit WordPerfect, your data disk will contain two files: REPORT.BK! will be the file as it was in the last generation, before this session of editing; REPORT will be the most current version of the file. If there was already a REPORT.BK! file, that version is deleted.

If you decide you want to return to the backup file REPORT.BK!, activate it with the Retrieve command, as you would any other file. Once you have retrieved REPORT.BK!, save it under a new name without the .BK! extension. Do not save it under the name REPORT unless you want the contents of REPORT.BK! to replace the contents of the existing REPORT file.

Even though WordPerfect automatically provides a backup, you should periodically copy important files to another disk. This protects you when you have one of those days when absolutely nothing goes right and you destroy not only your original but also the backup copy in a moment of panic.

HINTS/HAZARDS

Suppose you have been working on a file called REPORT for several sessions. In the current session, you want to discard the current on-screen version of the file. To do this, simply exit (F7) without saving. Then retrieve REPORT as it was as of your last Save command.

Suppose you have the backup feature on and you have been working on REPORT for several sessions. This time when you retrieve REPORT, you discover that you accidentally did something just before your last save that ruined the current version of REPORT. Don't panic. At this point, the REPORT file is useless, but the REPORT.BK! file is still good. Exit REPORT with F7, *without* saving the file, because if you save REPORT at this time you will be destroying the good version of REPORT.BK!. Once you have exited REPORT, retrieve REPORT.BK!, save it under a new name, and proceed to use the newly named file.

When you check to make certain that a disk has enough room for a document, remember that you are possibly dealing with *three* disk files. There must be enough room on the disk for the original file, the temporary file overflow (if needed), and the backup file.

DISK-FULL ERRORS

The message `Disk full - Strike any key to continue` may appear when you try to save a file, especially if you haven't checked the status of your data diskette lately. It means there is not enough disk space to save the file. Don't panic. Press any key to cancel the command. Then use the List Files (F5) command to look at your disk directory. See whether you can delete any unwanted files from the disk to make room for the save (.BK! files are likely candidates). After deleting some files, try the save again.

Unless your document is extremely large, it resides completely in RAM. In this case, you can also remove your current data disk, replace it with any formatted disk that has enough room for the file, and save to that disk. If you are trying to save to a hard disk that is full, save instead to a diskette in one of the floppy drives.

If a disk-full message appears when you are printing, it means you are trying to print a file from the screen that is too long to be printed this way. In this case, you must print the file using the Printer Control or List Files Menus.

PRINTING FILES

Shift + F7

Select Print from File Menu

You may want your output printed on good single-sheet rag bond paper, or you may not want to print the complete document, or you may want to print only "this" page. The Print (Shift + F7) command lets you give complete printing instructions. It produces the menu in Figure 2.1.

When WordPerfect prints a file, the margins on the paper will be as indicated when you were editing the file. Thus, WordPerfect automatically gives you a 1-inch left-hand margin on the printed output. This margin can be expanded simply by positioning the paper farther to the left in the printer.

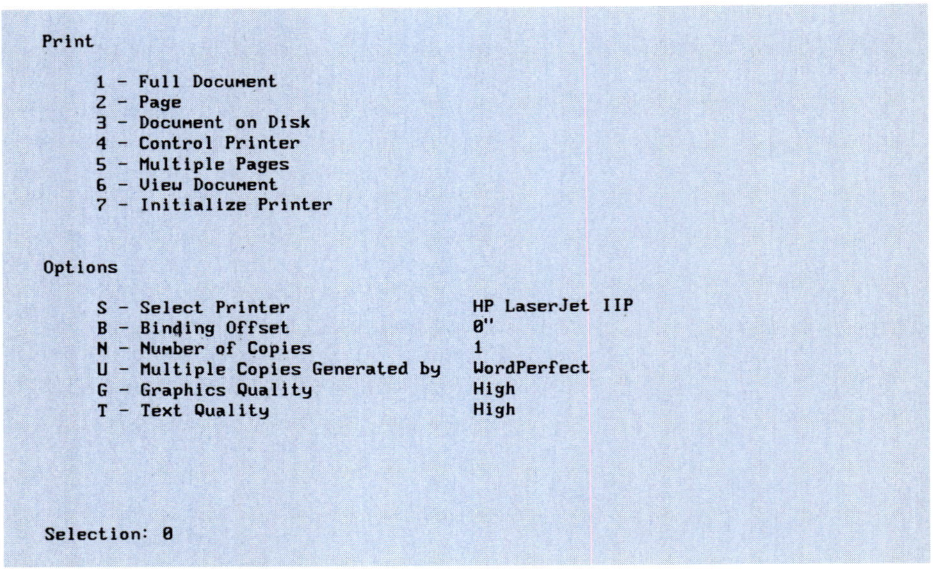

Figure 2.1
The Print Menu displayed on your screen when the Print (Shift + F7) command is issued.

PRINT PORTION OF THE PRINT MENU

NOTE WordPerfect usually provides the zero (0) entry of a menu as the default. If you press Enter, you are usually returned to the document or to a higher-order menu.

1 Full Document This "quick and dirty" method prints the entire document in RAM, using whatever print options you have defined.

2 Page This option prints only the page on which the cursor resides.

3 Document on Disk This option lets you print a file that resides on disk. After you enter the filename, press Enter. To print the entire file, press Enter. To print selected pages, use the following format:

N	Prints only page N.
N,M	Prints only pages N and M.
N-	Prints the file beginning at page N.
N-M	Prints pages N through M of the file.
-M	Prints the document through page M.

4 Control Printer Figure 2.2 displays this menu. From this menu, you can cancel, rush, or display print jobs and see what page is currently being printed.

1 Cancel Job(s) After choosing this option, enter the number of the print job that you wish to cancel. If you wish to cancel all print jobs, press *. Then press Y.

2 Rush Job This lets you change the priority of a document in the print-job list. You must first submit the job using either option 1 or 3 of the Print Menu (print Full Document or Document on Disk). Then select the Control Printer option and the Rush Job option. Enter the number of the print job that you want to rush.

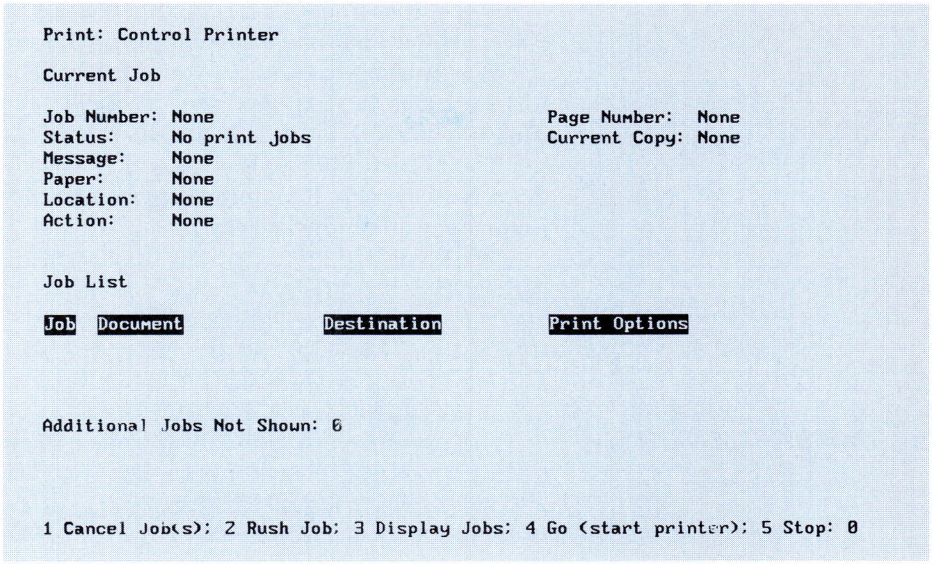

Figure 2.2
The Control Printer Menu.

WordPerfect now asks when you wish to print this job. If you press N, it will be printed after the current document. If you press Y, the interrupted job continues printing until the top of the next page is reached. The new document is then printed. After the rushed document is finished, the interrupted job resumes.

3 Display Jobs This lists the jobs that have been submitted for printing.

4 Go (start printer) This restarts printing if it has been interrupted.

5 Stop This lets you stop printing if a paper jam or other hardware problem occurs.

5 Multiple Pages This option lets you specify a range of pages to print from the document residing in RAM. You use the same conventions as those indicated in the Document on Disk option.

6 View Document This option lets you preview how a document will appear on the printed page without having to actually print. The document is displayed to the screen exactly as it will appear on the printed page. The quality of your video hardware is the only limit on the quality of this display. If your monitor does not display graphics, you cannot use this command.

7 Initialize Printer Use this option to load special sets of characters, or fonts, for the printer to use in printing a document.

OPTIONS PORTION OF THE PRINT MENU

The Options portion of the Print Menu (see Figure 2.1) lets you display status information about the selected printer or change selected print features.

Sometimes one microcomputer is linked to several different printers. The Select Printer option lets you choose which printer is currently active.

The Binding option lets you tell WordPerfect how much space you want text shifted to the right and the left on a page for binding on two-sided copies. This allows room for punched holes or other binding requirements.

The Number of Copies option lets you indicate how many copies of each document to print. If a multiple-page document is to be printed, the entire document is printed for each copy.

The remaining two options display self-explanatory menus that provide control over the quality of text and graphics.

HINTS/HAZARDS

When printing a document from a diskette, never remove the diskette from the drive. You cannot do this because WordPerfect creates a temporary file on disk that contains a copy of the file being printed. It is this temporary file that is accessed by WordPerfect during the print process.

SPECIAL TEXT-ENTRY COMMANDS

This section introduces several special-effects commands that are used in WordPerfect. To get the most benefit from the following discussion of special-effects text-entry commands, start WordPerfect or, if WordPerfect is running, clear the screen using the Exit command. After you have finished with the special text-command tutorial, you should have a screen that appears like that depicted in Figure 2.3.

Shift + F6

Select Align from the Layout Menu and Then Select Center

Center Command WordPerfect automatically centers text via the **Center** (Shift + F6) **command.** Once this command is entered, the cursor moves to the middle of the line, and you enter the text that you wish to have centered. When you have finished entering this text, press Enter to go to the next line and terminate centering.

F6

Select Appearance from the Font Option and Then Select Bold

Boldface Command The **Boldface** (F6) **command** results in dark, heavy print. The Boldface command is a toggle: The first command turns on the boldface feature, and the second turns it off. The characters to the right of the Pos indicator appear in high-intensity video when boldface is on.

F8

Select Appearance from the Font Option and Then Select Underline

Underline Command The **Underline** (F8) **command** underlines words. The Underline command is a toggle: The first command turns on the underline feature, and the second turns it off. Monitors vary in how they show underlining on the screen. A monochrome monitor displays the characters to the right of the Pos indicator as underlined when this option is on, but a color monitor may show highlighted text.

Alt + F6

Select Align from the Layout Menu and Then Select Flush Right

Flush Right The **Flush Right** (Alt + F6) **command** aligns text against the right-hand margin. It can be used to position dates, headings, and other data against the right margin. The Flush Right command, when used, jumps the cursor to the right-hand margin. Then type the text and press Enter when you are finished.

Shift + F5

Select the Date Option from the Tools Menu

Date Command The **Date** (Shift + F5) **command** accesses the system date information that has been stored by DOS during the boot process and changes

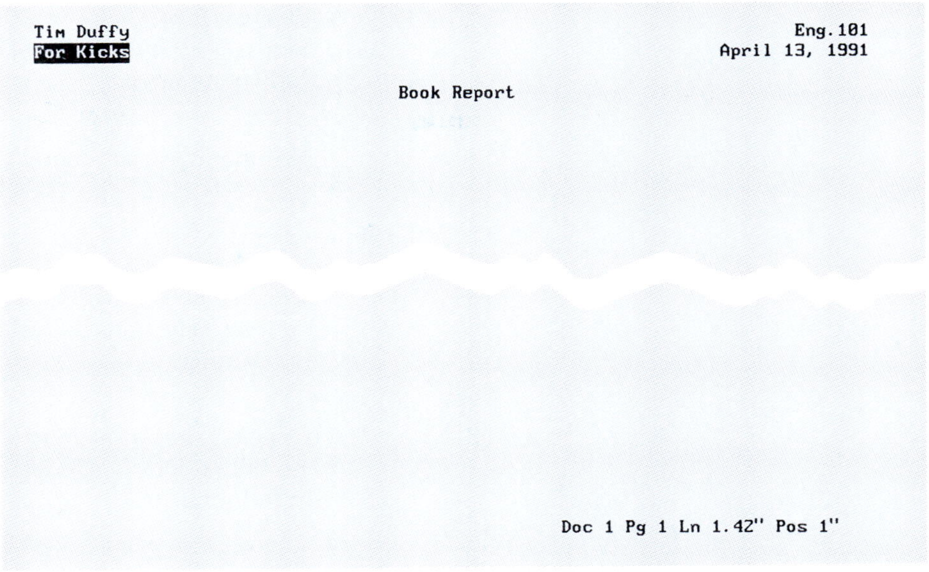

Figure 2.3
The screen that is generated via the special text tutorial.

it so that it is presented in a format such as January 7, 1992. The Date command displays these options:

```
1 Date Text; 2 Date Code; 3 Date Format
```

Option 1, Date Text, inserts the date at the cursor location. Option 2, Date Code, lets you "date stamp" a document. Then, no matter when you print or retrieve the document, the current date and time will be inserted. For example, if you type a document on January 7, 1992, and print it two days later, the printout will be dated January 9, 1992.

The Date Format option lets you build your own date format scheme, by following a special menu of choices.

If your text does not appear the way you want it in your document, use the **Reveal Codes** (Alt + F3) **command.** Centering codes are represented by [Center], boldface codes are [BOLD] and [bold], and underline codes are [UND] and [und]. Use Del or Backspace to delete the beginning or ending code to get rid of paired codes. Once one code of a paired code (for example, [BOLD] [bold]) is deleted, the text on your screen returns to normal.

You can also delete codes with other edit commands.

This hands-on WordPerfect exercise introduces a number of special-effects text-related commands.

1. Enter your name in boldface. Position your cursor to the beginning of the first line on a clear screen.

F6	(Or select the Appearance option of the Font option and then select the Boldface command) Turns on boldface.

   Type your name

F6	(Or select the Appearance option of the Font option and then select the Boldface command) Turns off boldface.

2. Right-justify the name of the class (Eng. 101).

Alt + F6	(Or select the Align option from the Layout Menu and then select the Flush Right command) Issues the Flush Right command.
Type `Eng. 101`	
Enter	Terminates the command.

3. Enter the name of the book (*For Kicks*) in underlined format.

F8	(Or select the Appearance option from the Font option and then select the Underline command) Turns on underlining.
Type `For Kicks`	
F8	(Or select the Appearance option from the Font option and then select the Underline command) Turns off underlining.

4. Right-justify today's date as text within the document.

Alt + F6	(Or select the Align option from the Layout Menu and then select the Flush Right command) Issues the Flush Right command.
Shift + F5	(Or select the Date Text option from the Tools Menu) Issues the Date command to embed text.
T	Selects the Date Text option.
Enter	Positions cursor to the next line.

5. Right-justify today's date as a code within the document.

Alt + F6	(Or select the Align option from the Layout Menu and then select the Flush Right command) Issues the Flush Right command.
Shift + F5	(Or select the Date Code option from the Tools Menu) Issues the Date command to embed text.
C	Selects the Date Code option.
Enter	Positions cursor to the next line.

6. Boldface and center the report title (*Book Report*).

Shift + F6	(Or select the Align option from the Layout Menu and then select the Center command) Issues the Center command.
F6	(Or select the Appearance option from the Font option and then select the Boldface command) Turns on boldface.
Type `Book Report`	
F6	(Or select the Appearance option from the Font option and then select the Boldface command) Turns off boldface.
Enter	Positions cursor to the next line.

Figure 2.4
The codes used by WordPerfect for the sample document.

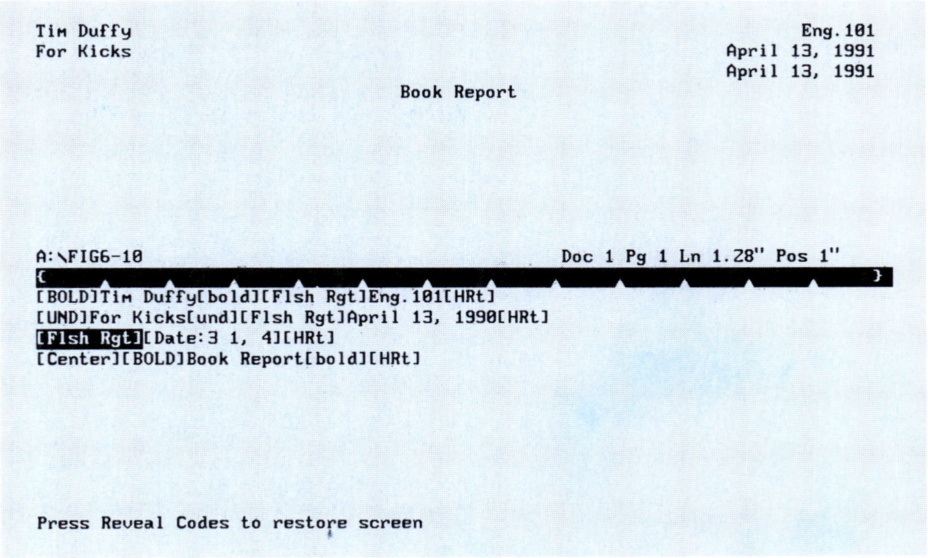

Let's now examine the effects of the various commands that we've entered in this sample document. Issue a Reveal Codes (Alt + F3) command and then issue several Up Arrow commands to see a display like that depicted in Figure 2.4. Notice that right-justified text is preceded by a [Flsh Rgt] code. Notice also that one of the April 13, 1991, dates appears as text, but the other date appears as the code [Date:3 1, 4]. The date April 13, 1991, will always appear in this document. The date code, however, will always put the current date (from DOS) in the document at that location. Notice also that the centered text uses a [Center] code and that triangles appear in the bar beneath the document status line. Each triangle represents a tab stop.

Issue Reveal Codes (Alt + F3) to return to the document.

MARGIN COMMANDS

The Line option of the WordPerfect Format (Shift + F8) command lets you reset the right- and left-hand margins. Once the Line Menu is displayed on the screen, choose the **Margin command.** The defaults are 1-inch right- and left-hand margins. If you wish to change the margins, you must indicate the new margin size in tenths of an inch. For example, if you wish to change the left-hand margin to 1½ inches, you would enter a margin size of 1.5. If you want to change one margin (for example, the right margin) but not the other, press Enter for the margin you do not wish to change.

The new margins that you set begin at the cursor location; if the cursor is not at the beginning of a line, a [Hrt] is inserted in the text by WordPerfect to place the margins at the beginning of a line.

Margins remain in effect until new ones are entered. To change the margins for another part of your document, position the cursor at the beginning of a new line and repeat the process. Because embedded codes are used, various margins can be used in different parts of the document without interfering with each other.

Retrieve the file called FRANCIS from your student data disk. Your screen should appear like that depicted in Figure 2.5. You are to change the left-hand

Figure 2.5
The FRANCIS file.

```
Dick Francis is the author of almost thirty mystery novels dealing
with all aspects of the racing industry.  He is an acknowledged
expert in this particular field based on many years of steeple
chase horse racing in England.  In his book, For Kicks, the main
character, Daniel Roke is a stud farm owner from Australia who is
persuaded to undertake an assignment in England to investigate a
horse-doping scandal.  He is persuaded to undertake this task by
the Earl of October after the original investigator was brutally
murdered.

Francis is known for the imagery and excitement that is evoked from
the reader by his writing.  A sample follows:

"In spite of the cold, I was sweating.  Dear heavens, I thought,
there was so much adrenalin pouring into my bloodstream as into the
horse's; and I realized that from the time Wilson started his
methodical walk around the track, I had been able to hear my own
heart thudding.

"Jud Wilson yelled at Kandersteg so close to my ear that it felt
like a blow.  The whip cracked...he was standing within feet of my
head.  The whip cracked again.  Jud shouted at the horse, stamping
his boot on the ground in encouragement.  He was a yard away,
perhaps, with his eyes on the horse.  He had only to turn his head.
A:\FRANCIS                                     Doc 1 Pg 1 Ln 1" Pos 1"
```

margin to 2 inches and the right-hand margin to 1.5 inches. Be certain that you position the cursor to the beginning of the file before you issue the following instructions:

Shift + F8	Issues the Format command.
L	(Or select the Line option from the Layout Menu) Selects the Line submenu.
M	Selects the Margin command.
2, Enter	Enters the left-hand margin.
1.5, Enter	Enters the right-hand margin.
F7 (2)	Exits the Format Menu and returns to the document.

Your screen should now appear like that depicted in Figure 2.6. Use the Reveal Codes command, find the [L/RMar:2",1.5"] code, and delete it.

F4

Select the Align Option of the Layout Menu and Then Select Indent

INDENT

From time to time, you might want to reset the left-hand margin for only a single paragraph of text. For example, it is a convention to indent a long quote five spaces into the document from the left-hand margin. This is accomplished by using the Left Indent (F4) command. The **Left Indent command** resets the left-hand margin to the next tab stop. The default tab stops occur every five spaces (0.5 inches) and operate like those on a typewriter. You have already used tabs in indenting the first line of a paragraph.

You are now going to indent the paragraph that starts with "In spite of the cold, ..." Make certain that you position your cursor to the beginning of that line before you issue the following commands.

F4	(Or select the Align option of the Layout Menu and then select the Indent command) Issues the Indent command.

Figure 2.6
The FRANCIS file with changed margins.

```
Dick Francis is the author of almost thirty mystery
novels dealing with all aspects of the racing
industry.  He is an acknowledged expert in this
particular field based on many years of steeple
chase horse racing in England.  In his book, For
Kicks, the main character, Daniel Roke is a stud
farm owner from Australia who is persuaded to
undertake an assignment in England to investigate a
horse-doping scandal.  He is persuaded to undertake
this task by the Earl of October after the original
investigator was brutally murdered.

Francis is known for the imagery and excitement
that is evoked from the reader by his writing.  A
sample follows:

"In spite of the cold, I was sweating.  Dear
heavens, I thought, there was so much adrenalin
pouring into my bloodstream as into the horse's;
and I realized that from the time Wilson started
his methodical walk around the track, I had been
able to hear my own heart thudding.

"Jud Wilson yelled at Kandersteg so close to my ear
A:\FRANCIS                                      Doc 1 Pg 1 Ln 1.17" Pos 2"
```

Figure 2.7
The FRANCIS file after the indent command is issued.

```
Dick Francis is the author of almost thirty mystery novels dealing
with all aspects of the racing industry.  He is an acknowledged
expert in this particular field based on many years of steeple
chase horse racing in England.  In his book, For Kicks, the main
character, Daniel Roke is a stud farm owner from Australia who is
persuaded to undertake an assignment in England to investigate a
horse-doping scandal.  He is persuaded to undertake this task by
the Earl of October after the original investigator was brutally
murdered.

Francis is known for the imagery and excitement that is evoked from
the reader by his writing.  A sample follows:

      "In spite of the cold, I was sweating.  Dear heavens, I
      thought, there was so much adrenalin pouring into my
      bloodstream as into the horse's; and I realized that from the
      time Wilson started his methodical walk around the track, I
      had been able to hear my own heart thudding.

"Jud Wilson yelled at Kandersteg so close to my ear that it felt
like a blow.  The whip cracked...he was standing within feet of my
head.  The whip cracked again.  Jud shouted at the horse, stamping
his boot on the ground in encouragement.  He was a yard away,
perhaps, with his eyes on the horse.  He had only to turn his head.
A:\FRANCIS                                  Doc 1 Pg 1 Ln 3.17" Pos 1.5"
```

Your document should now appear like that depicted in Figure 2.7. You can also indent a paragraph from both the left and right with the **L/R Indent** (Shift + F4) **command.**

TABS AND RESETTING TABS

Shift + F8

Select Layout from the Menu

The **tab stops** in WordPerfect work the same as tabs on a typewriter. Pressing the Tab key moves the cursor from one tab stop to the next and puts a [Tab] code in your document.

You can see your current tab settings with the Reveal Codes command. Each triangle beneath the status line represents a tab stop.

Figure 2.8
The Tabs Menu that appears at the bottom of your screen.

```
L.....L.....L.....L.....L.....L.....L.....L.....L.....L.....L.....L.....L.....L
|     ^     |     ^     |     ^     |     ^     |     ^     |     ^     |     ^
0"          +1"         +2"         +3"         +4"         +5"         +6"
Delete EOL (clear tabs); Enter Number (set tab); Del (clear tab);
Type; Left; Center; Right; Decimal; .= Dot Leader; Press Exit when done.
```

You can also see or change tab settings with the Format (Shift + F8) command. At the Format Menu, press 1 for Line, then 8 for Tabs. (If you are using a mouse, select the Line option from the Layout Menu.) A screen like that in Figure 2.8 now appears on your screen. Each L represents one tab stop on the ruler line, and as you can see, there is one tab stop every half-inch. The menu takes up five lines at the bottom of your screen. Issue the Exit (F7) command when all changes are finished.

To delete all tab stops, press Ctrl + End. This command is usually executed before the new tab stops are entered. Once the Delete to End-of-Line command has been issued, only periods remain on the ruler line. You can now press F7 (Exit) to return to your document, or you can create new tab stops. To create new tabs, simply move the cursor to the appropriate location and type *t* or *l* (Tab). An alternative method involves entering the tab location in inches from the keyboard (for example, 2.5 and 4).

HINTS/HAZARDS

When you incorporate lists in a columnar format within a document, it is to your benefit to incorporate such lists using tab stops. This provides much more flexibility if you wish to change margin settings or switch the print font (a topic covered later in the text). If you have not used tabs and make significant changes to a document, it may be easier to simply reenter that portion of the document rather than trying to fix it at the keyboard by inserting spaces.

Columns of numbers can be aligned with the **Tab Align** (Ctrl + F6) **command.** This command lines up text or numbers vertically on a character such as a decimal point. To change the **alignment character,** issue the Format (Shift + F8) command, take the Other option (4), select the Decimal/Align Character option (Figure 2.9), and enter the new character.

The decimal point (period) is the default alignment character (therefore, this command is not needed if you wish to align numbers that contain decimal fractions). You can change this character as often as you wish. For example, if you are dealing with whole numbers and wish to align positive numbers with negative numbers that are contained in parentheses, your **decimal align character** would be the right parenthesis. This allows the right parenthesis to appear to the right of any numbers, as in the example below:

```
65,000
 7,000
  (500)
99,567
```

Figure 2.9
The Format/Other/Decimal command allows you to change the decimal align character to fit your particular application.

```
Format: Other

     1 - Advance

     2 - Conditional End of Page

     3 - Decimal/Align Character       .
         Thousands' Separator          ,

     4 - Language                      US

     5 - Overstrike

     6 - Printer Functions

     7 - Underline - Spaces            Yes
                     Tabs              No

     8 - Border Options



Selection: 0
```

To realign the previous two-column example, each line has to be entered again: Enter the right-hand information at the first tab. Move the cursor to the second tab by pressing Ctrl + F6 (Tab Align), and entering the numeric text.

```
Men's     125.00
Women's    35.00
Boy's       5.00
Sports    123.50
```

Notice that the numbers align on the decimal point and that `Align char=.` appears on your screen. Typed text moves to the left until the alignment character is entered [a period (.) in this case] or until Tab, Tab Align, or Enter is pressed. Text typed after the Tab Align character is inserted normally.

You may find that you have difficulty in remembering to enter the Tab Align (Ctrl + F6) command to get the decimal tab stop to work properly. This is a relatively common problem because WordPerfect is using a text tab stop as a decimal tab only when the special command Tab Align is used. You can get around this problem by changing the L of a tab stop on the tab stop ruler line to a D. The D tells WordPerfect that this tab stop is to function as a decimal tab rather than as a text tab. Now, when you are entering numeric text, all that is required is to press Tab, and the `Align char=.` message appears at the bottom of the screen when the tab hits this decimal align tab.

You can use the following special characters on a tab stop line to determine how a tab stop operates:

- **L** Left-justifies at this tab stop.
- **C** Centers text at this tab stop.
- **R** Right-justifies text at this tab stop.
- **D** Issues a Tab Align command to justify this text according to the alignment character.
- 5.1 **T** The Type option of the Tab Stop Menu lets you decide what type of tab stop (absolute or relative to the left margin) a tab should be. The default is the relative tab stop (it is therefore the type most frequently desired by users). This means that, if you change the

Figure 2.10
A document containing dot leaders.

```
                       Campground Information

Color Map Section. . . . . . . . . . . . . . . . . . . . . . . . . 4
      USA. . . . . . . . . . . . . . . . . . . . . . . . . . . . 4-5
      Arkansas . . . . . . . . . . . . . . . . . . . . . . . . . . 7
      Illinois . . . . . . . . . . . . . . . . . . . . . . . . 20-21
      Texas. . . . . . . . . . . . . . . . . . . . . . . . . . 56-57
      Wyoming. . . . . . . . . . . . . . . . . . . . . . . . . . .63
RV Troubleshooting Charts. . . . . . . . . . . . . . . . . . . . .79
      Brakes . . . . . . . . . . . . . . . . . . . . . . . . . . .81
      Engines. . . . . . . . . . . . . . . . . . . . . . . . . . .85
      Roof Air-Conditioning Systems. . . . . . . . . . . . . . . .89
      Furnaces . . . . . . . . . . . . . . . . . . . . . . . . . .95
Rules of the Road. . . . . . . . . . . . . . . . . . . . . . . . 100
      Turnpike and Tollway Information . . . . . . . . . . . . . 103
      Weather Report . . . . . . . . . . . . . . . . . . . . . . 105
Following History's Footsteps. . . . . . . . . . . . . . . . . . 107
Advertisers' Index . . . . . . . . . . . . . . . . . . . . . . . 121
Manufacturers' Tours . . . . . . . . . . . . . . . . . . . . . . 125
Campgrounds. . . . . . . . . . . . . . . . . . . . . . . . . . . 129
      Arkansas . . . . . . . . . . . . . . . . . . . . . . . . 205-218
      Illinois . . . . . . . . . . . . . . . . . . . . . . . . 572-609
      Texas. . . . . . . . . . . . . . . . . . . . . . . . . 1206-1290
      Wyoming. . . . . . . . . . . . . . . . . . . . . . . . 1452-1469
Align char = .                          Doc 1 Pg 1 Ln 4.83" Pos 7"
```

5.1

left-hand margin, tab stops will still be at the same position relative to the new margin setting.

WordPerfect also lets you fill in blank areas between tab stops with periods called **dot leaders** (Figure 2.10). Using any tab stop, you can create a dot leader by first positioning the cursor to the desired location on the Tab Stop Menu and entering a period following the character for the desired type of tab.

The following exercise allows you to create the document depicted in Figure 2.10. If necessary, use the Exit (F7) command to clear the screen.

1. Enter the title:

Shift + F6	(Or select the Align option of the Layout Menu and then select the Center command) Issues the Center command.
Type `Campground Information`	
Enter (2)	Inserts a blank line.

2. Create the tab stops:

Shift + F8	Issues the Format command.
L	(Or select the Line option of the Layout Menu) Selects the Line submenu.
T	Selects the Tab command.
Ctrl + End	Deletes the tab stops.
.5	(Or position the cursor to the .5-inch position on the tab line)
L	Defines a left-justified tab stop.
6	(Or position the cursor to the 6-inch position on the tab line)
.	Establishes a dot leader.
D	Defines a decimal tab stop.
F7 (2)	Exits the Tab Stop Menu and returns to the document.

Figure 2.11

The tab line incorporated in the WordPerfect screen.

```
Color Map Section. . . . . . . . . . . . . . . . . . . . . . . . . 4
        USA. . . . . . . . . . . . . . . . . . . . . . . . . . . 4-5
        Arkansas . . . . . . . . . . . . . . . . . . . . . . . . . 7
        Illinois . . . . . . . . . . . . . . . . . . . . . . . 20-21
        Texas. . . . . . . . . . . . . . . . . . . . . . . . . 56-57
        Wyoming. . . . . . . . . . . . . . . . . . . . . . . . . .63
RV Troubleshooting Charts. . . . . . . . . . . . . . . . . . . . .79
        Brakes . . . . . . . . . . . . . . . . . . . . . . . . . .81
        Engines. . . . . . . . . . . . . . . . . . . . . . . . . .85
        Roof Air-Conditioning Systems. . . . . . . . . . . . . . .89
        Furnaces . . . . . . . . . . . . . . . . . . . . . . . . .95
Rules of the Road. . . . . . . . . . . . . . . . . . . . . . . . 100
        Turnpike and Tollway Information . . . . . . . . . . . . 103
        Weather Report . . . . . . . . . . . . . . . . . . . . . 105
Following History's Footsteps. . . . . . . . . . . . . . . . . . 107
Advertisers' Index . . . . . . . . . . . . . . . . . . . . . . . 121
Manufacturers' Tours . . . . . . . . . . . . . . . . . . . . . . 125
Campgrounds. . . . . . . . . . . . . . . . . . . . . . . . . . . 129
        Arkansas . . . . . . . . . . . . . . . . . . . . . . . 205-218
        Illinois . . . . . . . . . . . . . . . . . . . . . . . 572-609
        Texas. . . . . . . . . . . . . . . . . . . . . . . . 1206-1290
        Wyoming. . . . . . . . . . . . . . . . . . . . . . . 1452-1469
A:\TABSTOPS                                  Doc 1 Pg 1 Ln 4.83" Pos 1"
[       ▲                                                  ▲       ]
```

3. Enter the information.

Type `Color Map Section`	
Tab	Positions to tab stop. (Notice the periods.)
Type `4`	
Enter	Advances to next line.
Tab	Positions to first tab stop.
Type `USA`	Enters this text.
Tab	Positions to next tab stop.
Type `4-5`	
Enter	Ends line and advances to next line.

4. Continue entering the remaining lines using Figure 2.10 as a guide.
5. Save the file, using the name TABSTOPS.

HINTS/HAZARDS

If you wish to have the tab stop line appear on your screen like that depicted in Figure 2.11, enter the Window (Ctrl + F3) command and select the Window command. (The Window command will be discussed later in the chapter.) WordPerfect now displays a number next to the prompt `Number of lines in this window: 24`. Subtract 1 from that number and enter the number from the keyboard (23 in this example). Press Enter. Your screen should now have the tab stop line at the bottom of the screen. To return the screen back to normal, enter the above command, but add 1 to the number displayed next to the prompt.

BLOCK COMMAND

Using the **Block command** involves first marking the text to be included in the block and then telling WordPerfect what to do with it.

Alt + F4

Select the Block Command from the Edit Menu

MARKING A BLOCK OF TEXT

A **block** of text can be any contiguous group of characters, words, sentences, paragraphs, or pages of text.

To mark a block, position the cursor at the beginning of the text to be included in the block and issue the Block (Alt + F4) command. The message `Block on` then flashes on and off in the status line. Now move the cursor to the end of the text to be included in the block. As you move it, the text is "painted" and changes to reverse video on your screen.

You can use any of the cursor-positioning commands to enlarge or diminish the block. For instance, the Right Arrow extends the block one character at a time to the right, and the Down Arrow extends the block one line at a time. To cancel a block, press F1 (Cancel). After you have defined the block, you can issue any command that can use blocked text (Figure 2.12).

5.1

Using a Mouse You can also mark a block using a mouse. Position the cursor at the place in the document that you wish the block to start and then press the left-hand button. Expand the block by continuing to press this left-hand button and dragging the mouse. Canceling the Block command requires that you press again the left-hand button of the mouse.

Boldfacing (F6), Underlining (F8), and Centering (Shift + F6) Blocks One great advantage of the Block command is that you can add boldface, underlining, and centering to text after you have typed it. To try this out, type your name on the screen:

```
Tim Duffy
```

To boldface the name, place the cursor under the first character of the name. Press Alt + F4 (Block). Paint the entire name using the Right Arrow key. Press F6 (Bold). The name now appears in boldface.

Underlining and centering follow the same steps of marking the text with Alt + F4 and then giving the underline or centering command. (For the centering command, WordPerfect prompts you with `[Just Center]? No (Yes)`.) Press Y. If you want to both boldface and underline or center the same text, you can do so. Reblock the text by issuing the Block command and then press Ctrl + Home (Goto) twice to rehighlight.

Deleting Blocks With the Block command, you can delete any marked text by pressing Del. Clear the screen and retrieve the file called MOVE1 (it may not appear exactly like that depicted below). Suppose that you want to delete the last sentence in this paragraph:

```
    In the early 1960s, IBM introduced the mag typewriter, which used
a magnetic tape cartridge for sequential access to documents that had
been stored on the tape. This was hailed as a dramatic advance
because it allowed a user not only to store and then retrieve a
document but also to make immediate insertions, deletions, and
corrections on the original without having to change the entire
document manually.
```

To delete the sentence, place the cursor at the *T* of the word *This,* invoke the Block (Alt + F4) command, paint the sentence, press Del, and respond Y to the prompt `[Delete block]? No (Yes) N`. You should see the following text:

Figure 2.12
WordPerfect commands with which you can use the Block command.

Bold	Size (All)	Rectangle	Sort
Center	Format	Print	Spell
Delete	Macro	Replace	Switch
Font	Move	Save	Underline
Appearance (All)	Tabular Column	Search	Flush Right

```
   In the early 1960s, IBM introduced the mag typewriter, which used
a magnetic tape cartridge for sequential access to documents that had
been stored on the tape.
```

Block Shortcuts WordPerfect provides two shortcut methods of expanding a block to include all of a sentence or paragraph. If you want to include to the end of a sentence, enter a period (.) after issuing the Block command. If you want to include the rest of a paragraph in a block, press Enter. When either command is issued, the corresponding text is highlighted.

Save Block (F10) The **Save Block command** saves a block to a separate file on disk. This way you can place an often-used portion of a document on disk and retrieve it whenever it is needed.

Saving a block requires these steps: (1) Mark the text via the Block command; (2) press F10 (Save); (3) respond to the prompt `Block Name:_` by entering the name you want for the file and press Enter [if the file already exists, the message `Replace (filename)? No (Yes) N` appears]; and (4) press F1 (Cancel) to turn off the block.

You can add a block of text to the end of a disk file via the Append feature of WordPerfect. Issue the Move (Ctrl + F4) command after the text has been marked and select the Block option then the Append option. When WordPerfect displays the `Append to:_` prompt, name the file to which you want the text added and press Enter. The text is then added to the end of that file.

Print Block (Ctrl + F7) The **Print Block command** lets you print any blocked portion of a document. To print a block, mark it and press Shift + F7 (Print). WordPerfect now displays the prompt `Print Block? No (Yes) N`. Press Y to start printing. If necessary, cancel the block with F1 (Cancel).

OTHER COMMANDS THAT USE THE BLOCK FEATURE

Ctrl + F4

Select the Move Command from the Edit Menu

MOVE WITHOUT BLOCK

The **Move command** without block provides flexibility in copying chunks of text and moving them from one place to another. It also lets you delete the original text. Using the Move feature of WordPerfect is a two-step process that requires you first to indicate which text is to be moved or copied and then where it is to go. In the first step, the Move command (Ctrl + F4) displays the following menu:

```
Move: 1 Sentence; 2 Paragraph; 3 Page; 4 Retrieve: 0
```

The command executes at the current cursor location for a sentence, paragraph, or page of text. After you press the appropriate numeric key to indicate the amount of text that you want moved, the affected text is painted in reverse video (black on white) and a new menu appears:

```
1 Move; 2 Copy; 3 Delete; 4 Append: 0
```

1 Move This option of the Move feature removes the highlighted text from your document and places it in a temporary file.

2 Copy This leaves the original text in your document and copies it to a temporary file. The Copy feature works much like a duplicating machine, leaving the original intact.

3 Delete This removes the marked text from your document without saving it to a temporary file. [This text can, however, be restored by pressing F1 (Undelete).]

4 Append This lets you add the highlighted text to the end of an existing file on disk. WordPerfect asks you which file the text is to be added to via the prompt `Append to:_`. Type the filename and press Enter.

RETRIEVING TEXT

There are two ways to retrieve text following a Move or Copy command. The first method assumes that you are going to immediately retrieve the text at a new location. In response to the prompt `Move cursor; press Enter to retrieve,` position the cursor to the appropriate location in the document and press Enter. The text is then placed at the cursor location in your document. If you wish to perform other tasks now and retrieve the text later, you can cancel this "immediate move" by pressing F1 (Cancel).

If you have interrupted the Move command via a Cancel, use the following method of retrieving text. Position the cursor where you want to retrieve the block. Press Ctrl + F4 (Move) again to receive the following menu:

```
Move: 1 Sentence; 2 Paragraph; 3 Page; 4 Retrieve: 0
```

Select Retrieve by pressing 4. WordPerfect now displays the menu below to ask how you want this text moved:

```
Retrieve: 1 Block; 2 Tabular Column; 3 Rectangle: 0
```

Select the Block option (1) to copy the stored text to the cursor location.

The following example shows how the Move command (Move option) is used to move the second sentence to a new position behind the third sentence. Clear the screen and retrieve the file MOVE2. (Again, this file may appear differently on the screen.) The original order is as follows:

```
This is the first sentence. This is the second sentence. This is the
third sentence. This is the fourth sentence.
```

To mark the second sentence, position the cursor anywhere in that sentence. Press Ctrl + F4 (Move). Select the Sentence option (placing the sentence in reverse video). Select the Move option. The highlighted text is now deleted from the paragraph and saved to a temporary file, and WordPerfect knows what type of operation is to be performed. After re-forming, the text now appears like that below.

```
This is the first sentence. This is the third sentence. This is the
fourth sentence.
```

Move the cursor to the *T* at the beginning of the fourth sentence and press Enter. The text should now look like the following:

```
This is the first sentence. This is the third sentence. This is the
second sentence. This is the fourth sentence.
```

The Copy option of the Move command works in the same fashion as the Move option. The only difference is that the original text is left intact within the document.

USING MOVE WITH THE BLOCK COMMAND

One problem with the Move command is that it limits you to a sentence, paragraph, or page of text. You can circumvent this apparent limitation by first blocking the text that you want to manipulate via a Block (Alt + F4) command and then issuing the Move (Ctrl + F4) command.

Shift + F3

Select Convert Case from the Edit Menu

UPPERCASE/LOWERCASE CONVERSION

Have you ever entered text only to find later that the characters are all in upper case? The only way to correct this has been to erase the text and retype it.

WordPerfect has a **case conversion** feature that allows you to correct such errors. Clear the screen and retrieve the file CONVERT.

```
    STAND-ALONE WORD PROCESSORS ARE COMPUTERS WHOSE SOLE TASK IS WORD
PROCESSING.
```

To convert the text to lower case, block it with Alt + F4. Then use the Switch (Shift + F3) command, which displays the following menu:

```
Block: 1 Uppercase; 2 Lowercase: 0
```

The steps involved in switching the case of the characters are (1) block the text that you want to change (beginning with the *T* of *STAND*), (2) issue the Switch (Shift + F3) command, (3) select the appropriate option (lowercase), and (4) turn off the Block command with another Block (Alt + F4). The text should now appear like the following:

```
    Stand-alone word processors are computers whose sole task is word
processing.
```

SEARCH AND REPLACE COMMANDS

The Search and the Replace commands locate, change, or delete a word or phrase wherever it appears in your document.

F2

Select Forward from the Search Menu

SEARCH

The **Search** (F2) **command** locates all occurrences of a word or phrase. When the command is entered, the cursor moves to the right of the first occurrence of the word or phrase.

When you press F2 (Search), WordPerfect responds with the prompt → `Srch_`. Enter the desired word or phrase (up to 60 characters) and press F2 again to start the search. The cursor will advance to the first occurrence of the desired text; to find the next occurrence, press F2 again twice. The search operation has ended when you see the `* Not Found *` message displayed in the status line.

The regular Search command is a forward search, starting at the current cursor location and moving toward the end of the file. You can also use a **Reverse Search** (Shift + F2) **command,** which starts at the current cursor location and moves toward the beginning of the file.

Besides finding desired text, the Search command can also find embedded codes. For example, if you are interested in finding the next hard return, press F2. At the prompt → `Srch_`, press Enter. The search string is now a hard return [HRt].

You can also return the cursor to the position it had before the last Search (F2) command was executed by entering the Goto (Ctrl + Home) command twice.

REPLACE

Alt + F2

Select Replace from the Search Menu

The **Replace** (Alt + F2) **command** is used to find a word or phrase and then replace it with another word or phrase. When the Replace command is initially entered, you receive the prompt `w/Confirm? No (Yes) N`. If you respond N, every occurrence of the old word or phrase is replaced automatically. If you respond Y, WordPerfect will stop at each occurrence of the found word or phrase and prompt you with `Confirm? No (Yes) N`. Y replaces and moves to the next occurrence; N leaves the old word or phrase and moves the cursor to the next occurrence.

The search-and-replace process is as follows. Press Alt + F2. Answer the confirm prompt. Then WordPerfect prompts → `Srch:_`. Enter the text that you want to replace and press F2. You are prompted: `Replace with:_`. Type the replacement text and again press F2. The search-and-replace process proceeds as you indicated for all of the document that follows the initial cursor location.

The search-and-replace character strings can also be embedded codes.

If you want to find complete words such as *dog* rather than *dogma* or *dogmatic,* you must enter spaces before and after the word you want. Lowercase characters can be used to search for either uppercase or lowercase characters, whereas uppercase characters can be used to search only for uppercase characters.

DUAL-DOCUMENT CAPABILITIES

Shift + F3

Select Switch Document from the Edit Menu

Ctrl + F3

Select Window from the Edit Menu

You may recall that the WordPerfect screen status line contains the message `Doc 1` or `Doc 2`. This is because of the **dual-document feature,** which lets you work on two documents at a time.

Each document can take a full screen by itself, or the two documents can share one screen. To create a second full-screen document, use the **Switch** (Shift + F3) **command.** This command toggles back and forth between Document 1 and Document 2.

To display two documents on the same screen, issue the **Window** (Ctrl + F3) **command.** Select its option 1 Window. WordPerfect will ask how many of the 24 screen lines you want to give to the upper window. It will then create a bar that divides the screen into upper and lower areas and shows the tab settings for whichever document you are in. To move back-and-forth between the screens, press the Switch toggle (Shift + F3). To close the window, select the Window command again and give all 24 lines to one document.

Document 1 and Document 2 function separately, so any command you give in one document will not affect the other, and you can exit either document at any time. If both documents are still open when you exit WordPerfect, the program will remind you of this and prompt you on how to save each document.

One great convenience of the dual-document feature is that you can copy text from one document with the Block command, switch screens, and retrieve it to the other document.

HINTS/HAZARDS

The split-screen bar shows the tab stops for the active window (in which the cursor resides). If you are working with just one document and want to add a tab-settings bar at the bottom of the screen, simply create a window that gives 23 lines to the upper screen. The tab bar will then appear below your text.

CHAPTER REVIEW

When you are editing a file using WordPerfect, you are dealing with a temporary file that WordPerfect has copied from the original file. Temporary files residing in RAM and, if necessary, an overflow file provide for good error handling. If you really mess up the file that you are editing, all that you have to do is issue the Exit (F7) command. The original file remains intact, and the messed-up file is erased.

Another handy feature is the backup file, identified by its .BK! file extension. The backup file holds the contents of the file that existed on disk before the last save was executed. If you mistakenly erase your original file, you can re-create it from the backup version.

The Print (Shift + F7) command lets you print the file currently in memory. This command provides tremendous flexibility in how a document is printed. For instance, it lets you determine which printer to use as well as how many copies of the document to print. You can print only the page where the cursor is located. You also have control over which files to be printed, canceled, or rushed to printing.

WordPerfect provides the ability to center, boldface, or underline text. A code at the beginning of the text turns the selected feature on, and another code at the end of the text turns it off. Two or more of these codes can be used together.

WordPerfect also provides you with a number of commands that are used for resetting margins. (1) The Format (Shift + F8) Line command resets both the left- and right-hand margins. (2) The Left Indent (F4) command resets the left-hand margin to the next tab stop only for the current paragraph. (3) The L/R Indent (Shift + F4) command indents both the left- and right-hand margins of a paragraph by one tab stop.

WordPerfect provides a number of ways to position or rearrange data. (1) The Center (Shift + F6) command automatically centers any text between the right- and left-hand margins. (2) You can use the Tab (Shift + F8, 1) command to set tab stops in a way that is similar to tab stops on a typewriter or for creating columns of data. (3) Tabs can be set for text or numeric data. (4) The Tab Align (Ctrl + F6) command is used to align the decimal points of numerals.

Block commands let you mark text and then move, copy, or delete it; save it to a file on disk; or change its display characteristics.

Before you can issue block manipulation commands, you must mark the desired text by issuing a Block (Alt + F4) and painting with cursor movement commands.

The Move (Ctrl + F4) command lets you select a default option of sentence, paragraph, or page to be cut or copied from your document.

One real benefit of Block commands is that they let you store often-used pieces of text to disk for later use. This feature saves you a tremendous amount of time retyping the same text from one document to the next. Unless you use the Append command, data that you copy to an existing file will replace and destroy the data that are currently in that file.

WordPerfect gives you two ways to find text: The Search command merely locates text, which you can then manipulate or change in any way you please; the Replace command finds the text and replaces it with other text that you have previously chosen.

The dual-document feature lets you work with two WordPerfect files at the same time.

KEY TERMS AND CONCEPTS

align character
Append command
backup file
block
Block command
Boldface command
case conversion
center block
Center command
Copy command
Date command
decimal alignment
delete
dot leader
dual-document feature
Exit command
Flush Right command
Left Indent command
L/R Indent command
Margin command
Move command
Print Block command
Replace command
Reveal Codes command
Reverse Search command
Save Block command
saving files
Search command
Switch command
Tab Align command
tab stop
temporary file
Underline command
Window command

CHAPTER QUIZ

Multiple Choice

1. What is the key sequence for the Print command?
   a. F7
   b. Shift + F7
   c. F10
   d. Shift + F10

2. Which of the following commands is *not* a Save command?
   a. Exit
   b. Save
   c. Terminate
   d. All of the above

3. Which of the following statements is(are) false?
   a. When a block is moved into the current document, it is placed at the current cursor location.
   b. When a block is written to disk, it is placed at the end of existing data in that file via the Append option.
   c. The Move option causes two copies of the blocked text to appear in a document.
   d. All of the above statements are true.
   e. Both a and c are false.

4. Which of the following is *not* an option provided in the Print menu?
   a. Print only this page.
   b. Print the entire document.
   c. Change the font.
   d. All of the above are Print options.

5. Which of the following commands must be reissued for each paragraph when resetting margins?
   a. Center
   b. Left Indent
   c. Tab
   d. Margin

True/False

6. If you really mess up a file that you are editing, the safest thing to do is to issue the Exit command.

7. A major problem in using tabs is that the decimal points do *not* easily align in a straight column.

8. A block must be marked before you are allowed to use the Append command.

9. The printer can be interrupted simply by pressing the Cancel command.

10. The Center command centers text between the left- and right-hand margins.

Answers

1. b   2. c   3. c   4. c   5. b   6. t   7. f   8. t   9. t   10. t

Exercises

1. Define or describe each of the following:
   a. Temporary files
   b. Backup files
   c. Tab Align command
   d. L/R Indent command
   e. Tab stops

2. The ____________ command saves the file and exits WordPerfect.

3. The ____________ command saves the file and returns you to your document.

4. The ____________ command lets you abandon a file being created or edited.

5. When you are working with large documents, it is a good idea to use the ____________ command every 10 to 15 minutes.

6. Special effects command requires you to issue ____________.

7. You can interrupt any file that is printing by issuing the ____________ command.

8. If you are editing an existing file, the file that you are actually making the changes to is the ____________ file in RAM.

9. The ____________ command as well as the Print command lets you initiate the printing of a file.

10. The ____________ or ____________ command sets the right-hand margin.

11. The ____________, ____________, or ____________ command sets the left-hand margin.

12. The ____________ command underlines text.

13. The ____________ command centers text.

14. The ____________ command clears all tabs from the ruler line.

15. The ____________ symbol sets a regular text tab.

16. The ____________ command moves the cursor to the next tab location.

17. The ____________ type tab stop is to indicate that numeric information is being entered and directs WordPerfect to align the numbers on the decimal point.

18. The ____________ command resets the left-hand margin of only one paragraph.

19. Backup files automatically created by WordPerfect have a(n) ____________ file extension.

20. When two tab stops contain periods between them, this is known as a(n) ____________.

21. The command to mark a block of text is ____________.

22. A block of text is painted using ____________ commands.

23. The command that creates a copy of a block of text is the ____________ option of the Move command.

24. The command that moves a block of text to another location in a document and erases the original is the ____________ option of the Move command.

25. The block delete command is ____________.

26. The ____________ command records a marked block of text to disk.

27. The Search forward command is accessed by the __________ keys, and the Search backward command is accessed via the __________ keys.

28. The __________ command moves back to the prior cursor location in a Search command.

29. The maximum number of characters that can be included in a search string is __________.

30. The __________ command lets you change uppercase text to lowercase text and vice versa.

COMPUTER EXERCISES

Below is a summary of the WordPerfect commands covered in this chapter.

Print (Shift + F7) Prints a document.

Center (Shift + F6) Centers text on a line.

Boldface (F6) Boldfaces text.

Underline (F8) Underlines text.

Flush Right (Alt + F6) Right-justifies text on a line.

Date (Shift + F5) Converts the system date to various formats.

Format (Shift + F8) Line Sets margins and tabs.

Indent (F4) Indents the left-hand margin for a single paragraph.

L/R Indent (Shift + F4) Indents both the left- and the right-hand margins for a single paragraph.

Margin Release (Shift + Tab) Creates a paragraph with a hanging indent.

Block (Alt + F4) Marks a block of text in a document for use with another command.

Move (Ctrl + F4) Cuts or copies a unit or block of text in a document.

Case Conversion (Shift + F3) Converts upper case to lower case and vice versa.

Search (F2) Finds character strings in a document.

Replace (Alt + F2) Finds and replaces character strings in a document.

Screen (Ctrl + F3) Creates a window on your screen and specifies the number of lines in it.

Switch (Shift + F3) Moves the cursor between windows.

Tab Align (Ctrl + F6) Aligns numbers by a decimal point or text by any character.

1. Load the BOOKEXER file and then use the Exit command to clear the screen. Remain in WordPerfect.

2. Print out the entire BOOKEXER file, which is on the student data disk.

3. Print out only page 2 from the BOOKEXER file.

4. Using the BOOKEXER file, perform the following tasks:
   a. Position the cursor to the beginning of the file. Set the left-hand margin to 1.5 inches. Set the right-hand margin to 6.5 inches.

b. Position the cursor to the second paragraph of page 2. Indent the paragraph two tab stops from the left-hand margin.

c. Position the cursor to the third paragraph of page 2. Reset the left margin to 1.2 inches and the right margin to 7.5 inches. Re-form the document.

d. Position the cursor to the second paragraph of page 3. Issue a L/R Ident command and re-form the paragraph.

e. Use the Reveal Codes command to examine the beginning of the second paragraph of page 2. Note the [Indent] codes that have been embedded by WordPerfect.

Set the entire document for double spacing. Reset the margins to 2.5 inches for the left-hand and 6.0 inches for the right-hand.

Use the Exit (F7) command to quit the document. Do not save the file.

f. Reload the BOOKEXER file. Notice that the file is still in its original condition.

5. Clear the screen. Use the Center command to center the following text on separate lines.

```
Word Perfect
Using Centering Commands
Using Decimal Tabs
```

Delete all tab stops from the ruler line. Enter decimal tab stops at positions 2.5 inches and 5.0 inches. Enter the following columns of numeric data, the first column placed with the decimal alignment at the 2.5-inch location and the second column with the decimal alignment at the 5.0-inch location.

```
  12.76          7.65
 134.50           .531
1965.75         10.50
  12.65          9.6
```

Notice how the decimals are now lined up. Save the file using the name CH2EX5.

6. Clear the WordPerfect screen. Clear all tab stops. Set a regular tap stop at 1.0 inch. Set decimal tab stops at locations 2.20 inches, 3.5 inches, 4.70 inches, and 6.0 inches. Enter the document below. Save the file to disk using the name CH2EX6. Print the file.

The Basket Tree
Year-to-Date Sales Report

	Whls	Shows	Mail	Retail
Jan	750.00	3000.00	2300.00	0.00
Feb	600.00	3500.00	2000.00	0.00
March	1750.00	6000.00	2500.00	1750.00
Apr	3000.00	8500.00	4000.00	0.00
May	2500.00	9000.00	5400.00	2300.00
June	2000.00	7200.00	2000.00	1000.00

7. Clear the WordPerfect screen. Clear all tab stops. Enter a regular tab stop at location 0.5 inch and decimal tab stops at locations 2.5 inches, 4.0 inches, and 5.5 inches. Enter the document. Save the document to disk using the name CH2EX7. Print the file.

Ed's Microcomputer Store
Projected Profit Margin

Year	1	2	3
Sales	325,000.00	347,588.00	371,745.00
Cost	195,000.00	208,533.00	223,047.00
Margin	130,000.00	139,035.00	148,698.00

8. Clear the WordPerfect screen. Enter the following bibliography. Be certain that you include the appropriate boldfacing and underlining where it has been indicated. Save the file to disk using the name CH2EX8. Print the file.

BIBLIOGRAPHY

Albanese, Robert. Management: Toward Accountability for Performance. Homewood, Ill.: Irwin, 1975.

Cheit, Earl F. "Challenges Inherent in the Systematic Approach." In Appraising Information Needs of Decision Makers. Edited by Carl R. Adams, New Directions for Institutional Research, No. 15. San Francisco: Jossey-Bass, 1977.

Dauten, Carl A. and Valentine, Lloyd M. Business Cycles and Forecasting. Cincinnati: South-Western, 1974.

Drucker, Peter F. "Long-Range Planning Means Risk Taking." In Long-Range Planning for Management. Edited by David W. Ewing. New York: Harper & Row, 1972.

Naylor, Thomas H., ed. "The Age of Corporate Planning Models." In Simulation Models in Corporate Planning. New York: Praeger, 1979.

9. Clear the WordPerfect screen. This exercise requires you to develop a résumé suitable for use in a job search. How you present yourself on paper may determine whether you will be interviewed. Planning how to best present your strengths can therefore be extremely important.

    A good résumé usually has several distinct parts. The first part identifies the individual seeking the position. It is usually followed by job objectives that tell a prospective employer what type of job you are trying to find. The third area contains information about your educational background. The remaining topics to be covered are work experience, interests, references, and contact information.

    Under both the educational background and work experience headings, list your most recent experiences first. After these are given, list the others in descending order by date.

    Neatness and organization cannot be overemphasized in building your résumé.

    To help you with organizing your information and to provide you with ideas, two sample résumés are included on the following pages. Each uses a slightly different format for organizing and presenting personal information. Examine these sample résumés and borrow any conventions used.

As much as possible, try to keep your résumé to one page. Because some employers receive over 500 résumés each week, many do not like to read lengthy résumés; some even refuse to read more than one page. They feel that if you cannot summarize your accomplishments on one page, you will have difficulty summarizing information in reports later. Remember, this résumé provides employers with their first impression of you, which you want to make as favorable as possible. Save your résumé to a file called CH2EX9.

RITA D. COOLIDGE

CURRENT ADDRESS:	**PERMANENT ADDRESS:**
(until May, 1993)	250 W. Maywood
917 N. School	Des Plaines, Illinois 60013
Normal, Illinois 61761	(312)836-8374
(309)452-7778	

CAREER OBJECTIVE

Obtain an entry-level position in an accounting firm after passing the Certified Public Accountant examination in May, 1993.

EDUCATION

August, 1989– May, 1993	**Illinois State University,** Normal, Illinois Bachelor of Science degree in accounting Business Administration minor Overall GPA: 3.54 on a 4.0 scale Major GPA: 3.52 on a 4.0 scale

HONORS AND ACTIVITIES

Beta Gamma Sigma Business Honor Society, Golden Key National Honor Society, Dean's List (five semesters), Phi Eta Sigma Freshman Honor Society, I.S.U. Marching Band (Rank Leader).

WORK EXPERIENCE

All earnings have been applied toward college expenses

January 2, 1993– March 7, 1993	Arthur Young, Chicago, Illinois served as an intern in the Auditing Dept.
November, 1990– present	Oster Company, Milwaukee, Wisconsin (main office) Consumer Education Counselor duties: seasonal demonstration of appliances and education of consumers.
February, 1989– August, 1990	Woolworth Company, Lombard, Illinois Sales duties: handling money, training cashiers, ordering and stocking merchandise, and announcing advertisements.

Samuel R. Tick

CAREER OBJECTIVE	To secure an entry-level position in accounting that will provide challenge, excitement, and an opportunity to advance within the firm.
EDUCATION	ILLINOIS STATE UNIVERSITY, Normal, Illinois Bachelor of Science, Comprehensive Accounting Major, May, 1993 Cumulative GPA: 3.62/4.0
EXPERIENCE	
1993—spring	ARTHUR ANDERSEN & CO., Internship in Auditing.
1992—summer	GENERAL TELEPHONE CO., Internship in Internal Auditing.
1991—present	ILLINOIS STATE UNIVERSITY, Department of Accounting. Undergraduate Teaching Assistant to Mrs. Pat Arturo, Department Honors Coordinator and Instructor.
HONORS	OUTSTANDING UNDERGRADUATE/ College of Business—1991. RAYMOND ESWORTHY/ARTHUR ANDERSEN AWARD, 1991. BETA GAMMA SIGMA—1989. ALPHA LAMBDA DELTA HONOR SOCIETY—1989–present. DEAN'S LIST, 1989–present. HONORS PROGRAM—1989–present.
ACTIVITIES	STUDENT ACCOUNTING SOCIETY—President, 1992. STUDENT ACCOUNTING SOCIETY—Newsletter Committee—1990.
INTERESTS	Skiing, Sailing, Camping, and Music.
REFERENCES	Available on request.
CONTACT INFORMATION	819 Hillsdale Apt. #35 Normal IL 61761

10. Retrieve the following list of names and addresses from the disk file called CH2EX10. Using the Block commands, arrange the names and addresses in alphabetic order by last name. Save the sorted names and addresses to the file called CH2EX10A.

```
Reza Ghorbani
4033 N. Wolcott
Chicago, IL 60712

Debbie Acklin
408 E. Monroe
Bloomington, IL 61701
```

```
Harvey Posio
1013 Hillcrest
San Diego, CA 94307

Juan Decesario
1214 Flores
Miami, FL 12562

Arthur Adams
115 Ginger Creek Ct.
Bloomington, IL 61701

Russell Davis
707 Vale St.
Bloomington, IL 61701

Fred Ficek
1215 Tamarack
Normal, IL 61761
```

11. Retrieve the file called BOOKEXER. Using Block commands, save the first paragraph to a file called CH2EX11A. Save the third paragraph to a file called CH2EX11B. Append the fifth paragraph to the CH2EX11A file. Quit the BOOKEXER file using the Exit command without saving the file. Retrieve the CH2EX11x files that you just created in order. Be sure to position the cursor to the end of a "chunk" of text, before retrieving the next file. Using the List Files Delete commands, delete the CH2EX11x intermediate files. Save the file using the name CH2EX11.

12. Clear the screen and retrieve the CH2EX12 file. You will find text like that listed below. Using the Block command, perform each indicated task on the appropriate line. For example, the first line "Center this text" should be centered using the Block + Center commands. Save your work to the file CH2EX12A. Print the entire file.

    Center this text
    Center and boldface this text
    Center and underline this text
    Center, boldface, and underline this text
    Underline this text
    Boldface and underline this text
    Flush right this text
    Underline and flush right this text
    Delete this text
    CONVERT THIS TEXT TO LOWER CASE
    convert this text to upper case

    Use the Block command to print only the first five lines of the changed CH2EX12 file.

13. Use the Copy command from the List Files screen to copy the file EDTARTCL to a file called CH2EX13. For this project, assume you are working for a newspaper that has received a guest column on purchasing microcomputers. Your editor feels that the work submitted by the writer

is good but too long for a single column. Instead of being presented as one column, it is to be broken into two parts.

The editor has made a number of changes to the article for you to incorporate to prepare it for publication. The various editorial changes have been indicated on the written document. (The document follows these instructions.)

In indicating the changes to be made, the editor has used a number of common editing marks on the document. The marks, along with their meanings, are listed below:

- ¶ Start a new paragraph at this location.
- ℯ Delete this character(s).
- ∧ Insert a character(s) at this location.
- ⁀ Close up (get rid of unnecessary blank lines or blanks between characters).
-][Place the enclosed text centered at this location in the document.

Because the author originally prepared the article using WordPerfect, it was submitted on diskette. The name of the WordPerfect file is CH2EX13. You are to open the CH2EX13 file and make the changes indicated on the written document. Notice that the paragraphs are numbered on the written document but are not numbered on the diskette file. Perform any editing noted but not listed below. The paragraphs were numbered to make the instructions here easier for you to follow.

a. Change the original title to "Planning for a Computer Purchase." Center this title.
b. Delete the numbers in the first paragraph and make certain that there is only one space between the remaining words.
c. Delete the various section headings within the document.
d. In paragraph 2, make the term *micro processor* one word.
e. In paragraph 3, move the marked sentence to the end of the paragraph.
f. In paragraph 4, move the marked sentence to the end of the paragraph.
g. In paragraph 5, insert the comma at the indicated location.
h. In paragraph 6, insert an apostrophe.
i. In paragraph 8, move the word *also*.
j. Block paragraphs 1 through 10 and save them to a file named COLUMN1. Issue a Block Delete command to delete the first part of the file.

The file COLUMN1 now contains the first microcomputer column for the newspaper. You are now ready to make changes to the remainder of the document, which will be used for the second guest column.

k. The title for the second column is "Computer Stores Need Close Study." Be sure to center the title.
l. Insert the following introductory paragraph:

   Although home computers are readily available at a number of different types of outlets, consumers should be careful where they shop.

m. Delete the numbers from paragraph 11. Make certain that there is only one space between the words.

n. In paragraph 14, change *they are* to *he is.*
o. In paragraph 15, create a new paragraph beginning with the phrase *Used-computer stores.*
p. Delete the numbers from paragraph 16 and make certain that there is only one space between words. Change the indicated uppercase letters to lowercase letters.
q. In paragraph 17, change the capital *D* to a lowercase letter.
r. In paragraph 18, replace the % characters with the word *percent.*
s. Move paragraph 19 to the indicated position following paragraph 20.
t. Before paragraph 21, insert the following paragraph:

   Generic software packages combine word processing, spreadsheets, and database on one diskette. These packages may not have the capabilities of larger, more expensive packages but are ideal for home use. This software, along with documentation, typically costs less than $30.

u. In paragraph 21, change the word *ten* to the numeral *10.* Then delete the word *also.*
v. Block off this document and store it to a file named COLUMN2. Once COLUMN2 has been created on diskette, the existing file is no longer needed. You may now issue an Exit command without saving the file. This leaves the original EDTARTCL file unchanged.
w. Print out the COLUMN1 and COLUMN2 files.

Purchasing a Home Computer

1. This is the time of year when many consumers begin to ponder the idea of purchasing a microcomputer for home use. Over the past few years microcomputers have become fairly popular Christmas gifts either for children in the family or for the gift givers, themselves. A consumer must consider a number of important factors when purchasing a microcomputer for the home. The factors to consider are the (1.) the typical computer system, (2.) Compatibility, (3.) Special requirements, (4.) Where to purchase the hardware, (5.) Software considerations, and (6.) Hidden costs.

~~Typical Computer System Components~~

2. The typical microcomputer system is composed of four parts: (1.) The microcomputer itself, (2.) A storage device, (3.) An input device, and (4.) An output device. The microcomputer contains the internal memory (that portion available to the user), the actual micro processor, as well as all of the electronic components that are needed to make the device work.

3. The storage device for the computer is used to store programs (prewritten instructions to the computer) and data. The common storage medium used today is the diskette. Some computers use cassette tape, but this medium is extremely slow. There are a variety of sizes and types of diskettes on the market. Purchase only that type of disk for your system. All that you have to know is whether your computer is capable of recording on only one or both sides of the disk and whether the disk is single- or double-density (determines the quality of the surface).

4. The typical input device for giving instructions to the machine is the keyboard. No two manufacturers seem to make the same type of keyboard. Nothing can be more discouraging than getting a machine that has the keys arranged in a manner that is different from what you are accustomed to using. Before you buy a machine, make sure that you try out the keyboard.

5. The typical output devices are the monitor and the printer. The monitor is used to output any prompts to the user and for nonessential output that does not have to be saved. When you need information that has to be saved for historical purposes, the printer is used. There are a number of different types of monitors and printers. The cost of these devices is typically directly related to the quality of output. The higher the quality of output the higher the cost of the device.

~~Issue of Compatibility~~

6. The most important issue to address when purchasing a microcomputer is compatibility. Different manufacturers' computers cannot always easily "talk" with other manufacturers computers. You must therefore decide exactly why you want the machine. At this time, many consumers' purchasing decision becomes clouded by brand loyalty to some particular machine. This is the worst way to make a purchasing decision.

.
.
.

Special Requirements

8. Today's microcomputers, unlike minicomputers or mainframe computers, do not have many limitations on where they can be placed. They do not have any heat/cooling or humidity requirements that cannot be easily met within the typical household. Electrical requirements are minimal. You do not need a dedicated electrical circuit for the computer, but you do not also want to put it on the same circuit that already has the refrigerator, microwave oven, toaster, and coffee maker on it. A voltage/surge protector or lightning arrestor is also a good idea. Voltage/surge devices can cost upwards to $100, but a good lightning arrestor (all that is really needed) can be purchased for under $10 at your local hardware store.

.
.
.

Computer Stores Need Close Study

~~Where to Purchase the Machine~~

11. There are basically four different sources of computers: 1. local computer specialty shops, 2. department/discount stores, 3. mail order, and 4. used computers.

.
.
.

14. Mail-order shops also offer tremendous buys on hardware. The consumer is expected to be fairly knowledgeable about the equipment that they are purchasing. If something goes wrong with the equipment, it must be sent back for repair. Depending on the store, this can take anywhere from one to four weeks. Any questions that you have after the equipment arrives will usually cost a long-distance telephone call.

15. Used computers can be an exceptional buy. If the system is purchased from an individual, you may be able to purchase a complete system containing both hardware and software for a fraction of the original price. One disadvantage in purchasing such equipment is that the warranty has probably expired and it might be hard to get the equipment repaired if anything goes wrong with it. Another disadvantage is that the owner of the equipment may have unreasonable expectations about the value of the old equipment. Used-computer stores are also opening in large cities. These stores even provide a warranty for equipment purchased there.

Software Considerations

16. Once the machine has been purchased, the software (preprogrammed instructions) that allow you to make the machine useful must also be purchased. If you purchase name-brand software, you can easily invest one-half the cost of the hardware for programs. There are four basic sources for software: 1) Computer/Department stores, 2) Mail order, 3) Public domain software, and 4) Shareware.

17. Computer and Department stores typically stock many types of software packages. It is not uncommon to see literally hundreds of different packages in a store. Unless you purchase a name-brand or very popular software, the sales staff may not be able to answer questions that you have about its use. Also expect to pay close to full price for the programs.

18. Mail-order vendors often have anywhere from 20% to 60% discount on software prices. With such discounts, however, expect almost no support from the vendor. If you have any problems, you will probably have to call the manufacturer of the software.

19. Shareware is software that is typically available free to you for evaluation purposes. If, after using the software, you decide that you want to keep it, instructions are included that direct you where to send in a nominal charge for complete documentation and rights to enhancements or update. A number of good word processing and spreadsheet packages are available in this manner.

20. Public domain software is software that is available to you for about the cost of a disk. It is not pirated software but software that has been designed and developed possibly for a user's group. While some of this software is excellent, much of it is a waste. Many time this type of software is available to you by joining a local user's group for a specific type of computer.

Hidden Costs

21. There are a number of costs that are not always considered in making the decision to purchase a home computer. These hidden costs include software, disks, ribbon, paper, and computer furniture. Software, as mentioned previously, can easily reach one-half the cost of the hardware. Other costs include disks. It is not uncommon for a microcomputer

owner to have a number of boxes of disks. This cost mounts up when the disks can cost anywhere from $10 to $50 a box (ten). If you purchase a printer, you will have to buy ribbon and paper for it also. You may also find that the table that you had originally planned to use with the computer is not the right height (typically typing or 27 inches from the floor), so you may need to purchase a computer table.

Summary

22. Examining the various options available for purchasing the computer as well as software for the home allows a consumer to make a more intelligent purchase decision. Facing the issues of compatibility and special needs of microcomputers allows you to be more comfortable about using the computer as well as allow you to more completely enjoy the computer later on.

3

MACROS, SPECIAL PRINT FEATURES, AND DESKTOP PUBLISHING

CHAPTER OBJECTIVES

After completing this chapter, you should be able to

- ***Use the Macro feature of WordPerfect***
- ***Use WordPerfect's Format commands***
- ***Use WordPerfect's Font commands***
- ***Use the Columns command of WordPerfect***
- ***Incorporate graphics in a document***

This chapter introduces WordPerfect's Macro feature, which lets you perform repetitive tasks with fewer keystrokes. It also covers many of the formatting and printing features that make WordPerfect an effective desktop publishing tool, including how to use the Columns command and how to incorporate graphics in a document.

MACROS

WordPerfect can record an often-used string of keystrokes (called a **macro**) you enter, assign a name to, and then execute whenever you request it. Thus, you need perform a common task once only; therefore, you ask WordPerfect to simply replay the stored keystrokes. Any set of commands that you find yourself using frequently when building a document is a candidate for placing in a macro.

Ctrl + F10

Select Macro Option from the Tools Menu

CREATING A MACRO

You can create and execute a macro in six steps:

1. Begin the macro-definition process.
2. Name the macro.
3. Briefly describe the macro (up to 39 characters can be used).
4. Enter the keystrokes to be recorded.
5. End the macro-definition process.
6. Execute the stored macro keystrokes.

You begin the macro-definition process by entering the Define Macro (Ctrl + F10) command. If you are using the Menu Line, do this by selecting the Macro option from the Tools Menu. Once this command is executed, the prompt `Define Macro:` appears on the screen. Now enter the macro name, which can be done in any of four ways:

1. Type a name of two to eight characters.
2. Press Alt and type any letter from *A* to *Z*.
3. Type a name consisting of only one character (one key) to make a keyboard macro.
4. Press Enter. This bypasses the naming of the macro and is used when only a **temporary macro** is needed. You cannot save unnamed macros to disk.

If you define a macro using options 1–3, the macro can be retrieved from the disk whenever you are in WordPerfect. Option 4 creates a temporary macro that is erased when you exit WordPerfect. What you name a macro is important because **permanent macros** are saved to the default disk as separate files using the names that you entered plus a .WPM file extension. When you later tell WordPerfect to execute a macro, it looks for this file on the default disk and, on finding it, loads and executes the stored keystrokes.

Permanent macros are saved to the default (active) disk drive. If you want your macros saved to a different drive, be sure to use the List Files command to change the active disk/directory. If you enter a drive identifier and path before naming a macro, it is then saved to the specified disk/directory.

Once the macro has been named, you can record any keystrokes. WordPerfect lets you know that this recording process is in effect by displaying the blinking message `Macro Def` in the lower left-hand corner of the screen. After entering the keystrokes to be incorporated into the macro, issue another Define Macro (Ctrl + F10) command.

This temporary macro will place your name in boldface type within a document.

1. Create the macro name:

Ctrl + F10	(Or select the Macro option from the Tools Menu and then select the Define command) Issues the Define Macro command.
Enter	
F6	Issues the Boldface command.
Type your name [space]	
F6	Turns off boldfacing.
Ctrl + F10	Ends the macro definition.

2. Execute the macro:

Alt + F10	(Or select the Macro option from the Tools Menu and then select the Execute command) Issues the Macro command.
Enter	Executes the temporary macro.

You should now see your name appear on the screen in boldfaced type. Each time you execute the commands in step 2, your name will appear on the screen.

WordPerfect permits only one temporary macro at a time. If you issue a new type of command using steps 1 and 2, that set of commands replaces those used to write your name to the screen.

Repeating a Macro If you want a macro to repeat a specified number of time, press Esc, and enter the desired number of repetitions, the Macro (Alt + F10) command, and the name of the macro (press Enter if you want the temporary macro to execute). For example, if you want your name to print 100 times on the screen, enter the following commands:

Esc
100
Alt + F10
Enter

After the `* Please Wait *` message disappears, you should see 100 copies of your name.

ALT MACROS

To create macros that WordPerfect can execute anytime after they have been entered, you must use one of the naming options that creates a macro file on disk. Once one of these macros has been created, issue the appropriate command, and WordPerfect loads (from the .WPM file) and executes those instructions. If you created a macro using the Alt + a letter method, execute that macro by pressing Alt followed by the appropriate letter.

The following exercise creates a macro (Alt + L) that builds the letterhead for a letter to be printed on a plain piece of stationery. This letterhead, printed using boldface, italics, and very large print, is centered on the page. It contains your name, street address, city, state, and zip code. The current date should also be printed at the beginning of the fourth line following the letterhead.

1. Create and name the macro:

Ctrl + F10	(Or select the Macro option from the Tools Menu and then select the Define Macro command) Issues the Define Macro command.
Alt + L	Enters the name of the macro.
Type `Create a Letterhead`	Describes the macro.
Enter	Accepts the description.
F6	Issues the Boldface command.
Type your name	
Enter	Positions cursor to the next line.
Type your street address	
Enter	Positions to the next line.
city, state, and zip code	
F6	Turns off boldfacing.
Enter	Positions cursor to the next line.
↑ (3)	Gets to the beginning of your name.
Alt + F4	Issues the Block command.
↓ (3)	Extends the block.
Ctrl + F8	Issues the Font command.
S	Selects the Size option.
V	Selects the Very Large option.
Alt + F4	Issues the Block command.
Ctrl + Home (2)	Redefines the block.
Ctrl + F8	Issues the Font command.
A	Selects the Appearance command.
I	Selects the Italics command.
Alt + F4	Issues the Block command.
Ctrl + Home (2)	Redefines the block.
Shift + F6	Issues the Center command.
Y	Answers yes about centering lines.
End	Positions the cursor to the right of the embedded codes for Italic and Very Large options.
Enter (4)	Enters four blank lines.
Shift + F5	Issues the Date/Outline command.
C	Selects the Date Code command.
Ctrl + F10	Ends the macro definition.

2. Execute the macro:

Alt + F10	(Or select the Macro option from the Tools Menu and then select the Execute command) Issues the Macro command.
Alt + L	Executes Alt + L macro instructions saved in the ALTL.WPM file.

If your printer does not support italic or very large characters, these letters may appear as underlined text on your printed output.

BUILD MACROS TO SET TABS

Assume that you are using a word processing application in which you will be intermixing text and numeric information. You have projected that there will be about 15 to 20 of these numeric blocks. Each numeric block requires decimal tab stops at lineal positions 1.5 inches, 4.0 inches, 5.1 inches, and 6.2 inches. The text tab stops are to be at lineal positions of .5 inch, 1 inch, and 1.5 inches. This type of repetitious task of creating numeric and text tab stops is an ideal use of WordPerfect's macro feature.

Because the document will probably be generated at several sittings and there is need for two macros, the macros will be stored to disk files. The macro to create the numeric tabs is NTAB.WPM, and the macro to create the numeric tabs is TTAB.WPM.

The following exercise shows how to create and build these macros.

1. Create and build the TTAB macro:

Ctrl + F10	(Or select the Macro option from the Tools Menu and then select the Define Macro command) Issues the Define Macro command.
Type `TTAB`, Enter	Names the macro.
Type `Enter Text Tabs`	Describes the macro.
Enter	Accepts description of the macro.
Shift + F8	Enters the Format command.
L	Takes the Line option.
T	Selects the Tabs command.
Ctrl + End	Clears all tabs.
0.5, Enter	(Or use the cursor to position to the 0.5-inch position on the tab line and press L) Enters first tab stop.
1.0, Enter	Enters second text tab stop.
1.5, Enter	Enters third text tab stop.
F7 (2)	Exits Tab Menu and returns to the document.
Ctrl + F10	Ends the macro-definition process.

2. Create and build the NTAB macro:

Ctrl + F10	(Or select the Macro option from the Tools Menu and then select the Define Macro command) Issues the Define Macro command.

Type NTAB, Enter	Names the macro.
Type Enter Numeric Tabs	Describes the macro.
Enter	Accepts macro description.
Shift + F8	Enters the Format command.
L	Takes the Line option.
T	Selects the Tabs command.
Ctrl + End	Clears all tabs.
0.5, Enter, D	(Or use the cursor to position to the 1.5-inch position on the tab line and press D) Enters the numeric tab.
4.0, Enter, D	Enters second numeric tab stop.
5.1, Enter, D	Enters third numeric tab stop.
6.2, Enter, D	Enters the fourth numeric tab stop.
F7 (2)	Exits the Tab Menu and returns to the document.
Ctrl + F10	Ends the macro-definition process.

Anytime that you now wish to enter numeric data, issue the following commands:

Alt + F10	Enters the Macro command.
Type NTAB, Enter	Names the numeric tab macro.

After entering the numeric information and placing text tab stops at the pointer location, enter the following commands:

Alt + F10	Enters the Macro command.
Type TTAB, Enter	Names the text tab macro.

FORMAT Shift + F8

The **Format** (Shift + F8) **command** controls how a document appears on the screen and on the printed page. The Format menu (Figure 3.1) contains four submenus: Line, Page, Document, and Other. Once one of these is selected, a new menu appears on your screen.

Most of the commands in the Format Menu embed codes in your document to perform a desired task. If you want one of these options to affect the entire document, you must first position to the beginning of your document. If you want only an area of the document to be affected, position the cursor at the head of that area and enter the command. From the cursor location on, the document is now affected by this command. You may now have to position the cursor at the end of the area of your document to be affected and re-enter the original settings to return the rest of the document to its original settings.

The following discussion covers the most commonly used options of the Line, Page, and Other submenus.

HINTS/HAZARDS The position of the cursor in your document determines the point that most of the commands discussed in this chapter take effect.

Figure 3.1

The Format Menu.

```
Format

     1 - Line
              Hyphenation                     Line Spacing
              Justification                   Margins Left/Right
              Line Height                     Tab Set
              Line Numbering                  Widow/Orphan Protection

     2 - Page
              Center Page (top to bottom)     Page Numbering
              Force Odd/Even Page             Paper Size/Type
              Headers and Footers             Suppress
              Margins Top/Bottom

     3 - Document
              Display Pitch                   Redline Method
              Initial Codes/Font              Summary

     4 - Other
              Advance                         Overstrike
              Conditional End of Page         Printer Functions
              Decimal Characters              Underline Spaces/Tabs
              Language                        Border Options

Selection: 0
```

Figure 3.2

The Format: Line Menu.

```
Format: Line

     1 - Hyphenation                   No

     2 - Hyphenation Zone - Left       10%
                           Right       4%

     3 - Justification                 Left

     4 - Line Height                   Auto

     5 - Line Numbering                No

     6 - Line Spacing                  1

     7 - Margins - Left                1"
                   Right               1"

     8 - Tab Set                       Rel: -1", every 0.5"

     9 - Widow/Orphan Protection       No


Selection: 0
```

Shift + F8, L

Select Line from the Layout Menu

LINE

The Format: Line Menu (Figure 3.2) contains options that control line endings, spacing, numbering, grouping, length, and tab settings.

5.1

3 Justification This option determines how text is to align with respect to the margins. When this option is selected, the following menu appears on the screen:

```
Justification: 1 Left; 2 Center; 3 Right; 4 Full: 0
```

1 *Left* Left justification leaves a ragged right-hand margin.

2 *Center* Center justification centers all text. If you block several lines of

5.1

text and then center them using the Center (Shift + F6) command, WordPerfect inserts a [Just:Center] code at the beginning of the block and then inserts a code for whichever method of justification is in effect for the document.

3 Right Right justification aligns all text on the right-hand margin and leaves the left-hand margin ragged.

4 Full Full justification aligns the text on the printed page with smooth left- and right-hand margins. It is WordPerfect's default.

5 Line Numbering This option prints your document with a line number at the beginning of each line of text.

6 Line Spacing As described in Chapter 1, you can change the spacing of a WordPerfect document to any number of blank lines between each line of text. Single-, double-, or triple-space your document by changing this entry to 1, 2, or 3. Specify line-and-a-half spacing by entering 1.5.

7 Margins: Left/Right See Chapter 2.

8 Tab Set See Chapter 2.

9 Widow/Orphan Protection A **widow** is a first line of a paragraph that appears alone at the bottom of a page. An **orphan** is a last line of a paragraph that appears alone at the top of a page. The Widow/Orphan Protection option prevents their occurrence anywhere below where the code is entered.

Shift + F8, P

Select Page from the Layout Menu

PAGE

The Format: Page option (Figure 3.3) controls how text appears on a page, the amount of text that is to appear, paper changes, headers or footers, and page numbering.

3/4 Headers/Footers **Headers** and **footers** are lines of text printed in the top and bottom margins, respectively. Enter the command at the start of the file or at the beginning of the page on which you want headers or footers to start, and they will also appear on all subsequent pages. The default is no headers or footers.

The Headers or Footers command lets you create two different headers and two different footers, so that even and odd pages can be different. The Headers and Footers command menus let you choose which header you wish to use, which pages it will appear on (all, odd, even, or none), and what text it will contain.

To edit an existing header or footer, position your cursor just after the [Header/Footer] code, enter the Header or Footer command, and select the Edit option.

To prevent a header from appearing on the first page of a document, enter the header code after the first line but somewhere before the last line of the first page. The header line(s) will then begin to appear on the second page.

Use the command ^B (Ctrl + B) to automatically insert page numbers in a header or footer. The top line in Figure 3.4 would result in a page number appearing where you see ^B. If page numbers are printing twice on each page, it is probably because you are asking for a page number in a header or footer and in a Page Numbering command. Eliminate the Page Numbering command.

Figure 3.3
The Format: Page Menu.

```
Format: Page

     1 - Center Page (top to bottom)     No

     2 - Force Odd/Even Page

     3 - Headers

     4 - Footers

     5 - Margins - Top                    1"
                   Bottom                 1"

     6 - Page Numbering

     7 - Paper Size                       8.5" x 11"
               Type                       Standard

     8 - Suppress (this page only)



Selection: 0
```

Figure 3.4
A sample footer screen.

```
Four Software Tools Page ^B




Header A:  Press Exit when done                     Ln 1" Pos 3.25"
```

5 Margins: Top/Bottom This option sets new margins for the top and bottom of each page. The default margins are 1 inch.

6 Page Numbering This option displays the menu depicted in Figure 3.5. WordPerfect automatically controls the page numbering of a document. From time to time, however, you may want to alter this automatic numbering. For example, you may be working on a report that is composed of a number of different files—part 1 residing in the file REPORT1, say, and part 2 in the file REPORT2. Suppose part 1 has 10 pages, and you want the two parts to be numbered sequentially. The first page of REPORT2 should then be page 11.

Entering a **new page number** is a two-step process: (1) Enter the new page number and (2) specify its format. To do this, place the cursor at the beginning of the REPORT2 file. Press Shift + F8 (Format), select Page, and take option 6. Enter the new page number, in this case 11. If you wish to have roman numbering, simply enter the beginning page number as a roman numeral. The Roman option displays numbers as i, ii, iii, iv, and so forth. You can use the Roman option for such items as a preface, foreword, or table of contents.

As soon as you change the page number, the new number appears on the status line. When you print REPORT1, its pages will be numbered 1 to 10; when you print REPORT2, WordPerfect will number the first page of this document 11. Subsequent pages are numbered consecutively.

Figure 3.5
The Format: Page Numbering Menu.

```
Format: Page Numbering

     1 - New Page Number        1

     2 - Page Number Style      ^B

     3 - Insert Page Number

     4 - Page Number Position No page numbering


Selection: 0
```

HINTS/HAZARDS When you use page numbers, WordPerfect subtracts the line height of the page number font plus ⅙ inch from the text space on the page to provide a blank line between the text and the page number. The soft page breaks shown on your screen accurately depict where the printed breaks will occur as long as you do not incorporate headers and footers.

Page Number Position This option from the Page Numbering Menu specifies where to place page numbers according to the menu in Figure 3.6. The default is no page numbering. WordPerfect places the page number in the top or bottom margin and subtracts the line height of the page number font plus ⅙ inch from the text space on the page. This means that you get fewer lines of text printed per page. All page numbers are aligned on the margins.

Shift + F8, O
Select Order from the Layout Menu

OTHER

The Format: Other Menu (Figure 3.7) contains advanced formatting commands. Because your ability to use many of these commands depends on your printer, only the most important commands are covered here.

2 Conditional End of Page The **Conditional End of Page command** specifies that if a page break occurs in the next *x* lines a hard page break will occur. After entering the command, tell WordPerfect how many lines from the cursor location are to be "page-break protected" with the prompt `Number of lines to keep together: _`. This command is useful for protecting tables from page breaks that would otherwise leave half the table at the bottom of one page and place the other half at the top of the next page.

Suppose you want to keep the following six lines together:

```
Inflation During the 1980s

1980     9.9%
1981     8.5%
1982     6.0%
1983     4.5%
```

Figure 3.6

The Format: Page Number Position Menu.

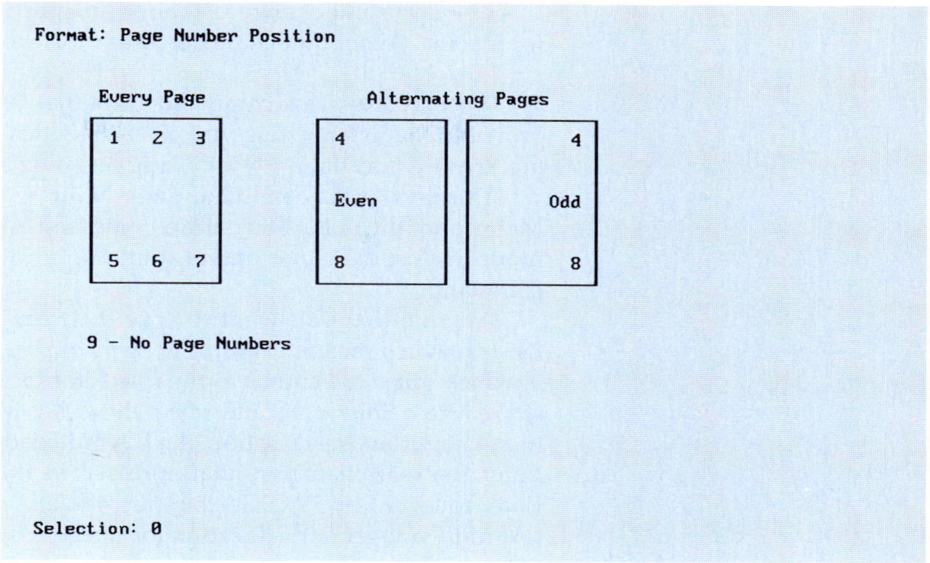

Figure 3.7

The Format: Other Menu.

```
Format: Other

     1 - Advance

     2 - Conditional End of Page

     3 - Decimal/Align Character       .
         Thousands' Separator          ,

     4 - Language                      US

     5 - Overstrike

     6 - Printer Functions

     7 - Underline - Spaces            Yes
                     Tabs              No

     8 - Border Options



Selection: 0
```

Place your cursor at the beginning of the text to be protected. Select the Format (Shift + F8) command and the Conditional End of Page command. Enter the number 6 to keep the six lines together.

3 Decimal/Align Character The decimal point (period) is the default alignment character. (Therefore, you do not need this command if you wish to align numbers that contain decimals.) You can change this character as often as you wish. For example, if you wish to align positive numbers with negative numbers shown by parentheses, your align character would be the right parenthesis. This allows the right parenthesis to appear to the right of any numbers, as in the example below:

```
65,000
 7,000
  (500)
99,567
```

If you wish to change the thousands separator from a comma to a period, for instance, enter that character after the decimal/align character is entered.

5 Overstrike This command combines two keyboard characters into one printable character, letting you place diacritics—accents (ˋ or ˊ), circumflexes (ˆ), macrons (-), and tildes (~), for example—over words.

To activate this command, press Shift + F8 (Format) and select the Other Menu and then the Overstrike command. Alternatively, if you are using a mouse, select the Other option from the Layout Menu and then the Overstrike command.

Assume that you want to type the Spanish phrase *Voy a pasar un año en España,* which means *I'm going to spend a year in Spain.* First type `Voy a pasar un a`, which takes the cursor to the character location that contains the first overstrike. Press Shift + F8 and select the Other Menu option, the Overstrike command, and the Create option. An [Ovrstk] code now appears on the status line. Enter the two characters that are used in the overstrike operation, `n~`. Press Enter followed by F7 (Exit) to return to your document. Continue entering the text until you get to the location for the next overstrike. Enter the same series of commands as above.

Your line on the screen should now look like this: `Voy a pasar un a~o en Espa~a`. You will not see all the characters on the screen, but they will print out correctly.

The Edit option finds the nearest overstrike code in a document to allow you to change it. In finding a code, WordPerfect moves backward within the file. If it is unsuccessful in locating a code in that direction, it moves forward.

You can enter up to 30 characters for an overstrike command. When the document is printed, all characters are printed on top of one another in the same character location.

FONT

Ctrl + F8

Select Font from the Menu

WordPerfect's Font command changes your current font and/or changes the size, appearance, or color of the text when the document is printed. This is the menu:

```
1 Size: 2 Appearance; 3 Normal; 4 Base Font; 5 Print Color: 0
```

The manner in which font attributes are displayed on the screen varies with the monitor screen that you are using.

CHARACTER FONT/PITCH

Pitch refers to how many characters are printed per horizontal inch of text. A pitch of 12 (also known as elite) results in 12 characters appearing per inch (cpi) of text; a pitch of 10 (also known as pica) results in 10 cpi. WordPerfect, unless told to do otherwise, defaults to 10-pitch (pica) text. Many impact letter-quality or dot-matrix printers only support characters printed in 10, 12, or 17 cpi. More advanced dot-matrix printers, and especially laser printers, support characters of many different character sizes as well as styles of types called fonts. A **font** is a specific style and size of character. Examples of different fonts include Times Roman, Helvetica, Letter Gothic, Elite, and Courier. You can also often specify how large the characters generated using a font are going to be. Font size is determined by a measurement called **points.** The more points in a character, the larger that character will be when it prints.

If you are using a printer with limited fonts, you may only be able to switch from 10 cpi to 12 cpi. If, however, you have a laser printer that supports different fonts, you may have many different fonts as well as different sizes of type from which to choose.

Proportional Versus Fixed-Pitch Fonts In a **fixed-pitch font,** each character that appears on a line takes up the same amount of space. This means that the character *M* requires the same amount of space as the character *I*. With fixed pitch, the output is usually designated in cpi. This means that if you are using a 12-cpi font, each inch of print will always contain 12 characters. The same holds true for 10 cpi, 5 cpi, or any other type style.

A **proportional font,** on the other hand, has larger characters occupying more space than smaller letters. This means that 1 inch of print may have as many as 12 or 13 characters, whereas another inch of print may have only 10 characters. Proportional fonts usually make text on a printed page look more balanced.

If you are using a proportional font, you can probably see why WordPerfect requires such things as margins and tabs to be entered in inch increments. Because different characters have different widths, tabs at character locations would result in "wavy" columns appearing on your page.

The Font Menu provides tremendous flexibility in printing your document. Various sizes of text can be included in a document (Figure 3.8). Make certain that you have first positioned your cursor where you wish to have the new font start.

When you select a new font size, WordPerfect automatically keeps track of the new line height, character size, and spacing and adjusts all spacing increments accordingly. This means that once you have set your margins, you don't have to worry about them even when you are printing larger characters. Page size is also automatically tracked so that page breaks occur at the correct locations.

When you select this option, be sure that you have selected the appropriate **base font.** If you want to change the size of the regular type that will appear in your printed document, select option 4 before making any other changes.

1 Size This option determines the amount of space characters are to take up on a line (see Figure 3.8). The menu looks like the following:

```
1 Suprscpt; 2 Subscpt; 3 Fine; 4 Small; 5 Large; 6 Vry Large; 7 Ext Large: 0
```

Select the size option that you wish. Depending on your printer, each size is slightly larger than the previous. Any text now selected appears in a specific color or shade based on the type of monitor attached to your computer.

Superscript/Subscript The Superscript/Subscript option prints a character or a block of characters one-third to one-half line above (superscript) or below (subscript) the current line of text.

Simple subscript:	A_2
Simple superscript:	2^2
Multiple subscript:	$\text{Chromium}_{\text{Dioxide}}$
Multiple superscript:	A^{23}

This is useful in scientific and academic environments.

These commands may not be supported (that is, the output cannot always be predicted) on dot-matrix printers, but they are supported by most letter-

Figure 3.8
The PRINTER.TST document provides a sample of various font sizes and an example of how WordPerfect 5.1 can intermix text and graphics.

WordPerfect 5.1 Printer Test

WordPerfect 5.1 has many new features such as labels, spreadsheet imports, tab sets relative to margins, pull-down menus, mouse support, and more advanced macro and merge functions. WordPerfect 5.1 also supplements your printer's available characters by graphically printing over 1,500 international, legal, math, scientific, and typographical characters.

Japanese ㇲ Copyright © Hand ☛ Greek Δ

Equations can be created using WordPerfect's Equation feature.

$$\int_0^\infty x^{n-1}e^{-x}dx = \int_0^1\left(\log\frac{1}{x}\right)dx = \frac{1}{n}\prod_{m=1}^{\infty}\frac{\left(1+\frac{1}{m}\right)}{1+\frac{n}{m}} = \Gamma(n),\ n\neq 0,-1,-2,-3,\ldots$$

The Tables feature in WordPerfect 5.1 creates, formats, and edits tables easily. The Tables Options[1] can be used to improve the appearance of the table.

Print Attributes	567,845.56	Centered	Right Aligned
	67,887.47	Shadow	SMALL CAPS
	635,733.03	Redline	~~Strikeout~~

Fine, Small, Normal, Large, Very Large, Extra Large, Superscript, and Subscript are some of the printing features that have made **WordPerfect the world's number one word processor.**

You can create ruled and numbered paper by using User Boxes with numbers and graphic lines as borders. Text size and ***appearance*** may be changed without affecting the numbers or lines.

Integrating Text and Graphics

Graphic images can be scaled, rotated, and moved. You can indicate the style of the border and include a caption.

MOUSE

The graphic image can be placed anywhere on the page, inserted in a line, tied to a paragraph, or included in a header or footer.

[1] Although only double and single lines are used in this table, many other border styles are available including dashed lines, dotted lines, thick lines, extra thick lines, and no lines at all.

This document printed in WordPerfect 5.1 - April 16, 1990 4:10 pm.

quality printers. The Superscript/Subscript is accomplished by first including the character(s) in a Block (Alt + F4) command, pressing Ctrl + F8 (Font), selecting the Size option, and then taking option 1 or 2.

Once the appropriate command has been issued, the text appears highlighted on the screen, but it does not appear as a subscript or superscript. To verify how the text will print, issue the Reveal Codes (Alt + F3) command. You turn off subscripting/superscripting by issuing the Font (Ctrl + F8) command and taking the Normal (3) option.

2 Appearance The Appearance option deals with the style of text. The following menu appears:

```
1 Bold 2 Underln 3 Dbl Und 4 Italc 5 Outln 6 Shadow 7 Sm Cap 8 Redln 9 Stkout: 0
```

Two of these options, Bold and Underline, are available using the F6 and F8 keys, respectively.

Redline and Strikeout These options mark text within a document to draw attention to added text or text that you think should be deleted. The Redline feature marks a line(s) of text by placing a vertical bar in the left margin. Invoke the Redline feature by the Font (Ctrl + F8) command and Appearance option.

Select Redline by pressing 8. Now enter the text that you desire to be redlined. When you are finished, press Ctrl + F8 (Font) again, select the Appearance option, and then select Normal (3). On a color monitor, the text will be displayed in red, whereas a monochrome monitor that has been specially configured for WordPerfect will display the text in some form of shaded video. On a printout, the text will look something like the following:

```
This is an example of text residing in a paragraph that has been marked via the Redline command.
```

The Strikeout command causes a dash (-) to be printed over every character in a portion of text, indicating that the marked text is not supposed to be there.

3 Normal The Normal option cancels any selected font features that have been turned on and returns any following text back to the base font.

4 Base Font This selects the font against which any other font options will be controlled. From the menu displayed, select the font as well as the beginning point size.

5 Print Color If you have a color printer, this option controls which colors to use in the document and how these colors will be shaded. Figure 3.9 shows the menu of possible colors. If you are using a regular printer, no color is assumed.

The following exercise generates the document shown in Figure 3.10, using a number of Font commands. It also assumes that you are using a font like Courier (10 cpi) or its equivalent.

1. Enter the text "Book Report" in very large print:

Alt + F6	Issues the Flush Right command.
Ctrl + F8	Issues the Font command.
S	Selects the Size command.
V	Selects the Very Large command.
Type `Book Report`	
→	Advances cursor beyond Very Large font code.
Enter	Moves cursor to next line.

2. Enter the text for the next two lines in large-style font:

Alt + F6	Issues the Flush Right command.
Ctrl + F8	Issues the Font command.
S	Selects the Size command.
L	Selects the Large command.
Type `English 101`	
Enter	Moves cursor to move to next line.
Type your name	
→	Moves cursor beyond Large font code.
Enter (2)	Inserts a blank line.

Figure 3.9
The Print Color Menu.

Print Color

	Primary Color Mixture Red	Green	Blue
1 - Black	0%	0%	0%
2 - White	100%	100%	100%
3 - Red	67%	0%	0%
4 - Green	0%	67%	0%
5 - Blue	0%	0%	67%
6 - Yellow	67%	67%	0%
7 - Magenta	67%	0%	67%
8 - Cyan	0%	67%	67%
9 - Orange	67%	25%	0%
A - Gray	50%	50%	50%
N - Brown	67%	33%	0%
O - Other			
Current Color	0%	0%	0%

Selection: 0

3. Place the book title in italics:

Ctrl + F8	Issues the Font command.
A	Selects the Appearance command.
I	Selects the Italics command.
Type `For Kicks`	
→	Moves cursor beyond Italics code.
Type `by Dick Francis`	

4. Save and print the document:

F10	Issues the Save command.
Type `FONT.DOC`	Names the file.
Enter	Executes the save.
Shift + F7	Issues the Print command.
F	Selects the Full Document option.

NEWSPAPER COLUMNS

Alt + F7

Select Columns Option from Layout Menu

Newspaper columns are most frequently used for club or organization newsletters. The Text Columns feature of WordPerfect creates a document in which the text flows from one column to the next on a page. Creating newspaper columns requires four steps: (1) defining the columns (column width and margins), (2) turning on the Columns feature, (3) entering the text, and (4) turning off the Columns feature.

Assume that you want to create a newsletter like that depicted in Figure 3.11 (you'll actually do this in a later exercise). This newsletter is built using the Columns feature of WordPerfect.

The various headings for this newsletter, the first paragraph, and the centered text "Topic of the Week" are entered in normal fashion. You are now ready to build the columns.

Figure 3.10
The output of the Font hands-on exercise.

Book Report
English 101
Tim Duffy

For Kicks by Dick Francis

Figure 3.11
The finished newsletter.

February 25, 1991 NEWSLETTER BIS Club

Current Events

A tour of the McDonald information center is planned for next Tuesday, March 1. At that time James A. Farentino, the director of the information center, will conduct a tour of McDonald Information Center as well as the Data Processing Operations Center. Sign-up sheets for the tour are available in Chalmers Hall, room 122. Refreshments will be served after the tour. Everyone is invited to attend.

Topic of the Week

Most people today must be able to express thoughts or needs via the written word, at least occasionally. It is often desirable to clarify written communication of what has already been committed to paper by refining, rephrasing, and restating it. Word processing can be defined as the manipulation of text data including creating a document, editing/changing it, storing and retrieving it, and printing it.

Word processing is generally accomplished by means of handwritten or typewritten page, but with either method, the process of revising text is difficult and time consuming. When using a typewriter, for example, you have to retype the entire page if it contains even one change. Or if time constraints disallow retyping, you must use scissors, correction tape, and correction fluid and then copy the patched document on a copy machine before anything approaching a professional looking document can be achieved.

Word processing software makes the process of changing a document much easier by automating the process of entering, editing, revising, storing, and printing documents. One of the most important aspects of computerized word processing is that you do not have to plan the original document carefully. Rather, you can compose the document while sitting at the keyboard; a rough outline is all that you need at the outset. Composing at the keyboard may require some practice on your part, but you will soon get used to composing documents as you enter them. You may also find that you don't forget to make points that somehow slip your mind when you are handwriting text. You can then print out or review the document and make changes. Thus, word processing greatly increases initial productivity.

Word processing began in the early 1900s with the introduction of the mechanical typewriter. The QWERTY keyboard on this device was designed to prevent keys from jamming, rather than to increase the speed of data entry by the user. The system was recognized as a vast improvement over handwriting; nonetheless, during the period from 1930 to 1950, various methods of automating the process of producing repetitive documents were attempted.

In the early 1960s, IBM introduced the mag typewriter, which used a magnetic tape cartridge for sequential access to documents that had been stored on the tape. This was hailed as a dramatic advance because it allowed a user not only to store and then retrieve a document, but also to make immediate insertions, deletions, and corrections on the original without having to change the entire document manually.

Line editors, the original word processors, are software development aids that allow a programmer to make changes in a line of program code. The program must be stored on some type of disk device, and only one line at a time can be changed and formatted in the program because line editors cannot deal with anything larger than an individual line.

During the late 1960s and early 1970s many large computer

Activate the Columns feature by first issuing the **Math/Columns** (Alt + F7) **command.** Once this command is issued, the Column Definition Menu depicted below appears on your screen:

```
1 Columns; 2 Tables; 3 Math: 0
```

Once the Columns command (1) is issued, the submenu below is displayed:

```
Columns: 1 On; 2 Off; 3 Define: 0
```

Now take the Define (3) option. The next task determines the type of column that you want to make. This is achieved by issuing the Define command and using the Text Column Definition screen depicted in Figure 3.12.

```
Text Column Definition

    1 - Type                                             Newspaper

    2 - Number of Columns                                2

    3 - Distance Between Columns

    4 - Margins

    Column     Left      Right     Column    Left      Right
     1:        1"        4"        13:
     2:        4.5"      7.5"      14:
     3:                            15:
     4:                            16:
     5:                            17:
     6:                            18:
     7:                            19:
     8:                            20:
     9:                            21:
    10:                            22:
    11:                            23:
    12:                            24:

Selection: 0
```

Figure 3.12
The Text Column Definition screen of WordPerfect for creating text columns.

For this particular example, leave the Type entry as Newspaper (1)—the default. Now tell WordPerfect that you want three columns of text, using the Number of Columns entry (2). Notice that WordPerfect automatically calculates the column width and the margins for each text column. Instead of using .5-inch margins, you want the margins to be .25 inches. Select option 3—Distance Between Columns—and make this change.

Once you have completed the columns-definition task, you are returned to the Columns submenu. You must now turn on the Columns feature by selecting the Column On (1) command. Continue entering information for the newsletter.

As you enter text for the newsletter and reach the end of a column, WordPerfect inserts a soft page code [Spg], and the cursor automatically moves to the top of the next column. When the last column on the page is filled, WordPerfect inserts another soft page code and moves the cursor to the first column at the top of the next page.

If you want to end a column before the end of the page, enter a hard return (Ctrl + Enter). The cursor then moves to the top of the next column. You can always tell which column you are in on a page because WordPerfect places a Col x entry in front of the Doc entry on the status line of the screen (Figure 3.13).

Instead of entering the text from the keyboard, you can also load text from a disk file using the Retrieve command. As this text is loaded, it is automatically placed in columns on the screen.

Once you have finished entering text, be sure to issue the Math/Columns command, select the Column option, and turn off the Columns feature using the Off command (2). Once that command is issued, you are placed at the left of the page, and you again have a single column of text on your screen.

EDITING TEXT

Editing text requires cursor movement within and between columns. Use regular cursor movement commands to move a cursor within a column. Cursor control keys simultaneously scroll all columns of text on a screen but reposition the cursor only within the column in which it resides. To position the cursor from one column to another, use the following **Goto commands:**

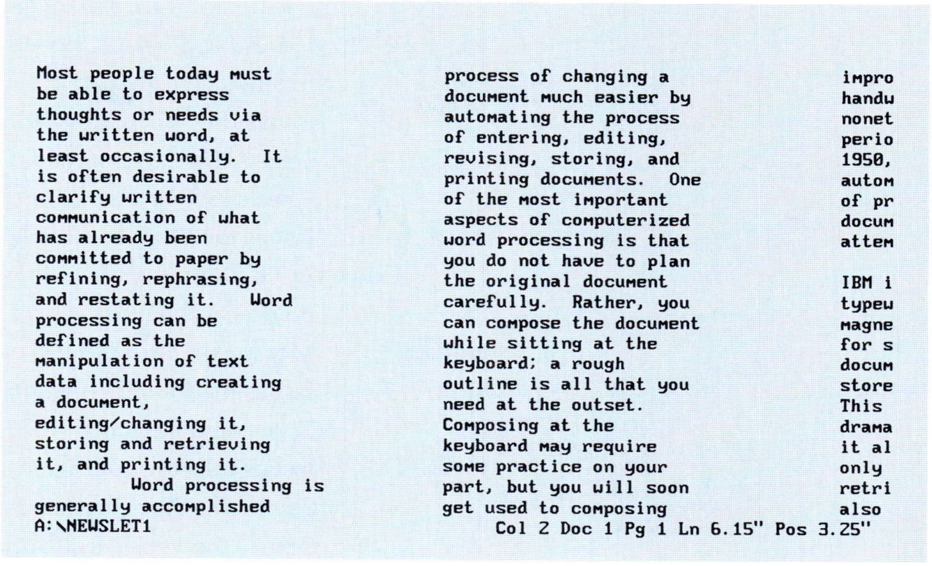

```
Most people today must           process of changing a            impro
be able to express               document much easier by          handw
thoughts or needs via            automating the process           nonet
the written word, at             of entering, editing,            perio
least occasionally.  It          revising, storing, and           1950,
is often desirable to            printing documents.  One         autom
clarify written                  of the most important            of pr
communication of what            aspects of computerized          docum
has already been                 word processing is that          attem
committed to paper by            you do not have to plan
refining, rephrasing,            the original document            IBM i
and restating it.   Word         carefully.  Rather, you          typew
processing can be                can compose the document         magne
defined as the                   while sitting at the             for s
manipulation of text             keyboard; a rough                docum
data including creating          outline is all that you          store
a document,                      need at the outset.              This
editing/changing it,             Composing at the                 drama
storing and retrieving           keyboard may require             it al
it, and printing it.             some practice on your            only
        Word processing is       part, but you will soon          retri
generally accomplished           get used to composing            also
A:\NEWSLET1                          Col 2 Doc 1 Pg 1 Ln 6.15" Pos 3.25"
```

Figure 3.13
The status line indicates in which column the cursor resides.

Ctrl + Home, ←	Moves cursor to previous column.
Ctrl + Home, →	Moves cursor to next column.
Ctrl + Home, Home, ←	Moves cursor to first column.
Ctrl + Home, Home, →	Moves cursor to last column.

Delete commands cause text to be deleted in the column where the cursor resides. Move commands also operate only on text within the column.

HINTS/HAZARDS

Newsletters often comprise numerous articles that are first written and stored as separate files. The newsletter is then constructed by using the Retrieve command to load each article into the newsletter document. This is a good practice because, if an article needs to be moved within the newsletter, it can simply be deleted where it is and then retrieved at the new location. This is easier and less risky than relying on the Undelete command because the article still exists as a separate file on disk.

In this exercise, assume that you are the editor of the newsletter depicted in Figure 3.11. Others who have worked on the newsletter have placed the introductory information in a file called INTRO.CH3 and the information for the first article in the file BOOKEXER. Your responsibility is to take these two files and create the newsletter. Start this exercise using a clear WordPerfect screen. Enter the first four lines of text depicted in Figure 3.11. Press Enter to place cursor on a new line.

Shift + F10	(Or select the Retrieve option from the File Menu) Issues the Retrieve command.
INTRO.CHO	Names the file to retrieve.
Enter	Retrieves INTRO.CHO.

↓, →	Positions cursor at *N* of Newsletter.
Alt + F4	Issues the Block command.
End	Extends block to end of line.
Ctrl + F8	Issues the Font command.
S	Selects the Size command.
V	Selects the Very Large option.
Alt + F4	Issues the Block command.
Ctrl + Home (2)	Redefines the previous block.
F6	Boldfaces the block.
Home (2), ↓	Moves cursor to the end of the file.
Shift + F6	Issues the Center command.
F6	Turns on boldfacing.
Ctrl + F8	Issues the Font command.
S	Selects the Size command.
V	Selects the Very Large option.
→ (2)	Moves cursor to the right of Size and Bold codes.
Type `Topic of the Week`	
Enter (3)	Inserts blank lines.
Alt + F7	Issues the Columns/Table command.
C	(Or select Columns option from Layout Menu) Selects the Columns option.
D	Selects the Column Definition screen (see Figure 3.12).
N	Selects the Number of Columns option.
3, Enter	Selects three columns.
D	Selects the Distance Between Columns option.
.25, Enter	Sets the distance as .25 inch.
F7	Returns to Column On/Off options.
O	Turns on columns.
Shift + F10	(Or select Retrieve from File Menu) Issues the Retrieve command.
BOOKEXER	Names the file to retrieve.
Enter	Retrieves BOOKEXER.

Now delete the blank lines between the paragraphs.

You should now see a screen like that depicted in Figure 3.14 on your monitor. Use the **View Document command** from the Print Menu to see how this file will print. Notice that the last page has unequal lines in the columns (Figure 3.15). This can be remedied in the following manner: To fix unequal lines in the columns, first determine how many lines are in the two columns. After examining the View Document screen and counting the lines, there are 77 total lines: 47 in the first column and 30 in the second (this number will vary depending on the type of printer and the font size that has been selected). To equally distribute the number of lines between the three columns, divide the 77 lines by the number of columns (3). Any fraction in this result must be rounded to a whole number (line). This gives the result of 26. This means that at the end of 26 lines in the first column press Ctrl + Enter to position to the next column. Then position

Figure 3.14
The beginning of the newsletter.

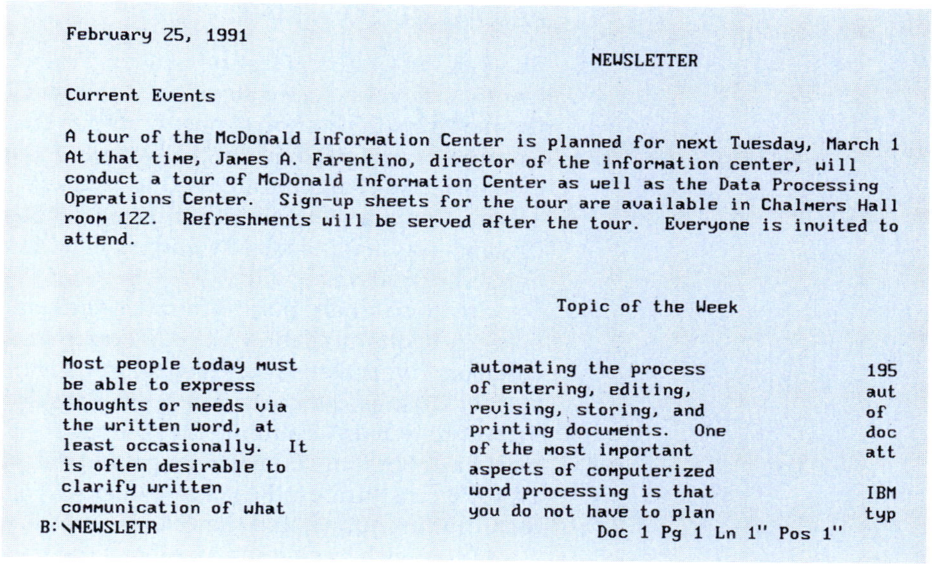

```
February 25, 1991
                              NEWSLETTER

Current Events

A tour of the McDonald Information Center is planned for next Tuesday, March 1
At that time, James A. Farentino, director of the information center, will
conduct a tour of McDonald Information Center as well as the Data Processing
Operations Center.  Sign-up sheets for the tour are available in Chalmers Hall
room 122.  Refreshments will be served after the tour.  Everyone is invited to
attend.

                           Topic of the Week

Most people today must          automating the process          195
be able to express              of entering, editing,           aut
thoughts or needs via           revising, storing, and          of
the written word, at            printing documents.  One        doc
least occasionally.  It         of the most important           att
is often desirable to           aspects of computerized
clarify written                 word processing is that         IBM
communication of what           you do not have to plan         typ
B:\NEWSLETR                          Doc 1 Pg 1 Ln 1" Pos 1"
```

Figure 3.15
The newsletter as it appears using the View Document command from the Print Menu.

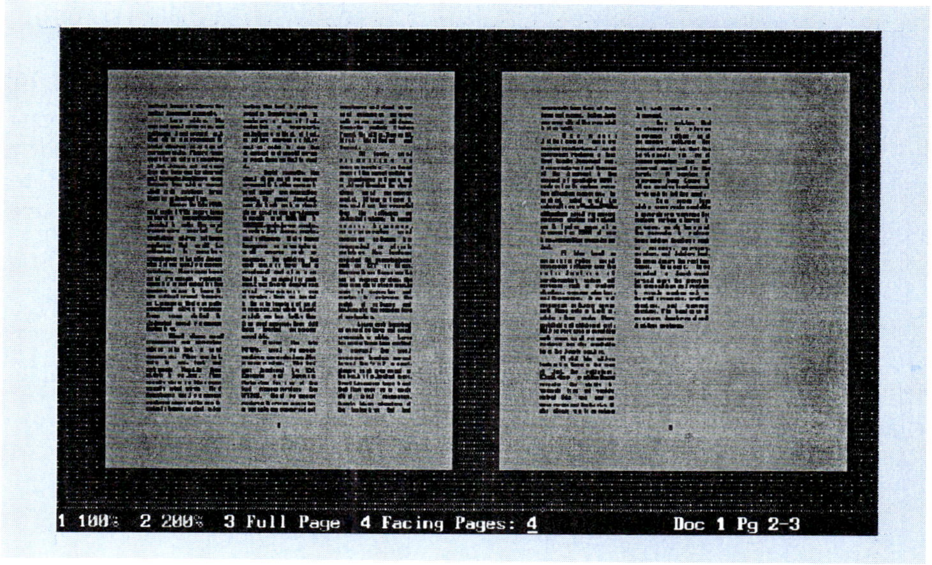

the cursor to the end of line 26 in the second column and again issue this command. You can now turn off the Columns feature using the commands below:

Alt + F7	Issues the Columns/Table command.
C	(Or select the Columns option from the Layout Menu) Selects the Columns option.
F	Selects the Off option.

You can now continue entering the newsletter with wide columns invoked. Save the file when you are finished.

PARALLEL COLUMNS

The Parallel Columns feature of WordPerfect lets you create columns to enter text that moves across columns in a group. Unlike newspaper columns, which "snake" from the bottom of one column to the top of the next, the text in **parallel columns** is independent. In the sample document (Figure 3.16) using parallel columns, three columns are used to compare mouse-pointing devices. The first column contains the manufacturer and mouse name information, the second contains the manufacturer's address, and the third contains some comments about the products.

Create parallel columns in much the same fashion as newspaper columns, using the Column/Table (Alt + F7) command. After issuing the Column/Table command, you then select the Columns entry from the menu and the Define option. Change the column type to Parallel Columns and indicate to WordPerfect how many columns are to appear on the screen. If you want column margins other than .5 inch, change that entry. Once you define the columns to WordPerfect, turn on the columns using the Columns/Table command, select the Columns option, and then choose the On option.

If you wish to page-break protect the lines for an item that stretches across several columns (Figure 3.17), select the **Parallel with Block Protect** entry when you select the Type option from the Define Menu. Once the columns are activated, if a page break is to occur inside the lines used by an item, the page break occurs at the first line (Figure 3.18).

Once you have activated the columns, the status line contains the column number in which the cursor resides. When you enter text, that text is only entered in the column in which the cursor resides. When you have finished entering text in one column and wish to enter text in the next column, issue a hard return (Ctrl + Enter) to move to the next column.

Figure 3.16
A document using Parallel Columns.

Mouse Comparison

Mouse	**Address**	**Comments**
Keytronic **Professional Series Mouse** Version 1.1	Keytronic P.O. Box 14867 Spokane, WA 99214 (509)927-5515 (800)262-6006	$109 -- This mouse has smooth tracking ability and an ergonomic design. The company has excellent support policies. The mouse comes with a limited pop-up menu. Requires MS DOS 2.0 or later.
Logitech **Logitech Mouse** Version 4.0	Logitech Inc. 6505 Kaiser Drive Fremont, CA 94555 (415)795-8500	$119 -- This mouse has a wide range of pop-up menus, comes with a long cord, and has an ergonomic design. The pop-up menus require use of MS DOS 3.0 or later and a minimum of 384K of RAM.
Microsoft **Microsoft Mouse 400** Version 7.0	Microsoft 16011 N.E. 36th Way P.O. Box 97017 Redmond, WA 98073 (206)882-8080	$150 -- This mouse has an ergonomic design as well as adjustable acceleration. It comes with a long cord and the documentation is excellent. This mouse is the one that serves as the industry standard.

Figure 3.17

A Parallel Columns document with a page break in the middle of the text for a column entity.

```
Logitech              Logitech Inc.          $119 -- This mouse has
                      6505 Kaiser Drive      a wide range of pop-up
Logitech Mouse        Fremont, CA 94555      menus, comes with a
                      (415)795-8500          long cord, and has an
Version 4.0                                  ergonomic design.  The
                                             pop-up menus require
                                             use of MS DOS 3.0 or
                                             later and a minimum of
                                             384K of RAM.


Microsoft             Microsoft              $150 -- This mouse has
                      16011 N.E. 36th Way    an ergonomic design as
-----------------------------------------------------------------------
Microsoft Mouse 400   P.O. Box 97017         well as adjustable
                      Redmond, WA 98073      acceleration.  It
Version 7.0           (206)882-8080          comes with a long cord
                                             and the documentation
                                             is excellent.  This
                                             mouse is the one that
                                             serves as the industry
                                             standard.

B:\COLUMNS                        Col 1 Doc 1 Pg 4 Ln 2.25" Pos 1"
```

Figure 3.18

The same document with the Parallel with Block Protect command in effect.

```
Logitech              Logitech Inc.          $119 -- This mouse has
                      6505 Kaiser Drive      a wide range of pop-up
Logitech Mouse        Fremont, CA 94555      menus, comes with a
                      (415)795-8500          long cord, and has an
Version 4.0                                  ergonomic design.  The
                                             pop-up menus require
                                             use of MS DOS 3.0 or
                                             later and a minimum of
                                             384K of RAM.


-----------------------------------------------------------------------
Microsoft             Microsoft              $150 -- This mouse has
                      16011 N.E. 36th Way    an ergonomic design as
Microsoft Mouse 400   P.O. Box 97017         well as adjustable
                      Redmond, WA 98073      acceleration.  It
Version 7.0           (206)882-8080          comes with a long cord
                                             and the documentation
                                             is excellent.  This
                                             mouse is the one that
                                             serves as the industry
                                             standard.

B:\COLUMNS                        Col 3 Doc 1 Pg 3 Ln 9.49" Pos 6.25"
```

The following exercise lets you build the document containing parallel columns depicted in Figure 3.16. If necessary, clear the screen using the Exit (F7) command.

1. Enter the title:

   Shift + F6 — Issues the Center command.

   Type `Mouse Comparison`

   Enter (2) — Inserts blank line.

2. Define and turn on columns:

Alt + F7	Issues the Columns/Table command.
	(Or select the Columns option from the Layout Menu)
C	Selects the Columns option.
D	Selects the Define option.
T	Selects the Type option.
B	Selects the Parallel with Block Protect option.
N	Selects the Number of Columns option.
3, Enter	Specifies three parallel columns.
Enter	Returns to the previous menu.
O	Turns on columns.

3. Enter the text for the first item in column 1:

Shift + F6	Issues the Center command.
Type `Mouse`	
Enter (2)	Inserts a blank line.
Type `Keytronic`	
Enter (2)	Inserts a blank line.
Type `Professional Series Mouse`	
Enter (2)	Inserts a blank line.
Type `Version 1.1`	
Ctrl + Enter	Moves cursor to the next column.

Using the text depicted in Figure 3.16, enter the rest of the document. When you get to the bottom of the text for an entity in a column, be sure to press Ctrl + Enter. This command moves you to the next column. Save to disk using the name COLUMNS.

GRAPHICS

Alt + F9

Select Graphics

WordPerfect can embed graphics either through its Grab command or from output generated by many popular programs such as Lotus 1-2-3 graphs in a document. A number of graphic-generation software packages and screen grabbers can also be used. Refer to the WordPerfect documentation for a listing of compatible packages.

This feature requires a graphics card and a printer that can generate graphics. If a graphics adapter card is not included in your computer, you can still use the graphics feature. The only way to verify that a graphic has been properly embedded within your document is to print the file.

Using the graphics feature involves a number of actions on the part of the user. First decide where you want to place the graphic. Then create a box that the text on the page wraps around and decide on the size of the box, the graphic image or text that is to reside in the box, and what description (caption), if any, should be included.

WordPerfect lets you include five different types of graphics images within your document: figure boxes, table boxes, text boxes, user-defined boxes, and horizontal and vertical lines. Because the procedures for generating the first four types of graphics are the same, most of this discussion focuses on generating figures. With each type of graphics, WordPerfect keeps track of the graphic-type number and the data to be included in the box.

Figure boxes usually hold graphic images, diagrams, or charts. **Table boxes** contain lists of numbers, maps, statistical data, or any other type of columnar numeric-oriented data involving numbers. **Text boxes** hold quotes that can be entered from the keyboard or loaded from a disk file. **User-defined boxes** hold any image in a document that does not fit the other categories. The Line option lets you draw a **horizontal** or **vertical line** anywhere on the page. The Equation option lets you enter equations that require Greek symbols.

Each box type, labeled and numbered within the document, has its own submenu for building the box, including graphics/text in the box. The default numbering mode for tables is roman numerals (for example, Table I, Table II, and so forth). Figures contain the abbreviation Fig. and an arabic number (1, 2, and so forth). The numbering mode, border style, and other options can be changed with the Graphics Options Menu.

The following example involves including two graphic symbols in a document about word processing. By the end of this discussion, it will contain two graphic images provided with WordPerfect (PC-2.WPG and CNTRCT-2.WPG). It will also contain a text box that is created using the file QUOTE.CH3, which is contained on your data disk.

Alt + F9 GRAPHICS COMMAND

Once you decide that a graphic image should be embedded within a document, position the cursor to the location (often the first line of a paragraph) where you want the graphic and issue the Graphics (Alt + F9) command. The menu depicted below is what now appears on your screen:

```
1 Figure; 2 Table Box; 3 Text Box; 4 User Box; 5 Line; 6 Equation: 0
```

Select the Figure option (1), and the Figure Menu depicted below appears at the bottom of your screen:

```
Figure: 1 Create; 2 Edit; 3 New Number; 4 Options: 0
```

Now select the Create option (1). The screen depicted in Figure 3.19 now appears on your monitor. If you want WordPerfect to place the figure in your document, select option 1 (Filename) and enter the name of the graphic file as it exists on disk. Be sure to enter any file extension that appears in the directory for the desired file. In this case, the filename CNTRCT-2.WPG was entered. When you return to the document, a border that is to contain the figure appears on your screen (Figure 3.20).

If you want to see how the graphic is going to appear when the file is printed, press Shift + F7 (Print) and take the View Document option. Press F7 (Exit) when you wish to return to the document. This page can now be printed (Figure 3.21).

Now you want to make several changes to your document. You decide that the figure is too large and want to make it smaller. Do this by pressing Alt + F9 (Graphics), selecting the Figure option, and taking the Edit option. WordPerfect now prompts you for the number of the figure that you wish to edit. Enter 1. Having decided to make the figure smaller, you take option 7 (Size). All that you have to know is how wide you want the figure to be. After this information is entered, the height is automatically readjusted. Select option 1 (Set Width Auto Height) and enter 2.75 to change the width to 2¾ inches. When you press Enter, WordPerfect will have adjusted the size to `2.75" wide x 1.99" (high)` on the screen.

Figure 3.19

The Graphic Definition Menu.

```
Definition: Figure

    1 - Filename

    2 - Contents                    Empty

    3 - Caption

    4 - Anchor Type                 Paragraph

    5 - Vertical Position           0"

    6 - Horizontal Position         Right

    7 - Size                        3.25" wide x 3.25" (high)

    8 - Wrap Text Around Box Yes

    9 - Edit



Selection: 0
```

Figure 3.20

The figure box as it appears on your screen.

```
     Word processing is generally      ┌FIG 1──────────────────────
accomplished by means of handwritten   │
or typewritten page, but with either   │
method, the process of revising text   │
is difficult and time consuming.  When │
using a typewriter, for example, you   │
have to retype the entire page if it   │
contains even one change.  Or if time  │
constraints disallow retyping, you     │
must use scissors, correction tape,    │
and correction fluid, and then copy    │
the patched document on a copy machine │
before anything approaching a          │
professional looking document can be   │
achieved.                              │
                                       │
     Word processing software makes    │
the process of changing a document     └───────────────────────────
much easier by automating the process
of entering, editing, revising, storing, and printing documents.  One of the mos
important aspects of computerized word processing is that you do not have to pla
the original document carefully.  Rather, you can compose the document while
sitting at the keyboard; a rough outline is all that you need at the outset.
A:\BOOKEXER                                      Doc 1 Pg 1 Ln 2.25" Pos 1"
```

You also decide to write a caption for this figure, so you select option 3 (Caption). A blank entry screen appears with the prompt `Figure 1`, and you enter "Word processing can be done manually." The caption fits the width of the figure. When you are finished entering the caption text, press F7 (Exit).

Once you make these changes, WordPerfect automatically adjusts the size of the graphic and the amount of text to be included on each line around the figure. To verify that changes will appear properly on the printed page, use the View Document option of the Print command.

Now you want to place the PC-2.WPG figure toward the bottom of the page. Position your cursor at the paragraph toward the bottom of the page where you wish to start the figure. Press Alt + F9 (Graphics); select the Figure option; select the Create option. Take the Size option and change the width to 2.75 inches. Take the Filename option and enter PC-2.WPG (make certain that the path for the filename is entered properly). Take the Caption option and enter

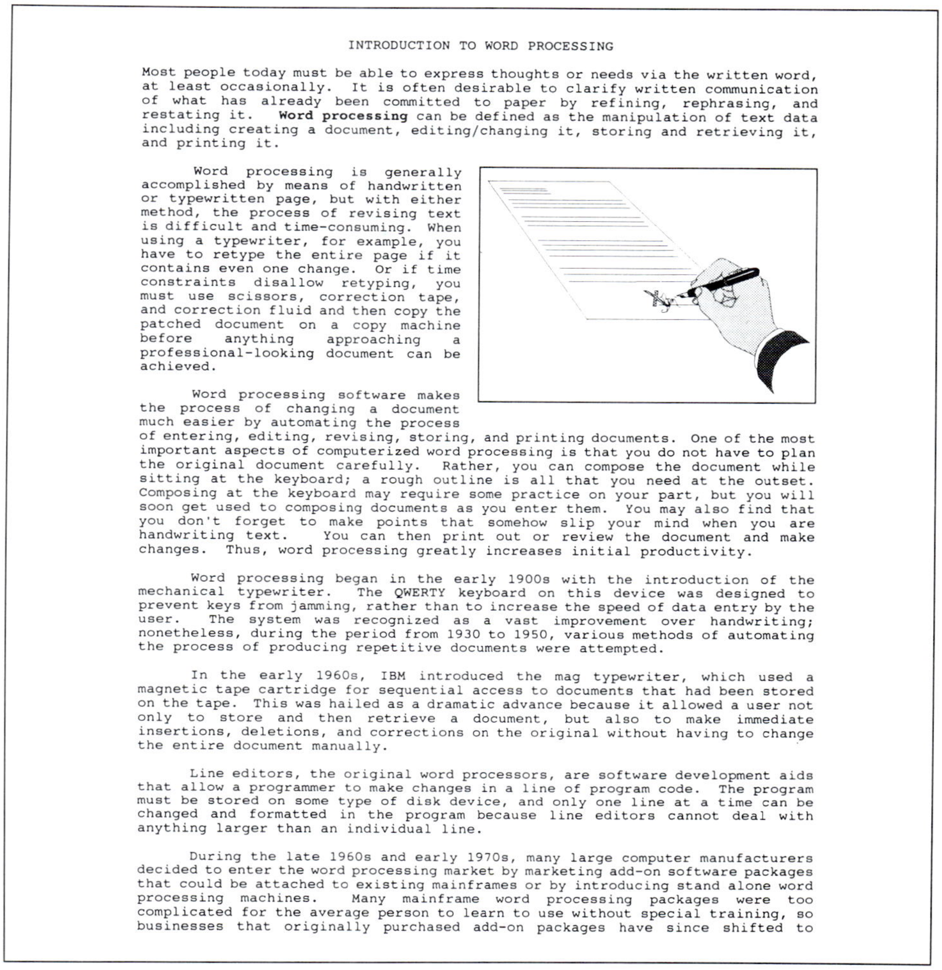

INTRODUCTION TO WORD PROCESSING

Most people today must be able to express thoughts or needs via the written word, at least occasionally. It is often desirable to clarify written communication of what has already been committed to paper by refining, rephrasing, and restating it. **Word processing** can be defined as the manipulation of text data including creating a document, editing/changing it, storing and retrieving it, and printing it.

Word processing is generally accomplished by means of handwritten or typewritten page, but with either method, the process of revising text is difficult and time-consuming. When using a typewriter, for example, you have to retype the entire page if it contains even one change. Or if time constraints disallow retyping, you must use scissors, correction tape, and correction fluid and then copy the patched document on a copy machine before anything approaching a professional-looking document can be achieved.

Word processing software makes the process of changing a document much easier by automating the process of entering, editing, revising, storing, and printing documents. One of the most important aspects of computerized word processing is that you do not have to plan the original document carefully. Rather, you can compose the document while sitting at the keyboard; a rough outline is all that you need at the outset. Composing at the keyboard may require some practice on your part, but you will soon get used to composing documents as you enter them. You may also find that you don't forget to make points that somehow slip your mind when you are handwriting text. You can then print out or review the document and make changes. Thus, word processing greatly increases initial productivity.

Word processing began in the early 1900s with the introduction of the mechanical typewriter. The QWERTY keyboard on this device was designed to prevent keys from jamming, rather than to increase the speed of data entry by the user. The system was recognized as a vast improvement over handwriting; nonetheless, during the period from 1930 to 1950, various methods of automating the process of producing repetitive documents were attempted.

In the early 1960s, IBM introduced the mag typewriter, which used a magnetic tape cartridge for sequential access to documents that had been stored on the tape. This was hailed as a dramatic advance because it allowed a user not only to store and then retrieve a document, but also to make immediate insertions, deletions, and corrections on the original without having to change the entire document manually.

Line editors, the original word processors, are software development aids that allow a programmer to make changes in a line of program code. The program must be stored on some type of disk device, and only one line at a time can be changed and formatted in the program because line editors cannot deal with anything larger than an individual line.

During the late 1960s and early 1970s, many large computer manufacturers decided to enter the word processing market by marketing add-on software packages that could be attached to existing mainframes or by introducing stand alone word processing machines. Many mainframe word processing packages were too complicated for the average person to learn to use without special training, so businesses that originally purchased add-on packages have since shifted to

Figure 3.21
Partial view of the printed document.

the text "Computers are now frequently used for word processing." for the caption. When printed, the document should resemble Figure 3.22.

Let's now examine in detail some of the options from the Definition: Figure Menu (see Figure 3.19). Anytime that you retrieve a file using the Filename option, the graphic in the current box is replaced by the new file's contents. If you wish to have multiple boxes on a page, they must be defined separately, and then a new graphic must be placed in that box.

DEFINITION MENU

The Definition Menu lets you control exactly how the graphic box and the resulting graphic file will appear on the printed page.

1 Filename The Filename option lets you retrieve data from a file and place it in the graphics box. If WordPerfect cannot read the file, an error message is displayed.

If you want to leave this box empty, do not load a file. If you want to enter text instead, select the Edit option and enter the text, along with any codes, in the text screen. After entering text, press F7 (Exit).

Figure 3.22
Partial document showing figure with caption.

INTRODUCTION TO WORD PROCESSING

Most people today must be able to express thoughts or needs via the written word, at least occasionally. It is often desirable to clarify written communication of what has already been committed to paper by refining, rephrasing, and restating it. **Word processing** can be defined as the manipulation of text data including creating a document, editing/changing it, storing and retrieving it, and printing it.

Word processing is generally accomplished by means of handwritten or typewritten page, but with either method, the process of revising text is difficult and time-consuming. When using a typewriter, for example, you have to retype the entire page if it contains even one change. Or if time constraints disallow retyping, you must use scissors, correction tape, and correction fluid and then copy the patched document on a copy machine before anything approaching a professional- looking document can be achieved.

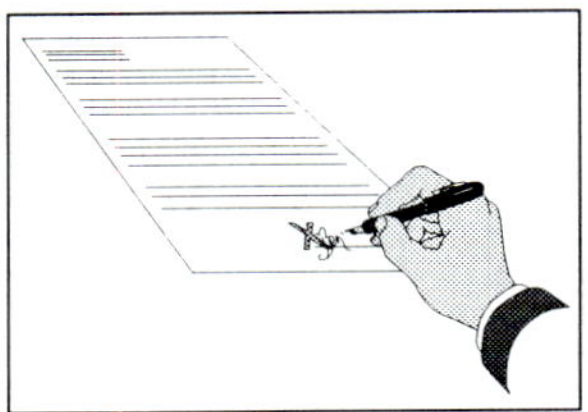

Figure 1 Word processing can be done manually.

Word processing software makes the process of changing a document much easier by automating the process of entering, editing, revising, storing, and printing documents. One of the most important aspects of computerized word processing is that you do not have to plan the original document carefully. Rather, you can compose the document while sitting at the keyboard; a rough outline is all that you need at the outset. Composing at the keyboard may require some practice on your part, but you will soon get used to composing documents as you enter them. You may also find that you don't forget to make points that somehow slip your mind when you are handwriting text. You can then print out or review the document and make changes. Thus, word processing greatly increases initial productivity.

Word processing began in the early 1900s with the introduction of the mechanical typewriter. The QWERTY keyboard on this device was designed to prevent keys from jamming, rather than to increase the speed of data entry by the user. The system was recognized as a vast improvement over handwriting; nonetheless, during the period from 1930 to 1950, various methods of automating the process of producing repetitive documents were attempted.

In the early 1960s, IBM introduced the mag typewriter, which used a magnetic tape cartridge for sequential access to documents that had been stored on the tape. This was hailed as a dramatic advance because it allowed a user not only to store and then retrieve a document, but also to make immediate insertions, deletions, and corrections on the original without having to change the entire document manually.

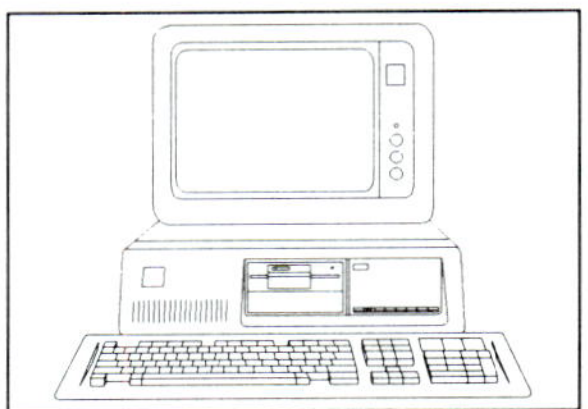

Figure 2 Computers are now frequently used for word processing.

Line editors, the original word processors, are software development aids that allow a programmer to make changes in a line of program code. The program must be stored on some type of disk device, and only one line at a time can be changed and formatted in the program because line editors cannot deal with anything larger than an individual line.

2 Contents This entry is controlled by the type of file loaded by WordPerfect.

3 Caption The Caption option displays text beneath the graphics box. Enter the text in a special captions screen that is displayed on your monitor. The word *Figure* and the figure number appear on the screen. The text of the caption wraps according to the width of the graphics box. Press F7 (Exit) when you have finished entering the caption text.

4 Anchor Type The Anchor Type option places three different types of boxes in your document. This option determines whether the graphics box moves with text. Once selected, it displays the following menu:

```
1 Paragraph; 2 Page; 3 Character: 0
```

Paragraph The Paragraph option (1) tells WordPerfect that the graphics box is to stay with its surrounding text. The function code for a paragraph box is placed at the beginning of the paragraph where the cursor resides. If the paragraph is too close to the bottom of the page for the graphics box to fit on the page, WordPerfect moves the box to the top of the next page.

Page The Page option (2), once selected, asks how many pages should be skipped before the graphic is to be printed. A 0 tells WordPerfect that the graphics box is to stay in the same position on the page. Insert the function code from the Page option at the cursor location. Also, insert this code before any text you want to wrap around the box, or else the box is moved to the next page. If you wish to have such a box at the top of a page, position the cursor to the top of the page and then issue the Graphics command.

Character The Character option (3) tells WordPerfect to treat the box as a single character regardless of the box size. When the line containing the character-type box code is wrapped, the next line starts below the box. This is the only type box allowed inside footnotes and endnotes.

5 Vertical Position The Vertical Position option depends on the type of box that you select. If you choose the Page option, place the graphic at the top, bottom, or center. If you choose the Paragraph option, enter an offset value such as 0 if you wish to have the box appear on the first line of the paragraph.

6 Horizontal Position The Horizontal Position option is tailored to the type selected. For example, if the Paragraph option is selected for type, the following menu appears:

```
Horizontal Position: 1 Left; 2 Right; 3 Center; 4 Both Left and Right: 0
```

7 Size The Size option determines the dimensions of the box used to hold the graphic. It displays the following menu:

```
1 Width (auto height); 2 Height (auto width); 3 Both; 4 Auto Both: 0
```

Width/Height The Width option (1) specifies the width for the box, and WordPerfect automatically calculates the box's height to maintain the proper scale for the graphic. The Height option (2) tells WordPerfect what height you want the box to be, and WordPerfect recalculates the properly scaled width. If you want total control, select the Set Both option (3) and enter the measurements.

8 Wrap Text Around Box Enter a no for this option if you want WordPerfect to ignore the graphics box and continue printing text from the left-hand margin to the right-hand margin. When this selection is set to no, the screen does not display the graphics box, but the graphic, along with overlayed text, appears when the document is printed. Use the View Document command from the Print Menu if you want to see how the box will appear when the document is printed.

9 Edit The Edit option rotates, scales, and moves the image in the box. If you have not placed a graphic or text in the box, this option lets you edit text in the box. If text or a graphic is loaded, the graphic appears within its graphic box along with the following menu at the bottom of your screen.

```
1 Move; 2 Scale; 3 Rotate; 4 Invert; 5 Black & White: 0
```

Move The Move option (1) moves the figure horizontally or vertically in the graphics box. The percentage amount is controlled via the arrow keys.

Scale The scale option (2) lets you enter a scale factor for increasing or decreasing the image size.

Rotate The Rotate option (3) lets you enter the degree increment that WordPerfect is to use to rotate the figure in a circle. The rotation amount is indicated in the lower right-hand corner. One hundred percent equals 360 degrees, whereas 25 percent equals 90 degrees.

Invert The Invert option (4) lets you specify that you want a mirror image of the graphic.

CONTROLLING THE GRAPHIC APPEARANCE

The Options entry of the Options: Figure submenu generates a menu (Figure 3.23) that provides a number of commands to control exactly how a graphic will be printed. While these default settings are sufficient for most users, the Gray Shading option (9) lets you make a graphic more striking. The document depicted in Figure 3.24 has a 10 percent gray shading for the graphic boxes.

LINE OPTION

The Line option of the Graphics Menu lets you, as the name implies, draw horizontal or vertical lines within a document. This option displays the following menu:

```
Create Line: 1 Horizontal; 2 Vertical; Edit Line: 3 Horizontal; 4 Vertical: 0
```

1 Horizontal The Horizontal option defines a horizontal line to WordPerfect. It displays a menu like that depicted in Figure 3.25. The Horizontal Position option (1) tells WordPerfect how wide the line is to be on the page. Once this option is selected, the following menu appears at the bottom of your screen:

```
Horizontal Pos: 1 Left; 2 Right; 3 Center; 4 Full; 5 Set Position: 0
```

Figure 3.23

The Options: Figure Menu for the Graphics command.

```
Options: Figure

     1 - Border Style
              Left                        Single
              Right                       Single
              Top                         Single
              Bottom                      Single
     2 - Outside Border Space
              Left                        0.167"
              Right                       0.167"
              Top                         0.167"
              Bottom                      0.167"
     3 - Inside Border Space
              Left                        0"
              Right                       0"
              Top                         0"
              Bottom                      0"
     4 - First Level Numbering Method     Numbers
     5 - Second Level Numbering Method    Off
     6 - Caption Number Style             [BOLD]Figure 1[bold]
     7 - Position of Caption              Below box, Outside borders
     8 - Minimum Offset from Paragraph    0"
     9 - Gray Shading (% of black)        0%

Selection: 0
```

Figure 3.24

A graphics box with 10 percent gray shading.

INTRODUCTION TO WORD PROCESSING

Most people today must be able to express thoughts or needs via the written word, at least occasionally. It is often desirable to clarify written communication of what has already been committed to paper by refining, rephrasing, and restating it. **Word processing** can be defined as the manipulation of text data including creating a document, editing/changing it, storing and retrieving it, and printing it.

Word processing is generally accomplished by means of handwritten or typewritten page, but with either method, the process of revising text is difficult and time-consuming. When using a typewriter, for example, you have to retype the entire page if it contains even one change. Or if time constraints disallow retyping, you must use scissors, correction tape, and correction fluid and then copy the patched document on a copy machine before anything approaching a professional- looking document can be achieved.

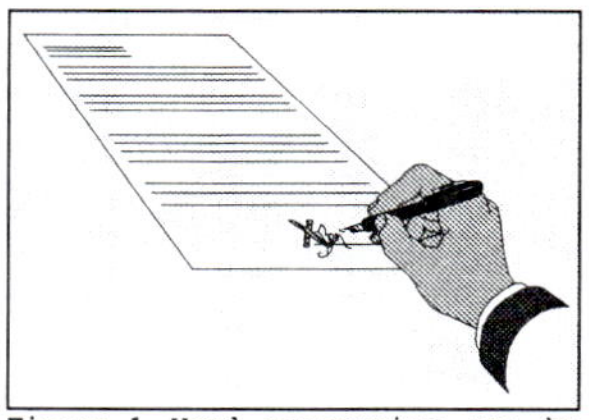

Figure 1 Word processing can be done manually.

Word processing software makes the process of changing a document much easier by automating the process of entering, editing, revising, storing, and printing documents. One of the most important aspects of computerized word processing is that you do not have to plan the original document carefully. Rather, you can compose the document while sitting at the keyboard; a rough outline is all that you need at the outset. Composing at the keyboard may require some practice on your part, but you will soon get used to composing documents as you enter them. You may also find that you don't forget to make points that somehow slip your mind when you are handwriting text. You can then print out or review the document and make changes. Thus, word processing greatly increases initial productivity.

Word processing began in the early 1900s with the introduction of the mechanical typewriter. The QWERTY keyboard on this device was designed to prevent keys from jamming, rather than to increase the speed of data entry by the user. The system was recognized as a vast improvement over handwriting; nonetheless, during the period from 1930 to 1950, various methods of automating the process of producing repetitive documents were attempted.

In the early 1960s, IBM introduced the mag typewriter, which used a magnetic tape cartridge for sequential access to documents that had been stored on the tape. This was hailed as a dramatic advance because it allowed a user not only to store and then retrieve a document, but also to make immediate insertions, deletions, and corrections on the original without having to change the entire document manually.

Line editors, the original word processors, are software development aids that allow a programmer to make changes in a line of program code. The program must be stored on some type of disk device, and only one line at a time can be changed and formatted in the program because line editors cannot deal with anything larger than an individual line.

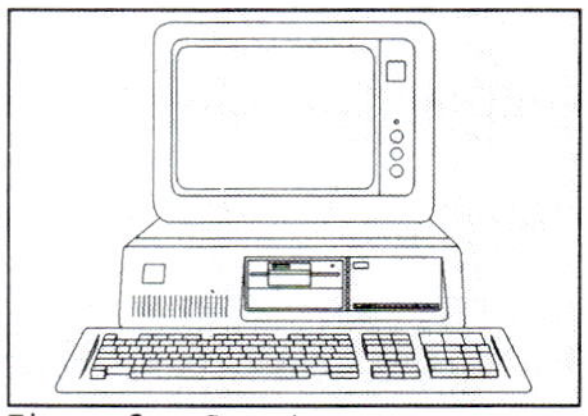

Figure 2 Computers are now frequently used for word processing.

These options position the line against the corresponding margin (Left or Right), center between margins (Center), and extend from the left-hand to the right-hand margin (Full) or set the exact beginning and ending location (Set Position).

The Vertical Position option (2) tells WordPerfect where the line is to start. WordPerfect defaults to the Baseline, which makes the bottom of the graphic line align properly with the bottom of text characters. Novice users should leave this setting as is.

The Length of Line option (3) tells WordPerfect to calculate the length of the line for Right or Left Lines from the cursor location to the right- or left-hand margin.

The Width of Line option (4) tells WordPerfect the width of the line to draw. If you change this option and you have the vertical position using the Baseline option, WordPerfect adjusts the line height upward from the text baseline.

The Gray Shading option (5) adjusts the darkness of the line. Leave this as is.

2 Vertical The Vertical option defines a vertical line to WordPerfect. It displays a menu similar to the Horizontal option (Figure 3.26). Only some of the different options are discussed. The Horizontal Position option (1) determines

Figure 3.25
The Graphics: Horizontal Line Menu.

```
Graphics: Horizontal Line

     1 - Horizontal Position        Full

     2 - Vertical Position          Baseline

     3 - Length of Line

     4 - Width of Line              0.013"

     5 - Gray Shading (% of black) 100%


Selection: 0
```

Figure 3.26
The Graphics: Vertical Line Menu.

```
Graphics: Vertical Line

     1 - Horizontal Position        Left Margin

     2 - Vertical Position          Full Page

     3 - Length of Line

     4 - Width of Line              0.013"

     5 - Gray Shading (% of black) 100%


Selection: 0
```

where on the page the vertical line is to be placed. It displays the menu depicted below:

```
Horizontal Position: 1 Left; 2 Right; 3 Between Columns; 4 Set Position: 0
```

This option places the line along the left- or right-hand margin and between columns or lets you set your own positioning.

The Vertical Position option (2) determines the line length and displays the menu depicted below:

```
Vertical Position: 1 Full Page; 2 Top; 3 Center; 4 Bottom; 5 Set Position: 0
```

The Full Page option (1) extends the line from the top to bottom margin. The Top (2) and Bottom (4) options extend the line from the cursor position on the page. The Center option (3) is used with the Length of Line option and centers the line between the top and bottom margins. The Set Position option (5) lets you tailor the line to your exact needs.

The Length of Line option (3), used after you have entered the line characteristics for the vertical line, lets you change the length of the selected line to meet your exact needs.

3/4 Edit Line The Edit Line options let you make changes to the previously embedded line codes. This prevents you from having to delete a code and rebuild the characteristics of the line. It results in the same type of menus being displayed.

The following exercise lets you create a document with graphic images like that discussed at the beginning of this section.

IMPORTANT! Before you can start, you must use the Copy command of the List Files screen to copy the BOOKEXER file to the file GRAPHIC.CH3. You must also have access to the CNTRCT-2.WPG file and the PC-2.WPG WordPerfect graphic image files that come with the WordPerfect 5.1 package. These should be in the directory containing your WordPerfect 5.1 files. If they are not there, consult your instructor. You will also need the student text file QUOTE.CH3 from your student data disk.

Clear your WordPerfect screen and retrieve the GRAPHIC.CH3 file. At the beginning of the document, press Ctrl + F8 (Font) and set the Base Font to 12 cpi.

1. Position the cursor to Pos 1″ of the second paragraph to build the first figure (CNTRCT-2.WPG):

Alt + F9	Issues the Graphics command.
F	Selects the Figure command.
C	(Or select the Figure command from the Graphics Menu and then select the Create command) Selects the Create command.
F	Selects the Filename option.
CNTRCT-2.WPG	Enters the filename. (You may have to enter the path if this file is not on your data disk.)
Enter	Gets the file.
F7	Exits and returns to the document.
↓ (5)	Makes the figure box visible on the screen.
Shift + F7	Issues the Print command.
V	Selects the View Document command. You should now see an image similar to that appearing in Figure 3.21.
F7	Returns to the document.

2. Change the size of the graphic image and place a caption on the graphic using the Edit command:

Alt + F9	Issues the Graphics command.
F	Selects the Figure command.
E	(Or select the Figure command from the Graphics Menu and then select the Edit command) Selects the Edit command.
1, Enter	Enters the graphic figure number.
S	Selects the Size option.
W	Selects the Width/Auto Height option.
2.75, Enter	Enters the new width.

C	Selects the Caption option.
Type [space] `Word processing can be done manually.`	
F7 (2)	Exits the Caption screen and returns to the document.
↓ (4)	Resizes the figure box on the screen.

3. Enter the second graphic toward the bottom of the page. Position the cursor to the beginning (Pos 1″) of the paragraph that begins with "In the early 1960s, IBM introduced . . .":

Alt + F9	Issues the Graphics command.
F	Selects the Figure command.
C	(Or select the Figure command from the Graphics Menu and then select the Create command) Selects the Create command.
F	Selects the File option.
PC-2.WPG	Enters the filename. (You may have to enter the path if this file is not on your data disk.)
Enter	Gets the file.
C	Selects the Caption option.
Type [space] `Computers are now frequently used for word processing.`	
F7	Exits the Captions screen.
S	Selects the Size option.
W	Selects the Width/Auto Height option.
2.75, Enter	Enters the new width.
F7	Returns to the document.

4. View the document:

Shift + F7	Issues the Print command.
V	Selects the View Document command. You should now see a screen that appears similar to that depicted in Figure 3.22.
F7	Returns to the document.

5. Change the shading for the figure boxes. Position the cursor to the beginning of the document:

Alt + F9	Issues the Graphics command.
F	Selects the Figure command.
O	(Or select the Figure command from the Graphics Menu and then select the Options command) Selects the Options command.
G	Selects the Gray Shading option.
10, Enter	Chooses 10 percent shading.
F7	Returns to the document.

6. Create a text box on the second page to hold the quotation from the file QUOTE.CH3. Position the cursor to the beginning (Pos 1″) of the paragraph that begins with "Until recently, the stand-alone word processor . . .":

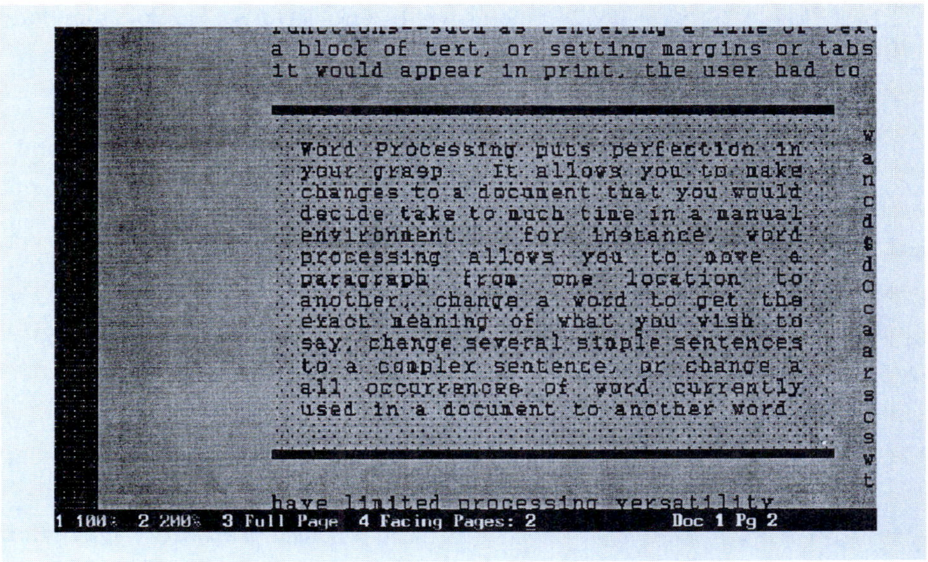

Figure 3.27
The View Document screen for the quotation.

Alt + F9	Issues the Graphics command.
B	Selects the Text Box command.
C	(Or select the Figure command from the Graphics Menu and then select the Text Box command) Selects the Create command.
F	Selects the Filename option.
QUOTE.CH3	Enters the filename. (You may have to enter the path if this file is not on your data disk.)
Enter	Gets the quote.
H	Selects the Horizontal Position option.
L	Selects the Left Justify command.
F7	Returns to your document.

7. View the document using the Print command:

Shift + F7	Issues the Print command.
V	Selects the View Document command. Select the 200% command. Use cursor-positioning commands to get the quote visible on the screen. You should now see a screen that appears similar to that depicted in Figure 3.27.
F7	Returns to the document.

8. Save the file.
9. If you have the printer capabilities, print the document. If you are using a dot-matrix printer, it may take some time to print.

The following exercise requires you to retrieve the file that was created in the preceding exercise—GRAPHICS.CH3 (Graphic Images). This exercise places a horizontal line in a header and footer to be used for each page of the document. It also resets the top and bottom margins.

1. Retrieve the GRAPHICS.CH3 document and make certain that the cursor is at the beginning of the document.
2. Reset the top and bottom margins:

Shift + F8	Issues the Format command.
P	(Or select the Page option of the Layout Menu) Selects the Page submenu.
M	Selects the Margins option.
.7, Enter	Sets new top margin.
.7, Enter	Sets the new bottom margin.

3. Enter the header.

H	Selects the Header command.
1	Selects the first header.
P	Selects the Every Page option.
Alt + F6	Issues the Flush Right command.
Type `Page`, Ctrl + B	Enters text Page ^B for the page number.
Enter	Positions to the next line.
Alt + F9	Issues the Graphics command.
L	Selects the Line option.
H	Selects the Horizontal command.
Enter	Executes the command.
F7	Exits the Header screen.
F	Selects the Footer command.
1	Selects the first footer.
P	Selects the Every Page command.
Alt + F9	Issues the Graphics command.
L	Selects the Line option.
H	Selects the Horizontal command.
Enter	Executes the command.
F7 (2)	Exits the Footer screen and returns to the document.

4. Use the View Document command from the Print Menu to verify that the headers and footers were entered properly.
5. Save the document to a file called GRAPHICS2.CH3.

Notice that this exercise required you to change the top and bottom margins to keep the same amount of text on a page. If these margins had not been changed, the second figure would have moved to the top of the next page. If text had been added to the footer, the margins would have to have been slightly smaller. Some experimentation may be required when you want lines in a header or footer. In such a situation, the View Document command of the Print Menu is indispensable.

The following exercise requires you to retrieve the file NEWSLETR.CH3 that was created in a previous exercise. This exercise places a vertical line between each column of the newsletter. Your final result should appear like the document depicted in Figure 3.28.

Figure 3.28

The newsletter with lines placed between columns.

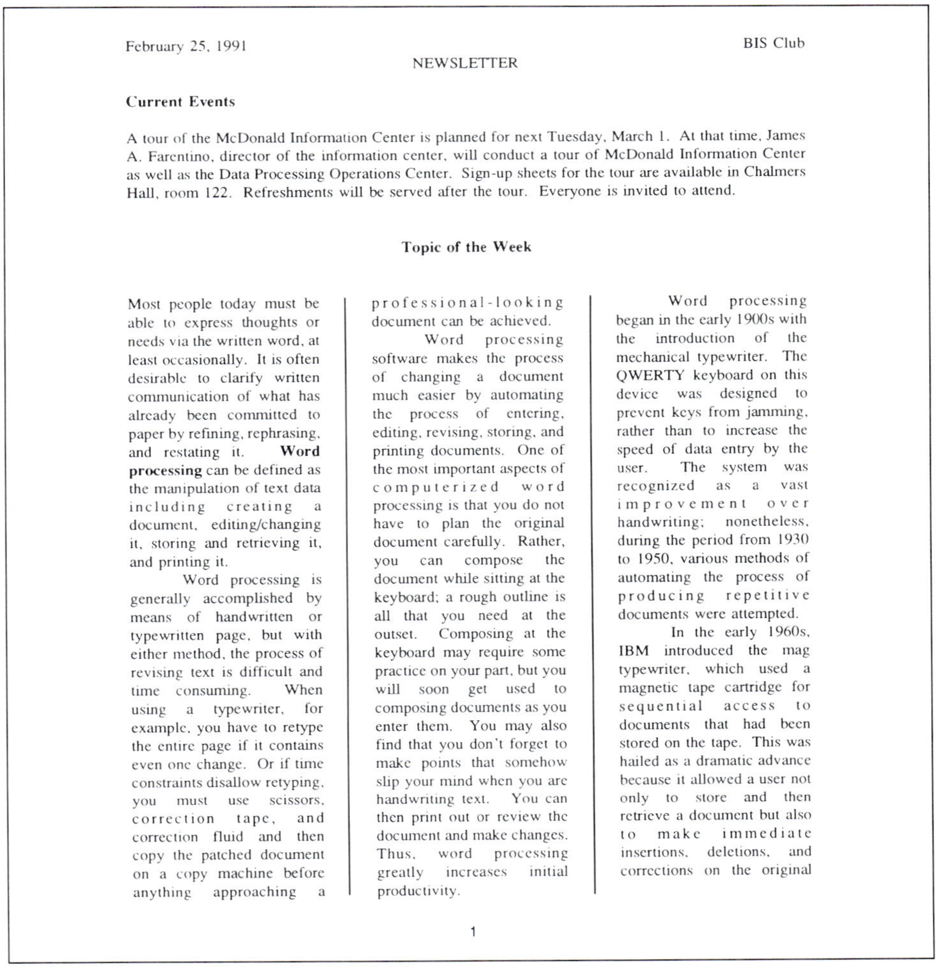

February 25, 1991 BIS Club

NEWSLETTER

Current Events

A tour of the McDonald Information Center is planned for next Tuesday, March 1. At that time, James A. Farentino, director of the information center, will conduct a tour of McDonald Information Center as well as the Data Processing Operations Center. Sign-up sheets for the tour are available in Chalmers Hall, room 122. Refreshments will be served after the tour. Everyone is invited to attend.

Topic of the Week

Most people today must be able to express thoughts or needs via the written word, at least occasionally. It is often desirable to clarify written communication of what has already been committed to paper by refining, rephrasing, and restating it. **Word processing** can be defined as the manipulation of text data including creating a document, editing/changing it, storing and retrieving it, and printing it.

Word processing is generally accomplished by means of handwritten or typewritten page, but with either method, the process of revising text is difficult and time consuming. When using a typewriter, for example, you have to retype the entire page if it contains even one change. Or if time constraints disallow retyping, you must use scissors, correction tape, and correction fluid and then copy the patched document on a copy machine before anything approaching a professional-looking document can be achieved.

Word processing software makes the process of changing a document much easier by automating the process of entering, editing, revising, storing, and printing documents. One of the most important aspects of computerized word processing is that you do not have to plan the original document carefully. Rather, you can compose the document while sitting at the keyboard; a rough outline is all that you need at the outset. Composing at the keyboard may require some practice on your part, but you will soon get used to composing documents as you enter them. You may also find that you don't forget to make points that somehow slip your mind when you are handwriting text. You can then print out or review the document and make changes. Thus, word processing greatly increases initial productivity.

Word processing began in the early 1900s with the introduction of the mechanical typewriter. The QWERTY keyboard on this device was designed to prevent keys from jamming, rather than to increase the speed of data entry by the user. The system was recognized as a vast improvement over handwriting; nonetheless, during the period from 1930 to 1950, various methods of automating the process of producing repetitive documents were attempted.

In the early 1960s, IBM introduced the mag typewriter, which used a magnetic tape cartridge for sequential access to documents that had been stored on the tape. This was hailed as a dramatic advance because it allowed a user not only to store and then retrieve a document but also to make immediate insertions, deletions, and corrections on the original

1

1. Retrieve the File NEWSLETR.CH3.
2. Position the cursor to the first line of the first column. This line starts with the text "Most people today must. . . ."
3. Place the line between the first two columns:

Alt + F9	Issues the Graphics command.
L	Selects the Line option.
V	Selects the Vertical command.
H	Selects the Horizontal Position option.
B	Selects the Between Columns option.
Enter	Accepts to the right of column 1.
V	Selects the Vertical Position option.
S	Selects the Set Position option, to use the cursor location within the line to set the vertical line length.
Enter (2)	Executes the command and returns to the document.

4. Place the line between the second and third columns:

Alt + F9	Issues the Graphics command.
L	Selects the Line option.
V	Selects the Vertical command.
H	Selects the Horizontal Position option.
B	Selects the Between Columns option.
2	Places the line to the right of column 2.
Enter	Accepts to the right of column 1.
V	Selects the Vertical Position option.
S	Selects the Set Position option, to use the cursor location within the line to set the vertical line length.
Enter (2)	Executes the command and returns to the document.

5. Use the View Document option of the Print command to verify that the lines were created correctly.
6. To create lines on other pages of the newspaper requires that you issue the commands listed in steps 3 and 4, after positioning your cursor to the first line of that page.

CHAPTER REVIEW

The coverage of features in this chapter is introductory: for more information, consult the WordPerfect documentation.

The macro feature of WordPerfect stores keystrokes entered from the keyboard and "replays" them later. Even simple macros can save many keystrokes in repetitious operations.

WordPerfect provides many features that qualify it as a desktop publishing tool. Some of the Format commands let you control page numbering, centering, the top margin, the occurrence of widow and orphan lines, headers, footers, and conditional end of page. The Font commands control pitch, font, underlining style, size of text, and other options.

The Column (Alt + F7) command creates either newspaper columns or block columns. Newspaper columns snake from one column to the next and are read left to right top down. Parallel columns are read by moving left to right across a page. Any column type must first be defined before it can be activated using an On command.

The Graphics (Alt + F9) command embeds graphic images that have been captured using the Grab command of WordPerfect or have been created by a WordPerfect-compatible software package. Graphic images appear on the screen in a marked rectangle and can only be seen using the View Document option of the Print command. WordPerfect also lets you create lines that can be placed at any location on the page.

KEY TERMS AND CONCEPTS

base font
bottom margin
Conditional End of Page command
figure box
fixed-pitch font
font
footer
Format command
Goto command
header
horizontal line
line spacing
macro
Math/Columns command
new page number
newspaper columns
numbering style
orphan
page number position
parallel columns
Parallel with Block Protect command
permanent macro
pitch
point
proportional font
redline
table box
temporary macro
text box
top margin
user-defined box
vertical line
View Document command
widow

CHAPTER QUIZ

Multiple Choice

1. Which statement(s) concerning columns is(are) false?
   a. A column must first be defined before it can be activated.
   b. A limit of four columns per page is imposed by WordPerfect.
   c. A ½-inch margin appears automatically between columns.
   d. Columns appear until they are deactivated using a Column Off command.

2. Which is the default for page numbering?
   a. Bottom center of every page
   b. No page numbers
   c. Top alternating left and right
   d. None of the above

3. What is the key sequence for invoking the Format command?
   a. Ctrl + F8
   b. Ctrl + F7
   c. Shift + F8
   d. Ctrl + F8
   e. None of the above

4. Which command(s) is(are) used to avoid widow and orphan lines?
   a. Size
   b. Print
   c. Font
   d. Conditional End of Page
   e. None of the above

5. Which command(s) is(are) used to place one or more lines of text at the top and/or bottom of each page?
   a. Conditional Page
   b. Top Margin
   c. Headers or Footers
   d. None of the above

True/False

6. The cursor does not play any role in issuing Font commands.

7. The letters *cpi* refer to a proportional font.

8. A graphic figure can only be tied to a paragraph.

9. A permanent macro actually resides on disk as a separate file.

10. WordPerfect does not let you change a header line; rather, you must delete the header and then re-enter it.

Answers

1. b 2. b 3. c 4. e 5. c 6. f 7. f 8. f 9. t 10. f

Exercises

1. Define or describe each of the following:
   a. Font
   b. Macro

2. The key sequence ____________ invokes the Font command.

3. The default pitch in WordPerfect is usually ____________ cpi.

4. The ____________ command of the Font Menu is used to print large or small characters.

5. The Columns Type command ____________ is used to page-break protect parallel columns.

6. A set of newspaper columns must be ____________ before they can be turned on.

7. The default margin between columns is ____________ inch.

8. The Column ____________ command deactivates columns anywhere on a page of text.

9. A WordPerfect graphic appears on the screen in a(n) ____________ .

10. The ____________ command of the Print Menu verifies graphic images before printing.

11. The ____________ key sequence invokes the Format command.

12. Many Format commands must be entered at the ____________ of a document.

13. The ____________ command is useful in starting the page numbering of a file with a value other than 1.

14. Widows and orphans can be avoided by using the ____________ command.

15. When ____________ is used on a header or footer line, page numbers appear.

COMPUTER EXERCISES

Below is a summary of the WordPerfect commands covered in this chapter.

Columns (Alt + F7) Creates newspaper columns or parallel columns.

Define Macro (Ctrl + F10) Creates a macro.

Macro (Alt + F10) Executes a macro.

Graphics (Alt + F9) Embeds a graphic image, a text box, or a vertical or horizontal line.

Format (Shift + F8) Determines how information will appear on each page

Font (Ctrl + F8) Determines how information will appear on the printed page.

1. From the List Files screen, copy the file BOOKEXER to a file called CH3EX1. Retrieve the CH3EX1 file. If you examine the file, move the cursor to the beginning of the document before starting this exercise.
   a. Tell WordPerfect to center the page number at the bottom of each page. Print the document. Compare this with the printout of this file from Chapter 2. Notice that there are two fewer lines of text per page.
   b. Decrease the top margin by .32 inch. Print the document and compare this to the printout that you generated above.
   c. Turn off page numbering. Create the following header: `BOOKEXER`. Tell WordPerfect to print this header at the top of each page. Now create a footer that prints the word *Page* followed by the current page number. Print the document and compare this printout with those from the previous printouts of this file.
   d. At the beginning of the document, tell WordPerfect to turn on widow/orphan protect. Again, print the document.
   e. Tell WordPerfect to use 5 as the beginning page number. Use arabic numbers. Print the file. Is the new numbering in effect?

2. Use the Reveal Codes command to examine codes now embedded at the beginning of your document. Identify which code was used for each task above.

3. Clear the screen. Retrieve the CH3EX1 file. Turn off right-justification and print the document using 12 pitch. Print the document again. Notice that 12 pitch packs more text per line.

4. Use the Block command to make the following font changes. Print the CH3EX1 file using the following font specifications. Exit without saving the file to disk, after you have printed the document.
   a. For paragraph 1 of page 1, use regular type.
   b. For paragraph 2 of page 1, use Fine size.
   c. For paragraph 3 of page 1, use Small size.
   d. For paragraph 4 of page 1, use Large size.
   e. For paragraph 5 of page 1, use Vry Large.
   f. For paragraph 6 of page 1, use Ext Large.
   g. For paragraph 1 of page 2, use the Base Font.
   h. For paragraph 2 of page 2, use the Shadow.
   i. For paragraph 3 of page 2, use the Outln.

5. Clear the screen. Retrieve the CH3EX1 file. Print the CH3EX1 file using 15 pitch (or 17 pitch if available). Print and then save the document.

6. Clear the screen. Retrieve the CH3EX1 file. Use the Reveal Codes command to display the codes from Exercise 1e. Delete these codes. Your text should now appear as the original.

7. Create the following macros and save them to the specified boldfaced macro name. Test them to make certain that they work, once you have created them.
   a. **CITY.** Create a macro named **CITY** that writes to the screen the name of the city in which you live. Make certain that there is a trailing space after the city name. Press Esc and execute this macro 150 times.
   b. **ITAL.** Create a macro named **ITAL** that executes all commands necessary to place WordPerfect in italic mode. (HINT: This is in the Font command.) After you have entered the italicized text, use the Right Arrow to position the cursor beyond the italics ending code.
   c. **NAME.** Create a macro named **NAME** that centers the cursor and then writes any text in boldface that you enter from the keyboard. When you press Enter, the cursor moves down two lines. (HINT: This requires an interactive macro.)
   d. **ADDR.** Create a macro named **ADDR** that will automatically enter your name, address, and date information left-justified for a letter like that depicted below. After the data has been entered, the cursor should position down two lines.

      Tim Duffy
      111 W. Vine
      Normal, IL 61761

      April 30, 1991

8. Create the newsletter depicted in Figure 3.29. This newsletter requires you to enter the top portion of the newsletter manually. Change the city information to the name of your city. At the location that you wish to start the columns portion of the newsletter, define the columns, turn on

Figure 3.29
The newsletter for the CH3EX8 file.

NEWSLETTER

Bloomington/Normal
PC User's Group

April 1, 1992 Edition

Tonight's Speaker

Mr. Ralph Johnson from Baxter Technologies, Inc., is making a presentation on the capabilities of the new 80746 chip technology. Mr. Johnson has been with the PC Resources Group of Baxter for the last 10 years. He has served as Baxter's liaison with leading hardware and software vendors. His role as liaison has been to convince these vendors to support Fortune 500 companies' hardware and software needs.

Topic of the Week
Data Protection

Once you purchase a microcomputer system, you are really dealing with three different assets: the hardware (the actual machinery), the software (preprogrammed sets of instructions that allow you to perform various processing tasks), and data (facts that you enter and store using the software). What happens if your computer system is stolen, destroyed in a fire, or you accidentally erase a key file or, much worse, all your data?

If you have properly insured your system, your investment is partially protected in the first two instances. You can purchase like hardware to replace the previous system. You can also purchase new copies of the software programs. You are not, however, usually covered in the third instance. Your computer's data, while extremely valuable to you, cannot be replaced by simply buying "new" data. Many times this leads to hours of work to replace the data. Some data, unfortunately, may be impossible to replace, and its loss may lead to very serious business problems.

The responsibility of protecting the data lies with the individual using a computer system. Protecting your data can involve any one of three possible operations: you can protect a single file via the Copy command; you can protect an entire diskette via the DiskCopy command; and, finally, you can protect large files on hard disk via the Backup command.

The simplest way to protect data from an accident or, more probably, an error on your part is to make a copy of important data files. This is known as the back-up process and is easily accomplished by using the Copy command found in any computer's disk operating system.

The Copy command lets you take a file, like a month-end status report, that is contained on a diskette or on a hard disk and transfer it to another diskette. Once the Copy command has been executed, two copies of the file exist, an original and a duplicate. The diskette with the duplicate copy should now be placed in a safe location where it cannot be harmed (desk, filing cabinet, etc.). These steps are performed after major changes or additions are made to the report.

Later, without realizing what you are doing, suppose you inadvertently erase the month-end status report from your diskette. What do you do? Your first impulse, of course, is to get the diskette with the duplicate copy of your report and start using that. This is absolutely the worst thing that you can do. If the file was indeed erased from the diskette, the erasure was performed at your direction. You are now concerned with protecting your valuable data from your own worst enemy, yourself.

Rather than using the duplicate copy of the data file, copy the file to another diskette. This leaves you with a usable copy and a backup. Thus, if you are having one of those days where absolutely everything goes wrong, you can at least partially protect yourself from your own actions. The process of reconstructing your data files is known as recovery. The

the columns, and retrieve the rest of the newsletter text from a file called PROTDATA. Your newsletter should now appear something like that depicted in Figure 3.29. Print the newsletter. Save it using the name CH3EX8.

9. Use the List Files command to copy the file called PROTDATA to CH3EX9. Retrieve the CH3EX9 file. Add the centered boldfaced title `Data Protection`. Incorporate the graphic files PC-2.WPG and FLOPPY-2.WPG in this file. These are graphic files that come with WordPerfect 5.1. Place them in the paragraph locations depicted in Figure 3.30. Enter the captions that appear in Figure 3.30. On the second page of this document, place the text file called CH3QUOT. Print and save the document.

10. Use the Parallel Columns command to create a document like that depicted in Figure 3.31. You need three columns. Leave the between-columns margins at .5 inch. Print and save the document using the name CH3EX10.

Data Protection

Once you purchase a microcomputer system, you are really dealing with three different assets: the hardware (the actual machinery), the software (preprogrammed sets of instructions that allow you to perform various processing tasks), and data (facts that you enter and store using the software). What happens if your computer system is stolen, destroyed in a fire, or you accidentally erase a key file or, much worse, all your data?

If you have properly insured your system, your investment is partially protected in the first two instances. You can purchase like hardware to replace the previous system. You can also purchase new copies of the software programs. You are not, however, usually covered in the third instance. Your computer's data, while extremely valuable to you, cannot be replaced by simply buying "new" data. Many times this leads to hours of work to replace the data. Some data, unfortunately, may be impossible to replace, and its loss may lead to very serious business problems.

Figure 1 All computers should have the hard disk backup performed at regular intervals.

The responsibility of protecting the data lies with the individual using a computer system. Protecting your data can involve any one of three possible operations: you can protect a single file via the Copy command; you can protect an entire diskette via the DiskCopy command; and, finally, you can protect large files on hard disk via the Backup command.

The simplest way to protect data from an accident or, more probably, an error on your part is to make a copy of important data files. This is known as the back-up process and is easily accomplished by using the Copy command found in any computer's disk operating system.

The Copy command lets you take a file, like a month-end status report, that is contained on a diskette or on a hard disk and transfer it to another diskette. Once the Copy command has been executed, two copies of the file exist, an original and a duplicate. The diskette with the duplicate copy should now be placed in a safe location where it cannot be harmed (desk, filing cabinet, etc.). These steps are performed after major changes or additions are made to the report.

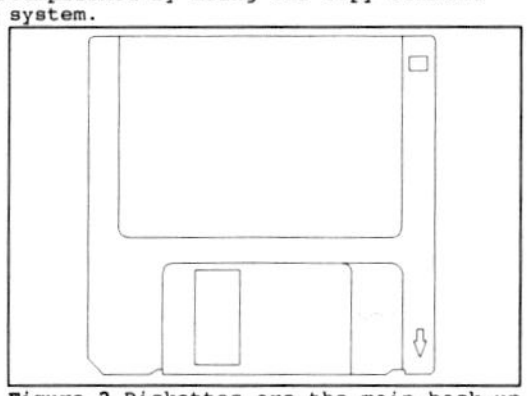

Figure 2 Diskettes are the main back-up mechanism for many PC users.

Later, without realizing what you are doing, suppose you inadvertently erase the month-end status report from your diskette. What do you do? Your first impulse, of course, is to get the diskette with the duplicate copy of your report and start using that. This is absolutely the worst thing that you can do. If the file was indeed erased from the diskette, the erasure was performed at your direction. You are now concerned with protecting your valuable data from your own worst enemy, yourself.

Rather than using the duplicate copy of the data file, copy the file to another diskette. This leaves you with a usable copy and a back-up. Thus, if you are having one of those days where absolutely everything goes wrong, you can at least partially protect yourself from your own actions. The process of reconstructing your data files is known as recovery. The back-up process saves copies of your files, and the recovery process returns these files to active use.

The Copy command is most appropriate when you have just one or two files that you wish to back-up. The Copy command, however, is inappropriate when you wish to make a backup copy of an entire diskette. Most disk operating systems provide a DiskCopy type of command for this process. The DiskCopy command cuts the time involved in copying an entire disk to about a minute-and-a-half.

> **If I had performed by backup procedure on a regular basis, I would have been able to recover my Accounts Receivable information after the file. Since I had not performed a backup in over four months, I was unable to reconstruct my most important file when the fire destroyed my business. Unfortunately, within two months I was forced to declare bankruptcy.**
>
> ---- An unfortunate user who didn't believe in regular backups.

The only thing that you have to keep track of using the DiskCopy command is the difference between a source diskette and a target diskette. The source diskette is the original diskette that you wish to back-up. The target diskette holds the copy, or back-up, of the original. Woe to the person that confuses these two. If you place a blank, formatted diskette in the source drive and your original in the target drive, you end up with two blank, formatted diskettes and a serious case of gastric distress.

In the above examples, the process of backup and recovery was simple and straightforward. For applications like word processing or spreadsheets that require files that fit easily on a diskette, the back-up and recovery process is easy. Applications like database management that require master/transaction file relationships, however, complicate the process of back-up and recovery.

Before we look at the back-up and recovery process, let's first describe the master and/or transaction file relationship through an inventory application. An inventory master file is a semipermanent file that holds data about all inventory items carried. The information about each inventory item is stored in a record. An inventory record contains such data as item number, item name, supplier name/reference, units on-hand, reorder point, as well as other pieces of data. Most of these data remains unchanged; hence the term semipermanent.

One of the pieces of datum (fields) that changes is the units-on-hand field. This particular piece of datum is affected by a number of possible actions: sales of existing inventory, returns of inventory, and purchase/arrival of more inventory. Each one of the possible above actions is recorded in a transaction file. A inventory transaction record then simply records one action that affects one item in the inventory master file.

This two-file relationship is typically further complicated by the size of the master file. Many master files are contained on hard disk and are of a size that will not easily fit on one diskette. In such a situation, the regular Copy command is of little use because it will result in an insufficient storage space error if it is used. How do you copy such a file?

In such a situation, use the Backup command or its equivalent. The Backup command results in a file back-up residing on two or more diskettes. To make such a file available for processing requires copying these various file parts using the Restore command or its equivalent. Once the Restore command has been executed, the sequential parts of the file have been "merged" back to the hard disk.

The above process may be too time-consuming for some applications. You may not want to take the time each day to perform this rather involved task.

Figure 3.30

The CH3EX9 file with the PC-2.WPG and FLOPPY-2.WPG graphic images.

Figure 3.31

The vacation itinerary for exercise CH3EX10.

Vacation Itinerary
Spring 1991

May 18	Shar-May Campground Newton, IA 62352 (516)792-2539	Travel - 287 mi. Visit Train Museum
May 19	Sioux Falls SOA Sioux Falls, SD 53432 (505)336-8876	Travel - 287 mi.
May 20	Grey Bull SOA Greybull, WY 82426 (207)756-2666	Travel - 400 mi.
May 21-31	Yellowstone Park W. Entrance West Yellowstone, MT 59758 (405)646-7077	Travel - 300 mi. Visit Old Faithful Travel around the park

SETUP MENU AND COMMAND SUMMARY FOR WORDPERFECT 5.1

SETUP MENU AND FILE BACKUP (Shift + F1)

The WordPerfect Setup Menu lets you control many options and initial settings that affect how WordPerfect employs the mouse and keyboard and how it displays information on your screen, prints documents, and handles files.

To activate the automatic Backup Files option, enter the menu (Shift + F1). Press 3 for the Environment option. Press 1 for the Backup Files option. Press 2 for Original Document Backup. Press Y and Enter to activate the backup. Exit the menu with F7 or F1. Now, when you save a file, a backup version will be placed in a file called FILENAME.BK!.

COMMAND SUMMARY

Alignment Character Shift + F8, 4, 3

Binding Width Shift + F7, B

Block Alt + F4 or F12

Block, Cut/Copy (Block on) Ctrl + F4

Bold F6

Cancel F1

Cancel Print Jobs Shift + F7, 4

Case Conversion (Block on) Shift + F3

Center Shift + F6

Center Page Top to Bottom Shift + F8, 2, 1

Change Directory F5, Enter

Change Print Options Shift + F7

Columns, Text Alt + F7

Conditional End of Page Shift + F8, 4, 2

Copy F5, Enter, 8

Create Directory F5, =

Date Shift + F5

Decimal Character Shift + F8, 4, 3

Delete Del

Delete Directory (List Files) F5, Enter, 2

Delete to End of Line (EOL) Ctrl + End

Delete to End of Page (EOP) Ctrl + PgDn

Delete to Left Word Boundary Home, Backspace

Delete to Right Word Boundary Home, Del

Delete Word Ctrl + Backspace

Display All Print Jobs Shift + F7, 4

Exit F7

Flush Right Alt + F6

Font Ctrl + F8

Format Shift + F8

Full Text (Print) Shift + F7, 1

Go (Resume Printing) Shift + F7, 4, 4

Hard Page Ctrl + Enter

Hard Return Enter

Headers or Footers Shift + F8, 2, 3

Help F3

Home Home

Indent (left) F4

Indent (left and right) Shift + F4

Justification On/Off Shift + F8, 1, 3

Line Numbering Shift + F8, 1, 5

Line Spacing Shift + F8, 1, 6

List Files F5, Enter

Look F5, Enter, 6

Macro Alt + F10
Macro Def Ctrl + F10
Margin Release Shift + Tab
Margins Shift + F8, 1, 7
Move Ctrl + F4
Name Search F5, Enter, N
New Page Number Shift + F8, 2, 6
Normal Text Ctrl + F8, 3
Number of Copies Shift + F7, N
Overstrike Shift + F8, 4, 5
Page Format Shift + F8, 2
Page Numbering Shift + F8, 2, 7
Page (Print) Shift + F7, 2
Preview a Document Shift + F7, 6
Print Shift + F7
Print (List Files) F5, Enter, 4
Print a Document Shift + F7, 4
Print Block (Block on) Shift + F7
Printer Shift + F7, 5
Printer Control Shift + F7
Redline Ctrl + F8, 2, 8
Rename F5, Enter, 3
Replace Alt + F2
Replace, Extended Home, Alt + F2
Retrieve Shift + F10
Retrieve (List Files) F5, Enter
Retrieve Column (Move) Ctrl + F4, C
Retrieve Text (Move) Ctrl + F4, T
Reveal Codes Alt + F3 or F11
Rush Print Job Shift + F7, 4, 2
Save F10
Screen Ctrl + F3
Search Backward Shift + F2
Search Backward Extended Home, Shift + F2
Search Forward F2
Search Forward Extended Home, Shift + F2
Select Printers Shift + F7, 5
Setup Shift + F1
Sort Ctrl + F9, 2
Spacing Shift + F8, 1, 6
Spell Ctrl + F2
Split Screen Ctrl + F3, 1
Stop Printing Ctrl + F7, 4, 5
Super/Subscript Ctrl + F8, 1
Suppress Page Format Shift + F8, 2, 8
Switch Shift + F3
Tab Tab
Tab Align Ctrl + F6
Tab Ruler Shift + F8, 1, 8
Tab Set Shift + F8, 1, 8
Top Margin Shift + F8, 4, 5
Typeover Ins
Undelete F1
Underline F8
Underline Style Shift + F8, 4, 7
Widow/Orphan Shift + F8, 1, 9
Window Ctrl + F3
Word Count Ctrl + F2
Word Search F5, Enter

CURSOR CONTROL

Go To Ctrl + Home (enter page number)
Word Left Ctrl + Left Arrow
Word Right Ctrl + Right Arrow
Screen Left Home, Right Arrow
Screen Right Home, Left Arrow
Screen Down +
Screen Up −
Page Down PgDn
Page Up PgUp

Beginning of Text Home, Home, Up Arrow
End of Text Home, Home, Down Arrow
Beginning of Line (Text) Home, Home, Left Arrow
Beginning of Line (Codes) Home, Home, Home, Left Arrow
End of Line Home, Home, Right Arrow

GLOSSARY

align character: WordPerfect character that indicates where numeric information is to align. The default is the decimal point (.).

Alt: Key label for the Alternate key.

Append command: WordPerfect Block command that lets you add text to the end of an existing disk file.

Backspace key: Key used to erase the last character typed. It is labeled with an arrow that points toward the left.

backup file: A file with a .BK! file extension that is automatically created by WordPerfect.

base font: The default font for a document that WordPerfect uses when no other font command is in effect.

block: Designated portion of text, consisting of one or more lines, that is to be copied, moved, or deleted.

Block command: WordPerfect command (Alt + F4) that lets you mark text that is to be used by a later command.

Boldface command: WordPerfect command (F6) that activates and deactivates the boldface feature.

boldface text: Darkened text, accomplished by striking or printing the same character three or four times.

bottom margin: The amount of blank space at the bottom of each page.

Caps Lock key: Key used to switch the case of letters *A* through *Z* on the keyboard. This key does not affect numbers and special characters.

case conversion: The ability to change uppercase text to lowercase or vice versa.

Center Block command: WordPerfect Center command (Shift + F6) that marks a block of text between the left and right sides of the page.

Center command: WordPerfect command (Shift + F6) that centers text between the left- and right-hand margins.

center page (top to bottom): The WordPerfect feature that centers information vertically on a sheet of paper.

character overprint: Function that creates text using diacritical marks such as tildes. It also creates special effects in printing.

character pitch: Number of characters printed per horizontal inch of space. Twelve pitch (elite) prints 12 characters per inch; 10 pitch (pica) prints 10 characters per inch.

clicking: Pressing the mouse button and releasing immediately.

Conditional End of Page command: The command that indicates to WordPerfect that if a page break will occur in the next specified number of lines, it should occur now.

Copy command: WordPerfect command that copies a block of text to another location in a document.

Ctrl: Key label for the Control key.

cursor control key: One of the four Arrow keys on the numeric keypad used to move the cursor left, right, up, or down on the screen.

cursor movement: Operation of moving the cursor over the text.

Date command: WordPerfect command (Shift + F5) that places the current date as text or a code within a document.

decimal alignment: Aligning numbers in a column according to the position of the decimal point.

Del: Key label for the Delete key.

delete: Ability of a word processing package to remove text from a document.

deleting text: The process of removing text from a document, worksheet, or command using the appropriate text deletion commands.

desktop publishing: The ability to merge text and graphics in a typeset-quality document.

dormant hard return: The ability to delete a hard return that appears between paragraphs at the top of a page.

dot leader: The ability to place evenly spaced periods to the next tab stop.

double-clicking: Pressing the button of a mouse twice, quickly in succession, to execute a command.

double word: Two like words that appear together (*took took,* for example).

dragging: Pressing and holding a button down, while moving the mouse.

dual-document feature: The ability of WordPerfect to have two different documents open at one time.

End key: Key used together with the Ctrl key to erase characters on the screen from the current cursor position to the end of the line.

Esc: Key label for the Escape key.

Exit command: The command that lets you exit WordPerfect.

figure box: The figure box indicates where a WordPerfect figure will appear within a document.

find and replace: Ability to find a character string and replace it with another character string.

fixed-pitch font: Any font that has the same number of characters per horizontal inch.

Flush Right command: WordPerfect command that right-justifies text entered against the right-hand margin for a single line.

font: Character set for printing. Pica, elite, Helvetica, Courier, and Orator are among the many common fonts.

footer: Line of text that appears at the bottom of every page of a document.

Format command: The WordPerfect command that allows you to determine how text is to appear in a documennt.

function keys: Ten keys (F1 to F10) that allow special functions to be entered with a single keystroke. WordPerfect uses these keys together with the Ctrl, Shift, and Alt keys.

Goto command: WordPerfect command (Ctrl + Home) that positions the cursor to a specific page within a document.

hard copy: Printed document on paper.

hard page break: Convention of word processing packages to show where one page ends and another page begins.

hard return: Special carriage return recorded in a document when Enter is pressed, usually at the end of a paragraph.

header: Line of text that appears at the top of every page of a document.

horizontal line: WordPerfect command that places a graphic line within a document.

Indent command: WordPerfect command (F4) that indents the left-hand margin of the current paragraph to the next tab stop.

Ins: Key label for the Insert key.

insert: The ability to move text to the right when new text is entered.

Insert key: Key used to tell the computer program that you want to insert characters to the left of the cursor. The Insert mode continues until you press the key again or until you press another special key (cursor arrows, Del, End) indicating that you want to go on to a different editing operation.

justification: Alignment of word processing text flush with the right (and left) margins. This produces straight margins on both the left- and right-hand sides of a document.

Left Indent command: The command that indents the left margin of a paragraph to the next tap stop.

line spacing: Number of filled and blank lines that are established with each generated line. Double spacing produces one blank line after each generated line.

Link option: The ability of WordPerfect to automatically include information from a changed Lotus 1-2-3 worksheet.

L/R Indent command: WordPerfect command (Shift + F4) that indents both margins inward one tab stop.

macro: The feature of WordPerfect that allows you to save keystrokes to a file and then execute them at any time.

main dictionary: The major dictionary of WordPerfect, which contains over 100,000 words. It is used in performing the spell-check process.

Margin command: The command from the Format Menu that resets the left- and right-hand margins.

merge feature: The ability to merge (combine) name and address information with text data to create individualized form letters.

Move command: WordPerfect command (Ctrl + F4) that repositions text within a document.

newspaper columns: The "snaking" columns that are read top-down and left to right.

orphan: Last line of a paragraph when it appears as the top line of a page.

page breaks: Marks that show where one page ends and another begins. In WordPerfect, they are represented by a line of dashes across the screen.

parallel columns: The columns that are read left to right.

Pg Dn: Key label for the Page Down key, which moves the cursor down to the top of the next page.

Pg Up: Key label for the Page Up key, which moves the cursor up to the top of the previous page.

pitch: The number of characters per inch (cpi) of a type style.

point: A measurement equal to $\frac{1}{72}$ of an inch.

Print Block command: WordPerfect command (Shift + F7) that prints a marked block of text.

Print screen: Function produced when the Print Screen (PrtSc) key is pressed while the Shift key is held down. When this key combination is pressed, the current information on your screen is printed.

proportional font: A font in which a character takes up only the amount of space that it needs in a line of text.

re-form: WordPerfect feature that automatically readjusts text within existing margins.

Replace command: WordPerfect command (Alt + F2) that finds one character string and replaces it with another.

Reveal Codes command: The WordPerfect command (Alt + F3) that displays codes that have been embedded within a document.

Reverse Search command: WordPerfect command (Shift + F2) that finds specified text anywhere farther toward the front of a document.

right justification: The smooth right-hand margin generated on a document.

Save Block command: WordPerfect command (F10) that saves a marked block of text to a newly created separate file.

saving files: The ability to place a file that has been created in memory on disk.

Search command: WordPerfect command (F2) that finds specified text anywhere below in a document.

Shift key: Key used to select the uppercase character on keys that have two characters or to reverse the case of letters *A* through *Z*, depending on the status of the Caps Lock key.

soft page break: A page break that is tracked by WordPerfect and moves forward or backward as text is added or deleted to the document.

soft return: Carriage return accomplished by the word-wrap feature.

Speller: The WordPerfect feature that checks for spelling, case, and double-word errors.

status line: The line at the bottom of the WordPerfect screen that indicates the filename, location of the cursor, and whether any special text commands are active.

supplementary dictionary: A dictionary that can be used by WordPerfect in addition to the main dictionary in performing the spell-check function for a document.

Switch command: WordPerfect command (Shift + F3) that moves the cursor from one window to the other.

Tab Align command: WordPerfect command (Ctrl + F6) that turns a regular tab stop into a decimal tab.

tab stop: Point on a line to which the cursor will position itself whenever the Tab command is issued. Tab stops are usually represented as marks in the ruler line of WordPerfect.

temporary file: File that is used temporarily in an application. Such a file will have a randomly assigned file extension such as .$$$ or .%%%. When the file is no longer needed, it is erased.

text box: WordPerfect graphics box that lets you load text from a file.

text window: That area of the WordPerfect screen in which document text appears.

Thesaurus: WordPerfect feature that obtains synonyms and antonyms for a specific word in the document.

toggle key: Key with two states, ON and OFF, that causes subsequent key operations to be processed in a predetermined manner. Toggle keys include the Caps Lock, Num Lock, and Scroll Lock keys.

top margin: The amount of blank space at the top of each page.

typeover: WordPerfect feature that replaces text in a document a character at a time as new text is entered at the keyboard.

Underline command: WordPerfect command (F8) that activates and terminates the underline feature.

user-defined box: WordPerfect graphics box that can contain any graphic image.

View Document command: The option from the WordPerfect Print Menu that lets you preview on the screen how a page will print.

widow: First line of a paragraph when it occurs at the bottom of a page.

wild cards: Characters that let you include a number of files or fields in an operation by using only one command.

Window command: The WordPerfect command that allows you to split the screen to see two documents at once on the screen.

window feature: The WordPerfect ability to split the screen so that two documents are visible on the same screen.

WordPerfect: The best-selling DOS word processing package on the market.

word processing: Automated manipulation of text data via a software package that usually provides the ability to create, edit, store, and print documents easily.

word wrap: Feature that automatically places a word on the next line when it will not fit on the current line.

INDEX

WordPerfect

Cursor Movement

GoTo	Ctrl + Home (enter page number)	Screen up	+	Beg. of line (text)	Home, Home, left arrow
Word left	Ctrl + left arrow	Screen down	-	Beg. of line (codes)	Home, Home, Home, left arrow
Word right	Ctrl + right arrow	Page up	PgUp	End of line	End or Home, Home, right arrow
Screen right	Home, right arrow	Page down	PgDn		
Screen left	Home, left arrow	Beg. of text	Home, Home, up arrow		

WordPerfect

Delete Text

Delete character at cursor	Del	Delete to End of Line	Ctrl + End
Delete character to left of cursor	Backspace	Delete to End of Page	Ctrl + PgDn
Delete to Left Word Boundary	Home, Backspace	Delete (List Files)	F5, D
Delete to Right Word Boundary	Home, Del		

WordPerfect

Special Features

Bold	F6	Flush Right	Alt + F6
Center	Shift + F6	Font	Ctrl + F8, F
Underline	F8	Spacing	Shift + F8, L, S
Date	Shift + F5, T		

Merge Codes

Merge	Ctrl + F9, M
End Record	Shift + F9, E
End Field	F9
Merge Codes	Alt + F9

WordPerfect

File Commands

Exit	F7
Save	F10
Retrieve	Shift + F10

Search/Replace Commands

Search Forward	F2
Search Backward	Shift + F2
Replace	Alt + F2

Special Commands

Block	Alt + F4
Reveal Codes	Alt + F3
Cancel	F1
Help	F3

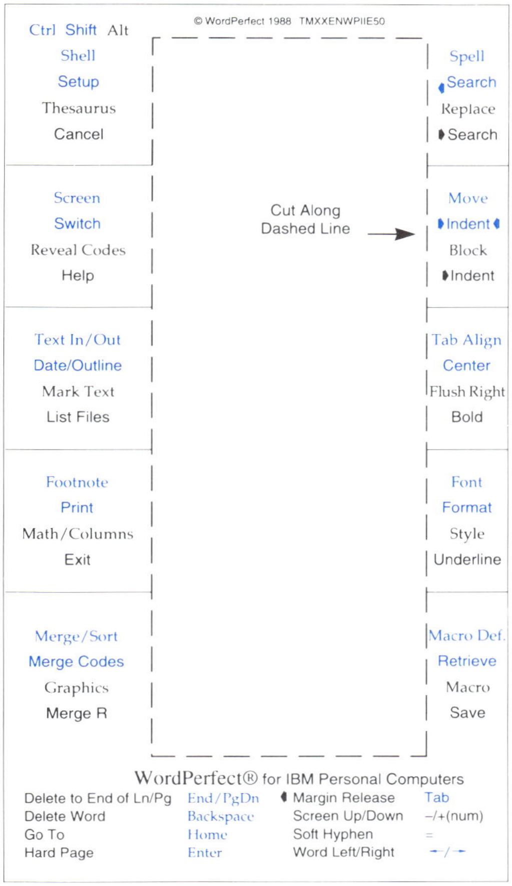

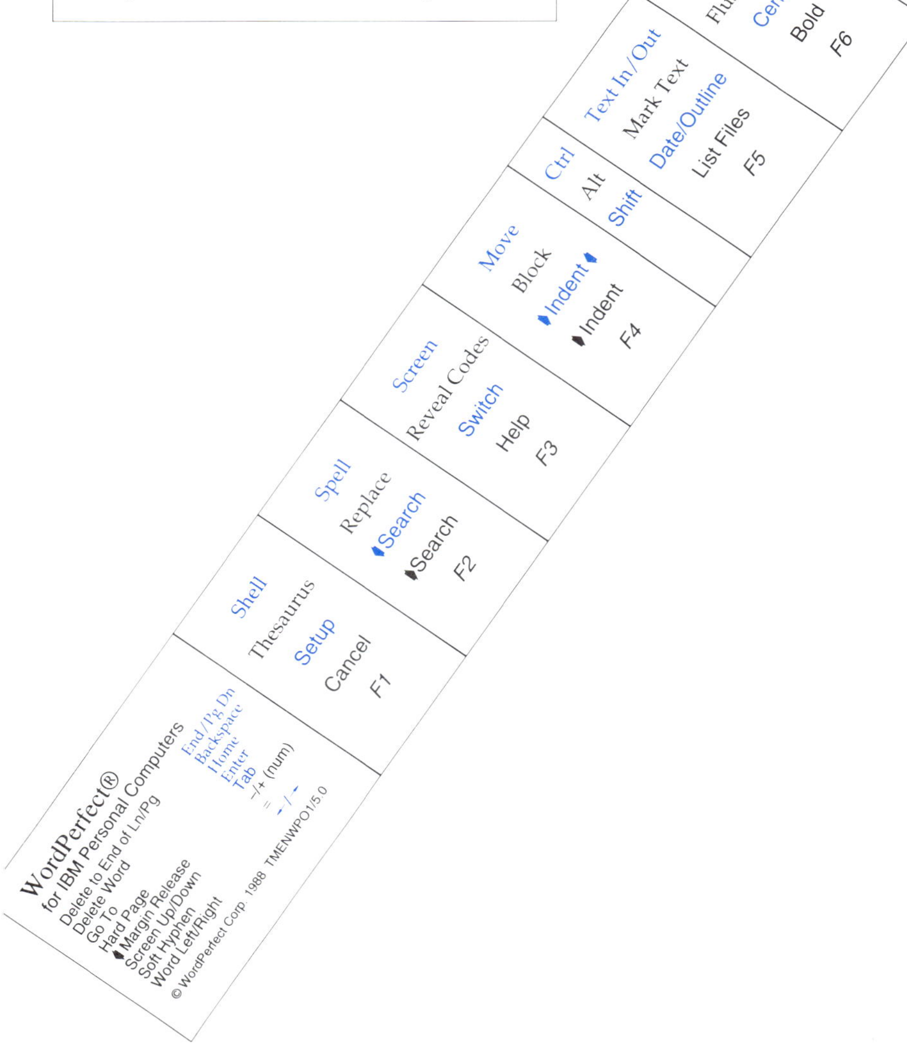

Function Keys Templates
for WordPerfect 5.0/5.1

ESSENTIAL LOTUS 1-2-3 (VERSION 2.2)

Tim Duffy
Professor of Accounting in Information Systems
Illinois State University

ESSENTIAL
Lotus 1-2-3 (Version 2.2)

Wadsworth Publishing Company
Belmont, California
A Division of Wadsworth, Inc.

Computer Science Editor: Frank Ruggirello
Developmental Editor: Alan Venable
Editorial Assistant: Rhonda Gray
Production: Hal Lockwood, Bookman Productions
Print Buyer: Martha Branch
Art Editor: Jane Brundage, Bookman Productions
Interior and Cover Design: Vargas/Williams/Design
Copy Editor: Betty Duncan
Photo Researchers: Sarah Bendersky, Darcy Lanham, Judy Mason, Monica Suder
Technical Illustrator: Illustrious, Inc.
Compositor: Graphic Typesetting Service, Los Angeles
Printer: Arcata Graphics, Kingsport, Tennessee

3 4 5 6 7 8 9 10—96 95 94 93 92
ISBN: 0-534-18724-2

To Wendy and Michael

CONTENTS

Chapter 4

Graphing with Lotus 1-2-3 L.124

PREFACE

PURPOSE

This *Software Essentials* book and its associated software training materials teach software competency. These materials are designed for both majors and nonmajors in a quarter or semester course that uses the microcomputer as the primary vehicle for introducing students to problem solving. As typically expected in this type of course, there are no prerequisites.

APPROACH

Students acquire software competency by completing a set of software-training chapters that focus on current releases of various major software packages. To achieve that competency, each software package is presented in a separate booklet emphasizing hands-on problem solving. Carefully prepared, hands-on tutorials are provided within each chapter. Closely related end-of-chapter exercises reinforce the tutorial learning and expand the student's mastery over a broader range of applications.

Software packages covered in this series include

- DOS 3.3 and 5.0.
- WordPerfect 5.0/5.1.
- Lotus 1-2-3 2.2 and 2.3.
- Quattro Pro 3.0.
- dBASE III Plus.
- dBASE IV 1.1.
- Paradox 3.5.
- Windows 3.1.

IMPROVEMENTS IN SOFTWARE INSTRUCTION

I have always made the greatest possible effort to make hands-on instruction direct and meaningful. For this series in *Software Essentials*, the hands-on passages have been extensively reviewed and revised to make the booklets in the series more effective for the teacher and learning easier for the beginning student. Important changes include the following:

- **Self-Contained Modules** Each software module is self-contained. Each has its own front matter, chapter numbering, glossary, and command summary.
- **Expanded Hands-On Learning** The number of hands-on exercises has been increased dramatically. Particularly, the number of shorter exercises has been increased.
- **Use of Second Color** All hands-on exercise commands in the text appear in second color. This allows the student to quickly identify what keystrokes to enter and to distinguish them from additional explanation about a software feature or command.

- **Hints/Hazards Boxes** Many Hints/Hazards boxes inform students about the tricks they can use and potential traps they may encounter when using a particular software tool.
- **Keyboard Icons** Keyboard icons appear frequently in headings and tables. These icons help the student identify and remember specific keystrokes.

WORKING IN A HANDS-ON ENVIRONMENT

Software Essentials and its allied materials work best in a hands-on environment. The step-by-step exercises make most sense when an individual is sitting at a computer and can immediately see the results of his or her actions. A symbol such as the one shown in the margin indicates hands-on material.

Each software package covered in this series is treated in enough detail to satisfy the requirement of a computer novice. However, each software booklet assumes that the software has already been configured for the student's use. If a package has not been configured for a specific machine, refer to the documentation for that package.

HARDWARE REQUIREMENTS FOR HANDS-ON SOFTWARE

An IBM PC or compatible computer with two disk drives and 320K of memory is required for most tools in this series. Note that you need 512K and a hard disk to run dBASE IV. You will also need a color monitor/graphics adapter board to properly display Lotus 1-2-3 graphics on the screen. A printer (with graphics capabilities if you wish to print Lotus graphs) is also required for printing documents, reports, graphs, and worksheets.

The hard disk (fixed disk) has resulted in many changes in the way computer concepts and use are taught in the classroom. During the past few years, the prices of hard disk technology have plummeted. Because this technology is now affordable for most colleges and universities, this text includes instructions for running software from a fixed disk.

LEARNING AIDS AND SAMPLE FILES

Exercises are provided at the end of each chapter to give students quick feedback on their progress. Besides the written exercises, hands-on computer exercises are included at the end of the software chapters to provide feedback through challenging applications of material covered in the chapter. A number of sample diskette files—including sample worksheets, text files, and database files—have been provided for use with text lessons and exercises.

ESSENTIAL LOTUS 1-2-3 (VERSION 2.2)

1

FUNDAMENTALS OF THE LOTUS 1-2-3 SPREADSHEET

CHAPTER OBJECTIVES

After completing this chapter, you should be able to

- **List the three parts of Lotus 1-2-3**
- **Understand the various aspects of the 1-2-3 screen**
- **Manipulate the 1-2-3 pointer**
- **Enter various commands using / keystrokes as well as various key combinations**
- **Enter and save a 1-2-3 worksheet**

INTRODUCTION TO SPREADSHEETS

An electronic spreadsheet program produces a file that is equivalent to a manual accounting worksheet. Both the electronic worksheet and the accounting worksheet consist of a matrix of rows and columns that let you organize information in an easy-to-understand format.

In spreadsheet software terminology, a **spreadsheet** is the set of program instructions, such as Lotus 1-2-3, that produces a worksheet; a **worksheet** is a model or representation of reality that is created using the spreadsheet software.

Electronic spreadsheet software greatly improves the user's accuracy, efficiency, and productivity. Once a worksheet has been prepared, other options (what-if alternatives) can be easily considered by simply making changes and instructing the spreadsheet to recalculate all entries to reflect these changes. This leaves more time for creative decision making.

MANUAL AND ELECTRONIC WORKSHEETS

Understanding the similarity between manual and electronic worksheets is important in learning how to use spreadsheet programs effectively.

Figure 1.1

(a) Manual worksheet containing labels and sales figures. (b) Manual worksheet with Change column calculated. (c) Manual worksheet with % Change calculation results shown. (d) Manual worksheet with totals shown.

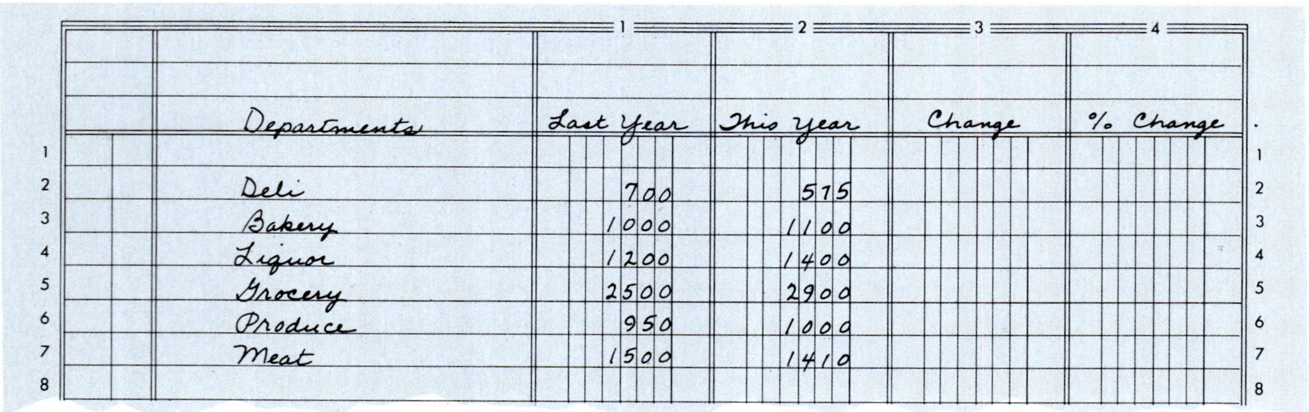

(a)

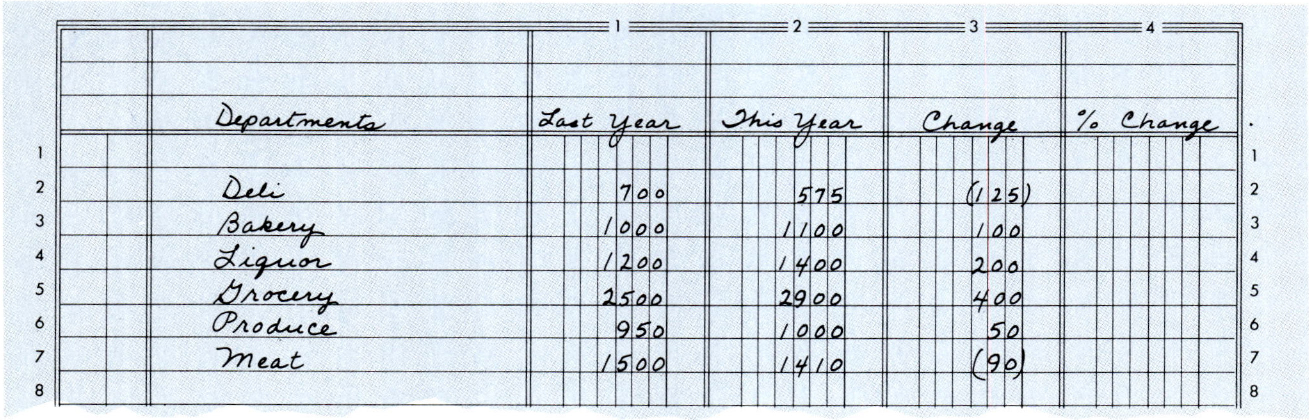

(b)

Suppose that you have a friend, Ed, who owns a grocery store with the following departments: Deli, Bakery, Liquor, Grocery, Produce, and Meat. It's the end of the year, and Ed wants to compare the sales of the various departments for last year and this year, finding the overall change in sales (positive or negative) and the percent change in sales for each department.

You have volunteered to help Ed develop this report manually. To ease the calculation process and ensure that the correct numbers are included in each calculation, you have decided to use some standard lined paper divided into a number of columns. This type of paper is often referred to as worksheet paper.

In designing the report, you decide that the easiest way to present the data is to have the names of the departments along the vertical axis of the report and the column headings along the horizontal axis. You can now enter last year's and this year's sales figures for each department (Figure 1.1).

Once you have entered the data properly, use your calculator to compute the change in sales from last year to this year by subtracting the sales for last year from the sales for this year and then record the difference for each department in the Change column. For example, to calculate the change for the Deli department, enter the equation 575 − 700 in your calculator and receive the

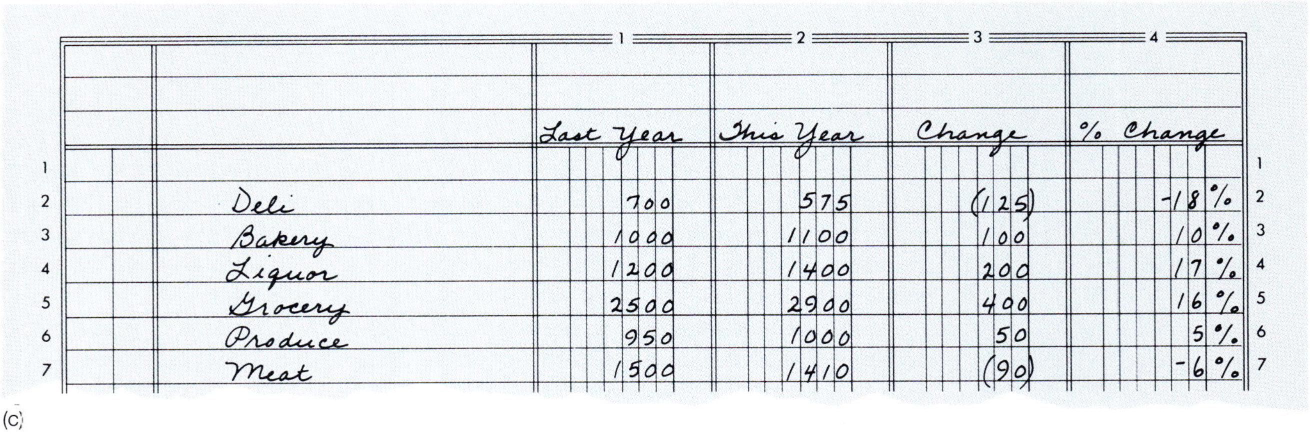

		1	2	3	4	
		Last Year	This Year	Change	% Change	
1						1
2	Deli	700	575	(125)	-18 %	2
3	Bakery	1000	1100	100	10 %	3
4	Liquor	1200	1400	200	17 %	4
5	Grocery	2500	2900	400	16 %	5
6	Produce	950	1000	50	5 %	6
7	Meat	1500	1410	(90)	-6 %	7

(c)

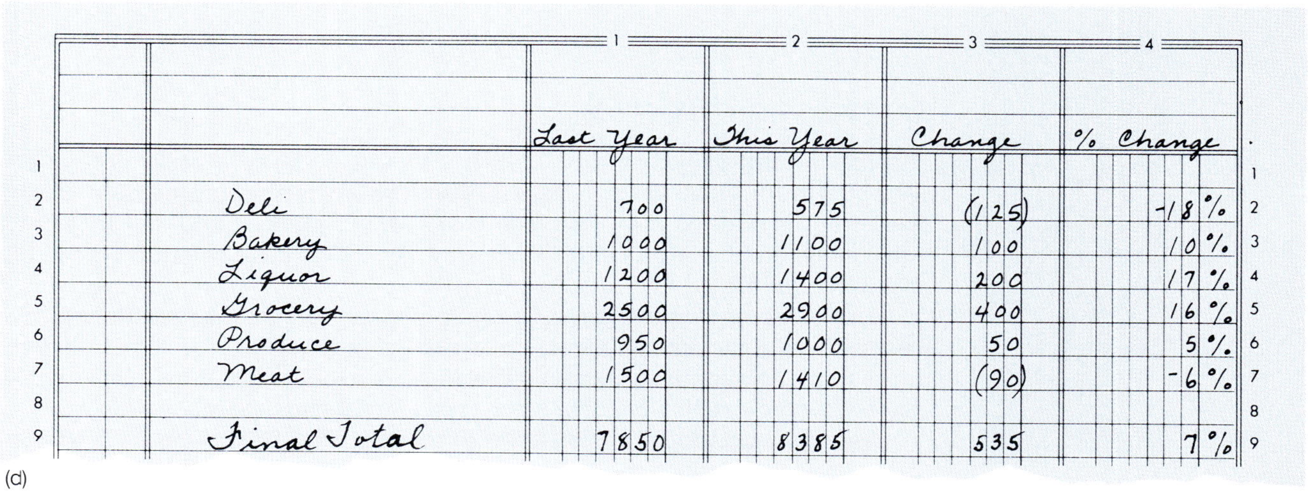

		1	2	3	4	
		Last Year	This Year	Change	% Change	
1						1
2	Deli	700	575	(125)	-18 %	2
3	Bakery	1000	1100	100	10 %	3
4	Liquor	1200	1400	200	17 %	4
5	Grocery	2500	2900	400	16 %	5
6	Produce	950	1000	50	5 %	6
7	Meat	1500	1410	(90)	-6 %	7
8						8
9	Final Total	7850	8385	535	7 %	9

(d)

answer, −125. In many business applications, negative numbers are represented within parentheses rather than with a minus sign. Enter the −125 as (125) on your report (Figure 1.1b).

You are now ready to compute the % Change entries. Do this by dividing the Change figure by the Last Year sales entry for each department and converting the result to a percentage (Figure 1.1c). For example, to arrive at the % Change for the Deli department, divide −125 by 700. The result, −.1786, must now be converted to a whole percentage. Because percentages are really just decimal fractions, the value to be placed in your report is −18%.

You must now generate a total for each of the four columns containing numbers: Last Year, This Year, Change, and % Change (calculate Change and % Change as before) (Figure 1.1d). For the first two columns, this involves adding all numbers in a column together, recording the sum value, clearing the calculator, and starting over for the next column of numbers. The last two columns are calculated as before.

Your report for Ed is now completed, and you can present it to him to use in his decision making. What if, however, the sales for three departments change? Then, to use the report effectively, you would have to entirely redo it. Or what if Ed wants you to determine the impact of a 10% increase in this year's sales for each department? The ability to respond quickly to changes and reflect them in a report, as well as to respond to various what-if questions, is what gives a spreadsheet package its tremendous power.

Suppose that instead of building this report manually you use a computerized spreadsheet package. The computer-generated report will appear to be amazingly similar to your manual report. All column headings, department names, and sales figures for each department must be entered. The calculation instructions (formulas) on how the spreadsheet package is to manipulate the figures are also entered. However, because the instructions are the same within a column, once a formula is entered, you can reuse it by copying it down the column. For example, you enter a formula for calculating the Change data once and then copy that formula down the column. Do the same for the % Change formula. All that is left is to tell your spreadsheet package to calculate the total for the Last Year column of numbers. Because the other columns also have to be summed, you can copy the formula to them. Figure 1.2 shows how the electronic version of Ed's worksheet would appear on your screen.

The real advantage of using a spreadsheet is that because it is formula-driven, when a change is made to any of the sales figures, the spreadsheet automatically recalculates the report and generates the appropriate answers without any additional work on your part. Spreadsheet software thus makes answering what-if questions easy.

SPREADSHEET SYNTAX

A spreadsheet package lets you identify a unique address, or **cell,** at the intersection of a row and a column. A **row** is horizontal; a **column** is vertical. Worksheet cells are referred to by their Column/Row designation, and each may contain a label, number, or formula. For example, in Figure 1.2, the number 535.00 appears in cell E12.

A **label** is alphanumeric text that provides headings for the rows and columns, to make the worksheet easier to understand. Labels may contain letters or numerals. A **number** is a numeric value entered in a cell. It may be either a constant or the variable result of some type of mathematical calculation.

A cell can also contain a **formula** that creates relationships between values

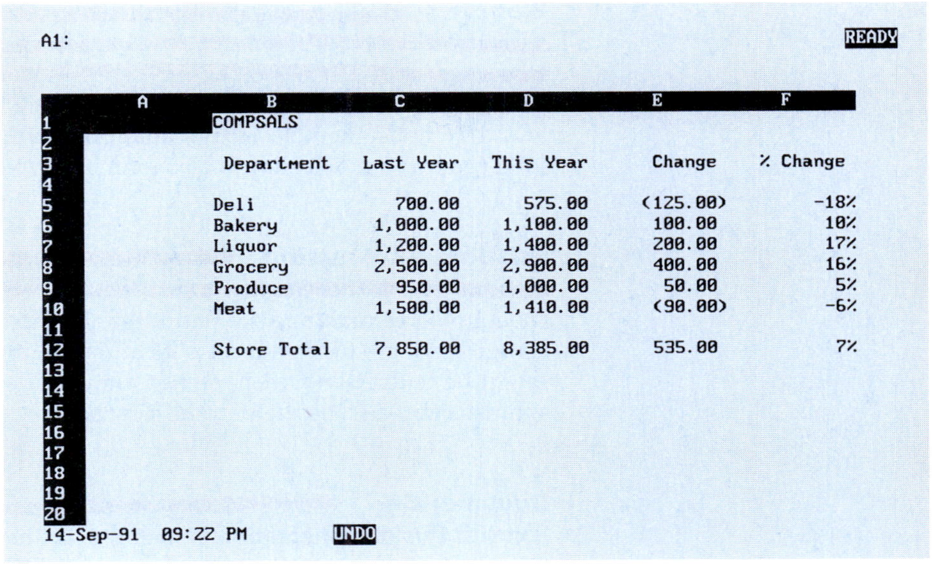

A1: READY

	A	B	C	D	E	F
1		COMPSALS				
2						
3		Department	Last Year	This Year	Change	% Change
4						
5		Deli	700.00	575.00	(125.00)	-18%
6		Bakery	1,000.00	1,100.00	100.00	10%
7		Liquor	1,200.00	1,400.00	200.00	17%
8		Grocery	2,500.00	2,900.00	400.00	16%
9		Produce	950.00	1,000.00	50.00	5%
10		Meat	1,500.00	1,410.00	(90.00)	-6%
11						
12		Store Total	7,850.00	8,385.00	535.00	7%
13						
14						
15						
16						
17						
18						
19						
20						

14-Sep-91 09:22 PM UNDO

Figure 1.2
The electronic worksheet equivalent of Figure 1.1.

in other specified cells. For example, in Figure 1.2, the final total figure 535.00 in cell E12 is generated by the following formula in that cell: +E5+E6+E7+E8+E9+E10. This formula tells the spreadsheet to add the numbers in cells E5 through E10 and place the sum in cell E12. Formulas used in cells can be more complex than just simple sums; they can contain financial calculations such as net present value or statistical expressions such as variance or standard deviation.

Anyone wishing to make effective use of spreadsheets must be able to express relationships in mathematical terms—for example, gross margin = sales − cost of goods sold, or taxes = gross income × 35%. Once such a relationship has been defined numerically, you can analyze any situation involving that relationship via an electronic worksheet.

You can use spreadsheets in two basic ways: with your own worksheet, if you have a unique application or just have the time and want the practice (and if the application to be modeled is not very complex), or with a template. A **template** is a worksheet predesigned by someone else. The individual using the template only has to enter some data and receive the results.

PROBLEM-SOLVING STEPS USING SPREADSHEETS

In approaching a problem, especially a complex one, try to develop a plan as early as possible. Much additional work can be avoided by prior planning, and your end product will look better. The planning process steps are (1) determining the purpose, (2) planning, (3) building and testing, and (4) documenting.

Determining the Purpose First, determine exactly what the purpose or goal of the worksheet is. What do you want it to do for you? What inputs will you need to provide to the worksheet? What outputs do you want the spreadsheet to generate? Will printed reports be needed?

Planning Second, plan a blueprint of your worksheet on paper. This blueprint should maintain the same rectangular format presented by the screen you are using and should include all screens that will have explanations to you or other users. Remember that you may be using this spreadsheet only once a year and may not remember all the nuances of your spreadsheet logic after such a long separation. You should also plan how you will manipulate your data.

Building and Testing Third, build and test your worksheet. If you have planned everything properly, this step should go smoothly. Testing the spreadsheet involves making sure that it manipulates the data correctly. Many things can go wrong—for instance, a formula might reference an incorrect cell, or it might be entered incorrectly—but a number of packages that you can process against a spreadsheet help in this procedure.

Documenting Finally, finish the documentation for using the worksheet. Some of this documentation is included within the worksheet itself, but many other concepts may have to be covered to allow another user to operate it effectively. In addition, limitations on inputs and outputs must be communicated, and, if the worksheet is to be used as a template within an organization, its date of creation and its author's name and telephone number must be provided.

INTRODUCTION TO LOTUS 1-2-3

As its name implies, the **Lotus 1-2-3** software package has three logical and totally integrated parts: spreadsheet, graphing, and data management. **Integration** means that you do not have to leave the spreadsheet program, for instance, to get to the graphing program.

The extremely powerful **Lotus spreadsheet** manipulates the tabular accountinglike data. You can enter numbers, labels, or formulas into the worksheet. For example, you can list 12 numbers in a column and define one cell to hold the sum of those numbers; thereafter, when any one of these numbers is changed, the sum is automatically updated to reflect the change.

The **graphics feature** takes information that you have entered in a worksheet and displays it graphically to the screen (assuming you have graphics screen capability) or to the printer. You can display information in the form of a pie chart, bar chart, stacked-bar chart, line graph, or XY graph. A regular monochrome monitor, however, will not display a graph; the computer will simply beep.

The **data management feature** of Lotus 1-2-3 sorts, summarizes, and extracts (makes reports of) portions of the individual records contained in a file. The major difference between this type of data management and other types is that in 1-2-3 the entire file is contained in a worksheet.

This text covers spreadsheets and graphing for Lotus 1-2-3 Versions 2.0, 2.1, and 2.2. Portions of the text that relate specifically to Version 2.2 are marked with the symbol **2.2**. Besides data management, two additional features are included with Version 2.2. The **Allways** feature is a spreadsheet publishing aid that creates presentation quality printouts of worksheets and graphics and merges text and graphics on one page. The **Macro Library Manager** creates libraries of macros that can be used in various worksheets.

STARTING LOTUS 1-2-3

Lotus is menu-driven, meaning that the screen displays lists of options *(menus)*. You can select an option by either entering the first character of the option at the keyboard or positioning the pointer using a Right or Left Arrow key and pressing Enter.

Diskette-Based Systems

1. Place your data disk in drive B.
2. If your Lotus system disk does not contain DOS, first boot the computer with DOS. Then place the Lotus system in drive A. At the A> prompt, type `LOTUS` and press Enter. If your Lotus system disk contains DOS, simply insert the disk in drive A, turn on the computer, type `LOTUS`, and press Enter.

Hard Disk–Based Systems

1. Issue the appropriate command to select the Lotus directory (that is, `CD \123` or `CD 123`).
2. Type `LOTUS` and press Enter.

Once you have entered Lotus, the computer displays the **Lotus Access System** (Figure 1.3). This is the first example of a Lotus 1-2-3 menu structure. The first line, with the 1-2-3, PrintGraph, Translate, and other entries, is the menu line containing the various options from which to choose. The second line contains a description of the highlighted menu option.

Press the Right and Left Arrow keys to move the pointer from one option to the next Note that the message line changes.

Move the pointer back to 1-2-3 and type `1` or press Enter.

After some disk processing, a copyright screen will appear indicating that you are in Lotus 1-2-3. After a short wait, the screen depicted in Figure 1.4 will be displayed, and the directory of the default disk drive will be read by the system.

LOTUS 1-2-3 SCREEN

At first, the worksheet screen may appear to contain little, but looks in this case are deceiving. The following pieces are part of the worksheet screen: control panel, mode indicator, border, worksheet with pointer/cursor, current date and time, error message area, and indicators.

Control Panel The **control panel** is contained on the top three lines of your screen and consists of (1) the status line, (2) the entry line, and (3) the prompt line. The **status line** tells where you are, displaying the cell address, data format

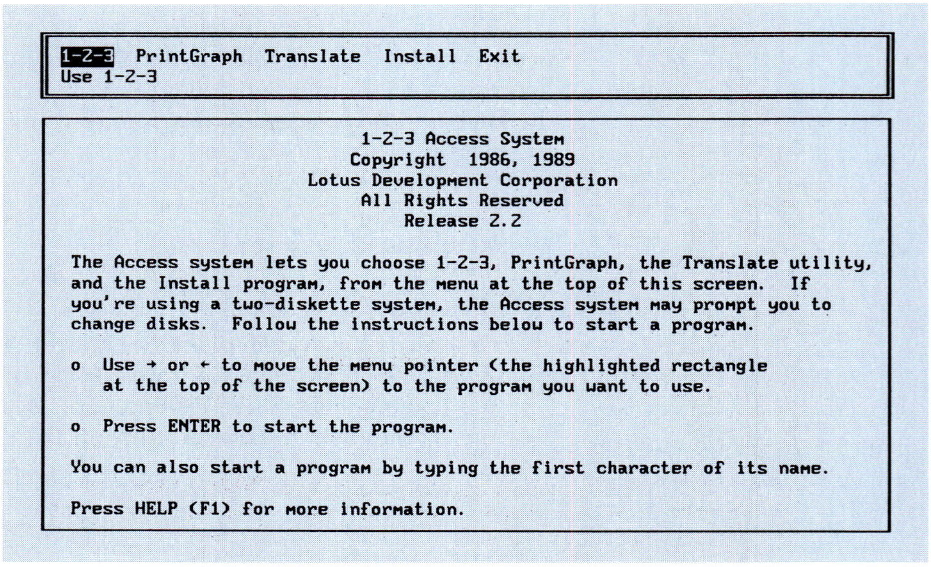

Figure 1.3
The Lotus Access System.

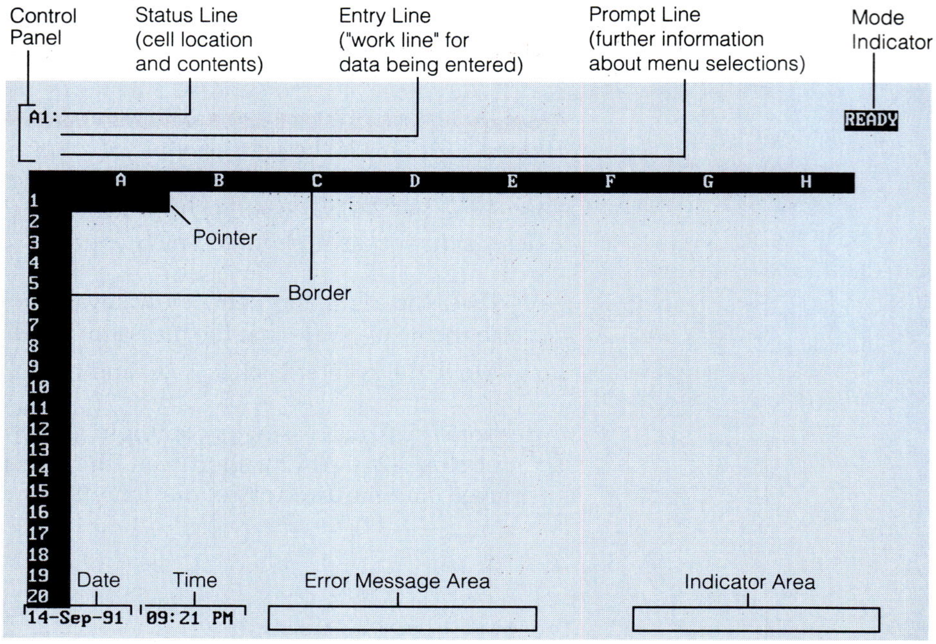

Figure 1.4
The 1-2-3 worksheet screen.

(if any), cell width, and cell contents. It also tells how the data in that particular cell are being processed and whether the cell contains a label, value, or formula. The status line has the following format:

- The cell address is always followed by a colon—A1:.
- Information about a cell formatted using the / Range Format command appears in parentheses—(C2).
- A cell that has a column width different from the rest of the worksheet appears within brackets—[W15].

- The protection status appears. If a PR appears in the cell, you cannot change this cell's contents. If a U appears, this cell's contents can be changed.
- The cell contents appear to the right of any of the above entries.

The **entry line** corresponds to a "scratch" area that contains any data you happen to enter. It also contains any "pre-entered" information destined for the cell location given in the status line. This information is not placed in either the cell or the status line until Enter is pressed. The entry line may also contain a menu of options for performing various operations on your worksheet. You can invoke the Main Menu anytime by entering the slash (/) command.

The **prompt line** contains further options or an explanation of a specific command when a 1-2-3 menu is displayed.

Mode Indicator The **mode indicator,** in the upper right-hand corner of the screen, displays status information about what 1-2-3 is doing. Table 1.1 lists some mode indicators you will see while you are working in this book.

Table 1.1 Mode Indicators

Mode	*Description*
READY	Lotus 1-2-3 is waiting for you to tell it to do something.
VALUE	You are entering a number of formula to be put in a cell.
LABEL	You are entering text information to be put in a cell.
EDIT	You are changing the contents of a cell via the Edit feature.
POINT	You are pointing to a cell or range of cells.
MENU	You are choosing from the menu that is displayed.
HELP	You are using the Help feature.
ERROR	Something went wrong, and 1-2-3 is waiting for you to press Enter or Esc to acknowledge the error.
WAIT	1-2-3 is busy and cannot accept commands.
FIND	The data management feature is performing a Find operation.
FILES	You are using a command that displays a listing of files.
LEARN	You entered the Learn (Alt + F5) command to turn on the Macro Learn feature to record your keystrokes in a specific grouping of cells.
MEM	The amount of unused computer memory has dropped below 4096 bytes. If you enter more data in this worksheet, you may receive a `"Memory full"` error message.
OVR	The Ins key is activated, so that characters entered from the keyboard will replace existing characters in the cell.
RO	This worksheet has a read-only status. You cannot save any changes you make unless some individual on the network that has write privileges saves this worksheet for you.
UNDO	The Undo feature is activated, allowing you to recover from errors committed in building or using the worksheet. This feature will be covered later in this chapter.

Border The **border** labels the rows and columns of your worksheet. Letters label the columns, and numbers label the rows.

Worksheet The **Lotus worksheet** contains whatever space is available for problem solving. It has three key parts: cell, pointer, and window. A cell is the intersection of a row and column and is referred to by its cell address Column/Row. For example, B5 refers to the cell located at the intersection of column B and row 5. A cell can contain either a label, a value, or a formula.

The **pointer** (or cursor) is the reverse-video bar (light background with dark characters). Its width depends on the width of the cell being referenced. The status line of the control panel displays the contents of the referenced cell.

The 1-2-3 worksheet contains 256 columns (A, B, C, D, . . ., IV) and 8192 rows for a grand total of 2,097,152 cells.

It goes without saying that all these cells cannot be displayed at one time on your small display screen. Instead, the screen displays only small, rectangular sections. The display, referred to as the **window,** always has 20 rows; the number of columns displayed depends on the column width.

Current Date and Time The **current date** and **current time** are displayed here. For this information to be correct, you must respond to the DATE and TIME prompts when you boot the system unless your computer has a built-in clock.

Error Message Indicator **Error messages** appear in the lower left-hand corner of the screen, giving a brief explanation of what has gone wrong. The computer also beeps when a 1-2-3 rule has been broken. After you have read the message and wish to return control to the worksheet, press Esc or Enter.

Indicators The 1-2-3 **indicators** show whether the Scroll Lock, Caps Lock, and Num Lock keys are on or off. If one of these keys is on, a message in reverse video is displayed in the lower right-hand corner of the screen. Other indicators, CALC and UNDO, will be discussed later.

NAVIGATING AROUND THE LOTUS 1-2-3 WORKSHEET

Because 1-2-3 was designed specifically for the old IBM PC, it makes full use of all keys on the keyboard—an especially important feature when it comes to moving the pointer quickly around the worksheet. Most pointer movement commands use the 10-key keypad found on the right-hand side of the keyboard (Figure 1.5). Lotus automatically places these keys in pointer movement mode rather than in numeric mode. Table 1.2 shows how the movement keys work.

A worksheet typically has blocks of cells with data, followed by blocks of blank, empty cells that are in turn followed by other cells with data. If the pointer is in a blank/empty region and End is pressed, followed by an Arrow key, the pointer moves to the first nonblank cell. If the same command sequence is entered again, the pointer moves to the last nonblank cell in that block. Entering the same command sequence moves the pointer to the next nonblank area. When there are no longer any *nonblank cells* remaining in one direction of pointer movement, one of 1-2-3's boundaries will have been reached (for example, row 8192 or column IV).

The above keys move the pointer across the worksheet. In contrast, the **Scroll Lock key** moves the *worksheet* under the cursor.

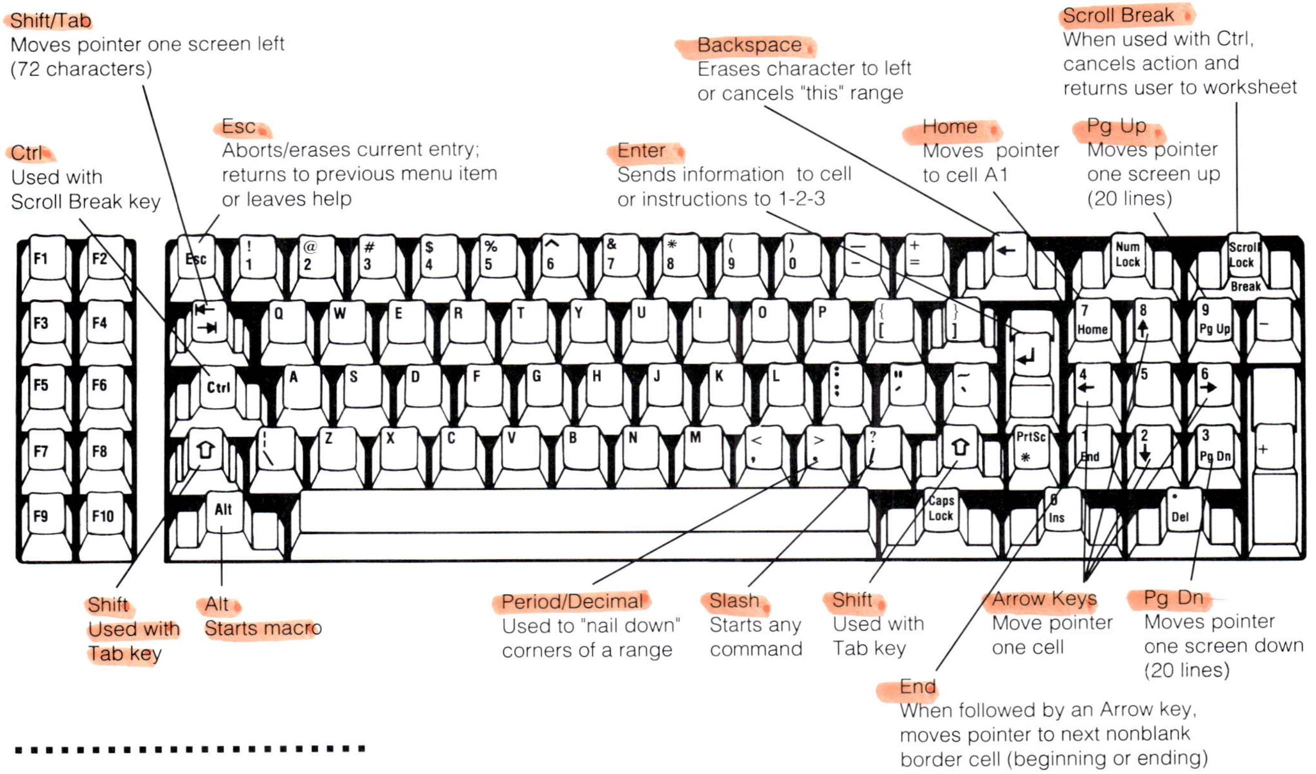

Figure 1.5
IBM PC keyboard labeled for use with Lotus 1-2-3.

The GoTo Command (F5) Besides the movement commands in Table 1.2, Lotus also lets you use a special GoTo command to move the pointer to a cell. To issue this command, press F5, type the address of the cell, and press Enter.

HINTS/HAZARDS

Many times throughout this text, you will be instructed to move the pointer to a particular cell. For instance, the instruction ↑ to D5 will tell you to use the Up Arrow key to go to cell D5. The phrase "Go to D5" will also tell you to move to cell D5, using the GoTo Command or whatever pointer movement commands are most convenient.

Practice using the Pointer Movement Commands and the GoTo Command (F5) to move around the worksheet. Select and use the most efficient command to move to each of the following cells:

A2 B2 B22 D75 CC75 A1

*Table 1.2 Pointer Movement Commands**

Key	*Pointer Movement*
↑ ↓	**Up Arrow/Down Arrow:** Moves up/down one cell position (one row).
→ ←	**Right Arrow/Left Arrow:** Moves right/left one cell position (one column).
PgUp PgDn	**PgUp/PgDn:** Moves up/down 20 lines in the same column.
Home	**Home:** Moves to cell A1.
Tab or Ctrl + →	**Tab or Ctrl + Right Arrow:** Moves right one screen (72 characters).
Tab + Shift ⇧ or Ctrl + ←	**Tab + Shift or Ctrl + Left Arrow:** Moves left one screen (72 characters).
End, → ←	**End, Right Arrow/Left Arrow:** Positions the pointer at the next nonblank boundary cell to right or left.

*Throughout this text, the following system is used to show how keystrokes are combined. When two or three keystrokes are separated by plus signs (for example, Ctrl + Del), hold down the first key while you press the remaining key(s). When two keystrokes are separated by a comma (for example F2, Del), simply press and release each key in sequence.

HOW LOTUS 1-2-3 USES OTHER KEYS

Other special-purpose keys work as follows (see also Figure 1.5):

/ **(Slash)** Invokes the 1-2-3 Main Menu. The Main Menu (Figure 1.6) invokes other menus or commands. The various menus used in 1-2-3 account for over 115 different commands. The menus and the command prompts appear in the control panel of the worksheet screen. Select a menu item by positioning the pointer to that item and pressing Enter or by entering the first character of the command. Pointing to an item yields a message in the prompt line that describes the command or displays a submenu that will be executed if this option is selected. The various menus contained in 1-2-3 can be seen in the appendix.

Esc **(Escape)** Lets you back out of a command sequence if you are in a menu. If you are entering data in a cell, Esc erases anything that appears on the entry line and leaves the original contents of the cell (if any) unchanged.

Ctrl + Scroll Break Cancels any action taking place and returns you to the worksheet. This key sequence cancels printing, sorting, or any other 1-2-3 operation.

Alt **(Macro key)** Lets you give letter keys alternative meanings. If you find yourself repeating certain sequences of keystrokes, you can have 1-2-3 save these keystrokes in a **keystroke macro;** then you can direct 1-2-3 to execute them by pressing Alt along with the coded one-letter name.

Figure 1.6
The 1-2-3 Main Menu invoked by pressing /.

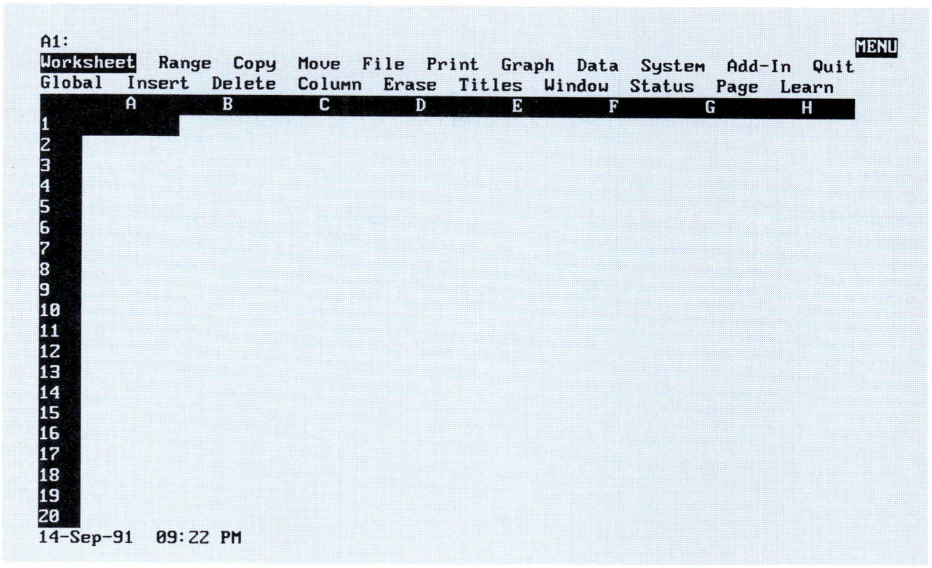

Table 1.3 Function Key Commands

Function Key	*Command*	*Task*
F1	Help	Displays a help screen.
F2	Edit	Edits the contents of a cell.
F3	Name	Displays defined range names.
F4	Abs	Defines a cell as an absolute value.
F5	GoTo	Moves the pointer to a cell.
F6	Window	Jumps from one window to another.
F7	Query	Performs the last query sequence.
F8	Table	Performs the last table sequence.
F9	Calc	Recalculates all formulas in the worksheet.
F10	Graph	Generates the graph last defined.

Enter — Tells 1-2-3 that you have finished typing and sends the information to the cell or gives 1-2-3 an instruction.

BackSpace — Deletes the character to the left of the pointer or cancels the current range.

2.2 **Function keys (F1 to F10)** See Table 1.3. Function keys can also be used in conjunction with Alt. This means that you can issue 10 additional instructions, using the commands in Table 1.4.

HINTS/HAZARDS

When you are issuing any of the above commands that require the Alt key, you can use Shift instead of Alt.

Table 1.4 Expanded Function Key Commands

Function Key	*Command*	*Task*
Alt + F1	Compose	In READY, EDIT, and LABEL modes, creates special characters that cannot be entered using the regular keys of the keyboard. Refer to 1-2-3 documentation to see these characters.
Alt + F2	Step	Turns on STEP mode, allowing you to execute a macro one keystroke at a time.
Alt + F3	Run	In READY mode, displays a list of range names so you can select the name of the macro you want to run.
Alt + F4	Undo	In READY mode, cancels any changes made to the worksheet since 1-2-3 was last in READY mode.
Alt + F5	Learn	Records keystrokes entered from the keyboard as text within a cell, which can then be used as a macro.
Alt + F7	App1	In READY mode, activates the add-in program that has been assigned to this key.
Alt + F8	App2	In READY mode, activates the add-in program that has been assigned to this key.
Alt + F9	App3	In READY mode, activates the add-in program that has been assigned to this key.
Alt + F10	App4	In READY mode, activates the add-in program that has been assigned to this key.

DATA ENTRY

Data entry is the process of placing values, labels, or formulas into the individual cells of a worksheet. The type of data stored in a cell dictates how that cell can be manipulated. For example, a label cell can be printed or listed onto the screen, but it cannot be involved in a calculation. The spreadsheet software must have some indication of the type of data you wish to store in a cell, and it is forced to make certain assumptions.

If you begin by entering an alphabetic character within a cell, the spreadsheet will assume that you wish to enter **label data** and will automatically place a single quote (') at the beginning. This presents a problem when you are entering formula-related information because the formula's reference to the cell location must start with an alphabetic character. You can solve the problem by placing a + symbol before the cell location, so that 1-2-3 recognizes the entry as a formula rather than as a label.

Numeric data are entered simply by typing the digits. Represent a negative number by placing a minus sign (−) before it. When you wish to have numeric data treated as a label, type a single quote (') before it. For example, if you enter the characters '1984, Lotus treats *1984* as a label.

Formulas explaining how numeric data are to be manipulated are entered as they would be processed algebraically. If the formula is entered properly, the spreadsheet will perform the operation; otherwise, an error message will be displayed in the lower left-hand corner of the screen, and the computer will beep. If this happens, the formula must be edited or re-entered.

HINTS/HAZARDS

Any numbers that are entered with a label prefix are treated as text by 1-2-3, and 1-2-3 assigns a numeric value of zero to such a cell. Any calculations that reference this cell may thus generate incorrect results.

ENTERING FORMULAS

Operators Formulas tell what mathematical manipulations you want to perform on specific cell contents. You can use the following symbols:

^	Exponentiation	+	Addition
*	Multiplication	–	Subtraction
/	Division		

Thus, to divide the contents of cell C3 by the contents of cell D3, you would enter the formula + C3/D3.

Precedence (Order of Operations) The order in which calculations are executed is called **precedence.** Operations are always performed in the following order, left to right within a formula:

1. First exponentiation
2. Then any multiplication and division, in the order that they occur
3. Then any addition and subtraction, in the order that they occur

For example, the formula + A7/A1 + B3*D4^3 results in the following:

1. The contents of cell D4 are raised to the third power.
2. The contents of cell A7 are divided by the contents of cell A1.
3. The contents of cell B3 are multiplied by the result of step 1.
4. The result of step 2 is added to the result of step 3.

Parentheses and Precedence Parentheses can be used to override the above order of operations. Operations inside parentheses are performed before those outside; within the parentheses, however, the order of operations is the same as that listed above. When multiple sets of parentheses are used, the operations within the innermost set are executed, followed by those within the next set.

For example, the formula + C3 – (A3 + D3) results in the following:

1. The contents of cell A3 are added to the contents of cell D3.
2. The result of step 1 is subtracted from the contents of cell C3.

For a more complex example, the formula + D3*D4 + (C7 + E4^3*F6 − (G6/F7 + D3^2) + A1) results in the following:

1. The calculation (G6/F7 + D3^2) is performed first because these operations reside in the innermost set of parentheses.
   a. The contents of cell D3 are raised to the second power.
   b. The contents of cell G6 are divided by the contents of cell F7.
   c. The result of step 1a is added to the result of step 1b.
2. The formula now logically appears as + D3*D4 + (C7 + E4^3*F6 − step 1 + A1), and the next part of the formula to be executed is (C7 + E4^3*F6 − step 1 + A1).
   a. The contents of cell E4 are raised to the third power.
   b. The result of step 2a is multiplied by the contents of cell F6.
   c. The contents of cell C7 are added to the result of step 2b.
   d. The result of step 1 is subtracted from the result of step 2c.
   e. The result of step 2d is added to the contents of A1.
3. The formula now logically appears as + D3*D4 + step 2.
   a. The contents of cell D3 are multiplied by the contents of cell D4.
   b. Finally, the result of step 3a is added to the result of step 2.

Circular References A **circular reference** is a formula in a cell that, directly or indirectly, refers back to the same cell. Lotus 1-2-3 does not allow circular references. A `CIRC` message at the bottom of the screen indicates a circular reference in the worksheet. When the circular reference is corrected, the message disappears. A `CIRC` message would appear if the following formula were entered in cell B12: @SUM(B1.B12). The formula is circular because the cell B12 is an operand in the operation as well as the cell designated to hold the answer. A cell cannot be both.

Built-In Functions **Built-in functions** are processes or formulas that are already programmed into the spreadsheet. In the Lotus spreadsheet, a function is designated by the @ symbol. To sum the values contained in cells A3, B3, C3, D3, and E3 and place the result in cell G3, the following formula would be required in cell G3: @SUM(A3.E3). Some of the more common 1-2-3 functions follow:

- *Mathematical:* Absolute value, arc cosine, arc sine, arc tangent, cosine, log, exponent, pi, random, round, integer, sine, square root, tangent
- *Logical:* True, false, if/then/else
- *Financial:* Internal rate of return, net present value, future value of an annuity, present value, payment
- *Statistical:* Average, minimum, maximum, standard deviation, variance

CORRECTING ERRORS ON THE WORKSHEET

Five basic methods, plus one start-over method, correct errors that you've made while using Lotus:

1. *Backspace:* If you make an error while typing in the "scratch" area of the control panel, use Backspace to erase the mistake and retype.
2. *Retype:* If you have entered something in the worksheet that you want to replace with other data, move the pointer to that cell, type the new data, and press Enter. The new entry will replace the old.

Table 1.5 Editing Keys

Editing Key	*Task*
Home	Places the cursor at the beginning of the line.
End	Places the cursor at the end of the line.
Del	Deletes the character at the cursor.
BackSpace ←	Deletes the character to the left of the cursor.
Esc	Returns the user to the worksheet without changes.
Ctrl + Break	Stops what is being done and returns you to the worksheet in READY mode.
← or →	Moves the cursor in the direction of the arrow.

3. */ Range Erase:* If you want to blank out the contents of a cell, move the pointer to that cell, type the sequence /RE, and press Enter to erase it.
4. *Esc:* If you start to enter data for a cell and then change your mind, press Esc, and the data will not be entered. If you are inside a menu, press Esc to get back to the previous level. If you want to return to the worksheet, press Ctrl + Break.
5. *F2 (Edit):* Suppose a cell that has an error in it contains a very long formula or label. You don't want to re-enter all the information because you will more than likely commit some other error in doing so. In this type of situation, **press F2 (Edit).** This places the cell contents on the entry line and status line. Use the keys shown in Table 1.5 to edit the cell contents. To insert information on a line, position the cursor one position to the right of where you want the new information to go and start typing.
6. */ Worksheet Erase:* If everything is totally wrong and you have a complete mess on your hands, you may just wish to start over with a new worksheet, erasing what's already on the screen. To erase the current worksheet, enter the following commands: `/ Worksheet Erase Yes`. This will erase both the screen and RAM. Unless the worksheet was already saved, you cannot recall anything, so use this command sequence carefully.

HINTS/HAZARDS

Many novices just starting out with 1-2-3 make the mistake of clearing a worksheet cell by positioning the pointer to the cell, pressing the Space Bar key, and then pressing Enter. Instead of clearing (blanking) the cell, however, this places a space in the cell. You can now see the single quote (') in the status line indicating a cell with text data. You must always clear a cell with the / Range Erase command. Any other method leaves something in the cell.

2.2 THE UNDO FEATURE OF LOTUS 1-2-3 (ALT + F4)

The **Undo feature** of 1-2-3, which could be referred to as the "oops" command, restores your worksheet as it existed before changes that were made since the

2.2

last time you were in READY mode. Undo can only be used if the Undo indicator appears at the bottom of your screen. If it does not appear, this feature has been disabled on your copy of 1-2-3. This may have been done to let you create a larger worksheet because the Undo feature divides available RAM memory into two parts, one for the present worksheet and the other for a copy of the contents prior to the last READY mode.

The Undo feature can save tremendous amounts of time when you are making changes to your worksheet. Suppose you have entered a complex segment of text or a formula in a cell. While the pointer is at that cell at a later session, you inadvertently press the Space Bar and then issue a pointer movement command to move the pointer, thus replacing the cell's prior contents with a single space. You can restore the worksheet to its prior contents with the Undo command.

Notes on Using Undo Undo works only when you are in 1-2-3 in READY mode. It does not work when you are in any other features of 1-2-3, such as PrintGraph, Translate, or Install, or while add-in programs are invoked.

The default for 1-2-3 is to have Undo invoked. You can, however, disable Undo by entering the command / Worksheet Global Default Update to modify the configuration file. Undo will now be off whenever 1-2-3 is started.

If Undo is not invoked, once you have started 1-2-3 and retrieved a worksheet or attached a 1-2-3 add-in, you cannot turn on Undo. Once memory has been allocated for a worksheet or add-in software, that memory cannot be used to create an Undo buffer (temporary storage area). In this type of situation, you would save the worksheet (/ File Save), erase RAM (/ Worksheet Erase), turn on the Undo feature (/ Worksheet Global Default Other Undo Enable), and then retrieve the worksheet (/ File Retrieve).

The Backup When you are using Undo, 1-2-3 creates a backup copy of the worksheet whenever you press a key that could lead to changes in the worksheet [for example, the slash (/) key]. Because this is done in RAM, it happens very quickly, and the user notices no delay. Once an undesired change is made, the original version of the worksheet (prior to the change) can be restored by pressing Alt + F4 (Undo). The commands listed in Table 1.6 automatically result in a **backup** of the worksheet.

Table 1.6 Backup Commands for Undo

Key	*Command*
Alt + F2	Step
Alt + F5	Learn
BackSpace ←	Delete character
Ctrl + Break	Interrupt
Del	Delete
Enter ↵	Enter
Esc	Escape
F1	Help
F3	Name
F4	Abs
F5	GoTo
F6	Window
Ins	Insert
/	Main Menu

Figure 1.7
Help screen for READY mode.

```
A1:                                                              HELP

1-2-3 Help Index

About 1-2-3 Help          Linking Files              1-2-3 Main Menu
Cell Formats              Macro Basics               /Add-In
Cell/Range References     Macro Command Index        /Copy
Column Widths             Macro Key Names            /Data
Control Panel             Mode Indicators            /File
Entering Data             Operators                  /Graph
Error Message Index       Range Basics               /Move
Formulas                  Recalculation              /Print
@Function Index           Specifying Ranges          /Quit
Function Keys             Status Indicators          /Range
Keyboard Index            Task Index                 /System
Learn Feature             Undo Feature               /Worksheet

To select a topic, press a pointer-movement key to highlight the topic and then
press ENTER.  To return to a previous Help screen, press BACKSPACE.  To leave
Help and return to the worksheet, press ESC.

14-Aug-91  05:45 PM
```

2.2

Limitations of Undo Although Undo lets you undo commands that affect the worksheet, it does not let you undo changes that affect files on disk. For example, Undo will not undo the results of issuing a / File Save command.

GETTING HELP (F1)

From time to time, you may forget where you are in a menu structure (see the appendix for 1-2-3 command structure), or you may not understand how a particular command operates. Because 1-2-3 has over 115 built-in commands, don't feel badly if you don't know all of them.

To aid you in learning and remembering these commands, 1-2-3 provides a built-in tutor, known as the **Help facility,** which is activated by pressing F1. This displays information about the current menu options or the current command on which you are working. To get out of Help and back to the worksheet, press Esc.

Check to see that your worksheet is at the READY mode. Then press the following keys:

F1	Displays the screen in Figure 1.7. Mode indicator says HELP.
Esc	Leaves the Help screen.
/	Selects the Main Menu.
F1	Displays the screen in Figure 1.8.
Highlight Move	Displays a Help screen for the Move command.
Esc	Returns to READY mode.

ENTERING A SAMPLE LOTUS 1-2-3 WORKSHEET

Recall our earlier example, in which your friend Ed owned a grocery store and asked you to design a report comparing sales of his various departments. Because Ed knows you are enrolled in a course that covers Lotus 1-2-3, he wants

Figure 1.8

Help screen for Main Menu.

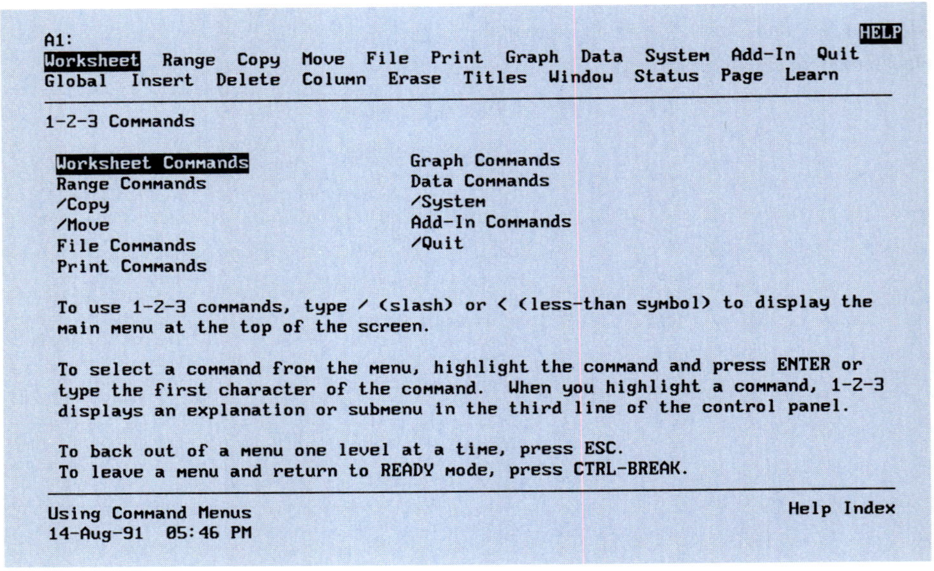

```
A1:                                                                    HELP
Worksheet  Range  Copy  Move  File  Print  Graph  Data  System  Add-In  Quit
Global  Insert  Delete  Column  Erase  Titles  Window  Status  Page  Learn

1-2-3 Commands

 Worksheet Commands                 Graph Commands
 Range Commands                     Data Commands
 /Copy                              /System
 /Move                              Add-In Commands
 File Commands                      /Quit
 Print Commands

 To use 1-2-3 commands, type / (slash) or < (less-than symbol) to display the
 main menu at the top of the screen.

 To select a command from the menu, highlight the command and press ENTER or
 type the first character of the command.  When you highlight a command, 1-2-3
 displays an explanation or submenu in the third line of the control panel.

 To back out of a menu one level at a time, press ESC.
 To leave a menu and return to READY mode, press CTRL-BREAK.

Using Command Menus                                               Help Index
14-Aug-91  05:46 PM
```

you to prepare a spreadsheet to perform the data manipulation. After carefully examining the problem, you decide that a worksheet like that shown in Figure 1.2 will present the information in an understandable format.

In completing this project, you will learn the following:

1. Basic pointer movement
2. Entering labels (text)
3. Using @SUM function
4. Entering 1-2-3 formulas
5. Changing column width for an entire worksheet
6. Changing global data format
7. Using Copy command
8. Using / Range Format command
9. Using / Range Erase command
10. Justifying text within a cell
11. Printing a worksheet

Format of Instructions In accomplishing the preceding objectives, you will have to perform a number of processing steps, which are detailed on the following pages. Any time you see a letter followed by a number (for example, B4), it signifies that you are to go to that cell location and enter the data or instruction that follows.

After you have finished entering data or an instruction in a cell, press Enter or an Arrow key. Pressing Enter takes the information from the entry line and places it in the cell, leaving the pointer on that cell. The pointer can then be moved to another cell via the appropriate Arrow key.

Pressing an Arrow key accomplishes the same task with one less keystroke. It both enters the data in the cell and moves the pointer to the next cell location.

Step-by-Step Instructions for Lotus 1-2-3 Sample Worksheet—COMPSALS

1. Enter the following row and column labels at the indicated cell. Don't worry if some of the labels won't fit in a cell. That will be taken care of later.

B1	COMPSALS	B6	Bakery
B3	Department	B7	Liquor
C3	Last Year	B8	Grocery
D3	This Year	B9	Produce
E3	Change	B10	Meat
F3	% Change	B12	Store Total
B5	Deli		

2. Change the column width to 12 for the whole spreadsheet (global). Lotus 1-2-3 brings up a blank worksheet with a column width of 9.

/W	Selects Worksheet from the Main Menu. You may select from a menu in either of two ways: (1) Move the pointer with Arrow keys to the selection and press Enter or (2) enter the first letter of the option desired. You will notice that, as you move the pointer along the options, the prompt line changes, giving you information about each option.
G	Tells 1-2-3 that the command will affect the entire worksheet.
C	Selects the Column Width command.
12	Changes the column width from 9 to 12 positions.
Enter	Executes the command.

3. Enter totals for the Last Year and This Year columns at the indicated cells. Don't enter the commas or decimal points yet. We will do this later.

C5	700	D5	575
C6	1000	D6	1100
C7	1200	D7	1400
C8	2500	D8	2900
C9	950	D9	1000
C10	1500	D10	1410

4. At C12, insert the @SUM function using the pointer method:

Go to C12	Positions the pointer at cell C12.
Type @SUM(	Enters the beginning of the formula.
↑ to C5	Marks the beginning of the range.
Type .	Establishes the beginning of the range.
↓ to C10	Marks the end of the range.
Type)	Stops the sum process.
Enter	Executes the @SUM function.

HINTS/HAZARDS

Note that when you moved the pointer from cell C5 to cell C10, you caused the intervening cells to also be included in the range. When you are using pointer movements to establish a range, always follow a path that covers only those cells you wish included in the range.

The above steps will produce the value 7850 in cell C12. This use of the @SUM function illustrates 1-2-3's ability to point to data and thereby enter its address into a formula. The @SUM function also introduces the concept of a **range.** As you no doubt noticed, the pointed range (adjacent cells included in the operation) appears in reverse video. This lets you see exactly which cells will be included in an operation.

Note carefully what happens as you total the This Year column.

5. At D12, use the @SUM function to add the This Year column:

Go to D12	Positions the pointer at cell D12.
Type `@SUM(`	Enters the beginning of the formula.
↑ to D5	Marks the beginning of the range.
Type `.`	Establishes the beginning of the range.
↓ to D10	Marks the end of the range.
Type `)`	Stops the sum process.
Enter	Executes the @SUM function.

The above steps will produce the value 8385 in cell D12.

6. Use a global change to put two positions to the right of the decimal point and to allow for commas between the hundreds and thousands digits:

/W	Selects Worksheet from the Main Menu (see task 2 above).
G	Indicates the command will affect the entire worksheet.
F	Indicates a format (the manner in which data are presented on the worksheet) will be selected.
Type `,`	Requests commas where you would logically expect them. (Negative numbers will be contained in parentheses; a fixed number of decimal places can also be specified.)
2	Requests that two decimal positions be displayed.
Enter	Executes the instruction.

7. At E5, calculate the change between This Year and Last Year (using the pointer method):

Go to E5	Positions the pointer at cell E5.
Type `+`	Indicates a formula.
← to D5	Positions the pointer at cell D5.
Type `-`	Indicates that the next cell is to be entered.
← to C5	Positions the pointer at cell C5.
Enter	Executes and places the result in cell E5.

You can use the pointer when entering a cell location in a formula. This works well when you don't remember the exact location.

8. Copy (replicate) this formula for the rest of the cells in the column. Copying the formula into the other cells in the column can save a tremendous amount of time and can eliminate typing errors. Make sure that the pointer is at E5.

/C	Selects the Copy option from the Main Menu.
Enter	Establishes the sending area. (You want to copy only the contents of cell E5.)
↓ to E6	Positions the pointer at the first cell in the range to receive the formula contained in E5.
Type .	Indicates that this is the first cell to be referenced in a range—"nailing down" the beginning.
↓ to E12	Positions the pointer at the last cell in the range to receive the formula contained in E5.
Enter	Executes the command.

Don't worry about the garbage in E11. You'll get rid of that later.

You will notice that the other cells now have answers in the change column that correspond to those at the beginning of this lesson. Move the pointer from one cell to another in the column. Notice that 1-2-3 automatically changes the cell addresses. This ability to change cell locations automatically during a copy or move is referred to as **relative addressing.**

9. Enter the formula to calculate the percent change. You'll change the format of the column later. Position the pointer to cell F5.

Type `+E5/C5`	Places this formula in cell F5.
Enter	Executes the instruction.

You should have the value (0.18) in cell F5.

This method demonstrates that you are not required to point if you know the cell addresses. The pointing method, although impressive at first, can actually mean extra work, especially if the cell locations are far away on the worksheet.

10. Copy this formula for the rest of the column, after first positioning the pointer at cell F5:

/C	Selects the Copy command from the Main Menu.
Enter	Establishes cell F5 as the only cell holding data to be copied to other cells.
↓ to F6	Positions the pointer at the first cell that is to receive the formula to be copied.
Type .	Indicates that this is the first cell to be referenced in a range.
↓ to F12	Positions the pointer at the last cell in the range that is to receive the formula from cell F5.
Enter	Establishes the range and executes the command.

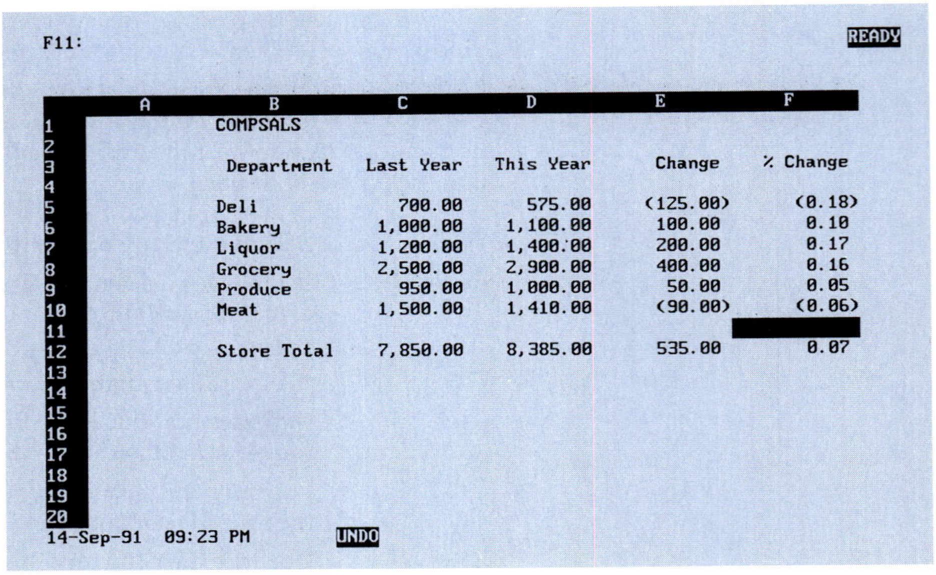
F11: READY

	A	B	C	D	E	F
1		COMPSALS				
2						
3		Department	Last Year	This Year	Change	% Change
4						
5		Deli	700.00	575.00	(125.00)	(0.18)
6		Bakery	1,000.00	1,100.00	100.00	0.10
7		Liquor	1,200.00	1,400.00	200.00	0.17
8		Grocery	2,500.00	2,900.00	400.00	0.16
9		Produce	950.00	1,000.00	50.00	0.05
10		Meat	1,500.00	1,410.00	(90.00)	(0.06)
11						
12		Store Total	7,850.00	8,385.00	535.00	0.07
13						
14						
15						
16						
17						
18						
19						
20						

14-Sep-91 09:23 PM UNDO

Figure 1.9
COMPSALS worksheet.

11. To get rid of the entries at E11 and F11, move the pointer to F11:

/R	Selects the Range option from the Main Menu. (The Range option should be used whenever you wish to perform operations on only a part of the worksheet.)
E	Erases the contents of a range of cells beginning with F11, not the entire worksheet.
← to E11	Moves the pointer to the last cell in the range.
Enter	Establishes the range and executes the command.

Your spreadsheet should now look like the worksheet in Figure 1.9.

12. Format column F for percentages, beginning with position F5:

/R	Selects the Range option from the Main Menu.
F	Selects the Format option to change a portion of the worksheet.
P	Uses the percent format to display data within a range.
0 (zero)	Establishes that no positions are to be used to the right of the decimal.
Enter	Marks cell F5 as the beginning of the range.
↓ to F12	Marks the rest of the cells in the range.
Enter	Establishes the range and re-formats for percentages.

13. To right-justify the column labels, position the pointer at F3:

/R	Selects the Range option from the Main Menu. (You want to right-justify only one row of labels—a range.)
L	Selects the Label Prefix command.
R	Right-justifies the label within the cell and starts the range with cell F3.

← to B3	Marks the range of cells whose labels are to be right-justified.
Enter	Establishes the range and executes the right justification.

14. Save the worksheet onto disk, using the name COMPSALS.

/F	Selects the File option from the Main Menu. (This option is selected anytime you wish to read or write data onto a disk.)
S	Begins the Save command to save a worksheet to the disk in drive B.
Type `COMPSALS`	Responds to the prompt for the filename. (If the file has already been saved before, 1-2-3 will ask if you want to cancel or replace: Cancel cancels the command; Replace overwrites the old file with the present worksheet in RAM.)
Enter	Executes the command.

15. Print the worksheet:

/P	Selects the Print option from the Main Menu.
P	Directs the output to the printer.
R	Tells 1-2-3 you wish to tell it what range of the worksheet is to be printed. (Remember that there are 2,097,152 cells.)
Home	Marks A1, the first cell location (upper right-hand corner).
Type .	Establishes the beginning of the range.
Go to F12	Marks the last cell location (lower right-hand corner).
Enter	Executes the command.
G	Begins printing.

16. Advance the printer to the next sheet, so the current page can be removed:

P	Tells 1-2-3 to go to the top of the next page.
A	Tells 1-2-3 that it is now at the top of the paper. (If you forget to align the printer with this command, your worksheet may have a wide gap in the middle.)

SAVING AND RETRIEVING WORKSHEET FILES (/FS and /FR)

The first time that you work on a worksheet, 1-2-3 prompts you to enter a name for the worksheet when you issue the command to save it to disk. Any worksheet file that you save to disk has the .WK1 file extension. The following commands are used to save a worksheet to disk:

/F	Selects the File option from the Main Menu. (Choose this option anytime you want to save or load a worksheet from disk.)
S	Saves a worksheet to the default drive.

The worksheet file can now be loaded at a later time and changes can be made to that worksheet. Use the following commands to load a worksheet:

/F	Selects the File option from the Main Menu.
R	Selects the Retrieve option to read a worksheet file from the disk in drive B. (You can now either manually enter the name of the worksheet to be loaded or simply "point" to the appropriate worksheet file using the pointer and Enter.)

Once you finish making any changes to the worksheet, you must again save it to disk. Because you indicated the name of the worksheet when you loaded it, 1-2-3 displays that name as the default when you issue the Save command. By pressing Enter, you accept that default. If you wish to enter another name, the current name disappears as soon as you press any other alphabetic or numeric key. Accepting the default name displays three menu options:

- *Cancel* stops this operation and returns you to READY mode.
- *Replace* saves the contents of this worksheet to disk. This process destroys the original worksheet file.
- 2.2 *Backup* saves the prior version of the worksheet (the one currently residing on disk) with a .BAK file extension and then saves the worksheet in RAM using the original filename.

Once you have saved a file to disk, you may want to verify that it actually was stored properly. There are two ways to do this. You can simply reload the worksheet file from disk using the / File Retrieve commands, or you can use the List command from the File Menu. The / File List command produces a menu display from which you select the type of file you wish to have displayed. In this case, you would enter the following commands:

/F	Selects the File option of the Main Menu.
L	Selects the List option.
W	Displays all worksheet files (those files with a .WK? file extension) to the screen (Figure 1.10).

Your worksheet should now look exactly like the worksheet at the beginning of this lesson. When you wish to return to 1-2-3, press Enter.

QUITTING LOTUS 1-2-3 (/Q)

The command for exiting from Lotus 1-2-3 is / Quit. If you try to exit 1-2-3 without saving changes to disk, 1-2-3 displays the menu prompt `WORKSHEET`
2.2 `CHANGES NOT SAVED! End 1-2-3 anyway?` This gives you the opportunity to respond with a no and then issue a / File Save command to save your worksheet. This precaution helps you avoid losing many hours of work by simply forgetting to save your worksheet to disk.

CHAPTER REVIEW

One of the most frequently used microcomputer applications in business is the electronic spreadsheet, which allows an individual to manipulate any data/information that can be placed in a row-and-column format. Most spreadsheet

Figure 1.10
Type of screen displayed when you enter the / Files List Worksheet instruction.

software packages have a number of features in common, including the ability to copy formulas or text, delete rows or columns, load worksheets from disk, insert rows or columns, change the format of data presentation, move text or formulas from one location to another, print the worksheet, save the worksheet, freeze portions (titles) of the worksheet, and split the screen.

When using a spreadsheet package, you must follow a number of logical steps in planning, developing, and testing your worksheet in order to ensure that the problem is properly modeled.

The Lotus 1-2-3 spreadsheet package is a menu-driven, integrated package composed of the functional parts of spreadsheet, graphics, and data management. Its screen consists of a control panel, border, mode indicator, special indicators, error message indicator, and worksheet area. Various keys of the keyboard are used to move the pointer around the worksheet area.

You can enter data and correct errors by making changes in the control panel area. After data are entered or changes made, they will be reflected in the appropriate cell if you press an Arrow key or Enter. Arithmetic manipulation of numeric data contained in cells can be accomplished by entering a formula or by telling 1-2-3 to use one of its built-in functions. A detailed example of worksheet formation involves the practical application of many of these functions.

KEY TERMS AND CONCEPTS

Allways
Alt
Backspace
backup
border
built-in function
cell
circular reference
column
control panel
Ctrl + Left Arrow
Ctrl + Right Arrow
Ctrl + Scroll Break
current date
current time
data entry
data management feature
Down Arrow
End
Enter
entry line
error message

Esc (Escape)
formula
F2 (Edit)
function keys (F1 to F10)
graphics feature
Help feature
Home
indicator
integration
keyboard macro
label
label data
Learn command
Left Arrow
Lotus Access System
Lotus 1-2-3
Lotus spreadsheet
Lotus worksheet
macro
Macro Library Manager
mode indicator
number
numeric data
Pg Dn
Pg Up
pointer
precedence
prompt line
range
relative addressing
Right Arrow
row
Scroll Lock key
spreadsheet
status line
Tab
Tab + Shift
template
Undo feature
Up Arrow
window
worksheet
/ (Slash)

CHAPTER QUIZ

Multiple Choice

1. Which of the following terms is *not* related to a worksheet?
   a. Row
   b. Column
   c. DOS prompt
   d. Pointer
   e. Border
   f. All of the above are related to a worksheet.

2. Which of the following items is *not* allowed in a cell?
   a. Formula
   b. Label
   c. Function
   d. Number
   e. All of the above are allowed in a cell.
   f. None of the above is allowed in a cell.

3. Which key sequence executes the Undo command?
   a. F1
   b. Alt + F3
   c. Ctrl + F3
   d. Alt + F4
   e. Ctrl + F4

4. Which of the following keystrokes does *not* result in cursor movement?
   a. Arrow key
   b. Pg Up
   c. Alt
   d. Tab

e. End + an Arrow key
f. All of the above result in cursor movement.

5. Which of the following items is *not* found in the control panel?
 a. Entry line
 b. Prompt line
 c. Error line
 d. Status line
 e. All of the above are part of the control panel.
 f. None of the above is part of the control panel.

True/False

6. Integrated packages let you pass information from one part to another without any real difficulty.

7. The mode indicator shows the current status of the worksheet.

8. A cell is referenced by using the row/column designation.

9. The built-in functions in 1-2-3 always start with a @ character.

10. When entering a formula, you need only enter the cell location and an operation symbol—for example, A2 − B7.

Answers

1. c 2. e 3. d 4. c 5. c 6. t 7. t 8. f 9. t 10. f

Exercises

1. Define or describe each of the following:
 a. Built-in function
 b. 1-2-3 graphics
 c. Lotus Access System
 d. Control panel
 e. Mode indicator
 f. Indicators
 g. Edit key (F2)
 h. Precedence
 i. On-line help

2. A spreadsheet is the software, whereas a(n) __________ is the work area.

3. Any cell can be referenced by referring to its corresponding __________ and __________.

4. The three types of contents a cell may have are __________, __________, and __________.

5. A(n) __________ is similar to a prepackaged program. You enter the data, and it computes the results.

6. The four steps involved in using a spreadsheet to solve a problem are __________, __________, __________, and __________.

7. The three integrated parts of Lotus 1-2-3 are __________, __________, and __________.

8. The three parts of the 1-2-3 control panel are ____________, ____________, and ____________.

9. The ____________ indicator identifies the current status of the Lotus 1-2-3 package.

10. The part of your worksheet that is visible on your screen is referred to as the ____________.

11. The second line of the control panel is the ____________.

12. Explain the use of each of the following cursor movement keys:
    a. Arrow key
    b. Pg Up
    c. Pg Dn
    d. End
    e. Home
    f. Tab

13. The ____________ key is used to quit an instruction or back up a step in the menu.

14. The ____________ and ____________ keys stop any spreadsheet process or function.

15. A cell that contains text automatically has a(n) ____________ placed in it.

16. Why is the concept of precedence important in entering formulas? Explain how 1-2-3 evaluates a formula and executes it using precedence. How can this order of precedence be changed?

17. Why are built-in functions so useful? List some functions with an application that you might find useful. (At least four.)

18. Explain how the use of each of the following keys changes when the EDIT mode is entered by pressing F2.
    a. Home
    b. Del
    c. Backspace
    d. End
    e. Esc
    f. Arrow keys

19. The four keystrokes ____________, ____________, ____________, and ____________ erase the entire worksheet.

20. Practice using the on-line help facility, which is activated by pressing F1.

21. The two add-in packages that are provided with Lotus 1-2-3 Release 2.2 are ____________ and ____________.

22. The ____________ add-in provides spreadsheet-publishing capabilities.

23. The ____________ feature of 1-2-3 lets you restore the contents of a worksheet using the Alt + F4 key sequence.

24. The ____________ key can be used in place of the Alt key when issuing a command requiring use of the Alt key.

25. The ____________ key sequence erases the contents of a cell.

COMPUTER EXERCISES

1. Use the / File Retrieve command to load the worksheet file CALENDAR, which contains an appointment calendar for keeping track of various appointments. Practice moving the pointer around the worksheet using the following commands.

   Part I

   a. Use the various Arrow keys to move the pointer.
   b. Press Home.
   c. Press Pg Dn twice.
   d. Press Pg Up three times; notice the beep.
   e. Position the pointer at 8:00.
   f. Press End, followed by Down Arrow.
   g. Press the same two keys again; the pointer should be at row 8192.
   h. Press End, followed by the Right Arrow key; the pointer should be at cell IV8192.
   i. Now enter any character at cell IV8192. You should receive a `Memory Full` error message. Even though 1-2-3 has a bountiful number of cell locations, the limited amount of RAM in your computer prevents you from using all of them. Press Esc to get rid of the error message.
   j. Press End, followed by Up Arrow. You should now see `'end of column` at cell IV1. Notice that there is a single quote mark in front of the text. This single quote tells 1-2-3 that the contents of this cell are text data. Although you can enter the single quote, 1-2-3 automatically places it in the cell for you.
   k. Press Home.
   l. Press Tab twice.
   m. Press Shift and Tab together (Shift + Tab).
   n. Position the pointer at cell A5. This cell contains the 1-2-3 function @NOW. This function is used to get the date that you entered when you started Lotus 1-2-3. If you did not enter a date, this cell contains 01-Jan-80 (the DOS default).

   Part II

   a. Press Scroll Lock.
   b. Use the various Arrow keys to move the pointer.
   c. Press Pg Dn twice.
   d. Press Pg Up once.
   e. Press Tab twice.
   f. Press Shift + Tab.

2. Use the / File Retrieve command to load the worksheet file PAYMENT, which is a template that allows you to enter the amount of a loan, the interest rate, and the number of years for the loan and then automatically calculates the amount of the payment and the total amount paid over the life of the loan.

   Before you do anything to the worksheet, let's explore some of its features. This worksheet has two areas: The first will hold information about various loans, and the second contains the information about a loan that you are permitted to change. The high-intensity (bright) cells' contents can be changed, but the others can't. If you try to change any but the high-intensity cells, the computer merely beeps and displays the error message `Protected Cell`. Press Esc to continue. Note the PR entry on the status line for protected cells and the U entry of the high-intensity unprotected cells.

You are therefore allowed to change the loan amount, the interest rate, and the life of the loan in years. Enter the loan amounts without using dollar signs or commas. For example, if a loan is for $10,000, enter it as 10000. The current interest rate is 12%, expressed as a decimal (.12). The final field that you are allowed to change is the length of the loan, which is currently set for 4 years. These two variables appear at the bottom of the screen.

Notice that as soon as you change the contents of one field the worksheet automatically recalculates itself.

Enter information about the following loans:

a. $10,000 at 12% for 4 years
b. $15,000 at 12% for 4 years
c. $25,000 at 14% for 6 years
d. $80,000 at 16% for 20 years
e. $120,000 at 13% for 15 years

3. Use the / File Retrieve command to load the worksheet file called ERRORS, which contains a number of mistakes that you should correct.
   a. Reenter the following mistakes:

      twilve
      cumpany

   b. Press F2 (Edit) to remedy the following errors:

      The dog jumped ovr the lasy cat
      The childrun sat at hoam

   c. Use the / Range Erase command to delete each of the following:

      xxxxxxxxx
      ****
      \\\\\\\\\

4. Create a student's budget schedule that will subtract total expenses from total income for a 4½-month period (one semester) and set net cash amounts for each month. In addition, the schedule should provide monthly totals for income and expense items, with grand totals as depicted in the example below.

   The dollar figures, along with the budget categories, are only illustrative. Pick categories and supply amounts appropriate to your particular situation. Use formulas or the sum function to calculate column and row totals as well as the net cash amount.

School Year Budget

TERM: FALL

NAME: YEAR: 1992

INCOME	JANUARY	FEBRUARY	MARCH	APRIL	MAY	TOTAL
WORK	175	400	400	400	200	1575
AWARDS	50	150	150	150	50	550
ALLOWANCE	35	75	75	75	75	335
OTHER	5	25	25	25	25	105
EXPENSES						
TUITION	250	550	550	550	250	2150
BOOKS	400	0	0	0	0	400
HOME	100	250	250	250	250	1100
CLOTHING	40	125	125	125	75	490
FOOD	40	90	90	90	40	350
TRANSPORT	20	35	35	35	100	225
OTHER	20	35	35	35	35	160
TOTALS	1135	1735				
INCOME	265	650	650	650	350	2565
EXPENSES	870	1085	1085	1085	750	4875
NET CASH	-605	-435	-435	-435	-400	-2310

Need to do calculations

Save the worksheet to a file called CH1EX4.

5. You are the manager of a car dealership. You have six salespeople working for you. Your boss has requested that you take the last 2 years of sales information for each sales rep and determine the difference between the 2 years in sales dollars. Your boss has requested the information in the format shown in Figure 1.11.

do calculations

A1: READY

	A	B	C	D	E	F
1						
2	Sales Rep.	Last Year	This Year	Change	% Change	
3						
4	Harry	125,000	178,000	53,000	42%	
5	Sally	190,000	260,000	70,000	37%	
6	Ben	76,000	68,000	(8,000)	-11%	
7	Marge	98,000	153,000	55,000	56%	
8	Felix	230,000	198,000	(32,000)	-14%	
9	Carol	78,000	163,000	85,000	109%	
10						
11	Totals	797,000	1,020,000	223,000	220%	
12						
13						
14						
15						
16						
17						
18						
19						
20						

14-Aug-91 05:53 PM

Figure 1.11
Car dealership worksheet.

Figure 1.12
Candy sales worksheet.

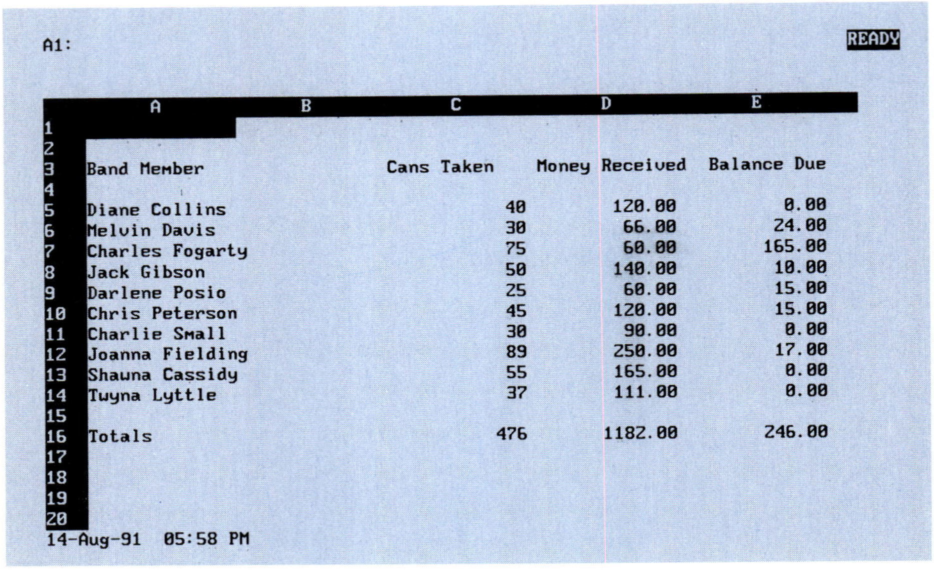
A1: READY

	A	B	C	D	E
1					
2					
3	Band Member		Cans Taken	Money Received	Balance Due
4					
5	Diane Collins		40	120.00	0.00
6	Melvin Davis		30	66.00	24.00
7	Charles Fogarty		75	60.00	165.00
8	Jack Gibson		50	140.00	10.00
9	Darlene Posio		25	60.00	15.00
10	Chris Peterson		45	120.00	15.00
11	Charlie Small		30	90.00	0.00
12	Joanna Fielding		89	250.00	17.00
13	Shauna Cassidy		55	165.00	0.00
14	Tuyna Lyttle		37	111.00	0.00
15					
16	Totals		476	1182.00	246.00
17					
18					
19					
20					

14-Aug-91 05:58 PM

Enter the formulas that will calculate the Change and % Change column entries. Place a total at the bottom of any column containing numeric information. Set the worksheet global column width to 12. Save the worksheet to a file called CH1EX5.

6. The bandleader has asked you to help in the record keeping for the high school band members' fund-raising drive. The band members are selling candy (at $3.00 per can) to pay for a trip to Washington, D.C. The bandleader has accounting information concerning the number of cans of candy checked out by each member and the money turned in by each member (Figure 1.12). You have been asked to determine how much, if anything, each member owes and to provide any information you can on totals. Save this worksheet file to disk using the name CH1EX6.

7. The head of the accounting department is interested in a comparative income statement for the last 2 years and has asked you to prepare the financial statement using the information that follows. You have also been asked to ascertain the dollar change between the various income statement entries. Be sure to calculate the margin by subtracting cost from sales.

ACE Inc.
Income Statement (unaudited)

	Last Year	This Year	Change
INCOME			
Sales	175,000	225,000	50,000
Cost	120,000	160,000	40,000
Margin	55,000	65,000	10,000
EXPENSES			
Materials	22,000	20,000	(2,000)
Supplies	3,000	3,100	100
Payroll	19,000	20,000	1,000
Utilities	950	975	25
Misc.	1,000	1,125	125
Rent	6,000	6,000	0
Total	51,950	51,200	(750)
NET INCOME	3,050	13,800	10,750

Don't worry too much about getting the headings exactly centered. Save this worksheet to a file called CH1EX7.

8. Prepare a worksheet that contains a quarterly summary report for the ABC Company by region, as shown in Figure 1.13. Each of the regions should have a column total. Set the global column width to 12 and right-justify the column headings using the Label Prefix command. Save as CH1EX8.

Figure 1.13

A1: READY

	A	B	C	D	E	F	G
1			ABC Company				
2		Quarterly Sales Report by Region					
3							
4		Jan.	Feb.	Apr.			
5	Region A	12,644.00	7,500.00	23,780.00			
6	Region B	45,623.00	8,750.00	21,960.00			
7	Region C	7,634.00	9,890.00	33,450.00			
8	Region D	12,575.00	3,256.00	28,750.00			
9	Region E	33,456.00	7,250.00	25,500.00			
10							
11	Totals	111,932.00	36,646.00	133,440.00			
12							
13							
14							
15							
16							
17							
18							
19							
20							

14-Aug-91 05:59 PM

Figure 1.14

A1: READY

	A	B	C	D	E	F	G
1				Nissan Motors			
2				Car Sales Report			
3			By Sales Representative and Auto Model				
4							
5							Sales Rep.
6		Sentra	Maxim	Pulsar	Pulsar XE	Pathfinder	Total
7	Fred	50,870	43,000	16,000	0	49,560	159,430
8	Harold	10,600	20,000	31,250	43,670	0	105,520
9	Jim	0	19,800	15,400	0	24,675	59,875
10	John	30,900	21,000	45,780	0	0	97,680
11	Madeline	43,000	62,500	30,790	47,760	0	184,050
12	Marie	22,000	19,450	0	18,900	72,450	132,800
13							
14	Total	157,370	185,750	139,220	110,330	146,685	739,355
15							
16							
17							
18							
19							
20							

14-Aug-91 05:59 PM

Figure 1.15

A1: READY

	A	B	C	D	E	F	G	H
1								
2								
3				XYZ Company				
4				Projected Profit Report				
5								
6		Year 1	Year 2	Year 3	Year 4	Year 5		
7	Sales	100,000	120,000	144,000	172,800	207,360		
8	Costs	60,000	72,000	86,400	103,680	124,416		
9								
10	Profit	40,000	48,000	57,600	69,120	82,944		
11								
12								
13								
14								
15								
16								
17								
18								
19								
20								

14-Aug-91 06:00 PM

9. Prepare a worksheet containing the car sales report by sales representative for Nissan Motors, as shown in Figure 1.14. You wish to track sales for six sales representatives and five car models. The global column width should be set to 10. The global column format should be comma with zero decimal positions. A total should be calculated using the @SUM function for each sales representative as well as for the total sales for each model of car. Save as CH1EX9.

10. Prepare a projected profit report for the XYZ Company for a 5-year period, as shown in Figure 1.15. The sales for each year should increase

20%. The costs should always be assumed to be 60% of sales, while the profit is always equal to the sales minus the costs. After the worksheet has been finished, plug in a first-year sales figure of $60,000. Save as CH1EX10.

2.2

11. Retrieve the CALENDAR worksheet. Once the screen displays the worksheet, issue the command / Worksheet Erase to erase the worksheet. Your screen should now be blank. Once a worksheet is erased, you can issue the Undo (Alt + F4) command to once again view the CALENDAR worksheet. Issue the Undo command again and you see the blank worksheet.

    With the screen showing the CALENDAR worksheet, issue a / File Retrieve command and load the worksheet file PAYMENT. The payment template should now appear on your screen. Issue the Undo command, and the CALENDAR worksheet appears on your screen. Again issue the Undo command, and the PAYMENT worksheet appears on your screen.

    Issue the Undo command to make the CALENDAR worksheet appear on your screen. Position the pointer to cell B3, issue the command / Range Erase, and press Enter. The text APPOINTMENT CALENDAR is now erased from your worksheet; to make this text reappear, issue the Undo command. Notice that, because you had made a change to the worksheet, the prior contents of the backup worksheet containing PAYMENT were replaced with the CALENDAR worksheet as it appeared before the / Range Erase command was issued.

2

MORE ON RANGES, COPYING, FORMATTING, PRINTING, AND FUNCTIONS

CHAPTER OBJECTIVES

After completing this chapter, you should be able to:

- **Use ranges effectively**
- **Use the Copy command**
- **Use the format conventions of 1-2-3 and know the differences between a range format and a global format**
- **Add and delete rows and columns**
- **Use the Move command**
- **Use the Print command to print a worksheet**
- **Use 1-2-3 built-in functions**

In this chapter, we cover the concept of ranges and the Copy, Format, Move, and Print commands in more detail. These commands give a 1-2-3 user additional power to simplify actions and to determine how output will appear.

RANGE

When you are using 1-2-3, a statement or a process you wish to perform may require your indicating a range of cells to 1-2-3. A **range** is any specially designated single cell or rectangular group of cells on a worksheet; it is defined by pointing to the cells with the pointer or by typing the addresses of cells at the opposite corners of the range. Remember that a range is a rectangle and therefore has only four corners.

Figure 2.1a displays a valid range containing three cells. Figure 2.1b would not be a valid range.

To define a range, you can give the cell locations of any pair of cells on opposite corners. For example, suppose you had a range containing a number of cells, and having as its four corners the cells A2, A5, C5, and C2. To define the range, you would only have to give the cell addresses of two opposite corners, in whichever order you like—A2 and C5, A5 and C2, C2 and A5, or C5 and A2. Any of these cell addresses will define the range depicted in Figure 2.2.

From time to time, a worksheet will contain range settings from a previous session with 1-2-3 that you no longer desire, such as print settings. You can cancel a previous print range and specify another. To cancel any range in any 1-2-3 command, press Backspace. A new range can now be entered.

Given the many commands involving ranges, a 1-2-3 novice may be uncertain when to first "nail down" the pointer with a period (.) and when to simply extend the range by moving the pointer. If 1-2-3 has not already nailed down the pointer for the command you are issuing, the prompt will contain only one reference to the cell (A1, for example). In this case, move the pointer to the correct starting cell, press period (.) to nail the range, and extend it. If 1-2-3 has already nailed the pointer, the prompt will look like `A1 .. A1`. In this case, simply extend the range. If the range displayed by a command is incorrect, press Backspace to cancel the range, move the pointer to the appropriate beginning cell, press period (.) to nail the range, and extend it with pointer movements.

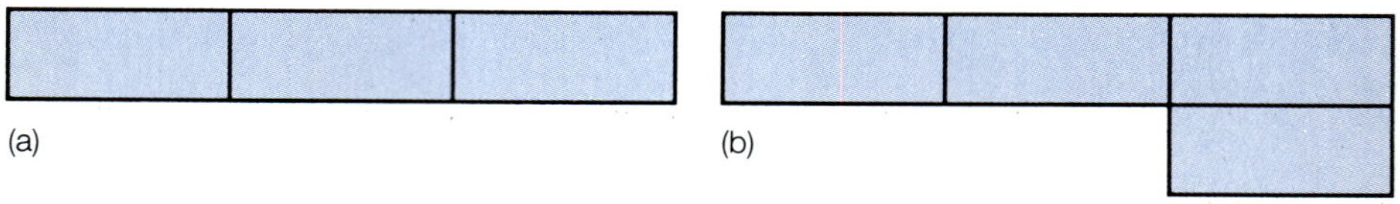

Figure 2.1
(a) A valid range and (b) an invalid range.

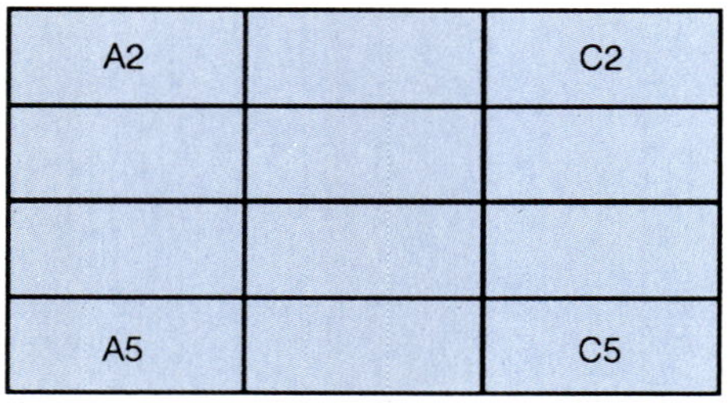

Figure 2.2
The cell addresses of any two corner cells can be used to define a range.

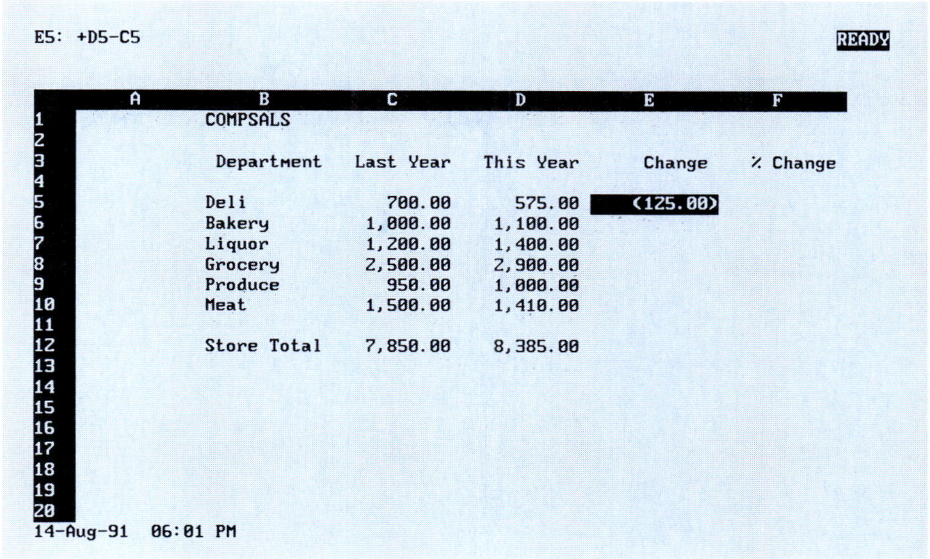

Figure 2.3
The cells to be copied identified to 1-2-3.

COPY COMMAND (/C)

The **Copy command** takes information that has been entered in one or more cells and copies it to other cells. This can save you many keystrokes and much time when you are building a worksheet. You may remember using the Copy command on the sample COMPSALS worksheet in the last chapter, but you may not yet understand everything that it was doing. The Copy command involves setting up a **sending** cell or cells that contain the data to be copied and then setting up a **receiving** range of cells to which the data will be copied. The following steps are required:

1. Position the pointer and select the Copy command from the Main Menu (/C).
2. Indicate which cells are in the "From" range—that is, which cells hold data to be copied onto other cells. If only one cell is involved, simply press Enter; if a range of cells is involved, extend the range [the two periods (..) indicate that the beginning of the range is already fixed] and then move the pointer to the last cell in the range (or enter the cell address) and press Enter (Figure 2.3).
3. Indicate which cells are in the "To" range—that is, which cells are to receive data held in the "From" cells. If only one cell is involved, press Enter. If a range of cells is involved, **nail down** the beginning of the range with a period (.). Move the pointer to the last cell in the range (or enter the cell address) (Figure 2.4). Once Enter is pressed, the indicated cells are copied (Figure 2.5).

HINTS/HAZARDS

Make certain that your "From" cell range does not overlap your "To" cell range. If this happens, 1-2-3 overwrites the previous contents of the cell(s), and the previous contents are irretrievably lost.

Figure 2.4
The cells to receive the outputs of the copied cell identified to 1-2-3.

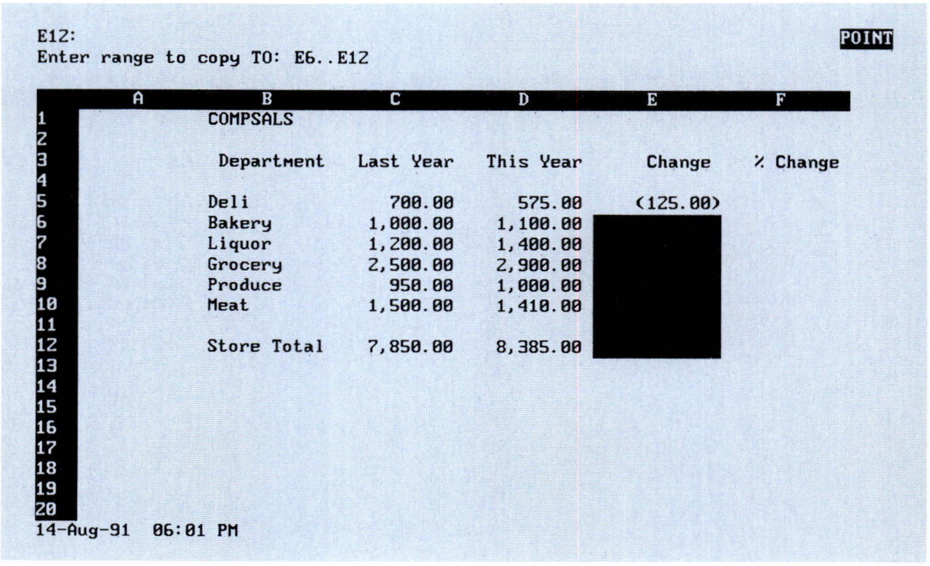

Figure 2.5
The worksheet after the Copy command has been executed.

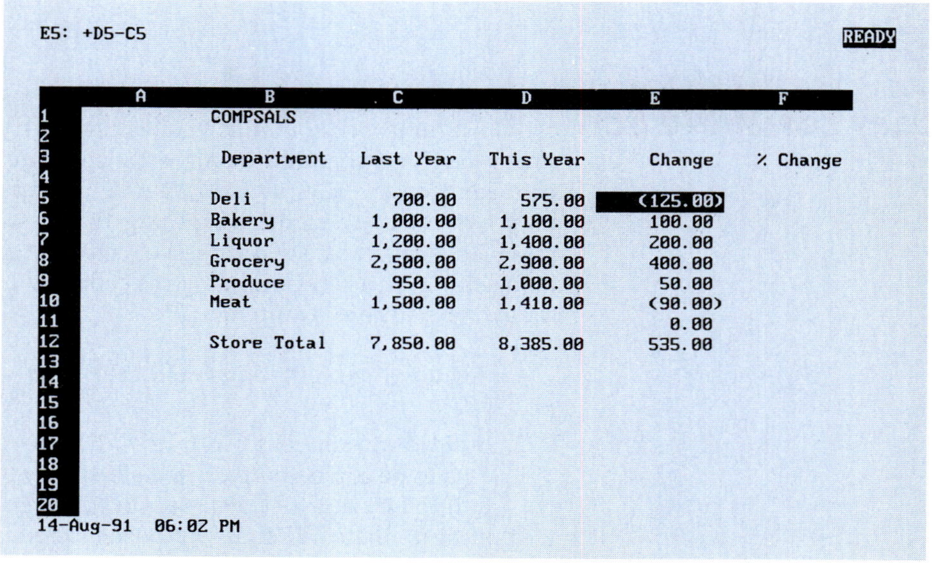

As noted in Chapter 1, 1-2-3 automatically changes the cell references in a formula it is copying to reflect the new cell location of the formula. This is an example of the concept of relative addressing. Other text data are copied from one cell to another exactly as they appear. For example, if a cell containing the label *Year* is copied to another cell, the receiving cell will also contain *Year;* and if the text in the sending cell is right-justified, the text in the receiving cell will also be right-justified.

The Copy command can copy a range of cells. Suppose you want to copy a range of cells two cells (columns) wide by 20 rows deep. You can establish the "From" range as before—by entering the cell addresses or by pointing—and 1-2-3 will then be informed that the sending range consists of two columns and 20 rows. When you tell 1-2-3 the "To" range, however, you can simply identify the address of the upper left-hand cell of the receiving range (or point to this cell) and press Enter. Because 1-2-3 retains in memory what the sending data look like, it assumes that you want it to move the whole range and does so.

FORMAT COMMANDS (/WGF OR /RF)

Lotus uses the Format command to control how numeric information appears in a cell. As you have already seen, you can **format** either the entire worksheet via the **/ Worksheet Global Format option** or a specific part of the worksheet via the **/ Range Format option.** It is important to note that the range format takes precedence over the worksheet global format, so only cells containing data not specifically formatted using the / Range Format command can be changed using the / Worksheet Global Format command.

Cell data can be formatted using the global or range options in various ways, including the following.

Fixed The **Format Fixed option** displays a fixed number of decimal places (0 to 15), specified by the worksheet user. Examples: 10, 10.5, −120.00. When this command is used in a / Range Format command, the message (Fx) appears in the status line. The x denotes the number of decimal positions.

Scientific The **Format Scientific option** displays data in the exponential scientific notation format. The worksheet user specifies the number of decimal places in the multiplier (0 to 15). The exponent (E) is expressed as a power of 10 from +99 to −99. Examples: 1.35E + 11, −7.5E −19. When this command is used in a / Range Format command, the message (Sx) appears in the status line. The x denotes the number of decimal positions.

Currency The **Format Currency option** places a dollar sign ($) before each numeric cell entry and places commas after the thousands and millions places in each entry large enough to have them. Negative numbers are placed in parentheses. The user specifies the number of positions to the right of the decimal. Examples: $13.50, ($6.75), $1.050. When this command is used in a / Range Format command, the message (Cx) appears in the status line. The x denotes the number of decimal positions.

, The **Format , option** is like the Currency option but without dollar signs. When this command is used in a / Range Format command, the message (,x) appears in the status line. The x denotes the number of decimal positions.

General The **Format General option,** the default numeric display, suppresses trailing zeros after a decimal point. Extremely large or small numbers are displayed in exponential notation format. Examples: 17.66, −4.3, 2.4 + 10. When this command is used in a / Range Format command, the message (G) appears in the status line.

+/− The **Format +/− option** displays a horizontal bar graph in which the number of symbols is the integer part of the value. Plus signs represent positive integers, and minus signs represent negative integers; if the value is zero, a period (.) is displayed. For example,

6	= + + + + + +
4	= + + + +
−3	= − − −
10	= + + + + + + + + + +
−5	= − − − − −
3.5	= + + +

When this command is used in a / Range Format command, the message (+) appears in the status line.

Percent The **Format Percent option** displays the numeric entry in a cell as a percentage (%). The user must specify decimal positions. The value contained in the cell is the decimal equivalent multiplied by 100 and followed by a percent sign. Examples: 45%, 12.5%, −23%. When this command is used in a / Range Format command, the message (Px) appears in the status line. The x denotes the number of decimal positions.

Date The **Format Date option** displays the date in one of five formats:

1	DD-MMM-YY	(Example:09-Sep-92)
2	DD-MMM	(Example:09-Sep)
3	MMM-YY	(Example:Sep-92)
4	(Long Intn'l)	(Example:09-09-92)
5	(Short Intn'l)	(Example:09-09)

The time entries provide you with more control when you wish to format a cell containing a date function:

1	(HH:MM:SS AM/PM)	(Example:11:18:53 A.M.)
2	(HH:MM AM/PM)	(Example:11:18 A.M.)
3	(Long Intn'l)	(Example:11:18:53)
4	(Short Intn'l)	(Example:11:18)

When the Date command is used in a / Range Format command, the message (Dx) appears in the status line. The x denotes the date format option selected. If the time format was selected, a (Tx) appears in the status line.

Text The **Format Text option** displays the formula, rather than the result of the formula, in a cell. Example: + D3/C3. When this command is used in a / Range Format command, the message (T) appears in the status line.

Hidden The **Format Hidden option** inhibits numbers, formulas, or text residing in a cell from being displayed in the cell. It is useful when you wish to embed comments or documentation concerning the worksheet but do not wish to have those comments appear when the worksheet is printed. When the pointer resides on the cell that has been hidden, its contents appear in the control panel, along with the range indicator (H). When you use the Hidden command in a / Range Format command, the message (H) appears in the status line.

Reset The **Format Reset option** changes the format of a cell or a range of cells from the existing range format back to the global format.

Remember that the general format option is the default format used by 1-2-3 to start a spreadsheet and that the default column width used by 1-2-3 is nine positions wide. You can determine other default values used by 1-2-3 by entering the / Worksheet Status command.

HINTS/HAZARDS

When you are trying to determine which global format to use, examine which format is used for the largest portion of the worksheet and make that your global format. Any exceptions to this global format can be addressed using the / Range Format command.

ADDING AND DELETING ROWS AND COLUMNS (/WI)

From time to time, you may want to add or delete one or more rows or columns on the worksheet. The pointer is used to show where you wish to add or delete the row or column. Columns are added to the *left* of the pointer position, and rows are added *above* the pointer position, using the Insert and Delete options.

HINTS/HAZARDS

Make certain that there are no important areas of the worksheet offscreen that may be affected by your deleting a row or column. Remember, the entire column or row will be completely destroyed, not just what appears on the screen.

Let's add a column to the COMPSALS worksheet, which currently appears as shown in Figure 2.6. First, position the pointer where the addition or deletion is to take place. For example, if you want to add a column between present columns B and C, place the pointer anywhere in column C. Then issue the following commands:

/W	Selects Worksheet from the Main Menu.
I	Selects the Insert option.
C	Selects the column command.
Enter	Executes the command.

The pointer in column C appears in reverse video, indicating that the range is only one column wide. When you press Enter, the old column C becomes the new column D. If you want to add two columns, press the Right Arrow one time and then press Enter. The COMPSALS worksheet now looks as shown in Figure 2.7.

Now let's add two rows between the Deli and Bakery lines. First position the pointer anywhere on the Bakery line; then issue the following commands:

/W	Selects Worksheet from the Main Menu.
I	Selects the Insert option.
R	Selects the row command.
↓	Extends the range to two rows.
Enter	Inserts the rows.

The COMPSALS worksheet now appears as shown in Figure 2.8. You are now free to use these new rows and columns to enter new departments and to enter summary information for sales from 2 years ago.

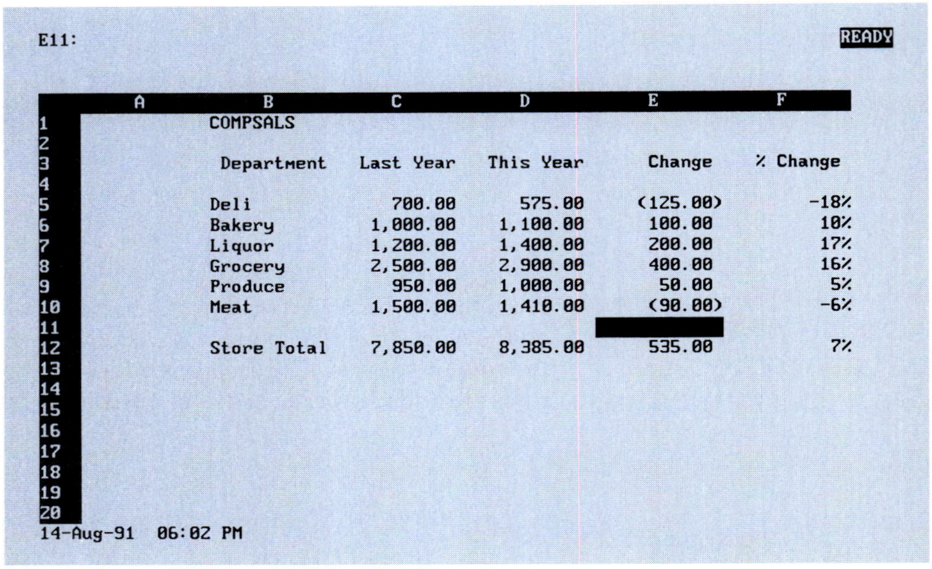

E11: READY

	A	B	C	D	E	F
1		COMPSALS				
2						
3		Department	Last Year	This Year	Change	% Change
4						
5		Deli	700.00	575.00	(125.00)	-18%
6		Bakery	1,000.00	1,100.00	100.00	10%
7		Liquor	1,200.00	1,400.00	200.00	17%
8		Grocery	2,500.00	2,900.00	400.00	16%
9		Produce	950.00	1,000.00	50.00	5%
10		Meat	1,500.00	1,410.00	(90.00)	-6%
11						
12		Store Total	7,850.00	8,385.00	535.00	7%
13						
14						
15						
16						
17						
18						
19						
20						

14-Aug-91 06:02 PM

Figure 2.6
COMPSALS worksheet.

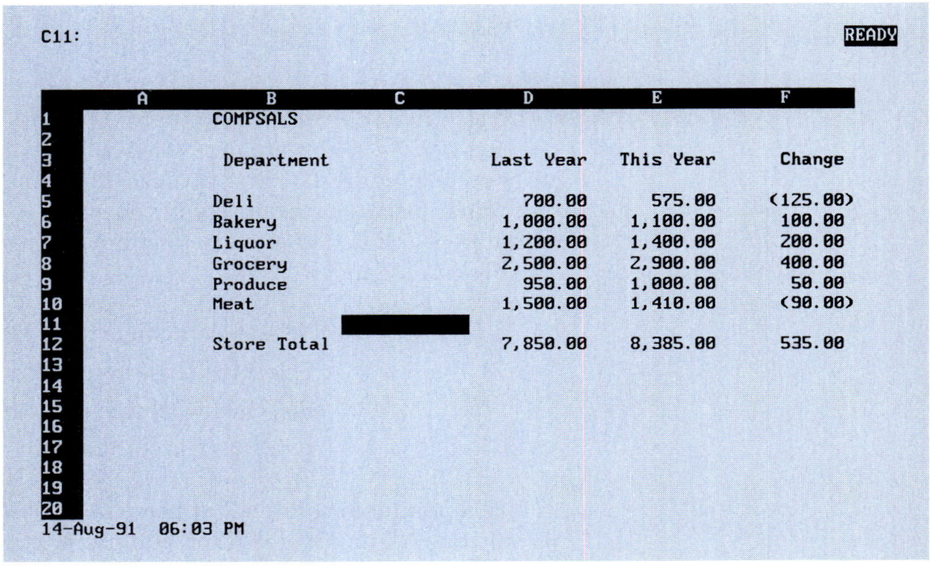

C11: READY

	A	B	C	D	E	F
1		COMPSALS				
2						
3		Department		Last Year	This Year	Change
4						
5		Deli		700.00	575.00	(125.00)
6		Bakery		1,000.00	1,100.00	100.00
7		Liquor		1,200.00	1,400.00	200.00
8		Grocery		2,500.00	2,900.00	400.00
9		Produce		950.00	1,000.00	50.00
10		Meat		1,500.00	1,410.00	(90.00)
11						
12		Store Total		7,850.00	8,385.00	535.00
13						
14						
15						
16						
17						
18						
19						
20						

14-Aug-91 06:03 PM

Figure 2.7
COMPSALS worksheet with column added.

Deleting rows and columns involves essentially the same process, except that you mark the actual ranges (rows or columns) to be deleted instead of inserted.

MOVING CELL CONTENTS (/M)

You may want to add or delete a column or row from your worksheet, only to discover that another area of your worksheet would be disastrously affected by such an action. This is the time to use 1-2-3's **Move feature,** which lets you relocate cell contents without disturbing other worksheet areas. The Move feature automatically retains all functional relationships of any formulas; it works by specifying sending and receiving areas on the worksheet (much like the Copy statement, except that in Move the sending contents are destroyed).

Figure 2.8
COMPSALS worksheet with rows added.

C6: READY

	A	B	C	D	E	F
1		COMPSALS				
2						
3		Department		Last Year	This Year	Change
4						
5		Deli		700.00	575.00	(125.00)
6						
7						
8		Bakery		1,000.00	1,100.00	100.00
9		Liquor		1,200.00	1,400.00	200.00
10		Grocery		2,500.00	2,900.00	400.00
11		Produce		950.00	1,000.00	50.00
12		Meat		1,500.00	1,410.00	(90.00)
13						
14		Store Total		7,850.00	8,385.00	535.00
15						
16						
17						
18						
19						
20						

14-Aug-91 06:03 PM

Figure 2.9
Loan amortization worksheet.

A2: 'Interest READY

	A	B	C	D	E	F	G
1							
2	Interest		12.00%				
3	Loan Amount		$1,200				
4	Months		20				
5	Beginning Date		May-90				
6							
7		TOTAL			BALANCE		
8	DATE	PAYMENT	PRINCIPAL	INTEREST	OUTSTANDING		
9	May-90	66.50	54.50	12.00	1145.50		
10	Jun-90	66.50	55.04	11.46	1090.46		
11	Jul-90	66.50	55.59	10.90	1034.87		
12	Aug-90	66.50	56.15	10.35	978.72		
13	Sep-90	66.50	56.71	9.79	922.01		
14	Oct-90	66.50	57.28	9.22	864.73		
15	Nov-90	66.50	57.85	8.65	806.88		
16	Dec-90	66.50	58.43	8.07	748.45		
17	Jan-91	66.50	59.01	7.48	689.44		
18	Feb-91	66.50	59.60	6.89	629.84		
19	Mar-91	66.50	60.20	6.30	569.64		
20	Apr-91	66.50	60.80	5.70	508.84		

14-Aug-91 06:06 PM

HINTS/HAZARDS

When using Move, make certain that the receiving range does not overlap any valuable cells in your worksheet. All cells in the receiving range will be destroyed, and you will not be able to retrieve the data previously contained in them.

Suppose that you have a loan amortization worksheet that looks like the one in Figure 2.9. Imagine that you want to center the lines at the top of the worksheet to give a more balanced look. To perform this task, which involves

Figure 2.10
Loan amortization worksheet with information centered.

A2: READY

	A	B	C	D	E	F	G
1							
2		Interest		12.00%			
3		Loan Amount		$1,200			
4		Months		20			
5		Beginning Date		May-90			
6							
7		TOTAL			BALANCE		
8	DATE	PAYMENT	PRINCIPAL	INTEREST	OUTSTANDING		
9	May-90	66.50	54.50	12.00	1145.50		
10	Jun-90	66.50	55.04	11.46	1090.46		
11	Jul-90	66.50	55.59	10.90	1034.87		
12	Aug-90	66.50	56.15	10.35	978.72		
13	Sep-90	66.50	56.71	9.79	922.01		
14	Oct-90	66.50	57.28	9.22	864.73		
15	Nov-90	66.50	57.85	8.65	806.88		
16	Dec-90	66.50	58.43	8.07	748.45		
17	Jan-91	66.50	59.01	7.48	689.44		
18	Feb-91	66.50	59.60	6.89	629.84		
19	Mar-91	66.50	60.20	6.30	569.64		
20	Apr-91	66.50	60.80	5.70	508.84		

14-Aug-91 06:06 PM

moving the information contained in eight cells one column to the right, execute the following steps:

Go to A1	Establishes the beginning of the "From" range by pointing.
/M	Selects the Move option from the Main Menu.
Type .	Nails down the beginning of the "From" range.
Go to C5	Marks the ending cell of the "From" range.
Enter	Establishes the "From" range.
Go to B1	Marks the beginning of the "To" range.
Enter	Moves the cell contents.

The worksheet now appears as shown in Figure 2.10.

SETTINGS SHEET

2.2

Some 1-2-3 commands, such as the Print, usually require various submenu commands to tell 1-2-3 exactly how to do something. In these situations, users are sometimes uncertain whether they have entered all the necessary commands. To alleviate this problem, 1-2-3 occasionally displays a special status screen called a **settings sheet** that helps keep track of which commands you have selected and 1-2-3's responses (Figure 2.11). Appearing above the settings screen, the control panel shows the contents of the cell at the pointer location and the current command menu. To change the settings, make selections from the menu. You cannot make changes directly on the settings screen.

With the Print command, for instance, you might want to change the right-hand margin, change the typesize, add a header, or specify a new print range. You can do these things using the commands in the Print Menu and its Options submenu. As you enter each command, the settings sheet reflects your changes.

Figure 2.11

A Print Settings screen that appears when the Print command is selected.

```
A1: 'FUNCTION                                                         MENU
Range  Line  Page  Options  Clear  Align  Go  Quit
Specify a range to print
 ------------------------------------- Print Settings ----------------------------
|  Destination:  Printer                                                          |
|                                                                                 |
|  Range:        A1..E25                                                          |
|                                                                                 |
|  Header:                                                                        |
|  Footer:       Page #|FUNCTION|@                                                |
|                                                                                 |
|  Margins:                                                                       |
|    Left 4    Right 76    Top 2    Bottom 2                                      |
|                                                                                 |
|  Borders:                                                                       |
|    Columns                                                                      |
|    Rows                                                                         |
|                                                                                 |
|  Setup string:                                                                  |
|                                                                                 |
|  Page length:  66                                                               |
|                                                                                 |
|  Output:       As-Displayed (Formatted)                                         |
 ---------------------------------------------------------------------------------
14-Aug-91  06:07 PM
```

Figure 2.12

The settings screen that appears any time that the / Worksheet Global command has been entered at the keyboard.

```
A1: 'FUNCTION                                                              MENU
Format  Label-Prefix  Column-Width  Recalculation  Protection  Default  Zero
Fixed  Sci  Currency  ,  General  +/-  Percent  Date  Text  Hidden
 ------------------------------- Global Settings ---------------------------------
|  Conventional memory:  337076 of 338784 Bytes (99%)                             |
|  Expanded memory:      (None)                                                   |
|                                                                                 |
|  Math coprocessor:     (None)                                                   |
|                                                                                 |
|  Recalculation:                                                                 |
|    Method              Automatic                                                |
|    Order               Natural                                                  |
|    Iterations          1                                                        |
|                                                                                 |
|  Circular reference:   (None)                                                   |
|                                                                                 |
|  Cell display:                                                                  |
|    Format              (G)                                                      |
|    Label prefix        ' (left align)                                           |
|    Column width        15                                                       |
|    Zero suppression    No                                                       |
|                                                                                 |
|  Global protection:    Disabled                                                 |
 ---------------------------------------------------------------------------------
14-Aug-91  06:07 PM
```

HINTS/HAZARDS

When a settings screen is active, your worksheet is not visible. To see the worksheet without leaving the command with which you are working, issue the Window (F6) command to make the settings screen disappear so that you can view your worksheet.

2.2

Another commonly viewed settings screen is the Global Settings screen (Figure 2.12), which appears any time you enter a / Worksheet Global command. This settings screen provides information about the status of several important commands that affect the entire worksheet. Many of these commands are covered later in the text.

PRINT COMMAND (/P)

The **Print command** prints either the whole worksheet or parts (ranges) of it. The output can be sent directly to a printer or placed in a disk file, from which it can later be used by a word processing program.

After you select the Print option from the Main Menu, 1-2-3 prompts you if you want the output to go to a printer (the Printer option) or onto a disk file (the File option). If you select the File option, enter the filename, to which 1-2-3 will add the extension .PRN. To access the file later, the filename you specify must include the .PRN extension.

PRINT MENU

Selecting the Print option from the Main Menu displays the following **Print Menu** in the control panel:

```
Range Line Page Options Clear Align Go Quit
```

Let's examine in turn what each option does.

Range The **Print Range option** lets you determine which part of the worksheet to print. You can enter the cell addresses of two opposite corners of the range that is to be printed, or you can use the pointer to identify the range.

Line The **Print Line option** tells the printer to advance the paper one line. This lets you leave some blank space between ranges that are printing out.

Page After 1-2-3 is finished printing a range of cells, it stops the printer at that location. The **Print Page option** advances the paper in the printer to the top of the next page. It is useful if you want printed output to start on a new sheet of paper. The Page option also results in the printing of any footer lines.

Options The **Print Options Menu** lets you put **header, footer,** borders, and so forth on the printout:

```
Header Footer Margins Borders Setup Pg-Length Other Quit
```

These options let you temporarily override defaults for printing information. The overrides remain in effect until you change them or restart Lotus 1-2-3. If you save your worksheet and later call it back, 1-2-3 will remember the overrides because they will have become part of the worksheet file.

Header/Footer The **Header** and **Footer options** let you enter one line of text to be used as a heading or footing on each page of printout. You will be prompted for the text and can place up to 240 characters on the line. In either a header or a footer line, the following special characters can be used to give printing instructions:

#	Numbers the pages beginning with 1.
¦	Split header/footer into sections as follows: The first part is left-justified. The second part is centered. The third part is right-justified.
@	Prints today's date

For example, you could place the following text in the footer of the sample worksheet COMPSALS:

```
Page #|COMPSALS|@
```

This input would develop a footer with the word *Page* and the page number in the first (left-justified) section. The word *COMPSALS* would appear centered in the center part of the footer. The date would appear in the third section (right-justified).

Lotus always leaves two blank lines between the worksheet and any header and footer. You can suppress headers and footers by selecting Options Other Unformatted and reinstate them by selecting Options Other Formatted.

Margins The **Margins option** changes **margins** (left, right, top, and bottom). It is especially important if you have a dot-matrix printer and want to print the worksheet using compressed print to get more characters per line. The maximum value allowed for resetting the right-hand margin is 240 characters.

2.2 The None option of the Margins command clears the current margins and resets the top, left, and bottom margins to 0 and the right margin to 240.

HINTS/HAZARDS

When you are printing on 8½-inch by 11-inch paper and you reset the right-hand margin to a setting greater than the default (76), you will usually want to use a smaller type to get more characters to print. In this instance, you must also remember to use the Setup command to change the type size.

Borders The **Borders option** displays horizontal or vertical borders text on each page of a printed report. For example, you may have a worksheet that develops a loan amortization table and generates one line of output for each month of the loan; in this case, use the Borders option to print column headings on each page. All you have to do is select the row or column (depending on where you want the labels) and then specify the range of cells containing the desired text. To clear the borders, enter the commands / Print Printer Clear Borders. The Borders option requires specifying a range for the border and a range for the data. When you use borders, do not specify any border cells in the print range; rather, specify them separately in the border range (Figure 2.13). Otherwise, the border cells print twice on the first page.

Setup The **setup option** tells your printer which escape code to use for printing the data. For example, for Epson FX or Epson-compatible printers, condensed printing (17.16 cpi) can be obtained by entering \015 as the setup string. To get back to pica (10 cpi) printing, enter / Print Printer Options Setup, followed by \018. If you wish to print in elite (12 cpi), enter \077 to turn on elite; to turn it off, enter \080. Depending on the setup string, you can print in 10-, 12-, or 17.1-character pitch.

Page Length The **Page Length option** changes the number of lines on a page. It becomes important when you use paper other than 11-inch paper.

Figure 2.13

Two ranges are required using the Borders option.

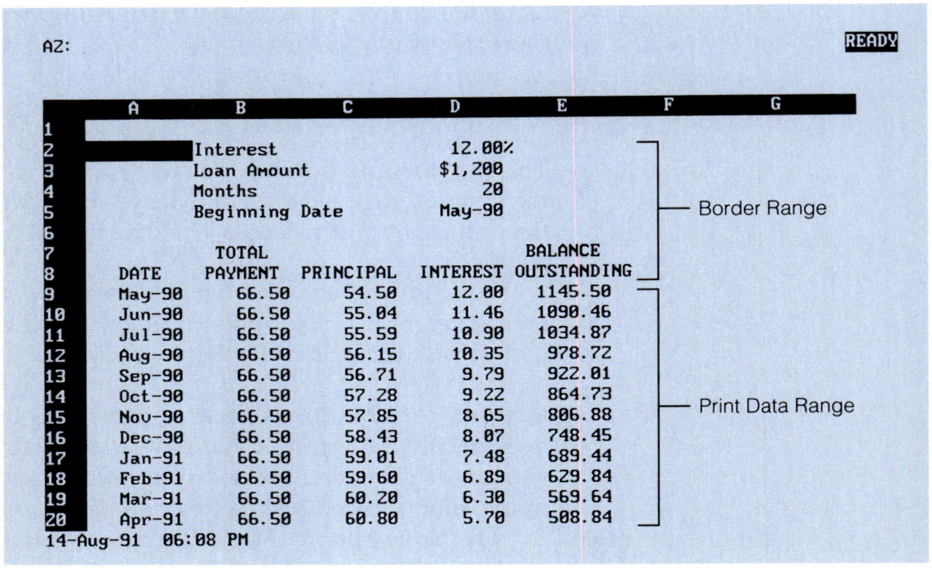

	A	B	C	D	E
1					
2		Interest		12.00%	
3		Loan Amount		$1,200	
4		Months		20	
5		Beginning Date		May-90	
6					
7		TOTAL			BALANCE
8	DATE	PAYMENT	PRINCIPAL	INTEREST	OUTSTANDING
9	May-90	66.50	54.50	12.00	1145.50
10	Jun-90	66.50	55.04	11.46	1090.46
11	Jul-90	66.50	55.59	10.90	1034.87
12	Aug-90	66.50	56.15	10.35	978.72
13	Sep-90	66.50	56.71	9.79	922.01
14	Oct-90	66.50	57.28	9.22	864.73
15	Nov-90	66.50	57.85	8.65	806.88
16	Dec-90	66.50	58.43	8.07	748.45
17	Jan-91	66.50	59.01	7.48	689.44
18	Feb-91	66.50	59.60	6.89	629.84
19	Mar-91	66.50	60.20	6.30	569.64
20	Apr-91	66.50	60.80	5.70	508.84

Other The **Other option** displays the following menu:

```
As-Displayed Cell-Formulas Formatted Unformatted
```

- *As-Displayed* prints the output exactly as it appears on the screen.
- *Cell-Formulas* prints one cell per line and displays the cell contents (text or formula).
- *Formatted* restores any footers, headers, or page breaks that might have been suppressed.
- *Unformatted* overrides any footer, header, or page breaks, printing the output without any of these features.

Clear As print specifications are entered, 1-2-3 stores them in RAM and uses them for any printing operations; in addition, it stores them to your worksheet file when the file is saved onto disk. Occasionally, you may not want these various print settings to be stored in memory; the **Print Clear option** returns print options to their default values, according to the following menu:

```
All Range Borders Format
```

- *All* resets all print settings to the default values.
- *Range* cancels the print range.
- *Borders* cancels the border range.
- *Format* returns margins, page length, and setup string to default values.

Align The **Print Align option** is used when 1-2-3 has lost track of where it is on a sheet of paper—for example, when a user turns the knob on the printer platen to roll the paper forward, rather than using the Line or Page options. When this happens, position the paper in the printer to the top of a new sheet and execute the Align command; Lotus will immediately assume that it is at the top of a new page.

Go The **Print Go option** sends the designated range as output to the printer or to the named disk file and returns you to the Print Menu. This lets you print other parts of the worksheet if you desire. If the printer is not on-line, 1-2-3 will try to print and find that it can't; it will then beep and display an error message. You must press Esc to continue.

What happens if you forget to enter the setup string or print the wrong range? To stop printing, press Ctrl + Break. This interrupts the printer and returns control to the Print Menu. Use the Page command to go to the top of the next page or position the paper to the top of the next page manually and enter the Align command.

Quit The **Print Quit option** terminates the print session and returns you to READY mode in the worksheet. When you are storing output data onto a disk file, you must use this command to close the file properly. If you do not, no data will be stored. When storing data onto a disk file, always follow these steps:

1. Name the file
2. Establish the range and any options.
3. Enter the Go command to store data onto the disk file.
4. Enter the Quit command to close the disk file.

PRINT DEFAULT SETTINGS

Lotus has a number of defaults for printing. Depending on the type of printer you have, some defaults may differ from those listed below. When a blank worksheet is started or when the Clear option is selected, 1-2-3 institutes or restores those default settings:

- Left margin is 4.
- Right margin is 76.
- Top margin is 2 lines from the top of the page.
- Bottom margin is 2 lines from the bottom of the page.
- Page length is 66 lines per page.
- Auto-line feed is no.
- Wait to insert a sheet of paper is no.
- Interface is parallel.
- Setup string is no.

PRINT LINE COUNTER

Lotus has an internal line counter that keeps track of the current printer position on a page. As it prints each line of a worksheet, 1-2-3 automatically adjusts this line counter. Three of the Print Menu commands—Line, Page, and Align—also affect this counter. The Line command not only issues a line feed for the printer but also increments the internal 1-2-3 line counter by a value of 1. The Page command tells the printer to go to the top of the next page and sets the line counter back to a beginning value. The Align command simply resets the line counter back to its beginning value.

It follows from the above that you should not manually adjust the position of the paper within the printer because 1-2-3 has no way of knowing that you have moved the paper. It remembers only the current line counter value.

If you print one worksheet and then manually position the paper at the top of the next page to print another, you will have a 10-line gap wherever 1-2-3 "remembers" to issue a page break command to the printer. To correct this, press Ctrl + Break and return to the Print Menu. Then manually move the paper to the top of the next page and issue an Align command. The line counter will be reset, and you will be ready to start printing.

FORCED PAGE BREAKS (/WP)

The / Worksheet Page command automatically forces a **page break** at the location in the worksheet in which it is entered. For example, if you wish to force a page break after the Liquor department line in the COMPSALS worksheet, first position the cursor to the Grocery line and enter the / Worksheet Page command. Once this command has been entered, a blank line appears within the worksheet with a :: entry. The :: entry tells 1-2-3 that when it reaches this line in the worksheet it should issue a page break and begin the next line at the top of a new sheet of paper.

HINTS/HAZARDS

Use the page break command carefully because parts of your worksheet that are not currently viewed on your screen can be affected. To get rid of an undesired page break, use the / Worksheet Delete Row command if you have just entered the page break command. If you have had this command embedded in your worksheet for some time, make certain that no worksheet entries are currently on this row. If text, numbers, or formulas reside there, use the Move command or possibly the Range Erase command.

PASSING PRINT FILES TO OTHER SOFTWARE PACKAGES

Lotus lets you easily create print files that can be passed along to other applications such as word processing software. This is done with the / Print File command. Once this command has been entered, 1-2-3 prompts you for the name of the file to created. Enter the name without specifying an extension, using regular DOS naming conventions. When you press Enter, an empty file with the specified name will be created on disk, and 1-2-3 will automatically place a .PRN file extension on the file. You are now placed in the Print Menu; you can specify any options that you want the report to contain, such as header, footer, margin changes, borders, and so on. After you have made all of the required entries, issue the Go command. You will note some disk activity as 1-2-3 saves the range to disk. You must now enter the Quit command to close the file on disk. You will again see some disk activity.

The steps involved in generating a .PRN file on disk that can then be accessed by another application program are as follows:

1. Tell 1-2-3 to store data to disk (/ Print File).
2. Tell 1-2-3 the name of the file and press Enter.

3. Make any changes using print commands in the Print Menu.
4. Issue a Go command to save the print range to disk.
5. Issue a Quit command to close the file.

HINTS/HAZARDS

Steps 2, 4, and 5 are absolutely required any time you wish to create a .PRN file. If the Quit command is omitted, the file allocation table will not be updated, and the file will be empty when it is accessed by another application program. Because the Quit command returns you to READY mode and is not used when multiple prints are sent to the printer instead of to a file, this portion of the command sequence is most frequently omitted. Remember that you must always end the process of creating a .PRN file by issuing the Quit command from the Print Menu and returning to READY mode.

LOTUS 1-2-3 FUNCTIONS

You have already used the 1-2-3 function @SUM. Functions save time and increase accuracy because they reduce the number of keystrokes and the chance for error. A function contains a preprogrammed set of instructions that you issue by using what 1-2-3 refers to as a **function call** (naming the function) and then telling 1-2-3 where to find the data to act on.

A typical 1-2-3 function consists of the following parts:

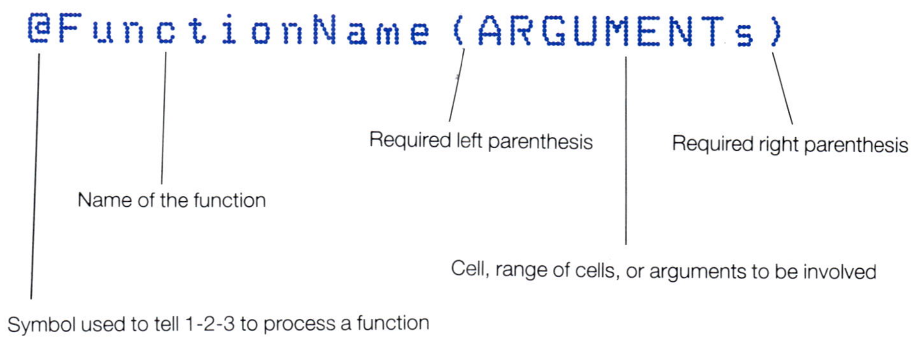

Table 2.1 lists some 1-2-3 functions used frequently in business and education.

A piece of datum that is used as input for a function is called an **argument.** Arguments are typed within parentheses. If a function has several arguments, they are separated by commas. Sometimes arguments may consist of a range of cells; at other times, they can have completely different roles. The point to remember is that the function itself has all of the built-in routines required for producing the correct answer.

Functions can be **nested,** meaning that one function references another function. Suppose, for example, that you want to get the number of the month from the system date (DOS). You could do this by using the nested function statement @MONTH (@NOW), which uses the output of the @NOW function as input to the @MONTH function.

Table 2.1 1-2-3 Functions for Business and Education

Function	*Task*
Date Functions	
@DATE (year, month, day)	Places the date for any day since 1/1/1900.
@DAY (date)	Gets the day number from this date.
@MONTH (date)	Gets the month number from this date.
@YEAR (date)	Gets the year number from this date.
@NOW	Gets the date from the DOS date register.
Statistical Functions	
@COUNT (list)	Counts the number of entries in the specified list (range).
@SUM (list)	Sums the values of all cell contents in the list (range).
@AVG (list)	Averages the values of all cell contents in the list (range).
@MIN (list)	Finds the smallest value from the cells listed in the range.
@MAX (list)	Finds the largest value from the cells listed in the range.
@STD (list)	Finds the standard deviation from the values of the cells listed in the range.
@VAR (list)	Finds the variance from the values of the cells listed in the range.
Miscellaneous Functions	
@IF (cond, x, y)	Indicates that if the condition is true the value or formula in x will be used; otherwise, the value or formula in y will be used.
@ROUND (x, n)	Indicates that number x will be rounded to n decimal positions. If the next position has a value of 5 or greater, the digit n will be rounded up; if that position has a value of 4 or less, the digit n will remain unchanged.

Another example of nesting is @ROUND (@AVG(F3..F6),1), which averages the numbers in the range F3 to F6 and then rounds the results to one decimal place. When you use nested functions, you must make certain that the number of left-hand parentheses equals the number of right-hand parentheses. If the numbers are not equal, the computer will beep, indicating an error.

MORE ON DATA ENTRY

CHANGING A COLUMN WIDTH (/WC)

When you are entering numeric data into a cell and receive asterisks (**********) in the cell, 1-2-3 is telling you that the column is not wide enough to display the number properly. You may also want to expand a column to provide sufficient room to display row labels properly. A column can be expanded via the **Column Width command:**

/W	Selects the Worksheet option from the Main Menu.
C	Selects the Column Width command.
S	Selects the Set Width command.
Type -	Enters the desired column width.
Enter	Executes the command.

To enter the new column width, either enter a number or adjust the column width a character at a time by pressing an Arrow key one or more times. The Right Arrow increases the width, and the Left Arrow decreases it. The new column width appears on the status line between brackets ([ ]). For example, a cell in a column set to a width of 15 would contain a [W15] on the status line of the control panel.

HINTS/HAZARDS

For a numeric cell, 1-2-3 always reserves the rightmost character position to hold a right-hand parenthesis [)] or a percent sign (%).

2.2 CHANGING THE WIDTH OF SEVERAL COLUMNS (/WCC)

Many times, after you have set a global column width size, you may have a number of adjacent columns that you wish to set to a common column width other than the original width. For example, in the worksheet in Figure 2.14 (you'll build this worksheet later in this chapter), you may wish to change the column width of all the columns containing numbers from 5 to 10. Rather than using the / Worksheet Column-width (/WC) command, it is easier to use the

Figure 2.14

A worksheet requiring column-width change in columns B through E.

```
B7: [W5]                                                          READY

           A          B    C    D    E        F            G
1  FUNCTION
2
3       14-Aug-91
4
5  Homework assignment for Business Statistics:
6  Examine the statistical characteristics of four sets of numbers.
7
8                 Set 1Set 2Set3 Set4
9                     9    8    1   69
10                   12   36   16   60
11                    7   16    4   59
12                    5    9    9   65
13                    2    4   36   56
14                    1    0   25   77
15                    3   12   16   81
16                    4        23   91
17                    8        17   85
18                ===================
19           Sum:    51   85  147  643
20       Average: 5.67 12.1 16.3 71.4
14-Aug-91  06:10 PM
```

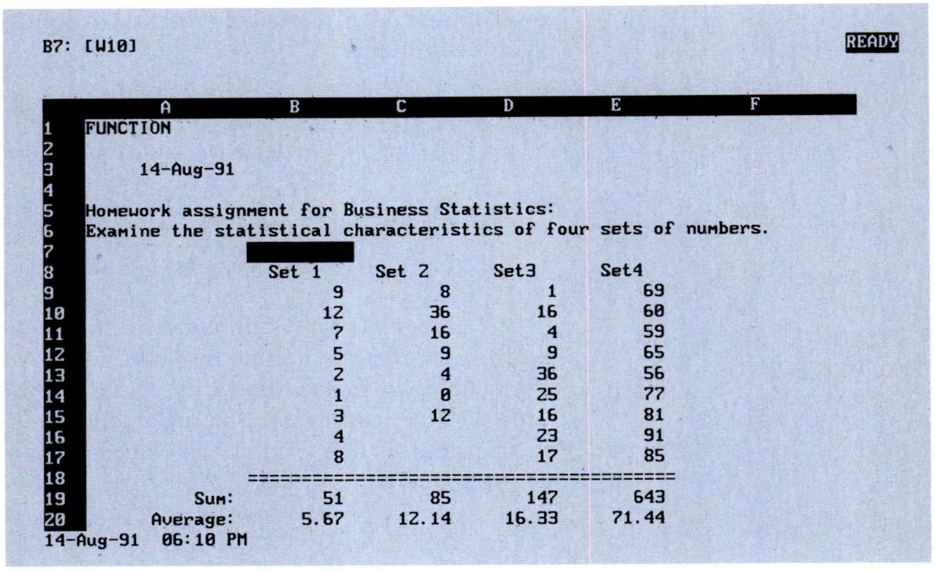

Figure 2.15
The worksheet after execution of the Column Range command.

2.2

/ Worksheet Column Column-range (/WCC) command. This means that instead of entering four different commands, you only have to enter a single series of commands.

After moving the pointer to cell B7, use the following command sequence:

/W	Selects the Worksheet option from the Main Menu.
C	Selects the Column Width command.
C	Selects the Column Range option.
S	Selects the Set option.
Go to E7	Positions the pointer at cell E7.
Enter	Establishes the range.
10	Establishes the column width.
Enter	Executes the command.

Figure 2.15 shows the changed worksheet.

DATES

Lotus handles dates as numeric values. Each of its date functions generates a number based on days elapsed since January 1, 1900. This number must then be converted to usable form via the / Range Format Date command. Because a date is really a numeric entry for 1-2-3, you cannot let it overflow to the next cell as with text data. Appropriate column width is essential no matter what date format you select. If the column is not wide enough to accept the text translation of the numeric-data entry, 1-2-3 displays asterisks (**********) in the affected cell.

TEXT

When you enter text data within a worksheet cell, 1-2-3 automatically assumes that the text is to be left-justified within the cell and embeds a single quote (') to accomplish this task. If you want text right-justified or centered within a cell, you must instruct 1-2-3 via a **label prefix** character how the data should be presented. The label prefix characters are as follows:

'	Left-justifies text.
"	Right-justifies text.
^	Centers text.

Although 1-2-3 automatically places the single quote in a cell for left-justifying text, you must manually enter a double quote (") or caret (^) as the first character within a cell when you want to right-justify or center text, respectively. For text to appear properly justified, the column width has to be greater than the text width. The text Last Year cannot be properly right-justified in a column whose width is nine.

HINTS/HAZARDS

Never use a label prefix for a number that is to be involved in a calculation. When 1-2-3 sees a label prefix of ', ", or ^, it assumes that this is text data exactly as you have indicated and as a result assigns a numeric value of zero to the cell. If you sum a column of numbers that all have a label prefix, a value of zero will appear.

REPEATING TEXT

When you want to enter a repeating character or string of characters within a cell, 1-2-3 requires you to use the backslash (\) as a shorthand notation to tell it to repeat the character. Any character or characters following this **repeat symbol** will then be repeated until the cell is filled. The following examples assume that a column width of nine has been used.

Cell Entry	*Cell Display*
_	_ _ _ _ _ _ _ _ _
\ABC	ABCABCABC
\DOG	DOGDOGDOG
\=	= = = = = = = = =

This shorthand method is frequently used to create subtotal lines (_ _ _ _ _ _ _) and total lines (= = = = = = = = =) within business reports.

LOTUS 1-2-3 SAMPLE FUNCTION WORKSHEET

Suppose you are taking introductory statistics and early in the semester the teacher asks that you examine four sets of numbers. For each set, you are to calculate the average, the standard deviation, and the variance; you are also to give the high, the low, the sum, and the number of entries for each set of numbers. You are aware that 1-2-3 would be an ideal aid in this homework assignment. The sets of numbers are as follows:

1. 9, 12, 7, 5, 2, 1, 3, 4, 8
2. 8, 36, 16, 9, 4, 0, 12

3. 1, 16, 4, 9, 36, 25, 16, 23, 17
4. 69, 60, 59, 65, 56, 77, 81, 91, 85

After careful analysis, you conclude that the following worksheet will solve the problem:

```
FUNCTION
10-Oct-92
Homework assignment for Business Statistics:
Examine the statistical characteristics of four sets of numbers.

               Set 1     Set 2     Set 3     Set 4
                   9         8         1        69
                  12        36        16        60
                   7        16         4        59
                   5         9         9        65
                   2         4        36        56
                   1         0        25        77
                   3        12        16        81
                   4                  23        91
                   8                  17        85

================================================
        Sum:      51        85       147       643
    Average:    5.67     12.14     16.33     71.44
Stand. Dev.:     3.4     10.86     10.26     11.83
   Variance:   11.56    117.84    105.33    140.02
    Maximum:      12        36        36        91
    Minimum:       1         0         1        56
      Count:       9         7         9         9
```

In doing this project, you will practice the following skills:

1. Using the @NOW and @DATE date functions.
2. Changing the column width of one column.
3. Using the F2 Edit function for correcting errors.
4. Using statistical functions.
5. Using the @ROUND function.
6. Using nested functions.
7. Copying a single-column range to multiple columns.
8. Handling blank cells and cells with a blank on functions.

Be sure to enter the date before you start 1-2-3. This will be important later on. If there is material on the worksheet screen, you can erase it by typing

/W	Worksheet
E	Erase
Y	Yes

LOTUS 1-2-3 SAMPLE FUNCTION SPREADSHEET

1. Enter the name of the worksheet:

Go to A1	Positions the pointer at cell A1.
Type `FUNCTION`	Enters the name of the worksheet.
Enter	Executes the command.

2. "Stamp" the worksheet with today's date at cell A3, using the @NOW function:

Go to A3	Positions the pointer at cell A3.
Type `@NOW`	Stamps the worksheet with today's date.
Enter	Executes the command.

In this sample worksheet, the @NOW function causes 33726 to be placed in the cell, signifying that 33,726 days have elapsed since January 1, 1900. That number must now be converted to a more useful format.

You could also enter today's date manually, using the @DATE (yy,mm,dd) function. In this example, enter @DATE (92,5,2). You would receive the same result of 33726 in cell A3, however, and you would still need to format that cell in order for the information to become useful.

3. Change the number in cell A3 to a standard business format:

/R	Selects the Range option from the Main Menu.
F	Selects the Format option.
D	Selects the Date command.
Enter (2)	Selects and executes the first option of Date (DD-MMM-YY).

4. You will notice that ********* (1-2-3's overflow indication) now appears in cell A3, indicating that the cell is not wide enough to display the data. This generally happens after some type of data manipulation; it does not happen with standard text data. To correct this, change the width of column A to 15—a size large enough for labels that are to be entered later.

/W	Selects the Worksheet option from the Main Menu.
C	Selects the Column Width command.
S	Selects the Set-Width command.
Type `15`	Enters the new desired column width for this column.
Enter	Executes the instruction.

5. Enter the text data exactly as shown below (you'll correct errors later). You will be using three commands that tell 1-2-3 how to position data within a cell. The three are

'	Left-justifies text within the cell.
"	Right-justifies text within the cell.
^	Centers text within the cell. The ^ character is found above the 6 key.

A5	Homework assignment for Business Statistics:
A6	Examine the statistical characteristics of fours sets of numbers.
B8	"Set 1
C8	"Set 2
D8	"Set 3
E8	"Set 4
A19	"Sum:
A20	"Average:
A21	"Stand. Dev.:
A22	"Variance
A23	Maximum
A24	"Minimum:
A25	"Count:

Notice that 1-2-3 handles text data and manipulated data differently. Text data are allowed to overflow cell boundaries. For example, if you enter "new text in cell B6," the words would appear in the middle of the text that was entered in A6.

6. You probably noticed that the text you entered above contains three errors: Cell A6 says *fours* instead of *four;* cell A22 lacks a colon after *Variance;* and cell A23 is not right-justified and lacks a colon. You can correct these errors by re-entering all data, but to be more efficient you could use the Edit function (F2) as part of the following procedure:

Go to A6	Positions the pointer to cell A6.
F2	Displays the contents of A6 on the status line and the entry line and positions the pointer at the end of the line. (The text is now available to edit.)
→ to *s* of *fours*	Moves the cursor.
Del	Erases the *s*.
Enter	Changes the data within the cell.
Go to A22	Positions the pointer at cell A22.
F2	Displays the contents of cell A22 for editing.
Type :	Enters the : at the end of the line.
Enter	Changes the data within the cell.
Go to A23	Positions the pointer at cell A23.
F2	Displays cell A23 for editing.
Home	Moves the pointer to the beginning of the line, under the quote (') mark.
Del	Deletes the single quote (').
Type "	Right-justifies the contents of the cell.
End	Moves the pointer to the end of the text within the cell.
Type :	Enters the colon (:) at the end of the line.
Enter	Changes the data within the cell.

7. Enter the four sets of numbers:

B9	9	C9	8	D9	1	E9	69
B10	12	C10	36	D10	16	E10	60
B11	7	C11	16	D11	4	E11	59
B12	5	C12	9	D12	9	E12	65
B13	2	C13	4	D13	36	E13	56
B14	1	C14	0	D14	25	E14	77
B15	3	C15	12	D15	16	E15	81
B16	4			D16	23	E16	91
B17	8			D17	17	E17	85

8. Go to cell B18 and enter the total line (double underscore):

\=	Repeats the equal sign throughout the cell.
Enter	Enters the data in the cell.

Lotus uses the backslash (\) as the repeat indicator. [Do not confuse the backslash key (\) with the slash key (/).] Any character or characters that appear after the backslash will be repeated throughout the cell. For example, \ABC would place ABCABCABC in the cell.

9. Beginning with the pointer at cell B18, copy the Total line to the cell locations of C18, D18, and E18:

/C	Selects the Copy command from the Main Menu.
Enter	Makes B18 the only cell in the "From" range.
Go to C18	Marks the beginning of the "To" range by pointing.
Type .	Nails down the beginning of the range.
Go to E18	Marks the last cell in the "To" range.
Enter	Executes the Copy command.

10. Enter the statistical functions for column B.

a. Enter the @SUM function at B19:

Type @SUM(	Begins the @SUM function.
Go to B9	Marks the beginning of the range.
Type .	Nails down the beginning of the "To" range.
Go to B17	Marks the last cell in the "To" range.
Type)	Enters the right parenthesis.
Enter	Executes the command.

This method demonstrates using the pointer to point addresses to a 1-2-3 function. Alternatively, you can type the locations as shown next.

b. Enter the @AVG function at B20 by directly entering the cell addresses of the cells involved. Because you already know the cell locations from having pointed out the @SUM locations, you now need enter only the cell location at the beginning of the range and the cell location at the end of the range. To execute the command, press Enter.

Type @AVG(B9.B17)	Inserts the @AVG function in cell B20.

c. Enter the remaining functions, either by pointing or by entering the cell addresses directly. Remember, enter the formulas only for column B; you'll be copying them to the other columns later.

@STD	Standard deviation
@VAR	Variance
@MAX	Maximum
@MIN	Minimum
@COUNT	Count

11. You can now see that the average, standard deviation, and variance entries all have several decimal positions; having this many positions to the right of the decimal point can be distracting to anyone wishing to use the information in report form. You could use the / Range Format command to change the output format of these three cells, but this situation provides an excellent opportunity to use nested functions. You will use the Edit (F2) feature of 1-2-3 and add the @ROUND function to the three cells containing average, standard deviation, and variance entries. First, position the pointer at cell B20:

F2	Invokes 1-2-3's EDIT mode.
Home	Positions the pointer at the beginning of the line.
Type `@ROUND(`	Inserts @ROUND(at the beginning of the existing line.
End	Positions the pointer at the end of the line.
Type `,2`	Specifies two positions to the right of the decimal.
Enter	Enters the data in the cell.

Instead of seeing 5.6666666 in cell B20, you should now see 5.67.

12. Repeat the steps in task 11 to change the entries in cells B21 and B22.

13. Copy the formulas for the calculations from column B to columns C, D, and E. Position the pointer at B19:

/C	Selects the Copy command from the Main Menu.
Go to B25	Marks the end of the "From" range.
Enter	Establishes the "From" range.
Go to C19	Marks the first cell in the "To" range.
Type `.`	Nails down the beginning of the "To" range.
Go to E19	Marks the last cell in the "To" range.
Enter	Establishes the "To" range and executes the command.

The reason you didn't have to give cell E25 as the last address has to do with how 1-2-3 remembers your definition of the "From" range. You defined the range as one column wide, from cell B19 to cell B25. Lotus 1-2-3 thus knows that the "From" range is seven rows of cells. Once you tell 1-2-3 in a Copy command where to put the first cell of the "From" range, it assumes that you also wish to copy the rest of the cells in that column.

You indicated three cells as the columns to receive the range. Because each of these cells was in a different column, 1-2-3 assumed that you wanted three copies of the "From" range—one for each column.

14. Examine the results of the calculations on the screen. Notice that column C has two blank entries and that the count is indeed equal to 7. Lotus 1-2-3 is capable of determining when to include a cell in a calculation, and when not to, based on its contents or lack of them. Now what will happen if you make a change in cell C16? Position your pointer at C16.

Space Bar	Adds a character space.
Enter	Enters the "data" in the cell.

Notice that, even though there is no value in C16, the results of the calculations on the screen have been altered dramatically. Notice also that a single quote (') appears in cell C16. Go back to cell C16 and enter the command / Range Erase. The results of the various statistical evaluations immediately return to their original values.

HINTS/HAZARDS

When using ranges that contain so-called blank cells, make certain that they really are blank. The single quote (') warns you that the contents of this cell will not work properly in any numeric calculation.

/F	Selects the File option from the Main Menu.
S	Selects the Save command.
Type `FUNCTION`	Enters the filename.
Enter	Executes the command.

16. Print the file and put the date, page, and name of the file in a footing.

/P	Selects the Print option from the Main Menu.
P	Directs the output to the printer.
R	Selects the Range command.
Go to A1	Marks the beginning of the print range.
Type .	Nails down the beginning of the print range.
Go to G25	Marks the end of the range (allowing all text to print).
Enter	Establishes the range.
O	Selects the Options Menu entry.
F	Selects the Footer option.
Type `Page #¦FUNCTIONS¦@`	Divides the footing into three parts, as follows: the page number left-justified in the left-hand part; the filename FUNCTION, centered in the middle part; today's date right-justified in the right-hand part.
Enter	Submits the footer to 1-2-3.
Q	Closes the Options Menu and returns to the Print Menu.
G	Prints the worksheet.
P	Prints the footer while going to the top of the next page.
Q	Quits and returns to the worksheet.

Your worksheet should now appear exactly like the one at the beginning of this Sample Worksheet section.

CHAPTER REVIEW

A range is any "box" of data cells that has four 90-degree corners. Various commands allow you either to point out a range of cells to be affected by a command or to specify addresses of two opposite corners of the range, thereby identifying it.

The Copy command copies contents of one or more cells (the sending area) to one or more other cells (the receiving area). The Copy command has two parts: specifying the sending area (the "From" range) and specifying the receiving area (the "To" range). Both areas are ranges that you can denote either by giving the cell addresses or by using the pointer.

The Format command works either in a range or globally. The Range option formats only a portion of the worksheet. The Global option formats the entire worksheet except any part that is currently under a / Range Format command. A number of format options are available, including Fixed, Currency, Date, Percent, or Scientific.

The Print command lets you specify exactly how to print all or part of your worksheet—the range to be printed and any options such as margins, header, or footer—and execute the print.

The built-in functions of 1-2-3 may be simple or compound (the nested functions, produced when one function is used as input to another function). A worksheet using a number of statistical functions can accommodate many of the spreadsheet concepts involved in these various commands.

Lotus lets you perform a number of special-purpose tasks to ensure that data are presented properly. You can add and delete rows and columns, move text from one position in a worksheet to another, and issue page breaks within the worksheet for later printing.

You can also control how data appear within a cell. For example, you can change the column width, right-justify text, center text, and repeat text within a cell.

KEY TERMS AND CONCEPTS

argument
Borders option
Column Width command
Copy command
footer
Footer option
format
Format Currency option
Format Date option
Format Fixed option
Format General option
Format Hidden option
Format Percent option
Format Reset option
Format Scientific option
Format Text option
Format , option
Format +/− option
function call
header
Header option
label prefix
margin
Margins option
Move feature
nail down
nested function
Other option
page break
Page Length option
Print Align option
Print Clear option
Print command
Print Go option
Print Line option
Print menu

Print Options Menu
Print Page option
Print Quit option
Print Range option
range
/ Range Format option
receiving ("To") range
repeat symbol
sending ("From") range
settings sheet
Setup option
/ Worksheet Global Format option

CHAPTER QUIZ

Multiple Choice

1. Which of the following statements about ranges is false?
   a. A range must be either a rectangle or a square.
   b. A range can be defined by "pointing."
   c. A range can be defined by giving the cell addresses of two opposite corners.
   d. A range can be defined by pointing to the first cell and entering the address of the second cell.
   e. All of the above methods can be used to define a range.

2. Which of the following statements about the Copy command is false?
   a. The first item to be defined is the sending cell/range.
   b. The second item to be defined is the receiving cell/range.
   c. The receiving range can overlap with the sending range without data being lost.
   d. The receiving range can be larger than the sending range.
   e. All of the above statements are true.

3. Which of the following is *not* involved in printing a worksheet to a file?
   a. Naming the file.
   b. Establishing the range and any options.
   c. Issuing the Go command.
   d. Issuing the Quit command to close the file.
   e. All of the above are necessary.

4. Which of the following is *not* available using the Print Menu?
   a. Specifying the right margin.
   b. Specifying the page length.
   c. Specifying the subtotal point.
   d. Specifying the header and/or footer for each page.
   e. Specifying the setup string for printing.
   f. All of the above are Print commands.

5. Which of the following statements is true for functions?
   a. It is difficult to nest functions.
   b. The character used to denote a function is *.
   c. The date functions are of relatively little use.
   d. The function @MONTH (@NOW) is used to get the month of the year when the date was entered after the boot process.

True/False

6. Functions can save you, the user, a tremendous amount of time.

7. Ranges are typically entered by using three cell addresses.

8. You can print a worksheet without specifying the print range.

9. The setup string allows you to print in 10, 12, or 17.1 cpi.

10. Print footers allow you to print out the page number, today's date, and some text data.

Answers

1. d 2. c 3. e 4. c 5. d 6. t 7. f 8. f 9. t 10. t

Exercises

1. Define or describe each of the following:
   a. Range
   b. Range Format
   c. Global Format
   d. Setup string
   e. Footer
   f. Align option
   g. Line option
   h. Page option
   i. Nested function

2. When using the Copy command, you must first define the ___________ range and then define the ___________ range.

3. When the receiving range overlaps the sending range, some data will be ___________ .

4. A(n) ___________ format affects the entire worksheet, whereas a(n) ___________ format affects only an area of the worksheet.

5. The ___________ format places a $ and any needed commas in a numeric cell.

6. Before the worksheet or a part of the worksheet can be printed, the print ___________ must be defined to 1-2-3.

7. Besides dumping output to a printer, 1-2-3 can also place it in a(n) ___________ .

8. The ___________ selection under the Options Menu changes the print pitch.

9. The ___________ command defines *top of page* to 1-2-3.

10. The ___________ command moves the paper a small increment, whereas the ___________ command moves the paper to the top of the next page.

11. How does the role of the Quit command in creating printer output differ from its role in creating disk output?

12. What is the advantage of nesting functions?

13. List the functions you consider to be useful at this time.

14. When a number will not fit in a cell, 1-2-3 fills that cell with ___________ .

15. The ___________ character tells 1-2-3 to repeat the text across the cell.

16. If you delete a row or a column, all of the ___________ in that row or column will be deleted.

17. The ___________ command sequence increases the width of a column.

18. The @NOW function results in ___________ appearing in the cell in which it resides.

19. The label prefix ___________ centers text.

20. The "repeat the following characters" command in 1-2-3 is the ___________ .

21. The screen that provides information about the options that you have selected as well as the defaults of command options is called a(n) ___________ sheet.

22. If you wish to set the width of several columns at one time, use the ___________ command sequence.

23. To make a settings screen disappear, use the ___________ command.

24. The ___________ of the Margins command resets all margins except the right-hand margin to zero.

25. The command sequence ___________ selects a printer other than the default.

COMPUTER EXERCISES

1. In this exercise, you are to prepare a payroll register. Enter the formulas that would be necessary to prepare the register shown in Figure 2.16. The Net Pay figure is calculated by subtracting the appropriate deductions and taxes from the Gross Pay figure that has been previously calculated. The deductions and taxes, for the sake of simplicity, are assumed to be 37%. The overtime rate is computed by rate * 1.5. Set column A to a width of 20. Set the remaining columns to a width of 11. Your worksheet will not appear so crowded. Save your worksheet file using the filename CH2EX1.

2. A teacher friend has asked your assistance in developing a worksheet for calculating grades (Figure 2.17). Your friend has developed the following criteria for the worksheet:
   a. The worksheet is to be stamped with today's date.
   b. The total possible points are to appear at the top of each column.
   c. The average, high grade, low grade, standard deviation, and variance statistics are to be calculated using 1-2-3 functions.
   d. The % of Total Points entry is to be calculated by dividing the average by total possible points.

   The following information contains the format for the worksheet.
   a. Set column A to a width of 15.
   b. Set the rest of the columns to a width of 11.

Figure 2.16
Payroll register worksheet.

A1: [W20] READY

	A	B	C	D	E	F	G
1		Total		Overtime	Overtime	Gross	
2	Employee	Hours	Rate	Hours	Rate	Pay	Net Pay
3							
4	James, Tony	40.00	6.50	2.00	9.75	279.50	176.09
5	Biel, Harry	40.00	6.50		9.75	260.00	163.80
6	Singlof, Don	25.00	6.50		9.75	162.50	102.38
7	Hall, Barry	40.00	6.50	3.00	9.75	289.25	182.23
8	Lele, Michelle	40.00	6.50		9.75	260.00	163.80
9	Kanter, John	33.00	6.50		9.75	214.50	135.14
10	Helmsley, Joanna	40.00	5.50		8.25	220.00	138.60
11	Sahara, Ohmar	40.00	5.50		8.25	220.00	138.60
12	Jerrod, Henry	40.00	4.25	10.00	6.38	233.75	147.26
13	Dixon, Yvonne	40.00	7.50		11.25	300.00	189.00
14							
15	TOTALS					$2,439.50	$1,536.89
16							
17							
18							
19							
20							

14-Sep-90 08:04 PM

Figure 2.17
Worksheet for calculating grades.

A1: (D1) [W15] @INT(@NOW) READY

	A	B	C	D	E	F	G
1	14-Aug-91						
2		Grading Template					
3		¦					
4	NAME	¦	Exam I	Anot. Bib	Exam II		
5	POSSIBLE POINTS	¦	150	45	130		
6	---------------	¦	----------	----------	----------		
7	Student 1	¦	113	44	110		
8	Student 2	¦	116	42	90		
9	Student 3	¦	129	42	85		
10	Student 4	¦	133	44	125		
11	Student 5	¦	121	42	76		
12	Student 6	¦	139	41	115		
13	Student 7	¦	120	42	115		
14	---------------	¦	----------	----------	----------		
15	Average	¦	124	42	102		
16	% of Tot. Pnts.	¦	82.67%	93.33%	78.46%		
17	High Grade	¦	139	44	125		
18	Low Grade	¦	113	41	76		
19	Std. Deviation	¦	9	1	17		
20	Variance	¦	77	1	291		

14-Aug-91 06:13 PM

c. Use the @NOW function to "date-stamp" the worksheet in cell A1.

d. The ¦ character is the uppercase character of the backslash (\) key. Save this worksheet file using the filename CH2EX2.

3. Print your CH2EX2 worksheet file. Specify a heading that has "Introduction to Microcomputers" as the text to appear at the top of the page. Specify a footing that has the page number, the name of the worksheet file, and the date at the bottom of the page. Refer to the Print command menu structure in the appendix if you have questions about how to get to a command.

4. Print your CH2EX1 worksheet file. Specify a condensed print setup so that the worksheet will print on one page of paper. Refer to the Print

Figure 2.18
Golf score worksheet.

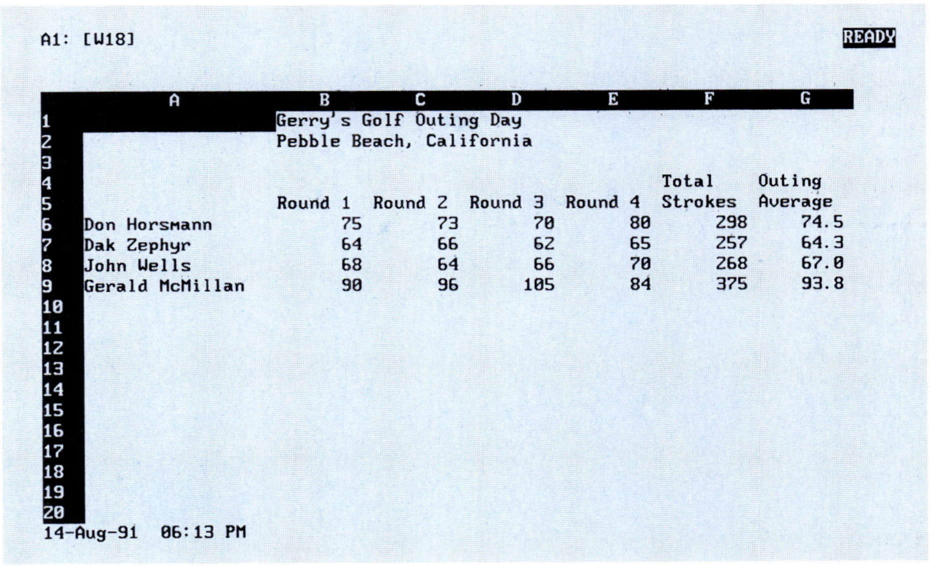
A1: [W18] READY

	A	B	C	D	E	F	G
1		Gerry's Golf Outing Day					
2		Pebble Beach, California					
3							
4						Total	Outing
5		Round 1	Round 2	Round 3	Round 4	Strokes	Average
6	Don Horsmann	75	73	70	80	298	74.5
7	Dak Zephyr	64	66	62	65	257	64.3
8	John Wells	68	64	66	70	268	67.0
9	Gerald McMillan	90	96	105	84	375	93.8
10							
11							
12							
13							
14							
15							
16							
17							
18							
19							
20							

14-Aug-91 06:13 PM

Menu in the appendix. You will also have to change the right print margin to 120.

5. Print your CH2EX2 worksheet to a disk file called TEST. Leave 1-2-3 and access the TEST.PRN file with your word processing software or use the DOS TYPE command to make sure that you created the file properly. Remember that 1-2-3 has placed the .PRN extension on the file.

6. Retrieve the worksheet CH2EX2. You have just received word that your teacher friend forgot to include a student named Student5a in the list. This individual's scores are 100 for Exam I, 41 for Anot. Bib., and 113 for Exam II. Add this individual to the existing grading worksheet, making any necessary changes. Store the changed worksheet to a file named CH2EX6.

7. You are now to add a column to replace the existing column A in the CH1EX5 file. This column should have a heading of "Dept." The two different sales forces in the business are the new-car sales staff (1) and the preowned-car sales staff (2). Ralph, Louise, and Caroline are in the Dept. 1 cells, whereas the others are in Dept. 2. Place a 1 or 2 in column A to indicate the department of each employee. Place the result in a file called CH2EX7.

8. Prepare a worksheet that Gerry can use for his golf outing day. Gerry is interested in tracking scores for golfers over four rounds. He is interested in not only calculating the total strokes over the four rounds of golf but also finding the average number of strokes for each golfer during the outing. Give the average score column a range format of fixed with one position to the right of the decimal (Figure 2.18). Save as CH2EX8.

3

MAINTAINING AND ENHANCING YOUR WORKSHEETS

CHAPTER OBJECTIVES

After completing this chapter, you should be able to

- **Discuss commands that allow you more control over your environment**
- **Use range names**
- **Use dummy rows and columns in ranges**
- **Use the Sort commnd**
- **Use the Titles option**
- **Know when to use relative and absolute addressing**
- **Use mixed-cell addresses**
- **Use absolute range names**
- **Use automatic worksheet recalculation**
- **Use the @PMT, @ROUND, and @IF functions**
- **Use the @DATE function**
- **Create some simple macros**

After you have initially built a worksheet, you are usually still not finished with it. You may wish to correct minor errors or add enhancements to give your worksheet a more professional appearance.

In this chapter, we cover the following topics: controlling your worksheet environment, range names, sorting, titles, absolute versus relative addressing, automatic recalculation, and more on the functions @PMT, @IF, and @DATE. We also discuss how macros can reduce the need to repeatedly type common sequences of keystrokes and create some simple macros.

CONTROLLING YOUR WORKSHEET ENVIRONMENT

Lotus gives you several options for more control over your worksheet environment. Some of these commands make it easier to generate reports with the exact columns desired, present numeric information in a specific manner, or change directories on a fixed disk.

/ WORKSHEET ZERO COMMAND (/WGZ)

The / Worksheet Global **Zero command** suppresses any zeros that occur within numeric cells, including zeros generated by a formula and those entered from the keyboard. The command / Worksheet Global Zero Yes tells 1-2-3 that no zeros are to be displayed in cells. The command / Worksheet Global Zero No reinstates the zeros.

2.2

The Label option of the Zero command tells 1-2-3 to place a character string in any cell that contains a zero value. This option displays the following prompt at the top of your screen:

```
Enter label (can include label prefix):
```

You now enter the desired characters, for instance, the text N/A. Now, whenever any cell contains a zero value, the N/A character string appears in that cell.

CHANGING THE DIRECTORY

Directory Command in Global Worksheet Default Submenu (/WGDD) When you use 1-2-3 on a fixed disk, 1-2-3 usually assumes that worksheet files are to be saved to the directory in which your 1-2-3 program files reside. You may, however, wish to save worksheet files to another directory or even to a diskette in a disk drive (for example, drive B). To do this, use the / Worksheet Global Default **Directory command** and then enter either the new directory path (for example, C:\wksfiles\school) or the disk drive followed by a colon (for example, B:).

Once you have entered the appropriate information, 1-2-3 returns you to the Default submenu. To make this change permanent so that 1-2-3 always uses the entity you have just described for storing any worksheet, issue the Update command. Most of the time, however, this change is temporary. In that case, issue the Quit command. The directory change will be in effect only for this worksheet session, and you will be returned to READY mode.

Directory Command in File Submenu (/FD) A second way to change the default directory involves the Directory command found in the File submenu. This command changes the default directory for this 1-2-3 session only but does not change this default in the configuration file. To execute this command, enter / File Directory and then type the drive identifier/path. To change the default drive to the A drive, enter A:.

/ WORKSHEET COLUMN HIDE COMMAND (/WCH)

In some situations, it is advantageous to print or display certain columns of a worksheet without printing or displaying other embedded columns. This is done with the / Worksheet Column **Hide command.** For example, suppose you wish to print and display your COMPSALS worksheet (Figure 3.1) without the Change column (column E). Position your pointer anywhere in column E and issue the following commands:

/W	Selects Worksheet from the Main Menu.
C	Selects the Column option.
H	Selects the Hide option.
Enter	Tells 1-2-3 that this is the only column to be hidden. (To hide multiple columns, expand the range.)

The screen now displays the worksheet depicted in Figure 3.2. Even though column F's entries are dependent on the hidden column E, the data are calculated properly. The only way to tell that column E has been hidden is to examine the column border labels. To make the hidden column reappear, issue the above commands but replace the Hide option with the Display option. Columns previously hidden reappear on the screen with an asterisk to the right of the column identifier in the column border (Figure 3.3). To "unhide" the column, place the pointer in the column marked with the asterisk (column E) and press Enter. The column has now been restored.

The real advantage of hiding columns is that you can hide intermediate results when it comes time to print a report. Only the columns that contain data meaningful for a specific report need be displayed on the screen and printed. This feature produces reports that are more easily understood by their users.

Figure 3.1
COMPSALS worksheet.

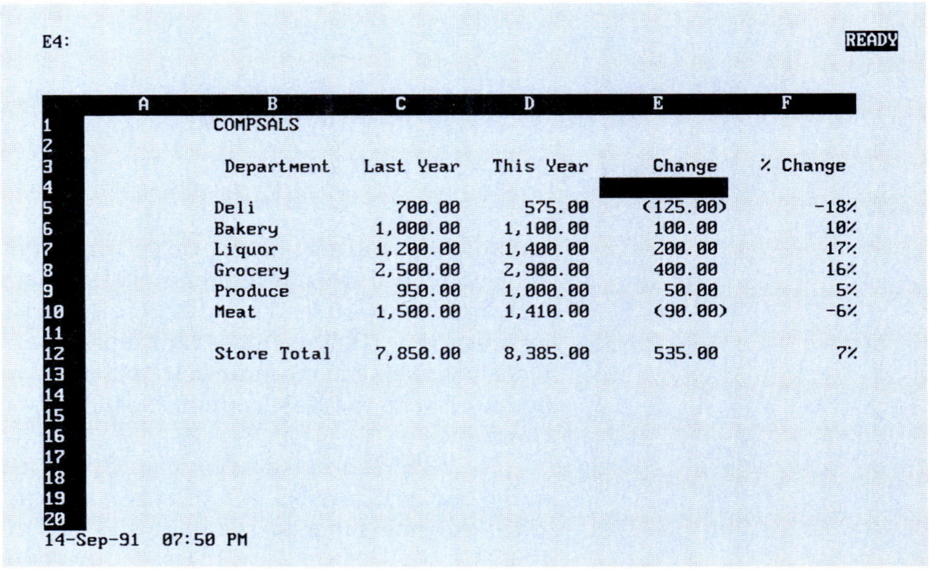

E4: READY

	A	B	C	D	E	F
1		COMPSALS				
2						
3		Department	Last Year	This Year	Change	% Change
4						
5		Deli	700.00	575.00	(125.00)	-18%
6		Bakery	1,000.00	1,100.00	100.00	10%
7		Liquor	1,200.00	1,400.00	200.00	17%
8		Grocery	2,500.00	2,900.00	400.00	16%
9		Produce	950.00	1,000.00	50.00	5%
10		Meat	1,500.00	1,410.00	(90.00)	-6%
11						
12		Store Total	7,850.00	8,385.00	535.00	7%
13						
14						
15						
16						
17						
18						
19						
20						

14-Sep-91 07:50 PM

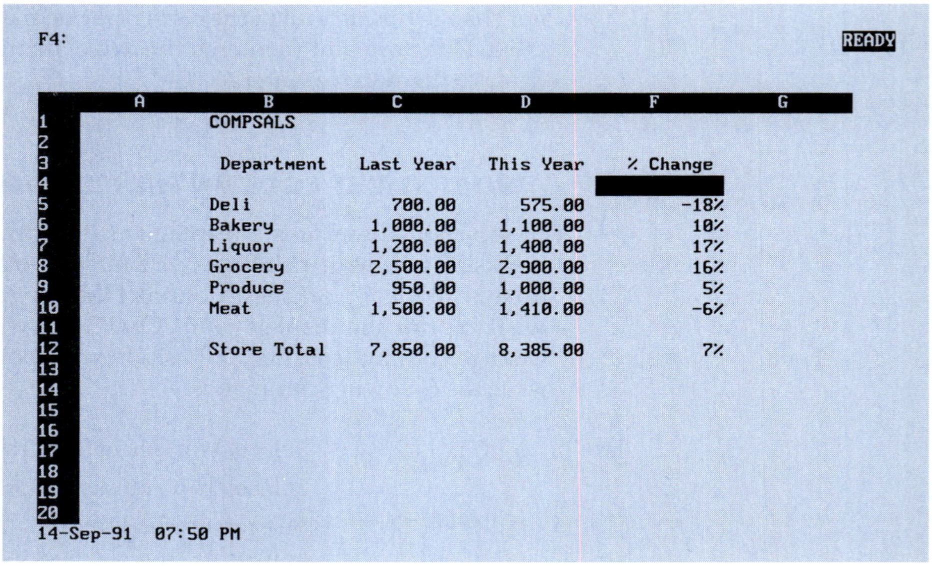
F4: READY

	A	B	C	D	F	G
1		COMPSALS				
2						
3		Department	Last Year	This Year	% Change	
4						
5		Deli	700.00	575.00	-18%	
6		Bakery	1,000.00	1,100.00	10%	
7		Liquor	1,200.00	1,400.00	17%	
8		Grocery	2,500.00	2,900.00	16%	
9		Produce	950.00	1,000.00	5%	
10		Meat	1,500.00	1,410.00	-6%	
11						
12		Store Total	7,850.00	8,385.00	7%	
13						
14						
15						
16						
17						
18						
19						
20						

14-Sep-91 07:50 PM

Figure 3.2

Worksheet with column E hidden.

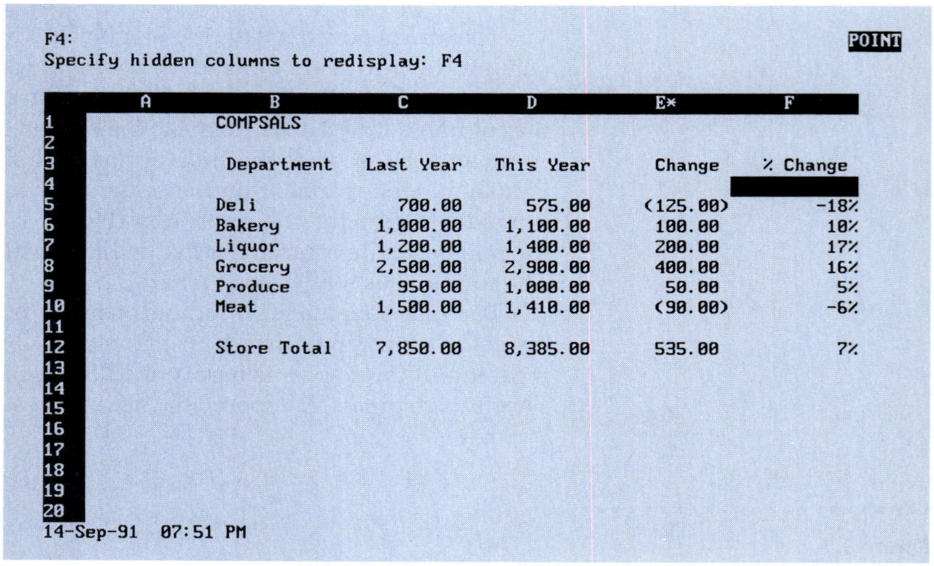
F4: POINT
Specify hidden columns to redisplay: F4

	A	B	C	D	E*	F
1		COMPSALS				
2						
3		Department	Last Year	This Year	Change	% Change
4						
5		Deli	700.00	575.00	(125.00)	-18%
6		Bakery	1,000.00	1,100.00	100.00	10%
7		Liquor	1,200.00	1,400.00	200.00	17%
8		Grocery	2,500.00	2,900.00	400.00	16%
9		Produce	950.00	1,000.00	50.00	5%
10		Meat	1,500.00	1,410.00	(90.00)	-6%
11						
12		Store Total	7,850.00	8,385.00	535.00	7%
13						
14						
15						
16						
17						
18						
19						
20						

14-Sep-91 07:51 PM

Figure 3.3

Worksheet hidden column marked with * using Display command.

FINDING CIRCULAR REFERENCES AND STATUS COMMANDS

Suppose that you are working on an application like the COMPSALS worksheet and suddenly a **circular reference** (`CIRC`) is indicated in your worksheet (Figure 3.4). You have no idea how this occurred. You don't even have any idea how long ago the CIRC reference indicator appeared on your screen because you were not looking at the indicators area of the worksheet. Circular references can be found with the least amount of difficulty by using the / Worksheet Status command.

The / Worksheet Status command produces a Global Settings screen similar to the one in Figure 3.5. It indicates that a circular reference exists in cell C12. After pressing Enter to return to READY mode, you find that the formula @SUM(C5. .C12) is in cell C12 (see Figure 3.4). The problem is that cell C12 has

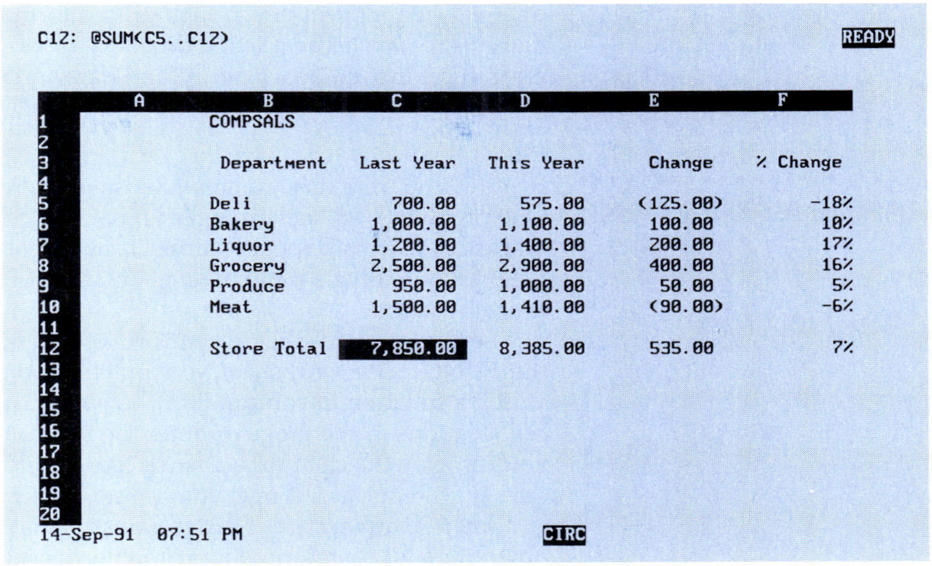

Figure 3.4
Worksheet with a circular reference.

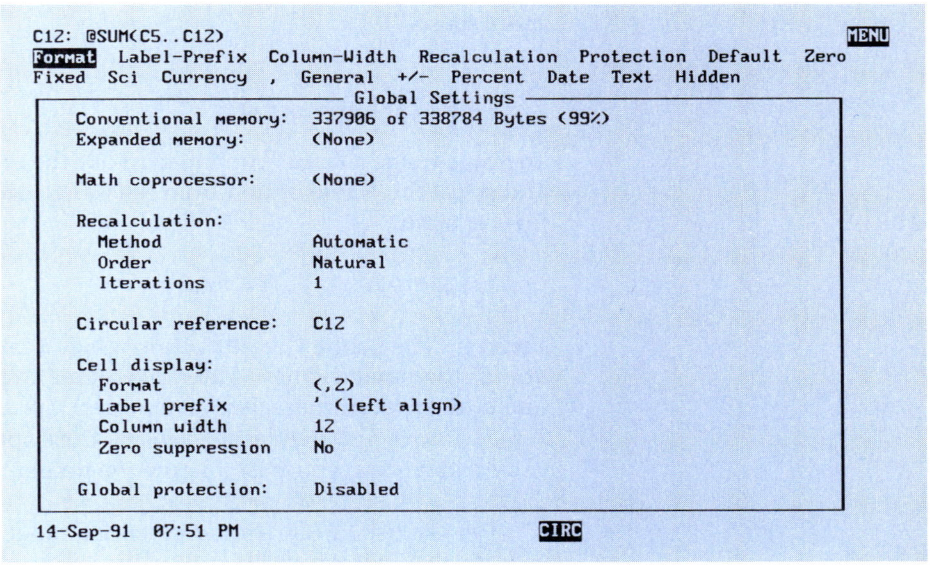

Figure 3.5
Status screen for COMPSALS worksheet.

been told not only to hold the answer but also to participate in the calculation. After you use Edit (F2) to change the 12 in the formula to 10, the circular reference disappears.

If multiple circular references occur within a worksheet, 1-2-3 finds only one at a time. Therefore, you must correct each as it is found and then issue another / Worksheet Status command to find the next.

Besides finding circular references, the / Worksheet Status command provides other valuable information. For example, it shows the amount of memory available for a worksheet as well as the amount used by your worksheet. It also reports on methods of recalculation, global format use, the current global column width, and whether or not zero suppression is in effect.

Another important settings screen can be invoked via the / Worksheet Global Default command. The report generated by this command also shows defaults currently in effect, including information about the printer interface, margins, page characteristics, directory in use, and various formats that are in effect for punctuation, currency, and date and time presentation.

RANGE NAMES (/RN)

By now, you have used ranges extensively in formatting, copying, and printing. One problem with using ranges is that you must always keep track of the cell addresses of two opposite corner cells in each range; to avoid this problem, 1-2-3 lets you give a **range name** to a range of cells and thereafter refers to that range by name.

Let's re-examine the procedure involved in setting up function formulas for the FUNCTION worksheet you practiced on in Chapter 2. Every time you added a function in column B of the worksheet, you either had to point to the cell locations in the range or enter the previously recorded cell locations. Now you can give the cell range a name like COLB (short for column B); then every time 1-2-3 requests a range, you can say COLB.

Another advantage of range names is that they make a worksheet self-documenting and therefore more readable. Setting up formulas to refer to a range name rather than merely a cell location, for example, can be very helpful. If you come back to a worksheet later, a formula using range names will make much more sense.

/ RANGE NAME MENU

To give a range a name, you must invoke the Range option from the Main Menu and select the Name option from the Range Menu (/RN). This displays the following menu:

```
Create   Delete   Labels   Reset   Table
```

Create The **Name Create option** names a range of cells or redefines the location of the named range. The range name can be 1 to 14 characters in length (including special characters and spaces); Lotus recommends that you use only *A* to *Z*, 0 to 9, and the dash (–) and not use spaces. The Create option prompts you for the name you wish to give the range. You are then prompted to define the range.

You can use F5 (GoTo) to reference a range name or a cell address. You can include a cell in many different named ranges. When the worksheet is saved, the range names are also saved.

Delete The **Name Delete option** drops a named range from memory. The contents of the individual cells involved remain unchanged. This option prompts you to point to the range or enter its name.

Labels The **Name Labels option** is like the Create option but takes the name for the range directly from an adjacent label entry. Make certain that the label to be used as the range name does not contain more than 14 characters.

For example, assume that you have two adjacent entries like those shown below. Position your pointer at cell D3 and enter the command / Range Name Labels. Press Enter (or, if there are multiple cells involved, indicate the end of the range). Now tell 1-2-3 whether the named cells are right, down, left, or up with respect to the labels.

```
  D3        E3
|Sales  |  $100.00|
```

Reset The **Name Reset option** drops all range names from memory.

Table The **Name Table option** constructs a report containing all range names and their appropriate cell addresses in your worksheet. The pointer location is used as the upper left-hand corner of the report. Because the report actually takes up space within the worksheet, make certain that you are in an unused area; otherwise, part of your worksheet may be lost.

NAMING INSTRUCTIONS

The steps needed to give the numbers in column B of the FUNCTION worksheet the range name COLB are as follows:

B9	Positions the pointer to cell B9.
/R	Takes the Range option from the Main Menu and displays the Range Menu.
N	Chooses the Name Menu.
C	Takes the Create option.
Type COLB	Specifies the range name to be used.
B17	Marks the last cell in the COLB range.
Enter	Executes the command.

You can now enter functions simply by referring to the range name COLB. For example, you could enter @SUM(COLB) without entering cell addresses or pointing. You can also copy this formula to the other columns, in which case 1-2-3 keeps track of the range but not the range name.

MORE RANGE NAME EXAMPLES

Load the COMPSALS worksheet and create the range names indicated in Figure 3.6. When you are finished, you should have the following range names:

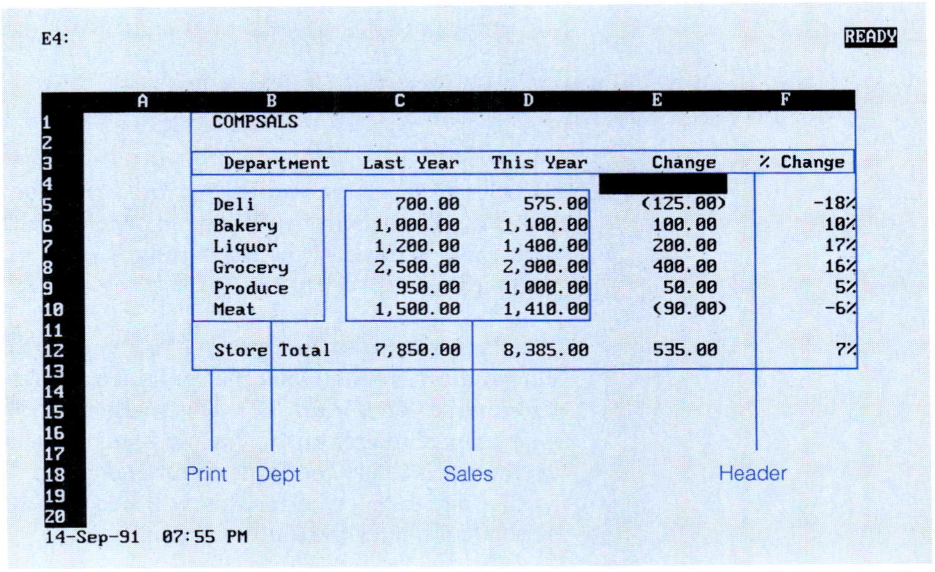

Figure 3.6
Cells included in the specified named ranges.

Figure 3.7

Named ranges in COMPSALS listed via the / Range Name Create command.

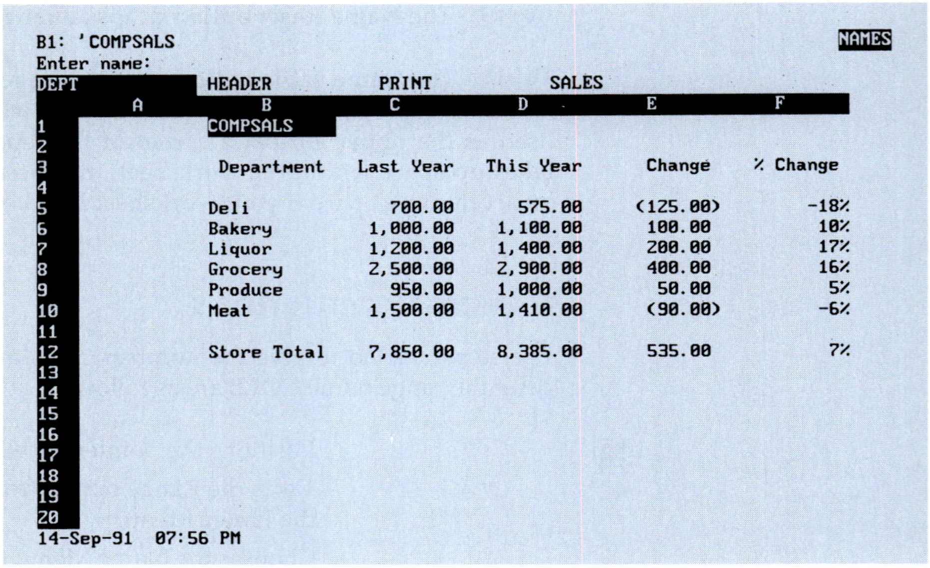

Figure 3.8

Verifying the named range Sales via the Create command.

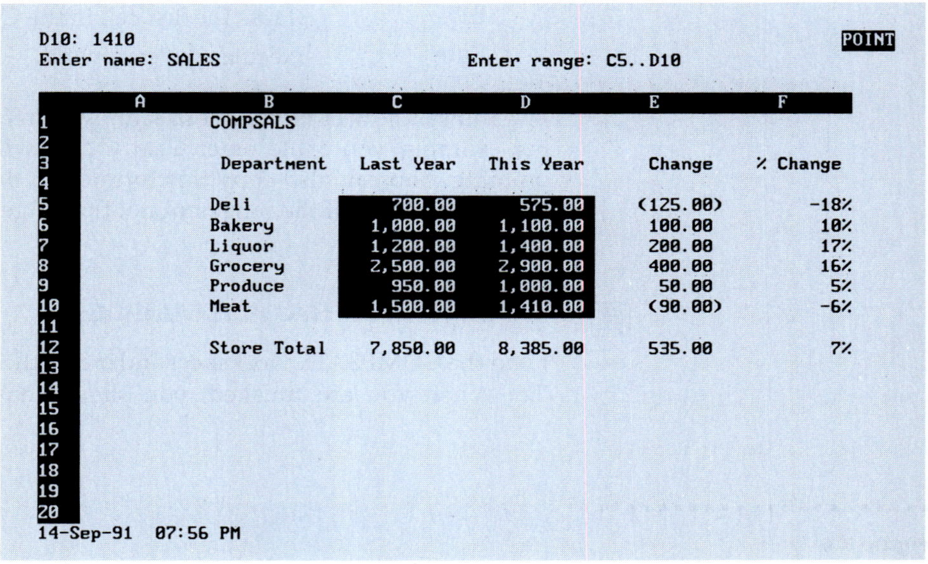

Header, Dept, Sales, and Print. Notice that as you are creating the range names 1-2-3 displays them in alphabetic order on the prompt line (Figure 3.7). Once you have created the named ranges, you can verify that each was created properly.

Verifying Named Ranges When you highlight a range name on the prompt line and press Enter, the cells contained in the named range will be highlighted on your screen (Figure 3.8). This method works well if you wish to verify only one named range, but if you wish to verify all your named ranges, the best technique is to use the Table command of the / Range Name submenu. Position your pointer to cell B16 (this will become the upper left-hand corner of the report) and enter the following commands:

/R	Takes the Range option from the Main Menu.
N	Takes the Name option.
T	Takes the Table option.
Enter	Creates the report.

Your worksheet should now appear like the one in Figure 3.9. Each range name appears on a separate line in the report, and the beginning and ending cell addresses are included in the report. Lotus always views the beginning cell as the upper left-hand cell and the ending cell as the lower right-hand cell. Therefore, for a named range composed of a single row, the first cell is really the upper left-hand corner of the range. Notice also that the entries generated by the Table option have actually become part of the worksheet and have been treated as labels by 1-2-3 (notice the 'DEPT entry in Figure 3.9).

Using Named Ranges Once you have created named ranges in your worksheet, you can use them in any command that requires a cell address or a range of cells. For example, you can use named ranges with the **GoTo** (F5) **command.** Press F5, enter the range name DEPT, and your pointer will move to cell B5, the upper left-hand cell.

Instead of actually entering the characters contained in a named range, you can also use the Names (F3) function key. If you are in a command that requires you to enter a cell address or a cell range and you want to use a named range, press F3 and highlight the named range to be included in the instruction. For example, F3 can be used with the Copy command. The following example will copy the DEPT named range to cell E15 (Figure 3.10) without extensive pointer movement. Position your pointer to cell E15.

/C	Takes the Copy command from the Main Menu.
F3	Specifies the Names function.
DEPT	Highlights the named range by pointing.
Enter (2)	Specifies the DEPT named range as the "From" cells and cell E15 as the "To" range.

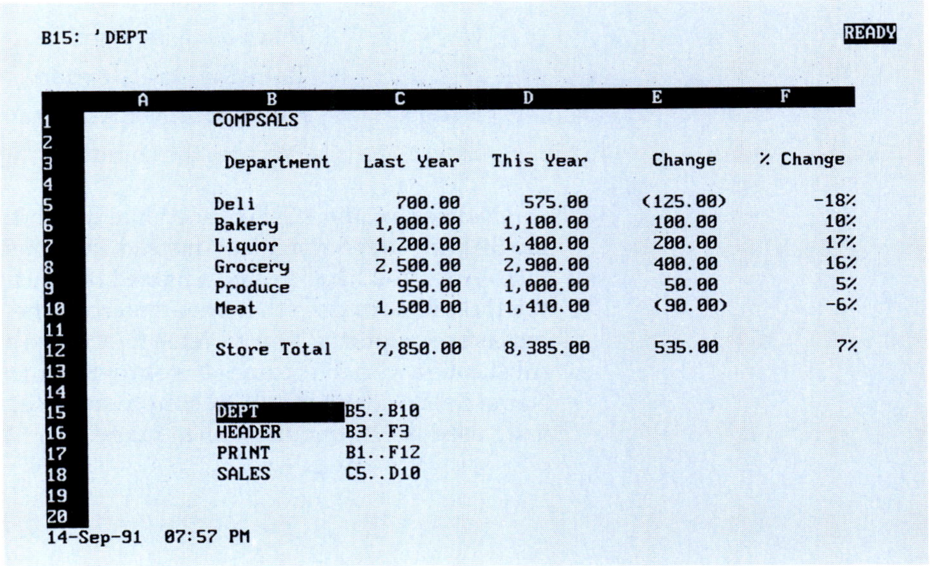

B15: 'DEPT READY

	A	B	C	D	E	F
1		COMPSALS				
2						
3		Department	Last Year	This Year	Change	% Change
4						
5		Deli	700.00	575.00	(125.00)	-18%
6		Bakery	1,000.00	1,100.00	100.00	10%
7		Liquor	1,200.00	1,400.00	200.00	17%
8		Grocery	2,500.00	2,900.00	400.00	16%
9		Produce	950.00	1,000.00	50.00	5%
10		Meat	1,500.00	1,410.00	(90.00)	-6%
11						
12		Store Total	7,850.00	8,385.00	535.00	7%
13						
14						
15		DEPT	B5..B10			
16		HEADER	B3..F3			
17		PRINT	B1..F12			
18		SALES	C5..D10			
19						
20						

14-Sep-91 07:57 PM

Figure 3.9
The output of the / Range Name Table command.

Figure 3.10
Result of a Copy command using the Names (F3) function key.

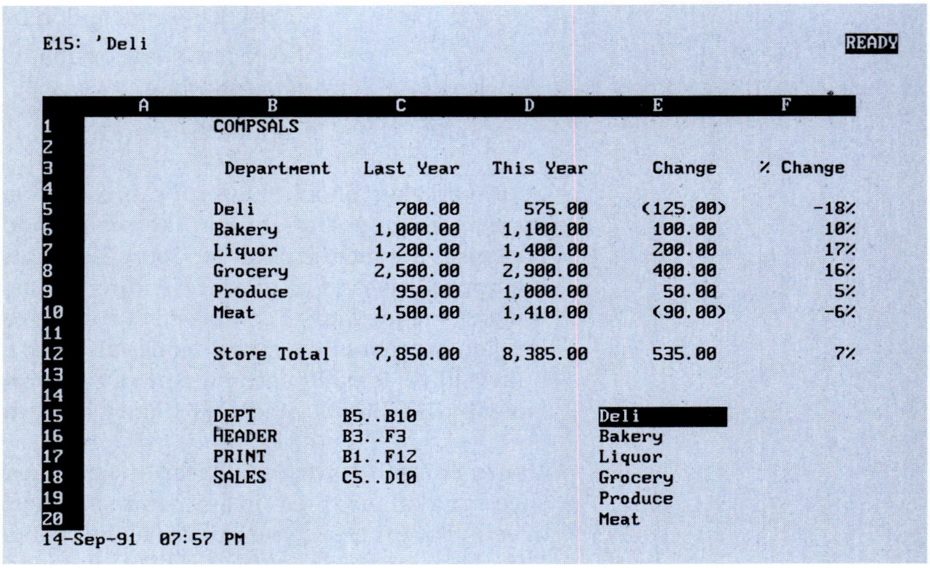

E15: 'Deli READY

	A	B	C	D	E	F
1		COMPSALS				
2						
3		Department	Last Year	This Year	Change	% Change
4						
5		Deli	700.00	575.00	(125.00)	-18%
6		Bakery	1,000.00	1,100.00	100.00	10%
7		Liquor	1,200.00	1,400.00	200.00	17%
8		Grocery	2,500.00	2,900.00	400.00	16%
9		Produce	950.00	1,000.00	50.00	5%
10		Meat	1,500.00	1,410.00	(90.00)	-6%
11						
12		Store Total	7,850.00	8,385.00	535.00	7%
13						
14						
15		DEPT	B5..B10		Deli	
16		HEADER	B3..F3		Bakery	
17		PRINT	B1..F12		Liquor	
18		SALES	C5..D10		Grocery	
19					Produce	
20					Meat	

14-Sep-91 07:57 PM

Notice that the cells contained in the DEPT named range (see Figure 3.10) have been copied without your positioning the cursor to cell B3, highlighting cells B3..F3, and then indicating that cell E15 is the destination cell. The Names function key technique is extremely useful when you have common text (such as lines of dashes used to indicate subtotals in a business report) required at multiple locations in a document.

Now use a named range to calculate the grand total for the This Year and Last Year columns. This calculation could be accomplished by the formula +C12+D12, but this method would not allow you to use a named range. Instead, enter the formula `@SUM(SALES)` in cell C13. Once this formula has been entered, the result, 16,235.00, is displayed in the cell. Notice that the entry in the status line shows `C13: @SUM(SALES)`. Now delete the named range called SALES using the following commands:

/R	Takes the Range option from the Main Menu.
N	Takes the Name option.
D	Takes the Delete option.
SALES	Highlights the SALES named range by pointing.
Enter	Executes the command.

Notice that the @SUM function entry in the status line no longer contains the SALES named range but, instead, contains the cell address C5..D10 (Figure 3.11). After you have created a named range, 1-2-3 still keeps track of that range via the cell addresses that were entered when the named range was created. Instead of requiring you to refer to a range via the addresses, 1-2-3 lets you substitute a variable name. If you delete the variable name via the / Range Name Delete command, 1-2-3 simply substitutes the cell addresses that you initially used in creating the named range.

Figure 3.11

Example of a formula after a named range is deleted.

```
C13: @SUM(SALES)                                                   READY

        A         B           C            D            E          F
1              COMPSALS
2
3              Department   Last Year    This Year      Change     % Change
4
5              Deli            700.00       575.00     (125.00)       -18%
6              Bakery        1,000.00     1,100.00      100.00        10%
7              Liquor        1,200.00     1,400.00      200.00        17%
8              Grocery       2,500.00     2,900.00      400.00        16%
9              Produce         950.00     1,000.00       50.00         5%
10             Meat          1,500.00     1,410.00      (90.00)       -6%
11
12             Store Total   7,850.00     8,385.00      535.00         7%
13                          16,235.00
14
15             DEPT          B5..B10               Deli
16             HEADER        B3..F3                Bakery
17             PRINT         B1..F12               Liquor
18             SALES         C5..D10               Grocery
19                                                 Produce
20                                                 Meat
14-Sep-91   07:58 PM
```

Figure 3.12

A typical worksheet tracking year-to-date totals.

```
D5: @SUM(B5..C5)                                                   READY

        A         B           C            D            E          F
1
2                                        Store
3                 January    February    Total
4
5       Deli       100.00       75.00    175.00
6       Bakery      75.00      125.00
7       Liquor     200.00      225.00
8       Grocery    120.00      150.00
9       Produce    110.00      115.00
10      Meat       220.00      245.00
11
12
13
14
15
16
17
18
19
20
14-Sep-91   07:58 PM
```

USE OF DUMMY COLUMNS OR ROWS IN EXPANDING RANGES

Dummy Columns Many times you will have an application in which you wish to create year-to-date sales totals for each department. You may also want to set up the report so that it automatically expands as you insert a column to enter the sales for a new month. Such a report requires a format similar to that in Figure 3.12. If you use the @SUM command as shown in Figure 3.12, you immediately have problems when you insert a new column for the figures for March. To generate the correct store totals, you must change the @SUM function each time you add a new month. Requiring this kind of change each month not only results in an inflexible worksheet but also produces a worksheet that

Figure 3.13
Worksheet with a dummy column D.

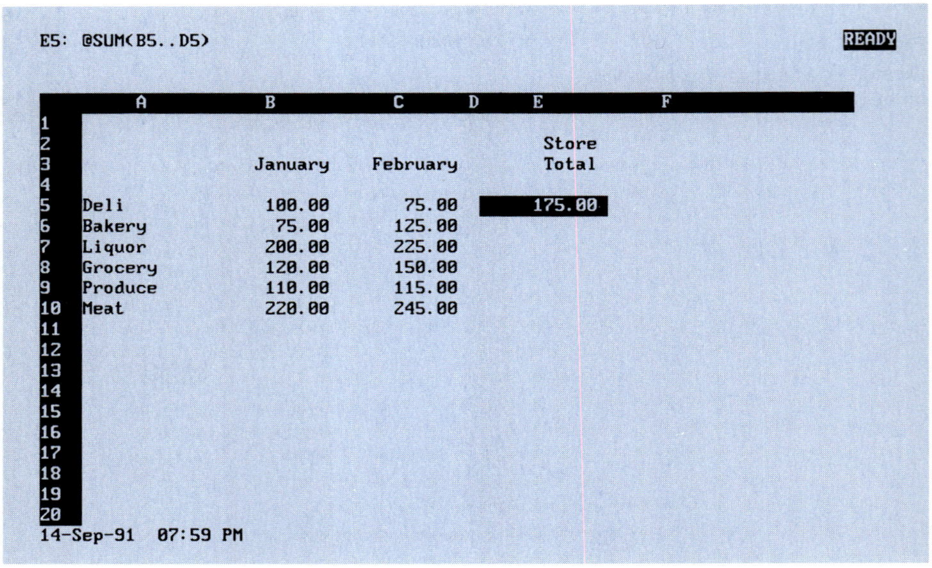
E5: @SUM(B5..D5) READY

	A	B	C	D	E	F
1						
2					Store	
3		January	February		Total	
4						
5	Deli	100.00	75.00		175.00	
6	Bakery	75.00	125.00			
7	Liquor	200.00	225.00			
8	Grocery	120.00	150.00			
9	Produce	110.00	115.00			
10	Meat	220.00	245.00			
11						
12						
13						
14						
15						
16						
17						
18						
19						
20						

14-Sep-91 07:59 PM

sooner or later is going to contain incorrect answers when someone forgets to change the @SUM function.

The solution to this problem is to use a **dummy column.** When you want to add and delete rows and columns and have this change reflected in any calculation that references a range, such as the @SUM function, your range must be set up so that any additions or deletions occur after the beginning cell in the range and before the ending cell in the range.

To incorporate this flexibility into the worksheet depicted in Figure 3.12, load the file COLSALES and make the following changes:

1. Insert a blank column (the dummy column to be referenced later) to the left of the grand total column (column D).
2. Set the new column D to a width of 1.
3. Edit the @SUM function so that the ending cell in the range is D5 [the function should now be @SUM(B5..D5)].

Your worksheet should now look like the worksheet in Figure 3.13.

Now when you want to add a new month and have the sales figures for that month automatically included in the Store Total, position the pointer to the dummy column, insert a new column, and enter the sales figures. Because the new column gets inserted to the left of the dummy column and therefore before the last cell in the @SUM function range, new data are automatically included in the store total. You can now copy this new sum formula down column F.

Dummy Rows Load the file COMPSALS. To adapt the concepts just covered to add new departments so that they are automatically included in the yearly total, change the @SUM functions to include the blank row entry after the Meat department. Your Last Year sum function in cell C12 should then be @SUM(C5..C11). Of course, you must make the same change to the This Year column @SUM function. To add a new department so that it can be included in the total, position your pointer to row 11, insert a new row, and enter the new sales figures. The newly entered sales figures are now included within the yearly total.

Expanding the range of the @SUM function for the COMPSALS worksheet was a straightforward task because a blank row existed that could be used as the **dummy row.** What happens, however, when you have an application like that depicted in Figure 3.14 that requires you to indicate subtotal lines with a cell of dashes (- - - - - -) and a total line with a cell of equal signs (= = = = = = =)? Recall that text entries are given the value of zero by 1-2-3. Because a value of zero does not affect the summation of a column of numbers, the dummy row can be the row containing the total or subtotal text indicators. However, you must never use such a dummy row for statistical functions like @AVG, @MIN, @STD, and @VAR because a cell with a zero value is included in these calculations. For example, an @AVG function that includes a text cell with a zero value has a deflated average.

Any time an application requires you to add several numbers together, you should use the @SUM function with a dummy ending cell. Later on, when you add numbers to that list, you won't have to change any formulas in order to include the new items in the list. Any range or named range including a dummy column or row will automatically expand and contract as columns are added to the left of a dummy column or above a dummy row. When the dummy row or column contains text data, make certain that you do not use functions that will be affected by a zero value.

HINTS/HAZARDS

When you are using lines of dashes (-) or equal signs (=) or a column of broken bars (¦) for a dummy entity, make certain that you are using only the @SUM function for mathematical manipulation. If you are using any other statistical function, this cell will have the value of zero and will result in functions such as @AVG, @MIN, @MAX, and so on generating incorrect results.

Figure 3.14
Worksheet with a dummy row containing equal signs (=).

```
A1:                                                              READY

     A        B           C           D           E          F
1          COMPSALS
2
3           Department   Last Year   This Year      Change    % Change
4
5          Deli             700.00      575.00    (125.00)        -18%
6          Bakery         1,000.00    1,100.00     100.00          10%
7          Liquor         1,200.00    1,400.00     200.00          17%
8          Grocery        2,500.00    2,900.00     400.00          16%
9          Produce          950.00    1,000.00      50.00           5%
10         Meat           1,500.00    1,410.00     (90.00)         -6%
11                     ----------------------------------------------
12         Store Total    7,850.00    8,385.00     535.00           7%
13                     ==============================================
14
15
16
17
18
19
20
14-Sep-91  07:59 PM
```

SORT COMMAND (/DS)

From time to time, you may want to rearrange data in a particular order within a column. Some spreadsheets perform such a task via the Move statement; Lotus, however, contains a **Sort command.** This feature lets one person construct a worksheet in a form that is logical for one purpose and lets another person rearrange it to a form that is logical for another purpose.

SORT MENU

The Sort command has its own settings screen and is found in the Data Menu, which is invoked from the Main Menu (/DS). The following is the Sort Menu:

```
Data Range  Primary Key  Secondary Key  Reset  Go  Quit
```

Data Range To perform a sort, you must first mark a range. The **Data Range option** lets you do this. Column headings and total lines are not included in the data range.

Primary Key The **Primary Key option** lets you select the column by which you want the data range to be sorted. Because the entire range has been described to 1-2-3, all you have to do is point to a cell in the column; Lotus then prompts you to select the sort order, either ascending (*A* to *Z*, 0 to 9) or descending (*Z* to *A*, 9 to 0).

Secondary Key The **Secondary Key option** lets you arrange data within the primary key according to a secondary column. For example, in a sort of name and address data, you could establish City as the primary column and Last Name as the secondary column; the data would then be sorted by city, and within each city the data would be sorted by last name.

Reset The **Reset option** drops all sort parameters from memory.

Go The **Go option** executes the sort.

Quit The **Quit option** returns you to your worksheet and READY mode.

HINTS/HAZARDS

When you have a large worksheet, you may want to set up a number of sorts for different data ranges. In such an application, it is advisable to use the Reset before the next sort, especially when you are going from an application that has both primary and secondary sort keys to an application that has only a primary sort. Unless you tell 1-2-3 to reset the sort parameters, it still remembers the secondary key. In this type of situation, you receive the error message `Key column outside of sort range.`

WORKSHEET PRACTICE WITH THE SORT COMMAND

Load the CH2EX1 worksheet you created in Chapter 2 and try some experiments with the Sort command. The loading process is accomplished via the following commands:

/F	Selects the File option from the Main Menu.
R	Selects the Retrieve option.
Type `CH2EX1`	Identifies the name of the worksheet.
Enter	Gets the worksheet.

You should now have the worksheet shown in Figure 3.15 loaded (some spaces have been deleted to make the worksheet fit within the figure).

Once the worksheet has been loaded, you must tell 1-2-3 how to sort the information with the following steps:

/D	Invokes the Data Menu from the Main Menu.
S	Takes the Sort option.
D	Selects the Data Range option to define the area of the worksheet to be sorted.
Go to A4	Marks the cell with the contents "Tony James".
Type .	Nails down the beginning of the range.
Go to G13	Marks the cell with the contents "189.00".
Enter	Defines the data range.
P	Selects the Primary Key option.
Go to A4	Marks the cell with the contents "Tony James". (Or go anywhere in column A inside the data range.)
Enter	Defines the primary column.
A	Chooses a sort in ascending order.
Enter	Indicates that the sort order is complete.
G	Executes the sort.

Figure 3.15
Payroll worksheet.

A1: [W20] READY

	A	B	C	D	E	F	G
1		Total		Overtime	Overtime	Gross	
2	Employee	Hours	Rate	Hours	Rate	Pay	Net Pay
3							
4	James, Tony	40.00	6.50	2.00	9.75	279.50	176.09
5	Biel, Harry	40.00	6.50		9.75	260.00	163.80
6	Singlof, Don	25.00	6.50		9.75	162.50	102.38
7	Hall, Barry	40.00	6.50	3.00	9.75	289.25	182.23
8	Lele, Michelle	40.00	6.50		9.75	260.00	163.80
9	Kanter, John	33.00	6.50		9.75	214.50	135.14
10	Helmsley, Joanna	40.00	5.50		8.25	220.00	138.60
11	Sahara, Ohmar	40.00	5.50		8.25	220.00	138.60
12	Jerrod, Henry	40.00	4.25	10.00	6.38	233.75	147.26
13	Dixon, Yvonne	40.00	7.50		11.25	300.00	189.00
14							
15	TOTALS					$2,439.50	$1,536.89
16							
17							
18							
19							
20							

14-Sep-91 08:05 PM

HINTS/HAZARDS

Before you perform your initial sort, it is a good idea to save your worksheet file. While you can specify descending order to place sorted data in a prior order, this is not possible if you have not already sorted the data.

TITLES COMMAND (/WT)

By this time, you have surely noticed that it is inconvenient to work with large spreadsheets, like CH2EX1, whose width exceeds the display on the screen—especially when you are interested in gross pay and net pay information for an employee. You can't see the net or gross pay numbers at the same time as the employee names. You may wish you could freeze a column of data or a row of text to act as labels for an off-screen row or column. Like many spreadsheet packages, Lotus lets you do this with its **Titles option.**

The pointer plays an important role in the Titles option. Any columns to the left of the pointer or any rows above the pointer that appear on the screen can be frozen to act as labels. You cannot move the pointer into a title area by using Arrow keys. To get the pointer into the titles area, you must press F5 and then enter the address of the cell. This causes the screen to display two copies of the title cells.

TITLES MENU

The Titles command is invoked from the Worksheet Menu (/WT). It presents the following menu:

```
Both  Horizontal  Vertical  Clear
```

Both The **Both option** freezes the rows above the pointer and the columns to the left of the pointer, creating a fixed border of headings for vertical and horizontal scrolling through the worksheet.

Horizontal The **Horizontal option** freezes the rows above the pointer, creating fixed headings for vertical scrolling through the worksheet.

Vertical The **Vertical option** freezes the columns to the left of the pointer, creating fixed-line labels for horizontal scrolling through the worksheet.

Clear The **Clear option** causes any rows or columns that have been frozen to return to unfrozen status. (Note that in order for a cell to be frozen on the screen it must appear on the screen at the time that the Titles option of the Worksheet Menu is selected. If a cell does not physically appear on the screen, it cannot be frozen on the screen.)

TITLES INSTRUCTIONS

The following steps will freeze employee names:

Go to B1	Marks cell B1.
/W	Selects Worksheet from the Main Menu.
T	Selects the Titles option.
V	Selects the Vertical Titles option.

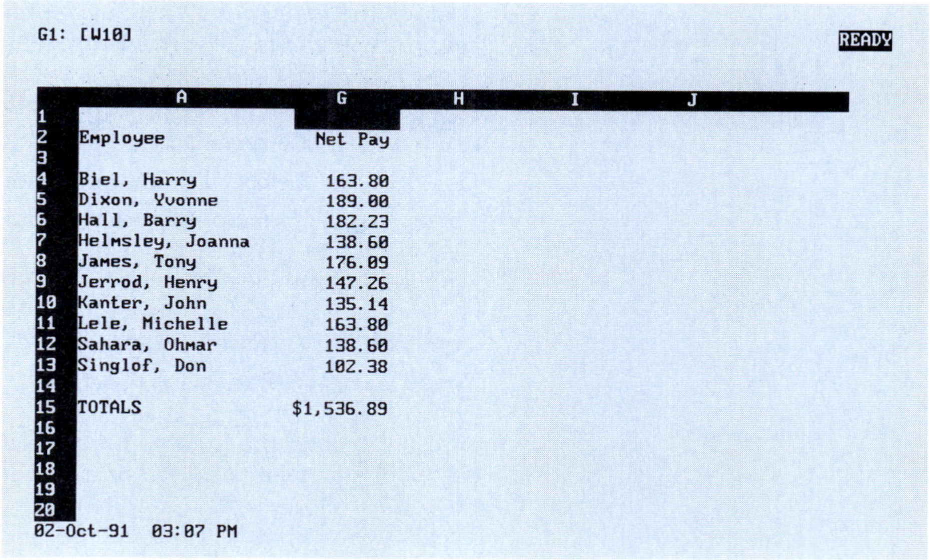

G1: [W10] READY

	A	G	H	I	J
1					
2	Employee	Net Pay			
3					
4	Biel, Harry	163.80			
5	Dixon, Yvonne	189.00			
6	Hall, Barry	182.23			
7	Helmsley, Joanna	138.60			
8	James, Tony	176.09			
9	Jerrod, Henry	147.26			
10	Kanter, John	135.14			
11	Lele, Michelle	163.80			
12	Sahara, Ohmar	138.60			
13	Singlof, Don	102.38			
14					
15	TOTALS	$1,536.89			
16					
17					
18					
19					
20					

02-Oct-91 03:07 PM

Figure 3.16
CH2EX1 worksheet showing Net Pay column.

When you move the pointer to the Net Pay column, the Employee column will remain on the screen and your display will look like that in Figure 3.16. Clear the titles using the / Worksheet Titles Clear command.

RELATIVE AND ABSOLUTE ADDRESSING

As you have already seen, a formula can be copied across a row or down a column, and 1-2-3 will automatically adjust the formula placed in each cell to reflect its new location and the location of any participating cells. This is the concept behind **relative addressing.** But what happens if you don't want 1-2-3 to change a formula automatically to reflect a new cell location? How do you tell 1-2-3, without directly entering a different formula in each cell, to refer to only one cell in a series of calculations?

Let's examine a concrete application of this question. How would you find out what percentage each individual's gross pay was of the total gross pay in the CH2EX1 worksheet? You could insert a column between the Gross Pay and Net Pay columns, but how could you enter a formula and copy it to the other cells in the column in such a way that it would always refer to the contents of the total gross pay cell in calculating the percentage?

The first possibility, manually entering the required formula for each row in the column, is feasible with the few employees currently in the worksheet, but it would require a tremendous amount of work if you were dealing with 100 employees. The easiest way to solve the problem is to use a technique referred to as **absolute addressing.**

An absolute cell reference is easy to distinguish from a relative cell reference because it appears with one or more dollar signs ($) in the cell reference—for example, $A$1, $A1, or A$1.

Let's begin by examining further why the relative addressing feature of 1-2-3 is inappropriate for this application.

Load the worksheet file CH2EX1, if it is not already on your screen.

1. Position the pointer anywhere in column G (Net Pay) and insert the new column, using the following instructions:

/W	Selects Worksheet from the Main Menu.
I	Selects the Insert option.
C	Selects the Column option.
Enter	Executes the Insert command.

2. Enter the column headings in cells G1 and G2:

Type `% of Total`	Enters text in cell G1.
Type `Gross Pay`	Enters text in cell G2.

3. At cell G4, enter the formula for calculating the percentage of total gross pay, using the relative addressing convention:

Type `+F4/F15`	Enters text in cell G4.

   When you press Enter, you should see 0.11 as the cell contents.

4. Select the column to a percent format with one decimal position:

/R	Selects the Range option from the Main Menu.
F	Selects the Format option.
P	Selects the Percent format.
1	Sets the number of decimal positions to one.
Enter	Finishes setting decimals.
Go to G13	Marks the last cell in the range.
Enter	Establishes the range and executes the command.

5. Copy this formula to the rest of the cells in the column:

Go to G4	Marks cell G4.
/C	Selects the Copy command from the Main Menu.
Enter	Indicates that cell G4 is the only "From" cell.
Go to G5	Marks the beginning of the "To" range.
Type `.`	Nails down the beginning of the "To" range.
Go to G13	Marks the last cell in the "To" range.
Enter	Executes the Copy command.

You should now see the worksheet shown in Figure 3.17 on your screen. Obviously, something is drastically wrong with this worksheet. What happened? When 1-2-3 copied the formula +F4/F15 to the other cells in the column, it automatically changed the formula for each cell as it proceeded down the column; as a result, cell G5 contains the formula +F5/F16, and cell G6 has the formula +F6/F17. But cells F16 and F17 do not contain any numeric values—hence the error message `ERR`.

Lotus did not use the contents of the total gross pay cell for each of the calculations after the Copy command was used because no absolute cell references were contained in the original formula entered in G4.

Go to cell G4 and enter the formula +F4/$F$15. Then use the instructions contained in step 5 above to copy the formula to the other cells in the column.

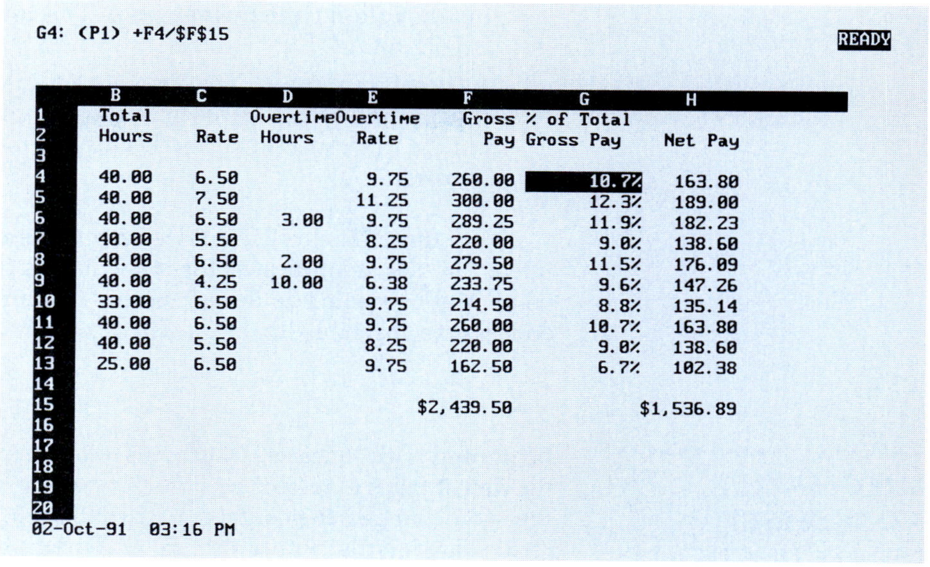

G4: (P1) +F4/$F$15 READY

	B	C	D	E	F	G	H
1	Total		Overtime	Overtime	Gross	% of Total	
2	Hours	Rate	Hours	Rate	Pay	Gross Pay	Net Pay
3							
4	40.00	6.50		9.75	260.00	10.7%	163.80
5	40.00	7.50		11.25	300.00	12.3%	189.00
6	40.00	6.50	3.00	9.75	289.25	11.9%	182.23
7	40.00	5.50		8.25	220.00	9.0%	138.60
8	40.00	6.50	2.00	9.75	279.50	11.5%	176.09
9	40.00	4.25	10.00	6.38	233.75	9.6%	147.26
10	33.00	6.50		9.75	214.50	8.8%	135.14
11	40.00	6.50		9.75	260.00	10.7%	163.80
12	40.00	5.50		8.25	220.00	9.0%	138.60
13	25.00	6.50		9.75	162.50	6.7%	102.38
14							
15					$2,439.50		$1,536.89
16							
17							
18							
19							
20							

02-Oct-91 03:16 PM

Figure 3.17
PAYSORT worksheet changed using relative addressing.

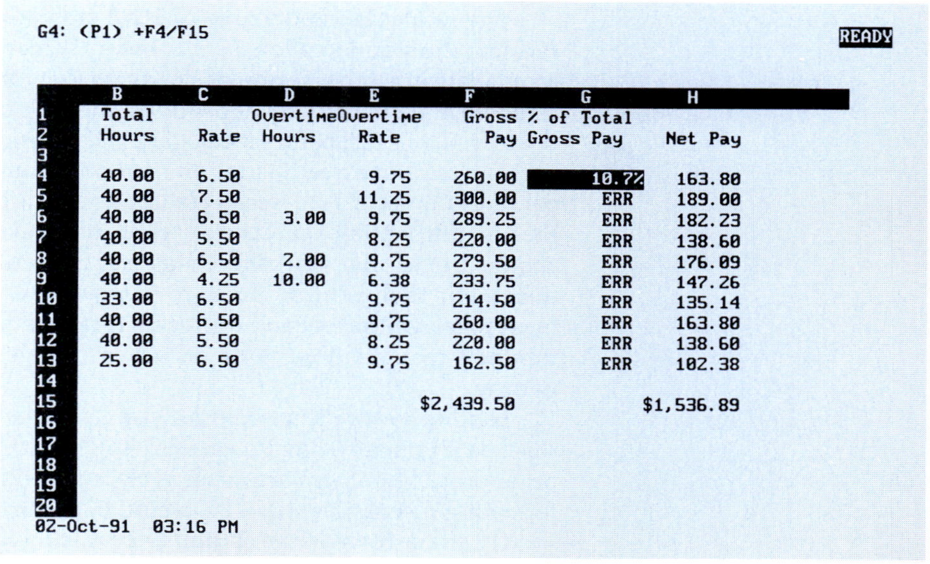

G4: (P1) +F4/F15 READY

	B	C	D	E	F	G	H
1	Total		Overtime	Overtime	Gross	% of Total	
2	Hours	Rate	Hours	Rate	Pay	Gross Pay	Net Pay
3							
4	40.00	6.50		9.75	260.00	10.7%	163.80
5	40.00	7.50		11.25	300.00	ERR	189.00
6	40.00	6.50	3.00	9.75	289.25	ERR	182.23
7	40.00	5.50		8.25	220.00	ERR	138.60
8	40.00	6.50	2.00	9.75	279.50	ERR	176.09
9	40.00	4.25	10.00	6.38	233.75	ERR	147.26
10	33.00	6.50		9.75	214.50	ERR	135.14
11	40.00	6.50		9.75	260.00	ERR	163.80
12	40.00	5.50		8.25	220.00	ERR	138.60
13	25.00	6.50		9.75	162.50	ERR	102.38
14							
15					$2,439.50		$1,536.89
16							
17							
18							
19							
20							

02-Oct-91 03:16 PM

Figure 3.18
PAYSORT worksheet changed using absolute addressing.

Afterward, your screen should have a display like that in Figure 3.18. The dollar signs in the amended formula tell 1-2-3 that it is to leave this part of the formula exactly the same as it copies it from one cell to another. Relative addressing will not affect any part of the formula containing dollar signs.

In the above example, the formula containing the absolute cell reference had a cell address of $F$15. As noted earlier, you can also use addresses like $A1 or A$1. This type of cell reference has elements of both absolute addressing and relative addressing and is called a **mixed-cell address.** The relative part of a mixed-cell address will change, and the absolute part will not, as described below:

$A1 **($columnrow)** The absolute address portion of this reference is the column portion of the reference, so the row can change within the address, but the column must remain as A. This formula could be read as "any row in column A."

A$1 **(column$row)** The absolute address portion of this reference is the row portion of the reference, so the column can change within the address, but the row must remain as 1. This formula could be read as "any column in row 1."

Note that mixed-cell addresses cannot be used with range names. If absolute addresses are indicated for range names (for example, $COLB), the range name will be treated as though both the column and the row portions of the address are absolute—that is, it will be wholly an **absolute range name.**

AUTOMATIC WORKSHEET RECALCULATION

Beginning with Release 2.2 of Lotus 1-2-3, you no longer have much delay in the time it takes to recalculate your worksheet. Previous to Release 2.2, anytime that you changed the contents of a single cell, the entire worksheet had to be recalculated. Now, with **minimal recalculation,** however, anytime a change is made to a cell in the worksheet, only those cells actually affected have to be recalculated.

The recalculation defaults of 1-2-3 are natural and automatic. The **natural recalculation** option allows 1-2-3, before it recalculates a particular formula, to recalculate any other formulas on which that formula depends. This means that if the formula in cell C23 depends on the formula in cell B23, 1-2-3 recalculates the formula in B23 before it calculates the one in C23.

2.2

The **automatic recalculation** method means that each time you change the contents of a cell, 1-2-3 recalculates any formulas affected by the change. With the default setting on natural, 1-2-3 recalculates only those cells that have changed since the worksheet was last recalculated, along with the cells that depend on them. This minimal recalculation feature optimizes the recalculation of cells in a worksheet and decreases recalculation time. There is no way to turn minimal recalculation on or off when the recalculation order is specified as natural.

Neither rowwise nor columnwise calculation is needed for any examples in this text if you are using Release 2.2. You may, however, need to do this for some other project (or if you are using a release of 1-2-3 prior to 2.2), in which case the following discussion might be useful. If, for example, you are using 2.01 or you specify either rowwise or columnwise calculation, 1-2-3 must recalculate every cell in your worksheet. This necessitates manual recalculation, which is accomplished by entering the following command sequence:

/W	Selects Worksheet from the Main Menu.
G	Selects the Global option.
R	Selects the Recalculation option.
M	Executes the Manual command.

If you make changes to any cell after this **manual recalculation** option has been selected, 1-2-3 displays a CALC message at the bottom of your screen next to the indicators area. To get 1-2-3 to recalculate the worksheet, you must press F9.

If you save the worksheet file onto disk, the manual recalculation setting is saved in the worksheet file. If you wish to reset the spreadsheet to automatic (that is, minimal), all you need to do is enter the above commands, replacing the M with an A (for automatic).

MORE ON FUNCTIONS

@PMT

Lotus has a financial function that is a true time-saver. The **@PMT** (principal, interest rate, periods)—payment per period—function calculates the payment of a loan or mortgage based on three pieces of information: principal, interest rate, and number of periods. Using this function avoids entering the following formula:

```
Prin*Inter/12/(1-1/(1+Inter/12)^Periods)
```

@IF AND LOGICAL OPERATORS

The **@IF** function checks for certain conditions and then takes actions based on the results of the check. The format of the @IF function is @IF (condition, true, false). The condition portion of the function lets you set up an equation to check for specific results or cell contents; the true portion contains instructions that will be executed if the condition is true; the false portion contains instructions that will be executed if the condition is false.

The operators allowed in a 1-2-3 @IF function are as follows:

Relational	
=	Equal to
<	Less than
<=	Less than or equal to
>	Greater than
>=	Greater than or equal to
< >	Not equal to
Logical	
#NOT#	Not (the opposite of any equation or relation must be the case before the true option is executed)
#AND#	And (both conditions must be true before the true option is executed)
#OR#	Or (either action can be true for the true option to be executed)

These operators can be used to set up a number of different conditions:

- +B1=60#OR#D17<20 The value contained in cell B13 is equal to 60, or the value contained in cell D17 is less than 20.
- +H14>0#AND#D19>1985 The value contained in cell H14 is greater than zero, and the value in cell D19 is greater than 1985.
- #NOT#(YEAR=1985) The value stored in the cell named YEAR is not 1985.
- (B15−C10)=D3#AND#C5>D7 The value of cell B15 minus the value of cell C10 is equal to the value contained in cell D3, *and* the value contained in cell C5 is larger than the value contained in cell D7.

These new conditions also have places in the order of precedence discussed earlier. The complete listing of this order is given in Table 3.1.

Table 3.1 The Operator Order of Precedence

Operator	*Meaning*	*Level*
^	Exponentiation	7
–	Negative	6
+	Positive	6
*	Multiplication	5
/	Division	5
+	Addition	4
–	Subtraction	4
=	Equal	3
<	Less than	3
<=	Less than or equal	3
>	Greater than	3
>=	Greater than or equal	3
<>	Not equal	3
#NOT#	Logical not	2
#AND#	Logical and	1
#OR#	Logical or	1

Applications of the @IF Function Assume that you have a worksheet that calculates the sales commission for the sales representatives of a manufacturing company. The extension (units sold multiplied by price) is contained in cell H4. Sales commissions are calculated based on the extension amount. If the extension is greater than $1000, the sales commission is 10% of the extension; otherwise, the commission amount is zero. The following @IF function might appear in cell I4:

```
@IF(H4>1000,H4*.1,0)
```

This function could be translated as follows:

```
If the sales extension (H4) is greater than 1000
    compute the sales commission as 10% of the extension
else
    enter 0 for the sales commission value
Endif
```

You could also set two levels of sales commissions. For example, in the situation above, you might have a commission of 10% for sales over $1000, a commission of 5% for sales equal to or less than $1000 but greater than $500, and a commission of zero for sales equal to or less than $500. This situation requires the use of a nested function. When you are using nested @IF functions, always start with the most inclusive entry and work down (in this case, first check for a commission greater than $1000 and then check for a commission of greater than $500).

```
@IF(H4>1000,H4*.1,@IF(H4>500,H4*.05,0))
```

This function could be translated as follows:

If the sales extension (H4) is greater than 1000
    compute the sales commission as 10% of the extension
else
    If the sales extension (H4) is greater than 500
        compute the sales commission as 5% of the extension
    else
        enter a commission rate of 0
    Endif
Endif

The @IF function also lets you perform string tests on data in a worksheet and then take actions based on the results of the comparison. If, for example, you wished to generate a Pass/Fail message in a grade book application with the message Pass displaying for a grade equal to or greater than 65 and a Fail message displaying for a grade less than 65, the @IF function depicted below would be used.

```
@IF(D27<=.65,"Fail","Pass")
```

Any text that is to be entered in the cell must be included within double quotes.

Suppose you ran a business that needed to collect taxes only on mail orders received from within the state of Illinois. The next example could be used to check the value of a cell (D7) containing a code for a state and calculate tax only if the value in the cell were Il or IL.

```
@IF(D7="IL"#or#D7="Il",D15*.0625,"No Tax")
```

This @IF function first checks to see if the state has been entered as IL or Il. If the state entry is equal to either of these values, the sales tax is computed; otherwise, the message "No Tax" is entered in the cell.

@DATE AND ARITHMETIC

You were introduced to some aspects of the **@DATE** function when you entered the FUNCTION worksheet in Chapter 2. The information returned by the @NOW and @DATE functions is numeric and represents the number of elapsed days since January 1, 1900. Thus, when 1-2-3 displays a date via one of the three formats listed below, it is merely formatting numeric information for display. Lotus displays date information in one of the following formats:

(DD-MMM-YY)	29-Jan-92
(DD-MMM)	29-Jan
(MMM-YY)	Jan-92

Displaying a date is a two-step process: First, you get the date via the @DATE or @NOW function (the @NOW function gets the date from DOS), causing a number to appear on the screen and in the cell; second, you use the / Range Format Date command on the cell to specify one of the above formats, causing a date display to appear on the screen.

The numeric method that 1-2-3 uses to display dates can be very beneficial in manipulating dates. Because the date is really numeric, any arithmetic operations can be performed on it. To generate the date for a week from today, for example, you simply add 7 to the existing numeric date. If you want to find out how many weeks there are between two dates, you can subtract the ending date from the beginning date, divide by 7, and round the result using the **@ROUND** or **@INT** functions.

With date arithmetic involving months, be careful. You can't simply convert a month to 30 days and expect it to work. Adding a number like 30.5 doesn't work well either, unless the period covered is small. The following method assumes that payment will occur on or before the twenty-eighth day of the month:

1. Add 31 to the previous date.
2. Subtract the current @DAY from the present number to bring you back to the present day of the prior month.
3. Add @DAY to the original number to move you forward to the proper day in the next month.

This method allows you to advance from one month to the next if the day of the month is 1 through 28.

You can also compare the value of the @NOW function with another date already entered on the worksheet or with a date in a formula. To do this requires using the command @IF(@NOW>@DATE(91,2,1),x,y). The x represents the action to be taken if the information is true, and the y represents the action to be taken if the condition is false.

INTRODUCTION TO MACROS

Lotus's macro feature sets it apart from other spreadsheets. Macros let you automate just about any part of your worksheet with a minimum of effort. You can store keystrokes as text in a cell and then execute those stored keystrokes.

A **macro** is a cell or group of cells of text that has a special name (range name) and acts as a repository of keystrokes; it is created by entering the keystrokes (or their representation) in a cell. Using some advanced 1-2-3 commands, macros can be made to resemble programs. A macro is capable of containing complex logic that controls how a worksheet executes and of building a menu from which users can select operations or tasks. Some of these advanced commands are similar to BASIC's If-Then-Else, GoTo, and GoSub commands.

Macros can have global effects on a worksheet and should be used with care. Complex macros are not recommended for the spreadsheet novice, but you do not have to know everything about 1-2-3 to use simple ones.

Complex macros that contain control logic may be easier to create if you have some programming background. It doesn't matter what language you have used. Prior programming experience enables you to solve a problem using a structured approach. Simple macros, however, can be created and used by any individual who understands how a spreadsheet's menu structure works.

Creating a Simple Macro If you are seated at a computer, prepare for the following example by loading (retrieving) the worksheet file COMPSALS. Set the global format of the worksheet to general.

Suppose you want to create a macro that will format any cell to contain currency data with two positions to the right of the decimal. Before you create the macro, let's review the keystrokes you would use from 1-2-3 to format a cell:

/R	Selects the Range option from the Main Menu.
F	Selects the Format option to change a portion of the worksheet.
C	Selects the currency format to display data within a range.
Enter (2)	Takes the default two positions to the right of the decimal point and tells 1-2-3 that this is the only cell in the range.

As you can see, the task of formatting a single worksheet cell to currency with two decimal positions requires six keystrokes. These keystrokes can be placed in a single cell and then executed. Position your pointer to any unused cell in your worksheet, such as H23. Now type `'/rfc~~` and press Enter. You thus enter a macro into a cell of the worksheet exactly the same way that you would enter any other label. First you type the label prefix ('). (Otherwise, the / will execute immediately to tell 1-2-3 to display the Main Menu in the control panel.) Any macro that begins with a nontext character must contain a label prefix (typically ').

The next four characters (/RFC) represent the commands to create this desired format: / Range Format Currency. The two characters at the end of the macro are called *tildes*. Each represents one Enter keystroke. In the preceding macro, Enter is pressed twice. It does not matter whether the keystrokes are entered in uppercase or lowercase.

Naming the Micro Once you have entered a macro into a worksheet cell, you must give it a special range name before it can be executed. Position the pointer to the cell containing the macro instructions and issue the / Range Name Create command. Beginning with Release 2.2 of Lotus 1-2-3, you can give a macro any range name, or it may consist of two characters (a method supported by earlier releases of 1-2-3). If a 1-2-3 macro name consists of two characters, the first character is always a backslash (\), which tells the spreadsheet that a macro is being created. The second character is a letter. Name the cell containing your macro \F (abbreviation for Format). Be sure to press Enter to tell 1-2-3 that this is the only cell in this range.

Executing the Macro You can now execute this macro by positioning the pointer to any numeric cell in the COMPSALS worksheet that you want to format and pressing Alt + F (hold down the Alt key and press F). The contents of the cell should now appear in the new format.

The Alt followed by any letter tells 1-2-3 that it should find the macro with that name and execute it. If there is no macro with that name, the computer will beep, indicating that 1-2-3 cannot find the macro on the worksheet.

2.2

If you gave the macro a range name such as *save*, execute the macro by using the Run (Alt + F3) command. Once you have issued the Run command, the screen displays a listing of the named ranges in your worksheet at the top (Figure 3.19). You can now either manually enter the name of the range containing the macro instructions or position the pointer to the appropriate named range and press Enter.

Note that if you name a macro with a backslash followed by another character, these macro names will appear at the end of the named-range listing. They can be easily accessed by pressing the Left Arrow key immediately following the Run command, which places you at the end of the listing of named ranges instead of at the beginning.

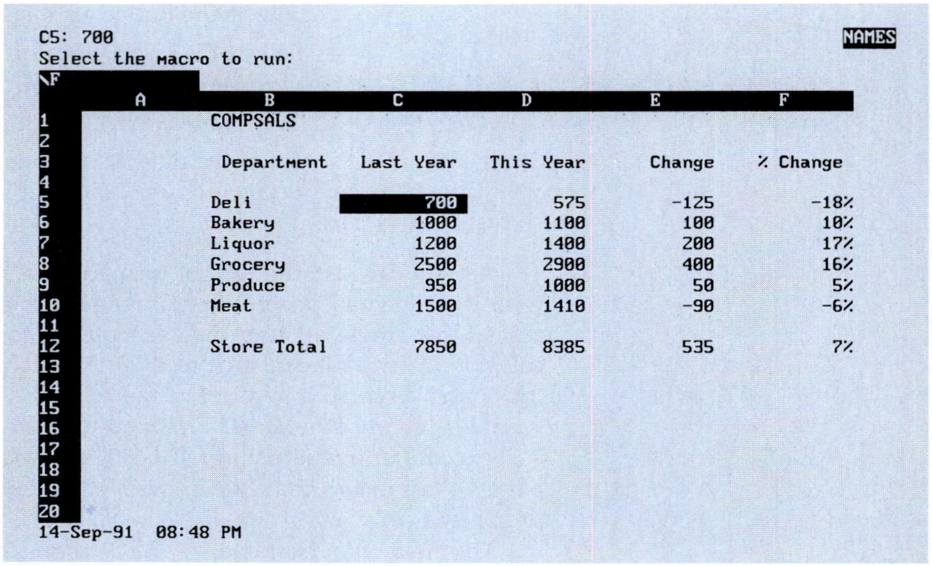

Figure 3.19

The listing of named ranges displayed via the Run command (Alt + F3).

SPECIAL KEYS

As shown above, the Enter key could not be stored in a cell as a macro command without using a special representation, the tilde (~), to signify this keystroke. Many other keys also have special representations. Table 3.2 shows a complete list of the special key representations for use in 1-2-3 macros. Each expression on the left must be typed as shown to produce the result shown on the right. The name of the key is always typed in braces. If you enclose in braces a phrase that is not a function or key name, 1-2-3 returns the error message `Unrecognized key named {...}`.

An important special key representation is {?}, which is similar to BASIC's Input command. When 1-2-3 encounters a {?} in a macro, it pauses and waits for you to enter data from the keyboard. Once you type in data and press Enter, the current cell stores the data.

Modifying the Macro Suppose you want to modify the macro that was just entered to format an entire column rather than one cell. You could enter the appropriate number of {down} commands to include the correct number of cells that appear in the column. This method, however, lacks the flexibility that is needed if you want to add or delete rows that might appear in the column to be formatted. Remember the role of the End key when you move the pointer from one position to another. In this case, the End key followed by a Down Arrow key positions the pointer from its current location to the last occupied cell in this group of cells (the bottom of the column). If you also want to include a TOTAL cell, you could add two Down Arrow commands. To include this ability, change the macro to the following:

```
'/RFC~{end}{down}{down}{down}~
```

Now to format a column of numbers, position the pointer to the beginning of the column and press Alt + F. It no longer matters how many cells are included in the column. The only limitation is that the column can have no blank cells (a blank cell marks the end of the range for the {end}{down} command).

Table 3.2 1-2-3 Macro Keys

Key	*Task*
Function Keys	
{EDIT}	Edits content of current cell (F2).
{NAME}	Displays a list of range names in the worksheet (F3).
{ABS}	Coverts relative reference to absolute (F4).
{GOTO}	Jumps cursor to cell coordinates (F5).
{WINDOW}	Moves the cursor to the other side of the window (F6).
{QUERY}	Repeats most recent query operation (F7).
{TABLE}	Repeats most recent table operation (F8).
{CALC}	Recalculates worksheet (F9).
{GRAPH}	Redraws current graph (F10).
{APP1}	Activates the add-in assigned to the key Alt + F7.
{APP2}	Activates the add-in assigned to the key Alt + F8.
{APP3}	Activates the add-in assigned to the key Alt + F9.
{APP4}	Activates the add-in assigned to the key Alt + F10.
Pointer-Positioning Keys	
{UP} or {U}	Moves pointer up one row.
{DOWN} or {D}	Moves pointer down one row.
{LEFT} or {L}	Moves pointer left one column.
{RIGHT} or {R}	Moves pointer right one column.
{Big Right}	Moves pointer to the right a screen at a time.
{Big Left}	Moves pointer to the left a screen at a time.
{PGUP}	Moves pointer up 20 rows.
{HOME}	Moves pointer to cell A1.
{END}	Used with an Arrow or Home key.
Other Special Keys	
{DEL}	Deletes a single character when used with {EDIT}.
{ESC}	Evokes the Esc command.
{BS}	Moves the cursor via the Backspace key.
{?}	Causes the macro to pause and wait for keyboard input; the macro resumes executing when you press Enter.
~	Represents one Enter keystroke.
{INS}	Makes changes between INSERT and OVERWRITE modes.
/ or {MENU}	Invokes the Main Menu.
{-}	Searches for data management wildcards.
{{ }	Represents the left brace.
{ }}	Represents the right brace.

BUILDING MORE MACROS

You are now going to build a macro that can be used to save an existing worksheet, COMPSALS, to disk. It will execute the same commands you do when you save a worksheet: / File Save Enter (accept the default filename) Replace.

Position the pointer to an unused cell (H25) in your COMPSALS worksheet. Now enter the following character string: '/FS~R. Make certain that there are no embedded blanks in the macro; a blank causes the macro to stop executing. Press Enter. The cell should contain the following: '/fs~r.

Use the / Range Name Create command and give this cell the name \S. Then press Alt + S to execute the macro. The worksheet should now automatically be saved to disk. The saved worksheet will contain the macros that you have created.

Next, build a macro that can be used to insert columns in the worksheet. Issue the following commands from the keyboard each time you want to insert a row in a worksheet: / Worksheet Insert Column Enter.

Position the pointer to an unused cell (J25) in your worksheet. Now enter the following character strong: '/WIC~. Make sure that there are no embedded blanks in the macro. Press Enter. The cell should contain this: '/wic~.

Use the / Range Name Create command to name this cell \C. Position the pointer where you want to insert a column and press Alt + C to execute the macro.

2.2

CREATING A MACRO WITH A REGULAR RANGE NAME

As you no doubt remember from the beginning of the chapter, you can, in addition to naming a macro with a backslash (\) and an alphabetic character, also use a regular range name. Remember, however, that a macro named by a regular range name must be invoked using the Run (Alt + F3) command.

The next macro sets a column to a width of 25. Position the pointer to an unused cell (L25) in your worksheet. Enter the following character string: '/WCS25~. Again, make certain that there are no embedded blanks within the macro. Press Enter. The cell should contain the following: '/WCS25~.

Use the / Range Name Create command to name this cell WIDTH. After positioning the pointer where you want to change the width of a column, press Alt + F3, highlight the named range WIDTH, and press Enter. The width of the column should now be changed.

Most macros can be stored in a single cell, but some complex macros require more than one cell. Any other cells in a column that make up the macro are automatically included in the macro. A macro executes instructions in a top-down, left-to-right fashion until it comes to a blank or a blank cell. There can be no embedded blanks between the commands in a cell (except label data). Any blank cell tells the spreadsheet that this is the end of the macro.

HINTS/HAZARDS

Check your macros to ensure that you have matching braces { } around any special words. Also, make certain that you have included tildes (~) to represent an Enter keystroke where 1-2-3 would normally expect to find them. Braces and tildes are the most frequently omitted characters in entering macros.

2.2

USING LOTUS'S LEARN MODE FOR ENTERING MACROS (/WL)

Up to this point, you have been recording macro instructions by manually entering them from the keyboard. Lotus also lets you place the spreadsheet in LEARN mode and automatically record keystrokes, at specified cells in the form of a macro, as you enter commands from the keyboard. The cells in which the keystrokes are recorded make up a **learn range.**

The **Learn feature** of 1-2-3 has the advantage that it lets you both record and test a macro at the same time. Because you are actually executing an instruction at the same time that you are recording the keystrokes, the screen appears as it will when the macro executes. The Learn feature also minimizes data-entry errors that can occur if you improperly spell one of the special key commands used in 1-2-3. Creating a macro using the Learn feature requires you to follow four steps:

1. Specify a learn range in which the keystrokes and instructions can be recorded in a worksheet. This range must be a series of cells within a single column.
2. Record keystrokes for a macro by executing 1-2-3 commands at the keyboard.
3. Use the / Range Name Create command to name the first cell in the learn range.
4. Execute the macro to make certain it works properly. If you entered some additional keystrokes that are not actually needed for proper execution, the macro can be edited and the unneeded keystrokes deleted. Make certain that there are no embedded spaces when you have finished making changes.

Creating a Learn Range To use the Learn feature, select the Learn option from the Worksheet submenu (/WL). This displays the following menu:

```
Range   Cancel   Erase
```

Range The Range option specifies a single-column range of cells to hold the macro. You must do this to use Learn.

Cancel The Cancel option turns off the Learn feature.

Erase The Erase option erases all cells containing macro commands in the learn range.

If you specify several columns as the learn range, 1-2-3 will take only the cells in the first column of the range. As a general rule, it is safest to include more cells than you think you will need for the macro instructions. A learn range for the COMPSALS file is created from cells N23 to N43 by issuing the following commands after you have positioned your pointer to cell N23.

/W	Selects Worksheet from the Main Menu.
L	Selects the Learn option.
R	Selects the Range option.
Type .	Nails down the beginning of the range.
Pg Dn	Extends the range to cell N43.
Enter	Executes the command.

Recording Keystrokes with Learn Once you have created the learn range, you can activate the Learn feature by issuing the Learn (Alt + F5) command. Any commands that are entered from the keyboard are placed in the learn range. If you record more keystrokes than can be held in the specified learn range, 1-2-3 automatically turns off the Learn feature and displays an error mes-

2.2

sage indicating that the learn range is full. In such a situation, you may have to make your learn range larger and erase the characters in the present learn range with the / Worksheet Learn Erase command.

Suppose you wish to create a range format macro that will do the following: When the pointer is placed at the first cell of a column of numbers, the macro will format the cells of all numbers except the total with commas (,) and two decimal positions. It will format the total cell for currency with two decimal positions. We will name this macro COLFORMT.

1. Use the Learn feature to record these keystrokes. Go to cell C5 and enter these commands:

Alt + F5	Invokes the Learn command to record keystrokes.
/R	Selects the Range option from the Main Menu.
F	Selects the Format option.
Type ,	Selects the Comma (,) command.
Enter	Selects two positions to the right of the decimal.
End, ↓	Moves pointer to bottom of column.
Enter	Executes the command.
End, ↓	Moves pointer to bottom of column.
↓ (2)	Positions the pointer on the total.
/R	Selects the Range option from the Main Menu.
F	Selects the Format option.
C	Selects the Currency command.
Enter (2)	Selects two positions to the right of the decimal, formats this cell only, and executes the instruction.
Alt + F5	Turns off the LEARN mode.
F5	Executes the GoTo command.
N23	Moves the pointer to cell N23 so that you can examine the macro (Figure 3.20).

2. Name the macro. First go to cell M23:

Type COLFORMT	Enters the macro name in cell M23.
N23	Positions the pointer to cell N23.
/R	Selects the Range option from the Main Menu.
N	Selects the Name option.
C	Selects the Create option.
Type COLFORMT	Enters the name of the macro.
Enter	Executes the command.

Remember, if you made any mistakes entering the macro, they can be corrected using the Edit (F2) command. As you edit the macro, make certain that you do not embed blanks or leave a blank cell.

To execute this macro, position the pointer to the first cell in a column, press Alt + F3 (Run), select the COLFORMT range name, and press Enter. Of course, if you had named this macro with a backslash (\) followed by an alphabetic character, you would have executed this macro with the Alt + _ command.

Be aware that 1-2-3 does not record keystrokes using the Learn feature

Figure 3.20
The macro created using the Learn command.

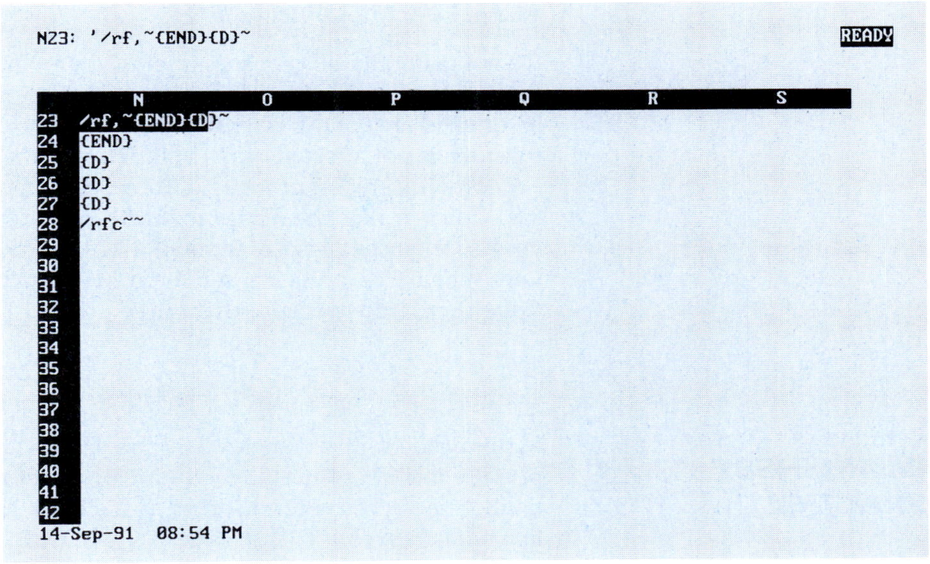

2.2 when you have not invoked the Learn command. Nor does it record any of the following keystrokes:

Compose (Alt + F1)	Print Screen
Run (Alt + F3)	Step (Alt + F2)
Undo (Alt + F4)	Scroll Lock
Num Lock	Help (F1)
Caps Lock	

Once you have finished creating a macro and want to create another macro using Learn, be sure to reset the learn range to another group of cells. Otherwise, these new macro instructions will be added to the existing macro in the specified learn range.

RULES FOR ENTERING MACROS

1. Use a comment to name the macro. Place a backslash (\) in the cell to the left of the macro location followed by the one-character alphabetic name of the macro or enter the name of the named range. Do not use the same character twice. Enter a single quote (') before the backslash (\).
2. Name the cell using / Range Name Create, or, if the name is already in a cell, using / Range Name Label Right.
3. Do not embed blanks in a macro (except within labels). A blank stops the macro.
4. A macro can occupy multiple cells in the same column. A blank cell in a column may stop the macro.
5. Unless an alphabetic character or brace ({) is the first character in a macro, the macro must be preceded by a label prefix (usually '). For example, numbers must be preceded by a single quote (').
6. A cell containing a macro can have a maximum of 240 characters (the limit for any cell). A macro is much more readable, however, if you keep the number of macro commands per cell small.

PLACEMENT OF MACROS

Do not generally place macros inside your worksheet model. Keep them outside the active area to help avoid erasing them accidentally. Generally, place them in an unused area of the worksheet to the lower right of your main model, because this area is not affected when you delete rows or columns.

Many users adopt a standard cell location in worksheets for starting macros, which makes them easy to locate later. You can also give the macro area of your worksheet a range name like MACROS. This lets you use the GoTo (F5) key. When you press F5 and type MACROS, your pointer will move to the upper left-hand corner of that range.

WORKSHEET PRACTICE

Many of the topics discussed in this chapter are used in the next few pages to prepare two worksheets. The first worksheet involves generating a loan amortization table; the second serves as the basis for evaluating various automobile loan alternatives.

LOAN AMORTIZATION WORKSHEET

The following loan amortization table requires you to enter the loan amount, the interest rate on the loan, the length of the loan in months, and the starting date of the loan. It will then generate a table that includes the amount of the payment, the month of the payment, the portion applied toward the principal, the portion applied to the interest, and the outstanding balance.

In doing this project, you will practice the following skills:

1. Using the @PMT function
2. Using the @IF function
3. Using date arithmetic
4. Using mixed-cell addressing

The completed worksheet is shown in Figure 3.21. To present the information in the format shown, you'll obviously have to use absolute addressing to allow each line of formulas to refer to the data at the top of the worksheet. In addition, you'll have to use date arithmetic to advance the date month-by-month from one line to the next; you'll have to use the @PMT function for easy calculation of the payment (you could place this piece of information at the top also); and later you'll have to use the @IF function to properly generate the worksheet.

The various column amounts are calculated as follows:

- The payment is calculated via the @PMT function.
- The interest is calculated by multiplying the outstanding balance by the interest rate and dividing that result by 12 (interest for 1 month).
- The principal is calculated by subtracting the interest amount from the payment amount.
- The new outstanding balance is calculated by subtracting the amount of the payment applied toward the principal from the old outstanding balance.

Now let's go through the individual tasks involved in creating this worksheet.

Figure 3.21
Loan amortization worksheet.

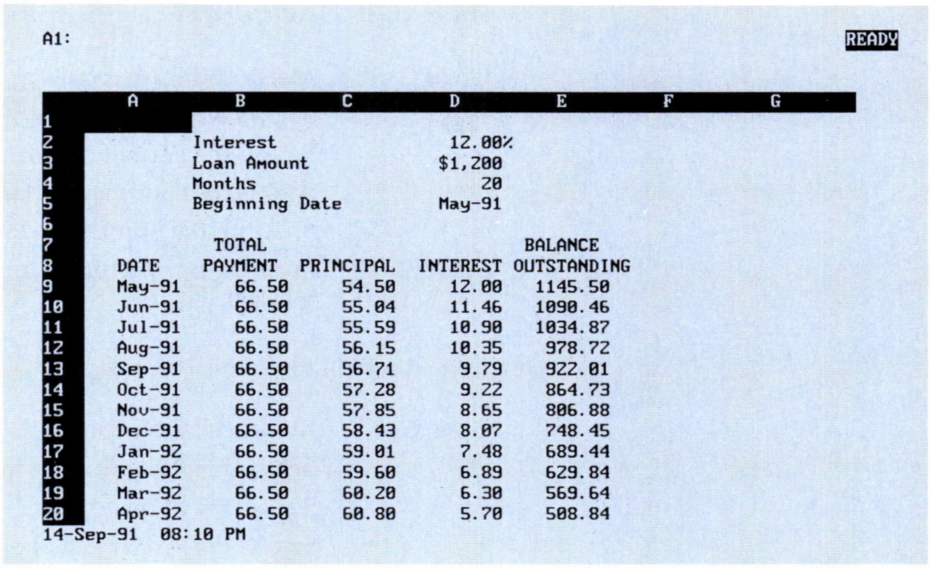

A1: READY

	A	B	C	D	E	F	G
1							
2	Interest			12.00%			
3	Loan Amount			$1,200			
4	Months			20			
5	Beginning Date			May-91			
6							
7		TOTAL			BALANCE		
8	DATE	PAYMENT	PRINCIPAL	INTEREST	OUTSTANDING		
9	May-91	66.50	54.50	12.00	1145.50		
10	Jun-91	66.50	55.04	11.46	1090.46		
11	Jul-91	66.50	55.59	10.90	1034.87		
12	Aug-91	66.50	56.15	10.35	978.72		
13	Sep-91	66.50	56.71	9.79	922.01		
14	Oct-91	66.50	57.28	9.22	864.73		
15	Nov-91	66.50	57.85	8.65	806.88		
16	Dec-91	66.50	58.43	8.07	748.45		
17	Jan-92	66.50	59.01	7.48	689.44		
18	Feb-92	66.50	59.60	6.89	629.84		
19	Mar-92	66.50	60.20	6.30	569.64		
20	Apr-92	66.50	60.80	5.70	508.84		

14-Sep-91 08:10 PM

1. Set the global column width to 10:

/W	Selects Worksheet from the Main Menu.
G	Selects the Global option.
C	Selects the Column Width option.
10	Specifies the new column width.
Enter	Executes the command.

2. Enter label information in the appropriate cells:

A2	Interest	B8	^PAYMENT
A3	Loan Amount	C8	^PRINCIPAL
A4	Months	D8	^INTEREST
A5	Beginning Date	E7	^BALANCE
A8	^DATE	E8	^OUTSTANDING
B7	^TOTAL		

3. Enter the loan information:

C2	.12
C3	1200
C4	20
C5	@DATE(91,5,1)

4. Format cell C2 for percentage, with two decimal positions:

Go to C2	Marks cell C2 by pointing.
/R	Selects the Range option from the Main Menu.
F	Selects the Format option.
P	Selects the Percent option.
Enter (2)	Takes the default of two decimal positions and formats only this cell.

5. Format cell C3 for currency, with zero decimal positions:

Go to C3	Marks cell C3 by pointing.
/R	Selects the Range option from the Main Menu.
F	Selects the Format option.
C	Selects the Currency option.
0	Specifies the number of decimal positions.
Enter (2)	Fixes the number of decimal positions and formats only this cell.

6. Format cell C4 for whole months:

Go to C4	Marks cell C4 by pointing.
/R	Selects the Range option from the Main Menu.
F	Selects the Format option.
F	Selects the Fixed Format option.
0	Specifies the number of decimal positions.
Enter (2)	Fixes the number of decimal positions and formats only this cell.

7. Format cell C5 for the date:

Go to C5	Marks cell C5 by pointing.
/R	Selects the Range option from the Main Menu.
F	Selects the Format option.
D	Selects the Date option.
3	Selects the (MMM-YY) option.
Enter	Formats only this cell.

Because the information on the first line of the schedule also represents the first payment, the formulas in this row will be a little bit different from those in subsequent rows.

8. Copy the beginning date onto the schedule:

Go to A9	Marks cell A9 by pointing.
Type `+C5`	Specifies the contents of cell C5 and places them here also. (If the contents of cell C5 change, the contents of this cell will also change.)
Enter	Enters the cell contents.

9. Format cells A9 and A10 for the date. You should already be at cell A9:

/R	Selects the Range option from the Main Menu.
F	Selects the Format option.
D	Selects the Date option.
3	Selects the (MMM:YY) option.
↓	Includes cell A10.
Enter	Executes the command.

10. In cell B9, enter the formula to calculate the monthly payment:

```
@PMT(C$3,C$2/12,C$4)
```

The first @PMT parameter gives the address of the cell containing the principal; the second gives the address of the cell containing the interest rate; the third gives the address of the cell containing the number of periods. Because each piece of information must be referenced in each row, absolute addressing is required; the absolute portion of each parameter freezes the location to a particular row. The formula can now be copied correctly.

11. In cell D9, enter the formula to calculate the interest portion of this payment. The amount must be divided by 12 to provide the amount of interest for this particular month rather than for the whole year:

```
+C$3*C$2/12
```

12. In cell C9, enter the formula to calculate the amount of the payment applied toward the principal:

```
+B9-D9
```

13. In cell E9, enter the formula to calculate the outstanding balance:

```
+C3-C9
```

14. Format the entire worksheet for two decimal positions.

/W	Selects Worksheet from the Main Menu.
G	Selects the Global option.
F	Selects the Format option.
F	Selects the Fixed command.
Enter	Takes the default and reformats the worksheet.

15. Copy the payment and principal formulas (which will stay the same) to the next line. (The cells will contain the correct results after the next steps are finished.)

Go to B9	Marks cell B9 by pointing.
/C	Selects the Copy command from the Main Menu.
Go to C9	Marks the last cell in the "From" range.
Enter	Establishes the "From" range.
Go to B10	Marks the beginning of the "To" range.
Enter	Copies the formulas.

16. In cell A10, enter the formula to advance the date incrementally:

```
+A9+31-@DAY(A9+31)+@DAY(A9)
```

This command lets you advance the date by the proper increment from one month to the next, as long as the loan begins on day 1 through 28. This formula can now be copied to the rest of the rows.

17. In cell D10, enter the new formula for calculating the interest:

```
+E9*C$2/12
```

You now have a formula that can be easily copied to other rows.

18. In cell E10, enter the new formula for calculating the outstanding balance:

```
+E9-C10
```

You now have a formula that can be easily copied to other rows.

19. Copy the formulas contained in row 10 down enough rows. (The number of rows depends on the maximum number of periods that you wish to allow in a loan; you'll copy this one down 40 rows. Remember, the more rows you have, the longer your worksheet will take to recalculate.)

Go to A10	Marks cell A10 by pointing.
/C	Selects the Copy command from the Main Menu.
Go to E10	Marks the last cell in the "From" range.
Enter	Establishes the "From" range.
Go to A11	Marks the first cell in the "To" range.
Type .	Nails down the beginning of the "To" range.
Pg Dn (2)	Moves the pointer down 40 rows.
Enter	Copies the formulas and recalculates the worksheet.

Now sit back and watch 1-2-3 do all the work! When you look at your worksheet, everything seems to have worked until about row 29—when negative numbers suddenly begin popping up in the worksheet. What happened? The loan was completely paid, but 1-2-3 wasn't aware of it, so the balance went from positive to negative.

Somehow you have to make 1-2-3 take appropriate action when the balance is completely paid to get rid of the negative numbers. Let's review the logic and determine which are the critical formulas.

The two most important calculations seem to be the outstanding balance and the payment. When the outstanding balance equals a few cents or less, the loan is paid off. (The outstanding balance never comes out to exactly zero because of rounding errors.) All other calculations are based on the contents of either the outstanding balance or the payment entry; if those fields zero out, the other fields will also contain zeros.

To examine the contents of a cell and check for a value, you must use the @IF function.

19.5. Enter the following instructions only if you are using a release of 1-2-3 prior to 2.2. Change the method of recalculation from automatic to manual to save waiting time.

/W	Selects the Worksheet option from the Main Menu.
G	Selects the Global option.
R	Selects the Recalculation option.
M	Selects the Manual command.

20. At cell E10, either re-enter the formula or use the Edit feature to enter changes. Your new formula should look like the following:

```
@IF(E9<=1,0,@ROUND(+E9-C10,2))
```

This formula can be translated as follows: If the result of the old balance is just a few cents, put a zero in this cell; otherwise, calculate the new rounded outstanding balance.

21. You also have to do something to make the payment column stop printing. At cell B10, either enter the new formula or press F2 to edit:

```
@IF(E9<=1,0,@PMT(C$3,C$2/12,C$4))
```

This formula can be translated as follows: If the contents of the outstanding balance cell are just a few cents, place a zero in the payment cell; otherwise, execute the payment function.

22. Copy these new formulas onto the rest of the worksheet, using the commands from step 19 above.

22.5. Enter this instruction only if you are using a release of 1-2-3 prior to 2.2. Recalculate the worksheet.

F9	Enters the Calc command (function key F9).

23. Center the information at the top of the spreadsheet to give it a more balanced appearance:

Go to A2	Marks cell A2 by pointing.
/M	Selects the Move command from the Main Menu.
Go to C5	Marks the first cell in the "From" range.
Enter	Establishes the "From" range.
Go to B2	Marks the first cell in the "To" range.
Enter	Executes the Move command.

24. Save the worksheet under the name LOANAMOR. It should look like the one in Figure 3.22.

Figure 3.22
LOANAMOR worksheet.

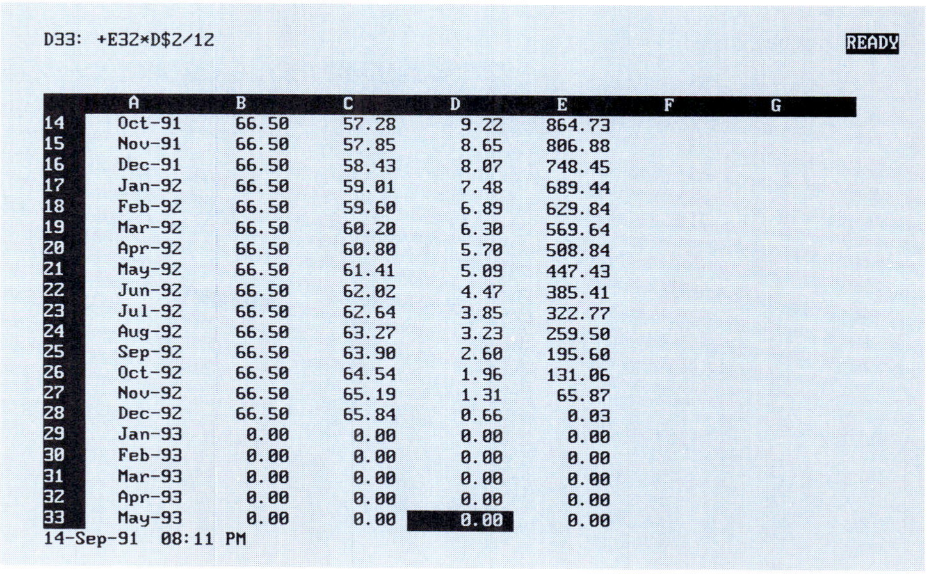

D33: +E32*D$2/12 READY

	A	B	C	D	E	F	G
14	Oct-91	66.50	57.28	9.22	864.73		
15	Nov-91	66.50	57.85	8.65	806.88		
16	Dec-91	66.50	58.43	8.07	748.45		
17	Jan-92	66.50	59.01	7.48	689.44		
18	Feb-92	66.50	59.60	6.89	629.84		
19	Mar-92	66.50	60.20	6.30	569.64		
20	Apr-92	66.50	60.80	5.70	508.84		
21	May-92	66.50	61.41	5.09	447.43		
22	Jun-92	66.50	62.02	4.47	385.41		
23	Jul-92	66.50	62.64	3.85	322.77		
24	Aug-92	66.50	63.27	3.23	259.50		
25	Sep-92	66.50	63.90	2.60	195.60		
26	Oct-92	66.50	64.54	1.96	131.06		
27	Nov-92	66.50	65.19	1.31	65.87		
28	Dec-92	66.50	65.84	0.66	0.03		
29	Jan-93	0.00	0.00	0.00	0.00		
30	Feb-93	0.00	0.00	0.00	0.00		
31	Mar-93	0.00	0.00	0.00	0.00		
32	Apr-93	0.00	0.00	0.00	0.00		
33	May-93	0.00	0.00	0.00	0.00		

14-Sep-91 08:11 PM

CAR LOAN EVALUATION WORKSHEET

In doing this project, you will practice the following skills:

1. Using mixed-cell addressing
2. Observing the effects of copying mixed-cell addresses

A friend of yours, Sandy, is trying to decide which vehicle to purchase, and a major part of the decision-making process involves the size of the monthly payment. Sandy wishes to finance the purchase over four years, but she also wants to easily change the loan length. The vehicles being considered, along with the amount to be financed, are as follows:

Conversion van	$18,000
Toyota pickup	8,000
Chrysler LeBaron	10,000
Ford Thunderbird	11,000

Sandy has also visited a number of financial institutions to find the interest rate offered. They are as follows:

Credit union	11%
Car manufacturer	15.5%
Bank 1	12.5%
Bank 2	13%

The spreadsheet shown in Figure 3.23 will let Sandy compare monthly payments.

The @PMT function is perfect for this application. Mixed-cell addressing (combining absolute and relative addressing) will also be useful.

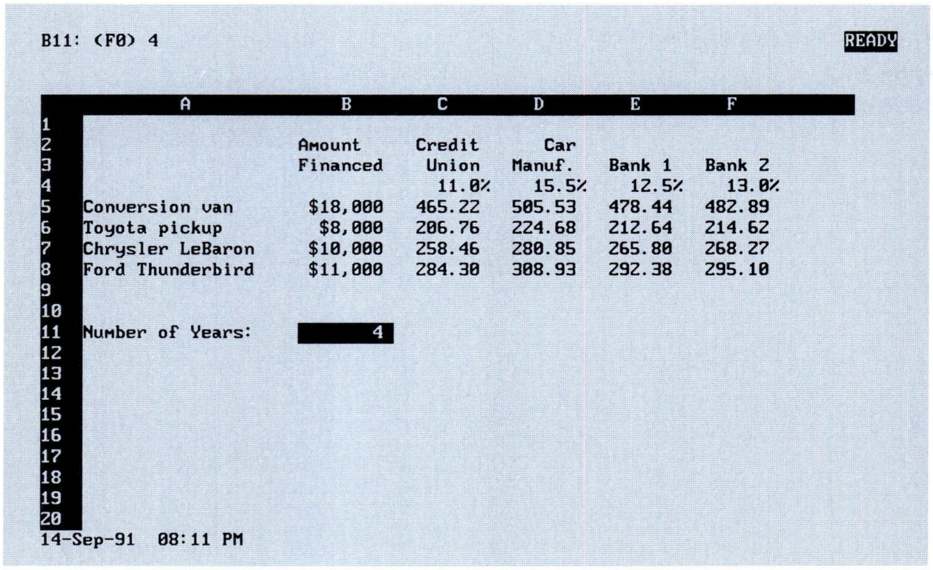
B11: (F0) 4 READY

	A	B	C	D	E	F
1						
2		Amount	Credit	Car		
3		Financed	Union	Manuf.	Bank 1	Bank 2
4			11.0%	15.5%	12.5%	13.0%
5	Conversion van	$18,000	465.22	505.53	478.44	482.89
6	Toyota pickup	$8,000	206.76	224.68	212.64	214.62
7	Chrysler LeBaron	$10,000	258.46	280.85	265.80	268.27
8	Ford Thunderbird	$11,000	284.30	308.93	292.38	295.10
9						
10						
11	Number of Years:	4				
12						
13						
14						
15						
16						
17						
18						
19						
20						

14-Sep-91 08:11 PM

Figure 3.23
Car loan spreadsheet.

Entering the spreadsheet involves a number of steps.

1. Go to column A and change its width to 20:

/W	Selects Worksheet from the Main Menu.
C	Selects the Column Width command.
S	Sets the column width.
20	Specifies the new width.
Enter	Executes the command.

2. Enter the label data at the indicated cell:

C1	Sandy's Loan Evaluation		
B2	Amount	F4	.13
C2	"Credit	A5	Conversion van
D2	"Car	A6	Toyota pickup
B3	Financed	A7	Chrysler LeBaron
C3	"Union	A8	Ford Thunderbird
D3	"Manuf.	B5	1800
E3	"Bank 1	B6	8000
F3	"Bank 2	B7	10000
C4	.11	B8	11000
D4	.155	A11	Number of Years
E4	.125	B11	4

3. Go to C4 and format the percentages:

/R	Selects the Range option from the Main Menu.
F	Selects the Format option.
P	Selects the Percent format.
1	Specifies the number of decimal positions.
Enter	Establishes the decimal positions.
Go to F4	Extends the range to cell F4.
Enter	Executes the format change.

4. Go to B5 and format the amount financed to currency:

/R	Selects Range from the Main Menu.
F	Selects the Format option.
C	Selects the Currency format.
0	Specifies the number of decimal positions.
Enter	Establishes the decimal positions.
Go to B8	Extends the range to cell B8.
Enter	Executes the format change.

5. Set the worksheet format to two decimal positions:

/W	Selects Worksheet from the Main Menu.
G	Selects the Global option.

F	Selects the Format option.
F	Selects the Fixed option.
Enter	Executes the format change.

6. Go to B11 and format the length of loan cell to fixed with zero decimal positions:

/R	Selects the Range option from the Main Menu.
F	Selects the Format option.
F	Selects the Fixed option.
0	Specifies the number of decimal positions.
Enter (2)	Establishes the decimal positions and executes the format change.

7. Enter the @PMT function for cell C5:

```
@PMT($B5,C$4/12,$B$11*12)
```

The principal entry $B5 keeps 1-2-3 returning to column B of "this" row. The interest entry C$4 keeps 1-2-3 returning to "this" column of row 4. It is divided by the 12 months of the year.

The periods entry $B$11 keeps 1-2-3 returning to cell B11. It is multiplied by the 12 monthly payments.

8. Go to C5 and copy this formula to the rest of the spreadsheet:

/C	Selects the Copy command from the Main Menu.
Enter	Establishes the "From" range.
Type .	Nails down the beginning of the "To" range.
Go to F8	Marks the end of the "To" range.
Enter	Executes the Copy command.

9. Save this worksheet to the file CARLOANS.

CHAPTER REVIEW

Lotus 1-2-3 provides several commands for controlling your worksheet environment. The Worksheet Zero command suppresses any cell that has a zero. The / System command temporarily leaves 1-2-3 and issues commands at the system (DOS) level. You can hide columns so that they appear neither on the screen nor in print. You can use the / Worksheet Status command to find circular references.

After a worksheet has been created, you will probably want to make a number of improvements to it. Making cell formulas self-documenting and easier to read can be accomplished easily by the use of range names. A single cell or a range of cells can be given a name and accessed under that name in such applications as calculations, uses of the Copy command, and printing a portion of your worksheet.

The Sort feature included with 1-2-3 lets you arrange data in an order that is logical for any given application. Another handy (and more common) feature is the Titles feature, which freezes column or row headings on the screen so that they are visible no matter where you are in the worksheet. This feature makes it much easier to track information in large worksheets.

Referencing a single cell over and over, even when the formula is copied down a column, is often useful. In 1-2-3, this technique is called absolute addressing. An entire address can be absolute, or only the row or column can be; the latter situation is referred to as a mixed-cell address.

The @IF function embeds logic within the worksheet that enables 1-2-3 to perform one action if a given condition is satisfied and another if it is not.

The macro feature of 1-2-3 stores instructions as keystrokes in a worksheet cell and later executes those instructions. The representations of the instructions must be preceded by a single quote ('); otherwise, the spreadsheet package will immediately start executing the instructions instead of storing them as text data. Once the keystrokes have been entered properly, a one-character alphabetic name preceded by a backslash (\) must be assigned to the cell with the keystrokes. The macro can now be executed by pressing Alt plus the alphabetic character.

Keystrokes are stored as they are used in entering a regular spreadsheet command, with the exception of a number of special commands such as the Enter keystroke. A representation of many keystrokes is enclosed in braces ({ }) and must be used for such a command.

KEY TERMS AND CONCEPTS

absolute addressing
absolute range name
#AND#
automatic recalculation
Both option
Cancel option
circular reference
Clear option
$columnrow
column$row
Data Range option
@DATE
Directory command
dummy column
dummy row
Erase option
Go option
GoTo command
Hide command
Horizontal option
@IF
@INT
Learn feature
learn range
macro
manual recalculation
minimal recalculation
mixed-cell address
Name Create option
Name Delete option
Name Labels option
Name Reset option
Name Table option
natural recalculation
#NOT#
#OR#
@PMT
Primary Key option
Quit option
range name
Range option
recalculation
relative addressing
Reset option
@ROUND
Secondary Key option
Sort command
Titles option
Vertical option
Zero command

CHAPTER QUIZ

Multiple Choice

1. Which of the following statements is false about range names?
   a. Range names can be used to enhance readability.
   b. Range names make cell formulas self-documenting.
   c. Using range names in formulas is better than using cell addresses.
   d. A range name created via the Labels option takes its name from the contents of an adjacent cell.
   e. All of the above statements are true.
   f. All of the above statements are true except d.

2. Which of the following statements is false about the Sort command?
   a. It is safest to save your worksheet before you do any sorting.
   b. Three levels of sorts or keys can be specified.
   c. All or part of a worksheet can be sorted.
   d. The Sort command allows you to rearrange data quickly within the worksheet.
   e. None of the above

3. Which of the following statements is false about an absolute address?
   a. It can have both the column and row absolute—CR.
   b. It can have only the column portion absolute—$CR.
   c. It can have only the row portion absolute—C$R.
   d. It can actually be a range name—$EXPENSES.
   e. All of the above responses are true.

4. Which command lets you freeze portions of the worksheet so that they can be used as column or row headings on the screen?
   a. Titles
   b. Labels
   c. Borders
   d. Legend
   e. None of the above

5. Which command lets you detect circular references within your worksheet?
   a. Worksheet Hide
   b. Directory Status
   c. Worksheet Status
   d. Worksheet Reference Hide
   e. None of the above responses is correct.

True/False

6. Using manual recalculation with Release 2.2 slows the operation of the spreadsheet.

7. The Titles command allows only horizontal text to be frozen on the screen.

8. Relative addressing is used whenever you want a formula that is to be copied down a column or across a row to refer to the identical cell.

9. It is impossible to create a mixed-range name by using a mixed-cell address.

10. The function @IF lets you embed sophisticated logic within your worksheet quickly.

Answers

1. e 2. b 3. e 4. a 5. c 6. t 7. f 8. f 9. t 10. t

Exercises

1. Define or describe each of the following:

a.	Range name	d.	Absolute address
b.	Titles	e.	Mixed-cell address
c.	Manual recalculation	f.	Date arithmetic

2. One of the greatest benefits of range names is that they allow a cell formula to be self-____________.

3. Positioning the pointer at a word (cell) and then making that word the range name is accomplished via the ____________ option of the Range Name Menu.

4. The Create and Delete commands reside in the ____________ Menu.

5. A hidden column is so indicated by a(n) ____________ when the / Worksheet Column Display command is issued.

6. The option of the Range Name submenu that is used to create a report of the various named ranges created within the worksheet is ____________.

7. The ____________ command resets the date or time without leaving 1-2-3.

8. A(n) ____________ key will have information sorted in order inside a(n) ____________ key.

9. The Sort option is found in the ____________ Menu.

10. Before you use the Sort command, it is probably wise to ____________ your worksheet file.

11. The ____________ command freezes rows and/or columns on the screen for use as headings.

12. ____________ addressing lets cell references change as they are copied; ____________ addressing maintains all or part of the cell address from one cell to the next.

13. ____________ cell addressing lets one part of the cell address change while keeping the other part intact.

14. With Lotus 1-2-3 Release 2.01, ____________ recalculation may cause you to wait for long spreadsheets to recalculate each time a cell is changed or a new cell is entered.

15. Press the function key ____________ when you wish 1-2-3 to recalculate a worksheet while you are in manual recalculation mode.

16. The message __________ appears at the bottom of the screen when a change has been made to the contents of some cell during manual recalculation mode.

17. The __________ function lets you embed logic in your worksheet.

18. The logical operators __________, __________, and __________ let you specify how comparisons are to interact.

19. The operators <, >, and <= are referred to as __________ operators.

20. The @DATE function is extremely useful because it lets you perform __________ to advance the date from one month to the next.

21. The __________ option lets 1-2-3 optimize how cells are recalculated.

22. The __________ format command changes the contents of cells to text.

23. The minimal recalculation method of 1-2-3 is disabled if either the __________ or __________ recalculation method is selected.

24. The keystrokes contained within a macro must always start with a(n) __________.

25. A macro name beginning with a backslash contains __________ characters.

26. A macro name may start with a(n) __________ and be followed by __________.

27. A macro executes from __________ to __________ in a cell.

28. One of the more common errors in building a macro is forgetting to enter the __________ command represented by a(n) __________.

29. The __________ option of the Range Name submenu is frequently used for creating a macro name from existing text.

30. Once the macro has been named, you can invoke it by holding down the __________ key and then some other alphabetic key or by entering the Run command.

COMPUTER EXERCISES

1. Ed has been approached to invest in a microcomputer store that will specialize in selling relatively low-cost microcomputers. Ed has done an excellent job of collecting information about this proposed business venture. He is interested in modeling the next 4 years of business activity. He wants a worksheet to present information in two basic areas—an input area and an income statement area—as appears below.* Apply the following criteria to the worksheet:
   a. The input area will start in column A. Set column A to a width of 25.
   b. The income statement will start in column F.
   c. Sales are expected to be 300 units the first year.

**Adapted from Arthur Andersen & Co. materials.*

d. Rent for each year is \$7500 per year.
e. Salaries are equal to 10% of sales (commission sales).
f. Supplies are 1.5% of sales.
g. Clerical costs are \$4000 the first year and 6% more each additional year.
h. Advertising costs are \$50,000 plus 7% of sales the first year, \$25,000 plus 7% of sales the second year, and 5% of sales in subsequent years.

INPUT AREA	
UNITS SOLD (YEAR 1)	300
COST PER UNIT	$650
ANNUAL SALES GROWTH	15.00%
ANNUAL PRICE REDUCTION	7.00%
PROFIT MARGIN	40.00%

ED'S MICROCOMPUTER SHOP

Projected Financial Statements

	1	2	3	4
Sales	325,000	347,588	371,745	397,581
Cost	195,000	208,553	223,047	238,549
Margin	130,000	139,035	148,698	159,032
Expenses:				
Advertising	72,750	49,331	18,587	19,879
Salaries	32,500	34,759	37,174	39,758
Rent	7,500	7,500	7,500	7,500
Supplies	4,875	5,214	5,576	5,964
Clerical	4,000	4,240	4,494	4,764
Other Costs	10,000	10,500	11,025	11,576
Total Expenses	131,625	111,544	84,357	89,441
Income b/f Taxes	(1,625)	27,491	64,341	69,591
Income Taxes	0	13,746	32,170	34,796
Net Income	(1,625)	13,746	32,170	34,796

i. There is a 50% tax rate.
j. Other costs are \$10,000 the first year and 5% more each additional year.
k. An @IF statement must be set up to check for a positive income before taxes.
l. The following range names will be used:

Units sold	UNITS
Costs per unit	COST
Annual growth	GROWTH
Annual price reduction	ANN.RED
Profit margin	MARGIN
First year sales	SALES

Year 1 net income	YEAR1
Year 2 net income	YEAR2
Year 3 net income	YEAR3
Year 4 net income	YEAR4

m. Column F will be set to a width of 16.
n. The global column will be set to a width of 11.
o. For year 1, the following sales formula will be used:

```
$UNITS*(COST/(1-$MARGIN))
```

p. For years 2–4, the following sales formula will be used:

```
+SALES*(1+$GROWTH)*(1-$ANN.RED)
```

q. The following is the cost formula for year 1:

```
$SALES*(1-$MARGIN)
```

r. Generate a report of named ranges and print it. Save this worksheet to a file called CH3EX1.

2. Retrieve the worksheet CH3EX2. Locate and correct all circular references contained in the worksheet. Be sure to use the GoTo command to position the pointer directly to each circular reference once you have located it.

3. Retrieve the CH1EX5 file. Use the 1-2-3 Sort command to place the rows of the worksheet in order by the names of the sales representatives. Don't include any total or heading lines in the sort. Save the sorted worksheet to a file called CH3EX3.

4. Load the worksheet CH1EX8. Set up the worksheet so that any additional monthly sales data are automatically included in the total for each region. Also set up the vertical totals such that a new region can be added at the bottom of the column. Enter sales for April and May. (You supply them.) A new region, F, is added in March. The sales figures are $4500 for March and $3700 for April for the new region.

5. Retrieve the CH2EX2 worksheet. To the right of the worksheet, enter a Final % column as depicted in Figure 3.24. Take the students' total earned points and divide them by the total possible points to calculate the current percent grade. Make certain you use some form of absolute cell reference. Save this worksheet using the name CH3EX5.

6. Develop a loan amortization schedule for a 15-year mortgage. The principal is $20,000. The interest rate is 13.5%. Select the beginning date. Each line in the amortization schedule should have the month, payment amount, principal reduction amount, amount applied toward interest, and remaining outstanding balance. [Remember that you must multiply the periods (years) by 12 when dealing with months.]

   In solving this problem and looking at the worksheet, you must use the Horizontal Titles option to keep the column headings on the screen.

Figure 3.24
Student grade worksheet.

A1: (D1) [W15] @INT(@NOW) READY

	A	B	C	D	E	F	G
1	15-Aug-91						
2		Grading Template					
3							
4	NAME		Exam I	Anot. Bib	Exam II	Final %	
5	POSSIBLE POINTS		150	45	130	325	
6	---------------		----------	----------	----------	----------	
7	Student 1		113	44	110	82.15%	
8	Student 2		116	42	90	76.31%	
9	Student 3		129	42	85	78.77%	
10	Student 4		133	44	125	92.92%	
11	Student 5		121	42	76	73.54%	
12	Student 6		139	41	115	90.77%	
13	Student 7		120	42	115	85.23%	
14	---------------		----------	----------	----------	----------	
15	Average		124	42	102	82.81%	
16	% of Tot. Pnts.		82.67%	93.33%	78.46%		
17	High Grade		139	44	125		
18	Low Grade		113	41	76		
19	Std. Deviation		9	1	17		
20	Variance		77	1	291		

15-Aug-91 09:36 AM

You must also design the worksheet so that it quits calculating and outputting negative numbers when the principal is completely paid.

Print this worksheet using the Borders option. This option will print the column headings at the top of each page of the printout, making the output more readable. Save this worksheet under the name CH3EX6.

7. Develop a worksheet that allows users to investigate a number of different principal amounts plotted against a number of different interest rates for home mortgages. Start with principal amounts of $20,000, $40,000, $60,000, $80,000, $100,000, and $120,000. Use interest rates of 11.5%, 12.5%, 13%, 14%, 14.5%, 15%, and 15.5%. Refer to the Car Loan Evaluation Worksheet for ideas. The loans are all for 25 years. Save this file using the name CH3EX7.

8. Load the CH2EX1 worksheet containing the payroll information. Sort it alphabetically by rate of pay—that is, so that rate of pay is the primary key and last name is the secondary key. Save this file using the name CH3EX8.

9. Load the CH3EX6 worksheet. Move the input labels to column A. Hide the Total Payment column. Print the first 3 years of payments.

10. Create a worksheet like that depicted in Figure 3.25. Save the worksheet to the file CH3EX10. Set column B to a width of 20. The extension is calculated by multiplying the units cells times the price cells. The commission is calculated as follows: Sales equal to or greater than $2000 receive a 12% commission; sales equal to or greater than $1000 and less than $2000 receive an 8% commission; all other sales receive a 4% commission.

11. Retrieve the CH3EX5 worksheet. Change it so that the letter grade is automatically entered, via a nested @IF function, based on the final

Figure 3.25

A1: READY

	A	B	C	D	E	F
1			Mort's Manufacturing			
2			Weekly Sales Report			
3						Sales
4	Employee	Item Description	Price	Units	Ext.	Comm.
5						
6	Fred					
7		Table 234	$25.00	10	$250.00	$10.00
8		Chair 23	$95.00	18	$1,710.00	$136.80
9		Desk 245	$350.00	5	$1,750.00	$140.00
10		Filing cabinet 23	$175.00	3	$525.00	$21.00
11	Mary					
12		Table 234	$25.00	1	$25.00	$1.00
13		Chair 23	$95.00	30	$2,850.00	$342.00
14		Desk 245	$350.00	8	$2,800.00	$336.00
15		Filing cabinet 23	$175.00	15	$2,625.00	$315.00
16						
17						
18						
19						
20						

14-Sep-91 08:21 PM

Figure 3.26

A1: (D1) [W14] @INT(@NOW) READY

	A	C	D	E	G	H
1	14-Sep-91					
2		Grading Template				
3						
4	NAME	Exam I	Anot. Bib	Exam II	Final %	Grade
5	POSSIBLE POINT	150	45	130	325	
6	----------	----------	----------	----------	----------	----------
7	Student 1	113	44	110	82.15%	B
8	Student 2	116	42	90	76.31%	C
9	Student 3	129	42	85	78.77%	C
10	Student 4	133	44	125	92.92%	A
11	Student 5	121	42	76	73.54%	C
12	Student 6	139	41	115	90.77%	A
13	Student 7	120	42	115	85.23%	B
14	----------	----------	----------	----------	----------	----------
15	Average	124	42	102		
16	% of Tot. Pnts	82.67%	93.33%	78.46%		
17	High Grade	139	44	125		
18	Low Grade	113	41	76		
19	Std. Deviation	9	1	17		
20	Variance	77	1	291		

14-Sep-91 08:19 PM

percent figure (Figure 3.26). Use the table below for generating the letter grade. Save the worksheet to the file CH3EX11.

90% and above	A
80%–89%	B
70%–79%	C
60%–69%	D
Less than 69%	F

12. To complete the following exercise, retrieve the CH2EX1 (payroll) worksheet file. Create an area called MACROS that will hold any macros

you build. Be sure to position this area in the lower right-hand quadrant of your worksheet.

a. Create a macro that you can use to add a blank row to receive a new employee.
b. Create a macro that, after you have positioned the pointer to the overtime rate cell for the new employee, will automatically position to the same cell of the prior row and copy the formulas for the overtime rate, gross pay, and net pay cells to the next row.
c. Save the worksheet file using the name CH3EX12.

4

GRAPHING WITH LOTUS 1-2-3

CHAPTER OBJECTIVES

After completing this chapter, you should be able to

- ***Use the various options contained in the Graph Menu***
- ***Build a graph***
- ***Generate various types of graphs using 1-2-3***
- ***Save graph settings for later use***
- ***Use additional items for graphs, such as Titles and Legends***
- ***Generate a table of graph names***
- ***Save a graph to disk for later printing***
- ***Use the PrintGraph utility***

This chapter is divided into three parts: The first deals with the various options provided in the Graph Menu, the second deals with generating graphs, and the third deals with printing graphs.

The information presented in the last three chapters demonstrates how 1-2-3 can manipulate information arithmetically through the use of formulas for processing data that have been entered on the worksheet. The worksheet is automatically updated and completely recalculated whenever information is entered in a cell, allowing you to play a number of what-if games to see how a change will affect the rest of the worksheet.

These characteristics alone may satisfy your needs when a worksheet containing small amounts of data is being used, but what happens when you have large amounts of data or when you cannot make sense of the small amount of data that is in the worksheet? The answer lies in the old maxim "a picture is worth a thousand words." Lotus lets you, with only a little effort, depict the data that have been entered in a worksheet on the screen in the form of a graph (Figure 4.1).

If you want to use this feature, your computer must have either an EGA, VGA, or color graphics board and a color (or regular) monitor or a board that makes it possible to display graphics on a monochrome monitor. If you don't have this hardware, your computer will only beep when you try to display the graph; in this case, you must save the graph onto a file and then print the graph via the PrintGraph feature of the Lotus Access System.

If your computer has both a monochrome monitor and a color monitor attached to it, 1-2-3 will use the monochrome monitor to display the worksheet and the color monitor to display the graph.

STEPS IN GENERATING AND PRINTING A GRAPH

Making and printing a graph with 1-2-3 involves the following easy steps:

1. Select and load in a worksheet file from disk or use the current worksheet.
2. Select the Graph Menu via the command sequence / Graph.
3. Select the type of graph to be used (line, bar, XY, stacked-bar, or pie).
4. Tell 1-2-3 which data ranges are involved in the graph (up to six ranges of data can be depicted in a graph).
5. Tell 1-2-3 to include any labels or extra information.
6. Display the graph on the screen.
7. Make any changes in the graph.
8. Save the graph onto disk for later printing, if desired (in which case 1-2-3 will place a .PIC extension on the graph file).
9. Save the worksheet to disk.
10. Print the graph with PrintGraph.

With a little practice, you can go through this process easily in 3 to 5 minutes. You can also enter what-if changes in your data and automatically regraph the new information via the **F10 (Graph) key,** without going back through the Graph Menu.

GRAPH MENU (/G)

Invoke the **Graph Menu** by entering a / Graph command sequence. Unless you wish to add information to a "naked" graph, you can build the entire graph from this menu, without entering any submenus; submenus let you dress up a

Figure 4.1
(a) Exploded pie graph; (b) side-by-side bar graph.

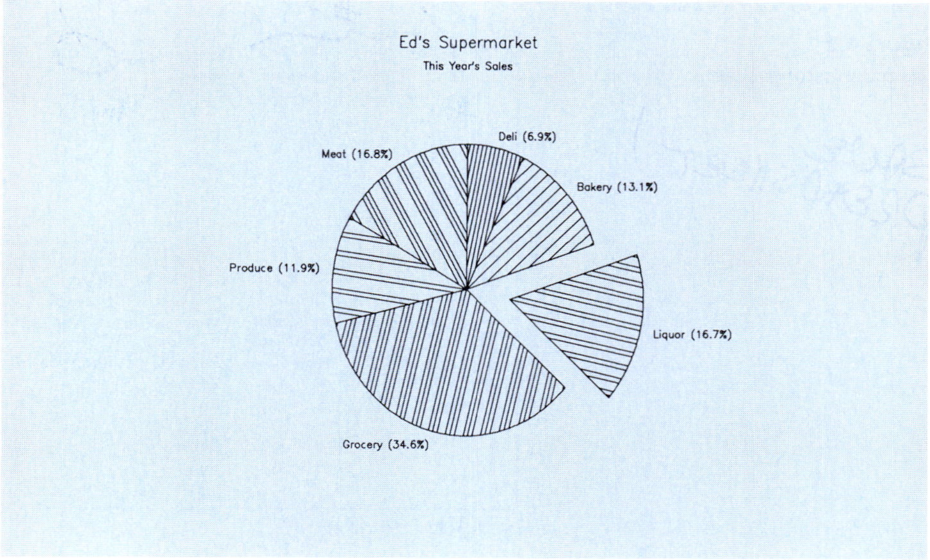

(a)

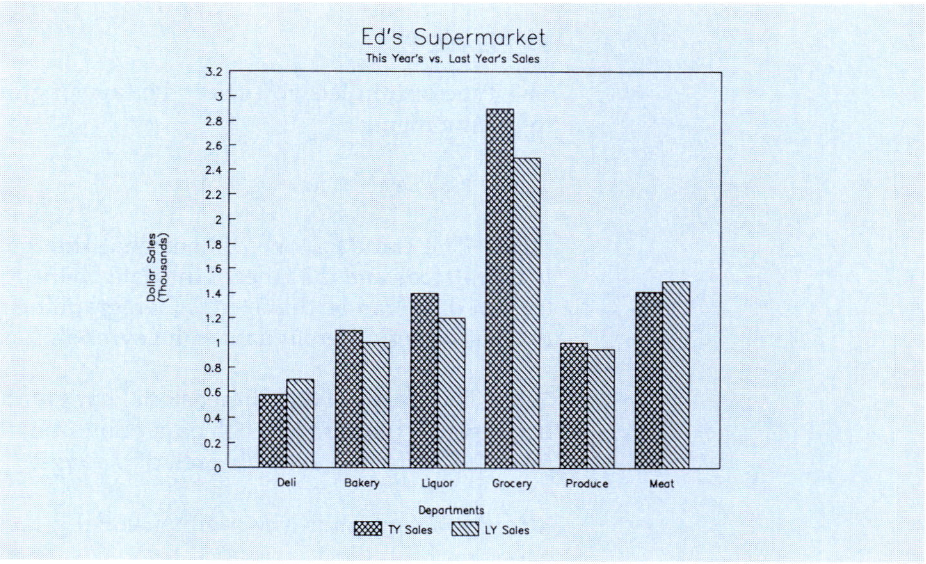

(b)

graph with meaningful, descriptive data. The appendix includes a chart of the Graph command structure.

Pressing the command sequence / Graph displays the following menu:

```
Type X  A B C D E F  Reset  View  Save  Options  Name  Group  Quit
```

Along with the Graph Menu appears a graph-settings sheet like that depicted in Figure 4.2. This settings sheet has data that have been generated from any commands in the Graph Menu that have been executed. It is an excellent summary of all the actions that you have taken in building a graph. The Graph Menu options work as follows.

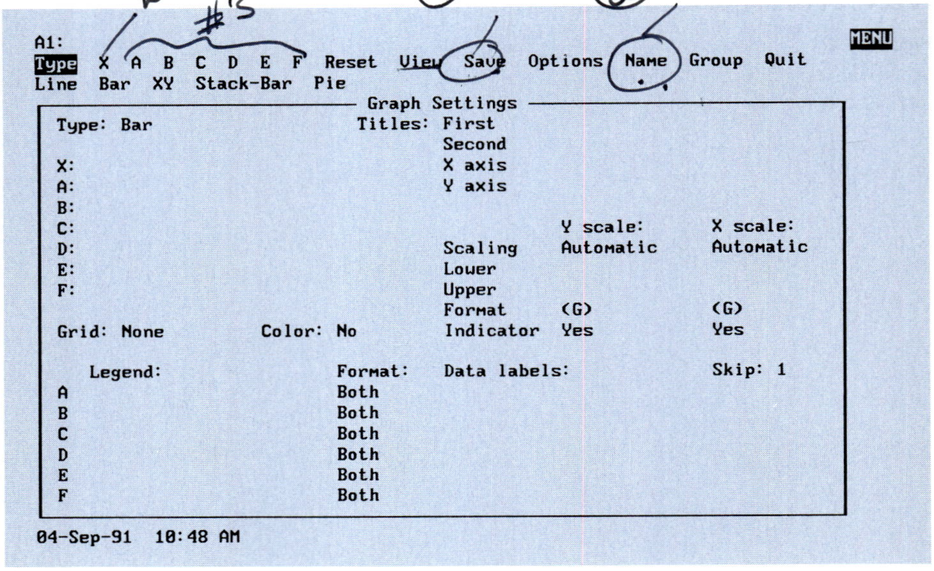

Figure 4.2
The graph-settings sheet.

TYPE (/GT)

The **Type option** lets you select the type of graph you wish to display from the following menu:

```
Line   Bar   XY   Stack-BAR   Pie
```

Line The standard one-dimensional **line graph** presents the data on the **Y (vertical) axis** and the label of the data on the **X (horizontal) axis.** Up to six lines (sets of data) can be depicted. When graphing multiple sets of data, 1-2-3 automatically uses different data-point symbols for each set.

Bar The standard one-dimensional **bar graph** (when multiple data ranges are used) places the bars for each data point from the data ranges side-by-side. Different shadings are used for each data range.

XY An **XY graph** is a two-dimensional graph with a set of data points referenced on both the X axis and the Y axis. For example, to graph a company's profits compared to inflation over a period of years, you would select this option. An example is included later in the chapter.

Stacked-Bar A **stacked-bar graph** stacks multiple ranges of data on top of each other instead of next to one another. Different shadings are given to each range of data to differentiate among them.

Pie The **pie chart,** as the name implies, is a circle divided into wedges; it is used to depict a single data range. Because of its nature, the pie chart cannot depict multiple data ranges.

X (/GX)

The **X option** defines a range of the worksheet to be used for a horizontal label of the graph. When you take the X option, you must give the addresses of or point to the cell(s) containing the label information. Often, these are row or column labels from the worksheet.

ABCDEF (/GA . . .)

The **ABCDEF options** specify up to six data ranges to be depicted on your graph. The first data range must be labeled A, the second B, and so on. You can enter the cell addresses or point to the cells to be included in each data range; press Enter when you have finished.

Lotus remembers each data range you specify; to respecify an existing range, reselect it and specify a new data range. To cancel a data range, use the Reset option. Lotus requires you to define at least one data range, regardless of the type of graph.

RESET (/GR)

The **Reset option** selects the Reset Menu for the graphing function. The following Reset commands cancel either the entire graph or portions of it.

```
Graph  X  A B C D E F  Quit
```

Graph The Graph command cancels the entire graph. If this option is taken, the entire graph will have to be respecified to 1-2-3.

X The X command cancels the labeling of the graph's horizontal axis.

ABCDEF The ABCDEF commands cancel one or more data ranges of a graph. If you cancel all of them, 1-2-3 acts as though you have not specified a graph.

Quit The Quit command returns you to the Graph Menu.

VIEW (/GV)

The **View option** displays the currently specified graph on the monitor, after which you can press any key to return to the Graph Menu.

You can also display a graph, showing the specified settings, while you are in the worksheet in READY mode. To do so, simply press F10, the Graph function key. Return to the worksheet by pressing any key.

SAVE (/GS)

The **Save option** stores the currently specified graph onto a disk file. Lotus refers to this file as a "graph" or "picture" file and gives it a .PIC extension.

Anyone with a regular monochrome monitor must use the Save command to save a graph file because this type of monitor cannot display a graph. The file must then be printed using the PrintGraph option from the Lotus Access System Menu.

OPTIONS (/GO)

The **Options option** lets you dress up a graph according to the following menu:

```
Legend  Format  Titles  Grid  Scale  Color  B&W  Data  Labels  Quit
```

Legend The **Legend command** lets you specify characters for the legend to be used to represent the various ranges of data. Up to 19 characters can be shown, but as few as possible should be used. The following menu is displayed:

```
A B C D F
```

From this menu, you select the appropriate data range, and 1-2-3 displays the current legend for it. To change the legend, enter the new characters; to leave it unchanged, press Enter. The legend is displayed beneath the X-axis title entry.

Format The **Format command** changes how the specified graph is displayed—that is, what characters are used to represent the displayed data points and how those data points are connected on the graph. The following menu is displayed:

```
Graph  A B C D E F  Quit
```

Graph This selection determines how the data are to be presented on the graph. The following menu is displayed:

```
Lines  Symbols  Both  Neither
```

- *Lines* connects each data point within a range with a line.
- *Symbols* displays each data point in a data range with the same character or symbol.
- *Both* uses both lines and symbols in representing data points in a data range.
- *Neither* uses neither lines nor symbols, requiring the legends for data points to be specified in the Legend commands.

ABCDEF This selection lets you choose a data range. When you have done so, 1-2-3 prompts you in exactly the same way it does when you select the Graph option in this menu.

Quit This returns you to the Options Menu.

Titles The **Titles command** labels the graph with up to two lines of text; these will appear at the top of the graph. You can also use it to enter a one-line text label for each axis. The following menu is displayed:

```
First  Second  X Axis  Y Axis
```

First This selection lets you enter the first line of text that is to be placed at the top of the page.

Second This selection lets you enter the second line of text that is to be placed (below the first line) at the top of the page.

X Axis This selection lets you enter one line of text to be displayed along the X (horizontal) axis.

Y Axis This selection lets you enter one line of text to be displayed along the Y (vertical) axis.

Grid The **Grid command** lets you choose grid lines for display on a graph. It displays the following menu:

```
Horizontal  Vertical  Both  Clear
```

Horizontal This selection places horizontal grid lines on the graph when it is displayed. Grid lines make the relative size of plotted points clearer.

Vertical This selection places vertical grid lines on the graph when it is displayed.

Both This selection places both horizontal and vertical grid lines on the graph when it is displayed.

Clear This selection clears any grid lines from the display.

Scale The **Scale command** sets the scaling and format of a graph for either the X or Y axis. When you have selected the axis, the following menu is displayed.

```
Automatic  Manual  Lower  Upper  Format  Indicator  Quit
```

Automatic With this selection, 1-2-3 automatically calculates the scaling on the graphs to keep the entire graph visible on the display.

Manual With this, you select the scaling.

Lower/Upper You must use these options if the Manual command was selected. They allow you to choose upper and lower scale limits, giving you more control over how data are presented. Small differences can be made to seem much greater.

Format This selection determines how numeric data will be used with scaling. Numbers will appear on the graph according to the format selected.

Indicator This selection turns on or off the scale indicators on a graph when it is displayed to the screen via the View command.

Quit This returns you to the Options Menu.

Color/B&W The **Color command** displays the information in colors that have been preselected by 1-2-3. The **B&W command** displays the data in standard black and white, with cross-hatching on the bars.

Data/Labels The **Data command** lets you specify a range of cells whose contents will be used to label the data points of a data range (A to F). First choose the range (A to F); then specify the cells to be included in the range; then, for line and XY graphs, select the alignment of the labels in relation to the data points (Centered, Left, Above, Right, Below), using the **Labels command.** Select Quit when you are finished to return to the Graph Menu. The next time the graph is displayed, the cell contents of the specified range(s) will be displayed as data points.

NAME (/GN)

The **Name option** loads in graph settings that were previously saved using the Create option of the Graph Name Menu, resets the graph options to those for this graph, and then draws the graph using the specified features. The Name option displays the following menu:

```
Use   Create   Delete   Reset   Table
```

Use The **Use command** retrieves graph file settings that are contained in RAM memory. To do this, enter the name or point to the file with the pointer. The selected graph will then be displayed.

Create The **Create command** saves the settings of the current graph. The graph can later be accessed via the Use command.

Delete The **Delete command** deletes any graph settings contained in memory. To do this, enter or point to the graph name and press Enter.

Reset The **Reset command** erases all named graphs from the computer's memory.

2.2

Table The **Table command** constructs a report of all the archived graphs in your worksheet. The pointer location is used as the upper left-hand corner of the report. Because the report actually takes up space within the worksheet, be sure that you are in an unused area; otherwise, a valuable portion of your worksheet model may be lost.

2.2

GROUP (/GG)

The **Group command** lets you specify all data ranges (A to F) and the X-label range at one time when these ranges are in adjacent rows or columns. Once you have specified the block of cells to be included in the range, 1-2-3 responds with the menu

```
Columnwise   Rowwise
```

You must tell 1-2-3 whether it is to divide the data in the range by columns or rows. If, for example, you had a worksheet like that depicted in Figure 4.3, to develop a graph of last year's and this year's sales data and have the department names at the bottom of the graph, you would include those highlighted cells in the range after the Group command was executed. In Figure 4.3, for example, a columnwise interpretation is to be used. The resulting graph is shown in Figure 4.4.

Quit The **Quit command** returns you to the Main Menu of 1-2-3.

GENERATING GRAPHS

SIMPLE BAR GRAPHS

This first exercise generates the simple bar graph shown in Figure 4.5, using the This Year information contained in the COMPSALS worksheet.

Figure 4.3

The cells to be included in the / Graph Group command.

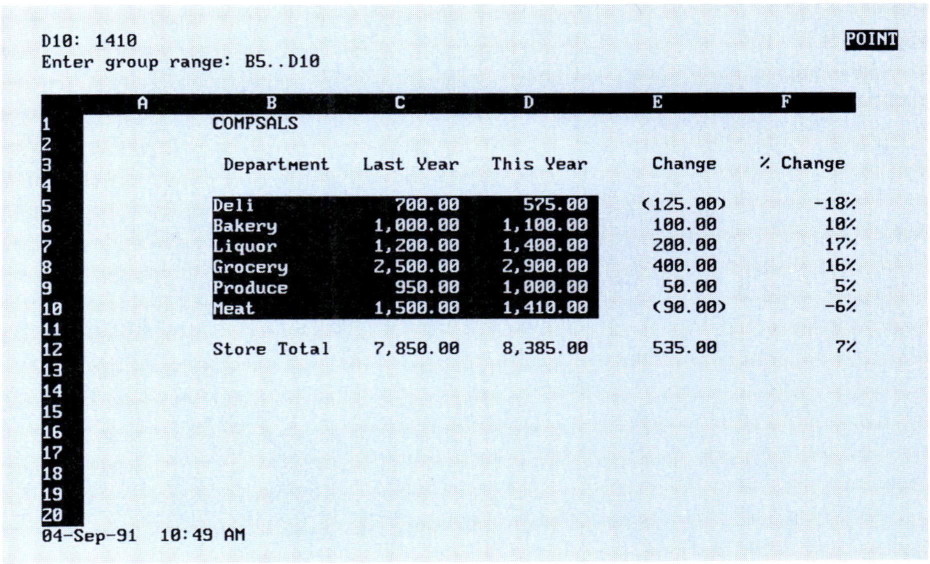

D10: 1410 POINT
Enter group range: B5..D10

	A	B	C	D	E	F
1		COMPSALS				
2						
3		Department	Last Year	This Year	Change	% Change
4						
5		Deli	700.00	575.00	(125.00)	-18%
6		Bakery	1,000.00	1,100.00	100.00	10%
7		Liquor	1,200.00	1,400.00	200.00	17%
8		Grocery	2,500.00	2,900.00	400.00	16%
9		Produce	950.00	1,000.00	50.00	5%
10		Meat	1,500.00	1,410.00	(90.00)	-6%
11						
12		Store Total	7,850.00	8,385.00	535.00	7%
13						
14						
15						
16						
17						
18						
19						
20						

04-Sep-91 10:49 AM

Figure 4.4

The graph generated by the / Graph Group command.

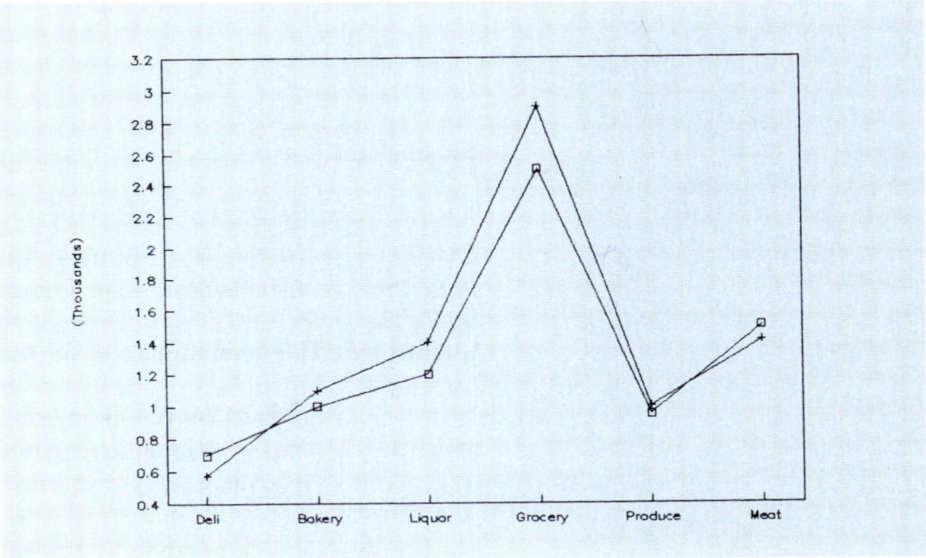

1. Load in the COMPSALS worksheet:

/F	Selects the File Menu from the Main Menu.
R	Selects the Retrieve option.
Type `COMPSALS`	Identifies the worksheet (or you can point to the worksheet name).
Enter	Executes the command.

2. Select the Graph Menu and tell 1-2-3 to generate a bar graph:

/G	Selects the Graph Menu from the Main Menu.
T	Selects the Type option.
B	Generates a bar chart.

Figure 4.5
Simple bar graph of the This Year information from the COMPSALS worksheet as it appears when printed.

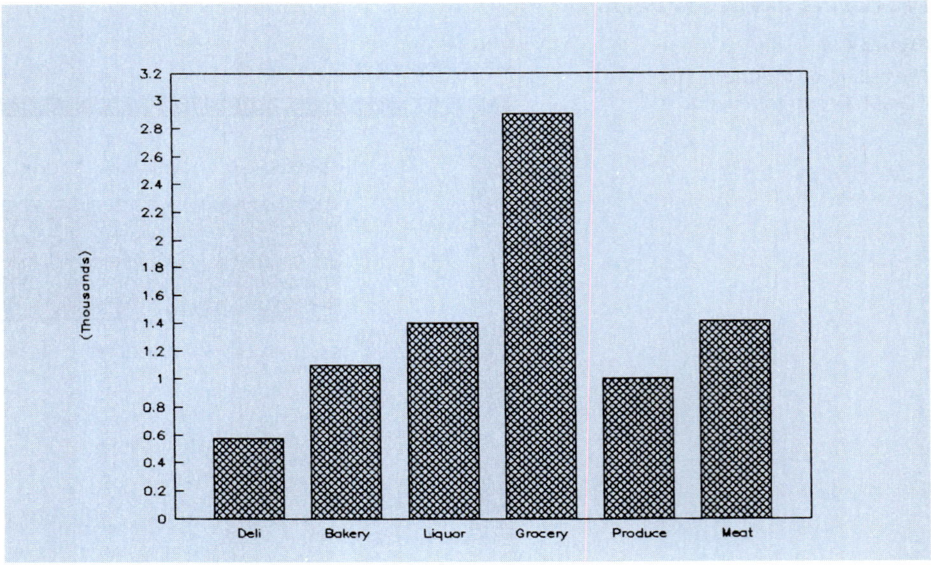

3. Establish the X-axis label range (department names):

X	Selects the X-axis label range.
B5.B10	Marks the range by pointing or entering addresses.
Enter	Establishes the label range.

4. Establish the This Year column as the A data range:

A	Selects the A data range.
D5.D10	Marks the range by pointing or entering addresses.
Enter	Establishes the range.

5. Execute the View command (V) to display the graph (Figure 4.5). The 1-2-3 program created the scale along the Y axis based on the data (option A) being graphed. Press any key to return to the Graph Menu.

ENTERING TITLES

Although the graph in the just-completed exercise looks okay, if you want it to mean anything at a later date, you should probably label it. Lotus lets you put a two-line title at the top of the graph and a one-line title on each axis. In this exercise, you will label a bar chart (Figure 4.6) as follows:

Title Line 1	`Ed's Supermarket`
Title Line 2	`This Year's Sales`
X axis	`Departments`
Y axis	`Dollar Sales`

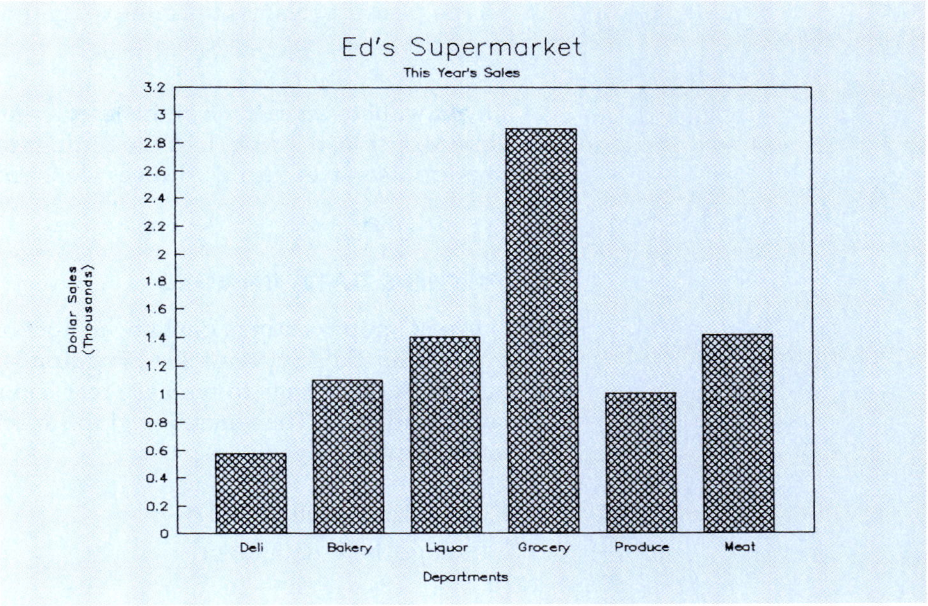

Figure 4.6
Printed bar graph of this year's COMPSALS sales, with graph and axis titles in place.

1. Use the Graph Options Menu to place labels on the bar chart:

O	Selects the Options Menu from the Graph Menu.
T	Selects the Titles option.
F	Selects the First line option.
Type `Ed's Supermarket`	Specifies the title.
Enter	Enters the title.
T	Selects the Titles option.
S	Selects the Second line option.
Type `This Year's Sales`	Specifies the title.
Enter	Enters the title.
T	Selects the Titles option.
X	Selects the X-axis title option.
Type `Departments`	Specifies the title.
Enter	Enters the title.
T	Selects the Titles option.
Y	Selects the Y-axis title option.
Type `Dollar Sales`	Specifies the title.
Enter	Enters the title.
Q	Quits Options and returns to the Graph Menu.

Ch4-ex1-42

2. Press V to view the graph. It should now look like the one in Figure 4.6.
3. Press any key to return to the Graph Menu.
4. Save the graph's settings onto the worksheet for later retrieval:

N	Selects the Name option of the Graph Menu.
C	Selects the Create option.

Type TYSALE	Names the group of graph settings.
Enter	Enters the settings.

If you want to take a look at this graph again, you don't have to re-enter all keystrokes; just load TYSALE as the settings to generate a graph. These graph settings are also saved to a worksheet file when a save operation is performed.

CHANGING DATA RANGES

The current graph settings contain instructions for creating a graph of this year's sales for Ed's Supermarket. To graph last year's sales, you will have to change the A data range to the Last Year column and put Last Year's Sales in the second title line. The remaining graph specifications can be left unchanged. The steps are as follows:

1. Get to the Graph Menu.
2. Change the A data range:

A	Selects the A option.
Backspace	Cancels the existing range.
C10.C5	Marks the A data range by pointing or entering addresses.
Enter	Establishes the range.

3. Change *This* to *Last* in the second title line:

O	Selects the Options Menu from the Graph Menu.
T	Selects the Titles option.
S	Selects the Second line option, displaying This Year's Sales.
Home	Moves the pointer under the *T* in *This*.
Del (4)	Deletes the word *This*.
Type Last	Inserts the word *Last*.
Enter	Enters the changed title.
Q	Quits Options and returns to the Graph Menu.

4. Press V to view the changed graph. It should now look like Figure 4.7.
5. Press any key to return to the Graph Menu.
6. Save these worksheet settings for later use:

N	Selects the Name option from the Graph Menu.
C	Selects the Create option.
Type LYSALE	Names the group of graph settings.
Enter	Executes this command.

SIDE-BY-SIDE BAR GRAPHS

You now have two bar graphs showing sales for this year and last year. Ed, however, wants to compare the 2 years in one bar graph. Because you saved the settings of the TYSALE bar graph, all you have to do is load in those graph

Figure 4.7

Printed bar graph of last year's COMPSALS sales, with graphs and axis titles in place.

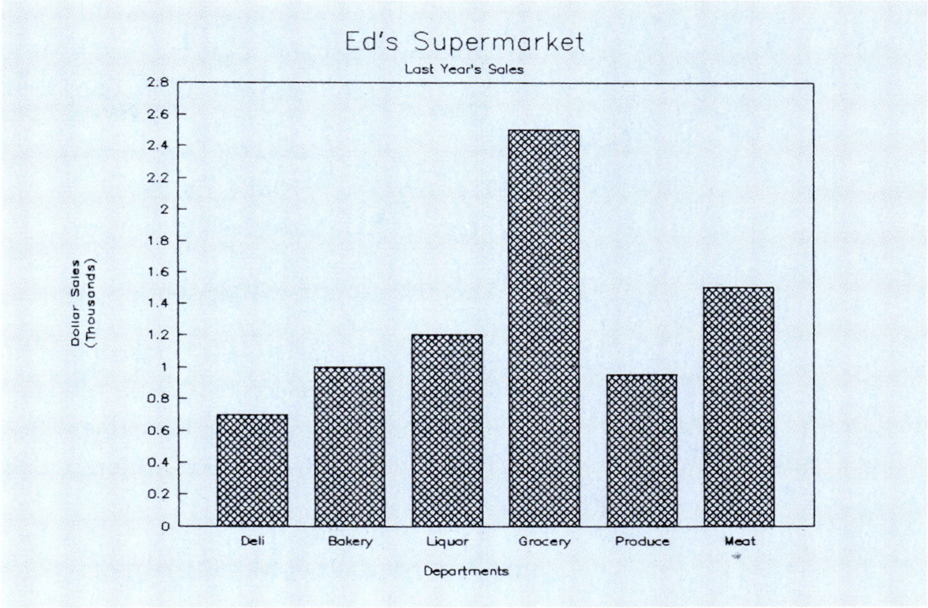

settings and change them in accordance with Ed's request. The following steps are required:

1. Get to the Graph Menu.
2. Replace the current graph settings with those contained in TYSALE (and stored in the spreadsheet):

N	Selects the Name option from the Graph Menu.
U	Selects the Use option, letting you replace current graph settings with previously stored settings.
Type `TYSALE`	Specifies the graph settings to be stored.
Enter	Executes the command.

3. The screen now displays the graph TYSALE. Press any key to return to the Graph Menu.
4. Establish the B range as the numbers in the Last Year column:

B	Selects the B data range.
C5.C10	Marks the B data range by pointing or entering addresses.
Enter	Establishes the range.

5. Change the second title line of the graph:

O	Selects Options from the Graph Menu.
T	Selects the Titles option.
S	Selects the Second line option.
←	Positions the pointer to the right of the *S* in *Sales*.
Type `vs. Last Year's`	Identifies new characters to be inserted.
Enter	Enters the new second title line.
Q	Quits Options and returns to the Graph Menu.

6. Press V to view the graph. It should now look like Figure 4.8.
7. Press any key to return to the Graph Menu.
8. Save the graph onto disk, so it can be printed later:

S	Takes the Save option.
Type `LYTYSALE`	Names the graph.
Enter	Executes the command.

9. Save these graph settings for later use:

N	Selects the Name option from the Graph Menu.
C	Selects the Create option.
Type `LYTYSALE`	Specifies the name of the graph settings to be saved.
Enter	Records these settings to the worksheet.

CONVERTING TO LINE GRAPHS

Ed would also like to see the bar graph information depicted as a line graph. The following steps are involved.

1. From the Graph Menu, change the graph type:

T	Selects the Type option from the Graph Menu.
L	Generates a line graph.

2. Press V to view the graph. It should look like Figure 4.9.

ENTERING LEGENDS

Now Ed is confused because he can't tell the difference between this year's sales and last year's sales on the line graph. You can solve this problem by providing a legend that tells which symbols represent which data ranges.

The following steps begin from the Graph Menu:

1. Add the legends:

O	Selects Options from the Graph Menu.
L	Selects the Legend option.
A	Selects the A data range to hold the first legend text.
Type `TY Sales`	Identifies the text of the legend.
Enter	Enters the text.
L	Selects the Legend option.
B	Selects the B data range to hold the second legend text.
Type `LY Sales`	Identifies the text of the legend.
Enter	Enters the text.
Q	Leaves Options and returns to the Graph Menu.

2. Press V to view the graph. It should look like Figure 4.10.

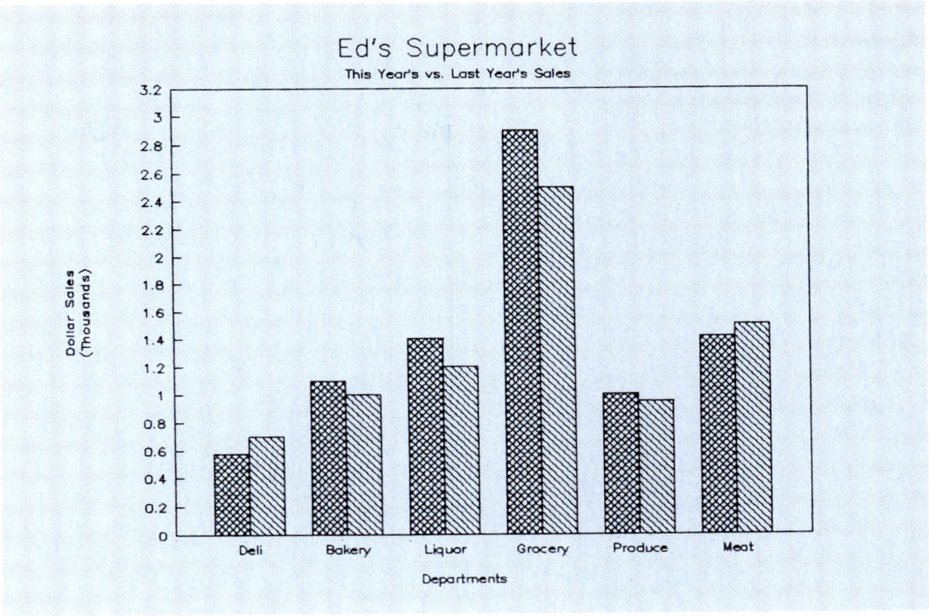

Figure 4.8
Printed side-by-side bar graphs of COMPSALS sales.

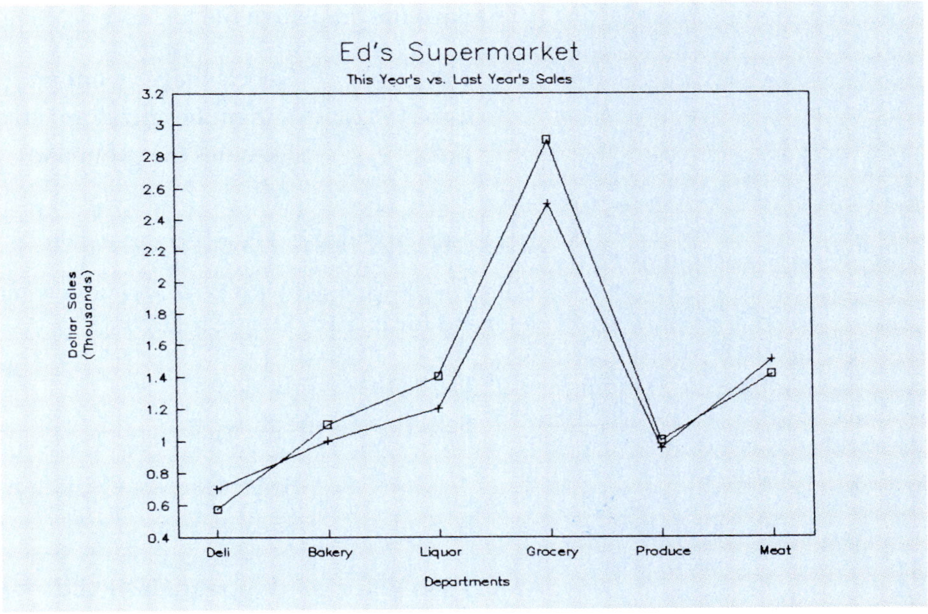

Figure 4.9
Printed line graph of this year's and last year's COMPSALS sales.

3. Press any key to return to the Graph Menu.
4. Save these graph settings:

N	Selects the Name option from the Graph Menu.
C	Selects the Create option.
Type `LYTYLINE`	Names the graph settings.
Enter	Saves the graph settings.

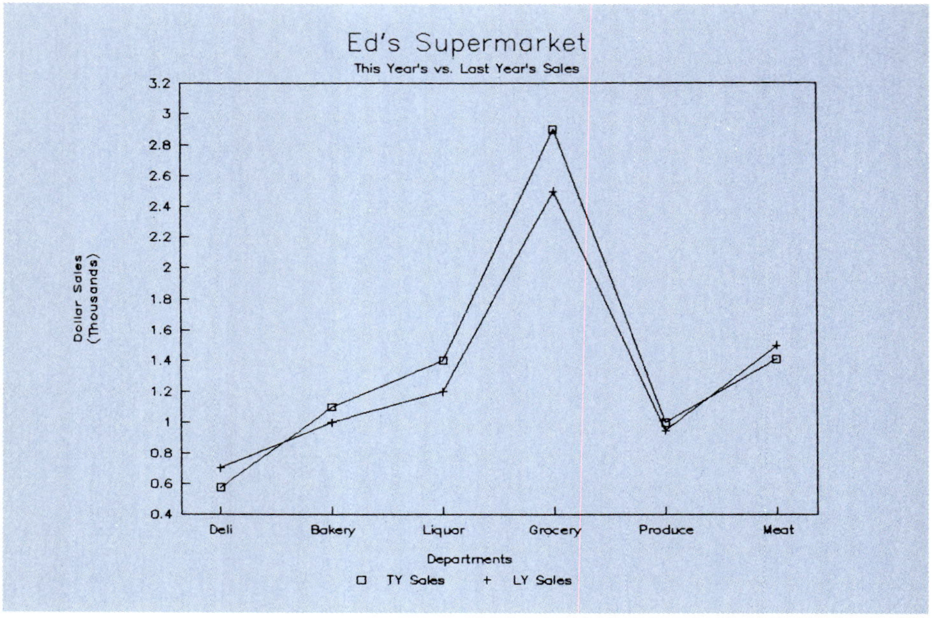

Figure 4.10
Printed line graph of last year's and this year's COMPSALS sales, with accompanying legend.

5. Save the graph to a file for later printing:

S	Selects the Save option from the Graph Menu.
Type LYTYLINE	Identifies the graph to be saved.
Enter	Executes the command.

RECONVERTING TO BAR GRAPHS

Ed is very impressed with 1-2-3 and now wants the double-bar graph to include a legend for its bars. Do the following:

1. Get to the Graph Menu.
2. Select a new graph type:

T	Selects the Type option from the Graph Menu.
B	Creates a bar graph.

3. Press V to view the graph. It should look like Figure 4.11.

PIE CHARTS

Ed wants more. Try to satisfy him by showing the original bar-chart information about this year's sales as a pie chart. Do the following:

1. Get to the Graph Menu.
2. Reset the graph settings to TYSALE:

N	Selects the Name option from the Graph Menu.
U	Selects the Use command, telling 1-2-3 which graph settings to use.

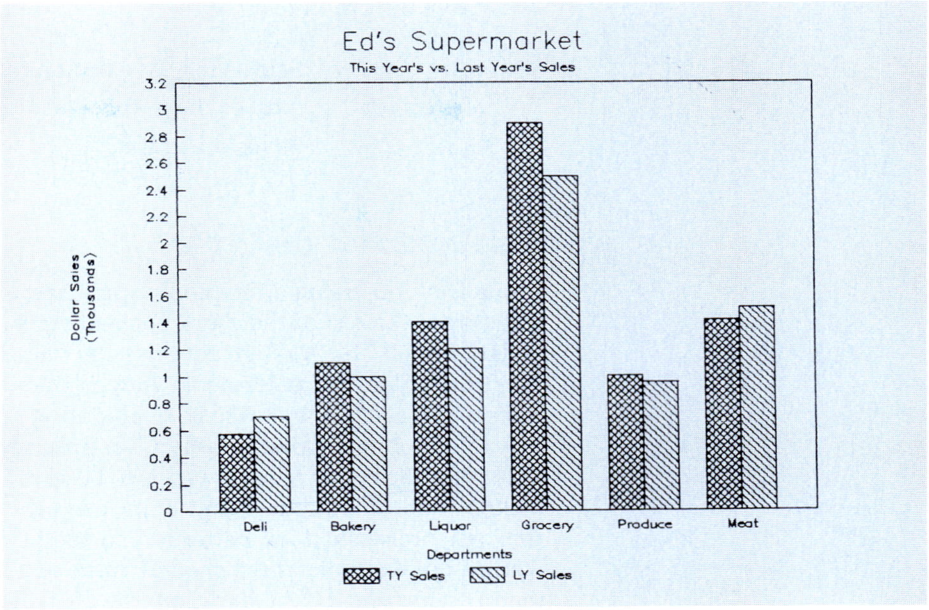

Figure 4.11
Printed bar graph of last year's and this year's COMPSALS sales, with accompanying legend.

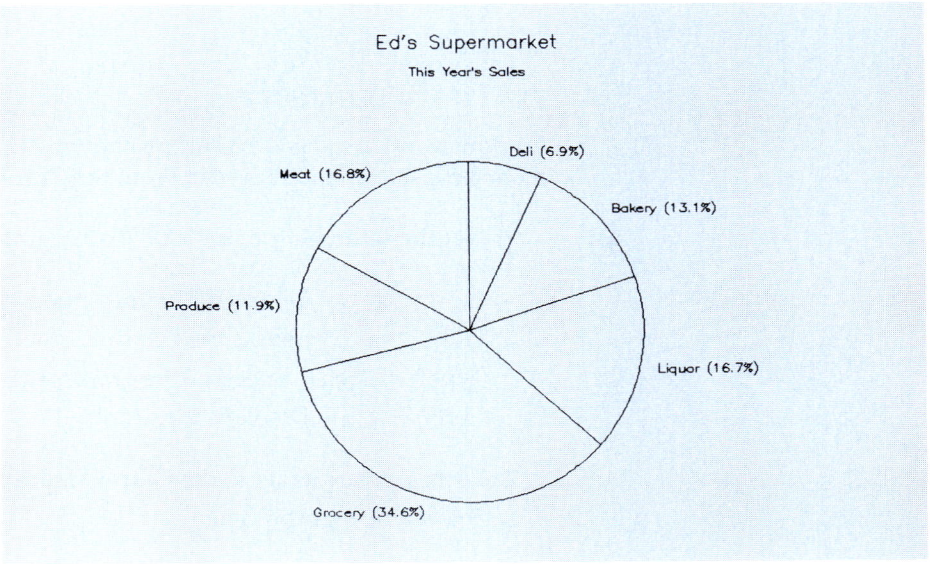

Figure 4.12
Printed pie chart of this year's COMPSALS sales.

Type TYSALE	Specifies the settings to use.
Enter	Changes the settings of the current graph.

3. Get to the Graph Menu and change the graph type:

T	Selects the Type option from the Graph Menu.
P	Draws a pie chart.

4. Press V to view the graph. It should now look like Figure 4.12. Lotus remembers all titles from the TYSALE graph settings.

5. Save the graph to a file:

S	Selects the Save option from the Graph Menu.
Type `TYPIE`	Names the graph.
Enter	Saves the graph.

EXPLODED PIE CHARTS

Lotus lets you create an exploded pie chart showing one or more slices separated from the rest of the chart. To create this effect, you must set up a separate B data range. The A range contains the values to be plotted. The B range tells 1-2-3 the colors (or patterns, if viewed on a noncolor screen) to be used and which wedges (if any) are to be exploded.

To plot an exploded pie chart, set up a new B data range in column G with values for the colors of each wedge to be plotted. These are given as single digits 0 through 8. The digits 0 and 8 are used for nonshaded wedges, the digits 1 through 7 for a shade or pattern. Add 100 to the shading values to explode the wedge. For example, if the shaded value of a wedge is 4 and you wish to have that wedge appear exploded from the pie, enter 104.

The worksheet displayed in Figure 4.13 generates the exploded pie chart shown in Figure 4.14. Don't worry if the graph appears a little "squashed"; it will appear fine when it is printed.

STACKED-BAR CHARTS

Ed now wants a stacked-bar graph showing the combined sales of each department for last year and this year. From the Graph Menu, take the following steps:

1. Get the settings from the LYTYSALE graph that you stored previously.

N	Selects the Name option from the Graph Menu.
U	Selects the Use option.
Type `LYTYSALE`	Specifies the graph settings to use.
Enter	Displays the graph.

2. Press any key to get to the Graph Menu.
3. Select a new graph type:

T	Selects the Type option from the Graph Menu.
S	Generates a stacked-bar graph.

4. Enter a new second title line for the graph:

O	Selects Options from the Graph Menu.
T	Selects the Title option.
S	Selects the Second title line.
←	Move the pointer under the *v* of *vs*.
Del (4)	Deletes the word *vs*.
Type `+`	Identifies the character to be added.
Enter	Enters the changed second line.
Q	Quits Options and returns to the Graph Menu.

Figure 4.13
Worksheet for generating the graph in Figure 4.14.

G5: 1 READY

	B	C	D	E	F	G
1	COMPSALS					
2						
3	Department	Last Year	This Year	Change	% Change	
4						
5	Deli	700.00	575.00	(125.00)	-18%	1.00
6	Bakery	1,000.00	1,100.00	100.00	10%	2.00
7	Liquor	1,200.00	1,400.00	200.00	17%	103.00
8	Grocery	2,500.00	2,900.00	400.00	16%	4.00
9	Produce	950.00	1,000.00	50.00	5%	5.00
10	Meat	1,500.00	1,410.00	(90.00)	-6%	6.00
11						
12	Store Total	7,850.00	8,385.00	535.00	7%	
13						
14						
15						
16						
17						
18						
19						
20						

15-Aug-91 08:45 AM

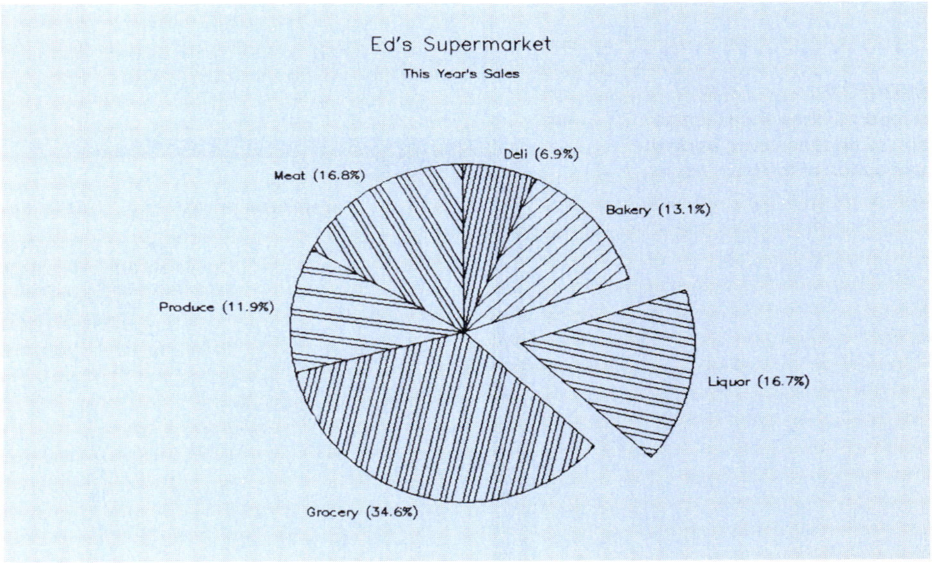

Figure 4.14
Printed exploded pie chart of the data depicted in Figure 4.13.

5. Press V to view the graph. It should look like Figure 4.15.
6. Press any key to return to the Graph Menu.

2.2

GENERATING A TABLE OF GRAPH NAMES (/GNT)

Ed would now like to see a table of the various graphs that have been archived to the worksheet using the Name Create commands. Do this by using the Name Table command. Once you have positioned the pointer to cell C14, enter the following commands:

N	Selects the Name option of the Graph Menu.
T	Selects the Table option.
C14	Positions the pointer to cell C14.
Enter	Generates the table.

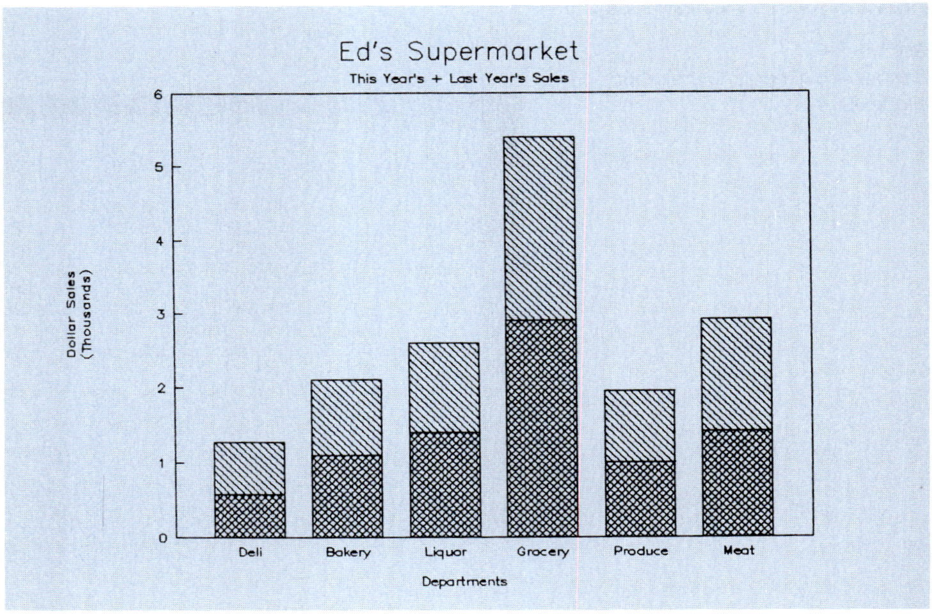

Figure 4.15
Printed stacked-bar graph of last year's and this year's COMPSALS sales.

Figure 4.16
The report of the various sets of graph settings achieved using the Name option of the Main Menu.

A1: READY

	A	B	C	D	E	F
1		COMPSALS				
2						
3		Department	Last Year	This Year	Change	% Change
4						
5		Deli	700.00	575.00	(125.00)	-18%
6		Bakery	1,000.00	1,100.00	100.00	10%
7		Liquor	1,200.00	1,400.00	200.00	17%
8		Grocery	2,500.00	2,900.00	400.00	16%
9		Produce	950.00	1,000.00	50.00	5%
10		Meat	1,500.00	1,410.00	(90.00)	-6%
11						
12		Store Total	7,850.00	8,385.00	535.00	7%
13						
14			LYSALE	Bar	Ed's Supermarket	
15			LYTYLINE	Line	Ed's Supermarket	
16			LYTYSALE	Bar	Ed's Supermarket	
17			TYSALE	Bar	Ed's Supermarket	
18						
19						
20						

04-Sep-91 11:05 AM UNDO

2.2 You should now see a report embedded within your worksheet like that in Figure 4.16. Now save the COMPSALS worksheet file to preserve the various changes.

XY GRAPHS

Up until now, Ed has been requesting only one-dimensional graphs—graphs in which only Y data points are plotted. Now Ed has come up with an application that requires you to plot a set of Y data points against a set of X data points. Ed has accumulated 7 years of profit figures that he would like to compare to each year's rate of inflation. To build such a graph, you must use the XY option from

Figure 4.17
PROFITS worksheet.

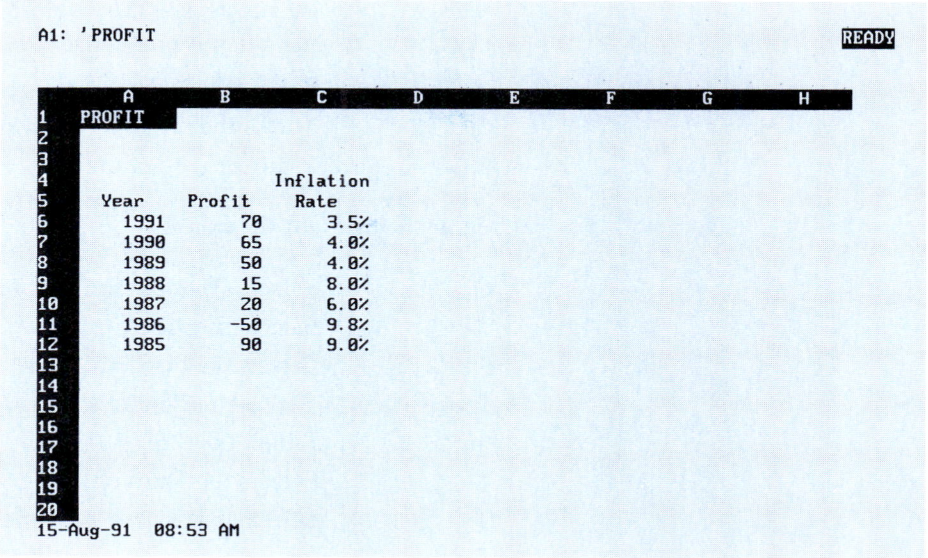
A1: 'PROFIT   READY

	A	B	C	D	E	F	G	H
1	PROFIT							
2								
3								
4			Inflation					
5	Year	Profit	Rate					
6	1991	70	3.5%					
7	1990	65	4.0%					
8	1989	50	4.0%					
9	1988	15	8.0%					
10	1987	20	6.0%					
11	1986	-50	9.8%					
12	1985	90	9.0%					
13								
14								
15								
16								
17								
18								
19								
20								

15-Aug-91   08:53 AM

Figure 4.18
Printed XY graph comparing profits to inflation over a 7-year period.

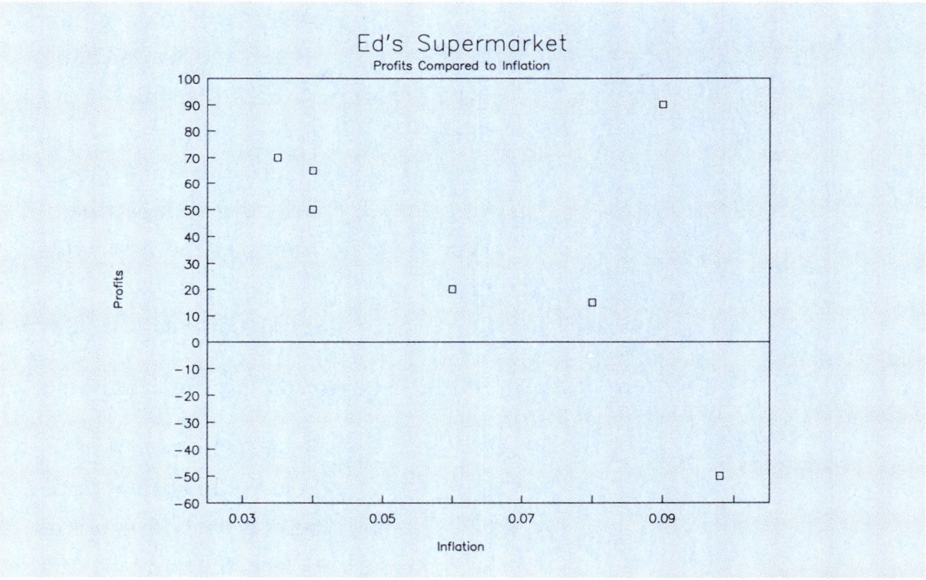

the Type Menu. Figure 4.17 shows Ed's figures, and Figure 4.18 shows a corresponding XY graph.

Ed's figures have been entered in a worksheet called PROFITS. The cell that contains 1992 is cell A6. Either load or create this worksheet. Then perform the following steps to generate the XY graph:

1. Get the Graph Menu:

/G	Takes the Graph option from the Main Menu.
T	Selects the Type option of the Graph Menu.
X	Prepares to generate an XY graph.
A	Selects the A data range option from the Graph Menu.

B6.B12	Marks the range by pointing or entering addresses.
Enter	Establishes the range.
X	Selects the X data range option from the Graph Menu.
C6.C12	Marks the range by pointing or entering addresses.
Enter	Establishes the range.

2. Enter the titles for the graph:

O	Selects Options from the Graph Menu.
T	Selects the Titles option.
F	Selects the First title line.
Type `Ed's Supermarket`	Identifies the first title line.
Enter	Enters the title.
T	Selects the Titles option.
S	Selects the Second title line.
Type `Profits Compared to Inflation`	Identifies the second title line.
Enter	Enters the title.
T	Selects the Titles option.
X	Selects the X-axis title.
Type `Inflation`	Identifies the X-axis title.
Enter	Enters the title.
T	Selects the Titles option.
Y	Selects the Y-axis title.
Type `Profits`	Identifies the Y-axis title.
Enter	Enters the title.
Q	Quits Options and returns to the Graph Menu.

3. Tell 1-2-3 not to connect the data points with lines:

O	Selects Options from the Graph Menu.
F	Selects the Format option.
G	Selects the Graph option.
S	Selects the Symbols option.
Q	Quits Format and returns to Options.
Q	Quits Options and returns to the Graph Menu.

4. Press V to view the graph. It should look like Figure 4.18.
5. Press any key to return to the Graph Menu; then save to a picture file called XY1GRA.

Formatting the X and Y Numeric Scaling

1. Change the format of the Y numeric scaling, that is, the manner in which the scale numbers are displayed:

O	Selects Options from the Graph Menu.
S	Selects the Scale option.
Y	Specifies the Y scale as the scale to be changed.

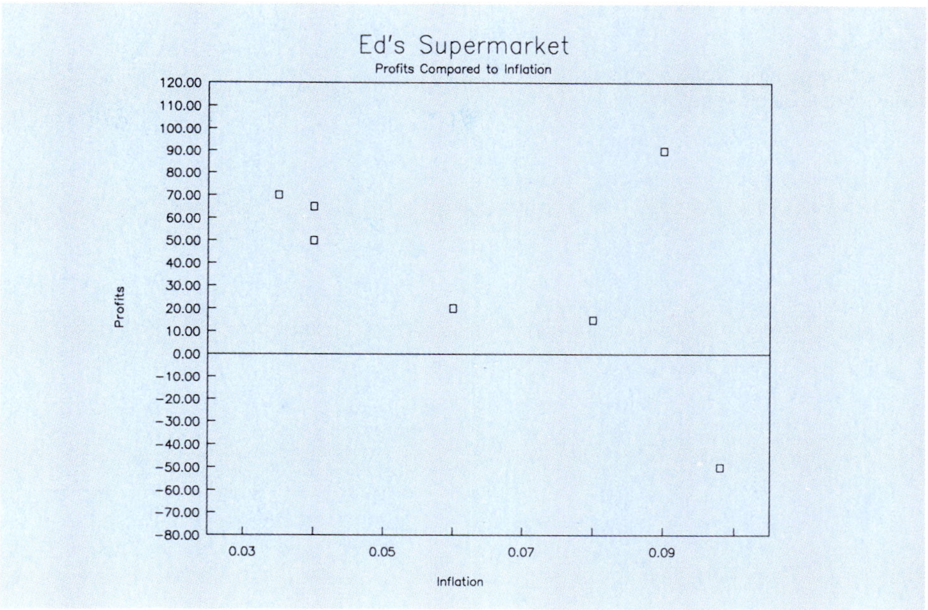

Figure 4.19
Printed reformatted XY graph comparing profits to inflation over a 7-year period.

F	Selects the Format option.
F	Selects the Fixed option.
Enter	Changes the format to two decimal positions.
M	Draws the graph based on user-specified upper and lower limits.
L	Selects the Lower limit entry.
Type `-80`	Specifies the new lower limit.
Enter	Enters the lower limit.
U	Selects the Upper limit entry.
Type `120`	Specifies the new upper limit.
Enter	Enters the upper limit.
Q	Quits the Scale Menu and returns to Options.
Q	Quits Options and returns to the Graph Menu.

2. Press V to view the graph, which should now look like Figure 4.19.
3. Save to a .PIC file called XY2GRAPH.

Labeling Graph Data Points XY Graphs can sometimes be hard to read, especially if data points are unlabeled. For instance, in Figure 4.18, each small square represents a different year, but which is which? Fortunately, data points can be labeled by using 1-2-3's Data Labels feature. This involves the following steps:

1. Establish the data labels:

O	Selects Options from the Graph Menu.
D	Selects the Data Labels option.
A	Selects the A data range option.
A6.A12	Marks the range by pointing or entering addresses.
Enter	Enters the range.

Figure 4.20
XY graph comparing profits to inflation with data labels added.

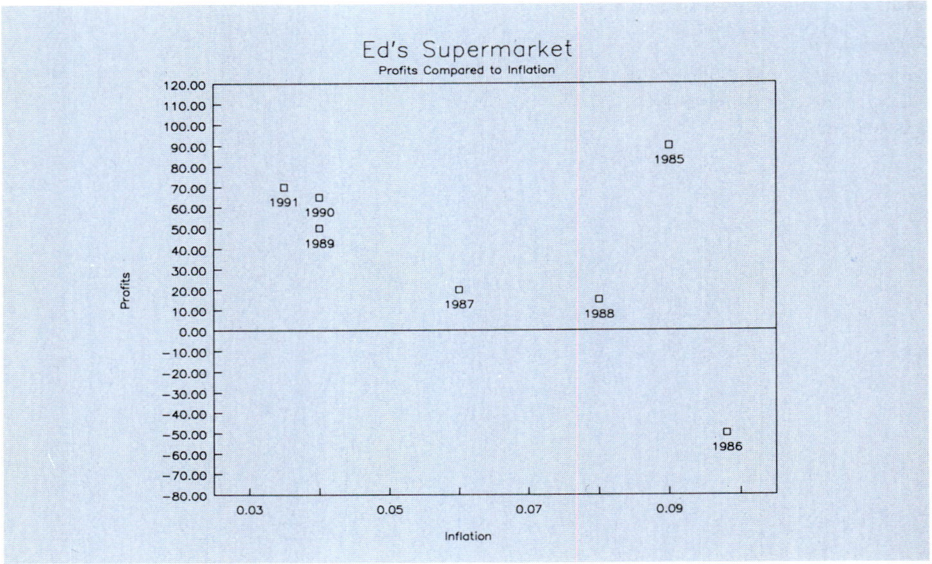

B	Places the labels below the data-point representation (square).
Q	Quits the Data Labels Menu.
Q	Quits Options and returns to the Graph Menu.

2. Display the graph shown in Figure 4.20.

INTRODUCTION TO GRAPH PRINTING

Lotus does not print your graphs directly from the spreadsheet program. This is one of the few areas in which Lotus's integration breaks down. If this feature were included, 1-2-3 would need much more RAM memory than it does.

To print a graph, you must leave the 1-2-3 spreadsheet, return to the Lotus Access System Menu, and take the **PrintGraph option.** If you have been using 1-2-3, you will be instructed to insert the PrintGraph disk in drive A. If you have previously saved your graph files and want to print them out, you can boot directly from the PrintGraph disk, which also contains a copy of the Lotus Access System.

Make certain that the disk containing the graphs you have saved is in the default drive. If 1-2-3 is already running, follow the instructions below. If the computer is off, boot the system, insert the PrintGraph disk in drive A, and start PrintGraph, skipping the instructions below. The steps to access PrintGraph from 1-2-3 are as follows:

/Q	Selects the Quit option from the Main Menu.
Y	Affirms leaving 1-2-3 and in a few seconds displays the Lotus Access System Menu.
P	Selects the PrintGraph option.

At this point, you will be directed to insert the PrintGraph disk in drive A (Figure 4.21a), unless you have a fixed disk. Once you have inserted the

Figure 4.21

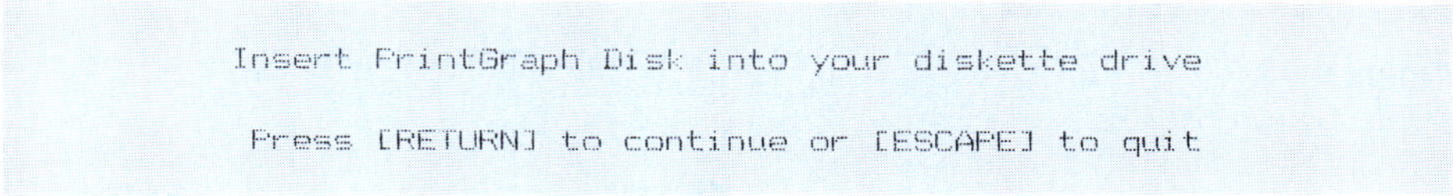

(a)

(b)

Figure 4.22
The PrintGraph Menu.

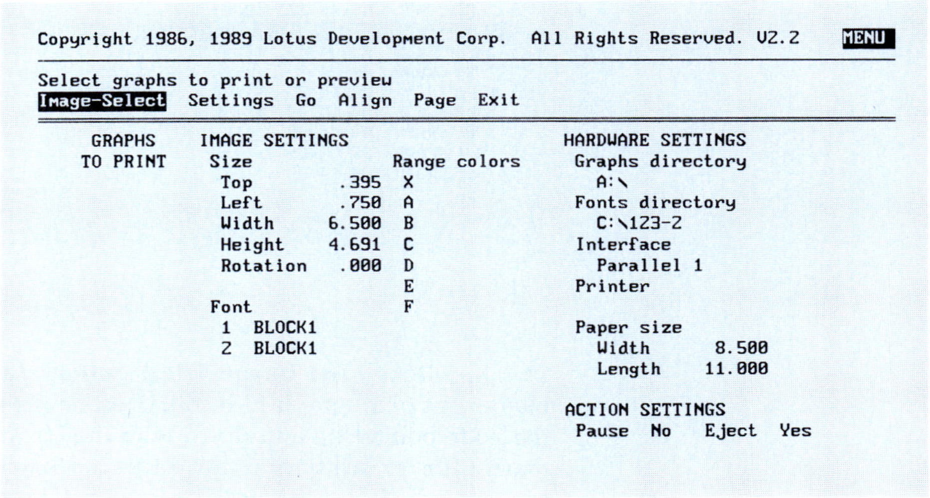

PrintGraph disk, the screen depicted in Figure 4.21b will appear. When PrintGraph is loaded, the PrintGraph screen shown in Figure 4.22 appears.

PRINTGRAPH MENU

The information displayed beneath the PrintGraph Menu details the status of its various options, including what paper sizes are expected, what fonts have been selected, where files are to be found, and what type of printer PrintGraph is currently configured for. The menu itself reads

```
Image-Select  Settings  Go  Align  Page  Exit
```

Figure 4.23
Menu of graph (.PIC) files.

```
Copyright 1986, 1989 Lotus Development Corp.  All Rights Reserved. V2.2   POINT
Select graphs to print

   GRAPH FILE  DATE      TIME      SIZE
   -----------------------------------       Space bar marks or unmarks selection
   BAR        09-04-89  10:52     5010       ENTER selects marked graphs
   EXPLOPIE   09-04-89  11:02     3201       ESC exits, ignoring changes
   LINE       09-04-89  10:58     1076       HOME moves to beginning of list
   LYSALE     09-04-89  10:56     5206       END moves to end of list
   LYTYBAR    09-04-89  10:59     6540       ↑ and ↓ move highlight
   LYTYLINE   09-04-89  10:59     1167         List will scroll if highlight
   LYTYSALE   09-04-89  10:57     6410         moved beyond top or bottom
   STACKEDB   09-04-89  11:02     4858       GRAPH (F10) previews marked graph
   TYPIE      09-04-89  11:00     1955
   TYSALE     09-04-89  10:55     5066
   XY1GRAPH   09-04-89  11:09      858
   XY2GRAPH   09-04-89  11:12     1005
   XY3GRAPH   09-04-89  11:13     1089
```

Figure 4.24
Graphs marked for printing.

```
Copyright 1986, 1989 Lotus Development Corp.  All Rights Reserved. V2.2   POINT
Select graphs to print

   GRAPH FILE  DATE      TIME      SIZE
   -----------------------------------       Space bar marks or unmarks selection
   BAR        09-04-89  10:52     5010       ENTER selects marked graphs
   EXPLOPIE   09-04-89  11:02     3201       ESC exits, ignoring changes
   LINE       09-04-89  10:58     1076       HOME moves to beginning of list
   LYSALE     09-04-89  10:56     5206       END moves to end of list
   LYTYBAR    09-04-89  10:59     6540       ↑ and ↓ move highlight
 # LYTYLINE   09-04-89  10:59     1167         List will scroll if highlight
   LYTYSALE   09-04-89  10:57     6410         moved beyond top or bottom
   STACKEDB   09-04-89  11:02     4858       GRAPH (F10) previews marked graph
 # TYPIE      09-04-89  11:00     1955
   TYSALE     09-04-89  10:55     5066
   XY1GRAPH   09-04-89  11:09      858
   XY2GRAPH   09-04-89  11:12     1005
   XY3GRAPH   09-04-89  11:13     1089
```

Image-Select The **Image-Select option** marks graphs for printing. It displays a list of all graph files contained on the default disk (Figure 4.23). Move the wide pointer up and down with the Up and Down Arrow keys. To tag or mark a file for printing, simply press the Space Bar; a **pound sign (#)** will then appear to the left of that graph-file entry (Figure 4.24).

Up to 16 graph files can be selected for printing. Pressing the Space Bar a second time will "unmark" the file. If more than one file is selected, they are printed in the order in which they appear, from top to bottom. The computer automatically prints each graph and advances the paper for the next graph. When you have selected all the files you wish to print, press Enter to return to the PrintGraph Menu.

This convenient feature, known as **batch printing,** lets you do something else (like catching up on your reading) while your graphs are being printed.

Settings The **Settings option** gives the following menu (Figure 4.25):

```
Image  Hardware  Action  Save  Reset  Quit
```

Figure 4.25
Settings Menu.

```
Copyright 1986, 1989 Lotus Development Corp.  All Rights Reserved. V2.2   MENU
Select graph size, fonts, and colors
Image  Hardware  Action  Save  Reset  Quit
  GRAPHS    IMAGE SETTINGS                       HARDWARE SETTINGS
 TO PRINT    Size               Range colors      Graphs directory
              Top         .395  X                   A:\
  TYPIE       Left        .750  A                 Fonts directory
  LYTYLINE    Width      6.500  B                   C:\123-2
              Height     4.691  C                 Interface
              Rotation    .000  D                   Parallel 1
                                E                 Printer
             Font               F
              1  BLOCK1                           Paper size
              2  BLOCK1                             Width       8.500
                                                    Length     11.000

                                                 ACTION SETTINGS
                                                  Pause  No    Eject  Yes
```

Figure 4.26
Image Menu.

```
Copyright 1986, 1989 Lotus Development Corp.  All Rights Reserved. V2.2   MENU
Specify size and orientation of printed graphs
Size  Font  Range-Colors  Quit
  GRAPHS    IMAGE SETTINGS                       HARDWARE SETTINGS
 TO PRINT    Size               Range colors      Graphs directory
              Top         .395  X                   A:\
  TYPIE       Left        .750  A                 Fonts directory
  LYTYLINE    Width      6.500  B                   C:\123-2
              Height     4.691  C                 Interface
              Rotation    .000  D                   Parallel 1
                                E                 Printer
             Font               F
              1  BLOCK1                           Paper size
              2  BLOCK1                             Width       8.500
                                                    Length     11.000

                                                 ACTION SETTINGS
                                                  Pause  No    Eject  Yes
```

Image The Image option displays the following submenu (Figure 4.26):

```
Size   Font   Range-Colors   Quit
```

Size lets you specify the height and width of the graph.

Font lets you select up to 2 fonts from 11 possible fonts in generating dot-matrix output. Font 1 is used only for the first line of the graph title, font 2 for any other text. Fonts are selected in the same way as files: Use a pointer to highlight the desired option and press the Space Bar to choose the font (Figure 4.27).

Range-Colors lets you assign a different color to each data range. Of course, you must have a color printer to use it.

Quit returns you to the Settings Menu.

Hardware This option configures 1-2-3 to the type of print that your printer is capable of printing and tells 1-2-3 where to find the graph files and font files.

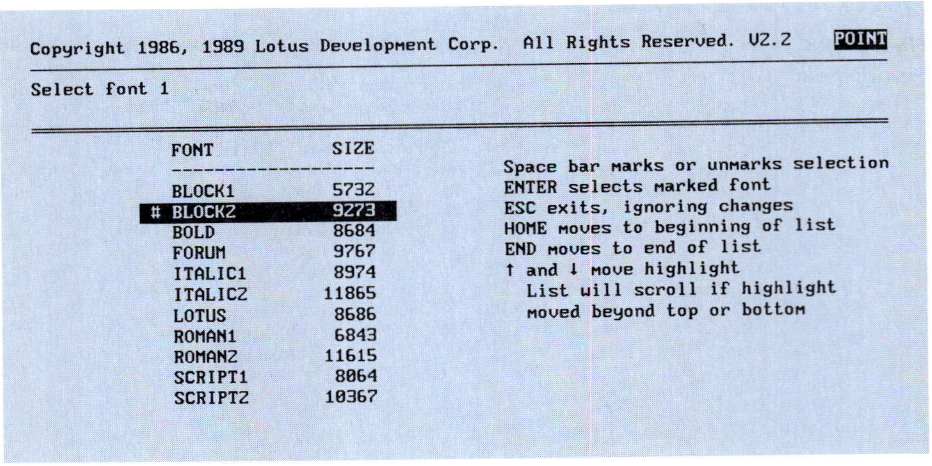

Figure 4.27
Font marked for use.

Most likely these tasks have already been done for readers of this textbook, so this option—as well as the remaining options—will not be covered here.

Quit This option returns you to the PrintGraph Menu.

Go The **Go option** results in the graph being printed.

Align The **Align option** resets the top-of-page. If the graph did not print properly (for example, if there is a blank area in the middle), simply move the paper manually to a perforation and select the Align option. PrintGraph now knows where the top of the page is.

Page The **Page option** moves the paper in the printer to the top of the next page.

Exit The **Exit option** ends a PrintGraph session. It displays the menu `No Yes`. When you select Yes, you are returned to the Lotus Access System Menu. You can now take the 1-2-3 option to return to the spreadsheet or take Exit again to end the overall session. If you select the 1-2-3 option and you are working in a diskette environment with 1-2-3 program disks, you will be prompted to insert the disk containing the 1-2-3 program in drive A.

STEP-BY-STEP PRINTGRAPH INSTRUCTIONS

To print the graph files TYPIE and LYTYLINE that were created earlier, start from the PrintGraph menu. Then perform the following steps:

1. Move the pointer to the Image-Select option (see Figure 4.23) and press Enter.
2. Move the pointer (via the Arrow keys) to each desired graph name (TYPIE and LYTYLINE). Mark it by pressing the Space Bar so that a pound symbol (#) appears to its left. Press Enter after both graph names have been marked (see Figure 4.24).
3. Take the Settings option.
4. Take the Image option.
5. Take the Font entry of the Image Menu. Select font 1 and choose BLOCK2 by pointing, pressing the Space Bar, and pressing Enter (see Figure 4.27).

Figure 4.28

(a) The printed pie chart and (b) the printed line graph.

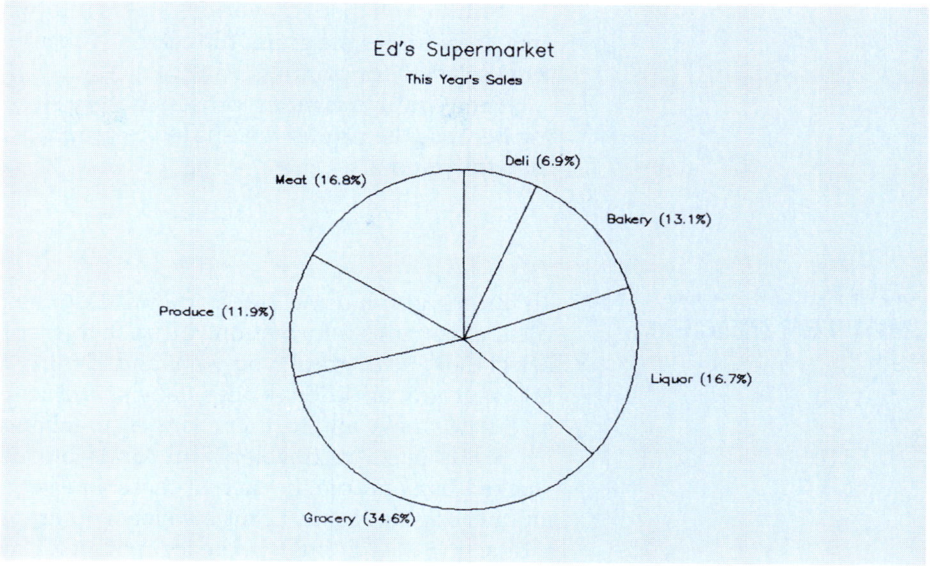

(a)

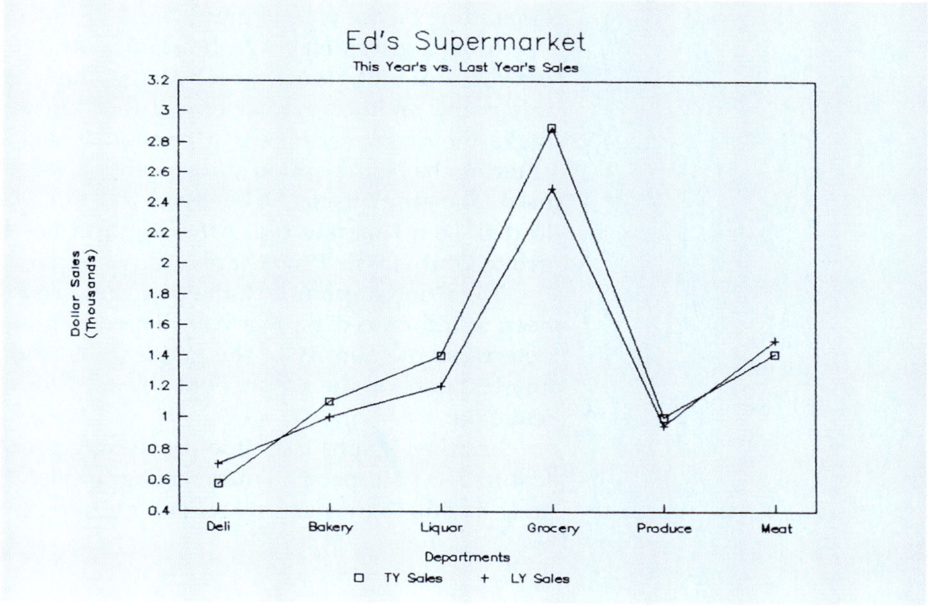

(b)

6. Take the Font entry of the Image Menu again. Select font 2 and choose BLOCK1 by pointing, pressing the Space Bar, and pressing Enter.
7. You've finished with the Image; now take the Quit option.
8. Quit the Settings Menu.
9. Make sure the printer is at the top of a page; then select the Align option.
10. You're going to accept all the defaults for printing. Take the Go option to start printing.

With the following options, PrintGraph

1. Loads the font files.
2. Loads the graph file and generates the picture.
3. Prints the graph file (Figure 4.28).

PrintGraph displays various status information while it prints. In the menu area, it identifies the graph file currently printing; below this it lists the files that were selected for printing.

PrintGraph's printing process is very slow in comparison to regular printing because the printer has shifted to graphics mode, which is generally slower than text mode.

CHAPTER REVIEW

To build a graph using 1-2-3, you must do the following: (1) select a worksheet file that contains information you wish to graph; (2) obtain the Graph Menu; (3) select the type of graph you want and identify the pieces of data to be included; (4) enter any additional titles, labels, and legends; (5) view the graph on the screen; (6) make any further changes or enhancements.

Lotus lets you develop four kinds of one-dimensional graphs: line, bar, stacked-bar, and pie. In each of these, one set of data points is arranged across an unchanging X axis. Lotus also lets you graph in two dimensions (two sets of interacting data points), in the form of an XY graph.

Each type of graph, except the pie chart, can use more than one set of Y data points. Each subsequent set of data points produces an additional line or bar, depending on the type of graph.

After a graph has been finished, you can save the settings for that graph onto an area of the worksheet by using the Name option of the Graph Menu. At this point, another graph, termed the "current" graph, can be built. You can make the graph settings you previously saved become the current graph by entering the Name option and specifying which group of graph settings is to be used. The graph itself can be saved, too, but it (unlike the graph setting) is saved to disk as a separate file. After a graph has been saved onto disk, it can be printed out via the PrintGraph utility supplied by Lotus.

The PrintGraph utility, the program used to print any 1-2-3 graph that has been saved onto disk, lets you (depending on the printer that you are using) determine the density of the graph to be printed and the fonts to be used for any text data on the graph. Font 1 is used for titles; font 2 is used for any other text data.

Printing graphs is a time-consuming process. PrintGraph's batch-printing feature lets you specify a number of graphs to be printed automatically, without your having to oversee any remaining steps in the printing process.

KEY TERMS AND CONCEPTS

ABCDEF options
Align option
bar graph
batch printing
B&W command
Color command
Create command
Data command
Delete command
Exit option
Format command
F10 (Graph) key
Go option
Graph Menu
Grid command
Group command
Image-Select option
Labels option
Legend command
line graph
Name option
Options option
Page option
pie chart
pound sign (#)
PrintGraph option
Quit command
Reset command

Reset option
Save option
Scale command
Settings option
stacked-bar graph
Table command
Titles command
Type option
Use command
View option
X option
X (horizontal) axis
XY graph
Y (vertical) axis

CHAPTER QUIZ

Multiple Choice

1. Which of the following graph types can have only one set of Y data points?
   a. Line
   b. Bar
   c. Pie
   d. Stacked-bar
   e. XY
   f. All of the above can have more than one set of Y data points.

2. Which of the following is *not* considered to be a title?
   a. The two lines at the top of the graph
   b. X-axis title
   c. Y-axis title
   d. Legends
   e. All of the above are titles.

3. What is ABCDEF?
   a. Grades assigned for this exercise
   b. X-axis data points
   c. Y-axis data points
   d. Data-point labels
   e. None of the above

4. Which of the following is *not* a feature of PrintGraph?
   a. Exists as a separate program available under the Lotus Access System.
   b. Allows you to specify up to four fonts in a graph
   c. Allows you to batch-print graphs
   d. All of the above are features of PrintGraph.

5. Which of the following statements is *not* true about the Name feature of the Graph Menu?
   a. The stored graph settings are all active.
   b. The current graph settings can be saved onto the worksheet using this option.
   c. When the worksheet is saved onto disk, any graph settings are also saved.
   d. You can delete selected graph settings individually or all at once.
   e. All of the above statements are true.

True/False

6. The PrintGraph utility is one of the nonintegrated features of 1-2-3.

7. Once a set of graph settings is selected via the Use option of the Name Menu, the graph built with these settings is automatically displayed.

8. It is possible to reset either selected parts of a graph or the complete graph.

9. Using legends lets you distinguish among the various sets of Y data points.

10. The XY graph is the only 1-2-3 graph type that lets you create a two-dimensional graph.

Answers

1. c, e 2. d 3. c 4. b 5. a 6. t 7. t 8. t 9. t 10. t

Exercises

1. Define or describe each of the following terms:
   a. X axis c. Legend e. Batch printing
   b. Y axis d. Scaling

2. The nine steps involved in building and then printing a graph are __________, __________, __________, __________, __________, __________, __________, __________, and __________.

3. Lotus 1-2-3 automatically places the extension __________ on the file of any graph that is saved onto disk.

4. The __________ labels each set of Y data points, in order to make a graph more readable.

5. Graph settings can be saved onto the worksheet using the __________ option of the Graph Menu.

6. The __________ command of the Graph Menu displays the graph.

7. The __________ command deletes a portion or all of the current graph settings.

8. The __________ command stores a graph onto disk.

9. Any range can be canceled by pressing the __________ key.

10. Using the __________ option controls the format in which numeric data appear on a graph.

11. The __________ axis is usually enlisted to produce labels across the bottom of the graph.

12. Explain the difference between a one-dimensional graph and a two-dimensional graph.

13. __________ bar charts combine entries into one set of Y data points; __________ bar charts let you see differences immediately by comparing bars.

14. __________ lets you specify a number of graphs to be printed and then leave to do whatever you want.

15. When you are using two fonts, use ____________ for the heading and ____________ for the rest of the graph.

16. Basically, ____________ sizes of graphs can be printed.

17. PrintGraph is separate from 1-2-3 because it takes up too much ____________.

18. Explain how graphs are selected for printing.

19. You can mark graphs for printing by pressing the ____________ key.

20. List the three actions that PrintGraph performs in printing a graph.

COMPUTER EXERCISES

In building the following graphs, referring to the Graph command structure in the appendix will help you greatly in locating the various graph commands.

1. Retrieve the CH1EX5 worksheet file.
   a. Generate a pie chart, using the This Year column data.
   b. Generate a bar graph, using the same data. Save these graph settings to a named area called TYEAR.
   c. Compare the two years of sales, using a line graph. Save these graph settings to a named area called TYLYSALE.
   d. Generate a bar graph of the named graph TYEAR, using all the stored graph settings but changing the column to be graphed to Last Year.
   e. Generate a line graph of the named graph TYLYSALE and enter legends at the bottom of the graph. Save these settings to a named area called LEGENDS.
   f. Using the TYLYSALE settings, change the graph type to a bar graph. Save this file to a picture file using the name BAR2SALE.
   g. Enter the following headings:

Line 1	`FRED'S AUTO SALES`
Line 2	`YEARLY SALES COMPARISONS`
X axis	`Sales Reps`
Y axis	`Dollar Sales`

   h. Save the graph to a picture file called BARTITLE.
   i. Save the graph settings to a named area BARTITLE.
   j. Exit from the Graph Menu. Change the contents of cells in the sales range. View the graph by pressing F10.
   k. Resave the worksheet file. This will also save the named graphs.
2. Retrieve the CH1EX7 worksheet file.
   a. Graph the expenses for each year, using a line graph. Enter appropriate headings, labels, and legends. Save the file to a graph picture file called EXPENSES.
   b. Generate a pie chart for each year's expenses. Save them to files called PIE1 and PIE2. You will have to reset the B data range to do this.
3. Use the PrintGraph utility to print the above graphs. Refer to the PrintGraph portion of the chapter for instructions on using this utility.

GLOSSARY

absolute address: Cell location that does not change in the course of copying a formula to other cells. In a cell marked for absolute address, the formula contains dollar signs.

accelerator keys: Key sequence commands of 1-2-3 that usually require Alt + some other character (for example, Alt + F3). These commands can take the place of commands that are issued via the menu.

add-in: A piece of software that provides 1-2-3 with capabilities not otherwise found in it.

Align: Command that tells 1-2-3 to expect the top of page at this page position.

Allways: An add-in for 1-2-3 that provides desktop/spreadsheet-publishing capability.

Alt: Key label for the Alternate key.

argument: Items continued between parentheses to pass data to a function.

automatic recalculation: Feature that enables the worksheet to automatically recalculate itself after any change.

available memory: Amount of RAM that is available for use by 1-2-3 in building a worksheet.

Backspace: Key used to erase the last character typed. It is labeled with an arrow that points toward the left.

backup file: .BAK-extension file that 1-2-3 automatically creates as protection against loss of an original file.

Big Left: The 1-2-3 command (Ctrl + Left Arrow) that moves you to the left a screen at a time.

Big Right: The 1-2-3 command (Ctrl + Right Arrow) that moves you to the right a screen at a time.

border: Set of labels for the rows and columns of a worksheet. The columns are labeled with letters, and the rows are labeled with numbers.

Borders option: The command of the / Print Options Menu that lets you add documenting text to a spreadsheet printout.

built-in function: A series of commands that are already resident in 1-2-3. A user simply references the function and passes parameters to the function in order to get the desired result.

cell: Intersection point of a row and a column. It is referenced by the cell address Column/Row.

centering command: Spreadsheet command that centers text in a document or cell.

circular reference: The situation that exists when a cell's effect depends on both its contents and the contents of other cells.

column: Cells aligned top to bottom on the screen.

command line: Third line of the Lotus 1-2-3 control panel. It contains the 1-2-3 commands that can be issued from the current menu.

control panel: Top three lines on the 1-2-3 worksheet screen, consisting of the status line, the entry line, and the prompt line.

Copy: Command that copies the contents of a cell into one or more other cells.

criterion range: Area of the worksheet on which you specify the records to be included in an operation.

Ctrl: Key label for the Control key.

Ctrl + Scroll Break: The interrupt command that returns 1-2-3 to READY mode.

data entry: Process of placing text, values, labels, or formulas into a text document, data file, or worksheet.

data management feature: The Lotus feature that allows you to perform rudimentary file manipulation on records held in the worksheet.

Directory command: The command from the 1-2-3 / File command that temporarily changes the default directory.

dummy: A row or column used to end a range. This lets you add another row or column and have that be inside the range specified by a 1-2-3 command referencing that range.

Enter: The key that is pressed to indicate to 1-2-3 you are finished with a command or entering data.

entry line: The second line of the control panel that lets you enter information or make changes to an existing entry in a cell.

error message: Message informing you that you did not type something the program can process or that some other system failure has occurred.

Esc: Key label for the Escape key.

execute: To perform the intent of a command or instruction; to run a program or a portion of a program.

font: Character set for printing. Pica, elite, Helvetica, Courier, and Orator are among the many common fonts.

footer: Line of text that appears at the bottom of every page of a document.

format: How data are stored in a worksheet cell, for example, as character or numeric data.

formula: Series of characters containing cell references and arithmetic operators for numeric data manipulation.

function key: One of 10 keys (F1 to F10) that allow special functions to be entered with a single user keystroke.

global: Spreadsheet command that allows changes entered thereafter to affect the entire worksheet.

Global Format command: The 1-2-3 command that specifies the most frequently desired numeric format for a worksheet.

GoTo command: The 1-2-3 command (F5) that positions the pointer directly to a specified cell.

Group command: Graph command that lets you specify the X and data ranges by indicating a range of cells in the worksheet.

header: Line of text that appears at the top of every page of a document.

Hide command: The 1-2-3 command that is used to hide a column so that it does not appear on the screen.

home: Upper left-hand corner screen position where the first printable character can be placed. This is also referred to as the initial cursor position.

Home key: Key used to send the cursor to the Home position. If used with the Control key, a clear screen results.

indicators: Signals that appear in the upper right-hand corner of the worksheet screen, telling the user which toggle keys are currently activated.

input line: Second line in the control panel, corresponding to a scratch area. The entry line contains any information you are currently entering for the cell location contained in the status line.

integration: Process that combines a number of applications under one software umbrella. For instance, 1-2-3 combines spreadsheets, graphing, and database applications.

label: Alphanumeric information used to identify a portion of a row or column.

label prefix: Tells 1-2-3 whether to left-justify ('), center (^), or right-justify (") text within a cell.

Learn command: A 1-2-3 command that records keystrokes of commands as they are entered and then places them in a cell as a macro.

Learn feature: The feature of 1-2-3 that automatically records any keystrokes entered from the keyboard into a specified range of cells within the worksheet.

Learn range: The range of cells that have been specified for use when the Learn command is active.

Legend command: Lotus 1-2-3 graph feature used to label sets of data so that a graph can be easily understood.

Lotus Access System: The menu and screen that appear when Lotus is first entered from DOS.

Lotus 1-2-3: An electronic spreadsheet program written for IBM and IBM-compatible computers.

macro: Entity that contains keystroke commands stored for later execution.

macro library: A range of cells that have been taken from a 1-2-3 worksheet by the Macro Library Manager, saved to disk as a library file with an .MLB file extension, and then loaded into memory in an area separate from any worksheet that is currently in RAM.

Macro Library Manager: An add-in for 1-2-3 that allows macro libraries to be loaded into memory and executed without being part of the worksheet.

manual recalculation: Functional mode in which a worksheet can recalculate itself only when the F9 key is pressed.

margin: Unused border around a page of a document.

minimal recalculation: Feature of Lotus 1-2-3 that recalculates only those cells affected by a change to a worksheet.

mixed-cell address: Address in which the row or column portion (not both) of the cell address can change to reflect a new cell location.

mode indicator: Status information that appears in the upper right-hand corner of the 1-2-3 worksheet screen.

Move feature: The 1-2-3 command that moves text from one part of the worksheet to another.

nail down: The process of anchoring the pointer by pressing the period (.) key.

natural recalculation: The default method used by 1-2-3 for recalculating a worksheet.

nested function: Function that resides inside another function. The innermost function must be executed before any outer ones.

numeric data: Data consisting of the digits 0 through 9.

password: A string of characters assigned to a worksheet that must be entered in order to gain access to the worksheet.

Pg Dn: Key label for the Page Down key.

Pg Up: Key label for the Page Up key.

pointer: Reverse-video bar, sometimes referred to as the cursor. Its width is dependent on the width of the cell it is referencing.

precedence: Order in which calculations are executed.

prompt line: Last line in the control panel. When a 1-2-3 menu is displayed, the prompt line contains a further explanation about a specific command.

protected cell: 1-2-3 cells that cannot be changed by the user. The worksheet has been globally protected by the Global Protection command.

protection: In 1-2-3, a way of prohibiting changes on either the entire worksheet or specific cells.

range: Rectangular or square area of a worksheet.

/ Range Format command: A 1-2-3 command that changes the format of a numeric cell to something other than the global format.

range name: Function used to give a specific name to a range of a worksheet; by using it, you can refer to formulas by meaningful names instead of by cell address only.

/ Range Search command: The 1-2-3 command that finds a character string and replaces it with another character string in any indicated worksheet cell.

/ Range Transpose command: The 1-2-3 command that transposes rows and columns.

recalculation: Process by which a spreadsheet changes all cell contents that are affected by a change to any other cell in a worksheet.

receiving range: Cells that will hold the information after a Move or Copy command is executed. Sometimes referred to as the "To" range.

relative addressing: Automatic changing of cell locations in a Copy or Move operation to reflect their new locations.

repeat symbol: In Lotus 1-2-3, the backslash (\). Any text following the backslash is repeated throughout the cell.

Reset: Command that usually results in the return of a piece of software to its original default values.

row: Horizontal axis on a spreadsheet or document.

scaling: Description of how data values will be displayed on a 1-2-3 graph.

Scroll Lock key: Key that is little used in modern programs but is intended for use as a lock-type key, causing displayed text (rather than the cursor) to move when a cursor control key is pressed.

sending range: Cells that hold the information before a Move or Copy command are executed. Sometimes referred to as the "From" range.

settings sheet: A screen displayed in many 1-2-3 commands that provides information about the current status of lower-level entries in a menu.

Setup option: The 1-2-3 option from the / Print Options Menu that specifies the size of type to be used for printing.

setup string: 1-2-3 feature used to vary the pitch of printed information.

Slash command: The command (/) that displays the 1-2-3 Main Menu to the screen.

Sort command: The 1-2-3 command that reorders the contents of row cells within a specified area of the worksheet based on the contents of one or more specified columns.

source file: A file that contains data that is to be linked to a target file in a 1-2-3 file link operation.

spreadsheet: Software package that can manipulate rows and columns of data.

status line: Top line of the control panel, which displays the cell address, the format of the data, and the cell contents.

system: The command that allows you to exit a software package to DOS, issue DOS commands, and then return to the software package previously exited.

tab: Point on a line (also called a tab stop) to which the cursor will position itself whenever the Tab command is issued.

target file: The file that is to receive information in a 1-2-3 file link operation.

template: Form that contains the prepackaged worksheet instructions needed to perform some type of application. It can be viewed as a piece of application software on which someone has already performed the planning, design, and implementation of the logic involved.

Titles: A 1-2-3 feature used to freeze text on the screen so that it will act as row or column headings.

Undo feature: A 1-2-3 command that restores a worksheet to its prior state, allowing you to recover from many mistakes that you might make.

window: Displayed portion of a worksheet or document. A window can be split into two or more smaller windows, horizontally or vertically.

worksheet: Model or representation of reality that is created using a spreadsheet software package. The worksheet is contained inside the spreadsheet border.

Zero command: The 1-2-3 command that lets you specify what value or text, if any, should be displayed in a cell that contains a value of zero.

INDEX

Lotus 1-2-3 Command Menus

WORKSHEET OPTIONS—LOTUS® 1-2-3™ COMMANDS

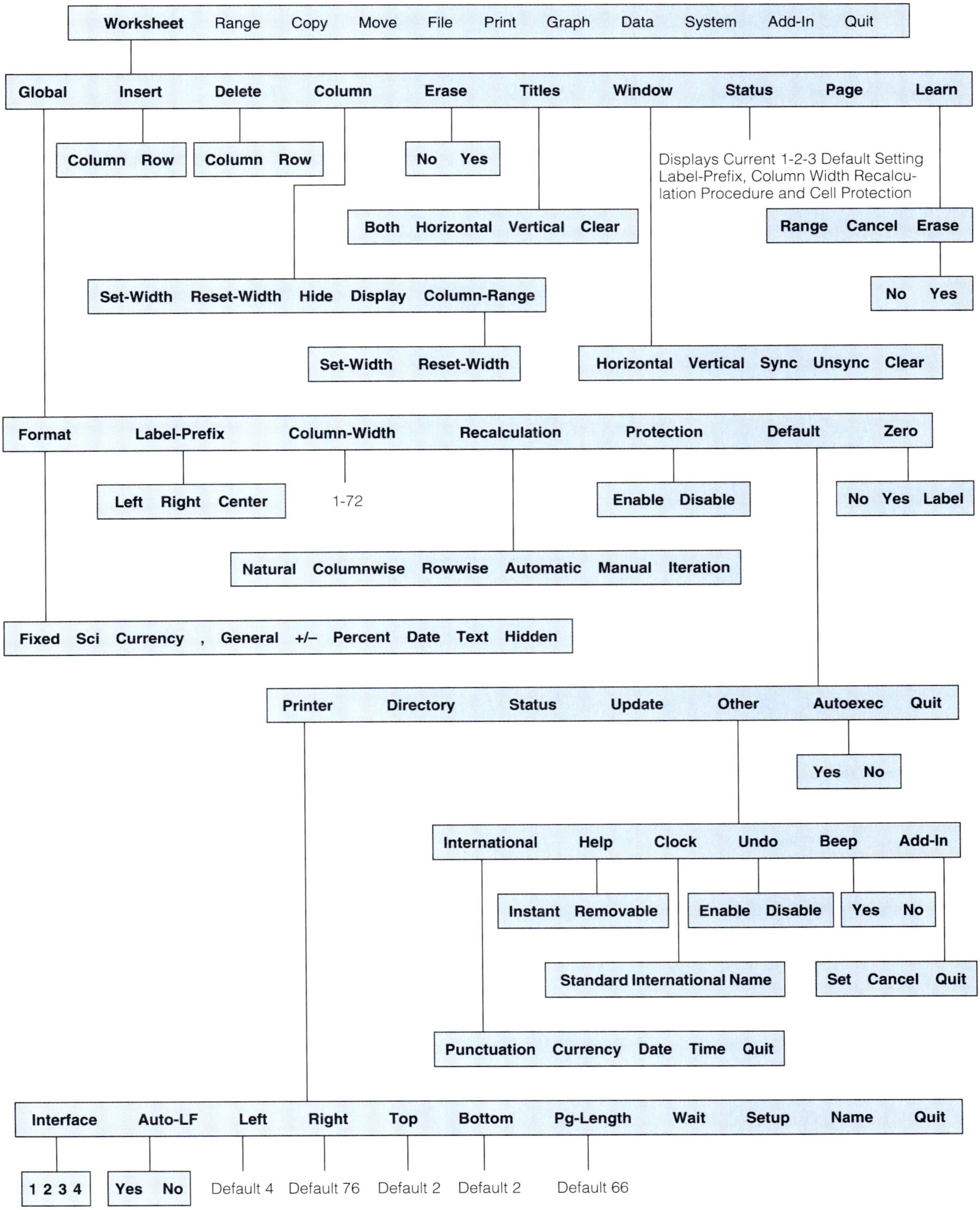

RANGE OPTIONS—LOTUS® 1-2-3™ COMMANDS

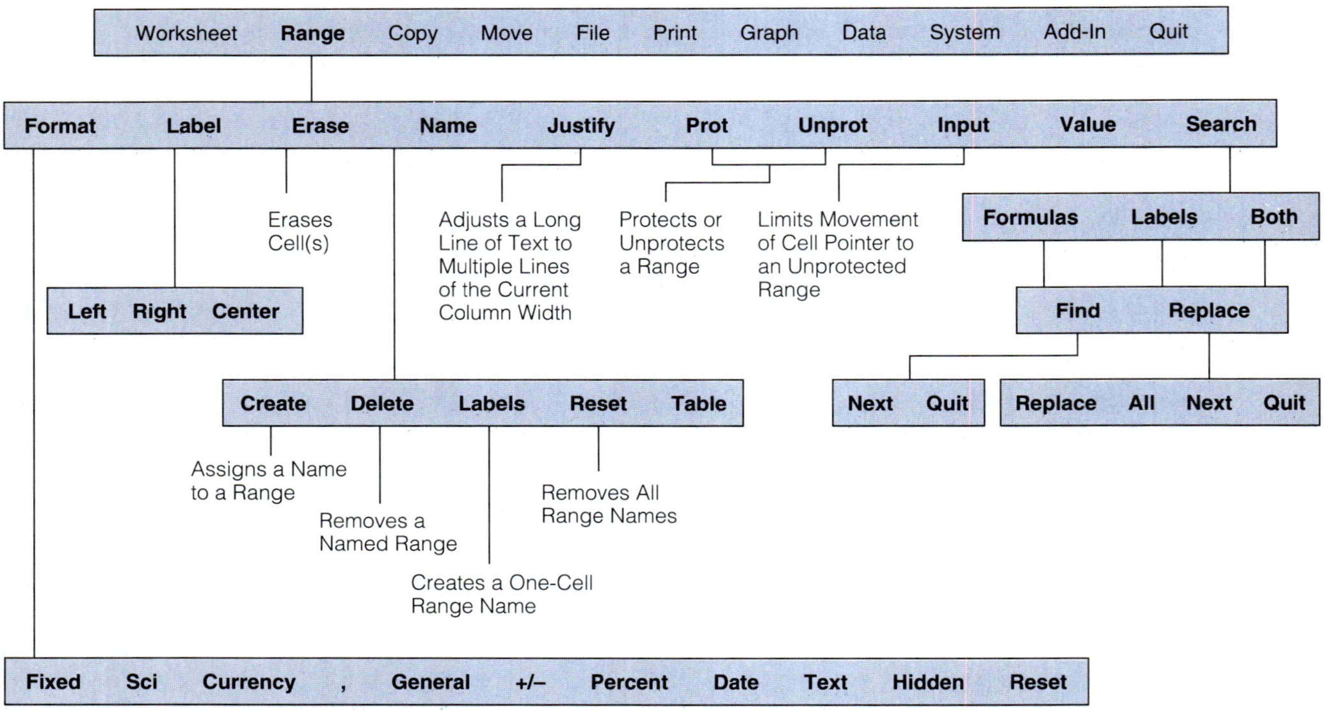

COPY, MOVE, ADD-IN OPTIONS—LOTUS® 1-2-3™ COMMANDS

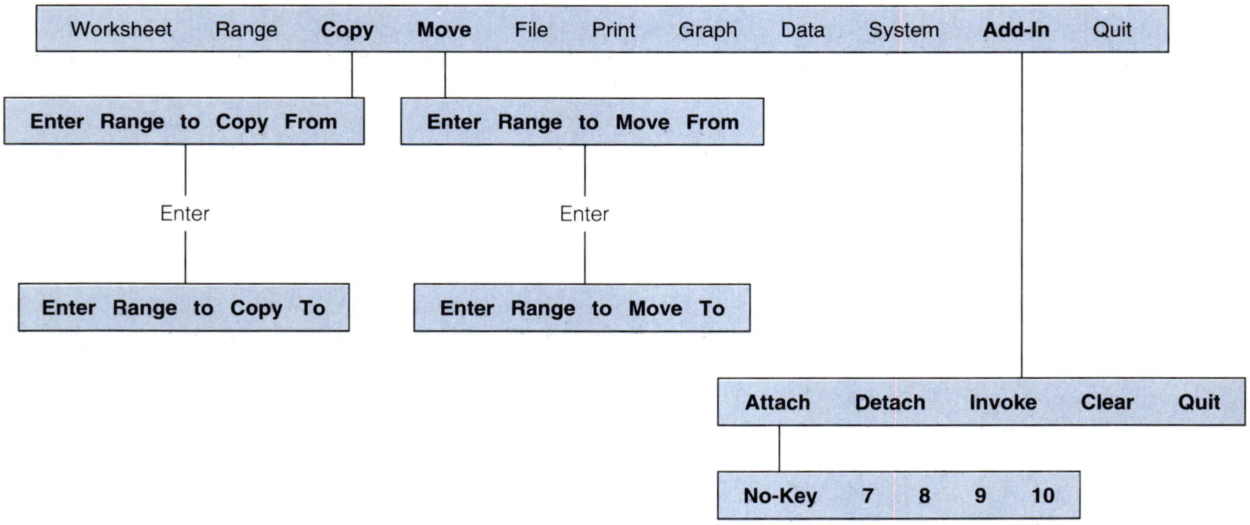

FILE OPTIONS—LOTUS® 1-2-3™ COMMANDS

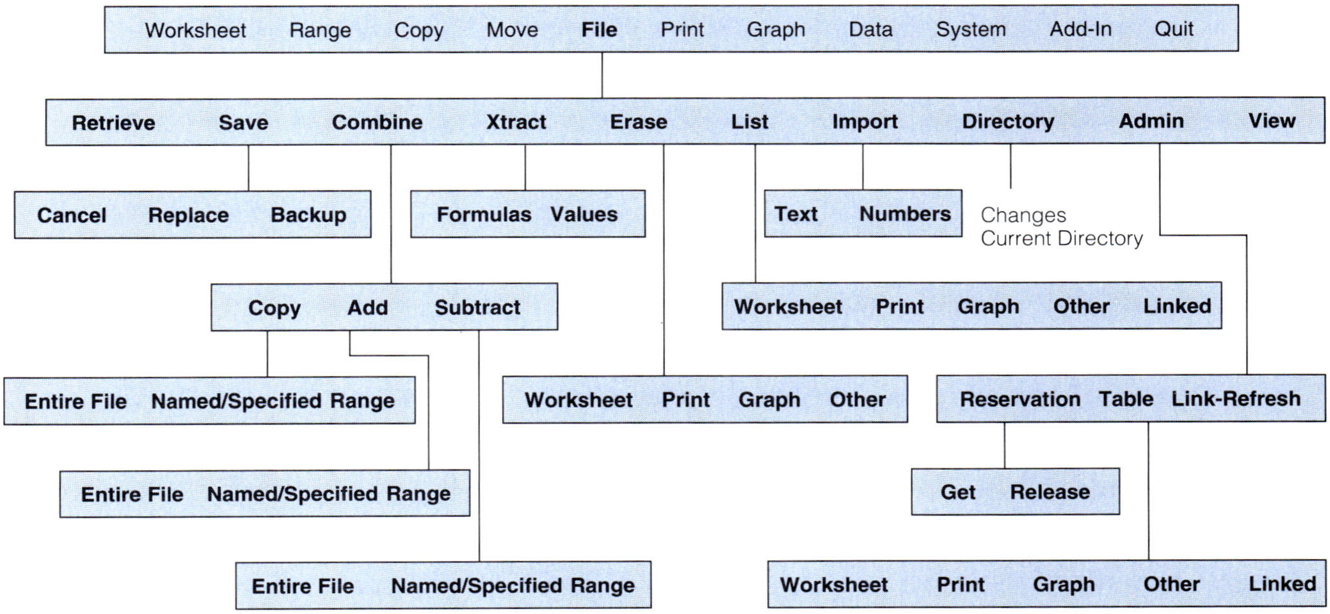

PRINT, QUIT OPTIONS—LOTUS® 1-2-3™ COMMANDS

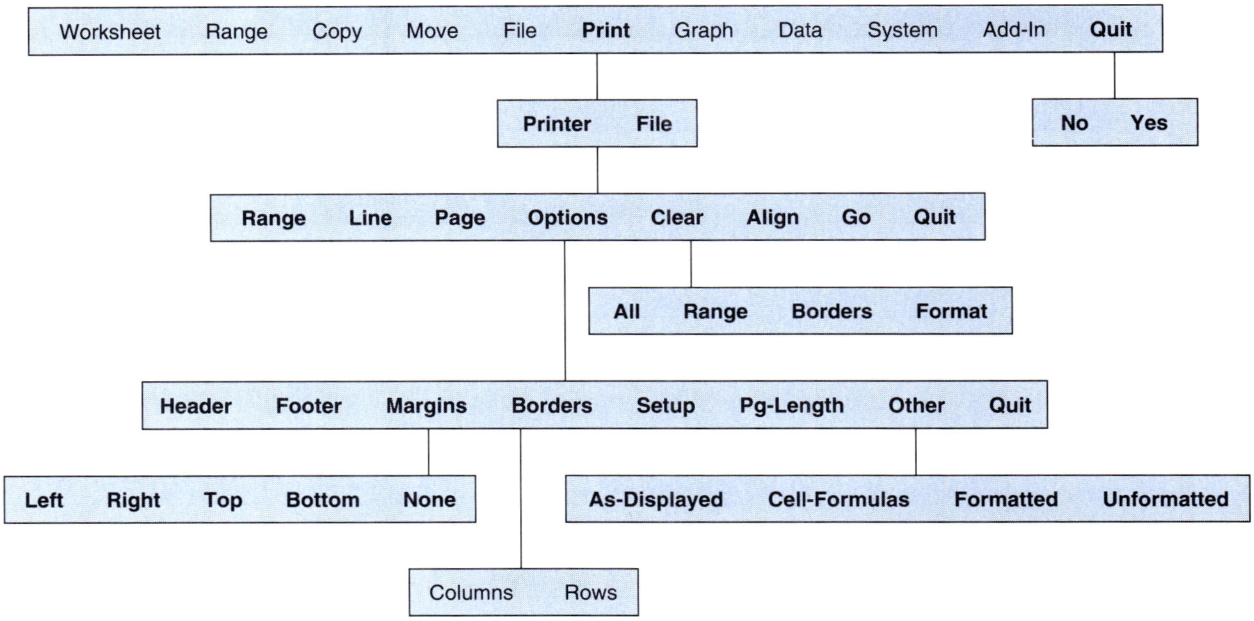

GRAPH OPTIONS—LOTUS® 1-2-3™ COMMANDS

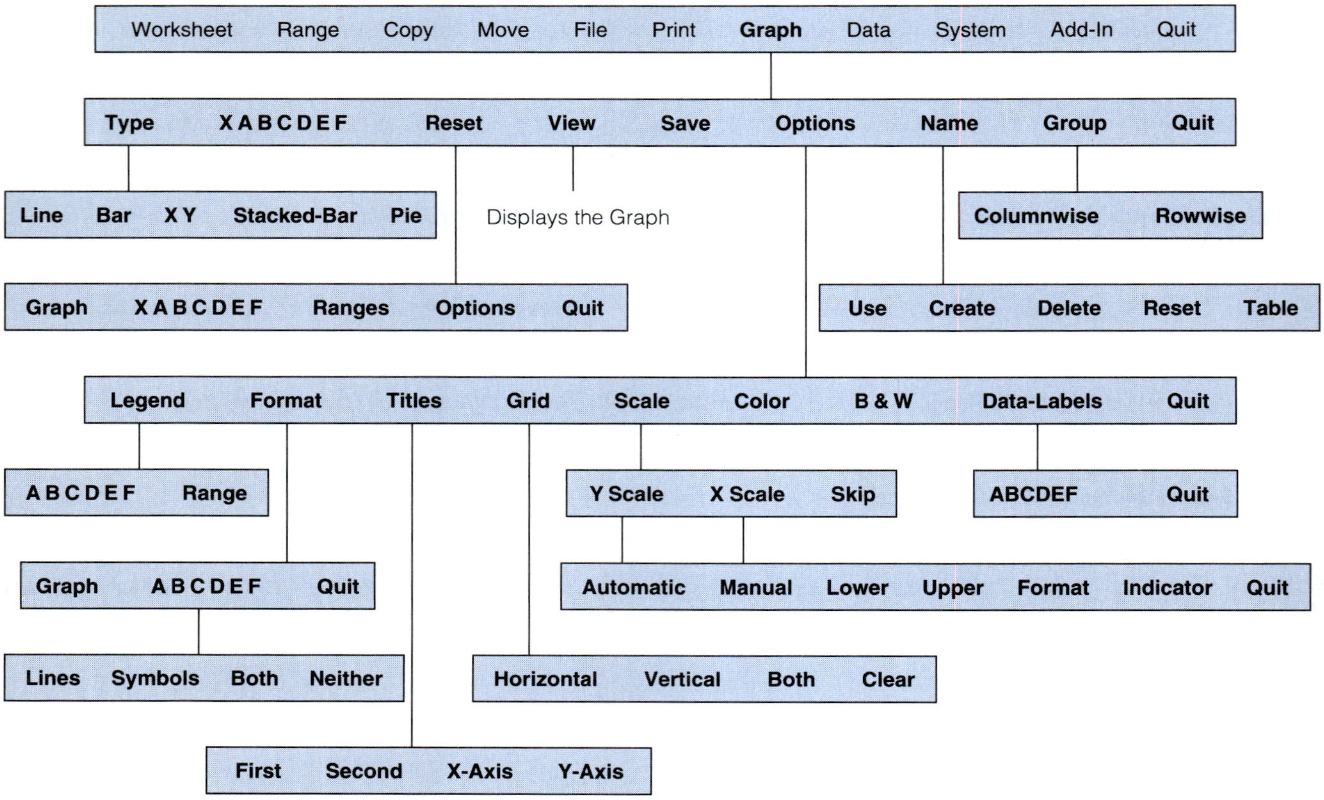

DATA OPTIONS—LOTUS® 1-2-3™ COMMANDS

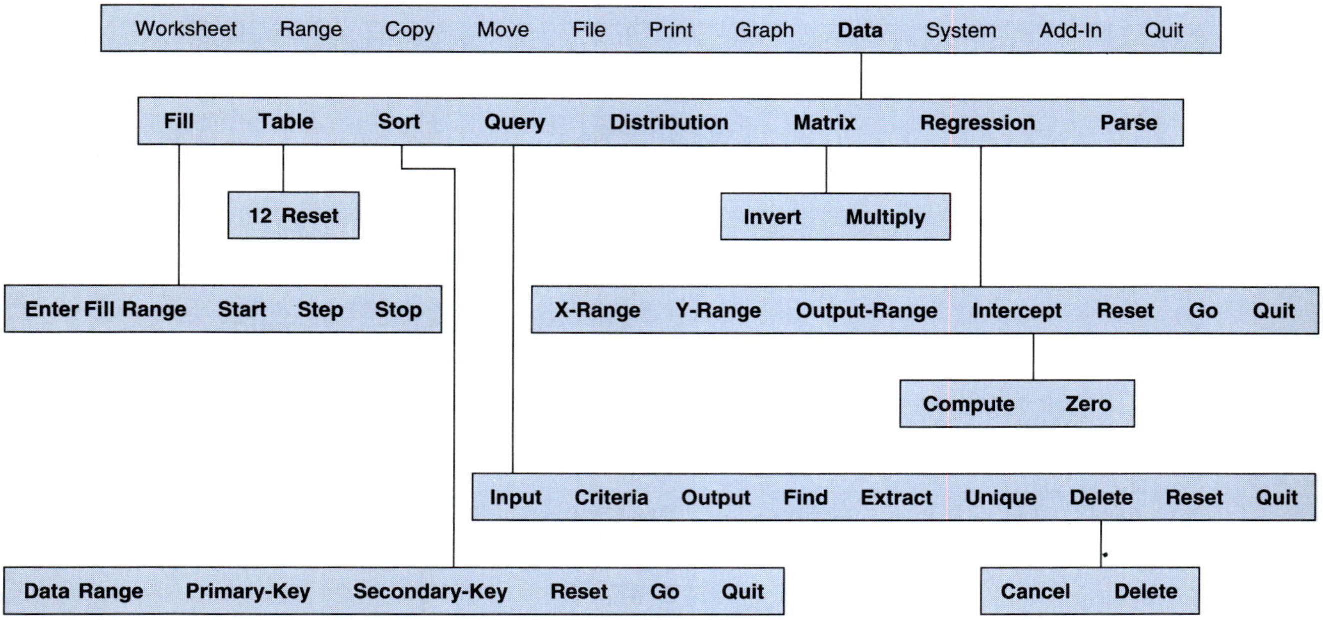

Lotus 1-2-3

Arithmetic and Logical Operators

+ Addition	= Equals
− Subtraction	< Less than
* Multiplication	> Greater than
/ Division	
^ Exponentiation	

Functions

@COUNT(range)	Number within a range	@STD(range)	Standard deviation
@SUM(range)	Sum of a range of values	@VAR(range)	Variance
@AVG(range)	Average of a range of values	@NOW	Today's numeric value
@MIN(range)	Smallest value	@DATE(yy,mm,dd)	Get number of a date
@MAX(range)	Largest value	@PMT(prn,int,term)	Payment amount

Lotus 1-2-3

Label Prefix

- ' Left justify text within a cell
- " Right justify text within a cell
- ^ Center text within a cell
- \ Repeating label

Absolute Cell References

CR	Always come back to the same row and column location (cell).
$CR	The row can change within the address, but the columns must always remain as specified. (Any row in this column)
C$R	The column can change within the address, but the row must remain the same. (Any column in this row)

Lotus 1-2-3

Function Keys

F1 Help	F5 Goto	F9 Calc
F2 Edit	F6 Window	F10 Graph
F3 Name	F7 Query	
F4 Abs	F8 Table	

Edit Keys

[Backspace]	Delete character to right of cursor	[Del]	Delete character at cursor
[ESC] or [Ctrl + Break]	Erase entry	[End]	Position cursor to end of line
right or left arrow	Move cursor one position right or left	[Enter]	Record/save the changes
[Home]	Position cursor to beginning of line		

Function Keys Templates
for Lotus 1-2-3
(Releases 2.2 and 2.3)

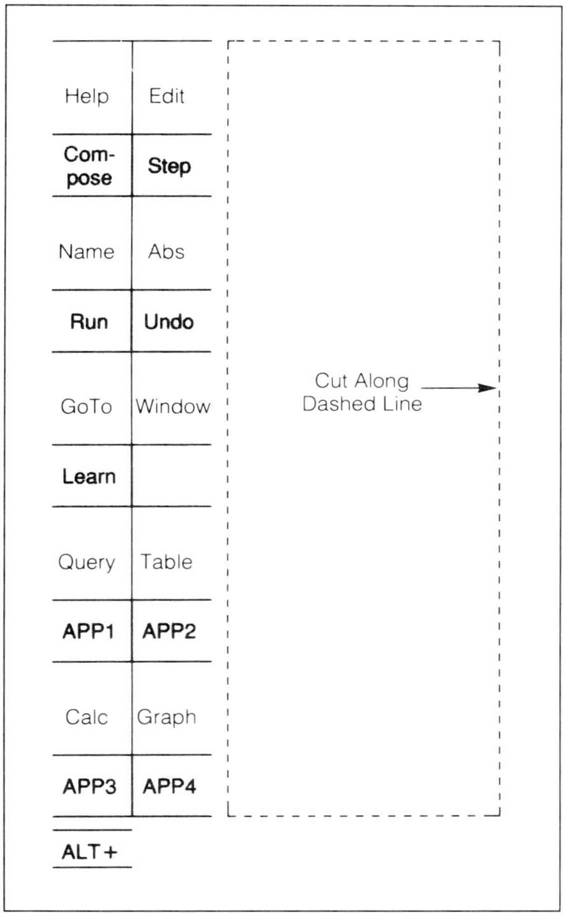

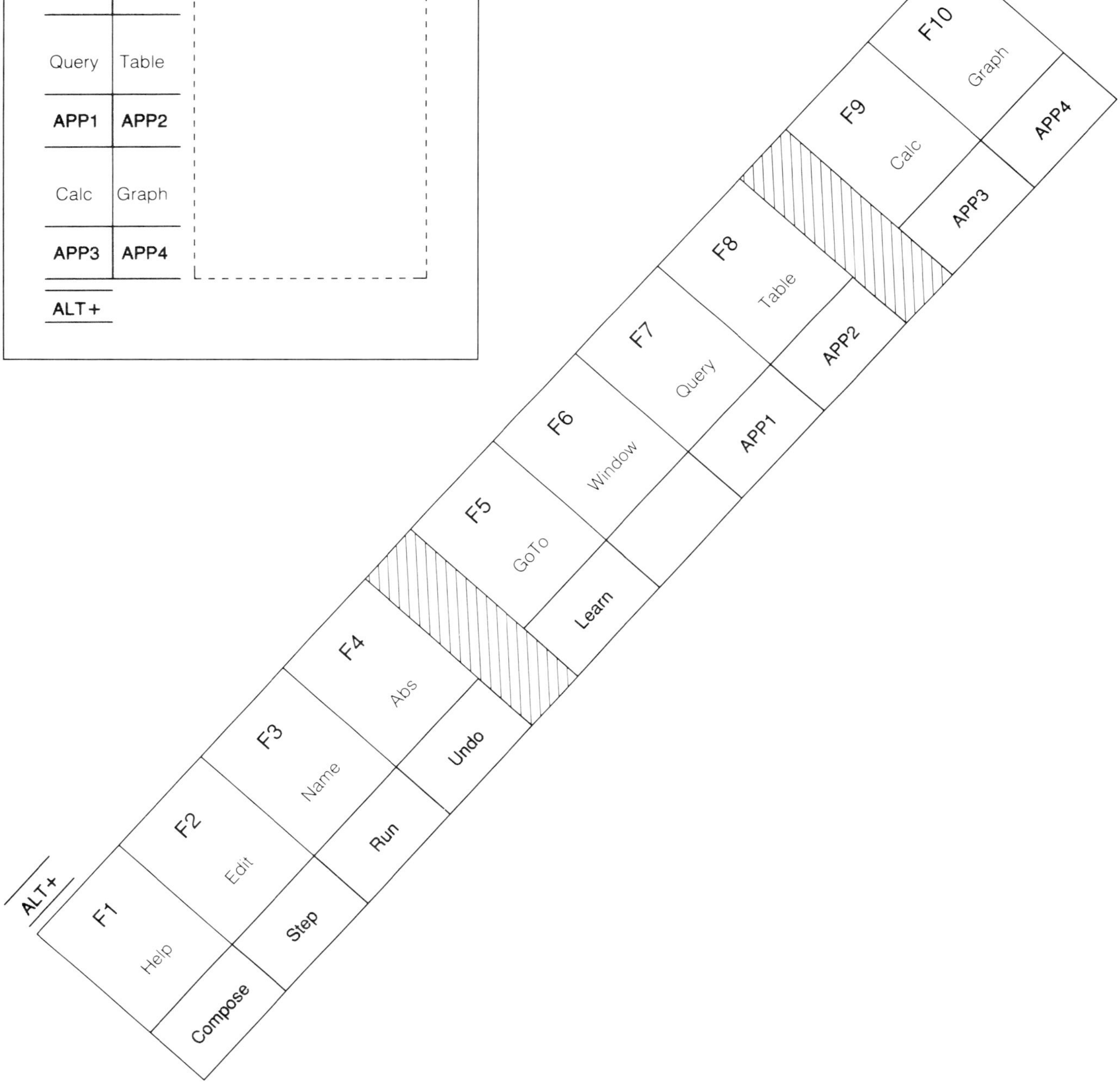

ESSENTIAL
dBASE III PLUS

Tim Duffy
Professor of Accounting in Information Systems
Illinois State University

ESSENTIAL dBASE III Plus

Wadsworth Publishing Company
Belmont, California
A Division of Wadsworth, Inc.

Computer Science Editor: Frank Ruggirello
Developmental Editor: Alan Venable
Editorial Assistant: Rhonda Gray
Production: Hal Lockwood, Bookman Productions
Print Buyer: Martha Branch
Art Editor: Jane Brundage, Bookman Productions
Interior and Cover Design: Vargas/Williams/Design
Copy Editor: Betty Duncan
Photo Researchers: Sarah Bendersky, Darcy Lanham, Judy Mason, Monica Suder
Technical Illustrator: Illustrious, Inc.
Compositor: Graphic Typesetting Service, Los Angeles
Printer: Arcata Graphics, Kingsport, Tennessee

2 3 4 5 6 7 8 9 10—96 95 94 93 92
ISBN: 0-534-18720-X

To Wendy and Michael

CONTENTS

PREFACE

PURPOSE

This *Software Essentials* book and its associated software training materials teach software competency. These materials are designed for both majors and non-majors in a quarter or semester course that uses the microcomputer as the primary vehicle for introducing students to problem solving. As typically expected in this type of course, there are no prerequisites.

APPROACH

Students acquire software competency by completing a set of software-training chapters that focus on current releases of various major software packages. To achieve that competency, each software package is presented in a separate booklet emphasizing hands-on problem solving. Carefully prepared, hands-on tutorials are provided within each chapter. Closely related end-of-chapter exercises reinforce the tutorial learning and expand the student's mastery over a broader range of applications.

Software packages covered in this series include

- DOS 3.3 and 5.0.
- WordPerfect 5.0/5.1.
- Lotus 1-2-3 2.2 and 2.3.
- Quattro Pro 3.0.
- dBASE III Plus.
- dBASE IV 1.1.
- Paradox 3.5.
- Windows 3.1.

IMPROVEMENTS IN SOFTWARE INSTRUCTION

I have always made the greatest possible effort to make hands-on instruction direct and meaningful. For this series in *Software Essentials,* the hands-on passages have been extensively reviewed and revised to make the booklets in the series more effective for the teacher and learning easier for the beginning student. Important changes include the following:

- **Self-Contained Modules** Each software module is self-contained. Each has its own front matter, chapter numbering, glossary, and command summary.
- **Expanded Hands-On Learning** The number of hands-on exercises has been increased dramatically. Particularly, the number of shorter exercises has been increased.
- **Use of Second Color** All hands-on exercise commands in the text appear in second color. This allows the student to quickly identify what keystrokes to enter and to distinguish them from additional explanation about a software feature or command.

- **Hints/Hazards Boxes** Many Hints/Hazards boxes inform students about the tricks they can use and potential traps they may encounter when using a particular software tool.
- **Keyboard Icons** Keyboard icons appear frequently in headings and tables. These icons help the student identify and remember specific keystrokes.

WORKING IN A HANDS-ON ENVIRONMENT

Software Essentials and its allied materials work best in a hands-on environment. The step-by-step exercises make most sense when an individual is sitting at a computer and can immediately see the results of his or her actions. A symbol such as the one shown in the margin indicates hands-on material.

Each software package covered in this series is treated in enough detail to satisfy the requirement of a computer novice. However, each software booklet assumes that the software has already been configured for the student's use. If a package has not been configured for a specific machine, refer to the documentation for that package.

HARDWARE REQUIREMENTS FOR HANDS-ON SOFTWARE

An IBM PC or compatible computer with two disk drives and 320K of memory is required for most tools in this series. Note that you need 512K and a hard disk to run dBASE IV. You will also need a color monitor/graphics adapter board to properly display Lotus 1-2-3 graphics on the screen. A printer (with graphics capabilities if you wish to print Lotus graphs) is also required for printing documents, reports, graphs, and worksheets.

The hard disk (fixed disk) has resulted in many changes in the way computer concepts and use are taught in the classroom. During the past few years, the prices of hard disk technology have plummeted. Because this technology is now affordable for most colleges and universities, this text includes instructions for running software from a fixed disk.

LEARNING AIDS AND SAMPLE FILES

Exercises are provided at the end of each chapter to give students quick feedback on their progress. Besides the written exercises, hands-on computer exercises are included at the end of the software chapters to provide feedback through challenging applications of material covered in the chapter. A number of sample diskette files—including sample worksheets, text files, and database files—have been provided for use with text lessons and exercises.

ESSENTIAL

dBASE III PLUS

1

INTRODUCTION TO DATABASE AND dBASE III PLUS

CHAPTER OBJECTIVES

After completing this chapter, you should be able to

- **List some of the basic concepts of database**
- **List the limitations of dBASE III Plus**
- **Use the dBASE III Plus Assist feature**
- **Know the parts of a dBASE III Plus screen**
- **Use the dBASE III Plus menu options**
- **Issue commands to dBASE III Plus**
- **Create dBASE III Plus files**
- **Add and edit data**
- **Use some elementary dBASE III Plus commands**

The concept behind a database is simple. A database is like a filing cabinet. Just as a filing cabinet stores information, so does a database. Just as the folders in the cabinet are arranged in some useful order, so are the records in a database. Searching the database for certain information is like searching in the cabinet. As you can change the order of the folders in the cabinet to suit your convenience, so you can also change the order of things in a database.

DATABASE, RECORD, AND FIELD

A **database** is a set of information related to some specific application. In the context of dBASE, a database is synonymous with *file.*

A **record** is a unit within the database. Each record in a database contains related information, such as the details of a single business transaction or a single customer's name and address.

A **field** is a smaller unit within a record. In a customer record, for instance, one field might contain the customer's last name, another his or her street address.

Information from one or more fields is used to define keys, which are used to order, identify, and retrieve the records in the database. Several keys are commonly used. The **primary key** is the unique identifier for a particular record, most often a unique record number. When a database is in primary key order, record number 5 occupies the fifth position in the database. A **secondary key** can also be defined by information from one or more other fields within the database. This key is used to arrange the database in some other order. For instance, you might create a secondary key containing a Social Security number field to put a file of employee records in order by that number.

The **structure** of a database is a set of instructions regarding the arrangement of information within each record, the type of characters (numeric or alphanumeric) used to store each field, and the number of characters required by each field. Once structured, the database can be managed, and the computer can be instructed to do such things as adding new records, changing existing records, sorting and arranging records into a new order, searching for and retrieving specific types of records, printing data, and deleting data.

INTRODUCTION TO dBASE III PLUS

The dBASE package is the best-selling relational database package on the market. The dBASE III version of dBASE evolved from dBASE II. Ashton-Tate originally developed dBASE II for 8-bit microcomputers that used the CP/M operating system. When IBM introduced the IBM PC, Ashton-Tate revised dBASE to run on the PC/MS DOS operating systems.

LIMITATIONS OF dBASE III PLUS

Anyone who wants to use the full version of **dBASE III Plus** should be aware of the following limitations: (1) It requires an IBM PC or compatible 16-bit computer with a minimum of 320K of memory (more memory is faster); (2) the system should have either two 360K diskette drives or a hard disk and one diskette drive; (3) no file can hold more than 1 billion records; (4) the maximum record size is 4000 characters and 128 fields; (5) a character field can have up to 254 positions, a numeric field 15 positions, a memo field 4096 positions; (6) no more than 10 database files can be open at one time; and (7) only seven indexes can be specified as active for a file at one time. Most applications are not affected by these limitations.

The version of dBASE III Plus covered in this and the following chapters is the student demonstration version. The only difference between the full version and the student version is that the student version limits file size to 31 records.

MODES OF dBASE III PLUS

The dBASE III Plus package provides three different modes. **ASSISTANT mode** is an easy-to-use menu-driven interface that lets you issue commands without an in-depth understanding of dBASE. **COMMAND mode** requires some understanding of dBASE because instructions are entered at the **dot prompt (.)** and Help Menus are not displayed for most commands. **PROGRAM mode** (also referred to as BATCH mode) lets you store instructions in a program file and execute all of them with one command.

STARTING dBASE III PLUS

How you start dBASE III Plus depends on your system.

Diskette-Based Systems

1. Boot the computer with the DOS system disk. Enter the date and time if you want this information in the directory of any files you create.
2. Unless your instructor tells you otherwise, place the first program diskette in drive A and your data diskette in drive B. Type `DBASE` at the DOS prompt A> and press Enter. Once the first diskette files have been loaded, follow the prompts to replace the first program diskette with the second diskette and press Enter.

Hard Disk–Based Systems

1. Turn on the system. At the DOS prompt, use the CD command to activate the directory containing the dBASE III Plus program files. For instance, if your dBASE III Plus directory is named DB3PLUS, type `CD \DB3PLUS` and press Enter.
2. At the DOS prompt, type `DBASE` and press Enter.

THE ASSISTANT SCREEN

Once you have started dBASE III Plus, the copyright screen appears. This screen disappears after a few seconds or when you press Enter, and the Assistant Menu takes its place (Figure 1.1).

Whether you start dBASE from a hard disk or a diskette, the Assistant Menu screens will be virtually identical. The Assistant Menu provides a number of options across the top of the screen. Select an option by either positioning the pointer (via the Arrow keys) or entering the first character of the command and confirm your selection by pressing Enter. As you make selections, the pull-down menus change. (For instance, compare Figure 1.1 with Figure 1.2.) Figure 1.3 shows all the menus. A pull-down menu may have a submenu with further options.

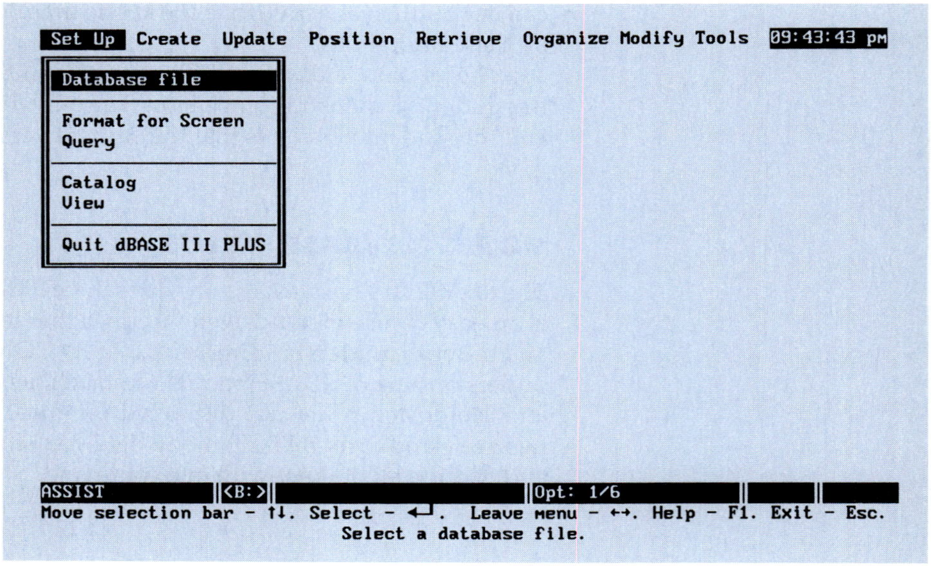

Figure 1.1
The dBASE III Plus screen with the Assistant Menu activated.

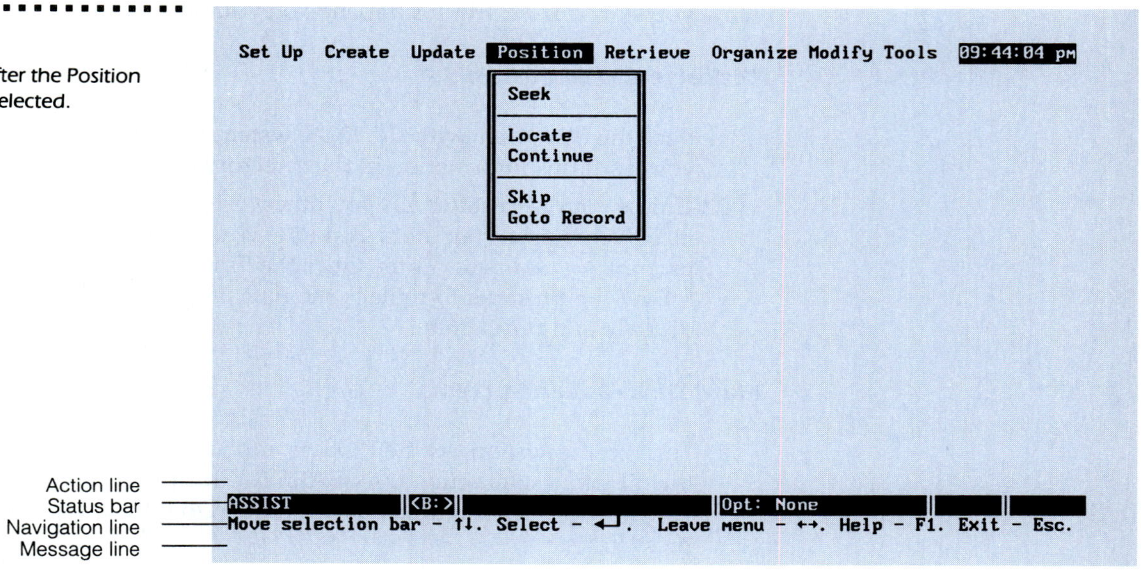

Figure 1.2
Assistant screen after the Position option has been selected.

Other components of the Assistant Menu include the following (see also Figure 1.2).

Action Line The **action line** (above the bar near the bottom of the screen) displays the command being generated by your menu or submenu selection.

Status Bar The **status bar** (in reverse video near the bottom of your screen) describes the current status of dBASE III Plus, for instance, the current drive, the file (if any) in use, the current record number or the option from the menu or submenu in use, whether the Ins or Del option is in use (during the edit process), and the status of the Caps Lock key (Caps if it is on).

Navigation Line The **navigation line** (just beneath the status bar) gives instructions for moving from one menu option to another or from one submenu to another.

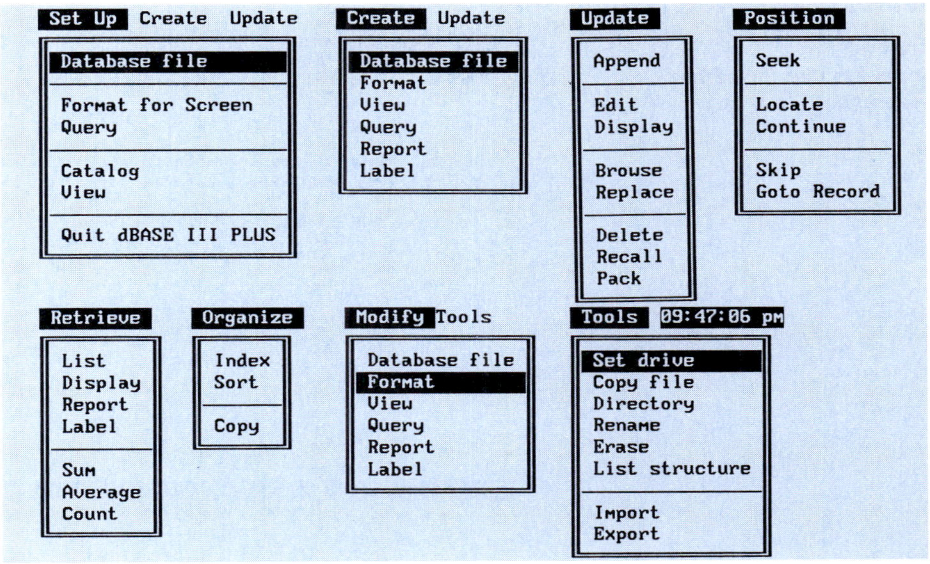

Figure 1.3
Various menus available from the Assistant Menu.

Message Line The **message line** (beneath the navigation line) states the current menu option and any action you are to take.

LEAVING THE ASSISTANT MENU

If you make a mistake on a menu selection, you can back up one level by pressing Esc. If you are at the menu line, however, upon pressing Esc you leave the Assistant Menu and drop to the dot prompt mode. In dot prompt mode, no menus are displayed; rather, the dot prompt (.) appears on the action line. The status bar and the message line are also visible. The message line contains the following prompt:

```
Enter a dBASE III PLUS command.
```

If you enter dot prompt mode by mistake, you can get back to the Assistant Menu (Figure 1.1) by typing the **Assist command** at the dot prompt and then pressing Enter.

THE HELP FACILITY (F1 OR .HELP)

Help is available by highlighting any item in the Assistant Menu or any submenu and then pressing the F1 function key. For instance, if you want help on the Create command, press F1 while that option is highlighted; a description of that command (Figure 1.4) will then be displayed. Another way to get help is pressing Y at the prompt.

```
Do you want some help? (Y/N) _
```

This prompt appears when you commit an error in entering a command at the dot prompt. Pressing Y displays the Help Main Menu (Figure 1.5).

You can also get help by entering the **Help command** (type HELP or press F1) at the dot prompt and pressing Enter. This displays the Help Main Menu.

Figure 1.4
The Help screen for the Create command.

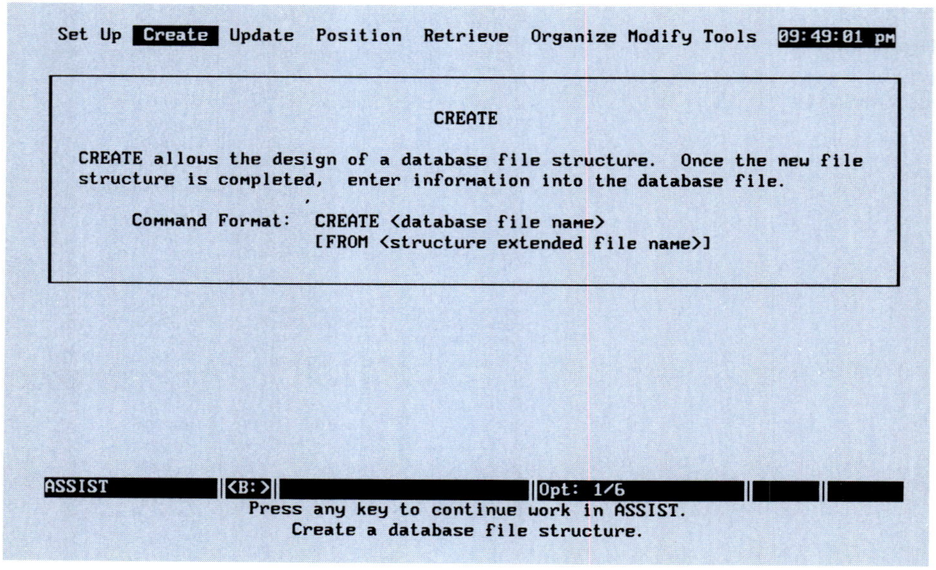

Figure 1.5
The Help Main Menu for the Report command.

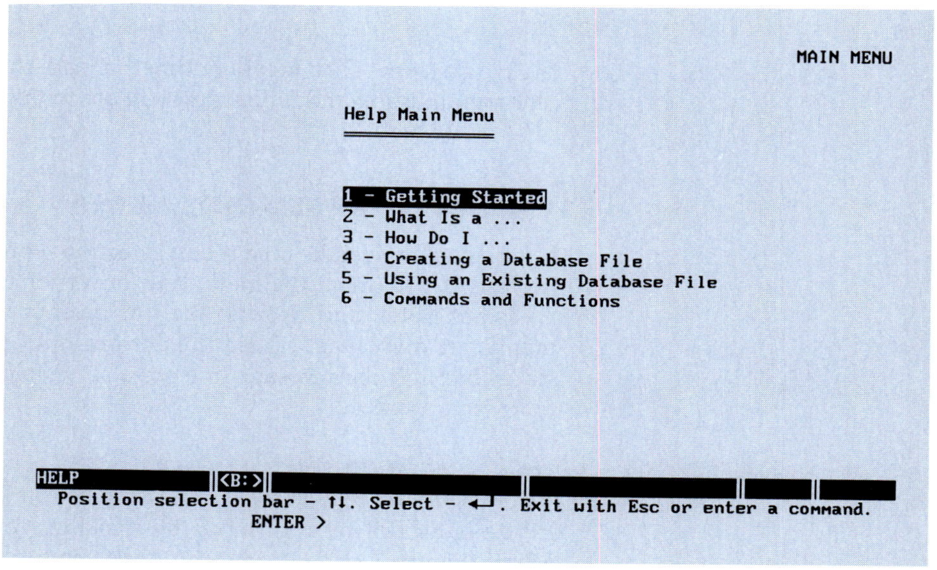

Select option 1, Getting Started, and enter the command about which you want additional information. For example, if you want information about the Report command, enter `REPORT` in the message line and press Enter. The information then appears (Figure 1.6).

Note that when you are in the Help Menus, the navigation line contains prompts about how to move from one screen to the next by pressing the Pg Up or Pg Dn keys. It also tells you to move to the previous menu by pressing F10 or to exit to the dot prompt by pressing Esc. If you want information about any other dBASE command, simply enter that command in the message line.

You can save yourself one step by entering the Help command and then the command about which you want the information. To get immediate information about the Report command (Figure 1.6), enter the following command at the dot prompt.

```
.HELP REPORT
```

Figure 1.6
The Help screen generated for the Report command.

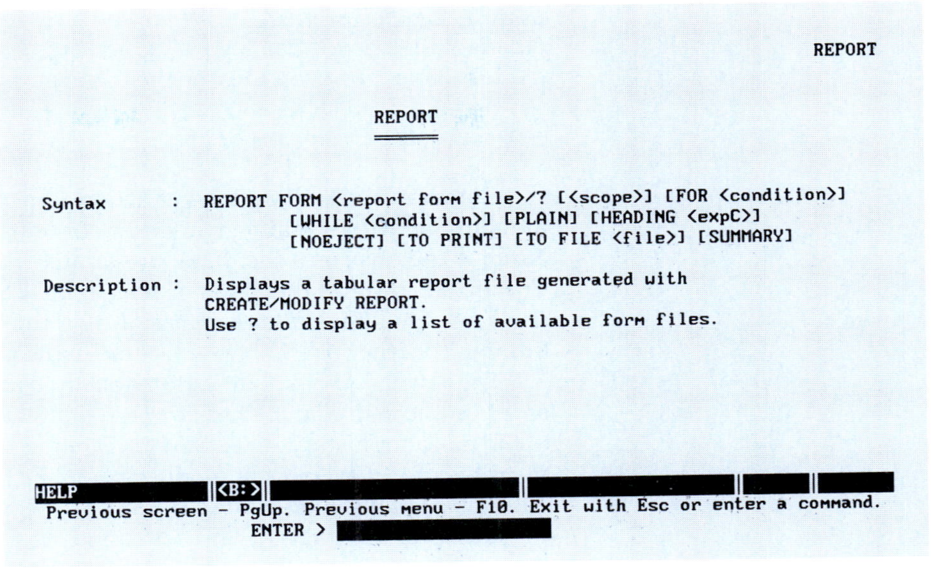

```
                                                                REPORT

                                   REPORT
                                   ======

Syntax       :  REPORT FORM <report form file>/? [<scope>] [FOR <condition>]
                        [WHILE <condition>] [PLAIN] [HEADING <expC>]
                        [NOEJECT] [TO PRINT] [TO FILE <file>] [SUMMARY]

Description  :  Displays a tabular report file generated with
                CREATE/MODIFY REPORT.
                Use ? to display a list of available form files.

HELP          <B:>
 Previous screen - PgUp. Previous menu - F10. Exit with Esc or enter a command.
                   ENTER >
```

LEAVING dBASE III PLUS (QUIT)

At the end of a dBASE III Plus session, you must use the **Quit command,** which closes any files that might still be open. If a file has had records added to it and is not closed properly, the end-of-the-file marker will be misplaced, and records may be lost. To quit from the Assistant screen, move the pointer to the Set Up command. Once the Set Up Menu is displayed, move the pointer bar to Quit dBASE III Plus and press Enter.

To quit from the dot prompt, press Esc once or twice to receive the dot prompt on the action line. Then type `QUIT` and press Enter. Whichever method you choose displays a message and the DOS prompt:

```
*** END RUN  dBASE III Plus
C>_
```

FROM ASSISTANT MODE TO COMMAND MODE

This section presents the ASSISTANT (menu-driven) and COMMAND (dot prompt) modes of dBASE III Plus. It also introduces some dBASE commands: Create, Use, Append, List, and Edit.

The ASSISTANT mode is an excellent tool for learning dBASE because it is **menu-driven** and does not require programming experience. For these reasons, we emphasize it in this and the following chapters.

Use the ASSISTANT mode to learn commands. Once the commands and their proper sequence are familiar, start trying the COMMAND mode. In the long run, this **command-driven mode** will be quicker because you will not have to view several menus before completing a command, and you will not have to return control to a previous menu before proceeding, as sometimes happens in the ASSISTANT mode.

At the computer, start dBASE III Plus as instructed in the previous section. Because the ASSISTANT mode is the dBASE default, you will see the Assistant Menu, which lists your initial options.

dBASE Sentence Rules When you use a series of menus to issue a command to dBASE, you can regard the series as a sort of sentence. The ASSISTANT mode menus cause you to issue the commands in correct grammatical order:

```
COMMAND SCOPE NOUN CONDITION
```

Command tells dBASE what action to perform. **Scope** limits the range of the command, determining whether all or only a part of the file is to be affected. **Noun** is the object—a file, field, or variable—on which the command will act. **Condition** specifies the fields or files to be acted upon. A dBASE III Plus sentence need not have all four parts; it may consist of the Command part alone. But if it has other parts, they will come in the above order.

The ASSISTANT mode automatically constructs sentences in the correct order on the action line. Once you are familiar with this order, you can switch to the more sophisticated COMMAND mode and type such sentences yourself. In using the COMMAND mode, remember that you must always sequence your instructions in this order: Command, Scope, Noun, Condition.

To switch from the ASSISTANT mode to the COMMAND mode, press Esc once or twice. This will cause the dot prompt (.) to appear on the action line. The dot (actually a period) is the dBASE III Plus COMMAND mode prompt and indicates that dBASE is waiting for you to enter a command. After each command, press Enter to tell dBASE to execute the command. To return to the ASSISTANT mode, type `ASSIST` at the dot prompt and press Enter.

COMMUNICATING WITH dBASE III PLUS

SETTING THE DEFAULT DRIVE

Unless told otherwise, dBASE assumes that data files are on the same disk as the dBASE III Plus program files. If you are using a diskette-based system, however, you will not want to record your data files on the limited space of the dBASE system disk. If your copy of dBASE does not default to drive B (look at your status bar), you must reset the default disk. The following steps instruct dBASE to record data files on a different disk. Begin from the Assistant Menu.

Tools	Highlight Tools from the Assistant Menu.
Set drive	Highlight Set drive.
Press Enter	Produces prompt `SET DEFAULT TO`.
B:	Highlight drive B.
Press Enter	Selects the designated drive (Figure 1.7).

Henceforth, commands entered with a drive specifier will automatically refer to files in drive B.

FULL-SCREEN CURSOR MENUS

Whenever dBASE offers you a full-screen menu like that in Figure 1.8, you will be able to move the cursor to various formatted locations on the screen, following instructions on the menu. The box of information on the screen describing cursor movement keystrokes can be turned on and off by issuing the **Set Menu On/Off command** at the dot prompt. On displays the cursor movement menu; Off suppresses it.

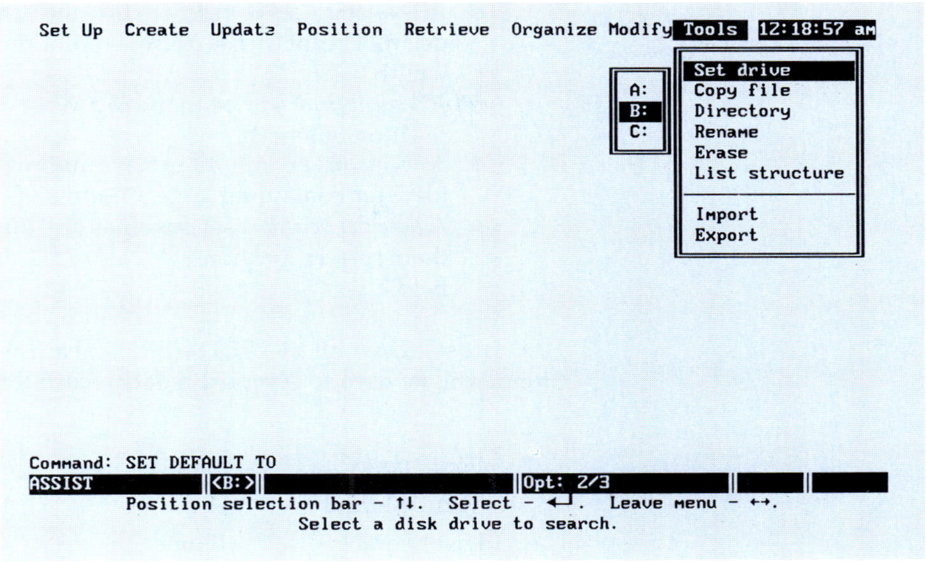

Figure 1.7
The Tools option used to set the default drive to B, and the dBASE command on the action line that has been generated by the menu selections.

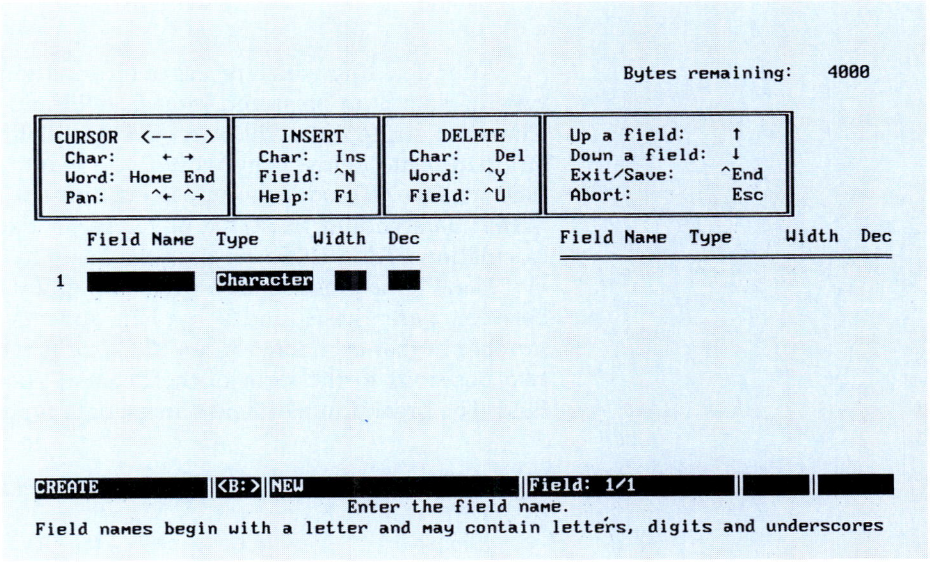

Figure 1.8
Example of a full-screen Cursor Menu.

CREATING A dBASE III PLUS FILE

Before dBASE III Plus can use a file, you must provide its name and information about its data fields (name, data type, and length), using the following rules:

1. A filename can contain up to 8 characters. Do not give the file an extension; dBASE III Plus automatically places a .DBF extension on all database files.
2. A field name consists of up to 10 characters. Acceptable characters are the letters *A* through Z, the digits 0 through 9, and the underscore mark (_). The data to be stored in a field determine the type of the field: character string (C), numeric (N), logical (L), memo (M), and date (D).
   a. A *character string field* can hold any alphanumeric character (number, letter, or special character).

b. A *numeric field* is restricted to the signs + or −, numerals, and the decimal point (.); the decimal point must be counted as part of the field length.
c. A *logical field* will be marked Y (yes) or N (no) and is always only one position in length.
d. A *memo field* can hold a maximum of 4096 characters and is therefore ideal for containing large amounts of text data.
e. A *date field* contains 8 positions and automatically has the slashes (/) in their correct locations; "__ / __ / __ indicates an empty data field."

Let's begin with a CUSTOMER database application. The following 10 data items will be used to compose a data record for each customer:

First Name	State
Middle Initial	ZIP
Last Name	Phone
Address	Amount Owed
City	Payment Date

After deciding which pieces of information to store, you must decide which type of data is to be stored in each field and how long each field should be. Character string data will be used for all fields except the Amount Owed and Payment Date fields. Why would you want to use character data for the ZIP field when a ZIP code is composed of numeric digits? A common rule of thumb is that data should be stored as character data unless they are to be used in calculations. Also, character data are easier to include in indexing.

The Phone field is also character data because the area code appears between parentheses and a hyphen appears between the exchange and the number in that exchange. Amount Owed is the only numeric field. It will have two positions to the right of the decimal point. Payment Date will be a date field. The breakdown of field names, data types, and field lengths is as follows:

Field	*Data Type*	*Field Length*
FIRST	C	10
INIT	C	1
LAST	C	12
ADDRESS	C	25
CITY	C	15
STATE	C	2
ZIP	C	5
PHONE	C	13
AMOUNT	N	8,2
DATE	D	8

It is important not to use too many fields in a record or to define fields that are too large to hold the data. The size of the fields determines how much space they will take on disk. Unused field positions are filled with blanks. Reserving too much room for a field wastes the disk storage space.

Hands-On Exercise: Building a File This exercise shows you how to build a dBASE data file and place records in the file.

1. Create the file:

Create	Selects the Create option from the Assistant Menu.
Enter	Selects the Database file option.
Enter	(Or highlight B or the desired drive and press Enter) Selects drive B (Figure 1.9).
Type CUSTOMER	Enters the filename.
Enter	Names the file (Figure 1.10).

2. Enter the fields from the Create screen (Figure 1.11). Notice that the status line contains four pieces of information: (1) the name of the instruction being executed (CREATE), (2) the disk on which it is to be recorded (B:), (3) the name of the file (CUSTOMER), and (4) the fact that the pointer is on field 1 of 1 (no others have been created). You are now ready to enter information about each field to be stored:

Type FIRST	Enters the name of the first field of data. Field names always appear in uppercase characters regardless of how they are entered.
Enter	Names the first field.
Enter or C	Accepts Character as the default data type for this field. [You can select other data types as appropriate by entering the first character of each possible type (Numeric, Date, Logical, and Memo). You can also press the Space Bar until you obtain the appropriate data type.]
Type 10	Selects the field width. When you are defining a numeric field, you will also be prompted regarding the number of decimal positions.
Enter	Establishes the field width.

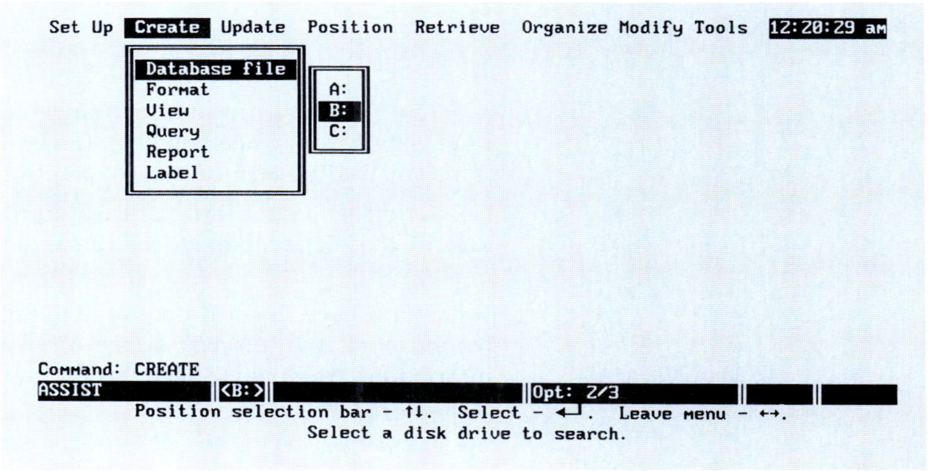

Figure 1.9
Selecting the disk drive on which the file is to be created.

Figure 1.10

Entering the filename of the file to be created.

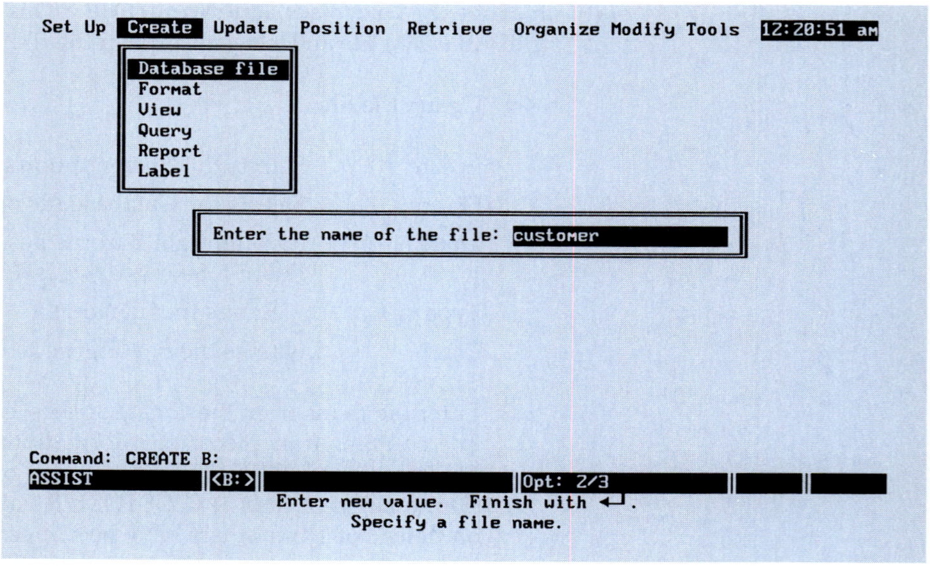

Figure 1.11

The Create screen that appears for a file to be created.

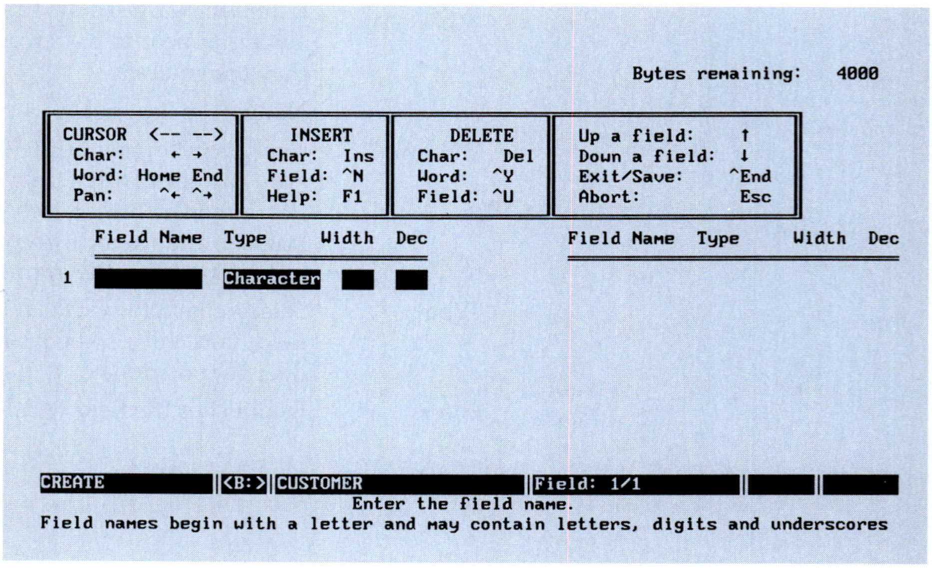

You have now finished defining Field 1. Continue by defining the remaining fields. When you enter the last field (date data type), the width is automatically assumed to be eight positions (Figure 1.12).

3. Correcting errors is a straightforward process. Use the cursor-positioning keys on the keypad to move the cursor to the desired field and re-enter the data.
4. When you have finished defining the fields in the record, press Enter in response to the prompt for a field name, without entering any information. You then receive this prompt.

```
Press ENTER to confirm. Any other key to resume. _
```

Figure 1.12
The completed Create screen for the CUSTOMER.DBF file.

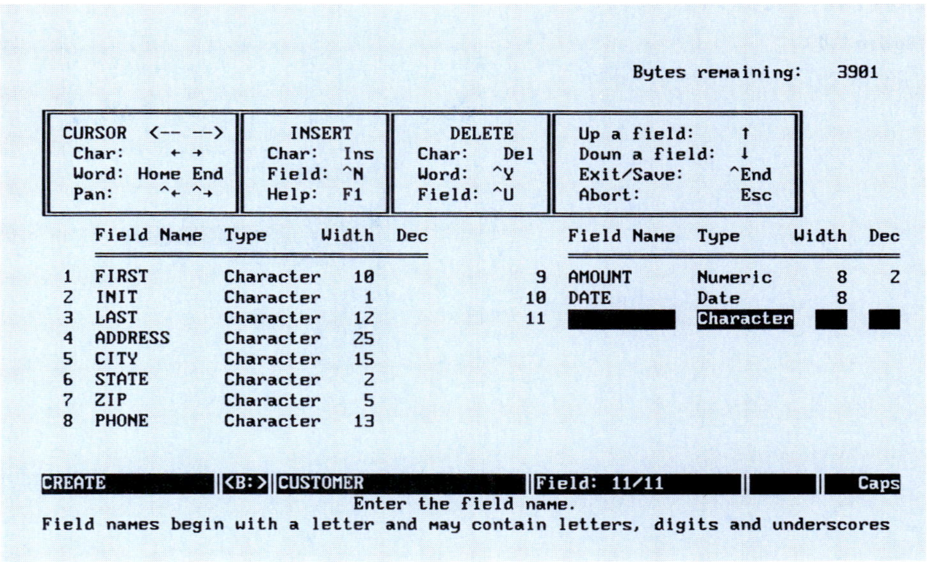

If you press Enter again, the file definition is finished. Pressing any other key lets you go back and make changes. You now see the message `Please Wait . . . .` as dBASE records this information to the disk. It then asks

```
Input data record now? (Y/N) _
```

Type Y. Then enter the five records below:

```
                    Name and Address Database
--------------------------------------------------------------------------
Last         First      Init          Address           City         St Zip
Ghorbani     Reza       R.     4033 N. Wolcott        Chicago        IL 60712
                                       (312)245-0324      125.00   01/17/92
Ghorbani     Ann        B.     4033 N. Wolcott        Chicago        IL 60712
                                       (312)245-0324      250.00   03/23/92
Acklin       Douglas    C.     408 E. Monroe          Bloomington    IL 61701
                                       (309)663-8976       55.00   04/01/92
Walters      Barbara    A.     1981 Crestlawn         Arlington      VA 13411
                                       (703)237-3727       75.00   12/23/92
Adams        Arthur     V.     115 Ginger Creek Ct.   Bloomington    IL 61701
                                       (309)828-7290       35.00   03/15/92
```

A blank record form now appears on the screen (Figure 1.13), with the full-screen Cursor Menu at the top. The status line shows the name of the file and the current record number. Each field name appears in the left-hand column next to the field itself, which is in reverse video to indicate its length. Fill in the appropriate blanks. When you have reached the end of a field, the computer beeps, and the cursor automatically advances to the next field. If you finish entering data before the end of the field is reached, simply press Enter. When the last field is filled or Enter is pressed, a new blank form appears.

When you enter numeric information, dBASE III Plus automatically right-justifies the number in the field when you press Enter. If the number does not

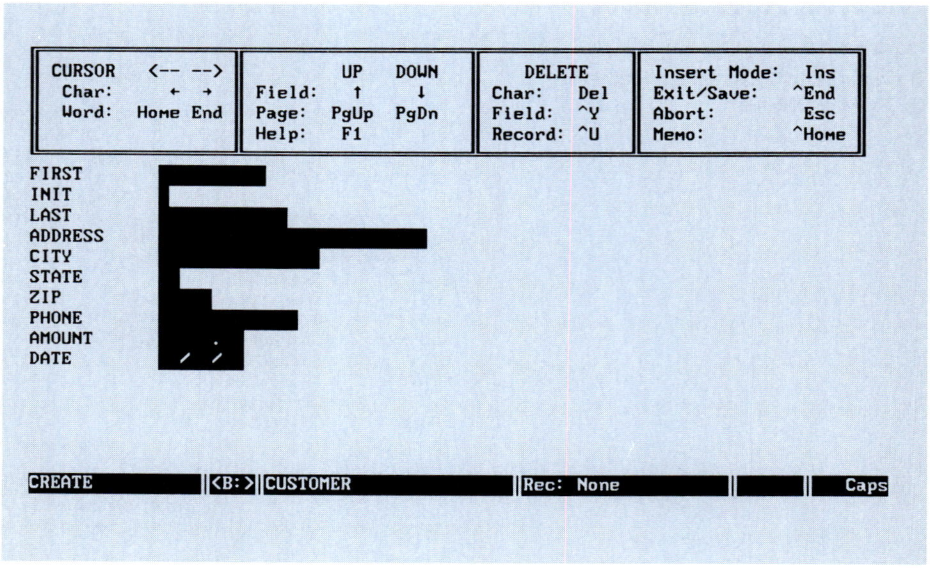

Figure 1.13
Blank record form for the CUSTOMER file.

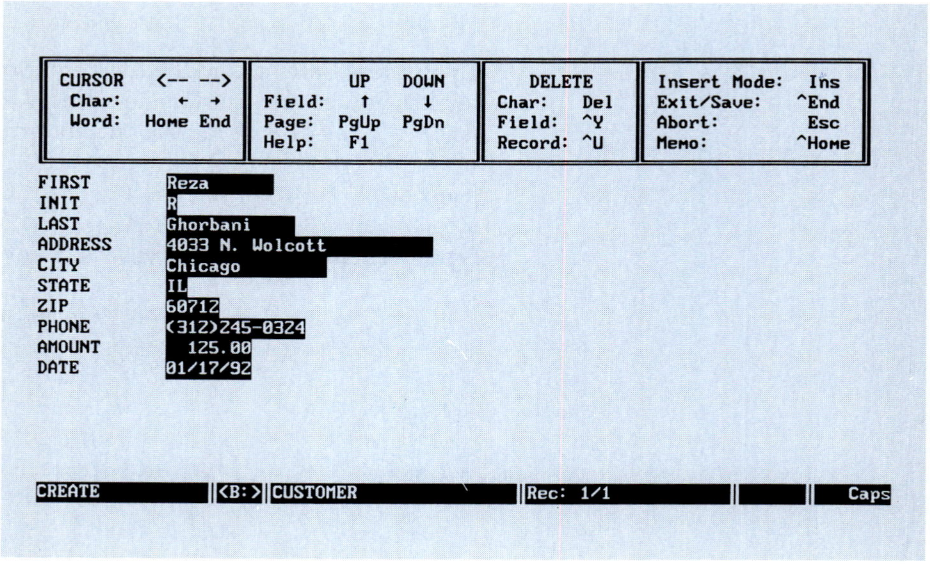

Figure 1.14
Filled-in form for the first data record of the CUSTOMER.DBF file.

have decimal positions, you do not have to enter a decimal point; dBASE will automatically place it in the appropriate location.

When this form has been filled with the data for the first record, it should look like the screen in Figure 1.14.

As each record is entered, dBASE raises the record number in the status bar of the screen. When you have finished entering all five of the records, press Enter at the next blank form. dBASE then assumes that you have finished entering data and returns you to the Assistant Menu. If you press Enter prematurely, leaving the process before you have entered all the records, select the Update command from the Assistant Menu and press Enter when the pointer is on the Append option. A new blank form is now displayed on the screen.

REACTIVATING A DATABASE

The previous section showed you how to enter dBASE and create a database file. Suppose that you quit the program at the end of that session and now wish to resume your work on the database. First, re-enter dBASE. Then perform the following steps:

1. Set your disk drives as necessary:

Tools	Selects Tools from the Assistant Menu.
Set drive	Selects the Set drive command.
Enter	Asks for the disk drive by prompting `SET DEFAULT TO`.
B:	Selects drive B, assuming you are using a data disk in drive B.
Enter	Sets the designated drive.

2. Activate the database file:

Set Up	Selects the Set Up option from the Assistant Menu.
Database file	Selects the Database file command.
Enter	Asks for the disk drive name.
Enter	Selects the drive specified above. Specify the drive if different from B.
`CUSTOMER.DBF`	Selects the file.
Enter	Selects the file (Figure 1.15).
N	Answers no to the prompt `Is the file indexed? [Y/N]` (Figure 1.16).

Looking at the Structure of a File Once the file has been activated, use the following commands to look at its structure:

Tools	Selects Tools from the Assistant Menu.
List structure	Selects the List structure command.
Enter	Executes the command.
N	Answers no to the prompt `Direct the output to the printer? [Y/N]`.

The screen in Figure 1.17 should now appear. As the message at the bottom of the screen tells you, you can now press any key to return to the Assistant Menu and continue working in ASSISTANT mode.

As Figure 1.17 shows, dBASE keeps track of the current number of records in the file and includes the .DBF extension in the filename. If you remembered to enter the date when you booted DOS, dBASE also keeps track of the date of the last update; if you forgot to do so, the date will be 01/01/80. You can also see the name, character type, and width of each field. The total bytes of storage used by each record is at the bottom of the display. The total number of bytes is one more than the sum of the individual field sizes, to reserve a position for the delete indicator (*).

Listing the Contents of a File Now that you've looked at the structure of the database, you should also list its contents to be sure they are correct. Do this with the Retrieve option of the Assistant Menu:

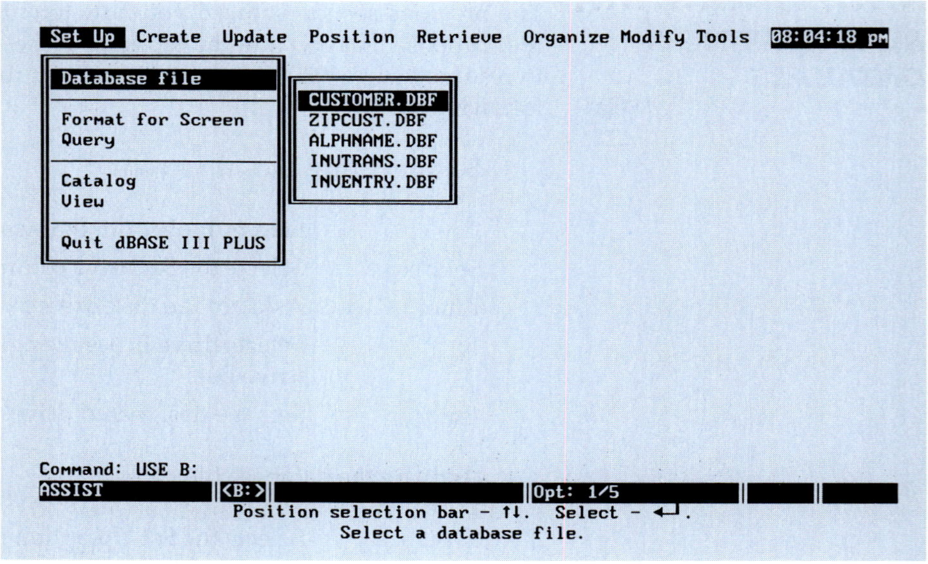

Figure 1.15
Specifying a database file to be opened.

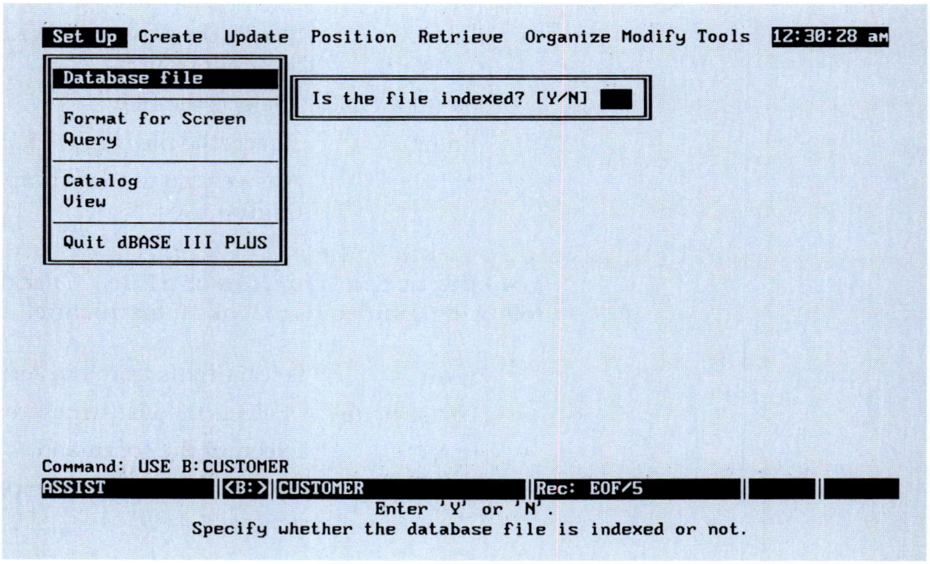

Figure 1.16
Specifying the database file to open.

Retrieve	Selects Retrieve from the Assistant Menu.
List	Selects the List command.
Enter	Displays the List submenu.
Execute the command	Selects Execute the command (Figure 1.18).
Enter	Completes the selection.
N	Answers the prompt `Direct the output to the printer? [Y/N]`.

The file contents should now appear on the screen, as shown in Figure 1.19. To return to the Assistant Menu, press any key.

The List command starts at the beginning of your data file and lists all records to the screen. For readability, dBASE lists the names of the fields above

Figure 1.17

Output of the List Structure command for the CUSTOMER.DBF database file.

```
 Set Up  Create  Update  Position  Retrieve  Organize Modify Tools  06:24:50 pm

Structure for database: B:customer.dbf
Number of data records:       5
Date of last update   : 05/10/92
Field  Field Name  Type       Width    Dec
    1  FIRST       Character    10
    2  INIT        Character     1
    3  LAST        Character    12
    4  ADDRESS     Character    25
    5  CITY        Character    15
    6  STATE       Character     2
    7  ZIP         Character     5
    8  PHONE       Character    13
    9  AMOUNT      Numeric       8      2
   10  DATE        Date          8
** Total **                    100

ASSIST           <B:> CUSTOMER           Rec: 1/5
                 Press any key to continue work in ASSIST.
```

Figure 1.18

Assistant screen to implement the List command.

```
 Set Up  Create  Update  Position  Retrieve  Organize Modify Tools  12:31:21 am
                                   List
                                   Display   Execute the command
                                   Report    Specify scope
                                   Label     Construct a field list
                                             Build a search condition
                                   Sum       Build a scope condition
                                   Average
                                   Count

Command: LIST
ASSIST           <B:> CUSTOMER           Rec: 1/5
                 Position selection bar - ↑↓.  Select - ↵.
             Perform the command displayed above the status bar.
```

the data, and it continues displaying records on the screen until the end of the file is reached. dBASE keeps track of where it is in a file by the use of a pointer, or **record number,** which is simply the file location of the current record being worked on by dBASE. The first record in a file is 1, the second is 2, and so forth.

ADDING RECORDS TO THE FILE

Adding records to an activated database file involves the Update Append command sequence:

Update	Selects Update from the Assistant Menu.
Append	Selects the Append command.
Enter	Executes the command.

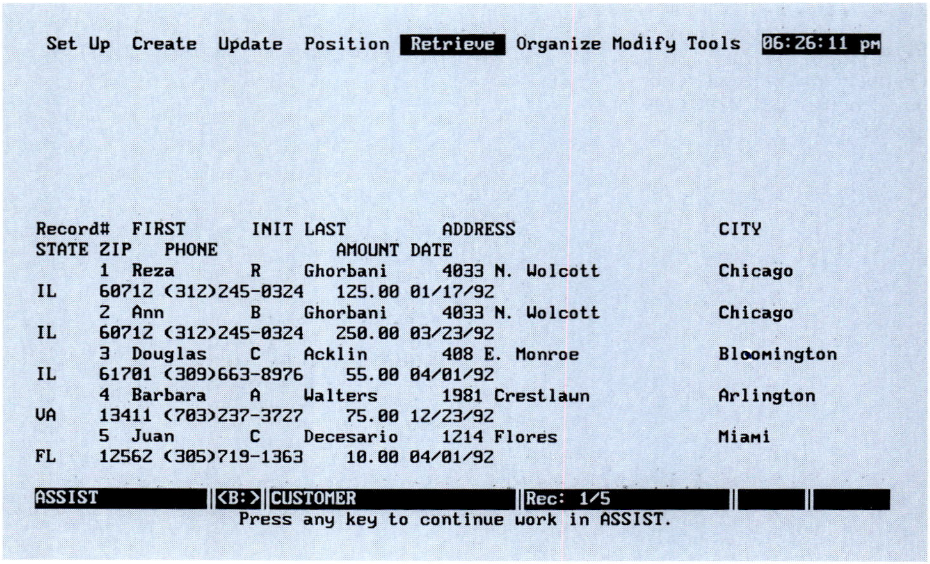

Figure 1.19
Output of the List command.

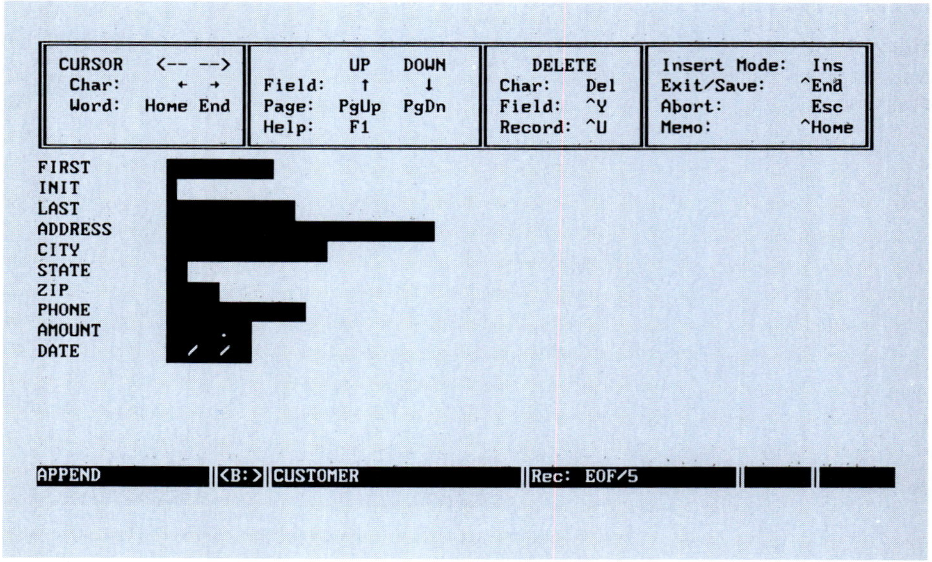

Figure 1.20
The Append screen.

The **Append command** causes dBASE to display a blank record form and places the number of the new record in the status bar (Figure 1.20). You can now enter new records, which will be added to the end of the file. As soon as you fill the last field of this form or press Enter when the cursor is in the last field, dBASE automatically displays the next blank record form.

When you have finished adding new records, indicate this by pressing Enter at the start of the next blank form.

Add the following records to the CUSTOMER.DBF file:

```
         Last       First    Init      Address           City       St Zip
Davis             Russell    B.    707 Vale St.       Bloomington    IL 61701
                                     (309)662-1759         35.00    02/27/92
Acklin            Debbie     C.    408 E. Monroe      Bloomington    IL 61701
                                     (309)827-1395         35.00    03/21/92
```

```
Posio        Harvey     B.    1013 Hillcrest       San Diego      CA 94307
                                    (619)271-9871      1250.00   04/03/92
Pietrowiak   Ben        A.    3334 N. Foster       Normal         IL 61761
                                    (309)452-9126        20.00   03/23/92
Acklin       Sandy      C.    408 E. Monroe        Bloomington    IL 61701
                                    (309)829-9901        35.00   02/25/92
Ficek        Fred       R.    1215 Tamarack        Normal         IL 61761
                                    (309)454-7123         0.00   04/05/92
Decesario    Juan       C.    1214 Flores          Miami          FL 12562
                                    (305)719-1363        10.00   04/01/92
```

When these records have been entered, check for errors by listing the file with the Retrieve List command sequence. It should look like the following:

```
Record#     FIRST     INIT         LAST              ADDRESS             CITY
    STATE ZIP    PHONE             AMOUNT  DATE
      1  Reza         R        Ghorbani     4033 N. Wolcott       Chicago
   IL     60712 (312)245-0324   125.00 01/17/92
      2  Ann          B        Ghorbani     4033 N. Wolcott       Chicago
   IL     60712 (312)245-0324   250.00 03/23/92
      3  Douglas      C        Acklin       408 E. Monroe         Bloomington
   IL     61701 (309)663-8976    55.00 04/01/92
      4  Barbara      A        Walters      1981 Crestlawn        Arlington
   VA     13411 (703)237-3727    75.00 12/31/92
      5  Arthur       V        Adams        115 Ginger Creek Ct.  Bloomington
   IL     61701 (309)828-7290    35.00 03/13/92
      6  Russell      B        Davis        707 Vale St.          Bloomington
   IL     61701 (309)662-1759    35.00 02/27/92
      7  Debbie       C        Acklin       408 E. Monroe         Bloomington
   IL     61701 (309)827-1395    35.00 03/21/92
      8  Harvey       B        Posio        1013 Hillcrest        San Diego
   CA     94307 (619)271-9871  1250.00 04/03/92
      9  Ben          A        Pietrowiak   3334 N. Foster        Normal
   IL     61761 (309)452-9126    20.00 03/23/92
     10  Sandy        C        Akclin       408 E. Monroe         Bloomington
   IL     61701 (309)829-9901    35.00 02/25/92
     11  Fred         R        Ficek        1215 Tamarack         Normal
   IL     61761 (309)454-7123     0.00 04/05/92
     12  Juan         C        Decesario    1214 Flores           Miami
   FL     12562 (305)719-1363    10.00 04/01/92
```

EDITING RECORDS IN THE FILE

There should be 12 records in the file. Examine each record for errors. Notice that in record 10 the last name is spelled incorrectly. To correct this, invoke the **Edit command** as follows:

Update	Selects Update from the Assistant Menu.
Edit	Selects the Edit command.
Enter	Executes the command.

The contents of the last record in the file should now be displayed. Use the Pg Up and Pg Dn keys to move from one record to the next. Use these keys to locate record 10 (Figure 1.21).

Figure 1.21
An Edit screen for record 10 of the CUSTOMER file.

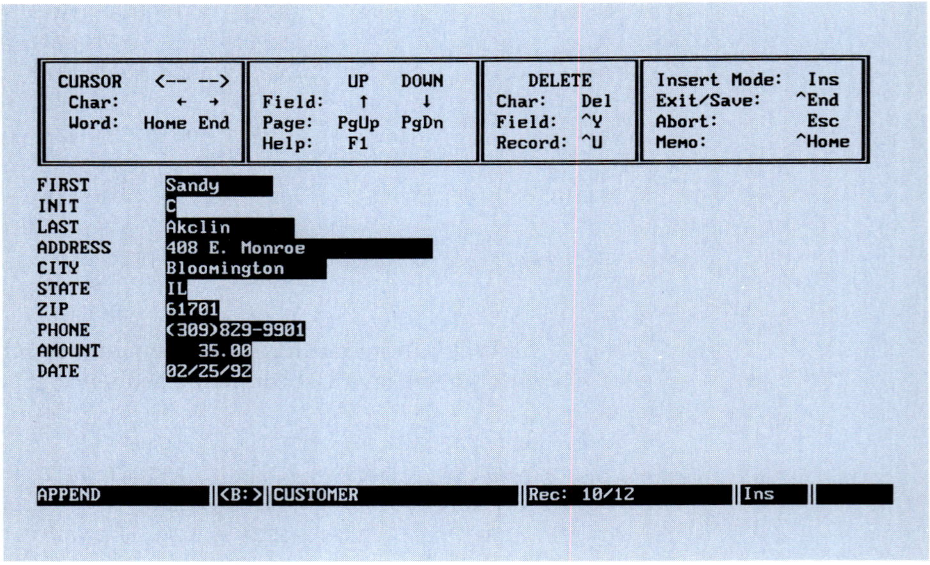

Cursor Movement Within a Record Various commands let you move around with a record to edit selected fields. To move the cursor from one field to the next, press Enter. You can also use the commands listed on the Edit screen. There are still other commands you can use, as shown in Table 1.1. Each control key command is performed by holding the control key while you press the alphabetic key. Now correct the error in record 10:

Enter (2) or ↓, ↓	Moves the cursor to last field.*
→	Positions the cursor at the *k*.
Type `ck`	Corrects the error.
Ctrl + End (or Ctrl + W)	Exits Edit and returns to Assistant Menu.

If you are a WordStar user, you may have noticed that the movement commands in column two of Table 1.1 are the same as those for WordStar.

CHAPTER REVIEW

Before creating a dBASE file, you must plan the field name, the field length, and the type of data to be used for each field. The Create command from the Assistant Menu builds a template for a database file. Once the template is created, you can enter records immediately; use the Append command to add records to the file later.

Accessing a file requires using the Set Up command from the Assistant Menu (this issues a Use command). The Tools option of the Assistant Menu

**Throughout this text, the following system is used to show how keystrokes are combined. When two or three keystrokes are separated by addition signs (for example, Ctrl + End), hold down the Ctrl key while pressing the End key. When two keystrokes are separated by a comma (for example, ↓, ↓), simply press and release each key in sequence—in this case, press the ↓ key twice.*

Table 1.1 Cursor Movement Within a Record

Cursor Control Key	*dBASE Command*	*Cursor Movement and Other Functions*
	Ctrl + A	Moves cursor one word to the left.
	Ctrl + F	Moves cursor one word to the right.
←	Ctrl + S	Moves cursor one position to the left.
→	Ctrl + D	Moves cursor one position to the right.
↑	Ctrl + E	Moves cursor up one line; at top line, displays prior record.
↓	Ctrl + X	Moves cursor down one line; at bottom line, displays next record.
Del	Ctrl + G	Deletes character at cursor position and moves text one position to the left.
	Ctrl + Y	Deletes contents of a field.
	Ctrl + W	Writes changes back to file and then returns you to Assistant Menu.
PgUp	Ctrl + R	Writes current record to disk and displays previous record.
PgDn	Ctrl + C	Writes current record to disk and displays next record.
Ins	Ctrl + V	Toggles between OVERWRITE and INSERT mode. (When you are in INSERT mode, the `INS` message is displayed in the status bar.)
	Ctrl + U	Deletes or undeletes a record. (When a record is undeleted, `Del` is displayed in the status bar.)
	Ctrl + End	Saves the file and returns to the Assistant Menu.

invokes the List structure command to display the structure of the file to show the field names, data types, and field size.

Listing the records to the screen requires selecting the Retrieve option from the Assistant Menu and then selecting the Execute the command option. The screen displays the field name, along with each field's contents of all records.

To change a record, select the Update option of the Assistant Menu and then position the pointer to the Edit option. The screen displays the last record accessed. Full-screen cursor movement commands, as well as WordPerfect cursor movement commands, can now be used to position the cursor and to move from one record to the next within the file.

KEY TERMS AND CONCEPTS

action line
Append command
Assist command
ASSISTANT mode
Command
command-driven mode
COMMAND mode
Condition
database
dBASE III Plus
dot prompt (.)
Edit command
field
Help command
menu-driven mode
message line
navigation line
Noun
primary key
PROGRAM mode
Quit command
record
record number
Scope
secondary key
Set Menu On/Off command
status bar
structure

CHAPTER QUIZ

Multiple Choice

1. Which of the following is *not* a true statement about dBASE III Plus?
   a. The package can be used only in MENU mode.
   b. No statements can be saved to a file and executed later.
   c. Once the dot prompt is reached, the Assistant Menu cannot be reactivated.
   d. All of the above statements are false.

2. Which of the following commands lets you place records in a database file?
   a. Use
   b. Create
   c. List
   d. Append
   e. Add

3. The List command is used for the following:
   a. Looking at records contained in a file
   b. Invoking a database file
   c. Displaying the structure of a database file
   d. Exiting the dBASE III program
   e. Making changes to a file

4. Which of the following commands lets you make a change to an existing database file?
   a. Edit
   b. List
   c. Use
   d. Create
   e. Quit

5. Which of the following are valid data types for use with dBASE III Plus?
   a. Character
   b. Numeric
   c. Memo
   d. Date
   e. Logical
   f. All of the above

True/False

6. dBASE III Plus in ASSISTANT mode is menu-driven.

7. dBASE III Plus uses the period (.) as the default user prompt.

8. It is advisable to use the Quit command from the dot prompt or the Quit dBASE III Plus from the Set Up option of the Assistant Menu to avoid data loss.

9. The dBASE III Edit command makes use of the cursor pad as well as WordStar-like commands for cursor manipulation.

10. The Edit and Append commands use the full-screen feature of dBASE III Plus.

Answers

1. d 2. b, d 3. a, c 4. a 5. f 6. t 7. t 8. t 9. t 10. t

Exercises

1. Define or describe each of the following:
   a. Command-driven
   b. Menu-driven
   c. Record number

2. The maximum number of records allowed in a dBASE III Plus file is ____________.

3. The line of the Assistant Menu that indicates the current disk drive and the name of the file in use is the ____________ line.

4. You can invoke the Help command by pressing the ____________ function key.

5. Before you turn off the computer, you must issue the ____________ command to avoid data loss.

6. To exit the Assistant Menu, press the ____________ key.

7. The default mode for dBASE is the ____________ Menu.

8. A dBASE record can have up to ____________ characters.

9. The ____________ command describes a record to dBASE.

10. To make a file available to dBASE, enter the __________ command.

11. The __________ gives the physical location of a record in a file.

12. Use the __________ command to exit dBASE.

13. Use the __________ command to look at the structure of a dBASE file.

14. Use the __________ command to add data to an existing database file.

15. The Append and Edit commands make use of the __________ screen editing feature of dBASE.

COMPUTER EXERCISES

1. Create a file called PAYMAST. It should have the following structure:

```
STRUCTURE FOR FILE:   A:PAYMAST .DBF
NUMBER OF RECORDS:    00012
DATE OF LAST UPDATE: 01/01/80
PRIMARY USE DATABASE
  NAME        TYPE WIDTH    DEC
EMPLOYID      N     004
FIRSTNAM      C     010
LASTNAM       C     012
PAYRATE       N     006      002
YTDGROSS      N     009      002
```

2. Enter the following records:

ID	NAME	RATE	GROSS
4908	Richard Payne	4.45	556.00
5789	Connie Reiners	3.35	450.00
5323	Pamela Rich	6.00	780.00
6324	Mark Tell	5.50	980.00
2870	Frank Terlep	3.80	670.00
4679	Kenneth Klass	4.90	780.00
8345	Thomas Momery	4.70	580.00

3. Use the List command to list the contents of the file.

4. Add the records below:

5649	Toni McCarthy	5.20	667.00
5432	Alan Monroe	5.20	1340.00
5998	Paul Mish	4.90	887.00
4463	Edward Mockford	4.90	775.00
456		0.00	0.00

5. Use the Edit command to correct any errors. Also use the Edit command to place your name in the name area for record #12.

2

dBASE III PLUS FILE MANIPULATION COMMANDS

CHAPTER OBJECTIVES

After completing this chapter, you should be able to

- **Use various dBASE III Plus file manipulation commands that can be issued from the Assistant Menu and from the dot (.) prompt**
- **Use pointer movement commands**
- **Use the Create Report command**

In this chapter, we describe some dBASE III Plus commands that let you see what files are available on disk, see the structure of selected files, see the contents of records within files, and change the records in a file with commands such as Replace and Delete. We also learn how to print a dBASE report.

COMMANDS FOR DISPLAYING AND GAINING ACCESS TO FILES

This section introduces the Directory, Use, List, List Structure, and Display commands; the ? character; and the RECNO( ) function. We will practice these commands on the CUSTOMER file.

Executing Commands from the Assistant Menu or the Dot Prompt You can enter most commands from either the Assistant Menu or the dot prompt (.), as mentioned in Chapter 1. In either case, dBASE shows the command on the action line as you enter it. You may want to use the Assistant Menu in first learning the commands. Then practice issuing the command by typing dot prompt commands.

The following exercises show how to use the Assistant Menu and the dot prompt commands. To enter commands via the Assistant Menu, move the pointer with the Up and Down Arrow keys to highlight each selection and press Enter. Typing in a response is sometimes required.

To use the dot prompt commands, press Esc one or more times to reach the dot prompt. This produces a blank upper screen with the dot prompt on the action line (Figure 2.1). The dot prompt requires you to type occasional punctuation, such as commas (the ASSISTANT mode inserts these automatically). To return to ASSISTANT mode, enter `ASSIST` at the dot prompt.

DIRECTORY

The **Directory (DIR) command** displays the names of database files already stored on disk. To see that the CUSTOMER file is present, do the following steps to list the files on disk. Assume that you are working with drive B.

Tools	Selects Tools from the Assistant Menu.
Directory	Selects the Directory command.
Enter	Executes the command. The prompt now asks for the default-drive name.
B:	Specifies the drive.
Enter	Selects the drive. The prompt on the action line reads `DIR B:` (Figure 2.2).
.dbf Database Files	Selects .dbf Database Files from the Directory submenu.
Enter	Displays the names of the .DBF files on disk.

When you have finished viewing the files, press Enter, and the screen clears.

The following is the dot prompt Directory command. Type it exactly as shown and press Enter. The files with the .DBF file extension are now listed to the screen.

(.) DIR: `.dir *.dbf`

Figure 2.1
The dBASE screen with dot prompt.

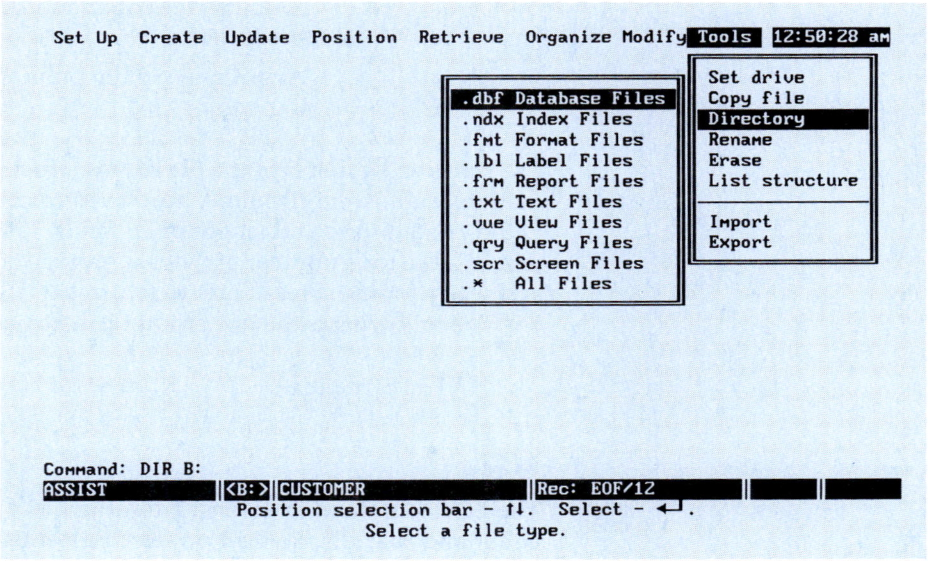

Figure 2.2
Screen for the DIR command.

USE

The **Use command** activates a file. *Use* is a dot prompt command word. The word does not appear in the Assistant Menu, though it will appear on the action line. Perform the Use command in ASSISTANT mode to activate the CUSTOMER file:

Tools	Selects Tools from the Assistant Menu.
Set drive	Selects the Set drive option.
Enter (2)	Executes the command and accepts the default drive (B:).
Set Up	Selects the Set Up option from the Assistant Menu.
Database file	Selects the Database file option.
Enter (2)	Executes the command, displays `USE` on the action line, and selects the default drive B. The action line now reads `USE B:`.
`CUSTOMER`	Specifies the file.
Enter	The action line now reads `USE B: CUSTOMER`.
N	Answers no to the prompt `Is the file indexed? [Y/N]`.

The CUSTOMER file is now activated and ready for use.

The following is the dot prompt Use command. Type it exactly as shown and press Enter after each line.

(.) Use

```
.set default to b:
.use customer
```

LIST STRUCTURE

The **List Structure command** lets you examine the structure of a file. Use it now to examine the CUSTOMER file:

Tools	Selects Tools from the Assistant Menu.
List Structure	Selects the List Structure command.
Enter	Executes the command. The action line now reads `DISPLAY STRUCTURE`.
N	Answers no to the prompt `Direct the output to the printer? [Y/N]`.

The screen now displays the file record structure (Figure 2.3). It provides information such as the filename, number of records, date of last update, and the names, data types, and length of all fields. The total figure at the bottom of the report is the total number of bytes of storage occupied by each record, activated and ready for use. Press Enter to return to ASSISTANT mode.

The following is the dot prompt List Structure command:

(.) List Structure	`. list structure`

LIST

The **List command** is distinct from the List Structure command. It is a **query command** that displays all or selected contents of a file. When the List command is executed, the pointer moves to the bottom of the file. The following is the procedure for listing the contents of the activated CUSTOMER file:

Retrieve	Selects Retrieve from the Assistant Menu.
List	Selects the List command.
Enter	Executes the command. The action line reads `LIST`, and the List Menu appears (Figure 2.4).
Execute the command	Selects Execute the command from the List submenu.
Enter	Executes the command.
N	Answers no to the prompt `Direct the output to the printer? [Y/N]`.

The following is the dot prompt List command:

(.) List	`. list`

The CUSTOMER file now scrolls down the screen (Figure 2.5). Press any key to return to ASSISTANT mode.

After you execute a List command, you can return the pointer to the top of the file with the following procedure (Figure 2.6):

Position	Selects Position from the Assistant Menu.
Goto Record	Selects the Goto Record command.
Enter	Executes the command.
TOP	Selects TOP from the Goto Record submenu.
Enter	Executes the command.

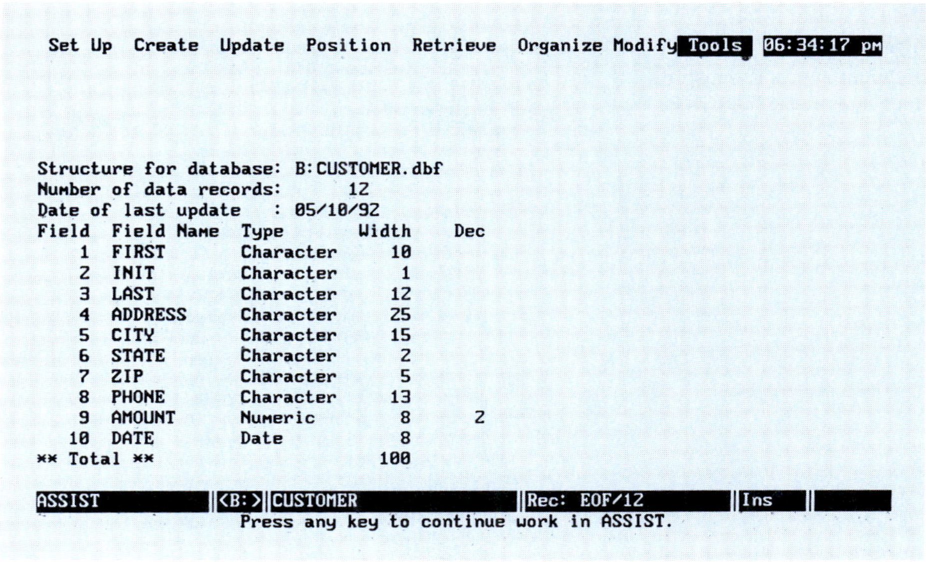

Figure 2.3
Output of the List-structure command accessed through the Tools option of the Assistant Menu.

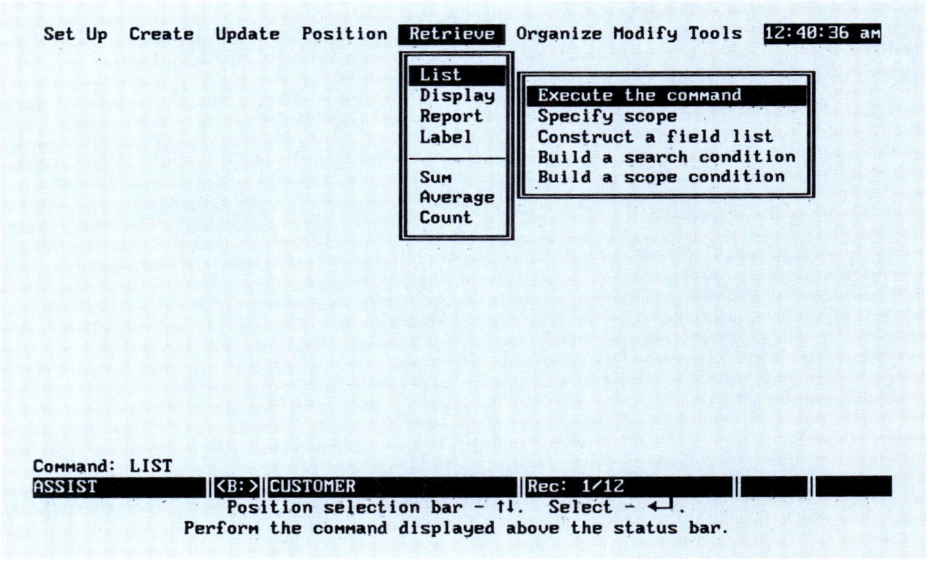

Figure 2.4
The List screen prompts.

List Field Rather than listing all contents of each record in the file, you can tell dBASE to list only the contents of certain fields by using the option Construct a field list from the List submenu (Figure 2.7). The following steps list first names, initials, and last names in the CUSTOMER file:

Retrieve	Selects Retrieve from the Assistant Menu.
List	Selects the List command.
Enter	Executes the command.
Construct a field list	Selects Construct a field list from the List submenu.
Enter	Displays the fields in CUSTOMER (Figure 2.7).

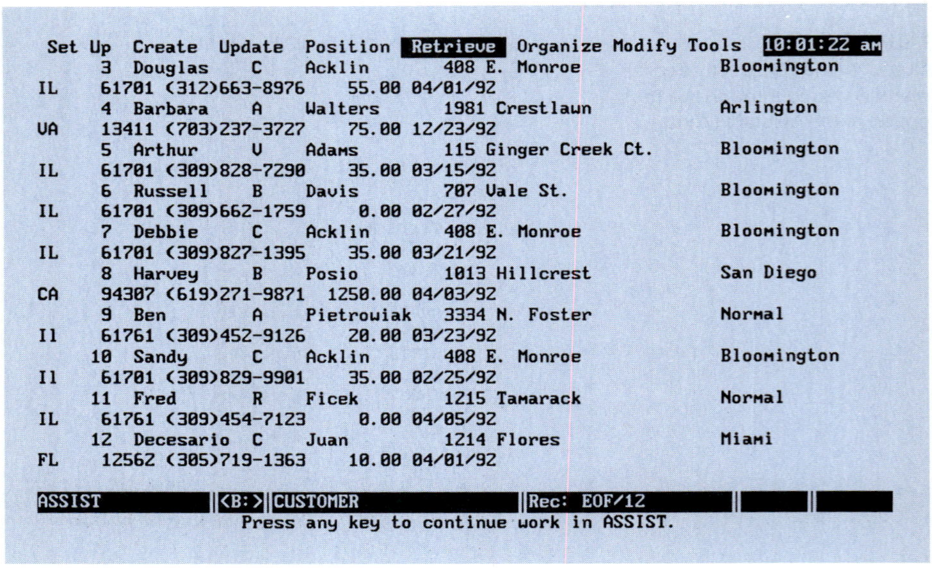

Figure 2.5
Output of the List command executed against the CUSTOMER file.

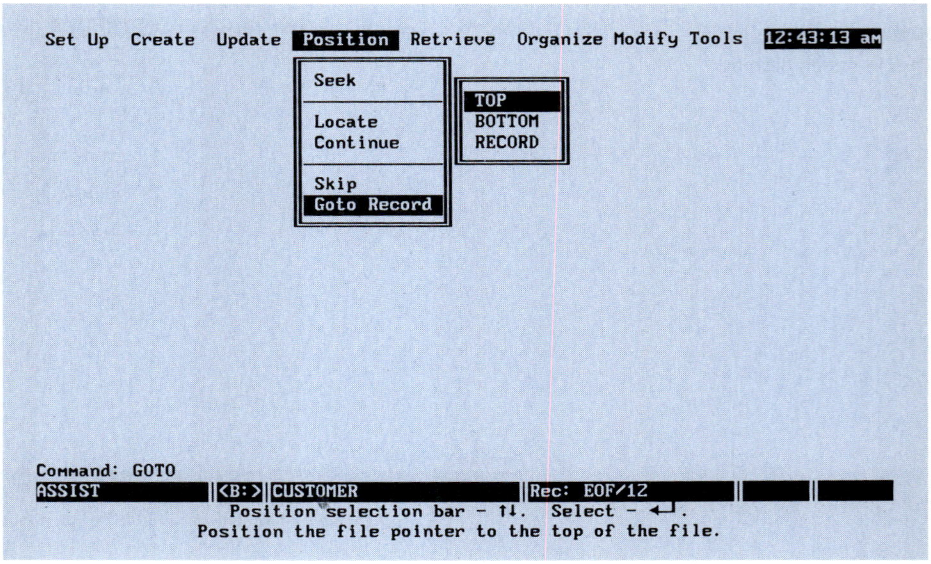

Figure 2.6
The Assistant screen for positioning the pointer at the beginning of the file.

Highlight and Press Enter for the fields FIRST, INIT, and LAST:

FIRST	Selects the FIRST field.
Enter	Executes the command.
INIT	Selects the INIT field.
Enter	Executes the command.
LAST	Selects the LAST field.
Enter	Executes the command.

As each field is selected, dBASE adds it to the List command. Moving the pointer with Up and Down Arrow keys highlights and lists each field and its

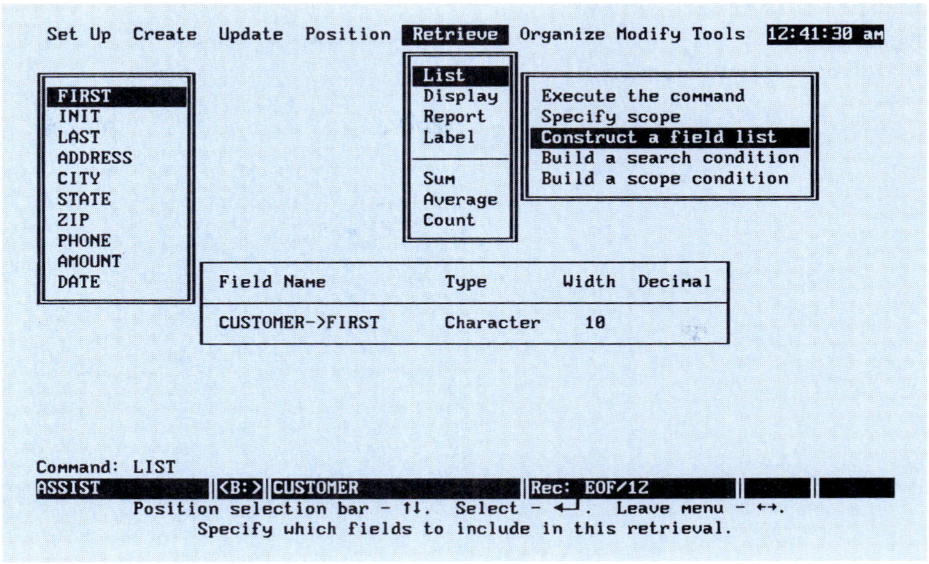

Figure 2.7
The Construct a field list screen.

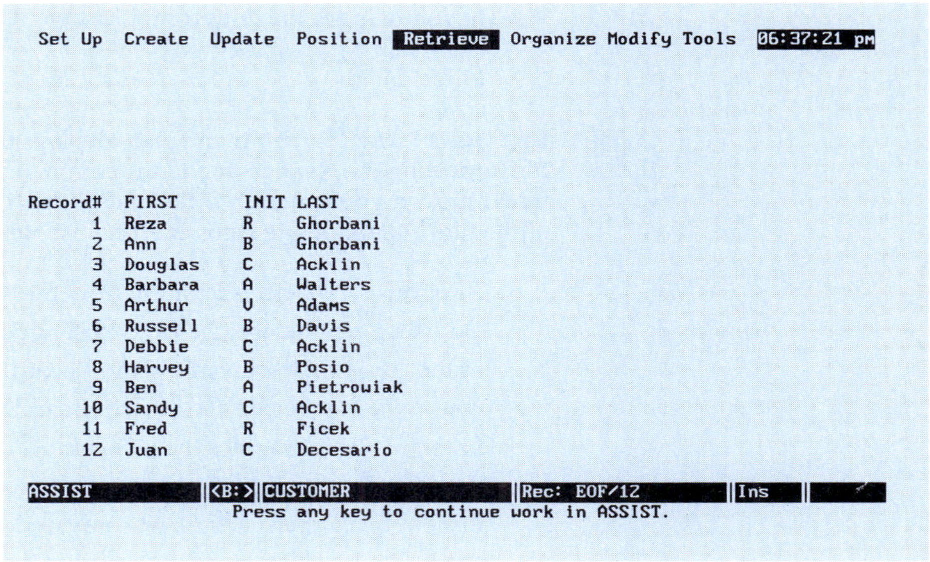

Figure 2.8
Output of the List command using selected fields.

characteristics in the box in the middle of the screen (Figure 2.7). The completed action line should read `LIST FIRST, INIT, LAST`.

← or →	Returns you to the List submenu.
Execute the command	Selects Execute the command from the List submenu.
Enter	Executes the command.
N	Answers no to the prompt `Direct output to the printer? [Y/N]`.

The screen now lists the records (Figure 2.8).

Try adding the AMOUNT field to the listing you just produced. The new command on the action line will be `LIST FIRST, INIT, LAST, AMOUNT`. The result should look like Figure 2.9.

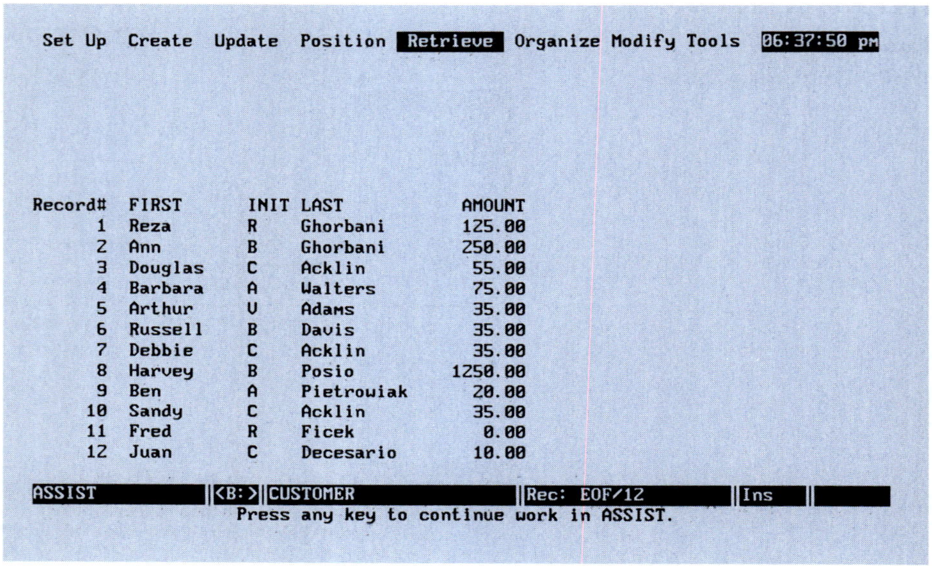

Figure 2.9
The List command with an additional field.

The following is the dot prompt List Field command:

(.) List Field `.list first, init, last`

List Next The List command also displays the next *x* number of records in a file by adding the **Next option** to the command. First, because the last List command moved your pointer to the end of the file, reposition it to the beginning of the file. The following steps execute List Next:

Position	Selects Position from the Assistant Menu.
Goto Record	Selects the Goto Record command.
Enter	Displays the Goto Record submenu.
Top	Selects the Top command.
Enter	Executes the command.
Retrieve	Selects Retrieve from the Assistant Menu.
List	Selects the List command.
Enter	Displays the List submenu.
Specify scope	Selects Specify scope.
Enter	Displays the Scope submenu.
NEXT	Selects NEXT.
Enter	Executes the command.
5	Enters a numeric value at the prompt `Enter a numeric value:` (Figure 2.10).
Enter	Enters the number and displays the List submenu.
Construct a field list	Selects Construct a field list.
Enter	Executes the command.
FIRST	Selects the FIRST field.
Enter	Executes the command.
INIT	Selects the INIT field.
Enter	Executes the command.

Figure 2.10
The Assistant screen for specifying the scope.

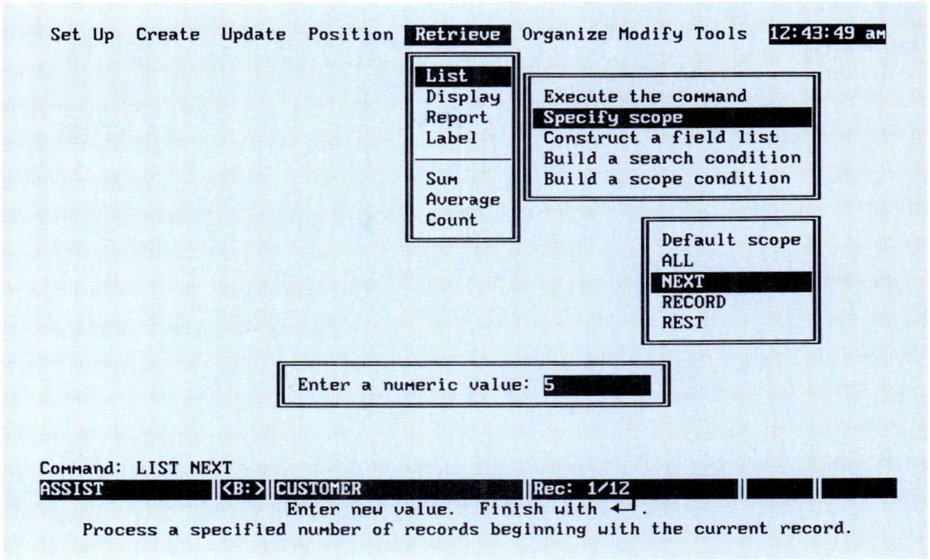

Figure 2.11
Output of the List Next command to list five records.

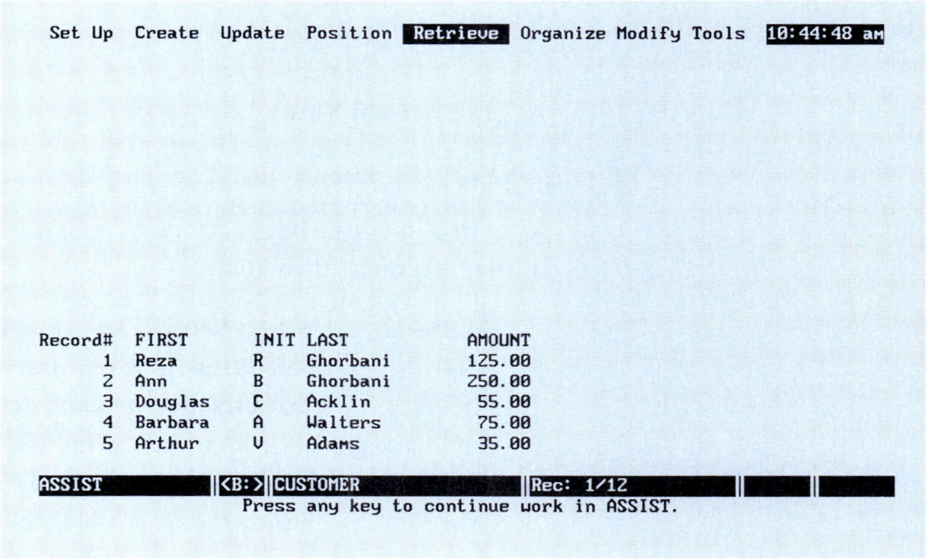

LAST	Selects the LAST field.
Enter	Executes the command.
AMOUNT	Selects the AMOUNT field.
Enter	Executes the command.
→ or ←	Returns you to the List submenu.
Execute the command	Selects Execute the command.
Enter	Executes the command.
N	Answers no to the prompt `Direct output to the printer? [Y/N]`.

The screen now displays the first five records (Figure 2.11)

The following is the dot prompt for the List Field Next command:

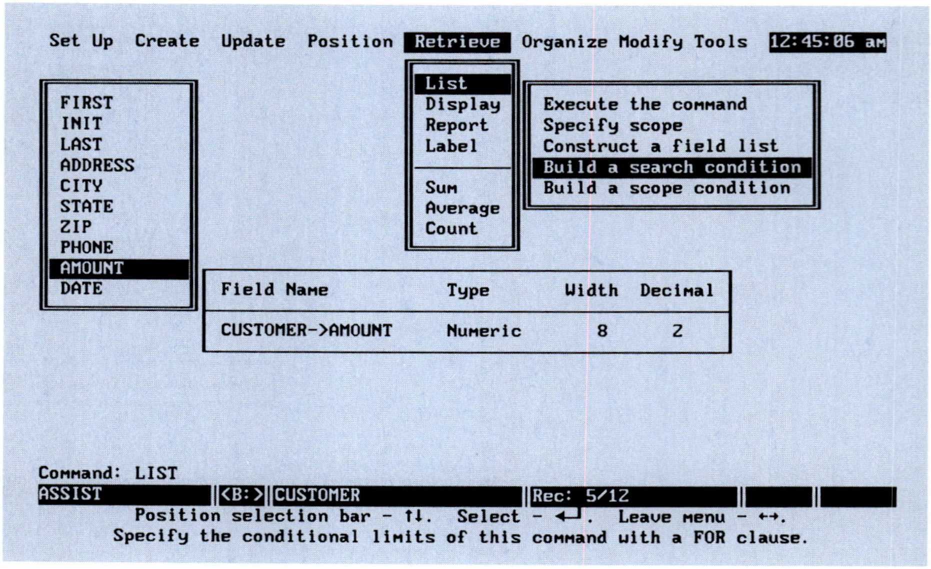

Figure 2.12
A field marked for a search condition.

(.) List Field Next: `list next 5 FIRST, INIT, LAST, AMOUNT`

List For The List command also displays records that meet a certain criterion by entering the **For parameter** and the selection criterion as part of the List command. For example, the following procedure would list all records containing an amount greater than $100:

Retrieve	Selects Retrieve from the Assistant menu.
List	Selects the List command.
Enter	Executes the command and displays the List submenu.
Build a search condition	Selects Build a search condition.
Enter	Displays the record fields (Figure 2.12).
AMOUNT	Selects the AMOUNT Field.
Enter	Executes the command and displays a condition box (Figure 2.13).
> Greater Than	Selects >Greater Than.
Enter	Executes the command.
100	Enters a numeric value at the prompt `Enter a numeric value.`
Enter	Enters the number and displays another condition box.
No more conditions	Selects No more conditions.
Enter	Executes the command. The action line now reads `LIST FOR > AMOUNT 100` (Figure 2.14).
Execute the command	Selects Execute the command from the List submenu.
Enter	Executes the command.
N	Answers no to the prompt `Direct output to the printer? [Y/N].`

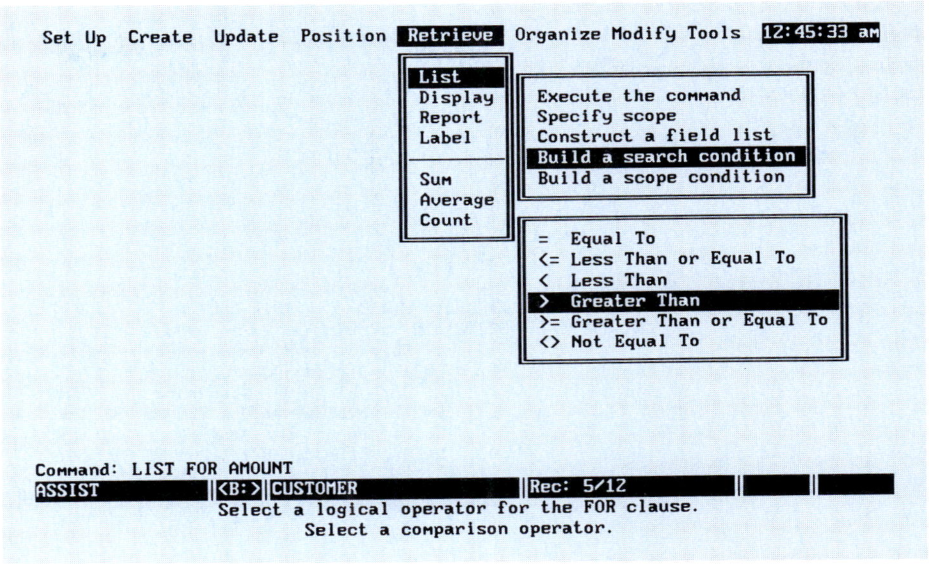

Figure 2.13
The condition screen.

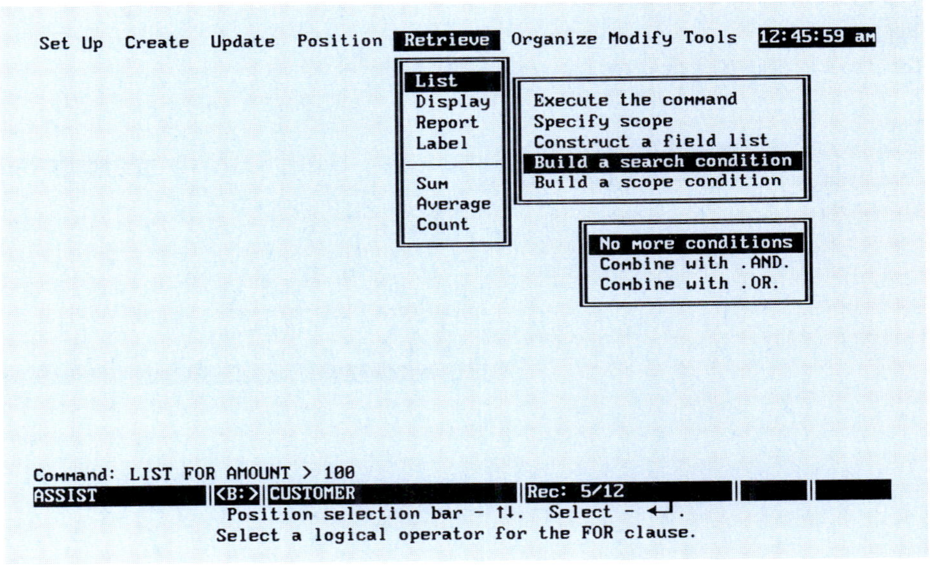

Figure 2.14
The prompt for more conditions.

Three records now appear (Figure 2.15).

This last command probably generated more output than you need or want. Fortunately, you can tailor the list by combining Field selection and For criteria within one List command. To do this, first reposition the pointer at the beginning of the file. Then, as you enter the List command, select fields with the Construct a field list option and select a criterion with the Build a search condition option. This process will produce a command such as LIST FIRST, LAST AMOUNT FOR AMOUNT > 100 in the action line—the same command you would enter from the dot prompt. List the records to the screen (Figure 2.16).

The following is the dot prompt List For command:

(.) List For `list for AMOUNT > 100`

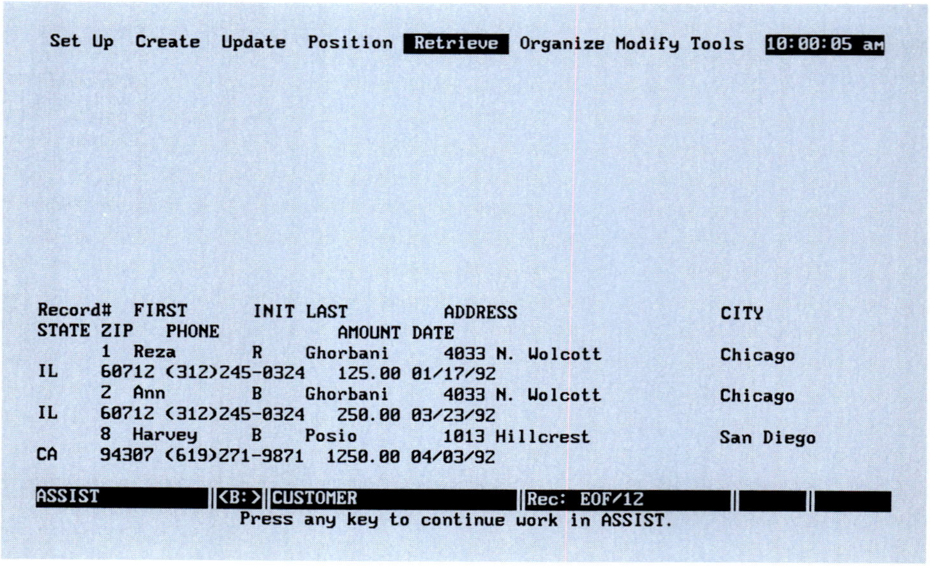

Figure 2.15
The records listed for the command List for Amount > 100.

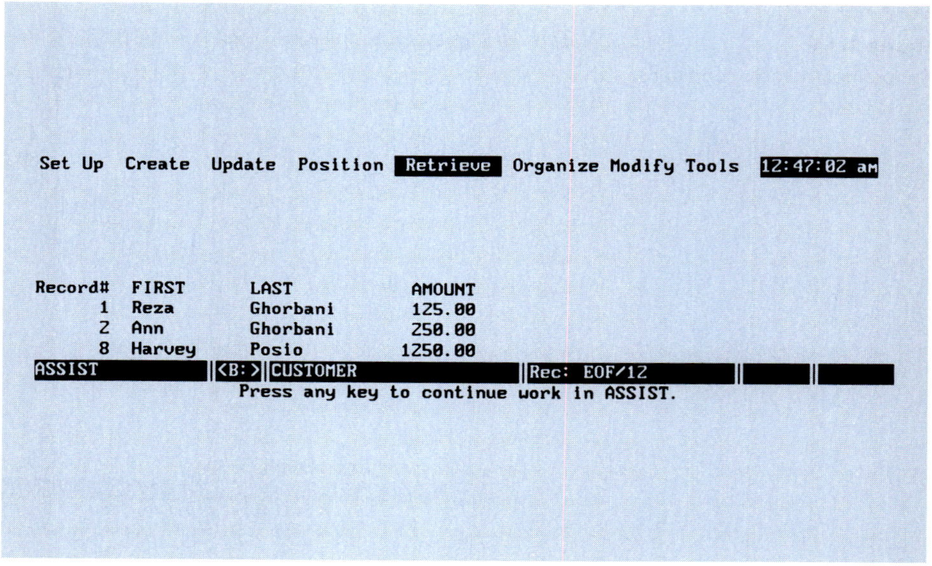

Figure 2.16
List of specific fields for a condition.

DISPLAY

The **Display command** is another form of query. It displays the record that is currently at the pointer location. If the pointer is at the bottom of a file (where it would be, for instance, after a List command), no record is displayed, but the field headings appear on the screen. In ASSISTANT mode, the command begins as follows:

Retrieve	Selects Retrieve from the Assistant Menu.
Display	Selects the Display command.
Enter	Executes the command and displays the Display submenu.
Execute the command	Selects Execute the command.
Enter	Executes the command.

Figure 2.17
The dBASE screen for specifying the ALL scope command.

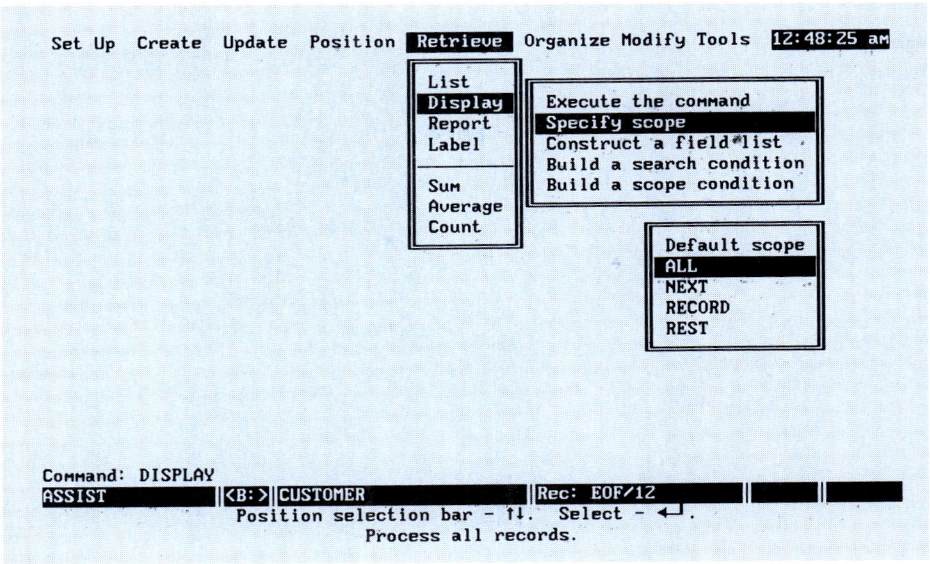

The record at the pointer location is now displayed.

The following is the dot prompt Display command:

(.) Display `. display`

Display All You can use the **All parameter** of the Display command to list all records onto the screen much as the List command will do. The advantage of Display All is that it displays only 16 lines at a time, rather than scrolling through the entire file. These are the steps in ASSISTANT mode (Figure 2.17):

Retrieve	Selects Retrieve from the Assistant Menu.
Display	Selects the Display command.
Enter	Executes the command and displays a Display submenu.
Specify scope	Selects Specify scope.
Enter	Executes the command and displays the Scope submenu.
All	Selects ALL.
Enter	Executes the command and returns to the Display submenu.
Execute the command	Selects Execute the command of the Display submenu.
Enter	Executes the command.

A screen like Figure 2.18 appears. Press any key to display the next 16 lines. The Display All command can use any of the Field List, Scope, or Conditions options used by the List command.

The following is the dot prompt Display All command:

(.) Display All: `. display all`

Printing Lists The List and Display All commands can generate and print crude reports. One way to do this is to respond Y when you see the prompt `Direct output to the printer? [Y/N]`. When the command sequence does not

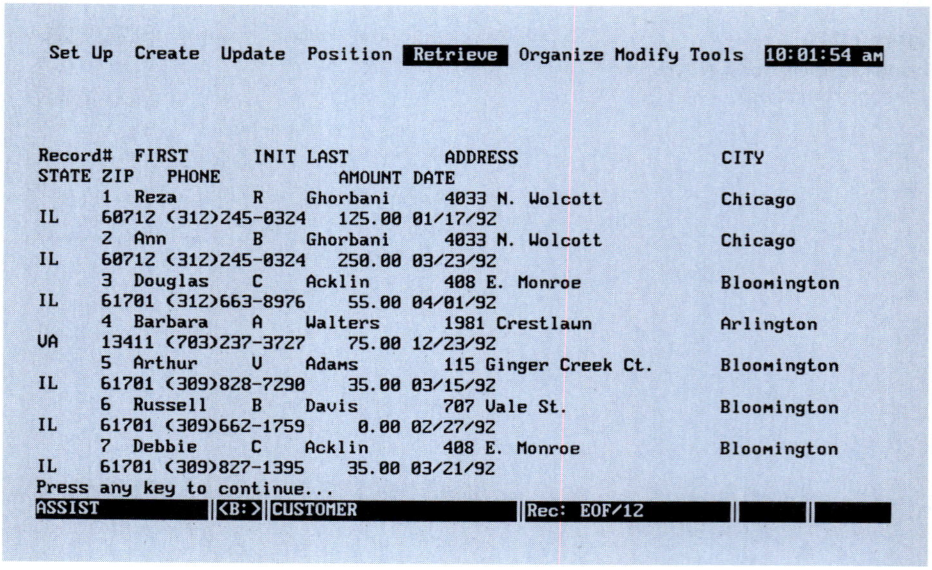

Figure 2.18
Output of the Display All command.

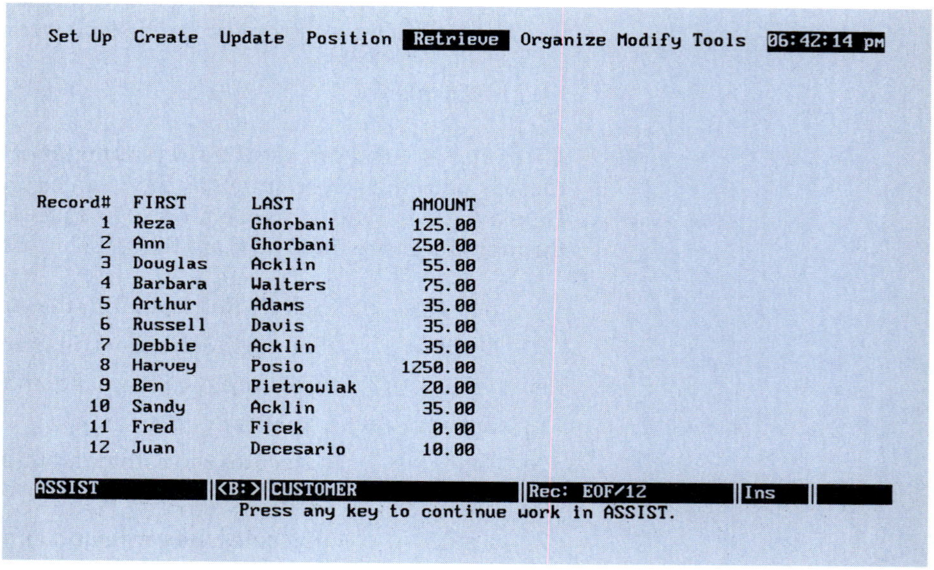

Figure 2.19
Output of the Display All First, Last, Amount command.

provide such a prompt, you can use another method. First, prepare to print with the dot prompt command `. set print on`. Next, execute your list or Display command. Finally, deactivate the printer with `. set print off`.

Display All Field This command restricts a listing to whatever fields you select. For instance, you can choose to list only the FIRST, LAST, and AMOUNT fields of the CUSTOMER file. Composing the command in ASSISTANT mode yields the command `DISPLAY ALL FIRST, LAST, AMOUNT` on the action line. Figure 2.19 shows the result.

The following is the dot prompt Display All Field command:

(.) Display All Field `. display all <field1, field2,...>`

ADDITIONAL POWERS OF THE DOT PROMPT

Some forms of the preceding commands can only be entered through the dot prompt. For example, you can use a version of the List/Display command(s) to search for rather loose criteria. Suppose you don't know how to spell someone's name exactly, but you do know how the name starts. In this situation, you can use the **substring function ($).** The following command could be translated as "list the first name and last name fields of any record that has the characters *Gho* in the last name field."

```
. list first, last for 'Gho' $last
Record# first   last
```

```
Record# first    last
      1 Reza     Ghorbani
      2 Ann      Ghorbani
```

The next command lists every record with a capital *A* in the first name field:

```
. List first, last for 'A' $first
```

```
Record# first    last
      2 Ann      Ghorbani
      5 Arthur   Adams
```

The next command lists every record with the characters *ar* in the first name field:

```
. list first, last for 'ar' $first
```

```
Record# first     last
      4 Barbara   Walters
      8 Harvey    Posio
```

? AND RECNO( )

Use the **? character** anytime that you want some piece of information displayed on the screen. Use the **RECNO( ) function** to obtain the printer location from dBASE. Using ? and RECNO( ) together produces a command to identify the location of the pointer and display that number on the screen as follows:

```
. ? recno( )
```

```
5
```

POINTER-POSITIONING COMMANDS

Pointer-positioning commands let you position the pointer at specific records within an activated file. These commands can be entered from the Position option of the Assistant Menu, but the process is cumbersome. The dot prompt method is more efficient. The positioning commands activate individual records for processing with commands such as Edit and Delete. Pointer-positioning commands include Goto, Go, Skip, Goto Top, and Goto Bottom. (Other commands, such as List and Display, also result in a change of pointer position.) Remember that the status line indicates the current record position of the pointer.

GOTO

The Go command and the **Goto command** can be used interchangeably. The following examples illustrate the joint use of the Goto and Display commands to let you examine the content of a record. Using ASSIST, the Goto command is located under the Position option and the Display is found under Retrieve. In each case, the Display command generates a display of the record pointed to by the Goto command, as shown below:

```
. goto 5
. display
```

```
Record#  FIRST          INIT     LAST           ADDRESS                  CITY
      STATE ZIP     PHONE               AMOUNT  DATE
       5  Arthur          V       Adams          115 Ginger Creek Ct.Bloomington
      IL     61701  (309)828-7290      35.00 03/13/92
```

```
. goto 10
. display
```

```
Record#  FIRST          INIT     LAST           ADDRESS                  CITY
      STATE ZIP     PHONE               AMOUNT  DATE
      10  Sandy           C       Acklin         408 E. Monroe            Bloomington
      IL     61701  (309)829-9901      35.00 02/25/92
```

The Goto portion of a pointer position command (except in cases of Goto Top and Goto Bottom) can be implied simply by entering the desired record number after the dot prompt. For example, the following command sequence suffices:

```
. 2
. display first, last, amount
```

```
Record#  first          last           amount
      2  Ann            Ghorbani       250.00
```

```
. list next 4 first,last
```

```
Record#  first          last
      2  Ann            Ghorbani
      3  Douglas        Acklin
      4  Barbara        Walters
      5  Arthur         Adams
```

SKIP

The **Skip command** moves the pointer to the next record in the file. It can be followed by a number (positive or negative). Using ASSIST, it is located in the Position Menu. A positive number moves the pointer forward that number of records, and a negative number moves the pointer backward that number of records. When you issue the Skip command, the screen displays the new record number. You can then use the Display command to show the contents of the record. For example, with the pointer currently situated at record 5 (as the result of the preceding file manipulation), the unmodified Skip command advances the pointer as follows:

```
. SKIP

  Record no.      6

. display first, last, amount
```

```
Record# first     last    amount
      6 Russell   Davis    35.00
```

From record 6, the following Skip command moves backward three records:

```
. skip -3
```

```
Record no.      3
```

```
. display
```

```
Record#  FIRST        INIT     LAST          ADDRESS              CITY
     STATE ZIP     PHONE              AMOUNT DATE
       3  Douglas       C      Acklin       408 E. Monroe        Bloomington
     IL     61701  (309)663-8976     55.00 04/01/92
```

With the pointer located at record 3, the following Skip command moves the pointer forward six records in the file:

```
. skip 6
```

```
Record no.      9
```

```
. display
```

```
Record#  FIRST        INIT     LAST          ADDRESS              CITY
     STATE ZIP     PHONE              AMOUNT DATE
       9  Ben           A      Pietrowiak   3384 N. Foster       Normal
     IL     61761  (309)452-9126     20.00 03/23/92
```

GOTO TOP

The **Goto Top command** positions the pointer at the first record in the file. The ? RECNO command confirms that you are at record number 1.

```
. GOTO TOP
. ?RECNO()
```

```
1
```

You can also use the Goto Top command with the Display command to position the pointer at the beginning (top) of the file and display that record, as follows:

```
. goto top
. display first, last, amount
```

```
Record#  first   last          amount
      1  Reza    Ghorbani      125.00
```

GOTO BOTTOM

The **Goto Bottom command** positions the pointer at the last record in the file, as follows:

```
. GOTO BOTTOM
. ?RECNO()
```

```
12
```

OTHER COMMANDS AND FUNCTIONS

DATE

If you want to access the system data while you are in dBASE, use the Date function. The screen now displays the date that you entered during the boot process; if you did not enter a date, the screen displays 01/01/80 below the dot prompt command. The command and display are as follows:

```
. ?DATE()
```

```
03/13/92
```

(The blank space between ? and DATE is optional.)

END OF FILE (EOF)

The **end-of-file (EOF) function** is a way of asking whether you are at the end of a file—the location beyond the "last" record.

```
. GOTO BOTTOM
. ?EOF()
```

```
.F.
```

Notice that the value returned is F (false), meaning that the end of the file was not detected. This is because the pointer is now at the beginning of the last record. Issue a Skip command to move past the last record.

```
.SKIP
```

```
Record no.       13
```

```
. ?EOF()
```

```
.T.
```

BEGINNING OF FILE (BOF)

The same technique applies to the **beginning-of-file (BOF) function;** as shown below, dBASE doesn't realize that it is actually at the top of the file until you try to access a record that isn't there.

```
. GOTO TOP
. ?BOF()
```

```
.F.
```

```
. SKIP -1
```

```
Record no.       1
```

```
. ?BOF()
```

```
.T.
```

SUM

dBASE can be directed to perform arithmetic via the **Sum command.** For instance, if you want to know the grand total owed, you can find out by using the Retrieve option of the Assistant Menu. You now select the Sum option and then the Construct a field list of option and point to any numeric fields that you want to sum (in this example, you can sum only the AMOUNT field). Once these commands have been given (see Figure 2.20), you are ready to execute the command. The steps are as follows:

Retrieve	Selects Retrieve from the Assistant Menu.
Sum	Selects the Sum command.
Enter	Executes the command and displays the Sum submenu.
Construct a field list	Selects Construct a field list.
Enter	Executes the command.
AMOUNT	Specifies the AMOUNT field.
Enter	Selects the field.
→ or ←	Returns you to the Sum submenu.
Execute the command	Selects Execute the command.
Enter	Executes the command.

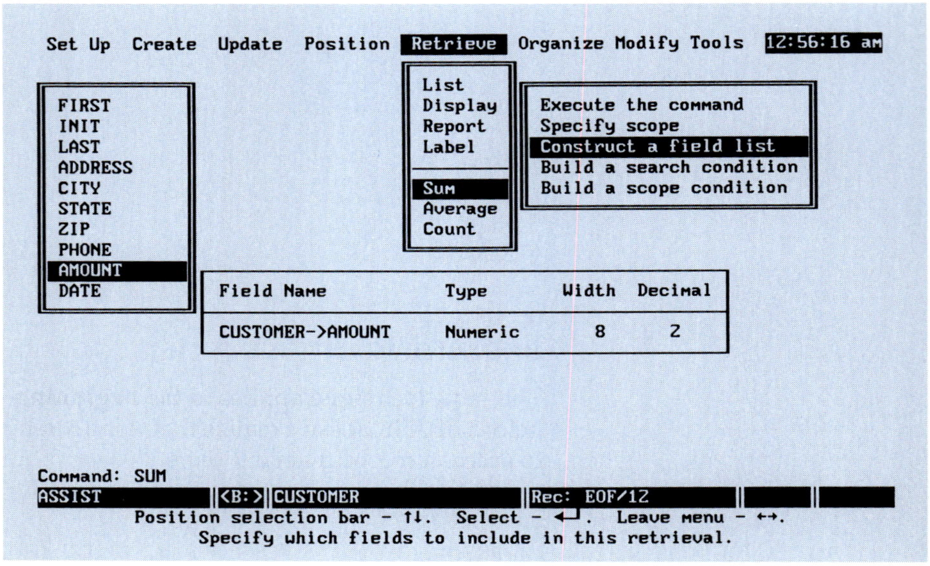

Figure 2.20
The Sum screen for summing the AMOUNT field.

Once control is returned to the Sum submenu, the command SUM AMOUNT appears on the action line. After the command has been executed, the following message appears:

```
 12 records summed
 amount
1925.00
```

The following is the dot prompt Sum command:

(.) Sum: `.sum amount`

Sum For You might also be interested in knowing the grand total for customers with a balance of $100 or more. You can set this and similar conditions on the Sum command by using its Build a search condition option (Figure 2.21). The ASSISTANT mode leads you through this process, which adds a For parameter to the Sum command. In its final form, the action line will read SUM FOR AMOUNT > 100. Executing the command yields the following message:

```
  3 records summed
 amount
1625.00
```

The following is the dot prompt Sum For command:

(.) Sum: `sum for amount > 100`

AVERAGE

dBASE can also generate the numeric average of a field. For instance, you can determine the average amount owed by people in the CUSTOMER file. Like Sum, the **Average command** is another option of Retrieve, and it requires the

Figure 2.21
Selects the Equal To relational parameter.

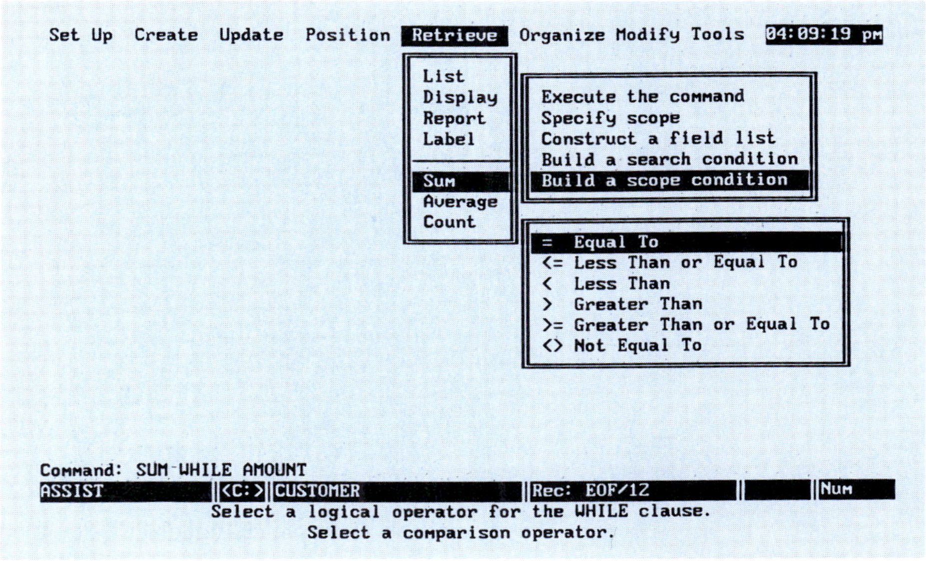

same process of selecting numeric fields via the Construct a field list option (see Figure 2.20). For the CUSTOMER file, the final action line will read `AVERAGE AMOUNT`. The following message should result:

```
  12 records averaged
average
160.42
```

RECORD ALTERATION COMMANDS

You have already seen how to make changes in a record with the Edit command. You can also make changes with the Replace, Delete, Pack, and Restore commands. The command-level dot prompt mode is used in the following examples. The Assistant Menu could be used in some of these examples.

REPLACE

Instead of accessing each record and displaying it for full-screen editing, you can use the **Replace command** to institute the change. (The Replace command is an option under Update on the Assistant Menu.) Suppose that Reza Ghorbani paid his bill in full. To change the amount in his record to zero, enter the Replace command shown below. A message telling you how many records were replaced will then be displayed. To verify that the Replace command has accomplished its task, enter the List command that follows it.

```
. replace amount with 0 for first = 'Reza'
```

```
1 record replaced
```

```
. list first, last, amount
```

Record#	first	last	amount
1	Reza	Ghorbani	0.00
2	Ann	Ghorbani	250.00
3	Douglas	Acklin	55.00
4	Barbara	Walters	75.00
5	Arthur	Adams	35.00
6	Russell	Davis	35.00
7	Debbie	Acklin	35.00
8	Harvey	Posio	1250.00
9	Ben	Pietrowiak	20.00
10	Sandy	Acklin	35.00
11	Fred	Ficek	0.00
12	Juan	Decesario	10.00

The above example changed only one record. If you want to change every record by the same amount, you can add the scope parameter All. For example, you could add five cents to each record's amount by issuing the Replace command shown below. Clearly, if you need to make a change that will affect all the records in a file, the Replace All command will do the job faster than the Edit command. The following example illustrates how it works:

```
. replace all amount with amount + .05
```

```
12 records replaced
```

```
. list first, last, amount
```

Record#	first	last	amount
1	Reza	Ghorbani	0.05
2	Ann	Ghorbani	250.05
3	Douglas	Acklin	55.05
4	Barbara	Walters	75.05
5	Arthur	Adams	35.05
6	Russell	Davis	35.05
7	Debbie	Acklin	35.05
8	Harvey	Posio	1250.05
9	Ben	Pietrowiak	20.05
10	Sandy	Acklin	35.05
11	Fred	Ficek	0.05
12	Juan	Decesario	10.05

You can easily return the file to its former status by issuing another Replace command.

```
. replace all amount with amount - .05
```

```
12 records replaced
```

```
. list first, last, amount
```

Record#	first	last	amount
1	Reza	Ghorbani	0.00
2	Ann	Ghorbani	250.00
3	Douglas	Acklin	55.00
4	Barbara	Walters	75.00
5	Arthur	Adams	35.00
6	Russell	Davis	35.00
7	Debbie	Acklin	35.00
8	Harvey	Posio	1250.00
9	Ben	Pietrowiak	20.00
10	Sandy	Acklin	35.00
11	Fred	Ficek	0.00
12	Juan	Decesario	10.00

The following example will place 125.00 back in the Reza Ghorbani record using the Assistant Menu of dBASE.

Update	Selects Update from the Assistant Menu.
Replace	Selects the Replace command.
Enter	Executes the command.
AMOUNT	Specifies the AMOUNT field.
Enter	
Type `125.00`	Gives the new amount for Reza.
Enter	Enters the amount.
→	Takes you to the Replace submenu.
Build a search condition	Selects Build a search condition.
Enter	
FIRST	Specifies the FIRST field.
Enter	
=	Specifies the equal (=) option.
Enter	
Type `Reza`	Enters Reza's first name.
Enter	
No more conditions	Selects No more conditions.
Enter	
Execute the command	Selects Execute the command.
Enter	

Press any key to return to the Assistant Menu.

DELETE, RECALL, AND PACK

From time to time, you will want to delete records from a database file. This is a two-step process: (1) The **Delete command** marks the records to be deleted, and (2) the **Pack command** recopies the file with all records that were marked for deletion left out and the rest "packed" together.

Delete Command Marking records for deletion is sometimes referred to as *logical deletion* because, although the record has been marked, it is not yet actually removed from the file and can still be read and processed.

The following example shows how to mark record 7 for deletion. First, position the pointer at the record; next the screen displays part of the record to verify that the right record has been located; then give the Delete command:

```
. 7
. display first, last
```

```
Record# first      last
      7 Debbie     Acklin
```

```
. delete
```

```
1 record deleted
```

```
. display
```

```
Record#  FIRST         INIT     LAST            ADDRESS                CITY
    STATE ZIP    PHONE             AMOUNT DATE
      7 *Debbie        C        Acklin          408 E. Monroe          Bloomington
    IL     61701  (309)827-1395     35.00 03/21/92
```

The **delete indicator (*)** now appears between the record number and the first field of the record. This mark takes up 1 byte of storage on a dBASE record and accounts for the extra position reserved for the fields in a record. The delete indicator makes the marked record easy to spot in a listing of file records:

```
. list first, last, amount
```

```
Record#  first     last           amount
      1  Reza      Ghorbani       125.00
      2  Ann       Ghorbani       250.00
      3  Douglas   Acklin          55.00
      4  Barbara   Walters         75.00
      5  Arthur    Adams           35.00
      6  Russell   Davis           35.00
      7  *Debbie   Acklin          35.00
      8  Harvey    Posio         1250.00
      9  Ben       Pietrowiak      20.00
     10  Sandy     Acklin          35.00
     11  Fred      Ficek            0.00
     12  Juan      Decesario       10.00
```

Recall Command Until you give the Pack command, you can still undelete a record that has been marked for deletion with the **Recall command.** To undelete a record, first position the pointer at that record and then give the Recall command. To undelete all marked records in a file, the command is **Recall All.** Because the pointer is still on record 7 in the present case, the pointer does not have to be repositioned, and the first line of the following command can be omitted:

```
. 7
. recall
```

```
1 record recalled
```

```
. display first, last
```

```
Record# first     last
      7 Debbie    Acklin
```

Notice that dBASE reports how many records have been undeleted.

Pack Command Prepare to practice the Pack command by using the Append command to add the following record to the file:

```
13  Eric C Wild  207 S. Broadmore  Felix  KS  34762  0.00
```

Now, with your pointer positioned at record 13, mark the file with the Delete command and list the files to confirm:

```
. delete
```

```
1 record deleted
```

```
. list first,last,amount
```

```
Record#  first    last           amount
      1  Reza     Ghorbani       125.00
      2  Ann      Ghorbani       250.00
      3  Douglas  Acklin          55.00
      4  Barbara  Walters         75.00
      5  Arthur   Adams           35.00
      6  Russell  Davis           35.00
      7  Debbie   Acklin          35.00
      8  Harvey   Posio         1250.00
      9  Ben      Pietrowiak      20.00
     10  Sandy    Acklin          35.00
     11  Fred     Ficek            0.00
     12  Juan     Decesario       10.00
     13 *Eric     Wild            10.00
```

HINTS/HAZARDS To find where you are when the record contents are not shown on the screen, consult the status line. At record 13 in a file containing 13 reports, the status line reads `Rec:13/3`.

Now give the Pack command and list the files:

```
. pack
```

```
12 records copied
```

```
. list first,last,amount
```

Record#	first	last	amount
1	Reza	Ghorbani	125.00
2	Ann	Ghorbani	250.00
3	Douglas	Acklin	55.00
4	Barbara	Walters	75.00
5	Arthur	Adams	35.00
6	Russell	Davis	35.00
7	Debbie	Acklin	35.00
8	Harvey	Posio	1250.00
9	Ben	Pietrowiak	20.00
10	Sandy	Acklin	35.00
11	Fred	Ficek	0.00
12	Juan	Decesario	10.00

REPORT TEMPLATE AND THE CREATE REPORT COMMAND

Having data stored in a computerized file is not worth much by itself; for the data to be useful in practical terms, they must be printed in report form on paper. This process begins with the **Create Report command** in dBASE. The Create Report command builds a **report template** on disk containing the report format, headings, and fields to be included in the report (see p. B.60).

After this general discussion of the Report command is a step-by-step exercise to build the report template. The template is created by filling in fields presented in dBASE screens that prompt you through the process. All you have to do is respond to the prompts on each screen.

To create a template, first open the database file from which the report will be taken.

Create	Selects Create from the Assistant Menu.
Report	Selects the Report command.

The following is the dot prompt Create Report command:

(.) Create Report: `. create report <filename>`

dBASE now asks for the drive where the report will be stored and the name of the report. If you don't have a database file open at this time, dBASE prompts for the name of a file to be used. For this example, you will enter the report name NAMEADDR. You would now see the Create Report Menu across the top of the screen:

```
Options    Groups    Columns    Locate    Exit
```

Begin with the Options submenu (Figure 2.22).

Options The Options Menu lets you enter a report heading (Page title) and change a number of print options.

Select the Page title option. A rectangular box appears, as shown in Figure 2.23. Enter any desired title. dBASE will automatically center these lines when it prints the report. You can enter up to four lines of titles. Once you have entered the title, press Ctrl + End (the End command) to return to the Options Menu.

Figure 2.22

Options screen of the Create Report command.

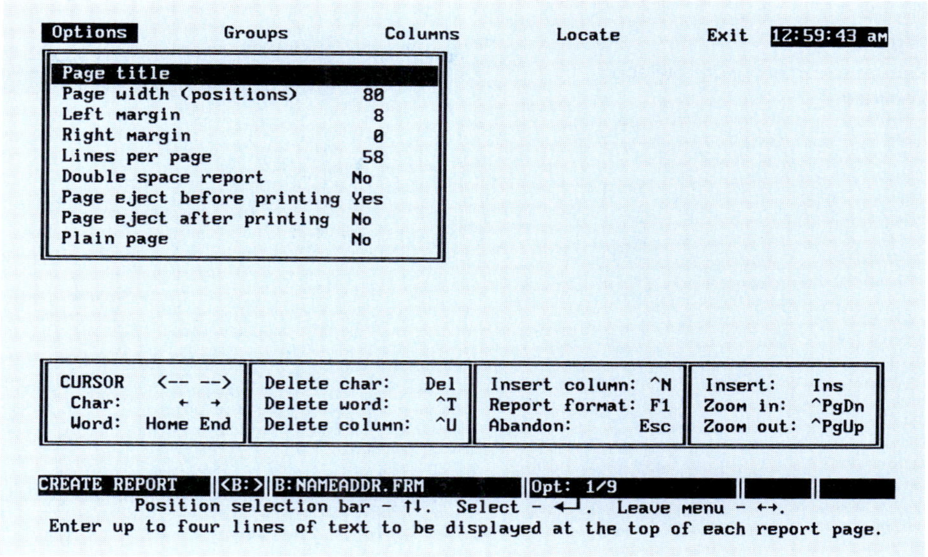

Figure 2.23

Report title box of the Options screen.

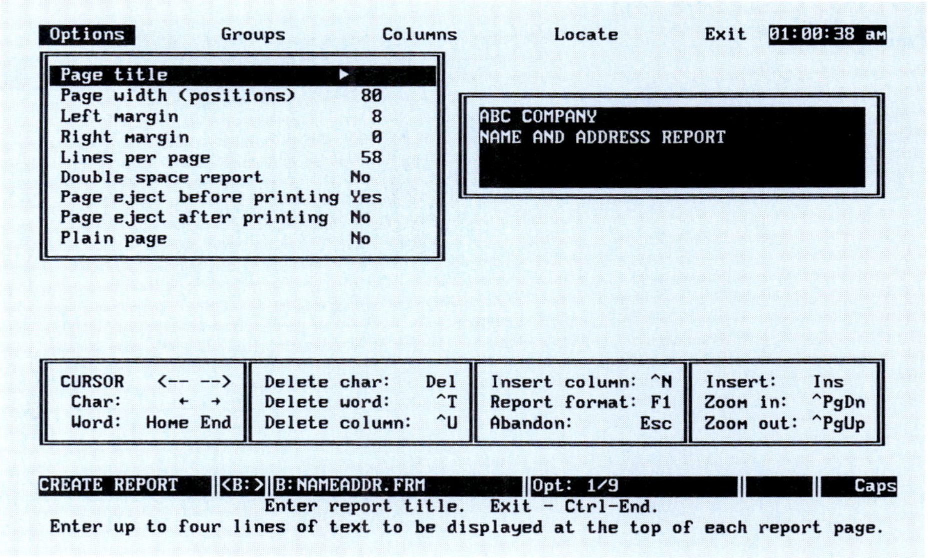

Some default and maximum values for the Options screen are as follows:

Page title. Up to four lines can be entered, with up to 500 characters per line.

Left margin. The default is eight characters.

Right margin. The default is zero characters.

Spacing. The default is single spacing.

Page eject before printing. The default is yes.

Page eject after printing. The default is no.

Plain page. The default is no. If yes, the page numbers and the system data are not printed. In such a situation, the report heading is printed only on the first page of the printout.

Press the Right Arrow key to move the next menu option (Groups).

Figure 2.24
Groups screen of the Create Report command.

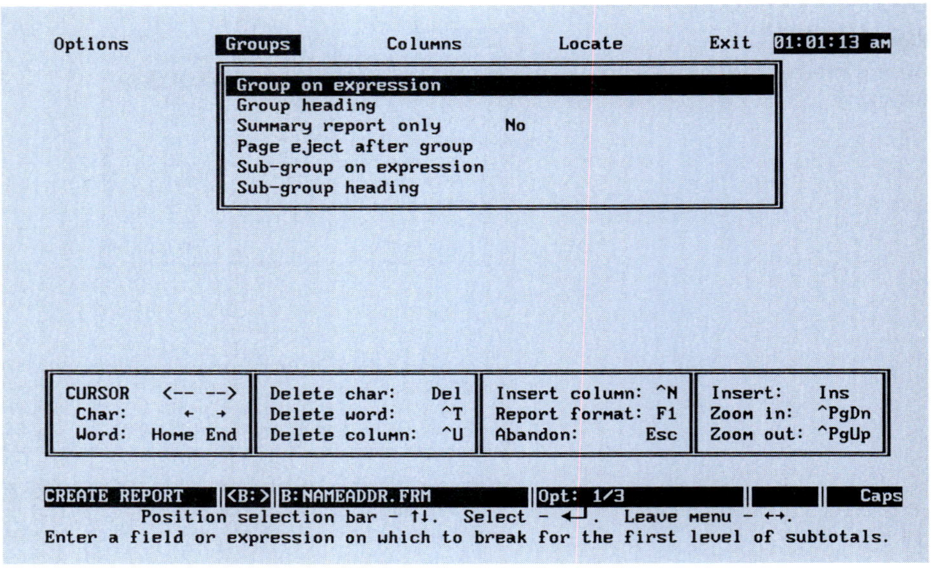

Figure 2.25
The Columns screen.

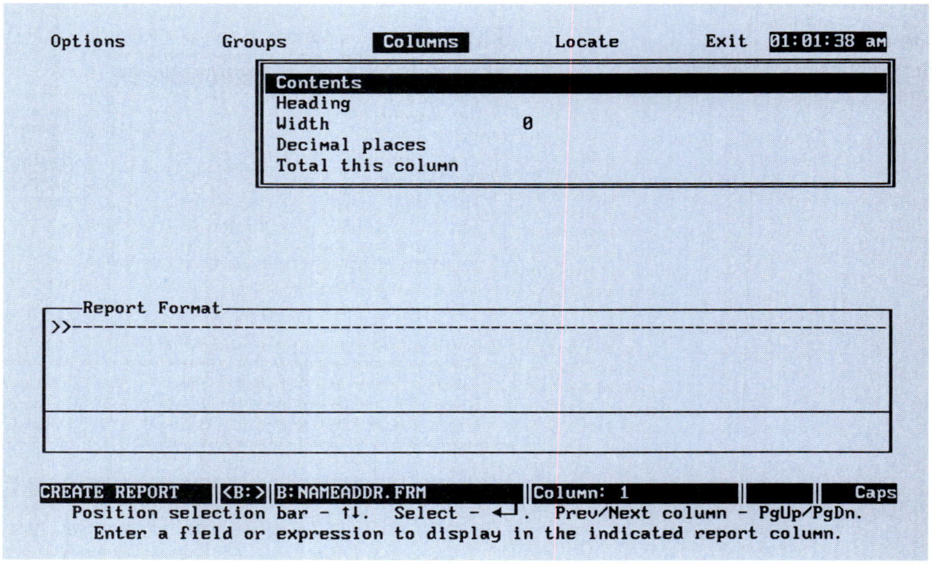

Groups The Groups screen (Figure 2.24) lets you establish subtotals for a report but only on a sorted or indexed file; because the CUSTOMER file is neither sorted nor indexed, you do not want to enter any information about subtotals. (You'll learn more about the Groups screen in Chapter 3.) Press the Right Arrow key to advance to the Columns screen.

Columns The Columns screen (Figure 2.25) lets you specify the file's field name that you want to print in this column of the report. You will use the top box of this screen to enter the name of the field for each column of the report. To do this, be sure that the pointer is positioned on Contents and press Enter. To obtain a list of the field names (in case you've forgotten them), press F10. This displays a box on the left side of the screen that lists the fields and a box on the right that describes each in turn (Figure 2.26). Select a field by pointing and

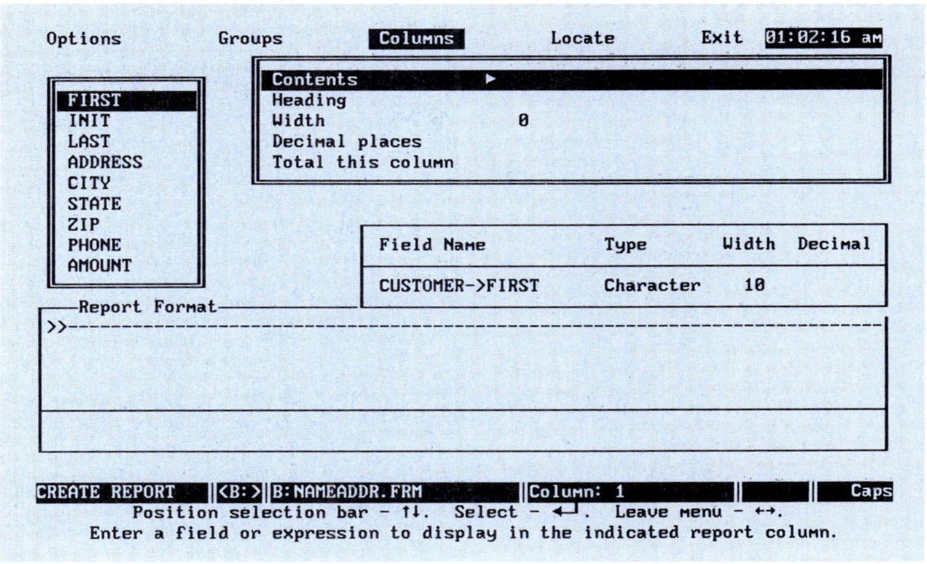

Figure 2.26

The dBASE F10 Help facility for fields displays both the field name and information about the data.

press Enter to unlock it. Press Enter once more to "unlock" the pointer and move it to the Heading line.

After you unlock this entry and lock the pointer by pressing Enter, a box appears in the middle of the screen, in which you can enter up to five lines of text as a heading for the field. Enter the heading and press Pg Dn when you are finished.

You can also enter a width for the field that is different than the size allotted in the record structure. If you are entering information about a numeric field, you will also be prompted to state the number of decimal positions and whether or not dBASE should total that column in the report. The box at the bottom of the screen depicts the report format. Press Pg Dn again to get back to the Columns screen and define the next field (column) to appear in the report.

Should you make an error in entering a valid field name, dBASE will beep, display an error message at the bottom of the screen, and direct you to press any key to continue.

After you have entered a field and have proceeded to the next field-definition box, dBASE shows you how the report will appear in the Report Format box (Figure 2.27). dBASE takes the previously specified column headings and places them at the top of the box. The width of a character field is indicated by XXXXs and the width of a numeric field by ###.##.

HINTS/HAZARDS

When you are entering data for the various entries in the Columns Menu, it sometimes becomes confusing about when you have to press Enter and when you can move the pointer. Before you can make a change to any entry, you must first activate or "unlock' that menu option by pressing Enter. Only after Enter is pressed does a little triangle appear at the beginning of the data item. If, when all menu or data-entry boxes are closed, the triangle still appears, you must again press Enter to "lock" this menu entry to allow the pointer to move using Up and Down Arrow keys. Otherwise, you can simply move the pointer.

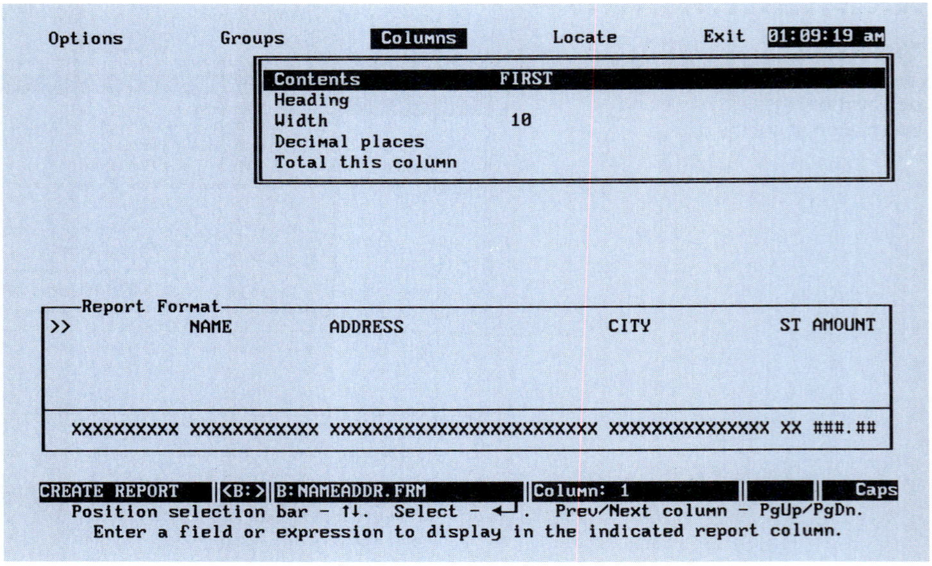

Figure 2.27
Completed Report Format box of the Columns screen.

dBASE automatically takes the field length from the record and places that number in the Width entry for each field. If you want to trim a column, simply decrease this number. This results in rightmost truncation for character fields. For example, if a field width that was 25 is changed to 18, characters to the right of position 18 will not print on this line but will wrap to the next line. Characters and entered blank spaces wrap to the next line, but unused, unentered spaces do not. dBASE also automatically places one space between each column.

Locate The Locate option of the Report Menu generates a screen containing all fields used by this report form. You can examine one of these fields by positioning the pointer to that field and pressing Enter. The report window for that field now appears.

Exit To save the report, simply issue the Exit command from the Report Menu. You now receive a two-prompt menu: `Save` and `Abandon`. To save this report form to disk, select Save. To exit the Create Report command without saving the template to disk, select Abandon. You then receive the prompt `Are you sure you want to abandon operation? [Y/N]`. Press Y to return to the Assistant Menu.

Build the dBASE report.

1. Create the report template:

Create	Selects Create from the Main Menu.
Report	Chooses Report from the Create submenu.
Enter	Selects the Report option.
B:	Selects the drive.
Enter	
Type `NAMEADDR`	
Enter	Executes the command.

2. Specify page titles and report characteristics (see Figure 2.22):

Options	Selects Options from the Main Menu.
Page title	Selects Page title from the Options Menu.
Enter	Opens the Page title box.
Type `ABC COMPANY`	
Enter	
Type `NAME AND ADDRESS REPORT`	Enters the first and second lines of the title. Don't worry about centering the title within the box. dBASE will automatically center the titles when it creates the report (see Figure 2.23).
Ctrl + End	Saves the heading and returns to the Options Menu.
Left margin	Selects Left margin from the Options Menu.
Enter	Opens the Left margin entry.
2	Enters the new margin of 2.
Enter	Executes the command.

3. Enter field specifications for the FIRST field:

Columns	Selects Columns from the Main Menu.
Contents	Selects Contents from the Columns submenu.
Enter	Opens the Contents option.
F10	Displays the field names of the CUSTOMER.DBF file (see Figure 2.26).
FIRST	Selects the FIRST field.
Enter (2)	Enters the FIRST field as the content of Column #1 and closes the Contents option.
PgDn	Enters the information defining Column 1. (Notice `Column: 2` now appears in the status line.)

4. Enter specifications for the LAST field:

Enter	Opens the Contents option for Column 2.
F10	Lists the fields available.
LAST	Selects the LAST field.
Enter (2)	Enters the LAST field as the content of Column 2 and closes the Content option.
Heading	Selects the Heading option from the Columns submenu.
Enter	Opens the Heading box.
Type `NAME`	Enters the heading for the second field in the Heading box.
Ctrl + End	Leaves the Heading box.
PgDn	Enters the information defining Column 2. (Notice `Column: 3` now appears in the status line.)

5. Define the remaining columns using the instructions from step 4. Information about the remaining fields follows. When you are finished, your screen should look like that in Figure 2.27.

Field	Heading	Total
ADDRESS	ADDRESS	
CITY	CITY	
STATE	ST	
AMOUNT	AMOUNT	Y

6. Save the report template.

Exit	Selects Exit from the Main Menu.
Save	Selects the Save command and saves the template to disk.

PRINTING A REPORT

Print reports by using the **Report Form command** together with the report template. Be sure your printer is turned on and properly linked to your computer. The following steps will print the report whose template you just created:

Retrieve	Selects Retrieve from the Assistant Menu.
Report	Selects the Report command.
Enter	Executes the command.

The following is the dot prompt Report Form command:

(.) Report Form: `. report form <drive:><filename>`

Indicate that the report form is on the default drive—drive B in this case. Select the NAMEADDR.FRM report form; you should now see the corresponding dot prompt commands on the action line: `REPORT FORM B:NAMEADDR.`

Execute the command	Selects Execute the command from the Report submenu.
Enter	
Y	Answers yes to `Direct the output to the printer? [Y/N].`

dBASE now appends the message `TO PRINT` on the action line. (If you do not respond Y, the output is sent to the screen.) The following report should now be printed:

```
Page No. 1
05/15/92
                          ABC COMPANY
                CUSTOMER NAME AND ADDRESS REPORT

        NAME       ADDRESS             CITY        ST   AMOUNT

Reza    Ghorbani   4033 N. Wolcott     Chicago     IL   125.00
Ann     Ghorbani   4033 N. Wolcott     Chicago     IL   250.00
Douglas Acklin     408 E. Monroe       Bloomington IL    55.00
Barbara Walters    1981 Crestlawn      Arlington   VA    75.00
Arthur  Adams      115 Ginger Creek Ct. Bloomington IL   35.00
Russell Davis      707 Vale St.        Bloomington IL    35.00
Debbie  Acklin     408 E. Monroe       Bloomington IL    35.00
Harvey  Posio      1013 Hillcrest      San Diego   CA  1250.00
Ben     Pietrowiak 3334 N. Foster      Normal      IL    20.00
Sandy   Acklin     408 E. Monroe       Bloomington IL    35.00
Fred    Ficek      1215 Tamarack       Normal      IL     0.00
Juan    Decesario  1214 Flores         Miami       FL    10.00
*** Total ***
                                                       1925.00
```

When dBASE executed the previous command, it accessed the disk for the NAMEADDR.FRM file and loaded it. It then accessed the CUSTOMER file.

Once you build a report template, you can use it over and over.

Selective Reports You can limit the records included in a report by using the For parameter of the Build a search condition option, much as you did with the Sum command earlier in this chapter. For example, you may want to print an exception report of those customers whose balance is over $100. To do this, begin by entering the same commands as in the previous example (Report Form B:Nameaddr). Before executing the command, however, select options and enter data as follows:

Build a search condition	Selects Build a search condition from the Report submenu.
Enter	Executes the command.
AMOUNT	Specifies the AMOUNT field.
Enter	Selects the field.
>Greater Than	Selects the >Greater Than option from the parameters box.
Enter	Executes the command.
Type 100	Enters the value 100.
Enter	Executes the command.
No more conditions	Tells dBASE that there are no more conditions. The corresponding dot prompt commands should now appear on the action line: REPORT FORM B:NAMEADDR FOR AMOUNT > 100.
Enter	Executes the command.
Execute the command	Selects Execute the command.
Enter (2)	Executes the command and tells dBASE to not direct output to the printer.

The following is the dot prompt command:

(.)
```
. report form <drive:><filename> for <numericfield><parameter><number>
. report form nameaddr for amount > 100
```

The following report should now print:

```
Page No.  1
05/15/92
                          ABC COMPANY
                  CUSTOMER NAME AND ADDRESS REPORT

          NAME       ADDRESS              CITY        ST   AMOUNT

Reza      Ghorbani   4033 N. Wolcott      Chicago     IL   125.00
Ann       Ghorbani   4033 N. Wolcott      Chicago     IL   250.00
Harvey    Posio      1013 Hillcrest       San Diego   CA  1250.00
*** Total ***
                                                          1625.00
```

You might also want to print a report of amounts owed by customers in a specific region. The following command entered at the dot prompt (.) produces a list of all customers who live in Bloomington and generates a grand total of the amount owed:

```
. report form nameaddr for city = 'Bloomington'
```

```
Page No. 1
05/15/92
                          ABC COMPANY
                 CUSTOMER NAME AND ADDRESS REPORT

        NAME          ADDRESS             CITY        ST   AMOUNT

Douglas Acklin    408 E. Monroe       Bloomington IL    55.00
Arthur  Adams     115 Ginger Creek Ct. Bloomington IL    35.00
Russell Davis     707 Vale St.        Bloomington IL    35.00
Debbie  Acklin    408 E. Monroe       Bloomington IL    35.00
Sandy   Acklin    408 E. Monroe       Bloomington IL    35.00
*** Total ***
                                                       195.00
```

You could also specify Build a search condition and specify the CITY field as the field to use in this operation. When prompted with `[Enter a character string (without quotes):]`, type `Bloomington` and press Enter. Tell dBASE there are no more conditions. Then tell it to execute the command.

Making changes to a report template requires selecting either the Create or Modify option of the Assistant Menu and then selecting the Report option. Once the drive and the template have been specified, you can change any of the screen information.

CHAPTER REVIEW

dBASE III Plus provides commands for manipulating data. The List command can display (a) the contents of an entire file, (b) selected records, or (c) selected fields of records. The Display All command works like the List command but stops when it has displayed 16 lines.

Pointer movement commands include the explicit and implied Go and Goto commands and the Skip command, which let you move forward or backward in the file, one or more records at a time.

The Replace command changes one record, selected groups of records, or all records in the field at one time, in accordance with selection criteria. This command provides another method, besides the Edit command, for changing the field contents of records.

The substring function ($) is a powerful command that lets you search for characters in a field of data. It can be used with commands such as Replace and List.

dBASE III Plus does not automatically delete a record from a file when you issue the Delete command. Instead, it marks the record with dBASE's delete indicator, the asterisk (*) for future deletion. After a record has been marked for deletion, it can be undeleted with the Recall command. Physically removing a record from a file requires the Pack command following the Delete command. The Pack command copies the entire file to a new location on disk, dropping any records marked for deletion, and deletes the previous file.

The Create Report command lets you format a report via a report template for information contained in a file. The Create Report feature provides a number of full-screen editing windows for you to use in describing the report, including screens for specifying report and column headings and any fields you want to print. The feature also generates totals for any numeric fields. The Report Form command prints the report.

KEY TERMS AND CONCEPTS

All parameter
Average command
beginning-of-file (BOF) function
Create Report command
Delete command
delete indicator (*)
Directory (DIR) command
Display command
end-of-file (EOF) function
For parameter
Goto Bottom command
Goto command
Goto Top command
List command
List Structure command
Next option
Pack command
query command
Recall All command
Recall command
RECNO( ) function
Replace command
Report Form command
report template
Skip command
substring function ($)
Sum command
Use command
? character

CHAPTER QUIZ

Multiple Choice

1. Which of the following dBASE commands can change records in a file?
   a. List
   b. Edit
   c. Report
   d. Replace
   e. Change

2. If you use the Set Print On command, reports could be generated using which of the following statements?
   a. List
   b. Report
   c. Display
   d. All of the above

3. The Report feature of dBASE III Plus lets you do which of the following?
   a. Establish a report title
   b. Print column headings
   c. Number each page
   d. Print totals
   e. All of the above
   f. Only a, b, and c

4. Which of the following commands does *not* move the record pointer?
   a. Skip
   b. Goto Bottom
   c. Goto Top
   d. .5
   e. Skip − 5
   f. All of the above commands move the record pointer.

5. Which of the following statements is true about the List and Display commands?
   a. Display does not let you display selected fields.
   b. Both List and Display prohibit arithmetic selection criteria.
   c. Display All shows the next 16 lines and then pauses.
   d. Display automatically lists all the records in the file.
   e. All of the above

True/False

6. The Display All command gives you more control than the simple List command.

7. The Delete command physically removes a record from the file.

8. The Recall command automatically unerases all deleted records within a file.

9. The Display command shows the record at the current pointer location.

10. The Sum command can total numeric fields from selected records.

Answers

1. b, d 2. d 3. e 4. f 5. c 6. t 7. f 8. f 9. t 10. t

Exercises

1. The command Display __________ displays all records in the file on the screen and pauses after 16 lines.

2. The __________ command displays the record at the current pointer location.

3. Three pointer positioning commands are __________, __________, and __________.

4. The Goto __________ command places the pointer at the end of the file.

5. Use the __________ command to move forward or backward in the file.

6. The __________ command displays the current record number.

7. The Goto __________ command positions the pointer at the beginning of the file.

8. The __________ command changes records in the file.

9. The function __________ finds a character string in a field.

10. The __________ command marks a record for deletion.

11. The __________ command undeletes a record.

12. The __________ command removes records from a file that have been marked for deletion.

13. The __________ command generates the total of a field from the records in a file.

14. The __________ command sends any output on the screen to the printer.

15. The __________ command builds a report template that can be used later.

COMPUTER EXERCISES

The following exercises require the PAYMAST file, created previously.

1. Look at the format of the database records.

2. Look at the employee and pay rate of each record.

3. Look at only those employees with a gross of more than $850.

4. Total the GROSS PAY field.

5. Total the GROSS PAY field for those with a gross of more than $900.

6. Give Mark Tell a raise of .50.

7. Give everyone a raise of .25.

8. Go to record 5 and display it to the screen.

9. Delete and recall record 9.

10. Delete record 5.

11. Pack the file.

12. Use the $ function to find any record with a *P* in the first or last name.

13. Create the following .FRM and print it.

```
 PAGE NO. 00001                PAYROLL SUMMARY                04/13/92
 ID        EMPLOYEE                PAY RATE         GROSS
4908 Richard     Payne                  4.45         556.00
5789 Connnie     Reiners                3.35         450.00
5523 Pamela      Rich                   6.00         780.00
6324 Mark        Tell                   5.50         980.00
2870 Frank       Terlep                 6.80         670.00
4679 Kenneth     Klass                  4.90         780.00
8345 Thomas      Momery                 4.70         580.00
5649 Toni        McCarthy               5.20         667.00
5432 Alan        Monroe                 5.20        1340.00
5998 Paul        Mish                   4.90         887.00
4463 Edward      Mockford               4.90         775.00
 456                                    0.00           0.00
** TOTAL **
                                                     8465.00
```

14. Use the report template you developed to generate a report for employees with a gross pay of more than $800.

15. Indicate which parts of the following commands correspond with the command, scope, noun, and condition portions of a dBASE command. For example, in the command `LIST NEXT 5 FIRST, LAST, ADDRESS FOR AMOUNT > 50`: the command is LIST; the scope is NEXT 5; the nouns are FIRST, LAST, and ADDRESS; and the condition is FOR AMOUNT > 50.
    a. DIR
    b. DIR *.DBF
    c. LIST FIRST, LAST, CITY, STATE
    d. USE ACCREC
    e. DELETE ALL
    f. REPLACE NAME WITH ADOLPH FOR LAST = 'HITLER'
    g. REPORT FORM NAMEADDR FOR AMOUNT > 100
    h. CREATE REPORT
    i. DISPLAY ALL FIRST,LAST
    j. REPLACE AMOUNT WITH 0 FOR STATE = 'Il'
    k. SUM AMOUNT FOR AMOUNT > 50
    l. LIST NEXT 7

3

MORE dBASE III PLUS COMMANDS

CHAPTER OBJECTIVES

After completing this chapter, you should be able to

- ***Use the dBASE III Plus Sort command***
- ***Use the dBASE III Plus Index command***
- ***Locate records in sequential and random files***
- ***Generate ordered reports***
- ***Use some miscellaneous file commands***
- ***Use the Browse command***

In this chapter, we introduce dBASE techniques for arranging, rearranging, and locating data in the manner most suitable to your application. The commands include Sort, Index, Locate, Seek, Delete, and Browse. We also introduce the Modify and Copy commands for changing existing files, creating new ones, and passing data to and from other application programs. We conclude with instruction on how to provide subtotals in a dBASE III Plus report.

ARRANGEMENT COMMANDS

SORT

The **Sort command** physically rearranges file records according to values contained in one or more specific fields of each record. To do this, Sort does not rearrange the records of the original file but produces a second output file with the contents in a different order.

Before you sort a file, you must first activate it. In the Sort command, you must designate the key fields for sorting and name the output file. Unless you state otherwise, this "To" file will have the .DBF extension.

You can specify up to 10 key fields for one sort. Enter the fields in order of importance, the most important first. Separate the fields by commas. You cannot sort logical or memo fields.

Unless you choose otherwise, sorts are in ascending order—alphabetically *A* to *Z* and numerically 0 to 9. Descending order is the reverse—*Z* to *A* and 9 to 0.

In the following example, we will sort the CUSTOMER file in zip-code order. To do this, first set the default drive to B (or the appropriate drive) and activate the CUSTOMER file. Now follow these steps:

Organize	Selects Organize from the Assistant Menu.
Sort	Selects the Sort command.
Enter	Executes the command. The action line now reads `SORT ON` and the fields in the CUSTOMER file are listed, along with information about the highlighted field (Figure 3.1).
ZIP	Specifies the ZIP field.
Enter	Selects the field.
→	Returns you to the Organize submenu and presents a menu of drives.
B:	Specifies the default drive (B) to hold the "To" file.
Enter	Selects the drive.
Type `ZIPCUST`	Answers the prompt `Enter the name of the file:`.
Enter	Enters the answer (Figure 3.2).

The Sort command now executes.

The following is the dot prompt Sort command:

(.) Sort: `Sort on zip to zipcust`

If you wish to have Sort execute in descending order, use the /D parameter. To execute the just-performed sort in descending order, go to the Command Menu (this cannot be done from the Assistant Menu) and enter the command

```
.sort on zip /D to zipdesc
```

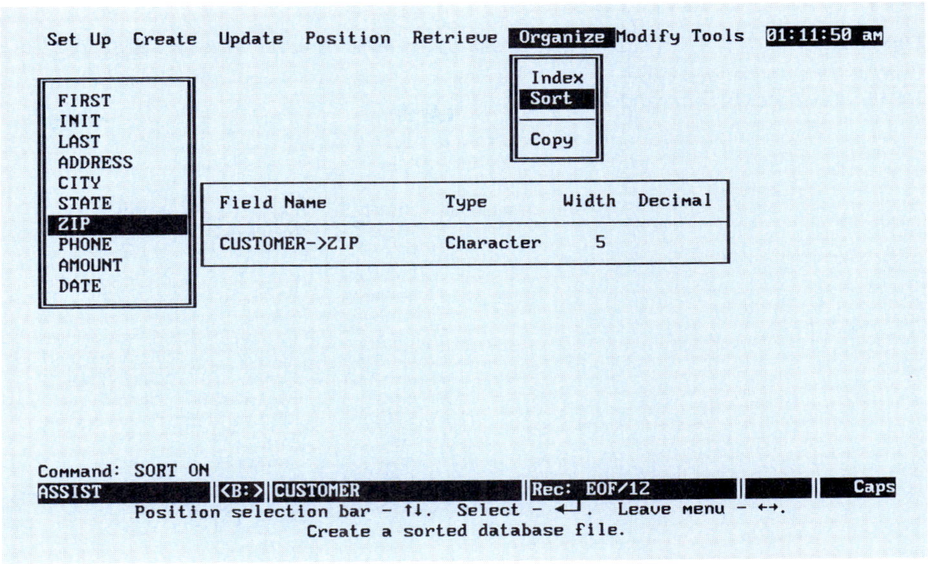

Figure 3.1
Field list for specifying key fields in a sort.

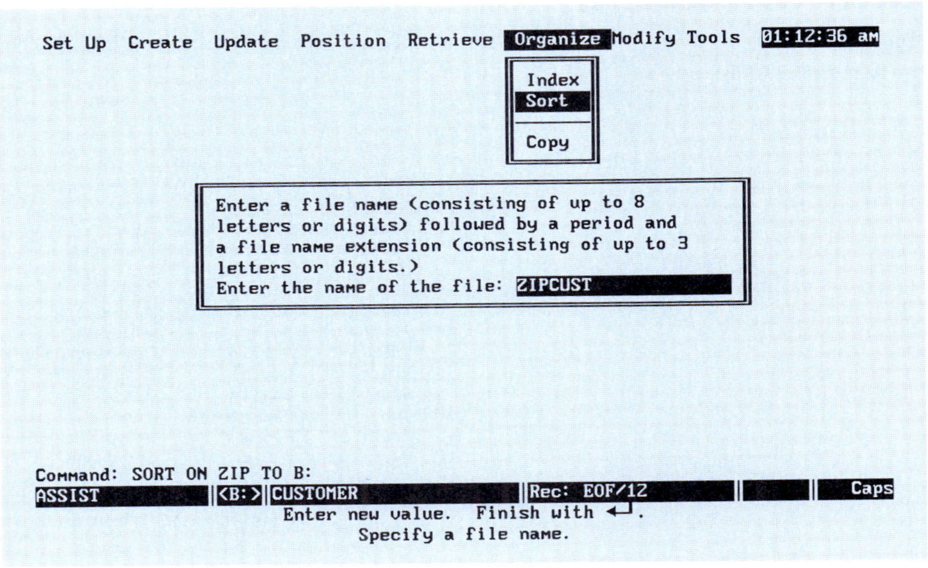

Figure 3.2
Screen for specifying the output file in a sort operation.

This command places the descending order sort in the ZIPDESC file.

Once the sort starts, dBASE displays the message `00%`. When the sort is completed, it says `100% 12 Records Sorted`.

The Sort command keeps you informed about how much of the file has been sorted. When the sort is completed, the screen displays the `100% xx Records Sorted` message. You now have two files: the original CUSTOMER file on disk, which remains unchanged, and the newly created ZIPCUST file, which contains the data from the CUSTOMER file arranged by the contents of the ZIP field. Because you have not changed the file activated via a Use statement, the CUSTOMER file remains active. You can confirm that its order has not changed by using the Retrieve command of the Assistant Menu and listing the file by the fields FIRST, LAST, CITY, STATE, and ZIP (Figure 3.3).

Figure 3.3
Output of the unchanged CUSTOMER file via the List command.

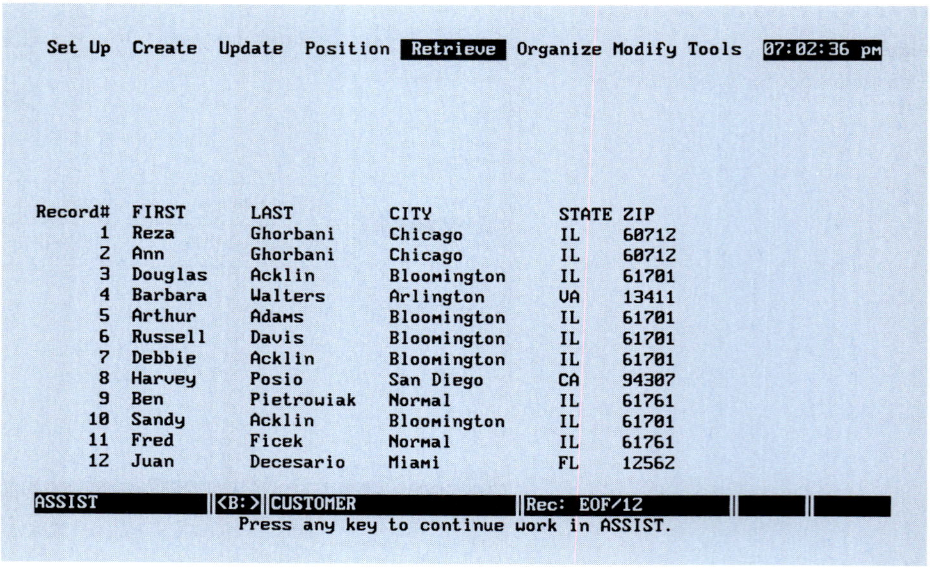

Figure 3.4
The sorted ZIPCUST file.

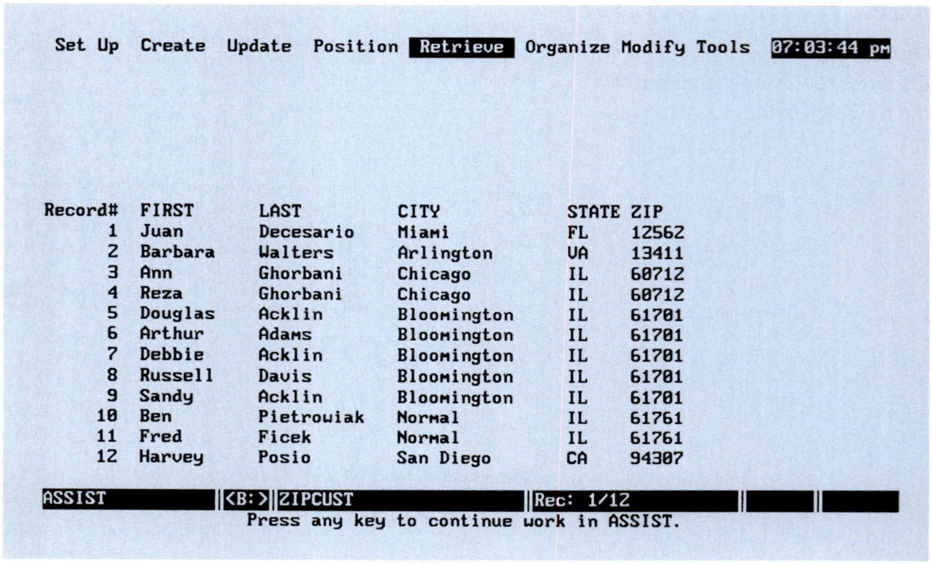

To verify that you have created the ZIPCUST file properly, issue the Set Up command from the Assistant Menu, activate the ZIPCUST file, select the Retrieve command from the Assistant Menu, specify the same fields, issue the List command, and execute (Figure 3.4). Notice that the records are not in the same order as in the CUSTOMER file but are arranged by the contents of the ZIP field. This means that the record numbers are also different, having been changed to reflect their new locations in the ZIPCUST file.

The process of sorting information by two fields is also straightforward. Suppose you want to sort the CUSTOMER file by name. When two customers have the same last name, you will want the first names to be in alphabetic order. In this case, the primary sort key (first field specified) is the last name, and the secondary sort key (second field specified) is the first name. Specify your sort

Figure 3.5
Result of a List command against the sorted ALPHNAME file.

```
 Set Up  Create  Update  Position  Retrieve  Organize Modify Tools  07:05:22 pm

Record#  LAST          FIRST        CITY             STATE ZIP
      1  Acklin        Debbie       Bloomington      IL     61701
      2  Acklin        Douglas      Bloomington      IL     61701
      3  Acklin        Sandy        Bloomington      IL     61701
      4  Adams         Arthur       Bloomington      IL     61701
      5  Davis         Russell      Bloomington      IL     61701
      6  Decesario     Juan         Miami            FL     12562
      7  Ficek         Fred         Normal           IL     61761
      8  Ghorbani      Ann          Chicago          IL     60712
      9  Ghorbani      Reza         Chicago          IL     60712
     10  Pietrowiak    Ben          Normal           IL     61761
     11  Posio         Harvey       San Diego        CA     94307
     12  Walters       Barbara      Arlington        VA     13411

ASSIST          ||<B:>||ALPHNAME         ||Rec: 1/12          ||     ||
                    Press any key to continue work in ASSIST.
```

fields in the manner previously indicated and place the output in the file ALPHNAME. (You can issue the Sort command in ASSISTANT mode or enter it via the dot prompt as `. sort on last, first to b:alphname.`) Once the Sort command has been executed, the information is placed in first-name-within-last-name order. Activate the ALPHNAME file and list it in LAST, FIRST, CITY, STATE, and ZIP order (Figure 3.5).

Using the Sort command is not usually the best way to arrange data within a file. Several restrictions apply to it:

1. It usually takes a lot of computer time. Although this is not evident with a small file such as CUSTOMER, an attempt to use Sort on a file containing 3000 records would make it obvious.
2. The Sort command creates a new file every time it is executed. This takes up a lot of disk storage when you sort large files.
3. The record numbers change from one file to another.

INDEX

The best way to reorder records is usually to use the **Index command,** which does not rearrange them physically but reorders them logically, without moving records. This is accomplished by an index file in which each specified field points to the appropriate record in the specified file. The contents of the original file remain unchanged, with the same physical file order and the same record numbers; the index file created by the Index command holds the logical order of the file. This command can generate two types of index files: single field and multiple field.

Single-Field Indexes A **single-field index** file is ordered by one field only.

To prepare for the following examples, activate the CUSTOMER file via the Set Up command in the Assistant Menu.

Zip Code	*Record Number*
12562	00012
13411	00004
60712	00001
60712	00002
61701	00003
61701	00005
61701	00006
61701	00007
61701	00010
61761	00009
61761	00011
94307	00008

Figure 3.6

Information contained in the ZIP.NDX file: the zip code and the location of each record.

The procedure below will index the CUSTOMER file in zip-code order:

Organize	Selects Organize from the Assistant Menu.
Index	Selects the Index command.
Enter	Executes the command and displays the Index submenu.
Type `ZIP`	Answers the prompt `Enter an index key expression:`.
Enter	Specifies the field to index and displays a menu of drives.
B:	Specifies the default drive.
Enter	Places the index file on this drive.
Type `ZIP`	Answers the prompt `Enter the name of the file:`.
Enter	Names the index file.

The following is the dot prompt Index command:

(.) Index:

```
. index on <field> to <.ndxfile>
.index on zip to zip
```

When the indexing process starts, dBASE displays the message `00%`. When the process is completed, it says `100% Indexed 12 Records Indexed`.

These steps generate the command `INDEX ON ZIP TO ZIP` in the action line. The result is an index file called ZIP.NDX; each record in the ZIP.NDX file contains the ZIP field for a record in the CUSTOMER file and the number of the record with that particular zip-code value (Figure 3.6). When the records are displayed, dBASE first accesses the ZIP.NDX file, which in turn points to the appropriate record from the CUSTOMER file.

Activating the ZIP index at a later time requires a number of steps:

Set Up	Selects Set Up from the Assistant Menu.
Select database file	Takes the Select database file option.
Enter	
B:	Specifies the drive.
Enter	
CUSTOMER	Highlights the file.
Enter	Specifies the file.
Y	Answers the prompt `Is the file indexed? [Y/N]`.
ZIP.NDX	Specifies the index file ZIP.NDX.
Enter	Selects ZIP.NDX and displays the word `Master` beside `ZIP.NDX`. The action line reads `USE CUSTOMER INDEX ZIP`.
→ or ←	Activates the index.
Retrieve	Selects Retrieve from the Assistant Menu.
List	Selects the List command.
Enter	Executes the command and displays the List submenu.
Construct a field list	Specifies the LAST, FIRST, CITY, STATE, and ZIP fields by highlighting each field and pressing Enter.
→ or ←	Returns you to the List submenu.
Execute the command	Directs the output to the screen.
Enter (2)	Executes the command and tells dBASE not to list to the printer.

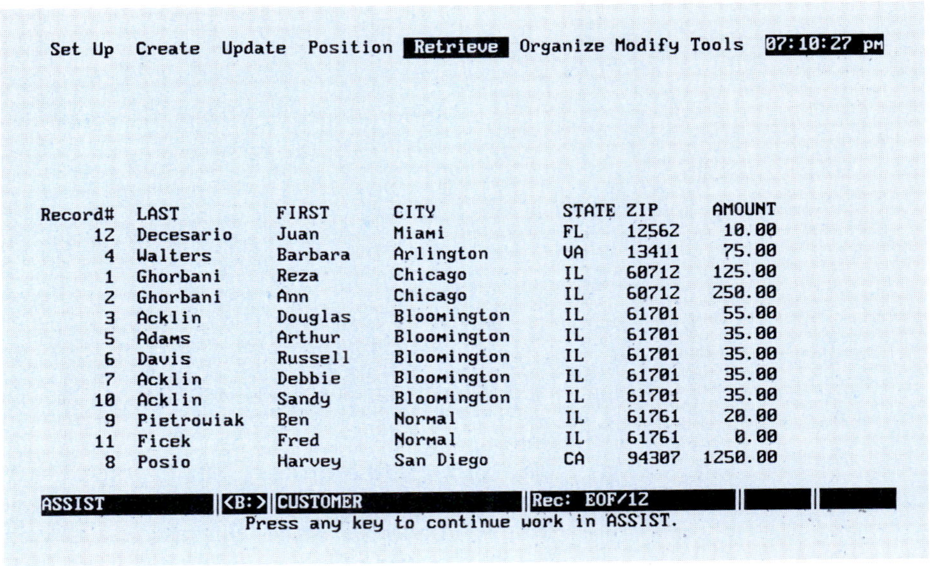

Figure 3.7
The CUSTOMER file listed via the ZIP.NDX index.

The screen now displays the information from the CUSTOMER file (Figure 3.7).

When dBASE lists the records from an indexed file, it performs a number of tasks automatically. First, it goes to the ZIP.NDX file (see Figure 3.6) and finds ZIP 12562. It also finds that record 12 of the CUSTOMER file holds the data for this index entry. dBASE now accesses records 12 of the CUSTOMER file. It then moves to the second index entry and repeats the process until all index entries have been processed.

As you can see from this example, using the Assistant Menu to create indexes and then invoke the file using that index requires a number of steps and even more keystrokes. Creating indexes and then verifying that you have created them correctly using the List command requires less time in COMMAND mode at the dot prompt (.). The remaining indexes will therefore be created using the COMMAND mode of dBASE III Plus.

Another bonus from using COMMAND mode is that after an index is created it is automatically invoked by dBASE. This means that you do not have to issue a Use <filename index> command to list the records from the file for the created index.

To verify that the contents of the CUSTOMER file remain physically unchanged, you could issue the following command:

```
. use customer
. list first,last,city,state,zip
```

If you want to see the file arranged in logical order of last name, issue the Index commands as follows:

```
. index on last to last
```

```
12 records indexed
```

```
. list last, first, city, state, zip, amount
```

Record#	last	first	city	state	zip	amount
3	Acklin	Douglas	Bloomington	IL	61701	55.00
7	Acklin	Debbie	Bloomington	IL	61701	35.00
10	Acklin	Sandy	Bloomington	IL	61701	35.00
5	Adams	Arthur	Bloomington	IL	61701	35.00
6	Davis	Russell	Bloomington	IL	61701	35.00
12	Decesario	Juan	Miami	FL	12562	10.00
11	Ficek	Fred	Normal	IL	61761	0.00
1	Ghorbani	Reza	Chicago	IL	60712	125.00
2	Ghorbani	Ann	Chicago	IL	60712	250.00
9	Pietrowiak	Ben	Normal	IL	61761	20.00
8	Posio	Harvey	San Diego	CA	94307	1250.00
4	Walters	Barbara	Arlington	VA	13411	75.00

Multiple-Field Indexes What if you want the file to appear in order by more than one field, for example, by first name and last name field contents? The Index command manages this task easily by enabling you to **concatenate** (join) fields in creating the index. The result is a **multiple-field index.** The first multiple-field index here will be created using the ASSISTANT feature of dBASE, but others will be created at the dot prompt.

Re-enter the ASSISTANT mode by entering `ASSIST` at the dot prompt and then pressing Enter.

With the CUSTOMER file activated (it already is unless you have just started dBASE), perform the following steps:

Organize	Selects organize from the Assistant Menu.
Index	Selects the Index command.
Enter	Executes the command and displays the Index submenu.
Type `Last+First`	Answers the prompt `Enter an index key expression:` (Figure 3.8).
Enter	Enters the LAST and FIRST name fields to be indexed.
B:	Selects default drive B and places the index there. The action line now reads `INDEX ON LAST+FIRST TO B:`.
Enter	Executes the command.
Type `LFNAME`	Answers the prompt `Enter the name of the file:` from the Index submenu.
Enter	Enters the index filename. The action line reads `INDEX ON FIRST+LAST TO B:LFNAME`. The command executes.

dBASE indexes the file, and the message `100% indexed 12 records indexed` appears on your screen.

The following is the dot prompt command:

(.) . index on <field1> + <field2> to <drive:ndxfile>

Now, from the Assistant Menu, select Retrieve and follow the prompts to list the CUSTOMER file, specifying the fields LAST, FIRST, CITY, STATE, ZIP, and AMOUNT. Execute the List command to the screen.

The screen now displays the file in alphabetic order by last name (Figure 3.9). Within the last name order, the screen now lists the Acklin and the Ghorbani records in alphabetic order by first name.

Figure 3.8
Screen used to concatenate fields for creating the LFNAME index file.

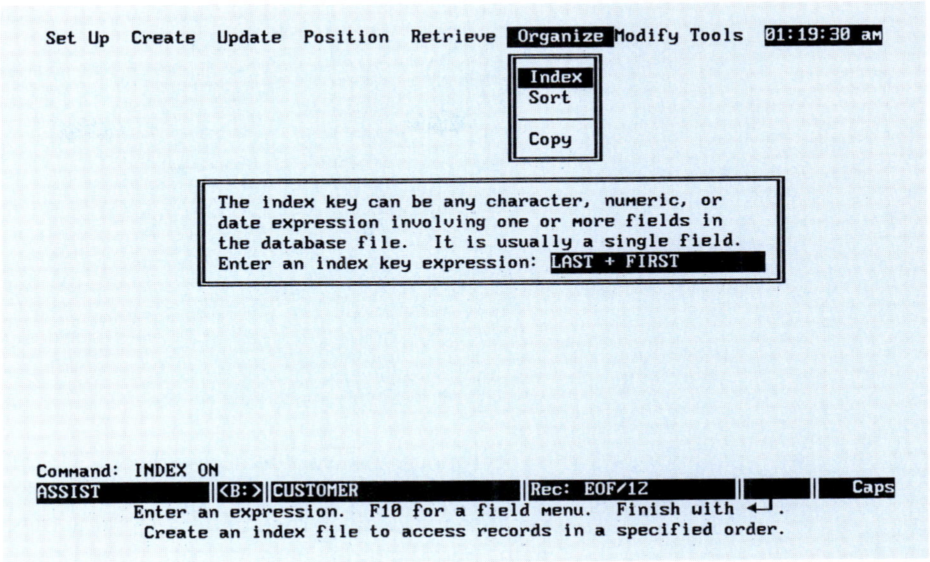

Figure 3.9
The listing of selected fields from the CUSTOMER file in alphabetic order via the LFNAME index.

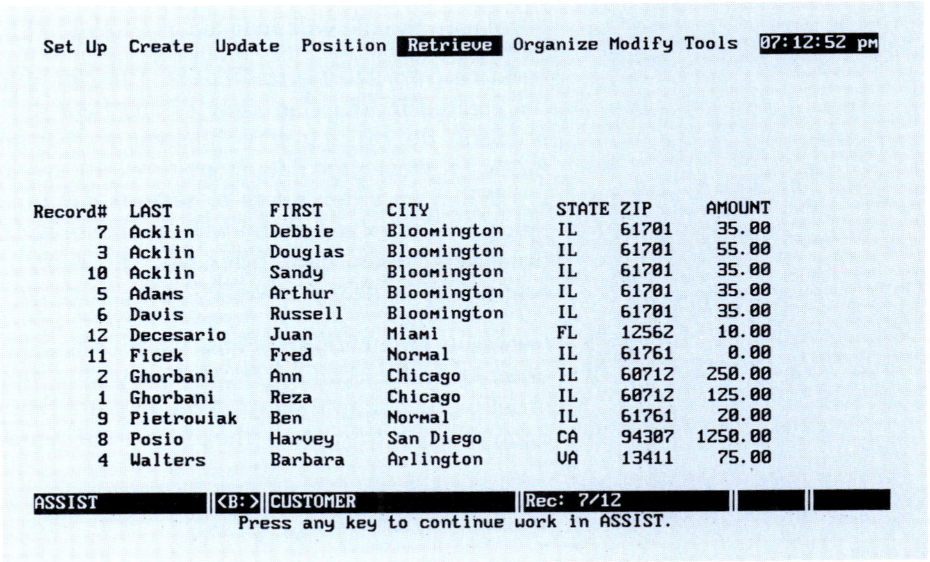

The remaining examples of multiple-field indexes will be entered via COMMAND mode at the dot prompt. Notice that you do not have to enter the drive identifier in front of the index filename because dBASE automatically creates it on the default drive (in these examples, drive B).

The following commands extend the index order to three fields and list the file in order by zip, last name, and first name:

```
. index on zip + last + first to ziplfnam
```

```
12 records indexed
```

```
. list last, first, city, state, zip, amount
```

Record#	last	first	city	state	zip	amount
12	Decesario	Juan	Miami	FL	12562	10.00
4	Walters	Barbara	Arlington	VA	13411	75.00
2	Ghorbani	Ann	Chicago	IL	60712	250.00
1	Ghorbani	Reza	Chicago	IL	60712	125.00
7	Acklin	Debbie	Bloomington	IL	61701	35.00
3	Acklin	Douglas	Bloomington	IL	61701	55.00
10	Acklin	Sandy	Bloomington	IL	61701	35.00
5	Adams	Arthur	Bloomington	IL	61701	35.00
6	Davis	Russell	Bloomington	IL	61701	35.00
11	Ficek	Fred	Normal	IL	61761	0.00
9	Pietrowiak	Ben	Normal	IL	61761	20.00
8	Posio	Harvey	San Diego	CA	94307	1250.00

Suppose you want to access the CUSTOMER file again at some future time by last name/first name order. You do not have to re-create the LFNAME index because it is now on disk under the name LFNAME.NDX. Simply type the filename and the index name as part of the Use command, as follows:

```
. use customer index lfname
. list last, first, city, state, zip, amount
```

Again the file will be listed as shown in Figure 3.9.

Indexing by Numeric Order You can also index data in numeric order. If the created index refers only to one field in the original file, and that field is numeric, the procedure is the same as that for creating any other single-field index. However, the data in an index file are always stored as character data.

When an index refers to several numeric or numeric and character data fields, the Index command will operate only on character data. To create a multiple-field, **mixed-data index,** you must first change the numeric fields in the original file to character data. Do this with the **STR (string) function.**

Index on One Numeric Field Only The following example creates an index ordered by the AMOUNT field only. The file can then be listed in ascending order by the amount owed. Keep in mind that the index entry is now character data, whereas the data in the original file remain numeric.

```
. use customer
. index on amount to amount
```

```
12 records indexed
```

```
. list last, first, city, state, zip, amount
```

Record#	last	first	city	state	zip	amount
11	Ficek	Fred	Normal	IL	61761	0.00
12	Decesario	Juan	Miami	FL	12562	10.00
9	Pietrowiak	Ben	Normal	IL	61761	20.00
5	Adams	Arthur	Bloomington	IL	61701	35.00
6	Davis	Russell	Bloomington	IL	61701	35.00
7	Acklin	Debbie	Bloomington	IL	61701	35.00
10	Acklin	Sandy	Bloomington	IL	61701	35.00
3	Acklin	Douglas	Bloomington	IL	61701	55.00
4	Walters	Barbara	Arlington	VA	13411	75.00
1	Ghorbani	Reza	Chicago	IL	60712	125.00
2	Ghorbani	Ann	Chicago	IL	60712	250.00
8	Posio	Harvey	San Diego	CA	94307	1250.00

STR Function Creating a mixed-data multiple-field index or multinumeric field index requires the use of the STR(string) function; otherwise, the screen displays an error message. The STR function requires providing the name of the field to be converted, the field length, and the number of positions to the right of the decimal point that are involved. The following commands create an index using the ZIP and AMOUNT fields:

```
. index on zip + str(amount,8,2) to zipamoun
```

```
12 records indexed
```

```
. list last, first, city, state, zip, amount
```

These commands result in the following list:

Record#	last	first	city	state	zip	amount
12	Decesario	Juan	Miami	FL	12562	10.00
4	Walters	Barbara	Arlington	VA	13411	75.00
1	Ghorbani	Reza	Chicago	IL	60712	125.00
2	Ghorbani	Ann	Chicago	IL	60712	250.00
5	Adams	Arthur	Bloomington	IL	61701	35.00
6	Davis	Russell	Bloomington	IL	61701	35.00
7	Acklin	Debbie	Bloomington	IL	61701	35.00
10	Acklin	Sandy	Bloomington	IL	61701	35.00
3	Acklin	Douglas	Bloomington	IL	61701	55.00
11	Ficek	Fred	Normal	IL	61761	0.00
9	Pietrowiak	Ben	Normal	IL	61761	20.00
8	Posio	Harvey	San Diego	CA	94307	1250.00

LISTING AND DELETING FILES

As you generate a variety of dBASE files, you will occasionally want to delete those that are no longer needed, such as the ZIPCUST file. Before you delete files, you may also want to list files on the screen in families. For this you can use the **List Files Like command.**

To list data (.DBF) files with the List Files Like command, you do not have to give an extension because, when no extension is given, dBASE automatically inserts .DBF. To list index files, you would need to specify the **.NDX extension.** You can use wild cards in List Files Like commands, as shown in the following examples:

```
(.)        .list files like *.DBF
```

```
. list files like *.ndx
```

```
ZIP     .NDX     LAST    .NDX     LFNAME   .NDX
ZIPLFMAN.NDX     ZIPAMOUN.NDX     AMOUNT   .NDX
   5120 bytes in     6 files.
330752 bytes remaining on drive.
```

```
. list files like *.dbf
```

```
CUSTOMER.DBF     PAYMAST.DBF     ALPHNAME.DBF
   3288 bytes in      3 files.
334848 bytes remaining on drive.
```

To delete database files, use the dot prompt **Delete File command:**

```
(.)        .delete file zipcust.dbf
```

```
File has been deleted
```

Managing Index Files One of the major conveniences of index files is that they do not have to be constantly re-created as you add or delete records from the original file. Any indexes that are specified following the Index portion of the Use statement are automatically **updated** when an Append, Delete, or Pack command is executed against the original file. You can specify as many as seven indexes in a Use statement. To make certain that all the indexes created in this chapter are updated to reflect all future changes in the CUSTOMER file, you would issue the following command.

```
use customer index ziplfnam,last,lfname,zipamoun,amount,zip
```

While the above command updates all indexes, it also **activates** the first index in the list. In the above example, the CUSTOMER file can now be accessed only via the active ZIPLFNAM index.

It is important to specify appropriate indexes after the filename when you are about to compress a file with the Pack command. If you do not specify the indexes before you pack the file, you will have to re-create each index separately. Should you forget to re-create any of the indexes and later try to use the old index to list the revised file contents, you will receive a `RECORD OUT OF RANGE` error message.

Reports Using Indexes When you are generating a report, you can use an index to specify the order in which records will be reported. For instance, to generate a report in zip-code, last-name, and first-name order, you would use the following commands:

```
. use customer index ziplfnam
. report form nameaddr to print
```

```
Page No.      1
05/10/92

                    ABC COMPANY
               NAME AND ADDRESS REPORT

         NAME        ADDRESS               CITY          ST    AMOUNT
Juan     Decesario   1214 Flores           Miami         FL     10.00
Barbara  Walters     1981 Crestlawn        Arlington     VA     75.00
Ann      Ghorbani    4033 N. Wolcott       Chicago       IL    250.00
Reza     Ghorbani    4033 N. Wolcott       Chicago       IL    125.00
Debbie   Acklin      408 E. Monroe         Bloomington   IL     35.00
Douglas  Acklin      408 E. Monroe         Bloomington   IL     55.00
Sandy    Acklin      408 E. Monroe         Bloomington   IL     35.00
Arthur   Adams       115 Ginger Creek Ct.  Bloomington   IL     35.00
Russell  Davis       707 Vale St.          Bloomington   IL     35.00
Fred     Ficek       1215 Tamarack         Normal        IL      0.00
Ben      Pietrowiak  3334 N. Foster        Normal        IL     20.00
Harvey   Posio       1013 Hillcrest        San Diego     CA   1250.00
*** Total ***
                                                              1925.00
```

The following commands would generate a report using the "numeric" (actually, character) AMOUNT.NDX index file:

```
. use customer index amount
. report form nameaddr to print
```

```
Page No.     1
04/15/92

                      ABC COMPANY
                 NAME AND ADDRESS REPORT

           NAME         ADDRESS                CITY         ST    AMOUNT
Fred       Ficek        1215 Tamarack          Normal       IL      0.00
Juan       Decesario    1214 Flores            Miami        FL     10.00
Ben        Pietrowiak   3334 N. Foster         Normal       IL     20.00
Arthur     Adams        115 Ginger Creek Ct.   Bloomington  IL     35.00
Russell    Davis        707 Vale St.           Bloomington  IL     35.00
Debbie     Acklin       408 E. Monroe          Bloomington  IL     35.00
Sandy      Acklin       408 E. Monroe          Bloomington  IL     35.00
Douglas    Acklin       408 E. Monroe          Bloomington  IL     55.00
Barbara    Walters      1981 Crestlawn         Arlington    VA     75.00
Reza       Ghorbani     4033 N. Wolcott        Chicago      IL    125.00
Ann        Ghorbani     4033 N. Wolcott        Chicago      IL    250.00
Harvey     Posio        1013 Hillcrest         San Diego    CA   1250.00
*** Total ***                                                     1925.00
```

LOCATION COMMANDS

Up to this point, you have used either the List or Display All command to locate a record. Both start at the beginning of a file and display all records that meet the specified search criteria. The Locate and Seek commands are other means for locating and displaying records, one or more records at a time. Because the COMMAND mode is more efficient than the ASSISTANT mode here, the following examples use the dot prompt.

LOCATE

The **Locate command** searches a file sequentially, starting at the beginning and progressing through until it "hits" a record whose contents meet the specified search criteria. Suppose you want to find all records of CUSTOMER file clients who live in Normal. Accomplishing this would require the following statements:

```
. use customer
. locate for city = 'Normal'
```

```
Record = 9
```

```
. continue
```

```
Record = 11
```

```
. continue
```

```
End of LOCATE scope
```

HINTS/HAZARDS When you are setting up the criteria for a character field, make certain that you enter the characters exactly as they appear in the field.

You can use any number of simple or complex search criteria to find records via the Locate command. dBASE displays the record number of the first record in the file that meets the search criteria. The **Continue command** sends dBASE looking for the next record. This process continues until the last record in the file is processed, at which point the message `End of LOCATE scope` is displayed. You can now use the Edit command to examine any or all of the displayed record numbers. For example, to edit record 9, enter the command `.edit 9`.

The preceding example can also be executed slowly from the Assistant Menu (via the Position option). The following discussion of the Seek command takes place from the dot prompt.

SEEK

You can use the **Seek command** only for accessing an indexed file. Both the file and the index must first be referenced in a Use statement.

The Seek command uses the index to find any records that match the search criteria. Because the information in the index is all character data, the search criteria must be contained inside single quotes.

The **Set Headings Off command** turns off the field headings for a displayed record and makes the resulting output more readable.

Activate the CUSTOMER file with the ZIP index and find those records that have a 61761 zip code:

```
. use customer index zip
. set headings off
. seek '61761'
. display
```

The display is the following:

```
   9  Ben         A Pietrowiak   3334 N. Foster              Normal
IL 61761 (309)452-9126     20.00  03/23/92
. skip
Record no.       11
. display
  11 Fred         R Ficek        1215 Tamarack               Normal
IL 61761 (309)454-7123      0.00  04/05/92
. skip
Record no.        8
. display
   8  Harvey      S Posio        1013 Hillcrest              San Diego
CA 94307 (619)271-9871   1250.00  04/03/92
```

When the Seek command is executed, the first occurrence of zip code 61761 is found in the index file (see Figure 3.6), and dBASE positions the pointer to that record (in this case, record 9). After accessing this 61761 record, dBASE advances to the next record. You have to manually ascertain if this is a 61761 record using the Display command. This is also a 61761 record. The second Skip command advances you (via the index) to a 94307 ZIP code, and you determine that there are no more 61761 records.

The Seek '61761' command directs dBASE to find the first occurrence of the 61761 zip code in the ZIP index. Unless the `NO FIND` **message** is displayed, dBASE positions the pointer at that record location. The record is displayed via the Display command. The next occurrence of the 61761 zip code is located via the **Skip command,** which positions the pointer at the next record that is pointed to in the ZIP index. This process is repeated until all the 61761 zip codes have been located.

The following commands use the AMOUNT index to find all customers in the CUSTOMER file who owe $35.00:

```
. use customer index amount
. seek 35.00
. display
```

```
     5  Arthur      V    Adams             115 Ginger Creek Ct.      Bloomington
 IL    61701 (309)828-7290    35.00   03/15/92
. skip
Record no.      6
. disp
     6  Russell     B    Davis             707 Vale St.              Bloomington
 IL    61701 (309)662-1759    35.00   02/27/92
. skip
Record no.      7
. disp
     7  Debbie      C    Acklin            408 E. Monroe             Bloomington
 IL    61701 (308)827-1395    35.00   03/21/92
. skip
Record no.     10
. disp
    10  Sandy       C    Acklin            408 E. Monroe             Bloomington
 IL    61701 (309)829-9901    35.00   02/25/92
. skip
Record no.      3
. disp
     3  Douglas     C    Acklin            408 E. Monroe             Bloomington
 IL    61701 (309)663-8976    55.00   04/01/92
```

Take care when you enter a seek specification involving criteria that involve a multiple-field relationship in the index. For example, suppose you seek records in the ZIPAMOUN index with the zip code 61701, but you enter the command as follows:

```
. use customer index zipamoun
. seek '6170135.00'
```

dBASE searches the entire file and responds with the message `NO FIND`. The program has "failed" to find the records you seek because your specification '6170135.00' failed to include the three blank spaces on the left side of the AMOUNT field. Whenever you use the Seek command using concatenated (joined) fields for the index, you must include as many positions for each field as there are in the field, including blanks. The following command finds any record with a zip code of 61701 and an amount of $35.00:

```
. seek '61701    35.00'
. display
```

```
      5  Arthur      V     Adams           115 Ginger Creek Ct.      Bloomington
  IL     61701 (309)828-7290    35.00    03/15/92
. skip
Record no.      6
. disp
      6  Russell     B     Davis           707 Vale St.              Bloomington
  IL     61701 (309)662-1759    35.00    02/27/92
. skip
Record no.      7
. disp
      7  Debbie      C     Acklin          408 E. Monroe             Bloomington
  IL     61701 (309)827-1395    35.00    03/21/92
. skip
Record no.     10
. disp
     10  Sandy       C     Acklin          408 E. Monroe             Bloomington
  IL     61701 (309)829-9901    35.00    02/25/92
. skip
Record no.      3
. disp
      3  Douglas     C     Acklin          408 E. Monroe             Bloomington
  IL     61701 (309)663-8976    55.00    04/01/92
```

As before, this process is continued until a record is displayed that does not meet the established criteria.

SKIP SEQUENTIAL PROCESSING

Aspects of random and sequential access can be combined to generate a listing of records that meet a certain criterion. This process is known as **skip sequential processing.** Suppose that you want to list only those records in the file that have a zip code of 61701. If you use the List command, dBASE will start at the beginning of the file and read through it sequentially to the end—a procedure that can consume a tremendous amount of time if you are dealing with a large file.

You can avoid this problem by using an index that incorporates the desired information in a continuous group. Tell dBASE to go to the beginning of the desired group of records via a Seek command and then issue a List command to list all records that meet the criterion. The statements that follow use the CUSTOMER file and the ZIP index. The beginning of the 61701 records is encountered, and all records are then listed as long as they match the 61701 zip-code criterion. As soon as the characteristics of the records in the index no longer match the search criterion, the search is stopped. You would use the following commands.

```
. use customer index zip
. seek '61701'
. list first, last, address, zip for zip = '61701'
```

```
3   Douglas    Acklin    408 E. Monroe           61701
5   Arthur     Adams     115 Ginger Creek Ct.    61701
6   Russell    Davis     707 Vale St.            61701
7   Debbie     Acklin    408 E. Monroe           61701
10  Sandy      Acklin    408 E. Monroe           61701
```

BROWSE

The **Browse command** lets you rapidly change data in specific fields of one or more records. Whereas the Edit command displays complete records, the Browse command displays and alters data by selected fields. This is especially useful for indexed files.

For example, you can use the Browse command for posting payments from customers in the CUSTOMER file. First arrange the payment-information paperwork in alphabetic order by last name. Next use the Browse command to display the records. Then use the FIRST and LAST fields to locate the correct record by customer name and the AMOUNT field to enter the new balance.

The procedure from the Assistant Menu is as follows. First, activate the CUSTOMER file with the LFNAME index:

Update	Selects Update from the Assistant Menu.
Browse	Selects the Browse command.
Enter	Executes the command and makes each entire record available to you for editing (Figure 3.10). Use the menu at the top of the screen for moving the cursor.

The problem with this Assistant Menu procedure is that you may be overwhelmed with data from each record. A much better method from COMMAND mode limits the number of fields displayed. The dot prompt command has the following format:

(.) Browse Fields: `. browse fields <field1>,<field2>,...`

The following commands activate the CUSTOMER file and let you browse three of its fields in alphabetic order by last and first names (Figure 3.11):

```
. use customer index lfname
. browse fields first,last,amount
```

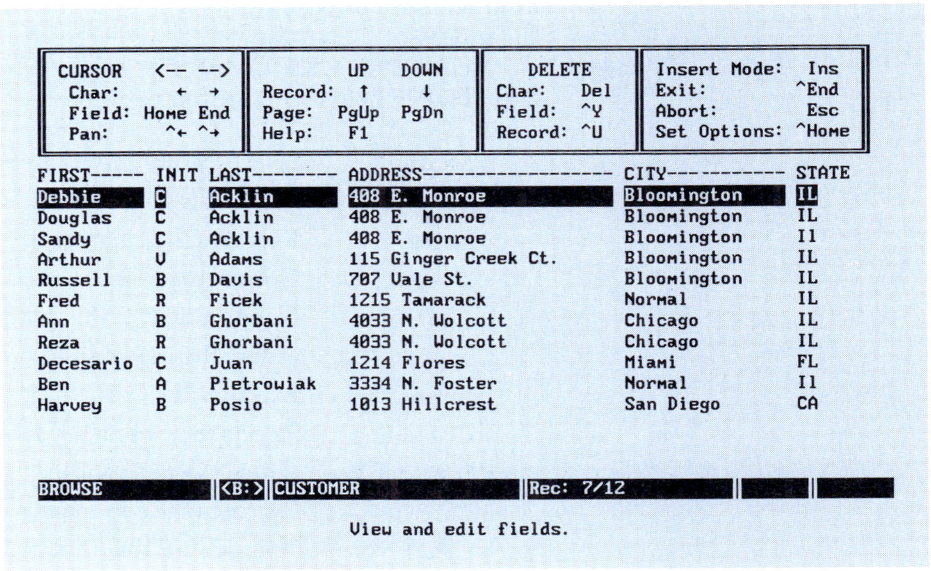

Figure 3.10
The Browse command as it is executed from the Assistant Menu.

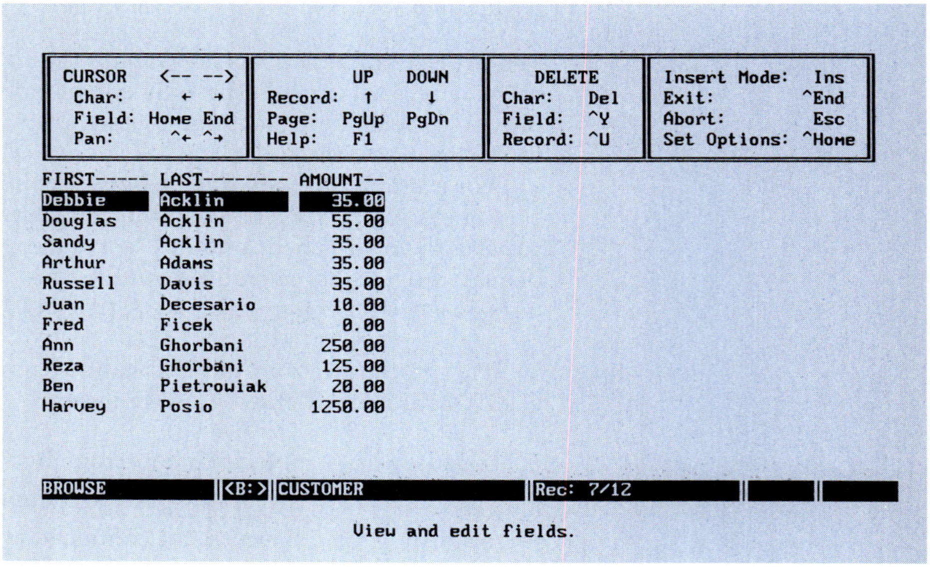

Figure 3.11
The Browse command used against selected fields.

The top of the screen shows the record number currently being changed. The top of each column shows the field names. The first record displayed (in this case, record 7) is in reverse video. Use the cursor movement keys to make changes. To move to the AMOUNT field, enter two Ctrl + F commands or just hold down the Right Arrow key. Each subsequent Ctrl + X (or Down Arrow) command moves you to the AMOUNT field of the next record. Clearly, this method is much faster than using the Edit command in making scattered changes in a file.

MODIFYING A STRUCTURE FILE

Suppose you decide that the existing CUSTOMER file does not provide enough geographic information; you would like to add a 1-byte REGION field (in character data) to each record, after the ZIP field. The **Modify Structure command** will do this. When you are using this command, Ctrl + N lets you insert a field at the cursor position; Ctrl + T lets you delete a field; and Ctrl + W concludes the process.

Activate the CUSTOMER file. Then add a REGION field between the ZIP and PHONE fields with the following steps:

Modify	Selects Modify from the Assistant Menu.
Database file	Selects the Database file command.
Enter	Executes the command.
↓	Goes to the PHONE field.
Ctrl + N	Inserts a field at this position.
Type `REGION`	Enters the field name.
Enter	Executes the command.
C	Selects the Character data type.
1	Enters the field width.
Enter	Executes the command.
Ctrl + W	Tells dBASE that the modifications are complete.
Enter	Confirms the command.

The following is the dot prompt Modify Structure command:

```
. use customer
. modify structure
```

The screen displays a message that indicates that the records have been added to the file.

Listing the file shows that the REGION field consists of blanks for each record. If you add a *numeric* field to a record, that field will contain zeros rather than blanks. You can now use the Edit or Browse command to add the appropriate REGION field information for each record.

CREATING FILES WITH EXISTING FILES

There are a number of ways to create dBASE files, apart from using the Create command. The following methods use the **Copy command** to create new files from existing files. The first illustrates the command in ASSISTANT and COMMAND modes. The rest are shown in COMMAND mode.

COPY COMMAND AND FILE BACKUP

The following steps use the Copy command to create a new, identical file ZIPCUST.FRM from the old file NAMEADDR.FRM:

Tools	Selects Tools from the Assistant Menu.
Copy file	Selects the Copy file command.
Enter	Executes the command.
C:	Specifies the drive.
Enter	Selects the drive.
NAMEADDR.FRM	Specifies file from Copy file submenu.
Enter	Selects the file.
A:	Specifies the drive.
Enter	Selects the drive.
Type `ZIPCUST.FRM`	Responds to `Enter the name of the file.`
Enter	Executes the command.

The following is the dot prompt command:

(.) `. copy file b:nameaddr.frm to b:zipcust.frm`

You can use the Copy command to create backup copies of .DBF files. For example, the following commands would copy the CUSTOMER file from drive A to drive B:

```
. use a:customer
. copy to b:customer
```

COPY STRUCTURE COMMAND

If you want to pick and choose from various fields that are currently on a record, use the **Copy Structure command,** which copies only the information from the header record to the receiving file. The field structures are copied, but data are not. You can then modify the new structure by adding and/or deleting fields. For example, you could issue the following commands in copying structures from the CUSTOMER file:

```
. use customer
. copy structure to temp
. use temp
. modify structure
```

The Copy Structure command can delete all records from a file by copying a bare structure over an existing file that contains both structure and records. This method is easier and faster than issuing a Delete All command followed by a Pack command. Suppose you have a transaction file TRAN whose records are deleted at the end of each day. Provided that you have previously copied its structure to a file called TEMPTRAN, you can empty the TRAN file with the following commands:

```
. use temptran
. copy structure to tran
```

COPY FIELD COMMAND

The **Copy Field command** will copy selected fields and their contents to another file. This lets you create intermediate files containing a portion of the data in a much larger file. This command lets you transfer a portion of a file on hard disk to diskette.

Suppose you want to create and list a name and address file from the CUSTOMER file. The following steps would do so:

```
. use customer
. copy field first,last,address,city,state,zip to newcust
```

```
12 records copied
```

```
. use newcust
. list
```

```
 1 Reza     Ghorbani   4033 N. Wolcott      Chicago     IL 60712
 2 Ann      Ghorbani   4033 N. Wolcott      Chicago     IL 60712
 3 Douglas  Acklin     408 E. Monroe        Bloomington IL 61701
 4 Barbara  Walters    1981 Crestlawn       Arlington   VA 13411
 5 Arthur   Adams      115 Ginger Creek Ct. Bloomington IL 61701
 6 Russell  Davis      707 Vale St.         Bloomington IL 61701
 7 Debbie   Acklin     408 E. Monroe        Bloomington IL 61701
 8 Harvey   Posio      1013 Hillcrest       San Diego   CA 94307
 9 Ben      Pietrowiak 3334 N. Foster       Normal      IL 61761
10 Sandy    Acklin     408 E. Monroe        Bloomington IL 61701
11 Fred     Ficek      1215 Tamarack        Normal      IL 61761
12 Juan     Decesario  1214 Flores          Miami       FL 12562
```

As you can see, only the information from the desired fields is copied to the receiving file.

CREATING ASCII FILES FOR OTHER PACKAGES

You can easily pass information contained in a dBASE file to application packages that accept (or are capable of translating) standard ASCII files. The basic process involves using the Copy command to change a .DBF or other dBASE file into a .DAT (data) file. This converts the data from the dBASE storage format to the standard ASCII format.

In ASCII files, a comma signifies the division of one field from another. Any dBASE field that contains a comma will normally be interpreted by ASCII as consisting of two fields. Thus, if there are any commas within a dBASE field, that field must be enclosed in double quotes ("..."). You can instruct dBASE to automatically place quotes around all fields by issuing a **Delimited parameter** (delimited with ") along with the Copy command. However, it is generally better practice, when possible, to design dBASE files so that commas are not necessary within fields.

The following commands would create an ASCII format file from the NEWCUST file:

```
. use newcust
. copy to names.dat delimited with "
```

```
12 records copied
```

You could then view the NAMES.DAT file with the command TYPE NAMES.DAT. The file would appear as follows:

```
. type names.dat
```

```
"Reza","Ghorbani","4033 N. Wolcott","Chicago","IL","60712"
"Ann","Ghorbani","4033 N. Wolcott","Chicago","IL","60712"
"Douglas","Acklin","408 E. Monroe","Bloomington","IL","61701"
"Barbara","Walters","1981 Crestlawn","Arlington","VA","13411"
"Arthur","Adams","115 Ginger Creek Ct.","Bloomington","IL","61701"
"Russell","Davis","707 Vale St.","Bloomington","IL","61701"
"Debbie","Acklin","408 E. Monroe","Bloomington","IL","61701"
"Harvey","Posio","1013 Hillcrest","San Diego","CA","94307"
"Ben","Pietrowiak","3334 N. Foster","Normal","IL","61761"
"Sandy","Acklin","408 E. Monroe","Bloomington","IL","61701"
"Fred","Ficek","1215 Tamarack","Normal","IL","61761"
"Juan","Decesario","1214 Flores","Miami","FL","12562"
```

Notice that fields are separated by a comma. The NAMES.DAT file is now a standard ASCII file; any program that can access an ASCII file can now process these data.

CREATING SUBTOTALS IN REPORTS

You can generate **subtotals** in reports when a file has been ordered into groups via sorting or indexing. Generating subtotals for groups of records is referred to as **control break,** or **level break,** processing.

Suppose that you want to create a report that shows the total number of records for each zip code in the CUSTOMER file. The new report will have the same format as the NAMEADDR.FRM report form, except it will include the subtotal instruction.

For the following example, activate the CUSTOMER file with the zip-code index ZIP.NDX. Use the Copy command to create a new ZIPCUST.FRM file identical to the NAMEADDR.FRM. Then use COMMAND mode to begin to modify the new report:

```
. copy file nameaddr.frm to zipcust.frm

    2048 bytes copied

. use customer index zip
. modify report zipcust
```

The monitor now displays the Modify command Options screen. Press the Right Arrow key to reach the Groups screen (Figure 3.12). Now press Enter and type `ZIP` (the name of the ZIP field) for the Group on expression entry. This names the field that is to be used for the subtotals. Position the pointer to the Group heading entry, press Enter, and enter `ZIP CODE TOTAL` (see Figure 3.12). Accept the N defaults for the subtotal, since Summary report only would print only one line per zip code and Page eject after group takes up too much paper for this application.

You are finished with the changes for this example. If there are other things that you want to do, take the appropriate option. You may now save the changes to disk by selecting the Exit option and then selecting Save. After the file has been saved to disk, return to the Assistant Menu. To print the report, select the Retrieve option, specify Report, specify the drive that the template

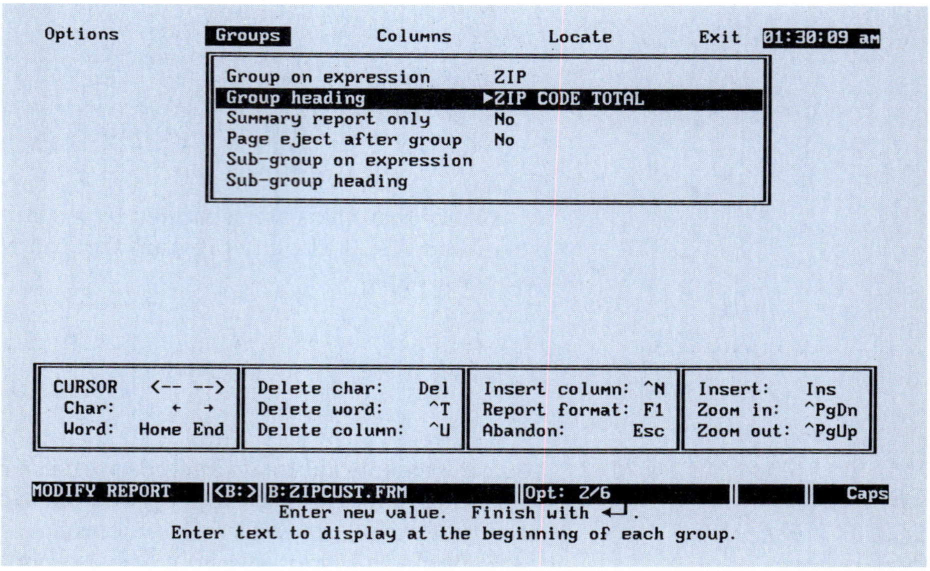

Figure 3.12
The changed entries for the Groups screen of the ZIPCUST.FRM report template.

resides on (B, in this example), tell dBASE to use the ZIPCUST.FRM template, and execute the command. The report is now generated, as follows:

```
Page No.      1
05/10/92

                              ABC COMPANY
                        NAME AND ADDRESS REPORT

          NAME        ADDRESS                  CITY         ST   AMOUNT

** ZIP CODE TOTAL 12562
Juan      Decesario   1214 Flores              Miami        FL     10.00
** Subtotal **                                                     10.00

** ZIP CODE TOTAL 13411
Barbara   Walters     1981 Crestlawn           Arlington    VA     75.00
** Subtotal **                                                     75.00

** ZIP CODE TOTAL 60712
Reza      Ghorbani    4033 N. Wolcott          Chicago      IL    125.00
Ann       Ghorbani    4033 N. Wolcott          Chicago      IL    250.00
** Subtotal **                                                    375.00

** ZIP CODE TOTAL 61701
Douglas   Acklin      408 E. Monroe            Bloomington  IL     55.00
Arthur    Adams       115 Ginger Creek Ct.     Bloomington  IL     35.00
Russell   Davis       707 Vale St.             Bloomington  IL     35.00
Debbie    Acklin      408 E. Monroe            Bloomington  IL     35.00
Sandy     Acklin      408 E. Monroe            Bloomington  IL     35.00
** Subtotal **                                                    195.00

** ZIP CODE TOTAL 61761
Ben       Pietrowiak  3334 N. Foster           Normal       IL     20.00
Fred      Ficek       1215 Tamarack            Normal       IL      0.00
** Subtotal **                                                     20.00

** ZIP CODE TOTAL 94307
Harvey    Posio       1013 Hillcrest           San Diego    CA   1250.00
** Subtotal **

                                                                 1250.00

*** Total ***
                                                                 1925.00
```

Notice that the zip code does not print on every line. Instead, a subtotal heading is printed for each group of records.

CHAPTER REVIEW

The dBASE package provides two commands for reordering records within a file: Sort and Index. The Sort command creates a file in which the records are sorted by one or more specified fields. For large files, it is a time-consuming command.

The Index command creates an index whose contents consist of the key field of each record and the location of each record on disk. The data file is left in its original order, whereas the index is arranged in the desired order. To access a record, dBASE first goes to the index file to find its location and then to the record in the data file. An index file can be built using a number of fields and can reorder the file in only one pass. For example, the file could be indexed in last-name/first-name order with only one statement. We call this a *logical reordering,* to emphasize that the original file remains in its original order; only the index file is arranged to reflect the changed relationship.

When you are using multiple-field indexes, you often want changes in the data file to be reflected in every index. Do this by placing the names of any indexes that you want updated after the Use statement. You can specify up to seven indexes. When a change is made that affects any of the specified indexes, the indexes will automatically be changed, too. However, only the first index can be used with a Seek command.

The dBASE package contains several commands that perform DOS-like actions. With them you can list files that meet certain criteria, or you can delete files from disk.

You can use the Report command with sorted or indexed files to generate reports that contain ordered data.

The Locate command searches sequential files (sorted files without indexes) for relevant records. When the end of the file is reached, the screen displays the `End of LOCATE scope` message. The Continue command locates the next occurrence of that record type.

The Seek command searches indexed files for relevant records. You must have specified the appropriate index on the Use statement beforehand. The Skip command locates the next occurrence of that record type. If no record of the desired type is found in the entire file, the screen displays the `NO FIND` message.

The Browse command lets you alter records with the full-screen editing feature of dBASE. Browse differs from Edit in letting you specify which fields to display on the screen. With the Browse command, you can quickly move through the file in an index file order and make changes to selected records.

The dBASE software makes it possible to build files in a number of different ways using data from existing files. The Copy command easily creates backup data files. The Copy Field command builds a new file with the data from only a few fields of the existing file. The Copy Structure command creates an empty file with a matching structure.

The Modify Structure command uses a straightforward method and automatically performs the steps for adding or deleting fields and then copying the records from the old files to the new, changed file.

The Copy command easily creates text files using the Delimited parameter. These files can then be used as input to application programs.

KEY TERMS AND CONCEPTS

active index
Browse command
concatenation
Continue command
Copy command
Copy Field command
Copy Structure command
Delete File command
Delimited parameter
Index command
level break (control break)
List Files Like command
Locate command
mixed-data index
Modify Structure command
multiple-field index
.NDX extension
`NO FIND` message
Seek command
Set Headings Off command
single-field index
Skip command
skip sequential processing
Sort command
STR(string) function
subtotals
updating multiple indexes

CHAPTER QUIZ

Multiple Choice

1. Which of the following statements about sorting is false?
   a. It takes more computer time than indexing.
   b. It takes up more disk space than indexing because an output life has to be created.
   c. A multiple-key sort is simply impossible.
   d. You are allowed to sort on only one field at a time.
   e. All of the above statements are true.

2. Which of the following statements is false about indexing?
   a. The original file is left the same.
   b. The index file that "logically" orders the file is created.
   c. First the index must be accessed and then the data file, if the records are desired in indexed order.
   d. The index holds the contents of each data record.
   e. All of the above statements are true.

3. Use a version of the ____________ command to list the files on disk to make changes.
   a. Display c. List e. Use
   b. Browse d. Index

4. Which of the following commands lets you make changes in a record?
   a. Browse d. All of the above
   b. Replace e. None of the above
   c. Edit

5. Which command locates records in an indexed file?
   a. Seek d. Continue
   b. Locate e. None of the above
   c. Skip

True/False

6. You must index a file before using the Locate command.

7. Use the Skip command to find the next record that meets the search criteria for a sequential search.

8. You can process an indexed file in sequential order by the indexed field.

9. When multiple indexes are specified, you can use only the first index name to find records.

10. Sorting files is usually faster than indexing them.

Answers

1. c, d   2. d   3. c   4. d   5. a   6. f   7. f   8. t   9. t   10. f

Exercises

1. Define or describe each of the following:
   a. Index d. Sequential file
   b. Multiple-field index e. Indexed file
   c. Active index f. Concatenation

2. Use the ____________ command to physically reorder the records within a file and create a new file.

3. You can sort the records in a file in either ____________ or ____________ order.

4. The Sort command sorts files using one or more ____________.

5. The ____________ file contains both the key field contents and the record location.

6. Listing records from an indexed file requires going to the ____________ file, which then points to the record ____________ in the file.

7. Indexing a file usually takes ____________ time than sorting a file.

8. The process of joining two or more fields to form one index is known as ____________.

9. You can include numeric fields in an index, but they must first be converted to ____________ characters.

10. Issue the command ____________ FILE ZIPCUST to erase the ZIPCUST file.

11. When several indexes follow the Use statement, you can use only the ____________ index to find records.

12. When several indexes follow the Use statement, the Pack command will result in ____________ index(es) being rebuilt.

13. You can generate an ordered report by using either a(n) ____________ or an indexed file.

14. You can incorporate totals in a report only when a field is ____________.

15. The ____________ command locates records via an index.

16. The ____________ command locates records in a sequential file.

17. When you are using the Seek command, the character string must appear inside ____________.

18. The ____________ command finds the next record in a sequential file search.

19. The ____________ command displays only desired fields when changing or updating records.

20. The Browse command makes use of the dBASE ____________ screen editing feature.

21. dBASE generates a(n) ____________ when the contents of a field change from one record to the next in a report.

22. dBASE generates subtotals only on ____________ data fields.

23. The command sequence ____________ inserts a blank line at the cursor location when you use the dBASE Modify Structure command.

24. The command sequence ____________ deletes the field at the cursor location when you use the dBASE Modify Structure command.

25. The simple ____________ command creates a backup of a data file.

COMPUTER EXERCISES

The following exercises require the PAYMAST file, created previously.

1. Sort the file by last name.

2. Sort the file by gross pay.

3. Index the file by employee ID. List the file.

4. Index the file by last name. List the file.

5. Index the file by gross pay. List the file.

6. Index the file by last name and first name. List the file.

7. Use the last-name index to list the file.

8. Find all employees who have a gross pay of $780.00. Use the Find command.

9. Use the Locate command to find all the employees that have a pay rate of $4.90.

10. Create a report using the last-name index.

11. Create a report using the gross pay index.

12. Use the Browse command to examine selected fields of your records.

13. Add the following fields to the PAYMAST file. Give each field an appropriate length.

    ADDRESS
    CITY
    STATE
    ZIP

14. Use the Browse or Edit command to fill in data for each record.

15. Using the DOS COPY command, make a copy of the .FRM report template that you created in Chapter 2, Exercise 13. Call the copy NEWPYREP.FRM (New Pay Report).

16. Use the Copy Field command to create a database file with the name and address information for each employee.

17. Create an ASCII text file with the information from Exercise 16.

dBASE III PLUS COMMAND SUMMARY

CONVENTIONS

Lower case User-supplied information

Upper case Explicit portions of dBASE III Plus commands

[. . .] Optional portions of dBASE III Plus commands

<. . .> User-supplied portions of dBASE III Plus commands

<cstring> Character strings

<exp> Valid item or group of items and/or operators

<exp list> List of expressions separated by commas

<field> Record field name

<field list> List of record field names separated by commas

<file> Name of a file to access or create

<index file> Name of an index file to create or access

<key> Portion(s) of a file used to create an index file

<n> Number that dBASE III Plus is to regard as a literal value

<numeric exp> An <exp> whose content is defined as numeric

<scope> Command option that specifies a range of records that dBASE III Plus must treat in executing a command; has three possible values: ALL records in the file; NEXT *n* records in the file; and RECORD *n* (default value varies from command to command)

<skeleton> Allows batch manipulation of files of the same type and/or having matching strings in filename

OPERATORS

LOGICAL OPERATORS (IN ORDER OF PRECEDENCE)

( ) Parentheses for grouping

.NOT. Logical not

.AND. Logical and

.OR. Logical or

$ Substring operator

ARITHMETIC OPERATORS

( ) Parentheses for grouping

/ Division

* Multiplication

\+ Addition

− Subtraction

RELATIONAL OPERATORS

< Less than

> Greater than

= Equal to

<> Not equal to

<= Less than or equal to

>= Greater than or equal to

STRING OPERATOR

\+ String concatenation

FUNCTIONS

* Delete indicator; identifies record marked for deletion.

$(exp,start,length) Substring; extracts the specified part of (exp) from the given starting position for the given length.

DATE( ) Invokes name of the system variable containing the system date.

EOF End-of-file function; evaluates as a logical true/false whether the last record of the file in use has been processed.

STR(exp,length,decimals) String function; converts the specified portion of (exp) to a character string.

TRIM(exp) Trim function; removes trailing blanks from a specified string variable.

SELECTED dBASE COMMANDS

ASSIST Activates the Assistant Menu.

AVERAGE <explist> [WHILE <condition>] [FOR <condition>] Calculates the arithmetic average for numeric fields.

BROWSE [FIELDS <field list>] Provides full-screen editing for changing a file.

CLEAR Erases the screen.

CLEAR ALL Closes all database files, index files, format files, and relations; releases all memory variables and selects work area one.

CONTINUE Continues a Locate command.

COPY TO <file> [FIELD <list>] Copies the file or fields from the file in use to the designated database file.

COPY TO <file> STRUCTURE [FIELD<list>] Copies the structure of the file in use to the designated file.

COUNT [<scope>] [FOR/WHILE<condition>] [TO<memvar>] Counts the number of records in the database that match the specified condition; if a memory variable has been specified, places the result there.

CREATE [<file>] Starts the creation process for a database file.

CREATE REPORT <.frm filename> Activates the Report Menu and lets you create a report template and store it to an .FRM file.

DELETE [<scope] [FOR <exp>] Marks record(s) for deletion.

DELETE FILE <file> Deletes the specified file.

DIR [<drive>] [<path>] Shows the files on the specified drive or path.

DISPLAY [<scope>] [<field list>] [FOR <exp>] [OFF] Displays selected records from the database file in use.

DISPLAY STRUCTURE Displays the structure of the file in use.

EDIT [n] Starts selective editing of the file in use.

EJECT Sends a form feed to the printer.

ERASE <filename> Deletes the specified file from the directory.

FIND <character string> Positions the record pointer to the first record with an index key that matches the specified character string, which does not have to be delimited.

GO or GOTO <n> or TOP, or <BOTTOM> Positions the pointer at a specific record or place in the file in use.

IF <condition> <statements>; ELSE <statements>; ENDIF The IF statement allows a condition to be evaluated and, if the condition is true, for the statements before the ELSE to be executed. Otherwise, the conditions following the ELSE are executed.

INDEX ON <key> TO <file> Creates an index for the file in use.

INPUT <'prompt'> TO <memvar> In command files, assumes that the data are numeric, unless enclosed in quotes, and places them in the memory variable specified by the TO parameter.

INSERT [BEFORE] [BLANK] Inserts a record into the database; if the BEFORE parameter is used, places the record before the current record; if the BLANK parameter is not used, invokes EDIT mode for the new record.

LIST [<scope>] [<field list>] [FOR <exp>] [OFF] Lists records from the file in use.

LIST FILES [ON <disk drive>] [LIKE <skeleton>] Lists files from disk.

LIST STRUCTURE Displays the structure of the file in use.

LOCATE [<scope>] [FOR <exp>] Finds the first record that satisfies the specified condition; the CONTINUE command is then used to locate the next record meeting the condition.

MODIFY REPORT <filename> Activates the Report Menu for changing .FRM report template parameters.

MODIFY STRUCTURE Allows structural modification of a database file.

PACK Eliminates records marked for deletion.

QUIT Terminates dBASE III and returns control to the operating system.

RECALL [<scope>] [FOR <exp>] Recovers records previously marked for deletion.

REINDEX Rebuilds existing active index files.

RENAME <oldfile> TO <newfile> Lets you rename a file.

REPLACE [<scope>]<field> WITH<exp> [FOR<exp>] Replaces the value of the specified field of specified records with stated values.

REPORT [FORM <filename>] [<scope>] [FOR <exp>] [TO PRINT] Generates or accesses an existing .FRM file for output of data in a defined format.

SEEK <expression> Positions the record pointer to the first record with an index key that matches the specified expression.

SELECT <workarea/alias> Activates the specified work area for accessing a file.

SET *See* SET commands.

SKIP [+ − n] Moves the pointer forward or backward within the file.

SORT ON <key> TO <file> [ASCENDING] or [DESCENDING] Creates another database file, sorted in the order specified by the named key.

SORT TO <new filename> ON <field list> [/A] [C] [/D] Creates an ordered copy of a database, arranged according to one or more fields.

STORE <expression> TO <memvar> Stores the results of the expression in the designated memory variable.

SUM <field list> [TO <memvar list>] [<scope>] [FOR <exp>] Computes and displays the sum of numeric fields.

TYPE <filename> [TO PRINT] Displays the contents of a file; TO PRINT parameter dumps a copy of the file to the printer.

USE <file> [INDEX <file list>] Opens a database file and (optionally) opens desired index files.

ZAP Removes all records from the active database file.

SELECTED SET COMMANDS

SET commands let you redefine the environment in which you are working with dBASE. The default value of each SET command of ON/OFF type is indicated by the order of presentation: OFF/ON indicates that the default is OFF; ON/OFF indicates that the default is ON.

SET ALTERNATE OFF Stops the echoing of output to the specified .TXT file and closes the file.

SET ALTERNATE ON In conjunction with a SET ALTERNATE TO command, starts the echoing of output to the specified .TXT file.

SET ALTERNATE TO <filename> Specifies the .TXT file that is to receive the echoed output to the screen (the .TXT contains standard ASCII output) and closes any currently open ALTERNATE files.

SET BELL ON/OFF ON rings the bell when invalid data are entered or a field boundary is passed; OFF turns off the bell.

SET CONFIRM OFF/ON Does not skip to the next field in the full-screen mode.

SET DATE TO <MM/DD/YY> Sets or resets the system date.

SET DECIMALS TO <expN> Sets the minimum number of decimals displayed in the results of certain operations and functions.

SET DEFAULT TO <drive> Commands dBASE III Plus to regard the specified drive as the default drive for all future operations.

SET DELETED OFF/ON ON prevents dBASE III Plus from reading/processing any record marked for deletion following a command that has <scope>; OFF allows dBASE III Plus to read all records.

SET EXACT ON Results in only those records being found whose characters exactly meet the criteria used in a SEEK command.

SET INTENSITY ON/OFF ON enables inverse video or dual intensity to appear during full-screen operations; OFF disables these features.

SET MARGIN TO <n> Sets the left-hand margin of the printer to <n>.

SET MENU ON/OFF Turns menus on or off.

FULL-SCREEN CURSOR MOVEMENT CODES

ALL COMMANDS

Ctrl + X Moves the cursor down to the next field (also Ctrl + F).

Ctrl + E Moves cursor up to the previous field (also Ctrl + A).

Ctrl + D Moves cursor ahead one character.

Ctrl + S Moves cursor back one character.

Ctrl + G Deletes character under cursor.

<Rubout> or DEL Deletes character to left of cursor.

Ctrl + Y Blanks out current field to right of cursor.

Ctrl + V Toggles between OVERWRITE and INSERT modes.

Ctrl + W Saves changes and returns to command (.) prompt.

IN EDIT MODE

Ctrl + U Toggles the record delete mark on and off.

Ctrl + C Writes current record to disk and advances to next record.

Ctrl + R Writes current record to disk and backs to previous record.

Ctrl + Q Ignores changes to current record and returns to command (.) prompt.

Ctrl + W Writes all changes to disk and returns to command (.) prompt.

IN BROWSE MODE

Ctrl + B Pans the window right one field.

Ctrl + Z Pans the window left one field.

IN MODIFY MODE

Ctrl + T Deletes current line and moves all lower lines up.

Ctrl + N Inserts new line at cursor position.

Ctrl + C Scrolls down one-half page.

Ctrl + W Writes all changes onto disk and returns to command (.) prompt.

Ctrl + Q Ignores all changes and returns to Assistant Menu or dot prompt.

IN APPEND MODE

Enter Terminates APPEND when cursor is in first position of first field.

Ctrl + W Writes record to disk and moves to next record.

Ctrl + Q Ignores current record and returns to command (.) prompt.

GLOSSARY

action line: The line appearing above the status bar that displays the dBASE command being generated by your menu or submenu selection.

active index: The index that will automatically be used to locate a record within an indexed dBASE file.

All parameter: The dBASE parameter that includes all records of a file in a command.

Append command: dBASE command that adds records at the end of an existing file.

Assist command: dBASE command that activates the Assistant Menu.

ASSISTANT mode: The menu interface through which the user builds dBASE commands from menus.

Average command: dBASE command that calculates the average of values in a numeric field in all records in a file.

beginning-of-file (BOF) function: dBASE command that checks to determine if the beginning of the file has been reached.

Browse command: dBASE command that displays a number of records on the screen at one time, letting you edit a file quickly.

character field: Field capable of holding any alphanumeric or special character. In dBASE, such a field can hold up to 254 characters.

Command: An instruction to dBASE to perform a task.

command-driven mode: Commands entered from the DOS prompt.

COMMAND mode: dBASE mode, indicated by the dot prompt (.), in which the user types a dBASE command.

concatenation: Process of joining two character strings, usually accomplished through use of the + sign.

Condition: The algebraic or logical means of controlling which records are to be affected by a dBASE command.

Continue command: dBASE command that finds the next record in a Locate command search.

Copy command: dBASE command that copies one or more files onto the current disk or onto another disk.

Copy Field command: dBASE command that creates a new file using specified fields from an existing file.

Copy Structure command: dBASE command that creates a new, empty file using the exact structure of the active file.

Create Report command: dBASE command that creates the report template by which printed reports are generated.

database: Collection of data related to one specific type of application. *Database* is often used synonymously with *file*.

dBASE II: Relational database package.

dBASE III: Updated version of dBASE II.

dBASE III Plus: The updated version of dBASE III.

Delete command: dBASE command that enables you to mark a record for later deletion.

Delete File command: dBASE command that deletes a specified .DBF file from disk.

delete indicator: Asterisk (*) that appears in a record when it has been marked for deletion.

delimited parameter: An instruction that is used with a Copy Field command to automatically enclose copied fields within desired characters. The instruction *delimited with "* would enclose each field within double quotes.

DIR: *See* **Directory command.**

Directory (DIR) command: dBASE command that lets you list specified files from disk.

Display command: dBASE command that displays the record at the pointer location.

dot prompt (.): The period that is displayed to the dBASE user indicating that dBASE is ready to evaluate another command.

Edit command: dBASE command that lets you make changes to a record.

end-of-file (EOF) function: dBASE command that checks to determine if the end of the file has been reached.

field: Subdivision of a record that holds one piece of data about a transaction.

Find: dBASE command that locates records in an indexed file, using the index.

For parameter: dBASE command that lets you specify which records are to be included in a command.

Goto Bottom command: dBASE command that positions the pointer to the last record at the end of a dBASE file.

Goto command: dBASE command that positions the pointer at a specific record in a file.

Goto Top command: dBASE command that positions the pointer to the first record at the beginning of a dBASE file.

Help command: dBASE command that invokes the dBASE Help feature.

index: dBASE feature that orders information logically within a file without physically reordering the records themselves. Indexes may be single- or multiple-field.

Index command: dBASE command that creates an index file on disk using information from one or more specified fields.

level break (control break): A term that indicates a

change in the contents of a field from one record to the next.

List command: dBASE command that displays records from a data file contained on disk.

List Files Like command: dBASE command that, with a file extension, lists all files from the default drive that have the desired extension.

List Structure command: dBASE command that lists the field names, data type, and field size for a dBASE file.

Locate command: dBASE command that finds data in a sequential file.

menu-driven mode: All commands can be entered from a menu.

message line: A line below the status line that tells what type of operation is to be performed using a menu option.

mixed-data index: An index created using text and numeric data. Unless the numeric data is converted to text, such a command will generate an error message.

Modify Structure command: dBASE command that is used to make changes to the structure of an existing dBASE file.

multiple-field index: An index created using two or more fields.

navigation line: The line at the bottom of the dBASE screen that shows which keys can be used for a particular menu item.

.NDX extension: The extension automatically placed on an index file by dBASE.

Next command: dBASE command that moves the pointer forward or backward in a file.

`NO FIND` **message:** The message displayed by dBASE if it cannot locate the record specified in either a Find or Seek command.

Noun: The part of a dBASE command that contains a file or field name.

Pack command: dBASE command that physically removes any records marked for deletion.

parameter: Modifying piece of information that constitutes part of a dBASE command. It might, for example, indicate which files or fields are to be included in an operation.

primary key: In dBASE, the record number; in sorting, the major sort field.

PROGRAM mode: Executing instructions that have been saved to a file.

? command: dBASE command that displays the result of a function or command to the default output device (screen or printer).

query: The process of asking a question and obtaining a response from a database.

Quit command: dBASE command that returns you to the operating system.

Recall All command: dBASE command that undeletes any dBASE records marked for deletion.

Recall command: dBASE command that retrieves or unmarks records that have been marked for deletion.

RECNO( ) function: dBASE function that is used to determine the location of the pointer within a file.

record: Entity that contains information about a specific business happening or transaction.

record number: Identification used by dBASE as the primary key for a record; the physical location in the file for a given record.

Replace command: dBASE command that changes several or all records within a data file quickly.

Report: dBASE command that creates or accesses a parameter file modifying how a specific printed report is to be generated.

Report Form command: dBASE command that generates a report using a report template.

report template: A dBASE file that contains all instructions needed for generating a printed report.

Scope: The part of a dBASE command that dictates which records are to be affected by a command. For example, *All* or *Next 5*.

secondary key: Defining key used to order information within the primary key.

Seek command: dBASE command that locates records in an indexed dBASE file.

Set Headings Off command: dBASE command that turns off field names for a List command.

single-field index: A dBASE index created using the contents of one field only.

Skip command: dBASE command that moves the pointer forward or backward within a data file.

skip sequential processing: Moving to a position in the file using a Seek command and then moving sequentially through the file from that point forward.

Sort command: dBASE command that reorders a database file physically.

status bar: The bar near the bottom of the dBASE screen that indicates the active file, the default drive, and the position of the pointer. It also displays information about the status of some of the toggle keys on the keyboard.

STR(string) function: The function that converts numeric data to string data. This is required for mixed-data indexes.

structure: The way information is allocated by records and fields for storage in a dBASE file.

substring function ($): The function that finds any character string at any location within a field.

subtotals: An intermediate total printed when a control break occurs.

Sum command: dBASE command that totals the contents of a field for all records within a file.

To Print option: The option used on a dBASE command to send the output to the printer.

Use command: dBASE command that makes a file available for manipulation.

INDEX

dBASE

File Commands			Pointer	Logical	Arithmetic	Relational	
Create	Append	Use	GOTO #	.OR.	+ Addition	< Less than	<= Less than or equal
Delete File	Edit	Modify	Skip	.AND.	− Subtraction	> Greater than	>= Greater than or equal
Copy File	Browse	Pack	Find	.NOT.	* Multiplication	= Equal	
Display Structure	Index		Locate		/ Division	<> Not equal	

dBASE

Selected Set Commands

Set Bell On/Off	On rings the bell when invalid data are entered or a field boundary is passed. Off turns off the bell.
Set Colon On/Off	On displays colons which delimit or bound input fields: Off hides the colons. (Only dBASE II)
Set Default to ⟨drive⟩	Commands dBASE to regard the specified drive as the default drive for all future operations.
Set Deleted Off/On	On prevents dBASE from reading/processing any record marked for deletion. Off allows dBASE to read all records.
Set Intensity On/Off	On enables inverse video or dual intensity during full-screen operations. Off disables these features.
Set Margin to ⟨n⟩	Sets the lefthand margin of printer to ⟨n⟩.

dBASE

Selected Full-Screen Cursor Movement Commands

^X	Moves DOWN to next field	⟨DEL⟩	Deletes character to left of cursor
^E	Moves UP to next field	^Y	Blanks out current field
^D	Moves RIGHT one position	^V	Toggle between overwrite and insert mode
^S	Moves LEFT one position	^W	Save changes and return to "." prompt
^G	Deletes character at cursor		

Other Common Commands

ESC	Cancel any command and return to "." prompt
^Q	Ignore any changes and return to "." prompt
^N	Insert a line at cursor's position (Modify)
^T	Delete current line and move text up (Modify)
^P	Toggle printer On/Off

Function Keys Template for dBase III Plus

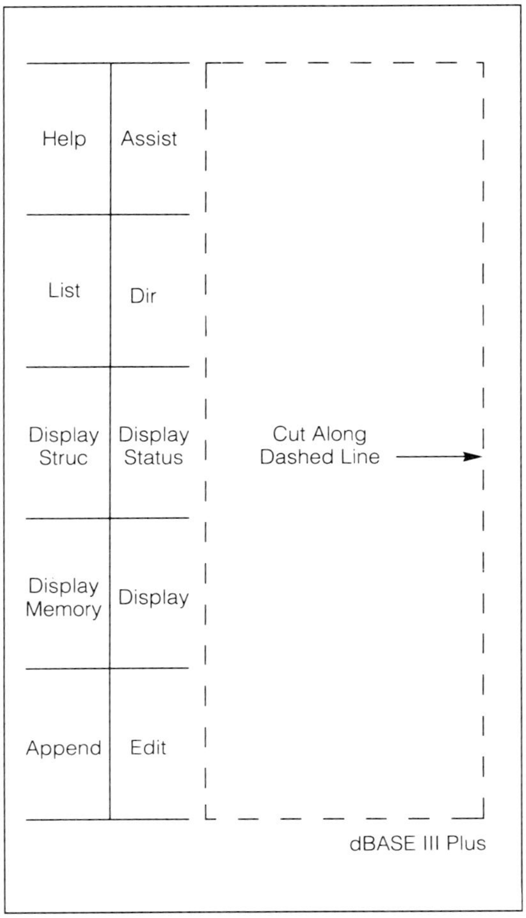